Forensic Psychology and Neuropsychology for Criminal and Civil Cases

Forensic Psychology and Neuropsychology for Criminal and Civil Cases

Edited by
Harold V. Hall

CRC Press
Taylor & Francis Group
Boca Raton London New York

CRC Press is an imprint of the
Taylor & Francis Group, an informa business

Cover Art: "Night Dread" by Steven W. Pollard, Ph.D. (www.abstract-art-wow.com)

CRC Press
Taylor & Francis Group
6000 Broken Sound Parkway NW, Suite 300
Boca Raton, FL 33487-2742

© 2008 by Taylor & Francis Group, LLC
CRC Press is an imprint of Taylor & Francis Group, an Informa business

No claim to original U.S. Government works
Printed in the United States of America on acid-free paper
10 9 8 7 6 5 4 3 2 1

International Standard Book Number-13: 978-0-8493-8173-7 (Hardcover)

Library of Congress Cataloging-in-Publication Data

Forensic psychology and neuropsychology for criminal and civil cases / editor, Harold V. Hall.
    p. ; cm.
    "CRC title."
    Includes bibliographical references and indexes.
    ISBN-13: 978-0-8493-8173-7 (hardcover : alk. paper)
    1. Forensic psychology. 2. Forensic neuropsychology. 3. Violence--Psychological aspects. I. Hall, Harold V.
    [DNLM: 1. Forensic Psychiatry. 2. Violence--psychology. W 740 F71497 2008]

RA1148.F5573 2008
614'.15--dc22
                                                       2007015246

Visit the Taylor & Francis Web site at
http://www.taylorandfrancis.com

and the CRC Press Web site at
http://www.crcpress.com

To Isidor "Sam" Steinfeld—a truly kind, creative, and intellectually curious person—whom I am proud to call father and friend

—HVH

Contents

Part II   Criminal-Forensic Evaluation

Part III   Civil-Forensic Evaluation

Preface

Forensic authors and researchers for the Pacific Institute for the Study of Conflict and Aggression have, in the past, carefully defined violence and aggression—building on the foundations of over a dozen previous well-received publications that have enriched the behavioral science literature. In this book, they go impressively beyond description of these unsettling topics to encompass extant civil and criminal issues with psychological and neuropsychological tools by directing the substance of the literature to each contributor's chapter in forensic cases. Readers will learn about a number of relevant topics from forensic evaluation to the ever-growing threat of methamphetamine-related violence. The increasing sophistication of neuropsychological assessments is also addressed in up-to-date presentations, clearly keeping the reader abreast of the field.

Clinicians, researchers, and psychologists practicing in any number of related fields will be able to address relevant questions from the civil area (e.g., How does the plaintiff attorney best address cerebral injury in his or her client? How does the psychologist address child care and protection issues from a neuropsychological and psychological perspective?). These are critical issues in today's world of forensics. Each chapter vigorously covers ethics, deception analysis, and the applied aspects of forensics, which are all firmly grounded in the growing body of empirical research.

The quality of each contributor's chapter in *Forensic Psychology and Neuropsychology for Criminal and Civil Cases* is superb, with several authors of national if not international stature. This latest edition in the impressive oeuvre of the contributors' expertise raises pertinent questions: Why is the neuropsychological status of parents associated with child abuse and neglect? What does methamphetamine-related violence teach us? Does possible cerebral injury in plaintiffs necessitate an analysis of malingering, and does the methodology in criminal-forensic evaluation apply in any way to civil cases? Can we predict violence with actuarial measures? How do we define victim-perpetrated violence? Can we truly discern faking good from faking bad, and both from truth telling? What are mitigating circumstances in murder? Does the MMPI predict violence? We must understand how to assess violence in criminal and civil issues if we are going to intervene with violent predators whose behavior disrupts the flow of a peaceful society. Michel Foucault suggests in his landmark 1995 book, *Birth of the Prison*, that if professionals are not careful, we may become part of the punishing machinery, the very architecture that continues to imprison the souls of men. These are wise words. Dr. Hall's latest edition offers professionals important answers to Foucault.

Sally Barlow
Brigham Young University
Provo, Utah

Acknowledgments

The editor's contribution to this book stands squarely on the shoulders of professionals and academics who have mastered some aspect of forensics and are willing to share their wisdom in an erudite and easily understood manner. A substantial percentage of the contributors are diplomates of the American Board of Professional Psychology (ABPP), with many years of quality forensic experience, and the remainder are renowned psychologists, psychiatrists, and attorneys who have established themselves as authorities and experts in the mental health–law interface.

The consulting editors for *Forensic Psychology and Neuropsychology for Criminal and Civil Cases* diligently blind-reviewed the chapters, each peer-reviewed three times, so that high-quality contributions resulted. The professional integrity and relevance of the book were thereby enhanced by consulting editors Sally Barlow, John A. Call, Robert J. Craig, Ronald S. Ebert, Jeffery S. Long, Geoffrey Marczyk, Sandra B. McPherson, Kris Mohandie, Joseph G. Poirier, and Steven W. Pollard.

Associate editors Sally Barlow of Brigham Young University and Jane Thompson of the University of Hawaii at Hilo were unflagging in their many efforts to produce a fine edited volume that was case oriented in focus. Special additional thanks are due to Jane Thompson who spent endless hours as managing editor for the work.

The editor would like to thank the American Psychological Association for authorization to reproduce in their entirety as appendices the *Ethical Principles of Psychologists and Code of Conduct* (2002) and the findings of the *Committee on the Revision of the Specialty Guidelines for Forensic Psychology* (2006).

Becky McEldowney Masterman, Senior Editor, Life Sciences, Taylor & Francis Group, CRC Press, a fine author in her own right, initially raised the notion of an edited work that incorporated the psychology and neuropsychology of criminal-forensic and civil-forensic settings and situations. Becky was gracious enough to provide counsel to Jill J. Jurgensen, Project Coordinator, Taylor & Francis Group, CRC Press, who spent prodigious amounts of time and effort in creating a book that will be truly enjoyed and helpful to the readership.

Much gratitude is directed to Steven W. Pollard, a clinical forensic psychologist and an artist of renown, who generously supplied the front cover artwork in addition to his duties as a consulting editor.

The editor is indebted to the Pacific Institute for the Study of Conflict and Aggression, a nonprofit scientific and educational organization that offers APA-approved training, consultation, and evaluation on individual and collective violence. To date, the Pacific Institute has produced a dozen books, a portion of the royalties from which are donated back to the organization for publications, training, and special projects. Most of the resources and financial support for this work were supplied by the Pacific Institute in its continuing efforts to address human violence and to serve the community at large.

Harold V. Hall
Pacific Institute for the Study of Conflict and Aggression
Kamuela, Hawaii

The Editor

Harold V. Hall, Ph.D., is the founder and director of the Pacific Institute for the Study of Conflict and Aggression in Kamuela, Hawaii. Dr. Hall is a diplomate in both forensic psychology and clinical psychology of the American Board of Professional Psychology, a fellow of the American Psychological Association, and a distinguished practitioner of the National Academy of Practice in Psychology. As a nongovernment organization (NGO), the Pacific Institute has presented and consulted on violence-related topics and situations in the U.K., Poland, the People's Republic of China, and the Republic of Palau, as well as provided consultation to local, state, and federal U.S. agencies. Dr. Hall has authored or edited 12 books and numerous articles on clinical-forensic issues, including the well-received second editions entitled *Violence Prediction: Guidelines for the Forensic Practitioner* (with Ronald Ebert), *Detecting Malingering and Deception: Forensic Distortion Analysis* (with Joseph Poirier), and *Methamphetamine Abuse: Clinical and Forensic Aspects* (with Errol Yudko and Sandra McPherson).

Royalties from these books as well as those written by expert consultants to the Pacific Institute, together with tuition from workshops and conferences, are donated to the Pacific Institute for training, consultation, and publication on individual and collective violence. Dr. Hall has served as a forensic consultant and trainer for issues such as the screening of public safety workers (police departments), profiling in serial-rape murder cases (Federal Bureau of Investigation), violence risk analysis for witness protection programs (National Bureau of Prisons), and bombing events associated with domestic terrorism (U.S. Secret Service). He has testified as an expert more than 200 times in murder and manslaughter cases in state, federal, and military courts. He was a Fulbright Scholar in 2003 at the University Marie Curie-Sklodowska, Lublin, Poland, focusing on the creation of a violence risk assessment device for a normal young adult population and the development of a genocide warning scale, and teaching the psychological aspects of terrorism. Through global competition, Dr. Hall was selected as a Rotary Cultural Scholar to attend the 2007 Peace and Conflict Study Program at Chulalongkorn University in Bangkok, Thailand.

Contributors

Lyle E. Baade
Department of Psychiatry and
  Behavioral Sciences
University of Kansas School
  of Medicine
Wichita, Kansas

Sally Barlow
Department of Psychology
Brigham Young University
Provo, Utah

Peter Bresciani
Office of the Public Defender
Kealakekua, Hawaii

John A. Call
Crisis Management Consultants, Inc.
Oklahoma City, Oklahoma

Deborah Chavez
Capella University
Minneapolis, Minnesota

Don Condie
Harvard Medical School
Boston, Massachusetts

Lois Oberlander Condie
Harvard Medical School
Boston, Massachusetts

Robert J. Craig
Department of Psychology
Roosevelt University
Chicago, Illinois

David DeMatteo
Drexel University
Philadelphia, Pennsylvania

Richart L. DeMier
U.S. Medical Center for
  Federal Prisoners
Springfield, Missouri

Ronald S. Ebert
Psychological Services, Inc.
Braintree, Massachusetts

Jay Finkelman
Alliant International University
Alhambra, California

Jonathan W. Gould
Child Custody Consultants
Charlotte, North Carolina

Kirk Heilbrun
Drexel University
Philadelphia, Pennsylvania

Robin J. Heinrichs
Department of Psychiatry and
  Behavioral Sciences
University of Kansas School
  of Medicine
Wichita, Kansas

Linda Knauss
Institute for Graduate
  Clinical Psychology
Widener University
Wilmington, Delaware

Josh Kutinsky
Institute for Graduate
  Clinical Psychology
Widener University
Wilmington, Delaware

Jeffery S. Long
Psychological Services, Inc.
Braintree, Massachusetts

James Manley
Independent Practice
Kona, Hawaii

Geoffrey Marczyk
Institute for Graduate
  Clinical Psychology
Widener University
Chester, Pennsylvania

David A. Martindale
Child Custody Consultants
Morristown, New Jersey

Sandra B. McPherson
The Fielding Graduate University
Santa Barbara, California
and
Independent Practice
Beachwood, Ohio

Kris Mohandie
Operational Consulting
   International, Inc.
Pasadena, California

Randy K. Otto
Mental Health Institute
University of South Florida
Tampa, Florida

Rolland S. Parker
Department of Neurology
New York University School of Medicine
New York, New York

Joseph G. Poirier
Independent Practice
Rockville, Maryland

Steven W. Pollard
Independent Practice
Hilo, Hawaii

Dana K. Soetaert
Department of Psychiatry and
   Behavioral Sciences
University of Kansas School
   of Medicine
Wichita, Kansas

Kurt Spohn
Criminal Justice Division
Office of the Attorney General
Honolulu, Hawaii

Jane Thompson
Department of Psychology
University of Hawaii
Hilo, Hawaii

Errol Yudko
Department of Psychology
University of Hawaii
Hilo, Hawaii

Part I

Foundational Issues

Criminal Responsibility Evaluation in a Methamphetamine-Murder Case

1

HAROLD V. HALL

Pacific Institute for the Study of Conflict and Aggression, Kamuela, Hawaii

PETER BRESCIANI

Office of the Public Defender, Kealakekua, Hawaii

KURT SPOHN

Criminal Justice Division, Office of the Attorney General, Honolulu, Hawaii

ERROL YUDKO

University of Hawaii, Hilo, Hawaii

Contents

Defendant John Smith is a 38-year-old, right-handed, single, construction supervisor who was charged with three counts of first-degree murder, attempted first-degree murder, burglary, kidnapping, and sexual assault, in addition to other charges, after an alleged home invasion and subsequent acts. He was referred by his court-appointed defense attorneys for a forensic evaluation of methamphetamine-related state of mind issues. In recounting the incident, he stated that he had a few beers at his job site with his boss after work. He and a friend then drove to a secluded spot and together smoked over 1 gram of methamphetamine ("ice"). After dropping off his friend, Defendant Smith went to his sister's home where he was staying. He found a syringe belonging to another family member and injected methamphetamine into his left arm. He then lay down in his room, feeling more intoxicated and thinking that he needed some fast money to buy more of the drug. He had $400 in his wallet at the time and the next day was payday. However, he had earmarked those funds for home improvements and automobile repairs. He then remembered an apparently vacant house on the route to work that would be a likely prospect to burglarize. He considered several options of places to rob such as a bank, store, or business, but decided to burglarize this particular house because it overall presented a low risk for apprehension.

He reported that after a few minutes, he felt energetic and had the need to act. He then drove straight to the victims' residence and parked outside the gate. (He estimated that the gate was 20 yards from the house, when measurements during the investigation revealed it was closer to 200 yards away.) After circling the periphery of the house three times to ensure that no one was present, he approached the house. On the second go around, he tripped on a "big log." He felt the ground and picked up a "stick" that he could use as a club in case a watchdog appeared. The "stick" was approximately 3 feet long and a few inches wide, with the hardness and general form of a baseball bat. He stated that he used his Phillips screwdriver to remove four screws in the frame of the window screen. He entered an unlit room, then proceeded into a lighted hall where, to his surprise, he encountered the parents of the victim family. He claimed that upon seeing them, he lost control and started swinging wildly with his "stick," repeatedly striking the man and the woman until they fell unconscious to the floor. He stated that at that time, he felt he was coming down from the methamphetamine and was "tweaking real bad," with intense fear and paranoia. He opined that he went into the "tweaking" stage immediately after sighting the victims. He then walked to the master bedroom and opened drawers looking for anything valuable to steal. He grabbed bed sheets, a comforter, blankets, and a pillow to cover the bodies and the blood on the floor. He stated that he wished to cover the blood because it was "making [him] sick." As he exited the master bedroom, he saw the woman lying on her back facing him, opening her eyes, and the man trying to sit up. This "freaked [him] out," and he clubbed them several more times on the head. He stated that he turned the woman on her left side (toward the eastern side of the house) and removed her short pants, thought of raping her, but then changed his mind.

Defendant Smith then returned to the master bedroom, thinking of removing computer equipment for resale. He then saw a young girl, the 9-year-old daughter of the family, standing in the hallway, staring at him. He thought of hitting her with the "stick," but could not because she was looking directly at him. Instead, he took her by the hand and led her out of the house. She followed obediently, and he then drove her to his residence for the purpose of having sex with her. He settled into his room, no one else being home. He stated that he first tried to get her to give him a "blow job," but the girl seemed in a daze and was not responsive. He set her face down on the bed because he did not want to look at her face and masturbated while feeling her buttocks. As he was masturbating, he inserted his right middle finger into her anus. He ejaculated on her back, then wiped his penis of semen, and dressed for work. He thought of killing her, but changed his mind. In the morning, he threatened to kill her if she left his room, locked the door, and left for work. He returned home that afternoon, picked up the girl, and drove to an isolated area. He again thought of killing her, but released her when she "kept looking" at him. Defendant Smith was arrested the next day.

Defendant Smith was found guilty of all charges and sentenced to multiple life terms of imprisonments without the possibility of parole. Through her extended family and attorneys, the daughter constructed a website to gather more information that was officially available and successfully litigated in civil court against various parties, including Defendant Smith, his ex-boss, and the owners of the house. Defendant Smith agreed to a (undisclosed) sizable settlement just before the civil trial was due to commence, rumored to be more than $6,000,000.

Introduction

This chapter opens this volume by examining a methamphetamine-murder case to illustrate the evaluation for criminal responsibility in Hawaii, the jurisdiction of the authors, and whose test of insanity is followed by the majority of other states, as discussed below (see Appendix A for the blinded report). A few thoughts and recommendations from the forensic literature and the authors' experiences are offered for a sound and successful forensic practice. Impressions are identified as such. Using this first chapter as a springboard, the contributors to this book discuss in detail and provide case material that clarifies and untangles the complex issues that characterize consultation services in the mental health–law interface. There is a heavy emphasis on basic issues in conducting a comprehensive forensic evaluation—knowing the relevant legal issues, being aware of the ethical issues involved, linking empirical research to evaluation findings as much as possible, clearly articulating the decision path of the evaluator, preparing a report that serves as a foundation for all forensic services, offering recommendations and expert testimony, and anticipating that criminal cases may later be civilly litigated.

Competency to Stand Trial

Legal fitness to face one's accuser, otherwise known as competency to stand trial, competency to proceed, or simply "fitness," is a foundational step in the evaluation of criminal responsibility. Simple in basic concept but demanding in rigor, discussions in the forensic literature on competency to proceed are found in Blau (1984); Curran, McGarry, and Shah (1986); Ewing (1985); Grisso, Borum, and Edens (2002); Gutheil and Appelbaum (1982); Melton, Petrella, Poythress, and Slobogin (1997); Shapiro (1984); Warren, Rosenfeld, and Fitch (1994); Weiner and Hess (1987); and Ziskin and Faust (1988). Works devoted exclusively to competency to stand trial include those of Frederick, DeMier, and Towers (2004); Grisso (1986, 1988); McGarry (1973); and Roesch and Golding (1980). Although none of these sources deals primarily with methamphetamine use, their content addresses means to assess and evaluate competency to stand trial based on competencies, regardless of interfering conditions that may reduce fitness. Several reliable and valid measures are available for use in evaluating trial competencies: the competency assessment instrument (Grisso, 1986, 1988), the Interdisciplinary Fitness Interview (Golding, Roesch, and Schreiber, 1984), the Competency Screening Test (McGarry, 1973), the Georgia Competency Test (Gothard, Rogers, and Sewell, 1995), and the MacArthur Competence Assessment Tool—Criminal Adjudication (1996). In Chapter 10 of this book, Randy Otto and Richart DeMier address the assessment of fitness. The forensic evaluator should utilize these measures within a broad-spectrum assessment approach that also evaluates psychopathology, skills, and response sets that may be associated with deception and distortion.

The legal requirement of competency to stand trial is an extension of the general rule that no one should be tried for a crime in his or her absence. If a defendant must be physically present to defend against criminal charges, that defendant must also be "mentally present." Disorders that interfere with the defendant's psychological participation in a trial may render that defendant incompetent to stand trial and require that the proceedings be postponed until effective participation can be assured. The effects of methamphetamine use may compromise the defendant's competency to stand trial. As discussed later, chronic methamphetamine abuse may cause severe confusion, apathy, short-term memory problems, executive dysfunction, auditory hallucinations, and other significant problems that may persist for a considerable length of time after abstinence commences.

Most jurisdictions use a variation of the rule articulated by the United States Supreme Court in *Dusky v. United States* (1960) to define competency to stand trial. *Dusky* requires that a defendant have the ability to (1) understand rationally and factually the legal proceedings and (2) cooperate with his or her attorney in proffering a defense. *Dusky* has been amplified in phraseology, as well as in concept, by case law and may include, at the discretion of the trial court, additional factors such as (1) whether or not the defendant has sufficient mental ability to consult with his or her defense counsel with a reasonable degree of rational understanding, (2) whether or not the defendant has the capacity to assist in preparing a defense, and (3) whether or not the defendant has a rational, as well as factual, understanding of the proceedings, and (4) whether there is freedom on the part of the defendant from interfering conditions that would prevent him or her in unspecified ways from mounting a defense (see *State of Hawaii v. Silverio Soares* (1996). A methamphetamine-induced disorder that interferes with any of these capabilities may be sufficient to render the defendant incompetent to stand trial. However, incompetency to stand trial is not to be equated with the mere presence of mental illness (*Feguer v. United States,* 1962; *United States v. Adams,* 1969), amnesia (*United States v. Wilson,* 1966), or need for treatment. The claimed disorder must be of the kind and severity that impairs the functional capacities outlined in *Dusky.*

Usually, the question of competency to stand trial is raised by the defense attorney, who has the most frequent contact with the defendant and who has the professional and legal obligation to raise the question in appropriate cases. However, case law suggests that the question must be raised, even by the prosecution or the court itself, whenever a "bona fide doubt" exists regarding the defendant's capacity to mount a defense (see *Drope v. Missouri,* 1975). The question of a defendant's competency to proceed may be raised at any time from the defendant's first appearance in court to the time of sentencing.

If found incompetent, the defendant cannot be held indefinitely but only for a reasonable period of time (*Jackson v. State of Indiana,* 1972); if competent, it is assumed that the defendant can "knowingly and voluntarily" waive constitutional rights, including the right to a jury trial and to be assisted by counsel (*Godinez v. Moran,* 1993). In actual practice, some mentally disturbed defendants are not difficult to identify. Those who are frankly psychotic, demented, and severely mentally retarded are often recognized by arresting officers, jail personnel, and defense attorneys, and they may be transferred to treatment facilities prior to any court appearances. In the authors' experience, criminal justice system personnel view the chronic methamphetamine abuser as one who looks malnourished, disheveled, and unhealthy; is reticent or loose in verbal responses; appears aphasic or has word-finding problems; is generally confused; and shows impulsiveness with a low frustration tolerance (see Yudko, Hall, and McPherson, 2003). Often, the individual exhibits a blank stare. He or she is often unable to answer simple questions that require orientation (to person, place, date, and circumstances of the evaluation), attention, and memory. Of course, these signs are impressionistically based and contain an unknown number of false-positives and false-negatives.

In summary, the question of competency to stand trial in methamphetamine cases involves three separate questions: (1) Does the defendant exhibit methamphetamine symptoms alone or in combination with other mental disorders sufficiently severe to justify a finding of incompetency? (2) Is the defendant unable (a) to understand rationally and factually the legal proceedings or (b) to assist counsel in defense? (3) Is this incapacity caused by the mental disorder? In the instant case, Defendant Smith was found fit to proceed because he met the *Dusky* and *Soares* criteria, and, in addition, he showed adequate intelligence, attentional, recall, and executive skills during the evaluation. He exhibited deception, which implies an awareness regarding what is actually true along with the implementation of a method to conceal the truth, and did not have any severely incapacitating conditions at the time he was evaluated.

Criminal Responsibility

Reviews of and methods for conducting criminal responsibility (i.e., insanity) evaluation can be found in Heilbrun, Marczyk, and Dematteo (2002); Melton et al. (1997); Rogers (1984); and Rogers and Shuman (2000), with focal applications of this century-old concept by the senior author and his colleagues to decision analysis (Hall, 1985), malingering and deception (Hall and Poirier, 2001; Hall and Pritchard, 1996), and cerebral injury (Hall and Sbordone, 1993). In Chapter 11 of this book, Sandra McPherson addresses aspects of criminal responsibility in regard to mitigatory defenses. Not surprisingly, forensic mental health evaluations for criminal responsibility, like competency to stand trial, are seen by these authors as involving both civil and criminal law.

Therefore, a forensic evaluator should know the relevant legal cases and statues in a given jurisdiction. As a bare minimum, the expert must be familiar with the statutorily defined test of insanity and surrounding case law for use in testimony. The conclusions proffered by an expert may be fatally flawed if he or she misuses or wrongly defines the extant test of insanity in court, or even displays an inability to articulate the exact wording in the statues.

There are several tests of insanity. First formulated by the Queen's Bench in 1843, the M'Naghten Rule traces its origin to the English case of that name. The M'Naghten Rule requires first that the accused suffer from a defect of reason arising from a disease of the mind. If the accused suffers from such a defect, then the accused is not held criminally responsible for an unlawful act if, as a consequence of the defect, at the time of the act in question the accused did not know either (a) the nature and quality of the act or (b) that the act was wrong (Lafave and Scott, 1986). Although initially popular in a majority of the states and in the federal circuits, criticism of the rule has been prevalent over the past few decades. One objection to the rule is that it singles out only one factor as a test of responsibility—cognition—relying on the ability of the accused "to know" what he or she was doing or "to know" the wrongfulness of his or her conduct. This compartmentalization of the mind and its functions ignores the reality that an individual is a complex being with varying degrees of awareness. In the past, 14 states and the federal jurisdictions recognized this defect in the M'Naghten Rule and supplemented the M'Naghten formula with what has been labeled as the "irresistible impulse" test. This second approach took into consideration the volitional aspects of an individual defendant in that a mental disease, disorder, or defect may produce an incapacity for self-control without impairing cognition. Therefore, this formulation recognized that a defendant whose volitional capacity is impaired as a result of a disease, disorder, or defect should be relieved of penal liability just the same as a defendant whose cognitive capacity is so impaired. However, a criticism of the irresistible impulse test is that it may be restricted to sudden, momentary, or spontaneous acts without recognition of mental illness characterized by brooding or reflection. More subtle criticisms of both the M'Naghten Rule and the "irresistible impulse" formulation are the requirements that the defendant completely lack the capacity for self-control. This legal requirement of total incapacity does not conform to modern medical knowledge or the clinical experience of mental health professionals.

A minority of jurisdictions have adopted a third approach, first set forth in *Durham v. United States* (1954). The test relieves an accused from criminal responsibility if his or her unlawful act was the product of a mental disease or mental defect. The criticisms of this test are twofold: the difficulty of mental health professionals to determine whether such impulses actually exist and the dangers of leaving the ultimate decision of criminal responsibility to the expert medical witness. Once the expert has decided the issue of causation and that the defendant's condition falls within a category of "mental disease or mental defect," the defendant must be acquitted. If medical experts have testified that a defendant's act was a product of a mental disease or defect, there is no standard by which a jury can determine whether the defendant should be held responsible (see Commentary to §704–400, Hawaii Revised Statutes; *Wade v. United States*, 1970). Thus, the problem with the *Durham* "product" test is that it gives the medical experts too much control, taking away the function of the jury who should ultimately determine criminal responsibility.

We now come to the fourth test that many jurisdictions have adopted through legislative enactment. The American Law Institute (ALI) Model Penal Code formulation for negating criminal responsibility has been widely accepted in all federal circuits, except the First Circuit, and by approximately 26 other states either through case law or by statute. Considered by many to be a significant improvement over M'Naghten and other formulations, it has numerous advantages. First, the test attempts to move toward a formulation that is more realistic and conforms to the practical experience of forensic psychologists and psychiatrists, recognizing that either the volitional or cognitive aspects of an individual's processes may be impaired. Thus, an individual would be relieved of criminal responsibility if he or she lacked substantial capacity either to appreciate the wrongfulness of his or her conduct or to conform his or her conduct to the requirements of the law. Second, the test moves away from the absolute requirement of total incapacity and toward one that permits substantial incapacity. Third, the test encourages maximum informational input from expert witnesses while preserving to the jury its role as the trier of fact and ultimate decision-maker. However, despite wide enthusiasm for the ALI standard in the various jurisdictions, it has been criticized by some based on vagueness and the lack of specificity in such terms as "appreciate" and "substantial impairment" (Lafave and Scott, 1986). (Definitional variation is allowed, but the forensic expert should explicitly define these terms prior to testifying.) Nevertheless, the ALI test of criminal responsibility leads to a three-part test of insanity: (1) a genuine, sufficiently severe mental disorder; (2) a substantial impairment in the capacity of the accused to appreciate the wrongfulness of his or her acts and in his or her ability to conform his or her conduct to the requirements of the law; and (3) a demonstrated link between the two.

The expert should consider mitigating defenses concomitantly with an analysis of insanity. There are several reasons. First, consider that the need for a diagnostic formulation and a clear articulation of the mental condition of the accused by the evaluator in specific cases is explicit or implied from all tests of insanity. In most jurisdictions, to be successful, the insanity defense must be the result or effect of a disease of the brain. Emotional insanity unassociated with the brain or mental disease is not considered a defense. In other words, where one does not act under the duress of a diseased brain, but from motives of anger, revenge, or other passion, he or she cannot claim to be shielded from punishment for crime on grounds of insanity. Although a mental derangement often coexists with a disturbance of the emotions, affections, or other moral powers, it must be distinguished from an overwhelming emotion not growing out of and connected with a disease of the brain. The reasoning goes that emotion as such is not a defense in that its presence neither prevents the forming of a criminal intent nor renders the defendant incompetent to discern the nature and criminality of his or her act. Of course, most jurisdictions have laws relating to mitigation of certain violent crimes due to heightened emotion or "heat of passion." For example, murder can be reduced to manslaughter. The forensic evaluator must ascertain whether such circumstances apply in a particular case and should anticipate that both insanity and mitigating defenses may be raised simultaneously, as most jurisdictions do not specifically disallow this practice. In Hawaii, extreme mental or emotional disturbance (EMED) which, when successful, mitigates murder to manslaughter, there is authority that a defendant's mental illness may be considered at least as a factor in this type of mitigation (Hall, Mee, and Bresciani, 2001). The authors point out that theoretically it is impossible to disentangle the volitional arm of ALI from loss of self-control inherent in mitigating defenses characterized by intense emotion and impulsivity on the part of the defendant. Criminal attorneys can and should analyze relevant cases simultaneously for insanity and mitigation, although the point at which such defenses may be introduced in the criminal proceedings vary from jurisdiction to jurisdiction as a matter of law and trial strategy.

In most jurisdictions (including the authors'), "pathological intoxication" means intoxication that is grossly excessive in degree, given the amount of the intoxicant, to which the defendant does not know he or she is susceptible and which results from a physical abnormality of the defendant. As we shall see, pathological intoxication may act as an exculpating disorder to relieve criminal responsibility and hence must be addressed by the forensic expert. Moreover, even ordinary (i.e., nonpathological) intoxication does not automatically inculpate the defendant, if coupled with sufficiently severe mental conditions, as shown by case law in most jurisdictions.

Despite the recent publicity that methamphetamine abuse has engendered and its relation to sanity issues, the interplay between substance abuse and insanity is not a new issue. The same issue has long been presented to courts in connection with the abuse of alcohol and other drugs. While voluntary intoxication is not generally recognized as a defense to criminal conduct, the majority of courts that have considered the issue have held that "insanity" caused by long-term drug use is a defense to criminal conduct. (In some jurisdictions with "specific intent" crimes, voluntary intoxication can reduce a specific intent crime to a general intent crime.) Two notable exceptions are Colorado and Hawaii. The exceptions notwithstanding, it is widely held that the long-term, consistent abuse of drugs or alcohol may result in permanent mental disorders that are symptomatically similar to mental disorders caused by brain diseases. This condition has been called "fixed" or settled insanity. Therein lies the key to exculpation, as the mental conditions can serve as a basis for lack of criminal responsibility. The parameters of this defense differ slightly from state to state.

In *Barrett v. United States* (1976), the court took a more restrictive approach to the time issue in "settled insanity." In *Barrett*, the defendant was convicted of arson and second-degree murder for setting fire to a house. The appeal centered on the exclusion of certain proffered evidence regarding the defendant's alleged insanity at the time of the offense. This evidence included expert testimony that the defendant was suffering from stimulant toxic psychosis at the time of the crime, as well as lay testimony that the defendant had been abusing drugs for a substantial period of time and, for several days prior to the arson, had been high on drugs and had ingested drugs including cocaine on the day in question. While not deciding the issue of "settled insanity," the court noted that there was dicta in that jurisdiction that recognized that the voluntary ingestion of alcohol that produced permanent mental disease amounting to insanity may relieve an accused of responsibility. However, the court noted that there was no evidence in that case as to how long the insanity lasted past the ingestion of the drugs and whether it left the defendant with a mental condition more severe than the one he had before. Hence, there was no showing of permanent or fixed insanity. The court also noted that there was insufficient evidence that the drugs the defendant had ingested exacerbated an underlying mental disorder into a psychosis.

In sum, in *Barrett*, the evidence demonstrated that the defendant suffered from some form of a mental illness that was aggravated by the abuse of alcohol and other drugs. In addition, the evidence indicated that the defendant may have suffered from toxic psychosis caused by the abuse of alcohol and drugs at the time of the incident. Thus, the defendant could not avail himself of the insanity defense because his alleged insanity was voluntarily achieved through the abuse of intoxicants, such as alcohol and drugs. Moreover, save the two-day spree culminating in the assaults, there was no evidence of permanent impairment of the mind induced by repeated bouts of drunkenness. Unfortunately, it is not clear from the opinion if and for how long the defendant's psychosis lasted after he was no longer "intoxicated." The court's position was that even if the defendant suffered from a preexisting mental illness, if the voluntary use of intoxicants is established, then the defense is not available. The court reasoned that the contrary rule "would allow one to steel his nerves, blanket his conscience, and fortify his resolve by taking drugs in preparation for a criminal enterprise."

Similarly, in *State of Arizona v. Cooper* (1974), the defendant was charged with kidnapping and assault with a deadly weapon. The experts testified at trial that at the time of the crime, the defendant was not sane. However, they also testified that without the use of drugs at the time, he would have been sane. According to the experts, the defendant was suffering from drug-induced toxic psychosis at the time of the crime. The trial court held that the evidence did not raise an issue as to the defendant's sanity and refused to instruct the jury on the defense. On appeal, the Arizona Supreme Court noted: "The authorities have distinguished between an existing state of mental illness and a temporary episode of mental incapacity caused by the voluntary use of liquor or drugs. In the first instance the defense of insanity is available even though the state of mind may have been brought about by excessive or prolonged use of liquor or drugs, but in the latter instance the defense is not available." The court went on to hold that the defendant voluntarily took amphetamines for several days prior to the conduct in issue and that he was sane prior to the ingestion of these drugs. Because his subsequent condition was the result of an artificially produced state of mind brought on by his own hand and of his own choice, the defense of insanity was not available to him.

The defense was completely rejected in *Bieber v. People of Colorado* (1993). In *Bieber*, the defendant was charged and convicted of first-degree murder, robbery, and aggravated theft. At trial, he argued that he was not intoxicated at the time of the murder but was legally insane. He contended that he suffered from amphetamine delusional disorder (ADD). ADD was described as a disorder caused by the chronic use of amphetamines, resulting in the person becoming very paranoid and delusional. This condition usually abates in few days or weeks. The prosecution's psychiatric expert conceded that it was possible that the defendant did suffer from ADD, but that in his opinion the defendant suffered from an antisocial personality disorder that did not prevent him from knowing right from wrong at the time of the shooting. The defendant proffered a jury instruction, indicating that insanity produced by long-term use of amphetamines affects responsibility in the same way as insanity produced by any other cause if the mental disease or defect causing the insanity is "settled." "Settled" does not mean permanent or incurable but means that the mental disease or defect resulting in insanity exists independently of the contemporaneous use of the drug. Intoxication at the time of the crime does not negate the defense. The instruction further contended that it was immaterial that amphetamines caused the insanity, so long as it was of a settled nature at the time. The trial court rejected the instruction and presented the jury with the standard insanity instruction. It also instructed the jury that intoxication in itself does not constitute a mental disease or defect within the meaning of the insanity plea. The *Bieber* court noted that the doctrine of "settled insanity" had its roots in early nineteenth-century British law and was recognized by a federal court in *United States v. McGlue* (1851). Noting that the doctrine of "settled insanity" draws a distinction between voluntary intoxication universally recognized as not constituting a defense and "insanity" arising from the long-term use of intoxicants but separate from immediate intoxication, the Bieber court acknowledged that the substantial weight of precedent from other jurisdictions is to recognize the defense. The court specifically held that the intoxication was "self-induced" because the defendant voluntarily took the drug knowing its effect on him in that he had previously sought treatment because he feared hurting someone. The court went on to note that of the jurisdictions with similar intoxication statutes, including Hawaii, all of the states that had addressed the issue had allowed "settled insanity" as a defense.

The forensic expert should be aware of key legal cases in the expert's jurisdiction. For instance, as a last example in this section, in *State of Hawaii v. Young* (2000), the defendant was convicted of murder in the second degree in a jury-waived trial. The defendant went to a fast food restaurant in Honolulu. He approached the victim-employee who was sweeping the patio and asked him for money. When the employee refused, the defendant swore at him and walked away. The defendant retrieved a hammer from his truck and returned to the restaurant's patio. He approached the victim, pulled the hammer out from behind his back, and struck the victim on the back of the head. The defendant repeatedly hit him and continued to hit him even after the victim had fallen to the ground. There was also evidence that the defendant stopped and assessed the damage between blows. The defendant fled after the attack. At trial, the defendant's girlfriend testified that the defendant drank about eight beers and smoked two joints of marijuana a day. She also admitted that they had tried cocaine and methamphetamine, but the last time she had seen him, a few days before the killing, he had only consumed alcohol and marijuana. The trial court found the defendant guilty of murder in the second degree. It found that Young voluntarily drank up to 12 beers per day, voluntarily smoked up to three marijuana joints per day in the weeks leading up to the incident, and had been using other illegal drugs during the time and that the psychosis caused by drugs can last for months after the drug use stopped.

Methamphetamine psychosis can be triggered by the use of other substances. The court found that, at the time of the offense, Young "(1) was not schizophrenic, (2) suffered from a mental disease or defect that was caused by drugs or alcohol, and (3) was not suffering from brain damage or impaired neurological functioning." The court held that the defendant's mental disease or defect did not cause him to lack the substantial capacity to appreciate the wrongfulness of his conduct or to conform his conduct to the requirements of the law.

On appeal, the Hawaii Supreme Court noted that insanity is an affirmative defense and must be proved by the defendant by a preponderance of the evidence. Because pathological intoxication had not been argued at trial, the court found that Young waived the argument. The court, in dicta, noted that even if the issue had been preserved, the evidence clearly establishes that Young's long-term, voluntary polysubstance abuse does not meet the Hawaii statutory definition of pathological intoxication.

Young argued that a drug-induced or exacerbated mental illness in and of itself constitutes a criminal defense as a matter of law. The appellate court noted that this case did not present the issue of a preexisting mental illness aggravated by drug use because the trial court had found that Young's mental disease, disorder, or defect was caused by substance abuse. The court rejected Young's arguments that a drug-induced mental illness is a defense because such a defense would be contrary to the legislative intent underlying the statutory scheme regarding pathological intoxication and insanity. The court noted that the Legislature had amended the intoxication statue specifically prohibiting self-induced intoxication as a defense except in limited circumstances. The rationale behind this legislative position is that, when a person chooses to drink, that person should remain ultimately responsible for his or her actions. If an intoxicated person cannot escape ultimate responsibility for his actions, neither should a defendant who chronically engages in substance abuse. The court went on to state that: "Only in the instance when intoxication causes the person to lack the ability to form the requisite state of mind is intoxication a defense. The same is also true of someone who has a drug-induced mental illness."

Given the parallel between the standard for "insanity" and "involuntary intoxication," the use of psychotropic substances could be argued to lead to a lack of penal responsibility because the defendant suffers from pathological intoxication or because the defendant's drug use has caused him or her to suffer from a mental disease, defect, or disorder that prevents the person from understanding the nature of his or her conduct or conforming his or her conduct to the requirements of the law. The *Young* case seems to preclude the latter. However, the defense of "pathological intoxication" requires the additional elements that the intoxication is "grossly excessive in degree, given the amount of the intoxicant, to which the defendant does not know the defendant is susceptible and which results from a physical abnormality of the defendant." In *Young*, the Hawaii Supreme Court interpreted the legislative intent underlying the intoxication and insanity statues to preclude drug-induced mental illness as a defense. The court specifically did not, however, rule on the issue of a preexisting mental illness that is aggravated by drug use.

In the case example presented at the beginning of this chapter, the defense attorneys determined that the defendant was at a decided disadvantage in claiming pathological intoxication as well as any form of mitigation, given the planning and preparation for the burglary. Their strategy focused on raising the issue of insanity of which methamphetamine abuse and intoxication were only two of several possible severe conditions for the time of the alleged offenses. They decided to drop pathological intoxication and EMED as trial strategies when the evaluator found clear evidences of a cerebral injury.

The foregoing is a brief introduction to the legal issues. Forensic professionals should study the relevant statutes regarding criminal responsibility in their jurisdiction. Board certification in forensics and other training are available. The legal review, necessary for all anticipated testimony, should be seen as an opportunity to enhance learning. Clearly, it is vitally important for the forensic expert to understand the defenses of insanity, mitigation, pathological intoxication, and any variants that may apply in a particular jurisdiction. By conducting a legal review, an expert can determine how the court is likely to reason prior to fielding questions during cross-examination. Thus, the expert can be more responsive to the needs of the court.

Ethics

Forensic psychologists should be keenly aware of the salient ethical principles in a particular case and, if asked in court, be prepared to demonstrate how they conformed to these principles in their evaluation of the accused. A single ethical misjudgment can compromise the expert's credibility and raises the risk of the opposing attorney moving to strike the expert's entire testimony. Preparation for this daunting task includes knowledge of the current Ethical Principles of Psychologists and Code of Conduct (American Psychological Association, 2002), the Specialty Guidelines for Forensic Psychologists (Committee on Ethical Guidelines for Forensic Psychologists, 1991; Committee on the Revision of the Ethical Guidelines for Forensic Psychologists, 2006), knowledge of other applicable APA specialty codes, for example, in assessment and intervention, as well as ethical codes of conduct promulgated by other organizations of which the professional is a member and which are relevant to the case. The contributors to this book discuss the myriad ways in which the principles of competence, integrity, professional and scientific responsibility, respect for persons' rights and dignity, concern for the welfare of others, and social responsibility, albeit difficult to apply precisely and evolving over time, can be applied in forensic settings and situations. Particularly impressive are the discussions of principle and empirically driven ethics and practices, comprehensively explored in detail in the next chapter on capital mitigation evaluations by Geoffrey Marcyzk, Linda Knauss, Josh Kutinsky, David Dematteo, and Kirk Heilbrun.

One gift of forensics is that it provides frequent opportunities for the evaluator to recognize and act upon ethical issues. In the senior author's experience, the retaining attorney in forensic cases is almost always biased in the direction of his or her client's vested interests. While defense attorneys are supposed to be the defendant's advocate, the line between ethical and unethical behavior is wide and gray. Moreover, the code of ethics for attorneys, as promulgated by the American Bar Association, is obviously different in scope, content, and mandate from the APA Code of Ethics. Prosecutors are the representatives of the state and, because their goal is to obtain a conviction, they may become overzealous in the performance of their duties. Retention of their job as well as promotion may depend on their performance. Forensic professionals need to understand and accept these attitudes, and even be aware that some attorneys act as if experts, even their own, are really overpaid "prostitutes" whose job it is to provide (helpful) conclusions in the direction of their vested interests. Experts must be alert to incomplete or distorted information provided to them by the retaining party and upon discovery of new or additional material revise their conclusions if warranted. They must also be willing to decline to be retained by attorneys who persist in unethical behavior.

Ethical principles are ethical imperatives in the sense that their implementation is preeminent over all other considerations in a forensic evaluation. Proactively, the expert should go beyond a mere adherence to principles. For example, to realize the spirit of the ethical code(s) to which the expert owes allegiance, and in addition to a variety of suggestions for the expert presented later in this chapter, a list can be constructed consisting of every criminal case for which the expert has been retained and the percentage of cases for which the expert was retained by the prosecution and by the defense. Experts who have testified almost exclusively for one side or the other would tend to avoid compiling such a list as it may indicate a bias. Yet, the trier of fact has a right to know such information as it goes to the weight of the proffered testimony.

Utilizing the Empirical Literature

For every case, the forensic professional should be cognizant of the relevant empirical literature to (1) generate hypotheses for inquiry, (2) conform to case law, and (3) maintain credibility when testifying as an expert. Why is this so? As discussed later, a prime purpose is to conform to the court's standards for admissibility as an expert. The *Frye* (1923) test calls for the expert's testimony to be based on methodology that is generally accepted in the field before it can be admitted. *Frye* is subjective in interpretation, extraordinarily inclusive, and may be headed for the bone yard in favor of a new cluster of standards that are stricter, more transparent, and less subjective. Under Rule 702 of the Federal Rules of Evidence, for example, "the trial judge must ensure that any and all scientific testimony or evidence admitted is not only relevant, but reliable" (*Daubert*, 1995). Pursuant to Rule 104(a) of the Federal Rules of Evidence, when faced with a proffer of expert scientific testimony, the trial judge must first determine "whether the expert is proposing to testify to (1) scientific evidence that (2) will assist the trier of fact to understand or determine a fact in issue. This entails a preliminary assessment of whether the reasoning or methodology underlying the testimony is scientifically valid and whether that reasoning or methodology can be properly applied to the facts in issue" (*Daubert*, 1995). Among the factors to be considered in making this determination are (1) whether a theory or technique can be and has been tested, (2) whether the theory or technique has been subjected to peer review and publication, (3) the known or potential rate of error and the existence and maintenance of standards controlling the technique's operation, and (4) whether the theory or technique is generally accepted within a relevant scientific community. The focus of the court's inquiry "must be solely on principles and methodology, not on the conclusions that they generate" (*Daubert*, 1995).

Let us probe the *Daubert* test further in order to gain a flavor of the nonvoluntary and rigorous standards imposed on experts. On remand, the Ninth Circuit noted that, pursuant to the United States Supreme Court's ruling, the court:

> Must engage in a difficult, two-part analysis. First, we must determine nothing less than whether the experts' testimony reflects "scientific knowledge," whether their findings are "derived by the scientific method," and whether their work product amounts to "good science." Second we must ensure that the proposed expert testimony is "relevant to the task at hand," i.e., that it logically advances a material aspect of the proposed party's case.

The Supreme Court referred to this second prong of the analysis as the "fit requirement." The court's task is "to analyze not what the experts say, but what basis they have for saying it." To perform their "gatekeeping role," courts must satisfy themselves that scientific evidence meets a certain standard of reliability before it is admitted. This means that the expert's bald assurance of validity is not enough. Rather, the party presenting the expert must show that the expert's findings are based on sound science, and this will require some objective, independent validation of the expert's methodology. The Ninth Circuit noted that one very significant fact to be considered is whether the experts are proposing to testify about matters growing naturally and directly out of research they have conducted independently of the litigation, or whether they have developed their opinions expressly for purposes of testifying. That an expert testifies for money does not necessarily cast doubt on the reliability of his testimony, as few experts appear in court merely as an eleemosynary gesture. But in determining whether proposed expert testimony amounts to good science, we may not ignore the fact that a scientist's normal workplace is the laboratory or the field, not the courtroom or the lawyer's office. The fact that an expert's testimony is based on research conducted independently of the litigation "provides important, objective proof that the research comports with the dictates of good science." If the proffered expert testimony is not based on independent research, the party proffering the testimony must come forward with other objective, verifiable evidence that the testimony is based on "scientifically valid principles."

Forensic neuropsychologists and other experts with knowledge of the biobases of behavior are expected to be knowledgeable about empirical findings relevant to a particular case within their area of expertise. Indeed, there is no preclusion to cross-examination in special domains. Experts should fully describe their training and experience while being qualified as an expert witness and should resist the temptation to opine beyond the limits of their competence. By this rule, clinical forensic psychologists may also testify on the methamphetamine literature which falls under their training and experience.

In methamphetamine cases, when testifying, an expert should be prepared for basic questions underlying the action of the drug, its attendant features, and how the expert applied findings from the literature to the instant case. Again, the forensic professional answers only those questions to which he or she can respond with competence. The expert should not assume that the trier of fact knows that methamphetamine is toxic for most users, that its effects vary widely in individual cases, and that the deleterious effects are often affected by use of other substances and may even be mediated by social interactive and interpersonal variables (Yudko et al., 2003).

Courts tend to be keenly interested in methamphetamine time-related data as it goes to whether the defendant or others may have been under the influence of the drug at the time of the alleged offense. An extensive review of the literature (see Yudko et al., 2003; Yudko et al., in press) reveals that methamphetamines are rapidly absorbed orally and have a rapid onset of action, usually within 30–40 min of oral ingestion. Methamphetamine may also be taken intravenously, whereupon it has an immediate effect. Certain forms, the so-called designer methamphetamines, may be inhaled. Crystal methamphetamine taken intranasally has an onset time of 5–20 min. When crystal methamphetamine is smoked, it has an onset time of several seconds, a subjective feeling of intoxication for up to 8 h, and a half-life of 12–36 h. Demethylation, or the biochemical breakdown process caused by the presence of methamphetamine in the body, is conclusive evidence that methamphetamine is being detected and not some harmless analog.

Information regarding tolerance and sensitivity to the effects of methamphetamine is often less well known by the courts but has implications for understanding the substance abuse history of the defendant. Tolerance is defined as a diminished response to a drug after repeated administration. Increased tolerance generally indicates longer usage, and increases in methamphetamine doses from 5 to 1000 mg/day in a single year are not uncommon as a reflection of rapid tissue tolerance in methamphetamine users (Yudko et al., 2003). In the case of methamphetamine, tolerance to anorexic, hypothermic, cardiovascular, and reinforcing effects has been reported (Lewander, 1971; Perez-Reyes, White, McDonald, Hicks, Jeffcoat, Hill, and Cook, 1991). Reports from chronic methamphetamine users confirm a significant amount of tolerance to the euphoric effects of the drug (Kramer, Fischman, and Littlefield, 1967; Grinspoon and Hedblom, 1975), which tends to result in tremendous dose increases by chronic abusers. The physiological mechanism for tolerance to amphetamine use is unclear but seems to occur at the cellular level. An interesting effect of chronic methamphetamine abuse with other substances is cross-reverse tolerance, or cross-sensitization, which was originally defined as a hypersensitivity to stress (Robinson and Becker, 1986), but has come to be associated with hypersensitivity to a number of drugs as well. Substances producing methamphetamine-like effects reported in the literature include phenobarbital (an antiseizure medication), theophylline (a stimulant found in tea), methylphenidate (a compound commonly found in diet pills which is structurally different from methamphetamine but with methamphetamine-like stimulant properties), L-dopa (used in treatment of Parkinson's disease), bromocriptine (a compound with antidepressant properties), morphine, benzphetamine (a mixture of benzedrine and other methamphetamine compounds), ephedrine (a component of methamphetamine), cocaine, and caffeine (Ando, Hironaka, and Yanagita, 1986; Tadokoro and Kuribara, 1986). Caffeine-related methamphetamine effects have been documented in the literature on both animals and humans (Ando et al., 1986; Chait and Johanson, 1988; Fujii, Kuribara, and Tadokoro, 1990; Griffiths, Evans, Heishman, Preston, Sannerud, Wolf, and Woodson, 1990; Holtzman, 1987; Kuribara and Tadokoro, 1989; Kuribara, 1994; Mumford, Evans, Kaminski, Preston, Sannerud, Silverman, and Griffiths, 1994; Oliveto, Bickel, Hughes, Shea, Higgins, and Fenwick, 1992; Oliveto, Bickel, Hughes, Terry, Higgins, and Badges, 1993; Stern, Chait, and Johanson, 1989; White and Keller, 1984). The first author has observed that a significant number of polysubstance abusers are aware of this phenomenon and will deliberately attempt to recreate the effects of methamphetamine by using these substances when methamphetamine is unavailable. In *State of Hawaii v. Michael Lawrence* (2001), the defendant drank coffee to reexperience a methamphetamine-like rush, including on the day he dismembered the murder victim, a Kirby vacuum cleaner salesman who came to his house to demonstrate his wares.

Whether a defendant knew or should have known of the unpredictable effects of methamphetamine is often a concern of the trier of fact. There are a variety of factors that may cause the effect of the methamphetamine to be unpredictable, even in chronic abusers. Methamphetamine manufactured in clandestine laboratories is frequently impure (Kram, Kruegel, and Kruegel, 1977; Sinnema and Verweij, 1981). Toxic chemicals can be used as the precursors from which methamphetamine can be formed (e.g., ephedrine and pseudoephedrine, benzyl chloride, benzyl cyanide, and methylamine), as reagents, substances that react with precursors (e.g., hydriodic acid, iodine, mercuric chloride, and sodium cyanohydridoborate), or as solvents (e.g., ethanol, ethyl chloroform, and acetone). Residues of these substances may contaminate the final product. The court may be interested in knowing that most methamphetamine is not the clear, pure hydrochloride salt typically associated with the drug but contains impurities that can be identified by their color as follows (Yudko et al., 2003):

- Red: Methamphetamine from pseudoephedrine; the red coloring of the tablet was not washed away
- Orange: Ephedrine sulfate was used; the sulfate was reduced to sulfur

- Purple: The iodine from the phosphorus–iodine reaction was not chemically washed
- Green: Copper somehow made its way into the mixture, possibly because of the mixing vessel
- Brown: A tabulating agent or oxidized red coloring was present in the reduction

It is the authors' impression that in individual cases, the courts usually appreciate knowing of neuroimaging data that amplify or clarify findings from the evaluation. Buffenstein, Coel, and Combs (1997) used single photon emission computed tomography (SPECT) scanning to show brain deterioration in methamphetamine abusers that continued for months after abstinence following incarceration for a serious felony (see Figure 1.1). The two top scans show frontal and (left) lateral damage in a 24-year-old methamphetamine abuser, while the bottom frontal view of a normal brain in a young adult male is presented for comparison.

Polydrug abuse is the rule rather than the exception in adult offenders (Kassebaum and Chandler, 1994). Addicts commonly use alcohol, a central nervous system suppressant, to decrease the effects of amphetamines, especially during withdrawal periods. For

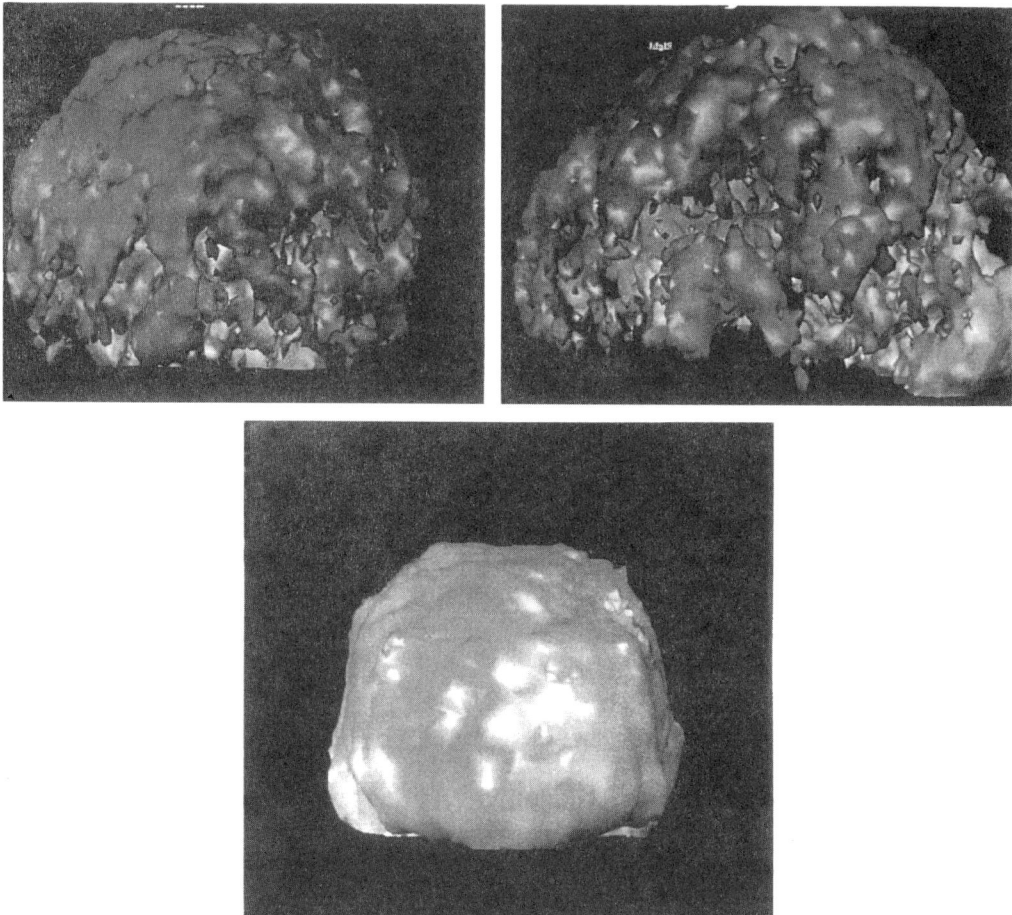

Figure 1.1 SPECT scans and methamphetamine use.

Defendant Smith, from 1972 to 1975, he smoked marijuana and inhaled glue and gasoline. Starting in 1968, he inhaled gasoline approximately 30 times. Starting at the age of 8,
he began smoking marijuana and estimates that, over his lifetime, he smoked marijuana
approximately 4000 times. He started drinking alcohol at the age of 12 and had been
drinking alcohol regularly since he was 14 years old. He drank at least a couple of beers
a day and more typically drank a six-pack of beer in combination with other drugs when
given the opportunity. Over the years, he passed out several times from drinking alcohol
(particularly vodka). He typically drank alcohol until he "dropped," or used alcohol to
come down after a methamphetamine high. In 1976, he lost consciousness after falling off
a motorcycle and hitting his head, not protected by a helmet. During that year, he started
abusing heroin by first inhaling and in later years injecting the drug. He overdosed on
heroin in 1980 and almost died. He estimated that he used heroin approximately 50 times
before stopping. In 1984, he also started using lysergic acid diethylamide (LSD) and estimated that he used LSD approximately 100 times between 1984 and 1996. From 1984 to
1985, he abused cocaine and mushrooms. Between 1984 and 1986, he used barbiturates
about 10 times and also got high on whipped cream by inhaling the gas to give him a giddy
feeling about 10 times. Defendant Smith reported that over the years, his auditory hallucinations worsened when he drank alcohol or ingested any kind of drug. He hastened to add
that he also heard voices when he was not high on any substance.

The trier of fact is naturally interested in what symptoms are associated with
methamphetamine both generally and for a particular defendant. The clinical symptoms
of methamphetamine use are primarily sympathomimetic in nature and are well documented in the empirical literature (Tadokoro and Kuribara, 1986; Rothrock, Rubenstein,
and Lyden, 1988; Sachdeva and Woodward, 1989; DeVito and Wagner, 1989; Tohhara,
Kato, and Nakajima, 1990; Beebe and Walley, 1995; Ando et al., 1986; Ashizawa, Saito,
Yamamoto, Shichinohe, Ishikawa, Maeda, Toki, Ozawa, Watanabe, and Takahata, 1996;
Chuck, Williams, Goldberg, and Lubniewski, 1996; Logan, Weiss, and Hurruff, 1996;
Peltier, Li, Lytle, Taylor, and Emmett-Oglesby, 1996; Wolkoff, 1997). At low doses, methamphetamine causes generally positive effects, such as increased alertness, energy, euphoria,
elevated self-confidence, persistent activity and work, increased talkativeness, increased
sexual pleasure and hypersexuality, a sense of well-being, increased strength, and a loss of
appetite. The ego-syntonic, pleasurable nature of methamphetamine intoxication explains
its persistence as well as the addictive cycle that usually emerges. The increase in violence
potential and the decrease in reality testing are associated with increasing dosages.

Higher doses of methamphetamine may result in negative symptoms such as disorganized or purposeless physical activity, tremors, muscle tics, slurred speech, muscle spasms
(hyperflexia), motor instability, incoordination, gait ataxia, bruxism (i.e., teeth grind-
ing), and athetosis (e.g., strange motor movements). Affective symptoms include agitation, restlessness, rage, panic, and anxiety. Somatic sensations include numbness of the
skin and limbs. Hallucinations may occur as well as strong feelings of paranoia with a
severe amphetamine-induced psychosis. Most high doses of methamphetamine are associated with a clear sensorium. Violent behavior toward others with increased risk-taking
behavior has been observed frequently. Hyperthermia (extreme rise in body temperature)
is common. At high dosages, difficulty with urination, irregular heartbeat, convulsions,
stroke, coma, and death have occurred.

Chronic use can have very different effects when compared with acute administration. This is because neurochemical changes occur in the brain after repeated drug

administration. Thus, chronic administration of a drug can lead to behavioral changes even when the user is not actively under the influence of the drug. Acute effects of a drug that has been administered chronically (i.e., when a chronic user stops using for a period of time and then starts again) can also have different effects from acute effects of a drug that has not been administered chronically. This sequence occurs potentially because the drug can alleviate withdrawal.

Chronic symptoms of methamphetamine use include motor problems, depression, irritability, fatigue, exhaustion, and formication (delusions of insects crawling on the skin). Persisting neuropsychological symptoms associated with chronic methamphetamine use have been noted in animal and human investigations. Symptoms include visual–spatial disturbances, memory encoding and retrieval problems, lowered attention and concentration (especially selective attention), and executive dysfunction such as delayed responses and perseveration. A long-lasting amotivational syndrome, probably associated with dopamine depletion, often sets in. Circadian variations upset the sleep–wakefulness cycle. Flashbacks associated with threatening stimuli have been noted. Symptoms similar to paranoid schizophrenia, a disorganized lifestyle, persistent delusions, poor judgment, and irresponsibility have been observed. As discussed earlier, the user may realize that visual and auditory hallucinations stem from methamphetamine use but will continue with the pathological behavior anyway. A diminished social life with compromised coping abilities is a natural consequence. Fatal liver, heart, kidney, and lung disorders, as well as brain injury due to cerebral bleeds and other factors, have been implicated. There is a lowered resistance to disease. Acne, sores, corneal ulcerations, and skin disorders such as dry, itchy skin may occur. As alluded to earlier, a chronic reverse tolerance (i.e., sensitivity) may develop. Weight loss is usually striking, along with malnutrition, avitaminosis, and other problems in nutrition and appetite.

There is a common belief among health-care providers and workers in the criminal justice system that amphetamine has a dose-dependent effect on aggressive behavior. Research shows, however, that D-amphetamine has quite different effects that vary in accordance with species, the dose of amphetamine, and the type of stimuli used. Varying quantities of amphetamine will have diverse effects on the treated subject, otherwise known as biphasic effects. It is interesting to note that the frequency of escape and defensive responses to threat during times of social conflict was increased in a dose-dependent manner in a much less ambiguous way (Miczek and Tidey, 1989). Aggressive and defensive responses are mediated by very different neurological systems. Thus, one possible explanation for the perception that amphetamine leads to aggressive behavior may be a misperception of the nature of aggressive behavior. Caseworkers may be calling "defensive" responses "aggressive" responses. Yet, in a self-report study involving amphetamine users from a metropolitan city in Australia, Vincent, Shoobridge, Ask, Allsop, and Ali (1998) reported that more than one-third of the sample comprising 100 participants had experienced symptoms of depression and anxiety prior to their amphetamine use, and nearly one-third had experienced previous mood swings and aggressive outbursts. In addition, some of the participants believed that their usage had intensified these conditions, and almost a quarter of the subjects felt symptoms of depression and anxiety attacks for the first time after they started using the drug, although not all of them associated these symptoms with their amphetamine use. However, other research shows decreases in fatigue, increases in vigor, no significant changes in anger or confusion, and a moderate decrease in depression (Cherek, Steinberg, Kelly, and Robinson, 1986). Different subjects from separate studies also show signs of excessive confidence and delusional paranoia (Wright and Klee, 2001). Thus, in individual cases, from a practical standpoint, it is important for the forensic evaluator to take into account the violence history of the defendant when using and not using methamphetamine or other drugs (Wright and Klee, 2001).

An individual's history of drug use, lifestyle, and social status and interactions are all possible influences on his or her drug habits and aggressive patterns of behavior. Wright and Klee (2001) reported some interesting points in the area of amphetamine-related human aggressive behavior. For instance, correlations between amphetamine use and aggression are strongly associated with drug dealing rather than intoxication. Moreover, in regard to the subjects' patterns of amphetamine use, there were no significant differences between those who reported aggression and the rest of the sample, and no straightforward relationship could be found between amphetamine use and one's potential for aggressive behavior.

This brief discussion of the literature indicates that the connection between amphetamine use and aggressive behavior or even other problems is ambiguous and complex, with no inviolate conclusions. Thus, the forensic expert cannot state with confidence that methamphetamine use always causes violence or any other effect but can state that use increases the risk of relevant symptoms. Because the possession, use, and distribution of amphetamine are illegal and because the compound causes brain damage, ethical concerns have prevented experimental research on the behavioral effects of amphetamine. The available literature on the effects of amphetamine in human participants is all correlational. Although there have been reports of high correlations between violent crime and amphetamine use, these studies may be confounded because other drugs such as alcohol are often involved, and users who commit these acts sometimes have aggressive tendencies beforehand (Wright and Klee, 2001). The existing literature does give some indication regarding the effects of various doses and the possible predictions one can make concerning the long-term effects on mental health, but until more research can be performed, our understanding of the relationship of amphetamine on human behavior is limited. These observations notwithstanding, the expert can utilize the literature to obtain hypotheses for study in individual cases and testify as to the results of that comparison. The trier of fact must still weigh the value of the evidence presented by the expert and is under no obligation to utilize the expert's testimony on methamphetamine to any significant degree. Nevertheless, the expert's obligation to educate the court in this area remains constant.

The Expert's Decision Path

In our opinion, the heart and soul of what mental health experts have to offer to the courts is the experts' reasoning about a particular case. As we have seen from the *Daubert* standards, courts are keenly interested in how experts came to their conclusions. This implies that a retrospective decision path or chain of reasoning for virtually every forensic opinion proffered by the expert can be formulated. To increase the chances of verdicts favorable to the party who retained the expert, we recommend that the expert's decision path be proactively presented in court and not have to be drawn out in cross-examination. The idea is to convince the trier of fact that the chain of reasoning is valid and, after competing hypotheses to explain the data are discussed, demonstrably superior to contrary expert opinions.

A decision path emerges regarding criminal responsibility evaluations. As we have seen, a simple three-part decision sequence is inherent in the ALI test of insanity: (1) a mental condition must be proffered; (2) a determination must be made as to whether a substantial impairment existed at the time of the alleged offense; and (3) to assert lack of criminal responsibility, a link must be established between the mental condition and any substantial impairment.

The *Rogers Criminal Responsibility Assessment Scales* (R-CRAS, Rogers, 1984; see also Rogers and Shuman, 2000), one of which addresses ALI standards in particular, presents an explicit decision path to include a determination as to whether malingering was present (if "yes," then a conclusion must be proffered that the accused was criminally responsible). Using the RCAS, a determination can be made as to whether the accused suffered from cerebral injury as differentiated from a nonorganic mental disorder, but both of these constitute a mental disorder. Likewise, a cognitive and volitional impairment can be differentiated from each other, but both are subsumed under the category of substantial impairment. Rogers showed correlational data indicating a 90%+ agreement between trial verdicts and outcomes from his empirically based decision tree with the recommended guidelines.

Rogers and his colleagues' retrospective decision path can be expanded to reflect forensic realities (Hall, 1985; Hall and Hall, 1987; Hall and Sbordone, 1993; Yudko et al., 2003; Yudko et al., in press). Put in the form of eight basic questions by the authors, these steps demand yes/no answers to the following:

1. Has an adequate forensic database been obtained?
2. Have unintentional distortion and deliberate deception been examined?
3. Was the defendant personally evaluated and able to reconstruct the incident?
4. Has long-term (i.e., historical) versus instant crime behavior been compared?
5. Has a sufficiently Severe Diagnostic and Statistical Manual, Fourth Edition, Text Revision (DSM-IV-TR) mental disorder(s) been diagnosed?
6. Were self-determination and choice of crime-related behaviors present?
7. Has a link between mental condition(s) and self-determination been established?
8. Are the proffered conclusions capable of replication by independent examiners?

The first recommended step involves the creation of a reliable and valid database, multisourced and interdisciplinary in nature, which forms the basis for all conclusions. Forensic examiners are limiting their database and therefore the soundness of their conclusions as well as their credibility if they ignore relevant information. A comprehensive database is obtained by examining the perpetrator, victim, and context of the alleged offense(s). As investigation reports are never perfect, it is highly recommended that experts examine the scene of the incident and personally inspect the evidence in the police property room.

Concerning methamphetamine issues, it is especially important to gather data from sources that the defendant may wish to conceal because of the likelihood of uncovering unfavorable information (e.g., juvenile records; "expunged" records, which are usually available in most jurisdictions in unredacted form at government archive centers and which experts are entitled to review; interviews with peers, ex-spouses, and mates; disciplinary actions in the military; information from other states or countries).

For Defendant Smith, the following significant/knowledgeable others were interviewed:

1. His mother
2. His maternal aunt
3. His maternal uncle
4. A friend of the victim family
5. His work supervisor
6. His previous probation officer
7. His girlfriend
8. His sister

In addition to inspecting the scene of the incident, Defendant Smith was examined four times with the following measures for a total of approximately 15 hours of direct contact:

1. Clinical Interviews and Mental Status Evaluation
2. Minnesota Multiphasic Personality Inventory-2 (MMPI-2)
3. Millon's Clinical Multiaxial Inventory-III (MCMI-III)
4. Multiphasic Sex Inventory
5. Stroop Color and Word Test
6. Standard Progressive Matrices (Ravens)
7. California Memory Test
8. Clock Draw
9. CEP Aphasia Screening
10. Wahler Physical Symptoms Inventory (twice for present and 1 week before the alleged offenses)
11. Sensory Perceptual Examination (Vision, Audition)
12. Wechsler Memory Test—Revised (Digit Span, Mental Control, Logical Memory I and II, and Recognition Testing)
13. Incomplete Sentence Blank (Rotter)
14. Boston–Rochester Neuropsychological Screening Test (Metaphors and Proverbs, Orientation, Repetition, Word List Generation, Praxis, Presidents, Visual Immediate, Delayed and Recognition Recall, Copy and Narrative Writing)
15. Tactile Performance Test
16. Cancellation Test
17. Psychopathy Checklist—Revised (PCL-R)
18. Shipley Institute of Living Scale
19. Suicide Probability Scale
20. Visual Organization Test (Hooper)
21. Wechsler Adult Intelligence Scale-III (WAIS-III)
22. California Verbal Learning Test (CVLT)
23. Cognitive Estimation Test
24. HCL-20 (Historical, Clinical, Risk Management)
25. Violence Risk Appraisal Guide (VRAG)
26. Hare Psychopathy Checklist—Revised
27. Stress Audit (completed as homework)
28. Mooney Problem Checklist (completed as homework)
29. Personal Problems Checklist for Adults (completed as homework)

The second step in the retrospective decision process in criminal responsibility evaluations consists of ruling out or accounting for unintentional distortion within (a) the evaluator, (b) the reporting person, and (c) the reported event. Unintentional distortion due to anxiety, fatigue, cerebral injury, psychosis, or other factors may largely explain both evaluation and crime behavior and is therefore considered before deliberate deception is analyzed. Nondeliberate distortion for the methamphetamine user at the time of the instant offense may consist of several simultaneously operating factors. As examples, time perception tends to speed up, resulting in unreliable estimates of time; short-term memory problems, including encoding and retrieval difficulties (Yudko et al., 2003). If distortion is suspected, observations should be cross-validated with other information. Data derived from the input of significant or knowledgeable others which indicate bias or a given motivational set (e.g., fear, desire for revenge, and desire to be reunited with the defendant) should be reported but likewise compared with other known facts.

Possible deception by the defendant is extraordinarily important in determining the accuracy of database information. Three chapters in this book are devoted to the issue of "faking" in clinical, criminal, and civil contexts, and other chapters address deception as it pertains to the focus of the chapter. There are two basic types of deception—malingering ("faking bad") and denial/minimizing ("faking good")—from which all other response styles stem, and literally dozens of methods to detect faking. Failure to perform a deception analysis may, in our opinion, fatally flaw an expert's opinions. To meet the demands of our decision path, a finding of deliberate deception should be ruled in by a positive and replicable demonstration of misrepresentation.

The evaluation of the defendant's self-reports in methamphetamine cases should be scrutinized for misrepresentation by examining third-party reports and material evidence of the crime. Psychometric testing of the accused by objective measures, such as the MMPI-2, California Personality Inventory (CPI), 16-PF, and the MCMI-III, are appropriate for assessing deception due to the embedded scales that measure response set. Clinical behavior, forced choice testing, arousal methods, and others can also be utilized. There are compelling reasons to suggest that the incidence of malingering may be high in methamphetamine cases. First, the chances of malingering increase with genuine deficiencies (Hall and Pritchard, 1996), and methamphetamine use creates significant cognitive and psychological deficiencies in many abusers. Second, it is our impression that most defendants know by the time they appear in court that substance intoxication or abuse will not remove penal responsibility. Thus, it is not in the best interests of most defendants to admit to substance intoxication or abuse at the time of the alleged offense. Instead, the defendant may, as seen by the authors in a number of cases, deliberately minimize methamphetamine use and exaggerate or fabricate psychotic features of his or her behavior.

In the Smith case, the defendant was oriented to time, place, person, and circumstance and exhibited a logical and coherent stream of thought during the four examination periods. He was focused and persistent on all tasks. Overall results indicated deception. Results on the validity scale on the Wahler Physical Symptoms Inventory suggested that he likely embellished his symptoms. There was no indication of malingering memory problems on the California Memory Test. On the Multiphasic Sex Inventory, he showed substantial deception in the areas of child molestation, rape, and exhibitionism, similar to testees who were "frankly dishonest." On the MMPI-2 validity indicia, he showed faking bad as the dominant response set. On the MCMI-III validity indicia, he scored in a similar manner, essentially endorsing items reflecting psychopathology that could not possibly be true (e.g., he endorsed "I hear voices 24 hours a day, even when I am asleep"; "I can run a mile in less than 3 minutes"). The clinical and historical information he presented on when the auditory hallucinations started appeared to have been fabricated. Importantly, he did not claim psychotic signs for the time of the alleged offenses.

As a third step in evaluating for criminal responsibility, contact with and knowledge of a defendant's recollection of an alleged crime is essential in inferring his or her state of mind. Although state of mind can often be inferred from eyewitness accounts, material evidence, and reports of third parties, the defendant's own description of events is critical in establishing mental condition, awareness of wrongdoing, and ability to conform his or her conduct to the requirements of the law. To diagnose an accused with a mental disorder, it is assumed in all versions of the Diagnostic and Statistical Manual that interviewing and testing by an expert has been conducted; otherwise in our opinion it would fatally compromise the credibility of the expert who diagnosed a mental disorder without first-hand contact with the accused. Reviews of the literature reveal that faked memories or loss of memories is common in homicide cases, especially when substance use or severe psychiatric conditions are involved, ranging up to 60% of the murder defendants (Hall and Pritchard, 1996; Hall and Poirier, 2002). A deception analysis should focus on suspected memory loss; for example, the test protocol and notes of the opposing expert can be obtained (by subpoena) and reexamined for the defendant's reconstruction of events.

The expert should be aware of whether, in the jurisdiction in which the case is tried, a defendant's statements can be admitted only as evidence of state of mind, or, in addition, as evidence that the accused committed the crime. Discussed in detail later, the accused should be informed of the purpose of the evaluation. If the accused declines to be evaluated by an expert, that professional must refrain from proffering conclusions relevant to criminal responsibility. The expert may, however, comment on the methodology of the other examiners, as in *Young*, and present information to the court from the literature on issues germane to the case at hand.

The fourth step involves conducting a historical analysis of relevant past behavior and comparing it with that shown by the accused during the instant offense. The goal is to determine whether the instant offense is typical or atypical of the defendant. Rare events are most likely triggered by high stress or an unusual combination of environmental or internal events. Frequent bad acts, especially those that are predatory or proactive in nature, suggest a habitual pattern—as in psychopathy—and are considered more inculpatory. For methamphetamine case, a key question is whether basal violence associated with the use of the drug, especially when that violence is similar to the instant offense, was a typical result of the use of methamphetamine or an isolated event under poor control. A difficulty emerges when the judge rules against bringing in prior bad acts. If such is the case, the expert must determine whether the same conclusions can be proffered, absent the disallowed history.

Defendant Smith's methamphetamine use started in 1984 and continued until 1996, during which period he estimated that he used methamphetamine a phenomenal 1800 times. He recalled injecting, smoking, inhaling, or drinking methamphetamine in juice almost every day when given the opportunity. He twice overdosed on methamphetamine and lost consciousness. When methamphetamine was not available, he drank coffee in prodigious amounts. Smith once left home because he was wanted by the police for drug-related activities. According to the defendant's mother, when he returned to his home state in approximately 1994, he lived at her house. She reported several instances where Smith threw objects at the wall (he once threw the telephone when she was talking to a friend), but stated that the defendant would never hurt her. She reported that he once punched his sister in the face. In 1995, Smith began serving six and a half years in prison for raping his "niece." His mother reported that he had threatened the victim's life if she told anyone of the sexual assault. When questioned about this incident, Smith stated that he was smoking "ice" with the victim (his adopted sister) and that he had indeed threatened her, stating, "Be quiet, or I'll kill you." The victim became isolatory and depressed and confined herself to her bedroom, which then alerted Smith's mother that something was wrong. Defendant Smith's mother also reported that she called the police on occasion due to her fear of her son. She stated that his ongoing substance abuse was a contributory factor to his going to prison. According to Defendant Smith, while in prison, he was involved in two "big" fights. During one of the fights, he was knocked unconscious and was choked.

As a fifth step, and the most straightforward and comfortable for the forensic evaluator, a diagnosis of the defendant for the time of the crime usually requires evidence in support of a DSM-IV mental condition. It is our impression that defense experts commonly offer dual or multiple diagnoses to the court, and that a diagnosis such as methamphetamine intoxication or abuse is rarely offered alone because the examiner (along with the accused) may have a vested interest in finding a lack of criminal responsibility and knows that voluntary substance abuse is not effective in achieving a favorable outcome. The possibilities for methamphetamine-related diagnoses in DSM-IV-TR (American Psychiatric Association, 2000) are listed under amphetamine or amphetamine-like disorders because of common properties and general arousal effects.

An expert's diagnosis of methamphetamine abuse or dependence for the time of an alleged offense does not imply that the affected person was under the influence of that drug during the commission of the alleged crime. A DSM diagnosis of methamphetamine intoxication for a particular time requires that the substance cause an altered state of consciousness, clinically significant maladaptive behavioral or psychological changes, and two or more focal signs (e.g., tachycardia or bradycardia, pupillary dilation, motor agitation, or retardation). Finally, the symptoms are not due to a general medical condition and are not better accounted for by another mental disorder. The diagnosis should specify whether delusions or perceptual disturbances (e.g., hallucinations and sensory illusions) occurred.

A diagnosis proffered for the time of the incident operates independently of whether or not it also existed prior to or after the crime. Evidence of a chronic mental disorder (e.g., schizophrenia, mental retardation, or cognitive disorder) in existence before the instant offense increases the likelihood that the disorder also existed at the time of the crime, but is not sufficient by itself to establish that it was present in its disabling forms during the incident. Some chronic mental disorders can be in remission or can be controlled with psychotropic medications. Evidence of a mental disorder (e.g., depression and anxiety disorder) that arose after the instant crime is irrelevant to a diagnosis at the time of the offense.

For Defendant Smith, the following mental conditions from the DSM-IV-TR (2000) were operative at the time of the evaluation (in DSM-IV-TR, methamphetamine disorders are listed as amphetamine-related conditions):

Axis I	Amphetamine Abuse, in institutional remission
	Cognitive Disorder NOS
	(Rule out) Pedophilia
	Depressive Disorder NOS
Axis II	Personality Disorder NOS, with psychopathic traits
Axis III	Status postcerebral injuries over the years from severe polysubstance abuse and closed head trauma from fighting/accidents
Axis IV	Severity of stressors: Extreme problems in general ability to function, financial, legal, and social problems
Axis VI	Current Global Assessment of Functioning (GAF) = 20 (danger of hurting himself inadvertently through accident proneness or deliberate injury)
	Highest GAF level over past year = 20

The diagnoses for the time of the alleged offenses were the same. In addition, Defendant Smith was retrospectively diagnosed as methamphetamine intoxicated, having smoked a considerable amount of ice for a prolonged period of time. At the time of the alleged offenses, he may have been mildly alcohol intoxicated.

Defendant Smith likely had some form of mild cerebral injury. His scores indicated borderline intelligence on the nonverbal, cross-culturally derived Ravens Test which presents different visual patterns of increasing difficulty (37R, seventh percentile). The Ravens is generally a good measure of intellectual "g," as well as a measure of visual organization. On the Shipley Institute of Living Scale, which correlates quite closely with overall WAIS-R results, he obtained an Estimated Full Scale WAIS-R IQ of 103. His Abstraction Score was above average (60T, 84th percentile), but his Vocabulary Score on this test was substantially lower (46T, 30–35th percentile). On the Halstead–Reitan Neuropsychological Test Battery (HRNTB), he obtained an impairment index of .6, meaning that approximately 60% of the test results were in the brain damaged range. The premorbid indicators on the WAIS-R and other tests showed some scatter but were overall in the average or above average range. Together with his impairment index, a mild, static, probably diffuse brain injury in a person who has a significant history of cerebral insult was suggested. Findings from the evaluation included (1) overall average verbal intelligence but borderline nonverbal intelligence; (2) adequate attention and concentration but with deterioration under increased complexity; (3) adequate and in fact above average verbal memory skills with particular problem in proactive inhibition; (4) average nonverbal memory for both simple and complex designs; (5) some deficiencies in his sensory-perceptual and motor abilities, for example, on the TPT, his total time in placing blocks in a form board and his left-handed performance, the mild impairment on this latter test suggesting right hemisphere involvement; (6) essentially spared speech and language skills, but his fund of information and knowledge of word meaning, probably a function of his impoverished education, were below expectation given his overall average intelligence. Verbal memory and nonverbal memory skills were also spared; mild impersistence in verbal fluency (i.e., word list generation), along with difficulty alternating between numbers and letters on a visual-spatial sequencing task; (7) borderline/low average abstraction skills. His cognitive estimation ability for numbers was mildly impaired. His Digit Symbol score was low average; and (8) maladjusted personality disorder along with current depression and stress. He was considered a moderate suicide risk, and antidepressant medication and supportive counseling were recommended.

The above patterns of strengths and deficiencies for Defendant Smith were consistent with the long-term effects of cerebral insult due to fighting and accidents, as well as from severe and chronic polysubstance abuse. Given these historical factors and his frequent use of a substance known to cause cognitive deficiencies, it would be surprising if he had shown no indicia of cerebral injury during testing. Overall, his brain impairment was considered to be mild on a scale of negligible, minimal, mild, moderate, and severe, but was at least moderately deficient in terms of judgment and adaptive level of functioning. The expert should note that the existence of a mental disorder at the time of the alleged offense may or may not shed any light on the defendant's (legal) blameworthiness. The severity of the disorder and its impairment of critical faculties at the time of the offense mediate its exculpatory effect.

Defendant Smith was diagnosed on Axis II with Personality Disorder NOS with psychopathic features. On the Hare Psychopathy Checklist—Revised, he showed historical and behavioral tendencies for the following: (1) need for stimulation/proneness to boredom (likes risky activities, may discontinue routine tasks); (2) poor behavioral controls, short temperedness, hypersensitivity; (3) early behavior problems as a child or young adolescent; (4) lack of realistic long-term goals (in the past, not overly concerned about the future, and living day-by-day); (5) impulsivity, acting before thinking because he felt like it, unreflecting; (6) irresponsibility (fails to honor obligations, commitments, problems with loyalty); (7) criminal versatility (applies to entire life pattern of law-breaking); (8) promiscuous sexual behavior, part and parcel of his previous lifestyle, along with several short-term relationships; (9) glibness, superficial charm along with low anxiety for this trait in mild amounts; (10) lying and prevarication, with minimal embarrassment when caught; (11) conning/manipulative behavior in many areas—drugs, sex, money, etc.; (12) some indications of lack of guilt or remorse. He experiences remorse but he has a tendency to project blame; (13) callous/lack of empathy for others, including victims, disregarding the feelings, thoughts or welfare of others; and (14) failure to accept true responsibility for his own actions. He used excuses or denied or minimized faults. His score of 28 placed him in the moderately elevated level of psychopathology.

As a sixth step, the analysis of self-control and choice exhibited by the accused is central to the determination of criminal responsibility. Intact self-regulation for the time of the alleged crime, which can exist along with delusional or hallucinatory behavior, often leads to a finding of criminal responsibility. When complex self-regulation is uncovered by the expert, the trier of fact is likely to ask: "How can the accused claim substantial impairment when there was a demonstrated ability to plan and orchestrate the incident?" Conversely, impaired self-control frequently results in exculpation or mitigation of responsibility for the instant offense. The evaluator should analyze the instant offense for the defendant's abilities and deficits in areas relevant to behavioral self-regulation, keeping in mind that a sole focus on a defendant's limitations and deficiencies is a fundamental mistake by limiting information in a case.

The alleged offenses can be analyzed for the defendant's abilities and deficits in areas relevant to behavioral self-regulation. For many of these self-regulatory parameters, statistically derived scores on an empirically validated, Likert-scale format can be obtained from the

Rogers Criminal Responsibility Scale (R-CRAS; Rogers, 1984). Using the R-CRAS variables, the following parameters were considered and results found for Defendant Smith.

1. Reliability of defendant's self-report under his voluntary control. This was rated a reliable self-report; Defendant Smith reported information in a factual, sincere manner. He also volunteered potentially self-damaging information but glossed over a few details. Within a reliable self-report, however, there were a few instances of suspected malingering. For example, his presentation of hearing "voices" did not conform to what is known about auditory hallucinations, and his offering that he "tweaked" just prior to attacking the victims was convenient but not congruent with his degree of reported consumption (i.e., it was too soon to "tweak," given the usual pattern).

2. Involuntary interference with defendant's self-report. This was rated a minimal involuntary interference, slight or suspected organic interference of doubtful clinical significance, to mild involuntary interference in terms of clear evidence of peripheral impairment. Even here, Defendant Smith answered most questions with a fair degree of accuracy. There was difficulty with details, especially with times and dates, and there were distortions in a few specific areas.

3. Level of intoxication at the time of the alleged crimes. This was rated severe, in that there was a major impairment in reasoning and actions due to methamphetamine intoxication.

4. Evidence of brain damage or disease. This was rated between suspected brain damage where there is fairly reliable evidence based on observation or marginal evidence from neuropsychological testing to definite brain damage of a mild degree, based on the neuropsychological test findings, history, and clinical presentation in its entirety.

5. Relationship of brain damage to the commission of the alleged crimes. The mild brain damage, if cross-validated, was not seen as having a relationship to the commission of the alleged offenses.

6. Mental retardation. No mental retardation.

7. Relationship of mental retardation to the commission of the alleged crimes. No mental retardation.

8. Observable bizarre behavior of the time of the alleged crimes. No bizarre behavior other than the alleged crimes themselves.

9. General level of anxiety of the time of the alleged crimes. Mild-to-moderate anxiety secondary to the effects of methamphetamine as well as the circumstances of the alleged offenses was indicated.

10. Amnesia for the alleged crimes. None. Defendant Smith recalled the entire incident in considerable detail.

11. Delusions at the time of the alleged crimes. Absent.

12. Hallucinations at the time of the alleged crimes. Absent.

13. Depressed mood at the time of the alleged crimes. Absent. He was intoxicated, not depressed.

14. Elevated or expansive mood at the time of the alleged crimes. Absent.

15. Defendant's level of verbal coherence at the time of the alleged crimes. No impairment in speech.

16. Intensity and appropriateness of affect during the commission of the alleged crimes. Strong-to-extreme expression of emotion, appropriate to the effects of methamphetamine.

17. Evidence of formal thought disorder at the time of the alleged crimes. None. However, symptoms associated with methamphetamine use often mimic paranoid schizophrenia.

18. Planning and preparation for the alleged crimes. Some planning which lacked specific details and time tables, little or no preparation.

19. Awareness of criminality during the commission of the alleged crimes. Relatively complete awareness of the criminality of the alleged offenses with a general understanding of the possible penalties. Defendant Smith made concerted efforts to avoid discovery and showed other indicia of awareness.

20. Focus of the alleged crimes in terms of how intentional the defendant was in choosing and selecting the purpose and situation of the alleged crimes. Markedly specific; Defendant Smith's actions were highly focused toward time, persons, and situation.

21. Level of activity in commission of the alleged crime. Moderate to marked. Required a concerted and high sustained level of activity.

22. Responsible social behavior during the week prior to the commission of the alleged crime. Average functioning at work and with friends, but with some physical problems and stresses as discussed below.

    For the week before the incident, Defendant Smith worked a heavy load, resided with his sister, and continued to abstain from methamphetamine use. He reported the following symptoms occurring nearly every day or at least twice weekly (see Wahler Physical Symptoms Inventory): (1) trouble with ears or hearing; (2) arm or leg aches or pains; (3) shakiness; (4) stuttering or stammering; (5) backaches; (6) aches or pains in the hands or feet; (7) excessive perspiration; (8) burning, tingling, or crawling feelings in the skin; (9) feeling tired; and (10) excessive gas. Interestingly, he did not report hearing voices or seeing visions, which he had previously stated was an almost daily occurrence.

23. Defendant's reported self-control over the alleged criminal behaviors. Severe impairment; Defendant Smith described himself as having lost control of his behavior when he was attacked by the victims in this case after choosing to initiate behavior with criminal intent.

24. Examiner's assessment of defendant's self-control over criminal behavior. This concerns Defendant Smith's deliberateness and self-control, regardless of the presence of other factors, such as stress. Defendant Smith was mildly impaired. He chose to commit the alleged offenses, although they were committed in an impulsive manner.

25. Was loss of control the result of a psychosis? Definitely not. Psychotic signs such as hearing voices or seeing visions, although affirmed in his history, were not presented or discussed at any time by Defendant Smith as he went through his version of the alleged offenses.

The last step calls for determining whether a link exists between mental condition and self-regulation at the time of the alleged offense. If substantial impairment is found in either cognition or volition, that impairment must result from the proffered mental conditions. All jurisdictions require that there be a demonstrated link between substantial impairments and the accused's diagnosed condition(s). Further, the cause must be direct, and not secondary.

For Defendant Smith, in spite of his mental conditions, there was no substantial impairment in his (cognitive) capacity to appreciate the wrongfulness of his acts or in his (volitional) capacity to conform his conduct to the requirements of the law.

The R-CRAS decision model for the ALI standard concludes on whether a link exists and is presented as follows for the instant case:

Psycholegal Criteria		Expert's Opinion
A-1	Does the defendant have definite malingering, in terms of intentionally fabricating symptomotology?	No (for time of incident)
A-2	Does the defendant have definite organicity?	Yes (mild impairment)
A-3	Does the defendant meet DSM criteria for a major psychiatric disorder?	Yes (Depressive Disorder NOS)
A-4	Was there definite loss of cognitive control? Did the defendant lack substantially the ability to comprehend the criminality of his behavior?	No
A-5	Was there definite loss of behavioral control? The defendant must have been unable to substantially change, monitor, or control his criminal behavior	No
A-6	If yes on A-4 or A-5, was the loss of cognitive or behavioral control over the criminal behavior directly resulting from a mental defect or a major psychiatric disorder?	N/A

Defendant Smith failed to meet the ALI standard for the insanity defense under the R-CRAS decision model because he showed no loss of cognitive or behavioral control. Therefore, there was no direct relationship or linkage between the diagnosed mental disorders and the cognitive or volitional control.

In criminal responsibility evaluations, it is our impression that forensic mental health professionals should not base their opinions exclusively on one measure, even one as impressive as the R-CRAS. In a manner of speaking, do not put all your forensic eggs in one basket. Every effort should be made to scrutinize other events that may suggest awareness of wrongdoing or ability to conform one's behavior to the requirements of the law.

In the sample case, Defendant Smith presented a full account of the incident and therefore there is no question of amnesia or loss of memory for the alleged crimes. Overall, indicia of choice, self-control, and awareness were present for the times before, during, and after the alleged offenses.

Defendant Smith showed a considerable amount of self-control, choice, and awareness for the time prior to the alleged violence against the victims. He generally planned the alleged burglary and showed other kinds of preparation for this event. During the commission of the killings of the three victims at their house, Defendant Smith showed choice, self-control, and awareness by retrieving the stick or club and aiming for the victims' heads. Although Defendant Smith claimed that he lost control just before the moment when the victims attacked and cornered him, his goal of striking them in the head with the stick is inconsistent with blind fear or emotion associated with simply trying to get out of the situation. He continued to strike the victims after they stopped resisting. The choice, awareness, and self-control for the time during the alleged sexual assault, kidnapping, and other acts toward the daughter were exceptionally strong and varied and continued over a prolonged period of time, thus removing any doubt as to whether Defendant Smith was aware of what he was doing or his ability to control his behavior. Moreover, in the alleged offenses toward the daughter, he embedded those events within the context of routine activities, such as going to work, eating, dressing, driving his vehicle, and so forth. For the time after the alleged offenses, he again showed considerable self-control. He told his work supervisor what he had done in considerable detail, thus displaying memory for the events. The remorse and guilt which he expressed were predicated on awareness and his memory of what transpired. The detailed description of the alleged offenses he gave to police stood unchallenged.

Considerable choice, self-control, and awareness were suggested for the times before, during, and after the alleged offenses. Although indicia of deception and malingering did occur, as discussed previously, Defendant Smith did not claim a psychosis for the time of the alleged offenses. He offered stress and intoxication from methamphetamine to explain his behaviors.

A defense psychiatrist testified that Defendant Smith was not criminally responsible. Analyzing his deficiencies, not his strengths, she opined that there was a substantial impairment in both his cognitive and volitional competencies. A third expert, a licensed clinical psychologist, was unable to determine criminal responsibility for Defendant Smith. He opined that although Defendant Smith showed obvious deficiencies, they appeared to be the result of voluntary substance intoxication. Neither of these experts used standardized testing or a deception analysis in arriving at their opinions.

Forensic Reports and Expert Witnessing

The chapters in this book, many with blinded cases, discuss the needs of the forensic report and subsequent testimony if called upon as an expert. The material is founded on clinical forensic training and experience of the contributors and a burgeoning forensic literature that will not be repeated here. Instead, this section focuses on what the trier of fact would like to see from the expert and how that might relate to criminal responsibility evaluation in methamphetamine cases.

Science is based on rigorous hypothesis testing, distinguishing it from other fields of human inquiry. In *Daubert* (1995), the United States Supreme Court held that vigorous cross-examination, presentation of contrary evidence, and consideration of error rates (as in Type 1 and Type 2 errors) while rejecting methodology that is not acceptable upon peer review further the goal of scientific hypothesis testing and the appropriate means of reaching the truth of the matter.

The expert should be prepared for *Daubert*-like questions prior to being allowed to testify. For methamphetamine-related issues as an illustration of the primary issues in a case, these questions may include the following:

1. Using your methods of generating findings from your database, what is the rate of error in coming to conclusions for each of the procedures you employed?
   The expert should have reliability and validity data for all measures employed.
2. Have you published any peer-reviewed articles on methamphetamine use? Have you published any peer-reviewed books or articles in your entire career?
   The expert should have an active publication program, especially in rapidly changing areas such as methamphetamine.
3. Are you aware of the empirical literature on the effects of methamphetamine on memory and perception?
   The expert should be able to cite several articles including recent research efforts.

4. What is a decision path or decision analysis? Does not a decision path illustrate retrospectively how the expert reasoned from gathered database to ultimate conclusions? What is your decision path in this case? What is the accuracy of that decision path, or is just something that you made up?

5. Is not hypothesis testing the essence of science? Describe all the data you have that support the competing hypothesis that Defendant Smith was substantially impaired. So why did you not come to that conclusion? By the way, what is the percentage of cases that you ever disagreed, in terms of criminal responsibility, with the side that retained you? Please give us the names of those cases (for defense cases where the experts assert privilege even regarding whether or not he or she was retained, ask for the name of the attorney, the year, and the general charges). You mean the number is zero (or 1, 2, 3, a few)? Does this have anything to do with you being paid by the side that retained you? Have you ever heard the saying as it applies to experts "Money talks and bullshit walks"? Is it not true that the vast majority of your cases have been referred to you by the defense (prosecution)? Where is your list of cases to show the court otherwise?

6. Is it not true that one way to validate competing hypotheses is by examination of corroborating or collateral data? Have you done that in this case? Why did you not talk with family members (or any significant/knowledgeable others that were not contacted)? How do you know that the information they may have revealed would have indicated that you were wrong in any of your conclusions?

9. Is it not true that the literature states that the purity of methamphetamine can vary widely as a function of precursor agents, additives, and other chemicals? To your knowledge, which precursor agents and additives were associated with the methamphetamine this defendant may have abused prior to the incident?

10. Did you cross-validate the accuracy of the memory of the child-victim in this case? How did you do that?

11. Is not another way of evaluating the impact of methamphetamine abuse to note its behavioral effects? What behavioral effects do you see in this case for Defendant Smith?

12. Given all of the above, how confident are you that you exhibited in coming to your conclusions a sound methodology that linked to the facts of this case?

13. Is it not true that your conclusions regarding methamphetamine in this case may be faulty if the database on which you relied is incomplete or flawed in some way? Like "garbage in, garbage out"? You did not even go to the scene in this case or the police property room. What assumptions are you making in failing to consider that data? What if I were to show you some errors in the investigation reports? Show us how the new facts would change your opinions.

The following conclusions (with notes following in parentheses) were proffered for Defendant Smith with *Daubert* considerations in mind:

1. In my opinion, the forensic database was sufficient to draw relevant conclusions to a reasonable degree of psychological probability. All conclusions were rendered independent of consultation with other experts in this case. (The database is deliberately kept all inclusive and is linked to the degree of overall accuracy mandated by the court in the jurisdiction in which the case is tried; the second sentence affirms the independence of the expert in formulating conclusions. Experts are under no obligation

to qualitatively or quantitatively assign relative weights to database sources, and it is not recommended that they do so. On cross-examination, attorneys may attempt, through hypothetical questions, to have the expert engage in such a weighting to show flawed reasoning and priorities.)

2. In my opinion, an analysis of nondeliberate and deliberate distortion suggests that the evaluation is an accurate representation of Defendant Smith for the time of the alleged offenses. The mental conditions of Defendant Smith for the time of the evaluation were Amphetamine Abuse, in institutional remission, a mild Cognitive Disorder, NOS; (Rule Out) Pedophilia; Depressive Disorder, NOS; and Personality Disorder, NOS, with psychopathic features. The mental conditions of Defendant Smith for the time of the alleged offenses in addition to the above include Amphetamine Intoxication. He has a number of Axis III physical problems secondary to multiple previous injuries and prolonged polysubstance abuse. The severity of psychosocial stressors (Axis IV) for the year before the alleged offenses is seen as moderate, using DSM criteria as shown manifested by his readjustment efforts upon returning to his home state, his lack of a social life, his poor living conditions, and other factors. The highest level of adaptive functioning was poor (Axis V GAF = 20–30 for both present and over the past years), which for Defendant Smith means that he has a serious impairment in his judgment, is episodically dangerous to self and others, and has exhibited major problems across several dimensions of behavior during the last year.

3. In my opinion, Defendant Smith is competent to legally proceed. He understands the nature and quality of the legal proceedings, understands the possible consequences to himself, and can cooperate with his attorneys in his own defense. Although he claims to hear voices daily, he has stated that he has learned to ignore them. These may not be genuine auditory hallucinations. He is currently depressed and moderately suicidal, scoring similar to 45% of the lethal responders group. His ability to rationally consult with his attorney is unimpaired. He has a clear understanding of the roles of the court officers. He sees no condition that would interfere with his ability to stand trial.

4. In my opinion, the extent to which the above-diagnosed conditions impaired Defendant Smith's cognitive ability to appreciate the wrongfulness of his acts was mild on a scale of negligible, minimal, mild, moderate, considerable, and substantial. (The expert should be prepared to show the court how the expert derived these labels, and that the conclusions were not based on any particular theory.) He knew that he was doing wrong at the time of the alleged offenses and had full recall for events.

5. In my opinion, and on the same scale as above, the extent to which the above-diagnosed conditions impaired Defendant Smith's volitional capacity to conform his conduct to the requirements of the law was mild. This rating was based on the interactive effects of demonstrated and intact choice and self-control for the times before, during, and after the alleged offenses.

It may be questioned whether methamphetamine intoxication by itself substantially impaired Defendant Smith in terms of his choice and self-control. Defendant Smith showed ample choice and self-control for the times before, during, and after the alleged offenses, despite claiming to have ingested a considerable amount of methamphetamine. He even decided not to kill the victim-daughter just a few moments after the violence against the other family members, and later decided to release her. Such an ability to stop and decide not to kill suggests that he possessed the ability to choose and self-regulate his behavior.

6. Risk of danger to self, others, and property and proposed intervention are usually offered only if an exculpating mental condition is proffered. In this case, the defense attorneys agreed to have the results of the violence risk analysis discussed in this report. The violence potential of Defendant Smith toward others, as shown on the VRAG, is a mild-moderate .58 over a 10-year period. This score is founded on the base rate for dangerousness for the sample which is approximately 33%. His score on the HCR also suggested a moderate risk of dangerousness toward others.

In addition to the primary forensic conclusions, the court may desire expert testimony on treatment. Across all interventions, the effect of treatment generally is modest for methamphetamine abuse. Although there are a variety of models that have been proposed for the treatment of methamphetamine addiction, none has been adequately supported with empirical evidence (for a review of these models, including the Matrix Program, which has been evaluated five times over 15 years, see Yudko et al., 2003, as well as Yudko et al., in press). Traditional treatment programs based on the Minnesota Model (28-day in-patient treatment) have been shown to be ineffective for the treatment of stimulant addiction. Both the National Institute of Drug Abuse (NIDA) and the Center for Substance Abuse Treatment (CSAT) have sponsored research into the efficacy of treatments for methamphetamine abuse. NIDA has published treatment guidelines for stimulant abusers that have been empirically tested and their efficacy validated. However, these manuals were developed and tested on a population of cocaine users. Rawson, Huber, Brethen, Obert, Gulati, Shoptaw, and Ling (2000) identified a variety of differences between methamphetamine and cocaine users. Methamphetamine users report more daily use of marijuana and hallucinogens, more headaches, depression, suicidal thoughts, and hallucinations than cocaine users. Further, methamphetamine users report spending less money on stimulants, using less drugs, consuming less alcohol, needing less treatment for co-morbid alcohol use, and, perhaps most importantly, a "significantly shorter length of longest abstinence prior to treatment entry" than do cocaine users. Moreover, methamphetamine users report more family problems, a larger number of friends who use drugs and more sex associated with drug use than do cocaine users. Because of these differences, we cannot assume that treatment strategies that work for cocaine users will also work to reduce or eliminate substance use in methamphetamine users.

A third program that has been put forward as a potentially useful model for the treatment of methamphetamine abuse is the Haight-Ashbury Outpatient Model (Inaba and Cohen, 2004). Although the components of this model are based on sound empirical evidence for the effective treatment of substance abuse, the model itself has not been evaluated for its efficacy in the treatment of methamphetamine abuse. That is, they all have a high level of face validity, including the highly touted Matrix Model (see Obert, McCann, Martinell-Casey, Weiner, Minsky, Brethen, and Rawson, 2000), but the lack of evidence for their usefulness is troubling.

Conclusions

This opening chapter presents a methamphetamine-murder insanity case that illustrates salient forensic issues that should be addressed by the competent forensic mental health professional and sets the stage for the chapters to follow. It is hopefully imparted that there is no escape from a thorough knowledge and application of the relevant law in a particular case. There must be a keen sensitivity and adherence to ethical principles as the driving force in every case, a difficult task given the pressures and monetary rewards in forensic work. Forensic experts should be prepared to share with the court, as it goes to the weight of the expert's testimony, a list of every criminal and civil case on which they have been retained. The empirical literature and utilization of scientific procedures must be the lodestone of the forensic evaluation. The methamphetamine literature was presented as an example of what the expert should be expected to discuss in court as the basis for proffered conclusions. Either a forensic neuropsychologist or a forensic psychologist can evaluate an accused and render ultimate conclusions in methamphetamine cases; however, while being qualified as an expert witness, both forensic professionals should present relevant training and experience and resist the temptation (or the entreaties of the cross-examiner) to go beyond the limits of their competence. In terms of standards for admissibility of expert testimony, the general acceptability standard of *Frye* has been largely replaced in most jurisdictions by the need for scientific methodology articulated in *Daubert*. The change has profound implications for forensic mental health experts in the direction of performing more rigorous, reliable, and valid measurement of behaviors in an attempt to address the referral questions. The expert's reasoning on a particular forensic issue, whether couched in terms of decision analysis, decision paths, or retrospective sequential steps/guidelines, is the primary contribution to the court and must be clearly articulated and capable of replication by independent evaluators. The deception analysis, only one of several the steps in the comprehensive forensic evaluation, emerges as an unavoidable application if evaluation data is not simply taken at face value. At the very least, the expert needs to take into account nondeliberate and deliberate distortion by the accused. Three chapters in this book are devoted to the deception analysis and the topic is addressed in virtually every other chapter. The analysis of self-regulatory behaviors in terms of strengths, abilities, and positive attributes of the accused, in addition to the traditional focus on problems, conditions, and symptoms, is likewise critically important and a key ingredient in garnering favorable verdicts. The forensic evaluator should treat every criminal case as if will culminate in a civil action, as occurred in the sample case. Forensic psychologists and neuropsychologists who tend to utilize standardized testing tend to fair better in terms of credibility and impact if they follow the above cautions and considerations.

References

American Psychiatric Association (2000). *Diagnostic and Statistical Manual of Mental Disorders* (DSM-IV-TR), Fourth Edition, Text Revision. Washington, DC: American Psychiatric Association.

American Psychological Association (2002). *Ethical Principles of Psychologists and Code of Conduct*. Washington, D.C.: American Psychological Association.

Ando, K., Hironaka, N., and Yanagita, T. (1986). Psychotic manifestations in amphetamine abuse—experimental study on the mechanism of psychotic recurrence. *Psychopharmacological Bulletin*, 22(3), 763–767.

Ashizawa, T., Saito, T., Yamamoto, M., Shichinohe, S., Ishikawa, H., Maeda, H., Toki, S., Ozawa, H., Watanabe, M., and Takahata, N. (1996). A case of amotivational syndrome as a residual symptom after methamphetamine abuse. *Nihon Arukoru Yakabutsu Igakkai Zasshi*, 31(5), 451–461.

Beebe, D.K. and Walley, E. (1995). Smokeable methamphetamine ("ice"): An old drug in a different form. *American Family Physician*, 51(2), 449–453.

Blau, T. (1984). *The Psychologist as Expert Witness*. New York: John Wiley & Sons.

Buffenstein, A., Coel, M., and Combs, B. (1997). Functional Neuroimaging of Chronic Crystal Methamphetamine Users. Unpublished grant application, University of Hawaii, John A. Burns School of Medicine.

Chait, L.D. and Johanson, C.E. (1988). Discriminative stimulus effects of caffeine and benzphetamine in amphetamine-trained volunteers. *Psychopharmacology*, 96(3), 302–308.

Cherek, D.R., Steinberg, J.L., Kelly, T.H., and Robinson, D.E. (1986). Effects of d-amphetamine on human aggressive behavior. *Psychopharmacology*, 88, 381–386.

Chuck, R.S., Williams, J.M., Goldberg, M.A., and Lubniewski, A.J. (1996). Recurrent corneal ulcerations associated with smokeable methamphetamine abuse. *American Journal of Ophthalmology*, 121(5), 571–572.

Committee on Ethical Guidelines for Forensic Psychologists (1991). Specialty guidelines for forensic psychologists. *Law and Human Behavior*, 15, 655–665.

Committee on the Revision of the Ethical Guidelines for Forensic Psychologists (2006). Specialty guidelines for forensic psychology. Retrieved May 21, 2006 from www.apa.org.

Curran, W., McGarry, A., and Shah, S. (Eds.) (1986). *Forensic Psychiatry and Psychology: Perspectives and Standards for Interdisciplinary Practice*. Philadelphia, PA: F. A. Davis.

DeVito, M.J. and Wagner, G.C. (1989). Functional consequences following methamphetamine-induced neuronal damage. *Psychopharmacology*, 28(a), 432–435.

Ewing, C. (Ed.) (1985). *Psychology, Psychiatry, and the Law: A Clinical and Forensic Handbook*. Sarasota, FL: Professional Resource Exchange, Inc.

Frederick, R., DeMier, S., and Towers, K. (2004). *Examinations of Competency to Stand Trial: Foundations in Mental Health Case Law*. Sarasota, FL: Professional Resources Press.

Fujii, W., Kuribara, H., and Tadokoro, S. (1990). Interaction between caffeine and methamphetamine by means of ambulatory activity in mice. *Yakubutsu Seishin Kodo*, 9(2), 225–231.

Golding, S., Roesch, R., and Schreiber, J. (1984). Assessment and conceptualization of competency to stand trial: Preliminary data on the Interdisciplinary Fitness Interview. *Law and Human Behavior*, 9, 321–334.

Gothard, S., Rogers, R., and Sewell, K. (1995). Feigning incompetency to stand trial: an investigation of the Georgia Court Competency Test. *Law and Human Behavior*, 19, 363–373.

Griffiths, R.R., Evans, S.M., Heishman, S.J., Preston, K.L., Sannerud, C.A., Wolf, B., and Woodson, P.P. (1990). Low-dose caffeine discrimination in humans. *The Journal of Pharmacology and Experimental Therapeutics*, 252(3), 970–978.

Grinspoon, L. and Hedblom, P. (1975). *The Speed Culture: Amphetamine Use and Abuse in America*. Cambridge, MA: Harvard University Press.

Grisso, T. (1986). *Evaluating Competencies: Forensic Assessments and Instruments*. New York: Plenum.

Grisso, T. (1988). *Competency to Stand Trial: Evaluations*. Sarasota, FL: Professional Resource Exchange, Inc.

Grisso, T., Borum, R., and Edens, J. (2002). *Evaluating Competencies: Forensic Assessments and Instruments*. Sarasota, FL: Professional Resource Exchange, Inc.

Gutheil, T. and Appelbaum, P. (1982). *Clinical Handbook of Psychiatry and the Law*. New York: McGraw-Hill.

Haight-Ashbury Training Manual (1997). In D. Inaba and W. Cohen, *Uppers, Downers, and All Arounders*. Ashland, OR: Cinemed, Inc.

Hall, H.V. (1985). Cognitive and volitional capacity assessment: A proposed decision tree. *American Journal of Forensic Psychology*, 3, 3–17.

Hall, H.V. and Hall, F.L. (1987). Post-traumatic stress disorder as a legal defense in criminal trials. *American Journal of Forensic Psychology*, 5, 45–53.

Hall, H.V., Mee, C., and Bresciani, P. (2001). Extreme Mental or Emotional Disturbance (EMED). *University of Hawaii Law Review*, 23(2), 431–478.

Hall, H.V. and Poirier, J. (2001). *Detecting Malingering and Deception: The Forensic Distortion Analysis*, Second Edition. Winter Park, FL: St. Lucie Press.

Hall, H.V. and Pritchard, D. (1996). *Detecting Malingering and Deception: The Forensic Distortion Analysis (FDA)*. Winter Park, FL: St. Lucie Press.

Hall, H.V. and Sbordone, R. (1993). *Disorders of Executive Functions: Civil and Criminal Law Applications*. Winter Park, FL: St. Lucie Press.

Heilbrun, G., Marczyk, G., and Dematteo, D. (2002). *Forensic Mental Health Assessment: A Casebook*. New York: Oxford University Press.

Holtzman, S.G. (1987). Discriminative stimulus effects of caffeine: Tolerance and cross-tolerance with methylphenidate. *Life Sciences*, 40(4), 381–389.

Inaba, D. and Cohen, W.E. (2004). *Uppers, Downers, and All Arounders: Physical and Mental Effects of Drug Abuse*, Fifth Edition. Ashland, OR: CNS Publications.

Kassebaum, G. and Chandler, S.M. (1994). Polydrug use and self control among men and women in prison. *Journal of Drug Education*, 24(4), 333–350.

Kram, T.C., Kruegel, B.S., and Kruegel, A.V. (1977). The identification of impurities in illicit methamphetamine exhibits by gas chromatography/mass spectrometry and nuclear magnetic resonance spectroscopy. *Journal of Forensic Science*, 22, 40–52.

Kramer, J.C., Fischman, V.S., and Littlefield, D.C. (1967). Amphetamine abuse: Pattern and effects of high doses taken intravenously. *Journal of the American Medical Association*, 201, 89–93.

Kuribara, H. (1994). Modification by caffeine of the sensitization to methamphetamine and cocaine in terms of ambulation in mice. *Life Science*, 55(12), 933–940.

Kuribara, H. and Tadokoro, S. (1989). Reverse tolerance to ambulation-increasing effects of methamphetamine and morphine in 6 mouse strains. *Japanese Journal of Pharmacology*, 49(2), 197–203.

Lafave, W.R. and Scott, A.W, Jr. (1986). *Substantive Criminal Law*. Minneapolis, MN: West Group.

Lewander, T. (1971). A mechanism for the development of tolerance in rats. *Psychopharmacologia*, 21, 17–31.

Logan, B.K., Weiss, E.L., and Harruff, R.C. (1996). Case report: Distribution of methamphetamine in a massive fatal ingestion. *Journal of Forensic Science*, 41(2), 322–323.

MacArthur Competence Assessment Tool—Criminal Adjudication (1996). Odessa, FL: Psychological Assessment Research, Inc.

McGarry, A. (1973). Competency to Stand Trial and Mental Illness (DHEW Publication No. ADM. 77-103). Rockville, MD: Department of Heath, Education and Welfare.

Melton, G., Petrella, R., Poythress, N., and Slobogin, C. (1997). *Psychological Evaluations for the Courts: A Handbook for Mental Health Professionals and Lawyers*. New York: Guilford.

Miczek, K.A. and Tidey, J.W. (1989). Amphetamines: aggressive and social behavior. *NIDA Research Monogram Series*, 94, 68–100.

Mumford, G.K., Evans, S.M., Kaminski, B.J., Preston, K.L., Sannerud, C.A., Silverman, K., and Griffiths, R.R. (1994). Discriminative stimulus and subjective effects of theobromine and caffeine in humans. *Psychopharmacology*, 115(1–2), 1–8.

Obert, J.L., McCann, M.A., Martinelli-Casey, P., Weiner, A., Minsky, S., Brethen, M.A., and Rawson, R. (2000). The matrix model of outpatient stimulant abuse treatment: History and description. *Journal of Psychoactive Drugs*, 32(2), 157–164.

Oliveto, A.H., Bickel, W.K., Hughes, J.R., Shea, P.J., Higgins, S.T., and Fenwick, J.W. (1992). Caffeine drug discrimination in humans: Acquisition, specificity and correlation with self-reports. *The Journal of Pharmacology and Experimental Therapeutics*, 261(3), 885–894.

Oliveto, A.H., Bickel, W.K., Hughes, J.R., Terry, S.Y., Higgins, S.T., and Badger, G.J. (1993). Pharmacological specificity of the caffeine discriminative stimulus in humans: Effects of theophylline, methylphenidate and buspirone. *Behavioral Pharmacology*, 4(3), 237–246.

Peltier, R.L., Li, D.H., Lytle, D., Taylor, C.M., and Emmett-Oglesby, M.W. (1996). Chronic D-amphetamine or methamphetamine produces cross-tolerance to the discriminative and reinforcing stimulus effects of cocaine. *The Journal of Pharmacology and Experimental Therapeutics*, 277(1), 212–218.

Perez-Reyes, M., White, W.R., McDonald, S.A., Hicks, R.E., Jeffcoat, A.R., Hill, J.M., and Cook, C.E. (1991). Clinical effects of daily methamphetamine administration. *Clinical Neuropharmacology*, 14, 352–358.

Rawson, R.A., Huber, A., Brethen, P.B., Obert, J.L., Gulati, V., Shoptaw, S., and Ling, W. (2000). Methamphetamine and cocaine users: differences in characteristics and treatment retention. *Journal of Psychoactive Drugs*, 32, 233–238.

Robinson, T.E. and Becker, J.B. (1986). Enduring changes in brain and behavior produced by chronic amphetamine administration: A review and evaluation of animal models of amphetamine psychosis. *Brain Research Review*, 1, 157–198.

Roesch, R. and Golding, S. (1980). *Competency to Stand Trial*. Urbana-Champaign, IL: University of Illinois Press.

Rogers, R. (1984). *R-CRAS: Rogers Criminal Responsibility Assessment Scales*. Odessa, FL: Psychological Assessment Resources, Inc.

Rogers, R. and Shuman, D. (2000). *Conducting Insanity Evaluations*. New York: Guilford Press.

Rothrock, J.F., Rubenstein, R., and Lyden, P.D. (1988). Ischemic stroke associated with methamphetamine inhalation. *Neurology*, 38(4), 589–592.

Sachdeva, K. and Woodward, K.G. (1989). Caudal thalamic infarction following intranasal methamphetamine use. *Neurology*, 39(2/1), 305–306.

Shapiro, D. (1984). *Psychological Evaluation and Expert Testimony*. New York: Van Nostrand Reinhold.

Sinnema, A. and Verweij, A.M.A. (1981). Impurities in illicit amphetamine: A review. *Bulletin of Narcotics*, 33, 37–54.

Stern, K.N., Chait, L.D., and Johanson, C.E. (1989). Reinforcing and subjective effects of caffeine in normal human volunteers. *Psychopharmacology*, 98(1), 81–88.

Tadokoro, S. and Kuribara, H. (1986). Reverse tolerance to the ambulation-increasing effect of methamphetamine in mice as an animal model of amphetamine-psychosis. *Psychopharmacology Bulletin*, 22(3), 757–762.

Tohhara, S., Kato, A., and Nakajima, T. (1990). Methamphetamine abuse by smoking. *Arukoku Kenkyuoto Yakubutsu Ison*, 25(6), 467–474.

Vincent, N., Shoobridge, J., Ask, A., Allsop, S., and Ali, R. (1998). Physical and mental health problems in amphetamine users from metropolitan Adelaide, Australia. *Drug and Alcohol Review*, 17, 187–195.

Warren, J., Rosenfeld, B., and Fitch, W. (1994). Beyond competence and sanity. The influence of pretrial evaluation on case disposition. *Bulletin of the American Academy of Psychiatry and Law*, 22(3), 379–388.

Weiner, I. and Hess, A. (1987). *Handbook of Forensic Psychology*. New York: Wiley.

White, B.C. and Keller, G.E. (1984). Caffeine pretreatment: Enhancement and attenuation of d-amphetamine-induced activity. *Pharmacology, Biochemistry, and Behavior*, 20(3), 383–386.

Wolkoff, D.A. (1997). Methamphetamine abuse: An overview for health care professionals. *Hawaii Medical Journal*, 56(2), 34–36.

Wright, S. and Klee, H. (2001). Violent crime, aggression and amphetamine: what are the implications for drug treatment services? *Drugs: Education, Prevention and Policy*, 8(1), 73–90.

Yudko, E., Hall, H.V., and McPherson, S.B. (2003). *Methamphetamine Use: Clinical and Forensic Aspects*. Boca Raton, FL: CRC Press.

Yudko, E., McPherson, S.B., and Hall, H.V. (in press). *Methamphetamine Use: Clinical and Forensic Aspects*, Second Edition. Boca Raton, FL: CRC Press.

Ziskin, J. and Faust, D. (1988). *Coping with Psychiatric and Psychological Testimony*, Fourth Edition. Los Angeles: Law and Psychology Press.

Legal References

Barrett v. United States, 377 A 2d 62 (D.C. 1976).

Bieber v. People of Colorado, 856 P.2d 811 (Colo. 1993).

Daubert v. Merrell Dow Pharmaceuticals, Inc., 113 S.Ct. 2786 (1993), on remand, 43 F.3d 1311 (9th Cir. 1995).

Drope v. Missouri, 420 U.S. 162 (1975).

Durham v. United States, 214 F.2d 862 (D.C. Cir. 1954).

Dusky v. United States, 362 U.S. 401 (1960).

Feguer v. United States, 302 F.2d 214 (1962).

Frye v. United States, 293 F. 1013 (D.C. Cir. 1923).

Godinez v. Moran, 509 U.S. 389 (1993).

Jackson v. State of Indiana, 406 U.S. 715 (1972).

State of Arizona v. Cooper, 111 Ariz. 332, 529 P.2d 231 (1974).

State of Hawaii v. Silverio Soares, First Circuit Court, Cr. No. 90-1068 (1996).

State of Hawaii v. Michael Lawrence, First Circuit Court, Cr. No. 99-675 (2001).

State of Hawaii v. Young, 93 Haw. 1224, 999 P.2d 230 (2000).

United States v. Adams, 297 F. Supp. 596 (1969).

United States v. McGlue, 26 Fed. Cas. 1093 (C.C. Mass. 1851).

United States v. Wilson, 263 F. Supp. 528 (D.D.C. 1966).

Wade v. United States, 426 F.2d 64 (9th Cir. 1970).

The Legal, Ethical, and Applied Aspects of Capital Mitigation Evaluations: Practice Guidance from a Principles-Based Approach

2

GEOFFREY MARCZYK

The Institute for Graduate Clinical Psychology,
Widener University, Wilmington, Delaware

LINDA KNAUSS

The Institute for Graduate Clinical Psychology,
Widener University, Wilmington, Delaware

JOSH KUTINSKY

The Institute for Graduate Clinical Psychology,
Widener University, Wilmington, Delaware

DAVID DeMATTEO

Drexel University, Philadelphia, Pennsylvania

KIRK HEILBRUN

Drexel University, Philadelphia, Pennsylvania

Contents

The overarching focus of this chapter is on forensic evaluations conducted in the context of capital mitigation and their associated practice challenges. The chapter begins with a brief discussion of relevant case law and statutory authority in this area, with special emphasis on legal developments following the *Atkins* decision. Next, that chapter turns to a discussion of the ethical contours and concerns related to conducting evaluations of this type. This discussion highlights ethical concerns in the broader realm of capital mitigation before moving to a more specific discussion of *Atkins*-specific issues, where the assessment of mental retardation is the overriding issue. An understanding of the relevant legal and ethical contours related to capital mitigation provides an excellent foundation and backdrop for discussing competent and effective forensic assessment practice in this area. Evaluations of this type are unique and present a number of correspondingly unique practice-related issues and challenges that might not be encountered in other types of forensic evaluations. Accordingly, the remainder of the chapter discusses these challenges and provides concrete recommendations from a principles-based framework for how to address them within the contours of existing support from relevant sources of authority within ethics, law, science, and standards of practice.

An Overview of Death Penalty Jurisprudence

The Modern Era

The modern era of death penalty jurisprudence began in 1972 when the Supreme Court of the United States abolished the death penalty in a series of cases, the most well known of which is *Furman v. Georgia* (1972). By a five-to-four vote, the Court in *Furman* held that the capital punishment statutes of Texas and Georgia violated the 8th Amendment's prohibition against cruel and unusual punishment and the Due Process Clause of the 14th Amendment. In a broadly written decision, the Supreme Court prohibited all death penalty statutes that left the sentencing decision to the unguided discretion of the sentencing jury. In response to the Supreme Court's decision in *Furman*, 35 states rewrote their death penalty statutes, with about half of the states removing jury discretion by making the death penalty mandatory in specified circumstances and about half of the states establishing guidelines to assist juries in making sentencing decisions in capital cases.

The moratorium on capital punishment imposed by the U.S. Supreme Court lasted for roughly 4 years after *Furman* was decided. Then, in 1976, the Supreme Court again considered the constitutionality of the death penalty in a series of cases (*Gregg v. Georgia*, 1976;

Jurek v. Texas, 1976; *Proffitt v. Florida*, 1976) and concluded that the death penalty would be constitutional under certain circumstances. Specifically, the 1976 cases, as well as several subsequent Supreme Court decisions, clarified the distinction between constitutional and unconstitutional state death penalty statutes. First, the Court prohibited mandatory death sentences because they do not allow for the particularized consideration of the defendant's character, the defendant's criminal record, and the circumstances of the offense (see *Lockett v. Ohio*, 1978; *Roberts v. Louisiana*, 1976; *Woodson v. North Carolina*, 1976). Second, the Court held that although juries could not be given unbridled discretion in reaching a sentencing decision, they must be allowed to consider all potentially mitigating evidence relating to the defendant's character and the circumstances of the offense (see *Eddings v. Oklahoma*, 1982). By these rulings, the Supreme Court sought to make the imposition of the death penalty less arbitrary and narrow the class of persons eligible for the death penalty.

In response to these Supreme Court decisions, modern death penalty statutes typically specify aggravating and mitigating factors that are designed to assist juries in reaching an appropriate sentencing decision. To impose a death sentence, the jury must find at least one aggravating factor (and must usually identify it in writing) and also find that any mitigating factors do not make the imposition of the death penalty inappropriate in the context of the particular case. The purpose of aggravating factors is to narrow the class of persons eligible for the death penalty and justify the imposition of a more severe sentence than is usually given for the crime of murder (see *Zant v. Stephens*, 1983). There are two categories of aggravating factors in most state death penalty schemes: aggravating factors relating to the offense and aggravating factors relating to the offender. Examples of aggravating factors relating to the offense include murdering certain categories of people (e.g., police officers, correctional officers, and judges); committing murder during the course of another felony (referred to as the "felony murder rule"); committing murder while imprisoned; committing murder for pecuniary gain; committing murder to avoid being arrested; and committing murder in a heinous, cruel, or vile manner. Examples of aggravating factors relating to the offender include a history of violent felonies and a high likelihood of being dangerous in the future. Specific aggravating factors differ from state to state, and the governing state statutes must identify an exhaustive list of aggravating factors that can be considered by the jury during the sentencing phase of a capital case. Juries are not permitted to consider aggravating factors not listed in the statutes. Moreover, the U.S. Supreme Court has held that a jury, not a judge, must make the findings necessary for a death sentence to be imposed in capital cases (i.e., determine the presence of aggravating factors; see *Ring v. Arizona*, 2002).

In contrast to aggravating factors, the list of mitigating factors in state death penalty statutes is not exhaustive, and juries are permitted to consider all relevant mitigating circumstances. The Supreme Court requires the sentencing jury to consider all relevant mitigating circumstances to ensure that (1) the decision to impose death is particularized to the defendant and the specific offense and (2) the punishment of death is not excessive or disproportionate under the specific circumstances of the case. In some cases, the presence of mitigating factors may render the imposition of the death penalty constitutionally inappropriate. For example, if a jury finds that mitigating factors outweigh or outnumber aggravating factors in a particular case, the jury may not recommend a sentence of death. Examples of mitigating factors include the following: the defendant was a "minor" participant in the offense, the murder was committed while the defendant was under extreme mental or emotional disturbance, the defendant acted under duress, the defendant's capacity to appreciate the wrongfulness of his or her conduct or conform his or her conduct to the requirements of the law was impaired due to mental disease or defect, the defendant believed the murder was morally justified, and a low likelihood that the defendant will be dangerous in the future. There is typically another mitigating factor that describes any other considerations that are relevant to mitigation.

Mental Retardation and the Death Penalty

When considering the relationship between mental retardation and the death penalty, the logical starting point is the U.S. Supreme Court's 1989 decision in *Penry v. Lynaugh*. In October 1979, 22-year-old Pamela Mosely Carpenter was raped, beaten, and stabbed to death with scissors in her home. Before dying, Carpenter provided a description of her attacker, who was subsequently identified as 22-year-old Johnny Paul Penry. At the time of the offense, Penry was on parole for a rape conviction. Penry subsequently confessed to the crime in two separate statements to the police and was charged with capital murder.

At the conclusion of his trial, a Texas trial court jury rejected Penry's insanity defense and found him guilty of capital murder. During the sentencing phase, the defense argued that the imposition of the death penalty would violate the 8th Amendment's prohibition against cruel and unusual punishment because of Penry's mental condition. Penry, who reportedly had organic brain damage resulting from a breach birth, had an IQ estimated to be between 50 and the low 60s (which when combined with his deficits in adaptive functioning would place him in the mild-to-moderate range of mental retardation). The jury concluded that the presence of aggravating factors justified the imposition of the death penalty, and Penry was sentenced to death. On appeal, the Texas Court of Criminal Appeals affirmed the trial court's conviction and the sentence of death, concluding that the death penalty is not prohibited based on Penry's mental retardation. Penry subsequently filed a habeas corpus petition in federal district court challenging the death sentence, but the district court denied relief. On appeal, the U.S. Court of Appeals for the Fifth Circuit affirmed the death sentence, rejecting Penry's claim that executing a mentally retarded offender would violate the 8th Amendment's prohibition against cruel and unusual punishment.

The Supreme Court of the United States granted certiorari to determine whether the 8th Amendment's ban on cruel and unusual punishment prohibits the execution of a defendant who is mentally retarded. The defense raised the following two arguments: (1) executing a mentally retarded defendant would violate the 8th Amendment because individuals with mental retardation do not possess a level of moral culpability sufficient to justify a death sentence, and (2) there is an emerging national consensus against executing the mentally retarded, which is an important consideration in the Supreme Court's 8th Amendment analysis. The prosecution countered by arguing that existing procedural safeguards (i.e., competence to stand trial proceedings, insanity, and diminished capacity defenses) adequately protect the interests of mentally retarded defendants, and that there is insufficient evidence of a national consensus against executing mentally retarded offenders.

The Supreme Court rejected the defense's arguments and held that executing mentally retarded defendants is not a per se violation of the 8th Amendment. In reaching its decision, the Supreme Court stated that mental retardation should be considered as a mitigating factor during the sentencing phase of a capital trial, which ensures the individualized sentencing decision required by prior Supreme Court cases. The Supreme Court also concluded that there was no national consensus against executing the mentally retarded, because only the federal jurisdiction and two states prohibited executing mentally retarded defendants. Accordingly, under *Penry*, mental retardation was viewed as a mitigating factor rather than as a basis for excluding a defendant from the reach of capital punishment.

In a more recent decision, *Atkins v. Virginia* (2002), the Supreme Court again considered whether the 8th Amendment's ban on cruel and unusual punishment prohibits the execution of a defendant who is mentally retarded. In August 1996, Daryl Atkins and William Jones carjacked Eric Nesbitt, an airman from Langley Air Force Base who had just walked out of a convenience store. Atkins and Jones robbed Nesbitt of $60, drove him to an automatic teller machine, and ordered him to withdraw more money. After driving Nesbitt to a secluded area, Atkins ordered Nesbitt out of the truck and shot him eight times with a semiautomatic handgun.

In 1998, a Virginia trial court found Atkins guilty of capital murder and related offenses. During the sentencing phase, the prosecution introduced evidence of two aggravating factors: future dangerousness (because Atkins had 16 prior felony convictions) and the vileness of the offense. The defense countered with the testimony of a psychologist, who diagnosed Atkins as being mildly mentally retarded. After weighing the aggravating and mitigating factors, the sentencing jury ultimately recommended a sentence of death for Atkins. Atkins appealed to the Supreme Court of Virginia, arguing that it is unconstitutional—i.e., a disproportionate punishment—to execute a criminal defendant with an IQ of 59. Citing the Supreme Court's decision in *Penry*, the prosecution argued that it does not violate the 8th Amendment's prohibition on cruel and unusual punishment to execute a defendant who is mentally retarded. Relying on *Penry*, the Supreme Court of Virginia rejected the defense's argument and affirmed the death sentence.

The Supreme Court of the United States granted certiorari to address the same question it had addressed 13 years earlier in *Penry*—i.e., whether executing a mentally retarded defendant would violate the 8th Amendment. The Supreme Court noted that it granted certiorari because of concerns expressed by the dissenting judges in the Supreme Court of Virginia and the dramatic shifts that occurred in the legislative landscape since *Penry* was decided. In a decision reversing its holding in *Penry*, the Supreme Court held in *Atkins* that executing a mentally retarded defendant is excessive in light of evolving standards of decency and therefore violates the 8th Amendment. The Court stated that although the deficiencies associated with mental retardation do not exempt the individual from punishment, they diminish personal culpability to the point where death is not an appropriate punishment. The Court concluded that executing a mentally retarded defendant would not further the primary goals of capital punishment—i.e., retribution and deterrence. Finally, the Court noted that there was now a national consensus against executing the mentally retarded that did not exist at the time *Penry* was decided. Specifically, the Court found that a national consensus existed because 18 states and the federal jurisdiction prohibited executing the mentally retarded, numerous secular and religious organizations opposed capital punishment for such individuals, and public opinion surveys suggested that the American public opposed executing the mentally retarded.

The *Atkins* decision effectively narrowed the class of offenders eligible for the death penalty by excluding all offenders who are mentally retarded. Given that recent estimates suggest that roughly 10% of all death penalty inmates are mentally retarded, the *Atkins* decision will likely have a dramatic effect on the death row population in the United States. Subsequent cases have added to the jurisprudence surrounding mental retardation and the death penalty and potentially further narrowed the class of offenders eligible for the death penalty. For example, in *Tennard v. Dretke* (2004), the U.S. Supreme Court held that a low IQ, regardless of whether it is in the range of mental retardation (i.e., <70), is a relevant mitigating factor at capital sentencing proceedings even if it is not directly related to the offense.

A particularly noteworthy aspect of *Atkins* was the Supreme Court's refusal to define mental retardation. Instead, the Supreme Court charged each state with the task of defining mental retardation in a manner that enforces the constitutional restriction on executing mentally retarded offenders. This is similar to what the Supreme Court did with respect to competence for execution in *Ford v. Wainwright* (1986), in which it left the task of defining specific standards for such competence to the states. An important question, therefore, is how states have responded to the Supreme Court's mandate in *Atkins*.

Perhaps most importantly, it appears that the states have responded to the *Atkins* decision by enacting legislation (or enforcing existing legislation) that excludes offenders with mental retardation from the reach of the death penalty. Eighteen of the 38 states that currently permit capital punishment had legislatively protected mentally retarded offenders from the death penalty prior to *Atkins*, and the remaining 20 states have since either enacted appropriate legislation or enforced existing legislation to exclude mentally retarded offenders from the class of offenders eligible for a death sentence (see DeMatteo, Marczyk, and Pich, 2006). Therefore, at least in this respect, it appears that the *Atkins* decision has successfully excluded mentally retarded offenders from the death penalty.

Importantly, however, the results of a recent 50-state legislative survey revealed that states use widely varying definitions of mental retardation (see DeMatteo et al., 2006). Although some states define mental retardation using accepted clinical standards, such as the diagnostic criteria contained in the American Psychiatric Association's diagnostic and statistical manual of mental disorders (DSM-IV-TR, 2000) or the diagnostic criteria promulgated by the American Association of Mental Retardation (AAMR), other states use overly broad and nonspecific definitions of mental retardation. Specifically, of the 38 states that currently permit capital punishment, four use the DSM-IV-TR criteria (with slight variation), 18 use the AAMR criteria (with slight variation), and the remaining 16 states define mental retardation in nonspecific and often vague ways (DeMatteo et al., 2006). For example, 11 of the remaining 16 states define mental retardation by mentioning all three elements found in the DSM criteria (i.e., significant intellectual impairment, deficits in adaptive functioning, and age of onset under 18) but do not define the elements in any meaningful manner (e.g., no IQ cut-off, no indication of what constitutes impaired adaptive functioning or how many deficits are required, and no specific age cut-off). It is also worth noting that one state (Kansas) defines mental retardation by including cognitive and volitional elements typically found in definitions of insanity. From a legal standpoint, these widely varying and vague definitions of mental retardation potentially raise important procedural due process concerns. From a forensic evaluation standpoint, the variation in definitions of mental retardation highlights the importance of being familiar with the particular definition of mental retardation being used in a jurisdiction. This point will be revisited in more detail later in this chapter. We will now turn to a discussion of prominent ethical issues encountered in capital litigation.

Ethical Dilemmas Facing Psychological Assessors: Ethical Principles and Hot Spots

Ethical considerations are central to any professional psychological undertaking but are especially crucial to assessments performed for the purpose of capital sentencing. Although all of psychology's ethical principles are relevant for psychologists assessing death-eligible defendants, without question the high stakes in such cases amplify the magnitude of a few critical concerns. The discussion below highlights a number of ethical issues that should unquestionably be considered by any psychologist involved in capital mitigation evaluations. These include "do no harm," boundaries of competence, informed consent, ethical use of psychometric testing, cultural fairness, and malingering. In addition, the *Atkins* ruling prohibiting the execution of the mentally retarded poses a number of unique ethical problems for psychologists. These include variability among IQ test results, test–retest phenomena, and problems in assessing adaptive functioning. Each of these issues is discussed in turn below.

The Ethical Context for Death Penalty Assessments

Many of the ethical quandaries arising in the death penalty context derive from the conflict between the legal system's demand for precision and bright-line determinations (such as whether a defendant is mentally retarded or has a mental illness that precludes basic understanding of his or her immediate situation), and the subtle and often muddy clinical realities involved in making such determinations. Diagnosis of mental retardation, for example, is not as simple as many judges and attorneys may presume it to be. Although criteria for a diagnosis of mental retardation vary depending on the authority, two common elements of a diagnosis of mental retardation include establishing an IQ score of below 70 points through standardized testing (allowing for some flexibility based on statistical standard error rates) and determining the presence of deficits in adaptive functioning (as defined by a person's ability to adapt to and function well across contexts) (American Association of Mental Retardation, 2002; American Psychiatric Association, 2000). Both of these determinations are less than exact, often requiring the application of subjective "clinical judgments," which may vary considerably by clinician (American Psychiatric Association, 2000, pp. 39–40). More specifically, the variability and cultural insensitivity of IQ scores are areas of deep ethical concern for psychologists, as is the need for the diagnosis to be made prior to age 18 for it to be considered valid (Kane, 2003).* Determinations regarding malingering (or "faking" for the purpose of achieving some secondary gain) are also notoriously unreliable in this context (Brodsky and Galloway, 2003). Assessments related to emotional or personality disturbance and the death penalty are also fraught with ethical concerns. The nature and legal significance of the relationship between a particular defendant's mental illness or mental disease or defect and his or her competence to be executed is notoriously ill defined and often leads different clinicians to very different conclusions, even when assessing the same defendant (Ackerson, Brodsky, and Zapf, 2005). Similarly, assessing the admittedly murky connection between mental illness and a defendant's ability to appreciate the wrongfulness of his or her conduct or conform his or her conduct to the requirements of the law often results in tremendous variability between expert opinions. Each of these concerns raises serious questions about just what constitutes the ethical practice and application of psychological assessment not only for forensic psychologists, but for the judges and attorneys involved in death penalty proceedings.

---

* It is also worth noting that the constructs of IQ and mental retardation are themselves the subjects of ongoing controversy. Some argue that these constructs are merely labels of convenience that are conceptually meaningless or fundamentally flawed (Greenspan and Switzky, 2003).

As these evaluations are literally a life-or-death matter, both the legal and psychological professions mandate that the highest standards of professionalism be adhered to and that a defendant be given every available opportunity to have mitigating evidence presented on his or her behalf (American Bar Association, 2004; American Psychological Association, 2002; American Psychological Association Council of Representatives, 2006). Although the legal and psychological professions agree on this particular point, a host of psychology-specific ethical issues are likely to emerge in this arena. Before discussing these in detail, it bears emphasizing that the conscience and moral convictions of the assessing psychologist are always superimposed on each of the ethical considerations discussed below. Practitioners considering a death penalty evaluation must thoroughly review their conscience and ethical position before agreeing to participate (American Psychological Association, 2002; Committee on Ethical Guidelines for Forensic Psychologists, 1991).

Do No Harm

Principle A of the current *Ethical Principles of Psychologists and Code of Conduct* (American Psychological Association, 2002) states that "[p]sychologists strive to benefit those with whom they work and take care to do no harm. In their professional actions, psychologists seek to safeguard the welfare and rights of those with whom they interact professionally…" (p. 3). This and other General Principles of the American Psychological Association (APA) Ethics Code are aspirational in nature and are meant to guide and inspire psychologists toward the highest ethical ideals of the profession. In the most general sense, these aspirational principles do not impose an enforceable duty upon psychologists working in this context. Nonetheless, any psychologist who feels that his or her work may compromise the welfare and rights of the individual that he or she working with has a responsibility to resolve this dilemma. What is unclear, unfortunately, is how to do that—particularly in the murky ethical waters of death penalty evaluations.

This dilemma may be amplified by the nature of the assessment process. For a psychologist performing an evaluation, the primary duty is to proceed through the assessment process in an objective, thorough manner that relies on accepted, well-validated measures and is grounded in structured clinical judgment. To accomplish this, a psychologist must enter into an assessment without any preconceived notions of what the conclusion "should" be. Under the current APA ethical guidelines, however, psychologists remain ethically responsible for the outcome of their assessments despite their necessary lack of foreknowledge or prejudgment (American Psychological Association, 2002, section 9). This places any psychologist in the unenviable position of having to take full responsibility for the life-and-death consequences of his or her assessment while simultaneously remaining deliberately ignorant of what his or her assessment may yield. This situation has the potential to ensnare even the most cautious psychologist in a truly vicious ethical dilemma.

A related concern involves a tradition of legal deference to certain judgments made by mental health professionals.* As a practical matter, legal determinations related to mental health or cognitive functioning are often based largely on the opinions offered by the

---

* See, for example, *Youngberg v. Romeo*, 457 U.S. 307, 1983, pp. 322–323: "In determining what is 'reasonable'… we emphasize that courts must show deference to the judgment exercised by a qualified professional … there certainly is no reason to think judges or juries are better qualified than appropriate professionals in making such decisions."

professionals conducting the assessments.* Although this tradition of professional deference may help circumvent attempts by courts and attorneys to influence or interfere with the assessment process, it may also impose additional risks upon psychologists. If an attorney's responsibility for establishing a patient is or is not incompetent or establishing whether a defendant is mentally retarded has been delegated to a mental health professional, then the risk of a "bad judgment" may arguably fall within the scope of the assessing psychologist's responsibilities. Attorneys defending their actions in a death penalty case may be able to plead professional deference as an "excuse" for a particular strategic decision or outcome. Such a risk further amplifies the need for psychologists working in this arena to be as cautious and methodologically rigorous as possible.

Boundaries of Competence

Another fundamental canon of ethical conduct demands that psychologists practice solely within the boundaries of their own professional competence. Section 2.01(a) of the APA Ethics Code limits a psychologist's scope of practice "based on their education, training, supervised experience, consultation, study, or professional experience" (American Psychological Association, 2002, section 2.01(a)). In the context of a psychological assessment, this guideline effectively prohibits a psychologist from engaging in any specific form of independent assessment unless the psychologist first acquires supervised experience assessing that particular type of referral question and has received appropriate, up-to-date training in the instruments used in the course of that assessment (American Psychological Association, 2002). Psychologists are obligated to refer a case to a competent professional in instances where they lack the training to provide the service themselves, although exceptions may be made to this rule where no other competently-trained psychologist is available to take the referral (American Psychological Association, 2002, section 2.01(b, d, e)). The ethics code further requires that any psychologist assuming a forensic role be "reasonably familiar with the judicial or administrative rules governing their roles" (American Psychological Association, 2002, section 2.01(f)).

The *Specialty Guidelines for Forensic Psychologists* (*Specialty Guidelines*) also requires practitioners to attend vigilantly to the boundaries of their own competence (Committee on Ethical Guidelines for Forensic Psychologists, 1991; Committee on the Revision of the Ethical Guidelines for Forensic Psychologists, 2006). As with the APA Ethics Code, the current *Specialty Guidelines* suggests that practitioners recognize and practice within the confines of their professional experience and training (Committee on Ethical Guidelines for Forensic Psychologists, 1991, section III). The *Specialty Guidelines* also imposes additional related obligations. In particular, any forensic psychologist who plans to testify as an expert is responsible for being able to demonstrate the factual bases (knowledge, skill, experience, training, and education) for his or her qualification as an expert, and the relevance of those factual bases to his or her qualification as an expert (Committee on Ethical Guidelines for Forensic Psychologists, 1991, section III(b)). These obligations also extend to the legal context. For example, forensic psychologists should possess a fundamental and reasonable level of knowledge and understanding of the legal and professional standards that govern their participation as experts in legal proceedings, understand the civil rights

---

* In fact, the *Atkins* decision cites the conclusions of a forensic psychologist to establish Atkins' claim of mental retardation (*Atkins v. Virginia*, 536 U.S. 304, 308–309 (2002)).

of parties in legal proceedings in which they participate, manage their professional conduct in a manner that does not diminish or threaten those rights, and maintain current knowledge of scientific, professional, and legal developments within their claimed areas of competence (Committee on Ethical Guidelines for Forensic Psychologists, 1991, sections III(b–d), section IV(a)). In places, the *Specialty Guidelines* goes so far as to demand degrees of competence that explicitly exceed those required of psychologists practicing in other, nonforensic settings. Specifically, the guidelines impose heightened expectations regarding proficiency in the most up-to-date methods and research, and an emphasis on the highest quality of documentation (Committee on Ethical Guidelines for Forensic Psychologists, 1991, section VI).

The need for psychological assessors to stay within the above-defined scope of their professional competence is never greater than in the death penalty context. This is true for two main reasons. First, the stakes simply could not be higher for the individual being assessed, and there may be only a very limited opportunity to rectify the unintended consequences of an inadequate or incompetent assessment.* Second, the nature of the legal questions posed in forensic contexts requires a thorough understanding of the standards governing the legal proceedings. To be effective, assessing psychologists must ensure their assessment procedures comport with legal requirements and that their findings are admissible and valid, while also clearly relating those findings to legally relevant factors.

Another crucial set of concerns is related to the heightened level of competence demanded by the challenging nature of death penalty assessments themselves. An individual who is the subject of a death penalty mitigation assessment may often present with multiple co-occurring problems (including mental illness, developmental delays, cognitive impairments, and substance abuse problems), whose nature and influence is further distorted and exacerbated by the harsh realities of prison life and stress of possible execution. Recent research has pointed to the importance of investigating a range of psychological factors in the course of such assessments (Cunningham and Reidy, 2001). Maintaining the integrity of the data-collection process, which is often challenging to begin with, is made still more difficult by the unusually pronounced possibility of malingering and the environmental disruptions that plague correctional settings. Thus, the complexity of the issues, the level of impairment, and the difficulties with data collection are often of the highest order. This set of circumstances requires the highest level of professional experience and training if they are to be handled appropriately and effectively as possible. It is therefore incumbent upon any psychologists considering such an undertaking to closely scrutinize their own training and experience beforehand to ensure that they can deliver a thorough, reliable, and valid assessment under challenging conditions.

Informed Consent

Informed consent generally refers to the requirement that assessing psychologists make available to their patients or clients any and all information that might reasonably affect that party's decision to seek services from the psychologist. This information must be made available prior to service delivery and must be delivered in a way that is reasonably understandable to the client (American Psychological Association, 2002, section 3.10;

---

* Although the death penalty appeals process may drag on for years, a defendant's opportunities to raise the inadequacy of his or her assessment as a legal issue may be quite limited.

Committee on Ethical Guidelines for Forensic Psychologists, 1991, section IV(a)). In forensic settings, the psychologist must also inform the individual being assessed of the nature of the anticipated services, including whether the services are court ordered or mandated and any limits of confidentiality (American Psychological Association, 2002, section 3.10(c)). These explanations must be provided even if the person being assessed is legally unable to give consent (American Psychological Association, 2002, section 3.10(b)). Informed consent disclosures must include an explanation of the nature and purpose of the assessment, fees, involvement of third parties, limits of confidentiality, and sufficient opportunity for the individual to ask questions and receive answers (American Psychological Association, 2002, section 9.03(a)). In addition, the *Specialty Guidelines* suggests that forensic psychologists have an obligation to ensure that individuals who will be evaluated are informed of their legal rights with respect to the anticipated forensic service, the purposes of any evaluation, the nature of procedures to be employed, the intended uses of any product of their services, and the party who has employed the forensic psychologist (Committee on Ethical Guidelines for Forensic Psychologists, 1991, section IV(e)). This last obligation requires that where an assessor is evaluating a defendant in a forensic context, he or she must make it clear that they are not there to provide therapy or advocate on the defendant's behalf, but are rather acting as a neutral evaluator (Heilbrun, 2001). Of course, the particular informed consent requirements necessary for a particular case will vary along with the specifics of that case, and it is the psychologist's responsibility to make certain that the disclosure provided is adequate for the task at hand.

In many forensic cases, psychologists may also be required to clarify the limits of their professional role with the attorneys and other relevant legal actors involved in the case. A psychologist may ethically act either as a consultant or as a testifying expert but may not fill both roles (Heilbrun, 2001). A psychologist-consultant may assist the defense or prosecution in developing trial strategy, but in doing so loses his or her ability to act as an impartial expert evaluator. Conversely, any psychologist called as an expert is ethically required to deliver his or her findings objectively and impartially, regardless of who is paying for those services (Committee on Ethical Guidelines for Forensic Psychologists, 1991, section VI). Informed consent requirements mandate that the psychologist make these facts clear to their clients prior to providing services.

Although informed consent always requires high levels of transparency and considerable forethought on the part of the psychologist, Cunningham and Reidy (2001) identify three other considerations that further heighten ethical expectations in death penalty cases. Their first argument is axiomatic and asserts that the greater the magnitude of the potential harm involved, the greater the individual's right to be fully informed. As a person's life is at stake, his or her corresponding right to be fully informed regarding his or her assessment is at its most extensive. Second, the complexity and sheer number of factors under assessment in death penalty cases can lead to an array of highly significant, but not readily apparent, repercussions, a feature that again mandates thoroughness during the informed consent process. Finally, because of the wide range of possible issues relevant to a capital mitigation assessment, there is a correspondingly wide breadth of matters that could conceivably affect an individual's decision to agree to such an assessment. Thus, the ethical requirement that the psychologist provide thorough and understandable informed consent disclosures is never greater than in the death penalty context (Cunningham and Reidy, 2001).

Psychometric Considerations

The use of psychometric tools, most commonly thought of as psychological testing, has become *de rigueur* for most forensic assessments. Psychometric instruments allow for systematic comparison to norm groups, assess response style, help ensure standardized assessment procedures, and can often help increase an assessment's perceived legitimacy and usefulness in the eyes of the court (Cunningham and Reidy, 2001; Heilbrun, 2001; Melton, Petrila, Poythress, and Slobogin, 1997). The decision to use psychometric instruments also brings with it a host of specific ethical obligations and concerns. Perhaps most salient among these for forensic psychologists is the requirement that any psychometric instrument used in the evaluation demonstrate adequate psychometric properties, most notably reliability (meaning the instrument is free of measurement error) and validity (meaning the instrument measures what it purports to measure) (Anastasi, 1988). Generally speaking, both the APA Ethics Code and the *Specialty Guidelines* require that all assessment tools selected for an evaluation be anchored by empirical research that establishes their sufficiency and appropriateness for the question under consideration (American Psychological Association, 2002, section 9.01-2; Committee on Ethical Guidelines for Forensic Psychologists, 1991, section VI). More specifically, the APA Ethics Code requires that assessment techniques be administered, adapted, scored, and interpreted in a manner and for purposes that are appropriate in light of the research on or evidence of the usefulness and proper application of the techniques (American Psychological Association, 2002, section 9.02(a)). Psychologists must also rely only on those assessment instruments whose validity and reliability have been established for use with members of the population tested. When such validity or reliability has not been established, psychologists describe the strengths and limitations of test results and interpretation (American Psychological Association, 2002, section 9.02(b)). These requirements are part of a larger obligation that any psychological assessment, as a whole, be based on accepted scientific and professional knowledge (American Psychological Association, 2002, section 2.04).

Interpretation of psychometric test results, however, must also take into account contextual and cultural factors that may affect test results in individual cases. For example, the APA Ethics Code requires that all assessment methods be appropriate to an individual's language preference and competence. In addition, interpretation of test results must take into account the purpose of the assessment and the various test factors, test-taking abilities, and other characteristics of the person being assessed, such as situational, personal, linguistic, and cultural differences, which might affect psychologists' judgments or reduce the accuracy of their interpretations (American Psychological Association, 2002, section 9.02(c)). On a related note, psychologists are required to indicate any significant limitations of their findings and interpretations (American Psychological Association, 2002, section 9.06). Finally, psychologists must take care to ensure that their chosen psychometric instruments are up to date for their intended purpose, and that their use is considered consistent with current clinical and scientific standards in the relevant professional communities (American Psychological Association, 2002, section 9.08; Committee on Ethical Guidelines for Forensic Psychologists, 1991, section VI(a)).

The use of psychometrically based assessment strategies, most notably testing, in the death penalty context presents a unique set of ethical dilemmas. Because of the stakes involved in such cases, any psychologist assessing a death-eligible defendant is ethically obligated to use every appropriate tool to perform his or her task effectively. Adding to the pressure to use psychometric testing is a widespread expectation on the part of the courts that psychological assessors will employ these instruments. Effective mitigation arguments in a capital context may often require a diagnosis of mental illness or mental retardation. Definitively making such diagnoses will, in turn, quite often require psychometric testing. For example, in the case of *Atkins* assessments, IQ testing is often required by law, or is a *de facto* requirement to make the necessary diagnosis of mental retardation. Thus, it is difficult, and inappropriate, for any psychologist involved in a death penalty assessment to avoid the use of psychometric instruments.

The ethical use of these instruments, however, requires a thorough understanding of each instrument's proper uses and limitations, along with scrupulous attention to accuracy and precision when describing their results. This is especially true in the death-penalty context, where life-or-death decisions could hinge on a particular test result. Unfortunately, most psychometric instruments are not normed on an incarcerated population, let alone a death-eligible population. As such, the generalizability (and, therefore, the accuracy) of psychometric test results may be somewhat limited in death-penalty cases (see DeMatteo and Edens, 2006). In addition, the precise meaning and accuracy of particular test results tend to change over time, again casting doubt on the reliability of particular test results (Clements, 1996; Flynn, 2006). Psychometric measures also generally provide only inferential data on the sorts of adverse developmental factors that are often the focus of death penalty mitigation arguments, and are therefore only loosely connected to many of the questions that are often the focus of capital sentencing hearings. In addition, they also reveal the presence of certain alarming pathologies, such as antisocial personality disorder, which may be unrelated to issues regarding culpability but may, absent a clear and thorough explanation, nonetheless influence legal decision-makers (Cunningham and Reidy, 2001). Given the gravity of death penalty proceedings, it is imperative that professional psychologists seek to uphold the highest scientific standards in selecting their psychometric measures, in interpreting their results, in clearly connecting those results to legally relevant questions, and describing the limitations of their instruments and subsequent interpretations.

Cultural Fairness of Psychological Measures

The need to ensure that any psychological assessment is culturally fair is a fundamental cornerstone of ethical psychological practice. By placing a premium on cultural fairness, professional psychology helps ensure the unbiased scientific integrity of psychological assessments while also honoring the profession's core humanistic values. This core value is codified as an aspirational goal in the APA Ethics Code, which requires psychologists to respect the dignity and worth of all people, and the rights of individuals to privacy, confidentiality, and self-determination (American Psychological Association, 2002, General Principle E). It further advocates that psychologists should be aware that special safeguards may be necessary to protect the rights and welfare of persons or communities whose vulnerabilities impair autonomous decision-making. Special attention is given to the importance of individual differences (e.g., age, gender, gender identity, race, ethnicity, culture, national origin, religion, sexual orientation, disability, language, and socioeconomic status) and the need to consider these factors when working with members of such groups. Finally, this aspirational guidance suggests that psychologists try to eliminate the effect of biases in their work based on those factors, and not knowingly participate in or condone activities of others based on such prejudices (American Psychological Association, 2002, General Principle E).

It is important to note that the above guideline is aspirational and not necessarily an enforceable mandate for ethical practice. Moving beyond aspirational principles, the Code of Conduct, which is enforceable, provides a number of important culturally related guidelines for ethical practice. For example, at the most general level of analysis, the Code of Conduct specifically prohibits discrimination of any kind based on the individual differences listed above and notes that an understanding of these factors is an important aspect of training and effective psychological practice (American Psychological Association, 2002, sections 2.01(b) and 3.01). The Code of Conduct specifically addresses the importance of cultural fairness in an assessment context by noting that any interpretation of test results should take into account the various test factors, test-taking abilities, and other characteristics of the person being assessed, such as situational, personal, linguistic, and cultural differences, which might affect the psychologists' judgments or reduce the accuracy of their interpretations (American Psychological Association, 2002, section 9.06). The Code of Conduct takes this statement one step further and requires psychologists to indicate any culturally based interpretive limitations on their data (American Psychological Association, 2002, section 9.06). Thus, the APA Ethics Code requires its practitioners to maintain the highest level of cultural sensitivity at all times, and to specifically consider those factors when interpreting psychometric test data and drawing related conclusions.

A similar principle was recently included in the second official draft of the *Revised Specialty Guidelines for Forensic Psychology* (*Revised Specialty Guidelines*). The *Revised Specialty Guidelines* closely mirrors the language and spirit of the APA Ethics Code by noting that forensic practitioners should be aware of and respect cultural, individual, and role differences, and consider these factors when working with members of such groups (Committee on the Revision of the Ethical Guidelines for Forensic Psychologists, 2006, section 4.08). Similarly, the *Revised Specialty Guidelines* states that forensic psychologists do not engage in unfair discrimination, take steps to correct or limit the effects of such factors on their work, and decline or limit their participation in such circumstances in a manner that is consistent with professional obligations (Committee on the Revision of the Specialty Guidelines for Forensic Psychology, 2006, section 4.08).

These mandates present a number of special ethical issues in the death penalty context. Accusations have long circulated charging that the administration of the death penalty is plagued by cultural, ethnic, and socioeconomic biases (Amnesty International, 2003). This can create an ethical conflict for those practitioners who believe that they are tacitly condoning a state-sanctioned system of retribution that is fundamentally unfair to certain groups by participating in a death penalty assessment. It is imperative, therefore, that psychologists come to terms with their personal feelings about these issues before agreeing to take on a death penalty assessment.

In addition, the cultural fairness of the psychological measures typically used in capital mitigation assessments has been a controversial topic for years. It has even been described as the most enduring controversy in the measurement of intellectual functioning (Kane, 2003). For racial and ethnic groups whose native language is English, IQ tests and personality inventories are believed to provide a reliable and valid measure of intellectual and personality functioning. Unfortunately, some evidence suggests that these measures are more relevant to the assessment of individuals from the industrialized world, making them far less reliable and valid with nonnative English speakers, poorly educated individuals, or individuals raised in non-Western or third-world cultures (Kaufman, 1994). As a result, the accuracy and relevance of our assessment approaches may be called into question. A few prominent personality and IQ measures have been translated into foreign languages. Nonetheless, a number of factors are thought to contribute to the cultural insensitivity of such measures even when foreign language differences are taken into account. Many IQ items are drawn from Caucasian, middle-class culture. Caucasian children often have more advantages and opportunities than children of color. The forms of spoken English used by African-American or Latino children may also not correspond to language used in IQ tests and personality measures (Kaufman, 1994).

Some commentators have cited these factors as evidence for cultural or racial bias, although a number of studies suggest that the effects of stereotypes, cultural differences, social class, and bias are negligible and cannot alone account for group differences (Kane, 2003). Nonetheless, this problem highlights the dangers inherent in using a single psychometric instrument as a primary criterion in making a critical life decision. A simple IQ score or personality profile cannot possibly represent the individual as a whole being within his or her unique life context. Indeed, a number of legally relevant diagnostic criteria within the DSM-IV, including mental retardation and antisocial personality disorder, specifically mandate the consideration of cultural and environmental factors in rendering a diagnosis (American Psychiatric Association, 2000). Similarly, the widely cited American Association of Mental Retardation's (2002) definition of its namesake disorder specifically mandates consideration of cultural, community, and peer contexts and suggests that a valid assessment must consider the impact of cultural and linguistic diversity as well as differences in communication, sensory, motor, and behavioral factors.

The possible cultural inequities inherent in many psychological measures thus create a rather ironic legal and ethical paradox, especially with regard to mental retardation. Measures of intellectual functioning are believed to systematically underreport the IQ of African Americans and Latinos because of the cultural biases inherent in IQ test construction. As a result, individuals from these minority groups are more likely than their Caucasian, English-speaking counterparts to be classified as mentally retarded using one of the standard measures of intellectual functioning. These same populations are proportionally far more likely to be convicted of a capital crime than are their Caucasian counterparts and are accordingly over-represented on America's death rows.* With the introduction of the *Atkins* doctrine, these two independent forms of cultural inequity may unexpectedly combine to protect a proportionally greater number of African-American and Latino inmates.

Malingering

Because of the seriousness and sometimes final consequences in capital cases, special attention needs to be directed toward the evaluation of response style as it relates to deception and malingering. In fact, the assessment of malingering has been described as the number one priority in forensic assessment (Brodsky and Galloway, 2003). Although attorneys might

---

* Although African Americans constitute 12.8% of the population of the United States, they make up approximately 43% of the inmates on death row and 35% of all executed inmates (Bureau of Justice Statistics, 2006; Ceci, Scullin, and Kanaya, 2003).

be more inclined to take their clients' presentation at face value, judges and psychologists are likely to be aligned in their heightened concern regarding potential malingering. No matter what their inclinations about a particular case may be, judges will certainly be very interested in what psychologists have to say about whether the subject of the assessment is presenting him- or herself accurately or attempting to malinger. The APA Ethics Code addresses the importance of assessing the accuracy of response style indirectly by noting that psychologists take into account the various test factors and characteristics of the person being assessed that might affect the psychologists' judgments or reduce the accuracy of their interpretations and indicate significant reservations they have about the accuracy or limitations of their interpretations (American Psychological Association, 2002, section 9.02(c)). Similarly, the *Specialty Guidelines* describes the role of third party and other sources of information, noting that an evaluation actively seeks information that will allow the psychologist to differentially test plausible rival hypotheses (Committee on Ethical Guidelines for Forensic Psychologists, 1991, section VI). In a capital context, malingering is always a rival hypothesis that must be tested to ensure the ethical obligation of accuracy in assessment.

Unfortunately, sorting real pathology and mental retardation from simulated pathology and mental retardation is one of the most challenging tasks in forensic assessment. Because the *Atkins* decision allows for mentally retarded offenders to avoid capital punishment, psychologists must be particularly well prepared to confront the issue in many death penalty assessments. Where a defendant's cognitive functioning is in question, at least one malingering strategy is quite obvious. Although one cannot do better on an IQ test than one is capable of doing, one can certainly do worse. For these reasons, psychologists performing capital mitigation assessments might consider using more than one psychological measure to assess the psychological factors at issue. In addition, assessment batteries should include general and specialized empirically based malingering-detection instruments.

Accuracy can also be an issue related specifically to the way in which mental retardation is classified and diagnosed. Because mental retardation is considered a developmental disability (i.e., present from childhood onward), formal diagnosis of mental retardation requires a history of onset prior to age 18; such a requirement does not typically exist for mental health diagnoses not related to developmental disabilities (American Psychiatric Association, 2000). Thus, a diagnosis of mental retardation usually requires examination of records created well before the defendant's incarceration. This can be a useful factor in helping to improve accuracy and distinguish malingerers from legitimately impaired individuals. Although anyone can do poorly in the present on an IQ test by not trying his or her best, a significant disparity in test scores will often be very difficult to explain absent an intervening head injury or other type of disease process. Because IQ is believed to be relatively static over time, a sharp, unexplained drop in IQ scores following incarceration can be strong evidence of malingering.

As a practical matter, collecting a thorough patient history and conducting a comprehensive records review is a necessary prerequisite to any competent forensic mental health assessment (FMHA) and is always invaluable in helping to parse real psychopathology from malingering. For defendants alleging mental retardation, the need for an evaluation of intellectual functioning for special education services will mean that previous school-based assessment results are available. To some degree, then, mental retardation may be relatively immune to malingering if a complete history is available to the diagnostician (Watt and McLean, 2003). Establishing an MR diagnosis is, of course, considerably more difficult when no such records exist. In those situations, taking a comprehensive developmental and educational history is crucial for accurate diagnosis. Although gathering appropriate historical information is indicated when diagnosing any developmental disability, a thorough review of the relevant clinical history is never more crucial than in the death penalty context. A detailed background check can reveal clues to a person's adaptive functioning outside of a structured penal environment, along with demonstrating the longevity and pervasiveness of any adaptive deficits.

Ethical Concerns Posed by *Atkins*-Type Evaluations

In addition to the concerns enumerated above, evaluations of cognitive functioning pursuant to the *Atkins* decision present a host of specific ethical concerns related to the accuracy of the results obtained during the evaluation. These include effectively interpreting the variability of IQ scores, the impact of repeated intelligence testing on the accuracy of findings, and difficulties in assessing and quantifying adaptive functioning (Knauss and Kutinsky, 2004). Although these unique concerns are relevant in any assessment where cognitive functioning is an issue, they take on a greater level of importance in the *Atkins* context where many states have operationalized mental retardation as a cut-off score on an IQ test. As with many areas of assessment, specific substantive guidance on these relatively specialized issues is not found in any existing code of ethics. Relevant codes of ethics do address them indirectly through the requirement that psychologists take into account the various *test factors* and characteristics of the person being assessed that might affect the psychologists' judgments or reduce the accuracy of their interpretations and indicate significant reservations they have about the accuracy or limitations of their interpretations (American Psychological Association, 2002, section 9.02(c); Committee on Ethical Guidelines for Forensic Psychologists, 1991, section VI). We will now turn to a discussion of special ethical considerations related to accuracy in the assessment of cognitive functioning in the wake of *Atkins*.

Variability of IQ Scores

As noted earlier, the *Atkins* decision left it up to individual states to determine their own criteria for mental retardation. Cited in footnotes to the *Atkins* decision were definitions of mental retardation from the American Association of Mental Retardation (AAMR; 2002) and from the fourth edition of the American Psychiatric Association's (1994) *Diagnostic and Statistical Manual of Mental Disorders*. Like many psychological disorders, assertions regarding the criteria for mental retardation have not been static over time. Both the AAMR and DSM-IV definitions of mental retardation have been revised quite frequently (Ceci, Scullin, and Kanaya 2003). The AAMR in particular has revised its definition nine different times over the last century (American Association of Mental Retardation, 1992, 2002). The consequences of these refinements have at times been quite significant. A lowering of the IQ cut-off in 1973, for example, changed the proportion of the American population classified as mentally retarded from 16 to 3% (Ceci et al., 2003). Given the frequency and significance of past adjustments, it seems all but certain that the definition of mental retardation could change again in the future.*

---

* In fact, the recently released Wechsler Intelligence Scale for Children, 4th edition (2003) (hereinafter "WISC-IV") redefines the domains of intellectual functioning seen as contributing to mental retardation. This represents a fundamental shift in the way the test conceptualizes mental retardation and is likely a harbinger of broader conceptual changes to come. The WISC-IV is discussed in greater detail in the next section.

By leaving the definition of mental retardation up to each state, however, the Supreme Court of the United States has given the states the ability to respond to changes in the state of the art, and legal definitions of mental retardation can be revised by those state legislatures willing to keep abreast of advances, and digressions, in the field of mental health. Unfortunately, it now appears that in addition to providing the states with much-needed flexibility, it has also created a legal landscape rife with definitional ambiguity and inconsistency (DeMatteo et al., 2006). Practitioners will have to carefully adjust their assessment approaches to take these idiosyncratic legal demands into account. This will be an ongoing challenge, especially considering that assessors are also ethically responsible for ensuring their assessment procedures are up to date and comport with the *Specialty Guidelines* (Committee on Ethical Guidelines for Forensic Psychologists, 1991).

The notion of whether mental retardation can be "treated" or show improvement has also undergone a great deal of rethinking. For years, the standard definitions emphasized the chronic, incurable nature of mental retardation (Smith, 1997). Although IQ is generally considered a static phenomenon, there is a growing focus on the power of a good support system to improve a person's adaptive functioning (Smith, 1997). If supports can help improve a mentally retarded individual's adaptive functioning, it may be possible to remediate or even eliminate a diagnosis of mental retardation. As the technology for doing so evolves, the "permanence" of *Atkins*-related mental retardation determinations may increasingly be called into question.

Another issue affecting the stability of mental retardation determinations is a phenomenon known as the "Flynn effect." This refers to a gradual, population-wide improvement in intelligence test performance that causes IQ test norms to become obsolete approximately every 20 years (Flynn, 1998, 2006). When this happens, IQ tests are "renormed" so that scores more closely reflect the population's true level of intellectual functioning. Each time an IQ test is renormed, there is a generalized lowering of IQ scores because the new norms recalibrate the average IQ to remove the increases that accumulated over the previous norming cycle. So, if 2.27% of the population is diagnosed as mentally retarded in the year an IQ test is normed (i.e., having an IQ of less than 70), then each subsequent year will find fewer and fewer people scoring below 70 due to the tendency for scores to rise, until new norms once again come into use. Thus, we can expect a spike in mental retardation diagnoses each time new IQ norms are published (Ceci et al., 2003; Flynn, 2006).

The newly released Wechsler Intelligence Scale for Children (4th edition) (WISC-IV) will have an especially important effect on this debate. The WISC-IV (which was published in 2003) redefined IQ by giving equal weight to four domains of intellectual functioning— verbal comprehension, perceptual organization, working memory, and processing speed (Dietzel, 2004). Previous versions of the WISC organized cognitive abilities into two general categories—verbal and performance IQ. Although the top 2.27% of the population will still be labeled "gifted," and the bottom 2.27% of the population will be labeled "mentally deficient," different people will fall into these categories than those identified by prior tests (Ceci et al., 2003). Thus, a child with excellent verbal and slow processing skills may be identified as gifted by the WISC-III but not by the WISC-IV, and a child with poor verbal skills and excellent processing speed may fall in the range of mental retardation on the WISC-III but not on the WISC-IV.

In the *Atkins* context, ethical dilemmas can be expected to arise when someone's IQ score was initially assessed above 70, but later appears below 70 because new norms come into use. Or someone's IQ can be simultaneously below 70 on one IQ test and above 70 on a different IQ test. Also, a person's IQ can be above 70 on a test that was administered in childhood, but the same person would have scored below 70 on a newer version of the same IQ test. Thus, someone's IQ score can fluctuate above and below the cut-off of 70 that many states use. Importantly, these documented changes in IQ scores occur in the absence of any meaningful change in the intellectual ability of the individuals affected—in short, any inconsistencies are likely to result not from actual changes in the individuals being tested, but rather from imperfections in our assessment tools and data. Determining how to interpret variability between test scores will require psychologists to stay abreast of changes in the state of the art, along with carefully reporting and counterbalancing of inconsistent information. More than ever, careful clinical judgment and reliance on convergent, overlapping data will be required for psychologists to discharge their duties competently and ethically.

Test–Retest Effects

The test–retest phenomena associated with assessments of cognitive functioning are also concerning in a capital context. Individuals who raise the issue of cognitive impairment as either a mitigating or exclusionary factor will often be required to take and retake the same IQ tests as different experts assess their cognitive functioning. This would not seem to be a problem at first, because a person's IQ is presumed to be static over time. It is well established, however, that repeated administrations of the same IQ tests often leads to artificial elevations in the overall IQ score (Wechsler, 1997). For example, the manual for the widely used Wechsler Adult Intelligence Scale-Revised (third edition) (WAIS-III) reports that the mean full-scale IQ score for adults 30–54 years old went up by approximately 5 points if those adults retook the same test within 12 weeks of the first administration. To prevent such an artificial inflation of IQ scores, the manual recommends that a minimum interval of 1–2 years occur between administrations (Wechsler, 1997).

The *Atkins* case illustrates the conundrum created by the legal system's need to allow different experts to administer and readminister IQ tests. In this case, the defendant produced a full-scale score of 59 on an IQ test administered in 1998. A defense expert who retested the defendant in 2004 found that his full-scale IQ score had improved to 74. The defendant's case was remanded to the trial court level for a hearing on whether he met the relevant legal tests for mental retardation (in Virginia, this required an IQ of 70 or below, among other things) after the Supreme Court of the United States ruled that the execution of mentally retarded offenders was unconstitutional in 2002. The defendant was then retested by prosecution experts in 2005, and that test yielded a full-scale IQ score of 76. Defense experts then countered that his scores had increased due to the "mental workout" his participation in years of litigation had given him (Liptak, 2005). A Virginia jury nonetheless found the defendant eligible to be executed (i.e., not mentally retarded) on the basis of the most recent IQ score (International Justice Project, 2005).

There are thus two related test–retest factors that an assessing psychologist must ethically consider when agreeing to evaluate the cognitive functioning of a death row inmate. The first is the interval effect or the expected practice-related increase in scores where a person has previously taken the same IQ test. The more recently and more often a person has been tested, then the more likely practice effects are to distort future test results. The second is the previously mentioned Flynn effect (Flynn, 1998, 2006). If a test has not been renormed, the forces that push the population's IQ scores up over time will also apply to individuals retaking the same test. This effect has been experimentally shown to raise an individual's IQ scores by around .3 points a year, or around 3 points a decade (Flynn, 2006). Taken together, these factors have the potential to seriously distort a defendant's IQ score. In the context of capital mitigation, a distortion of this type might make the difference between life and death.

A number of recommendations are therefore called for to help practitioners practice ethically under these circumstances. First, practitioners must determine whether a defendant has previously taken a particular IQ test. If so, it is critical to determine when this last occurred, and how many times. If the most recent previous administration occurred within the time frame proscribed by the IQ test's manual, then a different measure must be given, or assessment must be delayed until the appropriate time interval has passed. To account for any inflation in scores due to the Flynn effect, Flynn suggests a formula to convert IQ scores to a common metric. He suggests using the norms current at the time the test was taken to account for rising scores. To accomplish this, the standard practice suggested by Flynn is to deduct .3 IQ points per year (3 points per decade) to cover the period between the year the test was last normed and the year in which the individual in question took the test (Flynn, 2006).

Adaptive Functioning

The DSM-IV and AAMR definitions of mental retardation suggest that IQ scores alone should not determine a diagnosis of mental retardation (American Association of Mental Retardation, 1992, 2002; American Psychiatric Association, 1994). Individuals must also demonstrate significant limitations in adaptive living skills. A person's adaptive functioning serves as a measure of how well the individual copes with routine demands of life and whether the individual is able to achieve a level of independence consistent with his or her age, social and cultural background, or living situation (Watt and McLean, 2003). Limitations in these areas are usually determined by interviewing family members or caregivers who have seen the individual functioning in their day-to-day environment (Watt and McLean, 2003). The interviews can be supplemented by administering various inventories of adaptive living skills; however, no single assessment strategy can be used consistently across all settings or with all populations due to normative differences (Brodsky and Galloway, 2003). There is also latitude in determining at what point deficiencies in adaptive functioning become so clinically significant as to warrant a diagnosis of mental retardation. Ultimate discretion in making such determinations is typically left to the clinical judgment of the assessing psychologist, who must assess each individual based on the individual's interactions within his or her particular life context (American Psychiatric Association, 2000).

This sort of assessment is particularly challenging with incarcerated individuals because the structure and supports provided by a prison environment tend to reduce, or at least alter, the environmental demands placed upon inmates (Everington and Keyes, 1999). This again was raised as an issue in the *Atkins* case, where defense attorneys argued that the highly structured, safe environment of a prison allowed the defendant to appear more adaptive than he actually was (Liptak, 2005). Unfortunately, existing measures of adaptive functioning have not been designed or normed for use with a correctional population. Thus, adaptive functioning prior to incarceration should be the target for assessment.

Because of its necessarily inexact and idiosyncratic nature, it seems likely that the courts will be somewhat uncomfortable with the construct of adaptive functioning. Psychologists will almost certainly feel pressure either to diagnose mental retardation based solely on IQ score or to develop a more objective definition of adaptive functioning. The malleable nature of adaptive functioning assessments is, however, both deliberate and necessary. Mental retardation is not actually one discrete disorder. Rather, it is the final common pathway of various pathological processes and accordingly can affect an individual's intellectual functioning in myriad ways (American Psychiatric Association, 2000). It is difficulties with adaptive functioning (and not IQ) that typically bring mentally retarded individuals to the attention of psychologists and other mental health professionals. Those difficulties must necessarily be evaluated in light of each individual's education, personality, mental health, motivations, sociocultural background, and community setting. Because the assessment of these factors is so individualized, individual scores on existing adaptive functioning scales may vary considerably in terms of reliability (American Psychiatric Association, 2000). In making a diagnosis of mental retardation, courts must be educated about the need to look beyond IQ scores and to consider the defendant's actual abilities in relevant cases.

Practice Issues and Challenges: Guidance from a Principles-Based Approach

An understanding of the relevant legal and ethical contours related to capital mitigation provides an excellent foundation and backdrop for discussing competent and effective forensic assessment practice in this area. Evaluations of this type are unique and present a number of correspondingly unique practice-related issues and challenges that might not be encountered in other types of forensic evaluations. These challenges tend to fall into categories related to four broad steps within forensic assessment: preparation, data collection, data interpretation, and the communication of assessment results (Heilbrun, 2001). Accordingly, the remainder of this chapter discusses these challenges and provides concrete recommendations for how to address them within the contours of existing support from relevant sources of authority within ethics, law, science, and standards of practice. A consideration of these challenges within the context of relevant practice-related guidance should increase the quality of capital mitigation evaluations, which should in turn improve the quality of legal decision-making in this arena (Heilbrun, 2001; Heilbrun, DeMatteo, and Marczyk, 2004; Heilbrun, DeMatteo, Marczyk, Finello, Smith, and Mack-Allen, 2005; Heilbrun, Marczyk, and DeMatteo, 2002; Marczyk, Heilbrun, DeMatteo, and Bell, 2003).

The Distinction between Forensic and Therapeutic Assessment

A more basic point must be addressed before turning to a specialized discussion of practice issues related to capital mitigation evaluations. This point focuses on the distinction between therapeutic and forensic assessment. The process of forensic assessment differs substantially and in important ways from therapeutic assessment, and practice guidelines used in purely therapeutic assessments will be limited or insufficient when applied to forensic assessments (Heilbrun, 2001). As noted previously, forensic assessment differs from its more therapeutic counterpart in a number of important ways, and these differences call for a specialized approach to conducting evaluations of this type. The first main distinction focuses on the definition of each type of evaluation. Forensic assessment refers to psychological evaluations that are performed by mental health professionals to provide relevant clinical and scientific data to a legal decision-maker or the litigants in both civil and criminal proceedings (Heilbrun, 2001). This makes forensic assessment distinct from therapeutic mental health assessment, which is performed primarily for reasons such as treatment planning and diagnosis.

The second distinction between forensic and therapeutic assessment focuses on the purpose of each type of assessment. The primary purpose of forensic assessment is to assist either a legal decision-maker or litigant by providing scientifically based information about an individual's relevant capacities underlying the specific civil or criminal legal question at hand. Although a forensic assessment can address mental health needs, typically in the form of treatment recommendations, the primary purpose of a therapeutic evaluation is usually to meet the mental health needs of a wide variety of individuals and groups across different treatment contexts with respect to diagnosis and treatment planning (Heilbrun, 2001).

The third distinction between forensic and therapeutic assessment is related to the unique nature of the examiner–examinee relationship. In forensic assessment, the evaluator assumes an objective role that typically requires using a higher standard for the accuracy and relevance of information, and the emphasis is therefore not necessarily on the therapeutic interests of the client. In therapeutic assessment, by contrast, the evaluator assumes a helping role where the best interests of the client are paramount (Heilbrun, 2001). The nature of the examiner–examinee relationship also has a direct bearing on the notification of purpose for the assessment. Given that the evaluator is representing a third party and the results of the evaluation will not always be in the best interests of the examinee, all forensic evaluations should begin with a formal notification that clarifies the purpose of the assessment and the relationship between the examiner and examinee. This is in contrast to therapeutic assessment, in which the evaluator is working on behalf of the examinee with the purpose of providing information intended to enhance mental health functioning, guide treatment planning, or provide diagnostic clarity (Heilbrun, 2001). This is not to say that notification of purpose does not take place in the therapeutic assessment context. In this context, notification of purpose is typically driven by the ethical and legal mandates that require the practitioner to obtain informed consent before providing any type of mental health service (Marczyk and Wertheimer, 2001).

The fourth distinction between forensic and therapeutic assessment focuses on the relevant standards used in each type of evaluation. Forensic assessment often requires the evaluator to address both a mental health and legal standard. A common example of this can be found in the context of competence to stand trial evaluations. In such a context, the evaluator might have to address and document the existence and impact of certain types of mental illness and cognitive impairment (e.g., a mental health standard) on the examinee's ability to understand the nature of the charges against them and assist counsel in their own defense (e.g., a legal standard). Conversely, standards in therapeutic assessment tend to be concerned with classification and treatment; facilitate diagnosis and treatment; and serve organizing, condensing, and orienting functions (Heilbrun, 2001). As such, mental health standards that are concerned with these issues tend to be more circumscribed than the standards considered in forensic assessment.

The fifth distinction between forensic and therapeutic assessment highlights objectivity in terms of the difference between the sources of information used in each type of evaluation. Although distinct, the two kinds of evaluations do share some common data domains, including clinical data and psychosocial information. This type of data tends to come from self-report, psychological testing, and behavioral observations. Although these sources of information are typically sufficient for therapeutic assessment, additional information must be used in forensic evaluations. Specifically, the more rigorous requirements of forensic assessment require the use of collateral information, such as record review or interviews with relevant third parties, to assess the accuracy and consistency of information provided in the evaluation from more traditional sources typically employed in therapeutic assessment (Heilbrun, 2001). The use of collateral information is essential in two main aspects of forensic assessment in that it improves the overall quality of the evaluation and also allows the evaluator to assess the response style of the individual in question. Response style refers to the nature and accuracy of the information provided by the individual being evaluated regarding the individual's own thoughts, feelings, and behaviors (Rogers, 1984, 1997). In most types of therapeutic evaluations, it is not necessary to consider the possibility of deliberate distortion of self-report through exaggeration or minimization of certain symptoms or experiences. In forensic evaluations, however, there is a consistent expectation that the examinee might present in a manner that would have the most favorable impact on his or her current situation. It is this consistent presence of situational incentives in the context of civil and criminal litigation that distinguishes forensic from therapeutic evaluation in the importance of response style (Heilbrun, 2001).

The sixth distinction between forensic and therapeutic assessment is related to the process of clarifying the reasoning and the limits on knowledge used during the course of the assessment and to address the referral question. Therapeutic evaluations tend to be collaborative in nature, and there is little, if any, expectation that the assumptions and methods employed will be challenged, except under very unusual circumstances. Conversely, forensic evaluations are not collaborative in nature. They are conducted in an adversarial legal context and are subject to challenge through a number of mechanisms that include rules of evidence and cross-examination by opposing counsel. Accordingly, there is an expectation that relevant assumptions and methods will be challenged (Heilbrun, 2001).

A seventh and final distinction between forensic and therapeutic assessment occurs in the documentation and communication of results, typically via report writing and testimony. Given the wide range of theoretical approaches, choices of instruments, and levels of expertise present in today's practice environment, there are no well-established expectations about the structure, format, and content of the written report needed to document a therapeutic evaluation. Conversely, the expectations for the documentation and communication of forensic evaluations are far more demanding and extensive. Forensic reports tend to be lengthy and detailed because the legal issue being considered requires extensive documentation that clearly describes the procedures, findings, and reasoning used in the assessment (Heilbrun, 2001). Similarly, there is a comparable distinction between the two types of evaluation in terms of verbal communication of the results, or expert testimony. Only rarely will a therapeutic evaluation be entered into evidence in a legal proceeding, so the likelihood of having to provide testimony is small. By contrast, the forensic evaluator should always anticipate that testimony would be associated with the assessment (Heilbrun, 2001).

Given these distinctions, it is apparent that the process of forensic assessment differs substantially and in important ways from therapeutic assessment. It therefore follows that the approaches and practices related to therapeutic assessment have limited application to forensic contexts, broadly defined, let alone the special circumstances and conditions that surround capital mitigation evaluations. A similar analogy can be found when we look at the relationship between the broadest representation of forensic referral questions and the more specific context of capital mitigation evaluations. Although there are some common issues that seem to span all criminal and civil-forensic referral questions, each specific referral question might pose its own unique challenges and related considerations. For example, the process of conducting a sanity evaluation might include a heavy emphasis on reconstructing the individual's mental state at the time of the offense, or in the past, while an evaluation for civil commitment might emphasize current, or present, clinical condition as it relates to the intent to harm oneself or others. In other words, the specific procedures and approaches used in forensic assessment often vary by referral question. In a similar vein, the procedures and approaches used in capital mitigation evaluations are likely to differ somewhat from other types of forensic referral questions. So, just as one would not want to conduct a forensic evaluation in the same way as a therapeutic assessment, one would not necessarily want to conduct a capital mitigation evaluation in the same way as other types of sentencing or competence evaluations. If each forensic referral question generates its own unique challenges, then the obvious question is how the evaluator addresses the unique challenges and practice-related issues that arise in the context of capital mitigation evaluations, especially evaluations conducted in the wake of the *Atkins* decision.

A Principles-Based Approach to Capital Litigation Evaluations

Based on our previous discussion, it seems clear that the distinctions between forensic and therapeutic assessment require the forensic practitioner to assume enhanced obligations in terms of adopting a more rigorous standard of practice. Despite these enhanced obligations, a number of commentators have concluded that the practice of forensic assessment often falls far short of meeting these more stringent standards, and that there is significant variation in the practice and quality of forensic assessment across practitioners and referral questions (Borum and Grisso, 1995; Heilbrun and Collins, 1995; Horvath, Logan, and Walker, 2002; Melton et al., 1997; Nicholson and Norwood, 2000; Otto and Heilbrun, 2002; Ryba, Cooper, and Zapf, 2003; Skeem and Golding, 1998). Part of the problem seems to derive from the relative lack of officially sanctioned, issue-specific ethical and practice guidelines available to forensic practitioners (Elwork, 1992; Grisso, 1986; Otto and Heilbrun, 2002). This is particularly disturbing in the capital mitigation context, where the results of the forensic evaluation might be related to life-and-death decisions.

This state of affairs has prompted some commentators and scholars to call for "model" or "principles-based" approaches to forensic assessment, with the intent of providing general practice guidance that should improve the quality of forensic assessment across a wide range of civil and criminal referral questions (Heilbrun et al., 2002, 2004; Marczyk, De Matteo, Kutinsky, and Heilbrun, in press; Melton et al., 1997; Morse, 1978a,b). The earliest models were designed to provide guidance on how to effectively conduct forensic assessments, particularly in the areas of data collection, data interpretation, and the communication of results. Initial attempts in this area suggested that forensic evaluations must answer legally related questions pertaining to the existence of a mental disorder, whether the behavior in question was a product of the mental disorder, and how the individual in question might behave in the future (Morse, 1978a,b). This parsimonious model guides forensic assessment in that it highlights the importance of data collection in key areas such as mental health symptoms and deficits, capabilities and competencies that are directly related to the legal test, and how these characteristics affect functional capacities (Heilbrun, 2001; Morse, 1978a,b).

Although acknowledging the value of this approach, other commentators noted that although helpful, this relatively straightforward model might not account for other prominent and important influences that could affect the process of forensic assessment. In response to this concern, Grisso (1986, 2002) developed a model for forensic evaluations that consisted of six characteristics shared by "legal competencies." The six characteristics were termed functional, contextual, causal, interactive, judgmental, and dispositional. Although there is overlap between the two models, this model emphasizes the importance of context and interaction in forensic assessment, aspects that were not accounted for in previously articulated models (Heilbrun, 2001). Later efforts in this area focused on the differences between therapeutic and forensic assessment and recommended forensic assessment procedures that were also relevant to psychological testing, such as the role and importance of testing in hypothesis formulation and confirmation and the use of psychometrically sound assessment strategies (Greenberg and Shuman, 1997; Heilbrun and Collins, 1995, 2001; Melton et al., 1997). Subsequent efforts resulted in a detailed description of 29 "principles" of FMHA that appear to have broad applicability and utility across a wide range of legal questions and forensic issues, including capital mitigation contexts (e.g., Heilbrun, 2001, 2003; Heilbrun et al., 2002, 2003, 2004, 2005; Lander, Pich, Loiselle, and Heilbrun, 2006; Marczyk, Heilbrun, DeMatteo, and Bell, 2003) (Table 2.1).

Each of the principles was discussed in terms of the support that it received from four sources of authority relevant to forensic assessment: (1) ethics, (2) law, (3) science, and (4) standards of practice. The major sources of ethical authority were the ethical standards for psychology (*Ethical Principles of Psychologists and Code of Conduct*, American Psychological Association, 1992), the ethical guidelines for forensic psychology (*Specialty Guidelines for Forensic Psychologists*, Committee on Ethical Guidelines for Forensic Psychologists, 1991), the ethical standards for psychiatry (*Principles of Medical Ethics with Annotations Especially Applicable to Psychiatry*, American Psychiatric Association, 1998), and the ethical guidelines in forensic psychiatry (*Ethical Guidelines for the Practice of Forensic Psychiatry*, American Academy of Psychiatry and the Law, 1995). Support from legal sources of authority was analyzed by examining federal case law (federal appellate and U.S. Supreme Court cases), federal statutes and administrative regulations, and "model" mental health law (e.g., *Criminal Justice Mental Health Standards*, American Bar Association, 1989). Scientific support was assessed by reviewing the relevant behavioral science and medical literature, with particular attention to well-designed empirical studies. Finally, the practice criterion considered the extent to which each principle is recognized by various authors, organizations, and other contributors to the professional literature as being important or useful for the practice of FMHA. Based on an analysis using these sources of authority, Heilbrun (2001) classified each principle as either *established* or *emerging*. *Established* principles are largely supported by research, accepted in practice, and consistent with ethical and legal standards, while *emerging* principles are supported in some areas, but with mixed or absent evidence in others, or partly supported but with continuing disagreement regarding their application (Heilbrun, 2001).

The 29 principles of FMHA were organized sequentially around the four broad procedural steps within forensic assessment: (1) preparation, (2) data collection, (3) data interpretation, and (4) communication. The major consideration in the *preparation* stage relates to the focus of the evaluation, or the legal issue or issues that must be decided by the court. Determining the focus of the evaluation is a critical first step in the evaluation process because the legal question or questions should be used to identify the relevant functional

Table 2.1   Principles of Forensic Mental Health Assessment (Heilbrun, 2001)

Preparation

   Identify relevant forensic issues

   Accept referrals only within area of expertise

   Decline the referral when evaluator impartiality is unlikely

   Clarify the evaluator's role with the attorney

   Clarify financial arrangements

   Obtain appropriate authorization

   Avoid playing the dual role of therapist and forensic evaluator

   Determine the particular role to be played within the forensic assessment if the referral is accepted

   Select the most appropriate model to guide data gathering, interpretation, and communication

Data Collection

   Use multiple sources of information for each area being assessed

   Use relevance and reliability (validity) as guides for seeking information and selecting data sources

   Obtain relevant historical information

   Assess clinical characteristics in relevant, reliable, and valid ways

   Assess legally relevant behavior

   Ensure that conditions for evaluation are quiet, private, and distraction free

   Provide appropriate notification of purpose and obtain appropriate authorization before beginning

   Determine whether the individual understands the purpose of the evaluation and the associated limits on confidentiality

Data Interpretation

   Use third-party information in assessing response style

   Use testing when indicated in assessing response style

   Use case-specific (idiographic) evidence in assessing clinical condition, functional abilities, and causal connection

   Use nomothetic evidence in assessing causal connection between clinical condition, functional abilities, and causal connection

   Use scientific reasoning in assessing causal connection between clinical condition and functional abilities

   Do not answer the ultimate legal question

   Describe findings and limits so that they need change little under cross-examination

Communication

   Attribute information to sources

   Use plain language; avoid technical jargon

   Write report in sections, according to model and procedures

   Base testimony on the results of the properly performed forensic mental health assessment

   Testify effectively

abilities that will be the focus of the evaluation. This, in turn, has important implications for how the overall forensic assessment is defined and addressed (Heilbrun, 2001). The specific principles under the preparation category reflect this overarching purpose and include: (1) identify relevant forensic issue; (2) accept referrals only within area of expertise; (3) decline referral when evaluator impartiality is unlikely; (4) clarify role with attorney; (5) clarify financial arrangements; (6) obtain appropriate authorization; (7) avoid dual-role relationships of therapist and forensic evaluator; (8) determine the role to be played within forensic assessment if the referral is accepted; and (9) select and employ a model to guide data gathering, interpretation, and communication (Heilbrun, 2001).

    The focus of the *data-collection* phase is on the selection of data sources and assessment strategies, and the administration of those strategies. There are two related steps in this phase. The first step is conceptual and involves the selection of a model to guide the presentation of information and clarify the reasoning used by the evaluator. The second step focuses on the selection of relevant sources of data and the administration of the necessary procedures. An essential consideration in this second step is that data sources and procedures should be valid, reliable, and relevant to the legal question before the court. The specific principles under the data-collection phase reflect the importance of providing relevant data and include: (1) use multiple sources for each area being assessed; (2) use relevance and reliability (validity) as guides for seeking information and selecting data sources; (3) obtain relevant historical information; (4) assess clinical characteristics in relevant, reliable, and valid ways; (5) assess legally relevant behavior; (6) ensure that conditions for evaluation are quiet, private, and distraction free; (7) provide appropriate notification of purpose and obtain appropriate authorization before beginning; and (8) determine whether the individual understands the purpose of the evaluation and associated limits on confidentiality (Heilbrun, 2001).

The principles under *data interpretation* highlight two important points related to the quality and limitations of the data generated from a forensic evaluation. The first point is related to response style, defined in its most general terms as the accuracy of the self-report of the individual being evaluated. Self-report is a common and valuable source of data used across all types of forensic evaluations. Although valuable for gaining information related to most aspects of functioning, self-report data are also subject to various levels of distortion. In instances where distortion is likely or present then the evaluator should deemphasize self-report in favor of other sources of information such as collateral records and interviews. The second point calls for the consideration of the role of scientific reasoning and empirical data in the evaluation process. More specifically, this point emphasizes the importance of prioritizing data based on response style and relevance and clarifying the limits of the data and any related assertions or conclusions. The principles under this phase include: (1) use third-party information in assessing response style; (2) use testing when indicated in assessing response style; (3) use case-specific (idiographic) evidence in assessing clinical condition, functional abilities, and causal connection; (4) use nomothetic evidence in assessing clinical condition, functional abilities, and causal connection; (5) use scientific reasoning in assessing causal connection between clinical condition and functional abilities; (6) do not answer the ultimate legal question directly; and (7) describe findings and limits so that they need change little under cross-examination (Heilbrun, 2001).

The principles under *communication* address the issue of both written communication in the form of report writing and oral communication in the form of testimony. Regardless of format, the communication of results derived from the forensic evaluation is a crucial step in the overall assessment process. Whether the results are communicated in writing or orally, the perceived value and effectiveness of the entire assessment is affected by the way in which it is communicated. Effective written communication requires the detailed documentation of the evaluation process, including the sources of information, observations and results, conclusions, and reasoning process. Effective testimony requires an effective and convincing oral description of the entire assessment process, and the evaluator must be prepared for the challenges and questioning that are part and parcel of the adversarial context. As such, effective communication must consider the use of style and presentation techniques that enhance effectiveness and credibility in communication of the results of the assessment. The principles captured by this phase include: (1) attribute information to sources; (2) use plain language and avoid technical jargon; (3) write report in sections according to model and procedures; (4) base testimony on the results of the properly performed FMHA; and (5) testify effectively (Heilbrun, 2001).

In sum, the application of these principles can potentially enhance the quality of any forensic assessment from the initial referral, through data collection and interpretation, and to the final communication of results in the form of a report or testimony (e.g., Heilbrun, 2001, 2003; Heilbrun et al., 2002, 2003, 2004, 2005; Lander et al., 2006; Marczyk et al., 2003). The quality of assessments is obviously important because poorly conducted forensic assessments in an adversarial context can be especially problematic, given the importance and possible consequences of litigation. Specifically, poor assessments may fail to address the appropriate legal standard; exceed the scope of the evaluation and render opinions that are more appropriately left to the legal decision-maker; or fail to provide adequate, credible information consistent with the conclusions drawn from the results of the evaluation (Grisso, 1986, 2003; Heilbrun, 2001). This is especially problematic in the capital context, where the quality of legal decision-making can literally have life-and-death implications. Although all of the principles focus on producing high-quality forensic evaluations, some principles are especially important when conducting evaluations in the context of capital cases. Accordingly, the principles relevant to these areas would receive particular emphasis in the context of a capital case. The remainder of this chapter focuses on how aspects of this principle-driven framework might be helpful for addressing the special challenges that are intrinsic to evaluations conducted post-*Atkins*, and for capital cases more generally in which the presence of mental retardation is not necessarily the overriding issue. As we will now discuss, the application of these principles should help minimize arbitrariness in the decision-making process through promoting thoroughness, consistency, clarity, and impartiality.

The reader will note that, as with earlier sections, the structure of the following section makes a distinction between broader capital sentencing and mitigation evaluations and *Atkins*-based evaluations that emphasize the importance and role of cognitive functioning. This distinction is admittedly somewhat arbitrary because deficits in cognitive functioning are clearly mitigating under the broadly defined factors specified by most state statutes. Accordingly, even the broadest evaluation might include an evaluation of cognitive functioning. Nevertheless, we think the distinction is necessary because it serves to focus on relevant and important issues where cognitive functioning seems to be the primary issue. Such an emphasis can create a unique set of practice issues, and we have tried to make this point by treating referrals generated in response to the possible presence of mental retardation or specific statutory mandates as different from the typical capital mitigation or sentencing evaluation.

Preparation

The unique challenges presented by capital evaluations occur from the moment that contact is established with the referral source, typically an attorney or the court itself. Proper preparation during this initial phase helps establish the appropriate framework for later activities and can preempt future problems and challenges if handled appropriately. One of the initial issues that the evaluator must address is whether he or she possesses the expertise necessary to conduct this type of evaluation. In general, forensic evaluators should *accept referrals only within their areas of expertise* (Heilbrun, 2001). Although there are other relatively straightforward legal questions that might be more appropriate for less experienced evaluators, capital mitigation evaluations place special demands on the evaluator's skills and expertise. Specifically, both *Atkins* evaluations and broader capital evaluations demand a broad and a more specific expertise on the part of the evaluator. Practitioners evaluating defendants who may be mentally retarded should demonstrate training and professional experience with individuals who are developmentally disabled. Forensic clinicians conducting capital sentencing evaluations should have broader experience with offenders, as well as individuals with severe mental illness. For either kind of evaluation, the forensic expert should also have experience applying this expertise in a forensic context. Accordingly, it would be inappropriate for evaluators with more circumscribed experience to take on a capital case without intensive supervision. The issue of expertise frequently arises in the context of qualifying the expert during the adversarial process. Typically, the demonstration of such expertise might involve giving one's terminal degree, licensure, and board certification status. Further, the evaluator should be prepared to describe (through the CV and in testimony) relevant experience with the specific population of developmentally disabled individuals (for *Atkins* evaluations) and the broader populations of offenders and individuals with severe mental illness (for capital sentencing evaluations) (Heilbrun et al., 2005).

Impartiality is a hallmark of excellent forensic practice. It almost goes without saying that the evaluator should *decline the referral when evaluator impartiality is unlikely* (Heilbrun, 2001). The principle of declining the referral when impartiality is unlikely applies to all legal questions and related forensic issues. It is also the case, however, that the importance of this principle takes on a more urgent quality in the context of capital cases. In the broadest sense, when there is a substantial incentive—monetary, personal, or professional—for the forensic clinician to reach a conclusion in a certain direction, then the referral to conduct the evaluation should probably be declined. In capital contexts, such motivation is occasionally monetary (as when, for example, a forensic clinician is privately retained by defense counsel to conduct an evaluation for *Atkins* purposes or for capital sentencing more broadly). This, however, is not substantially different from the payment source for other kinds of forensic assessment and is handled by ensuring that the evaluator is paid for his or her time rather than for conclusions. Even more problematic would be taking the referral on a contingency basis, where payment is based on the outcome of the proceeding. Capital cases add an even more poignant and potentially dangerous threat to evaluator impartiality. Specifically, personal feelings or a professional position that is very strongly pro or con regarding capital punishment can give rise to evaluator bias. A forensic clinician with such reactions, or position, is well advised to seek consultation with experienced colleagues and avoid participating in either an *Atkins* evaluation or broader capital mitigation or sentencing assessment. The perceptions of judges and attorneys are likely to be that such an individual could not be impartial—and such perceptions are likely to be accurate (Heilbrun et al., 2005).

Related to the issue of impartiality is the ethical issue surrounding dual roles. In more traditional mental health settings, dual roles are not necessarily prohibited, provided they are not harmful to the client. In forensic contexts, it is always advisable to *avoid playing the dual roles of therapist and forensic evaluator* (Heilbrun, 2001). Fortunately, this set of circumstances would rarely arise in either *Atkins* assessments or broader capital mitigation or sentencing evaluations. The exception might involve a treating mental health professional (perhaps a former provider, or delivering services to the defendant in jail) being asked to render a forensic opinion regarding mental retardation, or broader questions of mitigation and aggravation. This is invariably a poor idea, for a variety of ethical and professional reasons (Heilbrun, 2001; Melton et al., 1997). The occasional instance in which it would be helpful to have a treating clinician provide information can be handled by having that clinician testify in the role of fact witness rather than forensic expert, assuming that any privilege associated with treatment information had been waived (Heilbrun et al., 2005).

Another aspect of preparation and deciding whether to accept or decline the referral involves *clarifying the evaluator's role and determining the role to be played within the forensic assessment if referral is accepted* (Heilbrun, 2001). Supreme Court jurisprudence states that the defendant in a capital case is entitled to an expert, typically at state expense, to assist the defense on the issue of sanity at the time of the offense, and at capital sentencing (*Ake v. Oklahoma*, 105 S. Ct. 1087 (1985)). Under the precedent of *Ake*, the role of the expert is described broadly as encompassing both evaluative and consultative roles. The evaluative role involves conducting the forensic assessment, while the consultative role might involve, for example, helping the defense attorney prepare the cross-examination of the opposing experts. This is another example of a dual role that should be avoided in a forensic context, however, because there are compelling ethical and professional reasons for the forensic clinician to avoid playing the roles of both impartial expert and consultant in the same case (Heilbrun, 2001). In both *Atkins* evaluations and broader assessments for capital mitigation and sentencing, these principles suggest that the forensic clinician should select the role of *either* impartial evaluator *or* consultant and retain that role for the duration of the case. In addition, the role of impartial expert (whether retained by either side or court ordered) and consultant should be identified and treated as distinct from the time the forensic clinician is retained, with only one role assumed in a given case. This is comparably applicable to both *Atkins* and broader capital mitigation and sentencing evaluations. The relative absence of bias or advocacy associated with the impartial expert role should be reflected in both the tone of the report and the tenor of the testimony. Specific reflections of this impartiality should include a description of all findings (e.g., if a test is administered, it should be scored, interpreted, and discussed as part of the overall pattern of findings), a thorough approach using multiple sources, an even-handed consideration of all reasonable possibilities, and communication in language that is clear but not hyperbolic or overly technical (Heilbrun et al., 2005).

Clarifying financial arrangements is another component of preparation that is typically addressed as role clarification is established (Heilbrun, 2001). When payment for an *Atkins* or capital mitigation or sentencing evaluation is provided by the defense (either through the defendant or the attorney's office), then the amount, timing, and other details of such payment should be clarified when the forensic clinician is retained. If necessary, these details should be memorialized in writing and made available to the relevant parties. Many evaluations in capital contexts, however, are publicly funded, with the mechanism for and amount of remuneration prescribed by relevant statute or administrative code. In such instances, it may be unnecessary to clarify the terms of payment if retained by one of the attorneys or ordered by the court to conduct either kind of evaluation. Both kinds of evaluation are very important and demand thorough and detailed collection of data across multiple sources. Significant time is needed, and the evaluator may be unwilling to conduct such evaluations without assurance that this time will be compensated. A court order authorizing payment up to an agreed-upon limit is an alternative to the evaluator's depending on the court to approve a postevaluation payment request that exceeds the statutorily imposed limit (Heilbrun et al., 2005).

Once the evaluator has grappled with issues surrounding expertise, impartiality, and role clarification, the next consideration under preparation is to *identify the relevant forensic issue* (Heilbrun, 2001). Clearly, the evaluator will be aware of the overarching purpose of the referral from other conversations surrounding role clarification. So, this principle does not simply refer to identifying the issue in a broad sense. Instead, identifying the relevant forensic issue requires the evaluator to identify the capacities underlying the ultimate legal question. Our earlier discussion of relevant Supreme Court jurisprudence suggests that, in a capital mitigation or sentencing evaluation, such capacities would be operationalized by the aggravating and mitigating factors that are appropriate for expert mental health evaluation. Common aggravating factors include history of offending and heinousness of the offense, while common mitigating factors include the presence of extreme mental or emotional distress at the time of the offense, an inability to appreciate the wrongfulness of the act, and characteristics related to the character of the defendant. This is far from an exhaustive list, and evaluators must familiarize themselves with jurisdiction-specific case law and statutory guidance because the definitions and conceptualizations of aggravating and mitigating factors can vary across jurisdictions.

Although a complete evaluation of aggravating and mitigating factors is typically involved, the *Atkins* decision has created the need for an evaluation that is at times more limited and solely diagnostic, because mental retardation per se is the basis under *Atkins* for exclusion from a death sentence. Despite this, care must be taken to identify the appropriate scope of the evaluation, especially in light of the variation across jurisdictions in defining mental retardation under *Atkins*. Accordingly, it is important to cite the legal question and relevant statutory guidance in the first section of the report. Specific case law and statutory guidance is typically obtained from the referral source. It is also helpful to cite the aggravating and mitigating factors applicable in that jurisdiction, identifying in particular those that will be the focus of the evaluation (Heilbrun et al., 2005).

The next two principles under preparation are less concerned with clarification and begin to transition into the next phase of an evaluation, or data collection. The evaluator should always *obtain appropriate authorization* before proceeding with the evaluation (Heilbrun, 2001). The nature of the required authorization can vary according to the forensic issues being evaluated and the role assumed by the forensic clinician. It is useful to distinguish between circumstances in which there is a legal demand or a legal right to refuse participation from those in which there is no such demand or right. In sum, notification of purpose is applicable in cases in which the evaluation is legally compelled, while informed consent applies when there is no such compulsion (Heilbrun, 2001). Court-ordered evaluations represent the former, with referrals from attorneys representing the later. Notification of purpose typically includes details such as the evaluator's name and profession, who requested the evaluation and why, the purpose(s) for which it may or will be used, the distinction between a specific forensic evaluation and a therapeutic evaluation, and the limits on confidentiality. When a defendant has a legal right to refuse to participate, as in cases in which the evaluation has been requested by the defense rather than ordered by the court, the defendant's consent to participate should also be obtained. Evaluators who are unclear about the required authorization, and deliver an inaccurate notification, can create a number of difficulties. The two most obvious difficulties include a request for consent when none is needed, or describing a process that does not require consent when it actually does. Accordingly, all individuals undergoing a forensic evaluation should, at a minimum, receive a notification of purpose concerning the evaluation before it begins. This holds true across all forensic referral questions (Heilbrun, 2001).

There are important distinctions in such notification and consenting between *Atkins* evaluations and broader capital mitigation and sentencing evaluations. These distinctions flow from the kind of information sought in each respective evaluation. Keeping in mind the variation in how various states have defined mental retardation discussed earlier in this chapter, the *Atkins* assessment typically seeks to determine whether the defendant is mentally retarded, and thus often requires data on intellectual functioning, adaptive functioning, and history of previous diagnosis of mental retardation. By contrast, the broader capital sentencing evaluation typically must address several factors associated with mental state at the time of the offense. Accordingly, the evaluator must seek information about the defendant's thinking, emotions, perceptions, and behavior at the time of the offense to evaluate these factors properly. Obtaining such information on a pretrial basis (when evaluations must be conducted, in order to allow sufficient time to gather appropriate information and write the report), however, is often difficult. Many defendants deny or minimize their culpability, so information regarding their mental state at the time of the offense cannot be obtained through self-report. The notification in capital sentencing cases must draw the complex distinction between the defendant's legal right to assert innocence until proven guilty, exercise preadjudication, and the defendant's interest in providing information regarding ment. state at the time of the offense, potentially useful in mitigation, which would nevertheless only be used at sentencing if the defendant is convicted. Not surprisingly, many defendants do not provide such information following this notification, even defendants for whom the evidence strongly suggests factual guilt, leaving the evaluator to draw more limited conclusions regarding applicable mitigating factors (Heilbrun et al., 2005).

The final principle under preparation requires the evaluator to *select an appropriate model to guide the data gathering, interpretation, and communication* that will occur in the next three phases of the evaluation (Heilbrun, 2001). As we noted earlier, there are a number of models available to guide forensic evaluations (Grisso, 1986; 2003; Heilbrun, 2001; Melton et al., 1997; Morse, 1978a,b). In addition to Heilbrun's model, there are two particular models that are useful in helping to structure the data gathering, interpretation and reasoning, and communication of results. These respective models were originally proposed by Morse (1978a,b) and Grisso respectively (1986, 2003). These models were mentioned briefly in our discussion of attempts to improve the overall quality of forensic practice. Although an exhaustive discussion of these models is beyond the scope of this chapter, some elaboration at this point would be informative.

Morse's model was based on the observation that the structures of many mental health laws are similar in that they focus on three broad questions: (1) the existence of a mental disorder, (2) the functional abilities related to the tasks that are part of the relevant legal question, and (3) the strength of the causal connection between the first and second areas (Morse, 1978a,b). The resulting assessment model parallels these basic legal questions in that it requires forensic assessment to answer questions related to the existence of a mental disorder, whether the behavior in question was a product of the mental disorder, and how the individual in question might behave in the future (Morse, 1978a,b). These questions guide forensic assessment in that they highlight the importance of data collection in key areas such as mental health symptoms and deficits, capabilities and competencies that are directly related to the legal test, and how these characteristics affect functional capacities (Heilbrun, 2001; Morse, 1978a,b).

Grisso noted that this relatively straightforward model might not account for other prominent and important influences that could affect the process of forensic assessment.

Accordingly, Grisso (1986, 2002) developed a model for forensic evaluations that consisted of six characteristics shared by "legal competencies." The six characteristics were termed functional, contextual, causal, interactive, judgmental, and dispositional. *Functional* abilities are those "that an individual can do or accomplish, as well as the specific knowledge, understanding, or beliefs" that are relevant to the particular legal competency (Grisso, 1986, p. 15). The *contextual* component describes the "general environmental context, which establishes the parameters for defining the relevance of particular functional abilities for the legal competency construct" (Grisso, 1986, p. 18). *Causal* inferences "explain an individual's functional abilities or deficits are related to a legal competency" (Grisso, 1986, p. 20). The *interactive* characteristic asks whether "this person's level of ability meet[s] the demands of the specific situation with which the person will be faced" (Grisso, 1986, p. 23). The *judgmental* aspect addresses whether the "person-context incongruency is of a sufficient magnitude to warrant a finding of legal incompetency and its disposition consequences" (Grisso, 1986, p. 26). Finally, the *dispositional* aspect refers to the consequences of a finding of incompetence, which may give the state "the authority to act in some way toward the individual" (Grisso, 1986, p. 27). Although there is overlap between the two models in that they emphasize the functional legal capacities underlying the legal question, the causal connection between deficits in such functional legal capacities, and the potential sources of these deficits, Grisso's model emphasizes the importance of context and interaction in forensic assessment, aspects that were not accounted for in Morse's original model (Heilbrun, 2001).

These models would apply quite differently to *Atkins* and capital mitigation and sentencing assessments. Typically, but with the exceptions noted previously, the sole question in an *Atkins* evaluation involves whether the defendant meets diagnostic criteria for mental retardation. Although this question requires intellectual, behavioral, and historical data to yield a proper answer, there is no demand for a description of functional legal capacities underlying the larger legal question. Considered differently, the diagnostic/symptomatic and the functional legal criteria are usually synonymous in *Atkins* evaluations.

By contrast, diagnostic/symptomatic criteria are distinct from functional legal criteria in a capital mitigation or sentencing evaluation, as they are in all other kinds of forensic evaluations. The Morse or Grisso model can help identify these two domains distinctly. Because there are a number of mitigating factors, and occasionally aggravating factors (e.g., the defendant's future dangerousness) that are appropriate for expert mental health evaluation, these models suggest that the data and reasoning applicable to each be described in a separate section of the report, with a number of subsections to delineate each factor separately (Heilbrun et al., 2005; Marczyk et al., 2003).

Data Collection

Data collection is the focus of the second phase in forensic assessment. The focus of the data-collection phase is on the selection of data sources and assessment strategies, and the administration of those strategies. Accordingly, the practice challenges that arise in this phase tend to be related to selecting the sources of information for use in the forensic assessment. Although these issues are common across all types of forensic referral questions, capital cases tend to produce their own unique set of challenges. Accordingly, the principles in this section highlight practical and effective approaches to data collection in both types of capital cases.

We emphasized the importance of obtaining the appropriate authorization in our discussion of important facets of preparation. In that discussion, we highlighted the importance of knowing the specific contours of the evaluation and the nature of the required authorization and distinguished between circumstances in which there is a legal demand or a legal right to refuse participation from those in which there is no such demand or right. The data-collection phase is typically the first time that the evaluator has contact with the evaluee, and the focus appropriately shifts from understanding the source and limitations of authorization to actually *providing appropriate notification of purpose or obtaining appropriate authorization before beginning and determining whether the individual understands the purpose of evaluation and limits on confidentiality* (Heilbrun, 2001). Both *Atkins* and capital mitigation and sentencing evaluations can have significant implications for subsequent legal proceedings. It is critically important, therefore, that the defendant have a basic understanding of the elements of the notification that were outlined in our discussion in the preparation section. The notification can be given in either written or oral form, or both formats if necessary. Of clinical note is that intellectual limitations are relatively common in this population (Cunningham and Goldstein, 2003). This should not be surprising in the *Atkins* context because the possible presence of mental retardation is what triggers the referral. For example, a number of investigations have documented intellectual functioning in the mentally retarded to borderline range for defendants in capital sentencing determinations, and many defendants have sufficient reading problems to make written material useless (Cunningham and Goldstein, 2003; Heilbrun et al., 2005; Lewis, Pincus, Feldman, Jackson, and Bard, 1986; Lewis, Pincus, Bard, Richardson, Prichep, and Feldman, 1988). As individuals with significant intellectual and academic limitations may have trouble understanding aspects of even a simple notification, language should be basic and the evaluator should ensure that there is a specific gauge of how well the notification is understood. Accordingly, the evaluator should make an immediate effort to determine how well the elements of notification have been understood, keeping in mind that it is also possible for the defendant to grasp the purpose of the evaluation even when he/she has significant cognitive limits. Given the complexity and the sensitive nature of some of the material addressed in the latter evaluation, however, it is very important for the evaluator to explain it carefully and document the extent to which this explanation has been understood.

In essence, how well the defendant can recall and describe the elements of the notification should reflect his or her basic awareness of the nature of the evaluation and why it is being conducted. This is typically accomplished by having the evaluee repeat back his or her understanding of the process and the use of the resulting information gained from the assessment. Such understanding should be documented in the body of the report. If the defendant does not understand the notification, then deficits that interfere with such understanding should be identified and described in fuller evaluation. Absence of fully informed consent, however, is not sufficient to stop the evaluation if the attorney, as the defendant's legal representative, wants it to proceed and the defendant is willing and provides what is basically assent rather than fully informed consent. The referring attorney should be made aware of the evaluator's reasons for asking detailed questions regarding mental state at time of offense, and for encouraging the defendant to describe some aspects of behavior that would be incriminating if conveyed to others (e.g., police and other inmates) (Heilbrun et al., 2005).

An accurate conveyance of the notification of purpose and the related understanding of that notification can also have a significant impact on response style of the defendant, particularly in capital sentencing evaluations where mental retardation is not the over-riding issue. Specifically, the defendant's discussion of thinking and feeling around the time of the offense may depend partly on the extent to which the complex notification regarding the value of information concerning mental state at the time of the offense is understood. The evaluator should make a concerted effort to explain why such questions are asked, and the limited circumstances under which the information obtained would be used. The essence of this aspect of the notification for a defense-requested capital assessment should make it clear that the material could be used as evidence at sentencing *if* the defendant is convicted of a capital offense and *if* the results are favorable to the defendant so the attorney decides to use them. Conversely, however, if there is no such conviction, or there is such a conviction but results of the evaluation are not favorable to the defendant, the material will not be used (Heilbrun et al., 2005).

Although important in the notification and consent process, the evaluator should take all necessary steps to ensure that *conditions for the evaluation are quiet, private, and distraction free* when moving into the actual assessment and data-gathering process (Heilbrun, 2001). A limited body of research suggests that a variety of environmental and situational factors can have an impact on general test performance (e.g., American Psychological Association, 1986b; Bell, Hoff, and Hoyt, 1964; Hofer and Green, 1985; Kelley, 1943; Sacks, 1952; Traxler and Hilkert, 1942). Although relevant for all types of assessments, this principle is particularly important in both an *Atkins* and a more general capital context. When assessing an individual's level of intellectual functioning, performance may be adversely affected by conditions that include distractions or other influences that might impair attention/concentration. Although this might seem like a minor point, its importance grows considerably when we consider that a number of states include an IQ cut-off score in their definition of mental retardation. For some states, the IQ score is the only relevant determining factor. Accordingly, in the *Atkins* context, a small deviation in performance can yield a very important difference in the conclusion regarding mental retardation, so this principle should be respected carefully when conducting an *Atkins* assessment. This principle is also important in capital mitigation and sentencing evaluations because sensitive information is sometimes divulged when the interview focuses on mental state at the time of an offense while the defendant is still preadjudication. It could be very damaging for such information to be overheard by another inmate, and such matters should never be discussed with jail staff. It is essential, therefore, that the conditions under which capital evaluations are conducted are fully private and do not permit sensitive information to be overheard. In both contexts, the evaluator should record unusual testing conditions, however minor, and take testing conditions into account when interpreting test results. Again, these limitations should be incorporated in the written report and discussed where relevant during testimony. If necessary, the evaluator should not begin the assessment, or proceed if initial favorable circumstances change (e.g., being moved from a private room to a general holding area) if the conditions are so poor that they might exert a significant confounding impact on the results of the assessment (Heilbrun et al., 2005).

Selecting the sources of information for use in the evaluation is also critically important in high-quality forensic assessment. As noted above, unfavorable testing conditions can introduce error into the assessment process. The same is true of data sources, and the evaluator should always attempt to *use multiple sources of information for each area being assessed* as part of the evaluation (Heilbrun, 2001). There are a variety of potential sources of information available to the evaluator, and it is often necessary to select and prioritize them given the overall context of the evaluation. Classic examples of data sources include the clinical interview and traditional forms of psychological testing. Other excellent sources of data include specialized forensic testing, institutional records, and third-party collateral interviews. Using multiple sources of information provides a number of related benefits. First, it allows the evaluator to gauge the consistency of results across sources, which can help reduce the degree of error associated with any single source (Podboy and Kastl, 1993). Second, it enhances the accuracy in measuring a given trait, symptom, or behavior as they relate to the constructs underlying the legal issue. Finally, it allows the evaluator to check hypotheses that may have been generated by observations from data-gathering procedures used in the evaluation (Elwork, 1984; Grisso, 1986; Heilbrun, 2001).

These benefits, however, must be weighed against some related concerns. Specifically, an underlying assumption of this approach is that forensic clinicians can integrate all data to produce more valid conclusions. Some commentators have noted that different sources of information have different levels of validity, and indiscriminate integration can produce conclusions that are less accurate (Faust, 1989; Heilbrun, 2001). Similarly, it can also be difficult to determine how much weight to give to any particular source of information used in the assessment. At this point in time, it appears that using a blend of actuarial and clinical approaches to data gathering, paying specific attention to the validity of each measure, and proceeding with caution (e.g., clearly attribute information to sources) when integrating information are appropriate safeguards when using multiple sources of information (Faust, 1989; Heilbrun, 2001). Despite these limitations and cautions, the importance of using multiple sources of information is almost axiomatic in forensic assessment, and the principle applies equally well to both *Atkins* assessments and the broader range of capital mitigation and sentencing evaluations. The scope of the referral question helps dictate the number and types of data sources used in the evaluation. For example, the focus of an *Atkins* evaluation might only require the assessment of IQ, adaptive functioning, or both. Accordingly, the focus of the evaluation would be relatively narrow and most likely utilize a limited number of data sources. Conversely, capital mitigation and sentencing evaluations can be quite broad in scope, requiring the evaluator to expand the scope of sources to an extent commensurate with this focus (Heilbrun et al., 2005). Elaborating on our discussion of the relative importance and quality of the various sources of data used in the evaluation, the evaluator should always use *relevance and reliability (validity) as guides for seeking information and selecting data sources and assess clinical characteristics in relevant, reliable, and valid ways.* At the broadest level, the selection of different sources of information in all types of forensic assessment should be guided primarily by relevance to the legal issue at hand and the validity and reliability of the different sources used in the evaluation (Heilbrun, 2001). As noted above, a source of information that has little relevance and accuracy can have a substantial negative impact on the overall quality of the evaluation. Relevance can be described qualitatively as the logical basis for a connection between a mental health construct and certain forensic issues. From an empirical standpoint, relevance can be described by citing empirical evidence about the strength of the relationship between these constructs in various types of available research. Reliability (having limited measurement error) and validity (established to measure what is intended) are typically operationalized in terms of the psychometric properties and related validation research that supports the use and application of a particular assessment strategy or instrument for particular forensic referral questions (Anastasi, 1988; *Daubert v. Merrell Dow Pharmaceuticals, Inc.,* 1993; Heilbrun, 2001).

Relevance, reliability, and validity play an important role in both *Atkins*-driven evaluations and the broader capital context. The *Atkins* evaluation is not only narrower in scope but largely employs conventional diagnostic measures (e.g., IQ tests and adaptive behavior scales) that have been developed and validated for assessing mental retardation. These measures make it more likely that the relevant clinical characteristics will be assessed in relevant, reliable, and valid ways. It is important to keep in mind that validation is a relative term, and even the best instruments and approaches have limitations. Accordingly, the evaluator should be aware of the normative basis and limitations of all instruments used in the evaluation. Our previous discussion of some of the ethical issues associated with cognitive testing also noted this issue and highlights the need to exercise caution even with some of the best-known and widely used measures of intelligence (Knauss and Kutinsky, 2004). Validation is an even more concerning issue in the context of broader capital mitigation and sentencing evaluations because they call for the assessment of clinical characteristics and data relevant to mental state at the time of the offense, and other domains that also encompass thinking, perception, and judgment, for which there are fewer and less well-validated tools available. Where relevant psychological instruments or specialized inventories are available (e.g., the Minnesota Multiphasic Personality Inventory-2 (MMPI-2), Butcher, Dahlstrom, Graham, Tellegren, and Kaemmer, 1989), it is appropriate to use the specialized norms applicable to correctional populations. Typically, the forensic clinician can compensate for this lack of standardized assessment procedures by employing more sources of information, judging the credibility of sources that have no formal validation (e.g., third-party interviews), and gauging the consistency of findings across sources rather than relying more heavily on fewer but well-validated sources (Heilbrun et al., 2005).

Other sources of data can be as, if not more, important than standardized testing, and the evaluator should always *obtain relevant historical information* regarding the person being evaluated when conducting evaluations in a capital context (Heilbrun, 2001). Historical information is often essential in interpreting results obtained from more structured types of assessment strategies. As with other data sources and assessment strategies, historical data should be relevant to the forensic issue at hand. This is an especially important consideration, given the large number of potential psychosocial and historical domains to choose from (e.g., social, vocational, medical, mental health, and family functioning). Reliability of historical information is established by establishing consistency across relevant sources of information used during the course of the evaluation (e.g., self-report, collateral interviews, and document review). Historical information serves three main functions in the context of forensic assessment. First, it is important for assessing patterns of behavior and the consistency of such behavior over time. Second, historical information can play a critical role in determining the truthfulness of self-reported facts, characteristics, and symptoms. Finally, historical information can be used in the course of a reconstructive evaluation where history must be used to provide information about relevant thoughts, feelings, and behaviors of the individual in question (Heilbrun, 2001). The use of historical information is therefore a critical component in all capital contexts. When assessing whether a criminal defendant is mentally retarded under *Atkins*, the evaluator must consider the possibility of exaggeration of cognitive deficits. Although specialized testing can be used in this determination (e.g., the Validity Indicator Profile (VIP), Frederick, 1997; the Test of Memory Malingering (TOMM), Tombaugh, 1997), a good history obtained from multiple sources can establish whether the defendant has been diagnosed as mentally retarded prior to age 18. This simultaneously helps establish the diagnosis, which requires such an initial diagnosis, and allows the evaluator to weigh the possibility that the defendant's deficits are exaggerated by comparing them with descriptions of such deficits from earlier in the defendant's life.

In the broader context of capital mitigation and sentencing evaluations, historical information is an essential component of a broad, longitudinal description of the defendant's functioning in particular areas. Self-reported information suggesting that a defendant suffered from symptoms of severe mental illness around the time of the offense, for example, can be weighed in the context of historical information regarding the presence of severe mental illness. In addition, other broad developmental influences that are often seen as mitigating, such as problems with childhood abuse or neglect, family, school, peers, neighborhood, and substance abuse, cannot be assessed without relevant historical information from multiple sources (Heilbrun et al., 2005).

Using relevance for selecting data sources and measuring clinical characteristics in reliable and valid ways are important considerations in capital contexts. These considerations, however, are insufficient in and of themselves unless the evaluator *assesses legally relevant behavior* (Heilbrun, 2001). This aspect of data collection highlights the importance of gathering the information that is directly related to the forensic issues, and more generally relevant to the legal question that is before the court. It is important to note that any forensic assessment must obtain information that clearly describes capacities relevant to the forensic issue while avoiding extraneous or irrelevant information. In both the *Atkins* and more general capital context, the evaluator must have an intimate knowledge of relevant jurisdictional authority, typically in the form of state statute and case law. Statutory guidance provides the framework and identifies the contours of the evaluation, while case law interprets the application of relevant statutory guidance. These sources of authority also provide direct guidance on what questions must be answered, and therefore identifies what behaviors and related constructs are the most relevant for evaluation. Once identified, it is up to the evaluator to identify appropriate strategies to capture and operationalize the behaviors. The importance of assessing legally relevant behavior cannot be overemphasized in a capital context. Our earlier discussion highlighted relevant case law and statutory guidance, which suggests that there is considerable variation in how states define mental retardation and operationalize aggravating and mitigating circumstances. As noted earlier, the assessment of legally relevant behavior under *Atkins* is usually, either in whole or in part, synonymous with establishing, or disconfirming, the diagnosis of mental retardation (DeMatteo et al., 2006). For capital mitigation and sentencing, however, the evaluator must consider factors that occur in a number of jurisdictions, such as whether or not the offense was committed while the defendant was under the influence of extreme mental or emotional disturbance; whether the defendant acted under extreme duress or under the substantial domination of another person; and whether at the time of the offense the capacity of the defendant to appreciate the criminality of his or her conduct or to conform that conduct to the requirements of law was impaired as a result of mental disease or defect (Heilbrun, 2001). There are few specialized tools that could combine the retrospective aspect of these factors with their functional legal focus, so the forensic clinician in the capital context must generally approach this aspect of the evaluation by combining multiple sources across multiple modalities (self-report, testing, and collateral information) to yield conclusions that are driven by comparable findings across sources.

When the defendant declines to report on mental state at the time of the offense by indicating the absence of any involvement in the offense, it becomes more difficult to establish the presence of mental or emotional disturbance, to appreciate criminality or conforming conduct, or to be influenced by extreme duress. There are two ways, however, in which the existence of such factors may be established (albeit less firmly): through collateral information, and because the deficits or symptoms involved are relatively static over time. In this respect, mental retardation (considered prior to *Atkins* as a mitigating factor rather than a basis for excluding the defendant entirely from a death sentence) is a factor that, when established through a verified history of diagnosis from an early age, would certainly have been present at the time of the offense. In a similar vein, if there is strong and consistent third-party evidence that an individual was behaving in a way that indicated the experience of symptoms of severe mental illness at the time of the offense, the evaluator may conclude that such symptoms were present—even when the defendant denies involvement in the offense (Heilbrun et al., 2005). One caveat is noteworthy here. This second approach is not an attempt to report on the actual psychological condition or "recreate the psychological life" of the defendant at the time of the offense. Instead, it is an attempt to address mitigating factors that may be both relevant (in the mitigating sense) and static. For example, psychotic symptoms (e.g., hallucinations and delusions) can vary over time and are therefore more difficult to "re-create" accurately through the use of collateral information, but mental retardation (assuming it is accurately diagnosed), which tends to be relatively enduring and stable, could be.

Data Interpretation

Data interpretation is the focus of the third phase in forensic assessment. This phase focuses on the integration of the nomothetic and idiographic data collected during the evaluation and highlights the use of scientific reasoning in assessing the relationship between clinical condition and relevant functional abilities (Heilbrun, 2001). Given the relatively high probability of malingering, fabrication, and exaggeration, a consideration of response style is always necessary in the context of forensic assessment. The assessment of response style is an important aspect of forensic assessment because of special incentives in forensic contexts and the corresponding perception of the legal decision-maker regarding whether the self-reported information is consistently accurate (Grisso, 1986). The perception of accuracy on the part of the decision-maker is among the most important types of validity in the legal decision-making context, and important implications follow from the conclusion about response style in any given evaluation. More specifically, a reliable response style adds credibility to self-reported information, and such information can be weighed along with other sources of information used in the evaluation. Conversely, a less reliable response style might require the evaluator to deemphasize or limit the role of self-reported information collected during the evaluation (Grisso, 1986; Heilbrun, 2001). As self-reported data are usually a key component in any forensic evaluation, it is important to assess the credibility of the respondent because a failure to do so can affect the overall accuracy and quality of the entire evaluation. Given the difficulty of determining the accuracy of response style when relying on clinical judgment alone (e.g., Ekman and O'Sullivan, 1991; Melton et al., 1997; Rogers, 1997) and the substantial incentive for the defendant to provide distorted information in capital contexts, the evaluator performing the assessment should *use third-party information and testing when indicated in assessing response style* (Heilbrun, 2001).

The use of third-party information and testing to assess response style is equally important and applicable in the context of all types of capital referral questions.

For example, when conducting an *Atkins* evaluation, the use of third-party information, most likely in the form of records and interviews with knowledgeable observers, provides a useful counterpoint to the possibility that a defendant might exaggerate intellectual deficits. When such information is used to construct a cross-checked, relevant history, there is little chance that inaccurate self-report might lead to a mistaken conclusion that the defendant is mentally retarded. A similar approach can be utilized in the broader capital context, where the defendant might attempt to fabricate or exaggerate symptoms of extreme mental or emotional distress, or other characteristics related to a broad range of mitigating factors. For example, a reported history of poor academic achievement could be cross-checked against school records while a claim of childhood abuse might be verifiable with records from relevant police, child protection, and social service reports.

In both contexts, the forensic clinician should describe the consistency of third-party information with self-reported information, and be particular cautious about self-report when it is significantly different from third-party accounts, using third-party information to cross-check potential exaggeration and potential defensiveness. It should be noted that third-party informants may have their own biases, affecting factual aspects of their descriptions of the defendant; such biases can be handled in a variety of ways, including focusing on observations rather than conclusions, providing memory prompts in non-sensitive areas, and asking about how the third party would like to see the case resolved (Heilbrun, Warren, and Picarello, 2003; Heilbrun et al., 2005).

Although third-party information is essential in gauging the accuracy of self-reported information, there are also specialized tests that are sensitive to response style. Some have been developed specifically to measure exaggerated or fabricated symptoms of different kinds (e.g., the Structured Inventory of Reported Symptoms (SIRS), Rogers, 1992; the VIP, Frederick, 1997; the TOMM, Tombaugh, 1997), or have "validity indicators" as part of the broader test (e.g., MMPI-2, Butcher et al., 1989; Personality Assessment Inventory (PAI), Morey, 1991). Although a discussion of each of these instruments is beyond the scope of this chapter, it might be helpful to note the relevance of how specialized testing such as the VIP and SIRS might be useful in a capital context (readers are encouraged to consult Rogers (1997) for a comprehensive discussion of this topic). Although testing might not always be required in the face of adequate historical and third-party information, the VIP might be particularly relevant in the *Atkins* context, where the question of mental retardation is the major issue. The VIP is a promising tool designed to distinguish between genuine and feigned cognitive deficits (Frederick, 1997). As such, it is a useful adjunct to achievement, cognitive, and neuropsychological testing, which tend to be common in *Atkins*-based evaluations. The VIP uses a forced choice methodology and measures performance across a series of verbal and nonverbal subtests. The norm group contains data from a mix of honest normals, brain injury patients, coached normals, suspected malingerers, random responders, and persons with mental retardation. Sensitivity (.67 and .74) and specificity (.83 and .86) rates for both subtests are reasonably good, with an overall classification accuracy reported between .75 and .80 (Frederick, 1997).

As noted earlier, a common mitigating factor in broader capital contexts across most jurisdictions is extreme mental or emotional distress, typically operationalized as the presence of severe psychopathology. Accordingly, it is often important to gauge the accuracy of self-reported symptoms in a format that is more rigorous and reliable than a clinical interview. Although there are a number of broad-based and specific measures that might be appropriate to detect exaggeration, the SIRS is a structured interview that was developed specifically for the evaluation of feigning psychopathology and includes eight primary scales that focus on base rates of symptom presentation and severity (Rogers, 1992). Each of the scales reportedly has a weighted mean interrater reliability coefficient greater than .90, and internal consistency (alpha) rates between .77 and .92. Effect size estimates (using Cohen's d) were calculated to describe the differences between clinical versus malingering subjects (using a known-groups design) and between clinical versus simulating subjects (using a simulation design), with a resulting mean effect size for both given as 1.74 (Heilbrun, 2001; Rogers, 1992). Accordingly, the SIRS holds considerable promise for aiding in the detection of symptom exaggeration and might be an excellent component of a two-stage malingering assessment strategy. The first stage of this strategy includes the use of the validity indicators of a broader test, such as the MMPI-2, with the addition of the SIRS when the validity indicators of the broader tests suggest the possibility of symptom exaggeration (Butcher, 2002; Rogers, 1997). Although we have highlighted this two-stage strategy under our discussion of broader capital mitigation issues, the approach might be just as relevant in the *Atkins* context, where these measures might provide a useful complement to the evaluation of response style beyond the consideration of cognitive functioning (Heilbrun et al., 2005).

The evaluation of response style is often the first step in considering other information obtained during the course of the assessment. As noted earlier, there are a wide variety of data sources to choose from when conducting a forensic evaluation, and these sources of data ultimately fall into one of two broad categories of classification. The first category of data is case specific, or idiographic in nature, and requires the evaluator to obtain information specific to the case circumstances and present functioning of the individual, and comparing it to that individual's capacities and functioning at other times. The second category of data is normatively based, or nomothetic in nature, and requires the evaluator to consider empirical data from groups similar to that of the defendant, typically through the administration of tests that have been validated on comparable populations. Each type of data is valuable and contributes to the overall accuracy and relevance of the evaluation. Accordingly, in a capital context, the evaluator should use both *case-specific (idiographic) and nomothetic evidence in assessing the causal connection between clinical condition and functional abilities* (Heilbrun, 2001).

Case-specific data typically involve information about the individual and the particular circumstances that are relevant to the forensic issues being assessed. There are three primary reasons for gathering case-specific data. The first is accuracy, which is critically important in the context of capital litigation. Typically, the data obtained during the course of the evaluation are used to generate and test hypotheses related to the defendant's functioning. Case-specific information plays a critical role in both the hypothesis generation and verification steps. Without case-specific information, the data, reasoning, and resulting conclusions are usually not as accurate. The second reason is related to the perception of relevance and accuracy of the assessment results by the legal decision-maker. Although face validity is the weakest form of validity in behavioral and scientific terms, it is often the strongest indication of relevance and accuracy in legal contexts (Grisso, 1986; Heilbrun, 2001). Specifically, the use of idiographic data makes it easier for the legal decision-maker to see the relationship between the defendant's functioning and the relevant legal issue under consideration. Finally, idiographic approaches to data collection are also consistent with the use of a model, with the emphasis on the causal connection between clinical and functional areas (Grisso, 1986; Heilbrun, 2001; Morse, 1978a,b).

The use of idiographic data in the *Atkins* context typically applies through an evaluation of present intellectual functioning, adaptive functioning, and a comparison with the individual's history of previously diagnosed mental retardation, if present. The use of idiographic data has greater applicability in the broader capital context. Consistent with the legal goal of individualized justice, as reflected in existing U.S. Supreme Court jurisprudence and corresponding state law, the evaluator attempts to describe the defendant's clinical condition (broadly conceived to include personality and behavioral attributes) and functional legal abilities in the context of the defendant's history of symptoms and demonstrated capacities (Heilbrun et al., 2005).

Nomothetic data are best exemplified by the use of empirical, group-level data applicable to and derived from populations similar to that of the individual being evaluated, and through forensic tools that have been developed and validated on similar populations (Heilbrun, 2001). As such, nomothetic data are driven by scientific research. The role of research and nomothetic data is important in forensic assessment in a number of ways. One is validation, and research can provide a wealth of information on the relative psychometric properties of various tools, procedures, and their relation to an outcome of interest to a legal decision-maker. Given the demands for both accuracy and relevance in legal contexts, it is important to be able to describe the degree of empirical scientific support that has been demonstrated for a particular assessment procedure. In addition, procedures used in forensic assessment should be reliable and valid to an extent adequate to the scope of statements, opinions, and conclusions resulting from the evaluation. Procedures lacking in appropriate levels of empirical support should be identified as such, used cautiously, and would be more appropriately categorized as another source of self-report data (Blau, 1984; Grisso, 1986; Heilbrun, 2001; Melton et al., 1997). Another benefit of scientifically derived nomothetic data lies in the area of prediction. Specifically, research can provide information on base rates and provide relatively sophisticated ways of constructing actuarial approaches and gauging the accuracy of these and other approaches to decision-making with measures of sensitivity and specificity. This aspect of science and nomothetic data is an indispensable part of the development of tools, the measurement of accuracy, and the determination of outcomes that are important in forensic assessment (Heilbrun, 2001).

Science also provides empirical data from groups similar to that of the defendant in a capital case and offers tests that have been validated on comparable populations. Using such tests allows the evaluator to compare measured capacities to those in "known groups." The use of nomothetic data is particularly valuable for promoting scientifically informed legal decisions. *Atkins* evaluations tend to be straightforward in this respect, using tests and measures that have been developed and validated for assessing individuals with different degrees of mental retardation and impairment in adaptive skills. It is important to note that the scientific aspects of such measures (reliability, validity, and other psychometric properties) should be scrutinized carefully, and only the strongest should be used as part of *Atkins*-driven assessments. The broader range of capital mitigation and sentencing evaluations tends to include the assessment of two broad domains, namely clinical condition and functional-legal capacities. As in *Atkins* evaluations, the importance of nomothetic data suggests that evaluators should carefully consider what tests and measures have been developed and validated for various aspects of each of these domains. The critical consideration of which tests are supported through nomothetic data, and how strongly they are supported, is a critical aspect of promoting quality, accuracy, and relevance in all types of assessments conducted in the course of capital litigation (Heilbrun, 2005).

As noted immediately above, scientific or empirical evidence is an important component of the evaluation process and therefore plays a critical role in improving the overall quality of forensic assessments. Higher quality evaluations should, in turn, lead to better informed legal decision-making. Although important, scientific data are difficult to interpret in the absence of a broader framework that can guide the overall reasoning process used in the evaluation process. Accordingly, the evaluator should *use scientific reasoning in assessing the causal connection between clinical condition and functional abilities* (Heilbrun, 2001). There are several aspects of scientific reasoning that are particularly relevant to forensic assessment. They include the operationalization of variables, hypothesis formulation and testing, falsifiability, parsimony in interpretation, and the awareness of limitations on accuracy and the applicability of nomothetic research to the immediate case (Heilbrun, 2001). In many respects, the forensic assessment process is similar to the process used in scientific reasoning and in the broader realm of research design and methodology. This is most apparent when applied to hypothesis testing. For example, multiple sources of information are used during the process of a thorough evaluation. One source of data can create a "hypothesis to be verified" through further information obtained from other sources. Accepting or rejecting hypotheses that account for the most information using the simplest explanation is consistent with the scientific principles of parsimony and falsifiability. At times, evidence appears mixed, or competing explanations seem to account comparably well for this available information. Competing explanations, or rival alternative hypotheses, should be communicated to the legal decision-maker. This type of approach to reasoning applies equally well in both *Atkins* and other types of capital assessments (Heilbrun et al., 2005).

Another important aspect of data interpretation can be found in the area of making assertions and clarifying limits. Although the use of many of the principles we have discussed so far can significantly enhance the overall accuracy and relevance of any forensic assessment, various issues and related considerations can affect the strength of the assertions that can be made in any given case. For example, the individual in question might not be well represented in the normative base for a particular assessment instrument. Similarly, the amount and quality of available idiographic data can vary considerably from case to case. Some limitations, as described above, are endemic to the assessment process itself, while others can be related to the structures and procedures of the law under which the assessment is performed (Heilbrun, 2001). For example, a legal decision-maker might expect or require the evaluator to address certain statutorily driven questions concerning cognitive functioning in an *Atkins*-based evaluation or mental state at the time of the offense in a broader capital mitigation or sentencing evaluation. Given the limitations inherent in any evaluation, this situation should be approached with caution. Accordingly, we recommend that the evaluator *should not answer the ultimate legal question* before the court (Heilbrun, 2001). It is important to note that there is disagreement within the fields of forensic psychology and forensic psychiatry concerning whether forensic evaluators should answer the "ultimate legal question" before the court (e.g., Bonnie and Slobogin, 1980; Grisso, 1986; Melton et al., 1997; Morse, 1978a,b; Poythress, 1982; Rogers and Ewing, 1989; Slobogin, 1989). Some judges and attorneys anticipate that the forensic clinician will answer the ultimate legal question in the course of the evaluation, while others emphasize the more appropriate focus on the relevant forensic capacities, because the ultimate legal decision includes moral, political, and community-value components and must apply these values to determining "how much is enough" when translating deficits into a dichotomous legal outcome (Heilbrun et al., 2005).

The ultimate legal issue in *Atkins* is whether the defendant should be excluded from a death sentence due to mental retardation, but there is little reasoning needed between this conclusion and the finding of mental retardation. Hence, an *Atkins* evaluator can draw a conclusion that is well supported by science and come close to the ultimate issue without injecting political or moral values. By contrast, the ultimate legal question in a capital mitigation or sentencing evaluation—whether the defendant should receive a death sentence—contains a broad mix of aggravating and mitigating factors that are not appropriate for expert evaluation because they are primarily fact based (e.g., number of prior convictions), and other aggravating and mitigating factors that are appropriate for expert evaluation. In addition, ethical guidance in this area suggests extreme caution in addressing the ultimate issue in the context of broader capital mitigation evaluations (Knauss and Kutinsky, 2004). It would seem best, therefore, to address the applicability of each factor that is part of the evaluation without coming close to combining them in the form of the ultimate legal decision (Heilbrun et al., 2005).

Another component of effective data interpretation involves how the limitations of the evaluation will be described in the context of written and oral communication. More specifically, the evaluator should *describe findings and limits so that they need change little under cross-examination* (Heilbrun, 2001). There are a variety of reasons why the data and reasoning associated with any evaluation may be limited in their accuracy. These include but are not limited to the unavailability of or inconsistency of relevant information, the application of testing instruments with limited psychometric properties and normative data, the response style of the individual, the common situation where the reasoning and related conclusions are not fully supported by the available data, and the existence of reasonable alternative explanations or conclusions. Given that these limitations on accuracy and applicability are always present, it is important for the evaluator to be open about them and acknowledge how they might impact the relevance of competing hypotheses for the main conclusions of the evaluation. Evaluators should therefore be proactive about acknowledging both limitations and the reasons for them in the context of both oral and written communication. Accordingly, the data and reasoning from the assessment should be described impartially, thoroughly, and with acknowledgment of appropriate limitations. This should apply comparably to both an *Atkins* assessment and broader capital mitigation and sentencing evaluations. When this approach is taken—when challenges that would be presented on cross-examination are considered and incorporated into the results of the evaluation—then it is not likely that the description of these results will change substantially during direct testimony or the cross-examination (Heilbrun et al., 2005).

Communication

The communication of evaluation results is the final step in the broader assessment process. Regardless of whether the results are communicated in oral or written form, the perceived value and the effectiveness of the evaluation are affected by the way in which it is communicated. Volumes have been written on this topic, and a complete discussion is beyond the scope of this chapter (Brodsky, 1991, 1999, 2004; Heilbrun, 2001; Melton et al., 1997). The remainder of this chapter, however, highlights a number of principles related to effective communication that might be particularly relevant in the context of capital litigation.

As noted earlier, relevance and reliability are directly related to the perceived quality of any forensic evaluation. Relevance and reliability are enhanced in the context of oral and written communication when the evaluator *attributes information to sources* (Heilbrun,

2001). There are several broad categories of information that are used in the context of any forensic assessment such as self-report, formal testing, and collateral information in the form of documents and third-party interviews. The relevance, reliability, and quality of any given source of data can vary in the face of a variety of factors, including the response style of the individual being evaluated. Accordingly, attributing information to sources is important because it allows a legal decision-maker or attorney to ascertain the origin of relevant information and the relative amount of support it might or might not have across multiple sources of information. A list of sources at the beginning of a written report is a must and should include sufficient information about each source so that it is clear to the reader what the source is, and where and when it was obtained. When attribution to sources occurs in the report (e.g., "According to school records, the psycho-educational evaluation conducted by Dr. X, self-report, and the results of current cognitive testing, Mr. Doe meets DSM-IV criteria for mental retardation."), the reader can then obtain the necessary information about the source from its description in the beginning of the report, facilitating access to that source if needed (Heilbrun, 2001). A similar approach can be adopted during the course of oral communication, specifically expert testimony. A challenge to findings should always be anticipated in the context of an adversarial proceeding. Source attribution in this context is necessary because findings across multiple sources may need to be deconstructed during testimony, and to allow the opposing attorney to prepare to challenge these results. Attribution to sources can also enhance the credibility of oral communication in the same way it enhances the credibility of written reports. For example, making a statement that notes three different sources of support for a diagnosis of mental retardation might have more impact than simply noting that the individual in question meets criteria for such a diagnosis. Accordingly, the evaluator should attribute information to sources when providing oral or written communication. This principle applies well to all types of capital referral questions (Heilbrun et al., 2005).

Many of the consumers (e.g., lawyers, judges, and juries) of forensic evaluations are not trained as mental health professionals. Accordingly, many lack formal training in the substantive content of psychology and its related terminology. Ironically, sometimes individuals with formal mental health training disagree on substantive issues and terminology. Accordingly, the forensic evaluator should strive to *use plain language and avoid technical jargon* when communicating in written and oral form with attorneys and other legal decision-makers (Heilbrun, 2001). This principle highlights the importance of a "common language" that emphasizes the elimination of as many technical terms as possible. Thus, it is important to use technical language only when absolutely necessary and to define technical terms parenthetically when they must be used. Communication of this type should minimize the potential for misunderstanding, which will promote more accurate decision-making. Accurate decision-making appears to be equally important in both an *Atkins* and broader capital mitigation and sentencing context (Heilbrun et al., 2005).

Often, the final report might be the sole product of the evaluation. It is therefore important that the report function as a form of communication that can stand alone in a way that facilitates understanding and avoids confusion. This can be accomplished by using an overarching structure, and the evaluator should therefore *write the report in sections according to model and procedures* (Heilbrun, 2001). Most, if not all, forensic reports can be written in sections that make it easy to apply many of the principles described earlier (e.g., use a model, use scientific reasoning, and use multiple sources). The most common structure that is consistent with these principles includes: (1) *Referral* (with identifying information concerning the individual, his/her characteristics, the nature of the evaluation, and by whom it was requested or ordered), (2) *Procedures* (times and dates of the evaluation, tests or procedures used, different records reviewed, and third-party interviews conducted, as well as documentation of the notification of purpose or informed consent and the degree to which the information was apparently understood), (3) *Relevant History* (containing information from multiple sources describing areas important to the evaluation), (4) *Current Clinical Condition* (broadly considered to include appearance, mood, behavior, sensorium, intellectual functioning, thought, and personality), (5) *Forensic Capacities* (varying according to the nature of the legal questions), and (6) *Conclusions and Recommendations* (addressed toward the relevant capacities rather than the ultimate legal questions) (e.g., Heilbrun, 2001; Grisso, 1998; Melton et al., 1997; Rogers and Shuman, 2000). These sections could guide the construction, conducting, and communicating of capital assessments. An *Atkins* evaluation could use all sections except Forensic Capacities, as the focus of *Atkins* is primarily on section four rather than the relationship between sections four and five. Conversely, all aspects of the framework would be applicable in the broader capital context (Heilbrun et al., 2005).

There is a relationship between a properly performed evaluation and the quality of expert testimony. Accordingly, the evaluator should *base testimony on the results of a properly performed forensic assessment* (Heilbrun, 2001). In essence, the foundation for effective expert testimony is the evaluation itself, which should be substantively accurate and documented in the report. If the quality of the evaluation and subsequent report is poor, then any related testimony will most likely be of similar quality. Obvious ethical issues aside, at an extreme, an improperly conducted evaluation will produce irrelevant, insufficient, and possibly invalid results. A substantively superior evaluation will consider forensic issues relevant to the legal question, be sufficiently detailed and thorough, and will use appropriate tools and reasoning to yield more accurate results. When the substantive aspects of the evaluation, whether an *Atkins* or capital mitigation or sentencing evaluation, are carefully documented in the report (and preferably performed consistent with the first 27 principles), then this creates a basis for testimony that allows the presenting attorney to use these findings more effectively, the opposing attorney to prepare to challenge them, the judge and jury to understand them, and the evaluator to communicate them (Heilbrun et al., 2005).

The final principle, *testify effectively*, refers to the substantive and stylistic aspects, respectively, of expert testimony (Heilbrun, 2001). The substantive component may be summarized by many of the principles already discussed in this section, while the stylistic component of expert testimony concerns how the forensic clinicians present as credible, interesting, understandable, and likeable through speech, dress, and other aspects of behavior without being deceptive. Volumes have been written on this issue, and a comprehensive discussion of this topic is beyond the scope of this chapter (for practical and comprehensive discussions of the stylistic and substantive aspects of expert testimony please see Brodsky, 1991, 1999, 2004). In short, when substance and style are both strong, expert testimony should be most effective. This principle would seem to apply comparably to *Atkins* assessments and broader capital evaluations (Heilbrun et al., 2005).

Conclusion

Although comparatively few in number, forensic assessments conducted in the context of capital contexts, either broadly or narrowly defined, are among the most important evaluations provided by psychologists and psychiatrists to the legal system. Evaluations of this type are unique and present a number of correspondingly unique practice-related issues and challenges that might not be encountered in other types of forensic evaluations. For example, the recent U.S. Supreme Court decision in *Atkins* created a somewhat different kind of assessment in the capital context, but the broad core of principles described in this article can be applied to both *Atkins* assessments and more traditional capital mitigation and sentencing evaluations. These principles provide a lens through which both kinds of evaluations can be viewed to make them more consistent, impartial, and attentive to the demands of the law, science, professional ethics, and standards for professional practice. This, in turn, should improve the quality of legal decision-making in this arena.

References

Ackerson, K. S., Brodsky, S. L., and Zapf, P. A. (2005). Judges' and psychologists' assessments of legal and clinical factors in competence for execution. *Psychology, Public Policy, and Law, 11*(1), 164–193.

American Academy of Psychiatry and the Law (1995). *Ethical Guidelines for the Practice of Forensic Psychiatry.* Bloomfield, CT: Author.

American Association on Mental Retardation (1992). *Mental Retardation: Definitions, Classification, and Systems of Supports* (9 ed.). Washington, DC: Author.

American Association on Mental Retardation (2002). *The AAMR Definition of Mental Retardation.* Retrieved July 8, 2006, from http://www.aamr.org

American Bar Association (1989). *Criminal Justice Mental Health Standards.* Washington, DC: Author.

American Bar Association (2004). *Model Rules of Professional Conduct.* Retrieved July 15, 2006, from http://www.abanet.org/cpr/mrpc/mrpc_home.html

American Psychiatric Association (1998). *Principles of Medical Ethics with Annotations Especially Applicable to Psychiatry.* Washington, DC: Author.

American Psychiatric Association (1994). *Diagnostic and Statistical Manual of Mental Disorders* (4th ed.). Washington, DC: Author.

American Psychiatric Association (2000). *Diagnostic and Statistical Manual of Mental Disorders* (4th ed., text rev.). Washington, DC: Author.

American Psychological Association (1986). *Guidelines for Computer-Based Tests and Interpretations.* Washington, DC: Author.

American Psychological Association (1992). Ethical principles of psychologists and code of conduct. *American Psychologist, 47,* 1597–1611.

American Psychological Association (2002). *Ethical Principles of Psychologists and Code of Conduct.* Retrieved May 26, 2006, from http://www.apa.org

American Psychological Association Council of Representatives (2006). *APA Policy Amendment Addressing Mental Illness and the Death Penalty.* Washington, DC: American Psychological Association.

Amnesty International (2003). *United States of America: Death by Discrimination—the Continuing Role of Race in Capital Cases.* Retrieved July 17, 2006, from http://web.amnesty.org/library/index/engamr510462003

Anastasi, A. (1988). *Psychological Testing* (6th ed.). New York: Macmillan.

Bell, F., Hoff, A., and Hoyt, K. (1964). Answer sheets do make a difference. *Personnel Psychology, 17,* 65–71.

Blau, T. (1984). *The Psychologist as Expert Witness.* New York: Wiley.

Bonnie, R., and Slobogin, C. (1980). The role of mental health professionals in the criminal process: The case for informed speculation. *Virginia Law Review, 66,* 427–522.

Borum, R, and Grisso, T. (1995). Psychological test use in criminal forensic evaluations. *Professional Psychology: Research and Practice, 26,* 465–473.

Brodsky, S. L. (1991). *Testifying in Court: Guidelines and Maxims for the Expert Witness.* Washington, DC: American Psychological Association.

Brodsky, S. L. (1999). *The Expert Expert Witness: More Maxims and Guidelines for Testifying in Court.* Washington, DC: American Psychological Association.

Brodsky, S. L. (2004). *Coping with Cross-Examination and Other Pathways to Effective Testimony.* Washington, DC: American Psychological Association.

Brodsky, S., and Galloway, V. (2003). Ethical and professional demands for forensic mental health professionals in the post-Atkins era. *Ethics and Behavior, 13,* 3–8.

Bureau of Justice Statistics (2006). *Capital Punishment Statistics.* Retrieved July 16, 2006, from http://www.ojp.usdoj.gov/bjs/cp.htm

Butcher, J. (2002). *Clinical Personality Assessment* (2nd ed.). New York: Oxford University Press.

Butcher, J., Dahlstrom, W., Graham, J., Tellegen, A., and Kaemmer, B. (1989). *MMPI-2: Manual for Administration and Scoring.* Minneapolis: University of Minnesota Press.

Ceci, S., Scullin, M., and Kanaya, T. (2003). The difficulty of basing death penalty eligibility on IQ cutoff scores for mental retardation. *Ethics and Behavior, 13,* 11–12.

Clements, C. (1996). Offender classification: Two decades of progress. *Criminal Justice and Behavior, 23,* 121–143.

Committee on Ethical Guidelines for Forensic Psychologists (1991). Specialty guidelines for forensic psychologists. *Law and Human Behavior, 15,* 655–665.

Committee on the Revision of the Specialty Guidelines for Forensic Psychology (2006). *Specialty Guidelines for Forensic Psychology.* http://www.ap-ls.org/links/currentforensicguidelines.pdf Retrieved May 21, 2006.

Cunningham, M. D., and Goldstein, A. M. (2003). Sentencing determinations in death penalty cases. In I. B. Weiner and A. M. Goldstein (Eds.), *The Handbook of Forensic Psychology* (vol. 11) (pp. 407–436). New York: John Wiley & Sons.

Cunningham, M., and Reidy, T. (2001). A matter of life and death: Special considerations and heightened practice standards in capital sentencing evaluations. *Behavioral Sciences and the Law, 19,* 473–490.

DeMatteo, D., and Edens, J. F. (2006). The role and relevance of the Psychopathy Checklist-Revised in court: A case law survey of U.S. courts (1991–2004). *Psychology, Public Policy, and Law, 12,* 214–241.

DeMatteo, D., Marczyk, G., and Pich, M. (2006). *A 50-State Survey of Atkins Legislation Defining Mental Retardation: Implications for Forensic Mental Health Professionals.* Paper presented at the 2006 Annual Conference of the American Psychology-Law Society (AP-LS)/Division 41 of the American Psychological Association (APA), St. Petersburg, FL.

Dietzel, L. (2004). *Didactic Presentation on the WISC-IV at Widener University.* Chester, PA: Widener University.

Ekman, P., and O'Sullivan, M. (1991). Who can catch a liar? *American Psychologist, 46,* 913–920.

Elwork, A. (1984). Psycholegal assessment, diagnosis and testimony. *Law and Human Behavior, 8(3/4),* 197–203.

Elwork, A. (1992). Psycholegal treatment and intervention: The next challenge. *Law and Human Behavior, 16(2),* 175–183.

Everington, C., and Keyes, D. W. (1999). Mental retardation: Diagnosing mental retardation in criminal proceedings: The critical importance of documenting adaptive behavior. *Forensic Examiner, 8(7–8),* 31–34.

Faust, D. (1989). Data integration in legal evaluations: Can clinicians deliver on their premises? *Behavioral Sciences and the Law, 7,* 469–483.

Flynn, J. (1998). WAIS-III and WISC-III gains in the United States from 1972 to 1995: How to compensate for obsolete norms. *Perceptual and Motor Skills, 86,* 1231–1239.

Flynn, J. (2006). Tethering the elephant: Capital cases, IQ, and the Flynn Effect. *Psychology, Public Policy, and Law, 12*(2), 170–189.

Frederick, R. (1997). *Validity Indictor Profile Manual.* Minnetonka, MN: NSC Assessments.

Greenberg, S., and Shuman, D. (1997). Irreconcilable conflict between therapeutic and forensic roles. *Professional Psychology: Research and Practice, 1,* 50–57.

Greenspan, S., and Switzky, H. (2003). Execution exemption should be based on actual vulnerability, not disability label. *Ethics and Behavior, 13*(1), 19.

Grisso, T. (1986). *Evaluating Competencies: Forensic Assessments and Instruments.* New York: Plenum Press.

Grisso, T. (1998). *Forensic Evaluation of Juveniles.* Sarasota, FL: Professional Resource Press.

Grisso, T. (2002). *Evaluating Competencies: Forensic Assessments and Instruments* (2nd ed.). New York: Plenum Press.

Grisso, T. (2003). *Evaluating Competencies: Forensic Assessments and Instruments* (2nd edition). New York: Kluwer Academic/Plenum Publishers.

Heilbrun, K. (2001). *Principles of Forensic Mental Health Assessment.* New York: Kluwer Academic/Plenum Press.

Heilbrun, K. (2003). Principles of forensic mental health assessment: Implications for the forensic assessment of sexual offenders. *Annals of the New York Academy of Sciences, 989,* 1–18.

Heilbrun, K., and Collins, S. (1995). Evaluations of trial competency and mental state at the time of the offense: Report characteristics. *Professional Psychology: Research and Practice, 26,* 61–67.

Heilbrun, K., DeMatteo, D., Marczyk, G., Finello, C., Smith, R., and Mack-Allen, J. (2005). Applying principles of forensic mental health assessment to capital sentencing. *Widener Law Review, 11,* 93–118.

Heilbrun K., DeMatteo, D., and Marczyk, G. (2004). Pragmatic psychology, forensic mental health assessment, and the case of Thomas Johnson: Applying principles to promote quality. *Psychology, Public Policy, and Law, 10,* 31–70.

Heilbrun, K., Marczyk, G., and DeMatteo, D. (2002). *Forensic Mental Health Assessment: A Casebook.* New York: Oxford University Press.

Heilbrun, K., Marczyk, G. R., DeMatteo, D., Zillmer, E., Harris, J., and Jennings, T. (2003). Principles of forensic mental health assessment: Implications for neuropsychological assessment in forensic contexts. *Assessment, 10,* 329–343.

Heilbrun, K., Warren, J., and Picarello, K. (2003). Use of third party information in forensic assessment. In I. Weiner (Editor-in-Chief), *Comprehensive Handbook of Psychology.* In A. Goldstein (Ed.), Volume 11, *Forensic Psychology* (pp. 69–86). New York: Wiley.

Hofer, P., and Green, B. (1985). The challenge of competence and creativity in computerized psychological testing. *Journal of Consulting and Clinical Psychology, 53,* 826–838.

Horvath, L. S., Logan, T. K., and Walker, R. (2002). Child custody cases: A content analysis of evaluations in practice. *Professional Psychology: Research and Practice, 33,* 557–565.

International Justice Project (2005). *Mental Retardation: Daryl Renard Atkins.* Retrieved July 15, 2006, from http://www.internationaljusticeproject.org/retardationDatkins.cfm

Kane, H. (2003). Straight talk about IQ and the death penalty. *Ethics and Behavior, 13*(1), 29.

Kaufman, A. (1994). *Intelligent Testing with the WISC-III.* New York: Wiley.

Kelley, T. (1943). Cumulative significance of a number of independent experiments: Reply to A. E. Teaxler and R. N. Hilbert. *School and Society, 57,* 482–484.

Knauss, L., and Kutinsky, J. (2004). Into the briar patch: Ethical dilemmas facing psychologists following *Atkins v. Virginia. Widener Law Review, 11,* 121–135.

Lander, T., Pich, M., Loiselle, K., and Heilbrun, K. (2006). *The Content and Quality of Forensic Mental Health Assessment in Pennsylvania: Validation of a Principles-Based Approach.* Paper presented at the annual conference of the American Psychology-Law Society, St. Petersburg, FL.

Lewis, D., Pincus, J., Feldman, M., Jackson, L., and Bard, B. (1986). Psychiatric, neurological, and psychoeducational characteristics of 15 death row inmates in the United States. *American Journal of Psychiatry, 143,* 838–845.

Lewis, D. O., Pincus, J. H., Bard, B., Richardson, E., Prichep, L. S., and Feldman, M. (1988). Neuropsychiatric, psychoeducational, and family characteristics of 14 juveniles condemned to death in the United States. *American Journal of Psychiatry, 145,* 584–589.

Liptak, A. (2005). Inmate's Rising IQ Score Could Mean His Death. *New York Times.*

Marczyk, G., DeMatteo, D., Kutinsky, J., and Heilbrun, K. (in press). Training in forensic assessment and intervention: Implications for principles-based models. In R. L. Jackson (Ed.), *Learning Forensic Assessment.* Mahwah, NJ: Lawrence Erlbaum Associates.

Marczyk, G. R., and Wertheimer, E. (2001). The bitter pill of empiricism: Health maintenance organizations, informed consent, and the reasonable psychotherapist standard of care. *Villanova Law Review, 46,* 33–94.

Marczyk, G., Heilbrun, K., DeMatteo, D., and Bell, B. (2003). Using a model to guide data gathering, interpretation, and communication in capital mitigation evaluations. *Journal of Forensic Psychology Practice, 3,* 89–103.

Melton, G., Petrila, J., Poythress, N., and Slobogin, C. (1997). *Psychological Evaluations for the Courts: A Handbook for Mental Health Professionals and Lawyers* (2nd ed.). New York: Guilford.

Morey, L. (1991). *Personality Assessment Inventory Professional Manual.* Odessa, FL: Psychological Assessment Resources.

Morse, S. J. (1978a). Crazy behavior, morals and science: An analysis of mental health law. *Southern California Law Review, 51,* 527–654.

Morse, S. J. (1978b). Law and mental health professionals: The limits of expertise. *Professional Psychology, 9,* 389–399.

Nicholson, R., and Norwood, S. (2000). The quality of forensic psychological assessments, reports and testimony: Acknowledging the gap between promise and practice. *Law and Human Behavior, 24,* 9–44.

Otto, R., and Heilbrun, K. (2002). The practice of forensic psychology: A look toward the future in light of the past. *American Psychologist, 57,* 5–18.

Podboy, J., and Kastl, A. (1993). The intentional misuse of standard psychological tests in complex trials. *American Journal of Forensic Psychology, 11,* 47–54.

Poythress, N. G. (1982). Concerning reform in expert testimony: An open letter from a practicing psychologist. *Law and Human Behavior, 6,* 39–43.

Rogers, R. (1984). Towards an empirical model of malingering and deception. *Behavioral Science and the Law, 2,* 93–112.

Rogers, R. (1992). *Structured Interview of Reported Symptoms.* Odessa, FL: Psychological Assessment Resources.

Rogers, R. (1997) (Ed.). *Clinical Assessment of Malingering and Deception* (2nd ed.). New York: Guilford.

Rogers, R., and Ewing, C. P. (1989). Ultimate opinion proscriptions: A cosmetic fix and a plea for empiricism. *Law and Human Behavior, 13,* 357–374.

Rogers, R., and Shuman, D. (2000). *Conducting Insanity Evaluations* (2nd ed.). New York: Guilford Press.

Ryba, N. L., Cooper, V. G., and Zapf, P. A. (2003). Juvenile competence to stand trial evaluations: A survey of current practices and test usage among psychologists. *Professional Psychology: Research and Practice, 34,* 499–507.

Sacks, E. (1952). Intelligence scores as a function of experimentally established social relationships between the child and examiner. *Journal of Abnormal and Social Psychology, 47,* 354–358.

Skeem, J., and Golding, S. (1998). Community examiners' evaluations of competence to stand trial: Common problems and suggestions for improvement. *Professional Psychology: Research and Practice, 29,* 357–367.

Slobogin, C. (1989). The ultimate issue. *Behavioral Sciences and the Law, 7,* 259–268.

Smith, D. (1997). Mental retardation as an educational construct: Time for a new shared view? *Education & Training in Mental Retardation & Developmental Disabilities, 32,* 167–173.

Tombaugh, T. N. (1997). *TOMM: Test of Memory Malingering Manual.* Toronto: Multi-Health Systems.

Traxler, A., and Hilkert, R. (1942). Effect of type of desk on results of machine-scored tests. *School and Society, 56,* 277–296.

Watt, M., and McLean, W. (2003). Competency to be sentenced and executed. *Ethics and Behavior, 13,* 35–36.

Wechsler, D. (1997). *Wechsler Adult Intelligence Scale, Third Edition—Administration and Scoring Manual.* San Antonio, TX: Harcourt Brace & Co.

Legal References

Ake v. Oklahoma, 105 S. Ct. 1087 (1985).

Atkins v. Virginia, 536 U.S. 304 (2002).

Daubert v. Merrell Dow Pharmaceuticals, Inc., 113 S. Ct. 2786 (1993).

Eddings v. Oklahoma, 455 U.S. 104 (1982).

Ford v. Wainwright, 477 U.S. 399 (1986).

Furman v. Georgia, 408 U.S. 238 (1972).

Gregg v. Georgia, 428 U.S. 153 (1976).

Jurek v. Texas, 428 U.S. 262 (1976).

Lockett v. Ohio, 438 U.S. 586 (1978).

Penry v. Lynaugh, 492 U.S. 302 (1989).

Proffitt v. Florida, 428 U.S. 242 (1976).

Ring v. Arizona, 536 U.S. 584 (2002).

Roberts v. Louisiana, 428 U.S. 325 (1976).

Tennard v. Dretke, 124 S. Ct. 2562 (2004).

Woodson v. North Carolina, 428 U.S. 280 (1976).

Youngberg v. Romeo, 457 U.S. 307 (1983).

Zant v. Stephens, 462 U.S. 862 (1983).

Detecting Malingering and Deception in Forensic Evaluations

3

HAROLD V. HALL

Pacific Institute for the Study of Conflict and Aggression, Kamuela, Hawaii

JOSEPH G. POIRIER

Independent Practice, Rockville, Maryland

JANE THOMPSON

University of Hawaii, Hilo, Hawaii

Contents

Introduction

Because of the critical importance of obtaining reliable and accurate information in forensic settings and situations, the evaluation of malingering and deception has assumed foundational if not primary concern for forensic mental health professionals (Brodsky and Galloway, 2003; Granhag and Stromwall, 2004; Hall and Poirier, 2001; Rogers, 1997). Forensic distortion analysis (FDA), articulated by Hall (1986), Hall and Pritchard (1996), and

Hall and Poirier (2001), is defined generically as a set of interlocking procedures designed to answer focal questions relevant to deception. The definitional inclusion of "forensic" in FDA refers to the application of psychological principles to civil and criminal law; the word "distortion" implies that nondeliberate distortion must be considered before offering statements regarding intentional deception. This chapter focuses on application guidelines relating to deception specifically and presents the view that all forensic evaluation, consultation, and expert testimony must take into account unintentional distortion and deliberate deception before findings are proffered in reports or forensic forums such as the criminal or civil court.

The purposes of FDA are as follows:

1. To examine the reliability and validity of database information.
2. To detect the possible existence of misrepresentation.
3. To determine the response style(s) utilized by the client.
4. To determine the magnitude of distortion.
5. To place symptoms, behaviors, or mental conditions associated with deception into clear perspective.
6. To offer a model of understanding and accounting for discrepancies and distortions.
7. To generate hypotheses for further evaluation/investigation.
8. To communicate the decision path and the findings of FDA to the referral source.
9. To eventually standardize the deception analysis process.

Applied Ethics and Moral Considerations and Pertinent Legal Cases

Ethical considerations are replete in deception analysis. The authors of this chapter are especially interested in applying the moral perspective to the methods used by professionals to detect deception and lying in others. Must clients be informed that one purpose of an evaluation is to assess the genuineness of their self-presentations? Should clients be informed that the sole purpose of a particular test is to detect malingering? Is it ethical for professionals to lie in order to detect deception in clients? Perhaps the published ethical statements of leading professional organizations will provide guidance on these questions. The ethical principles of psychologists (American Psychological Association, 1989) states:

Principle 8a. In using assessment techniques, psychologists respect the right of clients to have *full explanations of the nature and purpose of the techniques* (italics added) in language the clients can understand, unless an explicit exception to this right has been agreed upon in advance.

The ethical principles of psychologists (American Psychological Association, 1992) states:

Standard 1.07(a). When psychologists provide assessment, evaluation, treatment, counseling, supervision, teaching, consultation, research, or other psychological services to an individual, a group or an organization, they first provide the patient or client with *appropriate information about the nature of such service* (italics added), and they later provide appropriate information about results and conclusions.

Finally, most recently, the ethical principles of psychologists (American Psychological Association, 2002) states:

Standard 3.11. (a) Psychologists delivering services to or through organizations provide information beforehand to clients and when appropriate those directly affected by the services about (1) the nature and objectives of the services, (2) the intended recipients, (3) which of the individuals are clients, (4) the relationship the psychologist will have with each person and the organization, (5) the probable uses of services provided and information obtained, (6) who will have access to the information, and (7) limits of confidentiality. As soon as feasible, they provide information about the results and conclusions of such services to appropriate persons.

(b) If psychologists will be precluded by law or by organizational roles from providing such information to particular individuals or groups, they so inform those individuals or groups at the outset of the service.

The specialty guidelines for forensic psychologists (Committee on Ethical Guidelines for Forensic Psychologists, 1991) states:

IV.E. Forensic psychologists have an obligation to ensure that prospective clients are informed of their legal rights with respect to the anticipated forensic service, *of the purposes of any evaluation, of the nature of procedures to be employed* (italics added), of the intended uses of any product of their services, and of the party who has employed the forensic psychologist.

The American College of Physicians Ethics Manual (American College of Physicians, 1989), in discussing disclosures to patients, states:

In general, *full disclosure is a fundamental ethical requirement* (italics added). However, ethicists recognize the "therapeutic privilege," which is an exemption from the most detailed disclosure when such disclosure might inflict serious emotional damage, impair rational decision-making, or otherwise harm the patient or the assessor. On balance, *the therapeutic privilege should be interpreted narrowly* (italics added); if it is invoked without justification, it can undermine the whole concept of informed consent.

The 5th edition of the American College of Physicians Ethics Manual (American College of Physicians, 2005) states:

To make health care decisions and work intelligently in partnership with the physician, the patient must be well informed. Effective patient–physician communication can dispel uncertainty and fear and enhance healing and patient satisfaction. Information should be disclosed *whenever it is considered material to the patient's understanding of his or her situation* (italics added), possible treatments, and probable outcomes. This information often includes the costs and burdens of treatment, the experience of the proposed clinician, the nature of the illness, and potential treatments.

However uncomfortable for the clinician, one view from a reading of the above is that *information that is essential to and desired by the patient must be disclosed* (italics added). How and when to disclose information, and to whom, are important concerns that must be addressed with respect to patient wishes. Western tradition focuses on the rights of the individual and full and detailed disclosure. Some patients, however, may make it known that they prefer limited information, or disclosure to family members. But does this section apply to forensic types of evaluations, when the results may often be detrimental to the interests of the person being assessed? Perhaps not.

In addition, physicians should disclose to patients information about procedural or judgment errors made in the course of care if such information is material to the patient's well-being. *Errors do not necessarily constitute improper, negligent, or unethical behavior, but failure to disclose them may* (italics added).

These excerpts offer varying advice to the practicing professional. The 1989 statement by the American Psychological Association requires a "full explanation" of assessment services and techniques. This position would appear to prohibit both deceptive practices (e.g., nondisclosure) as well as outright lying to clients. However, the revised statement by the same organization (1992) requires only "appropriate information about the nature of such services," and the most recent revision (2002) similarly states that psychologists must "provide information … about the nature and objectives of the services." The trend is to allow more nondisclosure, a legitimate concern considering that a full explanation of the psychological tests to be employed in an evaluation would perforce invalidate for some the tests themselves. Presumably, the practitioner is to decide personally what is appropriate for disclosure and what is not. These revised statements appear to allow nondisclosure of information to a client, if the practitioner deems such nondisclosure appropriate, but does not specifically address the ethics of lying to a client, even if such lying is deemed appropriate. Nonetheless, the debate on the ethical use of deceptive practice in psychological research has had a measurable impact.

Nicks, Korn, and Mainieri (1997) reviewed journal articles in personality and social psychology from 1921 to 1994. They found rare use of deception in psychological research during the developmental years of social psychology into the 1930s; references to deception then occurred gradually and irregularly until the 1950s. From the 1950s to the 1970s, the use of deception increased dramatically. The authors attributed the increase to changes in experimental methods, the pursuit of realism in social research, and the influence of cognitive dissonance theory. Seeman (1997) offers a reprint of a 1969 assessment of deception in psychological research, corroborating the finding that the use of deception was on the rise in the 1960s.

Nicks et al. (1997) concluded that since the 1980s, there has been a decided decrease in the use of deception compared to the previous decades related to changes in ethical standards and related to federal efforts to regulate research. In another mid-1990s study, Sieber, Iannuzzo, and Rodriguez (1995) corroborate the Nicks et al. (1997) finding that the use of deception, identified as such, in psychological research has declined since its peak in 1969. They attribute the decline to changes in topics (e.g., attribution, socialization, and personality), however, rather than to ethics or outside influences. However, as with all such studies, they do not address deception by minimizing or denying critical information that is the focus of the investigations themselves. No such large-scale analyses on the use of deception in psychology have been conducted in the last decade.

The Forensic Psychologists' Ethical Standards statement obliges, without exception, the practitioner to inform clients of both the general purpose of an assessment and the general nature of procedures to be used. Specific purposes of specific tests and test questions are not disclosed to the assessee, thus evaluators purposely do not disclose how answering a specific question yes or no could or could not affect the outcome of the assessment results. This position leaves little room for either nondisclosure or lying.

This variety of opinion represents the full spectrum of moral positions on full disclosure, from categorical rejection of deception by a practitioner to utilitarian acceptance of deception depending on the judgment of the practitioner. There appear to be no easy answers to the moral questions posed by deception and no agreement among thoughtful practitioners. Perhaps the most that individual practitioners can do is (1) be sensitive to the moral issues involved in the detection of deception, (2) consult with colleagues on the ethics of particular practices, (3) adopt consistent procedures that address the ethical issues involved, and (4) maintain constantly updated knowledge of evolving ethical standards and practice guidelines.

The ethical perils of deceptive or perceived deceptive practice facing forensic mental health clinicians are also well documented (Bersoff, 1995, 1999; Canter, Bennett, Jones, and Nagy, 1994; Durante, 2005; Palermo, 2006; Poirier, 1999). This is particularly true when interfacing with, or utilizing information from, police and public safety personnel and agencies.

In the landmark *Miranda v. Arizona* (1966) case, the court was sufficiently concerned with the risks of interrogation to establish the still standing precedent of defendants being warned of their rights prior to interrogation. Defendants are advised that whatever they say could be used against them. We note that Miranda rights extend to all aspects of the pretrial process to include court-ordered evaluations by mental health clinicians. What does the individual forensic professional do when he or she believes forensic information was gathered by police when violating Miranda rights of the defendant?

Interrogation activities are another example of calculated deception by police. Gudjonsson and Petursson (1991) suggested that three primary factors contributed to suspect confession: internal pressures, external pressures, and supporting data as to the suspect's complicity. Leo (1996) reviewed data, conducted fieldwork observations, and participated in interrogation training courses; Leo concluded that the process of police interrogation could be best understood in terms of a confidence game. Interrogation was effective because of manipulation and the betrayal of trust. In spite of Miranda warnings and media exposure regarding interrogation tactics, defendants routinely succumb to police interrogation manipulations, raising a number of constitutional rights issues.

There is a substantial empirical database regarding the unreliability and lack of validity of police interrogation outcomes (Hartwig, Granhag, and Vrij, 2005; Kassin and Gudjonsson, 2004; Loftus, 2004). Interrogation tactics that employ trickery, manipulation, and deception are clearly subject to false-positive findings whereby innocent suspects will be deemed involved (Bering and Shackelford, 2005; Leo and Ofshe, 1998; Russano, 2004; Russano, Meissner, Narchet, and Kassin, 2005; Witt, 2005) and false-negative findings where complicit suspects will be judged not involved. For example, Russano (2004; Russano et al., 2005) found that minimization of blame and leniency increased the confession rate for both innocent and guilty subjects.

Additionally, untrained police and observers are not able to accurately distinguish truthful from deceptive suspects (Ekman, 1997; Ekman and O'Sullivan, 1991; Kassin, 1997; Kassin and Fong, 1999; McMahon, 1995). A recent study (Stromwall, Hartwig, and Granhag, 2006) found no differences in the nonverbal behaviors of samples of liars and truth tellers.

Interrogation efforts begin with the interrogators knowing a crime has occurred. The interrogators are, by definition, suspicious and have the expectation that interrogatees will engage in deception. This prejudiced posture clearly lends itself to outcomes of finding suspects guilty (Burgoon, Buller, Ebesu, and Rockwell, 1994).

Police research is relevant to the FDA in several respects. First, if information collected unethically is known to the forensic professional, then there is a moral obligation to make this observation known to the referring attorney or judge. It is critical for the evaluator to determine whether the deception employed by the police fatally compromised information collected from the suspect. In some cases, defendants have become suicidally depressed after being fed false information, which then affected the quality of information provided to the evaluator. Second, forensic professionals need to be able to reanalyze information after fatally compromised information is removed from their database, including the finding that no conclusions can be reached.

Empirically Based Methods and Applications

This chapter attempts to equip the evaluator with data and procedures to answer relevant questions concerning deception. Several critical questions in every assessment of deception that must be answered by the examining forensic professional are as follows:

1. Am I properly trained to conduct an FDA? Have ethical issues in this case been considered?
2. What events triggered a referral for a deception analysis? What happened at that time?
3. Did unintentional distortion occur during the critical forensic event or evaluation? What is the source of that distortion and how was it measured?
4. Has the assessee engaged in deliberate deception? How is that known? Is the deception associated with the past or the present, or both?
5. What is the magnitude of the faking? Quantitatively or qualitatively, how can I demonstrate the degree of faking uncovered?
6. Does present deception differ from that shown previously by the assessee? What is the assessee's history of deception in similar situations?
7. What are the possible inducements to deceive for this particular forensic situation?
8. What is the deception response style shown by the client? Behaviorally, which variation of malingering or defensiveness is shown?
9. Who were, are, or will be the most likely targets of deception?
10. Which feedback mechanism can I suggest to assist future evaluators of this person's possible deception?
11. How can I fairly and accurately represent this person's possible deception to the referring party or trier of fact?

The practitioner, concerned with detecting deception in particular cases, as an additional concern, needs to review the available research on deception. Only some of that research is immediately useful in the individual case. The following guidelines should be considered in evaluating research studies.

There continues to be a fundamental problem with how models of deception and malingering have been historically framed. In addressing this issue, Rogers (1990b, 1997) critiqued that all efforts to improve the reliability of clinical observation are significantly compromised if feigned psychological disturbance cannot be accurately ruled out. Rogers dismissed the diagnostic and statistical manual-III-revised (DSM-III-R) and currently the DSM-IV (which is nearly identical to DSM-IV-TR) definitions of malingering as "puritanical" because they embodied moralistic overtones. Furthermore, Rogers notes that the

DSM definitions of malingering were based on assumed criteria as opposed to being based on any empirical paradigm.

As alternatives, Rogers (1990a, 1990b, 1997) proposed an adaptation model and a detection model. In the adaptation model, as briefly discussed previously, malingering is the adaptive product of a perceived, aversive stressor. The stressor and the malingering response are variables that can be empirically measured. Another dependent variable is the mechanism of choice making in weighing the expected utility of a malingered response against the probability of a desired outcome. Rogers (1997, 2004) differentiated the pathogenic model (psychiatric disturbance), the criminological model (DSM), and the adaptation model as representing explanatory models. The explanatory models are distinct from detection or assessment models. Explanatory models characterize potential antecedent variables of malingering (Vitacco and Rogers, 2005), whereas the detection models take forensic assessment one step further and attempt to identify actual malingering incidents.

A significant relationship between a variable and deception does not necessarily indicate that the variable is a good predictor of deception. Some research findings bear on the processes of deception and deception detection rather than on the outcomes of deception detection. Research on impression management and self-presentation (e.g., Schlenker and Weigold, 1992) is clearly relevant to deception, but only some of the research is relevant to the accurate identification of individual deceivers (Pauls and Crost, 2004; Tyler and Feldman, 2005). Ekman (1985, 2001; Ekman and Rosenberg, 2005; Ekman, Friesen, and O'Sullivan, 2005) described how nonverbal behaviors, such as posture, tone of voice, and facial expression, may leak information about the truthfulness of a person. Such findings provide valuable information about the processes of deception but do not provide reliable clues to deception in individual cases (Frank and Ekman, 2004). Ekman (1985), for example, warned that these clues might be related in individual cases to genuine emotions or to the person's feelings about being suspected of lying. The practitioner is cautioned "behavioral clues to deceit should only serve to alert you to the need for further information and investigation" (Ekman, 1985, p. 189).

In general, research reports of mean differences between groups of "deceivers" and "nondeceivers" or of correlations between test scores and malingering do not provide justification for use of the reported measures for detection of deception in individual cases. Such group differences and correlations do not address the important question of predictive accuracy, reliability, or credibility. Group differences on Rorschach variables, for example, do not reflect the accuracy of predictions made with a particular cut-off score.

Even when a research finding focuses on individual prediction rather than group correlates, a statistically significant relationship does not necessarily indicate a good predictor. The value of a variable as a predictor of deception is determined by its effect size, not by its statistical significance (Cohen, 1977). Since the significance of a statistical relationship is determined in part by the sample size of the study, it is possible for a weak relationship (small effect size) to attain statistical significance. Such weak predictors will not prove useful in the prediction of individual cases. Good overall predictors of deception are those that show a large difference (effect size) between deceivers and nondeceivers.

Some good predictors of deception are "locally" rather than "generally" valid. Being bald is a good predictor that one is male, but having a full head of hair is not a good predictor of being female. Amount of head hair is a poor general predictor of sex, but being bald is a good local predictor of being male. In forensic settings, incarceration for repeated offenses is a good predictor of criminal attitudes, but living in the community is a poor predictor of psychopathy. Psychopathy is assessed with increased deception. In general, a variable may be unrelated to a criterion throughout its entire range, but still be related to the criterion within a local region of its range.

In deception research, a low value on a scale or the absence of a "sign" may be unrelated to truthfulness, while a high value or the presence of the "sign" may or may not indicate deception. A low Minnesota Multiphasic Personality Inventory (MMPI) F-scale score, for example, tells us nothing about deceptiveness, but a very high score, according to test norms, increases the likelihood of malingering.

Such asymmetrical relationships between predictors and deception function to lower overall tests of statistical significance, which are based on the entire range of values of the predictor. Thus, it is possible for research results, which yield nonsignificant or small effects, nonetheless to discover good predictors of deception.

These "local" predictors of deception are most clearly revealed in decision tables rather than in t-tests or correlation coefficients. Decision tables relate ranges of values on the predictor (e.g., high, medium, and low) to values on the criterion (e.g., deceptive and non-deceptive) (Wiggins, 1973). Often, however, this research does not specify the validity and reliability for the deception measures employed. Such classification tables, nevertheless, provide hypotheses on the relationship between successive local ranges of the predictor and the criterion rather than just the overall relationship between predictor and criterion.

Different research comparisons have differing practical implications. Published research on malingering typically involves group comparisons between (1) normal subjects instructed to "fake bad" and normal subjects instructed to respond normally, (2) normal subjects instructed to "fake bad" and genuine patients instructed to respond normally, or (3) patients suspected of malingering instructed to respond normally and genuine patients instructed to respond normally. These three types of comparisons yield widely varying accuracy rates and resulting scales, and the resulting patterns and cut-off scores are applicable to widely different evaluation situations.

For example, Leavitt (1987) reported that a measure of pain was 82% accurate in detecting normal subjects instructed to fake pain, but only 64% accurate in detecting genuine pain patients who were instructed to exaggerate their pain. Similarly, Berry, Baer, and Harris (1991) reported in a meta-analysis of MMPI indicators of malingering that the mean effect size for studies comparing normal subjects with normal subjects instructed to "fake bad" was 2.66. The mean effect size for studies comparing genuine patients with normal subjects instructed to "fake bad" was 1.86, the mean effect size for studies comparing genuine patients with patients instructed to exaggerate was 1.48, and the mean effect size for groups inferred to be malingering with other groups was .83. Thus, the accuracy of detection methods varies greatly with the type of discrimination being made.

Different tests also show variability in discrimination between honest responders and malingerers. For example, a meta-analysis by Vickery et al. (2001) reported that studies that used the Digit Memory Test (DMT), Portland Digit Recognition Test (PDRT), 15-Item Test, 21-Item Test, and the Dot Counting Test indicated that malingerers scored an *average* of 1.1 standard deviations below honest responders, but each test performed differently. The DMT performed best, separating the two groups by two standard deviations, the 21-item test was next with 1.5 standard deviations, the PDRT separated groups by 1.25 standard deviations, and the 15-item test and the dot counting test only separated groups by .75 of a standard deviation. The DMT also had the highest sensitivity and overall hit rate. The DMT, PDRT, and 15- and 21-item tests showed high specificity rates, but the PDRT and

15-item test showed only moderate sensitivity and the 21-item test showed poor sensitivity. The examiner always needs to keep in mind that detection of deception on these tests cannot be generalized to being deceptive regarding other, and perhaps more germane, issues (e.g., lying about committing a crime).

The results of studies that compare normal subjects with normal subjects instructed to "fake bad" are most relevant to evaluation situations that themselves involve this comparison (e.g., detecting malingerers among job applicants). The results of studies that compare genuine patients with normals instructed to "fake bad" are most relevant to situations where malingerers are seeking admission to patient status. The results of studies that compare genuine patients with other patients instructed to exaggerate their symptoms are most relevant to situations where current patients are seeking additional treatment-attention benefits. In terms of the MMPI results reported by Berry et al. (1991), MMPI indices of malingering are likely to be most accurate in situations where they are least needed (e.g., distinguishing genuine normals from faking normals) and to be less accurate in situations where they are needed most (e.g., distinguishing suspected malingerers from genuine patients). Being a patient or client in a medical setting often has little or nothing to do with many forensic assessments. The findings, however, from such nomothetic sources can be used in conjunction with idiosyncratic information to generate conclusions about an individual examined forensically.

As a final example, a study by Ekman, O'Sullivan, and Frank (1999) reported a group of federal law enforcement officers and a group of sheriffs to be significantly more accurate than other law enforcement peer groups in detecting laboratory deception. The greater prediction accuracy was attributed to the experience and special training of the federal officer group. In the same study, a group of psychologists "interested in deception" were more accurate in predicting deception than a control group of psychologists. The significance of the study was the selectively greater accuracy of two subsets of professionals in detecting deception. This finding supported earlier evidence (Ekman and O'Sullivan, 1991) that some professionals are very accurate in detecting deception. The current study demonstrated deception-detection accuracy with select psychologists. While an important study in the deception literature, the approach was a laboratory-based paradigm involving videotaped scenarios that were observed by the Ss. The Ss received financial bonuses if their enactments of truth or deception were believed. The bonuses were intended to ensure a "high-stakes" milieu. It was unknown, however, whether such bonuses would have significance in real life. There are limits to the practical utility of laboratory analog models.

A good predictor is not necessarily a useful one. Discovery of a good overall or local predictor of deception may be helpful but not sufficient for useful prediction of deception. It must also be shown that the predictor is useful in the situation in which it is applied. Meehl and Rosen (1955) discussed the influence of base rates (prior probabilities) on errors in prediction. If deception is very rare or very frequent in a particular situation, a good predictor will nevertheless produce a large number of incorrect predictions. Indeed, if the base rate is low enough, a good predictor with even a low error rate can produce more incorrect than correct predictions!

Even a predictor that produces more correct than incorrect predictions in a particular situation may not be useful. A false prediction in one situation is not necessarily as serious as a false prediction in a different situation. Falsely predicting malingering in a neurological case may have more dire consequences than falsely predicting dishonesty in hiring. Indeed, Swets (1992) has argued that the best decision rule for any given test is strictly a function of the base rate of the condition being evaluated and the relative costs of false-positive and false-negative decisions. Without knowing anything at all about the accuracy of a particular test, sign, or other decision rule, it is not possible to define its usefulness in given situations. In general, assessment procedures for malingering will be less useful in situations with a low base rate for malingering than in situations with a higher base rate for malingering. "That is, one should not make the positive decision very readily when the chances are great that the negative alternative will actually occur" (Swets, 1992, p. 525). In addition, conservative rules for predicting malingering will be more useful than liberal rules when the relative cost of falsely calling someone "malingering" is greater than the relative cost of falsely calling someone "genuine." These costs of misclassification may differ considerably from one situation to another, even when the assessment decision (e.g., neurological malingering versus genuine impairment) and base rates are the same. For example, it can be argued that the cost of falsely calling "malingering" is greater when the decision is irreversible (e.g., in courtroom testimony) than when the decision is reversible (e.g., in treatment where new information continuously updates treatment plans).

A final factor in determining the usefulness of a malingering assessment procedure is the cost of administering the procedure. A procedure that appropriately minimizes costs of misclassifications for a given situation may not be useful if it is prohibitively expensive to administer. Most clinicians would be unwilling to spend 3 h assessing the "genuineness" of a 1-h screening evaluation. However, the same 3-h assessment may be a bargain when the relative cost of a misclassification is high enough (e.g., selection of astronauts for long-term space missions). Similarly, equipment costs may offset the value of accurately classifying subjects. Buchwald (1965) presented a discussion of the impact of the cost of testing on decisions of whether or not to use a test at all. In some situations, the cost of detecting "malingering" may be greater than the cost of tolerating undetected "malingerers."

The accuracy of an individual prediction is all-or-none. Statistics on the accuracy of predictions and classifications (e.g., valid positive rates and positive hit rates) always reflect the results of a series of decisions as applied to norm groups and not to the specific person being assessed. An assessment procedure is used with a group of people, and the accuracy of the procedure is determined for the entire group (i.e., for the series of individual decisions). This type of accuracy information provides an empirical basis for deciding which procedures, cutting scores, signs, or other decision rules to use for particular purposes. For a particular purpose, the procedure with higher accuracy is preferable to one with lower accuracy; for a particular assessment situation, one cutting score is more accurate than another cutting score; for a given set of classificatory costs, a less costly procedure is preferable to a more costly procedure.

None of these statistics, however, reflects the accuracy of a prediction in an individual case. When an assessment procedure for "malingering" has a positive hit rate of 80% (for a particular base rate), the probability that a person with a positive score on the procedure is actually malingering is not .80. The probability of an individual prediction being correct is always either 1.0 or 0.0. A prediction in an individual case is always either correct or incorrect. The positive hit rate, valid positive rate, and so on associated with a particular procedure refer only to the relative frequency of correct decisions among a series of decisions, not to the probability of being correct in a particular case.

However, the accuracy statistics associated with a particular procedure in a particular situation can be used in a logical argument to support the decision in a particular case (Movahedi and Ogles, 1976). Given that 80% of persons with a positive score on a malingering test are in fact malingering and given that Mr Jones has a positive score on the test, it is "80% logical" that Mr Jones is malingering. In other words, the claimed probability is a measure of the logical relationship between the premises and the conclusion and not a measure of the empirical truth of the conclusion. Given the following premises—75% of persons with X, Y, and Z are malingering and Mr Jones possesses X, Y, and Z, the proper conclusion is not that "There is a 75% chance that Mr. Jones is malingering," but rather that "It is 75% logical that Mr Jones is malingering."

Alternatively, accuracy statistics can be regarded as a measure of the decision-maker's confidence in an individual conclusion rather than as a statement about reality. A rational decision-maker would have more confidence, for example, in an individual prediction based on a procedure with a positive hit rate of 80% than in an individual prediction based on a procedure with a positive hit rate of 50%. The proper conclusion in the above syllogism is that "I am willing to bet that Mr Jones is malingering."

With either interpretation, an individual decision is empirically either correct or incorrect, but the decision-maker has a rational basis for acting on the decision in this particular case.

In summary, research on deception is relevant to the actual detection of deception only when it presents results on the predictive accuracy of general or local predictors of deception in research groups similar to those with whom the detection method will actually be used. These results are best evaluated in decision or classification tables, which allow determination of the error rates associated with the predictor. Predictors with low error rates must then be evaluated in terms of their usefulness in particular situations. The usefulness of a procedure involves considerations of (1) the base rate of the condition being assessed in the situation where the procedure will be used, (2) the relative costs associated with false-positive and false-negative classifications, and (3) the cost of administering the procedure. The accuracy statistics for a given procedure can be used in a logical argument that assessment results in individual cases should be used as if they may be empirically true.

Basic Points to Consider in Clinical-Forensic Assessment

We now briefly present an applied model of deception shown in Figure 3.1 (see also Hall and Poirier, 2001, or Hall, Thompson, and Poirier, in press, for more detail). The evaluator

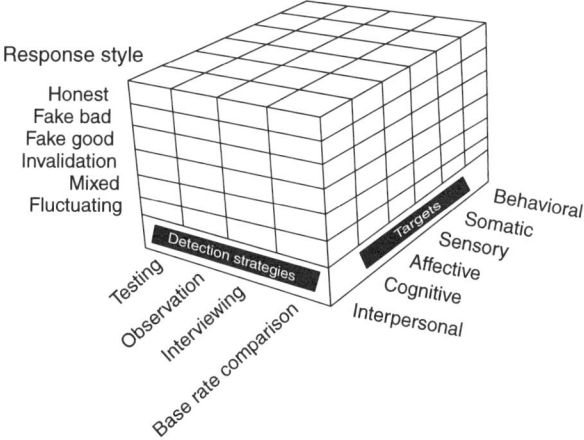

Figure 3.1 Three-dimensional model of deception analysis.

first needs to consider *target symptoms* of the faker selected in congruence with goal achievement on the right side of Figure 3.1. A veteran may malinger the intensity of his or her posttraumatic stress disorder (PTSD) in order to obtain a higher service-connected compensation. Another may deny a history of violence in order to receive a lighter sentence for assault. A plaintiff may fake memory loss in order to obtain a large monetary settlement. A defendant may fake insanity to achieve exculpation and, hence, avoid penal incarceration. The task for the evaluator is to tap into these cognitive targets in order to determine whether they have led to faked or honest behavior. Table 3.1 presents the target categories and examples of each.

As a rule, fakers choose target symptoms in accordance with the direction of their vested interests. People choose what they think will work in order to accomplish their goals. Much knowledge of psychological and medical conditions has been publicized in the media. Thus, actual neuropsychological symptoms may be selected for bogus head trauma. Amnesia may be chosen when a gap in memory is self-serving in a violent crime. Targets are not to be confused with goals—targets are short term in nature; goals represent the ultimate objective of the faker. Goals may include anything from avoiding prison to obtaining a monetary reward.

Table 3.1 Targets of Deception

Category	Examples
Behavioral	
Motor	Slowness/agitation
Verbal	Mutism, aphonia
Somatic/psychosomatic	
Central nervous system	Epileptic seizures, paralysis
Other systems	Factitious arthritis, muscle weakness
Sensation	
Visual	Visual hallucinations, partial blindness
Auditory	Hearing voices, deafness
Tactile	Intense or persisting pain
Taste	Gustatory insensitivity
Smell	Olfactory hallucinations, loss of smell
Imagery	
Perception	Flashbacks, illusions
Rapid eye movement sleep	Nightmares, night terrors
Affect	
Autonomic	Anxiety, rage
Emotional	Lability, major depression
Cognitive	
Attention	Stupor, unconsciousness
Memory	Amnesia, recall problems
Language	Aphasia, word salad
Thinking	Schizophrenia, dementia
Interpersonal	
Social	Imposture, Munchausen by proxy

Table 3.2 Response Styles

Honest	Attempts to be accurate within own frame of reference, may show nondeliberate distortion
Faking bad	Exaggeration or fabrication of symptoms and negative features, denial and minimization of positive traits/events, misattribution of deficit to false cause
Faking good	Minimization and denial of symptoms and behaviors, exaggeration or fabrication of positive points, misattribution of blame to outside source
Invalidation	Attempts to render the evaluation meaningless
Mixed	Combination of styles within same evaluation period
Fluctuating	Change of style within or between evaluation period(s)

Selecting a target means that the faker makes assumptions about both ground truth and distortion. For how can psychosis be faked without having an idea of how a psychotic person behaves? This gives the evaluator an advantage by putting the onus for performing on the deceiver.

Targets can change as a function of many factors such as opportunity, fatigue, and evaluator behavior. The goal, however, usually remains the same (e.g., wanting compensation for a back injury). Some targets are nonverifiable, particularly suicidal ideation, pain, hearing voices, and trauma-related nightmares. Finally, targets are often based on partially real deficits and represent an exaggeration of deficits rather than pure fabrication. The best lie is the partial truth.

A simple method for listing possible targets of the faker is presented in Table 3.1. All the major dimensions of deception in terms of targets are covered. The "behavioral" category includes verbal or motor acts as targets. "Somatic or psychosomatic" targets and symptoms include a broadband category of physical signs. "Sensation" refers to faked deficits in vision, hearing, smell, taste, touch, temperature, pressure, balance, and pain. "Affect" can involve autonomic or emotional events that may be distorted. "Cognitive" problems include deficits in attention, memory, language, and thinking. "Interpersonal" deficits involve faking when reporting upon the interaction with others. The right side of Table 3.1 presents clinical examples of target symptoms.

In sum, targets involve any short-term objectives which, when reached, are in the direction of the faker's stake. The targets (a) may change over time, during the evaluation, or subsequent to the evaluation; (b) may be specific or broadband in focus (e.g., tics or dementia); (c) are based on cognitive schemes, experience, sophistication, and available disguises; (d) must be differentiated from nonfaked behaviors; and (e) can be translated into discrete response styles that can be measured.

The second part of the model deals with the *response patterns or response styles* of the deceiver, which fortunately cluster into variations of concealing the real or presenting the fake. Response styles are behaviors exhibited by the faker to achieve some outcome (see Table 3.2 for a summary of response styles). The following response patterns seem most indicative of faking as indicated by comprehensive reviews of the literature (Hall and Poirier, 2001; Rogers, 1997):

1. A rapid improvement when external incentives change or when weak environmental triggers are presented. A waxing or waning of response intensity is suspicious when it

is in harmony with environmental events such as when the deceiver knows he or she is being observed.

2. Response patterns not congruent with neuropsychological or psychological conditions or symptoms. This often involves the violation of anatomical laws (e.g., loss of feeling across widely separated sites allegedly due to spinal injury rather than according to expected deficits). Neuropsychological principles may also be suspiciously disregarded (e.g., loss of crystallized knowledge in presence of ability to learn and short-term recall skills).

3. Critical behaviors during the interview such as absurd responses, unlikely combinations, and contradictory responses. While not definitive by themselves, these critical behaviors should alert the evaluator to conduct a more intensive search for indicators of deception.

The heart of FDA is in the analysis of response styles that are described in detail below. Only through behavior can we infer deception. Response styles are connected to targets in the nature of cause and effect even though targets can be quickly conceived of or yield poor (i.e., detectable) patterns of behavior.

Honest Responding

Despite the focus of this chapter, clinical-forensic experience indicates that most individuals may have built-in prohibitions against deliberate deception. In forensic intervention settings, many clients are distressed psychologically or physically and just want to be well again. Returning to work or a meaningful lifestyle is a powerful reinforcer; most clients seem to believe that nondeceptive behavior is proper and essential to achieve these goals.

In the criminal arena, defendants, witnesses, and significant others are reminded of their moral duty, which is reinforced by legal sanction, for truth telling. Possible charges relating to perjury and hindering prosecution add incentive to tell the truth. For defendants, malingering is strongly suspected in about 20% of the cases (Rogers, 1988, 1997). This means that the vast majority of defendants are not engaging in blatant deception, even when their liberty is at stake.

In the civil arena, the most notorious of settings with regard to eliciting deception for monetary gain, there may be a fear of being detected for one's fakery. Depositions are taken and oaths are administered in a judicial attempt to reduce deception. For some situations, such as workers' compensation, a theoretical question emerges as to why persons would fake in order to obtain a fraction of their normal pay.

Honest responding does not equal cooperation with the evaluator. Noncooperation can occur for a variety of reasons—from dislike of the evaluator to circumstances of the setting. Witnesses and significant others are often only minimally cooperative. They may claim that they are too busy, or make it clear that they do not want to become involved, or may be biased in favor of or against the accused.

Nondeliberate distortion can occur in the presence of truth telling. The brain-damaged or psychotic subject may give what he or she believes to be an accurate portrayal of events. Recall that nondeliberate distortion caused by stress may occur in the majority of people (Buckhout, 1980; Hall and Poirier, 2001).

The following excerpt from a report of a forensic case illustrates honest responding for a borderline retarded individual accused of attempting to sexually assault a 25-year-old school teacher. The purpose of the report was to comment on criminal responsibility, of which possible deception is of high concern to the criminal court:

> Mr. Tanaka displayed few evidences of deliberate deception as suggested by the following in their entirety: (a) the congruence between pathological test signs and clinical behavior (e.g., both showing perseveration and bizarre statements). Although both could be interpreted to be evidence of deliberate deception, the consistency of findings across settings renders that conclusion less likely; (b) acceptable range of responses on measures helpful in detecting faking bad and faking good (e.g., MMPI and forced choice testing). Although it cannot be generalized from these findings regarding credibility to any statement about sexual assault, it does shed light on possible malingering on this measure; (c) expected learning deficits with increased task difficulty (e.g., on neuropsychological testing), which, again, is not related to the sexual assault question, but is to the issue of deception; (d) similarity of scores on different subtests or test items of equal difficulty (e.g., digits forward and backward obtained on WAIS-R and Wechsler Memory Scale); (e) congruence of volunteered information with the physical evidence and victim and witness statements; (f) concordance of mental condition at the time of assessment with crime behavior, and (g) volunteering of much self-incriminating data.

There were suggestions of considerable nondeliberate distortion for both the time of the evaluation and the alleged offenses. Immediate, short-term, and long-term recall showed contamination with psychotic features when compared to cross-validating data. Concrete answers were given to many queries with prompting needed to extract responses, which were later determined to be correct. His sense of time was substantially impaired compared to cross-validating data. He further displayed an inability to see his mistakes during testing, corresponding to historical behavior which showed poor judgment at home and on the job. His Wechsler Adult Intelligence Scale-Revised (WAIS-R) score revealed borderline intelligence with deficits in all areas of intellectual functioning, including vocabulary, computational, informational, and verbal associational skills.

In general, for both the time of the evaluation and the instant offenses, the accused showed little deliberate, but considerable nondeliberate, distortion. Cross-validation with other database sources was necessary to determine credibility parameters.

Faking Bad

Faking bad, also known as malingering, deceit, prevarication, false imputation, and simulation, always involves fabrication of nonexistent problems or the exaggeration of actual pathology. Denial or minimization of good points in an attempt to look worse than one actually is may also occur. As with any response style, malingering can coexist with genuine deficits. The writers' experience is that malingering associated with real problems should alert the evaluator that we are not dealing with an either-or situation.

Many faking bad patterns are possible. Table 3.3 presents a dozen of the more common patterns of faking bad encountered in clinical-forensic evaluation.

Frequency data are lacking for most of these faking subtypes. Data on faked recall problems using a forced choice format, however, suggest that many of the subtypes are common among successful fakers (Hall and Shooter, 1989; Shooter and Hall, 1990). These include

Table 3.3 Faking Bad Response Styles

Style	Behavioral Strategy	Examples
Verbal fabrication	Claiming a nonexistent problem	"I have ringing in my right ear"
Verbal exaggeration	Amplifying real problem	"I'm more forgetful than usual"
Verbal denial	Disclaiming an ability	"I can't smell anything"
Verbal minimizing	Downplaying an ability	"I can walk only one block"
Misattribution	Stating deficit due to false cause rather than true etiology	Claiming developmental learning disability caused by a vehicular accident
Behavioral fractionalizing	Shows crudely estimated fraction of ability	Hand grip scores only 1/2 of ability
Behavioral approximating	Gets a close, but not exact, answer	"6 + 6 = 13; 7 x 3 = 22"
Behavioral infrequency	Sprinkles errors throughout performance on graduated scale	Errors on Wechsler Adult Intelligence Scale-Revised Comprehension and Vocabulary on initial items
Behavioral disengagement	Shows confusion and frustration—may give up	Claims total inability during blindfolded period of tactual performance test (TPT) testing
Impulsivity	Answering quickly, presents first thing on mind	Poor on Arithmetic and Block Design compared to untimed performance
Perseveration	Persists with one response mode regardless of feedback	Alternates errors on Wisconsin Card Sorting Test (WCST) or explicit alternative testing
Randomizing	No consistent pattern of errors	Speech perception test errors due to deliberate inattention

randomizing (28%), perseveration (19%), fabrication (16%), fractionalizing (9%), and disengagement (9%). For unsuccessful fakers, the same response subtypes emerged, but in a different order or magnitude. Results showed that randomizing (9%), perseveration (5%), fabrication (41%), fractionalizing (20%), and disengagement (13%) were clearly detectable as response strategies. For both successful and unsuccessful fakers, the full gamut of the subtypes presented in Table 3.3 was represented.

Faking Good

Also known as defensiveness and dissimulation, faking good is the exact opposite of faking bad. Faking good always involves denial or minimization of problems in the direction of one's vested interests. Fabricating and exaggerating positive points are also frequent. Second to honest responding, faking good is probably the most common distortion strategy utilized. Indeed, most people seem to minimize and deny or exaggerate their positive points to adapt to the social environment. Otherwise, most marriages, businesses, and other relationships involving people would not last. The adaptive function of deception has been noted for over a century (Triplett, 1900).

In faking good on tests of cognitive ability, the deceiver cannot do better than his or her true ability. For example, faking good cannot occur on intelligence, neuropsychological, and other ability tests. The exception to this rule is taking performance-enhancing drugs, such as anabolic steroids or stimulants, in order to increase vigilance and motor speed. Some substances, such as antianxiety drugs, are occasionally used to cover anxiety during an interview and to project an image of confidence to the evaluator.

It is possible to fake good on personality measures and in interviews. One may affirm a fraction of the pathological items on the MMPI, or engage in self-praise during an interview. In general, the five most commonly used methods of faking good are:

Denial	"I didn't drink alcohol." "I don't have a memory problem."
Minimizing	"I snort coke only on Wednesday nights with friends." "I do poorly on tests like this."
Fabrication	"I have run a mile in less than four minutes." "I have a parasensory ability which allows me to discern the truth."
Exaggeration	"Nobody cooks as good as I." "I'm considered a virtuous person."
Misattribution	"I beat my wife because I was grieving over my friend's death."

Faking good is difficult to demonstrate when it involves concealing the real. It places the onus on the evaluator to demonstrate the existence of that which is denied or minimized. Cross-validation is essential in these cases. The following excerpt illustrates defensiveness in a case involving violence risk for the purpose of sentencing a 26-year-old defendant accused of savagely beating his ex-girlfriend into a coma:

During the second interview on October 9, 1990, the defendant blamed the victim, acquaintances of the victim, his own attorney, and the court for slanting the "truth" and refusing to allow him to tell the whole story. He declined to take psychological tests, citing again issues of trust. Intellectually bright, verbal, and persistent in his efforts to dominate the interview, this male utilized cognitive strategies of minimization, denial, and withholding of information to convey a picture that this whole affair (i.e., the instant offense and events leading up to it) was a romantic feud that should best be simply forgotten by the court so he can go on with his life.

In regard to minimization and denial, examples include stating that (a) he hit the victim only once, consisting of an open-handed slap with his left hand, during the February 3, 1990, assault that caused brain damage to the victim, despite statements by two witnesses to the contrary; (b) he has never "attacked" the victim, only "hit" her on occasion. He affirmed the December 1988 assault, but stated that he hit the victim in the ribs two to three times at that time because she allegedly told him she had been sexually unfaithful with a previous boyfriend; (c) he placed an ice pick through a jacket on the victim's door, stating to the examiner that he was only returning the jacket and that no threat was intended. In retrospect, he can now see how the victim reacted with fright to this and other behaviors of his; (d) he threw a rock through the victim's window in October 1989 only to "wake her up," not to frighten her; (e) he never intended to pull the victim's hair out on October 6, 1989, and that he grabbed her head to get her attention; earlier in the day, the victim had reportedly walked into his apartment and destroyed two or three paintings with an umbrella. Even though he was angry at the victim, the hair-pulling allegedly occurred because the victim pushed his hand away, thus in essence pulling her own hair out; (f) he has never had a really serious drug problem; however, he stated later that while in California, he injected heroin 15 to 20 times, smoked it many other times, and committed crimes with eventual incarceration for those crimes that were related to drug procurement activities. Records from California revealed that his daily heroin addiction cost about $200.

Many other examples exist. Suffice it to say that the defendant may not be a credible source of information due to distortion methods of (a) minimization, (b) denial, (c) projection of blame, and (d) withholding information in order to project a positive picture of himself. He denied feelings of anger toward the victim. Finally, he stated that he did not want his relatives contacted in connection with this case.

Invalidation

The evaluator may not know the reasons for a client invalidating the evaluation by some tactic(s), thus rendering it meaningless. Conclusions cannot be reached when this occurs. Examples include (a) not reporting for the evaluation, (b) reporting for the evaluation, but having to leave after one-half hour to avoid being fired from work or because of a sick spouse, (c) showing up substance-intoxicated, (d) becoming nauseous and sick in the middle of an interview, or (e) leaving too many unanswered items on the MMPI-2. The evaluator must then perform the evaluation at another time or change data-collection strategies in order to counter attempts at invalidation.

Mixed Response Styles

Mixed response styles within one evaluation involve faking good and faking bad. How is it possible to have both malingering and defensiveness within one evaluation? The person may be extraordinarily sensitive about sexual behavior, for example, thinking (wrongly, of course) that this is none of the evaluator's business, yet attempting at the same time to exaggerate pain reactions in order to reap a financial reward in a civil suit. Clinically, the person may say, "I am here to assess my pain, not my lifestyle." On the MMPI-2, overendorsed depression and other traits associated with pain may be seen, but anger, distrust, and suspicion may be downplayed.

Fluctuating Response Styles

Suggestions have emerged that changes in response strategies occur within the same evaluation period (see Hall and Shooter, 1989; Hall, Shooter, Craine, and Paulsen, 1991). A common one, found in testing for feigned amnesia, is faking bad at the beginning of evaluation and showing honest responding, as fatigue sets in or as clients begin to believe that they have given themselves away. Honesty in the beginning of the interview, with faking bad as the evaluation progresses, is occasionally seen. This is a sign that the client may think the examiner can be duped.

A second fluctuating style involves presenting different styles during different time periods. The defendant may claim psychosis at the time of the instant offense in order to escape criminal liability, yet deny problems for the present in order to obtain release from hospitalization. A civil litigant may fake good concerning problems before an accident but fake bad for the present in order to assert damages. This suggests that evaluation procedures must be geared toward both the past and the present.

In general, there is no escape from considering possible deceptive responses, for it is only through behavior that faking can be understood and measured. Fakers select targets that serve overriding goals in the direction of their interest. By acting to achieve those targets, fakers create response patterns, which can be scrutinized by the evaluator.

Detection Strategies

Detection strategies are the third and last part of the FDA model. These include (a) variation from expected performance (e.g., errors on simple questions, violation of learning curves, and deviant scores on parallel testing), (b) validity indicators (e.g., random patterns and subtle versus obvious discrepancies), (c) failure on tests specifically designed to assess deception (e.g., explicit alternative testing (EAT) and tests of illusory difficulty), again, not related to the question of sexual assault, but important to a compensation claim, and (d) clinical intuition, which has been shown by research to be no better than chance under forensic information collected by structured approaches.

The last part of the FDA model deals with detection methods. The overall strategy of the evaluation is to gather information about the actor, the one acted upon, and the context of deception, all within a systematic, comprehensive approach, which is then tailored to the assessment needs of the individual examined.

For example, in testing for claimed cerebral deficits because of an auto accident involving the loss of specific sensory skills such as numbness and agnosia, the evaluator would first use a neuropsychological battery. Specific claimed problems not measured on the battery, such as loss of smell and "frontal" problems, would then be tested.

Nontesting approaches that yield high reliability can be utilized. Structured interviews and interviews of significant/knowledgeable others for cross-validation of claimed deficits, for example, are very helpful. Input from friends, relatives, and acquaintances, however, must be scrutinized for distortion before being accepted as truth. Observation, to determine whether or not claimed deficits correspond to actual behavior, may be utilized. The forensic community holds inpatient hospitalization for observation of deceptive response patterns in high regard. This method builds on multiple measures over time in order to evaluate the assessee. Figure 3.2 presents the authors' opinions of the clinical efficacy of selected methods for detecting deception.

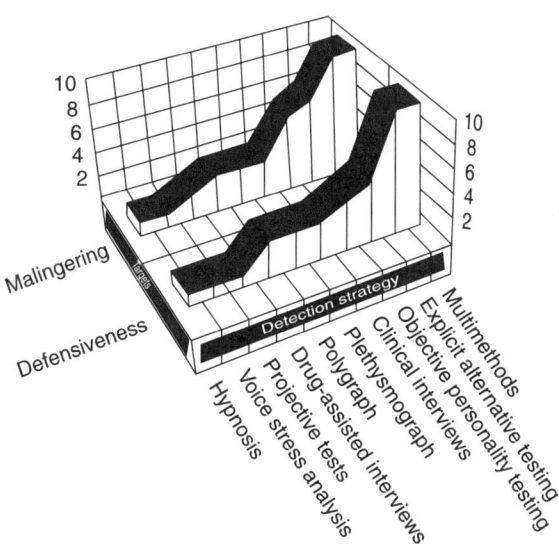

Figure 3.2 Clinical efficacy of deception detection methods.

In regard to detection methods, the evaluator should keep in mind that no one method is 100% accurate; they should be used in combination with one another. The examiner should use methods that are broadbanded, standardized, and flexible within the evaluation. Methods must eventually be geared specifically toward symptoms/targets. As discussed, they are operative for at least two periods of time. Few referral sources are particularly interested in deception only at the time of the evaluation. Last, built-in feedback and replication features are necessary to assess the effectiveness of the methods.

An adequate database for FDA requires information relevant both to the times of the evaluation and to the time of some past event. Thus, at the very least, the examiner must scrutinize two time periods. This is particularly important in light of the tendency of clients to fake differentially depending on the time period involved. Many criminal offenders, for example, fake bad for the time of the alleged crime only to fake good for the present, such as when the defendant applies for release from hospital incarceration. The database continues to expand until all referral questions are addressed. It is secured, protected against scrutiny, utilized again if needed, and eventually destroyed. Although the American Psychiatric Association (APA) recommends that data be kept for seven years, this standard is changing over time, and with revisions of the code, there is no preclusion to keeping data indefinitely.

As an initial step, the evaluator must gather information. Possible sources include:

1. Interviews of significant/knowledgeable others
2. Behavioral observations of the possible deceiver in individual and group, structured and unstructured, stressful and nonstressful situations
3. Functional analysis of previous (i.e., historical) deception
4. Analysis of validity indicators on psychological testing, with a statement of limitations on using it to generalize to other areas
5. Analysis of learning curves and expected performance in intellectual and neuropsychological methods
6. Competence assessment, vocational and ability testing
7. Medical and laboratory analysis
8. Neurological testing using PET, CAT, and MRI technologies
9. Semantic and transcript analysis
10. Body "leakage" (i.e., nonverbal behavior) analysis
11. Autobiographical materials (e.g., diaries and letters)
12. Records produced by others (e.g., military, school, and job)
13. "Expunged" records in the state or federal archives
14. Intervention paradigms designed to assess deceit by changing it
15. Base-rate analysis for traits of groups in which the deceiver holds membership

The analysis then proceeds to a synthesis of the findings. All known factors are considered; weights, if estimable, are given to the various factors, unless one has actuarial data. A judgment is rendered in terms of the evaluator's confidence in the findings and possible degree of accuracy, reliability, and credibility. Hopefully, the synthesis is verifiable and replicable by independent examiners. A good working rule is that deception must be demonstrated, not simply arrived at by ruling out other possibilities.

The evaluator should recognize that "ground truth" for any event, free of camouflage and faking, stands by itself and can be measured in the same manner as we confirm any reality. This comes with a consideration of actor, acted upon, and context. Adults caught up in disputed custody/supervision matters are subject to tremendous feeling states that may induce false statements and false accusations both on a voluntary and on an involuntary basis. Differentiating between what is voluntary distortion from involuntary distortion makes evaluation of disputed domestic matters extremely difficult.

Forensic events can be established even when deception is involved. Murders are an unfortunate reality and can be solved despite attempts by perpetrators to conceal or disguise the event. Auto accidents may cause genuine neurological damage for the plaintiff, who might exaggerate the symptoms in an effort to collect compensation. The perceptions of witnesses can be colored by many variables including excitement, stress, bias, and naiveté. Normal persons have faked their way into hospitals (and residential programs) for various reasons (Rosenhan, 1973); abnormal individuals have faked their way out of these settings. Some people even fake symptoms in others, for example, in Munchausen by proxy. In all of these situations, a reality exists separate from the faking. We call this reality "ground truth," and it is determined by establishing cross-validation data, as explained above. Deception manifests itself in the ways the deceiver attempts to fool others within a certain context. Ground truth always represents itself as an interaction of actor, acted upon, and context; deception represents a departure from what actually transpired in this three-entity interaction. Unfortunately, for the deceiver, deliberate deception takes energy, thought, and oftentimes reveals inconsistency. This can be uncovered with diligence and method.

Avoiding Evaluation and Consultation Errors

Most persons including many forensic evaluators are naive about deception. We believe that we can tell if someone is deceiving us and that it does not happen very often. Actually, people are lousy at lie-catching. That is why deception is generally successful. Although successive advances in distortion analysis have dispelled some misconceptions, others persist as follows:

Misconception 1 Most spoken words and behavior can be taken at face value. Actually, as we shall see, most people distort, either unintentionally or intentionally. For example, popular surveys reveal that over 90% of average Americans say that they lie regularly (Gates, 1991). Adolescents admit that they frequently lie to their parents (Jensen, Arnett, Feldman, and Cauffman, 2004). Finally, Roig and Caso (2005) reported that 72% of the college students in their study revealed that they had made up an excuse in college at least one time. Still, many forensic professionals believe that distortion does not usually occur (Hall and Poirier, 2001). They do not look for it. In the helping disciplines, false-negatives may be less of an issue, but it is a problem when forensic issues are involved, as are false-positives. Malingering has been confirmed or suspected in more than 20% of criminal defendants, with another 5% showing substantial unintentional distortion (Rogers, 1988, 1997). Based on experience, the deception rates for litigants in civil actions may be even higher, but this has to be empirically determined.

Misconception 2 Malingering, when it does occur, means that the faker is mentally sick. Desperate people often resort to desperate measures to survive or adapt. A person who fakes insanity is not necessarily mentally ill, but may want to avoid prison, a soul-destroying place under the best of conditions. As will be discussed, malingerers in general have good reality contact and are not psychotic. This myth may have been reinforced by the need to see psychopathology in liars when defendants or clients are misdiagnosed.

Misconception 3   The evaluator cannot be fooled (other people can). A favorite trick in cross-examination of experts is the following (Ziskin, 1981, p. 100):

Q. And it is possible for an individual to deceive you, isn't it?

A. Yes, it is possible, but I don't think that I am fooled very often.

Q. Well, if someone was successful in fooling you, you wouldn't know that he or she had fooled you, would you?

Melvin Belli, the famed litigator, recounts a case where a woman allegedly slipped on a greasy sauce on the floor of a restaurant, suffering a crippling hand injury. She was the ideal witness, "everybody's grandmother," giving a pitiful account about how she could no longer play the church organ until she bolted out of the courtroom when the defense attorney showed how she collected $500,000 on a similar case in Florida. Belli used this case to illustrate how honest his clients are, and how he was duped for the first time in 60 years of practicing law (*Honolulu Star-Bulletin*, January 25, 1991).

Traditionally, health and legal professionals have not been very good at detecting faking (Ekman and O'Sullivan, 1991). Worse yet, an inverse relationship has been suggested from research: the greater the confidence, the lower the accuracy in detecting faking. Investigations have raised promise, however, that with certain professional groups and with specialized training, deception detection can be significantly enhanced (Ekman et al., 1999).

Experts would like to believe that they are not fooled by forensic clients, given their experience and knowledge of the literature. The fact is that they would be fooled frequently without cross-validating data and standardized testing. Even with testing, they can and are regularly fooled.

Misconception 4   The DSM-IV criteria for malingering allow for deception analysis. DSM-IV states that malingering should be diagnosed if any combination of the following is shown (American Psychiatric Association, 1994, p. 683):

"(1)   medicolegal context of presentation, e.g., the person's being referred by his or her attorney to the physician for examination;
(2)   marked discrepancy between the person's claimed stress of disability and the objective findings;
(3)   lack of cooperation during the diagnostic evaluation and in complying with the prescribed treatment regimen;
(4)   the presence of Antisocial Personality Disorder."

However, these criteria are clinically inadequate. They fail to distinguish distorting influences such as evaluation-anxiety and fatigue from deliberate deception; they emphasize exaggeration and fabrication of symptoms to the neglect of denial and defensiveness; they associate deliberate deception with a personality type rather than with a person-in-a-situation.

Misconception 5   Some conditions, such as amnesia, hallucinations, and posttraumatic reactions, are easily faked and nearly impossible to prove. As will be presented, empirical methods can detect faked amnesia with promising degrees of accuracy (Hall and Poirier, 2001; Hall and Thompson, in press). Hallucinations are hard to disprove, yet base rates for comparison and decision criteria are available to assist the evaluator. PTSD, as with any mental condition, can be assessed by psychometrics or arousal methods with built-in features to assess deception.

Misconception 6 Detecting faking is an art and cannot be taught. Actually, the reverse appears to be true. Following a few simple rules increases the accuracy rate substantially. Deception analysis is a trainable skill. Workshops and clinical experiences over the years reveal that the average professional can be taught to adequately detect faking in a relatively short period. Detection tools include the MMPI, MMPI-2, and MMPI-A as part of a comprehensive evaluation (Shooter and Hall, 1989; Pope, Butcher, and Seelen, 2000). The caveat to trainees of course is that while deception may be noted as measured by these tests, it may not be generalized to other areas. Process guidelines for deception analysis as a specific focus of inquiry can also be taught (Hall, 1985; Paulsen and Hall, 1991). Another method is forced choice testing or EAT (Hall and Shooter, 1989; Shooter and Hall, 1990; Hall et al., 1991; Hall and Thompson, in press), with caution in generalizing cognitive distortion to criminal acts. Learning a few statistical decision rules allows the evaluator to obtain a high degree of accuracy in assessing faked memory deficits. A series of investigations highlight the ease of learning how to administer the procedure and to interpret results (Hall and Shooter, 1989; Shooter and Hall, 1990; Hall et al., 1991; Hall and Thompson, in press).

A dozen guidelines for avoiding mistakes should be considered:

1. Use multimodal methods. Standardized interviews, observation, review of records, and interviews of significant others can yield valid results; however, the evaluator should not rely on insight alone based on these traditional sources of information. If psychometric tests are administered, a battery of tests should be utilized. This addresses the issue of single tests versus a composite battery. Often, evaluators search for a quick sample of faking on a standardized instrument. It is highly unlikely that a single test instrument will cover all parameters of deception. In addition, an inordinate number of false-negatives and false-positives may be generated. The choice of a battery should typically include measures for possible genuine problems as well as for deliberate deception.

2. Start with the most valid information first. Data considered first most influence the evaluator. Premature closure or attempts to confirm what the evaluator already believes may lead to incorrect conclusions.

3. Adhere to validated decision rules even when tempted to abandon them for a particular case. Decision rules are more accurate than clinical judgment. The evaluator should ask why he or she is tempted to abandon the validated decision rules in the first place. What biasing factors may be operating? Remember that faking bad or good on cognitive functioning tests may not be associated with statements of risk or about criminal acts.

4. Think base rates. Knowledge of base rates alerts the evaluator of deception as to the general chances that certain events will occur. Literature will be cited later to provide base-rate information in deception analysis. It would be helpful, for instance, if the evaluator knew that between one-third and one-half of defendants malinger

memory problems in murder cases, with 25% overall rate of such malingering when pleading insanity.

Almost 50% of substances are verbally underreported compared to the results of urinalysis, yet the percentages differ depending on the particular locality and substance involved. On a test of remote memory, people generally do not err on autobiographical questions even if they are brain injured. Further, base-rate information is all that may be available to the evaluator in certain types of crimes, such as serial homicides where the perpetrator is unknown. For some types of unverifiable problems, such as suicide ideation and command hallucinations, base-rate information may be the only data available to the evaluator as a springboard for deception analysis.

5. Do not become overly focused on unique, salient, or unusual case features. Some evaluators consider the behavior in question to be genuine when a psychopath cries during the rendition of the instant offense. Conversely, evaluators have viewed a rape victim as not being credible because she was a prostitute and a belly dancer.

6. Do not fall prey to illusory associations between evaluation responses and supposed faking. These unfounded associations that have no empirical backing include the following:

   a. From the ancient literature, a burnt tongue from a hot sword indicates deception.
   b. Responses to white spaces on the Rorschach indicate oppositional tendencies.
   c. A lucid and reasonable account of the crime under hypnosis spells genuineness.
   d. The L (Lie) scale on the MMPI was developed as a measure of the test taker's credibility.

Evaluators should be wary of meaningless scores on tests measuring deception. Recall that:

   a. Scores regress toward the mean, with extreme scores showing the greatest change upon retesting.
   b. Small samples frequently misrepresent population parameters. Unfortunately, most of the specific tests for malingering fall into this category.
   c. Scatter can be due to chance and thus not indicate deception or other relevant dimensions.
   d. Chance occurrences can be seen as ordered.
   e. The year when a test is normed affects the scoring pattern. The normed population may be very different from the subject being evaluated.
   f. Reliance on highly intercorrelated measures is frequent. Evaluators tend to confirm the same problems when they use redundant testing.

7. Do not assess deception from DSM-IV-TR criteria (Rogers, 1990a; Hall and Poirier, 2001). Making incorrect associations between a diagnosis and certain traits may result in falsely attributing faking or honesty. For instance, a diagnosis of antisocial personality disorder does not always imply lying and a diagnosis of adjustment disorder does not automatically mean that the labeled person is telling the truth. In general, no mental condition automatically indicates deception or honesty.

As discussed in the *Introduction*, the DSM-IV-TR criteria for malingering are fatally flawed. Any forensic problem could be seen as malingered if the assessee was uncooperative or happened to be diagnosed as antisocial personality disorder. The need for a marked discrepancy between the subject's presented deficits and outside findings is important. Unfortunately, DSM-IV-TR provides no threshold criteria for evaluating such discrepancies.

8. Do not fail to consider triggers to ostensibly concealing or uncooperative behavior. Clients have bad days. The need to assess over several settings is important. Evaluators may have atypical days. Evaluators should consider that frustration or stress unrelated to the evaluation may be communicated to the assessee, who may show countertransference as a result. The evaluator, who may report distorted results, may overlook the cause-and-effect relationship.

   One trigger to distortion is commitment bias—the tendency to repeat a wrong answer if given a second chance to respond. It is operative when the subject wants to please the evaluator and believes that the assessor thinks a certain choice is correct. The client, for example, may pick out the wrong face again in a photo line-up due to this bias. Unconscious transference is another trigger. This occurs when a person seen in one situation is confused with another, such as when one sees the partial face of a person in a subway and concludes it was the defendant's face.

9. List alternative hypotheses and seek evidence for each. The evaluator should systematically list disconfirming and confirming data for each conclusion rendered. This may result in more accuracy; there is some evidence that evaluators who deliberate longer are most accurate (Hall and Poirier, 2001).

10. Do not fail to limit and operationalize conclusions. The evaluator should note the confidence in results as well as indicate the degree of defendant distortion that may have occurred. A feedback mechanism to reassess results should be specified—for example, a readministration of the same measures when a forensic issue reemerges.

11. Do not overload the referring party, trier of fact, or juries with data. The average working memory holds about seven bits of information at a time. There may be a decrease in accuracy in most people due to overload after that point. The writers try to give jurors no more than about one-half dozen critical points in their attempts to synthesize their overall presentation in court.

12. Make a deliberate effort to get feedback. At a bare minimum, cross-validating information should validate findings on deception. The forensic professional should know his or her "hit rate" in court for acceptance of conclusions regarding deception. Jurors can be questioned following either a civil or criminal trial. Normative data regarding distortion and deception for one's area, practice, or circumstances should be systematically collected. Age, sex, educational level, and ethnic differences should be noted.

Hindsight bias should be avoided. This occurs when an evaluator believes, after the fact, that the outcome could have been easily detected. It can be demonstrated by asking evaluators to estimate their own accuracy levels and comparing them with known results. Foresight in FDA focuses instead on what comes next in a deception problem.

Current Methods and Applications

FDA mandates a scrutiny of the actor, yourself as evaluator, and the context in which the distortion occurs. To comment upon possible faking by a murderer, you must be intimately familiar with the homicide. To state that cerebral insult stems from a car accident, you should know how the person typically behaved prior to the alleged trauma. To claim that a rehabilitation client is deliberately sabotaging therapy due to secondary motives, you must be aware of your own countertransference, an insidious and often overlooked source of self-deception.

Evaluation process guidelines have been articulated to assess deception for the time before, during, and after the forensic examination (Hall and Poirier, 2001; Paulsen and Hall, 1991). The traditional training of most mental health clinicians usually does not imbue the sense of caution and level of analytic inquiry that is necessary in forensic assessments. The effective FDA attitude is not skepticism, nor mistrust or antagonism, but rather one of neutrality and openness. Any of these negative clinician attitudes will inevitably convey to interviewees and result in distorted and biased findings. Such attitudes will also become predictable fodder for any later cross-examination designed to impeach the evaluator's credibility. The proper approach is one of constant but respectful wariness for the possibility of deliberate and nondeliberate distortion and the possibility that the person is not being deceptive, but truthful to the best of his/her ability. At the same time, there must be a vigilant effort to solicit the most accurate data possible. The evaluators must always respect the rights of interviewees to conduct themselves as they deem necessary during examinations. The forensic clinician is first a collector of data, which may later be evidentiary in nature; it is not his/her responsibility to conduct psychotherapy, to gather evidentiary information, or to correct the ills of the world (Greenberg and Shuman, 1997).

Armed with the proper attitude, effective FDA requires proper preparation for the evaluation, conducting a proper evaluation, and proper follow-up after the evaluation. It is very important to understand that the forensic evaluator's work product in most instances is the written report. Learning how to write professional, quality reports is a critical aspect of the forensic clinicians' training and ultimate working expertise.

The importance of careful and comprehensive preparation in any forensic assessment cannot be adequately stressed. By definition, every clinical/forensic assessment entails the probability of distortion, both deliberate and nondeliberate, as well as a combination of the two, as well as the probability of honesty and truthfulness. The vigilant clinician will be best prepared to detect distortion, but of course the effort is never foolproof. Preparation must involve a thorough review of all available background data and materials. If critical background information is known to be missing, then every effort should be made to access it. The final report should always have a listing of all materials reviewed, persons interviewed, data examined, and so on. Likewise, if there is known to be information that could not be accessed, that should be noted also. The effort is to document the clinician's database as accurately as possible.

The time to begin to prepare for standing up to cross-examination begins at the point of referral. The adversarial cross-examination means that the opposing attorney will make every possible effort to impeach the expert's testimony. The authors have had the experience of a comprehensive evaluation being cast in a dubious light with the opposing attorney's proffer that a prior report was not incorporated into the assessment. Another circumstance is not being able to access prior records because defense counsel advises the client not to provide consent. In this instance, the report should cite the reason for the inability to access material, and the trier of fact will then have to make a determination as to how to proceed.

Not having accurate or complete background materials is just one area in which the expert's testimony is subject to impeachment. Citing all background materials that were relied upon, as well as those materials that were inaccessible (and why they were inaccessible), is the safest approach for the potential expert witness. The primary reason for the thorough background review, however, is to prepare the clinician for FDA.

A set of evaluation process guidelines by Paulsen and Hall (1991) are recommended and presented in Table 3.4.

Table 3.4 Process Factors in Deception Analysis

Suggestion	Rationale
Prior to the Evaluation	
Remain vigilant to possibility of assessee distortion	Knowledge of high-risk groups and distortion literature is essential
Assess examiner distortion, including that which is unintended	Examiner distortion is common (e.g., wrong assumptions and bias)
Maintain independence from referral party	Closeness with referral party suggests bias
Gather source data relevant to subject/incident	Objective data must be reviewed in order to ask incident-specific questions
Prepare a standardized distortion	There is no substitute for battery evaluation completeness
Schedule the evaluation	Generally distortion increases with time since the incident
During the Evaluation	
Orient client to evaluation process and disposition	Written and signed orientation forms are recommended to refute later claims of evaluation bias
Tape the evaluation, with knowledge of client	This assists evaluator's recall and is the basis for possible replication
Conduct an open-ended interview	Broad questions force assessee to work out details
Eventually focus on critical distortion issues	Binary-type questions force assessee to take a stand
Sprinkle questions with known answers throughout interview	Known deviation from "ground truth" is helpful to assess distortion style
Use multiple assessment methods	Validity and examiner credibility will be increased
After the Evaluation	
Modify the evaluation as appropriate	Flexibility of examiner response may increase database (e.g., quickly presented questions)
Confront client with suggestions of distortion	Providing opportunity to change story may resolve discrepancies
Evaluate validity of each data source	Cross-validating sources are subject to distortion
Assess nondeliberate distortion of client	Rule out unintentional distortion before deception is ruled in
Rule in deliberate distortion	Deception should be explicitly demonstrated
Differentiate between incident and evaluation distortion	Distortion always refers to two different points in time
Identify distortion along different points of time subsequent to incident	Fluctuating response styles suggest deception
Report incomplete or invalid data	Referral source needs to know if complete database is utilized
Determine whether uncovered distortion is relevant to referral questions	Genuine impairments are often associated with deception
Reflect the decision process in the report	How the examiner arrived at conclusions is central to distortion
Describe adequacy of process	Explicitly stating that distortion data warrant the conclusions is helpful
Delimit scope of distortion-related conclusions	Degree of certainty and temporal limitations should be specified
Make recommendations for case disposition	Further evaluation may be indicated (e.g., inpatient observation)
Identify a feedback mechanism	Later retesting for distortion is a frequent issue
Retain all data regarding distortion	Baseline material may be used for reanalysis

Before the Evaluation

The following case, which won a $500,000 award for the plaintiff, illustrates errors on the part of the defendant, the State of Hawaii Health Department, which could have been avoided with proper preparation before an evaluation of a patient's readiness for discharge.

> A 28-year-old white male paranoid schizophrenic began hallucinating, hearing the voice of a spirit urging him to hurt people, particularly his family members who were responsible for his involuntary hospitalization. There was a history of repeated assaults on family members with threats to kill. After two weeks, the patient was partially stabilized on antipsychotic medication. However, episodic outbursts of rage, shown by head banging and chair throwing, continued. The patient was overheard saying that he belonged in the hospital and that, if released, he would physically hurt his family. For the next three days, he went to great lengths to deny and minimize symptoms, finally stating that he had "learned his lesson" and was ready to return home.

The psychiatrist noted that the patient had "achieved insight" and made arrangement for discharge, which unfortunately did not include informing the patient's parents of h return to the community. The patient went to his family's home unannounced, refused to take his medication, and quickly deteriorated. One week later, he stabbed his mother in the heart with a 12-inch kitchen knife, lacerated his niece and nephew on the legs and arms, and plunged the knife into his sister's torso, leaving the blade imbedded.

The forensic report submitted in this case concluded with the following:

> In sum, a prediction of violent behavior with a decision to continue preventive hospitalization was expected, required, and approved behavior by the authorities. There was no way for the State Hospital to escape the obligation of assessing the risk of violence prior to the patient's release from the hospital. Dr. Trevane should have been aware of a multitude of signals from the patient and from other sources that the patient posed a substantial risk of violence at the time of release. Dr. Trevane further ignored the extant professional literature on the subject, disregarded his own observations in deciding to release the patient, and used factors in his decision-making process that bore little, if any, relationship to whether future violence would occur.

The staff members did not have in their possession, or were otherwise not aware of, the contents of retrievable documentation regarding the patient's past violence and thus completely failed to uncover a history of dangerousness, escapes from previous inpatient psychiatric programs, noncompliance in taking medication, and other critical factors that must be considered in predicting dangerousness.

They believed the patient when presented with his falsehoods and did not believe or ignored him when he stated that he should not return to his family upon release. The staff should have known that he was a substantial risk of danger to his family in particular, that the opportunity to inflict violence through the use of a knife was available and precedented in both the patient's recent and remote history, and that consideration of inhibitory factors such as preparing or even notifying the family of his release and ensuring treatment compliance was important in preventing or controlling violence. The acute and chronic physical and mental trauma suffered by the victims were created by the patient's violence of May 15, 1988, in the nature of cause and effect.

In this case, a number of factors were neglected. First, hospital staff should have been alerted to the possibility of defensiveness, particularly after the patient changed his mind and stated that he wanted to go home. Florid psychosis usually does not disappear in several days; rather, it dissipates gradually. The basal history of violence was neglected, and there was strong evidence that the staff was unaware of the patient's previous dangerousness and future anticipated triggers of violence. No psychometric testing was conducted. Ward notes by nursing and social work staff did not appear to have been read by program planners. In sum, very basic errors in evaluating the patient's claim of readiness for release were made through inadequate preparation before the formal evaluation for release.

During the Evaluation

A forensic case illustrates factors to consider during a deception analysis. One of the factors to be dealt with during an evaluation is the occurrence of disruptions, distractions, and sabotage of the evaluation process.

> A 38-year-old white male defendant reported for the sanity evaluation with his (loud) wife, a neighbor, and a friend, despite specific instructions from the writer to come alone.
>
> A review of court records had revealed a lengthy criminal past with known attempts to manipulate evaluators in the direction of leniency.

The solution to this problem involved psychometrically testing the accused while his significant others were being interviewed individually. They were also given instructions to write down what they knew of the history of the accused and the instant offense involving an alleged assault on the wife. After 3 h of evaluation and the collection of much forensic data, the accused and his significant others were released from evaluation.

In matters where police authorities have been involved, the police reports can be very important sources of information. Oftentimes, police reports provide the only source of information as to the psychological state of the accused at the time of a critical incident. Clinicians must bear in mind that the police reports are investigation documents, and police are trained to write reports that will support anticipated prosecution.

Significant others are often given checklists to complete in addition to their other tasks. These include the Mooney problem checklist, posttraumatic stress disorder checklists, and a structured history form, all regarding the accused. Basic background information is collected about the party supplying the information in order to assess his or her credibility. Orientation procedures, of course, are followed in gleaning information from significant others in order to counteract later claims of examiner distortion. The evaluator is advised to outline clearly the evaluator's role and objectives, as well as the limits of confidentiality. If it becomes apparent during an assessment that the subject has lost sight of the evaluator's role, the subject should be reminded. A common problem is interviewees being lulled by the rapport of the assessment process and making incriminating statements or offering personal opinions that they would not make if they recalled, at the moment, the objective, impartial role of the forensic clinician. If interviewees complain later as they predictably will, the evaluator is portrayed as having a malevolent interest. Evaluators must treat all witnesses with the same rights and privileges as the defendant, including the right to cease questioning.

The evaluation may start on a general level in order to tap into the assessee's stream of consciousness and style of thinking. However, if the assessee insists on providing information out of order, it may be very productive to listen to him/her and later go back to cover information that may have been left out. Police commonly interrupt the interrogation of the accused before obtaining broadbanded information, thus losing the chance to observe the arrestee mentally working out details to the questions. Sometime during the initial part of the evaluation, the first in a pair of parallel test forms can be administered, followed by the second test toward the end of the session. These parallel test procedures include repeated measures of receptive vocabulary (e.g., Peabody picture vocabulary test), visual recall (e.g., California memory test), and auditory discrimination (e.g., auditory discrimination test), or other tests if the skills tapped by those tests are relevant to the issue of deception in a particular case. For example, the Shipley Institute of Living Scale or the Ravens Progressive Matrices can be administered to the accused in a sanity screening. This provides for parallel administration later or for comparison with WAIS-R scores. Regression equations permit prediction of WAIS-R IQ scores from both the Shipley and the Ravens tests.

Flexibility of response is especially important. One client refused to operate the hand dynamometer, claiming that it was a test for "physical therapy," but he agreed to do finger tapping. Although these tests are not sensitive to the same parts of the cortical motor system, both yield an indication of motor ability. Some individuals refuse a recommended CAT scan but are agreeable to the MRI, which actually shows more details in terms of cerebral encephalopathy.

The authors start with a structured interview format in order to lower threat. In sanity evaluations, the accused is oriented to the task, is asked about identifying information, is questioned on fitness to proceed, and is then asked to describe the day of the instant offense in detailed sequence. The instant offense is probed again to fill in missing time periods, behaviors, and other important details. It is during this stage of the process that data from the background information can be of immense value to the clinician. Posing hypotheticals, challenging the assessee's account, and confrontation can be utilized to allow the assessee a chance to resolve discrepancies. The evaluator should understand that the purpose of confrontation is to obtain more information, not to present an overview of evaluation findings to the defendant. Questioning in a friendly way, "Can you help me understand how this (whatever it was) happened?," is appropriate. Another caution is not to employ confrontation in a derogatory or oppositional manner such that the defendant complains, thereby setting the stage for dismissal or impeachment of the evaluation. Table 3.5 presents five methods of confrontation, and examples of each.

In sum, it is acceptable to ask the defendant to resolve discrepancies between the following:

1. What is written versus what is stated orally.
2. What was said or done earlier in evaluation versus what is being said or done now.

After the Evaluation

A retrospective check for completeness is essential before the assessee is dismissed. A common problem by examiners is failure to recognize that data about deception must be relevant to time periods other than that of the evaluation.

Table 3.5   Confrontation during Analysis for Deception

Assessor summarizes evaluation behaviors	"Are you saying that you do not recall anything about what happened on that night?"
Eliciting more complete information	"Tell me more about the reasons for your earlier [psychiatric] hospitalization."
Giving a chance to change self-report	"Looking back on what you said about the voices, do you obey them all the time? When don't you do what they say?"
Giving a chance to resolve discrepancies	"I'm wondering why you don't remember what you said yesterday about the accident."
Allowing client to admit to distortion	"If your ex-wife (boss, victim, and so on) were to describe your truthfulness, what would she say and why?"

Many forensic evaluations reviewed by the writers for various purposes have large amounts of data on distortion for the time of the evaluation but very little on that which connects to the critical event in question. In some instances, information about the defendant's behavior following the critical incident is essential. This is illustrated in the following case example involving an adolescent sexual offender.

Ivan was 17 years old and a senior in high school; he was identified as talented and gifted in the first two years of high school. During the summer between his sophomore and junior years he became heavily involved with cannabis and other hallucinogens. He also became involved with girls, something he had previously shunned. He solicited girls usually a year or two younger than himself with a punk rock image and free cannabis. A former girlfriend introduced Ivan to two of her girlfriends, both of who had no prior experience with drugs or sex.

Ivan and the three girls became a foursome and gradually they began to engage in hallucinogen induced weekend sexual orgies with Ivan being the focus of the girl's attentions. As with most adolescent dating, jealousy triangles emerged among the three girls and Ivan delighted in instigating bickering and actual physical altercations. Ivan then introduced bondage behavior into the sexual activities. One weekend Ivan took the youngest of the three girls for an evening drive. In addition to cannabis, Ivan brought alcohol, both the girl and Ivan were heavily intoxicated.

The evening ended in tragedy. The girl died from strangulation from implements used in an apparent bondage ritual; these implements were found with the body. The next day, police discovered the girl's nude body, partially submerged in a nearby stream. An autopsy showed strangulation to be the cause of death and reflected the victim's extreme intoxication.

The evening of the incident, police followed up on citizen complaints of a nude, male adolescent running through the neighborhood screaming, and had picked up Ivan. The police transported a bloodied and hysterical Ivan to an emergency room. He was sedated and treated for multiple abrasions and contusions.

The following day Ivan explained to the police that several adult males accosted him and the victim. The intruders haphazardly disrobed Ivan and beat him "to teach him a lesson." Ivan was not sure what the intruders did with his female friend. Police investigators determined that it was possible that intruders came upon the scene; the secluded area was well frequented by adolescents who engaged in the consumption of alcohol and illicit substances. Suspiciously, there was no evidence of Ivan's clothes or the victim's clothing. Ivan was charged in the matter.

The treating medical staff later testified that Ivan's injuries were more consistent with his running or being dragged through underbrush as opposed to his having been pummeled.

A defense-retained clinician opined that Ivan was not criminally responsible due to an acute psychotic state induced by chronic and habitual substance abuse. One of the authors was court-ordered to evaluate Ivan regarding the issue of criminal responsibility. During the course of the evaluation and while interviewing the investigating police detectives, the clinician was invited to visit the crime scene. The visit to the crime scene took place approximately two months after the incident. In the intervening period, the season had changed abruptly from summer to fall and the leaves had fallen from surrounding trees. After a fruitless hour and a half search and survey, one of the police detectives happened to look up into the surrounding trees and observed what appeared to be a plastic trash bag. The bag was almost 30 feet off the ground but readily retrieved by the officer by climbing a series of branches. The bag contained the victim's and Ivan's clothes. Subsequently Ivan confessed to the crime.

The discovery of the telling evidence in the Ivan case example was somewhat serendipitous. The case, nonetheless, illustrates the relevance of perpetrator behavior following the critical incident. The discovery of the well-hidden plastic bag dispelled the argument of a confused psychotic state, which purportedly had rendered Ivan not criminally responsible.

Information relevant to distortion about the critical incident includes (a) verbal statements about capacities versus self-control at the time of the instant offense, (b) blood alcohol concentration (BAC) versus self-reported alcohol ingestion, (c) comparing observations of witnesses to those provided by the client, and (d) statements about past behavior which violate known diagnostic criteria, or can be demonstrated to be false. Table 3.6 lists other process factors when assessing for deception.

Table 3.6 is an important tool for the forensic examiner of deception and distortion. Retrospectively, the examiner ensures that he or she has covered all the bases in deception analysis.

We have already stressed the importance of an adequate database prior to the clinical assessment. The evaluator must also approach the post-hoc decision tree with a firm grasp of the database. Next, nondeliberate distortion must be ruled out or taken into account.

Deliberate distortion must then be examined in witnesses and significant others, the accused, and the evaluator. Eventually, the subject's deception style must be identified. Last, conclusions regarding deception are presented.

The evaluator must opine that the database was sufficient to draw conclusions to a reasonable degree of psychological probability or certainty. If the assessment findings are not able to yield such a conclusion, then the report should

Table 3.6   Retrospective Forensic Decision Analysis Steps

Forensic Database
Multisourced
Interdisciplinary

Rule out/Account for Nondeliberate Distortion
Reporting person
Reported event
Evaluation errors

Rule in Deliberate Distortion
Examiner factors
Individual examined
Cross-validating sources

Determination of Response Style
No distortion
Faking good
Faking bad
Invalidation of results
Mixed style
Fluctuating style

Conclusions
Sufficiency of data
Degree of deception
Confidence in judgment
Likely targets of deception
Temporal limits
Feedback mechanism
Intervention recommendations

acknowledge this and not proceed with any pertinent opinions about deception. If the assessment findings cannot meaningfully address the issue of deception, then opinions regarding other ultimate issues must either be qualified or result in no opinion. Second, the degree of deception uncovered should also be specified.

Table 3.7 presents degree factors for faking bad and faking good. Whatever the response style, the degree of deception uncovered must be specified.

Third, the confidence level of the evaluator's judgment about deception needs to be specified. Base rates and empirical support, as Table 3.8 shows, should validate one's conclusions whenever possible.

Fourth, likely victims and contexts in which deception occurs should be considered. History is the best predictor. The best guesses are those types of victims and settings in which the assessee was rewarded for past deception.

Fifth, the temporal limits of the report, as well as a feedback mechanism to assess opinions, need to be stated, as the following illustrates: "The opinion that the accused is currently malingering psychotic symptoms to a moderate degree is valid for the time of

Table 3.7   Degree of Deception Uncovered

	Faking Bad	Faking Good
Negligible	No evidence of deception	No evidence of deception
Minimal	Basically honest but with some exaggeration of symptoms or minimization of strengths	Basically honest with some minimization of negative behaviors and exaggeration of positive attributes
Mild	Exaggeration of several critical symptoms and minimization of several positive behaviors	Minimization of several critical symptoms or exaggeration of several critical positive attributes
Moderate	Creation or fabrication of several critical symptoms or denial of several critical positive behaviors	Denial of several critical factors or fabrication of several critical positive attributes
Considerable	Creation or fabrication of a wide range of critical symptoms or denial of a wide range of positive behaviors	Denial of a wide range of critical behaviors or fabrication of a wide range of positive attributes
Extreme	Faked or denied behaviors are absurd with absolutely no basis in reality	Denied or fabricated behaviors are patently obvious and can be easily demonstrated

Table 3.8   Confidence in Evaluation Findings

Negligible	The examiner has no confidence in evaluation findings; the probability of valid findings in terms of classifying the person is 0–10%
Minimal	Findings are congruent with theory and yield some information about distortion, but there is much conflicting and insignificant data; the probability of valid findings in terms of accurately classifying the person is 11–25%
Mild	The probability of valid findings in terms of accurately classifying the person is 26–50%
Moderate	The probability of valid findings in terms of accurately classifying the person is 51–75%
Considerable	The probability of valid findings in terms of accurately classifying the person is 76–89%
Near certain	Findings are supported by research and theory and can be replicated upon reevaluation, using the same test procedures; accuracy is from 0–100%

the assessment only, after which a reassessment using inpatient observation and psycho-metric testing is recommended." It behooves evaluators to be very conservative with such temporal estimates, because human behavior can be very capricious. Intervention recommendations are given when appropriate. The assessee should be treated for nondeliberate distortion as deficits may affect the ability and motivation to deceive.

As pertinent to the situation (e.g., in court-ordered assessments), the defendant is always reminded of his or her Miranda rights. That is, the assessment is not confidential, and a report will be forwarded to the requesting judicial authority; the defendant has the right to remain silent, the right to have legal counsel if he or she cannot afford to retain an attorney, and the right to have his or her attorney present.

Treatment Considerations

Examples where treatment would be appropriate include:

1. Intensive psychotherapy for a child victim preempts assessment for deception. This holds true for all victims, but it is possible to question them during the treatment process.
2. Some fakers have severe associated problems such as psychosis, borderline retardation, and brain damage. They may need treatment for these disorders as well as assessment for deception.
3. Factitious disorders, variants of faking bad, are usually associated with severe psychopathology, such as willingness to chemically alter the body in order to assume the role of a hospitalized patient.

The literature offers very sparse validation of factitious disorders as an independent diagnosis as opposed to a specific variation of malingering. Rogers, Bagby, and Vincent (1994) compared Structured Inventory of Reported Symptoms (SIRS) records of Ss diagnosed with factitious disorders with primarily psychological symptoms to 25 suspected malingerers. There were no consistent differences between the records of the two groups. The authors suggested use of the factitious disorder diagnosis only on a provisional basis.

Evaluators should keep gathered data for as long as necessary—usually for a minimum of five to ten years after an evaluation. Clinicians must be aware of and abide by local statutory requirements for retention of records as well as the provisions of the APA Ethical Code, which now mandates keeping records for 7 years. Following a criminal or civil action, data should not be released to anyone unless written permission from the original referring party is obtained. A criminal case may have to be retried if an appeal is successful. Finally, we note that clinicians who do forensic work are highly vulnerable to ethical complaints and malpractice torts; the retention of forensic records must take into consideration statute of limitation provisions for ethical complaints and tort actions.

An interactional forensic case that illustrates two-person evaluation and related deception issues is presented in Appendix N. In general, findings from deception-detecting measures and methods are appropriate for use in both criminal and civil law settings. This blinded criminal case was utilized in a tort action brought by the victim-plaintiff against the perpetrator, the business in which the assault occurred, and other parties, and resulted in a favorable judgment.

References

American College of Physicians. (1989). American College of Physicians Ethics Manual. *Annals of Internal Medicine, 111*(3), 245–251.

American Psychiatric Association. (1994). *Diagnostic and Statistical Manual of Mental Disorders (4th ed., revised).* Washington, DC: Author.

American Psychological Association. (1989). Practice directorate: Expert testimony in mental health useful in courtrooms, Newman argues. *Psychological Practitioner, 3,* 12.

American Psychological Association. (1992). Ethical principles of psychologists and code of conduct. *American Psychologist, 47,* 1597–1611.

American Psychological Association. (2002). Ethical principles of psychologists and code of conduct. Washington, D.C.: American Psychological Association.

Bering, J. M., and Shackelford, T. K. (2005). Evolutionary psychology and false confession. *American Psychologist, 60*(9), 1037–1038.

Berry, D., Baer, R., and Harris, M. (1991). Detection of malingering on the MMPI: a meta-analysis. *Clinical Psychology Review, 11,* 585–598.

Bersoff, D. N. (1995). *Ethical Conflicts in Psychology.* Washington, DC: American Psychological Association.

Bersoff, D. N. (1999). *Ethical Conflicts in Psychology (2nd ed.).* Washington, DC: American Psychological Association.

Brodsky, S. L. and Galloway, V. A. (2003). Ethical and professional demands for forensic mental health professionals in the post-Atkins era. *Ethics and Behavior, 13*(1), 3–9.

Buchwald, A. M. (1965). Values and the use of tests. *Journal of Consulting Psychology, 29,* 49–54.

Buckhout, R. (1980). Eyewitness identification and psychology in the courtroom. In G. Cooke (Ed.). *The Role of the Forensic Psychologist* (pp. 335–339). Springfield, IL: Charles C Thomas.

Burgoon, J. K., Buller, D. B., Ebesu, A. S., and Rockwell. P. (1994). Interpersonal deception: II. The inferiority in deception detection. *Communication Monographs, 61,* 303–325.

Canter, M. B., Bennett, B. B., Jones, S. E., and Nagy, T. F. (1994). *Ethics for Psychologists: A Commentary on the APA Ethics Code.* Washington, DC: American Psychological Association.

Cohen, J. (1977). *Statistical Power Analysis for the Behavioral Sciences.* New York: Academic Press.

Committee on Ethical Guidelines for Forensic Psychologists. (1991). Specialty guidelines for forensic psychologists. *Law and Human Behavior, 15,* 655–666.

Durante, C. (2005). Ethical issues in forensic mental health research. *Journal of Mental Health, 14*(3), 311.

Ekman, P. (1985). *Telling Lies: Clues to Deception in the Market Place, Politics, and Marriage.* New York: W. W. Norton and Company.

Ekman, P. (Ed.). (1997). *Deception, Lying, and Demeanor.* New York: Oxford University Press.

Ekman, P. (2001). *Telling Lies: Clues to Deceit in the Marketplace, Politics, and Marriage.* New York: W. W. Norton and Co., Inc.

Ekman, P., Friesen, W. V., and O'Sullivan, M. (2005). *Smiles When Lying.* New York: Oxford University Press.

Ekman, P. and O'Sullivan, M. (1991). Who can catch a liar? *American Psychologist, 46,* 913–920.

Ekman, P., O'Sullivan, M., and Frank, M. G. (1999). A few can catch a liar. *Psychological Science, 10*(3), 263–266.

Ekman, P. and Rosenberg, E. L. (2005). *What the Face Reveals: Basic and Applied Studies of Spontaneous Expression Using The Facial Action Coding System (FACS) (2nd ed.).* New York: Oxford University Press.

Frank, M. G. and Ekman, P. (2004). *Nonverbal Detection of Deception in Forensic Contexts.* New York: Elsevier Science.

Gates, M. (1991). It's healthy to always be honest (Wait, we lied!). Newhouse News Service, *Honolulu Star-Bulletin,* Honolulu, HI.

Granhag, P. and Stromwell, L. (2004). *The Detection of Deception in Forensic Contexts*. New York: Cambridge University Press.

Greenberg, S. A. and Shuman, D. W. (1997). Irreconcilable conflict between therapeutic and forensic roles. *Professional Psychology: Research and Practice, 28(1)*, 50–57.

Gudjonsson, G. H. and Petursson, H. (1991). Custodial interrogation: Why suspects confess and how does it relate to their crime, attitude and personality? *Personality and Individual Differences, 12(3)*, 295–306.

Hall, H. V. (1985). Cognitive and volitional capacity assessment: A proposed decision tree. *American Journal of Forensic Psychology, 3*, 3–17.

Hall, H. V. (1986). The forensic distortion analysis: Proposed decision tree and report format. *American Journal of Forensic Psychology, 4(3)*, 31–59.

Hall, H. V. and Poirier, J. G. (2001). *Detecting Malingering and Deception: Forensic Distortion Analysis (2nd ed.)*. Boca Raton, FL: CRC Press.

Hall, H. V. and Pritchard, D. (1996). *Detecting Malingering and Deception: Forensic Distortion Analysis (FDA)*. Boca Raton, FL: CRC Press.

Hall, H. V. and Shooter, E. (1989). Explicit alternative testing for feigned memory deficits. *Forensic Reports, 2*, 277–286.

Hall, H. V., Shooter, E., Craine, J., and Paulsen, S. (1991). Explicit alternative testing for claimed visual recall deficits: A trilogy of studies. *Forensic Reports, 4(3)*, 259–279.

Hall, H. V. and Thompson, J. (2007). Explicit alternative testing (EAT): Application of the binomial probability distribution in clinical-forensic evaluations. *The Forensic Examiner, 16*, 38–43.

Hall, H. V., Thompson, J., and Poirier, J. G. (in press). Detecting deception in neuropsychological cases: Towards an applied model. *The Forensic Examiner*.

Hartwig, M., Granhag, P. A., and Vrij, A. (2005). Police interrogation from a social psychology perspective. *Policing & Society, 15(4)*, 379–399.

Jensen, L. A., Arnett, J. J., Feldman, S. S., and Cauffman, E. (2004). The right to do wrong: Lying to parents among adolescents and emerging adults. *Journal of Youth and Adolescence, 33(2)*, 101–112.

Kassin, S. M. (1997). The psychology of confession evidence. *American Psychologist, 52(3)*, 221–233.

Kassin, S. M. and Fong, C. T. (1999). "I'm innocent": Effects of training on judgments of truth and deception in the interrogation room. *Law and Human Behavior, 23(5)*, 499–516.

Kassin, S. M. and Gudjonsson, G. H. (2004). The psychology of confessions: A review of the literature and issues. *Psychological Science in the Public Interest. Special Issue: The Psychology of Confessions: A Review of the Literature and Issues, 5(2)*, 33–67.

Leavitt, F. (1987). Detection of simulation among persons instructed to exaggerate symptoms of low back pain. *Journal of Occupational Medicine, 29(3)*, 229–233.

Leo, R. A. (1996). Miranda's revenge: Police interrogation as a confidence game. *Law and Society Review, 30(2)*, 259–288.

Leo, R. A. and Ofshe, R. (1998). The consequences of false confessions: Deprivations of liberty and miscarriages of justice in the age of psychological interrogation. *Journal of Criminal Law and Criminology, 88*, 429–496.

Loftus, E. F. (2004). The devil in confessions. *Psychological Science in the Public Interest. Special Issue: The Psychology of Confessions: A Review of the Literature and Issues, 5(2)*, i–ii.

McMahon, M. (1995). False confessions and police deception. *American Journal of Forensic Psychology, 13(3)*, 5–43.

Meehl, P. and Rosen, A. (1955). Antecedent probability and the efficiency of psychometric signs, patterns or cutting scores. *Psychological Bulletin, 52*, 194–216.

Movahedi, S. and Ogles, R. (1976). Prediction and inference in criminology. *Criminology, 14(2)*, 177–188.

Nicks, S. D., Korn, J. H., and Mainieri, T. (1997). The rise and fall of deception in social psychology and personality research. *Ethics and Behavior, 7(1)*, 69–77.

Palermo, G. B. (2006). Forensic mental health experts in the court: An ethical dilemma. Thousand Oaks, CA: Sage Publications, Inc.

Pauls, C. A. and Crost, N. W. (2004). Effects of faking on self-deception and impression management scales. *Personality and Individual Differences, 37(6)*, 1137–1151.

Paulsen, S. and Hall, H. V. (1991). Common sense process factors in deception analysis. *Forensic Reports, 4*, 37–39.

Poirier, J. G. (1999). Violent juvenile crime. In H. V. Hall and L. C. Whitaker (Eds.). *Collective Violence: Effective Strategies for Assessing and Interviewing in Fatal Group and Institutional Aggression* (pp. 183–212). Boca Raton, FL: CRC Press.

Pope, K. S., Butcher, J. N., and Seelen, J. (2000). *The MMPI, MMPI-2, MMPI-A in Court: A Practical Guide for Expert Witnesses and Attorneys.* Washington, DC: American Psychological Association.

Rogers, R. (Ed.). (1988). *Clinical Assessment of Malingering and Deception.* New York: Guilford Press.

Rogers, R. (1990a). Development of a new classificatory model of malingering. *Bulletin of the American Academy of Psychiatry and the Law, 18(3)*, 323–333.

Rogers, R. (1990b). Models of feigned mental illness. *Professional Psychology: Research and Practice, 21(3)*, 182–188.

Rogers, R. (Ed.). (1997). *Clinical Assessment of Malingering and Deception.* New York: Guilford Press.

Rogers, R. (2004). Diagnostic, explanatory, and detection models of Munchausen by proxy: Extrapolations from malingering and deception. *Child Abuse and Neglect, 28(2)*, 225–238.

Rogers, R., Bagby, R. M., and Vincent, A. (1994) Factitious disorders with predominantly psychological signs and symptoms: A conundrum for forensic experts. *Journal of Psychiatry and the Law, 22(1)*, 91–106.

Roig, M. and Caso, M. (2005). Lying and cheating: Fraudulent excuse making, cheating, and plagiarism. *Journal of Psychology: Interdisciplinary and Applied, 139(6)*, 485–494.

Rosenhan, D. L. (1973). On being sane in insane places. *Science, 179*, 250–358.

Russano, M. B. (2004). *True and False Confessions to an Intentional Act: A Novel Experimental Paradigm.* (Doctoral dissertation, ProQuest Information & Learning). Dissertation Abstracts International: Section B: The Sciences and Engineering, 65(4), 2149.

Russano, M. B., Meissner, C. A., Narchet, F. M., and Kassin, S. M. (2005). Investigating true and false confessions within a novel experimental paradigm. *Psychological Science, 16(6)*, 481–486.

Schlenker, B. and Weigold, M. (1992). Interpersonal processes involving impression regulation and management (pp. 133–168) In Rosenzweig, M. and Porter, L. (Eds.). *Annual Review of Psychology.* Palo Alto, CA: Annual Reviews, Inc.

Seeman, J. (Ed.). (1997). *Deception in Psychological Research (1969).* Washington, DC: American Psychological Association.

Sieber, J. E., Iannuzzo, R., and Rodriguez, B. (1995). Deception methods in psychology: Have they changed in 23 years? *Ethics and Behavior, 5(1)*, 67–85.

Shooter, E. and Hall, H. V. (1989). Distortion analysis on the MMPI and MMPI-2. *Bulletin of the American Academy of Forensic Psychology, 10*, 9.

Shooter, E. and Hall, H. V. (1990). Explicit alternative testing for deliberate distortion: Towards an abbreviated format. *Forensic Reports, 4*, 45–49.

Strömwall, L. A., Hartwig, M., and Granhag, P. A. (2006). To act truthfully: Nonverbal behaviour and strategies during a police interrogation. *Psychology, Crime & Law, 12(2)*, 207–219.

Swets, J. A. (1992). The science of choosing the right decision threshold in high-stakes diagnostics. *American Psychologist, 47(4)*, 522–532.

Triplett, N. (1900). The psychology of conjuring deceptions. *American Journal of Psychology, 11(4)*, 439–510.

Tyler, J. M. and Feldman, R. S. (2005). Deflecting threat to one's image: Dissembling personal information as a self-presentation strategy. *Basic and Applied Social Psychology, 27(4)*, 371–378.

Vickery, C. D., Berry, D. T. R., Hanlon Inman, T., Harris, M. J., and Orey, S. A. (2001). Detection of inadequate effort on neuropsychological testing: A meta-analytic review of selected procedures. *Archives of Clinical Neuropsychology, 16(1)*, 45–73.

Vitacco, M. J. and Rogers, R. (2005). *Assessment of Malingering in Correctional Settings*. Washington, DC: American Psychiatric Publishing, Inc.

Wiggins, J. (1973). *Personality and Prediction: Principles of Personality Assessment*. Reading, MA: Addison-Wesley.

Witt, P. H. (2005). Interrogations and confessions: A manual for practice. *Journal of Psychiatry and Law, 33(1)*, 103–108.

Ziskin, J. (1981). *Coping with Psychiatric and Psychological Testimony (3rd ed., Vols. 1–2)*. Beverly Hills, CA: Law and Psychology Press.

Legal Reference

Miranda v. Arizona, 384 U.S. 336 (1966).

Parents with Brain Impairment: Care and Protection Matters

LOIS OBERLANDER CONDIE

Harvard Medical School, Boston, Massachusetts

DON CONDIE

Harvard Medical School, Boston, Massachusetts

Contents

Case Synopsis

Mr John Doe was investigated by the state child protective service (CPS) agency because of allegations that he digitally fondled his 5- and 7-year-old daughters. The allegations were supported, and he was referred for a sex offender evaluation to determine his risk of harm to his children and his need for sex offender treatment. He participated in the evaluation as a condition of pretrial probation for a parallel criminal charge. He was judged to be at moderate-to-high risk of reoffending. He agreed to move out of his home, and he was granted supervised visitation because the children's mother cooperated with the CPS agency, allowing Mr Doe to see the children only under supervised visitation conditions specified by CPS. Mr Doe was found to be in need of sex offender treatment, and he was diagnosed with alcohol dependence. He was unwilling to seek treatment, but he later agreed to do so as a condition of pretrial probation for his pending criminal matter. He entered and completed a 3-month residential substance-abuse rehabilitation program. He then sought outpatient group sex offender treatment and group substance-abuse relapse prevention treatment, two conditions of his CPS intervention plan. He completed a 3-month cycle of treatment in both groups, and his treatment providers wrote treatment summaries highlighting his progress but expressing concern about possible mental confusion. A few weeks later, one of the authors of this chapter saw him in an evaluation session relevant to the impact of chronic alcohol dependence on his mental state and parenting capacity. Having observed right-sided muscle weakness, mental confusion, and unusually poor comprehension of speech, the evaluation was delayed and the evaluator advised CPS to refer him for a neurological examination. The examination revealed he had suffered a cerebrovascular accident in the middle cerebral artery that damaged the left anterior temporal and parietal lobes. He entered a physical and cognitive rehabilitation program, and he was discharged after 3 weeks with residual motor and language impairment. During the interim, the children were removed from the mother's care on a supported neglect petition because she began cohabiting with a man who had a previous conviction of distributing child pornography. She relocated shortly thereafter, and her whereabouts were unknown for the remaining duration of the case. The evaluation of Mr Doe was resumed, with a modified referral question, to determine whether he was suffering from brain impairment secondary to chronic alcohol dependence or stroke, and whether the brain impairment compromised his mental state or parenting capacity in a manner legally relevant to his risk of harm to his children. His risk of sex offending had been addressed in a separate evaluation. Meanwhile, because the mother could not be located, the CPS agency delayed filing a termination of parental rights petition in favor of long-term foster placement and supervised paternal visitation. During paternal visitation, workers observed that Mr Doe sometimes seemed confused. There was a report that he had showered with his younger daughter during an extended visit that was monitored by an unauthorized supervisor. After receiving the neuropsychological evaluation report, the CPS agency separated the petitions (the parents were unmarried) and filed a petition for termination of the father's parental rights based on the findings of the neuropsychological evaluation report, the sex offender evaluation report of Dr Other-Evaluator, recent evidence that Mr Doe was seen drinking alcohol, the incident in which he showered with one of his children, and based on Mr Doe's behavioral disorganization and receptive language impairment witnessed during visitation by CPS workers. Termination proceedings went forward, and Mr Doe invoked the Americans with Disabilities Act (ADA) to protect his parental rights, without success. Termination of parental rights was granted.

Introduction

This chapter describes care and protection cases of parental and other caregiver risk of harm to children in which compromised caregiver functioning and existing risk of harm is further complicated by caregiver brain impairment. Cases in the legal system with brain impairment as a major risk factor include parents with mental retardation, chronic substance abuse, traumatic brain injury, early-onset dementia, and other medical conditions that affect the brain. Cases in which brain impairment due to mental retardation has been the central issue relevant to a petition for termination of parental rights include *In re Elijah R.*, 1993; *In re K.F.*, 1989; and *R. G. v. Marion County Office, Department of Family & Children*, 1995. Brain impairment unrelated to mental retardation that negatively affects parenting, even when relevant to risk of harm, rarely is persuasive to judicial fact finders as a sole rationale for terminating parental rights (*In the Interest of A.S.W.*, 2004) even though, in some states, when there are multiple grounds for termination, any one of those grounds is sufficient to sustain a judgment on appeal (*In the Interest of N.R.W.*, 2003). Although it is rarely a central factor in termination cases, brain impairment that affects parenting is cited in petitions favoring the initiation and continuation of care and protection. Because evaluation reports of neuropsychologists or neuropsychiatrists offer quantified assessment results, imaging results, or clinical observations of specific aspects of neurocognitive functioning, expert testimony is sought in legal proceedings in which there are questions about neurocognitive capabilities relevant to parenting and risk of child maltreatment. In this chapter, we focus on parental neurocognitive deterioration that is a function of brain impairment secondary to ischemic stroke and chronic alcohol dependence. For two reasons, we chose to highlight a case involving brain impairment that results from multiple etiological factors. First, care and protection cases rarely involve parents with only one disorder, the behavioral sequelae of which may be of legal relevance in child protection cases. Comorbidity of brain impairment, substance abuse, and mental illness are common. Assessment methodology that is based on legal realism must factor in the complications seen in cases of comorbidity. Second, studies have demonstrated that substance abuse is a high-frequency primary condition that is linked to child maltreatment or risk of maltreatment sufficient to merit care and protection involvement (Famularo, Kinscherff, and Fenton, 1992). As we describe a case example in this chapter, we illustrate how these factors may be of legal relevance in care and protection hearings when linked to risk or the exacerbation of risk of child maltreatment or parental incapacity. In our case example, these factors contributed considerably to already existing doubt that the parent in our case example would be able to refrain from inappropriate sexual conduct or meet the parenting needs of his children were he to regain custody of them. Substance abuse, brain injury or illness, or any other form of mental impairment must be linked to the harm that the parent caused to the child or might cause to the child in the future in order to be legally persuasive as relevant factors for care and protection jurisdiction and possible termination of parental rights.

Forensic consultation in care and protection matters requires an understanding of the CPS system and relevant policies and statutes. Forensic mental health expertise is sought to assist the court in understanding a parent's capacity to meet the needs of child, parental risk to the child, and parental benefit from services offered to remedy factors contributing to parental incapacity or risk. Public policy relevant to CPS requires mandatory reporting of child abuse or neglect and allows states to intervene on behalf of child victims of substantiated maltreatment. The prevailing standard for the care and protection of children is the *best interest* standard, the underlying philosophy that shapes and sets the tone and procedures for state intervention (Goldstein, 1999). Upon the court's granting of a care and protection petition, a parent may temporarily lose physical or legal custody of the child. The parent retains procedural rights to notice and to be heard regarding the child, along with presumptive substantive rights to services in support of reunification, visitation, communication, and eventual reunification. States have the authority to mandate that families make use of resources to promote the safety of children. Services aimed at improving parental deficits associated with risk of child maltreatment are specified in the context of a service plan. In the most serious cases, the law provides for termination of parental rights if certain risk factors are present. In termination proceedings, the court is concerned with the minimum level of parenting competence required to adequately care for and protect children. Within a termination of parental rights proceeding, the state alleges that even after the provision of relevant services, the parent remains unable or unfit to care for the child. The court is concerned with the behaviors and capacities of the adult in his or her role as parent, and the harm that may, or has, come to the child (Condie, 2003).

Forensic evaluation in care and protection matters takes place within a system designed to meet the care and safety needs of maltreated children while providing due process protections for the legal rights of parents. Cases typically are multifaceted. For reasons related to both confidentiality and the education of the reader, the case we review in this chapter represents an amalgam of cases that involved parental sexual offending, parental alcohol dependence, and parental brain impairment secondary to injury or illness. We focus on the combined effects of chronic alcohol dependence and stroke as causes of brain impairment. We provide a methodology relevant to alcohol dependence that can be adapted for other substances, as long as the evaluator has sufficient empirical data about the long-term impact of other substances. We provide a clinical example that follows empirically validated forensic neurocognitive evaluation methodology: interview and observational data, record gathering, multimodal assessment, emphasis on recently collected normative data in preference to older normative data, emphasis on data from large stratified population samples in preference to those with fewer participants, normative data with demographic adjustments in preference to those without breakdowns, and normative data in which the sample most closely resembles the demographic characteristics of the individual being evaluated (Condie, 2003; van Gorp, 2006). We review issues and methodology of relevance to evaluations that include chronic substance abuse and a complicating brain injury or illness, and we refer the reader to sources relevant to other forms of parental risk of harm to children (Ayoub and Kinscherff, 2006; Budd, 2005; Condie, 2003; Dubowitz, 1999; Hanson, 2004; Hanson and Thornton, 2000; Monahan, Steadman, Appelbaum, Robbins, Mulvey, Silver, Roth, and Grisso, 2000; Steadman, Silver, Monahan, Appelbaum, Robbins, Mulvey, Grisso, Roth, and Banks, 2000). For a broader spectrum of evaluation questions and methods relevant to termination of parental rights, other resources are available (Ayoub and Kinscherff, 2006; Condie, 2003; Condie and Condie, 2006).

Relevant Cases and Legal Standards

Parental rights have their basis in English common law and its subsequent manifestations in United States law as reflected in U.S. Supreme Court family privacy cases. Historically, parents have possessed relatively strong rights because of traditional views of children as the property of parents (Goldstein, 1999). The counterbalance to the U.S. Supreme Court cases protecting parental rights and family autonomy lies in statutes relevant to child safety and protection that allow for the temporary or permanent removal of a child from the family of origin. A review of relevant U.S. Supreme Court family privacy cases, and their counterbalances in cases brought forth to protect the interests of children, can be found in other sources (Condie, 2003; Condie and Condie, 2006). In those sources, one also finds landmark decisions on care and protection and termination of parental rights cases of the last 30 years. Cases of wide applicability that were specific to termination of parental rights did not appear until the 1980s. In *Lassiter v. Department of Social Services* (1981), the Court upheld a state's refusal to appoint publicly funded counsel for an indigent mother in a battle for reunification with her child, but the Court concluded that a state was free to provide counsel to indigent parents if it so wished. In *Santosky v. Kramer* (1982), the Court held that due process required a higher standard of proof than a fair preponderance of evidence, namely one of clear and convincing evidence, to support a state's allegations of parental unfitness leading to permanent removal of a child from the custody of an abusive or neglectful parent. After the inception of the Adoption and Safe Families Act of 1997, cases began to center upon statutory time frames. Because of financial incentives provided by the Adoption and Safe Families Act for states that demonstrated progress in moving children from foster care to adoption, many statutes incorporated statutory time frames within which successful rehabilitation of parents must occur. In cases with aggravated circumstances (i.e., substantiated abandonment, torture, chronic abuse, or sexual abuse), the Adoption and Safe Families Act removed the federal requirement that states must make reasonable efforts toward reunification of children with birth parents. Most states adopted provisions for an expedited process of early termination under conditions of severe maltreatment (Condie, 2003).

Grounds for termination are found in state statutes (in military and Native American cases, federal statutes may apply) and typically include: (a) parental incapacity to care for the child by reason of mental illness, substance abuse, or cognitive impairment; (b) extreme disinterest in or abandonment of the child; (c) extreme or repeated abuse/ neglect; (d) conviction of a crime carrying a sentence of long-term incarceration with early parole unlikely; (e) failure of the parent to improve in response to interventions; and (f) limitations on the length of time the child is in state-sponsored placement. Consideration is given to the child's significant relationships with parents, siblings, foster parents, and potential adoptive parents. Even when parents eventually address maltreatment, whether sufficiently or insufficiently, statutes may provide latitude for termination based on the quality and strength of the child's relationship to substitute caregivers and based on the length of time the child has been in an alternative placement. Most state statutes specify an obligation for the child protection agency to offer services intended to correct the conditions that led to the parenting breach. Those services must be reasonably available on a consistent basis (Condie, 2003; Goldstein, 1999). Some state statutes exclude conditions that are beyond the control of the parent, such as impoverishment, lack of the availability of relevant services, inadequate housing, low income, and inadequate medical care. Incarceration alone rarely is grounds for termination unless it is protracted, but some states specify categories of crime (e.g., murder, rape, sexual abuse of minors, and other charges) that may result in termination of parental rights regardless of length of incarceration (Goldstein, 1999).

Sexual Offending

In the case example that we describe in our chapter, a risk of parental sexual offending evaluation was completed by a different examiner. The evaluation described Mr Doe's history of offending, it described his risk of future offending, and it described the impact of his actions on his children's development and well-being. It made projections, over the course of the next six months to a year, of Mr Doe's likelihood of reoffending, relating that likelihood to his treatment participation and progress. It described some broader features of his strengths and weaknesses in his parenting competence. Because sex offending was a central issue in the case, we briefly review care and protection regulations and parallel criminal codes relevant to parental sexual abuse. State care and protection statutes often invoke criminal statutes in cases that involve sex offenses by caregivers. Cases involving intrafamilial sexual abuse of children draw upon a broader spectrum of criminal and civil sex offending cases. Most civil abuse reporting and jurisdictional statutes define sexual abuse by adopting the applicable criminal codes (Goldstein, 1999). The crimes of rape, statutory rape, and incest may require penetration as an element, whereas other sexual crimes do not (for example, lewd and lascivious acts, exhibitionism, and exploitation). Scholars argue that penetration should not be a significant factor in defining sexual abuse and its harm because a young child might not make a reasonable distinction between penetration and other forms of sexual and nonsexual touching (Walker, 1990). The differences between criminal code definitions and care and protection regulations often enter the discussion during hearings on care and protection jurisdiction and the content of service plans. Care and protection cases sometimes are complicated by settlement of criminal cases or decisions not to prosecute an alleged sex offender (related to youthfulness of and potential trauma to child witnesses), even though the child protection agency's allegations remain supported. With sufficient evidence of neglect, but lacking sufficient evidence to support sex offense allegations for a specific perpetrator, child protection agencies may support allegations of neglect by the nonoffending caretaker (more often than not a female) because of failure to protect the child from sexual abuse by a suspected or unknown perpetrator. *In re Glenn G.* (1992) was a case in which the court found a mother neglectful for "allowing" the father to sexually abuse the children even though the court also accepted her battered spouse defense. The court opined that neglect was "a matter of strict liability." Courts have found parents neglectful when they have failed to infer the sexual abuse of their children from observable evidence such as vaginal irritation or changes in behavior (*In re Scott G.*, 1986; *In re Jose Y.*, 1991). There are other mechanisms by which jurisdiction is retained when there is strong and justifiable suspicion of sexual abuse even though a perpetrator has not been criminally convicted. Examples include requesting a joint service planning process with the criminal prosecutor as the case is settled in criminal court and seeking treatment cooperation of the alleged offender as a condition of pretrial probation. Even when suspected offenders are exonerated in criminal court, there sometimes may be legally justifiable reasons, found in care and protection regulations or case law, to retain CPS jurisdiction. For example, when cases offer murky evidence of what took place or perpetrator intent, the legal path becomes thorny as courts interpret and apply criminal codes relevant to parental lewd and lascivious behavior or nonpenetrative sex crimes that include touching and nontouching offenses. The distinction in criminal law between sexual acts and those that depend upon proof of perpetrator intent is important in the context of family relationships. Families share physical intimacies that might be interpreted as sexual if engaged in by nonfamily members. The breadth of some definitions of lewd and lascivious conduct grants courts broad discretion to intervene (or not) in family life. Broad discretion might be a protective benefit to children who suffer from sexual abuse that does not fall within the specific but sometimes arcane boundaries of criminal definitions of sexual aggression. Criminal codes typically fail to provide clarification in the case of ambiguous behavior that might or might not be sexual or harmful to children, depending upon perpetrator intent (Goldstein, 1999).

Alcohol Abuse and Dependence

Legal cases involving the care and protection of children whose parents abuse alcohol illustrate that there must be a link between parental alcohol abuse or dependence and child maltreatment, and the risk of maltreatment must be current and demonstrable. Suboptimal parental compliance with recommendations is not persuasive in itself, provided the parent is making some modicum of relevant treatment progress. Evidence of treatment progress, even when incomplete or suboptimal, may be sufficient to persuade the court that the burden of clear and convincing evidence has not been met (*Adoption of Nancy*, 2004). Because of the unfortunate frequency of parental relapse, service plans and court proceedings typically are developed and changed in response to a pattern where parents show initial compliance that is followed by relapse (*Otey v. Roanoke City Department of Social Services*, 2006), and sometimes in response to repeated patterns of compliance and relapse. When parents capable of benefiting from treatment refuse or minimally follow recommendations and treatment, termination is a likely outcome as long as the state meets the burden of clear and convincing evidence of noncompliance that is coupled with a demonstrated link between the alcohol dependence and parental unfitness or risk of maltreatment (*Harris v. Campbell County Department of Social Services*, 2004). When substance abuse persists, but the harm to the child is no longer current or demonstrable, the court may not favor termination. For example, if the harm to the child is linked to domestic violence between the parents during drinking episodes, and the parents separate permanently, harm to the children may no longer be relevant even if one or both parents relapse (*D.P. v. Department of Children and Family Services*, 2006). If the harm persists, as in, for example, the case of substantially poor supervision of the children during episodes of parental intoxication, termination is likely to be successful and upheld on appeal (*E.T. v. State of Florida and Department of Children and Families*, 2006). The state must make a reasonable effort to provide services that are specified on the service plan (*State of Louisiana in the Interest of A.T., T.A., & J.A.*, 2006). The court may not rely on prior factors (past history of parental substance abuse and termination of parental rights to another child) without proof of current substantial risk to the child (*Florida Department of Children and Families v. F.L.*, 2004).

Brain Injury and Impairment

Impairment Secondary to Substance Abuse or Dependence
Parental brain injury and impairment, as a central factor in care and protection matters, is much less common than sex offending, domestic violence, substance abuse, or mental illness that interferes with parenting. Cases involving brain impairment secondary to

chronic substance abuse or dependence are complicated by the complex task of determining whether assessment results reflect fixed neurocognitive and behavioral deterioration related to chronic substance abuse or whether the deterioration might be reversible over time. If substance abuse alone, without demonstrable brain impairment, affects parenting competence in a legally relevant manner, the state would not need to rely upon statutory criteria relevant to brain impairment associated with prolonged substance dependence as a legally relevant contributing factor. The case would instead focus upon the current association between substance abuse and parental incapacity or risk. The case of *In re A.M.A.* (2006) captures the behavioral and social consequences of current substance abuse without the need for an associated finding of neurocognitive and behavioral deterioration: medical neglect of a newborn, an inadequate living environment for an infant, parental screaming and cursing, domestic violence, underemployment, and police involvement during drug raids of the home. During the tenure of the care and protection matter, the father tested positive for alcohol and drugs numerous times and he was convicted of several crimes. In a case such as this, substance abuse and its relationship to parenting problems would serve as sufficient evidence in a termination proceeding, without any evidentiary need for additional focus upon brain deterioration related to chronic use. When the state wishes to rely upon the statutory provision of unfitness due to brain impairment resultant from chronic substance abuse or dependence, there must be evidence, in addition to behavioral effects attributable to current substance abuse, to merit the use of that statutory provision. There must be a showing of evidence that the parent has demonstrable brain deterioration and associated deficits, and that those deficits cause or substantially contribute to behavioral effects relevant to the parenting problems. Because of symptom overlap, it may not always be possible to parse out the unique effects of brain damage due to chronic alcohol dependence. For example, an active user may be mentally disorganized, or a currently sober individual with a history of chronic substance abuse may be mentally disorganized due to residual neurocognitive effects of the historic substance abuse.

There is ample medical reason, however, to raise the question, when legally relevant, of the impact of chronic alcohol dependence on the integrity of brain functioning. Structural imaging of the brain by MRI or CT has revealed a consistent association between heavy drinking and physical brain damage, even in the absence of medical conditions that serve as clinical indicators of severe alcoholism, such as alcohol-induced dementia or chronic liver disease (Rosenbloom, Pfefferbaum, and Sullivan, 1995). Frontal lobe volume loss has been observed with magnetic resonance imaging in older chronic alcoholics (Pfefferbaum, Sullivan, Mathalon, and Lim, 1997). Brain gray and white matter volume loss accelerates with aging in chronic alcoholics (Pfefferbaum, Lim, Zipursky, Mathalon, Rosenbloom, Lane, Ha, and Sullivan, 1992). Brain deterioration, if clinically correlated with behavioral disorganization or deterioration of relevance to parental capacity or risk of child maltreatment, may take on legal significance. The state may wish to pursue termination using the cognitive impairment prong of the statute in combination with evidence for other relevant prongs of the statute. When there is serious deterioration that leads to suspicion of permanent parental incapacity, the evaluation of brain impairment might take on central relevance even if other factors also contribute to parental incapacity or risk of maltreatment.

Brain Impairment Secondary to Illness or Injury

A massive stroke may render a parent incapable of caring for a child to the degree that harm might result to the child, but without other factors relevant to care and protection jurisdiction, there would be other legal mechanisms for transfer of the child to a different custodian (*In re Rayvon T.*, 2006). When stroke or other relevant brain conditions occur in the absence of other factors relevant to care and protection, states tend not to assume jurisdiction under care and protection statutes. Even when jurisdiction is assumed, courts are unlikely to rule in favor of termination of parental rights. For example, the court ruled *In the Interest of Micah Alyn R.* (1998) that when a parent was unable to properly care for a child due to the parent's terminal illness, so that parental neglect was likely to persist, termination of parental rights was contrary to public policy even though there was no reasonable likelihood that the neglect would be corrected in the future. The court found that out of home placement was permissible, but that the relationship between the parent and child should be preserved. When brain impairment takes place in the context of already existing incapacity or risk, it may or may not be relevant to the care and protection matter. Relevance would depend upon whether the sequelae contributed to the parental incapacity or risk, whether the contribution was considerable, and the degree to whether the sequelae might be remediable versus permanent. Even when illness or injury leads to brain impairment that can be demonstrably linked to significant parenting problems, it tends not to be persuasive as central or primary evidence in favor of termination of parental rights. It may be relevant as a contributing factor. For example, when concern about significant parenting problems related to stroke is an accompaniment to other already existing risk to the child, as in the case of a parent who continues to deny, in the face of all supporting evidence, that a child has been molested, the stroke takes on more significance if its effects contribute to compromised cognitive or memory functioning that might be linked to the parental denial (*In re Gregory C.*, 2005). Parental brain damage may minimally affect global parenting skills, but when it specifically affects skills such as a parent's ability to make decisions about the necessity of medical appointments or emergency room consultation for a child with a life-threatening illness, the parental brain impairment takes on legal significance (*In re J.K.*, 2004). When brain damage interferes with a parent's ability to benefit from recommended services (e.g., violence reduction), it is relevant as evidence in termination proceedings (*In re J.K.*, 2002).

When substance abuse and stroke are comorbid, the effects of one might sometimes be mistaken for the other. For example, a mother with a history of substance abuse complained that she was having mini-strokes, and one side of her body was going numb. She was observed to have slurred speech during a visitation session with her child, and later on in her telephone voice messages. Because of the convincing nature of her symptoms, uncertainty existed as to whether she had suffered a stroke or whether her slurred speech was due to substance use (*In re Joshua J. et al.*, 2006). Symptoms common to both conditions include slurred speech, poor speech production or comprehension, incoordination, gait or balance problems, impaired attention, impaired memory functioning, mental confusion, impaired judgment, impaired social functioning, and impaired occupational functioning. The question of etiology has bearing on treatment recommendations and prognostications about recovery of functioning, but it may not always be possible to provide clear direction to the court. Should a referral question in the treatment planning phase contain questions relevant to treatment recommendations, the expected length of treatment, or expectations of recovery, ambiguity should be made clear, and it often is helpful to qualify recommendations by offering them in the context of relevant possible scenarios (Condie, 2003). The state has a duty to make reasonable efforts to reunify (*In re Adoption/Guardianship Nos. CAA92-10852 & CAA92-10853 in the Circuit Court for Prince George's County*, 1994), but guidance and consultation relevant to reasonable efforts best serves the CPS agency and the court when etiological ambiguity is described with candor in reports (Condie, 2003). It is up to the court and the parties offering evidence to grapple with the ambiguity in the context of the legal standards of relevance to the case (Goldstein, 1999).

In summary, evaluations of the impact of conditions such as chronic substance dependence or stroke on the integrity of brain functioning usually serve as a supplement to other evidence relevant to parental competence and risk of child maltreatment. Brain impairment may contribute minimally or substantially to parental functioning, but the impact must be legally relevant as defined by statutes governing care and protection regulations and termination statutes. Legal relevance may be seen in the form of cognitive dulling that might contribute to a failure to protect a child or to appreciate the impact of abuse on a child, cognitive or behavioral disorganization and deficits that prevent a parent from adequately providing for the child's educational or medical needs, cognitive inability to benefit from interventions relevant to risk reduction, or disinhibition that exacerbates already existing risk of maltreatment.

The ADA

In our case example, the parent argued, without success, that his parental rights should not be terminated because his brain impairment represented a disability of relevance to the ADA (1990). This section helps illustrate why the ADA sometimes has been invoked successfully in care and protection matters, and why it has been ruled either peripherally relevant or irrelevant in other cases. Parents with disabilities historically faced dark and drastic governmental measures to ensure that they did not reproduce. Although *Buck v. Bell* (1927) technically remains unchallenged, gone are the days of mandatory sterilization of deinstitutionalized mentally impaired or mentally retarded individuals. Even if it is not an articulated preventative policy, persons with mental disabilities may nevertheless have their parental rights terminated, and they tend to lose their appeals (Kerr, 2000). The courts seldom apply the ADA (1990) in determining parental rights, even though the ADA requires public entities to make reasonable modifications to their rules, policies, and practices to accommodate persons with disabilities who use their services. The ADA was designed to level the playing field by protecting the civil rights of disabled individuals. With proper implementation of the ADA, persons with mental disabilities might acquire adequate parenting skills so that they retain their parental rights. Although *Santosky* (1982) clarified that parental interest in the care and management of children is a fundamental liberty interest, the state must implement due process and meet the burden of clear and convincing evidence by balancing three distinct factors: the private interests of parties to the proceeding, the risk of error created by the potential inadequacy of a CPS agency service plan for addressing or providing relevance accommodations for remediation of the problem, and the countervailing governmental interest supporting the use of the service plan. In other words, courts must follow due process without falling prey to an unarticulated but practiced presumption that mentally disabled is synonymous with an inability to parent adequately (Kerr, 2000).

The ADA prohibits discrimination by any public entity, and its regulations apply to all services, programs, and activities of public entities. Services must be administered and provided in the most integrated setting appropriate to the needs of the individual with the disability (ADA, 1990). In care and protection matters, this means that disabled individuals must not be denied services or excluded from the provision of indicated services relevant to reunification of the parent and child. The services that agencies provide during the process of termination proceedings are subject to ADA scrutiny. Courts have routinely ruled in favor of parents who provide sufficient evidence that relevant services were never offered, and the rulings have been rendered with and without ADA scrutiny. Courts have specified in termination rulings that the CPS agencies did not meet the burden of proof required for termination when they made no offer of relevant and available services to parents, but they have allowed CPS agencies to maintain jurisdiction for protection of the child and for the purpose of then offering those services (Condie, 2003; Kerr, 2000). Cognitively impaired persons, however, are at risk of rulings that no services were necessary because of testimony or judgments that they would not benefit from them. For example, in *Orangeberg County Department of Social Services v. Harley* (1990), the parental rights of a mother diagnosed with borderline intellectual functioning were terminated before the offer of reunification services because of expert testimony that the mother was not competent to parent for a variety of reasons, and in *S.T. v. State Department of Human Resources* (1991), the court upheld the removal of a 2-day-old infant from her mother based on the testimony that parents with an IQ in the mild-to-moderate range of mental deficiency were incapable of caring for children. It remains to be seen whether parents might successfully invoke the ADA to argue the inappropriateness of offering no services to cognitively limited parents because of a presumed inability to benefit from them. Such as argument may have potential if combined with an assertion that not all cognitively impaired individuals have the same intellectual strengths and weaknesses, nor do they have the same parenting challenges. Some cognitively impaired parents do well if they have access to appropriate support services (Nurcombe and Parlett, 1994).

A common ADA challenge is the failure of the CPS agency or their contracted service providers to adequately or reasonably modify services for parents with mental disabilities. Services sometimes are offered with a one-size-fits-all, or boilerplate, mentality. In the case of *In re Torrence P.* (1994), an illiterate father facing termination of parental rights did not meet the conditions imposed upon him by court because he failed to respond to letters sent to him by the CPS agency's social worker. When he asserted his rights via an ADA defense, the court rejected the claim in the context of the termination proceeding, but the court left open the possibility of a separate cause of action under the ADA unrelated to the termination proceedings. In the case of *In re Victoria M.* (1989), the court reversed and remanded a termination case because the services provided by the state were not appropriately modified. The court found that there was nothing in the service plan that was tailored to the mother's limitations and that no accommodations were made for impairments that were a function of her disability. This is the type of ADA challenge in parental rights termination cases that has been the most successful in remanding the case for further services, but the challenge has not resulted in an immediate return of custody to the parents. When services have been modified appropriately, challenges are less successful. In an example of a case in which services were modified, a Washington state court ruled that the modifications were appropriate to the mother's learning disabilities, and the mandates of the ADA were applied appropriately. The court upheld the parental rights termination (*In re Joshua R. et al.*, 1998).

In summary, the ADA has been used to successfully challenge the appropriateness of services, but when services are modified in a manner reasonably consistent with the ADA, those challenges tend not to be successful. Parents have not been successful in their use of the ADA to argue that disability *per se* should preclude termination of parental rights.

In the case example that we provided, Mr Doe unsuccessfully made a *per se* challenge that his stroke was outside of his control, the resultant damage was outside his control, and therefore the effects of his brain impairment on his parenting risk and incapacity should not have been used as one of the determining factors in his termination case. The court was not persuaded by Mr Doe's assertion. Although Mr Doe's counsel made no assertion that services were not appropriately modified, that challenge possibly would have been unsuccessful for Mr Doe's substance abuse and sex offender treatment services because the agencies used treatment models that were routinely modified, when appropriate, for individuals with cognitive limitations. The treatment providers offered evidence at the termination hearing that they had used treatment approaches that included, among other strategies, the use of simplified language, session-by-session review of basic treatment principles and prevention plans, organizational assistance, slowly moving from one step to another in treatment, giving instructions in small segments or few steps, providing illustrations and examples of instructions, routinely checking for comprehension by Mr Doe, and repetition of instructions or statements when there was concern about Mr Doe's intermittent mental confusion. Whether those accommodations were sufficient would be a matter for the court to determine under an ADA challenge. In the next section of this chapter, we leave the topic of statutory and case law, and we review the ethical contours of expert consultation in care and protection matters.

Applied Ethics and Moral Considerations

Psychological assessment in forensic cases is an area of professional competence that is addressed by ethical standards. Ethical standards stem from basic philosophical notions and norms about the appropriateness of conduct within a professional sphere (Koocher and Keith-Spiegel, 1990). Primary sources for psychologists include the *Ethical Principles of Psychologists and Code of Conduct* (2002), *Standards for Educational and Psychological Testing* (1999), and *Record Keeping Guidelines* (1993), among other resources. Others have developed related ethical standards relevant to forensic practice (e.g., *Ethical Guidelines for the Practice of Forensic Psychiatry*, American Academy of Psychiatry and the Law, 1995). For more specific guidance, forensic psychologists who work with children and families consult the *Guidelines for Psychological Evaluations in Child Protection Matters* published in 1998 by the American Psychological Association, Committee on Professional Practice and Standards. Parties involved in care and protection matters come from a broad spectrum of backgrounds. The *Guidelines for Providers of Psychological Services to Ethnic, Linguistic, and Culturally Diverse Populations* (1990) contain valuable information to promote cultural sensitivity, and reliability and validity in the psychological assessment of specific populations. The application of ethical standards to forensic assessment is influenced by factors related to the case and factors related to the legal context. Factors related to the legal context have been reviewed elsewhere (Condie, 2003; Ogloff, 1999) and relevant clinical forensic practice is highlighted here.

In an evaluation that is tailored to the parent's need to participate in lengthy assessment procedures, the examiner varies the presentation of tests and appropriately plans and modifies the length of each session to ensure the individual's maximum productivity. Organization is required to allow the time needed for delayed trials on learning and memory tests. If testing the limits is used to determine maximum potential, it is done only after a test or test item in question has been completed according to standardized test instructions. If the parent has been examined historically for other reasons, the methodology is designed with practice effects in mind. Reasonable alternatives are used if standardized tests cannot be completed properly because the individual has sensory or motor deficits. Methods are paced appropriately to minimize the negative impact of reduced auditory attention, reduced mental tracking, distractibility, fatigue, motivational issues, frustration, or the interfering effects of mood disorders if relevant (Lezak, 1995). Our case example involved the need to shorten sessions as needed, to offer breaks or end sessions as needed, repeat instructions as needed, and to pace the sessions in order to optimize the individual's capacity to remain engaged in the assessment and to work at his best level of attention and motivation.

Ideally, there is a close and smooth correspondence between ethical principles and practice guidelines, legal standards relevant to the case, and clinical methodology. In cases involving complex comorbidity in a legal context, especially when two or more specialty areas overlap, relevant expertise is needed for all dimensions of the case. In our case example, areas of relevant expertise would include parenting competence, risk of maltreatment, brain impairment secondary to chronic alcohol abuse or dependence, brain impairment secondary to stroke, and other competing factors that may have contributed to the parent's current level of functioning. Using the comorbidity of chronic alcohol dependence and stroke as an example, one would use assessment measures and techniques appropriate to evaluating the impact of these conditions on brain functioning, with interpretation strategies that anticipate commingled effects of the two conditions along with other possible causal factors. There may be confounding risk factors associated with chronic substance dependence, such as unreported head trauma, which could have resulted from drinking behavior and alcohol-related disease or dysfunction. Alcohol dependence raises the risk of complications such as stroke, but family history of both alcoholism and stroke are relevant because of genetic vulnerabilities to both conditions. Diet plays a role in alcohol dependence because of the negative effects of malnutrition on cognitive functioning and in the development of neuropathogenic deficiency diseases (Lezak, 1995; Oscar-Berman and Schendan, 1999). In some cases, it may be possible to isolate symptoms related to chronic alcohol dependence or to stroke. More often, care and protection cases reflect the fact that multiple factors contribute to parenting problems, risk of child maltreatment, and amenability to interventions. For each contributing factor, it is important to examine the link, if any, to parenting concerns, and to consider whether those factors have the potential for amelioration.

Direct or indirect incentives for the examinee to skew the results in favor of socially desirable responses should be considered in care and protection evaluations. Individuals may feign or skew their results in cognitive, neuropsychological, or personality testing. There are many measures that have the potential to reveal social desirability responding in the examinee, but in the internet era, psychologists must consider whether the examinee has found a way to obtain a relatively sophisticated understanding of tests of social desirability responding (van Gorp, 2006). A final review of the examinee's overall test performance should be made to determine whether the actual scores make neuropsychological sense in light of the patient's presumed conditions. Communication between the expert and the referring party about the potential benefits and limits of the evaluation is critical, and problems can be avoided when there is open dialogue about the interface of legal standards and clinical forensic practice (Condie and Condie, 2006). In the next section, we review behavioral features relevant to alcohol dependence and stroke that might contribute to parental incapacity or risk of child maltreatment. We then turn to a summary of the evaluation methodology used in our case example, along with adaptations that can be made for similar cases.

Risk of Parental Incapacity and Child Maltreatment

Substance Abuse and Dependence

Concern about parental substance abuse is based on research relevant to its impact on children. Children of substance-abusing parents are at increased risk of maltreatment (Chasnoff, 1988; Murphy, Jellinek, Quinn, Smith, Poitrast, and Goshko, 1991). State CPS agency reporting records indicate that substance abuse is a factor in up to 90% of all reported cases, and research studies have estimated that up to 67% of CPS cases involve parental substance abuse (Famularo et al., 1992; Kelley, 1992; Miller, 1990; Murphy et al., 1991). Sustained paternal alcohol abuse is correlated with neglect, an exacerbation of existing risk of physical abuse, exacerbation of existing risk of domestic violence, and eventual child abandonment (Dube, Anda, Felitti, Croft, Edwards, and Giles, 2001; Jacob, Leonard, and Haber, 2001). Alcohol abuse does not lead to the same outcome in all families, but when antisocial behavior linked to risk of harm is present, alcohol abuse tends to potentiate the risk (Jacob et al., 2001). Families with at least one alcohol-abusing parent are described as lacking cohesion, emotional expression, attachment, and shared activities (Berlin and Davis, 1989), and parental substance abuse is correlated with less effective limit setting (Tarter, Blackson, Martin, Loeber, and Moss, 1993). Severity of paternal alcohol abuse is inversely associated with family competence, and it outweighs the predictive valence of other factors, such as socioeconomic status, family factors, and individual factors (Haugland and Havik, 1998). Lifetime alcohol problems predict the extent of child maltreatment (Muller, Fitzgerald, Sullivan, and Zucker, 1994). Family cohesion serves as a buffer against the effects of paternal alcohol abuse on distress, deviant behavior, and drinking patterns of adolescent children (Farrell, Barnes, and Banerjee, 1995).

In cases of suspected brain deterioration secondary to severe and chronic substance abuse/dependence, neuropsychological assessment is illustrative of deterioration (or lack thereof) of the integrity of brain functioning (Lezak, 1995; Moser and Frantz, 2004). Cognitive deterioration may develop from nutritional and vitamin deficiencies in individuals with chronic alcohol dependence. Memory impairment has been attributed to damage in the diencephalic midline, particularly in the mediodorsal nucleus of the thalamus and the mammillary nuclei (Shimamura, Jernigan, and Squire 1988). Cortical atrophy may account for some of the neurocognitive deficits that result from excessive chronic drinking. Deficits on tests of attention, problem solving, card sorting, metamemory, and temporal order have been noted. These deficits are associated with behavioral correlates that include memory dysfunction, impaired attention and concentration, impaired focus and working memory, decreased cognitive flexibility, impaired reasoning and decision-making abilities, compromised communication skills, and impaired visual spatial abilities. Long-term heavy alcohol use is associated with brain damage and consequent behavior changes that particularly affect visual spatial capabilities, short-term memory functioning, the ability to make plans and render sound judgments, behavioral flexibility, and emotional responsiveness and spontaneity (Oscar-Berman and Schendan, 1999). Autopsy results show that patients with histories of chronic alcohol dependence have smaller, less massive, and more shrunken brains than nonalcoholic individuals of the same age and gender. Brain shrinkage is especially extensive in the frontal lobe, the hypothesized location of higher cognitive functions in adults with normally developing brains. When existing child maltreatment risk is present, disinhibition secondary to impaired executive functions should be assessed due to its possible contribution to risk (Condie, 2003). Because indicators of structural pathology may lessen or disappear with long-term abstinence (Shimamura et al., 1988), length of sobriety may ameliorate frontal lobe factors contributing to risk.

Examples of parenting competencies that might be affected by chronic alcohol dependence include potential incapacity related to making logical decisions about the child's education and medical care, monitoring and responding to any special academic or medical needs of the child, keeping track of the child's school and activity schedule, providing nutritional meals and making sure the child has an adequate amount of sleep, interacting positively with the child, patiently responding to the child's demands for parental attention, maintaining sufficient physical energy to keep the child occupied, keeping the household and the weekly schedule organized, adequately supervising the child, reasoning with the child when setting limits on behavior, communicating with the child at a level appropriate to his or her development, and transporting the child to appointments and activities. When risk of maltreatment has been documented, there are additional demands upon the parent to attend relevant treatment appointments, adhere to treatment plans, update relapse prevention plans, take steps necessary to reduce risk of maltreatment, learn new behavior patterns, use new coping resources, and refrain from maltreatment. Whether any of these examples would contribute to parental incapacity or risk of child maltreatment would depend upon relevant case variables and the severity of the parent's relevant deficits (Condie, 2003).

Brain Impairment

Brain impairment secondary to brain injury or illness may have a significant impact on the parent–child relationship. After parental injury or illness, children may experience negative behavioral changes in the parent, and, in a relatively large percentage of cases, the impact on the relationship is significant (Pessar, Coad, Linn, and Willer, 1993). Parents with brain injury suffer a broad range of debilitating sequelae that include cognitive impairment, changes in mood, impulsive actions, and poor regulation of anger (Ducharme and Davidson, 2004). Depression is one of the most prominent emotional changes after a stroke, regardless of the location of the impact. There may be qualitative differences in the person's depression, depending upon the location of the impact. Indifference, restricted emotional expression, and apathy have been noted in individuals with left hemisphere involvement (Lezak, 1995). Parents may benefit from rehabilitation that focuses upon the parent–child relationship, but in many cases significant follow-up and support are needed (Ducharme and Davidson, 2004). Neuropsychological assessment is indicated in care and protection cases if the brain impairment of concern is hypothesized to have an impact on parenting behavior. It is less common and less necessary in cases involving substance abuse or mental illness without associated neurological or neurocognitive complications (Condie and Condie, 2006; Nayak and Milner, 1998). In cases of stroke, neuropsychological assessment helps illustrate whether there have been changes that are specific to the effects of the stroke. Results of measures of intelligence, attention, language abilities, learning and memory, visual spatial abilities, and executive functions are interpreted in terms of their consistency with estimates or existing data of the individual's premorbid level of functioning (van Gorp, 2006). The interpretation process is used to determine whether there is a link between the brain impairment and any parental incapacity or risk to the child (Grisso, Otto, Borum, Edens, and Moye, 2002; Nayak and Milner, 1998).

Records, if available, are of critical importance to establish a baseline of premorbid cognitive functioning, memory functioning, and mental and behavioral organization (Condie, 2003; Lezak, 1995). In this case, we gathered Mr Doe's educational records, we were granted access to two psychological evaluation reports from his adolescence that included cognitive and achievement testing, and we gathered rehabilitation data from the substance-abuse treatment agency and from the physical and cognitive rehabilitation program. We used collateral interview data, targeting credible reporters who knew Mr Doe from adolescence through his care and protection involvement, to analyze changes in Mr Doe's mental and behavioral presentation that were gradual and to differentiate them from changes that were sudden. The decision to conduct neuropsychological assessment was based on data relevant to the parent's observable neurological dysfunction, recorded observations of his functioning during supervised visits, rehabilitation records, and records from treatment providers expressing concern about his functioning (for a broader review of the use of neuropsychological assessment in forensic cases, see Sweet, 1999; van Gorp, 2006; Zilmer and Green, 2006). We cautioned the referring party (the court) that the premorbid data and the current assessment data would help us understand the parent's current functioning, but that any determination of etiological factors and their significance would be complicated by the dual impact of the stroke and the chronic alcohol dependence, along with any social-emotional impact of those conditions. We chose measures of relevance to stroke outcomes and to outcomes in cases of chronic alcohol dependence. Neuropsychological testing yielded data relevant to current functioning, but, as anticipated, the interpretation was complicated by comorbidity of the stroke and the chronic alcohol dependence (see below for a more detailed description). Linking the data to parental incapacity and risk of maltreatment required a further step.* The third critical component of our evaluation was to analyze and interpret data relevant to the link, if any, between hypothesized gradual brain impairment from chronic substance dependence, hypothesized brain impairment from stroke, and Mr Doe's parental incapacity and risk of child maltreatment. This determination was accomplished, in part, by considering the data in the context of an empirically derived risk assessment. A comparison to records describing the father's premorbid condition allowed us to extrapolate from baseline data, and a comparison of the data to that of interview data from relevant collaterals who knew him well over the course of adulthood provided further clarification of the gradual versus sudden onset and impact of symptoms and deficits. The assessment data were useful in describing the father's current strengths and weaknesses, along with factors that would mediate or potentiate risk (see below).

---

* The mechanics of violence risk assessment, sexual offending risk assessment, and risk of neglect are not described in this chapter. These topics are covered in depth in other chapters in this volume and in other resources (Condie, 2003; Condie and Condie, 2006; Dubowitz, 1999; Hanson, 2004; Hanson and Thornton, 2000; Monahan et al., 2000; Steadman et al., 2000).

Empirically Based Methods and Applications

Evaluation methodology consists of carefully selected techniques and measures that logically are connected to the referral question and that have reliability and validity consistent with the purposes of the assessment. After determining the appropriateness of the referral question for forensic and neuropsychological assessment, methodology should be individually crafted to address the referral question (Ayoub and Kinscherff, 2006; Condie, 2003; van Gorp, 2006). Evaluators choose the best available measures and then interpret them with appropriate caution. When used with appropriate caveats in the context of a multimodal assessment, measures provide meaningful information because they contribute to converging data (Wolfe, 1988). Although approaches to care and protection cases may take many forms, it is common for psychologists to use some form of psychological testing (Ayoub and Kinscherff, 2006; Budd, Poindexter, Felix, and Naik-Polan, 2001; van Gorp, 2006), along with a careful history taking, a review of all relevant and available documents, interviews, observations, and relevant assessment measures (Condie, 2003). The evaluation must produce sufficient substantiation for findings and opinions offered to the court (Ayoub and Kinscherff, 2006). The comprehensiveness of the clinical interview and evaluation methodology, in terms of both breadth and depth, is determined by the referral question (Condie, 2003). A strong evaluation balances inquiry into both positive and negative features of functioning (Schwartz, 1987).

Interview Data

In care and protection evaluation practice, typical areas of interview inquiry include the parent's perspective of the incidents and behaviors that led to his or her involvement with the CPS system (Crenshaw and Barnum, 2001), the parent's perspective of the child as an individual, and the parent–child relationship (Ayoub and Kinscherff, 2006). The parent's acceptance of the responsibilities involved in childrearing and the parent's account of other acts of maltreatment not found in the CPS records are also relevant (Condie, 2003). Because of the overlap, in this particular case, with a sex offender risk assessment, inquiry would be narrowed to the impact, if any, of brain atrophy, necrosis, or deterioration on parenting. Other interview content would depend upon the nature of the inquiry. In a case like that of our sample case, it would be important to inquire about the parent's view of his sex offender risk in light of his new neurocognitive limitations, his report of his history of alcohol use and abuse, his view of whether his alcohol dependence led to risk or actual harm to the children, his view of his treatment progress, factors that he views as potential triggers of future risk, and factors that might mediate future risk of incapacity or maltreatment. It would be important not to replicate the methodology of the sex offender evaluation, but to use it as a basis for determining Mr Doe's view of possible neurocognitive exacerbations of parental incapacity or sex offender risk. Because the impact of chronic alcohol dependence and stroke were not included in the sex offender evaluation, any new contribution to or exacerbation of risk would be included in the evaluation.

In the case example, Mr Doe had sought self-help group and relapse prevention treatment relevant to his alcohol dependence. The clinical interview included an inquiry into his candor in reporting his history of alcohol use, the correspondence between his report of alcohol use and the report of collaterals, the consistency of his report in the evaluation compared to his report to previous treatment providers, and his account of his treatment requirements and treatment progress. His report of alcohol use was relatively consistent with other accounts, reports by collaterals, and treatment providers. His report of the requirements of treatment was less clear. For example, when he informed the evaluator that he was on step four of a 12-step self-help program, the evaluator asked him to describe step four. He described steps one and two, but he did not recall step four, stating that it temporarily slipped his mind. When given ample time to think, he became embarrassed when he could cite only two of the 12 steps. Because of the otherwise relatively clear and rational quality of his thought process during this portion of the interview, because of the consistency of his account with guarded responding, and because it was later confirmed that his self-help attendance was inconsistent, the evaluator attributed his difficulty answering this and related questions to poor engagement in the self-help modality of treatment. The evaluator asked about his relapse prevention plan and found that it was incomplete, and he did not have a mechanism in place for continually updating it even though his outpatient counselor was monitoring the plan and reviewing the process carefully in each session. His difficulty with relapse prevention planning was related to both insufficient motivation and insufficient cognitive clarity. In the context of a semistructured interview, he was presented with a variety of scenarios known to increase risk of relapse. When he stated, in the context of each item, that he was 100% confident he would not drink alcohol in those situations, he was asked to justify his level of confidence. He gave two reasons for his confidence, both of which were external motivators of behavior (the legal context and a wish to impress his pretrial probation officer). The evaluator asked about his level of awareness of the disinhibiting effects of alcohol use on sex and aggression. The distinction between understanding and appreciation (Grisso et al., 2002) was relevant to his responses to interview questions on this topic. Although Mr Doe responded in a knowledgeable manner to questions relevant to disinhibition and alcohol use, he did not think he needed to worry about disinhibition as it applied to his alcohol use or its possible relationship to his risk of sex offending. He viewed the issue as irrelevant because he was 100% confident that he would not drink again. When it was brought to his attention that someone observed him drinking alcohol recently, he said he confidently regarded it as a one-time slip that would not recur.

For a parent with a history of alcohol dependence that is hypothesized to be linked, at least potentially, to risk of parental incapacity or child maltreatment, careful attention is given to the individual's history and duration of periods of use, alcohol abuse or dependence, and the length and success of periods of sobriety (Condie, 2003). Focus is placed upon factors that potentiated and hindered sobriety, the effectiveness of past rehabilitation, the individual's level of participation in rehabilitation, the individual's current stage of rehabilitation, the quality and nature (i.e., internal versus external) of motivating influences for remaining sober, options available for reducing urges to drink or use drugs, and the quality and realistic nature of relapse prevention plans (Bernardi, Jones, and Tennant, 1989; Hester and Miller, 1989; Miller, 1990). Interview questions vary according to the specific form of treatment offered to the individual. Because there is no single approach to treatment that is suitable for all individuals, flexibility and respect for cultural differences is required in the interview and assessment process. Treatment types include risk identification and management, spiritual direction, social sanctions, abstinence, identification and confrontation, education, relearning or disenabling, medical treatment, cognitive restructuring, skill training, and family therapy (Hester and Miller, 1989). It is often possible to match an individual to an optimal treatment approach using empirical knowledge to inform treatment choices, thereby increasing potential efficacy (Hester and Miller, 1989; Miller 1990). Effective evaluation of treatment outcome requires a flexible interview and assessment approach tailored to the substance(s) of relevance and the treatment approach that was used (Condie, 2003). The evaluation of the individual's response to treatment is tailored to the type of treatment offered, but it also requires knowledge of treatment approaches and motivational influences that might be more suitable if the treatment response has been suboptimal.

In the case example, another topic of relevance during the interview was the impact of the stroke. The evaluator inquired about the father's understanding of the impact of his stroke and its residual symptoms, along with their possible impact on his parenting. It was necessary to simplify questions relevant to this and other topics so that he would understand them. When the evaluator attempted to elicit his awareness of his lack of comprehension of more complicated questions, he showed a somewhat reduced awareness of the difference between reasonable questions and nonsense questions. He was able to recognize and laugh at simple nonsense questions, but he attempted to answer more complex nonsense questions. Mild confabulation in response to some questions was observed, regardless of whether they were reasonable questions or nonsense questions. Little emotional spontaneity was noted, and at times he appeared apathetic and emotionally flat. In response to questions about the impact of his stroke, Mr Doe expressed optimism for a full recovery and he was hopeful that the residual effects would subside in a matter of weeks. When documented and medically confirmed residual effects were discussed with him directly, he sometimes did not agree that he had residual effects. When he agreed that an effect was present, he tended to minimize the impact on his current functioning, and to wish away any impact on his future functioning. When interview techniques were used to address his guardedness, he was somewhat more realistic in his appraisal, but he continued to show a discrepancy between his understanding of the impact and his appreciation of the applicability to his individual circumstances. For example, he stated that he was aware that he was having difficulty with his organizational abilities and his schedule, but he said it would have "absolutely no impact" on his future ability to take his children to school, to activities, and to appointments. As he endorsed residual effects of relevance, he tended to emphasize effects that were less related to potential incapacity and exacerbation of risk, such as right-sided motor weakness, and to de-emphasize effects that might be more relevant, such as mental confusion about the time and location of his supervised visits with his children.

The evaluator asked about relevant highlights of the sex offender risk report in the interview of the father. The questions focused upon the potential for disinhibition secondary to chronic alcohol dependence, new episodes of drinking, and the residual effects of stroke. Mr Doe was asked about the impact of sex offender treatment on his understanding and appreciation of the behavioral consequences of disinhibition, and he was asked to describe how he was implementing preventive techniques. The evaluator asked Mr Doe about the relevance of neurocognitive factors, if any, to his need for supervision of paternal visitation, for how long Mr Doe thought supervision would be needed, and under what conditions Mr Doe thought visitation time could be increased and supervision could be curtailed. The evaluator asked about his strengths and supports. When the evaluator later tried to confirm them, the father was judged to be overconfident about the availability and willingness of some of his support sources. For example, Mr Doe said a female cousin planned to provide significant parenting support, but this information was not verified and the woman he identified as his cousin was later learned to be an ex-girlfriend of Mr Doe.

Interview data helped clarify Mr Doe's current thought processes relevant to possible parental incapacity and risk of child maltreatment. When those data were coupled with collateral interview data, records of premorbid functioning, and assessment data, it helped clarify the gradual versus sudden onset of factors that were relevant to parental incapacity and risk of child maltreatment. No new risk was identified, but a potential exacerbation related to disinhibition was noted. The disinhibition was thought to be related to both chronic alcohol dependence and stroke. The impact of Mr Doe's neurocognitive deterioration on his risk of sex offending, as an additional factor in his sex offender risk matrix, ultimately was judged to be relevant but mild in relation to other factors. It was judged to be linked in a relevant way to his risk of offending due to the likelihood of increased disinhibition, due to a recent decrease in his reasoning and logic about the impact of paternal sexual fondling of children (compared to the reasoning and logic documented in his sex offender evaluation report), and due to recently decreased awareness of when and how to seek help (compared to records and documented interview data relevant to his sex offender treatment progress prior to the stroke). Paradoxically, the evaluator also was impressed that Mr Doe might have fewer capabilities relevant to planning offenses and hiding his behavior from other individuals. Because of the combined effects of his disinhibition and his language processing issues, he was observed to talk at length in a somewhat disorganized fashion about incidents and behaviors that parents in his set of circumstances ordinarily would be inclined to hide. His risk of offending remained relevant, but the evaluator was of the opinion that it might be easier now for other adults to detect the father's planning, victim grooming, and other relevant behaviors in their early stages due to Mr Doe's increased disorganization and his likely tendency to discuss his offending plans without intending to do so. Because there was no guarantee that this set of behaviors would lead to early detection, however, there was a caveat about the secrecy of offending in most circumstances.

Records of Premorbid Functioning and Case Information

Records of premorbid functioning, in combination with interview data, were used to supplement the evaluation data to determine the etiological significance, if any, of chronic alcohol dependence and the stroke. Based on an analysis of the data in light of records and interview data relevant to premorbid functioning and changes in functioning over time, the evaluator concluded that some of Mr Doe's behaviors and cognitive variables had gradually deteriorated over time and likely were related, at least in part, to chronic alcohol dependence. Others changed rather suddenly, and the nature of the changes was consistent with hypothesized brain–behavior relationships in the region of the stroke. Because there is obvious controversy over brain lateralization, localization of specific brain functions, and specific brain–behavior relationships (Lezak, 1995), the evaluator made cautious conclusions with appropriate caveats about the state of the science. The impact of Mr Doe's cognitive deterioration on his potential for inadequate care and his potential for child neglect secondary to mental disorganization was judged to be moderate to severe. Although neglect was not the original allegation of concern to the CPS agency, it had taken on increasing significance as observers became worried about his cognitive and behavioral disorganization. The assessment results were consistent with those concerns. Without records of premorbid functioning and interview data relevant to changes in Mr Doe over time, conclusions would have been more descriptive, and there would have been less emphasis on the relevance of chronic alcohol abuse and stroke to his parental incapacity.

CPS records typically contain documentation of supported allegations of child maltreatment, investigation records, and an indication of why the allegations were supported.

When the records are descriptive and reliable, they may be used to gauge caregiver progress in acknowledging the frequency and severity of maltreatment, a necessary step toward meaningful intervention (Hanson, 1997). In addition, records usually contain a service plan for the caregivers and the children (Condie, 2003), making it possible to evaluate the caregiver's familiarity with and participation in the plan and whether the service plan included interventions relevant to the caregiver's level of cognitive functioning. Records may serve to clarify whether potentially effective interventions were included or neglected in the service plan. They may also be useful in determining whether prescribed interventions were relevant to the factors that led to the maltreatment. CPS records sometimes contain documentation of parental self-reports of child maltreatment, visitation records, parental adherence to visitation schedules, recorded observations of parental visitation of children, and observations of children's reactions to visitation commencement or termination. Records may contain information relevant to the parent–child relationship, the parent's participation in and response to interventions, and any past or pending criminal actions against the parent (Condie, 2003).

Other useful types of records include those documenting participation in or response to rehabilitation efforts, psychiatric treatment, prior psychological evaluations, substance-abuse rehabilitation, educational history, medical treatment, progress in rehabilitation, criminal history, visitation center adherence to appointments, and police investigations relevant to child maltreatment. Records may contain relevant maltreatment information that helps frame interview and follow-up interview questions. They may include documentation of the parent's attendance and participation in treatment, and the reasonableness of the caregiver's explanation for failure to attend or effectively use recommended interventions (Condie, 2003). Records should be complemented with interviews of relevant third parties. After obtaining appropriate releases to collect third-party information, the evaluator determines the scope of questions appropriate to each collateral contact. Possible sources of information include teachers, child care workers, foster parents, relatives, child maltreatment investigators for the state, physicians, mental health service providers, substance-abuse rehabilitation providers, and caregiver–child visitation supervisors (Condie, 2003). Treatment providers are a potentially valuable source of information when the parent's response to intervention is being examined. The evaluator should be alert to higher confidentiality standards for substance-abuse treatment providers, and to the possibility that not all collateral sources (e.g., relatives of the parent being evaluated) will be motivated to provide forthright information.[*]

Measures

Next, we describe the strategy for choosing measures of cognitive and neuropsychological variables in parenting evaluations. When choosing assessment measures, it is best to begin with theoretically or logically derived hypotheses and possible causal or explanatory variables that are relevant to the referral question. The evaluator carefully considers the degree to which each measure demonstrably corresponds to the behavior or set of behaviors of interest (Condie, 2003). Measures can be quite useful if their selection is based on research or theory supporting a relationship between the indices and specific parental behaviors of

[*] For a thorough discussion of the role of third-party information in forensic assessment, see Heilbrun, Warren, and Picarello, 2003.

concern (Budd, 2005). The use of global indices, such as intelligence quotient, diagnostic status, or personality functioning, may provide support for explanatory data related to parenting problems, maltreatment risk, or suitability of interventions if the data are linked to the parenting behaviors of concern (Grisso et al., 2002). Measures must be linked to the referral question and the context. For example, a cognitive assessment of an individual with limited intellectual functioning may not be needed unless there is no previous documentation of the limitations *and* if it is hypothesized that the limitations are linked to maltreatment risk. The intellectual limitations would be of little legal relevance if the maltreatment were related to some other factor or set of factors. When relevant, cognitive and intellectual assessment measures provide data relevant to the parent's overall abilities, differential strengths and weaknesses, capacity to communicate, and level of verbal and nonverbal knowledge. Nonverbal cognitive and intellectual assessment measures provide data relevant to the parent's nonverbal abilities and maturity, capacity for alternative modes of expression and understanding, and differential strengths and weaknesses in nonverbal communication. Neuropsychological assessment measures provide data concerning a parent's verbal abilities, organizational skills, behavior organization, planning and decision-making, abstraction abilities, capacity for attention and concentration, visual spatial abilities, memory functioning, and capacity for self-report narratives in the context of relevant treatment and communication with others about the children. They aid in differential diagnosis between brain injury or impairment and factors attributable to emotional or personality functioning. Assessment measures supplement other data that are integrated with objective information contained in the parent's history and assessment findings (Matarazzo, 1990).

In making a determination of the appropriateness of measures of overall functioning, it is important to remember that not all parents with brain impairment or substance-abuse problems have parenting deficits or engage in child maltreatment. Similarly, not all parents with parenting deficits or who engage in child maltreatment have brain impairment or substance-abuse problems. Risk might be a function of other factors such as negative learned and habitual behaviors, individual variables, or situational variables. If the parent's functioning is impaired in some fashion, the impairment is relevant only if there is a demonstrable link between the impairment and subsequent parental incapacity or child maltreatment (Grisso et al., 2002). Brain impairment, as illustrated by the results of cognitive and neuropsychological assessment, is insufficient by itself to warrant termination of parental rights, but global indices serve as a framework for understanding specific functioning limitations. If there is concern that brain damage is related to or exacerbates parental risk of harm to the child, assessment data would be relevant. For cases with strong documentation of the impact of the impairment, however, assessment might be indicated only if there is a need for clarification of specific strengths and weaknesses in current functioning or potential for a specific form of rehabilitation. Assessment data might clarify whether a caregiver would benefit from a particular type of training, support services, treatment, supervision, or substituted judgment (e.g., a limited-purpose guardian *ad litem*). Assessment measures are used to aid the process of differential diagnosis between neuropsychological deficits and other possible explanatory factors. Etiological distinctions may be important in determining the type of treatment to be offered, the severity of the condition, and chronicity of the condition. The choice of neuropsychological assessment measures should be drawn from reasonably formed hypotheses about possible causal variables that might partially or wholly account for sequelae related to parenting deficiencies or patterns of maltreatment.

In this assessment, the referral question was concerned with: (a) the impact, if any, of chronic alcohol dependence and stroke on the integrity of brain functioning; and (b) the impact of brain impairment, if any, on parental incapacity and risk of child maltreatment. The question of exacerbation of sex offender risk was a narrow one, but the question of possible parental incapacity was not. Because the question of brain impairment and its possible link to parental incapacity was relatively broad neuropsychological and parenting ground to cover, the evaluator used intellectual assessment measures and neuropsychological assessment measures that included scales relevant to receptive language, expressive language, verbal and nonverbal information processing, attention and concentration, learning and memory, executive functions, behavior control, and motor coordination and control. Scales of emotional functioning also were administered. No existing scales specific to parenting in the context of Mr Doe's circumstances were judged to be suitable for the evaluation, so data relevant to parenting were gathered in a semistructured interview format comparing Mr Doe's perspective of his parenting abilities to those of credible reporters who had known him for a long time, CPS caseworkers who met with him before and after the stroke, and visitation supervisors knowledgeable of his pre- and poststroke parenting behavior in the context of visitation sessions.

When the evaluation and semistructured interview data were compared to records relevant to premorbid functioning, it was concluded that Mr Doe had suffered significant deterioration in receptive language skills, mild deterioration in expressive language skills, new-onset emotional dulling, significant weakness in visual spatial processing, new-onset disorganization and intermittent mental confusion, gradual deterioration in executive functions, and new and more serious deterioration in executive functions. Although there had been gradual deterioration in Mr Doe's executive functions, based on interview data, there also was a sudden and much greater deterioration after the stroke. Cognitive, memory, and other neuropsychological variables hypothesized to be affected were described with appropriate caveats about Mr Doe's language comprehension throughout the assessment process. The remediability of the deficits was described in the form of three predictive scenarios. The first scenario anticipated cognitive recovery in an individual with a chronic drinking history who remained sober thereafter, the second anticipated cognitive recovery in that same individual in the context of a fairly severe alcohol relapse, and the third involved relapsing and remitting drinking behavior but with significant external support for recovery. This format was used to illustrate to the court the best and worst possible cognitive outcomes over the course of the next year. The state of the science relevant to stroke recovery was briefly described to provide appropriate caveats about the prognostications and the length of time needed for relevant treatment responses. The predictive scenarios were not extended beyond 1 year because of limitations in the long-term prediction of alcohol treatment outcomes, stroke rehabilitation outcomes, unknown variables such as new strokes, and sex offender treatment outcomes. When drawing logical inferences about the relationship between indices of functioning and parental risk to the child, it is important to do so after considering historical data about the individual. Historical data should be as complete as possible. The potential impact of Mr Doe's cognitive and neuropsychological status on his parenting abilities was described and is summarized below.

Intelligence and Achievement

Intelligence tests may be considered neuropsychological instruments in their own right. They provide scores of cognitive ability, verbal information processing, nonverbal information processing, working memory, and processing speed. In the absence of previous cognitive assessment scores, premorbid intellectual functioning may be estimated from demographic variables, such as highest level of education and occupational attainment, through the use of formulas that have been developed to compute estimated premorbid IQ (van Gorp, 2006). Achievement measures provide a useful supplement to intellectual assessment. Chronic alcohol abuse is hypothesized to affect certain cognitive functions but not others. Well-established abilities such as arithmetic and language remain relatively unimpaired (Lezak, 1995). The severity of specific deficits associated with chronic alcoholism has been related to intake quantity, duration of drinking problems, and sometimes to age. Age at which drinking began is a good predictor of conceptual level and efficiency (Oscar-Berman and Schendan, 1999). Binge drinkers are less prone to alcohol-related cognitive deficits than those with a heavy daily alcohol intake (Lezak, 1995).

Cerebrovascular accident, or stroke, may cause cognitive impairment by either of two mechanisms. Disruption of the supply of nutrients (oxygen and glucose) to the brain as a result of blockage of blood flow is seen in ischemic occlusive or thrombotic stroke. The most common cause of ischemic stroke is atherosclerosis that occludes an artery and deprives an area of the brain of oxygen. Symptoms of this type of stroke may progress over hours or days. Hemorrhagic strokes, on the other hand, are due to rupture of blood vessels, allowing blood to leak into brain tissues. This type of stroke carries a much higher risk of mortality, and damage is usually more extensive. Irreversible brain damage after stroke is rapid because of the inability of nervous tissue to survive more than several minutes of oxygen deprivation. Disruption of normal blood flow creates an area of damaged or dead tissue, called an infarct. The effects of infarctions vary from person to person due to a host of factors such as individual differences in the anatomical organization of cerebral circulation, the capacity to develop and utilize collateral brain circulation, and localization of brain functions such as language, which may differ from one individual to another (Lezak, 1995). Mr Doe suffered an ischemic stroke. Heavy drinkers of alcohol have been found to have a 45% greater risk of ischemic stroke compared to nondrinkers (Mukamal, Ascherio, Mittleman, Conigrave, Comargo, Kawachi, Stampfer, Willett, and Rimm, 2005).

Attention and Concentration
The prefrontal cortex is among the many anatomical brain structures implicated in attention. Significant frontal activation takes place during selective attention, and the prefrontal cortex mediates the capacity to make and control attention shifts. Conditions that affect frontal lobe functions, such as chronic alcohol dependence, may result in difficulty maintaining attention and focus, along with high susceptibility to distractions (Lezak, 1995). Some individuals who chronically abuse alcohol may show little or no disturbance in attention (Pfefferbaum et al., 1992). Because executive functions are implicated in chronic alcohol dependence, it is important to include measures of attention when evaluating the impact of sustained daily alcohol consumption. Many standardized measures of executive functions include scales of simple and sustained attention, along with scales of other executive functions (see below). Simple attention may be assessed through questions to which the individual ought to know the answer, immediate recall of simple information such as digits, continuous performance tests, and symptom checklists completed by self-report or by observers. With respect to the impact of stroke on attention skills, attention deficits are often more profound in conjunction with left hemiplegia relative to right (Lezak, 1995). Attention deficits would occur with sudden onset. Because neurological records localized

the region of the stroke, the evaluator considered the hypothesized nature of the impact in a right-handed individual (as was Mr Doe) when evaluating the impact of alcohol dependence versus stroke. Caveats were included that described the state of the science in making interferences based on brain lateralization and localization of impact.

Language

Language abilities are necessary for parental verbal and conceptual reasoning, comprehension of written and spoken instructions, and effective communication. Parents with language impairment that affects both expression and comprehension may have difficulty communicating with their children, their service providers, their probation officers, their case workers and case managers, and their attorneys. Assessment usually includes confrontation naming (i.e., naming of objects), verbal fluency, comprehension, repetition, controlled oral word associations, and other measures. Although not always the case, stroke tends to have one-sided effects. For aphasic stroke patients, speech fluency typically returns by 1 month if it returns at all, but confrontational naming recovers more slowly, usually after about 6 months. At 1 month poststroke, most patients with hemiglegia have perceptual deficits as well, regardless of the side of the lesion. More than half of right hemiplegic patients have aphasia since Broca's area is located on the left side of the cerebral cortex in most right-handed individuals. With left-sided infarcts, speech and language disorders are common residuals, but their specific nature depends upon the site and extent of the damage (Lezak, 1995). Chronic alcohol dependence affects verbal functions in a more gradual and less serious manner than a stroke that affects language functioning. On verbal learning tests, patients with long-term alcohol abuse differ from normal controls on immediate and delayed recall, and on recognition memory, but their learning curves have a similar slope over time to those of normal subjects. They are more susceptible than normal subjects to interference effects (Preston, Kramer, and Blusewicz, 1989).

Learning and Memory

Memory dysfunction is a fairly common outcome in a variety of neurological illnesses and injuries. It is usually assessed through a memory battery that includes scales of short-term verbal and visual memory functioning, immediate recall, delayed recall, recognition, and learning characteristics. Korsakoff's psychosis, due to lack of thiamine (vitamin B1), is an extremely rare disorder in which impairment of short-term memory prevents the formation of new memories and prevents learning. It can occur after years of heavy alcohol consumption due to the combined effects of poor nutrition and inflammation of the lining of the stomach, causing poor absorption of vitamins. Damage to a relatively circumscribed area of the brain is involved. Because of its overall infrequency and its occurrence relatively late in life, Korsakoff's would be an unusual outcome in a care and protection evaluation, and it should be distinguished from alcoholic dementia, which features widespread cognitive deterioration without the profound amnesic symptoms of Korsakoff's. Cerebral atrophy disproportionately affecting cerebral white matter causes memory deficits (Pfefferbaum et al., 1992). Strokes may also cause memory impairment, depending upon their location (Lezak, 1995).

Executive Functions

Executive functions are higher order cognitive abilities mediated by the frontal lobe. They are assessed through behavior and symptom checklists completed by observers or by self-report and by measures of executive functions designed to separate the effects of motor, verbal, and nonverbal inefficiency from frontal lobe inefficiency (Condie, 2003). These neurocognitive functions include planning, task initiation, cognitive flexibility, strategy formation, logic, reasoning, problem solving, judgment, and inhibition of inappropriate responses. Frontal lobe dysfunction is associated with inappropriate statements and behavior, impulsive actions, deficient self-awareness, disinhibition, inadequate problem solving and decision-making, and difficulty with novel tasks (Lezak, 1995). Lateralization of cognitive activity is less marked in patients with frontal damage compared to damage in other cortexes. Decreased verbal fluency and impoverishment of spontaneous speech may be seen in left frontal lobe lesions secondary to stroke. These problems are distinct from other verbal problems associated with left anterior damage such as disorganization of language, disrupted and confused narratives, simplified syntax, incomplete sentences and clauses, descriptions that are reduced to few or single words, misnaming, perseveration, and general impoverishment of language (Lezak, 1995). More diffuse damage is likely to be seen in cases of chronic alcohol abuse and dependence (Pfefferbaum et al., 1997).

Summary

Cognitive and neuropsychological indices, when combined with historic and interview data, confirmed Mr Doe's receptive language weakness of recent onset, mild expressive language weakness of recent onset, decreased spontaneous speech, decreased verbal fluency, difficulty learning new information, emotional dulling of recent onset, gradually declining organizational and memory abilities, gradual loss of interest in intellectual pursuits, significant weakness in nonverbal information processing of recent onset, significant intermittent mental confusion of recent onset, and significant weakness in executive functions of gradual onset but with a recent acute exacerbation in schedule organization and finding his way around. Clinical observations and collateral interviews were consistent with the assessment data and showed these deficits impacted parenting abilities in the following ways: Mr Doe had difficulty following the instructions of visitation supervisors, he sometimes forgot visitation appointments or arrived at the wrong time even though he had a history of consistent and timely visitation prior to his stroke, he sometimes needed cues to start a conversation with his children, he had difficulty following the conversational statements of his children, and he had difficulty keeping supervised visitation and treatment appointments as expected. He had difficulty remembering and following fairly straightforward treatment instructions given by his outpatient treatment providers. Although his verbal processing and memory had not been optimal prior to the stroke, it showed deterioration after the stroke that especially affected recall of information between treatment sessions. Mr Doe sometimes did not recall information that had been reviewed across several treatment sessions, he had difficulty keeping his relapse prevention plan organized and updated even with significant assistance and review, and he had trouble refraining from repeating himself within and across treatment appointments. He sometimes engaged in obvious confabulation during conversations with others, and he sometimes failed to complete his sentences or his thoughts. His children became frustrated and sometimes confused when he stopped mid-sentence during play activities with them. He sometimes engaged in coherent conversation that was interrupted by mental confusion. His children had difficulty understanding when he was speaking with cognitive clarity and when he was not, and so they had difficulty judging whether he would follow through on promises made to them or limits set by him.

Mr Doe showed difficulty expressing an expected repertoire of spontaneous emotions with his children and in other social situations. He had trouble understanding the bus schedule or taking bus and subway routes with which he previously had little difficulty. He had difficulty keeping his living space minimally organized and clean that predated the stroke but that was worse after the stroke. As part of his service plan, he was asked to monitor his children's academic progress by checking in weekly with his children's teachers. Although the children's caseworker had arranged a set weekly telephone appointment time with each teacher, the task frequently slipped his mind after his stroke. On two occasions, when asked the name of his children's pediatrician, he could not remember her name but he could describe the general location of her office. When one of his children developed an ear infection, he demonstrated a flat emotional reaction to the news that she vomited and had a fever for 24 h. He later asked if she had the flu and then he told a caseworker a somewhat confabulated story of how she contracted the flu. In the context of questions presenting various possible educational and medical decision-making scenarios involving his children, he had difficulty keeping their educational and health histories separate, and he had difficulty describing a rational basis for the educational and medical choices that he made in the context of the scenarios.

Mr Doe's strengths included his desire for appropriate contact for his children, his desire for them to eventually attend college, his consistent treatment attendance prior to the stroke, his participation in group treatment prior to the stroke, his interest in vocational rehabilitation with the hope of eventually finding suitable employment to better support his children in the future, his tendency to welcome helping resources even though he had difficulty determining how to best take advantage of those resources, his capacity to describe some relevant features of the impact of his substance abuse and sex offending on his children, his stated desire to refrain from drinking and sex offending, his growing respect for his pretrial probation officer and his treatment providers, his history of attending meetings with his caseworker whenever she scheduled them, and his compliance with random alcohol screening at a local substance-abuse treatment agency. After the termination hearing began, and despite these positive variables, it seemed likely to him over the pendency of the hearing that the case might result in termination of his parental rights. Prior to the final disposition, he met with his caseworker and he requested a final goodbye session with his children, annual school pictures of them, an opportunity to receive letters from them if they chose to send them to him in the future, and the possibility of post-termination supervised visitation if the court was willing to consider an open adoption arrangement for his children.

Avoiding Evaluation and Consultation Errors

1. Be prepared to demonstrate to yourself and others that you are professionally competent to render a relevant opinion and that no issues of ethics are involved. Know the relevant literature and be prepared to discuss it with the referring party and during direct and cross-examination.
2. Ascertain the referral question, and work with referring party to frame the question in a manner that is conducive to the assessment process, competent professional practice, and ethical practice.

3. Choose a methodology that addresses the referral question through multimodal assessment. Use multiple actuarial devices or modes of assessment, standardized testing, review of records, and interviews of knowledgeable individuals.
4. The evaluation of risk and exacerbation of risk should be based on documented historical factors. The sequence of maltreatment behaviors, including baseline behavior, the acceleration stage, the act of maltreatment, recovery, and return to baseline should be analyzed for all previous known acts of child maltreatment in order to determine commonalities and differences, as well as trends over time, for a particular individual. When factors have changed over time, be prepared to discuss both the usefulness and the limitations of predictions, especially in light of changing conditions.
5. Consider contributing factors related to future parental incapacity or maltreatment based on previous triggering stimuli and based on the presence of new or changed factors. Bear in mind that individual triggers may contribute minimally to a maltreatment act, and some classes of offenders may not need triggers in order to perpetrate maltreatment, only the opportunity to do so without being caught.
6. Consider conditions that would lead to opportunities for future maltreatment, such as access to victims and other factors.
7. Consider inhibitions to child maltreatment based on past inhibitory stimuli and responses for that individual, and based on new or changed factors that might be inhibitory.
8. Interview methods and data gathering relevant to parenting capacity should be appropriately broadened or limited to address the parenting behaviors of relevance to the evaluation. Be mindful of cultural variations in childrearing. Specific measures of parenting behavior should be used only when relevant to the parenting behaviors of concern, and only when group or supplementary norms are available that are suitable for the individual.
9. To enhance reader comprehension, present the findings for each assessment measure individually prior to synthesizing the data into an interpretive summary.
10. Synthesize your conclusions and account for discrepant findings.
11. Highlight the replicability of your conclusions.
12. Present risk factors, mediating factors, and conditional predictions rather than dichotomous conclusions when describing the link, if any, between chronic substance abuse or dependence, brain impairment, and risk of parental incapacity or child maltreatment.
13. Limit the temporality of the predictions to avoid the perception of an interminable prediction. Give the level of risk for different portions of the time period if variation is to be expected (e.g., a greater risk of substance-abuse recidivism within close temporal proximity to initial sobriety; likelihood of further recovery of functioning from brain impairment secondary to stroke).
14. Specify in summary form the factors that contribute to the risk of child maltreatment, and those that might lower or lead to desistance of the risk of maltreatment. A balanced report includes a synopsis of the positive abilities and characteristics of the individual.
15. Suggest feedback mechanisms to assist others with future predictors of child maltreatment potential (e.g., re-evaluation in 1 year with the same instruments).

Writing Forensic Reports and Acting as an Expert Witness

The forensic report is a work of scientific practice that demands good literary and organizational skills (Condie and Condie, 2006). Features of forensic psychological assessment reports include the circumstances of the referral, the purpose of the evaluation, the way in which informed consent was obtained, the interviewee's comprehension of the notification of the limits of confidentiality, and any means for compensating for a lack of comprehension of confidentiality limits, if relevant. Reports include sources of data, documentation of clinical interviews of the individual and any collaterals, and assessment measures. The body of the report includes a review of the aspects of each document that bear upon the referral question, a summary of interview data, psychological assessment results, data interpretation, and a summary and recommendations. The summary might include formal opinions if they are relevant and indicated. Some reports might include appendices of psychological assessment scores, expanded transcripts of interviews, and diagrams or drawings (Nurcombe and Parlett, 1994). The evaluation report is both a clinical and a forensic document, the primary purpose of which is to describe and interpret relevant data. The process of creating a report is a literary one requiring skill in organization, integration, and synthesis of data (Burns and Quintar, 2001). The process also is an inferential one, requiring a cautious and conservative approach to decisions about the appropriate level of interpretation and conclusion. The key to a relevant and thorough but cogent report is the integration and interpretation of data in light of the original referral question. Interpretation is made within a theoretical and situational context. The tone should be respectful of the audience of readers, and it should highlight both the strengths and weaknesses in the examinee's functioning.

One format for organizing data interpretation is to reiterate the referral question, review the reliability and validity of the assessment and interview data, address the referral question, entertain competing explanations or hypotheses, and offer a conclusion as to why competing hypotheses remain viable or why they were ruled out. The process would include consideration of possible influences on the evaluation process and results (e.g., social desirability responding in caregivers or others, intentional or unintentional overzealousness, or preconceived notions in some collaterals with protective motives). A quality report is cogent, but it contains relevant descriptive information. It is useful to follow a structure within which the interpretation of data is offered; for example, develop an outline of the main points, address one or two main points within each paragraph, and summarize the interpretation in a final paragraph. Enumeration of points may be useful when the referral question is broad and the conclusions cover significant ground. Depending upon the breadth of the referral question, main points in a case like our case example might include a synopsis of areas of functioning and their relevance to critical aspects of childrearing: (a) the caregiver's cognitive functioning; (b) the caregiver's mental and behavioral organization; (c) the caregiver's skill level for finding his way around the city as needed; (d) the caregiver's capacity to remember critical appointments and arrive on time; (e) the caregiver's language functioning; (e) the caregiver's pragmatic and motivational capacity for relevant and appropriate verbal exchange with the children; (f) the caregiver's initiative and follow-through on tasks relevant to critical aspects of childrearing; (g) the caregiver's capacity to make and act upon sound childrearing decisions; (h) the caregiver's capacity to comply with and benefit from relevant treatment that reduces risk of sex offending and that improves his parenting abilities; (i) whether the hypothesized etiological factors (brain impairment related to chronic alcohol dependence and residual impairment secondary to stroke activity) are related to or exacerbate the potential for future sex offending; and (j) whether the hypothesized etiological factors contribute to or exacerbate already existing concern about parenting competence (Ayoub and Kinscherff, 2006; Condie, 2003). Opinions that are based, in part, on psychological assessment scores are integrated with observations and reliable information contained in the individual's records. Records provide data relevant to baseline functioning for behaviors or constructs of concern. Multimodal assessment, using either records or other forms of assessment to bolster conclusions, will guard against measurement error. Conclusions withstand challenges to reliability and validity to a greater extent when they are gleaned objectively from multiple sources (Budd, 2005; Condie, 2003; Ayoub and Kinscherff, 2006). It is important to consider the cultural relevance of the data (Budd, 2005). Cultural context, socioeconomic status, and other potential influences on the meaning of the data should be considered.

Standardized cognitive and neuropsychological assessment results are thought to reflect an individual's current functioning and coping resources, approaches to problem solving, fluidity of thinking and language functioning, social-emotional strengths and weakness, level of organization, memory functioning, and perceptions of the world. Standardized testing may significantly enhance an assessment when interpreted in conjunction with other components of the evaluation. When applicable, sources describing premorbid functioning are used to illustrate areas that have remained static and those that have changed. If relevant to the referral question, the risks and benefits of parental reunification with the child would be viewed in light of all potentially contributing factors, not just those relevant to cognitive and neuropsychological functioning. If some of the factors were addressed by other evaluators, as in this case, appropriate limits would be placed on conclusions and recommendations. The structure of a permanent plan for the parent and child, if relevant, would be made in light of all contributing factors. An analysis of whether brain impairment contributes to the risk would be conducted in light of other possible complications and contributing factors. In writing a summary about the impact of chronic alcohol dependence and stroke on current functioning, the evaluator must use caution not to overstate or understate opinions. Opinions must be carefully defended by the information gathered in the body of the report. If there are ambiguities in the information, the evaluator would describe them and draw conclusions from clear and converging data and not mere assumptions (Budd, 2005; Ayoub and Kinscherff, 2006; Condie, 2003). When brain impairment is judged to contribute to parenting deficiencies or risk of future child maltreatment, it is important to include or rule out other possible contributing factors, such as the normal effects of aging, situational stress or crises, preexisting cognitive limitations, or other possible factors (Condie, 2003). Risk should be characterized in the context of caregiver strengths and weaknesses, and within the framework of the caregiver's need to respond to the child's level of development (Condie and Condie, 2006).

Judgments about amenability to treatment are based on what is known about the efficacy and predictive validity of various treatment methods, their applicability to child maltreatment, and their relevance in light of the individual's integrity of brain functioning, intellect, or level of education. Other relevant factors include the individual's attendance and participation in the rehabilitation, information from rehabilitation providers, the caregiver's self-assessment of rehabilitation impact, and the caregiver's ability to demonstrate or describe what they have acquired from rehabilitation (Condie, 2003; Condie and Condie, 2006).

Amenability may depend upon the availability of ongoing support, monitoring, or supervision (Mohit, 1996). Amenability judgments are based on supporting treatment outcome data, with appropriate caveats relevant to the fact that clinical outcome research typically is based on pure clinical samples, but care and protection samples usually contain individuals with complex comorbidity of mental health, medical, or substance-abuse issues (Condie, 2003). Outcome data frequently lack specificity to individuals with complex diagnostic concerns, or environmental complications, such as low socioeconomic status (Hipwell and Kumar, 1996). For example, much is known about expectations of treatment compliance and treatment progress in samples of substance abusers (Marlatt, Blume, and Parks, 2001), but less is known about expected treatment progress when substance abuse interacts with the stress of legal actions (Mejta and Lavin, 1996). Treatments that target specific behavioral indicators usually are more effective in the short term (Piper and Joyce, 2001). For some forms of cognitive rehabilitation, the duration of untreated symptoms is predictive of treatment outcome (Lezak, 1995). Character pathology and associated problems are predictive of poor outcomes, with antisocial characteristics having a particularly pronounced effect on risk of relapse (Galen, Brower, Gillespie, and Zucker, 2000). The predictive effect of addiction severity is mediated by employment (Marlatt et al., 2001). Positive outcomes in self-help treatment groups are linked to the individual's commitment to self-help practices, meeting attendance, and subjective impressions of the principles of the approach (Tonigan, Miller, and Connors, 2000). Amenability to treatment is described in the context of individual variables and theories and supporting data about expected treatment outcomes. Judgments about expected time frames for treatment should be addressed with appropriate caveats. Opinions as to whether a parent has demonstrated adequate treatment benefit should be rendered with cautionary comments about the limitations of the predictive validity of treatment outcome studies (Condie, 2003).

The report must be carefully planned, and it must be meaningful to the reader (Burns and Quintar, 2001). Awareness of legal decision-making patterns also is important. Reports that place too much emphasis on diagnoses, personality characteristics, or general intellectual functioning of parents neglect the law's concerns about the impact, if any, of those factors on parenting abilities. The concept of competence requires a description of how limitations relate to parenting, if at all (Grisso et al., 2002). Cognitive and neuropsychological assessment data may reveal a variety of deficits, but if they are irrelevant to the parenting abilities of concern, then it is essential to acknowledge this directly in the report. When the data are relevant to parenting abilities of concern, the relevance should be described logically and cogently. A systematic approach to report structure and content promotes clarity, thoroughness, and meaningfulness. The most common readers of care and protection evaluation reports are attorneys and judges. From the standpoint of the reader, what is required is thoroughness without wordiness, relevance to the legal issues in question, logic, comprehensible language, and a report structure that is standardized when indicated because of jurisdictional requirements (Nurcombe and Parlett, 1994). Attorneys commonly review the report with their client prior to court hearings. Comprehensible language facilitates this process and minimizes the possibility of miscomprehension of the report (Condie, 2003).

Expert testimony involves a preparatory phase of reviewing credentials and an offer of the suitability of the expert as a proper subject for expert testimony. A copy of the expert's resume or summary of professional credentials and qualifications is usually requested. The process of *voir dire* serves the purposes of questioning the witness about his or her credentials and qualifications. Direct examination is used to enhance the expert's credibility in the eyes of the trier of fact, and questions are aimed at qualifying the witness as an expert so that he or she may offer opinion testimony. The process provides an opportunity for opposing counsel to question the qualifications of the witness or to raise doubt as to the basis for the expertise of the witness. The judge has the discretion to refuse to allow the witness to offer expert or opinion testimony (Ewing, 2003). Preparation for court testimony includes preparation for this process, and it also includes a variety of techniques related to the content of testimony: using contact sheets to document conversations, telephone calls, and procedures; keeping records of all interviews, assessment measures, dates, and duration of contact; and keeping billing records current. Some evaluators find it useful to keep case records in folders with tabbed sections for copies of laws, statutes and regulations, scientific articles relevant to the case, legal documents relevant to the case, other documents, psychological assessment raw data and results, letters pertinent to the case, informed consent documents and release of information forms, and the forensic evaluation report (Nurcombe and Parlett, 1994). Some evaluators find it useful to schedule a pretrial conference with the retaining attorney. Some judges will call pretrial conferences. The process of pretrial participation and court testimony is facilitated by preparation and organization, and the evaluator is best served by learning his or her optimal strategies (Condie, 2003). Testimony, whether given at deposition or trial, is given under oath or affirmation. The expert witness is first questioned by the attorney who issued the subpoena for testimony, and then the expert is subject to cross-examination. Cross-examination is limited to the scope of questions asked on direct examination, but the scope often is interpreted liberally. After cross-examination, there may be a redirect examination. Redirect is limited to the scope of the preceding cross-examination. There may be further recross and redirect until the attorneys have exhausted their questions. Afterward, the witness is usually excused, but judges sometimes exercise the prerogative to question witnesses. If judicial questioning occurs, there may be further redirect and recross. The rules dictate what types of questions are allowed on direct and cross-examination. Most rules of evidence, whether based on statutory or common law, require experts to specify the bases for their opinions (Ewing, 2003).

Summary

The case example highlights the complexity and the relevance of referral questions that require the expert to integrate specialized knowledge and experience relevant to forensic clinical assessment, neuropsychological assessment, cognitive assessment, and the relationship between indices of functioning and parenting competence. Although there are isolated cases in which risk changes remarkably (for better or worse) because of changing parental mental status, it is rare that these indices, by themselves, substantially change the outcome of an overall risk matrix relevant to parental risk of maltreatment. If relevant to risk of child maltreatment, the contribution of these factors more often is mild to moderate. Even when factors have been identified as empirically related to future maltreatment, it is rare that any single factor is highly predictive. An analysis of cumulative risk is required, but with appropriate caveats about the state of the science. Expertise from professionals in psychology and medicine is needed to clarify the relevance and significance of cognitive and neuropsychological factors in the context of other relevant risk factors, in light of the case circumstances, and in the context of recommended interventions or reunification plans for the parent. Clinicians who assist courts in addressing a parent's capacities in relation to care and protection or termination standards are advised to engage in the following procedures: (a) know the relevant legal standards and how they have been used in law and translated into psychological constructs that bear a conceptual relation to the legal standards as they have been interpreted and applied by the courts; (b) rely upon a theoretical and empirical foundation, appropriate assessment methods, and adequate professional training; (c) use methods to collect data relevant to the psychological constructs derived from the application of those legal standards; and (d) interpret and communicate the evaluation results in a manner that aids the court in understanding their relevance to the legal standards that guide judicial decisions.

References

American Academy of Psychiatry and the Law. (1995). *Ethical Guidelines for the Practice of Forensic Psychiatry.* Bloomfield, CT: Author.

American Psychological Association. (1990). *Guidelines for Providers of Psychological Services to Ethnic, Linguistic, and Culturally Diverse Populations.* Washington, DC: Author.

American Psychological Association. (1993). Record keeping guidelines. *American Psychologist, 48,* 984–986.

American Psychological Association. (1999). *Standards for Educational and Psychological Testing* (2nd ed.). Washington, DC: Author.

American Psychological Association, Committee on Professional Practice and Standards. (1998). *Guidelines for Psychological Evaluations in Child Protection Matters.* Washington, DC: Author.

American Psychological Association. (2002). *Ethical Principles of Psychologists and Code of Conduct.* Washington, DC: Author.

Ayoub, C., and Kinscherff, R. (2006). Forensic assessment of parenting in child abuse and neglect cases. In S. Sparta and G. Koocher (Eds.), *Forensic Mental Health Assessment of Children and Adolescents* (pp. 330–341). New York: Oxford.

Berlin, R., and Davis, R. B. (1989). Children from alcoholic families: Vulnerability. In T. F. Dugan and R. Coles (Eds.), *The Child in Our Homes: Studies in the Development of Resiliency* (pp. 81–108). New York: Brunner/Mazel.

Bernardi, E., Jones, M., and Tennant, C. (1989). Quality of parenting in alcoholism and narcotic addicts. *British Journal of Psychiatry, 154,* 677–682.

Budd, K. (2005). Assessing parenting capacity in a child welfare context. *Children and Youth Services Review, 27,* 429–444.

Budd, K. S., Poindexter, L. M., Felix, E. D., and Naik-Polan, A. T. (2001). Clinical assessment of parents in child protection cases: An empirical analysis. *Law and Human Behavior, 25,* 93–108.

Burns, W. J., and Quintar, B. (2001). Integrated report writing. In W. I. Dorfman, and M. Hersen (Eds.), *Understanding Psychological Assessment: Perspectives on Individual Differences* (pp. 353–371). New York: Kluwer-Plenum.

Chasnoff, I. J. (1988). Drug use in pregnancy: Parameters of risk. *Pediatric Clinics of North America, 35,* 1408–1412.

Condie, L. (2003). *Parenting Evaluations for the Court* (Vol. 18, Perspective in Law and Psychology). New York: Kluwer-Plenum.

Condie, L., and Condie D. (2006). Termination of parental rights. In A. M. Goldstein (Ed.), *Forensic Psychology: Emerging Topics and Expanding Roles* (pp. 294–330). New York: Wiley.

Crenshaw, W., and Barnum, D. (2001). You can't fight the system: Strategies of family justice in foster care reintegration. *Family Journal: Counseling and Therapy for Couples and Families, 9,* 29–36.

Dube, S., Anda, R., Felitti, V. Croft, J., Edwards, V., and Giles, W. (2001). Growing up with parental alcohol abuse: Exposure to childhood abuse, neglect, and household dysfunction. *Child Abuse & Neglect, 25,* 1627–1640.

Dubowitz, H. (1999). The families of neglected children. In M. E. Lamb (Ed.), *Parenting and Child Development in "Nontraditional" Families* (pp. 327–345). Mahwah, NJ: Erlbaum.

Ducharme, J., and Davidson, A. (2004). Ameliorating the effects of violent behavior in a mother with brain injury: Intervention to improve parent–child cooperation. *Clinical Case Studies, 3*, 95–106.

Ewing, C. (2003). Expert testimony: Law and practice. In A. Goldstein and I. Weiner (Eds.), *Handbook of Psychology* (pp. 55–66, Vol. 11, Forensic Psychology). New York: Wiley.

Famularo, R., Kinscherff, R., and Fenton, T. (1992). Parental substance abuse and the nature of child maltreatment. *Child Abuse & Neglect, 16*, 475–483.

Farrell, M., Barnes, G., and Banerjee, S. (1995). Family cohesion as a buffer against the effects of problem-drinking fathers on psychological distress, deviant behavior, and heavy drinking in adolescents. *Journal of Health and Social Behavior, 36*, 337–385.

Galen, L. W., Brower, K. J., Gillespie, B. W., and Zucker, R. A. (2000). Sociopathy, gender, and treatment outcome among outpatient substance abusers. *Drug & Alcohol Dependence, 61*, 23–33.

Goldstein, R. D. (1999). *Child Abuse and Neglect: Cases and Materials.* St. Paul, MN: West.

Grisso, T., Otto, R., Borum, R., Edens, J., and Moye, J. (2002). *Evaluating Competencies: Forensic Assessment and Instruments.* (2nd ed.; Vol. 16, Perspective in Law and Psychology). New York: Kluwer-Plenum.

Hanson, R. K. (1997). *The Development of a Brief Actuarial Risk Scale for Sexual Offense Recidivism* (User Report 97-04). Ottowa: Department of the Solicitor General of Canada.

Hanson, R. K. (2004). Evaluating community sex offender treatment programs: A 12-year follow-up of 724 offenders. *Canadian Journal of Behavioural Science, 36*, 87–96.

Hanson, R. K., and Thornton, D. (2000) Improving risk assessments for sex offenders: A comparison of three actuarial scales. *Law and Human Behavior, 24*, 119–136.

Haugland, B., and Havik, O. (1998). Correlates of family competence in families with paternal alcohol abuse. *Psychological Reports, 83*, 867–880.

Heilbrun, K., Warren, J., and Picarello, K. (2003). Third party information in forensic assessment. In A. Goldstein and I. Weiner (Eds.), *Handbook of Psychology* (pp. 69–86, Vol. 11, Forensic Psychology). New York: Wiley.

Hester, R., and Miller, W. (Eds.). (1989). *Handbook of Alcoholism Treatment Approaches.* New York: Pergamon.

Hipwell, A. E., and Kumar, R. (1996). Maternal psychopathology and prediction of outcome based on mother-infant interaction ratings (BMIS). *British Journal of Psychiatry, 169*, 655–661.

Jacob, T., Leonard, K., and Haber J. R. (2001). Family interactions of alcoholics as related to alcoholism type and drinking condition. *Alcoholism: Clinical and Experimental Research, 25*, 835–843.

Kelley, S. J. (1992). Parenting stress and child maltreatment in drug-exposed children. *Child Abuse and Neglect, 16*, 317–328.

Kerr, S. (2000). The application of the Americans with Disabilities Act to the termination of the parental rights of individuals with mental disabilities. *Journal of Contemporary Health Law and Policy, 16*, 387–426.

Koocher, G. P., and Keith-Spiegel, P. C. (1990). *Children, Ethics, & the Law: Professional Issues and Cases.* Lincoln: University of Nebraska Press.

Lezak, M. (1995). *Neuropsychological Assessment* (3rd ed.). New York: Oxford.

Marlatt, G. A., Blume, A. W., and Parks, G. A. (2001). Integrating harm reduction therapy and traditional substance abuse treatment. *Journal of Psychoactive Drugs, 33*, 13–21.

Matarazzo, J. D. (1990). Psychological assessment versus psychological testing: Validation from Binet to the school, clinic, and courtroom. *American Psychologist, 45*, 999–1017.

Mejta, C. L., and Lavin, R. (1996). Facilitating health parenting among mothers with substance abuse or dependence problems: Some considerations. *Alcoholism Treatment Quarterly, 14*, 33–46.

Miller, B. A. (1990). The interrelationships between alcohol and drugs and family violence. *National Institute on Drug Abuse Research Monograph Series, 103*, 177–207.

Mohit, D. L. (1996). Management and care of mentally ill mothers of young children: An innovative program. *Archives of Psychiatric Nursing, 10,* 49–54.

Monahan, J., Steadman, H. J., Appelbaum, P. S., Robbins, P. C., Mulvey, E. P., Silver, E., Roth, L. H., and Grisso, T. (2000). Developing a clinically useful actuarial tool for assessing violence risk. *British Journal of Psychiatry, 176,* 312–319.

Moncher, F. J. (1996). The relationship of maternal adult attachment style and risk of physical child abuse. *Journal of Interpersonal Violence, 11,* 335–350.

Moser, R., and Frantz, C. (2004). The neuropsychological consequences of alcohol and drug abuse. In J. Brick (Ed.), *Handbook of the Medical Consequences of Alcohol and Drug Abuse* (pp. 49–83). New York: Haworth.

Muller, R., Fitzgerald, H., Sullivan, L., and Zucker, R. (1994). Social support and stress factors in child maltreatment among alcoholic families. *Canadian Journal of Behavioural Science, 26,* 438–461.

Mukamal, K. J., Ascherio, A., Mittleman, M. A., Conigrave, K. M., Camargo Jr., C. A., Kawachi, I., Stampfer, M. J., Willett, W. C., and Rimm, E. B. (2005). Alcohol and risk for ischemic stroke in men: The role of drinking patterns and usual beverage. *Annals of Internal Medicine, 142, 1,* pp. 11–22.

Murphy, J. M., Jellinek, M., Quinn, D., Smith, G., Poitrast, F. G., and Goshko, M. (1991). Substance abuse and serious child mistreatment: Prevalence, risk, and outcome in a court sample. *Child Abuse & Neglect, 15,* 197–211.

Nayak, M., and Milner, J. (1998). Neuropsychological functioning: Comparison of mothers and high- and low-risk for child physical abuse. *Child Abuse & Neglect, 22,* 687–703.

Nurcombe, B., and Parlett, D. F. (1994). *Child Mental Health and the Law.* New York: Free Press.

Ogloff, J. R. P. (1999). Ethical and legal contours of forensic psychology. In R. Roesch, S. D. Hart, and J. R. P. Ogloff (Eds.), *Psychology and Law: The State of the Discipline* (Perspectives in Law and Psychology, Vol. 10, pp. 405–422). New York: Kluwer-Plenum.

Oscar-Berman, M., and Schendan, H.E. (1999). Asymmetries of brain function in alcoholism: relationship to aging. In L. Obler and L.T. Connor (Eds.), *Neurobehavior of Language and Cognition: Studies of Normal Aging and Brain Damage.* New York: Kluwer Academic Publishers.

Pessar, L., Coad, M., Linn, R., and Willer, B. (1993). The effects of parental traumatic brain injury on the behaviour of parents and children. *Brain Injury, 7,* 231–240.

Pfefferbaum, A., Lim, K., Zipursky, R., Mathalon, D., Rosenbloom, M., Lane, B., Ha, C., and Sullivan, E. (1992). Brain gray and white matter volume loss accelerates with aging in chronic alcoholics: A quantitative MRI study. *Alcohol Clinical Experimental Research, 16,* 1078–1089.

Pfefferbaum, A., Sullivan E., Mathalon, D., and Lim, K. (1997). Frontal lobe volume loss observed with magnetic resonance imaging in older chronic alcoholics. *Alcohol Clinical Experimental Research, 21,* 521–592.

Piper, W. E., and Joyce, A. S. (2001). *Psychosocial Treatment Outcome.* In W. J. Livesley (Ed.), *Handbook of Personality Disorders: Theory, Research, and Treatment* (pp. 323–343). New York: Guilford.

Preston, K. A., Kramer, J. H., and Blusewicz, M. J. (1989). Prose memory in chronic alcoholics: Performance on the California Discourse Memory Test. *Journal of Clinical and Experimental Neuropsychology, 11,* 61–62.

Rosenbloom, M., Pfefferbaum, A., and Sullivan, E. (1995). Structural brain alterations associated with alcoholism. *Alcohol Health Research World, 19,* 266–272.

Shelman, E. A., and Lazoritz, S. (2005). *The Mary Ellen Wilson Child Abuse Case and the Beginning of Children's Rights in 19th Century America.* Jefferson, NC: McFarland.

Shimamura, A. P., Jernigan, T. L., and Squire, L. R. (1988). Korsakoff's syndrome: Radiological (CT) findings and neuropsychological correlates. *Journal of Neuroscience, 8,* 4400–4410.

Steadman, H. J., Silver, E., Monahan, J., Appelbaum, P. S., Robbins, P. C., Mulvey, E, P., Grisso, T., Roth, L. H., and Banks, S. (2000). A classification tree approach to the development of actuarial violence risk assessment tools. *Law & Human Behavior, 24,* 83–100.

Sweet, J. (1999). *Forensic Neuropsychology: Fundamentals and Practice.* Rotterdam, the Netherlands: A. A. Balkema.

Tarter, R. E., Blackson, T., Martin, C., Loeber, R., and Moss, H. B. (1993). Characteristics and correlates of child discipline practices in substance abuse and normal families. *The American Journal on Addictions, 2,* 18–25.

Tonigan, J. S., Miller, W. R., and Connors, G. J. (2000). Project MATCH client impressions about alcoholics anonymous: Measurement issues and relationship to treatment outcome. *Alcoholism Treatment Quarterly, 18,* 25–41.

van Gorp, W. (2006). Neuropsychology for the forensic psychologist. In A. M. Goldstein (Ed.), *Forensic Psychology: Emerging Topics and Expanding Roles* (pp. 154–168). New York: Wiley.

Walker, L. E. A. (1990). Psychological assessment of sexually abused children for legal evaluation and expert witness testimony. *Professional Psychology: Research and Practice, 21,* 344–353.

Wolfe, D. A. (1988). Child abuse and neglect. In E. J. Mash and L. G. Terdal (Eds.), *Behavioural Assessment of Childhood Disorders* (2nd ed., pp. 627–669). New York: Guilford.

Zilmer, E., and Green, H. (2006). Neuropsychological assessment in the forensic setting. In R. Archer (Ed.), *Forensic Uses of Clinical Assessment Instruments* (pp. 209–227). Mahwah, NJ: Erlbaum.

Legal References

Adoption of Nancy, 61 Mass. App. Ct. 252; 809 N.E.2d 554 (2004).

The Americans with Disabilities Act (ADA), 42 U.S.C. section 12101 *et seq.* (1990).

Buck v. Bell, 274 U.S. 200 (1927).

D.P. v. Department of Children and Family Services, 930 So.2d 798, Fla. App. (2006).

E.T. v. State of Florida and Department of Children and Families, 930 So.2d 721, Fla. App. (2006).

Florida Department of Children and Families v. F.L., 880 So.2d 602, Fl. App. (2004).

Harris v. Campbell County Department of Social Services, Records No. 0741-0403, Va. App. (2004).

In the Interest of A.S.W., 137 S.W.3d 448 453 (Mo. Banc 2004).

In the Interest of Micah Alyn R., 202 W. Va. 400, 504 S.E.2d 635 (1998).

In the Interest of N.R.W., 112 S.W.3d 465 469 (Mo. App. 2003).

In re Adoption/Guardianship Nos. CAA92-10852 & CAA92-10853 in the Circuit Court for Prince George's County, 103 Md.App. 1, 651 A.2d 891 (1994).

In re A.M.A., No. COA05-1472, Ct. App. North Carolina (2006).

In re Elijah R., 620 A.2d 282, 284 (Me. 1993).

In re Glenn G., 154 Misc.2d 677, 587 N.Y.S.2d 464 (N.Y.Fam.Ct.1992).

In re Gregory C., San Diego County Health and Human Services Agency v. Beatriz Q., D044252, Ct. App. Cal., 4th App. Dist. (2005).

In re J.K., Siskiyou County Dept. of Human Services v. G. K. et al., C036314, C036844, Ct. App. Cal., 3d App. Dist. (2002).

In re J.K., Siskiyou County Dept. of Human Services Dept. v. Gary F. et al. C043702, Ct. App. Cal., 3d App. Dist. (2004).

In re Jose Y., 177A.D.2d 580,576 N.Y.S.2d 297 (1991).

In re Joshua J. et al., Orange County Social Services Agency v. Jason S., G036186, G036298, Ct. App. Cal., 4th App. Dist. (2006).

In re Joshua R., Sharon R., and Marty R. v. the Department of Social and Health Services, 91 Wash. App. 1073 (1998).

In re K.F., 437 N.W.2d 559 (Iowa 1989).

In re Rayvon T., Los Angeles County Dept. of Children and Family Services v. Rayvon T., Sr., B188251 Ct. App. Cal., 2d App. Dist. (2006).

In re Scott G., 124 A.D.2d 928, 508 N.Y.S.2d 669 (1986).

In re Torrence P., 522 N.W.2d at 243, Wis. Ct. App. (1994).

In re Victoria M. v. Carmen S., 207 Cal. App.3d 1317 (1989).

Lassiter v. Department of Social Services, 452 U.S. 18 (1981).

Orangeberg County Department of Social Services v. Harley, 393 S.E.2d 597, S.C.Ct. App. (1990).

Otey v. Roanoke City Department of Social Services, Record No. 2558-0503, V. App. (2006).

R. G. v. Marion County Office, Department of Family & Children, 647 N.E.2d 326 (Ind. Ct. App. 1995).

S.T. v. State Department of Human Resources, 579 So.2d 640, Ala. Civ. App. (1991).

Santosky v. Kramer, 455 U.S. 745 (1982).

State of Louisiana in the Interest of A.T., T.A., & J.A., No. 2006-CJ-0501, Sup. Ct. Louisiana (2006).

Violence in the Family: Including Lethal Outcome

5

JOSEPH G. POIRIER

Independent Practice, Rockville, Maryland

Contents

Synopsis of Case

The Brown family consisting of Mr and Mrs Brown and four children lived in a subsided farmhouse in a rural area with just over three acres of land. Neither parent worked, Mr Brown was disabled with a work-related back injury; he had been employed as a truck driver. The family subsisted on various sources of welfare. Police involvement arose when neighbors complained about heavy traffic in and out of the Brown's property and "loud parties" once or twice a week. Upon investigation, police discovered a well-cultivated patch of thriving cannabis plants in a small garden. In contrast, hundreds of photos taken by the police reflected multiple forms of animal excrement, rotting food dirty laundry, and, generally, unbelievably filthy living conditions. The police confiscated 11 huge garbage bags of mostly adult-oriented pornographic books, magazines, and movies. In addition, police confiscated a life-size male store manikin with plaster-exaggerated genitals and glued-on pubic hair. Splotches of what appeared to be dried semen covered the manikin.

Child welfare service (CWS) removed the children from the home, and Mrs Brown went to stay at neighbors near where the children were in temporary placement. On the evening following the initial investigation, alarmed neighbors notified police of multiple gunshots coming from the location of the Brown's home. Investigation revealed an unconscious and gravely wounded Mr Brown. Mr Brown's upper body had multiple gunshot penetrations; the police recovered no weapon.

Initially, police theorized that one or more individuals who had purchased illicit substances from the Browns had returned fearing their identity would be disclosed in any investigation. Continued investigation, however, cast suspicion on Mrs Brown. Eventually, Mrs Brown confessed, and she was initially charged with attempted first-degree murder (plea-bargaining later resulted in a reduced charge of attempted second-degree murder). Mrs Brown described that in her distress with her circumstances, she returned to the home to find a stash of cocaine that she had hidden. Mrs Brown searched several places in the home, and she found a stash of cocaine, several hundred dollars, and a handgun under an attic floorboard. Mrs Brown stated to police that she snorted the cocaine. When she attempted to leave, Mr Brown interfered and Mrs Brown fatally shot him. Mrs Brown stated that she was already angry with Mr Brown over what had happened. The police report indicated that nine of 12 rounds from the handgun struck Mr Brown in the upper torso. Fortunately, Mr Brown eventually recovered from his wounds.

A juvenile court-ordered psychological evaluation on behalf of the children reflected the obvious disarray in the family matrix. Most striking was the impact of the parents' behavior on the children. The two older children spoke with disdain about the family circumstances noting that when they were younger, "it wasn't so bad." The two younger siblings complained of ongoing ridicule by peers at school because of their poor hygiene, and because of their worn and out-of-style clothing. The court placed the children temporarily with a paternal aunt and uncle.

In the criminal trial, defense experts had argued that Mrs Brown suffered from an involuntary, acute, drug-induced psychosis, rendering a lack of criminal responsibility. The prosecution successfully counter-argued that by Mrs Brown's own admission, she was voluntarily and acutely intoxicated immediately prior to the tragic event. A jury returned a guilty verdict. The bench ordered a presentencing psychological evaluation to generate dispositional recommendations to include a risk assessment of Mrs Brown's potential for spousal abuse recidivism.

Introduction

This chapter updates the 10 years of research regarding the problem of family violence since our chapter of the same title (Poirier, 1996) in the first edition of this book. Lethal family violence in the family is fortunately only a small part of the much broader problem of intimate partner and other family member violence. Different studies have adopted different definitions of family violence ranging from physical violence to acts of forced sex, or a combination of both. This inconsistency of definitions has only served to confuse the landscape of domestic violence. All domestic violence involves components of victim psychological humiliation and personal disparagement that can be long lasting and incapacitating (Campbell, 2002).

Lethal violence connotes circumstances of actual death or the potential for death. In nonfamily circumstances, lethal violence incidence and prevalence data are captured in statistics citing the number of victims, the number of offenders, and victim and offender characteristics. Violence in the family, however, is a significantly more complicated matter. Some readers may share the author's more-than-occasional contemplations of how the traditional structure and meaning of the family have undergone a major metamorphosis in contemporary western culture. Nevertheless, the family remains the core social institution in present-day society. All families have extended intergenerational histories, they have vibrant current existences, and they have futures that will determine and maintain future society and culture. Family violence, lethal or otherwise, is an event that jeopardizes healthy and normal evolution of family process.

Any professional who has worked with troubled families can attest to how families can maintain torrid, anger-laden stability for weeks, months, and even years, but then as with our Brown family case history above, something happens to trigger a violent incident. As with the Brown family, the precise dynamics of violence within a family are not always immediately apparent, but in most instances, the vulnerable family will have a history of conflict that was not well managed. That history often serves as a backdrop to an episode of explosive, aggressive behavior. There are, of course, instances of family violence perpetrated by a mentally ill family member, or secondary to substance abuse, but even in these situations, there is usually a discernable history of ongoing mounting personal tension and ultimately domestic violence.

Statistical data regarding arrests, convictions, and sentencing of domestic violence offenders can provide the reader with a quick snapshot as to the magnitude of the problem. Not revealed in such demographic data, however, are the social, psychological, and economic costs of domestic violence (Dutton and Kropp, 2000). Unfortunately, there is no single source of data that accurately or comprehensively documents the scope and extent of domestic violence. The reasons for this are varied, but the inadequate data are principally due to the logistical problem of collecting and analyzing the massive amount of ever-accumulating national data in a timely way. In addition, peculiar to domestic violence as compared with other forms of violence, caring family members notoriously underreport domestic violence. No one knows the actual extent of unreported domestic violence. Similarly, investigating local police officials are often more sympathetic to circumstances of domestic violence compared to their sentiments with stranger-to-stranger violence. For these reasons, the array of family violence data that is available can be misleading in its shortcomings.

A primary source of all violence data nationwide is the U.S. Bureau of Justice [Bureau of Justice Statistics (BJS), 2002]. The Bureau of Justice data regarding domestic violence is categorized into five areas: (1) physical or (2) sexual assault of adult family members, (3) physical or (4) sexual abuse of children, and (5) physical abuse of the elderly. We will utilize these five categories as one basis for the organization of this chapter. In the author's experience of conducting hundreds of court-ordered assessments of family matters, actual or potential violent behavior is a disturbingly common denominator with troubled family situations.

During the period 1993 to 2002, the rate of family violence dropped by more than half (Durose, Harlow, Langan, Motivans, Rantala, and Smith, 2005). This decrease represented a drop from an estimated 5.4 victims to 2.1 victims per 1000 U.S. residents who were 12 years or older. The decrease reflected a general drop in crime against persons for the same period. Data from the Bureau of Justice indicated that from 1998 to 2002 family violence represented an estimated 11% of all reported and unreported violence. Of these offenses, 49% were crimes against a spouse, 11% were a parent attacking a child, and 41%

were against another family member. In 73% of the family violence incidents, the victims were females and in 76% of the incidents, the perpetrators were males. In 39% of the incidents, drugs or alcohol were involved and in 20% of the cases, the offender had a weapon.

The most recent BJS on family violence (Durose et al., 2005) were compiled in 2005 and based on family violence occurring in 2002. "This compendium contains the most recent family violence statistics from these sources: surveys conducted by the Bureau of Justice Statistics (BJS), the BJS database of federal statistics, and two statistical databases maintained by the FBI" (p. 1).

Table 5.1 presents highlights from the 2002 family violence statistics compiled by BJS. Among other findings, the Table 5.1 data reflect that as in previous years, females were the majority of family violence victims and males were the majority of family violence offenders. The majority of family violence victims and offenders are white, and most family violence occurs in or near the family residence. Spouses, then other family members, then children comprise the order of frequency of victims of family violence.

Table 5.2 presents highlights of BJS family violence data as staged through different points of the adjudication process including local, state, and federal courts and detention facilities. The data in Table 5.3 present a summary of demographics from BJS compiled data specifically regarding lethal family violence.

Table 5.1   Highlights from the 2005 Bureau of Justice Statistics (BJS) Data Regarding Family-Based Violence[a]

From 1993 to 2002

The rate of family violence fell from an estimated 5.4 victims to 2.1 victims per 1000 U.S. residents 12 or older. Family violence accounted for 1 in 10 violent victimizations.

From 1998 to 2002

Family violence accounted for 11% of all reported and unreported violence.

Of these 3.5 million violent crimes committed against family members, 49% were crimes against spouses, 11% were sons or daughters victimized by a parent, and 41% were crimes against other family members.

Simple assault was the most frequent type of family violence offense. Murder was less than half of 1% of all family violence.

About 75% of all family violence occurred in or near the victim's residence.

The majority (73%) of family violence victims were females and the majority (75%) of family violence perpetrators were males.

Most family violence victims were white (74%) and the majority between ages 25 and 4 (65.7%). Most family violence offenders were white (79%) and most were age 30 or older (62%).

In 2002

About 22% of murders were family murders. Nearly 9% were murders of a spouse, 6% were murders of sons or daughters by a parent, and 7% were murders by another family member.

Females were 58% of family murder victims. Of all the murders of females, family members were responsible for 43%.

Children under age 13 were 23% of murder victims killed by a family member and just over 3% of nonfamily member murder victims.

The average age among sons or daughters killed by a parent was 7 years, and four of five victims killed by a parent were under age 13.

Eight in 10 murderers who killed a family member were males. Males were 83% of spouse murderers.

Parents were the least likely family murderers to use a firearm (28%), compared to spouses (63%), or other family members (51%).

Among incidents of parents killing their children, 19% involved one parent killing multiple victims.

Note: Adapted from Durose et al., 2005 (see text).

[a] These BJS statistics are collective for the years 1998 through 2002 (see text).

Table 5.2   Highlights of Bureau of Justice Statistics (BJS) Data Regarding Family Violence Matters at Different Points in the Adjudication Process[a]

Family Violence Reported to Police

Approximately 60% of family violence victimizations reported to police. There were no significant differences in reporting rates by female or male victims.

The most common reason for a family violence incident not being reported to police was the incident was a "private/personal" matter (34%).

Another 12% of victims stated that reports were not made to police in order to "protect the offender."

Of the 2.1 million incidents of family violence reported to police, 36% resulted in arrests.

A weapon was used in 16% of family violence compared to 21% of nonfamily violence.

Forty-nine percent of family violence cases resulted in an arrest.

State Prosecution of Family Assault

In state courts, 84% of defendants charged with family violence had at least one prior arrest.

Nearly half of defendants charged with family violence were released pending case disposition.

Family assault defendants had greater probability of conviction (71%) compared to nonfamily assault defendants (61%).

Sixty-eight percent of family assault sentences were to incarceration compared to 62% of nonfamily assault cases.

Forty-five percent of persons sent to prison for family assault received a sentence of more than 2 years compared to 77% of nonfamily assault offenders sent to prison.

Federal Prosecution of Domestic Violence

Persons suspected of domestic violence made up 4% of the total suspects referred to U.S. attorneys for alleged violent crimes from 2000 to 2002.

Most domestic violence suspects referred to U.S. attorneys were firearm-related domestic violence offenses rather than interstate domestic violence offenses between 2000 and 2002.

The Bureau of Alcohol, Tobacco, Firearms, and Explosives accounted for 80% of all referrals for firearm-related domestic violence.

The FBI accounted for 72% of all interstate domestic violence referrals.

Federal courts convicted 90% of defendants adjudicated for an interstate domestic violence offense.

Of the federal court convictions, 79% were the product of a guilty plea and the remaining 21% were the product of a conviction following a trial.

Most convictions were of male offenders (96%), under age 40 (67%), white (72%), and non-Hispanic.

Four in five defendants had a prior adult conviction.

Family Violence Offenders in Prison

In 1997, of the nearly 500,000 men and women in state prisons for a violent crime, 15% were there for a violent crime against a family member.

In 1997, nearly half of all the family violence offenders in state prisons were serving a sentence for a sex offense against a family member.

More than three-quarters of parents convicted of a violent crime against their son or daughter were in prison for a sex offense.

About 90% of offenders in state prisons for family violence had injured their victim.

Fifty percent of family violence victims were either raped or sexually assaulted.

Twenty-eight percent of the victims of family violence were murdered.

Family Violence Offenders in Local Jails

In 2002, convicted family violence offenders made up about 22% of the nearly 86,500 convicted violent offenders in local jails.

Seventy-nine percent of the victims of local jail inmates convicted of family violence were females.

Nearly 30% of the victims were under age 18.

Local jail inmates convicted of family violence injured 55% of their victims.

Most local jail inmates convicted of family violence (81%) did not use a weapon.

Forty-five percent of local jail inmates convicted of family violence had prior histories of a restraining order and 18% were under an active restraining order at the time of admission to jail.

Note: Adapted from Durose et al., 2005 (see text).

[a] These BJS statistics are collective for the years 1998 through 2002.

Table 5.3   Summary of 2005 Bureau of Justice National Family Lethal Violence Demographics[a]

Demographics of Family Murder Victims and Offenders	
Total number of violence victims	32 million
Total number of family violence victims	3.5 million
Total number of all family murder victims in 2002	9102
Total number of family murder victims/family member perpetrator	1.95%
Family member perpetrator	21.5%
Spouse perpetrators	8.6%
Parent perpetrators	5.5%
Family member perpetrator other than spouse or parent	7.4%
Victim Gender	
Females in U.S. population	50.9%
Female family victims	57.5%
Female family victims of family member perpetrator	43.1%
Victim Race	
White	65.9%
Black	29.7%
Other	4.4%
Victim Age	
Under 13	23.4%
Under 18	26.2%
13–17	2.8%
18–24	8.1%
25–34	15.4%
35–54	32.5%
55 or older	17.7%
Perpetrator Gender	
Male	79.2%
Female	20.8%
Perpetrator Age	
Under 13	0.8%
Under 18	5.5%
13–17	4.7%
18–24	17.3%
25–34	26.9%
35–54	38.9%
55 or older	11.4%
Perpetrator Race	
White	65.3%
Black	30.7%
Other	3.9%
Perpetrator Weapon Use	
Family murders involving a weapon	50.1%
Nonfamily murders involving a weapon	67.7%

Note: Adapted from Durose et al., 2005 (see text).

[a] Data based on police murder statistics compiled by the FBI in the 2002 Supplementary Homicide Reports (SHR) for the year 2002.

Pertinent Legal Cases

Case law addressing domestic violence cuts a wide swath from local, to state, and federal courts, and ultimately to the U.S. Supreme Court. Table 5.4 provides a sampling of landmark cases regarding domestic violence from different jurisdictions and different courts.

Table 5.4   Landmark Legal Cases Regarding Domestic Violence Issues

Case Citation	Synopsis of Case
Blondin v. Dubois, 2001	Under The Hague Convention, child taken from his or her home country must be returned, unless there is "a grave risk of harm." The Second Circuit affirmed the district court that return of the children to the place where they witnessed and experienced serious domestic violence presented a grave risk of psychological harm under The Hague Convention, and return was therefore not warranted.
Crawford v. Washington, 2004	A Supreme Court case, which held that testimonial statements in criminal prosecutions are prohibited by the confrontation clause of the Sixth Amendment. The decision bars admission of out-of-court "testimonial" statements by witnesses who are not testifying at trial and who have not been previously cross-examined by the defendant. The *Crawford* decision has had a devastating impact on domestic violence cases. Previously, prosecutors had used an innovative approach called evidence-based prosecution, which relied on victim's statements' to 911 operators, police, and medical personnel. The approach was used to make a case against a batterer when the victim is traumatized, terrified, or otherwise unable to testify. After *Crawford*, many courts have held that statements such as 911 calls are "testimonial" and therefore not admissible (see *Davis v. Washington; Hammon v. Indiana*, below).
Davis v. Washington; Hammon v. Indiana (currently under Supreme Court review)	These two cases are to be heard in tandem. The question posed by these cases is whether out-of-court statements are to be considered "testimonial" (see *Crawford v. Washington*, 2004, above).
DeShaney (a minor) v. Department of Social Services, 1989	Child severely beaten by father; mother sued Department of Social Services for failure to protect. Supreme Court ruled the State does not have to ensure freedom from "private violence," only has to attempt to help.
Gonzales-Valdes v. Florida, 2003	Plaintiff was a battered Florida woman who was convicted of murdering her common-law husband. Retrial requested because of alleged tainted prosecution because of repeated baseless suggestions that plaintiff had worked as a prostitute. The FL Supreme Court denied review.
Ibn-Tamas v. U.S., 1979	Ibn-Tamas married to husband who beat her often and had a history of violence toward women. She was pregnant; her husband beat her; she shot and killed him. The wife was charged with murder, and she argued self-defense. Witnesses said he begged her not to shoot. A psychologist testified on "battered woman syndrome." Judge refused to let the testimony be heard, saying victim was not on trial. The Appeals Court reversed and said "expert can testify even to ultimate question, where subject matter is beyond the understanding of the average layman."
Landeros v. A. J. Flood, MD et al., 1976	Plaintiff child was born in 1970, beaten a lot. In April 1971, the child was taken to San Jose Hospital and seen by Dr Flood. Child had multiple fractures, but Dr Flood took no x-rays, made no report. Later, a different hospital diagnosed "battered child syndrome"; parents were prosecuted. Action against flood was based on negligence, pain, and suffering. Trial court dismissed, saying "negligence is not malpractice." CA Supreme Court reversed, said further inquiry was foreseeable, a jury should decide. This type of statute exists in every state. There is always a question as to where therapeutic alliance ends and duty to warn/protect begins, but failure to report child abuse is a crime.
Marvin v. Marvin, 1976	An early case that wrestled with the problem of resolving community property with the dissolution of nonmarital relationships. In this instance, the court ruled that each case must be resolved by the court based on a judgment of whether the couple had a "express contract."
The National Child Protection Act of 1993	The Act established a background check system that enables childcare providers to determine whether employees and prospective employees have criminal records involving child-abuse offenses.

continued

Table 5.4 (continued)

Case Citation	Synopsis of Case
Nicholson v. Scopetta, 2003 *Nicholson v. Williams,* 2004	A battered woman's failure to prevent her children from witnessing her own abuse does not automatically give protective agencies license to remove the child. Each case has to be judged on its own merits. In *Nicholson v. Williams,* lower court decision (of *Nicholson v. Scopetta*) upheld by the NY State Court of Appeals.
People v. Stritzinger, 1983	Defendant had sexual contact with 14-year-old stepdaughter. Defendant agreed for himself and stepdaughter to see a psychologist. Psychologist reported stepdaughter's comments to sheriff. Psychologist also reported defendant's statements and testified to same at trial. Stepdaughter was excused from trial because her mother stated stepdaughter was too upset. Supreme Court said: (1) defendant's statements were privileged, and (2) the matter required medical testimony to determine that stepdaughter was unable to testify.
Santosky v. Kramer, 1982	Children removed form home because of neglect by parents. New York law said that Preponderance of Evidence (PoE level of proof = 51%) was the appropriate determination for loss of parental rights. Family appealed as they lost all contact with children forever. Family argued the matter was too serious for PoE. Court agreed noting that 35 states used Clear and Convincing (C&C level of proof = 75%), and federal courts used Beyond a Reasonable Doubt (BRD level of proof = 95%), and, therefore, in the current matter C&C was appropriate.
Thing v. La Chusa, 1989	A vehicle driven by La Chusa injured Ms Thing's son. Mother did not witness incident but arrived shortly after and perceived that her son was dead. Mother sued for Negligent Infliction of Emotional Distress (NIED). Court said NEID requires plaintiff to observe injury. Original decision was "hopelessly arbitrary." Most states use "Zone of Danger" principle. Issue remains legally ambiguous.
Thurman v. City of Torrington, 1984	Jury awarded $2.3 million in favor of wife who sued police department after they failed to arrest her abusive husband.
USA v. Kafka, III, 2000	Defendant Kafka appealed conviction for firearm possession while under a domestic violence restraining order. Kafka contended violation of due process because no notice was given that while under a state restraining order he was prohibited from possessing a firearm by state law. Appeals Court ruled no violation because ignorance of the law carried no merit.
United States ex rel. Alvera v. C.B.M. Group, Inc., 2001	This was the first legal case challenging discrimination against domestic violence survivors as sex discrimination under the Fair Housing Act. In a consent decree settling the suit, the property owner agreed not to evict Mrs Alvera.
Violence against Women Act (VAWA), 2005	The act reauthorized federal remedies for abused immigrant spouses and children. Battered women are now eligible to apply for permanent resident status for themselves and their children and are no longer forced to rely on their abusive husbands to apply for such status.

Applied Ethics and Moral Considerations

Clinicians who work with disturbed families must be familiar with applicable legal and ethical requirements. federal codes, ethical standards, and state laws do not always align with the special circumstances of working with families. Examples of unique applications of requirements could include reporting requirements for suspected abuse/neglect, and the availability of legal interventions such as protective orders. Another example is confusion over procedures for handling disclosures by individual family members regarding sensitive issues (e.g., fatal illness, sexually transmitted diseases, criminal activity, and substance abuse) that could negatively affect the family as a whole if not managed appropriately (Southern, Smith, and Oliver, 2005).

The American Psychological Association's "Ethical principles of psychologists and code of conduct" (2002) is the ethical standard for psychologists. For forensic psychologists, the "Specialty guidelines for forensic psychologists" (Committee on Ethical Guidelines for Forensic Psychologists, 1991) is also pertinent. In addition, other mental health discipline associations, local professional associations, and state and national professional groups have ethical codes that apply to clinicians from different disciplines.

As might be expected, working with problem families can present difficult issues with confidentiality both intrinsic and extrinsic to the family. For example, what information divulged by children and adolescents can be shared with the parents and vice versa? If potentially dangerous circumstances are discovered with a given family, how should that information be managed? Other confidentiality quagmires occur concerning collaterally involved parties and of course by any court involvement with the family or family members. There are no simple answers to any of these situations; each circumstance must be addressed on an individual, case-by-case basis. We note that one effective way to resolve questionable situations is to confer with colleagues and to document such collaboration. A formal plan of prevention strategies is the best way for the clinician to avoid stepping into circumstances likely to lead to ethical complaints (Thomas, 2005).

The ethical standards for family work are still in evolution. In recent years, practitioners have described a number of emerging ethical issues unique to working with families. The APA ethics code (2002) carefully distinguishes between the *personal* and *professional* roles of the psychologist (Pipes, Holstein, and Aquirre, 2005). Conceptually, the APA ethics code does not apply to the purely private life of the psychologist. The distinction, however, is not always clear. For example, if a clinician who has worked with a disturbed family elects to attend the wedding or a funeral of one of the family members, is the clinician's role personal or professional? It takes only a small amount of deliberation to envision that the proposed scenario could turn out to be an ethical disaster for the clinician. The clinician may perceive his or her role one way and the family perceives it another way. We could envision an ethical complaint over the fact that the clinician imbibed or danced at the wedding, or that the clinician's presence at the funeral demonstrated that the clinician felt in some way responsible for the death of the family member.

Merely conducting research with families conveys a host of ethical cautions (Margolin, Chien, Duhman, Fauchier, Gordis, Oliver, Ramos, and Vickerman, 2005). Clinical work with families often will entail working outside the private office, or office in a clinic, hospital, or similar traditional setting. Service delivery outside of traditional settings creates opportunities for professional boundary problems for the clinician (Knapp and Slattery, 2004). Entering a family home or seeing family members in unconventional settings (e.g., detentions centers, bars, recreational facilities, and places of worship) does not afford the clinician the usual veil of professionalism of the office setting. Appropriate professional boundaries serve to provide both necessary structure and safety to the consumer as well as to the clinician.

Patient-initiated boundary crossings in family matters can present as very delicate situations, but can also serve as data to explore in ongoing treatment. Consider the circumstance of a clinician conducting a home visit evaluation and a child showing the clinician a weapon from the parent's bedroom, or the circumstance of a young attractive mother who has just learned of a family member's tragic death and collapses into the arms of a male clinician. Many boundary-crossing situations occur spontaneously and without forewarning. Other forms of boundary crossings are somewhat predictable (Bewsey and Odulate, 2003; Lamb, Catanzaro, and Moorman, 2004). The prudent clinician makes every effort to anticipate potential boundary problems with families and manage circumstances accordingly. Beyond the cautions for the clinician working with families, all clinical work with children imposes an additional agenda of ethical implications. Current thinking is that all applicable ethical standards of working with children and adolescents by implication extend to family work also (Hoagwood, Jensen, and Fisher, 1996).

One problem area is the quality of mother/child relationship when mothers have been domestic violence victims. Tragically, statistics indicate that in 30–80% of cases of mothers who have endured spousal abuse inflict abuse on their children (Lewis, 2003). An ethical dilemma evolves from an effort to work with a mother who has been a victim of domestic abuse and who now discloses that she has been abusing her children. The statutes of most jurisdictions would unequivocally require reporting of the disclosed abuse, but, of course, such reporting will compromise the effort to work therapeutically with the mother (Bartens, 2004; Buchbinder and Elisikovits, 2004; Sullivan and Cain, 2004).

An emerging area of work for family psychologists is end-of-life care (Haley, Larson, Kasil-Godley, Neimeyer, and Kwiloz, 2003). In some instances, end-of-life clinical care will involve family member victims of violence. Gerontology involves another emerging area of work families. The American Psychological Association (APA, 2004) has issued practice guidelines for psychologists who work with the elderly. In the guidelines, APA estimated that while a large number of psychologists acknowledge working with the elderly, only 30% have actually completed formal graduate coursework in geropsychology.

Family circumstances often embody multicultural/multiethnic circumstances. The American Psychological Association (APA, 1993, 2003) also has established guidelines to assist clinicians in working with these family circumstances. APA and numerous other professional mental health organizations require graduate programs to provide training in multicultural issues. Smith, Constantine, Dunn, Dinehart, and Montoya (2006) utilized meta-analytic methodology to examine the quality of multicultural graduate training. A primary finding was that teaching programs that based multicultural interventions on formal theory and research offered the most effective training.

One aspect of the multicultural issue is family members who comprise subgroups of handicapped individuals, for example, deaf, wheelchair-bound, or quadriplegic family members (Olkin, Abrams, Preston, and Kirshbaum, 2006; Williams and Abeles, 2004). Each of these groups has its own cultural makeup. In a broad sense, other multicultural subgroups consist of gay, lesbian, bisexual, and transgendered (GLBT) family members (Janson and Steigerwald, 2002; Steigerwald and Janson, 2003). Each of these subgroups can present with special challenges to clinicians in terms of understanding the psychology and culture of each subgroup and how diversity in family makeup affects family functioning. Another consideration is how transference/counter transference issues can significantly interfere with effectiveness in attempting to work with families of diversity (Hansen, Randazzo, Schwartz, Marshall, Kalis, Frazier, Burke, Kershner-Rice, and Norvig, 2006; Stuart, 2004). Finally, contemporary society is struggling with the needs of subgroups of family members afflicted with HIV/AIDS. This circumstance presents still additional ethical challenges for clinicians (Yarhouse, 2003).

Clinicians who work with families coping with domestic violence should anticipate calls to testify as expert witnesses, or to function as family advocates, or both. It is imprudent to participate in courtroom proceedings without being thoroughly aware of one's specific role, and without being well versed in the both the allure and the potential pitfalls of participating in the adversarial process.

Empirically Based Methods and Applications[*]

For a variety of reasons, the evaluation of families is a significantly more complicated matter than evaluation of an individual (Poirier, 1991a). Evaluation of the family cannot be meaningfully perceived as merely a collection of individual evaluations of family members. The goal of family evaluation is to capture the existential style of the family as a unit, and as a component of the larger social community. Family evaluation should entail evaluating all the family members both individually and in most instances collectively. Compared to evaluation of a single individual, family work is more labor intensive and therefore more expensive. Another aspect of working with families is the considerable amount of case-management effort. This includes gathering prior records, which sometimes can be voluminous, accessing collateral contacts, coordinating with other involved professional and agencies, and so on. Frequently, accessibility to individual family members can be problematic because of travel, incarceration, illness, or similar issues. The more distressed a family, the greater the likelihood of a lack of communality of perceptions among family members. As suggested earlier, the family is an organism in itself; every family has a history that will often involve at least consideration of multigenerational dynamics.

Tarasoff (1976) circumstances, wherein a potential family member perpetrator indicates intent to harm another family member, can be extremely difficult for clinicians to manage. Unlike nonfamily member Tarasoff scenarios, the option of effecting creative barriers between family member perpetrators and victims is more difficult to achieve. Incidents of lethal family violence are most usually after the fact events for the clinician. Typically, clinician involvement in nonlethal and lethal family violence begins after an incident has occurred, and the need is for assessment, treatment, and management of the family after a tragic incident.

Domestic Spousal Violence Risk Assessment

Formal risk assessment instruments for criminal violence have been in use for a number of years, although there is a long parallel history questioning the general validity of violence prediction (Cocozza and Steadman, 1974; Grove and Meehl, 1996; Harris, Rice, and Quinsey, 1998). Borum (1996) observed that, in spite of the controversy, the courts have continued to rely on risk assessment data by mental health clinicians. Through it all, researchers and clinicians have employed actuarial instruments to assist with effective management of violent criminal offenders (Dutton, 1995; Harris, Rice, and Quinsey, 1998; Hilton, Harris, Rice, Lang, Cormier, and Lines, 2004; Hilton and Harris, 2005; Rice and Harris, 2003).

The violence literature has described three essential models of risk assessment. The models are: (1) *unstructured clinical decision-making*, (2) *actuarial decision-making*, and (3) *structured professional judgment* (Kropp, Hart, and Belfrage, 2004a, 2004b). Although *unstructured clinical decision-making* is probably the most widely applied method in violence risk assessment, it is the most empirically unsound approach. Unstructured clinical decision-making is little more than the best intuitive guess on the part of the clinician (Monahan, 1996). The approach is laden with problems of clinician bias and interpretation

---

[*] The concept of "empirically based" is broader than the concept of "evidence-based practice" (EBP) as recently adopted by the APA Council of Representatives (APA, 2005). The intent of the EBP concept is to capture the notion that "... doctoral psychologists should be trained as both scientists and practitioners..." (p. 1). The Task Force adopted the following definition: "Evidence-based practice in psychology (EBPP) is the integration of the best available research with clinical expertise in the context of patient characteristics, culture, and preferences" (p. 5). This chapter espouses this definition of EBP.

and therefore has especially limited value in forensic matters. According to Kropp et al. (2004a), with this method, "Recommendations for management strategies—if they are made at all—might be based more on the training preferences, and biases of the evaluator rather than on: (1) well-reasoned consideration of dynamic and criminogenic (i.e., crime relevant) risk factors; and, (2) intervention strategies that are either empirically valid or well accepted in the field" (p. 35).

It has been only in the past 15 years or so that risk factors for spousal abuse have been identified (Hilton et al., 2004). As a result, spouse abuse risk assessment remains at a relatively experimental stage. In these circumstances, clinicians essentially have no other options but to utilize the unstructured clinical decision-making approach in effort to assist with assessment of spouse abuse risk.* Such assessments must clearly outline the limitations of the clinical effort and be frugal with interpretive findings and conclusions.

Actuarial measures are dependent on base rates of violent behavior and the selection ratio, or both. Base rates essentially reflect the *prevalence* of the type of violence, and the selection ratio is the proportion of people predicted to evidence the violence (Rice and Harris, 1995). A basic problem is the vulnerability of predictive instruments generating false-negative or false-positive estimates.

A recent advance in violence prediction was the application of a measure derived from receiver operating characteristics (ROCs) (Beech, Fisher, and Thornton, 2003; Harris et al., 2003; Quinsey, Harris, Rice, and Cormier, 2006). The ROC concept was originally developed to assist with (radar) signal detection years ago. ROC is the best index of the predictive accuracy of an assessment method. ROCs can also compare the predictive performance of different instruments (Rice and Harris, 1995). ROC has the additional advantage of not being distorted by variations in the base rates of recidivism. Beech et al. (2003) succinctly characterized the ROC concept: "In general, it can be interpreted as the probability that a randomly selected recidivist would have a more deviant score than a randomly selected nonrecidivist. This varies from .5 (no predictive accuracy) to 1.0 (perfect predictive accuracy)" (p. 341).

The purpose of the *actuarial assessment* model is to provide an approach that improves on the lack of reliability and validity of the unstructured clinical approach. Actuarial assessment compares the violence risk of an individual by comparison of the individual's "totaled risk factors" to a reference group of known offenders.

One limitation of actuarial assessment is its fixed temporality. That is, the estimated risk factor estimates are for fixed time intervals. Their predictive value is limited to specified intervals. Heilbrun (1997) noted the practical utility of pursuing "management"-oriented models of risk assessment over "prediction" models of risk assessment. A management model of risk assessment strives to match offender needs with available resources as opposed to attempting to "predict" offender risk in some quantified way. The latter quest is decidedly more elusive. The defining aspect of an actuarial risk scale is "...that items are weighted and combined according to a fixed and explicit algorithm" (Kropp, Hart, Webster, and Eaves, 2001, p. 103). Thus, with an actuarial risk scale, it is unimportant whether the content of the scale was empirically derived or derived based on clinical intuition. When using the

---

* As an example of the still early stage of spousal abuse risk assessment, the case example in this chapter involved wife-perpetrated, lethal spouse violence. None of the available risk assessment instruments for spouse abuse has been specifically normed for female perpetrators; the author had to accommodate use of available actuarial instruments.

actuarial approach, the clinician considers a fixed set of risk factors and cannot consider other parameters. Because actuarial methods are based on a sum of scores of risk factors subjected to an algorithmic approach, they are likely to be more accurate than clinical judgment alone (Grove and Meehl, 1996). The latter characteristic is arguably the actuarial approach's strength and at the same time its point of vulnerability.

The *structured professional judgment* approach is an attempt to combine the relative strengths of unstructured clinical assessment with the strengths of actuarial assessment (Douglas and Kropp, 2002). Kropp et al. (2004a, 2004b) characterized the *structured professional judgment* approach as follows:

> Here, the evaluator must conduct the assessment according to guidelines that reflect current theoretical, professional, and empirical knowledge about violence. Such guidelines provide the minimum set of risk factors that should be considered in every case. The guidelines will also typically include recommendations for information gathering (e.g., the use of multiple sources and multiple methods), communicating opinions, and implementing violence prevention strategies (p. 36).

The structured professional judgment approach does not eliminate the intuition of the clinician but augments it with consideration of multiple sourced, actuarially based, risk factor data. According to Douglas and Kropp (2002), the primary objective of the structured professional approach to risk assessment is the prevention of violence. Violence prevention is accomplished by systematic identification of static (i.e., fixed over time, such as gender, ethnicity, and so on) and dynamic (i.e., changeable such as mental illness and environmental conditions) risk factors (Kropp et al., 2004a, 2004b).

Table 5.5 lists a number of the essential risk factors that research has identified as being associated with risk for spousal violence. It is important to recognize that risk factors are not necessarily causal predictors, but rather they represent factors that consistently co-occur with spousal abuse (Dutton and Kropp, 2004).

Table 5.6 presents a number of risk assessment instruments that have been developed for spousal violence. Each instrument in Table 5.6 is identified as an example of one of the three risk assessment approaches that we have described above. Of the instruments identified in Table 5.6, the Spousal Assault Risk Assessment (SARA) Guide and the Brief Spousal Assault Form for the Evaluation of Risk (B-SAFER) instruments have received the most attention.

Table 5.5   Research-Identified Categories of Risk Factors for Spousal Assault

- Age
- Severity of prior violence
- Duration of prior violence
- History of antisocial/asocial behavior
- History of violence in the offender's family of origin
- History of hostile attitude
- History of substance abuse
- Stability of relationships
- Stability of employment
- Psychological health and personality disorder
- Childhood abuse
- Attitudes toward women
- Motivation for treatment

Source: Adapted from Dutton and Kropp (2000) and Hilton et al. (2004).

Table 5.6　Empirically Based Risk Assessment Instruments for Partner/Spouse Violence

Instrument	Assesses	Description	References	Type
Spousal Assault Risk Assessment (SARA)	Spousal assault by male perpetrators	SARA utilizes 20 research-identified risk factors. Factors 1–10 are specific to violence risk in general and factors 11–20 are specific to spousal violence. Each factor is rated according to detailed guidelines. The SARA manual notes that the factor ratings ultimately rely on the discretion of the evaluator and as such, the process is not an *actuarial* method. Study evaluated reliability and validity of judgments made using SARA with a large sample ($N = 2681$) of male offenders. Interrater reliability was high. SARA convergent and discriminant validity was good with respect to other measures related to risk for general and violent criminality. SARA ratings significantly discriminated between offenders with and without a history of spousal violence, and between recidivistic and nonrecidivistic spousal assaulters.	Kropp, Hart, Webster, and Eaves, 1994, 1995, 1998, 1999; Kropp et al., 2001	Structured professional judgment
The Danger Assessment (DA)	Risk of lethal wife assault	Structured list that assesses risk based on wife or victim self-report and 15-item scale regarding perpetrator characteristics. Perpetrator characteristics include history of violence in the relationship and other violence, perpetrator availability of weapons, substance abuse, suicidality, and jealousy.	Campbell, 1986; Stuart and Campbell, 1989	Author described as actuarial, but based on retrospective estimates from female victims as to prior severity of partner violence raising interpretive problems (see Dutton and Kropp, 2000)

Instrument	Measures/Predicts	Description	Reference	Type of Assessment
The Ontario Domestic Assault Risk Assessment (ODARA)	Wife assault recidivism	The ODARA consists of a 13-item scale that predicts new assaults against legal or common-law wives or ex-wives. Includes consideration of victim's vulnerability to violence.	Hilton et al. (2004)	Actuarial / Based on established psychological assessment techniques
Various self-report instruments (i.e., MMPI-2, Lifetime History of Aggression Questionnaire, Barratt Impulsiveness Scale, Buss-Perry Aggression Questionnaire, State-Trait Anger Expression Inventory, and Eysenck Personality Questionnaire	Men accused of domestic violence employing willful impression management on self-report instruments	This retrospective study utilized a sample of male domestic violence offenders. The Ss were classified into three groups based on neuropsychological measures of impulse control or executive functioning: (1) documented risk, (2) high risk, and (3) low risk. The authors found that the majority in all three groups utilized "impression management" (i.e., deceptive self-presentation) on self-report methods.	Helfritz, Stanford, Conklin, Greve, Villemarette-Pittman, and Houston, (2006)	Unstructured clinical assessment
Violence Risk Appraisal Guide (VRAG)	Risk of violence posed by offenders in general / Predicted violent wife assault recidivism	High interrater reliability when scored according to instructions ($r > .90$). VRAG scores positively related to the likelihood and severity of violent reoffending. Requires extensive knowledge of offender history and therefore is not useful for rapid risk assessment.	Harris et al., 1993; Hilton et al., 1998, 2001; Grann and Wedin, 2002	Structured professional judgment

Table 5.7   Spousal Assault Form for the Evaluation of Risk (SAFER)-Derived Spousal Abuse Risk Factors and Instrument Basic Instructions

Section One—Spousal assault risk factors

1. Serious physical/sexual violence
2. Serious violence threats, ideation, or intent
3. Escalation of physical/sexual violence or threats/ideations/intent
4. Violations of criminal or civil court orders
5. Negative attitudes about spousal assault

Section Two—Psychosocial adjustment (violence in general) risk factors

1. Other serious criminality
2. Relationship problems
3. Employment or financial problems
4. Substance abuse
5. Mental disorder

B-SAFER Instructions: The B-SAFER is a guide for the assessment and management of risk for spousal assault. It helps users exercise their best judgment. The administration procedures and risk factors included in the B-SAFER were determined from a review of hundreds of scientific and professional publications on spousal violence. There are no cut-off scores or other rules that can be used to determine the nature or degree of risk posed by an offender; the presence of a single risk factor may justify a conclusion that the person opposed a high risk for future spousal violence.

Note: The authors caution that proper use of the B-SAFER requires specialized training. The interested reader who desires more information, and copies of the instrument manual and forms, should contact The British Columbia Institute against Family Violence, Suite 551, 409 Granville Street, Vancouver, British Columbia V6C 1T2, Canada. Tel: (604) 669-7055; Fax (604) 669-7054; E-mail: publications@bcifv.org; URL: www.bcifv.org.

Source: Material adapted from Kropp et al., 2004a, 2004b.

The B-SAFER was derived from the SARA in an attempt to draw on earlier research and to develop a briefer risk assessment tool (Kropp et al., 2004a, 2004b). It is instructive to review the process of the development of the B-SAFER. Based on the assumption that the SARA may have redundant or overlapping items, the authors conducted statistical analyses of the SARA factors. Seven factors were derived that served as an initial framework for the B-SAFER. Subsequent pilot studies expanded the number of factors to 10. Table 5.7 presents these final 10 factors and the basic B-SAFER instructions.

Spousal Physical Abuse

Marital relationships regardless of issues of gender makeup, and regardless of any legal sanctions, are the nuclei of family constellations. The lack of health in a marital relationship is an important contributing risk factor to family violence (Farr, 2002). The extent of trauma from spousal abuse is extensive, including negative impact on physical, psychological, and social well-being on family members (Ehrensaft, Moffitt, Caspi, 2006; Goulding, 1999; Gwinn, McClane, Shanel-Hogan, and Strack, 2004; Karpel, 1994; McCormack, Burgess, and Hartman, 1988; O'Leary and Maiuro, 2001). "The linkage of relationship distress to disruption of individual and physical well-being further emphasizes the importance of integrating empirically based strategies for assessing couple distress as an adjunct to effective intervention strategies with individuals" (Snyder, Heyman, and Haynes, 2005, p. 288).

The rate of divorce among married couples in the United States approaches 50% (Kreider and Fields, 2002). That datum itself speaks volumes as to the difficulties inherent in marital relationships and indirectly to the extent of violence within families. Domestic adjudication involving divorce matters and associated contested custody matters have become popular vehicles for physical and sexual violence assertions by spouses (Poirier, 1989, 1990, 1991).

Given the high rate of underreporting of spousal abuse (Ehrensaft and Vivian, 1996), an important aspect of combating the problem is careful screening for any abuse/neglect of family members (Bograd and Mederos, 1999; Jory, 2004; McCloskey and Grigsby, 2005). Smith and Winokur (2004) cautioned that many battered women are skeptical and resistant regarding mandatory reporting laws, and clinicians should be mindful that many battered women remain highly ambivalent about leaving the home even after instances of severe violence (Stanko, 1997).

Screening efforts for domestic violence should include prenatal evaluations of pregnant mothers who have been victims of violence (Renker and Tonkin, 2006). An established risk factor for spousal violence is family of origin abuse in the histories of male perpetrators (Murphy, Meyer and O'Leary, 1993). Routine screening for family of origin abuse may help clinicians identify a families potential for domestic violence. Single parenthood and teenage pregnancies are other risk signs of domestic circumstances that may be violence prone (Tan and Quinlivan, 2006). Families that have special needs family members or unusual ethnic or cultural configurations may also present as potential risks for domestic violence (Vanamo, Kauppi, Karkola, Merikanto, and Rasanen, 2001; West, 2004).

The potential for deceit and distortion with family members involved in domestic violence circumstances is ever present. Accordingly, all data reported by victims and witnesses of spousal violence must be held suspect by the clinician (Schuller, Wells, Rzepa, and Klippenstine, 2004). Perhaps the single greatest source of deceit and distortion, however, is the self-report of perpetrators (Helfritz et al, 2006). The significantly higher rates of spousal violence compared to other forms of domestic violence can afford evaluators an initial impetus as to where scrutiny can begin with troubled family matters. Additional clues are inherent in the Bureau of Justice data that the majority of abused family member adults are women and the majority of family member perpetrators are men.

There is ongoing research examining spousal gender differences in the expression of anger; this research may eventually lead to better understanding of why the majority of spousal violence perpetrators are men (Archer, 2004; Ehrensaft, Moffitt, and Caspi, 2004). This research has yet to clarify the age-old debate of the roles of heredity versus environmental influences affecting anger expression. Substance abuse plays a central role in a majority of spousal abuse cases (Bennett, Tolman, Rogalski, and Srinivasaraghavan, 1994). Table 5.8 data regarding spousal abuse clearly and consistently reflect the pivotal role of substance abuse.

One interesting chain correlation evidenced in the Table 5.6 across-study data was that posttraumatic stress disorder (PTSD) was a risk factor with *partner abuse by men*. In turn, *exposure to childhood abuse* was a risk factor for adult PTSD. The data, however, were from separate studies with different proband groups, and therefore a causal relationship between the two risk factors cannot be assumed. That is, the observation could reflect two independent risk factors with no overlapping relationship; the finding points to the complexities involved in understanding what identified risk factors actually signify. Table 5.8 data also reflect that a number of early studies of family partner violence were with Veteran's Administration (VA) populations. These studies explored the hypothesis that PTSD was a contributing factor to spousal abuse; the data suggest at least a comorbid relationship.

Table 5.8 Evidence-Based Findings Regarding Spousal Physical Abuse

Study	Findings
Bennett et al., 1994	Men who engage in partner violence have elevated substance abuse scales on psychometrics.
Bollinger, Riggs, Blake, and Ruzek, 2000	15% of posttraumatic stress disorder (PTSD) combat veteran inpatients have comorbid antisocial personality disorders.
Bremmer, Southwick, Johnson, Yehuda, and Charney, 1993	Childhood abuse is a predictor of PTSD in Vietnam veterans.
Campbell, 2002	Intimate partner violence causes a large variety of mental and physical health consequences. The physical health consequences include injury, chronic pain, and gastrointestinal and gynecological symptoms signs. Also documented in controlled research are sexually transmitted diseases, depression, and PTSD.
Linder and Collins, 2005	Partner violence predictors included early childhood physical abuse and witnessing of parent/partner violence, features (i.e., parent–child boundary violations) of parent/child interaction at age 13 years.
	Quality friendships at age 16 predicted lower levels of victimization and perpetration and poor-quality relationships predicted the inverse.
	Friendship quality at age 16 predicted over and above familial predictors. The latter finding raises the question that familial and peer predictors vary in their relative impact.
Maiuro and Cahn, 1988	Men who engage in partner violence have elevated depression scales on psychometrics.
McCormack et al., 1988	Childhood abuse is a predictor of PTSD in men.
Murphy et al., 1993	Risk for adult perpetration of violence related to exposure to violence in the family of origin, particularly childhood abuse and the witnessing of interparental violence.
	Men who engage in partner violence have elevated antisocial scales on psychometrics.
Swindle et al., 2000	Survey indicating most frequently cited causes of emotional stress were relationship difficulties, including divorce, separation, and other marital strains.
Taft, Pless, Stalans, Koenen, King, and King, 2005	In National Study of Vietnam Veterans, the authors identified potential risk factors for partner violence ($N = 109$).
	Partner violent (PV) men with PTSD were compared to PV men without PTSD. The PTSD-positive PD men evidenced highest levels of risk factors.
	Significantly higher levels of major depressive episode.
	Significantly higher levels of substance abuse.
	Poorer marital adjustment.
	Higher levels of exposure to atrocities.
Weisz, Tolman, and Saunders, 2000	Compared domestic violence survivor's prediction of reassault to research risk factors. Survivor's predictions significantly added to accuracy of risk factor predictions.

Spousal Sexual Abuse

Table 5.9 presents evidence-based studies regarding adult family member sexual abuse. Many sources do not distinguish between spousal physical and spousal sexual violence, but rather lump the two into one category. We have separated the two to maintain consistency with the BJS categories of domestic violence. One legal intervention intended to help prevent domestic violence is protective orders. Unfortunately, protective orders offer protection only to the point that they are immediately enforceable. Spouses who are victims of sexual abuse are particularly vulnerable because what may begin as an attempt to reconcile with a violent partner can conclude with further sexual abuse (Cole, Logan, and Shannon, 2005).

Table 5.9 Evidence-Based Findings Regarding Spouse/Intimate Other Sexual Assault

Study	Findings
Bachman, 1992	Rape injuries more severe when assailant is a stranger compared to when assailant is a partner.
Campbell, 2002	Numerous studies from around the world cite intimate partner violence in 3–13% of pregnancies.
	Chronic and serious gynecological problems are the most prominent difference between battered and nonbattered women.
Cole et al., 2005	Multivariate analysis showed that women with no partner sexual victimization has significantly fewer mental health problems than women who had experienced sexual insistence and women who had been threatened or forced to have sex.
Golding, 1999	Meta-analysis study reflects intimate partner violence poses risk for depression and posttraumatic stress disorder. The symptom risk is greater than trauma stemming from childhood sexual assault.
Koss et al., 1994	Intimates inflict most sexual assaults of women.
Negrao, Bonnanno, Noll, Putnam, and Trickett, 2005	Compared a population of survivors of childhood sex abuse to matched control group. Authors coded shame, anger, and humiliation from narrative transcripts. Verbal humiliation was found to be associated with nonverbal displays of shame. Verbal humiliation and facial shame among nondisclosers of childhood sex abuse was associated with increase of PTSD symptoms.

Research has consistently demonstrated a negative correlation between a woman spouse being sexually abused and her subsequent psychosexual development. The sexually victimized woman subsequently has difficulty maintaining a life of healthy sexual outlook or attitude (Meston, Rellini, and Heiman, 2006). A particular problem area of spousal sexual violence involves the woman victim who is pregnant or who becomes pregnant following the abuse (Samuelson and Campbell, 2005).

Domestic Physical Abuse of Child/Adolescent Family Members

Many of the available data regarding the problem of domestic child abuse/neglect are derived from administrative sources as opposed to data based on cases actually reported to authorities (McCurdy and Daro, 1994). There is agreement in professional circles that these data significantly underreport the magnitude of the child-abuse/neglect problem (Federal Interagency Forum on Children and Family Statistics, 2006). A more effective but also prohibitively costly approach would be data based on sample surveys. Even this approach, however, holds a host of new problems beginning with how such sensitive information could be reliably elicited. A related question is whether individuals collecting abuse/neglect survey data have a statutory obligation to report acknowledged or suspected cases of abuse/neglect.

For a number of reasons, child abuse and child neglect are often hidden problems (Cicchetti, 2004). Because of their youth, their limited cognitive development, and their emotional naiveté, children can be attractive victims to older family members looking for victim outlets for anger issues. Because of their youth, children are especially vulnerable to the potentially lethal consequences of chronic neglect (Knight and Collins, 2005; Pollanen, Smith, Chiasson, Cairns, and Young, 2002). The research on the effects of early childhood experience on later life abilities indicates a complex interplay of family and peer experiences (Carlson, Sroufe, and Egeland, 2004).

Perhaps one of the most insidious and traumatic forms of child abuse/neglect is children witnessing spousal abuse or abuse of other siblings (Campbell and Lewandowski, 1997; Cui, Conger, and Frederick, 2005). Researchers have explored the hypothetical cycle of a child-abuse victim who then later becomes a perpetrator (Glasser, Kolvin, Campbell, Glasser, Leitch, and Farrelly, 2001; Goldblatt and Eisikovits, 2005). Similarly, researchers have explored the impact of negative childhood experience and later being a less than effective parent or caring partner (Linder and Collins, 2005). The best data suggest that there is a victim/perpetrator link, but that relationship is not causal or predictable.

The physical abuse and neglect of children is sometimes severe enough to result in death (Fieguth, Gunter, Kleemann, and Troger, 2002; Fulton, 2000). In other instances, the death of a child is the result of frank homicide (Keenan and Runyan, 2001; Vanamo et al., 2001). Jones, Finkelhor, and Halter (2006) noted that although often not recognized with the same emphasis, the ravages of neglect could be as equally severe as abuse. A subtle and frequently ignored form of domestic abuse is trauma caused by sibling rivalry dynamics (Butler, 2006). In serious cases, sibling rivalry can have devastating impact on a victim's subsequent development.

In a longitudinal study of 451 adolescents, Cui et al. (2005) found that that increases in marital distress as well as in marital conflict were predictive of harm to adolescent development. Goldblatt and Eisikovits (2005) reported a conceptual study with interesting implications. The authors worked with a small sample of adolescents who were exposed to interparental violence. The adolescents assumed a variety of roles (e.g., gatekeeper, pacifier, judge, mediator, educator, and savior) in efforts to cope and attempt to intervene. The assumed roles permeated the adolescent's self-presentation and in some instances hampered the adolescent's ability to mature through usual identity formation. The roles assumed by the adolescents were linked to the temporal and physical characteristics of the parental violence. The authors suggested that while the adolescents experience with their parents' difficulties had potential learning value, in the end, any positive gain was negated by the exposure to the violence. The findings in this study also suggest the need to expand the scope of family therapy interventions when dealing with domestic violence. Adolescents in conflict/violence-ridden families can have major impact on their parents' behavior. To understand the dynamics of a violent family, "… it is important to consider the youths' subjective perspective of events in their families" (p. 654).

Table 5.10 presents evidence-based studies regarding child/adolescent family member physical abuse.

Domestic Sexual Abuse of Child/Adolescent Family Members

Table 5.11 presents evidence-based studies regarding domestic sexual abuse of children and adolescents. Child sexual abuse is a culturally onerous behavior. The cultural taboo results in child sexual abuse being one of the most difficult forms of child abuse to detect. Today, the problem is widely recognized by clinicians, parents, and the public, but this awareness does not serve to protect against every instance of child sexual abuse. One suggestion has been to attempt to monitor potential child abuse in community locations where children spend time away from their families. Thus, daycare centers, schools, and recreational facilities could be resources for monitoring the problem assuming proper training of childcare providers (Halikias, 2004). This, however, would not be an approach without difficulties. If the monitoring were conducted too aggressively, there would be flagrant issues of confidentiality and informed consent. On the other hand, the proposal has merit because careful, well-moderated observation of children in neutral settings could lead to early detection of potential abuse circumstances.

Table 5.10   Evidence-Based Findings Regarding Physical Abuse of Child/Adolescent Family Members

Study	Findings
Campbell and Lewandowski, 1997; Diamond and Muller, 2004	Children in households fraught with conflict and violence do not have to be actual physical abuse trauma. The mere witnessing of intimate partner violence by children can induce symptoms (i.e., depression and posttraumatic stress disorder) characteristic of actual child-abuse victims.
Cicchetti, 2004	Research with event-related potential responses to emotion stimuli, neuroendocrine regulation, and acoustic startle was consistent in demonstrating aberrations in maltreated children.
National Crime Victimization Survey (NCVS), 2004	Teens experience the highest rates of violent crime (i.e., murder, rape and sexual assault, robbery and assault).
U.S. Department of Health and Human Services, Health Resources and Services Administration, Maternal and Child Health Bureau, 2005	There is a need for regular, reliable estimates of the incidence of child abuse and neglect. Also needed are regular, reliable estimates of the incidence of child abuse and neglect that are based on sample surveys rather than administrative records. Since administrative data are based on cases reported to authorities, it is likely that these data underestimate the magnitude of the problem. Estimates based on sample survey data could potentially provide more accurate information; however, a number of issues still persist, including how to effectively elicit this sensitive information, how to identify the appropriate respondent for the questions, and whether there is a legal obligation for the surveyor to report abuse or neglect.
Skowron and Reinemann, 2005	The authors conducted a meta-analysis of the effectiveness of psychological interventions for child maltreatment. Treated children on average demonstrated 71% better adjustment compared to untreated children.

Domestic Abuse of Elderly Family Members

In Western culture, the welfare of the elderly as a social concern is a relatively recent phenomenon. The elderly are the fastest growing segment of our population. Recognition of this statistic as well as a progressive increase in political influence by the elderly has spawned interest in their needs (Aravanis et al., 1993; Aravanis, 2002). Clinicians who work with the elderly should be familiar with the American Psychological Association's "Guidelines for psychological practice with older adults" (2004).

Uetch and Garrett (1992) suggested that if child abuse was discovered in the 1960s, then elder abuse was discovered in the 1970s. The authors also concluded that initial attempts to apply definitional content from child-abuse research to elder abuse research were unfruitful. Likewise, early efforts to utilize data-collection procedures designed for child abuse were not appropriate for gathering data regarding elder abuse.

Compared to children, the elderly are usually autonomous in their living status and are not victims in the characteristic passive or silent way that children are. Unlike child victims, abuse of the elderly is frequently related to circumstances of financial control, or other forms of control, that elders may have over perpetrator family members. As adults, the elderly can be more deliberately clever and manipulative in not revealing abuse compared to children.

Stein (1991) described an effort to assemble a group of 10 researchers from a variety of disciplines to establish a national research agenda for elder abuse. According to Stein,

Table 5.11   Evidence-Based Findings Regarding Sexual Abuse of Child/Adolescent Family Members

Study	Finding
Cinq-Mars, Wright, Cyr, and McDuff, 2003	The study investigated the sexual at-risk behaviors of sexually abused adolescent girls. Severity of abuse was linked to greater number of at-risk behaviors. For example, adolescents with a history of sexual abuse involving penetration were 13 times more likely to have been pregnant.
Cyr, McDuff, Wright, Thèriault, and Cinq-Mars, 2005	The study investigated self-harming behaviors in female adolescent girls who were victims of sexual abuse. Rates of nine types of self-mutilating behaviors were compared at different intervals. At 9-month follow-up, one in four Ss reported moderate-to-high level of self-harming.
Cyr, Wright, McDuff, and Perron, 2002	A study of the victim abuse characteristics, which were due to due to interfamilial sexual abuse. The study compared the abuse characteristics of victims of brother–sister, father–daughter, and stepfather–stepdaughter incest. The abuse characteristics were similar across the three groups. Penetration was much more frequent in sibling incest group. Brother incest perpetrators were raised in families with more children and more alcohol abuse compared to father/stepfather perpetrators.
Glasser et al., 2001	The article identified perpetrators of child sexual abuse who had been victims of pedophilia or incest. The clinical case notes of 843 Ss (747 male and 96 female victims) were reviewed retrospectively. Having been a victim was a strong predictor of becoming a perpetrator, as was an index of parental loss in childhood. The data supported the notion of a victim-to-victimizer cycle in a minority of male perpetrators but not among the female victims studied. Sexual abuse by a female in childhood may be a risk factor for a cycle of abuse in males.
Lev-Wiesel, 2006	Study addressing the intergenerational transmission of sexual abuse through girls who were victimized by incest and who are now mothers.
Meston et al., 2006	Female child sex abuse (CSA) survivors as adults perceived themselves as less romantic and passionate compared to those who were not abused. CSA survivors displayed an inverse relationship between romantic/passionate sexual feeling and negative sexual affect during sexual arousal. The relationship between CSA and negative sexual affect was independent of symptoms of depression and anxiety, suggesting that the impact of CSA on sexual self-schemas may be independent from any impact the abuse may have in other areas of the survivor's life.
Seto, Lalumière, and Kuban, 1999	Men tend to adjust mating interests as a function of access to partners. Thus, men who are not attractive to adult females may be more prone to sexual contact with less preferred partners, e.g., prepubescent females.
Snyder, 2000	Presents Bureau of Justice statistical data based on the National Incident-Based Reporting System from 1991 through 1996.
	The age profile of juvenile sex assault victims by all perpetrators varied with the nature of the crime. Juveniles were the large majority of the victims of forcible fondling (84%), forcible sodomy (79%), and sexual assault with an object (75%). In contrast, juveniles were the victims in less than half (46%) of forcible rapes.
	About one-quarter (27%) of all perpetrators were family members of their victims. The offenders of young victims were more likely than the offenders of older victims to be family members. Almost half (49%) of the offenders of victims under age 6 were family members, compared with 42% of the offenders who assaulted youth aged 6 through 11, and 24% of offenders who sexually assaulted juveniles aged 12 through 17.
	Compared with young male victims, a greater proportion of female victims under age 12 were assaulted by family members. For male victims under age 12, 40% of the offenders were family members compared with 47% of the offenders of females under age 12.

in spite of extensive preparation by the program participants, they could not arrive at a consensus regarding even basic definitions of elder maltreatment. Stein concluded that the struggle to achieve basic, consistent working definitions was indicative of a broader problem of collecting meaningful data regarding elder abuse.

The first Bureau of Justice data regarding elder abuse were reported in 1987 (Bureau of Justice, 1987). Bachman (1992), a Bureau of Justice statistician, reviewed violent crime victimization rates for the period 1987 through 1990. Bachman found that the elderly were less likely than younger age groups to be victims of crime and, in particular, violent crime. For violent crime victims under the age of 25, the rate was 64.6 per 1000; for violent crime victims over the age of 65, the rate was 4.0 per 1000. When the elderly victimization did occur, however, elderly victims were more likely to incur serious injuries compared to younger victims.

Bachman's findings further reflected that, as a group, elderly victims were more likely than other age groups to report perpetrators as strangers. The death rates of the elderly due to felonious assault reflected their greater likelihood to suffer a lethal outcome by stranger assailants; the data, however, did not explain why. Presumably, the typically isolated living circumstances of many elderly and their more agile physical health were factors.

In reviewing statistics reflecting annual domestic violence homicide rates, Bachman found that, as a family member aged, the statistical likelihood of homicide death by another family member diminished. In comparison to younger family members, the elderly had a greater likelihood of homicide death by an acquaintance than by a family member, or by a stranger.

The elderly, especially the female elderly, are susceptible to sexual assault or rape, but the full scope of the problem is not well determined (Burgess, Hanrahan, and Baker, 2005). Clinicians involved in the care of the elderly should be vigilant in observing possible signs of abuse/neglect and taking steps to initiate appropriate intervention (Kennedy, 2005). Table 5.12 presents evidence-based studies regarding the physical abuse of elderly family members.

Basic Points to Considering Clinical Forensic Assessment

Clinicians need to remain cognizant of the potential impact their interventions can have on the health and integrity of a family both in the short and in the long term. Crisis intervention may occur on an emergent basis to deal with an immediate concern, but the needs of every family must be viewed in the long term. An immediate intervention intended to deal decisively with a violent perpetrator must take into consideration the eventual likelihood that the family will want to reintegrate that wayward family member.

The author has had the experience with hundreds of family situations whereby a father/father figure is forced to leave the family home because of a concern of violence potential. In some instances, the father/father figure is incarcerated. In one fell swoop, the family loses its primary source of income, the marital relationship is compromised, and the child/father relationship(s) is severely stressed. All too frequently, these circumstances traumatize family relationships irretrievably. Obviously, in some instances, the risk is so severe that there is no alternative but to remove potentially violent family members (who, of course, are not always fathers). Our caution to clinicians, in these situations, is to tread cautiously. The effort should be to avoid feeding into the emotional frenzies that family

Table 5.12   Evidence-Based Findings Regarding Physical Abuse of Elderly Family Members

Study	Finding
Bureau of Justice Statistics (BJS), 1987	Persons aged 50 or older made up 30% of the population, are 12% of murder victims, and are 7% of all serious crime victims.
Burgess et al., 2005	Study describing forensic markers of sexual abuse of elderly female victims.
Dawson and Langan, 1994	Among murders of victims over age 60, their offspring were the killers in 42% of the cases. Spouses were the perpetrators in 24% of family murders of persons over age 60.
Kennedy, 2005	Two million elderly are abused or neglected every year. Elderly visit their physicians five times per year, yet physicians initiate only 2% of reported cases of abuse and neglect.
National Center on Elder Abuse, 1994, 1996, 1998	At least one-half million older persons in domestic settings were abused, or neglected, or experienced self-neglect, and that for every reported incident of elder abuse, neglect, or self-neglect, approximately five go unreported.
	After accounting for their larger proportion in the aging population, female elders are abused at a higher rate than males.
	The nation's oldest elders (80 years or older) are abused and neglected at two to three times their proportion of the elderly population.
	In almost 90% of the elder abuse and neglect incidents with a known perpetrator, the perpetrator is a family member, and two thirds of the perpetrators are adult children or spouses.
	In 1994, the incidence of specific types of elder abuse were as follows: physical abuse, 15.7%; sexual abuse, 0.04%; emotional abuse, 7.3%; neglect, 58.5%; financial exploitation, 12.3%; all other types, 5.1%; and unknown, 0.06%.
	In most states, specific professionals are designated "mandatory reporters of elder abuse" and are required by law to report suspected cases of elder maltreatment. Members and their relatives reported 14.9% of reported cases. In 1994, 21.6% of all elder abuse reports came from physicians and other health care professionals, while another 9.4% came from service providers. Family members and relatives of victims reported 14.9% of reported cases of domestic elder abuse.
National Crime Victimization Survey (NCVS), 2004	From 1993 to 2002, persons aged 65 or older experienced less violence and fewer property crimes compared to younger persons.
	About one in five of personal crimes against the elderly were thefts compared to about one in 33 for persons aged 12–49.
	Property crime, not violence, provided the highest percentage of crime against persons aged 65 or older.
Oh, Kim, Martins, and Kim, 2006	15,230 elderly Koreans were interviewed. The rate of elderly who experienced any one category of abuse was 6.3%. Emotional abuse was the most frequent and physical abuse was the least frequent. A number of personal characteristics were associated with the likelihood of abuse including age, gender, educational level, and economic dependency. In addition, family characteristics such as type of household, family economic level, and quality of family relations were associated with the presence of elder abuse.
Tatara, 1996	Nationally, nearly 70% of Adult Protective Service agencies caseloads involve elder abuse.

circumstances can generate for the family and for interveners. Typically, adversarial proceedings inflame the emotional volatility still further.

Family histories go before, and beyond, what may be immediately apparent. A marital relationship, for example, can have a history of infidelity; an incident of violence occurs and pent-up feelings from the past are unleashed. Such dynamics can occur transgenerationally (Lev-Wiesel, 2006). A parent can have unresolved issues from childhood relationships with siblings, which brim over into current circumstances (Butler, 2006; Linder and Collins, 2005). Above all, the clinician must balance any intervention with the need to protect those who could be harmed by ineffective interventions both within and external to the family. Other basic points to keep in mind when working with violence-prone families are as follows:

1. As with any specialized clinical work, clinicians must have competence in the area of proficiency by virtue of training, supervision, research, or a combination of the above. The burden of responsibility to demonstrate competence is on the clinician. With families prone to violence, clinicians should have expertise in the assessment of marital relationships, parenting and childcare issues, and working with family members individually and conjointly. Additionally, clinicians should have expertise regarding the assessment and management of physically and sexually aggressive behavior.

2. When doing forensic work, it is very important for the clinician to know his or her precise role and make a concerted effort to maintain the boundaries of that role. The clinician must convey what that role is to family members as thoroughly as possible and as frequently as necessary. When there are multiple family members, there are bound to be different points of view to include different views of the role of the clinician. The author's experience is that this issue can be a flashpoint of complaints brought against clinicians. There are so many points of interest and competing players that clinicians can be unwittingly seduced into assuming a compromised role or violating appropriate boundaries. For example, a clinician can complete a court-ordered assessment of a family. All parties concerned can be initially pleased with the clinician's work. Later, however, a given family member can perceive that the clinician unjustifiably sided with another family member and problems unfold. The forensic evaluator must maintain objectivity and help every family member understand that focus.

3. As a follow-up to the above point, if the clinician is conducting a court-ordered evaluation of a family, the clinician must explicitly indicate that he or she will not be serving in a treating capacity with the family, with any family member, or coalition of family members.

4. The assessment of violence-prone family situations for forensic purposes must include accessing as many individual family member and collective family member domains of functioning as possible. In addition to usual clinical and developmental history information, this may include the following domains: physical health, educational, employment, military, police/arrest/court, psychosexual, marital, parenting, military, mental health, substance abuse, and violent behavior.

5. Forensic data collection regarding the family should involve as many data resources as deemed relevant. Examples would be clinical interviews, psychological tests and instruments, behavioral observations (in multiple settings if possible), and thorough review of all referral information including prior reports and case records.

6. Data for the forensic database should be obtained from as many collateral resources as deemed relevant. These would include but not be limited to information from the all family members and possibly extended family members. Other resources include the police, probation officers, child welfare caseworkers, and other collaterally involved professionals.

7. Whatever data are gathered must be scrutinized carefully; the clinician must be ever mindful of the possibility of distortion and deceit.

8. Clinicians should be up to date with demographics and other research regarding domestic violence, abuse, and neglect.

9. One essential aspect of every risk assessment should be application of empirically validated risk instruments, assuming empirically based instruments are available for the type of risk in question. We note that at least one researcher has questioned the validity of combining the findings of multiple risk instruments on the assumption that this increases predictive validity (Seto, 2005).

10. It is important for clinicians to be aware of reliability and validity coefficients with risk assessment instruments as well as applicable longitudinal research. At the current time, these data regarding domestic violence prediction are still experimental. These limitations should be acknowledged explicitly in written reports and in expert testimony.

11. Clinicians should also acknowledge that risk assessments, particularly those utilizing dynamic risk factors, are time limited as to period of predictive application. A given risk assessment may be rendered obsolete with the passage of time or change in risk factor status. A prudent approach is to always recommend follow-up evaluation within a reasonable period based on the applicable time periods from the research data. In most instances, this would be for no more than 24 months.

12. Given the still experimental nature of domestic violence risk instruments, opinions regarding the assessment of risk should be carefully worded. Statements in the absolute (i.e., "…this spouse will not be violent again"; "…this father presents no risk") are not appropriate. Opinions should be expressed qualitatively (i.e., minimal, moderate, substantial risk, etc.) or in terms of established risk factors being present (e.g., "…a number of risk factors known to coexist with spousal abuse are evidenced by this spouse").

13. All opinions regarding assessment of risk should include recommendations for a safety plan as well as risk-management strategies. These recommendations should be realistic in terms of clinical need and in terms of available and accessible resources.

Avoiding Evaluation and Consultation Errors

Clinical work with families is more challenging and complex compared to working with an individual. Clinical work with families also offers clinicians the possibility of special satisfaction when troubled families survive trauma and are able to move on in a healthier manner. Failure to recognize the complexity of family work can render clinicians vulnerable to a number of problems. Compared to the lengthy and established history of mental health intervention with individual patients, family work is comparatively rudimentary. The ethics involved in working with individuals have some application to working with families, but family work involves its own set of ethical principles, many of which are still undergoing conceptual development. Clinician forethought and careful statement and restatement of one's role is one basic strategy to avoid difficulties as work with a family proceeds.

Treatment Considerations

Treatment with perpetrators and victims of family violence must incorporate family and individual family member safety as a foremost consideration. There is no stock management plan that will apply in circumstances of family violence. Stuart (2005) recently suggested the strategy of initially identifying domestic abusers who can be helped from those who are not likely to be helped. Thus, rather than a "one-size-fits-all" approach to treatment, resources could be better allocated to those families most likely to profit from treatment. Marital and couples therapists should screen on an ongoing basis for indications of abusive dynamics in spousal relationships. Screening at this level is one of the most fundamental means of identifying spousal violence potential (Aldarondo and Strauss, 1994). Unfortunately, partners in the majority of troubled spousal relationships never seek treatment (Rathus and Feindler, 2004).

In some instances, an appropriate plan will entail ensuring that the perpetrator will have no further contact or only supervised contact with family member(s) deemed to be at risk. In other cases, safeguards within the home may be sufficient. An example of this might be arranging a residence bedroom plan so that the parent's bedroom is in between the bedrooms of an adolescent and a younger sibling who is at risk. Another treatment issue is the attempt to treat women who have been subjected to severe domestic trauma in the community (Chaikin and Prout, 2004). One issue is the safety status of the woman-victim; another issue is whether community-based treatment will be sufficiently intensive to achieve treatment goals. If there are children involved, then further considerations include the prospect of separating the children from the mother even for brief intervals.

Treatment of problem families is a popular area of interest judging by the amount and variety of literature the topic generates (Gilgun, 2005; Henggeler, Halliday-Boykins, Cunningham, Randall, Shapiro, and Chapman, 2006; Hogue, Dauber, Stambaugh, Ceccero, and Liddle, 2006; Robbins, Liddle, Turner, Dakof, Alexander, and Kogan, 2006). Investigators have addressed the presence of different violence-propensity risk factors as affecting treatment efficacy (Dutton, Bodnarchuk, Kropp, and Hart, 1997a; Dutton, Bodnarchuk, Kropp, Hart, and Ogloff, 1997b). There is also a surge of interest in the applicability of different therapeutic modalities with different cultural groups (Chen and Davenport, 2005).

Writing Forensic Reports and Acting as an Expert Witness

The writing of forensic reports and offering expert testimony are acquired skills. Expert testimony must follow applicable ethical proscriptions, must be grounded in a sound, empirically based database, must be creative, and must be persuasive (Poirier, 1993). This is a hefty mix of requirements. Achieving the mix can be a challenge to consistently master.

Clinicians must remember that the ultimate legal issues (e.g., guilt, custodial fitness, dangerousness, and so on) are the final prerogative of the bench. At the same time, clinicians are asked routinely to render opinions about these very issues, which of course is not the same as making the final determination. There is a lengthy legal history to this delicate mix of roles and limits between mental health and the law (Heilbrun, 2001). Our point for the moment is that the expert witness contribution must steadfastly respect this area of the legal/mental health interface. Forensic reports and testimony must be crafted so that respect for these areas of sensitivity is conveyed. Once the expert is on the witness stand, it is too late to undo what may have been a moment of lapse of judgment, indiscretion, or arrogance when writing a report.

There is perhaps no better example of attempting to offer an unswerving opinion while at the same time maintaining an appropriate balance of constraint than with expert opinion as to estimation of risk. In the body of this chapter, we have attempted to underscore the empirically tentative nature of risk assessment in general. Whittemore and Kropp (2002) described four general principles that should guide the use of SARA:

1. Risk assessment should consider risk factors supported in the literature.
2. Risk assessment should employ multiple sources of information.
3. Risk assessments should be victim-informed.
4. Risk assessments can be improved by using tools or guidelines.

The study of risk assessment has enjoyed immense and rapid development, but remains far from having accuracy even approximating 90% (i.e., approaching the legal "beyond a reasonable doubt" level of proof). Forensic clinicians need to bear in mind that the degrees of freedom embodied in field research with risk assessment tools are fundamentally different from taking risk assessment data into the courtroom. The language of forensic reports must have precision and follow accepted risk assessment schema embraced by the scientific community.

Novel Applications of Forensic Evidence and Knowledge

The future will see many refinements of spousal assault risk instruments and adaptations for additional classes of perpetrators beyond adult male spouse abusers. There will also be likely expansion of new areas of domestic violence and risk assessment instruments (i.e., child abuse/neglect, physical and sexual abuse, elder abuse, and so on). There has been preliminary work in the development of risk assessment instruments to identify potential family member domestic violence victims. Identification of potential victims will be an important first step toward implementing prevention measures with family members at risk. The development of risk assessment instruments for potential domestic violence victims, however, will add a number of new ethical issues. Prior to domestic violence actually occurring, no matter how many latent risk factors a family may present with, there would be implied assumption of a possible perpetrator. This, of course, is a legally untenable assumption. With families where there has been at least an initial violence event, the ethical concern may be moot because risk assessment would be part of a relapse prevention effort. The intent would be to identify at-risk victims, and then to work with family member victim(s) and perpetrator to help ward off future violence.

There is a growing body of research on the neurobiology of aggressive behavior (de Almeida, Ferrai, Parmigiani, and Miczek, 2005; Gollan, Lee, and Coccaro, 2005; Goodman, New, and Siever 2004; Turecki, 2005). One neurobiology study specifically examined deficits with domestic violence offenders; the authors found specific impairments with frontal lobe executive functions (Westby and Ferraro, 1999). Although still preliminary, this is fascinating data with far-reaching implications for the broad problem of violence. The author anticipates that future neuropsychological research will have significant bearing on assessment and intervention strategies with domestic violence.

A significant problem in any assessment effort of families at risk for violent behavior is the likelihood of distortion and deception (Hall and Poirier, 2001). Deception is an inherent issue in all-forensic evaluations. Because of family bond dynamics, family members will often protect perpetrators by denial, or minimization of risk, even when there has been an episode(s) of serious violence. This will likely be a continued area of ongoing research. From one perspective, an implied purpose of risk assessment is to sift through available data and circumvent the likelihood of domestic violence perpetrators utilizing deception. Risk assessment instruments, however, rely on the presence of risk factors that, in turn, rely on family member report. Perpetrators and colluding family members can simply be deceptive about acknowledging the presence of critical risk factors. There will undoubtedly be future research to identify subtle and implied risk factors that will not be directly reliant on family member or perpetrator report. The development of risk assessment tools for identifying actual or potential domestic violence victims may then provide assistance with the problem of deception/distortion.

References

Aldarondo, E., and Strauss M. (1994). Screening for physical violence in couple therapy. *Family Process, 33*, 425–439.

de Almeida, R. M. M., Giovenardi, M., da Silva, S. P., de Oliveira, V. P., Stein, D. J. (2005). Maternal aggression in Wistar rats: Effect of 5-HT-sub(2A/2c) receptor agonist and antagonist microinjected into the dorsal periaqueductal gray matter and medial septum. *Brazilian Journal of Medical and Biological Research, 38*(4), 597–602.

American Psychological Association. (1993). Guidelines for providers of psychological services to ethnic, linguistic, and culturally diverse populations. *American Psychologist, 58*, 45–48.

American Psychological Association. (2002). Ethical principles of psychologists and code of conduct. *American Psychologist, 57*, 1060–1073.

American Psychological Association. (2003). Guidelines on multicultural education, training, research, practice, and organizational change for psychologists. *American Psychologist, 58*, 377–404.

American Psychological Association. (2004). Guidelines for psychological practice with older adults. *American Psychologist, 59*(4), 236–260.

Aravanis, S. (2002). A profile of the National Policy Summit on elder abuse: Perspective and advice on replication. *Journal of Elder Abuse and Neglect, 14*, 55–69.

Aravanis, S., Adelman, R., Breckman, R., Fulmer, T., Holder, E., Lachs, M. et al. (1993). Diagnostic and treatment guidelines on elder abuse and neglect. *Archives of Family Medicine, 2*(4), 371–388.

Archer, J. (2004). Sex differences in aggression in real-world settings: A meta-analytic review. *Review of General Psychology, 8*(4), 291–322.

Bachman, R. (1992). *Elderly victims* (Tech. Rep. No. NCJ-138330). Washington, DC: U.S. Department of Justice.

Bartens, J. (2004). If a threat of violence is presented, when does the law require family mediators to break confidentiality? Guiding family mediators through the application of Tarasoff principles. *Family Court Review, 42*(4), 641–654.

Beech, A. R., Fisher, D. D., and Thornton, D. (2002). Risk assessment of sex offenders. *Professional Psychology: Research and Practice, 34*(4), 339–352.

Bennett, L., Tolman, R. M., Rogalski, C. J., and Srinivasaraghavan, J. (1994). Domestic abuse by male alcohol and drug addicts. *Violence and Victims, 9*, 359–368.

Bewsey, K., and Odulate, A. (2003). Therapist dilemmas: A discussion paper. *Counseling Psychology Review, 18*(4), 30–37.

Bograd, M., and Mederos, F. (1999). Battering and couples therapy: Universal screening and selection of treatment modality. *Journal of Marital and Family Therapy, 25*, 291–312.

Bollinger, L., Riggs, D. S., Blake, D. D., and Ruzek, J. I. (2000). Prevalence of personality disorders among combat veterans with post-traumatic stress disorder. *Journal of Traumatic Stress, 130*, 255–270.

Borum, R. (1996). Improving the clinical practice of violence risk assessment: Technology, guidelines, and training. *American Psychologist, 51*, 945–956.

Bremmer, J. D., Southwick, S. M., Johnson, D. R., Yehuda, R., and Charney, D. S. (1993). Childhood physical abuse and combat related posttraumatic stress disorder in Vietnam veterans. *American Journal of Psychiatry, 150*, 235–239.

Buchbinder, E., and Elisikovits, E. (2004). Reporting bad results: The ethical responsibility of presenting abused women's parenting practice in a negative light. *Child & Family Social Work, 9*(4), 359–367.

Bureau of Justice Statistics. (1987). *Elderly victimization.* Washington, DC: U.S. Department of Justice.

Bureau of Justice Statistics. (2002). *National crime victimization survey.* Washington, DC: U.S. Department of Justice.

Burgess, A. W., Hanrahan, N. P., and Baker, T. (2005). Forensic markers in elder female sexual abuse cases. *Clinical Geriatric Medicine, 214*(2), 399–412.

Butler, K. (2006). Beyond rivalry, a hidden world of sibling violence [Health and Fitness]. *The New York Times (New York), Late ed.,* Final, Section F, p. 1.

Campbell, J. C. (1986). Nursing assessment for risk of homicide with battered women. *Advances in Nursing Science, 8*(4), 36–51.

Campbell, J. C. (2002). Health consequences of intimate partner violence. *The Lancet, 359*, 1331–1336.

Campbell, J. C., and Lewandowski, L. A. (1997). Mental and physical health effects of intimate partner violence on women and children. *The Psychiatric Clinics of North America, 20*(2), 353–374.

Carlson, E. A., Sroufe, L. A., and Egeland, B. (2004). The construction of experience: A longitudinal study of representation and behavior. *Child Development, 75*(1), 66–83.

Chaikin, N. D., and Prout, M. F. (2004). Treating complex trauma in women within community mental health. *American Journal of Orthopsychiatry, 74*(2), 160–173.

Chen, S. W., and Davenport, D. S. (2005). Cognitive-behavioral therapy with Chinese American clients: Cautions and modifications. *Psychotherapy: Theory, Research, Practice, Training, 43*(1), 101–110.

Cicchetti, D. (2004). An odyssey of discovery: Lessons learned through three decades of research on child maltreatment. *American Psychologist, 59*(8), 731–741.

Cinq-Mars, C., Wright, J., Cyr, M. U., and McDuff, P. (2003). Sexual at-risk behaviors of sexually abused adolescent girls. *Journal of Child Sexual Abuse, 12*(2), 2–18.

Cocozza, J. J., and Steadman, H. J. (1974). Some refinements in the measurement and prediction of dangerous behavior. *American Journal of Psychiatry, 131*(9), 1012–1014.

Cole, J., Logan T. K., and Shannon, L. (2005). Intimate sexual victimization among women with protective orders: Types and associations of physical and mental health problems. *Violence and Victims, 20*(6), 695–715.

Committee on Ethical Guidelines for Forensic Psychologists. (1991). Specialty guidelines for forensic psychologists. *Law and Human Behavior, 15*, 655–666.

Cui, M., Conger, R. D., and Frederick, O. (2005). Predicting change in adolescent adjustment from change in marital problems. *Developmental Psychology, 41*(5), 812–823.

Cyr, M., McDuff, P., Wright, J., Thèriault, C., and Cinq-Mars, C. (2005) Clinical correlates and repetition of self-harming behaviors among female adolescent victims of sexual abuse. *Journal of Child Sexual Abuse, 14*(2), 49–68.

Cyr, M., Wright, J., McDuff, P., and Perron, A. (2002). Intrafamilial sexual abuse: Brother-sister incest does not differ from father-daughter and stepfather-stepdaughter incest. *Child Abuse and Neglect, 26*(9), 957–973.

Dawson, J. W., and Langan, P. A. (1994). *Murder in families.* Washington, DC: U.S. Department of Justice, Bureau of Justice Statistics.

Diamond, T., and Muller, R. T. (2004). The relationship between witnessing parental conflict during childhood and later psychological adjustment among university students: Disentangling confounding risk factors. *Canadian Journal of Behavioural Science, 36*(4), 295–309.

Douglas, K., and Kropp, P. R. (2002). A prevention-based paradigm for violence risk assessment: Clinical and research applications. *Criminal Justice and Behavior, 21,* 617–658.

Durose, M. R., Harlow, C. W., Langan, P. A., Motivans, M., Rantala, R. R., and Smith, E. (2005). *Family violence statistics: including statistics on strangers and acquaintances* (Tech. Rep. No. NCJ 207846). Washington, DC: Bureau of Justice Statistics.

Dutton, D. G. (1995). A scale for measuring propensity for abusiveness. *Journal of Family Violence, 10*(2), 203–221.

Dutton, D. G., and Kropp, P. R. (2000). A review of domestic violence risk instruments. *Trauma, Violence, & Abuse, 1,* 171–181.

Dutton, D. G., Bodnarchuk, M., Kropp, R., and Hart, S. D. (1997a). Wife assault treatment and criminal recidivism: An 11-year follow-up. International *Journal of Offender Therapy and Comparative Criminology, 41,* 9–23.

Dutton, D. G., Bodnarchuk, M., Kropp, R., Hart, S. D., and Ogloff, J. P. (1997b). Client personality disorders affecting wife assault post-treatment recidivism. *Violence and Victims, 12,* 37–50.

Ehrensaft, M., Moffitt, T. E., and Caspi, A. (2004). Clinically abusive relationships in an unselected birth cohort: Men's and women's participation and developmental antecedents. *Journal of Abnormal Psychology, 113*(2), 258–271.

Ehrensaft, M. K., Moffitt, T. E., and Caspi, A. (2006). Is domestic violence followed by an increased risk of psychiatric disorders among women but not among men? A longitudinal cohort study. *American Journal of Psychiatry, 163,* 885–892.

Ehrensaft, M., and Vivian, D. (1996). Spouses' reasons for not reporting existing physical aggression as a marital problem. *Journal of Family Psychology, 107,* 443–453.

Farr, K. (2002). Battered women who were "being killed and survived it": Straight talk from survivors. *Violence Victims, 17*(3), 267–281.

Federal Bureau of Investigation. (2002). *Supplemental homicide reports (SHR).* Washington, DC: Author.

Federal Interagency Forum on Child and Family Statistics (Forum). (2006) *America's children: key national indicators of well-being.* Available from the Forum web site, http://childstats.gov.

Fieguth, A., Gunter, D., Kleemann, W., and Troger, H. (2002). Lethal child neglect. *Forensic Sciences International, 130*(1), 8–12.

Fulton, D. (2000). Shaken baby syndrome. *Critical Care Nursing Quarterly, 23*(2), 43–50.

Gilgun, J. F. (2005). Qualitative research and family psychology. *Journal of Family Psychology, 19*(1), 40–50.

Glasser, M., Kolvin, J., Campbell, D., Glasser, A., Leitch, I., and Farrelly, S. (2001). Cycle of child sex abuse links: links between being a victim and becoming a perpetrator. *British Journal of Psychiatry, 179,* 482–494.

Goldblatt, H., and Eisikovits, Z. (2005). Role taking of youths in a family context: Adolescents exposed to interparental violence. *American Journal of Orthopsychiatry, 75*(4), 644–657.

Golding, J. M. (1999). Intimate partner violence as a risk factor for mental disorders: A meta-analysis. *Journal of Family Violence, 14*(2), 99–132.

Goodman, M., New, A., and Siever, L. (2004). Trauma, genes and the neurobiology of personality disorders. *Annuals of the New York Academy of Science, 1032,* 104–116.

Goulding, J. M. (1999). Intimate partner violence as a risk factor for mental disorders. *Journal of Family Violence, 14*, 99–132.

Grann, M., and Wedin, I. (2002). Risk factors for recidivism among spousal assault and spousal homicide offenders. *Psychology, Crime, and Law, 8*, 5–23.

Grove, W. H., and Meehl, P. E. (1996). Comparative efficiency of informal (subjective, impressionistic) and formal (mechanical, algorithmic) prediction procedures: The clinical-statistical controversy. *Psychology, Public Policy, and Law, 2*(2), 293–323.

Gwinn, C., McClane, G., Shanel-Hogan, K., and Strack, G. (2004). Domestic violence: No place for a smile. *Journal of the California Dental Association, 32*(5), 399–409.

Haley, W. E., Larson, D. G., Kasil-Godley, J., Neimeyer, R. A., and Kwiloz, D. M. (2003). Roles for psychologists in end-of-life care: Emerging models of practice. *Professional Psychology: Research and Practice, 34*(6), 626–633.

Halikias, W. (2004). School-based risk assessments: A conceptual framework and model for professional practice. *Professional Psychology: Research and Practice, 35*(6), 598–607.

Hall, H. V., and Poirier, J. G. (2001). Detecting malingering and deception: Forensic distortion analysis (2nd ed.). Boca Raton, FL: CRC Press.

Hansen, N. D., Randazzo, K. V., Schwartz, A., Marshall, M., Kalis, D., Frazier, R., Burke, C., Kershner-Rice, K., and Norvig, G. (2006). Do we practice what we preach? An exploratory survey of multicultural psychotherapy competencies. *Professional Psychology: Research and Practice, 37*, 66–74.

Harris, G. T., Rice, M. E., and Quinsey, V. L. (1993). Violent recidivism of mentally disordered offenders: The development of a statistical prediction instrument. *Criminal Justice and Behavior, 20*(4), 315–335.

Harris, G. T., Rice, M. E., and Quinsey, V. L. (1998). Appraisal and management of risk in sexual aggressors: Implications for criminal justice policy. *Psychology, Public Policy, and Law, 4*(1–2), 73–115.

Heilbrun, K. (1997). Prediction versus management models relevant to risk assessment: The importance of legal decision-making context. *Law and Human Behavior, 21*, 347–359.

Heilbrun, K. (2001). *Principles of forensic mental health assessment.* New York: Kluwer Academic.

Helfritz, L. E., Stanford, M. S., Conklin, S. M., Greve, K. W., Villemarette-Pittman, N. R., and Houston, R. J. (2006). Usefulness of self-report instruments in assessing men accused of domestic violence. *Psychological Record, 56*(2), 171–180.

Henggeler, S. W., Halliday-Boykins, C. A., Cunningham, P. B., Randall, J., Shapiro, S. B., and Chapman, J. E. (2006). Juvenile drug court: Enhancing outcomes by integrating evidence-based treatments. *Journal of Consulting and Clinical Psychology, 74*, 42–54.

Hilton, N., and Harris, G. (2005). Predicting wife assault: A critical review and implications for policy and practice. *Trauma Violence Abuse, 6*(1), 3–23.

Hilton, N. Z., Harris, G. T., Rice, M. E., Lang, C., Cormier, C. A., and Lines, K. J. (2004). A brief actuarial assessment for the prediction of wife assault recidivism: The Ontario domestic assault risk assessment. *Psychological Assessment, 16*(3), 267–275.

Hoagwood, K., Jensen, P. S., and Fisher, C. B. (Eds.) (1996). *Ethical issues in mental health research with children and adolescents.* Hillsdale, NJ: Lawrence Erlbaum Associates, Inc.

Hogue, A., Dauber, S., Stambaugh, L. F., Ceccero, J. J., and Liddle, H. A. (2006) Early therapeutic alliance and treatment outcome in individual and family therapy for adolescent behavior problems. *Journal of Consulting and Clinical Psychology, 74*(1), 121–129.

Janson, G. R., and Steigerwald, F. J. (2002). Family counseling and ethical challenges with gay, lesbian, bisexual, and transgendered (GLBT) clients: More questions than answers. *Family Journal: Counseling and Therapy for Couples and Families, 107*(4), 415–418.

Jones, L. M., Finkelhor, D., and Halter, S. (2006). Child maltreatment trends in the 1990s: Why does neglect differ from sexual and physical abuse? *Child Maltreatment: Journal of the American Professional Society on the Abuse of Children, 11*(2), 107–120.

Jory, B. (2004). The intimate justice scale: An instrument to screen for psychological abuse and physical abuse in clinical practice. *Journal of Marital & Family Therapy, 30*(1), 29–44.

Karpel, M. A. (1994). *Evaluating couples: A handbook for practitioners.* New York: Norton.

Keenan, H., and Runyan, D. (2001). Shaken baby syndrome. Lethal inflicted traumatic brain injury in young children. *North Carolina Medical Journal, 62*(6), 340–343.

Kennedy, R. D. (2005). Elder abuse and neglect: The experience, knowledge, and attitudes of primary care physicians. *Family Medicine, 37*(7), 481–485.

Knapp, S., and Slattery, J. M. (2004). Professional boundaries in nontraditional settings. *Professional Psychology: Research and Practice, 35*(5), 553–558.

Knight, L., and Collins, K. (2005). A 25-year retrospective review of deaths due to pediatric neglect. *American Journal of Forensic Medical Pathology, 26*(3), 221–228.

Koss, M. P., Heise, L., and Russo, N. F. (1994). *Psychology of Women Quarterly, 18*(4), 509–537.

Kreider, R. M., and Fields, J. (2002). Number, timing, and duration of marriages and divorces: 1966. In *Current population reports* (Tech. Rep. No. P70-80). Washington, DC: U.S. Census Bureau.

Kropp, P. R., Hart, S. D., and Belfrage, H. (2004a). *The development of the Brief Spousal Assault Form for the evaluation of risk (B-SAFER): A tool for criminal justice professionals* (Research and Statistics Division/Family Violence Initiative No. rr05fv-le). Canada: Department of Justice.

Kropp, P. R., Hart, S. D., Webster, C. W., and Eaves, D. (1994). *Manual for the Spousal Assault Risk Assessment Guide.* Vancouver, BC: British Columbia Institute on Family Violence.

Kropp, P. R., Hart, S. D., Webster, C. W., and Eaves, D. (1995). *Manual for the Spousal Assault Risk Assessment Guide, 2nd ed.* Vancouver, BC: British Columbia Institute on Family Violence.

Kropp, P. R., Hart, S. D., Webster, C. W., and Eaves, D. (1998). *Spousal Assault Risk Assessment: User's Guide.* Toronto, Canada: Multi-Health Systems, Inc.

Kropp, P. R., Hart, S. D., Webster, C. W., and Eaves, D. (1999). *Spousal Assault Risk Assessment Guide User's Manual.* Toronto, Canada: Multi-Health Systems Inc. and B. C. Institute of Family Violence.

Kropp, P. R., Hart, S. D., Webster, C. W., and Eaves, D. (2001). The Spousal Assault Risk Assessment (SARA) Guide: Reliability and validity in adult male offenders. *Law and Human Behavior, 24*(12), 101–118.

Kropp, P. R., Hart, S. D., Webster, C. W., and Eaves, D. (2004b). *Brief Spousal Assault Form for the Evaluation of Risk (B-SAFER) User Manual* (The British Columbia Institute on Family Violence). Vancouver, British Columbia, Canada: Department of Justice.

Lamb, D. H., Catanzaro, S. J., and Moorman, A. S. (2004). A preliminary look at how psychologists identify, evaluate, and proceed when faced with possible multiple relationship dilemmas. *Professional Psychology: Research and Practice, 35*(3), 248–254.

Lev-Wiesel, R. (2006). Intergenerational transmission of sexual abuse? Motherhood in the shadow of incest. *Journal of Child Sexual Abuse, 15*(2), 75–101.

Lewis, N. (2003). Balancing the dictates of law and ethical practice: Empowerment of female survivors of domestic violence in the presence of overlapping child abuse. *Ethics and Behavior, 130*(4), 353–366.

Linder, J. R., and Collins, W. A. (2005). Parent and peer predictors of physical aggression and conflict management in romantic relationships in early adulthood. *Journal of Family Psychology, 19*(2), 252–262.

Maiuro, R. D., and Cahn, T. S. (1988). Anger, hostility, and depression in domestically violent versus generally assaultive men and nonviolent control subjects. *Journal of Consulting and Clinical Psychology, 56,* 17–23.

Margolin, G., Chien, D., Duhman, S. E., Fauchier, A., Gordis, E. B., Oliver, P. H., Ramos, M. C., and Vickerman, K. A. (2005). Ethical issues in couple and family research. *Journal of Family Psychology, 19*(1), 157–167.

McCloskey, K., and Grigsby, N. (2005). The ubiquitous clinical problem of adult intimate partner violence: The need for routine assessment. *Professional Psychology: Research and Practice, 36*(3), 264–275.

McCormack, A., Burgess, A. W., and Hartman, C. (1988). Familial abuse and post traumatic stress disorder. *Journal of Traumatic Stress, 1,* 231–242.

McCurdy, K., and Daro, D. (1994). *Current trends in child abuse reporting and fatalities: The results of the 1993 annual fifty state survey* (Tech. Rep. No. Working paper number 808). Chicago, IL: National Center on Child Abuse Research.

Meston, C. M., Rellini, A. H., and Heiman, J. R. (2006). Women's history of sexual abuse, their sexuality, and sexual self-schemas. *Journal of Consulting and Counseling Psychology, 74*(2), 229–236.

Monahan, J. (1996). The past twenty and the next twenty years. *Criminal Justice and Behavior, 23,* 107–120.

Murphy, C. M., Meyer, S., and O'Leary, K. D. (1993). Family of origin violence and MCMI-II psychopathology among partner assaultive men. *Violence and Victims, 8,* 165–176.

National Center on Elder Abuse. (1994). *Findings from a national study of domestic elder abuse reports.* Washington, DC: Author.

National Center on Elder Abuse. (1996). *Older battered women: Integrating aging and domestic violence services.* Washington, DC: Author.

National Center on Elder Abuse. (1998). *The National Elder Abuse Incidence Study 1996: Final report.* Washington, DC: U.S. Department of Health and Human Services, Administration for Children and Families, and the Administration on Aging.

Negrao, C., Bonnanno, G. A., Noll, J. G., Putnam, F. W., and Trickett, P. K. (2005). Shame, humiliation, and childhood sexual abuse: Direct contributions and emotional coherence. *Child Maltreatment: Journal of the American Professional Society on the Abuse of Children, 10*(4), 350–363.

Oh, J., Kim, H. S., Martins, D., and Kim, H. (2006). A study of elder abuse in Korea. *International Journal of Nursing Studies, 43*(2), 203–214.

O'Leary, K. D., and Maiuro, R. D. (2001). *Psychological abuse in violent domestic relations.* New York: Springer.

Olkin, R. Abrams, K., Preston, P., and Kirshbaum, M. (2006). Comparison of parents with and without disabilities raising teens: information from the NHIS and two national surveys. *Rehabilitation Psychology, 51*(12), 43–49.

Pipes, R. B., Holstein, J. E., and Aguirre, M. G. (2005). Examining the personal–professional distinction: Ethics codes and the difficulty of drawing a boundary. *American Psychologist, 60*(No. 4), 325–334.

Poirier, J. G. (1989). Contested custody and allegations of violence. Paper presented at the American Psychological Association, Divisions 29, 42, and 43 Mid-Winter Convention, Orlando, FL.

Poirier, J. G. (1990). Disputed custody and concerns of parental violence: Ethical considerations. Paper presented at the American Psychological Association, Divisions 29, 42, and 43 Mid-Winter Convention, Palm Springs, CA.

Poirier, J. G. (1991a). Assessing the potential for violence in troubled families. Paper presented at the National Organization of Forensic Social Work, Eighth Annual Conference, Washington, DC.

Poirier, J. G. (1991b). Disputed custody and concerns of parental violence. *Psychotherapy in Private Practice, 9*(3), 7–23.

Poirier, J. G. (1993). Domestic violence and the ethics of expert testimony. In A. Austria (Chair), *Domestic violence and sexual harassment: ethical issues in expert testimony.* Symposium presented at the annual convention of the American Psychological Association. Toronto, Ontario, Canada.

Poirier, J. G. (1996). Violence in the family. In Harold V. Hall (Ed.), *Lethal violence 2000: A sourcebook on fatal domestic, acquaintance, and stranger aggression* (pp. 259–292). Kamuela, HI: Pacific Institute for the Study of Conflict and Aggression.

Pollanen, M., Smith, C., Chiasson, D., Cairns, J., and Young, J. (2002). Fatal child abuse-maltreatment syndrome. A retrospective study in Ontario, Canada, 1990–1995. *Forensic Sciences International, 126*(2), 101–104.

Quinsey, V. L., Harris, G. T., Rice, M. E., and Cormier, C. A. (2006). Methods and measurement. In Quinsey, Vernon L., Harris, Grant T., Rice, Marnie E., and Cormier, Catherine A. (Eds.), *Violent offenders: Appraising and managing risk* (2nd ed.). (pp. 49–60). Washington, DC: American Psychological Association.

Rathus, J. H., and Feindler, E. L. (2004). *Assessment of partner violence: A handbook for researchers and practitioners.* Washington, DC: American Psychological Association.

Renker, P., and Tonkin, P. (2006). Women's views of prenatal violence screening: Acceptability and confidentiality issues. *Obstetrics and Gynecology, 107*(2), 348–354.

Rice, M. E., and Harris, G. T. (1995). Violent recidivism: Assessing predictive validity. *Journal of Consulting and Clinical Psychology, 63,* 737–748.

Rice, M. E., and Harris, G. T. (2003). What we know and don't know about treating adult sex offenders. In Winick, Bruce J., La Fond, John Q. (Eds.), *Protecting society from sexually dangerous offenders: Law, justice, and therapy* (pp. 101–117). Washington, DC: American Psychological Association.

Robbins, M. S., Liddle, H. A., Turner, C. W., Dakof, G. A., Alexander, J. F., and Kogan, S. M. (2006). Adolescent and parent therapeutic alliances as predictors of dropout in multidimensional family therapy. *Journal of Family Psychology, 20,* 108–116.

Samuelson, S. L., and Campbell, C. D. (2005) Screening for domestic violence: Recommendations based on a practice survey. *Professional Psychology: Research and Practice, 36*(3), 276–282.

Schuller, R. A., Wells, E., Rzepa, S., and Klippenstine, M. A. (2004) Rethinking battered woman syndrome evidence: The impact of alternative forms of expert testimony on mock jurors' decisions. *Canadian Journal of Behavioural Science, 36*(2), 127–136.

Seto, M. C. (2005). Is more better? Combining actuarial risk scales to predict recidivism among adult sex offenders. *Psychological Assessment, 17,* 156–167.

Seto, M. C., Lalumière, M. L., and Kuban, M. (1999). The sexual preferences of incest offenders. *Journal of Abnormal Psychology, 108*(2), 267–272.

Skowron, E., and Reinemann, D. H. S. (2005). Effectiveness of psychological interventions for child maltreatment: A meta-analysis. *Psychotherapy: Theory, Research, Practice, Training, 42*(1), 52–71.

Smith, A., and Winokur, K. P. (2004). What doctors and policymakers should know: Battered women's views about mandatory medical reporting laws. *Journal of Criminal Justice, 32*(3), 207–221.

Smith, T. B., Constantine, M. G., Dunn, T. W., Dinehart, J. M., and Montoya, J. A. (2006). Multicultural education in the mental health professions: A meta-analytic review. *Journal of Consulting Psychology, 53*(12), 132–145.

Snyder, D. K., Heyman, R. E., and Haynes, S. N. (2005). Evidence-based approaches to assessing couple distress. *Psychological Assessment, 17,* 288–307.

Snyder, H. N. (2000). *Sexual assault of young children as reported to law enforcement: Victim, incident, and offender characteristics.* NCJ No. 182990. Washington, DC: Bureau of Justice Statistics.

Southern, S., Smith, R. L., and Oliver, M. (2005). Marriage and family counseling: Ethics in context. *Family Journal: Counseling and Therapy for Couples and Families, 13*(4), 459–466.

Stanko, E. (1997). Should I stay or should I go? Some thoughts on the variants of intimate violence. *Violence Against Women, 3*(6), 629–635.

Steigerwald, F., and Janson G. R. (2003). Conversion therapy: Ethical considerations in family counseling. *Family Journal: Counseling and Therapy for Couples and Families, 11*(12), 55–59.

Stein, K. F. (1991). A national agenda for elder abuse and neglect research: Issues and recommendations. *Journal of Elder Abuse and Neglect, 3*(3), 91–108.

Stuart, E., and Campbell, J. C. (1989). Assessment of patterns of dangerousness with battered women. *Issues in Mental Health Nursing, 10,* 245–260.

Stuart, R. B. (2004). Twelve practical suggestions for achieving multicultural competence. *Professional Psychology: Research and Practice, 35*(12), 3–9.

Stuart, R. B. (2005). Treatment for partner abuse: Time for a paradigm shift. *Professional Psychology: Research and Practice, 36*(3), 254–263.

Swindle, R., Heller, K., Pescosolido, B., and Kikuzawa, S. (2000). Responses to nervous breakdowns in America over a 40-year period: Mental health policy implications. *American Psychologist, 55*(7), Jul 2000, 740–749.

Sullivan, C. M., and Cain, D. (2004). Ethical and safety considerations when obtaining information from or about battered women for research purposes. *Journal of Interpersonal Violence, 19*(5), 603–618.

Taft, C. T., Pless, A. P., Stalans, L. J., Koenen, K. C., King, L. A., and King, D. W. (2005). Risk factors for partner violence among a national sample of combat veterans. *Journal of Consulting and Clinical Psychology, 73*(12), 151–159.

Tan, L. H., and Quinlivan, J. (2006). Domestic violence, single parenthood, and fathers in the setting of teenage pregnancy. *Journal of Adolescent Health, 38*(3), 201–207.

Tatara, T. (1996). Elder abuse in domestic settings. *Elder Abuse Information Series (1)*: 19. Washington, DC: National Center on Elder Abuse.

Thomas, J. T. (2005). Licensing board complaints: Minimizing the impact on the psychologist's defense and clinical practice. *Professional Psychology: Research and Practice, 36*(4), 426–433.

Turecki, G. (2005). Dissecting the suicide phenotype: the role of impulsive-aggressive behaviors. *Journal of Psychiatry and Neuroscience, 30*(6), 398–408.

U.S. Department of Health and Human Services, Health Resources and Services Administration, Maternal and Child Health Bureau. (2005). *Child Health USA 2005*. Rockville, MD: U.S. Department of Health and Human Services, 2005.

Utech, M. R. and Garrett, R. R. (1992). Elder and child abuse. *Journal of Interpersonal Violence, 7*(3), 418–428.

Vanamo, T., Kauppi, A., Karkola, K., Merikanto, J., and Rasanen, E. (2001). Intra-familial child homicide in Finland 1970–1994: Incidence, causes of death and demographic characteristics. *Forensic Science International, 117*(3), 199–204.

Weisz, A. N., Tolman, R. M., and Saunders, D. G. (2000). Assessing the risk of severe domestic violence: The importance of survivor's predictions. *Journal of Interpersonal Violence, 15*(1), 75–90.

West, C. (2004). Black women and intimate partner violence: New directions for research. *Journal of Interpersonal Violence, 19*(12), 1487–1493.

Westby, M. D., and Ferraro, F. R. (1999). Frontal lobe deficits in domestic violence offenders. *Genetic, Social and General Psychology Monographs, 125*(1), 71–102.

Whittemore, K. E., and Kropp, P. R. (2002). Spousal assault risk assessment: A guide for clinicians. *Journal of Forensic Psychology Practice, 2*(2), 53–64.

Williams, C. R., and Abeles, N. (2004). Issues and implications of deaf culture in therapy. *Professional Psychology: Research and Practice, 35*(6), 643–648.

Yarhouse, M. A. (2003). Working with families affected by HIV/AIDS. *American Journal of Family Therapy, 31*(2), 125–137.

Legal References

Blondin v. Dubois (2001), 19 F. Supp. 2d 123 (S.D.N.Y. 1998). *Vacated and remanded for further proceedings*, 189 F.3d 240 (2d Cir. 1999), *On rehearing*, 78 F. Supp. 2d (S.D.N.Y. 2000), aff'd 238 F.3d 153 (2d Cir. 2001).

Crawford v. Washington 541 U.S. 36 (2004).

Davis v. Washington (Nos. 05-5224 and 05-5705) No. 05-5224, 154 Wash. 2d 291, 111 P. 3d 844, affirmed; No. 05-5705, 829 N. E. 2d 444, reversed and remanded (2006).

DeShaney (a minor) v. Department of Social Services, 109 US Supreme Court WI (S. Ct. 1989).

Gonzales-Valdes v. Florida, 834 So. 2d 933 (Fla. Dist. Ct. Appeal 2003), petition for review denied, 851 So. 2d 728 (Fla. 2003).

Hammon v. Indiana 829 N. E. 2d 444 (2004).

IBN-Tamas v. U.S. (1979) 407 Atl Rpt 2d 626 U.S. Circuit Ct of Appeals for DC.

Landeros v. A. J. Flood, MD et al. (1976) 131 California 69 CA Supreme Court, CA.

Marvin v. Marvin, 18 Cal. 3d 660 (Cal. 1976).

Nicholson v. Scopetta, 344 F3d 154, 164 ([2d Cir] 2003.

Nicholson v. Williams (also known as *Nicholson v. Scopetta*) File No. Court and Date Filed, 00-CV-2229, 00-CV-5155, 00-CV-6885 (E.D.N.Y., Apr. 17, 2000) Citations 205 F. R.D 92 (E.D.N.Y. 2001); 181 F. Supp. 2d 182 (E.D.N.Y.).

People v. Stritzinger (1983). 688 P.2d 738 CA Supreme Court CA.

Santosky v. Kramer (1982). 102 S. Ct. 1388 US Supreme Court NY.

Tarasoff v. Regents of the University of California, 551 p.2d. 334 (1976).

The National Child Protection Act of 1993, 107 Stat. 2490, Pub. L. 103-209 (1993).

Thing v. La Chusa, 1989 CA. 48 Cal 3d 644. CA Supreme Court.

Thurman v. City of Torrington, 595 F. Supp. 1521 (Conn., 1984).

U.S 9th Circuit Court of USA v. Kafka, III, No. 99-30305 (2000).

United States ex rel. Alvera v. C.B.M. Group, Inc., No. CV 01-857-PA (D. Or. 2001) (favorable consent decree).

Violence against Women Act (VAWA), 1994; 2005. (Public Law No: 109-162).

Violence Prediction and Risk Analysis

HAROLD V. HALL

Pacific Institute for the Study of Conflict and Aggression, Kamuela, Hawaii

Contents

Synopsis of Case

Defendant Jones was convicted of kidnapping and vaginally assaulting a 9-year-old girl and was referred for violence risk assessment by the state to determine whether he should be sentenced to an extended term of imprisonment. Utilization of a variety of actuarial and qualitative violence risk measures revealed a basal history of predatory sexual violence as well as significant minimizing and denial of events and behaviors associated with violence. Evidence also emerged of an extensive drug abuse history, psychopathy, and attitudes supportive of crime. Testimony in criminal court involved the sharing of results, which showed a significant history of dangerousness to others resulting in criminally violent and predatory conduct, and that such a history rendered him a serious danger to others. Defendant Jones was sentenced to an extended term of imprisonment based on evaluation findings.

Introduction

This chapter focuses on advances in violence risk analysis—also termed dangerousness assessment and violence prediction—and provides a sample report for use with clinical forensic settings and situations. The focus is on quantitatively derived methods and decision analysis. Little doubt exists that violence risk assessment based on statistically derived empirical factors and decision analysis is superior to a purely clinical assessment (Breiman, Friedman, Olshen, and Stone, 1984; Gottfredson and Gottfredson, 1988; Grove and Meehl, 1996). In regard to sex-offender recidivism across various studies and investigations, for example, Hanson and Bussiere (1998) found strong support for statistical assessment ($r = .46$) as opposed to clinical assessment ($r = .10$), the last not much better than chance. Hanson's finding actually reflects a trend favoring quantitative methods regarding violence prediction over the last five decades involving a wide variety of subpopulation groups (Bonta and Hanson, 1994; Bonta, Law, and Hanson, 1998; Borum and Otto, 2000; Garnder, Lidz, Mulvey, and Shaw, 1996; Hall, 1987; Quinsey, Rice, and Harris, 1995).

Let us consider the evolution of risk analysis. The first generation of violence prediction methods, from an applied perspective, consisted of unstructured clinical opinion, a method that did not come close to meeting the rigorous standards demanded in forensic settings and situations. A second generation consisting of structured clinical opinion did not fare much better because of low reliability and validity of the methods employed. A proliferation of research in the 1980s provided the basis for a third generation of violence prediction methods—empirically guided evaluation (Becker and Coleman, 1988; Hall, 1987; Hall, Catlin, Boissevain, and Westgate, 1984; Klassen and O'Connor, 1989; Menzies, Webster, and Sepejak, 1985; Webster, Harris, Rice, Cormier, and Quinsey, 1994). A variety of findings were empirically established relating to history (e.g., multiple, recent violence; a past history of different kinds of violence; reinforcing results from violence; child abuse; and violent parent or sibling models), opportunity factors associated with violence (e.g., recent purchase of a lethal weapon; cessation of psychotropic medication; and release into the community), and triggering stimuli (e.g., substance intoxication and breakup of the central love relationship). Many, if not most, forensic professionals currently utilize empirically guided evaluation methods for a variety of reasons. Not only are the methods mantled in scientific methodology, and in fact they are more accurate than clinical opinion, they are also usually well received by referral sources and the criminal courts.

A fourth generation consisting of pure actuarial measures began to appear in the mid-1990s and continues to this day (Hanson and Thornton, 2000; Quinsey, Harris, Rice, and Cormier, 1998; Quinsey, Rice, and Harris, 1995). These scales yielded quantitative degrees of certainty for violent recidivism, ranging from 1 year to 10 years. As such, the actuarial measures represented a quantum advancement in violence prediction. Researchers are no longer vexed by violence representing a low base-rate phenomenon. Rather, the problem has been resolved through the use of statistical methods such as receiver operating characteristics (ROCs), first developed in communications technology and in signal detection theory in psychophysics, which looks at the trade-off between hit rate and false alarm rate in predicting violent events. ROCs permit an estimate of the true accuracy of a test, yielding an effect size that is unaffected by different selection ratios and base rates, and have been utilized extensively in the creation of actuarial devices to predict violence. Some test developers allow for the forensic professional to clinically adjust the fourth-generation actuarial measure (e.g., due to the predictee developing a sudden debilitating illness, incorporating verified violence that did not result in arrest or conviction), so long as the modifications are slight and do not violate the measure's underlying statistical assumptions (e.g., see Hanson, 1997, 1998; Hanson and Bussiere, 1998). Others discourage this practice if the predetermined probabilities associated with given scores are to be utilized (e.g., see Quinsey et al., 1998).

A fifth and most recent generation consists of combinations of the above and is commonly advocated by leading forensic practitioners who routinely predict violence in the course of their forensic work (e.g., Meloy, 2000; Salter, 1988). A variety of actuarial and other empirically based methods are typically employed along with reporting the findings for each measure in the risk analysis report. The evaluator then usually opines on the overall risk of violent recidivism within a given time period, citing the basis for the proffered conclusion.

A projected sixth generation may consist of violence prediction measures that attempt to reflect the real-life clinical thinking and the overall, sometimes mind-boggling, complexity in individual cases. Prior to 2000, only two such empirically derived decision paths were available: the assaultive risk screening sheet of the State of Michigan, reported by Monahan (1981), for use in prison assignment and parole decision making, and the dangerousness prediction decision tree (Hall, 1987), discussed later, which offers a short-term violence prediction for a 3-month period.

A 40% accuracy, denoting a 40% recidivism (true-positive) rate for 4.7% of the sample of 2200 inmates released on parole, was obtained by the Michigan group simply by noting whether (a) the crime description fit robbery, sex assault, or murder; (b) the inmates showed serious institutional misconduct; and (c) the inmates were first arrested before their fifteenth birthday. A 98% (true-negative) rate, denoting a very low risk, was obtained by 19.7% of the sample (a) by no serious type of crimes committed—robbery, sex assault, or murder; (b) by no juvenile felony; (c) by no assaultive felonies; and (d) if the inmate was ever married. This decision analysis is simple to utilize, merely following the path to its assigned risk category (Monahan, 1981, see p. 61).

Table 6.1 presents the extant empirical methods. The empirically based violence prediction systems from Table 6.1, available in the mental health–law interface today, are presented in the following pages. The reader should again keep in mind that development of empirically based violence prediction scales has been vigorously addressed by investigators only in the last 15 years (e.g., Hall, 1987; Hanson, 1998; Hanson and Bussiere, 1998; Monahan and Steadman, 1994; Quinsey et al., 1998). At this stage, statistical analyses in validation studies show that the systems are far less than perfect in terms of sensitivity (e.g., percentage of true positives) and specificity (i.e., percentage of true negatives). The use of multiple measures and methods to predict violence is therefore strongly recommended, along with presenting the appropriate caveats and limitations in the forensic report.

Table 6.1 Promising Empirically Based Violence Prediction Systems

Test or Method	Predictor Variables	Application or Findings	References
Seriousness Scoring System	History of harm/injury, sex acts, and intimidation based on survey responses of 60,000 Americans	Identifies high seriousness scores for possible intervention; demonstrates escalation over time for individuals	Wolfgang, Figlio, Tracy, and Singer (1985)
Meta-Analysis of Predictors of General and Violent Recidivism	Objective risk assessment, juvenile delinquency, family problems, and other factors (based on 52 studies and 16,191 persons)	Recidivism factors for mentally disordered offenders same as for nondisordered offenders; Criminal history best predictor; Clinical factors worst	Bonta, Law, and Hanson (1998)
Psychopathy Checklist-Revised (PCL-R)	Factors suggesting exploitation of others and chronically unstable lifestyle; few violence-related items	PCL-R scores are the best single predictor of violence, although scale was not designed for such; for adult males only	Hare (1991)
Violent Risk Appraisal Guide (VRAG)	Developmental, personality, and nonviolent and violent history items; includes PCL-R score	Predicts for 7 and 10 years the risk of violent (nonviolent) acts, yielding percentiles; for adult males only	Quinsey et al. (1998)
Sex-Offender Risk Appraisal Guide (SORAG)	Developmental, personality, nonviolent and violent history, and deviant sexual preferences	Predicts for 7 and 10 years the risk of violent (sexual) assaults, yielding percentage scores; for adult males only	Quinsey et al. (1998)
Meta-Analysis of Predictors of Sexual Violence	Deviant sexual arousal, violence history, and personality factors (based on 61 studies; 28,972 persons)	15- to 30-year follow-up showed 77% chance of reoffending for previous sex offenses, boy victims, and never married status, as one finding	Hanson and Bussiere (1998)
Rapid Risk Assessment for Sexual Offense Recidivism (RRASOR)	Includes victim and victim-relationship factors, prior sexual offenses, and age of release (total sample size of 2592 persons)	Predicts recidivism rates for 5- and 10-year periods based on four factors gleaned from review of administrative records	Hanson (1997)
Minnesota Sex-Offender Screening Test-Revised (MnSOST-R)	History, victim, substance use, and other factors	Predicts for 6 years high- versus low-risk sex offenders	Epperson, Kaul, and Huot (1995)
Static and Dynamic Risk Assessment Tools	History of sex offenses and demographic factors, attitudes	Provides for low, medium and high risk of sexual offenses	Hanson (1997); Hanson, Scott, and Steffy (1992)

Instrument	Description	Notes	References
Dangerousness Prediction Decision Tree	Remote and recent history of violence, opportunity, and triggers (HOT) after inhibitions are taken into account	Predicts for 3 months whether individual is more likely than not to be at high risk for violent acting out using a 5-step decision path	Hall (1987); Hall and Ebert (2002)
Spousal Assault Risk Assessment Guide (SARA)	Spousal assault, criminal history, psychosocial adjustment, and alleged most recent (based on 2309 adult male offenders)	Summary ratings include risk of violence toward partner, as well as toward others in general; risk-management strategies associated with SARA scores	Kropp, Hart, Webster and Eaves (1999)
Sexual, Violence, Risk (SVR-20)	Professional guidelines for the assessment of risk for sexual violence are presented	SVR-20 has been researched in Europe and translated into several languages	Boar, Hart, Kropp and Webster (1997)
Historical, Clinical, Risk Management (HCR-20, Version 2)	Risk factors include 10 historical, five clinical, and five risk-management items presented within a set of professional guidelines rather than a test or scale	HCR-20 has been researched in Europe and translated into several languages	Webster, Douglas, Eaves, and Hart (1997)
California Actuarial Risk Assessment Tables (CARAT)	Victim and sex offense history factors	Yields percent reoffenses within 5 years for both child molesters and rapists	Schiller and Marques (1999)
Level of Service Inventory-Revised (LSI-R)	Risk/needs assessment tool prompts data in almost all areas of offender's life	LSI-R score related to institutional problems, likelihood of early release, recidivism and self-reported criminal activities, parole outcome, and halfway house success	Andrews and Bonta (1995)
The Workplace Violence Risk Assessment Checklist (WVRAC)	Risk factors include historical, recent critical events, and work attitudes and traits; the checklist yields guidelines and does not represent a standardized scale	For use in workplace or vocationally related areas; takes into account characteristics of the worksite or work institution that may be associated with increased risk of violence	Hall and Pritchard (2002)
STATIC-99	Utilizes historical risk factors only by a stepwise regression approach to classify offenders as high, medium, or low risk	Developed by a merging of database for RRASOR and the SACJ (Grubin, 1998)	Grubin (1998); Kramer and Heilbrun (2000)

Pertinent Legal Cases

The foundational case for dangerousness that is followed in basic substance by most states is *Tarasoff v. Regents of the University of California* (1976) in which the Supreme Court ruled that a therapist has a duty to exercise "reasonable care to protect the foreseeable victim" if by applicable professional standards that therapist has determined that a patient poses a "serious danger of violence to others." The dozens of legal cases relevant to Tarasoff will not be reviewed here except to note that the forensic professional—whether therapist, evaluator, consultant, or trainer—to avoid professional liability and the destruction of a career must include relevant safeguards, documents, and procedures designed to ensure that a competent, comprehensive, and timely violence assessment has been performed.

Applied Ethics and Moral Considerations

To avoid malpractice, forensic professionals performing violence risk analyses cannot simply rely on their good intentions and judgment in regard to the relevant issues, what should be avoided and what ought to be done. They must be thoroughly familiar with the relevant portions of the Ethical Principles of Psychologists and Code of Conduct (1992) as well as the Specialty Guidelines for Forensic Psychologists, or a similar section in another professional discipline's ethical code.

Those who read the dangerousness report or listen to testimony of an expert who proffers a prediction involving harm to others or self have a right to know that professional's specific degree of competence in violence risk analysis, above and beyond a mere recitation of one's credentials. For this reason, it is recommended that the forensic professional keep a list of cases where he or she made a prediction and received feedback on outcome and present that list in terms of true-positives and true-negatives. In addition, the competency of predictors can be assessed by their knowledge of the literature on this topic, as shown in *Basic Points to Consider*.

Empirically Based Methods and Applications

Seriousness Scoring System

The seriousness scoring system shows the degree of harm resulting from violence by adding up the statistically derived values for each act of previous violent behavior within a given time period. The scoring system stems from the U.S. Department of Justice's *National Survey of Crime Severity* by Wolfgang et al. (1985). Based on the responses of over 60,000 Americans, this system, for the first time, provides an easily derived, quantitative score for the amount of harm that an individual has perpetrated during a particular act, a circumscribed time period (e.g., 1, 5, or 10 years), or even over the lifetime of the individual, if that is of interest. The following sections, summarized in Table 6.2 and described by the National Institute of Justice in its publication (1985), demonstrate how to calculate point values and utilize the system.

A. Number of persons injured. Each victim receiving some bodily injury during an event must be accounted for. Physical injuries typically occur as a direct result of assaultive events, but can be caused by other events as well. The four levels of bodily injury are:
1. Minor harm—An injury that requires or receives no professional medical attention. The victim may, for instance, be pushed, shoved, kicked, or knocked down, and receive a minor wound (e.g., cut and bruise).
2. Treated and discharged—The victim receives professional medical treatment but is not detained for further medical care.
3. Hospitalized—The victim requires inpatient care in a medical facility, regardless of its duration, or outpatient care for three or more clinical visits.
4. Killed—The victim dies as a result of the injuries, regardless of the circumstances under which they are inflicted.
B. Sexual intercourse by force. This event occurs when a person is intimidated and forced against his or her will to engage in a sexual act (e.g., rape, incest, and sodomy). Such an event may have more than one victim, and the score depends on the number of such victims.

A forcible sex act is always accomplished by intimidation. Thus, the event must also be scored for the type of intimidation involved (see Table 6.2). Intimidation is scored for all victims in a forcible sexual act. The victim of one or more forcible sexual acts is always assumed to have suffered at least minor harm during the event. Even when medical examination may not reveal any injuries, the event must be scored

Table 6.2 Serious Scoring System[a,b]

Score Sheet _____

Name and Identification Number(s): _____

Component Scored	Number of Victims	×	Scale Weight	=	Total
I. Injury					
(a) Minor harm	_____		1.47		
(b) Treated and discharged	_____		8.53		
(c) Hospitalized	_____		11.98		
(d) Killed	_____		35.67		
II. Forcible sex acts	_____		25.92		
III. Intimidation					
(a) Verbal or physical	_____		4.90		
(b) Weapon	_____		5.60		
IV. Premises forcibly entered	_____		1.50		
V. Motor vehicle stolen					
(a) Recovered	_____		4.46		
(b) Not recovered	_____		8.07		
VI. Property theft/damage (optional)	_____				
Total Score					

[a] U.S. Department of Justice (June 1985). *National Survey of Crime Severity*. NCJ-96017, Washington, DC: Superintendent of Documents.
[b] $\log 10Y = .26776656 \log 10X$, where Y = crime severity weight and W = total dollar value of theft or damage.

for minor harm. This level of injury should also be scored when the victim is examined by a physician only to ascertain whether a sexually transmitted disease has been transmitted or to collect evidence that the sexual act was completed.

C. Intimidation. Intimidation occurs when one or more victims are threatened with bodily harm (or some other serious consequences) for the purpose of forcing the victim(s) to obey the request of the offender(s) to give up something of value or to assist in a criminal event that leads to someone's bodily injury, the theft of or damage to property, or both. Ordinary assault and battery, aggravated assault and battery, or homicide are not to be scored for intimidation merely because someone was assaulted or injured. The event must also have included the threat of force for intimidation to have been present. With the exception of forcible sexual acts, criminal events involving intimidation are scored only once, regardless of the number of victims who are intimidated. The types of intimidation are:

1. Physical or verbal—Physical intimidation means the use of strong-arm tactics (e.g., threats with fists and menacing gestures). Verbal intimidation means spoken threats, not supported by the overt display of a weapon.

2. Intimidation by weapon—This involves display of a weapon (e.g., firearm, cutting or stabbing instrument, and blunt instrument) capable of inflicting serious bodily injury.

The scoring on property offenses is optional and, if deleted, will not change the independently derived violence scores. If included, the evaluator should note that the total score would provide information about escalating seriousness but not necessarily violence, as the offenses in this category are considered nonviolent.

The relevance of a total severity score (net harm) for global sentencing considerations should not be overlooked. Total net harm represented by an instant offense, for example, can be linked to victim restitution criteria or to sentencing procedures, thus adding a quantitative dimension to a notoriously subjective task.

Forensic professionals may wish to determine whether an individual's violence is escalating over time. A declining slope suggests deceleration, much as an upward slope suggests escalating violence. The author has used acceleration/deceleration data in court but always in conjunction with other predictive methods (Hall, 1987, 1999; Hall and Pritchard, 1996; Hall and Sbordone, 1993). The key question is whether the violence act under scrutiny represented an ongoing trend or the last gasp of a fading propensity. Only additional clinical forensic information can answer this question.

Violence Meta-Analysis

The meta-analysis by Bonta et al. (1998), involving 52 studies and 16,191 persons, was conducted to determine whether the predictors of recidivism for mentally disordered offenders were different from the predictors for nondisordered offenders. They were the same. Effect sizes were calculated for 27 predictors of violent recidivism. Criminal history variables were the best predictors and clinical variables the worst. Bonta et al. (1998) suggested that risk assessment of mentally disordered offenders can be enhanced with a focus on the criminological literature, and less reliance on notions of psychopathology. The predictors for violent recidivism are presented in Table 6.3. This author uses predictors of effect sizes equal to or greater than .10 or −.10, a practice with some statistical support.

Table 6.3   **Predictors of Violent Recidivism**[a]

Predictor	Violent Recidivism	N	k
Objective risk assessment	.30	2186	9
Adult criminal history	.14	2163	8
Juvenile delinquency	.20	985	3
Antisocial personality	.18	1634	3
Nonviolent criminal history	.13	1108	4
Institutional adjustment	.14	711	4
Hospital admissions	.17	948	3
Poor living arrangements	NR		
Gender (male)	NR		
Substance abuse (any)	.08	2013	4
Family problems	.19	1481	5
Escape history	NR		
Violent history	.16	2878	9
Drug abuse	NR		
Marital status (single)	.13	1068	4
Weapon	.12	716	2
Mixed Relationships			
Days hospitalized	−.09	850	4
Alcohol abuse	NR		
Employment problems	.22	1326	5
Clinical judgment	.09	786	3
Education	−.02	1066	4
Intelligence	−.02	1873	4
Socioeconomic status	NR		
Race (minority)	.09	999	3
Negative Relationships			
Mentally disordered offender	−.10	2866	6
Homicide index offense	NR		
Age		−.18	1519
Violent index	−.04	2241	6
Violent index (broadly defined)	.08	1950	7
Sex offense	.04	1636	3
Not guilty by reason of insanity	−.07	1208	3
Psychosis	−.04	3891	11
Mood disorder	.01	1520	3
Treatment history	NR		
Offense seriousness	.06	1879	5

[a]   Adapted from Bonta et al. (1998).

Psychopathy Checklist-Revised (PCL-R)

Hare's (1991) well-received PCL-R is commonly embedded in several validated predictive systems (e.g., see VRAG, SORAG, HCR-20, and SVR-20 in Table 6.1), and hence, the abbreviated and other versions of the PCL will not be discussed in this chapter. The PCL-R yields information on two main factors that comprise psychopathology: Factor I, the selfish, callous, and remorseless use of others (e.g., items reflecting superficial charm, pathological lying, manipulation, lack of remorse, failure to accept responsibility for own actions); and

Factor II, a chronically unstable, antisocial, and socially disruptive lifestyle (e.g., items reflecting a high need for stimulation, early behavior problems, parasitic lifestyle, and poor behavioral controls). Hare recommends a cut-off score of 30 to diagnose psychopathy. Others use a lower cut-off score, such as ≥ 26, to operationally define a high PCL-R score and therefore determine whether psychopathy is present (e.g., see Grann, Langstrom, Tengstrom, and Kullgren, 1999).

According to Zinger and Furth (1998), Canadian courts have encountered three problems with the PCL-R, all of which the author has observed in American courts. First, experts frequently render substantially different PCL-R scores for the same defendant. Defense experts typically present lower scores on the PCL-R for the defendant compared to their prosecution counterparts. Second, some forensic mental health professionals use the PCL-R on populations other than the normative base (e.g., women and adolescents). Third, Canadian courts have been provided with PCL-R scores based solely on a records review, which generally slightly underestimates the total scores. Hare (1991, 1996) points out that omitting the interview is acceptable only if "extensive" collateral information is available.

Violence Risk Appraisal Guide (VRAG)

The best extant measure of violent recidivism is the VRAG (Quinsey et al., 1998). The VRAG is the culmination of 25 years of research at a psychiatric facility at Penetanguishene, Ontario, Canada, with mentally disordered offenders. A sample of over 600 males, all of whom had a basal history of serious violence, were followed over a 10-year period once released. Correlation between VRAG scores and violent recidivism was .44 and, by utilizing the 80th percentile, classification accuracy was 74%, with a sensitivity of .40 (true-positives) and a specificity of .88 (true-negatives). Probabilities of violent recidivism are presented by the authors for both 7 and 10 years.

The 12-item measure consists of the following predictors, with score weightings available in the Quinsey et al. (1998) text:

1. Lived with both biological parents to age 16
2. Elementary school maladjustment
3. History of alcohol problems
4. Marital status
5. Criminal history score for nonviolent offenses
6. Failure on prior conditional release
7. Index offense
8. Victim injury in index offense
9. Any female victim in index offense
10. Meets diagnostic and statistical manual-III (DSM-III) criteria for any personality disorder
11. Meets DSM-III criteria for schizophrenia
12. PCL score

Support for the VRAG's reliability and validity, as well as its applicability to other populations, continues to mount (e.g., see Barbarbee and Seto, 1998; Grann, Belfrage, and Tengstrom, 2000; Hanson and Harris, 1999; Kroner and Mills, 1997; Nadeau, Nadeau, Smiley, and McHattie, 1999; Nichols, Vincent, Whittemore, and Ogloff, 1999).

The forensic clinician should note that the VRAG for adults can be used without directly measuring psychopathy through PCL-R scores. The PCL-R is simply scored zero, and the same probability table is utilized to calculate risk of violent recidivism (Quinsey, 2000). If the predictee is a psychopath, however, the obtained probability of risk may be lower than otherwise. In cases where psychopathy is suspected, therefore, the actual PCL-R score should be derived and included in the VRAG scoring. Alternatively, the Child and Adult Taxon Scale (CATS), discussed below, can replace the PCL-R in its entirety.

As stated, the PCL-R score in the VRAG can be replaced in its entirety by the Child and Adolescent Taxon Scale (CATS) (Quinsey et al., 1998). The CATS illustrates the static nature of the VRAG and supports the author's speculation that psychopathology is a life-history strategy. Importantly, such replacement allows the forensic clinician to calculate risk from the same probability table used in the original measure. The univariate correlation for the CATS is essentially the same as the PCL-R ($d = 1.04$, ROC area $= .75$; in a separate study, $r = .975$, with 54 mentally disordered offenders). The CATS has many of the same items, with the CATS more heavily loaded on Factor II of the PCL-R, reflecting a disruptive, conflictual lifestyle. The CATS items, with illustrated scoring in Quinsey, et al. (1998), include (1) several VRAG items and, in addition, (2) more than three DSM-III conduct disorders symptoms, (3) ever suspended or expelled from school, and (4) arrested under the age of 16.

Quinsey et al. (1998) stated the following:

The practical and theoretical significance of this result (if borne out in cross validation) is profound. First, from a practical point of view, actuarial appraisal of the risk of violent recidivism may be accomplished without reference to a restricted psychological test which, in some jurisdictions, requires a licensed professional for its administration. We would argue that a more appropriate approach to qualifying risk appraisers lies in the evaluation of the reliability and validity of predictions, irrespective of general professional certification. Second, from a theoretical perspective, we would argue that a measure of psychopathy might be necessary for the prediction of violent recidivism, but that the PCL-R might not be. That is, although the two PCL-R factors are highly correlated ($r = .50$, approximately; see Harpur, Hakstian and Hare, 1988), there is considerable theoretically motivated debate about which PCL-R factor better predicts violence. The results showing that the entire PCL-R can be replaced by variables pertaining only to antisocial childhood behavior imply that PCL-R Factor I items reflecting apparently adult personality (e.g., glibness, grandiosity, lying, conning, remorselessness, shallowness, callousness) do little or nothing to reduce uncertainty about the likelihood of violent recidivism. This is not to say that these characteristics are not associated with psychopathy. It is also possible that our records-based measurement was not the ideal way to measure these interpersonal behaviors. (pp. 167–168)

The reader is encouraged to use the CATS whenever gathering of the information necessary to derive a PCL-R score is not practical or warranted.

The possibility even likelihood that the VRAG can be accurately calculated without directly interviewing the predictee is raised by the foregoing discussion. The items on the VRAG can be obtained from a records review or significant/knowledgeable others. The author recommends, however, interviewing the predictee whenever possible. The courts and other forensic entities seem to assign greater credibility to those experts who have met with the predictee. The notion of fairness—allowing the predictee to explain past behavior and events—may be inextricably bound up with the perception of accuracy of the instrument.

The forensic professional who predicts violence in the absence of interviewing the assessee is well advised to obtain a strong multisourced database. Possible sources of information include, but are not limited to, the following:

1. Interviewing or testing of previous victims and significant/knowledgeable others
2. Behavioral observations of the predictee in both social and nonsocial contexts
3. Behavioral observations of the predictee in both structured and nonstructured situations
4. Behavioral observations in both stress/intoxicated (e.g., alcohol electroencephalogram (EEG)) and tranquil/nonintoxicated circumstances
5. A functional analysis of previous violence-related responses
6. Environmental assessment to include culture-bound stimulus factors
7. Description of probable but unknown behavioral traits from actual demographic traits observed by others
8. Use of relevant violence base-rate data
9. Medical, neurological, and laboratory examination results by others
10. Inspection of crime scenes or sites where violence was previously exhibited
11. Various intrusive medical procedures (e.g., alcohol EEG)
12. Semantic and transcript analysis, if available
13. Results from instrumentation such as the polygraph
14. Records produced by the predictee (diaries, letters, and so on)
15. Records produced by others (e.g., military, school, and job)
16. "Expunged" records usually available to court examiners in the state or federal archives
17. Relevant psychological mathematical models which are then used as a basis for further inquiry (e.g., geographic profiling).

Sex-Offender Risk Appraisal Guide (SORAG)

The SORAG predicts for both 7 and 10 years and was developed with the same methodology as the VRAG (Quinsey et al., 1998). The 14 items in the SORAG consist, in part, of similar factors as the VRAG (i.e., living with biological parents to age 16, elementary school maladjustment, history of alcohol problems, marital status, criminal history of nonviolent offenses, failure on prior conditional release, age at index offense, meeting the DSM-III criteria for any personality disorder or for schizophrenia, and the PCL-R or CATS score). In addition, the score is computed from new items (i.e., criminal history of violent offenses, number of previous convictions for sexual offenses, history of sex offenses only against girls under 14, and phallometric test results).

The SORAG has a greater than chance but only modest ability to predict sexual recidivism, with a correlation of about $r = .20$ between predictor and criterion variables (approximately 4.5% of the variance accounted for). Still, the SORAG has done as well as other sexual recidivism scales that other investigators have produced (e.g., see Firestone, Bradford, Greenberg, Nunes, and Broom, 1999; Hanson and Thornton, 2000).

Quinsey (2000) importantly observed the following:

We developed the SORAG as an enhancement of the VRAG for sex offenders but have been unable to show so far that the SORAG is more accurate than the VRAG for sex offender subjects in predicting violent or sexual recidivism. We ordinarily do not score both because they are highly correlated. The omission of the plethysmograph item slightly degrades accuracy on the SORAG but, as I mentioned above, these instruments are quite robust. Missing data move the estimated probability of a subject toward the base rate of the construction sample (emphasis added).

These points made by Quinsey (2000) are far reaching in their implications. The VRAG may be more accurate than the SORAG because sexual assaults may reflect a propensity and desire to harm rather than seek sexual gratification, an argument long raised by feminists and those who treat sex victims. Alternatively, the extra items in the SORAG relating specifically to sexual assaults may not be all that sensitive, despite the research findings upon which their inclusion was based. The finding that omitting the plethysmograph only slightly degrades accuracy on the SORAG, together with the finding that the VRAG is more accurate than the SORAG, suggests that the plethysmograph may not be necessary in order to accurately predict sexual recidivism. Yet research findings show that the plethysmograph is the single best predictor of sexual violence (Hanson and Bussiere, 1998, $r = .32$; there was a 46% chance of reoffending with deviant arousal and a 14% likelihood without deviant arousal). The answer may lie in the higher correlation of the VRAG with both physical and sexual recidivism ($r = .44$). Until more cross-validation is available, the forensic professional is advised to utilize the VRAG to predict sexual recidivism. It only takes a moment to compute both. In addition, the author has encountered cases where SORAG data were available, but the defense mental health professional chose to compute VRAG probabilities only because by doing so, results showed a lower probability (especially when phallometric data were ignored).

Sexual Recidivism Meta-Analysis

The Meta-Analysis of Predictors of Sexual Recidivism by Hanson and Bussiere (1998) stands as a superb statistical achievement in sex-offender research, involving 87 articles, 61 datasets, a median follow-up period of 4 years, and 28,972 sexual offenders. The base rate for reoffending was about 30% across all offenders. Among other findings, a combination of previous sex offenses, boy victims, and never married equaled a 77% chance of reoffense in the 15- to 30-year follow-up period. The likelihood of any new offense for this group was 42%. For the 4- to 5-year follow-up period, the likelihood of any offense was 37 and 13% for a new sex offense. Importantly, treatment did not reduce the chances of sexual recidivism.

Forensic professionals can include from this meta-analysis the following useful factors, with correlations on the right side, into their risk analyses (i.e., correlations equal to or greater than +.10 or −.10):

Phallometric preference for children	.32
Masculinity/femininity scale of MMPI	.27
Deviant sexual preference	.22
Prior sexual offense	.19
Personality disorder	.19
Negative relationship with mother	.16
Paranoia scale—MMPI	.16
Low motivation for therapy	.15

Stranger versus acquaintance victim	.15
P-graph preference—boys	.14
Antisocial personality	.14
Victim female child	−.14
Age	−.14

Evaluators should realize that there was no scientific basis from Hanson and Bussiere's (1998) meta-analysis for the following and should gear their reports and court testimony accordingly:

Classified mentally disordered sex offender	.07
Degree of sexual contact	−.03
Empathy	.03
Social skilled	−.04
Prior violent behavior unrelated to sex offenses	.05
Young child versus older child as victim	.05
Phallometric arousal to rape scenes	.05
Alcohol abuse	.00
Prior nonviolent	.00
Force/injury	.01
Psychological problems	−.01
Sexually abused as a child	.02

Some of these factors strongly correlate with sexual offenses in actuarial devices (e.g., nonviolent behavior and alcohol abuse on VRAG). In such cases, the evaluator should utilize factors from both approaches and report upon contradictions in the forensic report.

Rapid Risk Assessment for Sexual Offense Recidivism (RRASOR)

The RRASOR was based on a sample size of 2592 persons and predicts recidivism for 5- and 10-year periods. The measure does not require interviewing the predictee, and knowledge of the measure's four factors is commonly available from a review of administrative records. The RRASOR has a modest correlation with recidivism (.27). The factors and their scoring are presented below:

Prior sexual offenses
None = 0
1 conviction and 1–2 charges = 1
2–3 convictions and 3–5 charges = 2
4 or more convictions and 6 or more charges = 3
Age at release
25 or more years of age = 0
Less than 25 years old = 1
Victim gender
Only female victims = 0
Any male victims = 1
Relationship to victim
Only related = 0
Any nonrelated = 1

The total of four factors are broken down into 5- and 10-year periods. For 5 years, the estimated recidivism rates by obtained score (in parentheses) are: 0 (4.4%), 1 (7.6%), 2 (14.2%), 3 (24.8%), 4 (32.7%), and 5 (49.8%). For 10 years, the likelihood of recidivism is 0 (6.5%), 1 (11.2%), 2 (21.1%), 3 (36.9%), 4 (48.6%), and 5 (73.1%). The finding, that roughly three-quarters of sex offenders who score positive on all four factors recidivate within 10 years, should caution those who recommend interventions that sexual offending, especially with boy victims, is generally recalcitrant to change. A more meaningful statement about recalcitrance to change in this subgroup compares those who had undergone specialized treatment to those who dropped treatment, or never started intervention in the first place, if these data are available.

Minnesota Sex-Offender Screening Test-Revised (MnSOST-R)

The MnSOST-R by Epperson et al. (1995) and Epperson, Kaul, and Hesselton (1998) predicts for 6 years using a contrived base rate of reoffense of 35%. The 16 factors are as follows:

1. Sex-related convictions
2. Duration of sex-offending history
3. Supervisory status when committed a sex offense for which they were charged or convicted
4. Whether the sex offense was in a public place
5. Threat of force in any sex offense for which they were charged or convicted
6. Multiple acts on a single victim during one contact event
7. Age groups victimized
8. Offenses against a 13- to 15-year-old victim (perpetrator more than 5 years older than victim)
9. Stranger victim for any sex-related offense
10. Adolescent antisocial behaviors
11. Substance abuse in the year preceding index offense
12. Employment history
13. Documented discipline or infractions while incarcerated
14. Substance abuse treatment while incarcerated
15. Sex-offender treatment while incarcerated
16. Age at release or discharge from incarceration

These investigators provide cutting scores from +8 to +17, using their scoring on the above factors. Cutting scores correspond to percent correctly classified as high risk, ranging from 70 to 92%, to low risk, ranging from 68 to 75%.

Static and Dynamic Risk Assessment Tools

Static and dynamic risk assessment tools yield low-, medium-, and high-risk predictors for sexual offenses (Hanson, 1997; Hanson et al., 1992). Static measures consist of factors that cannot be altered history, demographic variables (except for age), and characteristics of past offenses. Hence, static factors cannot be utilized by programmers and treaters to either gauge change over time or as a basis for intervention. Dynamic risk assessment, on the other hand, consists of sexual interests, socioaffective functioning, response to treatment, and other factors that can be used for risk/reduction/management.

Dangerousness Prediction Decision Tree

The author and his colleagues developed a measure of both dynamic and static violence risk factors with adequate sensitivity (75%) and specificity (75%) for a 3-month predictive period (Hall, 1987; Hall et al., 1984). In this prospective project, young adult military males were followed over the 90 days in their on-post and off-duty behavior. The following strategies of prediction were yielded by data analysis.

The best predictor of short-term violence was at least two stimulus triggers, short term in duration (less than 1 month), high in impact, superimposed on multiple acts of past violence, one act of which occurred recently within the preceding year. This prediction presupposes victim availability and a context within which to act out.

a. The most potent external trigger seemed to be environmental stress, particularly actual or threatened breakup in the central love relationship. The second most potent external trigger was a deteriorating work environment or work conflict. Peer pressure to aggress, institutional commands to perform sanctioned violence, and other factors emerged from the literature as potential triggers but were not isolated in this study.

b. The most potent internal trigger was substance intoxication. The trigger was considered likely if substance abuse occurred within the month previous to the prediction using DSM-III criteria, the extant classification system at the time. Other important internal triggers from the literature were command hallucinations, some organic and paranoid states, and obsessive thoughts of revenge or violence.

Predict up to substantial short-term violence based on the strength of your data for the above category

The second best predictor of short-term violence was one trigger superimposed on a past history of violence. The literature suggests that conditions that are associated with violence should also be noted in the forensic report or expert testimony. These could be long-term in nature and define the form (topography) of violence.

a. The most important dynamic conditions were age (young), socioeconomic status prior to the military (lower class, lower middle-class), and substance abuse or dependence (particularly alcohol and opiates).

b. Other important static and dynamic conditions were sex (male), subcultural acceptance of violence, belief that certain types of violence will go unpunished (e.g., child abuse and spouse abuse), deficits in verbal skills, violent peers, and a weak community support base.

Predict moderate to considerable risk depending on the strength of your data for the above

The third best predictor of short-term dangerousness was relevant personality traits, superimposed on a history of violence. These traits included current high hostility, low frustration tolerance, hypersensitivity, and high distrust of others.

Predict mild risk, at most

The fourth best predictor of short-term violence, in the absence of having current information on the subject, was past violence standing alone.

a. Relevant dimensions were severity, frequency, recency, and a history of reinforcing results for violence.
b. Associated developmental events included abuse as a child, relevant school problems (e.g., fights, threats, fire setting, vandalism, and insubordination), and spontaneous or concussion-related loss of consciousness before age 10.

Predict minimal to mild dangerousness at most unless the base rate for recidivism exceeds this degree of possible violence

The fifth best predictor of violence was stress and intoxication, without a history of past dangerousness to others.

Predict negligible dangerousness

Spousal Assault Risk Assessment (SARA)

The SARA guide by Kropp et al. (1999) was developed in Canada using over 2300 male offenders, including criminal court referrals, probationers, and inmates. The similarity of factors compared to those obtained in the U.S. suggest that users of the SARA in that country can rely on the provided norms. Like the HCR-20 and SVR-20, the SARA is not a test with cut-offs, but simply a clinical checklist of risk factors for assault identified in the empirical literature. Nevertheless, norms were obtained on two large groups totaling 2309 offenders, with probation and correctional staff making the SARA ratings. Generally, probationers had lower scores than inmates. Many inmates had a known history of spousal assault. Overall, about 20–35% of offenders were judged by evaluators to be at high risk for spousal assault. Structural reliability analyses suggested that SARA has at least moderate internal consistency and item homogeneity (e.g., Cronbach's alpha for corrected item total correlations = .78 for total scores and .75 for number of factors present). Interrater reliability was impressive (e.g., $r = .84$ and .91 for the two subsamples and $r = .83$ and .91 for number of factors present). Criterion-related validity was examined in three ways, with the analyses offering strong support and a multitude of significant findings for the overall validity of the measure. SARA ratings of inmates can be proffered for those with and without a history of spousal assault and has concurrent validity with the PCL-SV. The SARA can be used for comparing men who did and did not recidivate following referrals for group treatment.

Presented in a condensed fashion, the risk factors from the SARA included items regarding (1) past assault, (2) violations of conditional release or supervision, (3) problems in work or primary relationship, (4) victim of abuse, (5) substance abuse, (6) psychological problems or conditions to include suicidal behavior and personality disorder, (7) use of weapons, (8) violation of no-contact orders, or minimizing/denial of violence history, and (9) attitudes that support spousal assault.

Sexual, Violence, Risk (SVR-20)

The SVR-20 was developed by Boar et al. (1997) for professionals rather than researchers as a set of guidelines to evaluate risk of sexual offending. No probability of recidivism is generated.

Factors in the SVR-20 include those reflecting psychosocial adjustment (e.g., presence of mental disorders, victim of child abuse, and relationship problems), sexual offenses (e.g., those offenses escalating in frequency/severity, time clustering of events, and physical harm to victims), and future plans (e.g., presence of future plans and attitude toward intervention). Scores above the median (19) show an incremental chance of reoffending.

The SVR-20 can be utilized for intervention, according to the authors, as it contains both static and dynamic factors.

Historical, Clinical, Risk Management (HCR-20)

The HCR-20 was developed by Webster, Douglas, Eaves, and Hart (1997) as a set of guidelines to prognosticate violence. Factors include historical items (e.g., previous violence, early maladjustment, and substance use problems), clinical items (e.g., lack of insight, negative attitude, and impulsivity), and risk-management items (e.g., exposure to destabilizers, lack of personal support, and noncompliance with remediation efforts). Research has demonstrated increased risk with increased number of items (e.g., scores above the median, 19, show four times the likelihood of future violence). The HCR-20, like some other measures of risk, contains both dynamic and static factors. This means that outcomes can be linked to risk-management strategies.

California Actuarial Risk Assessment Tables (CARAT)

The CARAT, developed by Schiller and Marques (1999), present the base-rate percentage of reoffenses within 5 years for both child molesters and rapists. For rapists, the range is from minimal risk (e.g., 21.5% for average IQ, acquaintance victim, has prior felonies, and age 25–35 at release from incarceration) to substantial (91.8% for average IQ, acquaintance victim, sexually abused as a child, and under 25 at release). For child molesters, the range is more restricted, from a mild risk (46.3% for stranger victim, victim age <6, has prior felonies, and age 25–35 at release) to moderate risk (e.g., 70.4% for one prior sex offense, has prior felonies, molests boys only, and age 15–35 at release). Keep in mind Hanson's (1998; Hanson and Bussiere, 1998) overall estimate that the base rate for reoffense for child molesters is about 30%. Thus, the use of these combinations of factors can significantly improve the accuracy of prognostication beyond that expected by the base rate. Further, the base rates for both rapists and child molesters do not include offenses for which the perpetrator avoided detection/apprehension, where the charges were dropped, or where a judicial alternative was imposed such as mental health treatment in lieu of prosecution. Thus, a deception analysis should be performed to avoid either an underestimate or an overestimate of basal violence and therefore future risk (Hall, 1986, 1987; Hall and Poirier, 2001; Hall and Pritchard, 1996).

Level of Service Inventory-Revised (LSI-R)

The LSI-R by Andrews and Bonta (1995) is considered a risk reduction/management tool that is based on information based on almost all areas of an offender's life—criminal history, education/employment, financial, family/marital, leisure/recreation, companions, substance use, emotional/personal, and attitudes. For both individual and programmatic change, the LSI-R can assign *a priori* risks for (1) institutional maladjustment, (2) likelihood of early release, (3) recidivism and self-reported criminal activities, (4) parole outcome, and (5) halfway house success. The presence of dynamic factors makes the LSI-R a particularly appealing management tool.

The Workplace Violence Risk Assessment Checklist (WVRAC)

The WVRAC developed by Hall and Pritchard (2002) includes factors from the clinical empirical literature on history, recent events, and work attitudes and traits, as reported in Table 6.4. The WVRAC consists of factors associated with workplace violence (Feldmann and Johnson, 1996; Hall, 1996; Hall and Whitaker, 1999; Vanden, Bos, and Bulatao, 1996). Additionally, the WVRAC has been applied by the author to clinical forensic cases of workplace violence, with a general finding that increased violence potential is associated with a greater number of endorsed items. The items are not exhaustive, fixed, or mutually exclusive, and the entire checklist should be considered a work in progress and a list of warning signs. Differing from other measures of risk, the checklist is meant for an interdisciplinary audience such as human resource managers, probation officers, and mental health personnel. Readers are cautioned that a simple sum of risk factors and the use of specific cut-offs does not automatically equate to varying degrees of risk. This must be determined by cross-validating research. Importantly, some form of previous threatened, attempted, or consummated violence to others, self, or property must be present to reasonably predict future violence from the predictor variables. The final summary ratings are judgments by assessors, which may lead to comprehensive assessment and intervention, if appropriate. The inclusion of both dynamic and static factors, as well as factors associated with organizational problems, suggests that the WVRAC may be utilized as a management/risk-reduction tool.

STATIC-99

The STATIC-99, designed to predict sexual recidivism by using a stepwise regression approach to classify offenders as high, medium, or low risk, was developed from a merging of the database for the RRASOR and a tool called the SACJ from a British database (Grubin, 1998). However, the reader should keep in mind that the STATIC-99 was not significantly more accurate than either the RRASOR or the SACJ and was outperformed by the VRAG (Kramer and Heilbrun, 2000).

Other Measures

Some extant methods of determining violence recidivism were not included in the list of promising tests/measures because of a lack of a norm base, the failure to report reliability/validity data, or even a listing of empirically based factors for those devices. The analysis of aggressive behavior (e.g., see Kramer and Heilbrun, 2000) falls into this category. Likewise, no objective or projective psychological test (e.g., MMPI-2, MCMI-III, CPI, BPI, and Rorschach) is listed, as Megargee's (1970) observation still holds true that no psychological test or subtest will postdict, let alone predict, violence.

**Table 6.4 Workplace Violence Risk Assessment Checklist (WVRAC),
Harold V. Hall, PhD, ABPP**

The following items comprise a research instrument that is a first step toward identification of factors associated with workplace violence reported in the clinical empirical literature. The items are not exhaustive, fixed, or mutually exclusive, and the entire checklist should be considered a work-in-progress. The checklist is meant for an interdisciplinary audience such as administrative supervisors, human resource managers, vocational counselors, and mental health personnel. Readers are cautioned that a simple sum of risk factors and the use of specific cut-offs do not equate to varying degrees of risk. The presence of one or two factors may suggest high risk of workplace violence. Generally, some form of previous threatened, attempted, or consummated violence to others, self, or property must be present to reasonably predict future violence. Finally, the final summary ratings are judgments by assessors, which may lead to a referral for comprehensive assessment and intervention, if appropriate.

Today's Date _____ Employer _____

Employee's Name _____ Date of Birth _____

Rater's Name and Title _____

HISTORICAL AND DEMOGRAPHIC ITEMS   Check If Present

19. Previous violence toward others   _____
20. Past use or threatened use of weapons outside work   _____
21. Previous damage or destruction of work-related property   _____
22. Male sex   _____
23. Substance abuse or dependence (alcohol or drugs)   _____
24. Poor compliance with company attempts to remediate worker   _____
25. Belligerence toward customers or clients   _____
26. Reckless or hazardous behavior on the job   _____
27. Previous direct or veiled threats to harm other employees   _____
28. History of major mental illness   _____
29. Early maladjustment   _____

RECENT EVENTS   Check If Present

30. Any of the above items for last 6 months (specify by numbers)   _____
31. Stress or desperation in workplace, domestic, or financial matters   _____
32. Acquires firearms or related lethal equipment or weapons   _____
33. Signs of rehearsal and preparation (e.g., practice at firing range, assembles weapons)   _____
34. Exposure to or increased use of destabilizers (e.g., alcohol or drugs)   _____
35. Fascination with or statements about other incidents of workplace violence   _____
36. Poor compliance with recent directives of management   _____
37. Lost job or perceives that job will be lost soon   _____
38. Stalking, including repeated harassment, of other employees   _____
39. Threats of suicide or homicide   _____
40. Ongoing fantasies of hurting co-workers   _____
41. Wishes to harm co-workers or management   _____

WORK ATTITUDES AND TRAITS   Check If Present

42. Sees self as victimized by management or treated unfairly by other employees   _____
43. Sense of identity wrapped up in job   _____
44. Does not take criticism well; hypersensitive to perceived slights   _____
45. Authority issues regarding control from others present   _____
46. Tends to be a loner on or off the job   _____
47. Hostile attitudes or behaviors toward aspects of work   _____
48. Erratic or irresponsible work traits   _____
49. Attitudes that condone or support workplace violence   _____
50. Minimizes or denies past maladaptive work behaviors   _____
51. Creates, fosters, or allows a work atmosphere of fear and intimidation   _____

Table 6.4   (continued)

52. Tends to have poor assertiveness skills	_____
53. Meets the criteria for psychopathy	_____

ORGANIZATIONAL DEFICIENCIES	**Yes or No**
54. Failure to screen work applicants for violence potential and mental problems	_____
55. Failure to implement physical security measures to protect employees and clients/customers	_____
56. Failure to implement a prevention-of-violence plan for relevant employees	_____
57. Failure to act immediately to direct, implied, or veiled threats of violence	_____
58. Failure to create a crisis plan for ongoing violence	_____
59. Failure to have an employees' assistance program (EAP), stress control, and anger-management programs	_____
60. Failure to have an out-referral program to community providers	_____
61. Failure to train employees in the warning signs of violence	_____
62. Failure to have in place outplacement services for laid-off or fired employees	_____
63. Failure to have clear policies for harassment, prejudice grievance resolution, and discriminatory behavior	_____
64. Failure to train employees to negotiate and communicate effectively with peers and management	_____
65. Organization is in a state of flux, such as downsizing	_____
66. Organization has a history of violence on worksite	_____
67. Organization has reduced or eliminated positive reinforcers such as secure pension benefits	_____
68. Organization employs intrusive methods to monitor employees, especially electronic monitoring	_____
69. Organization has top-down style of management that is perceived as highly controlling	_____
70. Organization allows employee conflicts to occur without immediate intervention and follow-up	_____
71. Organization uses inconsistent disciplinary actions	_____
72. Management is perceived as unfair, disrespectful, or discourteous to staff	_____
73. Management forces staff to wait before interaction, combined with noxious characteristics of management	_____
74. The worksite is physically uncomfortable	_____
75. Organization is moderate or large in size (more than 40 employees)	_____
76. Performance standards are not linked to employee expectations	_____
77. Performance standards do not have built-in employee input	_____
78. The organization does not have written and regularly reviewed procedures for all of the above	_____

Final risk judgment   Low   ☐
                        Moderate   ☐
                        High   ☐

LIST SUGGESTIONS OR RECOMMENDATIONS FOR FURTHER ASSESSMENT OR INTERVENTION HERE

_____

_____

_____

SPECIFY DATE AND STAFF MEMBER(S) TO REEVALUATE RISK STATUS

_____

_____

_____

ADDITIONAL RELEVANT COMMENTS

_____

_____

_____

Basic Points to Consider

Practice guidelines as basic points that every evaluator of dangerousness should be aware of include the following:

1. Be prepared to demonstrate that you are professionally competent to render a violence prediction and that no issues of ethics are involved. Know the literature on risk assessment and that you have been trained in the methods.
2. Ascertain the referral question, whether the task is assessment, intervention, consultation, or some combination.
3. Start with the most valid information first; do not be biased by recent data or by hindsight bias.
4. Never predict violence in the absence of previous significant threatened, attempted, or consummated violence. Most extant actuarial devices assume a previous history of violence and hence are really measures of violence recidivism. You should predict that violence will not occur if no significant basal violence is uncovered.
5. Remember that the perpetrator, victim, and context must all be analyzed in order to understand a particular violent event. Also use a multisourced database such as multiple actuarial devices, standardized testing, review of records, and interview of knowledgeable/significant others for each of these interactive factors.
6. Retain validated decision rules even when tempted to abandon them for a particular case. This is particularly true when your referral source desires a different conclusion other than the findings generated by your decision rules.
7. Use multiple, empirically derived, predictive measures or factors and present the finding for each individual prior to a synthesis of all the data into a risk judgment (see Table 6.1).
8. Remember to rule out or account for unintentional distortion as well as deliberate deception on the part of the predictee for both the time of the evaluation and previous violence. You must also take into account possible deception and distortion by witnesses and other third parties if they are utilized in your database.
9. The sequence of violence baseline—behavior, acceleration stage, the violent act, recovery, and return to baseline—should be analyzed for all previous acts of violence in order to determine commonalities and differences, as well as trends over time, for a particular individual.
10. Think in terms of base rates unless using predictive devices that focus on decision analysis for prediction (e.g., classification tree method). Even in this case, however, base rates are commonly used at each step of the decision path. The results of the MacArthur iterative classification tree, for example, are presented in terms of the base rate of the sample.
11. You can use empirically supported clinical opinion so long as it is identified as such (e.g., pain cues from the victim acting as a positive reinforcer for predictee violence). In fact, there is no escape from judgment in violence prediction (even purely actuarial devices like the VRAG are composed of items involving clinical judgment as, for example, if the predictee meets the criteria for schizophrenia).
12. Do not fall prey to illusory associations, unsupported by the empirical literature, between evaluation data and supposed violence potential (e.g., poor cooperation or

antagonism toward evaluator, physical stigmata, poor self-esteem, nonviolence during institutionalization, and white space responses in the Rorschach).

13. Consider triggers to possible future violence based on previous triggering stimuli. Keep in mind that triggers contribute only slightly to the violent act (e.g., <5% in Hall, 1987; Hall et al., 1984). Some classes of offenders such as psychopaths appear not to need triggers in order to perpetrate violence, only the opportunity to do so without being caught.

14. Consider opportunities for future violence given the availability of weapons, victims, and other factors.

15. Consider inhibitions to violence based on past inhibitory stimuli and responses for that individual.

16. List alternative hypotheses to explain exhibited violence and seek evidence for each, especially those contrary to your own interests or the vested interest of your referral party.

17. Synthesize your conclusions and account for discrepant findings. Keep in mind that your synthesis is essentially a clinical forensic judgment.

18. Operationalize your conclusions and make them capable of replication.

19. Present conditional predictions, if possible; avoid dichotomous conclusions unless using a classification tree approach.

20. Limit the temporality of the predictions to avoid the perception of an interminable prediction. Give the level of risk for different portions of the time period if variation is to be expected (e.g., a greater risk of violent recidivism within 2 years of release from prison).

21. Specify in summary form the factors that formed the proffered conclusions. The factors which lower the risk of violence, as well as the positive aspects of the predictee, should be presented in order to achieve a balanced report.

22. Suggest feedback mechanisms to assist future predictors of violence potential (e.g., reevaluation in 1 year with the same instruments).

Avoiding Evaluation and Consultation Errors

These include commonly known dangerousness prediction pitfalls reported over the decades (Hall, 1987; Hall and Ebert, 2002) as follows: (1) Failure to see the relevance of risk analysis in various settings and situations (e.g., bail setting and criminal responsibility evaluation when an exculpating condition is found); (2) Lack of an adequate database upon which to draw conclusions; (3) Failure to account for retrospective and current distortion; (4) Predicting violence in the absence of past violent behavior; (5) Falling prey to illusory correlations between evaluation responses and supposed dangerousness; (6) Predicting from clinical diagnosis alone; (7) Failure to account for anticipated triggering stimuli; (8) Failure to take into account opportunity variables; (9) Failure to take into account inhibitory factors; (10) Ignoring relevant base rates; (11) Using arrest, conviction, or incarceration for a violent crime, alone or in combination with psychiatric hospitalization, as the only outcome measures to violence; (12) Failure to both limit and operationalize proffered conclusions (especially rendering predictions without specific time limits).

Treatment Considerations

Given your database findings, be prepared to fairly and accurately represent the predictee's possible violence potential, as well as practical and effective interventions that are linked to the findings. Link recommended interventions with discrete predictor variables. Table 6.5 links specific methods of intervention with findings regarding violence risk.

Table 6.5   Examples of Proposed Interventions Associated with Predictor Variables

Predictor Variable	Intervention
Past violence	Intensive supervision Family treatment Parenting skills training Anger management Correctional treatment for violence
Any violations of conditional release or community supervision	Incarceration Intensive supervision Correctional recidivism program
Central love relationship problems	Divorce counseling Dispute resolution Spousal assault group therapy Couples counseling
Employment problems	Vocational counseling Drug/alcohol treatment
Substance abuse/dependence	Transitional house placement Drug/alcohol treatment (OPC) Court-ordered abstinence Urine or blood screening
Recent homicidal ideation/intent	Crisis counseling Psychiatric hospitalization Psychotropic medication Cognitive behavioral therapy Weapon restrictions Individual treatment Drug/alcohol restrictions
Mental illness	Hospitalization Psychotropic medication Individual psychotherapy Drug/alcohol restrictions
Personality disorder with anger, impulsivity, or behavioral instability	Group/peer approaches Intensive supervision Specialized therapy for personality disorders
Past use of weapons or credible threats of death	Incarceration Intensive supervision Weapon restrictions Notification of intended victims Crisis intervention
Extreme minimization or denial of violence history	Peer/group treatment Psycho-educational group
Attitudes that support or condone violence	Group treatment Psycho-educational group

Avoid recommending aversive interventions if at all possible. In particular, punitive interventions to violent behavior often lead to aversive cycles between perpetrator, victim, and, unfortunately, other innocent parties.

Writing Forensic Reports and Testifying as an Expert

The basic rule here is to communicate effectively. Kramer and Heilbrun (2000) present guidelines for effective risk communication to include (a) using plain language and avoiding jargon; (b) describing the results of risk assessment in regard to consistency with other sources; (c) identifying dynamic factors that can be used for management for intervention; (d) distinguishing imminence, risk and nature, frequency, and possible severity of violence; and (e) referring to the language of the report when asked if the predictee will act out or is dangerous, thus preventing the misrepresentation of report findings.

Violence predictions are usually proffered in terms of degree of likelihood or confidence in one's prognostication when, in fact, future violent behavior will either occur or not occur. As a convention, the following degrees of certainty for violence prediction are suggested for synthesized data for the forensic report.

1. Negligible—In your professional opinion, future significant violence will not occur within the specified time period. This term is used for average people with no history of serious violence. The probability of violence is 0–10% within the predicted time span. Numerical probability figures, as in all these degrees of certainty, are always tied to base-rate data (Frederick, 1978; Hall, 1987; Monahan, 1981; Stone, 1975). This degree of certainty is within the legal meaning of nondangerousness.

2. Minimal—In your opinion, within the specified time period, the likelihood of violence is very low. This term is used for average people, perhaps under high stress or showing some maladaptive behavior, with no significant history of violence. The probability of occurrence is 11–25% within the predicted time span, but only when numerical probability is tied to base-rate data. This degree of certainty is also within the legal meaning of nondangerousness.

3. Mild—In your opinion, significant violence may occur within the specified time period, but your evidence is weak. This term is used for people with or without a history of serious violence. You are saying there is a fair likelihood that violence will occur. This degree of certainty is within the legal meaning of "nondangerousness," even though there is some chance it will occur. The suggested range of probability associated with this legal term is 26–50%, but only when numerical probability is tied to base-rate data.

4. Moderate—In your opinion, it is more likely than not that violence will occur within the specified time period. This term is limited to persons with a violence history. The probability of occurrence is 51–75%, but as usual only when base-rate data are considered. This corresponds to the suggested legal definition of "preponderance of evidence."

5. Considerable—In your opinion, there is a strong likelihood that violence will occur within the specified time period. This term is limited to people with a violence history. Control may be institutional combined with community programs (e.g., residential facilities and transition houses). The probability of occurrence is 76–90%, but

only when base-rate data are considered. This corresponds to the legal meaning of "clear and convincing evidence."

6. Substantial—In your opinion, violence will occur within the specified time period if measures for intervention are not taken. This term is limited to people with a violence history. Institutional control may be necessary if the expected violence is to be controlled. Probability of occurrence is 91–100%, but only when base-rate data are considered. This corresponds to the suggested legal definition of "beyond a reasonable doubt."

A blinded report using several of the empirically guided methods and above practice guidelines is presented in Appendix A.

Novel Applications and New Directions

The previously discussed sixth-generation classification tree approach of decision analysis, rather than a main effects regression approach, may provide an opportunity to assist the forensic professional in a user-friendly, direct fashion. Steadman, Silver, Monahan, Appelbaum, Robbins, Mulvey, Grisso, Roth, and Banks (2000) elucidated how the classification tree approach can employ two decision thresholds for identifying high- and low-risk cases. This approach is congruent with the findings from the MacArthur violence risk assessment study. In this way, conclusions can be directly tied into proposed treatment and risk-management strategies. The reader may also note that the classification tree approach is highly compatible with artificial intelligence methodology.

A direction by the author is the attempt to increase prediction accuracy by increasing the degree to which a corrective factor for under reporting violence may be built into the process of risk analysis. Generally, the use of such "corrective factors" has been discouraged (Monahan, 1985), yet, at this point, true-positive accuracy in particular is poor, about 40% for the best measures such as the VRAG.

References

Andrews, D., and Bonta, J. (1995). *The Level of Service Inventory-Revised: User's Manual*. Toronto, Ontario: Multi-Health Systems, Inc.

Barbarbee, H., and Seto, M. (1998). *Empirical Evaluation of the WSBC Multifactorial Assessment of Sex Offender Risk for Reoffense*. 2nd Annual Research Day, Forensic Psychiatry Program, Department of Psychiatry, University of Toronto.

Becker, J., and Coleman, E. (1988). Incest. *Handbook of Family Violence*. V. B. Van Hasselt, R. Morrison, A. Bellack, and M. Hersen (Eds.). New York: Plenum.

Boar, D., Hart, S., Kropp, P., and Webster, C. (1997). *Manual for Sexual Risk-20*. Burnaby, British Columbia: Mental Health, Law and Policy Institute, Simon Fraser University.

Bonta, J., and Hanson, R. (1994). *Gauging the Risk for Violence: Measurements, Impact and Strategies for Change*. Ottawa: Ministry Secretariat, Solicitor General Canada.

Bonta, J., Law, M., and Hanson, K. (1998). The prediction of criminal and violent recidivism among mentally disordered offenders: A meta-analysis. *Psychological Bulletin, 123,* 123–142.

Borum, R., and Otto, R. (2000). Advances in forensic assessment and treatment: An overview and introduction to the special issue. *Law and Human Behavior, 24* (1), 1–7.

Breiman, L., Friedman, J., Olshen, R., and Stone, C. (1984). *Classification and Regression Trees.* Pacific Grove: CA: Wadsworth and Brooks/Cole.

Epperson, D., Kaul, J., and Hesselton, D. (1998). *Final Report of the Development of the Minnesota Sex Offender Screening Tool-Revised (MnSOST-R).* Presentation at the 17th Annual Research and Treatment Conference of the Association for the Treatment of Sexual Abusers, Vancouver, British Columbia, Canada.

Epperson, D., Kaul, J., and Huot, S. (1995). *Predicting Risk for Recidivism for Incarcerated Sex Offenders: Updated Development on the Sex Offender Screening Tool (SOST).* Poster session presented at the Annual Conference of the Association for the Treatment of Sexual Offenders, New Orleans, LA.

Feldmann, T., and Johnson, P. (1996). Workplace violence: A new form of lethal aggression. In H. V. Hall (Ed.), *Lethal Violence 2000: A Sourcebook on Fatal Domestic, Acquaintance and Stranger Aggression* (pp. 311–338). Kamuela, HI: Pacific Institute for the Study of Conflict and Aggression.

Firestone, P., Bradford, J., Greenberg, D., Nunes, K., and Broom. (1999). *A Comparison of the Sex Offender Risk Appraisal Guide (SORAG) and the Static-99.* Paper presented at the Association for the Treatment of Sexual Abusers Annual Convention, Orlando, FL.

Frederick, C. (1978). *Dangerous Behavior: A Problem in Law and Mental Health.* NIMH, DHEW Publication No. (ADM) 78-563. Washington, DC: Superintendent of Documents, U.S. Government Printing Office, 153–191.

Garnder, W., Lidz, C., Mulvey, E., and Shaw, E. (1996). A comparison of actuarial methods for identifying repetitively violent patients with mental illness. *Law and Human Behavior, 20,* 35–48.

Gottfredson, M., and Gottfredson, D. (1988). *Decision-Making in Criminal Justice: Toward the Rational Exercise of Discretion* (2nd ed.). New York: Plenum.

Grann, M., Belfrage, H., and Tengstrom, A. (2000). Actuarial assessment of risk for violence: Predictive validity of the VRAG and historical part of the HCR-20. *Criminal Justice and Behavior, 27,* 97–114.

Grann, M., Langstrom, N., Tengstrom, A., and Kullgren, G. (1999). Psychopathy (PCL-R) predicts violent recidivism among criminal offenders with personality disorders in Sweden. *Law and Human Behavior, 23,* 205–217.

Grove, W., and Meehl, P. (1996). Comparative efficiency of informal (subjective, impressionistic) and formal (mechanical, algorithmic) prediction procedures: The clinical-statistical controversy. *Psychology, Public Policy, and Law, 2,* 293–323.

Grubin, D. (1998). *Sex Offending Against Children: Understanding the Risk.* Police Research Series Paper 99. London: Home Office.

Hall, H. (1986). The forensic distortion analysis: A proposed decision tree and report format. *American Journal of Forensic Psychology, 4,* 31–59.

Hall, H. (1987). *Violence Prediction: Guidelines for the Forensic Practitioner.* Springfield, IL: Charles C. Thomas.

Hall, H. (1996, 1999, Ed.). *Lethal Violence 2000: A Sourcebook on Fatal Domestic, Acquaintance and Stranger Aggression.* Kamuela, HI: Pacific Institute for the Study of Conflict and Aggression. Republished Boca Raton, FL: CRC Press.

Hall, H., Catlin, E., Boissevain, A., and Westgate, J. (1984). Dangerous myths about predicting dangerousness. *American Journal of Forensic Psychology, 2,* 173–193.

Hall, H., and Ebert, R. (2002). *Violence Prediction: Guidelines for the Forensic Practitioner* (2nd Ed.). Springfield, IL: Charles C. Thomas, Publisher.

Hall, H., and Poirier, J. (2001). *Detecting Malingering and Deception: Forensic Distortion Analysis,* Second Edition. Boca Raton, FL: CRC Press.

Hall, H., and Pritchard, D. (1996). *Detecting Malingering and Deception: Forensic Distortion Analysis (FDA).* Winter Park, FL: PMD Publishers Group, Inc.

Hall, H. V., and Pritchard, D. A. (2002). *Workplace Violence Risk Analysis: Effective Prediction and Intervention Strategies*. Kamuela, HI: Pacific Institute for the Study of Conflict and Aggression.

Hall, H., and Sbordone, R. (1993). *Disorders of Executive Functioning: Civil and Criminal Law Applications*. Winter Park, FL: PMD Publishers Group, Inc.

Hall, H., and Whitaker, L. (Eds., 1999). *Collective Violence: Effective Strategies for Assessing and Interviewing in Fatal Group and Institutional Aggression*. Boca Raton, FL: CRC Press.

Hanson, R. (1997). *Development of a Brief Actuarial Risk Scale for Sexual Offense Recidivism*. Department of the Solicitor General of Canada. Public Works and Government Services Canada. Cat. No. J54-1/1997-E; ISBN: 0-662-26207-7.

Hanson, R. (1998). What do we know about sex offender risk assessment? *Psychology, Public Policy, and Law, 4,* 50–72.

Hanson, R., and Bussiere, M. (1998). Predicting relapse: A meta-analysis of sexual offender recidivism studies. *Journal of Consulting and Clinical Psychology, 66* (2), 348–362.

Hanson, R., and Harris, A. (1999). Where should we intervene? Dynamics predictors of sex offense recidivism. *Criminal Justice and Behavior, 1,* 1–20.

Hanson, R., Scott, H., and Steffy, R. (1992). A comparison of child molesters and nonsexual criminals: Risk predictors and long-term recidivism. *Journal of Research in Crime and Delinquency, 32* (3), 325–337.

Hanson, R., and Thornton, D. (2000). Improving risk assessments for sex offenders: A comparison of three actuarial scales. *Law and Human Behavior, 24* (1), 119–136.

Hare, R. (1991). *The Hare Psychopathy Checklist-Revised*. Toronto: Multi-Health Systems.

Hare, R. (1996). Psychopathy: A clinical construct whose time has come. *Criminal Justice and Behavior, 23* (1), 25–54.

Harpur, T. J., Hakstian, A., and Hare, R. (1988). *The Violence Prediction Scheme: Assessing Dangerousness in High Risk Men*. Thousand Oaks, CA: Sage Publications.

Klassen, D., and O'Connor, W. (1989). Assessing the risk of violence in released mental patients: A cross-validation study. *Psychological Assessment, 1,* 75–81.

Kramer, G., and Heilbrun, K. (2000). Decade of advances in risk assessment: Implications for corrections. *Correctional Mental Health Report, 2,* 17–32.

Kroner, D., and Mills, J. (1997). *The VRAG: Predicting Institutional Misconduct in Violent Offenders*. Paper presented at the Annual Convention of the Ontario Psychological Association, Toronto.

Kropp, P., Hart, S., Webster, C., and Eaves, D. (1999). *Spousal Assault Risk Assessment Guide User's Manual*. Toronto, Canada: Multi-Health Systems, Inc. and B.C. Institute Against Family Violence.

Megargee, E. (1970). The prediction of dangerousness. *Criminal Justice and Behavior, 3,* 1–21.

Meloy, J. R. (2000). *Violence Risk and Threat Assessment*. Workshop presented to the State of Hawaii Judiciary, Honolulu, HI.

Menzies, R., Webster, C., and Sepejak, D. (1985). The dimensions of dangerousness: Evaluating the accuracy of psychometric predictions of violence among forensic patients. *Law and Human Behavior, 9,* 49–70.

Monahan, J. (1981). *Predicting Violent Behavior: An Assessment of Clinical Techniques*. Beverly Hills, CA: Sage.

Monahan, J. (1985). Personal communication.

Monahan, J., and Steadman, H. (Eds.) (1994). *Violence and Mental Disorder: Developments in Risk Assessment*. Chicago, IL: University of Chicago Press.

Nadeau, J., Nadeau, B., Smiley, W., and McHattie, L. (1999). *The PCL-R and VRAG as Predictors of Institutional Behaviour*. Paper presented at conference on "Risk assessment and risk management: Implications for the prevention of violence," Vancouver, British Columbia, Canada.

Nichols, T., Vincent, G., Whittemore, K., and Ogloff, J. (1999). *Assessing Risk of Inpatient Violence in a Sample of Forensic Psychiatric Patients: Comparing the PCL:SV, HCR-20, and VRAG*.

Paper presented at the conference on "Risk assessment and risk management: Implications for the prevention of violence," Vancouver, British Columbia, Canada.

Quinsey, V. (2000). Personal communication.

Quinsey, V., Harris, G., Rice, M., and Cormier, C. (1998). *Violent Offenders: Appraising and Managing Risk*. Washington, DC: American Psychological Association.

Quinsey, V., Rice, M., and Harris, G. (1995). Actuarial prediction of sexual recidivism. *Journal of Interpersonal Violence, 10* (1), 85–105.

Salter, A. (1988). *Treating Child Sex Offenders and Victims: A Practical Guide*. Newbury Park, CA: Sage.

Schiller, G., and Marques, J. (1999). *California Actuarial Risk Assessment Tables (CARAT)*. Presented at A. Salter Predicting Sexual Recidivism. Honolulu, Hawaii, 1999. Available from Gary Schiller, Program Development and Evaluation, 1600 Ninth Street, Sacramento, CA 95814.

Steadman, H., Silver, E., Monahan, J., Appelbaum, P., Robbins, P., Mulvey, E., Grisso, T., Roth, L., and Banks, S. (2000). A classification tree approach to the development of actuarial violence risk assessment tools. *Law and Human Behavior, 24* (1), 83–100.

Stone, A. (1975). *Mental Health and the Law: A System in Transition*. National Institute of Mental Health. DHEW Pub. No. (ADM) 76-176. Washington, DC: Superintendent of Documents, U.S. Government Printing Office.

Vanden Bos, G., and Bulatao, E. (Eds.) (1996). *Violence on the Job: Identifying Risks and Developing Solutions*. Washington, DC: American Psychological Association.

Webster, C., Douglas, K., Eaves, D., and Hart, S. (1997). *HCR-20: Assessing Risk of Violence*. Burnaby, British Columbia: Mental Health, Law, and Policy Institute of Simon Fraser University. (To order: Mental Health, Law, and Policy Institute; Simon Fraser University; Burnaby, British Columbia, Canada V5A 1S6.)

Webster, C., Harris, G., Rice, M., Cormier, C., and Quinsey, V. (1994). *The Violence Prediction Scheme: Assessing Dangerousness in High Risk Men*. Toronto: Centre of Criminology, University of Toronto.

Wolfgang, J., Figlio, R., Tracy, P., and Singer, S. (1985). *The National Survey of Crime Severity*. Superintendent of Documents, U.S. Government Printing Office, Washington, DC, 20402. NCJ-96017.

Zinger, I., and Furth, A. (1998). Psychopathology and Canadian criminal proceedings: The potential for human rights abuse, *Canadian Journal of Criminology, 2*, 237–276.

Legal Reference

Tarasoff v. Regents of the University of California, 17 Cal. 3d 425, 551 P.2d 334, 131 Cal. Rptr. 14 (Cal. 1976).

Part II

Criminal-Forensic Evaluation

Forensic Psychological Issues in Officer-Involved Shooting, Use of Force, and Suicide by Cop Cases

KRIS MOHANDIE

Operational Consulting International, Inc., Pasadena, California

Contents

Synopsis of Case

On an early summer evening, officers responded to a 911 call by the subject's mother who indicated that the subject was threatening to kill himself. In the background of the 911 call, the subject could be heard yelling "go ahead call the police, I don't care, I'm going to make them kill me and it will be your fault!" Upon arrival, police encountered the 25-year-old man who was holding what appeared to be a small revolver. The subject screamed "fuck you" at the police and walked slowly toward them several times before backing away. He alternated between tucking the weapon in his pants and pulling it out without pointing it. At one point, he attempted to walk to the back of his apartment complex toward the alleyway—an avenue of potential escape because the perimeter had not yet been established—but then turned and again approached the officers. One of the first responding officers attempted to establish dialogue with the man, while other officers attempted to evacuate apartments and establish a perimeter. After approximately 15 min, the man ran toward the police officer who had been communicating to him from cover, while reaching for his waistband, making "intense eye contact," and screaming unintelligibly. He was shot six times by two officers and died at the scene. It was determined that at the time he was shot, he was not in possession of the gun (which was loaded and operational). It had apparently been dropped by the subject at some point prior to his rapid approach. The subject tested positive for marijuana and methamphetamine. He was on probation and had a history of multiple arrests for gang-related behavior such as vandalism, theft, and felon in possession of a loaded firearm. The judge had told him he would be sent to state prison if he violated his probation. The gun—which was stolen—had been obtained several days prior to the incident. Ultimately, his family sued the police department in Federal Court for excessive force and wrongful death. The various causes for action included: (i) improper tactics for a mentally ill person, (ii) the subject was suicidal and did not pose any risk to officers, (iii) failure to deploy a negotiation team, and (iv) police officers knew he was unarmed when they shot him.

Introduction

The use of force by law enforcement—especially deadly force—has important implications for forensic psychological analysis and practice. This chapter focuses on several forensic psychological issues that may arise in the aftermath of deadly force incidents. These issues—suicide by cop (SBC), crisis management techniques, and the impact of trauma upon responding officers—can impact criminal and civil cases, necessitating psychological expertise to assist the trier-of-fact. This expertise and methodology is different from the more common diagnostic/evaluative strategy utilized by forensic mental health professionals—strategies that typically rely upon psychological testing and clinical interviewing of litigants or criminal defendants. Although these techniques may sometimes be appropriate, the forensic questions that arise in police deadly force cases are often different, and the subject of the review is frequently deceased. This chapter provides an overview of how expertise pertaining to SBC, crisis management, and the psychological impact of deadly force incidents upon responding officers can be utilized in the forensic arena. Current scholarly literature, relevant legal statutes and case law affecting admissibility of such expertise, and ethical and methodological considerations in the forensic review process will also be presented.

Suicide by Cop

History

Suicide is the eighth leading cause of death in the United States (Moscicki, 1995), and while there is evidence that completed suicides are underreported due to social stigma, emotion, and family impact, the extent of such underreporting is debated. The topic of suicide has long been within the purview of mental health professionals who are tasked with assessing and intervening with potential suicide situations. There is a body of scientific and scholarly literature that addresses warning signs, known risk factors, and evaluation of suicide and suicide potential (Litman, 1989; Moscicki, 1995; Shneidman, 1996).

SBC is a particular method of suicide of more recent attention and occurs when a subject engages in threatening behavior in an attempt to get law enforcement to kill him or her (Mohandie and Meloy, 2000). California Peace Officer Standards and Training (POST) defines it as when a subject "engages in behavior which poses an apparent risk of serious injury or death, with the intent to precipitate the use of deadly force by law enforcement personnel toward that individual (1999)."

The term *SBC* was coined in 1983 by Karl Harris, an LA County medical examiner (Homant, Kennedy, and Hupp, 2000). However, the first published scholarly reference pertaining to SBC was by Noesner and Nolan (1992), who identified SBC as a risk that first responding police officers face in responding to barricade and hostage situations. Since that time, SBC, as a particular method of suicide, has been subject to growing and significant scholarly inquiry. It is now generally accepted by law enforcement and mental health professionals that certain individuals will engage in this form of suicide.

There has been some minor debate within the field of law enforcement and crisis negotiations regarding the appropriateness of the term SBC. Some have expressed concern that it might be confused with the issue of police suicides, while others wanted to make clear the fact that the offender has involved other unwilling parties—the police—in the suicide. Homant and Kennedy (2000) offered the term *police-assisted suicide*, while others suggested the term *victim-precipitated homicide* and *hetero-suicide* (Foote, 1996). Hutson, Anglin, Yarbrough, Hardaway, Russell, Strote, Canter, and Blum (1998) argued that the most appropriate term for this phenomenon is *law enforcement-forced-assisted suicide*, because law enforcement officers are forced to assist suicidal individuals in attempting or committing suicide. While this is a very accurate description of what occurs, it is a cumbersome phrase which has not found its way into any additional publications. *Victim-precipitated homicide* refers to a more general category of behavior that includes SBC and represents the suicidal subject as "victim" and the police officer by implication the "suspect," which is not an accurate reflection of the dynamics of these events. In another scholarly publication, Mohandie and Meloy (2000) adopted the term SBC since it was commonly used and represented a universally understood expression for these types of events, embraced by law enforcement, public, and media. Thus, this term will be used throughout the chapter.

There are occasions, as with any method of suicide, where the person does not complete the suicide but sustains injurie or is taken safely into custody. SBC is a method of suicide, and as with any method it may or may not lead to a completed suicide. As with other methods of suicide, it is proper to refer to suicides as either completed or not completed, as those who study suicide prefer from a values standpoint to avoid reference to a completed suicide as "successful." Unfortunately, some authors (Lord, 2005) persist in the use of the term "successful" to describe a completed SBC.

As a phenomenon, SBC falls within the larger rubric of *victim-precipitated homicide*, cases where the decedent somehow contributes to his/her death at the hands of another (Foote, 1996; Wolfgang, 1958, 1990). This larger category might include circumstances where the decedent exacerbates a situation, challenges an aggressor, or even coerces another person to kill them. The last type is exemplified by a stalker turned hostage taker who took his female victim hostage demanding that since he could not have her, she would have to kill him. After several hours of negotiations conducted through the victim because the offender refused to pick up the phone and talk with negotiators, the woman eventually relented, pulling the trigger of the second handgun the offender brought to the scene. He pointed his own gun at the victim, threatening to kill her unless she pulled the trigger (Mohandie, 2005). This case example shares much in common with SBC situations where the officer is similarly coerced by threat into participating in the subject's suicide.

The author prefers the updated *subject-precipitated homicide* to the 1958 term *victim-precipitated homicide* because the term *victim* is specific and reserved for those subjects who are truly victims as opposed to those who play a significant role in his/her own demise, as in the prior case. Clearly, the victim in the above example was the woman who was compelled, at the point of a gun, to defend herself by ending her perpetrator's life. Conceptually, it is more accurate to apply the term *victim* to the individuals subjected to threatening behavior by the precipitator in these cases.

Research

Empirical research into SBC commenced some time after the term was coined. This research has been important to establish the presence and frequency of the phenomenon, as well as the context, indicators, and dynamics of these high-risk encounters. These studies form the basis for sound forensic psychological analysis and review. An early empirical study of suicidal ideation among subjects during police intervention was conducted by Harruff, Llewellyn, Clark, Hawley, and Pless (1994). They examined firearm suicides during confrontations with law enforcement, something they termed "police-associated deaths." In this study, they identified from Indiana 14 cases of such suicides of 1203 total suicides that occurred between 1984 and 1992. They found that these subjects were exclusively males, primarily in the 20- to 39-year-old age range, 29% were wanted for a crime, 57% of the initial calls for police service originated as a relationship disturbance, and half tested positive for alcohol or drugs. While this study focused exclusively upon those who turned a gun upon themselves as the culmination of police intervention and not on those who used the police to commit suicide, it established that subjects who encounter police officers sometimes exhibit suicidal behavior in response to police intervention.

The first, and to date, best empirical study of SBC was published in 1998 (Hutson et al., 1998). The researchers examined all shooting cases ($n = 437$) handled by the LA County Sheriff's Department between 1987 and 1997 and determined that 13% of all fatal officer-involved shootings (OISs) and 11% of all OISs, fatal and nonfatal, were SBC situations. They also noted a trend in the last year of the sample: cases that could be categorized as SBC accounted for 25% of all OISs and 27% of all fatal OISs in 1997, suggesting that the prevalence was increasing. Further, their rigorous inclusion criteria may have omitted up to a third more cases. SBC as a method of suicide accounted for 2% of suicides in the region of the study during 1997.

Nearly all of the subjects were males (98%), 70% had a criminal record, 65% had drug or alcohol problems, 63% had a known mental health history, 39% had a history of domestic violence, and 65% had communicated suicidal intent. Forty-eight percent had guns, most of which were loaded and operative, while others had what appeared to be a lethal weapon (replica pistol, knife, or blunt object) during their confrontation with police. Thirty-nine percent of the cases involved a domestic violence call, 20% were despondent over a relationship breakup, and 9% involved a "three strikes" individual facing capture and immediate incarceration. To provoke the police to shoot them, 50% pointed their firearm at officers, 26% lunged at them with a knife, 15% fired their weapons at officers, 4% threw a knife at officers, and 4% continued to assault civilians with a lethal weapon after being ordered to drop their weapon. Seventy-eight percent of the suspects verbally indicated that they wanted to commit SBC, 58% asked officers to shoot them, 6.5% told someone else they would have officers shoot them, 6.5% told officers afterward that SBC was why they had pointed their weapons at the officers, 2.2% thanked officers for shooting them, 2.2% left a written note, and 2.2% called officers prior stating they wanted to commit suicide. Twenty-two percent demonstrated their suicidal intentions via behavior only: 15.2% continued to point their weapon after being told they would be shot and 6.5% lunged at officers with a knife, knowing they would be shot. Seventy percent of the shootings took place within 30 min of police arrival, while the median time until the shooting was only 15 min. Verbal dissuasion as a tactic was used in 96% of the cases to no avail and less lethal force (Arwen, bean bag gun, pepper spray, etc.) was not successful in the 24% of cases where it was deployed. The events were fatal to the subject 54% of the time. The fact that a substantial proportion of cases involved a history of alcohol or drug abuse, as well as past psychiatric histories or suicide attempts, is not surprising, as all of these factors have been associated with suicide generally (Wilson, Davis, Bloom, Batten, and Kamara, 1998; Moscicki, 1995; Hirschfeld and Russell, 1997).

Wilson et al. (1998) reviewed the deaths of 15 suicidal individuals who provoked officers to kill them in Oregon and Florida. They were concerned about the categorization or certification of the death by coroners, an issue that is subject to debate, with many opining that the appropriate categorization by coroners in these cases is suicide not homicide, as traditionally occurs. In that context, they examined 21 variables that seemed to be relevant in terms of classifying the death as a suicide. They noted that all subjects were males, all resisted arrest and threatened homicide during the fatal incident, two-thirds of the subjects took hostages, all possessed an apparent handgun or other weapon (knife and iron bar), all subjects posed their weapon and threatened others during the incident, 60% actually used the weapon with apparent intent to hurt others, 40% were intoxicated with alcohol, 47% had prior suicide attempts, 40% had medically documented psychiatric diagnoses, 60% had reasonable historical evidence of psychiatric diagnoses, and the most common psychiatric conditions were depression and substance abuse. They opined that "a person who points a gun at a law enforcement officer usually knows with reasonable certainty that the officer will shoot to kill (p. 51)." This point is reaffirmed by Best, Quigley, and Bailey (2004) who note "an awareness of the likely police response" should be a component of any analysis of the subjects in these incidents. Wilson et al. (1998) noted that "it is not unusual for people to look to others to help them commit suicide. Physicians are often recruited with or without their conscious knowledge … just as some individuals look to the authority and power of physicians to assist them in ending their lives, it should not be unexpected that some would look to law enforcement with the same motivation. A common denominator is that physicians and police have the power to end lives in their legally sanctioned roles (p. 51)."

Kennedy, Homant, and Hupp (1998) reported their findings of a review of 240 police shootings cases identified in 22 newspapers from an electronic library search from the years 1980 to 1995. They determined that 16% of the 240 incidents had probable or possible suicidal motivation. When they refined their analysis to 80 cases with sufficient detail to classify, they found that 46% contained some evidence of possible or probable suicidal motivation. They conducted a follow-up review of 33 cases taken from *Detroit Free Press* between 1992 and 1993 and determined that 46% had possible suicidal motivation. They obtained only 74% interrater agreement on categorization however. Sixty-nine percent of these cases resulted in the subject's death. These data, while not rigorously collected and subject to numerous report-ing biases (not the least of which is relying upon unreliable news reporting sources) and other significant data-collection problems, provided some initial evidence that suicidal motivation (although not specifically SBC) might occur at a rate of 16–46% of police shooting cases.

Homant et al. (2000) examined 123 completed or averted SBC cases that had been culled from 10 separate sources: a prior master's thesis study of 28 cases, cases from prior studies by the authors and others, expert witness consultations by the authors, the Internet, a SBC segment on the ABC TV show 20/20, the Federal Appellate Court case *Palmquist v. Selvick*, a Lexis-Nexis database search, and a local police department. This study is also limited by significant data-collection problems that stem from questionable or soft data sources that could lead to a multitude of potential reporting biases. They focused on the dangerousness of SBC incidents and found that 56% of the incidents posed a serious threat to police or bystanders. Fifty percent of the time, the subject confronted the police with a loaded firearm. In 22% of the cases, the threat appeared to be less severe, and in another 22% of the cases, the subject's behavior was nonexistent, but bluffed. In 22% of the cases, the suicide was successfully averted. They found that the use of deadly force was correlated with the *perceived* danger, not the actual or real danger. They also reported that the pres-ence of other people placed in potential danger by the subject increased the risk of police deadly force. They astutely observed that "the fact that the subject is suicidal is not relevant until the person is safely contained (p. 50)." Homant et al. (2000) noted that "suicide by cop situations are usually dangerous and that police are generally unable to distinguish the less dangerous incidents from the dangerous ones until after the fact (p. 50)." Further, they observed that "many individuals, bent on suicide by cop, are dangerous … suicide by cop situations are unpredictably dangerous and require at least the same level of caution as any other type of police intervention with potentially violent persons (p. 50)."

This particular study (Homant et al., 2000) was useful because it outlined multiple potential motivations among those who would use the police to commit suicide. They indi-cated that "any given individual may exhibit one or more" of these motives. These included *psychodynamic motives* such as a need for attention to compensate for feelings of inad-equacy or to publicize some delusional claim, a character structure based in being a victim, guilt feelings that require violent death by authorities for cleansing, final catharsis of inner rage by acting out a fantasy of dying in a lethal shootout and taking as many people as pos-sible, a desire to punish the authority figure with guilt feelings, and acting out a conflicted relationship with a parent figure. *Social value motivations* include the belief that "normal" suicide by one's own hand is not acceptable or a serious sin, seeking the sanctioned author-ity of the police to end one's life, and preferring a blaze of glory rather than facing prison or other forms of defeat. *Practical motivations* were outlined: lacking the nerve to pull the trigger on oneself, believing the police will do it effectively, concern about insurance pay-out exclusions for traditional suicide, or being physically incapable of committing the act.

Manipulative motivations were also identified such as wanting to make the police look bad, create civil or community unrest, or to provide one's heirs with a possible lawsuit. The latter motive might help the suicidal person alleviate guilt feelings over being a perceived failure as a spouse or parent.

Mohandie and Meloy (2000) differentiated motivation for SBC into three primary or "meta-goals" of a potential SBC: homicide-suicide, suicide only, or cry for help. They indicated that an officer facing a potential SBC generally might not be able to distinguish which meta-goal is operative in the subject. In addition, they opined that all suicide behavior is goal directed and identified instrumental (functional) and expressive (emotional) goals for SBC. The potential SBC may want to escape consequences of his/her behavior, use a confrontation with police as a tool (e.g., sympathy plea) for reconciling a lost or strained relationship, avoid the exclusionary clause for suicide in an insurance policy, avoid the religious or moral responsibility of suicide, or force another person to kill them because they are not capable, all instrumental motivations with clear functionality. Or, they may use SBC to communicate helplessness and hopelessness, make a statement about being the ultimate victim, save face by dying rather than surrendering, communicate an extreme need for power and control over a situation, express pent-up rage and exact revenge, or provide a forum to communicate about an important personal issue, all expressive motivations.

Homant and Kennedy (2000) did a follow-up to their earlier study, in which they added additional incidents to their original sample of 123 cases from the aforementioned sources for a total of 143 SBC events. They also included 29 cases that were not SBC as a methodological technique, allowing the assessment of how well an independent judge could reliably exclude the cases. They obtained 96.5% agreement in terms of these ratings, yielding a reliability coefficient of .87. This study also introduced a typology of SBC cases: (1) *direct confrontations*, in which suicidal subjects initiated attacks on police; (2) *disturbed interventions*, where potentially suicidal subjects took advantage of police intervention to attempt or commit suicide via SBC; and (3) *criminal interventions*, in which subjects facing arrest preferred death to submission. In the criminal interventions category, they found the cases equally distributed between those facing arrest for serious versus minor crimes, indicating that perception of seriousness, shame, and aversion to arrest and incarceration are from the perspective of the subject. They divided these three categories further into nine subtypes. Thirty percent of the cases were found to be direct confrontations, 57% disturbed interventions, and 12% criminal interventions. Homant and Kennedy found 78% interrater agreement for placement into the three main categories, yielding a reliability coefficient of .74, but only 60% agreement for placement into the nine subtypes, yielding a coefficient of .58. Examining their findings from another perspective, only 30% of the events were preplanned, while the majority, nearly 70%, represented SBC events that spontaneously emerged during the police intervention situation. There were only 13 females in the overall sample, which was not surprising; however, all were categorized as SBC—none was excluded. This suggests that when a female is shot by police, an examination of potential suicide motivation is indicated. The greater representation of men in SBC samples is consistent with the observation that men tend to choose methods with greater intent and lethality, which may account for their higher mortality from suicide attempts (Moscicki, 1995). SBC should be viewed as a highly lethal and violent method of suicide. This study was an important contribution to the literature as it assessed and established that categorization of SBC versus those that were excluded could be reliably accomplished, yet suffered from the same methodological weaknesses of the author's earlier work.

Lord (2005), researched 64 SBC cases derived from 32 North Carolina law enforcement agencies between the years 1991 and 1998. No comparison group was used. Lord found that 16 were killed by police, five subjects committed suicide, and 43 survived the attempt, making these attempts lethal 33% of the time. Fifty-four percent were found to have a mental health history (often bipolar and schizophrenia), 64% were considered substance abusers, 74% were under the influence of drugs or alcohol at the time of the incident, most were not socially isolated, 62% were not employed, and most were experiencing what could be perceived as a stressful event prior to the incident. Forty-one percent had recently lost significant people in their lives or were experiencing a major family problem, while 16% were having stressors related to their mental illness and 9.5% were experiencing multiple stressors such as domestic, financial, or consequences related to their criminal activity. Interestingly, Lord found that those addicted to hard drugs like cocaine were more likely to complete their suicide, while those who abused alcohol during the incident were less likely to complete.

Twenty percent of the subjects had suicidal histories. Those who attempted suicide once before were three times more likely to be injured or killed by officers than those who never before attempted suicide. Fifty-six percent of the subjects had communicated suicidal intent either verbally or through changes in their behavior. Very little planning occurred with half of the subjects. Seventy-three percent of the subjects possessed a gun and 21% had a knife during the incident, the presence of such weapons increasing the likelihood that they could compel law enforcement to shoot them. Ninety-two percent of those with a firearm were shot by officers, while only 8% of those with knives were shot by officers. Twenty percent of the subjects mentioned a desire to kill someone besides themselves during the incident. Thirty-six percent of the subjects evidenced both homicidal and suicidal intent. This latter point is noteworthy, as the overlap between homicidal and suicidal ideation has been observed in other violent crime contexts such as mass murder, school violence, and terrorism, as well as domestic violence (Mohandie, 2000; Meloy, Mohandie, Hempel, and Shiva, 2001; Hempel, Gray, Mohandie, Shiva, and Richards, 2004; Hempel, Meloy, and Richards, 1999).

California POST (1999), with the input of 14 multidisciplinary subject matter experts, identified "10 key points to remember about suicide by cop incidents."

1. A suicidal person can and may kill. Therefore, these incidents are dangerous, high-risk events that demand sound officer safety tactics.
2. Some suicidal persons want officers to kill them and may harm others to make it happen.
3. These events are increasing in frequency and magnitude.
4. Officers are often surprised by the behaviors of the precipitator in these situations.
5. The event often involves a precipitator who is armed and violent and whose behavior is irrational, threatening, noncompliant, defiant, and defies logic.
6. The actions of the precipitator are intended to remove the nondeadly force options available to the officer.
7. The event involves a planned or spontaneous "trap" created by the precipitator to manipulate the officer into using deadly force against him/her.
8. The violence and extreme dynamics of these situations and the resulting publicity and lawsuit increase the potential for adverse psychological impact on the officer and other involved law enforcement personnel.

9. In a "suicide by cop" incident, the officer is truly the victim, although the incident is often incorrectly portrayed in the media as the result of excessive force or improper tactics.

10. Thorough investigations are crucial in revealing the truth about the incident.

At the time of this writing, the largest empirically sound study of SBC is well under way (Mohandie, Meloy, and Collins, 2007). The study has already validated Hutson et al.'s (1998) suspicion that the prevalence of SBC cases among police deadly force encounters was much higher than their original conservative 10-year estimate. More than 700 cases derived from OIS investigations conducted by homicide units around the United States and Canada have been reviewed, with approximately one-third of all shootings, fatal and nonfatal, being categorized as SBC. Data collection and analysis from this study continues and will be disseminated in forthcoming peer-reviewed publications.

Suicide Risk Factors and Indicators

Shneidman (1996) observes that there are ten commonalities among suicidal individuals: (1) solution seeking—a way out, (2) cessation of consciousness, (3) unbearable psychological pain, (4) frustrated psychological needs, (5) the common emotion is hopelessness/helplessness, (6) cognitive state is ambivalence, (7) perceptual state is constriction, (8) common action is escape, (9) common interpersonal act is communication of intent, (10) consistency of lifelong styles.

While a few of these commonalities are self-explanatory, several merit further clarification. *Solution seeking* refers to the fact that although normal people would consider suicide to be dysfunctional, nonetheless it is an attempt by the subject to solve some problem. *Cessation of consciousness* means that the person wants to cease to be and no longer wants to perceive, feel, or think about the circumstances they have been dealing with or with which they are confronted. *Ambivalence* reflects the reality that most suicidal individuals have mixed feelings about living versus dying, and that their suicidal impulses may wax and wane. The person may want to die or may simply be ambivalent about living. *Constriction* means that suicidal subjects have a limited ability to see other options and choices for solving their problem—they often experience some degree of tunnel vision. Suicide is a form of running from a problem or problems—it is an *action of escape* among several that the subject may use concurrently or have previously exhausted. It is not uncommon in some SBC cases for the subject to initially flee police, then when they are facing capture, to compel the police to kill them. Both behaviors represent actions of escape with the permanent solution selected during moments of hopelessness while facing imminent arrest. Most subjects *communicate intent* of suicide prior to actually doing so—Shneidman reported that in 90% of actual suicide cases, people had given verbal or behavioral clues within the week or so before they committed suicide. *Consistency of lifelong styles* means that people will usually go about their suicide the way they went about their life—if they are impulsive, they will do it impulsively, for example.

Mohandie and Meloy (2000) outlined generic suicide and violence risk factors from the scholarly literature, as well as those specific to SBC, which could be applied during forensic psychological review. Suicide is a form of violence directed toward oneself. Like other forms of violence, male gender raises risk for suicide completion: women attempt suicide more than men, but because men choose more violent and lethal means (firearms, jumping off a building, etc.) of committing suicide, they are more likely to complete their suicide. Further, there is evidence that women are more likely to use self-inflicted injury as an expression of distress and cry for help (Moscicki, 1995). The prevalence of violence is more than five times higher among people who meet criteria for a diagnostic and statistical manual of mental disorder-III (DSM-III) axis I diagnosis than those who are not diagnosable, 12 times higher for those who have a diagnosis of alcoholism, and 16 times higher for those diagnosed as abusing drugs (Monahan, 1992). Similarly, diagnoses of schizophrenia, major depression, and mania/bipolar disorder are well represented among those who commit and attempt suicide (Moscicki, 1995; Best et al., 2004). Aggressive behavior disorders such as conduct and antisocial personality disorders have been found to relate to completed suicides in adolescent populations. Moscicki reports that 90% of completed suicides in all age groups in the United States and Sweden are associated with mental or addictive disorders.

Weapon availability in the home has been identified as a strong risk factor for suicide and homicide (Kellerman, Rivara, Somes, Reay, Francisco, Banton, Prodinsky, Fligner, and Hackman, 1992, Kellerman, Rivara, Rushforth, Banton, Reay, Francisco, Locci, Prodzinski, Hackman, and Somes, 1993). Other factors include family history of mental illness and substance abuse, family history of violence and child abuse, and seizure disorders or brain dysfunction. Exposure to suicidal behavior of others may lead to suicidal behavior in those at risk (Moscicki, 1995)—such exposure can be through family members or can even originate in the media, as sometimes occurs with suicide clusters. Family dysfunction may partly account for the increased risk among biological relatives of suicidal subjects, and it may also reflect some biological loading for depression or impulsivity (Moscicki, 1995).

A dysfunctional intimate relationship, including separation, divorce, or family violence, is another significant risk factor for suicide (Jobes, Casey, Berman, and Wright, 1991; Moscicki, 1995; Best et al., 2004). The threat of incarceration, incarceration, or finding oneself in jail is another potent risk factor (Hutson et al., 1998; Moscicki, 1995). Prior suicide attempts are also highly related to completed suicides as well as to future suicide attempts (Wilson et al., 1998; Moscicki, 1995; Hirschfeld and Russell, 1997).

Hopelessness has been identified as a strong indicator of suicidal potential. The author has additionally observed that those with antisocial, borderline, and narcissistic personality disorders and traits may be at increased risk for suicidal behavior. The DSM-IV-TR (APA, 2000) specifies that those with antisocial personality disorder are more likely to die by violent means, including suicide. Polysubstance abuse is frequently observed among the suicidal, and intoxication at the time of death is a highly significant correlate of suicide (Moscicki, 1995; Best et al., 2004). Seventeen to 25% of all completed suicides were intoxicated at the time of their suicide (Litman, 1989; Rosenberg, Davidson, Smith, Berman, Busbee, and Ganter, 1988).

Crisis Management Techniques

In civil and criminal matters, the reasonableness of the officers' actions, adequacy of his/her training, and use of special tactics may be called into question. Many departments train their officers about how to respond to suicidal, distraught, and mentally ill citizens, and psychologists are often subject matter experts in the development of such curricula, teach or collaborate in training efforts, and respond in the field to events in progress as evaluators on psychiatric emergency teams and consultants to crisis negotiation teams.

There is a body of expertise and scholarly knowledge pertaining to crisis management techniques for dealing with the suicidal, distraught, and mentally ill. While an extensive review of this subject is beyond the scope of this chapter, several main points about crisis management from McMains and Mullins (2001) and other sources are worthy of mention. These issues may be important assessment topics. Attorneys in these matters may attempt to assign liability or responsibility based on the presence or absence of crisis negotiators or other specially trained personnel. They may indicate that the absence of such resources is evidence of a policy and practice of resorting too quickly to force, the so-called "action imperative."

McMains and Mullins (2001) reported eight characteristics of a negotiable incident gleaned from the FBI's work: (1) There must be a need to live on the part of the subject; (2) there must be a threat of force on the part of the authorities; (3) there must be demands by the subject; (4) the negotiator must be seen by the subject as a person who can hurt the subject but is willing to help him; (5) there must be time to negotiate; (6) a reliable channel of communication must exist between the subject and the negotiator; (7) both the location and the communications need to be contained in order to encourage negotiation; and (8) the negotiator must be able to deal with the subject making the decisions (pp. 50–51).

It is the threat of force that sometimes comes up as an issue during litigation, with some purported experts offering the narrow view that "force and negotiations are incompatible." However, McMains and Mullins (2001) articulate that "the tactical team's presence is essential to successful negotiations. They provide containment and a visible threat, without which the subject has no reason to negotiate (p. 309)."

Ultimately, McMains and Mullins (2001) opine that "special care needs to be taken with subjects who are suspected of entertaining the idea of SBC, because they will kill others to achieve their ends. Additionally, they will threaten with deadly weapons. If officers do not have appropriate cover or if the subject is putting others at risk, appropriate force is the response of choice (p. 263)."

In 2001, the National Council of Negotiation Associations (NCNA and CNU) issued a set of guidelines pertaining to crisis negotiation and crisis management practice. Their input represented the expertise of 13 different U.S. negotiator associations and three negotiator conferences representing 5000 members nationwide. Here is a summary of their recommendations:

1. They opine that negotiations are the preferred method for resolving potentially violent crisis situations but clearly indicate that "the method by which any crisis situation is resolved is ultimately determined by the subject's behavior (p. 3)."
2. Tactical resolution is reserved for those situations in which the subject appears likely to engage in future violence despite negotiation efforts. Any department large enough to have a tactical team should have a negotiation team.
3. All departments should have a negotiation capability, and for smaller agencies this might take the form of mutual aid response.
4. Negotiation teams should be adequately trained and have the equipment necessary to perform their jobs. Adequate initial training is a 40-h course that covers basic concepts and techniques, abnormal psychology, active listening and suicide intervention, role playing drills, and case studies. Negotiators should also attend a recommended minimum of 5 days of recurrent training per year.
5. Staffing levels may vary by department due to perceived and demonstrated needs.

6. Negotiation teams should consider having a consultative relationship with a mental health professional for input not to perform the actual negotiation.
7. They report data from the FBI's Hostage Barricade Database (HOBAS) that 92% of all incidents are emotion driven. They recommend that "when practical agencies should employ a low profile response scheme for emotion driven situations."
8. The passage of time (buying time) is typically the most important tool of the negotiation team.

As a note, "buying time" is often cited as desirable in negotiation situations, as well as situations identified as having SBC risk. However, there are several downsides to the passage of time in crisis management circumstances including the fact that it may provide the subject increased opportunity for acting out behavior in certain situations (Mohandie and Albanese, 2006). Ultimately, it is up to the subject as to whether he/she will allow such time for peaceful resolution.

HOBAS, as mentioned by NCNA, is a tremendous asset to the forensic expert. This growing database, with thousands of negotiation incidents from around the United States, provides an empirical foundation for assessing the common practices and outcomes in jumper, barricade, and hostage situations. This database provides statistics about how incidents are typically resolved, duration, frequency of violence, use of specialized resources and equipment, and other pertinent information. It may be obtained by contacting the chief negotiator at the FBI's critical incident response group (CIRG).

These guidelines, and text books and training regarding crisis management, crisis negotiation, suicidal subjects, and dealing with the mentally ill, are available and provided to specialists such as negotiators, teams of police officers and mental health professionals (such as psychiatric emergency teams), and first responders. This training and these guidelines represent ideals that, in the real world, require time to deploy. As demonstrated by prior research (Hutson et al., 1998), most SBC events are over within 30 min, many in 15 min or less of officers first arriving, primarily due to the subject rapidly escalating the encounter through perceived or actual dangerousness. Many of the subjects who attempt or commit SBC have been observed to be unresponsive to verbal dissuasion techniques. Further, special resources such as SWAT, negotiation, and PET teams typically take at least 45 min to an hour or more from notification to on-scene arrival. These realities are important factors to consider when involved in forensic psychological assessment of such cases.

Related Scholarly Issues

Traumatic Response

Perceptual distortions, memory problems, and other psychophysiological effects such as tunnel vision are often observed among officers involved in traumatic events such as shootings and other use of force events. In fact, these kinds of experiences appear normative. Published scientific studies of over 1000 police officer involved in shootings (Honig and Roland, 1998; Artwohl, 2003; Lewinsky, 2002; Honig and Sultan, 2004) demonstrate that 90% of officers involved in such events will experience perceptual distortions, 22–52% will experience memory loss for part of the event, and up to 79% will experience tunnel vision. This information can be critical to civil and criminal trials where the accuracy of an officer's recall or initial perceptions is called into question. It can provide a documented, scientific reason for such inaccuracies that otherwise might be misinterpreted as purposeful omission. Lewinsky (2002) reports that there is a physiological basis for part of the distortion: the eye functions differently under conditions of stress-related adrenaline (and resultant tunnel vision), becoming jumpy (saccadic movements) in its scanning of the environment, resulting in input deficits. Further, the eye under normal conditions allows the perception of visual information only within five degrees of the focal point, and this area of focus diminishes under conditions of stress and low light. Thus, if an officer is highly stressed during a use of force encounter, and focused on the eyes of the subject as sometimes occurs, he/she could fail to receive sensory input about what the subject is doing with his or her hands, for example.

Reaction Times

There is a growing body of literature documenting the threat posed by individuals attempting or appearing to draw a weapon, whether moving or stationary, facing or turned away from an officer. Published studies of the psychophysiology of reaction times by Lewinsky (2000, 2002) show that an untrained person can draw a weapon from the waistband and fire off a round while moving as quickly as 9/100's of a second. These same studies have shown that if an officer waits to have complete positive identification of an actual weapon at the conclusion of the person's movement, an untrained person could fire at least two rounds before the officer could return fire due to the phenomenon of lag time. Different positions of weapon draw and response have been tested by Lewinsky (2000, 2002). Such information supports that officer perception of threat in response to certain movements in subjects suspected of being armed is real and justified.

Pertinent Legal Cases

Admissibility of Expert Testimony

Courts vary in terms of how they apply and interpret case law, allowing the admissibility of expert testimony. In Federal Court, the admission of expert testimony is governed by Rule 702 of the Federal Rules of Evidence (FRE), which states that "if scientific, technical, or other specialized knowledge will assist the trier-of-fact to understand the evidence or to determine a fact in issue, a witness qualified as an expert by knowledge, skill, experience, training, or education, may testify thereto in the form of an opinion or otherwise."

FRE, Rule 702, requires that the specialized testimony be reliable. Pursuant to Rule 702, an opinion's reliability is established by showing that: (1) the testimony is based on sufficient facts or data, (2) the testimony is the product of reliable principles and methods, and (3) the witness has applied the principles and methods reliably to the facts of the case. These principles also apply to technical and other specialized knowledge. (*Kumho Tire Co., Ltd. v. Carmichael*, supra.) The reliability requirement of Rule 702 is judged by examining "whether the reasoning or methodology underlying the testimony is scientifically valid." (*Daubert*, supra, 509 U.S. at 592–593.) Expert opinion testimony is deemed sufficiently reliable if the expert has "good grounds" for the expert's testimony. (*Daubert*, supra, 509 U.S. at 589; *Kumho Tire Co., Ltd. v. Carmichael*, supra, 526 U.S. at 147–148.) The Supreme Court has explained that "this condition goes primarily to *relevance*" (*Daubert v. Merrell Dow*

Pharmaceuticals, 509 U.S. 579, 589, 1993), which is defined in FRE 401 as "Evidence having any tendency to make the existence of any fact that is of consequence to the determination of the action more probable or less probable than it would be without the evidence." In *Daubert*, the Supreme Court, in addressing the admissibility of scientific expert evidence, held that FRE 702 imposes a "gatekeeping" obligation on the trial judge to "ensure that any and all scientific testimony … is not only relevant, but reliable." (Id. at 589.) While holding that the trial court has substantial discretion in discharging its gatekeeping obligation, it suggested a number of factors that the court may consider: (1) whether a theory or technique can be tested, (2) whether it has been subjected to peer review and publication, (3) the known or potential error rate of the theory or technique; and (4) whether the theory or technique enjoys general acceptance within the relevant scientific community. (Id. at 592–594.)

In *Kumho Tire Co., Ltd. v. Carmichael*, 526 U.S. 137, 147–148 (1999), the Court clarified that the gatekeeping function is not limited to "scientific" expert testimony, but applies to all expert testimony. In considering the admissibility of testimony based on "some other specialized knowledge," Rule 702 is generally construed liberally. (*United States v. Hankey*, 203 F.3d 1160, 1168 (9th Cir. 2000) [holding trial court properly discharged gatekeeping function in admitting police gang expert's testimony about gangs' "code of silence."]) Thus, trial judges are not required to mechanically apply the *Daubert* factors or the like to both scientific and nonscientific testimony; rather, judges are entitled to broad discretion with discharging their gatekeeping function. (*Kumho Tire*, supra, 526 U.S. at pp. 152–153.) Indeed, not only must the trial court be given broad discretion to decide whether to admit expert testimony, it "must have the same kind of latitude in deciding how to test an expert's reliability." (Id. at 152.) Thus, the *Daubert* factors are neither intended to be exhaustive, nor are they even intended to be applied in every case. (*Hankey*, supra, 203 F.3d at 1168.) A trial court may consider them when they are reasonable measures of the reliability of the proffered expert testimony. (Id. at 1168 [citations omitted].) Ultimately, the admissibility of expert opinion testimony generally turns on the following preliminary question of law determinations by the trial judge under FRE 104(a)(1):

1. Whether the opinion is based on scientific, technical, or other specialized knowledge
2. Whether the expert's opinion would assist the trier-of-fact in understanding the evidence or determining a fact in issue
3. Whether the expert has appropriate qualifications, i.e., some special knowledge, skill, experience, training, or education on that subject matter
4. Whether the testimony is relevant and reliable
5. Whether the methodology or technique the expert uses "fits" the conclusions (the expert's credibility is for the jury)
6. Whether its probative value is substantially outweighed by the risk of unfair prejudice, confusion of issues, or undue consumption of time. (Hankey, 203 F.3d at 1168 [citations omitted].)

Expert opinion testimony is appropriate when the factual issue is one that the trier-of-fact would not ordinarily be able to resolve without technical or specialized assistance. (*Daubert*, supra, 509 U.S. at 591; *Kumho Tire*, supra, 526 U.S. at 156.)

Rule 702's requirement that the evidence or testimony "assist the trier-of-fact to understand the evidence or to determine a fact in issue" goes primarily to relevance.

"Expert testimony which does not relate to any issue in the case is not relevant and, ergo, non-helpful." (Internal quotations and citations omitted.) (*Daubert*, supra, 509 U.S. at 591.) Relevance is evaluated based on "whether [that] reasoning or methodology can be applied to the facts in issue." (Ibid. at 593.)

Excessive Force Case Law

Pursuant to *Graham v. Connor*, 490 U.S. 386, 388 (1989), claims that law enforcement officers have used excessive force, deadly or not, in the course of an arrest, investigatory stop, or other seizure of a person are properly analyzed under the Fourth Amendment's "objective reasonableness" standard. The "'reasonableness' inquiry in an excessive force case is an objective one: the question is whether the officers' actions are 'objectively reasonable' in light of the facts and circumstances confronting them, without regard to their underlying intent or motivation." (Ibid. at 397.) The proper application of the test of reasonableness "requires careful attention to the facts and circumstances of each particular case, including the severity of the crime at issue, whether the suspect poses an immediate threat to the safety of the officers or others, and whether he is actively resisting arrest or attempting to evade arrest by flight. (See *Tennessee v. Garner*, 471 U.S., 1, at 8–9 [the question is 'whether the totality of the circumstances justifies a particular sort of … seizure'].") (Ibid. at 396.)

Applied to use of force cases involving potential SBC and officer stress responses, arguments in response to attempted motions *in limine* articulate that testimony about these issues could assist the trier-of-fact in understanding more clearly the "facts and circumstances" and "totality of the circumstances" confronting the officers at the time. This would include an explanation of what precipitated a suicidal subject's aggressive behavior.

The determination by the finder of fact as to whether the responding officers' conduct was reasonable depends upon the totality of the circumstances, including a subject's behaviors, and a qualified explanation as to the cause and effect of such behaviors. The trier-of-fact cannot determine the issue of reasonableness in a vacuum without regard to a subject's behaviors and the effect such behaviors would have on the responding officers. An expert's opinion to the effect that, for example, a plaintiff's injuries were "subject precipitated," along with an explanation of the effect of these behaviors on the responding officers, could arguably assist the trier-of-fact in understanding what the officers were dealing with, and whether their actions were objectively reasonable.

Forensic Interest in Suicide

Suicide determination for death certification has been of some forensic interest. Massello (1986) underscored the application of common law tradition. He identified the need for clear and convincing evidence for suicide in a given case that then could justify a medical examiner opinion that is reasonable and probable. In 1985, the California Supreme Court ruled that the standard of proof is a preponderance of the evidence that there is suicidal intent and that the subject is "shown to have performed the self-destructive act with an understanding of its physical nature and consequences (*Searle v. Allstate 31703*)." Homant et al. (2000) extrapolated three ways in which the issue of SBC could be legally relevant in a wrongful death (excessive force) lawsuit as they examined the 1997 federal appellate case, *Palmquist v. Selvik*. First, if the police officer (defendant) was aware of the decedent's suicidal motivation, then this might have a bearing on what tactics and level of force would be reasonable.

Second, if there is a dispute of the facts—such as the type of movement the decedent made—then a finding of suicidal motivation might have probative value. Third, the extent to which a decedent was suicidal is likely to be relevant to determining damages (p. 51).

It is important to note, however, exactly what occurred in *Palmquist v. Selvik*, 111 F.3d 1332 (7th Cir. 1997). This was an excessive force case, and the trial court initially ruled that defendants could present the suicide by police evidence under the FRE 404(a)(2) "first aggressor" exception to the inadmissibility of character evidence stating the suicide evidence could be used to determine Palmquist's motive and intent. The trial court subsequently clarified its evidentiary ruling by limiting the admission of the "death wish" evidence for the limited purpose of corroborating or rebutting factual eye witnesses. (Id. at 1338–1339.) The trial court further trimmed its initial ruling on the suicide evidence by allowing a cautionary jury instruction to the effect that the "death wish" evidence was irrelevant to the excessive force claim. (Id. at 1339.) After reconsideration of the suicide evidentiary ruling, the trial court excluded all "suicide by police" and "death wish" evidence, and limited the defense's evidence to the officers' personal knowledge—their experiences and observations—during the morning in question. (Id. at 1339.)

On appeal, the 7th Circuit essentially agreed with the logic of the trial court's ruling and upheld the award insofar as it pertained to the excessive force claim. (Id. at 1334–1346.) The 7th Circuit took care to note, however, that much testimony concerning "suicide by police" had in fact been admitted. (Id. at 1341.) All of the testimony concerning the decedent's asking the officers to shoot him had been admitted as known to the officer at the time of the shooting. (Ibid.) It is crucial to note that both sides' experts, in commenting on the appropriateness of the police response, described the case as being about "suicide by police." (Ibid.) The appellate court asserted that such testimony would have been cumulative and prejudicial, and if excluded improperly by the trial court, the exclusion would amount to harmless error. (Id. at 1342.)

The *Palmquist* Court also noted that the SBC evidence would be admissible in the damages phase. "Evidence that Palmquist wanted the police to kill him is directly relevant to his life expectancy…. Statements that Palmquist wanted to die certainly affected how long he would be expected to live, and thus what amount of money to award his mother and his estate." (Id. at 1342.)

Justice Ripple dissented to the majority's opinion, noting that they had overlooked the relevancy of the SBC evidence:

> "The evidence proffered in this case is probative of the situation Sergeant Selvik faced at the crucial moment (under *Sherrod* [*v. Berry*, 856 F.2d 802 (7th Cir. 1988)] that he fired the fatal shots: *Mr. Palmquist's prior expressions of his desire to die at the hands of the police make it more likely that his physical behavior at the scene that night was sufficiently aggressive to create a reasonable belief in Sergeant Selvik's mind that deadly force was necessary.* The majority's formalistic application of *Sherrod*, by which it absolutely forbids the admission of this powerfully relevant evidence, makes little sense…. Yet if pre-seizure evidence of intoxication is admissible to show that Mr. Palmquist acted as the officer claimed, then pre-seizure evidence of his fixed desire to commit suicide by police should be admissible to show the same. The majority's characterization of Mr. Palmquist's mental state, demonstrated by his prior statements and behavior, as 'character' evidence is simply unrealistic. See generally 22 Charles Alan Wright and Kenneth W. Graham, Jr., Federal Practice and Procedure § 5233 n1. This mischaracterization and the resulting inconsistency will confuse even further this area of the law." Id. at 1348 (emphasis added).

Justice Ripple went on to emphasize the need for a more flexible approach to the admission of preseizure evidence such as the SBC evidence:

"In my view, we need to adopt a more flexible approach to the admissibility of pre-seizure evidence, *an approach that recognizes that some evidence may be so probative (and not unduly prejudicial) that it is permissible to admit it to prove the nature of the situation faced by the officer at the time the shot was fired.* We need to leave this matter in the hands of the trial judiciary and allow it to make common-sense judgments as to the admissibility of this evidence." Id. at 1348 (emphasis added).

Courts properly have allowed expert psychiatric or psychological testimony regarding whether a plaintiff's behavior is consistent with someone suffering from a particular condition. See, e.g., *S.M. v. J.K.*, 262 F.3d 914, 920-922 (9th Cir. 2001) [expert testimony of his diagnosis that plaintiff was suffering from posttraumatic stress disorder ("PTSD") properly was admitted]. The court found that objections to testimony went to weight of the testimony and not its admissibility. In *S.M. v. J.K.*, supra, 262 F.3d at 921, fn. 4, the 9th Circuit refers to *Isely v. Capuchin Province*, 877 F.Supp. 1055, 1067 (E.D.Mich.1995) for its holding that "experts 'may testify as to [their] theories and opinions concerning PTSD … [and] as to whether [the patient's] behavior is consistent with someone who is suffering' from PTSD." While both cases address PTSD, and not the condition of "subject-precipitated" injuries or "suicide by cop," the reasoning adopted by the 9th Circuit supports the allowance of the other testimony as might be related to SBC. An expert could be allowed to testify as to theories and opinions concerning "suicide by cop," and as to whether plaintiff's behavior was consistent with someone who manifests the same type of behaviors. "Under *Daubert*, trial courts have broad discretion to admit expert testimony … A court may admit somewhat questionable testimony if it falls within 'the range where experts might reasonably differ, and where the jury must decide among the conflicting views….'." (*S.M. v. J.K.*, supra, at 262 F.3d 921, citing *Kumho Tire Co., Ltd. v. Carmichael, supra*, 526 U.S. at 153.) In *S.M. v. J.K.*, the 9th Circuit observed, "As commentators have repeatedly observed, 'mental health professionals involved in everyday practice may disagree more than half the time even on major diagnostic categories such as schizophrenia and organic brain syndrome.'" (Id. at 921, citing Christopher Slobogin, Doubts About *Daubert*: Psychiatric Anecdata as a Case Study, 57 Wash. and Lee L. Rev. 919, 920, 2000.) The *S.M.* court found the doctor's testimony on PTSD to fall within that range of reasonable disagreement. While offered testimony explaining a subject's behaviors at the time of the incident is not "questionable testimony," it does fall "within the range where experts might reasonably differ, and where the jury must decide among the conflicting views." While an expert's offered testimony explaining plaintiff's behaviors at the time of the incident is not "questionable testimony," particularly if a plaintiff argues that the defendants failed to properly assess the situation as a "suicide by cop" scenario, it does fall "within the range where experts might reasonably differ, and where the jury must decide among the conflicting views." As such, it could be argued that any plaintiff's objection to expert testimony in this arena goes to the weight of the testimony and not its admissibility. The 9th Circuit has suggested the proper way for a plaintiff to attack such expert testimony—as the court wrote in *S.M. v. J.K.*, following *Daubert*, "'vigorous cross-examination, presentation of contrary evidence, and careful instruction on the burden of proof are the traditional and appropriate means of attacking shaky but admissible evidence.'" (Ibid. 921–922, quoting *Daubert*, supra, 509 U.S. at 596.)

Applied Ethics and Moral Considerations

The APA Ethical Principles (APA, 2002) and the Forensic Specialty Guidelines (Committee on the Revision of the Specialty Guidelines for Forensic Psychologists, 2006) are especially relevant for this kind of forensic expertise. Forensic Specialty Guideline 4.01 *Scope of Competence* indicates that "Competent provision of services includes the psychological and legal knowledge, skill, throughness, and preparation reasonably necessary for provision of those services." Forensic Specialty Guideline 4.02 *Gaining and Maintaining Competence* specifies that "Forensic Practioners provide services only within the boundaries of their competence." Knowledge about SBC, phenomena such as the effect of trauma on perception and memory in police officers as well as crisis management techniques used by police officers in responding to suicidal and mentally ill citizens are very specific content knowledge areas. Such expertise is often acquired in highly specialized settings, such as police departments, and the training and education will be in venues most psychologists do not routinely traverse.

Forensic Specialty Guideline 4.02 *Gaining and Maintaining Competence*, additionally states that "Forensic practitioners undertake ongoing efforts to develop and maintain their competencies. To maintain the requisite knowledge and skill, forensic practitioners keep abreast of developments in the fields of psychology and law, engage in continuing study and education, and comply with any continuing education requirements to which they may be subject." Professionals practicing in this arena must stay on top of developments and changes so that their skills are sharp and their opinions contemporary.

Empirically Based Methods and Applications Methodology

Assessment of police deadly force case requires a different methodology than traditional psychodiagnostic assessment. There are numerous sources of data that can and should be considered: police reports, 911 tapes and transcripts, transcripts of witness interviews, photographs and videotapes of the scene(s) of the incident, criminal history, grand jury transcripts, depositions, trial testimony transcripts, medical records including toxicology reports, autopsy reports, crime scene investigation reviews, and reports, formal OIS investigative finding reports (often completed by district attorney investigators with a final report completed and signed by the DA), and mental health records. Occasionally, there will be videotape of the incident provided by police car mounted cameras, citizens, or local news sources. It is particularly useful to visit the scene of the incident for a formal *walk-through*, particularly while having it narrated by the responding officer(s). Often primary involved officers will provide information not present in the initial reports, and first-hand observations of locations will usually provide an appreciation for issues not gleaned by simply reviewing two-dimensional materials. Court records from the subject's other contacts with the legal system can be potentially useful—there are often details of family conflict and strife contained in divorce and child custody paper trails that counter surviving plaintiff's contention of blissful happiness until contact with the law enforcement officers. Medical records of the decedent or injured subject may also shed light on contributory issues, as well as family dynamics that are absent in other discovery of the litigation process. Depositions, while useful to review and often loaded with rich information, may also suffer from their lack of freshness, coaching by trial attorneys, and the tendency for involved parties to minimize negative information about their loved one who is now deceased.

Additionally, there may be information available about the involved police officers' disciplinary and training history. Such material, where mandated and admissible, should be reviewed for patterns that could be relevant to the issues at hand, such as prior poor responses to stress or excessive force complaints. This is consistent with the Forensic Guideline of "examining the issue at hand from all reasonable perspectives."

Basic Points to Consider in Clinical Forensic Assessment

Distortion of Collateral Data

In assessing the data available in use of force and potential SBC cases, particularly in the adversarial context of civil litigation or a criminal matter, it is generally recommended that statements made by family members, the subject (if he or she survived), and others should be obtained immediately following the incident. Such statements are often more accurate and honest than those obtained during depositions or at later points when individuals may be motivated by financial gain, to avoid or lessen criminal charges, or because of a desire to protect family members or the decedent's or subject's reputation (POST, 1999). Delay in the acquisition of statements often results in inadequate or inaccurate information due to these influences. Wherever possible, recordings of these statements are desirable as such witnesses may, for a variety of reasons, fail to recall or change statements. Reviewing such recorded material rather than just transcripts can help the forensic reviewer appreciate the emotionality, tone, and context of the communication. When deposition testimony conflicts with such initial reports, for example, the author suggests that the original statements be weighed more heavily.

Other Experts

There are usually other experts retained in police use of force cases including toxicologists, coroners, crime scene reconstructionists, and police procedure experts. Toxicologists can help detect, specify, and understand the presence and impact of drugs, alcohol, and medications. Coroners via autopsy reports will provide opinions regarding the types of injuries sustained by the decedent and may identify disease processes such as terminal or chronic illnesses such as AIDS or Hepatitis C that may have impacted the decedent's level of desperation or hopelessness. Police procedure experts, usually current or former police officers with substantial experience in OIS investigation, homicide investigations, and use of force policy and practice will review and render opinions about standards of care in training and practice. Access to the expertise and professional opinions of these other experts may be helpful when formulating opinions. Care should be taken, however, to recognize that some "experts" may not be as objective as desirable. The author has observed some variance in adherence to forensic consultation ethics among the professional groups. Some groups, such as police practice experts, may not have any entity to regulate their practice, leading to substantial variability in quality of opinions. Nonetheless, it behooves the forensic psychologist to be thorough in his/her review, as this enhances adherence to the Forensic Specialty Guidelines (Committee on the Revision of the Specialty Guidelines for Forensic Psychologists, 2006) *11.02, Methods and Procedures*, "forensic practioners maintain integrity by examining the issue at hand from all reasonable perspectives."

Avoiding Evaluation and Consultation Errors

Evaluation and consultation errors often stem from partisan blindness, bias, failing to understand the issues at hand, lack of competence in the area, and failing to establish clear boundaries with the consultee about what can and cannot be provided during the consultation. Cases should be initially screened for appropriateness, and areas where the expert can and cannot provide input should be identified.

Preparation is the key to effective consultation and avoiding consultation errors. It is imperative that the expert collaborate with the attorney about topics and areas for direct and redirect testimony, as well as discussing likely topics and issues that could arise during cross-examination. Full disclosure of the potential limitations of the expertise and testimony should be articulated, as well as any qualification or restricted topics.

Basic Points to Consider

There are several issues that usually should be addressed in forensic psychological consultations pertaining to police use of force cases.

1. *Expertise.* Expertise should be demonstrated, relevant to the issues at hand, and outlined in any generated reports, declarations, prepared testimony outlines, or other material. Professional backgrounds that provide such a nexus include extensive practical, clinical, and field experience with suicidal individuals; in-depth knowledge of the scholarly literature pertaining to suicidality and methods of suicide including SBC; professional presentations, research, publications pertaining to suicide, police response to mentally ill or suicidal individuals; and clinical experience with police officers postcritical incident. Prior work with psychiatric emergency teams conducting involuntary hospitalizations, or consulting to police crisis negotiation teams, is especially helpful.

2. *Multidisciplinary, Hands-on Perspective.* Expect to be more multidisciplinary and hands-on in approaching this kind of forensic review. Information from search warrants, vehicle and other property searches, toxicologists, coroners, crime scene reconstructionists, and walk-throughs or reenactments of the event are commonly available and useful, and often fill in important gaps in the assessment.

3. *Independence.* Be independent—request information. It is not uncommon for some attorneys to steer opinions through information control, leading to embarrassing moments on the witness stand or during deposition. While some attorneys may believe this to be a good tactic, it only serves to hurt them in the long run, and more importantly undermines credibility of the expert.

4. *Foundation.* Any opinion should be supported by clear foundation from the database. Direct quotes from source material, and appropriate qualifications or clarification of any contradictions, should be included.

5. *Openness.* Be open to new information as it becomes available.

Treatment Considerations

If the subject has survived his or her encounter with law enforcement, it is likely that treatment would be recommended to avoid a repetition of the problematic dangerous conduct. Common disorders include various DSM-IV axis I problems such as depression and substance abuse, as well as various axis II personality traits and disorders. Generally speaking, if conducting a forensic psychological review, it would be inappropriate, if not unethical, to provide treatment to the individual (Committee on the Revision of the Specialty Guidelines for Forensic Psychologists, 2006). However, it may be an appropriate recommendation that the individual be provided counseling or other appropriate treatment. Treating mental health professionals should be well versed in the issue of suicidality, and recognize the seriousness of an attempt to die at the hands of law enforcement (that this is a very violent, lethal method, as in other gunshot suicides) despite any minimization or blaming of others by the subject. Treating professionals should also have a thorough understanding of what exactly occurred during the encounter with police. Such an understanding should not exclusively rely upon the subject's potentially self-serving or psychologically protective statements about what occurred, but may be enhanced by obtaining collateral information such as police reports, witness statements, or even the subject's spontaneous admissions immediately following the event. The treating mental health professional should recognize that he or she might get records subpoenaed, or be compelled to testify at deposition or trial. In the event that such documents are requested, the provider should obtain an appropriate release from the subject. If confidentiality is limited from the outset by virtue of the therapist's role, then those limitations must be clearly articulated and understood by the subject, with appropriate written documentation to that effect. Thus, documentation should take these factors into account, consistent with the Specialty Guidelines for Forensic Psychologists (Committee on the Revision of the Specialty Guidelines for Forensic Psychologists, 2006).

Writing Forensic Reports and Acting as an Expert Witness

A forensic psychologist will be well served in his or her report writing and expert witness work when guided by and in compliance with the Forensic Specialty Guidelines and APA Ethical Principles. The Forensic Specialty Guidelines mandate competence, documentation, objectivity, and impartiality in forensic work. When reports are submitted as part of the professional work, as may be mandated under Federal Rules of Civil Procedure, Rule 26, the effective forensic mental health professional writes a timely, thorough, and well-documented report addressing the issues for which he or she is competent to testify about. It is critical not to allow oneself to be spoon fed information from one side so that one is blind to key points and issues. That can lead not only to embarrassment on the witness stand or during deposition, but to inaccurate conclusions and opinions. When known, caveats and qualifications to the data and conclusions should be articulated. Reports should identify all sources of information, and each opinion should clearly indicate the supporting foundational material.

Expert witness work in these matters ranges from behind-the-scenes review and consultation to deposition and courtroom testimony. The effective expert witness operates within the intent of professional ethics and is current with new developments in the literature pertaining to the issues. He or she avoids the appearance of bias or slant and states opinions and presents materials objectively and clearly so as not to mislead. A nondefensive, conversational, professional, egalitarian tone that avoids arrogant talking down to the court is helpful. Source material should be organized and readily available to support points of contention (such as when attorneys selectively cross-examine on a point, ignoring or omitting key contextual items). Ultimately, the expert appreciates his/her role as educator and performs the job accordingly. One should be able to anticipate likely topics of cross-examination, and to think on one's feet in responding to the varied topics that come up.

The effective expert works with the attorney client in anticipating potential motions *in limine* to his/her testimony and prepares his or her work on the case with this likelihood in mind. Such an approach ensures that information helpful to respond to such actions will have been developed and be available during the discovery process.

Novel Applications of Forensic Evidence and Knowledge

There is at least one objective technique that has been used to help distinguish suicides versus accidental deaths and holds promise for application to SBC cases. The empirical criteria for the determination of suicide (ECDS) was developed by Jobes et al. (1991) and consists of 16 empirically derived items with a cut-off scoring system for determining suicide and accident manner of death. The ECDS was derived from the lengthy and some-what cumbersome operational criteria for the determination of suicide (Rosenberg et al., 1988). The measure was constructed and validated by using 126 suicide and accident cases obtained from 70 medical examiner participants. In analysis of its concurrent validity, the ECDS instrument predicted 100% of the suicides and 83% of the accidents, thus correctly identifying 92% of all cases. A large ongoing empirical study of SBC cases conducted by Mohandie et al. (2007) is exploring the use of the ECDS and has initially replicated its application to SBC cases. Further research will be done to apply cut-offs specific to SBC that enhance true-positives and reduce false-positives, as the primary developer of the ECDS concedes that the original system was intended to be overly inclusive (D. Jobes, personal communication, May 15, 2006).

Final Comments

SBC is a method of suicide that has been subject to scholarly study and research over the last decade and a half. The use of police deadly force is often in response to such cases, and psychological expertise pertaining to this phenomenon, as well as the impact of trauma upon police officer perceptions, can be useful to criminal and civil proceedings.

References

American Psychiatric Association. (2000). *Diagnostic and statistical manual of mental disorders, fourth edition, text revision (DSM-IV-TR)*. American Psychiatric Association: Washington, DC.

American Psychological Association. (2002). *Ethical principles of psychologists and code of conduct*. American Psychologist, 57, 1060–1073.

Artwohl, A. (2003). No recall of weapon discharge. *Law Enforcement Executive Forum, 3, 41–49*.

Best, D., Quigley, A., and Bailey, A. (2004). Police shooting as a method of self-harming: A review of the evidence for suicide by cop in England and Wales between 1998 and 2001. *International Journal of the Sociology of Law, 32, 349–361*.

Committee on the Revision of the Specialty Guidelines for Forensic Psychologists. (2006). Specialty guidelines for forensic psychology-second official draft. Retrieved October 5, 2006.

Foote, W.E. (1996). Victim-precipitated homicide. In H.V. Hall (Ed.), Lethal violence 2000: A sourcebook on fatal domestic, acquaintance and stranger aggression (175–202). Kamuela, HI: Pacific Institute for the Study of Conflict and Aggression.

Harruff, R.C., Llewellyn, A.L., Clark, M.A., Hawley, D.A., and Pless, J.E. (1994). Firearm suicides during confrontations with police. *Journal of Forensic Sciences, 39, 402–411*.

Hempel, A.G., Meloy, J.R., and Richards, T.C. (1999). Offender and offense characteristics of a non-random sample of mass murderers. *Journal of the American Academy of Psychiatry and the Law, 27, 213–225*.

Hirschfeld, R.M., and Russell, J.M. (1997). Assessment and treatment of suicidal patients. *New England Journal of Medicine*, 337, 910–915.

Homant, R.J., and Kennedy, D.B. (2000). Suicide by police: A proposed typology of law enforcement officer assisted suicide. *Policing: An International Journal of Police Strategies & Management*, 23, 339–355.

Homant, R.J., Kennedy, D.B., and Hupp, R.T. (2000). Real and perceived in police officer assisted suicide. *Journal of Criminal Justice*, 28, 43–52.

Honig, A., and Roland, J. (1998). Shots fired: Officer involved. *The Police Chief*, 65, 116–120.

Honig, A., and Sultan, S. (2004). Reactions and resilience under fire: What an officer can expect. *The Police Chief*, 71.

Hutson, H.R., Anglin, D., Yarbrough, J., Hardaway, K., Russell, M., Strote, J., Canter, M., and Blum, B. (1998). Suicide by cop. *Annals of Emergency Medicine*, 32, 665–669.

Jobes, D.A., Casey, J.O., Berman, A.L., and Wright, D.G. (1991). Empirical criteria for the determination of suicide manner of death. *Journal of Forensic Sciences*, 36, 244–256.

Kellerman, A.L., Rivara, F.P., Rushforth, N.B., Banton, J.G., Reay, D.T., Francisco, J., Locci, A.B., Prodzinski, J., Hackman, B.B., and Somes, G. (1993). Gun ownership as a risk factor for homicide in the home. *New England Journal of Medicine*, 329, 1084–1091.

Kellerman, A.L., Rivara, F.P., Somes, G., Reay, D.T., Francisco, J., Banton, J.G., Prodinsky, J., Fligner, C., and Hackman, B.B. (1992). Suicide in the home in relation to gun ownership. *New England Journal of Medicine*, 327, 467–472.

Kennedy, D.B., Homant, R.J., and Hupp, R.T. (1998). Suicide by cop. *FBI Law Enforcement Bulletin*, August, 21–27.

Lewinsky, W. (2000). Why is the suspect shot in the back: Finally hard data about how fast the suspect can be in eleven different shooting scenarios. *The Police Marksman*, November/December, 20–28.

Lewinsky, W. (2002). Stress reactions related to lethal force encounters. *The Police Marksman*, May/June, 23–28.

Litman, R.E. (1989). 500 psychological autopsies. *Journal of Forensic Sciences*, 34, 638–646.

Lord, V.B. (Ed.) (2005). *Suicide by cop: Inducing officers to shoot.* Flushing, NY: Looseleaf Law Publications.

Massello, W., III (1986). The proof in law of suicide. *Journal of Forensic Sciences*, 31, 1000–1008.

McMains, M. and Mullins, W. (2001). *Crisis negotiations: Managing critical incidents and hostage situations in law enforcement and corrections.* Cincinnati, OH: Anderson.

Meloy, J.R., Hempel, A.G. Gray, T.B., Mohandie, K., Shiva, A., and Richards, T.C. (2004). A comparative analysis of North American adolescent and adult mass murderers. *Behavioral Sciences and the Law*, 22, 291–309.

Meloy, J.R., Mohandie, K., Hempel, A.G., and Shiva, A. (2001). The violent true believer: Homicidal and suicidal states of mind (HASSOM). *Journal of Threat Assessment*, 1, 1–14.

Mohandie, K. (2000). *School violence threat management.* San Diego: STS Publications.

Mohandie, K. (2005). *Stalking and crisis negotiation.* Presentation to Baltimore Hostage Negotiation Annual Training Conference, Baltimore, MD.

Mohandie, K., and Albanese, M. (2006). Advanced crisis negotiations. Unpublished manuscript.

Mohandie, K., and Meloy, J.R. (2000). Clinical and forensic indicators of suicide by cop. *Journal of Forensic Sciences*, 45, 384–389.

Mohandie, K., Meloy, J.R., and Collins, P. (2007). An analysis of a large sample of North American suicide by cop cases. Presentation to the American Academy of Forensic Sciences, San Antonio, Texas.

Monahan, J. (1992). Mental disorder and violent behavior: Perceptions and evidence. *American Psychologist*, 47, 511–521.

Moscicki, E.K. (1995). Epidemiology of suicidal behavior. *Suicide and Life-Threatening Behavior*, 25, 22–35.

x

x

x

National Council of Negotiation Associations (NCNA) and FBI Crisis Negotiations Unit (CNU). (2001). *Recommended negotiation guidelines and policies.*

Noesner, G., and Nolan, J.T. (1992) First responder negotiation training. *FBI Law Enforcement Bulletin,* August, 1–4.

Police Officer Standards and Training. (1999). *Suicide by cop: A satellite telecourse for law enforcement.* July 15.

Rosenberg, M.L., Davidson, L.E., Smith, J.C., Berman, A.L., Busbee, H., Ganter, G. et al. (1988). Operational criteria for the determination of suicide. *Journal of Forensic Sciences,* 33, 1445–1456.

Shneidman, E.S. (1996). *The suicidal mind.* New York: Oxford University Press.

Wilson, E.F., Davis, J.H., Bloom, J.D., Batten, P.J., and Kamara, S.G. (1998). Homicide or suicide: The killing of suicidal persons by law enforcement officers. *Journal of Forensic Sciences,* 43, 46–52.

Wolfgang, M.E. (1958). *Patterns in criminal homicide.* Philadelphia, PA: University of Pennsylvania Press.

Wolfgang, M.E. (1990). Suicide by means of victim precipitated homicide. *Journal of Clinical* and *Experimental Psychopathology and Quarterly Review of Psychiatry and Neurology,* 20, 335–349.

Legal References

Daubert v. Merrell Dow Pharmaceuticals, 509 U.S. 579, 589 (1993).

Graham v. Connor, 490 U.S. 386, 388 (1989).

Kumho Tire Co., Ltd. v. Carmichael, 526 U.S. 137, 147–148 (1999).

Palmquist v. Selvik, 111 f.3d 1332 (7th Cir. 1997).

Searle v. Allstate, L.A. 31703 Sup.Ct. No. 405535 (April 1985).

S.M. v. J.K., 262 F.3d 914, 920–922 (9th Cir. 2001).

Tennessee v. Garner, 471 U.S. 1 (1985).

United States v. Hankey, 203 F.3d 1160, 1168 (9th Cir. 2000).

Psychological Consultation in Hostage/Barricade Crisis Negotiation

JOHN A. CALL

Crisis Management Consultants, Inc., Oklahoma City, Oklahoma

Contents

Introduction

This chapter focuses on advances in hostage/barricade crisis negotiation. In particular, this chapter examines how mental health consultants can provide assistance to law enforcement negotiators. Therefore, the following discussion concentrates, in part, on the ways in which a crisis incident can be classified, discusses different negotiation techniques and methods of negotiation analyses, explores the empirical bases that currently support these findings, and, finally, examines the impact, on the victims, of being taken hostage and how best to ameliorate that impact.

March 1972 is usually considered the watershed moment in modern history regarding hostage incidents. It was in that month, during the 1972 Olympic games, that the "Munich Massacre" occurred. Palestinian terrorists took hostage 11 Israeli athletes. At the conclusion of the incident, 22 people were dead: a policeman, 10 terrorists, and all the hostages (Soskis and Van Zandt, 1986). Following this and similar incidents, law enforcement policy specialists sought an alternative to the traditional use of force in hostage/barricade situations. For example, in 1973 the New York City Police Department began using detectives trained as negotiators in hostage/barricade incidents (Bolz and Hershey, 1979; Schlossberg, 1980). Shortly thereafter, the FBI developed a hostage negotiation program (Soskis and Van Zandt, 1986).

Over the past 25 years, law enforcement agencies' use of trained crisis negotiators has increased dramatically. Research performed in 1993 suggested that a majority of law enforcement organizations in the United States (68% of state police agencies, 96% of large municipal agencies, and 30% of the small municipal agencies) employed trained negotiators (Butler, Leitenberg, and Fuselier, 1993). Later investigation found that most of these specialists were deployed approximately 11 times a year, worked part-time as negotiators having other law enforcement duties, and received about 32 h of negotiation training a year (Bahn and Louden, 1999). As the years have gone by, hostage/barricade crisis negotiation has, more and more, been accepted as a worthwhile tool. Noesner (1999, p. 6) writes that crisis negotiation is "one of the most important [instruments] available in law enforcement to peacefully resolve crisis events." In accord, Regini (2002, p. 1) states, "Crisis negotiation is one of law enforcement's most effective tools. The successful resolution of te.. of thousands of hostage, barricade, attempted suicide, and kidnapping cases throughout the world repeatedly has demonstrated its value." In fact, recent analysis of the hostage barricade database system (HOBAS) data maintained by the FBI supports these assertions. Data analyses from 2002 to 2003 indicate that 82% of the reported hostage/barricade incidents were resolved without death or injury to the perpetrator or the victim (Flood, 2003).

There are three types of crisis situations where a negotiator can be used: (1) hostage incidents, (2) barricade-victim incidents, and (3) barricade-no victim incidents. Traditionally, hostage situations occur when one or more hostage takers hold one or more hostages against their will, threatening them harm, unless a third party meets the hostage taker's demands. Thus, traditional hostage taking is a triadic event—an event that involves three participants (Soskis and Van Zandt, 1986; Call, 1996, 2003).

In a barricade-victim incident, the captor holds one or more victims against their will, threatening them harm but has no interest in negotiating with a third party. Instead, the hostage taker holds the victim for an expressive purpose. Thus, this incident is, initially, a dyadic rather than a triadic event. Expressive hostage taking is motivated by internal emotions and impulses rather than a desire to achieve an objective goal (Miron and Goldstein, 1979; Call, 2003). Technically, the person held is not a hostage but a victim who is captured and restrained to express anger at him or her, a situation, or events (Noesner, 1999; Call, 2003; Royce, 2005).

In a barricade-no victim incident, the perpetrator is armed and barricaded, but there is no hostage or captive. Examples of this type of crisis situation range from a trapped criminal who has the clear instrumental goal of escape to a mentally ill person who is in the midst of a personal crisis and is suicidal.

Crisis negotiation is a team endeavor. One should never negotiate alone. Depending on the circumstances, teams may range from three to six persons staged in three shifts (Fuselier and Van Zandt, 1987; Lancely, 1999). Given the emotional and behavioral complexity associated with crisis negotiation, the use of a behavioral science consultant as a team member is recommended (Butler et al., 1993).

Pertinent Legal Cases

Legal issues most relevant to crisis negotiation are those related to application of the fourth amendment as it applies to unreasonable searches and seizure; admissibility into evidence of a perpetrator's statements made during negotiation; enforceability of negotiator's promises; use of surveillance equipment; use of force; and controlling the media during negotiations (Higginbotham, 1994). Guidance regarding these six issues is as follows.

Fourth-Amendment Issues

The police may enter a dwelling in a crisis situation without a warrant. However, the purpose of the entry must be to provide immediate aid to victims, to arrest the perpetrator, or to provide such other services immediately required to resolve the emergency (*Mincey v. Arizona*, 1978).

Statement-Admissibility Issues

A perpetrator's statements made during negotiation are admissible as evidence at trial. The *Miranda* rule does not apply since during negotiations the perpetrator is neither in the custody of the police nor being subjected to interrogation (*People v. Gantz*, 1984).

Negotiator's Promise Issues

Although during a crisis negotiation, a negotiator may promise the perpetrator certain things in an attempt to successfully mediate surrender, the government is under no obligation to enforce the promise(s). Such action is void as against public policy (*State v. Sands*, 1985).

Surveillance Issues

Generally, federal law prohibits the electronic interception of telephone conversations or oral conversations, where the speakers have a reasonable expectation of privacy, without a court order or without the consent of one of the parties to the conversation. However, federal law permits electronic surveillance in emergency situations, such as those instances where there exists a danger of death or serious injury, as long as the emergency interception has been approved by a senior prosecutorial personnel and the application for a court order is made within 48 h of the first interception.

Use-of-Force Issues

Even though negotiations are in progress, it is permissible to use deadly force if the police have a probable cause to believe that the perpetrator poses a threat of serious physical harm, either to the police or to others. Further, it is permissible to use deadly force to prevent escape if there is probable cause to believe that the perpetrator has committed a crime involving the infliction of serious physical harm or the threat of serious physical harm and, if feasible, some warning has been given (*Tennessee v. Gardner*, 1985). However, the U.S. Court of Appeals for the Sixth Circuit chastised the FBI's use of deadly force during negotiations in a hijacked airliner incident, finding that they had turned "what had been a successful 'waiting game,' during which two persons safely left the plane, into a 'shooting match' that left three persons dead" (*Downs v. United States*, 1975, p. 1002).

Control-of-Media Issues

The media have the right to gather news from any source within the law but do not have a constitutional right of special access. Thus, the media have no guaranteed right of access to disaster or crime scenes where the general public has been excluded (*Branzburg v. Hayes*, 1972).

Applied Ethics and Moral Considerations

To date, there are no accepted guidelines as to best practice with respect to providing psychological consultation to law enforcement crisis negotiators. Even so, the *Ethical Principles of Psychologists and Code of Conduct* § 2.01 (e) (American Psychological Association, 2002, p. 5) states that even in those "emerging areas in which generally recognized standards for preparatory training do not yet exist, psychologists nevertheless take reasonable steps to ensure the competence of their work and to protect clients/patients, students, supervisees, research participants, organizational clients, and others from harm." Thus, it is incumbent upon the psychologist who consults with law enforcement crisis negotiation teams to take steps to ensure competence.

At a minimum, ensuring such competence would include attending the same crisis intervention courses as the law enforcement negotiator as well as being conversant with the existing scientific and law enforcement literature regarding crisis negotiation. Furthermore, Butler et al. (1993) noted that the psychological consultant must demonstrate adequate clinical training and experience, be familiar with applicable forensic issues, understand the organization and structure of law enforcement agencies, and be willing to work within the law enforcement system.

Likewise, the American Psychological Association has made it clear that when psychologists serve in *any* position by virtue of their training as a psychologist, the APA Ethics Code is applicable to their conduct (American Psychological Association, 2005). Thus, the argument that the code does not apply to psychologists acting in roles other than traditional health service provider relationships holds no weight. Of course, this means that the psychologist consultant must consider every section of the code and ask himself or herself how it might apply to his or her actions in various crisis situation scenarios. For example, one of the principal functions of a psychological consultant is to provide the negotiator with a diagnosis and assessment of the hostage/barricade subject (Feldmann, 2004). Such information can be crucial in formulating negotiation strategy as well as helping the negotiator and crisis commander assess negotiation progress and the threat of imminent lethality. But what if that information is ultimately used, in part, to implement a tactical solution to the crisis, one that results in the injury or death of the perpetrator? Recently, the American Psychological Association stated that psychologists must not use health care–related information to the detriment of an individual's well-being and safety even when providing consultation in interrogation or information-gathering processes for national security–related purposes. The basis for this decision was Principle A, "do no harm," and Principle B, which addresses the psychologist's responsibilities to the society. In other words, psychologists should do no harm and, in fact, should use their expertise to aid in the prevention of harm.

Does this decision mean that a psychologist cannot provide his or her law enforcement teammates with health care–related information regarding a hostage taker because it might, ultimately, be used in a way to physically harm the individual? As of yet, the American Psychological Association has not made a formal ruling on this issue. Debatably, there exist crucial differences between the ethical duties a consulting forensic psychologist owes a prisoner undergoing interrogation versus a hostage taker holding a gun to the head of a victim. First, the hostage taker is not in the custody of the authorities, but is a free agent. Second, the perpetrator is not undergoing interrogation, but is in the act of committing a felony. Third, there exists no professional relationship between the hostage taker and the consulting psychologist, not even a vicarious relationship since the perpetrator is not being held by the authorities. Fourth, the perpetrator is an imminent deadly threat to innocent third parties; if the crisis situation is not resolved, people are going to die. Arguably, because of these differences, Principles A and B would not prevent the psychologist from providing his or her law enforcement teammates with health care–related information regarding the hostage taker.

Empirically Based Methods and Applications

Ten years ago, Call (1996) lamented the fact that there was no ongoing nationwide collection of information regarding hostage incidents and that there was little, if any, empirical research regarding the effectiveness of specific negotiation techniques. With respect to the latter, Vecchi, Van Hasselt, and Romano (2005, p. 549) note that even after 10 years, "investigative efforts to prescriptively apply the most efficacious negotiation strategies based on empirically grounded decision-making have yet to be conducted." Thus, the title of this section is obviously somewhat misleading. In significant part, the training of crisis negotiation techniques continues to be guided by experienced negotiators passing on skills to their younger colleagues. Therefore, what will be discussed in the following three sections is a synopsis of the current level of professional opinion based upon both the anecdotal and the existing empirical literature.

Crisis Event Classifications

To successfully negotiate a crisis situation, the negotiator must, eventually, interact with the perpetrator using normative bargaining techniques (Donohue, Ramesh, Kaufmann, and Smith, 1991). Thus, a key initial question the negotiator must ask and answer is whether there exists a bargaining range. One way to investigate this question is to understand the classification or typology of the crisis incident. In other words, some types or classes of crisis events have, by their very nature, a greater bargaining range than other types. Knowing this at the outset can help the negotiator craft a negotiating strategy as well as predict success or failure.

There are five different typologies, or ways, to systematically classify a crisis incident, none of which are mutually exclusive. These are (1) crisis incident typology, (2) demand typology, (3) siege typology, (4) victim location versus perpetrator demand typology, and (5) hostage taker typology.

The first classification scheme was discussed in the introduction section. This scheme divides crisis incidents into three types: hostage situations, barricade-victim situations, and barricade-no victim situations. In the traditional hostage situation, the hostage taker makes substantive demands, usually instrumental, of a third party threatening harm to the hostages if the demands are not met. Typical characteristics of a hostage incident are (1) the hostage taker is, to a significant degree, goal oriented; (2) the hostage taker makes substantive demands; (3) the hostage taker's primary goal is having the demands met; (4) the hostage taker realizes that he or she needs the police to help obtain his or her goal; and (5) the hostage taker realizes that keeping the hostages alive prevents a tactical response by the police.

In the barricade-victim situation, the perpetrator does not make substantive demands of a third party. The perpetrator already has what he wants—the victim. Typical characteristics of a barricade-victim situation are (1) no substantive demands or objective goal; (2) perpetrator's action is directed against the victim; and (3) absence of rational thinking and prominence of expressive and emotional ventilation.

In the barricade-no victim situation, the perpetrator may or may not be willing to bargain. The existence of a bargaining range depends on whether the barricaded individual has substantive demands.

Understanding a perpetrator's demand type is another way to classify a crisis situation. There are four general types of demands: instrumental, expressive, substantive, and nonsubstantive. An instrumental demand is best described as objective, goal oriented, and substantive. For example, demands for money, a getaway car, or the release of political prisoners are instrumental demands. An expressive demand is also goal oriented but is subjective in nature, one that is unique to the mind-set of the perpetrator. Examples of expressive demands are a perpetrator wanting to talk to an ex-wife or a perpetrator demanding that a boss apologize for alleged wrongdoing. Substantive demands are those that have obvious value, at least to the perpetrator. Substantive demands may be either expressive or instrumental. Nonsubstantive demands are those that, in actual fact, have no real value, even to the perpetrator or are not related in any way to the victim. A nonsubstantive demand also includes those situations where no demands are made.

Another way to profile crisis events is to classify the incident as to whether the location of the victim and perpetrator is known and contained (a siege) or whether this information is unknown, a nonsiege or kidnapping (Lancely, 1999). At one end of this continuum, where the location is known and the perpetrator is making substantive demands, the ability to bargain exists. On the other end of this continuum, where the location is unknown and the perpetrator is making nonsubstantive demands, including no demands, the ability to bargain does not exist.

Sieges can be further classified into three types: deliberate siege, spontaneous siege, and anticipated siege. In a deliberate siege, the perpetrator intentionally initiates the siege situation. The negotiator may or may not have bargaining ability depending on whether the incident is a hostage situation, barricade-victim situation, or barricade-no victim situation and whether substantive or nonsubstantive demands are made.

A spontaneous siege occurs inadvertently, such as when an armed robbery goes awry. Victims may or may not be present. Substantive demands may or may not be made. Again if the perpetrator makes substantive demands, particularly if the demands are instrumental in nature, a bargaining range is believed to exist.

An anticipated siege is one where the perpetrator and law enforcement expected that, at some point in time, the authorities would attempt to arrest the former. Examples

Table 8.1 Hostage Taker Typologies

General Category	Possible Subtypes
Emotionally disturbed	1. Brain damaged
	2. Elderly/senile
	3. Depressed, various types
	4. Paranoid, various types
	5. Schizophrenic
	6. Substance abuser
	7. Personal/family disputes
Political extremists	1. Reluctant captors
	2. Deliberate hostage takers
Religious fanatics	
Criminals	1. Antisocial personality disorder/trapped criminal
	2. Antisocial personality disorder/kidnapper
Prison inmates	Antisocial personality disorder
Combination	

Source: Call, J. A. in *Lethal Violence 2000: A Sourcebook on Fatal Domestic, Acquaintance and Stranger Aggression*, Pacific Institute for the Study of Conflict and Aggression, Kamuela, HI, 1996, 561–588. With permission.

are the siege and negotiations that occurred in the early 1990s between the FBI and the Branch Davidians in Waco, Texas and, some years later, between the FBI and the Montana Freemen. Substantive demands are usually not made in a barricade-no victim situation. Substantive demands may or may not be made if the siege is a hostage situation.

Hostage taker typology is one last way a negotiator can classify the crisis situation (Call, 1996, 2003; Table 8.1). Six major types of hostage takers are enumerated: emotionally disturbed, political extremist, religious fanatic, criminal, prison inmate, and a combination of two or more of these types. Further, there are multiple subtypes. Under the emotionally disturbed category, there are seven subtypes: brain damaged; elderly/senile; depressed, various types; paranoid, various types; schizophrenic; substance abuser; and personal/family disputes (Pearce, 1977; Gist and Perry, 1985; Strentz, 1986; Fuselier, 1988; Kennedy and Dyer, 1992).

Knutson (1980) described two types of political extremist hostage takers: the reluctant captor and the deliberate hostage taker. Her research suggested that the former were best described as dreamers and philosophers whose violent act was part of an attempt to right a wrong and who indicated that they were unwilling to kill their hostages. The deliberate hostage taker, on the contrary, was described as perfectly willing to kill his or her captives.

Perhaps a better way to understand political extremist hostage takers is to use Ferracuti's (1982) conceptualization—the subcultural theory. He argued that the best approach to understanding this type of perpetrator is to examine and understand the unique self-imposed value system and mores within which the political extremist exists. Global theories applicable to all political extremists are probably unobtainable. True understanding can only come via thorough investigation of each subculture.

An example of the results of such an investigation is provided by Ferracuti and Bruno (1981). They studied right-wing Italian terrorists and then conceptualized a set of traits that they termed the "authoritarian-extremist personality." Note that these traits are only relevant to the political extremists studied, i.c., the right-wing Italian terrorists. Ferracuti and Bruno (1981) described this particular terrorist personality style or subtype in the following manner:

1. Ambivalent feelings toward authority
2. Lack of psychological insight
3. Conventional behavior patterns
4. Emotionally detached from the consequences of their actions
5. Sexual identity disturbances
6. Superstitious and magical thinking
7. Self-destructive
8. Below-normal educational experiences
9. Fetish for weapons and belief in violent subcultural norms

Cooper (1981) first discussed the religious fanatic hostage taker. To better understand the possible subtypes of this category, the advice of Ferracuti (1982) regarding the examination of a particular cult's internal mores and values should be followed.

The criminal category is generally held to include, primarily, the trapped criminal or the kidnapper. The major subtype is the criminal psychopath. The criminal psychopath is believed to be a major subtype in the prison category as well. Finally, the last category is reserved for those hostage takers who obviously belong to two or more of the five earlier categories (see Table 8.1).

Crisis Event Databases

Systematic nationwide collection of hostage incident information did not begin until 1996. In that year, the FBI initiated the use of the hostage/barricade report (HOBAS). HOBAS is a hostage/barricade incident data-collection questionnaire. Local law enforcement is requested to complete this questionnaire and forward it to the FBI after each crisis incident. The HOBAS questionnaire requests data as they relate to the incident, the nature of contacts made by law enforcement during the incident, resolution of the incident, postincident information, ancillary information regarding the negotiator and SWAT interaction and training, subject data, and hostage/victim data. Vecchi et al. (2005) report that the HOBAS database now contains over 3800 hostage/barricade incidents.

Prior to the initiation of HOBAS, a thorough review of the literature revealed the existence of only five earlier hostage incident databases. These are the ITERATE database developed by Micklous (1976), the HEAD database developed by Head (1990), the New York Police Department Hostage Recovery Program database analyzed by Head (1990), a small database developed by Friedland and Merari (1992), a database developed by Butler et al. (1993), and a database developed by Feldmann (1998, 2001).

Mickolus (1976) developed a database of over 3329 international terrorist incidents that took place from 1968 to 1977. He termed this database ITERATE, which stood for international terrorism: attributes of terrorist events. A subset of this database (539 events), which occurred between January 1970 and July 1974, was analyzed by Corsi (1981). Head (1990) performed a more thorough analysis of the ITERATE data, using all 3329 incidents, and published his results in 1990. Given that the ITERATE data are over 30 years old, exclude all hostage events that occurred in the United States, and have been thoroughly reported elsewhere (Call, 1996), these data will not be examined in detail in the present chapter.

Friedland and Merari (1992) investigated 69 incidents of international and domestic political extremist hostage taking that occurred between 1979 and 1988. They excluded cases of kidnapping from their database. Their results suggested that hijacking of airplanes and barricade incidents occurred with equal frequency (46.4% each). The average number of hostages in a barricade incident was 35 and the average number of hostages in a hijacking incident was 131. There were five or fewer hostage takers in 63.3% of the cases. Hostage takers used teams of between 6 and 10 in 15% of the cases and teams of 10 or more in 23.3% of the cases.

The results also indicated that the hostage situation lasted 24 h or less (43.8%). The most frequent outcome was violence, i.e., assault by the authorities (31.1%). Violence was more likely when the hostage situation was a barricade situation, a trained rescue team was available, and no attempts at negotiation were made.

Unconditional surrender occurred in 19.7% of the incidents. In 36% of the incidents, the event concluded after the authorities met the hostage takers' demands in full or in part.

In 1990, Head reported his analysis of 3330 incidents of domestic hostage taking that occurred between 1973 and 1982. He termed this database the hostage event analytic database (HEAD). In summary, the analysis indicated the following:

1. The majority of the perpetrators fit the criminal or prison inmate typology (52%).
2. The second-largest typology of perpetrators was the political extremist/religious fanatic (21%) followed by the emotionally disturbed (18%).
3. The majority of perpetrators were young (25% below age 30), white (61%), and male (80%) and acted alone.
4. The usual number of victims captured was one (47%) or two (15%).
5. The most common location for the crisis event was a form of transportation (35%) followed by a home (20%).
6. The most common motivation for the perpetrator's actions was political/publicity (33%) followed by money (23%).
7. The most common weapon used was a firearm (31%).
8. The most common event duration was one day or less (53%).
9. The majority of incidents were nonlethal (87%). However, hostages were more at risk for injury than the hostage taker.
10. The majority of incidents were negotiated (64%).

Head also analyzed 137 incidents recorded by the New York Police Department Hostage Recovery Program which occurred between 1973 and 1982. In summary, the analysis indicated the following:

1. The majority of the perpetrators fit the criminal or prison inmate typology (58%).
2. The second-largest typology of perpetrators was emotionally disturbed (26%).
3. The majority of perpetrators were young (46% below age 30), white (35%), and male (87%) and acted alone.
4. The usual number of victims captured was one (43%) or two (26%).
5. The most common location for the crisis event was a home (41%) followed by a public place (28%).
6. The most common motivation for the perpetrator's actions was money (39%) followed by family dispute (16%).

7. The most common weapon used was a firearm (41%).
8. The most common event duration was one day or less than a day (72%).
9. The majority of incidents were nonlethal (91%). However, hostages were more at risk for injury than the hostage taker.

Butler et al. (1993) studied 410 hostage incidents that occurred between 1986 and 1988. These researchers found the following:

1. The majority of the perpetrators fit the emotionally disturbed typology (71% large police departments, 88% small police departments, 38% state police).
2. The second-largest typology for the large and small police departments was criminal (15% large police departments, 6% small police departments) and, for the state police, prison inmates (22%).
3. The majority of incidents were nonlethal (>90%).
4. Negotiators were used in every incident.

Feldmann (1998, 2001) analyzed a database of 120 hostage/barricade incidents that occurred in Kentucky. In summary, his data indicated the following:

1. The majority of the perpetrators fit the personal/family dispute typology (31%).
2. The second-largest typology of perpetrators was criminal (26%) followed by the emotionally disturbed (19%).
3. The majority of perpetrators were young (below age 30) and male and acted alone.
4. The most common motivation for the perpetrator's actions was an interpersonal dispute complicated by an underlying psychiatric disorder as well as alcohol or drug use.
5. The most common weapon used was a firearm (75%).
6. The majority of incidents ended in injury or death to either some of the hostages or the perpetrator (88%).
7. The majority of incidents were negotiated, but negotiations were successful in less than 40% of the time.

Of further interest in the Feldmann database are the unique characteristics observed with respect to the personal/family dispute category, the criminal category, the emotionally disturbed category, and the workplace violence category. Characteristics of the personal/family dispute category were the following:

1. The perpetrator was usually a white male in his early 30s or late 20s.
2. The victim was usually a current or former spouse, girlfriend, or child.
3. The victim was stalked prior to the incident (66% of the cases) and threatened or harassed prior to the incident in 80% of the cases.
4. The incident usually occurred in a home.
5. Negotiations were successful in only a minority of cases (33%) and injuries or death occurred in 95% of the cases.

These results obviously support the anecdotal observation that barricade-victim incidents are much more deadly than the traditional hostage situation.

Characteristics of the criminal category were the following:

1. The perpetrators were primarily African-American males in their mid-20s.
2. The incident was most often the result of a failed robbery attempt (74%).
3. Negotiations were successful in 68% of the cases and injuries or death occurred in 45% of the cases.

Once again these results support the observation that hostage incidents, opposed to a barricade-victim incident, provide the negotiator with greater bargaining range, which results in increased negotiation success and fewer injuries and deaths.

Characteristics of the emotionally disturbed category were the following:

1. The perpetrators were typically in their mid-30s.
2. The most common location was a public place.
3. The incident was usually a barricade-no victim situation.
4. Demands were expressive, bizarre, and nonsubstantive in nature.
5. Negotiations were usually unsuccessful with most incidents resolved with a tactical assault.
6. There was a relatively low injury or fatality rate.

These results suggest that negotiating with a severely mentally ill individual is a difficult process.

Distinctive characteristics observed in the workplace violence category were the following:

1. The perpetrators were typically older individuals, usually in their mid-40s.
2. The perpetrators had often served in the military (50%) and had an excessive interest in weapons (>60%).
3. Negotiations were typically unsuccessful, with a high likelihood of injury and death and a high likelihood of suicide.

Workplace violence can be conceptualized as one form of the personal/family dispute category where the incident is a barricade-victim situation and not a traditional hostage situation. Thus, once more, the data support the idea that such incidents inherently provide the negotiator with less bargaining ability and are inherently more lethal.

In line with Feldmann's (1998, 2001) findings, recent analysis of the HOBAS database indicates that over 90% of all reported hostage/barricade incidents were in fact nonhostage or barricade-victim situations (Flood, 2003). In other words, the victim was taken captive for expressive reasons and was, in fact, a "homicide-to-be."

Crisis Negotiation Technique

Historically, law enforcement negotiators utilized only problem-solving techniques to respond, manage, and resolve crisis incidents. For example, many negotiators were taught to use Fisher, Ury, and Patton (1991) negotiation model that taught to concentrate on separating the person from the problem, to focus on mutual interests instead of individual positions, to generate options for mutual gain, and, finally, to insist on using objective criteria to judge the effectiveness of the agreement. The problem with such an approach is that it assumes the perpetrator enters into the negotiation process with his or her rational cognitive processes intact. Usually this is just not the case.

Even in those incidents in which the perpetrator has planned or anticipated the hostage/barricade situation, he or she will almost always be in a state of autonomic nervous system hyperarousal. Therefore, it should be expected that, initially, the perpetrator will display above-average emotionality, below-average attention span, and narrow, constricted, and disorganized thinking. Further, if one considers the database analyses discussed in the preceding section, in particular the recent HOBAS results that suggest that over 90% of reported incidents are nonhostage crisis situations, then the immediate use of problem-solving techniques is not appropriate (Vecchi et al., 2005).

Therefore, the negotiator must expect that, more often than not, the perpetrator in a crisis incident is experiencing a crisis state. According to Vecchi et al. (2005), the characteristics of a crisis state are the following: the perpetrator is behaving in an emotional and irrational manner as opposed to a cognitive and rational fashion in response to an event or situation the perpetrator perceives as overwhelming—a threat to his or her psychological well-being, physical well-being, or both; the precipitating event is recent, usually having occurred only within the past 24–48 h.

Vecchi et al. (2005) further argue that there are four phases of a crisis. These are termed precrisis, crisis, accommodation/negotiation, and resolution. It is during the crisis stage that the incident, be it barricade-victim or barricade-no victim, happens and the law enforcement negotiator is asked to intervene. Further, the goals of crisis intervention are to establish communication and develop rapport, buy time, defuse intense emotions, and gather intelligence and information so as to determine the negotiation strategies and techniques to use.

Initially, the negotiator should attempt to develop a relationship with the perpetrator (Rogan, Donohue, and Lyles, 1990; Schlossberg, 1980). This is conceived of as a negotiation within a negotiation (Donohue and Roberto, 1993). The behavioral change stairway model (BCSM) is the method taught by the FBI's Crisis Negotiation Unit and is designed to achieve this relationship-building process between the perpetrator and the negotiator. The BCSM process occurs in five phases: active listening, empathy, rapport, influence, and behavioral change. To achieve rapport, the negotiator must use and maintain active listening and empathy throughout the negotiation process. Then, with the establishment of the necessary rapport, the negotiator can utilize his or her new-found influence to effect behavioral change and, hopefully, successful resolution of the incident (Vecchi et al., 2005).

Active listening is the primary tool of the BCSM process, particularly in the early stages of negotiation. Active listening consists of core and supplemental skills (see Tables 8.2 and 8.3).

Table 8.2 Active Listening Techniques: Core Skills

General Category	Description
Emotion labeling	Negotiator identifies the perpetrator's emotions, e.g., "you sound angry."
Paraphrasing	Negotiator restates the content of the perpetrator's statements.
Mirroring	Negotiator repeats the perpetrator's last few words or the gist of what the individual was saying.
Summarizing	Negotiator restates both the content and the expressed emotion of the perpetrator's statements, e.g., "so what you're saying is that Ruth left you for no apparent reason and you're angry and hurt about that."

Table 8.3   Active Listening Techniques: Supplemental Skills

General Category	Description
Minimal encouragers	Negotiator uses verbal cues demonstrating attentiveness, e.g., "Go on, okay, then what."
"I" messages	Negotiator makes a personal statement to help further rapport, e.g., "I've been through a divorce too, so I know how hard that can be... ."
Open-ended questions	Negotiator asks questions that cannot be answered with a yes or no, e.g., "Tell me more about that... ."
Silence	Negotiator responds with pauses just before or after meaningful comments, e.g., "Am I understanding you correctly... (pause) ... you're angry with Ruth because... ."

Donohue et al. (1991) compare and contrast crisis bargaining, also known as distributive bargaining, versus normative bargaining, also known as integrative bargaining. These authors write that initially, the hostage taker typically uses crisis bargaining. This style of bargaining is manifested by

1. Coercion and threats
2. High stakes and feelings of urgency
3. Elevated emotionality
4. Seeking only one alternative
5. Reliance upon incomplete information
6. Overabundance of and overconcern with face or ego issues
7. Failure to develop detailed plans

The negotiator attempts to move the hostage taker away from crisis bargaining and toward normative or cooperative bargaining. This style of bargaining attempts to

1. Slow down the negotiation process
2. Decrease and control emotions
3. Develop multiple options or alternatives
4. Create informational resources
5. Avoid face issues
6. Use detailed plans

Donohue et al. (1991) argue that the negotiation occurs in five stages: intelligence gathering, introduction and relationship development, problem clarification and relationship development, problem solving, and resolution. Donohue and Roberto (1996) note that negotiation may progress in a stepwise fashion from crisis bargaining to normative bargaining; negotiation progress may be intermixed, sometimes integrative and sometime distributive; and negotiation may not progress at all but remain fixed with the perpetrator continuing in the crisis mode while the negotiator attempts to bargain normatively.

According to Vecchi et al. (2005), there are four stages in crisis negotiation. These are as follows: dealing with emotions, establishing communication, identifying the precipitating event, and solving problems. Problem solving is further broken down into six tasks: describing the problem, brainstorming alternative resolutions, purging unacceptable resolutions, selecting and agreeing upon an acceptable resolution, putting the plan in place, and executing the plan.

Giebels, Noelanders, and Vervaeke (2005) approached the exploration of negotiation strategy from a different point of view—that of the hostages themselves. These researchers interviewed 11 ex-hostages, of whom seven had been held in sieges and four had been kidnapped. More about the hostages' experiences will be discussed later. However, with respect to negotiation technique, Giebels et al. (2005) concluded that "little attention is paid to opportunities to promote the psychological well-being of the hostages during their captivity" (p. 249). Thus, they urged that in the future, negotiators address this issue in a more systematic manner and seek psychological consultants' advice in this area. Finally, Giebels et al. (2005) provided the following general guidelines for estimating and promoting the hostages' psychological well-being during captivity:

1. The negotiator should let the hostages know that they matter.
2. Hostages need to believe that the negotiators are experienced and proficient.
3. Hostages should appreciate frequent contact between the negotiator and the perpetrator. Those who have not been physically abused should listen carefully to the negotiations. Those who have been physically abused should utilize these periods as times to relax.
4. In kidnapping situations, it is psychologically important for the hostage to know that the negotiator has sought proof of life. This knowledge reduces the hostages' uncertainty, provides moral support, and reinforces the victims' social identity.
5. Negotiators should anticipate that the captives will develop both positive and negative feelings toward the perpetrators, particularly if they are not physically abused or if the incident is prolonged. Negotiators should also anticipate that as the time goes by, victims' feelings of uncertainty will increase.
6. Negotiators should analyze the social dynamics of multiple hostages and hostage takers as it may impact victims' survival. Areas of investigation and concern are the development of hostage-to-hostage support and hostage-to-hostage anger, in-group (hostages) versus out-group (perpetrator) dynamics, which could be detrimental to victim survival, and the possible existence of less violent perpetrators who may act as protective buffers between the victims and the more violent hostage takers.
7. Negotiators should analyze the possible role expectations of the hostages and how that may impact victim survival. For example, do one or more of the hostages have a law enforcement or military background, and, if so, will they precipitate a confrontation with the perpetrator or attempt an escape?
8. Negotiation team members should anticipate that the victims' families are also victims. Thus, actions should be directed to help them cope, for example, keeping a diary, writing letters to the victims, or discussing what is happening.

In any crisis negotiation, the negotiator must continually assess negotiation progress and the likelihood of imminent lethality. The literature suggests that there are 11 factors that signify negotiation progress and 14 factors that suggest imminent lethality (Call, 2003; Crisis Management Consultants, Inc., 2002; Fuselier and Romana, 1996; Fuselier and Van Zandt, 1987; Lancely, 1999; Soskis and Van Zandt, 1986). Factors that suggest progress are the following:

1. No additional injuries have occurred since negotiations have started.
2. Threats have decreased.
3. Instrumental demands have decreased.

4. The perpetrator's conversation level has increased.
5. The perpetrator makes more personal statements.
6. The perpetrator is behaving and conversing less emotionally and more rationally.
7. Some level of rapport has developed between the perpetrator and the negotiator.
8. Normative, or integrative, bargaining has increased and crisis, or distributive, bargaining has decreased.
9. Deadlines have passed with no injuries.
10. Some hostages have been released.
11. Surrender discussions have begun between the perpetrator and the negotiator.

Factors that suggest imminent lethality are the following:

1. Additional injuries have occurred since negotiations have started.
2. Threats have increased.
3. The incident was a deliberate confrontation between the perpetrator and the police, and there has been no escape attempt.
4. The captive is known to the perpetrator and was selected by the perpetrator, and there is a history of interpersonal problems between the captive and the perpetrator.
5. The perpetrator has committed similar incidents in the past.
6. The perpetrator believes that he or she has suffered a recent overwhelming life stressor.
7. The perpetrator believes that he or she has lost a significant amount of face and control of their life.
8. The perpetrator lacks social support or believes that he or she lacks social support.
9. The perpetrator is making no demands.
10. The perpetrator's conversation level has decreased.
11. The perpetrator is behaving and conversing less rationally and more emotionally.
12. No level of rapport has developed between the perpetrator and the negotiator.
13. Normative, or integrative, bargaining has decreased or has never been achieved.
14. Suicide threats or cues are apparent.

Recent empirical research has provided support for many of the concepts discussed in the first part of this section. In particular, Taylor (2002a) has developed an elegant but rather complex model of crisis negotiation, which he terms a cylindrical model of crisis communication. In this model, he argues that negotiation behavior can be understood in a number of different ways, all of which interact with one another. More specifically, he notes that there are three general levels of negotiation behavior ranging from avoidance, to distributive, to integrative levels of interaction. This conceptualization is analogous to the crisis bargaining/normative bargaining continuum discussed by Donohue et al. (1991) and Donohue and Roberto (1993). Next, he observes that there are three different motivational emphases in negotiation behavior. One motivational theme is instrumental in nature, such as making offers. The two other themes are expressive and include the relational theme and the identity theme. The relational theme captures the concept of negotiator/perpetrator interdependence and affiliation, or lack thereof. The identity theme captures the negotiating parties' concern, or lack thereof, for their own self-presentation, or face, or that of the other party. Finally, Taylor discusses the role of negotiation behavior intensity. Here, intensity refers to affect, in particular, as it is manifested in negotiation participant verbalizations.

Using data from nine actual hostage incidents, Taylor (2002a) found empirical support for his model. The cylindrical model posits the existence of nine different regions of behavior that can occur during crisis negotiations. These are termed as follows:

1. Integrative-instrumental
2. Integrative-identity
3. Integrative-relational
4. Distributive-instrumental
5. Distributive-identity
6. Distributive-relational
7. Avoidance-instrumental
8. Avoidance-identity
9. Avoidance-relational

Taylor further argues that different periods of the negotiation will be dominated, though not exclusively, by one of these nine regions. A region is manifested by the expression of concrete verbalizations of a like class. For example, a perpetrator's verbalization "I don't want to talk about that!" or "No, no, I didn't touch that girl!" are both avoidance statements. The first is an avoidance-instrumental communication behavior, with an intensity rating of 1, and is coded as Avoid. The second is an avoidance-identity communication behavior, also with an intensity rating of 1, and is coded as Denial. Taylor enumerates 37 different classes, or communication behaviors, each of which is separately categorized by orientation, motivation, and intensity.

More specifically, Taylor (2002a) contends that during the avoidance phase of interaction, one may observe the perpetrator involved in direct attempts to dissociate himself from any responsibility or even knowledge of crisis events (identity theme), or one may observe the perpetrator unwilling to attempt to develop a relationship with the negotiator (relational theme), or one may observe the perpetrator using tactics designed to minimize any problem-solving discussion (instrumental theme).

Next, during the distributive phase of interaction, one may observe the perpetrator communicating in a highly critical and insulting manner (identity theme) or one may observe the perpetrator attempting to justify or excuse his actions endeavoring to persuade the negotiator to accept this view as correct (relational theme), or one may observe the perpetrator making demands, threatening, and rejecting negotiator proposals (instrumental theme).

Finally, during the integrative phase, one may observe the perpetrator agreeing with the negotiator's perspective and even complimenting the negotiator (identity theme), or one may observe the perpetrator, the negotiator, or both encourage, reassure, and express confidence in the other's abilities (relational theme), or one may observe the perpetrator, the negotiator, or both make offers, accept offers, and compromise (instrumental theme).

An intriguing outcome of Taylor's research is his suggestion regarding the concept of entrainment (McGrath and Kelly, 1986). Entrainment relates to the negotiator adjusting his or her communication patterns in an attempt to shift the approach adopted by the hostage taker. Taylor states that the cylindrical model indicates that any attempt to induce movement away from one particular mode of communication should focus on behaviors associated with an adjoining region rather than upon the region ultimately desired. In other words, successful negotiations more often than not proceed in little steps as opposed to large ones.

In another piece of research, Taylor (2002b) empirically demonstrated that negotiation progress and ultimately negotiation success can be judged by the extent competitive, crisis bargaining is supplanted by a more normative, problem-solving approach. He studied 189 interaction episodes and found that episodes associated with unsuccessful negotiation were ranked higher on a partially ordered scale of competitiveness as opposed to those episodes associated with successful negotiations.

Bilsky, Muller, Voss, and Von Groote (2005) studied perpetrator and negotiator affect during negotiation phases, specifically during periods of escalation and de-escalation. According to the authors, an escalation phase is characterized by behaviors such as threats or irrevocable commitments, whereas de-escalation phases are characterized by behaviors that are supportive of problem solving, compromise, and attempts at resolution. Therefore, an escalation phase is analogous to the distributive or crisis bargaining phase as noted in the cylindrical model, whereas the de-escalation phase is similar to the integrative, or normative, bargaining phase. Likewise, it appears that the concept of affect, which Bilsky et al. (2005) measure via a hostility scale and a message affect scale, is quite similar to negotiation behavior intensity as described by Taylor (2002a). The results indicated that the overall level of arousal was higher for the perpetrator as opposed to the negotiator throughout the negotiation process; both the perpetrator and the negotiator experienced higher levels of affect during periods of escalation as opposed to periods of de-escalation; and change in affect was more pronounced for the perpetrator as opposed to the negotiator when moving from an escalating phase to a de-escalating phase.

Basic Points to Consider

Crisis negotiation is a team enterprise. The smallest acceptable team is composed of a primary negotiator, secondary negotiator, and a team leader. A more inclusive team is composed of a primary negotiator, secondary negotiator, negotiation team leader, tactical liaison, resource coordinator, and a behavioral science consultant (Fuselier and Van Zandt, 1987; Butler et al., 1993; Lancely, 1999; Feldmann, 2004). Research performed by Butler et al. indicated that 55% of the large police departments, 25% of the small police departments, and 59% of the state police agencies employed mental health consultants. The three most common roles of the behavioral science consultant were perpetrator assessment, negotiation technique consultation, and postincident counseling.

Butler et al. (1993) also reported that agencies that used behavioral science consultants during hostage and barricade-victim negotiation incidents reported greater number of successful negotiations and fewer incidents where the perpetrator was killed or hostages injured. However, this trend was not observed in the barricade-no victim incidents studied.

Basic guidelines for the behavioral science consultant hostage negotiation team member to bear in mind are as follows:

1. Be able to demonstrate that you are cognizant of the literature regarding crisis negotiation, that you have attended crisis negotiation courses, and that you have participated in mock crisis negotiations as a part of the law enforcement negotiation team with which you are associated.
2. Be prepared and willing to work within the established organizational structure of the law enforcement organization with which you are consulting.

3. Recognize that the role of the primary and the secondary negotiator is the one filled by specially trained law enforcement personnel, not the behavioral science consultant.
4. Recognize that appropriate duties for the psychological consultant are to
   i. Diagnose and assess hostage/barricade perpetrators.
   ii. Interview significant others during crisis incidents regarding the backgrounds and personalities of the perpetrator and victims (a guide to questions the consulting psychologist should ask during these interviews is presented in Appendix A).
   iii. Evaluate negotiation tactics and strategies.
   iv. Help document and record negotiation events as they occur, in particular factors related to the perpetrator, the victim, demand, and negotiation progress.
   v. Monitor participant stress during hostage/barricade incidents.
   vi. Train negotiation team members regarding mental health issues.
   vii. Develop and participate in hostage/barricade training scenarios.
   viii. Perform research into the characteristics of hostage/barricade incidents as well as the success or failure of negotiation tactics and strategies (Butler et al., 1993; Feldmann, 2004). This, in large part, can be done by developing and maintaining a database of all hostage/barricade incidents that the negotiation team encounters.
5. Remember that crisis negotiation is a five-stage process. These stages are termed (a) intelligence gathering, (b) introduction and relationship development, (c) problem clarification and relationship development, (d) problem solving, and (e) resolution. The goal of negotiations is the surrender of the hostage taker and the release of the hostages.
   i. During stage 1, the negotiators gather intelligence, develop a negotiation strategy, and attempt to predict any problems or difficulties that may arise.
   ii. Stage 2 starts when the primary negotiator makes contact with the hostage taker. The negotiator attempts to build a relationship, uses active listening techniques, and attempts to defer action on demands until some level of trust and rapport is developed.
   iii. During stage 3, the negotiator continues to build the relationship and at the same time attempts to understand the problem from the hostage taker's point of view. The primary goal for stage 3 is an implied agreement between the hostage taker and the negotiator to bargain normatively rather than using brinkmanship.
   iv. Thus, stage 4 is taken up with the hostage taker and the negotiator attempting to solve the problem. The negotiator, while continuing to build trust, becomes more directive in his communications. He or she develops proposals and seeks compliance.
   v. During the final stage of negotiations, the negotiator purposely slows down the pace of communication to ensure that no mistakes are made. The negotiator carefully and explicitly establishes the details of the hostages' release and the hostage taker's surrender by over and over reviewing the proposed scenario in his or her conversation with the perpetrator. Likewise, the negotiator continually assesses the strength of the fragile bond of trust that he or she has developed to make sure that the working relationship remains intact with the hostage taker (Call, 1996).
6. Remember the behavioral change stairway
   i. Employing active listening skills leads to
   ii. Empathy, which leads to

    iii. Rapport, which leads to
    iv. Influence, which leads to
    v. Behavioral change

7. Remember to continually assess negotiation progress and the risk of imminent lethality. To this end, record keeping is vital. Negotiation teams should use dedicated software programs to track and analyze negotiation events or keep detailed handwritten notes.
8. Remember to reinforce a negotiation strategy that reinforces the psychological well-being of the captives.
9. Be prepared to provide or arrange for the psychological support to the captives' families during the incident and to provide or arrange for the psychological support to the captives following their release.

Avoiding Evaluation and Consultation Errors

One of the most significant evaluation and consultative blunders to avoid in hostage negotiation is the *action imperative* (Vecchi, 2002). This problem occurs when decision makers decide they need to end a crisis incident *now*, either because the incident has become too lengthy or the incident has not yet resulted in any clear-cut resolution. Such a decision usually results in the implementation of a tactical solution, not always with success, and is initiated even though negotiations are in progress. For example, Noesner (1999) argues that the barricade incidents related to Ruby Ridge, Idaho and the Branch Davidians in Waco, Texas are examples of the *action imperative*, where the eventual high loss of life could have been prevented if the on-scene decision makers had a better understanding of the negotiation process. From the negotiation team's point of view, the passage of time is a positive rather than a negative occurrence. This interpretation is based upon the opinion that the effects of time passing usually result in

1. Lowered perpetrator emotionality
2. Increased perpetrator rationality
3. Reduced perpetrator stress
4. Reduced perpetrator expectations
5. Greater opportunity for building rapport between the negotiator and the perpetrator
6. Greater opportunity for gathering intelligence
7. Better decision making on everyone's part
8. Increased likelihood of negotiation success

Therefore, whenever the negotiation team is asked to consider an option that deviates from recommended negotiation protocol, the team members should ask themselves the following questions:

1. Is the action really necessary? Why?
2. Is the action risk effective? Why?
3. Is the action acceptable? Why?
4. Should this action be taken now? Why?

5. In particular, what conditions have changed since the beginning of the crisis incident that support the decision the action should be taken now?
6. Finally, have less risky alternatives been tried?

Unless acceptable answers can be developed for each of these questions, the team should seriously consider that the *action imperative* is at work.

Treatment Considerations

The following discussion focuses on the impact, upon the hostages, of captivity both during and after the incident. Being captured, threatened with death, and, perhaps, being physically abused is a severely traumatic experience. More than likely, at first, the captive experiences frozen fright (Fuselier, 1991; Symonds, 1980a, 1980b). Cognitive ability decreases while emotionality increases and the phenomenon of "traumatic psychological infantilism" can occur (Symonds, 1980b, p. 40). The victim sample investigated by Giebels et al. (2005) all reported experiencing feelings of helplessness. However, whereas the kidnapped victims also reported feelings of uncertainty and isolation, by far the majority of siege victims did not. Thus, there was a distinct difference noted between victims of siege and kidnapped victims. This difference is hypothesized to be related to the duration of captivity—kidnapping incidents last longer—and to the isolation the kidnapped victim experiences as opposed to the victim of a siege.

Subsequent to this initial phase, a number of identifiable sets of behaviors and emotions have been observed in hostages. In the past, the present author, as well as others, has used the word syndrome as part of the name of these observable behavioral clusters (Call, 2003). However, Giebels et al. (2005) have criticized the use of this word arguing that it suggests the victims are displaying an abnormal psychological process or manifesting a psychological defect. The present author disagrees with this reasoning. Different people react differently to severe stress and crises. However, it would seem more logical to expect a victim to display nontypical, or abnormal, behavior as opposed to typical, or normal, behavior when he or she is placed in an abnormal, life-and-death situation. Demonstrating such nontypical behavior under such circumstances does not mean that the victim possesses a psychological defect; rather, such behavior can be explained as a not uncommon reaction to an abnormal event.

In the past, seven emotional and behavioral clusters have been noted in hostages by various authors. These have been termed the Stockholm syndrome (Hacker, 1976), the common sense syndrome (Strentz, 1977), the survivor identification syndrome (Schlossberg, 1980), the hostage response syndrome (Wesselius and DeSarno, 1983), the hostage identification syndrome (Turner, 1985), the London syndrome (Olin and Born, 1983), and the "hysterical-whiner" syndrome (Fuselier, 1991). The first five phenomena refer to those situations in which the hostage develops positive feelings for the perpetrator(s) and is typically referred to by Hacker's designation—the Stockholm syndrome. This phenomenon is oftentimes associated with the victim developing negative feelings toward the authorities.

Recently, Lancely (1999) and others have argued that the Stockholm syndrome is relatively rare and that it requires both time and positive contact between the victim and the perpetrator. If there is no contact between the hostage and the hostage taker or if the hostage is abused, it is highly unlikely that such a phenomenon will develop. Furthermore, if the hostage has had a previous relationship, such as being the ex-wife of the perpetrator, it is unlikely that the Stockholm syndrome will arise. Finally, as noted by Turner (1985), the difference in cultural values, language, and racial, ethnic, religious, or ideological beliefs between the hostage taker and the captive can actually thwart the development of positive bonding between the captive and the captor. In fact, in such situations, the passage of time can work to increase the hostages' risk of harm. An example of this phenomenon is reported by Jacobson (1973). Jacobson, along with 148 other airline passengers, was held hostage for one week in September 1970 by members of the Popular Front for the Liberation of Palestine. The passengers were primarily westerners of Jewish ancestry. An Arab physician was assigned by the hostage takers to provide medical assistance to the captives. However, as the time progressed, the hostages noted that the initially kind and helpful Arab physician became increasingly hostile and rejecting.

Giebels et al. (2005) note that most of victims in their sample reported both positive and negative feelings toward their captors. As predicted by earlier researchers, those victims who were abused reported only negative feelings. It is generally believed that fostering positive feelings within the perpetrator for the victims increases the latter's survivability. Thus, Strentz (1980) argues that the negotiator should promote positive transference between the perpetrator and the victim. To help accomplish this, he suggests asking the hostage taker about the victims' health and to provide messages for the victims' families.

An example of an instance where a perpetrator perceiving the victim as human probably saved the latter's life is documented by Ochberg (1978). This author reported the experience of Gerald Vaders, who was held hostage by South Moluccans in December 1975 on a train in Holland. Vaders was selected to be executed. Before his execution, Vaders asked to speak with a fellow hostage. With the hostage takers listening, Vaders discussed the various problems in his family life leaving instructions for his wife regarding how to deal with a foster child. However, after Vader was through, his captors decided not to kill him. Instead, the perpetrators selected another man and shot him. Vaders had ceased to be a nonentity but had become a person. Nevertheless, hostage takers who are psychopaths do not care and never will.

The London syndrome and the hysterical-whiner syndrome are instances where the captive acts in a manner that culminates in his or her premature selection for being killed by the hostage takers. In the former, the hostage is verbally aggressive and provocative, whereas in the latter, the hostage is overly tearful and frightened. An example of the London syndrome occurred in 1986 in California. A failed jewelry store holdup turned into a hostage situation. During the incident, the perpetrator shot and killed the store security guard even though the victim was tied and lying facedown on the floor. Afterward, the hostage taker explained that he killed the guard because "he was talking back to me" (Fuselier, 1991, p. 714).

An example of the hysterical-whiner syndrome occurred in 1985 in New York. An African-American male held a group of white and African-American men and women hostage. The motivation for the incident was to protest against racial discrimination. During the incident, after a demand deadline passed, the perpetrator killed a black female. Afterward, the hostage taker explained that he had selected the woman because he was irked by her continual crying and pleading.

After rescue, the hostages will require psychological first aid and mental health screening. Past research indicates that a significant proportion of rescued victims will suffer diagnosable mental disorders (Allondi, 1994; Villa, Porche, and Mouren-Simeoni, 1999; Easton and Turner, 1991; Wesselius and DeSarno, 1983). For example, Easton and Turner observed 25–50% in their sample of those rescued suffering from emotional problems and Villa et al. (1999) observed 72% in their sample. The principal disorder observed is posttraumatic stress disorder, although phobia, major depression, and separation anxiety have also been noted. Even if a victim does not develop a diagnosable disorder, almost all will demonstrate, at least initially, symptoms of PTSD, usually cluster B and cluster D symptoms.

Likewise, the research indicates that the victims' psychological problems will last for some time (Desivilya, Gal, and Ayalon, 1996; Van der Ploeg and Kleijn, 1989; Terr, 1983). For example, Van der Ploeg and Kleijn noted that 32% of their sample reported symptoms after 9 years. Terr reported that 100% of her sample reported continued symptoms after 4 years. Finally, Desivilya et al. (1996) reported that even 17 years after the barricade/hostage incident, 39% of the survivors reported four symptoms, 52% reported five to eight symptoms, and 9% reported nine or more symptoms. The data also indicate that witnessing physical violence, suffering physical abuse, and not receiving psychological help after release are factors correlated with increased risk of long-term mental health problems (Bisson, Searle, and Srinivasan, 1998; Desivilya et al., 1996; Villa et al., 1999).

When providing psychological services to rescued hostages, the following goals should be considered:

1. Reassure the victims that their behavior during captivity was acceptable.
2. Educate the victims and their families regarding the after effects of captivity.
3. Attempt to restore feelings of power within the victims.
4. Work to reduce feelings of isolation.
5. Attempt to diminish feelings of helplessness.
6. Encourage feelings of control.
7. Foster a supportive social network among the victims.
8. Prevent others, particularly the media, from intruding upon the victims (McDuff, 1992; Symonds, 1983).

Writing Forensic Reports and Testifying as an Expert

Psychologists who consult with law enforcement negotiation teams do not typically write forensic psychological reports for court purposes or testify as an expert witness. That is not their primary role. However, it is quite possible that a negotiation team's behavioral science consultant may be called as a witness either in a criminal matter or in a civil action. In such cases, the basic guidelines for effective and ethical courtroom presentation should be followed.

Novel Applications and New Directions

The principal new directions for psychological consultants in crisis negotiation are in the areas of research and training. With the development of the HOBAS database 10 years ago, there now exists the ability to explore, in detail, the dynamics of crisis incidents and negotiation strategy. Utilizing HOBAS data in conjunction with in-depth interviews of incarcerated hostage takers as well as employing such conceptualizations as the cylindrical model of crisis communication and the study methodology used by Taylor (2002a), it may now be possible to accomplish significant research. Van Hasselt, Baker, Romano, Sellers, Noesner, and Smith (2005) outline one such ambitious project involving the comprehensive analysis of crisis negotiation in those incidents where the perpetrator has taken or captured a significant other, such as a spouse, ex-spouse, child, or partner. Other serious scientists should follow in their footsteps.

Developing and empirically validating the effectiveness of negotiation training techniques is also an important area that is ripe for future endeavors. To date, role-playing techniques have been a primary method for negotiator training but little empirical research has been done to validate such methodology (Vecchi et al., 2005). One exception is that reported by Van Hasselt, Flood, Romano, Vecchi, de Fabrique, and Dalfonzo (2005). These researchers describe an attempt to validate a role-playing technique as an assessment tool to evaluate crisis negotiation skills.

Also of interest is the work of Taylor and Donald (2004). These researchers, utilizing the cylindrical model of crisis communication and the multidimensional scaling technique of smallest space analysis, reported significant differences in simulated negotiations versus actual crisis negotiations. For example, they found that in simulated crisis negotiations, the participants used a greater number of avoidance-relational and distributive-instrumental behaviors than in actual negotiations. Knowledge of such differences is crucial to skillful design of future training aids.

Finally, even though the HOBAS database has been developed, it remains vital that psychological consultants initiate and maintain their own local and regional databases. Such work will help both to obtain important information regarding local hostage/barricade incidents and to analyze negotiation style and effectiveness. To this end, detailed record keeping is key. Record keeping is important not only for research purposes but also for on-site analysis of the crisis event.

In conclusion, although, in the recent past, there has been significant scientific study of crisis negotiation, much more remains to be accomplished. Furthermore, because of his or her scientific training, the crisis negotiation team's psychological consultant is best placed to realize this goal.

References

Allondi, F. A. (1994). Post-traumatic stress disorder in hostages and victims of torture. *Psychiatric Clinics of North America, 17*, 279–288.

American Psychological Association. (2002). *Ethical Principles of Psychologists and Code of Conduct.* Washington, DC: Author.

American Psychological Association. (2005). APA task force advises psychologist in national security to heed Ethics Code. *Monitor on Psychology, 36(8),* 16.

Bahn, C. and Louden, R. J. (1999). Hostage negotiation as a team enterprise. *Group, 23,* 77–85.

Bilsky, W., Muller, J., Voss, A., and Von Groote, E. (2005). Affect assessment in crisis negotiation: An exploratory case study using two distinct indicators. *Psychology, Crime & Law, 11(3),* 275–287.

Bisson, J. I., Searle, M. M., and Srinivasan, M. (1998). Follow-up study of British military hostages and their families held in Kuwait during the Gulf War. *British Journal of Medical Psychology, 71,* 247–252.

Bolz, F. and Hershey, E. (1979). *Hostage Cop.* New York: Rawson, Wade.

Butler, W. M., Leitenberg, H., and Fuselier, G. E. (1993). The use of mental health professional consultants to police hostage negotiation teams. *Behavioral Sciences & the Law, 11,* 213–221.

Call, J. A. (1996). The hostage triad: Takers, victims, and negotiators. In H. V. Hall (Ed.), *Lethal Violence 2000: A Sourcebook on Fatal Domestic, Acquaintance and Stranger Aggression* (pp. 561–588). Kamuela, HI: Pacific Institute for the Study of Conflict and Aggression.

Call, J. A. (2003). Negotiating crises: The evolution of hostage/barricade crisis negotiation. *Journal of Threat Assessment, 3,* 69–94.

Cooper, H. H. A. (1981). *The Hostage Takers.* Boulder, CO: Paladin Press.

Corsi, J. R. (1981). Terrorism as a desperate game. *Journal of Conflict Resolution, 25,* 47–85.

Crisis Management Consultants, Inc. (2002). *Crisis Negotiator 1.0 Manual.* Oklahoma City, OK: Author.

Desivilya, H. S., Gal, R., and Ayalon, O. (1996). Extent of victimization, traumatic stress symptoms, and adjustment of terrorist assault survivors: A long term follow-up. *Journal of Traumatic Stress, 9,* 881–889.

Donohue, W. A., Ramesh, C., Kaufmann, G., and Smith, R. (1991). Crisis bargaining in intense conflict situations. *International Journal of Croup Tensions, 21,* 133–153.

Donohue, W. A. and Roberto, A. J. (1993). Relational development as negotiated order in hostage negotiation. *Human Communication Research, 20,* 175–198.

Donohue, W. A. and Roberto, A. J. (1996). An empirical examination of three models of integrative and distributive bargaining. *The International Journal of Conflict Management, 7,* 209–229.

Easton, J. A. and Turner, S. W. (1991). Detention of British citizens as hostages in the Gulf War—Health, psychological and family consequences. *British Medical Journal, 303,* 1231–1234.

Feldmann, T. B. (1998). *Characteristics of Hostage and Barricade Incident: Implications for Negotiation Strategies and Training.* Unpublished manuscript, Department of Psychiatry and Behavioral Sciences, University of Louisville School of Medicine, Louisville, KY.

Feldmann, T. B. (2001). Characteristics of hostage and barricade incidents: Implications for negotiation strategies and training. *Journal of Police Crisis Negotiations, 1(1),* 3–33.

Feldmann, T. B. (2004). The role of mental health consultants on hostage negotiation teams. *Psychiatric Times, 21(14),* 4.

Ferracuti, F. (1982). A sociopsychiatric interpretation of terrorism. *The Annals of the American Academy of Political and Social Sciences, 463,* 129–140.

Ferracuti, F. and Bruno, F. (1981). Psychiatric aspects of terrorism in Italy. In I. L. Barak-Glantz and C. R. Huff (Eds.), *The Mad, the Bad and the Different: Essays in Honor of Simon Dinitz* (pp. 199–213). Lexington, KY: Lexington Books.

Fisher, R., Ury, W., and Patton, B. (1991). *Getting to Yes: Negotiating Agreement Without Giving In* (2nd ed.). New York: Penguin.

Flood, J. J. (2003). *A Report of Finding from the Hostage Barricade Database System (HOBAS),* Crisis Negotiation Unit, Critical Incident Response Group, FBI Academy, Quantico, VA.

Friedland, N. and Merari, A. (1992). Hostage events: Descriptive profile and analysis of outcomes. *Journal of Applied Social Psychology, 22,* 134–156.

Fuselier, G. D. (1988). Hostage negotiation consultant: Emerging role for the clinical psychologist. *Professional Psychology: Research and Practice, 19,* 175–179.

Fuselier, G. D. (1991). Hostage negotiation: issues and applications. In R. Gal and A. D. Mangelsdorff (Eds.), *Handbook of Military Psychology* (pp. 711–723). New York: John Wiley & Sons, Ltd.

Fuselier, G. D. and Romana, S. (1996, October). *Behavioral Aspects of Hostage Negotiation.* Symposium conducted at the University of Colorado Health Sciences Center, Denver, CO.

Fuselier, G. D. and Van Zandt, C. R. (1987). *A Practical Overview of Hostage Negotiation.* Unpublished manuscript, FBI Academy, Quantico, VA.

Giebels, E., Noelanders, S., and Vervaeke, G. (2005). The hostage experience: Implications for negotiation strategies. *Clinical Psychology and Psychotherapy, 12,* 241–253.

Gist, R. G. and Perry, J. D. (1985). Perspectives on negotiation in local jurisdictions: Part I. A different typology of situations. *FBI Law Enforcement Bulletin, 54(11),* 21–24.

Hacker, F. J. (1976). *Crusaders, Criminals, Crazies: Terror and Terrorism in Our Time.* New York: W. W. Norton Company.

Head, W. B. (1990). *The Hostage Response: An Examination of the U.S. Law Enforcement Practices Concerning Hostage Incidents* (Doctoral dissertation, State University of New York at Albany). *Dissertation Abstracts International, 50,* 4111-A. University Microfilms International No. DA9013316.

Higginbotham, J. (1994, June). Legal issues in crisis management. *FBI Law Enforcement Bulletin, 63,* 27–32.

Jacobson, S. R. (1973). Individual and group responses to confinement in a skyjacked plane. *American Journal of Orthopsychiatry, 43,* 459–469.

Kennedy, H. G. and Dyer, D. E. (1992). Parental hostage takers. *British Journal of Psychiatry, 160,* 410–412.

Knutson, J. N. (1980). The dynamics of the hostage taker: some major variants. *Annals New York Academy of Sciences, 347,* 117–128.

Lancely, F. L. (1999). *On-Scene Guide for Crisis Negotiation.* Boca Raton, FL: CRC Press.

McDuff, D. R. (1992). Social issues in the management of released hostages. *Hospital and Community Psychiatry, 43,* 825–828.

McGrath, J. E. and Kelly, J. R. (1986). *Time and Human Interaction: Toward a Social Psychology of Time.* New York: Guilford Press.

Mickolus, E. (1976). Negotiating for hostages: A policy dilemma. *Orbis, 19,* 1309–1325.

Miron, M. and Goldstein, A. (1979). *Hostage.* New York: Pergamon Press.

Noesner, G. W. (1999). Negotiation concepts for commanders. *FBI Law Enforcement Bulletin, 68(1),* 6–14.

Ochberg, F. (1978). The victim of terrorism: psychiatric considerations. *Terrorism, 1,* 147–168.

Olin, W. R. and Born, D. G. (1983). A behavioral approach to hostage situations. *FBI Law Enforcement Bulletin, 52,* 19–24.

Pearce, K. I. (1977). Police negotiations: A new role for the community psychiatrist. *Canadian Psychiatric Association Journal, 22,* 171–175.

Regini, C. (2002). Crisis negotiation teams: Selection and training. *FBI Law Enforcement Bulletin, 71,* 1–5.

Rogan, R. G., Donohue, W. A., and Lyles, J. (1990). Gaining and exercising control in hostage negotiations using empathic perspective-taking. *International Journal of Group Tensions, 20,* 77–91.

Royce, T. (2005). The negotiator and the bomber: Analyzing the critical role of active listening in crisis negotiations. *Negotiation Journal, 21(1),* 5–27.

Schlossberg, H. (1980). Values and organization in hostage and crisis negotiation teams. *Annals of the New York Academy of Sciences, 347,* 113–116.

Soskis, D. A. and Van Zandt, C. R. (1986). Hostage negotiation: Law enforcement's most effective nonlethal weapon. *Behavioral Sciences & the Law, 4,* 423–435.

Strentz, T. (1977). Survival Adaptation…the Common Sense Syndrome. Unpublished manuscript, FBI Academy, Quantico, VA.

Strentz, T. (1980). The Stockholm Syndrome: law enforcement policy and ego defenses of the hostage. *Annals of the New York Academy of Sciences, 347,* 137–150.

Strentz, T. (1986). Negotiating with the hostage-taker exhibiting paranoid-schizophrenic symptoms. *Journal of Police Science and Administration, 14,* 12–17.

Symonds, M. (1980a). Victims' responses to terror. *Annals New York Academy of Sciences, 347,* 129–136.

Symonds, M. (1980b). Acute responses of victims to terror. *Evaluation and Change,* Special Issue, 39–41.

Symonds, M. (1983). Victimization and rehabilitative treatment. In B. Eichelman, D. Soskis, and W. Reid (Eds.), *Terrorism: Interdisciplinary Perspectives* (pp. 69–81). Washington, DC: American Psychiatric Association.

Taylor, P. J. (2002a). A cylindrical model of communication behavior in crisis negotiations. *Human Communications Research, 28(1)*, 7–48.

Taylor, P. J. (2002b). A partial order scalogram analysis of communication behavior in crisis negotiation with the prediction of outcome. *The International Journal of Conflict Management, 13(1)*, 4–37.

Taylor, P. J. and Donald, I. (2004). The structure of communication in simulated and actual crisis negotiations. *Human Communication Research, 30(4)*, 443–478.

Terr, L. C. (1983). Chowchilla revisited: The effects of psychic trauma four years after a school-bus kidnapping. *American Journal of Psychiatry, 140*, 1543–1550.

Turner, J. T. (1985). Factors influencing the development of the hostage identification syndrome. *Political Psychology, 6*, 705–711.

Van der Ploeg, H. K. and Kleijn, W. C. (1989). Being held hostage in the Netherlands: A study of long-term after effects. *Journal of Traumatic Stress, 2*, 153–169.

Van Hasselt, V. B., Baker, M. T., Romano, S. J., Sellers, A. H., Noesner, G. W., and Smith, S. (2005). Development and validation of a role-play test for assessing crisis (hostage) negotiation skills. *Criminal Justice and Behavior, 32(3)* 345–361.

Van Hasselt, V. B., Flood, J. J., Romano, S. J., Vecchi, G. M., de Fabrique, N., and Dalfonzo, V. A. (2005). Hostage-taking in the context of domestic violence: Some case examples. *Journal of Family Violence, 20(1)*, 21–27.

Vecchi, G. M. (2002). Hostage/barricade management: A hidden conflict within law enforcement. *FBI Law Enforcement Bulletin, 73*, 1–6.

Vecchi, G. M., Van Hasselt, V. B., and Romano, S. J. (2005). Crisis (hostage) negotiation: Current strategies and issues in high-risk resolution. *Aggression and Violent Behavior, 10*, 533–551.

Villa, G., Porche, L.-M., and Mouren-Simeoni, M.-C. (1999). An 18-month longitudinal study of posttraumatic disorders in children who were taken hostage in their school. *Psychosomatic Medicine, 61*, 746–766.

Wesselius, C. L. and DeSarno, J. V. (1983). The anatomy of a hostage situation. *Behavioral Sciences & the Law, 1*, 33–45.

Legal References

Branzburg v. Hayes. (1972). 408 U.S. 665.

Downs v. United States. (Sixth Cir. 1975). 522 F.2d 990.

Mincey v. Arizona. (1978). 437 U.S. 385.

People v. Gantz. (N.Y. Sup. Ct. 1984). 480 N.Y.S.2d 583.

State v. Sands. (Ariz. App. 1985). 700 P.2d 1369.

Tennessee v. Gardner. (1985). 471 U.S. 1.

Deception in Criminal Contexts

9

HAROLD V. HALL

Pacific Institute for the Study of Conflict and Aggression, Kamuela, Hawaii

JOSEPH G. POIRIER

Independent Practice, Rockville, Maryland

JANE THOMPSON

University of Hawaii, Hilo, Hawaii

Contents

Introduction

Defendant Stardowsky, examined for criminal responsibility, stated to the examiner that the glow in the right side of his brain was quite clearly unequal to that in his left cerebral hemisphere. Forces of good (FOG) and forces of the enemy (FOE) operated in the jail where he was incarcerated for robbery. "The police hacked off my arms and legs; it's a good thing I didn't try to get away." Visual hallucinations of personages were claimed, providing the basis for his antipsychotic medication and diagnosis of schizophrenia by the correctional facility medical staff. Several days later, the investigating probation officer revealed that the defendant's mental problems had never been raised as an issue in his 100-plus burglaries and robberies over the last 8 years. Stardowsky's parents pointed out that the accused had been playing the FOG and FOE story since the fourth grade, but only when he wanted to get out of trouble.

Criminal Responsibility and Deception

This chapter addresses deception in criminal contexts, focusing on criminal responsibility (i.e., insanity) evaluations and testimony in terms of neuropsychological deficiencies, psychosis, and substance intoxication/abuse and further discusses considerations in the assessment of deception by use of psychological and neuropsychological test batteries. A review of which tests and methods are considered acceptable for forensic evaluations is encouraged (e.g., see Granhag and Stromwall, 2004; Hall and Poirier, 2001; Lally, 2003; and the now-classic but highly relevant Rogers, 1997).

Most readers of this chapter will have a grasp of the all-important history of the insanity defense (for historical reviews see Shapiro, 1999; Slovenko, 1973). Most of the commentary and investigation centers around psychosis, yet the insanity defense has undergone substantial changes in recent years. Based on the mistaken arguments that the insanity defense is easily "faked" and that many guilty criminals are unjustly spared from punishment by use of the insanity defense, several state legislatures have abolished the defense. Other states and the U.S. Congress have severely curtailed their definitions of legal insanity and still others have introduced an alternate verdict ("Guilty but Mentally Ill") in hopes of persuading courts to find fewer defendants legally insane (Melville and Naimark, 2002; Palmer and Hazelrigg, 2000).

Varying definitions of legal insanity exist. Some jurisdictions will excuse criminal behavior if it is the product of a mental disorder (Durham defense); others require that the perpetrator, at the time of the offense, was so mentally impaired that he could not appreciate the criminality of his conduct or could not conform his conduct to the requirements of law (Ali test of insanity); a few require that the accused could not tell the difference between right and wrong in regard to the criminal act (M'Naghten defense).

Shapiro (1999) summarized the impact of the Insanity Defense Reform Act of 1984, which followed the furor over the not guilty by reason of insanity defense of John Hinckley in 1982. A year earlier, Mr Hinckley attempted the assassination of President Reagan. The Act is the requirement in Federal courts and has also been incorporated into the statutory codes of several states. The Act essentially removes the volitional prong (i.e., the lack of substantial capacity to conform one's behavior to the law) of the American Law Institute (ALI) Model Penal Code, leaving intact only the cognitive prong (i.e., appreciation of the wrongfulness of one's behavior).

Within this historical context, various forensic investigators have attempted to standardize criminal responsibility evaluations. Rogers and his colleagues analyzed malingering along the decision path of the evaluator (Rogers, 1984a, 1984b; Rogers and Cavanaugh, 1981; Rogers, Seman, and Wasyliw, 1983). In offering the Rogers Criminal Responsibility Assessment Scales (RCRAS), Rogers (1984b, p. 24) stated the following in the test manual:

Malingering The authenticity of the symptoms, presented by the patient-defendant in the retrospective account of the time of the crime, forms a necessary prerequisite to subsequent psycholegal decisions. Although rare, the forensic examiner must consider the possibility that the patient-defendant is both malingering and had a bona fide mental disorder at the time of the crime.

The RCRAS asks the examiner to judge the severity of deception on the RCRAS five-part Likert scale:

Reliability of patient's self-report under his/her voluntary control

0 No information.
1 Highly reliable self-report; examiner is impressed by the patient's openness and honesty which may include volunteering potentially self-damaging information.
2 Reliable self-report; the patient reports in a factual, sincere manner. He/she may not volunteer potentially self-damaging information and may gloss over a few incidental details.
3 Self-report with limited reliability; the patient answers most of the questions with a fair degree of accuracy (volunteers little or nothing and distorts or evades a few specific areas).
4 Self-report without reliability; the patient, through guardedness, exaggeration, or denial of symptoms, convinces the examiner that his/her responses are inaccurate. There may be suspected malingering.
5 Definite malingering.

The evaluator is then asked to integrate the reliability of self-reports with other information and to compare the total information with the applicable legal definition of insanity. As an illustration, the RCRAS sequentially analyzes (1) malingering, (2) brain injury, (3) mental disorder(s), (4) loss of cognitive control, (5) loss of behavioral control, (6) whether the loss of cognitive or behavioral control resulted directly from brain injury or from a nonorganic mental disorder, and (7) conclusions regarding "insanity" using the ALI and M'Naghten definitions of insanity.

Empirical studies using the RCRAS have been generally favorable regarding construct validity (Rogers and Sewell, 1999), reliability (Rogers and Ewing, 1992), consistency with *a priori* hypotheses (Rogers, Seman, and Clark, 1986), generalizability (Rogers et al., 1983), and interrater reliability (Rogers, Dolmetsch, and Cavanaugh, 1981), but the RCRAS has been criticized for failing to satisfy the Frye test for admissibility of novel scientific evidence (Goldstein, 1992).

Decisions using the RCRAS have shown high agreement with actual court outcomes (Rogers, 1984b). Rogers' system is databased, flexible in terms of definition of insanity, and represents a clear advancement in assessment for criminal responsibility.

There is a general judicial resistance to accepting criterion-based or statistical approaches in favor of the qualitative analysis of each criminal case (Hall, 1982, 1985, 1987; Hall and Poirier, 2001). The senior and second authors when testifying as experts have observed in both state and federal courts that courts may or may not follow the implications of empirically derived conclusions for a relevant legal issue. This argues for a wide database upon which the evaluator should rely. There is also reluctance by clinicians to embrace actuarial prediction technology even though the accuracy of existing assessment tools improves predictive ability well beyond chance (Steadman, Silver, Monahan, Appelbaum, Robbins, Mulvey, Grisso, Roth, and Banks, 2000).

The RCRAS is focused on malingering (faking bad), yet other response styles also need to be considered. The RCRAS procedure considers malingering as preclusion to criminal responsibility. Even though there is a provision in the RCRAS for mentally ill defendants who malinger, many evaluators may not seriously consider that defendants who blatantly malinger can still be genuinely mentally ill. In the first author's experience, the most mentally disturbed defendants are sometimes the ones most likely to malinger, contrary to Rogers' (1984) assertion. It is also necessary to rule out or account for nondeliberate distortion within (a) the reporting person and (b) the reported event. Nondeliberate distortion due to anxiety, fatigue, or other factors may largely explain both evaluation and crime-related behavior and is therefore considered first.

Deliberate distortion should be ruled in by a positive and replicable demonstration of misrepresentation. Deliberate distortion may be shown by the examiner, the client, and all cross-validating sources. Examiners can and do deliberately distort for various reasons. The authors know of some forensic examiners who appear to thrive on the drama and publicity of court work and whose judgment and decisions are clearly influenced by a personal desire to "stir up controversy." It is not inappropriate to look at the evaluator's track record for particular types of forensic assessments (e.g., percentage of time for which he or she testifies for the defense versus for the prosecution), rate of court agreement with rendered opinions, and whether or not proffered findings can be replicated by equally competent examiners.

The evaluation of the defendant's self-reports should be scrutinized for misrepresentation by examining third-party reports and material evidence of the crime. Psychometric testing is very appropriate for assessing distortion in victims and other parties. Data derived from the input of significant or knowledgeable others, which indicate bias or a given motivational set (e.g., desire for revenge and to rejoin defendant), should be excluded from the data pool or placed into proper perspective by being compared with other known data.

Faked Brain Damage

Detection strategies employed by the evaluator have been investigated both for their effectiveness at detecting particular response patterns of the faker and for characteristics of standardized tests utilized to assess deception. As a measure of response set, most neuropsychologists employ personality tests in addition to specific tests of malingering.

The most widely used personality test in the world is the Minnesota Multiphasic Personality Inventory-2 (MMPI-2; Butcher, 2006). The original MMPI has been a mainstay component of neuropsychological test batteries (Lezak, 1995), and the MMPI-2 has been demonstrated to have comparable utility to the MMPI with neurological populations (Miller and Paniak, 1995; Mittenberg, Tremont, and Rayls, 1996). The MMPI-2 provides the neuropsychologist with valuable information about the patient's noncognitive functioning to include behavioral, emotional, and psychiatric issues. Also particularly useful in forensic circumstances are the MMPI-2 scales designed to indicate response bias. Lamb, Berry, Wetter, and Baer (1994) noted that the MMPI-2 is vulnerable to simulated closed head injury; MMPI-2 findings alone, however, should not be relied upon as the sole indicator of malingering of head injury.

Detection strategies to measure specific areas of neuropsychological faking outside the domain of personality fall into several categories (Craine, 1990a; Freedland and Craine,

1981; Hall, Shooter, Craine, and Paulsen, 1991). These include (1) assessing lack of neuro-logical fit, (2) retesting or comparison strategies, (3) assessing certain test characteristics, and (4) searching for departures from expected levels of accuracy on forced-choice tests.

1. *Lack of neurological fit*
   Reported history, presenting symptoms, or responses on neuropsychological tests or on individual test items must make sense compared to what is known about the functional neurological systems involved. Otherwise, there exists a lack of neurologi-cal fit. For single items or symptoms, does the assessee present signs that do not make sense neurologically, such as glove amnesia or hemiparesis ipsilateral, to a supposedly involved hemisphere? On multidimensional tests, does the assessee produce a pattern of scores (profile) that is consistent with known neuropsychological syndromes?
2. *Retesting or comparison strategies*
   a. Easy versus difficult versions of similar tests. The faker may not understand that a second testing may be easier or more difficult than the first. Thus, fakers may perform similarly on the two versions, whereas nonfakers would perform differently.
   The Dot Counting Test (DCT) illustrates this method. Cards A, B, and C (consist-ing of massed dots) are more difficult than their counterparts, Cards, D, E, and F (consisting of clusters of dots), even though the two sets have the same number of dots to count. Administration of the two sets of the DCT may yield such inconsistent results that only a conscious attempt to control performance can explain them. In a meta-analytic review of selected malingering detection procedures, Vickery, Berry, Hanlon Inman, Harris, and Orey (2001) found that, on the DCT, malingerers scored .75 standard deviations below honest responders. In analyzing 32 studies of com-monly researched neuropsychological malingering tests, Vickery et al. (2001) found that the Digit Memory Test (DMT) and the Portland Digit Recognition Test (PDRT) could effectively discriminate honest responders from fakers, separating the two groups by approximately two standard deviations.

   Another test with built-in easy versus difficult items is the Auditory Discrimination Test (ADT) (Language Research Association, 1958). Initial administration of the ADT involves informing the assessee that words will be read, two at a time, and that the task is to say whether the two words are the same or different (e.g., tub–tub, lack–lack, web–wed, leg–led, and chap–chap). A second form presents same or different word pairs of similar difficulty and number ($n = 40$) as the first form (e.g., gear–beer, cad–cab, and bug–bud). In terms of threshold values, the faker may not realize that normals can miss many of the "same" items (<15), but should miss only a few of the "different" items (>4) before the performance appears suspicious. Comparison of the "hit rates" for same ver-sus different items may detect a suspicious asymmetry in the types of items missed.

   Caution should be exercised, however, in deciding that failures of "easy" items within a test are more characteristic of deliberate distortion than of genuine respond-ing. Mittenberg, Hammeke, and Rao (1989) examined the distribution of intratest scatter among brain-damaged and normal subjects on the vocabulary, compre-hension, and similarities subtests of the Wechsler Adult Intelligence Scale-Revised (WAIS-R). Their results suggested quite high cut-off scores (e.g., more than six failed items interpolated among passed items) for distinguishing brain-damaged subjects from normal subjects. If intratest scatter is to be used as an index of "faking bad" as well as an index of brain damage, then the cut-off scores for distinguishing actual brain damage from malingered brain damage would have to be even higher than those for distinguishing brain-damaged subjects from normal subjects.

In another study, Mittenberg, Theroux-Fichera, Zielinski, and Heilbronner (1995) compared selected WAIS-R subtest score differences between a group of recruited simulators and a mild head injury group. A significant discriminant function was identified and the cut-offs differentiated the two groups. The traumatic brain injury (TBI) group showed negligible differences between vocabulary and digit span subtest performance. The simulators performed better on vocabulary compared to digit span. The authors acknowledged the limitation of their experimental cut-off scores being utilized with actual clinical populations.

  b. Parallel testing. Repeat administrations of the same test or administration of a parallel form of a test should yield similar performances. The faker may not understand that a repeat of the test will be given and, therefore, may have difficulty replicating the previous performance. Faked scores in general are less stable than genuine scores.

The Peabody Picture Vocabulary Test (PPVT) as a test of receptive vocabulary is an example. Clients often have difficulty obtaining the same score on a parallel form even when the testing is administered a short time later.

  c. Deviations from predicted scores. The evaluator can compare performance on predicted scores on a test with actual performance on that test. For example, regression equations have been developed to predict WAIS-R scores from scores on the Shipley–Hartford Institute of Living Scale (Zachry, 1986; Weiss and Schell, 1991), Ravens Progressive Matrices (O'Leary, Rusch, and Gudstello, 1991), and the National Adult Reading Test (Wilshire, Kinsella, and Pryor, 1991). A faker's obtained score on the WAIS-R may fall outside the confidence interval predicted from one of these three other tests.

The Shipley–Hartford and Ravens Progressive Matrices in particular are useful screening measures of intelligence because they take only a short time to administer. In addition, the Shipley–Hartford provides alternate forms that will yield information on test–retest performance as well as giving an estimated WAIS-R IQ. Impaired nonfaking subjects should obtain WAIS-R IQ scores similar to those predicted by these two tests.

3. *Certain test characteristics*

  a. Inconsistencies across similar items or tasks. Within the same test, the faker may not pay attention to item similarity and, therefore, not perform in an identical fashion. A less stable performance on similar items is frequently seen in fakers, just as with parallel tests. On tests with repeated trials of the same task (e.g., finger tapping and dynamometer), intertrial variability also increases with faking. However, it should be remembered that the reliability of item-level scores is much lower than the reliability of scale-level scores. Therefore, less confidence should be placed in item-level or trial-level inconsistencies than in scale-level inconsistencies.

  b. Failure to show learning. Fakers often do not show expected learning curves (or may perhaps even show deterioration) across repeated trials of a task. The mirror tracing test (Andreas, 1960; Millard, 1985) illustrates this expectation. The subject is told to trace the path between the two solid lines of a maze while viewing the maze in a mirror. An error is counted each time the subject's pencil touches a guideline. If the subject crosses the line, he/she must reenter at the same point; otherwise, a reentry counts as a second error. Faking may be suspected if the expected bilateral transfer of training (improved performance with the opposite hand after training with one hand) does not occur, if the expected improvement over trials (learning curve) is not apparent, or if the total time exceeds 5 min.

4. *Departures from expected accuracy*

Forced-choice testing and forced-choice reaction time testing provide powerful methods of assessing deception of deficits. These tasks are all so easy that even severely impaired persons should perform satisfactorily. Departures from expected levels of performance provide a measure of a conscious attempt to manipulate performance.

Symptom Validity Testing (SVT) or Explicit Alternative Testing (EAT) attempt to measure faked sensory and recall deficits (Grosz and Zimmerman, 1965; Hall and Shooter, 1989; Hall and Thompson, 2007; Pankratz, 1979, 1983, 1988; Pankratz, Fausti, and Peed, 1975; Theodor and Mandelcorn, 1973). EAT involves the presentation of stimuli whose perception or recognition is either affirmed or denied by the assessee. An interference period may be added if recall, rather than sensory perception, is the target of evaluation.

Almost no one should miss the presented items unless a genuine impairment exists. In the case of total impairment (e.g., total blindness or deafness), one's performance should approximate chance responding (50% accuracy with two-choice tasks). A significant deviation from chance responding is defined as an accuracy score with a probability less than some specified level (e.g., $p < .05$ or $p < .01$) as determined by the binomial distribution. For example, the one-tailed probability of obtaining fewer than 40 correct responses in 100 trials of a two-choice task is less than 2% ($p = .0176$). Achieving fewer than 36 correct answers would occur by chance less than twice in a thousand tests ($p = .0018$).

Fakers usually assume that impaired performance requires less than 50% accuracy (Haughton, Lewsley, Wilson, and Williams, 1979; Pankratz, 1988). Persons genuinely impaired will usually guess randomly on EAT testing. Fakers do worse than chance because they intentionally suppress the correct answers on items to which they know the answers.

The Smell Identification Test (SIT) provides an illustration of forced-choice testing of faked sensory deficits. Developed by Doty and colleagues (Doty, Shaman, and Dann, 1984a; Doty, Shaman, and Kimmelman, 1984b) at the University of Pennsylvania, the 40-item SIT provides a quantitative measure of olfactory dysfunction in less than 15 min. The authors note that problems with the sense of smell are frequently associated with genuine head trauma, with anosmia found in between 7 and 8% of cases.

The SIT may be useful when the assessee is suspected of malingering with regard to his or her sense of smell, such as when a criminal defendant claims a variety of signs of brain damage in order to bolster chances of obtaining mitigation or exculpation. Four choices of smells are presented upon release of an odorant, yielding a 25% chance of accuracy in correctly identifying the designated smell, given total anosmia (10 of 40). Most nonfaking patients will correctly identify 35 or more of the 40 odorants, with females generally outscoring males at all age levels. Zero was the modal number of correct guesses for 158 men and women instructed to fake bad in the Doty et al. (1984b) study. Doty (1991) notes that under the assumption that $p = .25$, the probability of obtaining a score of zero by chance is one in 100,000; the chance of obtaining five or less correct on the SIT is less than 5 in 100. Those with genuine problems reflecting total loss of smell (i.e., anosmia) generally score around 10 at chance level due to essentially random responding. Patients with partial dysfunction have intermediate SIT scores. Patients with multiple sclerosis yield scores slightly above average; Parkinson's or Alzheimer's patients surprisingly produce scores that are significantly lower than average, but that are still substantially above the expected range for random responding.

Frederick (1997) described the Validity Indicator Profile (VIP), a two-alternative forced-choice (2AFC) procedure designed to identify when the results of cognitive and neuropsychological testing may be invalid because of malingering or other problematic response styles. The instrument consists of 100 problems that assess nonverbal abstraction capacity and 78 word-definition problems. The VIP attempts to establish an S's performance as representative of the S's overall capacity (i.e., valid or invalid). A valid performance is classified as "compliant," an invalid performance is subclassified as "careless" (low effort to respond correctly), "irrelevant" (low effort to respond incorrectly), or "malingering" (high effort to respond incorrectly). Frederick and Crosby (2000) reported a cross-validation study with 152 nonclinical Ss, 61 brain-injured Ss, 49 Ss considered to be at risk for malingering, and 100 randomly generated VIP protocols. The nonverbal and verbal subtests of the VIP demonstrated overall classification rates of 79.8% (73.5% sensitivity and 85.7% specificity) and 75.5% (67.3% sensitivity and 83.1% specificity), respectively. The VIP is another promising instrument for the detection of malingering. Its author suggested that the instrument's fourfold classification scheme (i.e., cross-classification of high to low motivation and high to low effort) reduces problems with false-positive classifications.

The Victoria Symptom Validity Test (VSVT) (Slick, Hopp, Strauss, and Thompson, 1997) is a forced-choice instrument. The VSVT was designed to address the validity of reported cognitive impairments. The VSVT is computer administered and consists of five-digit numbers of varying difficulty. One feature of the VSVT is an administration time of 10–15 min, another is its production of probability values (scores for valid, questionable, and invalid profiles). The test manual has a table of binomial probability values that is used to estimate the probability of obtaining the number of items correct of the total number of items completed. The VSVT was found to be effective at detecting feigned memory impairment (Slick, Hopp, Strauss, and Spellacy, 1996; Slick, Tan, Strauss, Matter, Harnadek, and Sherman, 2003; Bauer and McCaffrey, 2006; Loring, Lee, and Meador, 2005). Overall, validity and reliability data are encouraging (see review by Lees-Haley, Dunn, and Betz, 1999).

Another instrument is the widely used Rey 15-Item Memory Test (FIT, Rey, 1964; Liff, 2004). The FIT is a screening instrument designed to identify malingered memory complaints. To the examinee, the FIT initially appears to be more difficult than it actually is. The redundancy of simple character sets makes the memory task relatively simple, such that significant memory problems are necessary to generate actual deficit performance. Twenty years of studies (for a review, see Hart, 1995), mostly consisting of cut-off score refinements and adjustments, have indicated the FIT to be vulnerable to false-positive findings. The FIT is unique in its simplicity and brevity, but these same attributes render it not able to yield meaningful discriminant functions. In Vickery et al.'s (2001) study, they found that the FIT separated the two groups by .75 of a standard deviation.

Importantly, the evaluator should note that empirically designed tests of deception are likely to meet the *Daubert* standards for admission of scientific evidence (Hall and Poirier, 2001; Hall and Thompson, 2007).

Caveats

Neuropsychologists, first, should understand that their training, especially in clinical settings, poorly prepares them for deception analysis. An emerging literature discussed above suggests that only recently has the typical neuropsychological practice incorporated deception analysis. Likewise, in actual clinical practice, a multidimensional view is necessary in that genuine symptoms may be distorted or exaggerated in intensity, frequency, and duration (Zielinski, 1995).

A second caveat is that the evaluator should be wary of the traditionally accepted signs of hysteria and malingering, which actually may reflect cerebral dysfunction. In one study, Gould, Miller, Goldberg, and Benson (1986) surveyed the literature and found that the majority of clients (60–80%) thought to be hysteric or presenting neurological problems due to secondary gain actually suffered brain damage.

A third caveat concerns the need for multiple measures of distortion. When evaluating neuropsychological patients for forensic purposes, the authors use specific devices for detecting deception, in addition to a composite neuropsychological battery and as much historical and premorbid information as is available.

A fourth caveat involves the array of factors that are reviewed in assessing neuropsychological symptoms. In a study of base-rate data regarding postconcussive syndrome (PCS) with a large sample ($n = 1,116$), neurological, psychological, and environmental variables were found to affect symptom presentation (Fox, Less-Haley, Earnest, and Dolezal-Wood, 1995). The authors observed that neuropsychological test data must be reviewed in the context of a broad range of factors before PCS complaints are used as a basis for brain damage.

A fifth caveat notes that the effects of coaching or priming by others, particularly criminal defense attorneys, should be carefully scrutinized. The senior author has encountered several forensic cases where the adversarial attorneys made available to their clients books and journal articles on deception and distortion. The implicit aspects of coaching in these situations were impossible to demonstrate but were suspected. In these cases, ironically, the clients were detected in their faking by a battery of tests, suggesting as a testable hypothesis that even with knowledge of the literature on faking, deceptive persons can nevertheless be identified.

But this may not be true. Despite widespread use of malingering instruments, few if any empirical studies have been published determining the vulnerability of malingering measures to explicit coaching. Dunn, Shear, Howe, and Ris (2003) studied two commonly utilized measures of deception (the computerized assessment of response bias-97 and the word memory test) with participants aged 18–30 years. They found that both tests could detect malingering, but neither test differentiated between naïve and coached participants. They also found that response times and items correct were the two best indicators of participants not giving their full effort. Borckardt, Engum, Lambert, Nash, Bracy, and Ray (2003) found similar results on the cognitive behavioral driver's inventory for 98 student subjects. The students were divided into a coached group and an uncoached group; the coached students performed indistinguishably from the uncoached students on the measure.

In an attempt to detect malingering on the Ravens Standard Progressive Matrices, McKinzey, Prieler, and Raven (2003) found that all but 2 of 44 subjects (aged 7–17 years) could produce lower scores when asked to malinger on the test. Yet a simple rule involving missing any of three very easy items (i.e., A3, A4, or B1) yielded 5% true-positives and true-negatives and an overall hit rate of 95%.

A sixth caveat rests on the necessity of the examiner's attempting to reconstruct the malingering experience from the perspective of the suspected faker. Alban (2003) found that subjects who were asked to malinger were unable to maintain faked responses under cognitive overload for reaction time measures, but this finding did not hold true for other neuropsychological domains. We can speculate that for timed tasks, fakers would have difficulty determining which temporal limitation was associated with impairment.

As a last concern, the evaluator who provides expert testimony in court should be cognizant of *Daubert* standards for admissibility of evidence. Relevant questions for a deception analysis may include those designed to reveal the sensitivity and specificity of the measures employed, as well as the degree of error associated with the different procedure's steps employed (e.g., order of administration). Findings that stem from empirical studies on deception may be more helpful to the trier of fact (as well as less painful to the expert who is cross-examined!) than subjectively based findings or clinical judgment. The expert who opines on deception in a particular case should be prepared to share with the courts his or her own accuracy level in attempting to detect deception in forensic cases.

Neuropsychological testing in criminal settings and situations lends itself well to deception analysis. Fruitful areas of inquiry are plentiful within a composite battery consistent with an applied model as discussed above. Tests for cerebral functioning can be combined with personality tests, clinical observation and cross-validating sources to provide conclusions regarding faking.

The following list presents cross-validated signs suggestive of deception:

1. Failure on specific measures adapted to assess faking of cerebral impairment (e.g., illusorily difficult tests)
2. Goodness of neurological fit
    a. Inconsistency between clinical/test behaviors and known neuropsychological syndromes
    b. Failure to exhibit impaired function outside the context of evaluation
3. Skill performance changes on parallel testing
4. Anterograde better than retrograde memory
5. Approximate answers in interviews when concurrent testing reveals adequate skills
6. Neuropsychological test results consistent with statistical rules for detecting malingering
7. Similar or better performance on easy compared to difficult versions of the same test
8. Less than accurate performance on forced-choice sensory, recall and reaction-time tests
9. No improvement where expected (e.g., absence of learning curve)
10. Test scores outside of predicted confidence intervals (e.g., actual WAIS-R full-scale IQ outside the confidence interval predicted by the score on the Shipley)

While not definitive in themselves, these factors are suggestive enough of distorted performance to justify a more intensive investigation of the possibility of deliberate deception. Clinically based empirical research in this fascinating area is strongly encouraged for the following reasons.

First, much is unknown concerning the dimensions of faking, under what conditions it most likely will occur, its magnitude and direction, the role of motivation and vested interest in given outcomes by the faker, and, importantly, interventions that could reduce deliberate deception while simultaneously offering a reliable and valid evaluation of the forensic client. Practically, a deception analysis could be applied to every criminal-forensic examination by integrating measures of faking good and faking bad into the battery of tests employed. Thus, all forensic professionals, not only neuropsychologists and psychologists, who utilize evaluation findings corrected for deception would benefit from its application. Finally, the proposed model lends itself well to research that ultimately will lead to an empirically based theory of human deception.

Psychological Testing Approaches to Deception Analysis

M Test

A short test for measuring malingering in schizophrenic persons has been developed by Beaber, Marston, Michelli, and Mills (1985). The M Test consists of three scales: (a) confusion (C) scale where subjects were expected to respond in a particular way (e.g., "I believe that cancer is a horrible disease"); (b) schizophrenia (S) scale where items reflect Diagnostic and Statistical Manual III-Revised (DSM III-R)-associated features of schizophrenia (e.g., "Periodically, I am bothered by hearing voices that no one else hears"); and (c) malingering (M) scale or indicators of malingered schizophrenia.

The M scale showed the largest absolute mean difference between normals ($M = .36$; $SD = .83$), schizophrenics ($M = 2.07$; $SD = 2.83$), and fakers ($M = 8.07$; $SD = 4.94$). The M scale consists of items that cannot be true because they consist of nonexistent entities (e.g., "I believe that God has appointed me to teach the Zolan beliefs to all people that I meet"). Atypical hallucinations, even for genuine experiences, are presented in this scale (e.g., "Sometimes after waking up in the morning, I am bothered by seeing colored triangles in my field of vision"). Items reflecting extreme severity not characteristic of schizophrenia are also included (e.g., "Sometimes my need to be alone and my fear of people are so powerful that I will spend hours in a closed closet by myself"). Other items reflect atypical delusions (e.g., "There have been times when I have found myself thinking that as a teenager, I was the chairman of the board of a major corporation"). The M Test identified 87.3% of 65 schizophrenics (true-negatives) and 78.2% of 104 normal persons who were in fact malingering (true-positives).

Smith and Borum (1992) attempted to cross-validate the M Test with 23 malingerers and 62 nonmalingering inmates referred for a forensic evaluation but were able to achieve only a 67% overall hit rate. Gillis, Rogers, and Bagby (1991) were able to identify only 40% of suspected malingerers with the M test and therefore proposed a revised M Test (Rogers, Bagby, and Gillis, 1992), which was able to screen more than 80% of suspected malingerers. Smith, Borum, and Schinka (1993) cross-validated the revised test and identified 72.7% of malingerers, but unfortunately found a false-positive rate of 50.8%.

MMPI and MMPI-2

A large field of literature on the MMPI and MMPI-2 shows that normals who fake psychosis, and psychotics who feign normality or exaggerate their disorder, can be detected with some degree of accuracy. Throughout this literature, however, it is important to distinguish the specific contrasting groups used to support the detection of distorted responding. MMPI scores and indices are better at discriminating between normal MMPI profiles and those of normal subjects instructed to feign psychopathology (normal pseudo-malingerers) than they are at discriminating between genuine patients and normal pseudo-malingerers (Berry, Baer, and Harris, 1991; Schretlen, 1988).

MMPI indices of malingering are even less accurate in distinguishing genuine, honest patients from genuine patients who are exaggerating. Furthermore, some indices of distortion on the MMPI are consistently more effective compared to others. For example, Berry et al. (1991) concluded that "the largest mean effect size [for discriminating genuine from malingered MMPI profiles] was T-scaled F ... followed by raw F ... the original dissimulation scale ... F minus K ... obvious item scales ... obvious minus subtle scales ... subtle item scales ... and the revised dissimulation scale" (p. 593).

Table 9.1   MMPI and MMPI—Validity Indicators

Validity Indicators	MMPI	MMPI-2
1. Item omissions	a. Present	a. Present
2. Consistency	b. Test–retest (TR) index	b. & c. Replaced with two new scales based on the same rationales: variable response
	c. Carelessness (CLS) scale	Inconsistency (VRIN), 49 pairs of items; true response inconsistency (TRIN), 20 pairs of items indicating a true or a false set
	d. Sum of TR and CLS	d. Eliminated and replaced by above scales
	e. Weiner and Harmon	e. Present obvious and subtle scales
	f. Gough Dissimulation Scale-Revised	f. Information not available
	g. Lochar and Wrobel critical items	g. Present with minor revision (4–5 items)
	h. F scale	h. Present
	i. Absent	i. F(B) or back-page F scale Designed to assess the validity of responses to the latter part of the MMPI (e.g., random responding after tiring)
	j. Positive malingering	j. Present
	k. L and K scales	k. Present
	l. F-K	l. Present
	m. Individual item endorsement vs. cross-validated historical behavior	m. Present

Berry et al. (1991) noted that the search for a universal cut-off score for distinguishing genuine from faked MMPIs on any of these indices is ill advised. Cutting scores must be locally determined according to the base rate of malingering in the population of interest and according to the costs of classification errors. For example, in order to achieve a given level of false-positive errors, cut-off scores would need to be higher when differentiating exaggerating patients from genuine patients than when differentiating malingering normals from genuine normals. Consistent with this observation, Sivec, Lynn, and Garske (1994) assigned undergraduate students ($n = 237$) to three instructed groups (somatoform disorder, paranoid psychotic, and general "fake-bad") and administered the MMPI-2. Each instructed group differed from a control group on the majority of the MMPI-2 clinical and validity scales. The simulated paranoid psychotic and "fake-bad" groups did not differ from each other, although the somatoform disorder group differed from both. The F scale appeared to be the most effective validity indicator in this study.

The MMPI-2 was introduced in 1989. Shooter and Hall (1989) compared the various validity indicators available on the MMPI and the MMPI-2 (Table 9.1) based on extant information (Anderson, 1989; Butcher, 1990).

Over a decade and a half later, the MMPI-2 has now withstood the rigors of time and usage. Pope, Butcher, and Seelen (1993, 2000) described the MMPI, MMPI-2, and MMPI-A as widely relied upon forensic instruments; their reasons for using these instruments in court are summarized in Table 9.2.

During the 1990s, there was an unprecedented increase of studies investigating the application of the MMPI-2 and the MMPI-A in forensic matters. Beginning with the original MMPI, research suggested that the instrument is less useful in discriminating malingering from genuine psychopathology than in discriminating malingering from

Table 9.2   The MMPI, MMPI-2, and the MMPI-A in Court

The MMPI is the most frequently used clinical test. Many courts accept it as a source of personality
information about defendants or litigants.

The instrument is relatively easy to administer and is available in a variety of formats.

The test is self-administering, under monitored conditions. A minimum of sixth-grade reading level is
required to understand statements that test-takers simply respond as being "true" or "false" as applies
to them.

The tests are relatively easy to score. The answer sheets can be scored manually or by a number of
computerized scoring programs. The computerized scoring programs are quick, provide expanded scoring
options, and offer greater reliability with fewer errors.

The tests are available in a variety of languages (e.g., Spanish, Thai, Vietnamese, Chinese, Norwegian,
Japanese, etc.), and appropriate national norms are available.

The tests incorporate a number of response attitude measures.

The tests are objectively interpreted on empirically validated scales.

The test scales have been demonstrated to be reliable (stable over time).

The tests offer valid interpretations of patient symptoms, problems, and characteristics.

The test scores enable clinicians to predict anticipated responses to treatment and rehabilitation approaches.

In court, the test findings are reasonably easy to explain and are reasonably understood.

Source: Adapted from Pope, K. S. et al., *The MMPI, MMPI-2, & MMPI-A in Court: A Practical Guide for
Expert Witnesses and Attorneys* (2nd ed.), APA, Washington, DC, 1993.

normalcy (Berry et al., 1991). In acknowledgment of the central role of malingering in forensic
matters, the development of the MMPI-2 involved an effort to retain from the original test a
number of measures to assess negative response approaches to the test items. There was also
an effort to develop new measures. These MMPI-2 measures are summarized in Table 9.3.

Pensa, Dorfman, Gold, and Schneider (1996) described a study investigating the utility of the MMPI-2 and the detection of malingered psychosis. Male Ss ($n = 20$) diagnosed
with psychosis were matched in age and education with 20 male volunteers. The volunteers
received training materials on psychosis along with instructions and monetary incentives to
malinger. All Ss were administered the MMPI-2. The results reflected significant differences
between the groups on the F-Fb index, which yielded a hit rate of 70%. Additional t-tests
revealed significant group differences on scales infrequency (F), bizarre mentation (BIZ),
obvious-subtle difference score, and the F-Fb Index. Discrimination with the additional
t-test scores improved hit rates to the 80–90% range. A discriminant function with scales
F, Fb, F-K, BIZ, and S-O yielded a hit rate of 92.5%. In a study with a group of forensic
psychiatric patients ($n = 353$), Roman, Tuley, Villanueva, and Mitchell (1990) found traditional cut-offs for validity indicators (L, F, K, F-K, and O-S) to be of questionable validity in
distinguishing malingerers. In addition to deliberate efforts to deceive, validity indicator
elevations could be attributable to a variety of comorbid psychopathology.

An important variable affecting malingering detection with psychological tests is the level
of test-taker knowledge of specific psychopathologies. For example, across different studies
with the MMPI and MMPI-2, Ss are variously asked to "fake bad" or to simulate a specific psychiatric disorder. Bagby, Rogers, Nicholson, Cameron, Rector, Schuller, and Seeman (1997b)
investigated two groups of student fakers who completed the MMPI-2 with instructions to
feign schizophrenia. Their responses were compared to the responses of a group of outpatient
schizophrenics. The first group of simulators was undergraduates with no clinical training.
The second group consisted of clinical psychology graduate students and psychiatry residents.
The sophisticated group produced generally lower scores on the clinical scales and validity
indicators compared to the undergraduate students. Both groups had higher scores for the

Table 9.3 Dissimulation Measures on the MMPI-2

Measure	Assessed Behavior
Cannot say score (CS)	Total number of unanswered or answered both true and false; the overall profile is attenuated as the total number increases
Lie scale (L)	Tendency to deliberately deceive the evaluator
Subtle defensiveness scale (K)	Tendency to posture in a socially favorable light; corrects some clinical scales for defensiveness
Superlative self-presentation scale (S)—scale has 5 subdimensions: S1 Belief in human goodness S2 Serenity S3 Contentment with life S4 Patience/denial of irritability/anger S5 Denial of moral flaws	Tendency to present in a highly virtuous manner
Infrequency scale (F)	Tendency to exaggerate symptoms
Infrequency scale (FB)	Derivative of F, but measures F responses only on the last half of the test to provide a comparison between front and rear test performance of symptom exaggeration
Dissimulation index (F-K)	K > F not empirically useful; F > K empirically demonstrated to indicate faking
Fake bad scale (FBS)	Originally designed to measure "fake bad" tendency in personal injury cases, has not been adequately validated for forensic use
F(p) scale	Tendency to extreme endorsement (symptom exaggeration); most useful with psychiatric inpatients; original F and F(B) scales were not normed with psychiatric population
Variable response inconsistency scale (VRIN)	Tendency not to be consistent in responding to pairs of similar questions
True response inconsistency scale (TRIN)	Tendency to respond inconsistently by endorsing too many items in the same direction (either true or false) when the same response is semantically inconsistent

Source: Adapted from Pope, K. S. et al., *The MMPI, MMPI-2, & MMPI-A in Court: A Practical Guide for Expert Witnesses and Attorneys* (2nd ed.), APA, Washington, DC, 1993.

clinical scales 6 (paranoia) and 8 (schizophrenia) when compared to the schizophrenic sample. The largest validity indicator effects were observed on F and F-K.

In a follow-up study, Bagby, Rogers, Nicholson, Buis, Seeman, and Rector (1997a) investigated this issue with respect to whether divergent validity scales and indicators were differentially effective depending on what psychopathology Ss simulated. The investigators looked at simulated depression and simulated schizophrenia. Overall, the MMPI-2 indicators were better at detecting feigned schizophrenia than feigned depression. The investigators suggested that familiarity with depressive symptoms was probably more commonplace in comparison to schizophrenia. The study also reflected the F, Fb, and F(p) validity scales to best differentiate schizophrenic patients from Ss feigning schizophrenia and F and Fb to best distinguish depressed patients from Ss feigning depression.

More recently, Bagby, Marshall, and Bacchiochi (2005) found that the Fb and F/F(p) scale combination of the MMPI-2 are still the best single predictors of feigned depression and that the malingering depression scale (Md) is also able to discriminate fake depression from real depression, but that the Md scale only minimally adds incremental validity over the F scales.

Also recently meta-analyzed was the MMPI-2 fake bad scale (FBS; Nelson, Sweet, and Demakis, 2006). This study computed effect sizes across 19 studies for the validity scales of the MMPI-2. The FBS was found to perform as well as or better than other validity scales in differentiating between groups that overreport symptoms compared to other groups. For a review of MMPI-2 validity scales, see Bagby, Marshall, Bury, Bacchiochi, and Miller (2006).

PAI

Like the MMPI, the Personality Assessment Inventory (PAI) is another multiscale inventory; it lacks, however, the many validity referents of the MMPI. The Negative Impression (NIM) Scale of the PAI was found to successfully discriminate psychology graduate students with 1-week preparation simulating specific disorders (Rogers, Ornduff, and Sewell, 1993). The NIM cut-off score was found to be effective with feigned schizophrenia, moderately effective with feigned depression, and ineffective with feigned generalized anxiety disorder. Rogers, Sewell, Morey, and Ustad (1996) investigated the PAI's effectiveness at detecting Ss feigning specific disorders. Two levels of simulating Ss were utilized: 166 naïve (undergraduates with minimal preparation) and 80 sophisticated (doctoral psychology students with 1-week preparation). The student Ss results were compared to persons with the designated disorders: schizophrenia ($n = 45$), major depression ($n = 136$), and generalized anxiety disorder ($n = 40$). The PAI was moderately effective with naïve simulators but only modestly effective with their sophisticated counterparts. Subsequently, a two-stage discriminant analysis yielded a moderately high hit rate (>80%). This hit rate was maintained in the cross-validation sample, irrespective of the feigned disorder or the sophistication on the simulators.

More recent comparisons between the MMPI-2 and the PAI have generally found that the MMPI-2 validity scales outperform those of the PAI in the detection of malingering (Blanchard, 2001; Blanchard, McGrath, Pogge, and Khadivi, 2003; Greene, 2005). These studies also found that prediction accuracy increased when using validity indicators from both the MMPI-2 and the PAI together. For more information about the PAI, see Morey (2003, 2004), Morey and Boggs (2004), and Morey and Quigley (2002).

Psychological Testing

Schretlen, Wilkins, Van Gorp, and Bobholz (1992) developed and cross-validated a three-test battery on samples of prison inmates and alcoholic inpatients instructed to "fake bad" and samples of prison inmates, alcoholic inpatients, and psychiatric inpatients who took the tests under standard instructions. The three tests were the MMPI, a specially scored Bender Gestalt, and a specially developed malingering scale (Table 9.4). A discriminant function* of three scores from these tests correctly classified 80% of the "fakers" with no false-positive errors among their original subjects and 95% of the "fakers" with no

---

* The discriminant equation was (2.5 + (.06 * (MMPI F(raw) − K(raw))) − (.17 * (VOCABULARY(malingering scale)) + (.11 * Bender Gestalt score)). Scores greater than 1 have a 100% probability of faking, while scores less than 1 have a 92% probability of not faking.

Table 9.4   Malingering Scale

Name_____   Age_____

VOCABULARY

Circle the word that means the same thing as the word in CAPITAL letters.

Sample: LAW	book	(rule)
(1) PENNY	money	candy
(2) STEP	write	walk
(3) STREET	road	path
(4) SAUCER	spoon	dish
(5) COUCH	sofa	glass
(6) FABRIC	cloth	shirt
(7) ENORMOUS	huge	gentle
(8) FIDDLE	story	violin
(9) REMEMBER	recall	number
(10) EVIDENT	separate	obvious
(11) HAT	coat	cap
(12) DONKEY	dreadful	mule
(13) THIEF	robber	driver
(14) REPAIR	fix	rest
(15) TUMBLE	dress	fall
(16) FURIOUS	angry	noisy
(17) SHIP	jump	boat
(18) MANY	several	coins
(19) FRY	cook	eat
(20) APPLE	fruit	berry
(21) PARDON	divide	forgive
(22) IMMUNE	diseased	protected
(23) TALK	speak	sleep
(24) GAMBLE	join	bet
(25) DIAMOND	follow	jewel
(26) LIKE	new	same

ABSTRACTION

Circle the answer that should go in the blank (___) space.

(1) A B C ___	D	R
(2) 1 2 3 4 ___	5	4
(3) Scape Cape Ape ___	Ca	Pe
(4) North South East ___	Winter	West
(5) A AB ABC ___	DEF	ABCD
(6) 56/65 24/42 73/___	37	10
(7) Mouth/Eat Eye/See Hand/___	Smell	Touch
(8) AB AC AD ___	AE	BC
(9) Over/Under In/Out Above/___	Below	Behind
(10) A1 B2 C3 ___	D4	E5
(11) White/Black Fast/Slow Up/___	Side	Down
(12) Bus Car Ship ___	Truck	Table
(13) 2 4 6 ___	5	8
(14) Red Blue Green ___	Yellow	Chair
(15) Monday Friday Sunday ___	March	Tuesday
(16) 5 10 15 ___	50	20
(17) Candy/Bar In/Side Light/___	Bulb	Ball

Table 9.4   (continued)

(18) Dog Bird Cat ___	Tree	Horse
(19) Bread Fruit Meat ___	Cheese	Fork
(20) * ** *** ___	****	*

ARITHMETIC

1. How much is 6 divided by 2?
2. A woman has 2 pairs of shoes. How many shoes does she have altogether?
3. How much does 19 minus 5 equal?
4. How much is 50 cents plus 1 dollar?
5. If you have 3 books and give 1 away, how many will you have left?
6. How much does 1 plus 1 plus 3 equal?
7. If you have 18 dollars and spend 7 dollars and 50 cents, how much will you have left?
8. How much is 20 cents plus 5 cents?
9. How much does 6 divided by 3 equal?
10. A boy had 12 newspapers, and he sold 5 of them. How many did he have left?
11. How much is 4 dollars plus 5 dollars?
12. How much does 1 times 8 equal?
13. If I cut an apple in half, how many pieces will I have?
14. Raffle tickets cost 25 cents each. How much will 6 tickets cost?
15. How much does 3 times 9 equal?
16. If you buy 6 dollars worth of gasoline and pay for it with a 10-dollar bill, how much change should you get back?
17. How much does 7 plus 4 equal?
18. How many hours will it take a person to walk 24 miles at the rate of 3 miles per hour?
19. A girl had 1 dollar in change. She lost 50 cents. How much did she have left?
20. How much does 10 minus 5 equal?

INFORMATION

1. What are the colors of the American flag?
2. How many months are there in a year?
3. How many things make a dozen?
4. What must you do to make water boil?
5. Who discovered America?
6. How many pennies make a nickel?
7. From what animal do we get bacon?
8. Why does oil float on water?
9. What is the capital of Italy?
10. What is a thermometer?
11. How many days make a week?
12. Where does the sun rise?
13. Name the two countries that border the United States.
14. Who wrote Hamlet?
15. Name the four seasons of the year.
16. Who invented the electric light bulb?
17. Name the month that comes next after March.
18. What does the stomach do?

continued

Table 9.4   (continued)

19. What is the shape of a ball?
20. In what direction would you travel if you went from Chicago to Panama?
21. How many weeks are there in a year?
22. Who runs a courtroom?
23. Who was president of the United States during the Civil War?
24. How many legs does a dog have?

Note: Vocabulary ____ Abstraction ____ Arithmetic ____ Information ____
Total ____
Score +1 for each correct answer on each of the four subtests.

Source: Reprinted with permission from Schretlen, D., *Malingering Scale.*
Johns Hopkins University, Baltimore, MD, 1990. Copyright 1990,
David Schretlen, PhD. The Johns Hopkins Hospital, Meyer 218, 600
North Wolfe St., Baltimore, Maryland 21205.

false-positive errors among their cross-validation subjects. These results were substantially higher than those obtained from any of the three tests used singly.

Schretlen et al. (1992) used a 2AFC format for their vocabulary and abstraction subtests of their malingering scale. This permitted them to examine how many of their subjects scored significantly below chance based on the binomial distribution. Since scoring correct on less than 18 of the 46 items on these two subtests would occur by chance with $p < 05$, they examined how many of their faking and nonfaking subjects scored below this cut-off. Twenty-six percent of the faking subjects scored below 18 and 100% of the non-faking subjects scored above 18. Thus, this paper-and-pencil application of EAT showed results comparable to other applications of EAT: when a person performs below chance level, one can be confident that they are faking, but few genuine fakers do so.

Smith and Burger (1997) described a new instrument called the Structured Inventory of Malingered Symptomatology (SIMS). The SIMS was designed as a paper-and-pencil screening measure to detect malingering. Test items were constructed from a combination of revised validity questions from existing instruments and characteristics of malingerers captured in existing research. The test items were organized on one of five subscales (psychosis, amnestic disorders, neurologic impairment, affective disorders, and low intelligence) by experienced clinical psychologists. College students ($n = 476$) were assigned to one of various simulation conditions (each of the subscales and fake bad) or an honestly responding group. All Ss were administered the SIMS, the F and K scales of the MMPI-2, 16PF faking bad scale, and portions of the malingering scale. The SIMS total score demonstrated the highest sensitivity rating (95.6%) for detection of dissimulation compared to the other indices. Subsequent studies using the SIMS have found the inventory to be useful as a screening tool for malingering (Cima, Hollnack, Kremer, Schellbach-Matties, and Klein, 2003; Jelicic, Hessels, and Merckelbach, 2006; Lewis, 2001; Merckelbach and Smith, 2003).

Lewis (2001) calls the structured interview of reported symptoms (SIRS) "the best available instrument for detecting malingering." In a study by Hayes, Hale, and Gouvier (1998), the SIRS instrument alone produced a 95% overall classification accuracy for discriminating between malingered psychiatric and neuropsychological dysfunction. The Ss in this study were initially classified by a multidisciplinary team as nonmalingerers

($n = 12$) and known malingerers ($n = 9$). When scores on the DCT, memory for FIT, and the M test were added to the analysis, 100% of the Ss were correctly classified. As with most forensic assessment efforts utilizing psychometrics, there is wisdom in not relying on any single test or instrument. Although more costly and more time consuming, the advisability of employing a battery of relevant tests in forensic assessments, especially when malingering is suspected, is an often repeated recommendation in the literature (Fauteck, 1995; Hayes et al., 1998; Roman et al., 1990).

Psychosis and Deception

Most probably, malingered psychosis (a) varies according to context—faked psychosis may be more frequent in criminal cases when there is a history of mental illness; (b) varies in degree within the same individual in his or her attempts to be consistent or inconsistent; (c) is more frequently engaged in by those who are already maladjusted; and (d) is encouraged by widespread dissemination of information on genuine psychosis, the move by deinstitutionalized people to return to the state hospitals, and the increasing mood of the judiciary to imprison felons.

Diverse circumstances and mental conditions are associated with faked psychoses. Ritson and Forrest (1970), in common with others, suggested that the malingering of psychosis is more serious than the condition faked, meaning that faking psychosis can be considered an illness in itself, although it should be noted that Adetunji, Basil, Mathews, Williams, Osinowo, and Oladinni (2006) state that malingering is *not* a form of mental illness, in keeping with others (e.g., Hall and Poirier, 2001). Ritson and Forrest's patients had a number of reasons for faking, including (a) not wishing to leave the hospital, (b) being criminally charged, (c) financial problems or seeking a new residence, (d) manipulating unsympathetic doctors, and (e) escaping from an intolerable domestic situation. They proposed we go beyond the unconscious versus conscious dichotomy, in the fashion of Freud and the neodynamically oriented, and focus on the communication or message that the faked behavior represents. The real problem may be the outrage and the indignation shown by the clinician. In the Ritson and Forrest study, most of the 12 fakers originally had personality disorders (or features thereof), but later showed schizophrenic symptoms, a finding cross-validated by Pope, Jonas, and Jones (1982) in their study of factitious psychosis among hospitalized patients. Like Ritson and Forrest, Pope et al. found that their fakers of psychosis had a poor prognosis. Almost one-half of their malingering patients were hospitalized 4 to 7 years later. Resnick (1999) offers a different perspective, noting that when the malingerers are defendants, failure to diagnose malingered psychosis causes injustice in the legal system and allows misuse of the mental health system.

Targets

The long-range targets or goals of the faker of psychosis typically include a desire to avoid the unpleasant (e.g., imprisonment) or to obtain a desired goal (e.g., drugs, transfer within institutional settings, such as protective custody).

Table 9.5   Targets of Faked Psychosis

Targets	Examples
Behavior	Bizarre motor behavior, audible self-talk
Somatic	Internal body changes, physical disease processes
Sensation	Vivid hallucinations, strange illusions
Imagery	Terrifying nightmares, uncontrollable flashbacks
Affect	Immobilizing fear, suicidal depression
Cognition	Delusions of persecution, grandiosity, looseness of thought
Interpersonal	Inability to respond: mutism, sexually inappropriate questions

Feigned behaviors chosen at the time of evaluation include alterations in speech, motor changes, the presentation of unexpected behavior, and the withholding of expected responses. As with all faked conditions, the faker of psychosis selects targets designed to accomplish a particular goal. Responses that the faker chooses should leave him or her blameless or, at least, point to uncontrollable forces beyond the ability to initiate, modulate, or stop. To assist the evaluator, the faker of psychosis often calls attention to faked symptoms. This does not necessarily imply consistency of responding or a desire to be detected. Rather, the examiner must be aware of psychotic symptoms in order to respond to them.

The faker of psychosis may present faked symptoms in writing, only to repudiate the symptoms when questioned orally. Presumably, the stress of verbal inquiry may be greater than with written expression. The evaluator should be prepared for both the presentation of moving targets and a wide variation in response styles. Some fakers will suggest that any variability or inconsistency in their presentation is due to the purported mental illness that they are experiencing.

Targets of faked psychosis with examples are presented in Table 9.5.

Research on forensic subjects may yield important guidelines to the detection of disingenuous psychosis. A unifying theme of these investigations is that, given motivation to fake, malingerers of psychosis appear to exhibit patterned responses and can be detected by conformance to an inner logic (Bash, 1978; Bash and Alpert, 1980). These investigators determined that increased specificity of response style is associated with less involvement of the faker's own personality. Conversely, the more adaptive and widespread the malingering is to a variety of situations, the greater the likelihood that the faker's own enduring personality traits and lifestyle come into play. This finding has important implications for the assessment of deception.

Response Styles

Malingerers tend to overendorse clinical symptoms when compared to normals and when compared to individuals with specific diagnoses (Bagby et al., 1997b; Wetter, Baer, Berry, Robison, and Sumptor, 1993). Malingering is often combined with defensiveness, as when the faker denies symptoms when arrested and asserts severe symptoms before and during the trial proceedings. Often overlooked, clients may deny genuine psychosis for various motives, for example, to preserve the ego. Diamond (1956) speculates that simulating sanity occurs very frequently. He encourages the clinician to investigate simulated sanity actively instead of waiting for the client inadvertently to reveal psychosis.

Even severely maladjusted persons can fake bad or good, depending on their vested interests and opportunities for deception. Braginsky and Braginsky (1967) showed, in a now classic study of 30 long-term schizophrenics, that subjects could present themselves as "sick" or "healthy," depending on their goals. The former response set was presented when the subjects were faced with discharge, while "healthy" behaviors were shown when their open ward status was challenged. Three staff psychiatrists who blindly reviewed tapes of interviews with patients were erroneously convinced by the patients' impressions. The importance of assessing for all response styles, even among persons with well-documented histories of psychopathology, is thus strongly indicated.

A standing question is whether certain diagnostic categories have comorbidity with malingering efforts. Lewis and Bard (1991) described the comorbid relationship of multiple personality disorder (MPD) in a variety of forensic circumstances. Noting a similarity between MPD symptoms and those of antisocial personality disorders, the authors suggested that MPD was often overlooked in forensic assessments. Osran and Weinberger (1994) described the prevalent role of personality disorders in criminal responsibility defenses. More recently, however, Poythress, Edens, and Watkins (2001) found no empirical support for the notion that individuals with higher levels of psychopathy are better malingerers.

Detection Methods

By understanding the phenomenology of genuine psychosis, the clinician's skill in detecting fake symptoms is measurably enhanced (Pollock, 1998; Resnick, 1999; Schlesinger, 1996). Resnick (1984, 1988, 1997, 1999) has extensively described baseline techniques for detecting malingered psychosis. Resnick's approach is based on known clinical presentation patterns and prevalence rates of real psychotic symptomatology. This essentially means that the clinician must have a thorough working understanding of real hallucinations, delusions, and affective symptoms.

Rogers (1984a, 1987, 1988) presented a structured interviewing approach to the problem of malingered psychosis. He analyzed the schedule of affective disorders and schizophrenia (SADS; Spitzer and Endicott, 1978), which stems from a 1978 study on depression but which measures a wide variety of psychiatric symptomatology (Endicott and Spitzer, 1978). He next developed the SIRS (Rogers, 1992), which is intended for the identification of unreliable or inconsistent presentations during clinical interviews.

The discriminating ability of the SIRS is shown by the frequent and significant differences between malingerers and genuine patients. Symptom combinations are endorsed on Form A of the SIRS by only 2.4% of the patient population but were endorsed by 28.9% of malingerers (Form B, 6.8 and 18.8%, respectively). Symptom combinations in the SADS which were rare (all endorsed by less than 10% of genuine patients) included reporting (a) an adequate appetite together with current feelings of inadequacy, discouragement, distrust, and anger; (b) agitation together with anxiety or discouragement;

and (c) persecutory delusions together with worrying, discouragement, insomnia, and anger.

Rogers (1988) suggested a number of criteria for detecting malingering which formed the basis for the development of the SIRS. The criteria, which are empirically validated, included the following:

Descriptor	Malingerers Endorse
Symptom subtlety	More blatant than subtle symptoms
Severity of symptoms	Items reflecting extreme or unbearable severity
Rare symptoms	Infrequent symptoms
Improbable or absurd symptoms	Items of fantastic or preposterous quality
Symptom combinations	Symptoms unlikely to coexist
Consistency of symptoms	Inconsistent items when repeated
Nonselective endorsement	More nonselective in choosing psychiatric symptoms

However, even rare items sometimes are seen in psychotics. These include symptoms such as (a) thought withdrawal, (b) delusions of guilt, (c) somatic delusions, (d) loosening of associations, (e) incoherence during the past week, and (f) neologisms (Rogers, 1988). As Rogers noted, contradictory symptoms are seen in cyclothymic or bipolar disorders such as (a) depressed and elevated mood, (b) worthlessness and grandiosity, (c) insomnia and hypersomnia, (d) decreased and increased energy, (e) decreased and increased appetite, (f) decreased and increased interests, and (g) psychomotor retardation and agitation.

Rogers' approach to structured interviewing has demonstrated impressive discriminant and concurrent validity across a number of follow-up studies and with a number of laboratory and clinical populations (Rogers, Gillis, and Bagby, 1990; Rogers, Gillis, Bagby, and Monteiro, 1991a; Rogers, Gillis, Dickens, and Bagby, 1991b; Rogers, Kropp, Bagby, and Dickens, 1992). Two primary drawbacks with the SIRS are that it must be administered individually and its administration time is lengthy.

Norris and May (1998) described the development of the screening structured interview of report symptoms (SSIRS), an abbreviated version of the SIRS. In a counterbalanced design, the SSIRS and the SIRS were administered to 75 inmates. The SSIRS discriminated significantly better than chance when compared to the classification analysis of the SIRS. The authors suggested that the screening procedure may help facilitate optimal allocation of resources in correctional settings where classification requirements can be demanding. Story (2001) also administered an abbreviated version of the SIRS to 50 pretrial forensic inmates and 30 pretrial nonforensic inmates. The abbreviated SIRS exhibited a mean alpha coefficient of .86, interrater reliability of .99, moderately high positive correlations with malingering indices from the MMPI-2, and an overall correct classification of 85.7%.

For the assessment of retrospective malingering, Goodness (2000) modified the SIRS by creating two new versions called the retrospective structured interview of reported symptoms (R-SIRS) and the concurrent-time structured interview of reported symptoms (CT-SIRS). Initial validation indicated that these two new inventories exhibited classification rates of malingerers and nonmalingering patients similar to the SIRS.

Available research suggests that the following may indicate manufactured or exaggerated psychosis:

1. Production of psychotic symptoms is apparently under voluntary control and is understandable in terms of pay off and environmental circumstances.
2. Psychotic symptoms worsen when being observed or when being interviewed, are bizarre for the circumstances, involve quick shifts to nonpsychotic behavior when not being observed, or symptoms cease under mild environmental stimulation.
3. Patient has a history of faked mental problems.
4. Patient admits to faking psychosis, and his or her behavior can be explained in terms of environmental events.
5. Patient uses an alias, is unwilling to allow access to old records, displays evidence of a severe personality disorder, has a history of substance abuse to include possession of paraphernalia, etc., which explain psychotic symptoms.
6. Laboratory testing suggests malingering (e.g., as a factitious disorder).
7. Psychological tests suggest deception in regard to psychosis.
8. Patient has rapid remission of symptoms.
9. Crime is associated with accomplices; crime fits into history of defendant's criminality; defendant has nonpsychotic motives for the crime.

There are caveats for forensic clinicians who conduct evaluation for malingered psychosis. The performance of schizophrenic patients was investigated on cognitive malingering instruments (Back, Boone, Edwards, Parks, Burgoyne, and Silver, 1996). The study evaluated the effect of a diagnosis of schizophrenia on test performance and its relationship between severity of psychosis-associated cognitive impairment and psychiatric disturbance. The Ss ($n = 30$) were administered the Rey 15-Item Memory Test (FIT), Rey Dot Counting Test (RDCO), and Hiscock Forced-Choice (FC) method to detect malingering of cognitive symptoms. The Ss also completed the Mini Mental State Exam and the Brief Psychiatric Rating scale. The results showed that 13% of the Ss failed the FIT and the RDCO, and 27% failed the FC measure. The investigators noted that performance on the FIT appeared to be significantly lowered by lesser educational levels. By comparison, the RDCO and the FC performances were related to the presence of cognitive impairment and the RDCO was also significantly affected by increasing age. The relatively high failure rates of the Ss implicate caution in forensic assessments of malingering when there is any history of schizophrenic symptoms. A number of investigators (Ganellen, Wasyliw, Haywood, and Grossman, 1996; Roman et al., 1990) have pointed out that positive psychometric indicators of malingering do not necessarily rule out the presence of a comorbid psychiatric disorder such as characterological features, substance abuse, or acute or severe psychopathology. Any malingering assessment requires careful analysis by the clinician and an appreciation for all possibilities of clinical presentation.

Neuropsychologists are confronted by particular problems with maladjusted patients who nevertheless may be malingering. Patients may have reported histories of neurological trauma, but also present with varied psychiatric symptoms or effects of medications, all of which confound meaningful neuropsychological assessment. Schwartz (1991) described the particular problem of neuropsychological assessment when the patient presents with possible malingering or paranoia approaching psychosis.

Cultural factors can influence the apparent presentation of a malingering effort. In a study with ultra orthodox Jewish military inductees, 24 Ss who had been diagnosed as malingering were reexamined (Witztum, Grinshpoon, Margolin, and Kron, 1996). The reexamination found 21 Ss to evidence severe psychopathology (i.e., psychosis, personality disorder, and mental retardation), but none was diagnosed as malingering. The investigators attributed the discrepancies in diagnosis to the ignorance, cultural bias, and countertransference of the original examiners.

As a final comment, we note the extensive use of studies in which Ss are instructed/coached to engage in deception and malingering. As Ben-Porath (1994) commented, it is important for psychologists who interpret psychometric validity to understand the susceptibilities of psychometrics to malingering. Additionally, the use of experimental models of deception is subject to misappropriation and misunderstanding. Forensic psychologists must subscribe to the requirements of professional ethics codes regarding the validity, integrity, and security of tests and test data.

Much is owed to Resnick for his base-rate approach. In generically addressing the issue of malingered psychosis, Resnick (1993) cites a series of clinical indicators:

1. Overacting
2. Calling attention to illnesses
3. Lack of the subtle signs of residual schizophrenia
4. Sudden onset of delusions
5. Contradictions in patient's account of illness

With specific regard to feigned hallucinations, Resnick suggests a "Threshold Model" (1988, p. 47). Faking hallucinations is suspected if any of the following occur:

1. Continuous rather than intermittent hallucinations
2. Vague or inaudible hallucinations
3. Hallucinations not associated with delusions
4. Stilted language reported in hallucinations
5. Inability to state strategies to diminish voices
6. Self-report that all command hallucinations were obeyed

Item 6 is especially helpful to evaluators because, as Resnick points out, command hallucinations are generally ignored. Further, they can be actively made to temporarily disappear altogether by interpersonal contact, motor activity (e.g., working and exercising), taking psychotropic medication, and even passive activities such as watching TV and lying down.

Some caution is needed with Resnick's approach, however. Hallucinations can occur in the absence of delusions, particularly in organic states and substance intoxication (item 3). Stilted language is occasionally used to describe actual hallucinations (item 4), especially if there is psychotic recall of the hallucinations and the person is reporting a nonverbal event with familiar verbal labels. Likewise, the inability to state strategies to diminish voices (item 5) may be a function of the severity of a mental condition, poor verbal skills, or resistance toward the evaluation.

Congruent with Resnick's (1988) findings, instructions to aggress within a hallucinatory experience probably do not contribute to dangerousness (Hellerstein, Frosch, and Koenigsberg, 1987). Contrary to clinical lore, investigators' study of 789 sequentially admitted inpatients showed no significant differences between patients with command and patients without command hallucinations on such variables as assaultiveness, suicidal behavior (or ideation), time in seclusion, use of restraints, and length of hospitalization.

In this important study, Hellerstein et al. (1987) found that about 19% of the patients reported auditory hallucinations, with about 7% of the total sample (58 of 789 patients) experiencing command auditory hallucinations. About 38% of the patients with hallucinations experienced such commands.

Interestingly, all cases of borderline personality disorder experienced command hallucinations. Of the schizophrenic subjects, those with command hallucinations ($n = 29$) had significantly shorter (less than 15-day) hospitalizations than those with noncommand hallucinations. Hellerstein et al. (1987) opine that command hallucinations may be a risk factor only when superimposed upon a previous history of violence. This last point is repeatedly supported by the literature (e.g., Hall, 1987). The foregoing findings were essentially replicated in a more recent investigation (Kasper, Rogers, and Adams, 1996). This study compared psychotic patients with command hallucinations ($n = 27$) to patients with other hallucinations ($n = 27$) and with other psychotic patients ($n = 30$). The investigators reported that the three groups did not differ on aggressive behavior or most nonhallucinatory symptoms. However, most patients (84.0%) with command hallucinations reported having recently obeyed the hallucinations. Among those with command hallucinations, almost one-half had heard and attempted to obey messages on self-harm during the preceding month.

Genuine hallucinations in the present do not imply that previously reported hallucinations were genuine. The two time periods (e.g., offense and evaluation) must be considered separately. One can fake for the present and still have had genuine hallucinations at the time of the alleged crime. Perhaps the accused (now stabilized and not experiencing hallucinations) feels the need to remain consistent with previous behaviors. In sum, both current and previous time periods can involve fake or genuine hallucinations.

Signs of faked hallucinations include the following: (1) The person admits to faking or is inconsistent in symptom presentation, along with confirming evidence; (2) The hallucination cannot be explained by any known condition or event, along with the ability of the examiner to show faking in testing or observation; (3) Knowledgeable/significant others or the evaluator report complex, purposeful behavior while the accused is allegedly subject to hallucinations; (4) Alleged command hallucinations occurred when behavior can be explained by secondary gain or an identifiable goal.

Deception Regarding Substance Abuse and Intoxication

Substance abuse or intoxication may produce disabling symptomatology and therefore must be ruled out or accounted for in any criminal-forensic evaluation. A vast literature exists on the causes, associated features, and effects of substance intoxication, abuse, and dependence (e.g., see Armor, Polich, and Stanbul, 1976; Bailey, 1961; Bean, 1981; Blane, 1968; Chait and Perry, 1992, 1994; Fals-Stewart, 2005; Jellinek, 1952, 1980; Mulhaney and Trippett, 1979; Nace, 1982, 1987; Rutherford, Cacciola, and Alterman, 1999; Sobell, Toneatto, and Sobell, 1994).

Criminal-forensic clinicians will encounter the issue of substance-abuse denial at any point in criminal adjudication and beyond. Commonly, defendants deny substance intoxication during a criminal proceeding such as a trial because most jurisdictions typically hold the accused responsible for acts while substance intoxicated. Following criminal sentencing, the issue of substance abuse is a common feature in sentence reconsideration, and violation of probation/parole hearings (Bonczar, 1997; Mumola, 1999). A significant percentage of probationers/parolees are stipulated to maintain abstinence or be involved in ongoing substance-abuse treatment. Clinicians and others who work with these populations on a follow-up assessment or treatment basis are constantly confronted with deception regarding substance abuse.

Targets

The DSM criteria for substance intoxication are generally known by the lay community. Drug and alcohol intoxication is commonly understood to be characterized as (a) a recent ingestion of a particular substance; (b) maladaptive behavioral changes such as poor judgment, labile behavior, or physical or sexual aggression, without which it would not matter from a legal viewpoint whether the person was intoxicated; and (c) critical physical and psychological signs that will vary according to the substance.

The deceiver may try to hide these symptoms in an attempt to hamper an investigation (e.g., by field testing and urinalysis). Typically, noncooperation with police involving alcohol intoxication takes the form of belligerence and aggressiveness. The range of reactions with drugs other than alcohol is wide ranging from aggressiveness to almost catatonic immobility.

The person who has a stake in denying or minimizing substance use may selectively hide symptoms. Symptoms chosen for denial depend on the faker's understanding of what constitutes a substance-abuse problem. Any of the following for psychoactive substance dependence, polysubstance dependence (DSM-IV, 1994), or psychoactive substance dependence not otherwise specified may be targeted for denial:

1. Substances ingested in larger amounts or over a longer period than the person intended
2. At least one unsuccessful effort to cut down or control substance use, or continuing desire to quit
3. Much time devoted to procurement, actually ingesting the substance (e.g., frequent smoking of "ice"), or in recovery from the substance
4. Interference with work, school, or home obligations when intoxicated or in withdrawal, or when intoxication is imminently dangerous (e.g., while driving)
5. Substance use leading to decreased involvement in work, play, or social activities
6. Continued use with awareness of a medical or other problem that is created because of it (e.g., alcohol use with cirrhosis, "ice" use with heart problems)
7. Substantial tolerance with at least a 50% increase to attain the same level of intoxication, or a decrease in positive effects as experienced by the individual over time
8. Withdrawal symptoms with discontinued use
9. Withdrawal symptoms are avoided on purpose by reuse of substance

Response Styles

Faking good is the dominant response style. Exaggeration of substance use occurs in some cases. Mixed styles are common—the faker may deny substance use for drugs but admit to depression, marital problems, and alcohol use. Usually the substance abuse is justified by blaming outside problems (e.g., loss of a job) or other people (e.g., "bad influences").

Fluctuating response styles are also seen. The faker may deny substance-use problems during a criminal trial in order to reduce culpability, but admit or even exaggerate the problems in order to obtain a sentence to a community treatment setting rather than prison.

Detection Methods

The traditional method for establishing substance abuse is the gathering of cross-validating material. The data gathering involves a search for substance-related behaviors and events from significant others, neighbors, bartenders, friends, and family. Supporting material should be collected if available (e.g., DUI arrest reports, mental health treatment records). If available, prior and current urinalysis records should be accessed as they provide the most reliable hard data of all. The evaluator should always review the material before questioning the person. The alternative is to return for a second session in order to ask pinpoint questions about the civil or criminal event.

Critical events that should raise the suspicion that alcohol (or other substance) abuse has occurred are reported by Nace (1987):

1. Any person with a history of substance abuse.
2. Referrals from corporations or industry secondary to job-related problems. Nace cites base rates that suggest that about one-half of job-related problems are alcohol related. Drugs are often interchangeable with alcohol, as some abusers seek different intoxicants after alcoholism has been identified as a problem.
3. Hospital and emergency room consultations. The high rate of substance abuse in hospital populations is well known. Nace states that about 40% of the persons in emergency rooms in urban settings have recent detectable alcohol use, and this is in a setting that generally underdiagnoses substance use.
4. DUI or DWI history. Scrutinizing the actual police reports will often reveal more information relevant to the pattern of abuse.
5. Persons with a history of divorce, especially multiple divorces. Substance abuse generally deteriorates social relationships of all sorts. Separation and divorce occur seven times more frequently among alcoholics than normals (Paolino and McCrady, 1977).
6. Persons who express even minimal concern that they may be substance abusers. In light of the pervasive problem of denial, any admission of substance use should be the springboard for further inquiry.

Chronic alcoholic behaviors can serve as signals (Jellinek, 1952, 1980). The more easily verified ones include (a) drinking a technical product, (b) multiple benders, (c) loss of tolerance, (d) tremors, (e) psychomotor inhibition, (f) verbally admitting defeat, (g) impairment of cognition, (h) alcoholic psychosis, and (i) continual drinking after the problem has been identified.

Laboratory methods and results can be utilized to indicate substance intoxication. Blood, breath, and urine analyses have long been used to detect substances in the body, despite controversy on their efficacy and intrusiveness. Generally, the tests are carefully controlled and have high accuracy rates. There are several common problems with urinalysis, and clinicians should always be on the lookout for defective specimen collection procedures. Substance abusers can employ ingenious methods to submit false or doctored specimens. For example, specimens from nonusers can be secreted into the collection room using a balloon-type apparatus hidden in the armpit; the specimen bottle can be dipped into the commode, etc. The proper procedure for specimen collection must be the immediately supervised flow of urine into the specimen bottle.

Urine specimens are typically evaluated, for example, by booking facilities in American cities as follows (O'Neil, Wish, and Visher, 1990):

> Urine specimens are analyzed by EMIT for 10 drugs: cocaine, opiates, marijuana, PCP, methadone, benzodiazepine (Valium), methaqualone, propoxyphene (Darvon), barbiturates, and amphetamines. Positive results for amphetamines are confirmed by gas chromatography to eliminate positives that may be caused by over-the-counter drugs. For most drugs, the urine test can detect use in the prior 2 to 3 days. Exceptions are marijuana and PCP, which can sometimes be detected several weeks after use. (p. 2)

A relatively new laboratory procedure, but one with considerable promise in terms of accuracy and efficiency, is radioimmunoassay of hair (RIAH) (Rogers and Kelly, 1997). The metabolites of illicit substances become imbedded in the hair shaft; the shaft is a record of substance abuse and nonuse. The main drawbacks of RIAH are that it is not effective with alcohol abuse and laboratories do not yet utilize standardized procedures thereby preventing cross-laboratory comparisons.

Denial of substance abuse on testing has sometimes been associated with relatively positive traits. Rohsenow, Erickson, and O'Leary (1978) found that lower levels of psychopathology were related to the use of denial and intellectualization as ego defenses on the Defense Mechanism Inventory (DMI). Reviewing the locus of control research, Rohsenow and O'Leary (1978) found that internality was related to better social functioning and the defenses of denial, intellectualization, and repression. Last, Pekarik, Jones, and Blodgett (1986) found that denial scores on the MMPI were positively correlated with intelligence, but only for completers of an alcohol treatment program.

The MMPI MacAndrew Alcoholism (MAC) Scale (MacAndrew, 1965) has been traditionally considered an index of substance-abuse tendencies. However, in a comprehensive review of the empirical literature, Gottesman and Prescott (1989) concluded that the scale makes so many false-positive errors that the use of the scale should be suspended. They reviewed 74 studies on the MAC published between 1976 and 1987. They calculated that the positive hit rate (percent of positive scorers who are actually alcoholic) in the general population is only 15% and that 85% of persons called alcoholic by the test are, in fact, not alcoholic.

In a study of 63 white, male forensic patients, Wasyliw, Grossman, Haywood, and Cavanaugh (1990) stated the following:

> While the MacAndrew Alcoholism Scale is the most widely used MMPI measure of vulnerability to alcohol abuse, its accuracy has not been studied in patients intrinsically motivated to exaggerate or minimize psychopathology. We examined the accuracy of the MAC in forensic patients with high rates of response-bias. Results indicated: (1) MAC scores were correlated positively with exaggeration and negatively with minimization for subjects with histories of alcohol abuse. (2) MAC scores were related to exaggeration or minimization of psychopathology rather than to admission or denial of alcohol abuse. (3) MAC scores were only moderately more accurate in valid than in exaggerated or minimized MMPI protocols. (4) Validity scale cut-off scores generated by discriminant function analyses were effective in identifying MAC misclassifications. Results suggest that the MAC should be used cautiously, particularly when motivation to minimize psychopathology is suspected.

There is now a revised version of the MAC: The MAC-R. In the most recent review of 71 MAC and MAC-R studies from 1989 to 2001, the MAC and MAC-R were found to correlate significantly with measures of alcohol and substance abuse for adolescent and adult substance abusers (Craig, 2005). The two measures performed best at discriminating substance abusers from nonclinical nonabusing groups, but were not as effective when used with psychiatric and medical patients.

The MMPI-A incorporates two new scales to assist with the assessment of substance abuse in adolescents (Pope et al., 2000). These scales are the Alcohol or Drug Problem Scale (PRO) and the Alcohol or Drug Problem Acknowledgement Scale (ACK). Micucci (2002) administered the ACK, PRO, and MAC-R scales from the MMPI-A to 79 adolescent psychiatric inpatients. At least one of the three scales was able to accurately identify 89.9% of the cases, but the three scales were better able to screen out cases of substance abuse than to identify individuals who were using substances.

Tirrell (2005) also administered the MMPI-A's ACK, PRO, and MAC-R scales to a sample of 100 substance-abusing adolescents, 100 nonsubstance-abusing psychiatric patient adolescents, and 100 normal adolescents. The three scales performed best at separating adolescent substance abusers from the normal adolescents. The scales, especially the ACK, were also deemed "statistically useful" at differentiating the substance abusers from the psychiatric patients who did not show evidence of active current use.

There have been studies using psychometrics correlating psychoactive substance abuse with a variety of personality characteristics to particularly include personality disorder symptoms (Lather, Vasudeva, and Verma, 1997; Sigurdsson and Gudjonsson, 1995). It is difficult, however, to know precisely what these findings implicate. Correlation is not causation, and once illicit substance abuse becomes an established pattern the abuser, by necessity, falls into a behavioral pattern that may partially explain the psychometric scale elevations indicative of the personality issues.

First, the PAI (Morey, 1991) has been touted as having psychometric advantages over other instruments (Rogers et al., 1993). Fals-Stewart (1996) described that the PAI items can be answered on a four-point Likert format (e.g., very true, mostly true, slightly true, and false), which offers quantitative response variability as opposed to the more limited dichotomous (i.e., true or false) scale that is most commonly used. Second, the PAI scales do not share items like the MMPI-2 and the MCMI-III. The argument is that this affords more discriminative validity to the PAI. The PAI has two scales relevant to substance-abuse deception—alcohol problems (ALC) and drug problems (DRG). The PAI also has a potentially useful validity scale—the positive impression scale (PIM)—that is designed to detect the degree of positive impression management by Ss. Fals-Stewart (1996) observed that unlike the nonobvious items on the MMPI-2 and the MCMI-III drug and alcohol subscales, the PAI subscale items were all obviously related to substance-abuse issues. This same issue with obvious subscale items was also the case with the popular Michigan Alcoholism Screening Test (MAST) (Selzer, 1971). The implication is that the PAI and the MAST may be useful in settings where substance-abusing patients are motivated to seek help and whose credibility can be generally assumed. When credibility cannot be assumed, these instruments will have clear limitations. The original PAI normative data (Morey, 1991) was derived exclusively with self-identified substance abusers, and this is another significant limitation of the instrument.

Parker, Daleiden, and Simpson (1999) compared the PAI to the Addiction Severity Index (ASI; McLellan, Kushner, Metzger, and Peters, 1992), a semistructured interview, with 103 male veterans who were being treated to chemical dependence. The ALC and DRG scales of the PAI demonstrated convergent validity with the ASI and substance-abuse diagnosis. The ALC was superior to the DRG regarding discriminant validity.

Fals-Stewart (1996) investigated the use of the PAI with substance abusers. One treatment group was asked to respond honestly ($n = 59$), another group was instructed to respond defensively ($n = 59$), a third group was a nonclinical control group ($n = 59$), and a fourth group was referred by the criminal justice system ($n = 59$). The findings indicated that the PAI validity scales (DRG and ALC) designed to measure positive dissimulation were prone to making false-positive and false-negative errors depending on the cut-off utilized. The author concluded that the findings were expected, given the high face validity of the content of the subscale items. The foregoing findings warrant extreme caution when utilizing the PAI with substance abusers when there is any question of deception potential.

In a follow-up study, a similar experimental paradigm (Fals-Stewart, 1996) utilized a classification analysis (i.e., a method similar to discriminant function analysis). An optimally weighted multivariate combination of the DRG, ALC, and PIM was developed to classify more accurately the experimental groups. This analysis resulted in an 82% correct identification of the groups. A third cross-validation study (Fals-Stewart and Lucent, 1997) replicated the design and used two separate sample groups in order to reduce validity shrinkage (i.e., caused by sampling bias and random variability by not using an independent comparative sample). In this study, the overall accuracy of the PAI subscales differentiating the experimental groups fell to 68%. The study did identify <80% of the substance abusers with standard instructions (i.e., with Ss in treatment and motivated to not dissimulate). Once again, the findings underscored the difficulties of second-guessing the response of forensic populations who are presumably motivated to dissimulate both in actual forensic application and in empirical studies. In both instances, and assuming no independent source of verification (e.g., urinalysis), there is no way of knowing with this population when dissimulation is in effect.

The following criteria should be used for a diagnosis of substance abuse or dependence:

1. A history of maladaptive behavior and substance abuse as suggested by DSM-IV-TR criteria, and evidenced by cross-validating sources to include:
   a. Significant/knowledgeable others
   b. Medical/psychological records of evaluation or treatment
   c. Criminal history data involving maladaptive behavior associated with substance abuse
   d. Prior and preferably concurrent urinalysis records
2. Psychological test scales if accompanied by a, b, or c
3. Admission of substance use if accompanied by a, b, or c
4. Withdrawal symptoms if accompanied by (1) or (2)

Summary

This chapter has explored deception-related issues relevant to neuropsychological deficiencies, psychosis, and substance abuse in criminal settings and situations. To assist the readership, an applied model of deception analysis is proposed which systematically scrutinizes the targets of the faker, response styles employed, and deception-detecting measures utilized. Research in deception and deception detecting has proliferated in the last decade, resulting in a substantial revision of the clinical forensic lore and heretofore acceptable practice. A core finding across applied forensic research is that a deception analysis must be an integral part of every case analysis. Failure to conduct a deception analysis results in accepting information as true without corroboration or cross-validation and renders, in our opinion, the evaluation itself as fatally flawed. Research in this fascinating area is strongly encouraged.

References

Adetunji, B. A., Basil, B., Mathews, M., Williams, A., Osinowo, T., and Oladinni, O. (2006). Detection and management of malingering in a clinical setting. *Primary Psychiatry, 13(1),* 61–69.

Alban, A. D. (2003). *Neuropsychological malingering and cognitive load: Disrupting deception of neuropsychological measures through cognitive overload.* (Doctoral dissertation, www.il. proquest.com/umi.) Dissertation Abstracts International: Section B: The Sciences and Engineering, *63(9-B),* 4358.

Anderson, K. (1989). Personal communication.

Andreas, B. G. (1960). *Experimental psychology.* Oxford, England: John Wiley.

Armor, D. J., Polich, J. M., and Stanbul, H. B. (1976). *Alcoholism and treatment.* Santa Monica, CA: Rand Corporation.

Atlas, R. (1982). Crime site selection for assaults in four Florida prisons. *Man-Environment Systems, 12,* 59–66.

Back, C., Boone, K. B., Edwards, C., Parks, C., Burgoyne, K., and Silver, B. (1996). The performance of schizophrenics on three cognitive tests, 15-Item Memory Test, Rey Dot Counting, and Hiscock Forced-Choice Method. *Assessment, 3(4),* 449–457.

Bagby, R. M., Marshall, M. B., and Bacchiochi, J. R. (2005). The validity and clinical utility of the MMPI-2 malingering depression scale. *Journal of Personality Assessment, 85(3),* 304–311.

Bagby, R. M., Marshall, M. B., Bury, A. S., Bacchiochi, J. R., and Miller, L. S. (2006). Assessing underreporting and overreporting response styles on the MMPI-2. In J. N. Butcher (Ed.), *MMPI-2: A practitioner's guide.* (pp. 39–69). Washington, DC: American Psychological Association [URL:http://www.apa.org/books].

Bagby, R. M., Rogers, R., Nicholson, R. A., Buis, T., Seeman, M. V., and Rector, N. (1997a). Does clinical training facilitate feigning schizophrenia on the MMPI-2? *Psychological Assessment, 9(2),* 106–112.

Bagby, R. M., Rogers, R., Nicholson, R. A., Cameron, S. L., Rector, N. A., Schuller, D. R., and Seeman, M. V. (1997b). Detecting feigned depression and schizophrenia on the MMPI-2. *Journal of Personality Assessment, 68(3),* 650–664.

Bailey, M. B. (1961). Alcoholism and marriage: A review of research and professional literature. *Quarterly Journal of Studies on Alcohol, 22,* 81–97.

Bash, I. (1978). Malingering: A study designed to differentiate between schizophrenic offenders and malingerers. Unpublished doctoral dissertation. New York University, New York.

Bash, I., and Alpert, M. (1980). The determination of malingering. *Annals of the New York Academy of Science, 347,* 86–98.

Bauer, L., and McCaffrey, R. J. (2006). Coverage of the test of memory malingering, Victoria symptom validity test, and word memory test on the internet: Is test security threatened? *Archives of Clinical Neuropsychology, 21(1),* 121–126.

Beaber, R., Marston, A., Michelli, J., and Mills, M. (1985). A brief test for measuring malingering in schizophrenic individuals. *American Journal of Psychiatry, 142,* 1478–1481.

Bean, M. H. (1981). Denial and the psychological complications of alcoholism. In M. H. Bean and N. E. Zinberg (Eds.), *Dynamic approaches to the understanding and treatment of alcoholism* (pp. 55–96). New York: The Free Press.

Ben-Porath, Y. S. (1994). The ethical dilemma of coached malingering research. *Psychological Assessment, 6(1)*, 14–15.

Berry, D., Baer, R., and Harris, M. (1991). Detection of malingering on the MMPI: A meta-analysis. *Clinical Psychology Review, 11*, 585–598.

Blanchard, D. D. (2001). A comparison of the MMPI-2 and PAI as predictors of faking bad. (Doctoral dissertation, www.il.proquest.com/umi.) Dissertation Abstracts International: Section B: The Sciences and Engineering, *61(7-B)*, 3831.

Blanchard, D. D., McGrath, R. E., Pogge, D. L., and Khadivi, A. (2003). A comparison of the PAI and MMPI-2 as predictors of faking bad in college students. *Journal of Personality Assessment, 80(2)*, 197–205.

Blane, H. J. (1968). *The personality of the alcoholic: Guises of dependency.* New York: Harper & Row.

Bonczar, T. P. (1997). *Characteristics of adults on probation, 1995* (U.S. Department of Justice, NCJ-164267). Washington, DC: Office of Justice Programs.

Borckardt, J. J., Engum, E. S., Lambert, E. W., Nash, M., Bracy, O. L., and Ray, E. C. (2003). Use of the CBDI to detect malingering when malingerers do their "homework." *Archives of Clinical Neuropsychology, 18(1)*, 57–69.

Braginsky, B., and Braginsky, D. (1967). Schizophrenic patients in the psychiatric interview: An experimental study of their effectiveness at manipulation. *Journal of Consulting Psychology, 31*, 543–547.

Butcher, J. N. (1990). *User's guide to the Minnesota clinical interpretive report for MMPI-2.* Minneapolis, MN: University of Minnesota Press.

Butcher, J. N. (2006). *MMPI-2: A practitioner's guide.* Washington, DC: American Psychological Association.

Chait, L. D., and Perry, J. L. (1992). Factors influencing self-administration of, and subjective response to, placebo marijuana. *Behavioural Pharmacology, 3(6)*, 545–552.

Chait, L. D., and Perry, J. L. (1994). Effects of alcohol pretreatment on human marijuana self-administration. *Psychopharmacology, 113(3–4)*, 346–350.

Cima, M., Hollnack, S., Kremer, K., Knauer, E., Schellbach-Matties, R., and Klein, B. et al. (2003). The German version of the structured inventory of malingered symptomatology/ "Strukturierter Fragebogen Simulierter Symptome": Die deutsche Version des "Structured Inventory of Malingered Symptomatology: SIMS." *Nervenarzt, 74(11)*, 977–986.

Craig, R. J. (2005). Assessing contemporary substance abusers with the MMPI MacAndrews Alcoholism Scale: A review. *Substance Use and Misuse, 40(4)*, 427–450.

Craine, J. (1990a). Minimizing and denying: A testing approach to feigned amnesia. In *Truth or lies: Guidelines for detecting malingering and deception.* Workshop by Psychological Consultants and Forest Institute of Professional Psychology, Honolulu, Hawaii.

Diamond, B. (1956). The simulation of insanity. *Journal of Social Therapy, 2*, 158–165.

Doty, R. L. (1991). Personal communication. University of Pennsylvania Smell and Taste Center, Philadelphia, PA.

Doty, R. L., Shaman, P. S. and Dann, M. (1984a). Development of the University of Pennsylvania Smell Identification Test: A standardized microencapsulated test of olfactory function. *Physiology & Behavior, 32*, 489–502.

Doty, R. L., Shaman, P. S., Kimmelman, C. P. (1984b). University of Pennsylvania Smell Identification Test: A rapid quantitative olfactory function test for the clinic. *Laryngoscope, 94*, 176–178.

Dunn, T. M., Shear, P. K., Howe, S., and Ris, M. D. (2003). Detecting neuropsychological malingering: Effects of coaching and information. *Archives of Clinical Neuropsychology, 18(2)*, 121–134.

Endicott, J., and Spitzer, R. L. (1978). A diagnostic interview: The schedule of affective disorders and schizophrenia. *Archives of General Psychiatry, 35*, 837–844.

Fals-Stewart, W. (1996). The ability of individuals with psychoactive substance abuse disorders to escape detection by the Personality Assessment Inventory. *Psychological Assessment, 8*, 60–68.

Fals-Stewart, W. (2005). Substance use disorders. In J. E. Maddux, and B. A. Winstead (Eds.), *Psychopathology: Foundations for a contemporary understanding* (pp. 301–324). Mahwah, NJ: Lawrence Erlbaum Associates.

Fals-Stewart, W., and Lucente, S. (1997). Identifying positive dissimulation by substance-abusing individuals on the Personality Assessment Inventory: A cross-validation study. *Journal of Personality Assessment, 68(2),* 455–469.

Fauteck, P. K. (1995). Detecting the malingering of psychosis in offenders: No easy solutions. *Criminal Justice & Behavior, 22(1),* 3–18.

Fox, D. D., Lees-Haley, P. R., Earnest, K., and Dolezal-Wood, S. (1995). Base rates of postconcussive symptoms in health maintenance organization patients and controls. *Neuropsychology, 9(4),* 606–611.

Frederick, R. I. (1997). *Validity Indicator Profile Manual.* Minnetonka, MN: NCS Assessments.

Frederick, R. I., and Crosby, R. D. (2000). Development and validation of the Validity Indicator Profile. *Law and Human Behavior, 24(1),* 59–82.

Freedland, K., and Craine, J. (1981). Personal communication.

Ganellen, R. J., Wasyliw, O. E., Haywood, T. W., and Grossman, L. S. (1996). Can psychosis be malingered on the Rorschach? An empirical study. *Journal of Personality Assessment, 66(1),* 65–80.

Gillis, J. R., Rogers, R., and Bagby, R. M. (1991). Validity of the M test: Simulation-design and natural-group approaches. *Journal of Personality Assessment, 57(1),* 130–140.

Goldstein, R. L. (1992). Dr Rogers' "insanity detector" and the admissibility of novel scientific evidence. *Medicine & Law, 11(5–6),* 441–447.

Goodness, K. R. (2000). Retrospective evaluation of malingering: A validational study of the R-SIRS and CT-SIRS. (Doctoral dissertation, www.il.proquest.com/umi.) Dissertation Abstracts International: Section B: The Sciences and Engineering, 60(9-B), 4888.

Gottesman, I., and Prescott, C. (1989). Abuses of the MacAndrew MMPI Alcoholism Scale: A critical review. *Clinical Psychology Review, 9,* 223–242.

Gould R., Miller, B., Goldberg, M., and Benson, D. (1986). The validity of hysterical signs and symptoms. *Journal of Nervous and Mental Diseases, 174,* 593–597.

Granhag, P. A., and Stromwall, L. (2004). The detection of deception in forensic contexts. Cambridge, UK: Cambridge University Press.

Greene, C. (2005). A direct comparison of the MMPI-2 and the PAI in the detection of malingering. (Doctoral dissertation, www.il.proquest.com/umi.) Dissertation Abstracts International: Section B: The Sciences and Engineering, 65(8-B), 4285.

Grosz, H., and Zimmerman, J. (1965). Experimental analysis of hysterical blindness: A follow-up report and new experiment data. *Archives of General Psychiatry, 13,* 255–260.

Hall, H. V. (1982). Dangerous predictions and the maligned forensic professional: Suggestions for detecting distortion of true basal violence. *Criminal Justice and Behavior, 9,* 3–12.

Hall, H. V. (1985). Cognitive and volitional capacity assessment: A proposed decision tree. *American Journal of Forensic Psychology, 3,* 3–17.

Hall, H. V. (1987). *Violence prediction: Guidelines for the forensic practitioner.* Springfield, IL: Charles C Thomas.

Hall, H. V., and Poirier, J. G. (2001). *Detecting malingering and deception: Forensic distortion analysis.* (2nd ed.). Boca Raton, FL: CRC Press.

Hall, H. V., and Shooter, E. A. (1989). Explicit Alternative Testing for feigned memory deficits. *Forensic Reports, 2,* 277–286.

Hall, H. V., Shooter, E. A., Craine, J., and Paulsen, S. (1991). Explicit Alternative Testing: A trilogy of studies on faked memory deficits. *Forensic Reports, 4(3),* 259–279.

Hall, H. V., and Thompson, J. (2007). Explicit Alternative Testing (EAT): Application of the binomial probability distribution in clinical-forensic evaluations. *The Forensic Examiner, 16,* 38–43.

Hart, K. (1995). The assessment of malingering in neuropsychological evaluations: Research-based concepts and methods for consultants. *Consulting Psychology Journal: Practice and Research, 47(4),* 246–254.

Haughton, P. M, Lewsley, A., Wilson, M., and Williams, R. G. (1979). A forced-choice procedure to detect feigned or exaggerated hearing loss. *British Journal of Audiology, 13,* 135–138.

Hayes, J. S., Hale, D. B., and Gouvier, W. D. (1998). Malingering detection in a mentally retarded forensic population. *Applied Neuropsychology, 5(1),* 33–36.

Hellerstein, D., Frosch, W., and Koenigsberg, H. (1987). The clinical significance of command hallucinations. *American Journal of Psychiatry, 144,* 219–221.

Jelicic, M., Hessels, A., and Merckelbach, H. (2006). Detection of feigned psychosis with the Structured Inventory of Malingered Symptomatology (SIMS): A study of coached and uncoached simulators. *Journal of Psychopathology and Behavioral Assessment, 28(1),* 19–22.

Jellinek, E. M. (1952). Phases of alcohol addiction. *Quarterly Journal of Studies on Alcohol, 13,* 673–684.

Jellinek, E. M. (1980). *The disease concept of alcoholism.* New Haven: College and University Press.

Kasper, M. E., Rogers, R., and Adams, P. A. (1996). Dangerousness and command hallucinations: An investigation of psychotic inpatients. *Bulletin of the American Academy of Psychiatry & The Law, 24(2),* 219–224.

Lally, S. (2003). What tests are acceptable for use in forensic evaluations? A survey of experts. *Professional Psychology Research and Practice, 34(5),* 491–498.

Lamb, D. G., Berry, D. T. R., Wetter, M. W., and Baer, R. A. (1994). Effects of two types of information on malingering of closed head injury on the MMPI-2: An analog investigation. *Psychological Assessment, 6(1),* 8–13.

Language Research Association (1958). *The Auditory Discrimination Test.* Chicago, IL: Author.

Lather, A., Vasudeva, P., and Verma, P. (1997). A study of drug abuse among students as related to personality variables. *Journal of the Indian Academy of Applied Psychology, 23(1–2),* 43–49.

Lees-Haley, P. R., Dunn, J. T., and Betz, B. P. (1999). Test review: The Victoria Symptom Validity Test. *American Psychology-Law Society Newsletter, 19(3),* 12–16.

Lewis, J. L. (2001). Detection of malingering in a forensic population: The utility of the SIMS. (Doctoral dissertation, www.il.proquest.com/umi.) Dissertation Abstracts International: Section B: The Sciences and Engineering, *61(11-B),* 6140.

Lewis, D. O., and Bard, J. S. (1991). Multiple personality disorders and forensic issues. *Psychiatric Clinics of North America, 14(3),* 741–756.

Lezak, M. (1995). *Neuropsychological assessment* (3rd ed.). New York: Oxford University Press.

Liff, C. D. A. (2004). *The detection of neuropsychological malingering.* (Doctoral dissertation, www.il.proquest.com/umi.) Dissertation Abstracts International: Section B: The Sciences and Engineering, *64(9-B),* 4623.

Loring, D. W., Lee, G. P., and Meador, K. J. (2005). Victoria Symptom Validity Test performance in non-litigating epilepsy surgery candidates. *Journal of Clinical and Experimental Neuropsychology, 27(5),* 610–617.

MacAndrew, C. (1965). The differentiation of male alcoholic outpatients from nonalcoholic psychiatric outpatients by means of the MMPI. *Quarterly Journal of Studies on Alcohol, 26,* 238–246.

McKinzey, R. K., Prieler, J., and Raven, J. (2003). Detection of children's malingering on Raven's Standard Progressive Matrices. *British Journal of Clinical Psychology, 42(1),* 95–99.

McLellan, A. T., Kushner, H., Metzger, D., and Peters, R. (1992). The fifth edition of the Addiction Severity Index. *Journal of Substance Abuse Treatment, 9(3),* 199–213.

Melville, J. D., and Naimark, D. (2002). Punishing the insane: The verdict of guilty but mentally ill. *Journal of the American Academy of Psychiatry and the Law, 30(4),* 553–555.

Merckelbach, H., and Smith, G. P. (2003). Diagnostic accuracy of the Structured Inventory of Malingered Symptomatology (SIMS) in detecting instructed malingering. *Archives of Clinical Neuropsychology, 18(2),* 145–152.

Micucci, J. A. (2002). Accuracy of MMPI-A scales ACK, MAC-R, and PRO in detecting comorbid substance abuse among psychiatric inpatients. *Assessment, 9(2),* 111–122.

Millard, R. W. (1985). Application of Selected Measures for Detecting Neuropsychological Impairment Among Alcoholics. Unpublished doctoral dissertation, University of Hawaii, Manoa.

Miller H. B., and Paniak, C. E. (1995). MMPI and MMPI-2 profile and code type congruence in a brain-injured sample. *Journal of Clinical and Experimental Neuropsychology, 17(1),* 58–64.

Mittenberg, W., Hammeke, T., and Rao, S. (1989). Intrasubtest scatter on the WAIS-R as a pathognomonic sign of brain injury. *Psychological Assessment: A Journal of Consulting and Clinical Psychology, 1,* 273–276.

Mittenberg, W., Theroux-Fichera, S., Zielinski, R. E., and Heilbronner, R. L. (1995). Identification of malingered head injury on the Wechsler Adult Intelligence Scale-Revised. *Professional Psychology: Research and Practice, 26(5),* 491–498.

Mittenberg, W., Tremont, G., and Rayls, K. R. (1996). Impact of cognitive function on MMPI-2 validity in neurologically impaired patients. *Assessment, 3(2),* 157–163.

Morey, L. C. (1991). *Personality assessment inventory: Professional manual.* Tampa, FL: Psychological Assessment Resources.

Morey, L. C. (2003). *Essentials of PAI assessment.* Hoboken, NJ: John Wiley & Sons.

Morey, L. C. (2004). The personality assessment inventory (PAI). In M. E. Maruish (Ed.), *The use of psychological testing for treatment planning and outcomes assessment: Volume 3: Instruments for adults* (3rd ed.). (pp. 509–551). Mahwah, NJ: Lawrence Erlbaum Associates.

Morey, L. C., and Boggs, C. D. (2004). The personality assessment inventory (PAI). In M. J. Hilsenroth, and D. L. Segal (Eds.), *Comprehensive handbook of psychological assessment, vol. 2: Personality assessment* (pp. 15–29). Hoboken, NJ: John Wiley & Sons.

Morey, L. C., and Quigley, B. D. (2002). The use of the personality assessment inventory (PAI) in assessing offenders. *International Journal of Offender Therapy and Comparative Criminology, 46(3),* 333–349.

Mulhaney, J. A., and Trippett, C. J. (1979). Alcohol dependence and phobias: Clinical description and relevance. *British Journal of Psychiatry, 135,* 565–573.

Mumola, C. J. (1999). *Substance abuse and treatment, state and federal prisoners, 1997* (U.S. Department of Justice No. NCJ 172871). Washington, DC: Office of Justice Programs.

Nace, E. P. (1982). The role of craving in the treatment of alcoholism. *National Association of Private Psychiatric Hospitals Journal, 13(1),* 27–31.

Nace, E. P. (1987). *The treatment of alcoholism.* New York: Brunner-Mazel.

Norris, M. P., and May, M. C. (1998). Screening for malingering in a correctional setting. *Law & Human Behavior, 22(3),* 315–323.

O'Leary, U., Rusch, K., and Guastello, S. (1991). Estimating age-stratified WAIS-R Iws from scores on the Ravess Standard Progressive Matrices. *Journal of Clinical Psychology, 47(2),* 277–284.

O'Neil, J., Wish, E., and Visher, C. (1990). *Drug use forecasting: July to September 1989.* Rockville, MD: National Institute of Justice.

Osran, H. C., and Weinberger, L. E. (1994). Personality disorders and "restoration to sanity." *Bulletin of the American Academy of Psychiatry & the Law, 22(2),* 257–267.

Palmer, C. A., and Hazelrigg, M. (2000). The guilty but mentally ill verdict: A review and conceptual analysis of intent and impact. *Journal of the American Academy of Psychiatry and the Law, 28(1),* 47–54.

Pankratz, L. (1979). Symptom validity testing and symptom retraining: Procedures for the assessment and treatment of functional sensory deficits. *Journal of Consulting and Clinical Psychology, 47,* 409–410.

Pankratz, L. (1983). A new technique for the assessment and modification of feigned memory deficits. *Perceptual and Motor Skills, 57,* 367–372.

Pankratz, L. (1988). Malingering on intellectual and neuropsychological measures. In R. Rogers (Ed.), *Clinical assessment of malingering and deception* (pp. 169–192). New York: Guilford Press.

Pankratz, L., Fausti, S. A., and Peed, S. (1975). A forced-choice technique to evaluate deafness in a hysterical or malingering patient. *Journal of Consulting and Clinical Psychology, 43,* 421–422.

Paolino, T., and McCrady, B. (1977). *The alcoholic marriage: Alternative perspectives.* New York: Grune & Stratton.

Parker, J. D., Daleiden, E. L., and Simpson, C. A. (1999). Personality assessment inventory substance-use scales: Convergent and discriminant relations with the addiction severity index in a residential chemical dependence treatment setting. *Psychological Assessment, 11(4),* 507–513.

Pekarik, G., Jones, D. L., and Blodgett, C. (1986). Personality and demographic characteristics of dropouts and completers in a nonhospital residential alcohol treatment program. *International Journal of Addiction, 21,* 131–137.

Pensa, R., Dorfman, W. I., Gold, S. N., and Schneider, B. (1996). Detection of malingered psychosis with the MMPI-2. *Psychotherapy in Private Practice, 14(4),* 47–64.

Pollock, P. (1998). Feigning auditory hallucinations by offenders. *Journal of Forensic Psychiatry, 9(2),* 305–327.

Pope, K. S., Butcher, J. N., and Seelen, J. (1993). *The MMPI, MMPI-2, & MMPI-A in court: A practical guide for expert witnesses and attorneys.* Washington, DC: APA.

Pope, K. S., Butcher, J. N., and Seelen, J. (2000). *The MMPI, MMPI-2, & MMPI-A in court: A practical guide for expert witnesses and attorneys* (2nd ed.). Washington, DC: APA.

Pope, H. G., Jonas, J. M., and Jones, B. (1982). Factitious psychosis: Phenomenology, family history, and long-term outcome of nine patients. *The American Journal of Psychiatry, 139(11),* 1480–1483.

Poythress, N. G., Edens, J. F., and Watkins, M. M. (2001). The relationship between psychopathic personality features and malingering symptoms of major mental illness. *Law and Human Behavior, 25(6),* 567–582.

Resnick, P. J. (1984). The detection of malingered mental illness. *Behavioral Sciences and the Law, 2(1),* 21–38.

Resnick, P. J. (1988). Malingered psychosis. In R. Rogers (Ed.), *Clinical assessment of malingering and deception* (Chapter 3). New York: Guilford Press.

Resnick, P. J. (1993). Defrocking the fraud: The detection of malingering. *Israel Journal of Psychiatry & Related Sciences, 30(2),* 93–101.

Resnick, P. J. (1997). Malingered psychosis. In R. Rogers (Ed.), *Clinical assessment of malingering and deception* (2nd ed.) (pp. 47–67). New York: Guilford Press.

Resnick. P. J. (1999). The detection of malingered psychosis. *Psychiatric Clinics of North America, 22(1),* 159–172.

Rey, A. (1964). *L'examen clinique en psychologie [The clinical examination in psychology].* Paris: Presse Universitaires de France.

Ritson, B., and Forrest, A. (1970). The simulation of psychosis: A contemporary presentation. *British Journal of Medical Psychology, 43,* 31–37.

Rogers, R. (1984a). Towards an empirical model of malingering and deception. *Behavioral Sciences and the Law, 2,* 93–112.

Rogers, R. (1984b). *RCRAS: Rogers Criminal Responsibility Assessment Scales.* Odessa, FL: Psychological Assessment Resources, Inc.

Rogers, R. (1987). The assessment of malingering within a forensic context. In D. N. Weisstub (Ed.), *Law and psychiatry: International perspectives (Vol. 3).* New York: Plenum.

Rogers, R. (1988). *Clinical assessment of malingering and deception.* New York: Guilford Press.

Rogers, R. (1992). *Structured Interview of Reported Symptoms (SIRS).* Odessa, FL: Psychological Assessment Resources.

Rogers, R. (1997). *Clinical assessment of malingering and deception.* New York: The Guilford Press.

Rogers, R., Bagby, R. M., and Gillis, J. R. (1992). Improvements in the M test as a screening measure for malingering. *Bulletin of the American Academy of Psychiatry & the Law, 20(1),* 101–104.

Rogers, R., and Cavanaugh, J. (1981). The Rogers Criminal Responsibility Assessment Scales. *Illinois Medical Journal, 160(3),* 164–166.

Rogers, R., Dolmetsch, R., and Cavanaugh, J. L. (1981). An empirical approach to insanity evalua- tions. *Journal of Clinical Psychology, 37(3)*, 683–687.

Rogers, R., and Ewing, C. P. (1992). The measurement of insanity: Debating the merits of the R- CRAS and its alternatives. *International Journal of Law & Psychiatry, 15(1)*, 113–123.

Rogers. R., Gillis, J. R., and Bagby, R. M. (1990). The SIRS as a measure of malingering: A validation study with a correctional sample. *Behavioral Sciences & The Law, 8(1)*, 85–92.

Rogers, R., Gillis, J. R., Bagby, R. M., and Monteiro, E. (1991a). Detection of malingering on the Structured Interview of Reported Symptoms (SIRS): A study of coached and uncoached simulators. *Psychological Assessment, 3(4)*, 673–677.

Rogers, R., Gillis, J. R., Dickens, S. E., and Bagby, R. M. (1991b). Standardized assessment of malingering: Validation of the Structured Interview of Reported Symptoms (SIRS). *Psychological Assessment, 3(1)*, 89–96.

Rogers, R., and Kelly, K. S. (1997) Denial and misreporting of substance abuse. In R. Rogers (Ed.), *Clinical assessment of malingering and deception* (pp. 108–129). New York: Guilford Press.

Rogers, R., Kropp, P. R., Bagby, R. M., and Dickens, S. E. (1992). Faking specific disorders: A study of the structured interview of reported symptoms (SIRS). *Journal of Clinical Psychology, 48(5)*, 643–648.

Rogers, R., Ornduff, S. R., and Sewell, K. W. (1993). Feigning specific disorders: A study of the personality assessment inventory. *Journal of Personality Assessment, 60(3)*, 554–560.

Rogers, R., Seman, W., and Clark, C. R. (1986). Assessment of criminal responsibility: Initial validation of the R-CRAS with the M'naghten and GBMI standards. *International Journal of Law and Psychiatry, 9(1)*, 67–75.

Rogers, R., Seman, W., and Wasyliw, O. (1983). The RCRAS and legal insanity: A cross-validation study. *Journal of Clinical Psychology, 39*, 554–559.

Rogers, R., and Sewell, K. W. (1999). The R-CRAS and insanity evaluations: A re-examination of construct validity. *Behavioral Sciences & The Law, 17(2)*, 181–194.

Rogers, R., Sewell, K. W., Morey, L. C., and Ustad, K. L. (1996). Detection of feigned mental disorders on the personality assessment inventory: A discriminant analysis. *Journal of Per- sonality Assessment, 67(3)*, 629–640.

Rohsenow, D. J., Erickson, R. C. and O'Leary, M. R. (1978). The defense mechanism inventory and alcoholics. *International Journal of Addictions, 13*, 403–414.

Rohsenow, D. J. and O'Leary, M. R. (1978). Locus of control research on alcoholic populations: A review. *International Journal of Addictions, 13*, 231–236.

Roman, D. T., Tuley, M. R., Villanueva, M. R., and Mitchell, W. E. (1990). Evaluating MMPI validity in a forensic psychiatric population: Distinguishing between malingering and genu- ine psychopathology. *Criminal Justice & Behavior, 17(2)*, 186–198.

Rutherford, M. J., Cacciola, J. S., and Alterman, A. I. (1999). Antisocial personality disorder and psychopathy in cocaine-dependent women. *The American Journal of Psychiatry, 156(6)*, 849–856.

Schlesinger, L. B. (1996). *Explorations in criminal psychopathology: Clinical syndromes with forensic implications*. Springfield, IL: Charles C Thomas.

Schretlen, D. (1988). The use of psychological tests to identify malingered symptoms of mental disorder. *Clinical Psychology Review, 8(5)*, 451–476.

Schretlen, D., Wilkins, S., Van Gorp, W., and Bobholz, J. (1992). Cross-validation of a psychological test battery to detect faked insanity. *Psychological Assessment, 4(1)*, 77–83.

Schwartz, M. L. (1991). Sometimes safe, sometimes out: Umpire gives split decision. *Clinical Neuropsychologist, 5(1)*, 89–99.

Selzer, M. L. (1971). The Michigan Alcoholism Screening Test: The quest for a new diagnostic instrument. *American Journal of Psychiatry, 127*, 89–94.

Shapiro, D. (1999). *Criminal responsibility evaluations: A manual for practice*. Sarasota, FL: Profes- sional Resource Press.

Shooter, E., and Hall, H. V. (1989). Distortion analysis on the MMPI and MMPI-2. *Bulletin of the American Academy of Forensic Psychology, 10*, 9.

Sigurdsson, J. F., and Gudjonsson, G. H. (1995). Personality characteristics of drug-dependent offenders. *Nordic Journal of Psychiatry, 49(1)*, 33–38.

Sivec, H. J., Lynn, S. J., and Garske, J. P. (1994). The effect of somatoform disorder and paranoid psychotic role-related dissimulations as a response set on the MMPI-2. *Assessment, 1(1)*, 69–81.

Slick, D. J., Hopp, G. Strauss, E., and Spellacy, F. J. (1996). Victoria Symptom Validity Test: Efficiency for detecting feigned memory impairment and relationship to neuropsychological tests and MMPI-2 validity scales. *Journal of Clinical and Experimental Neuropsychology, 18(6)*, 911–922.

Slick, D. J., Hopp, G., Strauss, E., and Thompson, G. B. (1997). *Victoria Symptom Validity Test, Version 1.0., Professional Manual*, Odessa, FL: Professional Resource Press.

Slick, D. J., Tan, J. E., Strauss, E., Mateer, C. A., Harnadek, M., and Sherman, E. M. S. (2003). Victoria Symptom Validity Test scores of patients with profound memory impairment: Nonlitigant case studies. *Clinical Neuropsychologist, 17(3)*, 390–394.

Slovenko, R. (1973). *Psychiatry and the law*. Boston, MA: Little, Brown & Co.

Smith, G. P., and Borum, R. (1992). Detection of malingering in a forensic sample: A study of the M test. *Journal of Psychiatry & Law, 20(4)*, 505–514.

Smith, G. P., Borum, R., and Schinka, J. A. (1993). Rule-out and rule-in scales for the M test for malingering: A cross-validation. *Bulletin of the American Academy of Psychiatry & the Law, 21(1)*, 107–110.

Smith, G. P., and Burger, G. K. (1997). Detection of malingering: Validation of the Structured Inventory of Malingered Symptomatology (SIMS). *Journal of the American Academy of Psychiatry & the Law, 25(2)*, 183–189.

Sobell, L. C., Toneatto, T., and Sobell, M. B. (1994). Behavioral assessment and treatment planning for alcohol, tobacco, and other drug problems: Current status with an emphasis on clinical applications. *Behavior Therapy, 25*, 533–580.

Spitzer, R. L., and Endicott, J. (1978). *Schedule of affective disorders and schizophrenia*. New York: Biometric Research.

Steadman, H., Silver, E., Monahan, J., Appelbaum, P. S., Robbins, P. C., Mulvey, E. P., Grisso, T, Roth, L., and Banks, S. (2000). A classification tree approach development of actuarial violence risk assessment tools. *Law and Human Behavior, 24(1)*, 83–100.

Story, D. L. (2001). Validation of a short form of the structured interview of reported symptoms (SIRS). (Doctoral dissertation, www.il.proquest.com/umi.) Dissertation Abstracts International: Section B: The Sciences and Engineering, *61(9-B)*, 5049.

Theodor, L. H., and Mandelcorn, M. S. (1973). Hysterical blindness: A case report and study using a modern psychophysical technique. *Journal of Abnormal Psychology, 82*, 552–553.

Tirrell, C. A. (2005). *Concurrent validity of the MMPI-A substance abuse scales: MAC-R, ACK, and PRO*. (Doctoral dissertation, www.il.proquest.com/umi.) Dissertation Abstracts International: Section B: The Sciences and Engineering, *65(9-B)*, 4893.

Vickery, C. D., Berry, D. T. R., Hanlon Inman, T., Harris, M. J., and Orey, S. A. (2001). Detection of inadequate effort on neuropsychological testing: A meta-analytic review of selected procedures. *Archives of Clinical Neuropsychology, 16(1)*, 45–73.

Wasyliw, O., Grossman, L., Haywood, T., and Cavanaugh, J. (1990). *Is the MacAndrew Alcoholism Scale related to response-bias: A forensic study*. Presented at the American Psychological Association, Boston, Massachusetts.

Weiss, J., and Schell, R. (1991). Estimating WAIS-R IQ from the Shipley Institute of Living Scale: A replication. *Journal of Clinical Psychology, 47(4)*, 558–562.

Wetter, M. A., Baer, R. A., Berry, D. T. R., Robison, L. H., and Sumptor, J. (1993). MMPI-2 profiles of motivated fakers given specific symptom information: A comparison of matched patients. *Psychological Assessment, 5(3)*, 317–323.

Wilshire, D., Kinsella, G., and Pryor, M. (1991). Estimating WAIS-R IQ from the National Adult Reading Test: A cross-validation. *Journal of Clinical and Experimental Neuropsychology, 13(2),* 204–216.

Witztum, E., Grinshpoon, A., Margolin, J., and Kron, S. (1996). The erroneous diagnosis of malingering in a military setting. *Military Medicine, 161(4),* 225–229.

Zachry, R. (1986). *Manual for Shipley Institute of Living Scale.* Los Angeles, CA: Western Psychological Services.

Zielinski, J. J. (1995). Malingering and defensiveness in the neuropsychological assessment of mild traumatic brain injury. *Clinical Psychology: Science and Practice, 1(2),* 169–184.

Suggested List of Relevant Legal Cases

Barefoot v. Estelle, 463 U.S. 880 (1983).

Buckler v. Sinclair Ref. Co., 68 Ill.App.2d 283, 216 N.E.2d 14 (1966).

Cohn v. State, 849 S. W.2d 817 (Tex. Crim. App. 1993).

Daubert v. Merrell Dow Pharmaceuticals, Inc., 509 U.S. 579 125 L Ed 469 113 S. Ct. 2786 (1993).

Ducket v. State, 797 S. W.2d 906 (Tex. Crim, App. 1990).

Estelle v. Smith, 404 U.S. 494 (1981).

Frye v. United States, D.C., 54 App D.C. 46, 293F. 1013 (1923).

Gregory G. Sarno, Annotation, Admissibility of Expert Testimony as to Criminal Defendant's Propensity toward Sexual Deviation, 42 A.L.R. 4th 937 (1985 & 1996 Supp.).

Hall v. State, Ark. App. 309, 692 S.W. 2d 769 (1985).

Jenkins v. United States, 307 F.2d 637, 651, 652 (D.C. Cir. 1961).

Maryland v. Craig, 110 S. Ct. 3157, 3169 (1990).

Pennell v. State Del., Supr., 602 A. 2d 48 (1991).

People v. Stoll, Cal. Supr,. 49 Cal. 3d 1136, 738 P 2d. 698, 265 Cal. Rptr. 111 (1989).

People v. Watkins, Mich. App., 176 Mich. App. 428, 440 N. W. 2d 36, 37 (1989).

Powell v. Texas, 57 U.S.L.W. 3857 (1989).

State v. Cavallo, N. J. Supr., 88 N.J. 508, 443 A.2d 1020, 1023 (1982).

State v. Clements, Kan. Supr. 770 P.2d 447 (1989).

State of Delaware v. Floray, 715 A.2d 855,*,1997 Del. Super. LEXIS 272.

State v. Maule, Wash. App., 15 Ark. App. 287, 667 P. 2d 96 (1983).

State v. Michaels, 642 A.2d 1372 (NJ 1994).

State v. Michaels, N. J. Super. App. Div., 264 N. J. Super. 579, 625 A. 2d 489, 508 (1993).

State v. Percy, Va. Supr. 146 Vt. 475, 507 A.2d 955 (1986).

State v. Screpesi, Del. Supr., 611 A.2d 34 (1991).

State v. Tucker, App., 165 Ariz. 340, 798 P.2d 1349 (1990).

Tarasoff v. Regents of the University of California (Cal. 1976) (551 P.2d. 334).

Turgate v. Commonwealth, Ky. Supr., 901 S. W. 2d 41 (1995).

United States v. Beyers, 740 F.2d 1104 (D. C. Cir. 1984) certiorari denied 104 S. Ct. 717, p. 465.

United States v. Powers, 4th Cir., 59F. 3rd 1460, 1470 (1995), cert. denied, 116 S. Ct. 784 (1996).

United States v. St. Pierre, 8th Cir., 812 F.2d 414, 420 (1987).

Utah v. Rimmasch, 775 P.2d 388, Sup. Ct. of Utah (May 17, 1989).

Wheeler v. U.S., 159 U.S. 523 (1895).

Williams v. State of Texas, 895 S. W.2d 363,*, 1994 Tex. Crim. App. LEXUS 135.

Assessment of Competence to Proceed in the Criminal Process

10

RANDY K. OTTO

University of South Florida, Tampa, Florida

RICHARD L. DeMIER

U.S. Medical Center for Federal Prisoners, Springfield, Missouri

Contents

Introduction

The requirement that defendants be able to assist in their defense and participate in criminal proceedings against them can be traced to at least fourteenth-century England, when common law prohibited prosecution of defendants whose abilities were impaired as a result of mental disorder or defect (Melton, Petrila, Poythress, and Slobogin, 1997). Following Grisso's (2003) recommended approach to forensic assessment in our discussion of evaluating criminal defendants' competence to proceed,* we begin with a review of the legal framework, followed by a discussion of the clinical assessment and report writing.

Legal Framework

Common Law Conceptions

As noted above, courts have long required that criminal defendants have the capacity to understand and participate in the legal process. This competence requirement serves multiple purposes. Requiring that defendants understand and have the capacity to participate in the criminal proceedings against them is essential to ensure the dignity and fairness of the criminal justice system. Trying defendants who are so impaired that they cannot assist in their defense, or who are unaware of the nature and purpose of the criminal proceedings against them, threatens the dignity of the legal process and is inconsistent with conceptions about fundamental fairness (Melton et al., 1997; Roesch, Zapf, Golding, and Skeem, 1999; Wulach, 1980).

Society's investment in accurate decision-making and just legal outcomes precludes active prosecution of defendants who cannot assist in preparation of a defense. A defendant's ability to provide information relevant to his or her defense and challenge the state's allegations may be compromised by an underlying mental disorder, which, in turn, can result in less accurate verdicts and outcomes. The law's recognition that it is ultimately the accused who must make decisions about important legal strategies and decisions (with the assistance of an attorney) also requires that criminal defendants have the capacity to do so.

Constitutional Contours

Only the legal issues most pertinent to conducting competence-to-proceed evaluations are reviewed below, as a comprehensive review of this legal construct is beyond the scope of this chapter (for such discussions see Bonnie, 1993; Melton et al., 1997; Poythress, Bonnie, Monahan, Otto, and Hoge, 2002; Roesch et al., 1999). Consistent with common law underpinnings, the Constitution requires that defendants be competent to participate in the criminal justice process. In *Dusky v. United States* (1960), the Supreme Court ruled that a defendant must have "… sufficient present ability to consult with his lawyer with a reasonable degree of rational understanding … [and have a] rational as well as factual understanding of the proceedings against him." *Dusky* identified that which the Constitution requires as a *minimum* in order for a criminal prosecution to proceed, and most states have adopted some variant of the *Dusky* language and approach (Grisso, 2003). However, this does not preclude states from establishing higher or more demanding standards. It is therefore essential for clinicians to fully comprehend the specific laws applicable in the jurisdictions in which they practice.

As is often the case, analysis of the legal standard enunciated in *Dusky* suggests a more complicated landscape than a quick review of the holding might indicate. Perhaps most significant is that the standard does not delineate or describe any predicate conditions

---

* Although the reader may be more familiar with the concept of "competence to stand trial" the term used to refer to this issue throughout this chapter will be "competence to proceed" since this more accurately reflects the legal requirement that a criminal defendant have the capacity to participate in the legal proceedings throughout, from the time of his or her detention and arrest, until the time of disposition.

(e.g., mental illness, mental retardation, or normal "limitations" associated with youth) that must be in place and responsible for any deficits in capacity. Although the large majority of states limit findings of incapacity to those that result from a mental impairment of some type (i.e., mental illness or mental retardation), there is considerably more variability across jurisdictions regarding how incapacity attributable to youth and developmental maturity factors should be treated. Careful analysis of the *Dusky* language provides additional guidance in interpreting this standard. The legal test requires only "sufficient" ability and a "reasonable" degree of understanding; this suggests that the defendant's abilities need not be complete or without impairment. Reference to "present" ability makes clear that considerations should be based on a defendant's competence-related abilities in the present and the immediate future, while use of the term "capacity" indicates that factors such as a mere lack of knowledge about the legal proceedings or process, or an unwillingness to participate in the proceedings or work with one's attorney do not necessarily render a defendant incompetent to proceed. The core issue is the individual's ability or capacity, rather than the choice to use those skills—competent defendants are free to refuse to participate or to otherwise exercise bad judgment. Finally, the test's reference to both a "factual" and "rational" understanding indicates that the defendant must demonstrate not only more than simple knowledge of facts and factors relevant to the proceedings, but also a presumably deeper ability to appreciate, consider, and manipulate those facts that are not significantly impaired by mental disorder.

Finally, most legal authorities and mental health professionals would agree that competence is context-specific (Bonnie, 1993; Melton et al., 1997). For example, a defendant might be incompetent to stand trial on one charge (e.g., an allegation of sophisticated securities fraud) but, at the same time, be competent to stand trial on a less complicated offense (e.g., a simple charge of driving with a suspended license).

The Legal Process

Questions regarding a defendant's competency can be raised by defense counsel, the prosecution, or *sua sponte* (on the court's own initiative). Once the issue of the defendant's competence to proceed is raised, the court can appoint a mental health professional to conduct a competency evaluation. A defendant can be required to submit to an evaluation of his or her competence to proceed, but statements made by the defendant during the examination or subsequent competency hearing cannot be admitted into evidence against the defendant on the issue of guilt in any criminal proceeding (unless first introduced into evidence by the defendant). This protection has important implications for the evaluation process that are discussed more fully below.

Disposition of Defendants Adjudicated Incompetent to Proceed

Although rates vary from study to study and across jurisdictions, it is generally agreed that between 20% and 30% of all defendants who are assessed after their compet-ence to proceed is questioned are eventually adjudicated incompetent (Melton et al., 1997; Nicholson and Kugler, 1991). These findings indicate that the threshold or bar for raising issues of competence is low, and this is certainly consistent with constitutional law directing that such matters should be considered whenever there is a "bona fide doubt" about the defendant's capacity to proceed (*Pate v. Robinson*, 1966).

Incompetent defendants are typically diagnosed with more severe disorders such as schizophrenia, bipolar disorder, and schizoaffective disorder (Nicholson and Kugler, 1991). A small minority of defendants (i.e., less than 10%) who have been adjudicated incompetent and are committed for treatment have a diagnosis of mental retardation. It is noteworthy that these data are considerably different for juveniles who have been adjudicated incompetent to proceed. Research indicates that as many as half of youth adjudicated incompetent to proceed in juvenile court may suffer significant intellectual limitations (McGaha, Otto, McClaren, and Petrila, 2001).

In *Jackson v. Indiana* (1972), the Supreme Court held that the state can only detain as incompetent those persons who have a reasonable expectation of restoration to competence. Thus, defendants determined to be incompetent and unrestorable cannot be held or treated under that section of the law that provides for commitment or treatment of incompetent defendants. In such cases, the criminal proceedings may not move forward, and the state may either keep the charges in place or dismiss them. The state, of course, could also pursue alternative dispositions for the defendant (e.g., civil commitment, guardianship) that he or she would otherwise be subject to, but such proceedings are independent of the criminal process.

The Clinical Forensic Evaluation of Competence to Proceed

Provided below is a recommended format for conducting competence evaluations. Because approaches and styles for competency evaluations can vary considerably, the format suggested below is simply offered as one approach for the reader to consider.

Gather Relevant Third-Party Information

Before meeting with the defendant and starting the evaluation, the prudent examiner should gather any relevant third-party information that may be helpful in assessing the defendant and his or her involvement in the legal system. Review of third-party information is especially important in all forensic evaluations because examinees may be less than completely candid in an attempt to gain a desired legal outcome, and assessment of response style is particularly important.

Criminal justice records, including the arrest report and the criminal indictment or complaint, are helpful in informing the examiner about the nature of the charges and allegations. These documents are typically made available to the examiner by the court or retaining attorney. After all, if the examiner does not know and appreciate the charges and allegations, how can he or she assess the defendant's capacity in this regard? Medical, mental health, and school records are often valuable in identifying underlying conditions that might be responsible for any competence-related deficits that are observed, and they also provide a way of assessing the accuracy of the defendant's self-report with respect to a variety of important issues. A brief conversation with the party who initiated the evaluation (almost always the defense attorney) also provides important information regarding the specific behaviors, symptoms, or deficits in capacity that resulted in the competence evaluation referral. The defense attorney can also provide other information regarding the nature and quality of interactions with the defendant, which may provide some insight into the examinee's ability to work and communicate with counsel. At this point, it can also be helpful to ask that the defense attorney instruct the defendant to cooperate with the evaluation process.

Ideally, the retaining attorney will gather much of this third-party information, but in some cases the examiner may have to seek such information. Although a detailed discussion of use of third-party information is beyond the scope of this chapter, it is noteworthy that accessing third-party information is sometimes more complicated than it appears (see Otto, Slobogin, and Greenberg, 2006 for a detailed discussion). This effort can be affected by a variety of factors including how the examiner is retained in the case (e.g., appointed by the court or confidentially retained by the defense attorney and thus covered under the umbrella of privilege as a result) and the type of information that is sought (e.g., confidential medical records versus a correctional officer's passing observations of the defendant in the jail mess hall).

Notification

Once armed with necessary background information, the examiner is ready to meet the defendant. Prior to initiating the evaluation, the examiner is obligated by law and ethics to notify the defendant of the nature and purpose of the evaluation. This task is best conceptualized as one of *notification* rather than informed consent or a *Miranda* warning as some describe it. Informed consent is not an accurate description because, in some cases, competence evaluations are completed over the objections and without the consent of the defendant. Referring to notification as providing the defendant with a *Miranda* warning is another misnomer for a number of reasons. First, the examiner is not a law enforcement officer interrogating or questioning the examinee who is in his or her custody. But more importantly, description of this notification as a "*Miranda*-like warning" (e.g., "... you have the right to remain silent, anything you say can and will be used against you in a court of law ...") is inaccurate in many cases since the defendant can be required to submit to an evaluation. Moreover, statements made by the defendant during the competence examination *cannot* be admitted into evidence against the defendant on the issue of guilt in any criminal proceeding, unless first introduced into evidence by the defendant, as noted in the section "The Legal Process" (also see Roesch et al., 1999; Melton et al., 1997; *Estelle v. Smith*, 1981).

During the notification, the examiner should instruct the defendant about how he or she is involved in the case, how the results of the examination will be used, and who will have access to the information that is gathered. Discussion of the lack of confidentiality, privilege (when indicated), and the nontherapeutic nature of the encounter is also required. In addition to documenting this disclosure in the written report, examiners would do well to describe the defendant's understanding and appreciation of this information. Examiners may consider use of a written notification form to ensure a comprehensive disclosure and to document that notification occurred. When utilized, however, such forms must be accurate and employ language that is comprehensible by criminal defendants, many of whom have quite limited reading abilities. Of course, a brief narrative in the report that describes the notification process is more helpful than the mere existence of a signed notification form.

In some cases, the examiner may have questions about the defendant's capacity to understand the notification and consent to the evaluation. The appropriate response depends, in part, on how the examiner is involved in the case. If the examination has been ordered by the court, then the defendant's inability to understand or consent to the evaluation does not bar the examination from going forward, because it has been ordered by the court and could even be conducted over the objections of the defendant. If, however, the examination has not been ordered by the court but has been requested by the attorney, the examiner could consider going forward on the basis of the assumption that the attorney is acting on behalf of the defendant. Absent such an approach, the examiner would be forced to return to the retaining attorney and request that either a court order be issued directing the evaluation to occur, or proceedings be initiated to have the defendant declared incapacitated to consent to or refuse the evaluation (perhaps via guardianship). As indicated above, the notification and consent process, regardless of the examinee's abilities, should be documented in the report.

Although it is rare, a defendant may be encountered who understands the notification but simply refuses to participate. In such cases the examiner should try to identify the defendant's concerns and allay them if possible. The examiner can have the defendant contact his or her attorney to discuss the evaluation in order to gain cooperation, or inform the defendant about implications of refusing to participate in the evaluation. Of course, those examiners who have previously asked the defense attorney to direct the defendant to cooperate with the evaluation process may avoid some of these difficulties.

Social History

Once the defendant has been apprised of its nature and purpose, and agrees to participate, the evaluation can begin. It is recommended that examiners start by collecting a social history that includes relevant information regarding the defendant's family, medical, academic, mental health, substance abuse, and criminal justice experience. As this information is provided by the defendant, the examiner can begin to (1) assess the defendant's general mental status, cognitive functioning, and communication abilities, (2) identify possible mental disorders or cognitive impairments that might be responsible for any competence-related deficits that are later observed, and (3) assess the defendant's response style and candor by comparing this self-report to accounts available in previously accessed third-party sources. Information regarding the defendant's history of mental disorder and successful treatments may be particularly helpful if competence-related deficits are observed, and the examiner must draw some conclusions about whether the defendant can be treated in order to restore his or her competence to participate in the process. An additional benefit of beginning the competence evaluation with a social history is that, as a general rule, review of much of the information included in the history may be less threatening and anxiety-arousing than discussion of the index offense, associated charges, and the upcoming legal proceedings. This may assist in establishing rapport early in the process and reducing any general anxiety the examinee may be experiencing.

Assessment of Competence to Proceed

Once the social history has been gathered, the examiner can begin to focus on assessment of the defendant's competence to proceed. Before discussing the evaluation process in detail, it is important to review three overriding issues that have been addressed in the section "Constitutional Contours."

First, the test of competence is one of capacity, as distinguished from knowledge or willingness. Thus, defendants who are simply ignorant about their charges, possible penalties, or the legal system and its operation are not incompetent to proceed *providing* that they are able to incorporate and utilize such information in their decision-making process once it is made available to them. An important corollary, of course, is that simple rote knowledge does not equate to capacity given the requirement of a rational, as well as factual, understanding (see the section "Constitutional Contours"). Some defendants with limited intellectual abilities may answer questions about the legal system correctly but may still show no true or meaningful understanding or appreciation of the topic at hand. Similarly, defendants who exhibit disordered thought content (i.e., delusional thinking) may be able to offer organized factual accounts and depictions, but their appreciation of the same factors may be limited by specific delusions. Second, defendants who are capable of working with their attorneys or otherwise participating in the legal process, but who choose not to do so for reasons other than those that might be attributed to mental disorder, mental retardation, or other impairment nevertheless have the *capacity* to participate. And finally, the capacity required to be competent to proceed is not absolute, as indicated by the language in *Dusky* suggesting "*sufficient* present ability" and "*reasonable* degree of rational understanding."

Given the complexity and importance of the evaluation, the beginning examiner is well advised to use a device designed to structure the competence evaluation and ensure that the examiner addresses and considers all potentially relevant issues (e.g., Competence Assessment Instrument, Laboratory of Community Psychiatry, 1973; Interdisciplinary Fitness Interview—Revised, Golding, 1993; Fitness Interview Test, Roesch, Zapf, and Eaves, 2006; Juvenile Adjudicative Competence Interview, Grisso, 2005).

It may be easiest and least threatening to begin the specific competence inquiry with an assessment of the defendant's understanding of the legal process, those involved in it, and its adversarial nature. This inquiry may be started by assessing the defendant's ability to identify the various actors in the legal process (e.g., defense attorney, prosecutor, witnesses, judge, jury) and their roles, the operation and stages of the legal process, and one's rights as a defendant. Impaired capacity may be manifested by defendants whose ability to understand and relay this information is limited as a function of a disordered thought process, or mental retardation or other cognitive impairments. Defendants whose thought content is affected by a mental disorder (e.g., a defendant with paranoid or grandiose delusions) may also show impaired capacity in understanding the motivations of those in the process, their rights and entitlements, and the likely outcomes. Given that in excess of 90% of criminal defendants never go to trial but enter a plea, assessment of the defendant's appreciation of the plea agreement process, the rights that are relinquished, and the factors that are of most relevance when considering a plea (e.g., likelihood of conviction, quality of the state's evidence, sanctions associated with a conviction versus a plea) is also essential.

Next, the examiner may consider assessing the defendant's understanding of courtroom procedure and protocol, and his or her ability to participate in and understand any future legal proceedings. In addition to specific inquiries focused on the above, the examiner should be able to draw some conclusions about the defendant's abilities in this sphere on the basis of behavior observed during the interview. For example, does the defendant understand information provided by the examiner? Does the defendant behave during the interview in a way that would be acceptable in legal proceedings? Of course, it is important that the examiner keep in mind, whenever making inferences about legally relevant behaviors on the basis of the defendant's behavior during the evaluation, that the contexts of the evaluation and legal proceedings vary in important ways. An examinee may be much more anxious during the trial process than he or she is in a one-on-one interview with the mental health professional, who may act in a way to maximize the defendant's comfort and performance. To take these differences into account, the examiner, at some point during the evaluation, may choose to approximate more closely the more challenging conditions a defendant may face in a variety of ways and gauge the examinee's response (e.g., by speaking more rapidly or using more sophisticated language, by confronting the defendant, by adopting a more adversarial approach). Adoption of a more adversarial or anxiety-arousing tone or stance should be attempted during the latter part of the evaluation, so as not to risk alienating or upsetting the defendant before important information is gathered.

Assessment of the examinee's understanding and appreciation of the charges, allegations, and possible penalties requires that the examiner have a sound understanding of these factors, on the basis of review of the arrest reports, indictment or criminal information, and discussion with the defense attorney or prosecutor. Sophisticated examiners know that charges listed by law enforcement officers in their arrest reports are sometimes dismissed by prosecutors, and others are sometimes added. Thus, there may be discrepancies between the charges listed in the arrest report(s) and those in the criminal indictment. When in doubt about the charges and allegations that are current, examiners should contact the defense attorney or prosecutor.

During the evaluation process, it is important to distinguish between charges (i.e., the formal offense) and allegations (i.e., the defendant's alleged specific behaviors that resulted in the more general charges). Oftentimes, defendants may be aware of what they are accused of, but not know the specific charges. In such cases, simply informing them about the charges may be adequate. Some less sophisticated defendants may refuse to discuss the charges or allegations on the basis of the belief that acknowledging them constitutes an admission of responsibility, whereas other defendants may simply repeat that they are not guilty of anything with which they are charged. In such cases, it may be helpful to distinguish for the defendant between acknowledging awareness of the charges and admitting responsibility by simply stating to the defendant, "I know you are telling me that you did not do anything wrong, but what do the police *say* you did?"

Determining the sanctions that may be imposed (so that one can assess the defendant's understanding of these) is almost always more complex than identifying the charges and allegations since penalties often vary as a function of a number of factors including the defendant's criminal history, the defendant's willingness to admit wrongdoing and enter a plea, and the actual offense for which the defendant is convicted. Although sentencing guidelines or other rules of thumb operating in some jurisdictions may provide some direction (e.g., the maximum penalty for a misdemeanor is 1 year in county jail; the minimum penalty for capital murder is 25 years or life in prison), it may be helpful for the examiner, before meeting with the defendant, to contact the defense attorney or prosecutor to gain an idea of possible or likely sanctions.

In many cases, examinees will offer that they have little idea of possible penalties because they have had minimal opportunity to meet with the defense attorney. Again, such lack of knowledge, in and of itself, does not indicate that the defendant lacks the capacity to understand and appreciate possible sanctions. As is always the case, when the defendant reports a lack of knowledge, the examiner should provide relevant information and assess the defendant's ability to incorporate and make sense of it. A follow-up inquiry into these same issues later in the interview to assess the defendant's ability to retain and understand that information provides helpful information about the defendant's capacities.

It is important to remember that a factual understanding of the charges, allegations, or penalties may not necessarily reflect a rational understanding. A paranoid defendant may fully understand what he is accused of and with what offense he is charged, yet delusions that he is being conspired against by the police department and district attorney's office may color his appreciation of why he was arrested and charged. Similarly, a manic defendant may know that she could receive a prison sentence of up to 10 years, but her grandiose beliefs that she will finally be recognized as the next Daughter of God in 2 years, be crowned Queen of the World, and immediately be released from prison may color her true appreciation of the sentence she is facing.

Crucial to participating in the criminal process is effective interaction with one's attorney. Ideally, defendants can provide their attorneys with information about offense-related events (e.g., their whereabouts and actions, the behaviors of the alleged victim or arresting officers) that is helpful in considering defenses and responding to the prosecution's evidence and witnesses. Defendants should also be able to consider a variety of legal strategies with the assistance of counsel (e.g., whether to testify, whether to enter a guilty plea to a lesser charge) and make an informed decision about the best course of action in their case. These abilities, however, can be limited by mental illness, mental retardation, or other cognitive impairments. For considering these issues, it is often beneficial to talk with the attorney and gain his or her opinion about the nature and quality of interactions with the defendant. It may even be helpful to observe the attorney and defendant interaction.

The examiner can also make inferences about the defendant's ability to work and cooperate with his or her attorney on the basis of behavior observed during the assessment. With limited exceptions (e.g., the defendant harbors paranoid ideation about the attorney), the examiner may reasonably infer that a defendant who is able to assess and consider various legal strategies during the evaluation could do the same when meeting with the defense attorney. Similarly, the examiner may reasonably infer that a defendant who is able to provide an account of his behavior and that of relevant third parties at and around the time of the alleged offense, or who is able to raise questions about the state's witnesses and allegations during the evaluation process, should be able to do so with his or her attorney.

In many cases, a defendant may claim lack of memory for the events surrounding the arrest. Some defendants may erroneously expect that this precludes their prosecution. In the event that the amnesia is legitimate, however, it could preclude the defendant from providing potentially exculpatory information or otherwise challenging the prosecution's allegations (Frederick, DeMier, and Towers, 2004). Forensic examiners must understand that the mere presence of amnesia for events surrounding the alleged offense is not an automatic bar to competence, although it may render a defendant incompetent to proceed. In many cases, the role of the evaluator involves an examination of the nature of the amnesia complaint. Although the examiner may be able to offer some expert opinion regarding whether a reported amnesia might be expected given a particular insult, injury, or impairment that is alleged to cause it, the decision regarding whether the reported amnesia renders the defendant incompetent to proceed is ultimately left to the legal decision maker. The appellate court's decision in *Wilson v. United States* (1968) provides guidance to legal decision makers facing this issue by way of its delineation of six factors that may be considered in cases of reported amnesia including: (1) the extent to which the amnesia affected the defendant's ability to consult with and assist his or her attorney, (2) the extent to which the amnesia affected the defendant's ability to testify, (3) the extent to which relevant evidence could be extrinsically reconstructed despite the defendant's amnesia, (4) the extent to which the prosecutor assisted the defense in reconstructing relevant information that may not be otherwise available because of the amnesia, (5) the strength of the prosecution's case, and (6) any other factors of relevance operating in the case at hand. Although a clinician's opinion may shed light on some of these matters, others (e.g., the strength of the prosecution's case) are legal matters about which the evaluator should offer no opinion.

Related to the above inquiry is assessment of the defendant's ability to testify, should he and his attorney decide that it is in his best interests to do so. Like the above, assessment of this capacity may primarily be based on the defendant's behavior and responses during the interview. With some exceptions, the examiner may reasonably infer that a defendant who is able to answer questions about his behavior and that of relevant third parties at and around the time of the alleged offense should be able to do so when on the witness stand. As noted above, of course, it is important to remain cognizant of differences between the forensic examination and testimony contexts, and consider them accordingly. A defendant who is able to answer an examiner's questions about his or her behavior at and around the time of the alleged offense may show diminished ability when facing the stressors associated with undergoing direct or cross examination in a courtroom. Thus, as described above, the examiner may choose to approximate more closely the more challenging conditions a defendant may face during the evaluation (e.g., by using a more challenging tone, confronting the defendant and any inconsistencies or weaknesses displayed in response to questions) and assess his or her response accordingly.

Assessment of Current Mental State

Once the defendant's competence-related abilities have been assessed, a more formal mental status examination should be conducted to aid in identification of symptoms and assist in diagnostic decision-making. Although the examiner may have developed some diagnostic impressions on the basis of observations of the defendant and review of relevant third-party records, a mental status examination and more focused inquiry into the defendant's current adjustment and functioning will be necessary to assess the defendant's current functioning.

Accessing Additional Third-Party Information

During the course of the evaluation, the examiner may identify other sources of third-party information that will prove beneficial in the overall assessment. In some cases the defendant's assistance can be garnered (e.g., providing the phone number of a spouse, signing a records release authorizing access to medical records or mental health records that were not previously available for review). At this time, the examiner may also wish to access third-party information from informants not previously available but readily available at the time of the evaluation (e.g., the jail officer assigned to the defendant's unit, the parent who accompanied the defendant to the evaluation, the jail log).

Special Issues in Competence Assessment

Utility of Diagnosis

Diagnosis, in and of itself, provides little information about a defendant's competence to participate in the criminal process, and decisions about competence based solely on diagnosis are likely to result in considerable errors. Although persons with more severe disorders (e.g., schizophrenia, bipolar disorder, schizoaffective disorder) are over-represented among persons who have been adjudicated incompetent to proceed, the majority of persons with these diagnoses are competent to proceed. Evaluators of a generation ago have been faulted for placing too much emphasis on diagnosis alone. Research indicates that few evaluators today make this basic mistake, but instead focus on the specific deficits in competence-related abilities that may be attributed to underlying mental disorder (Skeem and Golding, 1998; Christy, Douglas, Otto, and Petrila, 2004).

Although decisions about competence cannot be based simply on diagnosis, diagnosis is not wholly irrelevant to the competency question. The diagnostic picture may be important for the examiner when considering prognosis or making specific treatment recommendations. Diagnosis has important implications for restorability (i.e., persons whose incompetence is attributable to more static or unremitting disorders may require a different disposition from those whose predicate disorders are more responsive to treatment and show a better prognosis).

Persons diagnosed with mental retardation may demonstrate specific competence-related deficits, and some issues related to defendants who are considered to be incompetent due to mental retardation deserve special attention. Persons with mental retardation may be more likely to acquiesce and claim they possess knowledge that they do not, in an attempt to appear in control and capable (Stafford, 2003). Additionally, they may be particularly vulnerable to displaying a *factual* understanding or knowledge (particularly after rote training) without an accompanying *rational* understanding and appreciation. As a result, those assessing defendants with mental retardation should be particularly careful to avoid "yes/no" questions and be sure not to simply infer rational appreciation of legal issues on the basis of an ability to simply recite factual material or information.

Because many of the basic deficits associated with mental retardation are considered to be static and nonchanging, the term "treatment" is typically not used when referring to interventions designed to bring about capacity. However, persons with mental retardation can show greater and lesser abilities, depending on the training, education, and habilitation opportunities provided to them. Thus, in the case of a defendant who is adjudicated incompetent to proceed due to mental retardation, "treatment" designed to result in "restoration" is not an accurate depiction of what is occurring since the underlying deficits are not being "treated" and the defendant may never have had the necessary capacity. Although some persons with severe mental retardation may show deficits that cannot be habilitated, others with significant intellectual limitations can show improvement in competence-related abilities with appropriate and specialized interventions.

Inquiring about the Defendant's Behavior at and around the Time of the Alleged Offense(s)

There exists some disagreement in the field regarding whether mental health professionals conducting competence evaluations should query defendants about their behavior at and around the time of the alleged offense(s), as well as the behavior of relevant third parties (e.g., the alleged victim, the arresting officers, witnesses). A more conservative approach dictates that examiners not address these issues with defendants because gaining such information may result in revelation of incriminating information. An alternative approach suggests that such an inquiry is appropriate and necessary because it typically provides helpful information about the defendant's ability to provide the defense attorney with relevant information or testify, collaborate with the attorney, identify inaccurate claims made by the prosecution, and challenge adverse witnesses. It is also argued that this latter approach is permissible since the law precludes use of incriminating information gained in the competence context for purpose of proving guilt. Such inquiries and discussions should not provide the prosecution with incriminating information if the examiner, when writing a report or testifying, simply summarizes the defendant's communication capacity rather than the specific details that have been related (e.g., "The defendant offered a coherent, logical, and time sequenced account of her behavior at and around the time of the alleged offense, as well as the behavior of others including the arresting officers and alleged victim. Her responses to questions about the arrest-related events were informative, and she was able to distinguish relevant from irrelevant information.").

Those uncomfortable with the above approach but who nonetheless recognize the need to assess the defendant's capacity to relate information about the events in question to the defense attorney, as well as testify, may choose to ask the defendant about his or her ability to relate such events to defense counsel and testify about such, and follow this up with a discussion with the attorney, who can apprise the examiner of the defendant's abilities in this arena, on the basis of their prior interactions.

Utility of Psychological Testing in Competence Evaluations

Historically, psychologists conducting competence evaluations relied heavily on clinical assessment instruments (i.e., measures that assessed general clinical constructs such as intelligence, psychopathology, and academic achievement) (Melton et al., 1997). As discussed above, there is no clear or direct relationship between any clinical construct and competence to proceed in the criminal process. Because the test for competence is a functional one, mental health professionals should consider the use of clinical assessment instruments carefully. To the degree that a clinical assessment instrument validly measures and helps the examiner identify or understand a construct (e.g., depression, intelligence) that may be causally related to and help explain functional competence deficits that the defendant displays, then that measure may be of some value. The potential utility of clinical assessment instruments is limited, however, because they will not prove of any use with respect to assessing the specific competence abilities of the defendant.

Some clinical assessment instruments and "forensically relevant instruments" (i.e., instruments that assess constructs that are most relevant in forensic contexts, such as response style and psychopathy) may also prove of some value with respect to assessment of the examinee's response style. As noted above, in all forensic assessments, including competence-to-proceed evaluations, the examiner must pay special attention to the response style of the examinee, given the increased likelihood of a less than candid approach to the evaluation process.

Over the past 40 years, a number of "forensic assessment instruments" have been developed to assist forensic examiners in their assessment of criminal defendants' competence-related abilities (Heilbrun, Rogers, and Otto, 2002). These measures range from checklists or structured assessment instruments simply designed to ensure a comprehensive consideration of all competence-related abilities (e.g., Competence Assessment Instrument, Laboratory of Community Psychiatry, 1973; Interdisciplinary Fitness Interview—Revised, Golding, 1993; Fitness Interview Test, Roesch et al., 2006; Juvenile Adjudicative Competence Interview, Grisso, 2005) to tests that have been developed and normed on a number of relevant populations (e.g., defendants adjudicated incompetent to stand

Table 10.1 Specialized Competence Assessment Measures

Measure	Purpose	Administration (min)	Scoring	Available Norms
Competence Screening Test[a]	Screening	30	Yes	Yes (cutoff)
Competence to Stand Trial Assessment Instrument[b]	Comprehensive	45	No	No
Georgia Court Competency Test[c]	Screening	15	Yes	Yes (cutoff)
Competence Assessment for Standing Trial—Mental Retardation[d]	Comprehensive	45	Yes	Yes
MacArthur Competence Assessment Tool—Criminal Adjudication[e]	Comprehensive	45	Yes	Yes
Evaluation of Competency to Stand Trial—Revised[f]	Comprehensive	45	Yes	Yes

[a] Laboratory of Community Psychiatry (1973).
[b] Laboratory of Community Psychiatry (1973).
[c] Wildman, Batchelor, Thompson, Nelson, Moore, and Patterson (1978).
[d] Everington and Luckasson (1992).
[e] Poythress, Nicholson, Otto, Edens, Monahan, Bonnie, and Hoge (1999).
[f] Rogers, Tillbrook, and Sewell (2004).

Source: Adapted from Melton, G.B., Petrila, J., Poythress, N., and Slobogin, C. in *Psychological Evaluations for the Courts: A Handbook for Attorneys and Mental Health Professionals* (2nd edition). Guilford, New York, 1997.

trial, defendants with a mental disorder for whom competence was not raised as an issue). All of these measures are best described as "forensic assessment instruments" because they are specifically designed to assess a psycholegal issue. Although a comprehensive review of these instruments is beyond the scope of this chapter, some of these measures are described in Table 10.1.

When considering the use of competence assessment instruments, it is important to understand that none of the measures can be used to classify defendants as "competent" or "incompetent." The most any of these measures do is provide normative information about the defendant's competence abilities or structure the examiner's inquiry and judgments in some way. Use of any of these instruments, therefore, must be incorporated into the broader clinical competence evaluation incumbent upon the examiner.

Ultimate Issue Issues

Too much ink has been devoted to discussing the "ultimate issue issue" in a variety of contexts. For the uninitiated, some in the field argue that mental health professionals should avoid offering opinions about legal issues (e.g., whether a defendant is competent, whether a defendant is sane) because these issues are ultimately moral-legal (not scientific) ones that are to be decided by the legal decision maker (i.e., judge or jury) (Melton et al., 1997). In contrast, other authorities claim that such advisory opinions are not harmful as long as the mental health professionals offering them remember that the ultimate decision maker is the judge or jury, and make clear to the decision maker the rationale and reasoning underlying their opinion (e.g., Rogers and Ewing, 1989). Those who see nothing wrong with mental health professionals offering such opinions also argue that, in some jurisdictions, mental health professionals are required by law to form and offer opinions about legal issues.

The "ultimate issue issue" debate will likely never be settled. Most important for the mental health professional conducting competency to proceed evaluations is to be aware of the issue and debate, recognize that the decision about competence is ultimately a legal one (that is informed by the expert opinions of mental health professionals), avoid offering only conclusory opinions in reports and testimony, and always make clear the facts and rationales underlying advisory opinions that may be offered regarding the defendant's competence.

Report Writing

Whether the examiner will write a report summarizing his or her findings depends on the rule and law of the jurisdiction, as well as the nature of his or her involvement in the case. Although report content can vary by jurisdiction (some states require that certain aspects of the competency question be addressed explicitly), there are considerable commonalities. In most courts, a comprehensive competency evaluation report will include (1) an opinion about the defendant's competence, (2) identification and discussion of any specific issues referred to the examiner by the court, (3) documentation of appropriate disclosures made to the defendant about the evaluation and the report, (4) a listing of procedures, techniques, and tests used in the evaluation and the purposes of each, (5) a rich description of the defendant's competence-related abilities and any limitations, and (6) if the defendant is considered by the expert to be incompetent, a description of the deficits and their relationship to the functional abilities required for competence, as well as treatment recommendations for "restoring" the defendant's competence (see Table 10.2 for a sample outline).

The examiner should also keep in mind the audience when writing reports and testifying. Because judges, attorneys, and jurors typically know little about mental health issues, jargon should be avoided when possible and explained when its use is necessary. By the

---

Table 10.2   Competence Report Format

Identifying information/referral question/notification
Relevant history
   Social and family history
   Educational history
   Employment history
   Medical history
   Mental health and substance use history
   Criminal history
Mental status/current clinical functioning
Competence to proceed
   Appreciation of charges and allegations
   Appreciation of the range and nature of possible penalties
   Understanding of the legal process and its adversarial nature
   Capacity to work with attorney and provide relevant information
   Ability to manifest appropriate courtroom behavior
   Ability to testify relevantly
Opinion regarding competence to proceed and need for treatment/restoration

time the reader comes to the end of the examiner's report, the conclusions regarding the defendant's competence, restorability (when indicated), and treatment needs (when indicated) should be obvious (Skeem, Golding, and Emke-Francis, 2004).

Summary

Given the stakes involved in criminal proceedings, and the justice system's investment in accuracy, fairness, and autonomy, all defendants who are subject to criminal proceedings must be competent to proceed. Although competence to proceed with the criminal process is ultimately a legal issue, mental health professionals can be of considerable assistance to legal decision makers by: (1) assessing and describing the defendant's capacity to understand and participate in the legal proceedings, (2) identifying and describing any mental disorders and impairments, broadly defined, that may be responsible for impaired capacities, and (3) in that subset of cases in which a finding of incapacity may occur, determining if the mental disorder or impairment that may be responsible for the reported deficits can be treated or habilitated so as to restore the defendant's capacity (and identify those treatments). The examiner should make clear in any reports or testimony provided, the assessment techniques utilized and the factual basis and reasoning underlying any opinions.

Assessment of a defendant's competence to proceed requires knowledge of the law, as well as expertise with respect to mental conditions that may affect competence-related abilities, and interventions designed to treat and habilitate these underlying conditions. The mental health professional conducting competence evaluations must rely on traditional clinical assessment techniques, as well as approaches that are unique to forensic practice so as to best inform the legal decision maker about the defendant's capacities and needs.

References

Bonnie, R. (1993). The competence of criminal defendants: A theoretical reformulation. *Behavioral Sciences and the Law, 10,* 291–316.

Christy, A., Douglas, K., Otto, R. K., and Petrila, J. (2004). Juveniles evaluated incompetent to proceed: Characteristics and quality of mental health professionals' evaluations. *Professional Psychology: Research and Practice, 35,* 380–388.

Everington, C., and Luckasson, R. (1992). *Competence Assessment to Stand Trial for Defendants with Mental Retardation (CAST-MR) Manual.* Worthington, OH: International Diagnostic Services.

Frederick, R., DeMier, R., and Towers, K. (2004). *Examinations of Competency to Stand Trial: Foundations in Mental Health Case Law.* Sarasota, FL: Professional Resource Press.

Golding, S. (1993). *Training Manual for the Interdisciplinary Fitness Interview—Revised.* Salt Lake City, UT: Author.

Grisso, T. (2003). *Evaluating Competencies: Forensic Assessment and Instruments* (2nd edition). New York: Kluwer/Plenum.

Grisso, T. (2005). *Evaluating Juveniles' Adjudicative Competence: A Guide for Clinical Practice.* Sarasota, FL: Professional Resource Press.

Heilbrun, K., Rogers, R., and Otto, R. K. (2002). Forensic assessment: Current status and future directions. In: J. R. P. Ogloff (Ed.), *Psychology and Law: Reviewing the Discipline* (pp. 119–146). New York: Kluwer/Plenum.

Laboratory of Community Psychiatry. (1973). *Competency to Stand Trial and Mental Illness.* New York: Aronson.

McGaha, A., Otto, R., McClaren, M., and Petrila, J. (2001). Juveniles adjudicated incompetent to proceed: A descriptive study of Florida's competence restoration program. *Journal of the American Academy of Psychiatry and Law, 29,* 427–437.

Melton, G. B., Petrila, J., Poythress, N., and Slobogin, C. (1997). *Psychological Evaluations for the Courts: A Handbook for Attorneys and Mental Health Professionals* (2nd edition). New York: Guilford.

Nicholson, R., and Kugler, K. E. (1991). Competent and incompetent criminal defendants: A quantitative review of comparative research. *Psychological Bulletin, 109,* 355–370.

Otto, R. K., Slobogin, C., and Greenberg, S. (2006). Legal and ethical issues in accessing and utilizing third-party information. In: A. Goldstein (Ed.), *Forensic Psychology: Emerging Topics and Expanding Roles* (pp. 190–205). New York: Wiley.

Poythress, N., Bonnie, R., Monahan, J., Otto, R. K., and Hoge, S. (2002). *Adjudicative Competence: The MacArthur Studies.* New York: Kluwer/Plenum.

Poythress, N., Nicholson, R., Otto, R. K., Edens, J. F., Monahan, J., Bonnie, R., and Hoge, K. (1999). *Manual for the MacArthur Competence Assessment Tool—Criminal Adjudication.* Odessa, FL: Psychological Assessment Resources.

Roesch, R., Zapf, P., Golding, S., and Skeem, J. (1999). Defining and assessing competency to stand trial. In: A. K. Hess and I. Weiner (Eds.), *The Handbook of Forensic Psychology* (2nd edition, pp. 327–349). New York: Wiley.

Roesch, R., Zapf, P. A., and Eaves, D. (2006). *Manual for the Fitness Interview Test—Revised.* Sarasota, FL: Professional Resource Press.

Rogers, R., and Ewing, C. P. (1989). Ultimate opinion prescriptions: A cosmetic fix and plea for empiricism. *Law and Human Behavior, 13,* 357–374.

Rogers, R., Tillbrook, C., and Sewell, K. (2004). *Professional Manual for the Evaluation of Competency to Stand Trial—Revised.* Odessa, FL: Psychological Assessment Resources.

Skeem, J., and Golding, S. (1998). Community examiners' evaluation of competence to stand trial: Common problems and suggestions for improvement. *Professional Psychology: Research and Practice, 29,* 357–367.

Skeem, J., Golding, S., and Emke-Francis, P. (2004). Assessing adjudicative competency: Using legal and empirical principles to inform practice. In: W. O'Donohue and E. Levensky (Eds.), *Forensic Psychology: A Handbook for Mental Health and Legal Professionals* (pp. 175–211). New York: Academic Press.

Stafford, K. P. (2003). Assessment of competence to stand trial. In: A. Goldstein (Ed.), *Forensic Psychology, Handbook of Psychology* (pp. 359–380). New York: Wiley.

Wildman, R., Batchelor, E., Thompson, L., Nelson, F., Moore, J., and Patterson, M. (1978). The Georgia Court Competency Test. Unpublished manuscript, Milledgeville, Georgia.

Wulach, J. (1980). The incompetency plea: Abuses and reforms. *Journal of Psychiatry and Law, 8,* 317–328.

Legal References

Dusky v. United States, 362 U.S. 402 (1960).

Estelle v. Smith, 451 U.S. 454 (1981).

Jackson v. Indiana, 406 U.S. 715 (1972).

Miranda v. Arizona, 384 U.S. 436 (1966).

Pate v. Robinson, 383 U.S. 375 (1966).

Wilson v. United States, 391 F.2d 460 (1968).

Mitigatory Defenses: Degrees and Aspects of Criminal Responsibility

SANDRA B. McPHERSON

The Fielding Graduate University, Santa Barbara, California, and Independent Practice, Beachwood, Ohio

Contents

Synopsis

Current conceptualization in science has been moving toward more and more inclusion of an orientation that recognizes the futility of applying linear formulas to the task of understanding and predicting behavior. This approach, referred to as complexity or sometimes chaos theory, is in distinct contrast to the traditions characteristically associated with both science and law. In fact, both disciplines have operated in the past on the notion that there is predictability that will approach perfection if the values for the predictors are successfully ascertained. Nonetheless, as scientific observations have become more refined, newer perspectives, which are both mathematically and theoretically based, are replacing traditional thinking.

In approaching forensic work in the area of mitigation of criminal responsibility, complexity theory is applied from two perspectives. First of all, it is argued that explanations of behavior and bases for functioning in this area will be best conceptualized within a complexity framework. Beyond that, however, it is further argued that complexity theory, in combination with evolving potentials to gather and analyze data, will allow the emergence of much more sophisticated and realistically based ways of predicting and controlling outcomes in a variety of human systems and specifically in forensic work.

In Waldrop's (1992) discussion of what is known variously as chaos or complexity theory, he articulated that complex systems are prone to "spontaneous self-organization" (p. 11). The notion was that adaptive systems—systems that adjust to complex changing demands—undergo massive reorganizations to accommodate to the conditions that will allow life to continue and move forward. In effect, he stated that those systems that do survive, "have somehow acquired the ability to bring order and chaos into a special kind of balance" (p. 12). He has been quite willing to apply these concepts to psychological and social systems. In common with others' writing in this area, he pointed to certain principles as characteristic of system adaptations.* Those principles include the following:

1. There is a network of operating agents in parallel process.
2. Control is dispersed rather than residing in some central place.
3. There are varying levels of organization with connections.
4. As a function of interacting with the external world, which is called experience, there are functional adaptations.
5. Large systems "anticipate the future" (p. 146).
6. Complex systems are always changing; the only stable system is a dead one (Waldrop, 1992).

The notion is that in complex systems small inputs can make for significant adjustments. Operational patterns have periods of relative stability (linear predictability), but there is uniqueness within each organization and the potential for periodic drastic readjustments (Bűtz, 1997; Waldrop, 1992).

In the particular case of mitigatory factors, the issue is one of degrees of responsibility. A simple way to approach criminal justice is to determine whether an individual has transgressed a given statute and, if so, to apply a consequence. As soon as one introduces the notion that the reasons for the transgression rather than the fact of the act should play some part in society's response, a whole arena of complex and often unpredictable, or predictable only in limited ways, features are introduced. The task of the forensic psychologist in providing data to the court system is only justified if this type of complexity is contemplated to be part of the criminal justice system. To the extent that only act and statute are considered, there is no need for forensic assessment and its attendant problems.

Many sources of complexity exist when it comes to criminal responsibility assessments. Among others, these factors include variations of time, memory, and motivation. There are limitations of psychological data, lack of operational definitions in law, and psychological factors involving both group and individual dynamics that are part of the responses that juries, attorneys, and judges make to cases. Additional complication is also introduced by the Heisenberg principle of indeterminacy—the act of measurement (or data collecting) impacts the behavior that is being studied.

---

* For those interested in looking for in-depth applications of this kind of approach, the work of Lacan, as discussed and integrated into the field of criminal law and complexity theory, can be found in the study by Williams and Arrigo (2002). Lacan has approached from a neo-psychoanalytic viewpoint questions of language, self, and social systems that fit well within this area.

Scope

This chapter will look at mitigation at several levels and contexts. The issue is one of degree of criminal responsibility that may be assigned, and the implication is that the outcome of being found guilty of a specific act (*actus rea*) should vary as a function of these factors. Specific areas of criminal responsibility that will be considered include the following:

1. Not guilty by reason of insanity (NGRI). This affirmative defense is a fully exculpatory one. There are a couple of jurisdictions that do not have the sanity issue as an option but, for the most part, historically, beginning with *M'Naghten* (1843) and continuing to date, some form of insanity plea has existed in Western legal systems.

2. Diminished capacity/diminished responsibility. In diminished capacity, a partial exculpation is involved. In jurisdictions that have this option, there is the opportunity to show that by virtue of a mental condition the individual lacked some of the necessary capabilities for assuming full responsibility for what occurred. The practical effect of a diminished capacity defense is to reduce the penalty but not completely remove it. The related category of diminished responsibility involves the notion that due to reduced culpability the level of crime charged is reduced with resulting lowered level of punishment. Legal scholarship notwithstanding, the practical differences between diminished capacity and diminished responsibility are not substantial. Furthermore, the terms cause confusion by being used interchangeably in some writing.

3. Battered spouse defense. In this special affirmative defense, if certain criteria are met, the individual is viewed as having lacked the ability to perceive options that were, in fact, present, or having held the belief that those options could not possibly work to protect or save the individual. This defense is essentially a psychological self-defense argument.

4. Obsessive compulsive defense. In this approach, it is argued that the presence of obsessive compulsive disorder (OCD) has resulted in an individual's inability to refrain from the act committed. This defense is rarely, if ever, successful and, in effect, rests on a two-prong NGRI, which has been dropped in most jurisdictions.

5. Multiple personality disorder defense. This defense, reflecting what is now in the *Diagnostic and Statistical Manual*, Fourth Edition, Text Revision (DSM-IV-TR, 2000) nosology as dissociative identity disorder (DID), has been only somewhat successfully used and more often than not rejected in courts. It is obviously open to self-serving misrepresentation to the effect that the act was committed by another personality residing within the body that now, with a different self present, is facing punishment.

6. Mitigation in sentencing, including capital cases. This category ranges from the nuisance behavior that can bring mentally ill persons to the attention of the criminal court (who then are given treatment *in lieu* of criminal sanctions by virtue of the mitigation report) to the very serious and singular system of capital justice in the United States, which involves a bifurcated trial. Upon finding of guilt during the first phase, a second phase takes place in which the defendant may present to the court mitigatory factors. Expert testimony regarding psychological state, social factors, and related psychosocial data is typically a part of the mitigation phase of a capital case. Testimony may be directly related to the crime or may reflect a general view of the psychology of the defendant.

History

Although periodically there have been voices raised for what has been termed a strict liability approach to criminal justice (see, for example, Huckabee, 2006), in fact, law from ancient time to the present has involved notions of mitigation. The act alone was not the determiner of outcome but rather some consideration has always been given to the intent and context. Thus, a review of the earliest legal history would include the Code of Hammurabi who lived about 1700 BC. Codification of law reduced arbitrariness. The code included that an act that occurred as a function of an accident should not be punished in the same way as an act that occurred intentionally. No punishment was prescribed if the accident did not involve carelessness or neglect. In the case of murder, degree of intent defined what would be currently called first-degree murder versus a lower level homicide. Similar kinds of concepts are found in the Talmud, in biblical sources, in the Code of Dracos, the Roman Code, and subsequently in Christian theological expositions (Buchanan, 1992; Danesh-Khoshdoo, 1991; Sinsheimer, 1947). In Eastern cultures, similar concepts are found; Gautama Buddha provided guidelines in 500 BC which reference mitigation (Kyokai, 1992).

Mitigation, whether accomplished by specific defenses or by consideration of more general factors, has been incorporated into codes and case law. It has been construed narrowly, as with the Hammurabi Code that focused only on context of act and actor. However, the return of the death penalty led to decisions, notably *Lockett v. Ohio* (1977), that resulted in almost any factors being acceptably presented. The sentencing guidelines for federal offenses, themselves reflecting an evolution from minimal discretion to the current at least partial return to more judicial freedom (see *United States v. Booker*, 2005), still represent rather narrowly defined windows for presentation of mitigation.

The infusing of religious thought into the development of legal systems and philosophy has always been characteristic of civilizations. In many respects, of course, religious structures were the primary sources of social control, and a more civil or public system of law was a later development. In the case of European and U.S. systems of law, one can see the blending and, ultimately, the emergence of a legal system at least formally independent of the religious establishment. At present in the Middle East, there are dual systems but the influence and even the predominance of Shariah or religious law are frequently present.

In the case of English jurisprudence, it is interesting to note that in the thirteenth century, Brackton, who was a jurist and high churchman, infused into civil law concepts of morality which included intentionality as an important factor in determining criminal behavior. At that time, in King's law, there was the stricter approach of whether a prohibited act occurred. The notion of *mens rea* came from Brackton's work (Gerber, 1984). However, the quest then became one of determining who should be exculpated due to the lack of intentionality and thus began a legal journey that continues to reflect pendulum swings favoring extenuation and the needs of the individual versus protection and the needs of society.

In 1724, the trial of Edward Arnold took place. At that point, to be considered NGRI, one had to be so deprived of reasoning that one was unable to count to 20 or give the name of one's mother. Called the "wild beast test," this definition meant that no person fell into the category. Over a hundred years later in 1843, the *M'Naghten* test developed, which required that by virtue of mental illness the defendant not be able to understand the nature of the criminal act. The so-called irresistible impulse prong arose in an 1887 case (*Parsons v. State*), which allowed that even if the nature of the act was known, if the individual did not have the ability to refrain from doing it there would be exculpation.

Seventy-seven years after that, in 1954, the *Durham* test provided that if the act was viewed as the "product" of mental disease, there could be exculpation. *Durham* did not have significant longevity. It was so vaguely worded that it soon fell into disfavor.

Proposed in 1955 and ultimately published in its final form in 1962, the American Law Institute test was a two-prong approach involving lack of knowledge of wrongfulness, or inability to refrain, both occurring as a function of mental illness. The tenor of the times through the 1960s and 1970s was such that this broader approach to dealing with mental illness and criminal responsibility seemed somewhat settled. However, the attempt on the life of President Reagan became the lynchpin for a return to what was essentially a *M'Naghten* standard. The Insanity Defense Reform Act of 1984 (IDRA) specified for federal crimes that the only standard would be mental illness or defect that caused an inability to appreciate the wrongfulness of the act. Over time, most of the states with two-prong insanity defenses moved to enact statutes that conformed to the federal approach.

Definitions are always an issue. The legal specifications of mental health and mental defect have been no exceptions. In both psychology and law there has been significant disputation regarding the nature and impact of mental disability. In general, however, in regard to criminal responsibility, the requirements reduce to the presence of a psychotic condition or such substantial impairment of intellect that significant retardation is present. In Michigan, mental illness is a "substantial disorder of thought or mood" but there is a further elaborated description. The Ohio definition is "substantial disorder of thought, mood, perception, orientation, or memory, that grossly impairs judgment, behavior, the capacity to recognize reality, or ability to meet the ordinary demands of life."

In the mental health world, official definitions and criteria are found in the system developed by the American Psychiatric Association. The initial edition of the *Diagnostic and Statistical Manual* (DSM) was published in 1952 with iterations to the current DSM-IV-TR. As of the third edition in 1980, the system came to specify differences between Axis I conditions (which are clinical and a focus of treatment) and Axis II conditions (which are personality disorders and often viewed as relatively, but not entirely, resistant to intervention). At this point, certain case law or statutory law has specifically excluded personality disorders, particularly referencing antisocial personality disorder. This category is unique in that it is essentially behavioral and it is defined by reference to criminal or antisocial behavior. However, there have been difficulties in developing and refining this nosology, which reflects the fact that knowledge about the human brain, its development, and human personality are subjects of emerging findings.

Another aspect in the current evolution of criminal responsibility is the concept of burden of proof. IDRA reversed the burden from prosecution to defense, thus defining insanity as affirmative (defendant has the burden of proving what is asserted). Following suit and in common with most states, Ohio, which had relied on case law (*Staten*, 1971), passed legislation in 1990 to place the burden on defense (and to instate a *M'Naghten* single-prong approach). The standard, however, was that of preponderance, meaning more likely than not, which is the lowest of the standards required by courts. Another approach to narrowing the door for exculpation was Michigan's 1976 guilty but mentally ill (GBMI) category. However, this approach, which allowed a finding that the individual was criminally responsible but the act involved significant contribution of mental illness, did not reduce the number of "true" NGRI cases (Roberts and Golding, 1991). The effect was essentially to formalize that mentally ill persons who were found guilty and responsible should receive mental health assistance.

Finally, it is interesting to note that the history of chaos or complexity theory has an intriguing recursive property of itself being complex. In common with many other developments in scientific thought, complexity theory is the coming together of many strands in many areas. Thus, there was the work of Brian Arthur in economics in the 1980s, concurrent findings in biology, which were incorporating DNA and other cellular complexities, and work in physics and even in weather prediction which was revolutionized by the ability to look at large and complex systems from outer space. The focal points of all of these different levels of scientific observation and the development of the mathematics of complexity theory came together. The result was the notion that an explanation of any complex system had to rest on the observation of the patterns that were created, the interrelationships and interdependencies of those patterns, and on principles of self-organization. Complexity began to sound much like the modern equivalent of very old notions of free will (but there were some essential differences as well) (Bütz, 1997; Waldrop, 1992).

In summary, the development of complexity theory, a very modern phenomenon, is a formalization of what has been intuitively present in many aspects of the history of law, social systems, and philosophy, including its religious foundations. Furthermore, as pointed out by Waldrop (1992), the primary function of science is to provide explanations of phenomena. Prediction is secondary and always probabilistic. Consistently, when experts enter the complex system of the courtroom, and are asked for predictions, they are only capable of providing limited probabilistic statements. (Sometimes this scientifically necessary limitation is viewed as offending against the purpose of law, which is to make determinations on the basis of a specific person and a specific act.)

Pertinent Legal Cases

In general, when NGRI does not apply, diminished capacity is not supported as a desirable alternative. Rather, it has been held that mitigation can be presented at the time of sentencing on behalf of a defendant. The point is nicely illustrated in *Jackson v. The State of Texas* (April 13, 2005). In this case, the appellant, Jackson, had a history of mental illness. He and his brother arrived home, became involved in an argument, with verbal and physical interaction. Although their mother had been warned by mental health authorities to call the police should the defendant become aggressive with anyone in the household, she did not do so since there had been little to gain from prior episodes in which the police were involved. The appellant and brother went to sleep but some hours later, Jackson killed his brother using hammer blows to the head. The issue of mental illness was raised belatedly and the trial court limited testimony regarding mental state to a description of the problems that Jackson had, to the fact that he was not mentally retarded, to the opinion that he was competent to stand trial, and that he did not meet the *M'Naghten* standard for insanity. Subsequently, defense counsel tried to raise the argument that Jackson "lacked the mental capacity to intentionally or knowingly cause bodily injury." The state raised objections to that argument, which was sustained, and Jackson was found guilty and sentenced to 60 years of imprisonment. The appeal raised issues of diminished capacity, indicated that there had been a confusion in past case law between diminished capacity and diminished responsibility, maintained that diminished capacity was recognized in Texas, and suggested that the constitutions of both the United States and Texas contained provisions that allow a defendant to present a diminished capacity defense.

In parsing the issues, the court first of all indicated that the fact that Jackson was para-noid did not reach the level of a negation of a *mens rea* because, in effect, it was the motive for what the court saw as an intentional act. With respect to diminished capacity, reference was made to a prior case (*Wagner v. State*, 1985). However, this case included the element of "sud-den passion," which was not in evidence in this act even if the doctrine existed. However, the court then also supported the state in the conclusion that there was no "diminished capacity as an affirmative defense." The opinion stated that evidence could be presented to a jury to negate a *mens rea* element, which could sometimes include defendant's mental illness. In so stating, it was found that the potential for a kind of diminished capacity defense did exist on a case-by-case basis, at the discretion of the judge. In the instant case of *Jackson*, however, the judge had ruled that the evidence was not admissible. The appeals court then went on to point out that such evidence could be admitted at the point of sentencing.

The above case is interesting for several reasons. First of all, it illustrated some of the almost tortuous reasoning that can be found in mitigatory defenses. It also illustrated that the general status of diminished capacity is not clear even where appeals courts have affirmed that it does not exist. These kinds of ambiguities in law not only give rise to interesting legal scholarship and discourse but also enhance uncertainty about outcome in situations where human factors alone are complicated and interwoven in ways that make coming to solid and simple conclusions difficult. For forensic experts, this lack of clarity creates shifting grounds on the basis of which evaluations and testimony must be prepared.

Other relevant and significant case law and statutory findings are presented below by category of interest.

The primary sources for legal definitions of NGRI include importantly the original *M'Naghten* (1843) case, the now generally discredited *Durham* (1954), the American Law Institute test (1962), and the IDRA (1984). The progression of these conceptualizations illus-trates the swing to the conservative approach that is currently favored. Huckabee (2006) has written extensively over a considerable period of time in favor of that kind of tightening and generally took the position that the best approach has a fairly strict *mens rea* requirement. From his perspective, only severe mental illnesses of a nature that entirely disrupt thinking to the point that inability to understand the act committed is involved will satisfy a reason-able constitutional and societal approach. At the same time, he noted that there needs to be some room for a case-by-case consideration of unusual mental states other than psycho-sis, without losing sight of the strict wrongfulness aspect. Huckabee, predictably enough, favored only a full sanity defense and not the inclusion of diminished capacity.

Support for the conservative approach is certainly found in contemporary cases. Thus, in Utah, in *State v. Bishop* (1988), the defendant presented that he was a pedophile who was unable to refrain from his activities with young children, he needed to avoid being caught for this intractable behavior, and therefore had to kill his victims. On that basis, he felt that he should receive a reduction from intentional to unintentional homicide. The court was unim-pressed. In fact, in Utah, as in Idaho and Montana, there has been a partial abolition of NGRI (however, as with Michigan's GBMI, the practical impact has been insubstantial since mental state evidence is still considered on a case-by-case basis). As already illustrated in *Jackson*, in the arena of diminished capacity (and diminished responsibility), both case law and statu-tory law provide for a confusing *mélange* of findings. Thus, there are jurisdictions that accept variants of this defense, such as West Virginia, Tennessee, Hawaii, New Mexico, and New York. Other states have specifically rejected diminished capacity either by case law (Ohio: *State v. Wilcox*, 1982; Maryland: *Johnson v. State*, 1983) or by statute in the case of California

(California Penal Code, 2002). On the contrary, Washington state, by statute, sets forth seven conditions that define the presentation of diminished capacity evidence and are clearly aimed at restricting the court to information that would pass a current *Daubert* (1993) challenge.

Specific case information gives a flavor of further kinds of confusions, solutions, and inequities that can present. Thus, in *State v. Hall* (1997) in Tennessee, a defendant was allowed to introduce reduced serotonin, alcohol use, brain injury, mental retardation, and the diagnosis intermittent explosive disorder to sustain a diminished capacity defense. However, when he was unsuccessful and appealed the case, the appeals court not illogically took the position that the jury did not have to be given options for other charges (the classic diminished responsibility approach). Rather, the panel was appropriately instructed about the requisites for full criminal responsibility in terms of *mens rea* and was given an adequate opportunity to evaluate evidence whether that *mens rea* was present.

In another case, the issue of whether the requirements of an affirmative defense was presented in the state of New Jersey, but the appeals court ruled that if a diminished capacity issue was raised, the prosecution had the burden to prove beyond reasonable doubt (the highest standard) that the condition did not exist (*State of New Jersey v. Moore*, 1991). This ruling represented a most permissive or promental health approach in this arena and was in significant distinction to the general trend seen throughout the country in recent years.

In the category of special affirmative defenses, there are three very specific assertions and one of a more general nature. Specifically, battered spouse defense, obsessive/compulsive disorder defense, and multiple personality/dissociative identity disorder defense all involve presenting expert evidence to the court that indicates the presence of an identified mental condition with behavioral implications. These defenses further assert that by virtue of that condition, the degree to which the individual is responsible for what he or she has done in the criminal context should be at least reduced.

In regard to the OCD condition, there are limited cases and no particular success has attended this strategy. A recent case, *People v. Moore* (2002), involved an appeal of a premeditated murder based on the notion that the jury should have been instructed about a partial defense on the basis of an obsessive/compulsive disorder. However, there was no expert evidence offered in regard to that condition or its relationship to the crime. In general, an OCD defense would require that the expert be able to support, and the jury or fact finder determine, that the individual was unable to restrain from the act due to the presence of this compelling behavioral problem. However, it is relatively easy to show that individuals afflicted with OCD vary depending on the degree to which their symptoms are manifest and do, in fact, have at least some control. Furthermore, the behaviors involved tend to be focal and ritualistic, if not symbolic, and do not include the complex and varying behaviors that are necessary to plan and carry out an isolated act of murder.

Multiple personality disorder, or DID, has received a fair amount of legal attention. Often the issues have focused on competency rather than responsibility, with the argument being that the individual is literally not "all there" and due to lack of presence cannot assist counsel at trial. In general, this approach to competency has not been successful (Elkins, 2005; Slovenko, 1993). From the standpoint of psychological theory, several problems present. First of all, there is lack of agreement that DID involves fully formed multiple personalities (see Brown, Scheflin, and Hammond, 1998; and Spanos, 1994, 1996 for varying perspectives). It has been demonstrated that the diagnosis tends to be made at high rates by therapists who specialize in its treatment and, otherwise, is rarely seen, particularly by therapists and diagnosticians who are skeptical (Spanos, 1996). To add further to the problems of this diagnostic category, there is the notion that in some cases one or more personalities are aware of the others while other ego states are existing unaware. Research and clinical assessment have demonstrated behavioral differences in different states, but critics have noted that social role behavior combined with need to avoid responsibility could easily explain such findings. At the same time, there is now support from functional magnetic resonance imaging research that different conscious states are associated with different brain patterns (see, for example, Lanius, Williamson, Boksman, Dersome, Gupta, Nerfeld, Gate, and Menon, 2002; she and colleagues have done significant work in this area). Taking an insecure conceptualization of how an individual's personality is organized into a courtroom, where the question is whether a heinous act was performed, and, if so, what should be the consequence, creates all kinds of tensions.

A recent case, *People v. Mendez* (2003), is illustrative. Forensic evaluation addressed the issue of competency to stand trial and the finding was for the state. The DID diagnosis did not support inability to assist in her defense. However, after being found competent, the defendant then raised and pled to the New York State extreme emotional disturbance, which is a type of diminished responsibility. Apparently, this defendant had a long history of psychiatric problems with hospitalizations, which included a diagnosis of DID. The fact picture involved an argument between herself and her boyfriend about his unfaithfulness. The argument came to some kind of preliminary conclusion, after which the couple went to bed; she then left, came back, and asked him if he was tired; he indicated he was and she told him that he would rest for a long time. She proceeded to stab him to death with the knife she had retrieved from the kitchen. Although reduction of culpability might seem questionable, the presence of the statutory conditions for this defense may indeed have been adequately met.*

A somewhat notorious exception involving a successful DID defense was the Ohio case of *Milligan* (1978; also see especially Keyes, 1981) was a media event and one of few where a finding of exculpation (NGRI) occurred in consequence of this diagnosis. Milligan's 23 personalities were accepted as the basis for nonresponsibility as a person.

In the case of battered spouse defenses, a number of very special circumstances have to be met. There are states that have the battered spouse defense as part of statutory law and there are case laws as well that support this defense. However, the defense largely rests upon subjective data and requires professional opinion on not only subjective state of mind but also special limitations of perception. A number of cases, beginning with *Ibn–Tamas v. United States* (1979), exist that established criteria. In Ohio, there is a statutory provision that, among other things, spells out the requirements for expert evidence (Ohio Revised Code 2901.06, 1990). Essentially, states explicitly permitting evidence in this area require that there be a foundation for the defendant having arrived at a state of learned helplessness, high anxiety, and the inability to perceive alternatives to death including those that may present to more rational view (such as going to a women's shelter). The picture that can be successful needs to document, preferably by way of information from multiple sources, the existence of a terroristic environment over an extended period of time. Classically, the batterer has not only engaged in periodic severe beating of the partner but also threatened

---

* In New York State law, extreme emotional disturbance may or may not involve diagnosed conditions. There is generally presented evidence of a build up of tension over an extended period of time with the individual either on the basis of pre-existing psychological vulnerability or by virtue of the particularity of the situation, suddenly acting with lethal violence, in effect discharging what is a delayed response to accumulated affronts. Triggers to the action are usually identifiable as well as ensuing compromised judgment and rationality.

children, may have killed animals as a way to demonstrate power, and has forced various indignities upon the family. Additionally, there is usually some degree of isolation of the partner from other sources such as family and friends.

In a case in which the present author provided a third opinion on request of prosecution (but the outcome of which actually favored defense), the woman's behavior and the context met all the requirements. Her essential psychological functioning indicated cognitive deficits from both physical and psychological traumas. She had been repeatedly head injured, the children had been threatened, and all the children's pets were killed in front of them. She and the children had been forced to eat dog food. There had been significant isolation of the woman from other sources of input and the family lived in a remote area. Interestingly, one of the behaviors often found in cases of this sort, turning oneself in, was in place in this particular case. The husband after abusing her told her he was going to sleep and would kill her and the children when he awoke. The woman, after killing her husband, who had passed out from his latest drinking bout, called a sister to come get the children and called the police to come get her.

One of the most important kinds of evidence to collect in repeatedly battered women involves neuropsychological assessment. Chronic brain injury can result in a condition associated with boxing often referred to as being "punchdrunk." The individual may be impaired for planning, perceiving options, and initiating action effectively. In battering cases, some of the contribution may be due to chronic stress impacts, but it can also reflect the fact that a favorite target of beatings is the head since bruising is invisible. The reverberations of the brain inside the skull create subtle and diffuse brain insults (Chitra, Ganghadar, Rao, and Hezck, 1989; Gayford, 1975; McMillan and Glucksman, 1987; Strut and Black, 1988; Uma and Shobhini, 1987).

There are a number of existing references that detail the primary case law in death penalty mitigation starting with *Furman v. Georgia* (1972), and continuing with cases that have defined the scope of mitigation and the acceptable kinds of evidence that can be brought to bear (*Gregg v. Georgia*, 1976; *Jurek v. Texas*, 1976; *Lockett v. Ohio*, 1978). A new set of factors was introduced when the Supreme Court allowed victim impact statements to be initiated by the state (*Payne v. Tennessee*, 1991). Most recently, there were the cases of *Simmons v. Roper* (2003), which eliminated the application of the death penalty to persons under the age of 18, and *Adkins v. Virginia* (2002), which ended its use with retarded persons. In *Adkins*, the problem then became one of psychological evaluations to determine which defendants were in fact retarded and which defendants might be malingering retardation. Subsequently, the so-called "Flynn effect" was raised, which in essence involved the notion that IQ tests taken at different times give different scores because individuals are being measured against a set of norms that were established at an earlier period. Significant disputation has ensued with much chatter over professional Internet list serves about the ethical and scientific implications for using Wechsler IQ tests, normed at prior times, on current defendants claiming to be exempt from the death penalty on the basis of retardation. Flynn (2006), who in the 1980s brought this anomaly to the attention of psychological science, took the following position: "No defense attorney should be allowed … [as a basis for exemption from capital punishment] … to argue that a person who today scores 71 (against current norms) would probably score 65 against norms of 20 years hence" (p. 186). He went on to point out that the Supreme Court,

… rightly undermines such arguments by setting as a criterion of M.R. that a person should be two or more standard deviations below the mean—if we add the corollary that the mean refers to the average performance of Americans at the time the person was tested. The prosecution should not make the unwarranted assumption that the defendant will gain ground on his or her cohort, in terms of IQ, as the defendant ages ... (p. 186)

Flynn then concluded his argument by pointing out that while intelligence tests are a necessary component to evaluation, IQ scores "are not like a loaf of bread that simply is what it is" (p. 187) and suggested that interpretation is a necessity. Thus, he illustrated yet another nonrandom but individually varying factor into the application of psychological science in the courtroom.

Applied Ethics and Moral Considerations

In general, psychological work in the mitigation context does not potentially offend against the specific ethical principles of good practice. These directives go to proper scientific foundations, appropriate delineation of roles and observation of boundaries, and the general accountabilities involved in record keeping, advertising, financial arrangements, delivery of services, and constraints in the work of teaching and research. Individuals may act in breach in any of these areas, of course, but doing mitigation work *per se* does not specifically create an inordinate potential for such lapses. Forensic work in many respects is not different from clinical or organizational work in the expectations represented by the ethical standards.

However, in the case of the overriding aspirational principles, which articulate the "very highest ethical ideals of the profession" (American Psychological Association, 2002, p. 3), significant discourse presents with respect to forensic work in mitigation contexts, only a limited portion of which can be developed in this section as follows:

a. Beneficence and nonmaleficence. In the area of death penalty work, the instruction to do no harm immediately leads to the issue of whether psychologists should engage in competency to die evaluations. However, even work in death penalty mitigation implicitly supports the system that can act to kill or severely cause suffering to an individual. Similarly, in any contribution to sentencing, including downward adjustment of penalty or diversion to mental health or substance abuse courts, while it may benefit the individual assessed, it also precipitates an often unwanted experience. Furthermore, "successful" contribution of mitigation evidence may lead to reduction of penalty with the potential for the defendant to return to offensive behavior with further harm to society and its membership. Arguably, the psychologist who recommended alternatives has contributed to those problems.

b. Fidelity and responsibility. It can be argued that the potentials for breaches of trust are far higher in much forensic work, especially where there may be ambiguities, or at least confusions in the mind of those being served regarding the loyalties and obligations of the psychologist. It is for this reason that forensic practice requires explicit statements of confidentiality or the lack thereof and some assurance that the individual is knowledgeably participating in the process. Even witnesses or ancillary contacts in psychological investigations are often not only instructed in the reasons for their participation but also asked to sign statements of understanding and permissions to proceed in recognition of the hazards of this area. A dilemma arguably presents where severe psychosis or deficiency of intellect may not allow the individual to understand the purpose and limitations of the evaluation. In some cases, obtaining written permission from a court-appointed legal guardian may be necessary.

c. Integrity. Forensic psychologists are often called upon to assess whether there is likely malingering or other impression management taking place. To do that, there are specific tests that are themselves deceptive regarding their purpose and individuals agreeing to be assessed are not, and cannot be, informed about the nature of the examination or it could not be carried forward. Thus, the structured interview of reported symptoms (SIRS) (Rogers, Bagby, and Dickens, 1992) is one example of a test that includes, by necessity, deception in its process.

d. Justice. Psychologists are enjoined to practice without prejudice. However, any participation in the criminal justice system in the United States supports a system wherein there is ample evidence that the poor and minorities are overrepresented (U.S. Department of Justice, 2005). For every trial of O. J. Simpson type, where a team of attorneys and multiple experts including psychologists worked to obtain an acquittal, there are thousands of cases where limited resources ensure limitations of potential outcomes. An additional caution is warranted because psychological instrumentation is known to have some deficits when applied to minority and nonclinical populations.

e. Respect for people's rights and dignity. This principle, as well, is confronted by the inequities of the criminal justice system, with hazards to the psychologists working in the area.

Forensic psychology training and literature have emphasized that practitioners should enter the courtroom on behalf of their data and should offer only opinions that are fully supportable in an objective way. However, the tools with which we work have many weaknesses, especially as they get transplanted from the clinic to the jail or prison and on to the forum. At a more subjective level, it is recognized that the person who is hired by an attorney is going to have a sense of alliance or loyalty, which can be biasing. Law in the United States is based on the adversarial system and, while in many forensic contexts the court may call for independent expertise, in mitigation cases it is not uncommon for there to be a request for services from defense. Conversely, where presentence work is generated through a court clinic, there is some identification of the psychologist with the state. In many jurisdictions, there is no court clinic and the state or defense counsel hires experts. There is some tendency to develop favorite sources who then become overidentified with their employers.

The best forensic attitude to have is that of skepticism toward everyone (including the individual retaining the psychologist). The present author approaches instruction of graduate students in forensic work with the somewhat overstated following direction:

> In clinical work, you ally with the patient and assume him or her to be telling you the truth as best as the individual can; in forensic work you must assume the potential for deceit and be surprised and delighted when you have determined it not to be present.

Empirically Based Methods and Applications

Assessment for mitigatory purposes, whether in capital cases or in lesser penalty contexts, involves reliance on a full range of both empirically validated but also nonnormative and nonstandardized procedures. Empirically validated procedures would include such measures as the Minnesota Multiphasic Personality Inventory-2 (MMPI-2), the Millon

Clinical Multiaxial Inventory III (MCMI-III), the Wechsler tests, and the personality assessment inventory among others. Significant research and normative data underlie these instruments, particularly in the case of the MMPI-2 series and the Wechslers, provided they are used to reflect case-specific and statute-based variables such as mental deficiency and mental illness. However, there is a weakness in that these methods were essentially developed to identify and measure problems of people presenting themselves in the clinical setting. The goal of assessment was generally one of contributing to an intervention or therapy plan. These approaches were then moved to the courtroom with the very real possibility that the norms may not fully support accurate interpretations.

Even tests developed for the forensic arena are not without problems. Instruments such as the SIRS (Rogers et al., 1992), the Gudjonsson Suggestibility Scales (Gudjonsson, 2003), and a variety of malingering approaches (Rogers, 1997) have been developed secondary to specific legal concerns or, in some cases, based on the content of legal statutes. In criminal responsibility, an approach known as the Rogers Criminal Responsibility Assessment Scales (R-CRAS) introduced structure but incorporated data from a variety of sources; although it has some psychometric properties, it is also vulnerable to significant criticism due to normative and other weaknesses (Rogers and Ewing, 1992). The development of normative bases is at beginning stages and, thus, the empirical foundations are not yet at impressive levels.

In addition to tests that have a lot, or at least some, empirical foundation, there are nonnormative, nonstandardized procedures, notably the interview, which is a stalwart of both clinical and forensic work. There are highly structured interviews which allow a certain amount of standardization, but they are rarely appropriate for the purposes of the courtroom. Furthermore, the assessment of criminal defendants is a highly case-driven, idiographic process that requires an unstructured interview which can follow the subject and the leads that the overall complexly presenting case situation offers.

The use of projective techniques has been debated with many cautioning against their use (Goldstein, 2003; Grove and Barden, 1999; Grove, Barden, Garb, and Lilienfeld, 2002; Melton, Petrilla, Poythress, and Slobogin, 1997), but substantial support is also found (Gacono, Evans, and Viglione, 2002; Gacono and Meloy, 1994; Hilsenroth and Stricker, 2004; McCann, 1998; Meloy, 2005; Ritzler, Erard, and Pettigrew, 2002a, 2002b; Rosenthal, Hiller, Bornstein, Berry, and Brunell-Neuleib, 2001). The present author would suggest that the negative side of the controversy has been fed by inappropriate use of projectives. There is rarely, if ever, a good reason to use such devices to second guess or even fortify a DSM-IV diagnosis based on MMPI-2, carefully collected third-party information, and carefully preserved interviews. Furthermore, in most criminal responsibility cases, mental health condition at a past time is the focus; psychological testing at the time of the act is usually not available and testing post the act is not relevant (except perhaps to document an ongoing condition for which there is prior evidence). It should also be noted that the ever-popular MMPI-2, and other supposedly objective tests like it, are based on group norms and may be biased for evaluation of persons from some sectors of the society. Even where the MMPI-2 is consistent with the presence of a mental illness, the proper conclusion is a statement that persons with similar profiles have been described with the condition, but this individual may or may not fall into that classification. It is basic to all assessment and to forensics in particular that diagnostic and related opinions are based on multiple sources of data.

However, in certain areas of mitigation work, where an explanation of the psychology of the individual in its broadest sense is desirable, projectives can reasonably be part of the data pool. In mitigation to sentencing, relational aspects are relevant to treatment recommendations—and treatment planning is a significant part of risk reduction. Projectives are more often than not used in the context of death penalty mitigation, where the task is to provide a narrative that details the life and the personality of the defendant and then relates that information to the criminal context.

As already referenced, use of ancillary sources and the collection of third-party information is part of the process. However, such data contain all kinds of problems from an empirical standpoint. For example, in doing presentence investigations, usually the province of parole officers but sometimes an activity in which psychologists become involved, there is contact with victims. Complex motives and even credibility issues can sometimes be raised, just as are generally raised when it comes to the self-report of the defendant. Death penalty mitigation procedures in particular rely heavily on not only statements of the defendant and his family or friends or associates but also records review. The reliability of the way in which the records were created and maintained, the mixed motives that may have gone into some of those records, even including school and prison reports, and the addition of interpretive responding on the part of the forensic psychologist add to the potentials for a challenge to reliability and, therefore, to validity of the methods that are necessarily used.

Table 11.1 provides a guide to the limitations of these data.

Basic Points to Consider in Clinical-Forensic Assessment

The following guidelines may be of assistance in enhancing the independence of forensic practitioners in their work:

1. The first task of the forensic practitioner is to clarify roles and relationships. Steps to take include.
   a. Determining who is retaining the psychologist (defense, the court, prosecution).
   b. Determining under what legal strictures the motions have been made with copies of said motions obtained.
   c. Obtaining agreement concerning payment with advance retainer being the preferred mode (specifics regarding retainer policies should be in writing and provided to retaining counsel—in some cases, motions specify later payment, particularly when the psychologist is responsible to the court but also in assigned cases where the court is the source of defense support).
   d. Establishing clear understanding about limits of confidentiality or lack thereof.
2. Once the above details are in place, the next task of the forensic practitioner is to determine the legal question and the law that is governing what will be considered by the court system and what is considered relevant. This information often can be obtained from the retaining attorney but should be augmented by independent review of the relevant statutes.
3. Once the target of the investigation is identified, decisions should be made about strategies for appropriate data collection. Each of these sources should be evaluated with respect to scientific respectability à la Daubert (1993) inquiry.
4. As indicated in item 1 above, clarification of confidentiality status must be made from the outset. Private consultation is completely protected and takes place between the attorney and the psychologist. If the consultation involves evaluation of a defendant,

Table 11.1 Evaluating Third-Party Information (TPI)

Category	Source	Reliability	Validity	Type of Data	Degree of Relationship to the Instant Offense	Contents Multilevel[a]
School records	Administrators, teachers, and counselors	Varies—good to poor	Varies; significant bias sources	Objective and subjective	Usually none	Sometimes
Juvenile, adult criminal records, and prison records	POs, COs, educators, counselors, and mental health workers	Varies—good to poor	Varies; significant bias sources	Objective and subjective	Often none	Sometimes
Treatment records	Mental health treatment providers and tests	Varies—good to moderate	Generally good	Objective and subjective	Often none	Sometimes
Medical records and medical examiner reports	Medical professionals	Generally good	Generally good; exceptions exist	Objective with some subjective	Medical records usually none; medical examiner report directly related	Usually not
Family sources	Family of defendant	Questionable and high variation	Varies; high sources of bias	Subjective	Highly related or not related	May or may not
Victim statements	Victim	Victim statements high to low	Varies; bias sources exist	Subjective	Usually highly related	May or may not
Crime scene data	Police, investigators	Generally high; depends on procedural integrity	Generally high but some variation	Objective with some subjective	Highly related	Usually not
Media reports	Newspapers, TV, etc.	Highly variable	Highly variable	Subjective and objective	Highly related	Often

a Not only reflects the informant or source's experience but also incorporates by extension of other sources.

the defendant must be fully informed about the way in which any data collected will be used. It is recommended that signed releases be obtained, even where defendants understand that only their attorneys will be recipients of information. If the consultation is court ordered, even though on motion of defense, unless that motion has specified and the court has agreed to a private consultation, the results are not confidential and signed releases are a desirable component to completing the evaluation. Results are then made available to court, to defense, and to prosecution see Appendix L for one model of a consent form.

5. Confidentiality of communications with attorneys in criminal court cases is generally protected by the mutual privileged communication provisions in state laws. However, some ongoing disputation is occurring in civil arenas; it is wise not to put into writing anything that is likely to contain unsupportable conclusions, even as a work product memorandum.

6. Many practitioners have taken the position that proper forensic procedure best involves nonconfidential evaluations, the results of which are made available to both prosecution and defense (see, for example, Melton, Petrilla, and Poythress, 1997). There are, however, specific legal contexts where such an approach is not possible or appropriate. One of these is death penalty mitigation and another exception involves providing defense counsel with consultation about the viability of some defense, such as an NGRI or other mitigatory plea. Results are communicated to defense counsel for purposes assisting in the question whether to go forward with a motion versus discounting that strategy.

7. In the special case of death penalty work, two approaches have been taken. One involves complete separation of psychologist as the expert witness from the broad-based mitigation effort. This separation allows the expert to be retained by defense but not function as a team member. In such an approach, the psychologist may not be privy to all of the mitigation information. The role involves evaluation of defendant and testimony if desired by defense. The other approach involves integration into the defense team,* participation in planning for the mitigation trial, and work with the defendant and family that can include a variety of activities. Prior to trial, there is collection of sensitive information, often of a type that has been kept secret in families. Sometimes there is a request to assist the defendant and family in the process of evaluating plea offers that are available. At the point at which the mitigation hearing looms, the psychologist engages in a consulting role in terms of determining whether to present the information that has been developed or whether to stay out of the courtroom. The psychologist may also contribute to decisions about who should be brought forward as witnesses for the defense and may provide input about how to handle the task of testifying. The psychologist may become involved in assisting the defendant in presenting whatever statements he wishes to make on his own behalf. Clearly, there are pitfalls in this kind of multiple role functioning. However, a strict appreciation for the legal constraints, the absolute requirements of honesty, and the

---

* Goldstein (2003) takes exception to such a posture, maintaining that the psychologist's need for objectivity is too imperiled by identification with the defense team. The present author does not concur and sees the duty of the psychologist as that of honesty in testimony but as aligned with goal of a life sentence. It is acknowledged that there may be multiple roles involved with consultation, evaluation, and even a kind of intervention occurring.

need for self-monitoring for both the appearance and actuality of improper influence allow avoidance of ethical error.

8. It is important that forensic psychologists know the basic law in the areas in which they are practicing and particularly understand what the laws request of them. There is then a decision that has to be made in any instant case assignment whether what the psychologist can present in a scientifically respectable fashion is germane to the specific questions that have been raised.

Avoiding Evaluation and Consultation Errors

The primary obligation in any forensic task is to answer a question of relevance to the legal system using methods of data collection that meet the highest levels of scientific respectability available at the time. Forensic psychologists have the ethical obligation to provide only information warranted by their data regardless of who may be retaining them. However, it is also known that the loyalties that develop between an attorney and the expert whom he or she retains can operate both consciously and unconsciously in how the expert sees and interprets data with ambiguous aspects. It is perhaps reassuring that there is some evidence that psychologists can resist bias and operate with a fair amount of independence. For example, in a study of responses to the draw-a-person, a technique well known for ambiguity and insecurity of interpretive schemes, a particular method for identifying emotional disturbance was evaluated in a fairly special way. Clinicians were given information about abuse status, both true and false, in a randomized model, and then scored the protocols. Analysis of results showed that the system was applied without impact of knowledge, either accurate or inaccurate, regarding the background factor of abuse (Bruening, Wagner, and Johnson, 1997). What can be said at this point is that while alliances between retaining attorneys and experts can easily lead to confirmatory bias and other sources of lack of objectivity, clinicians are capable of exercising self-imposed controls that limit the degree to which conscious and unconscious sources of error creep into their work. To the extent that they operate on a self-aware basis for the underlying sources of noncase-related factors and impose appropriate organized schemes for proceeding, they operate at the necessary ethical and forensically responsible levels.

In areas where there will be substantial reliance on actual behavior in interview, it is generally important to create a veridical record. In cases where dissociative disorders including DID are involved, and in spite of the very fragile legal status that currently exists (or in response to it), some specific guides have been created. Savitz (1990), an attorney, recommended an approach reminiscent of death penalty mitigation in its scope (broad, including ancillary interviews from varying sources, complete mental health assessment especially referencing prior history and records) but quite different in the role of the psychologist. In his scheme, the examining expert would have no other involvement in the case and no prior knowledge of the case except that which would be written down and given to him or her. It was his opinion that a person trained in forensic hypnosis who would follow the established guidelines would be necessary and would be best appointed by order of the court (and therefore would be performing a nonconfidential evaluation). Obviously, while the recommendations are consistent with good forensic practice, the hazards from a defense standpoint may make counsel reluctant to endorse same.

Much has been written about problems of risk assessment, an area in which forensic clinicians are often called on to provide evaluation and ultimately testimony. The problems of that kind of prediction have been, and continue to be, a matter of substantial discussion with ethical concerns raised whether such predictions should be made on the basis of the instrumentation available to the practitioner. At the same time, and consistent with the present author's reliance on complexity concepts, models and instruments that move beyond simple linear statistical approaches are showing promise for present and future work (Borum, 1996; Hanson, 1998; Hiday, 2006; Sjostedt, 2002; Westen, 2004).

Mitigatory work also involves, in some cases, specific references to dangerousness. In the case of death penalty mitigation, a review of capital statutes determined that 21 included dangerousness as an aggravating factor (McPherson, 1998). Certain laws, notably the Texas statute, explicitly ask for an assessment of dangerousness, which is to be considered by the jury in formal decision making. The unconscionable performance of forensic psychiatrist Grigson in his willingness to pronounce individuals likely to reoffend in dangerous ways even without seeing them (see *Barefoot v. U.S.*, 1983) notwithstanding, it is still possible to raise serious concerns where far more ethical and scientific constraints have been observed.

In mitigation, the use of actuarial instruments has been a focus of concern. At best, these approaches (the Psychopathy Checklist Revised (PCL-R), the Static 99, Violence Risk Assessment Guide, and others) give probability estimates that lead to significant questions when their results are the basis for decisions about the future—even the life—of a defendant (see, for example, Walsh and Walsh, 2006, for a discussion of adequacies and limitations of the PCL-R in the courts). The most reliable approaches are least dependent on subjective data. However, the only basis that generates opportunity for intervention and changes requires systematic consideration of "softer" and more subjective sources of information about variables that can respond to inputs. Furthermore, from a scientific standpoint, recidivism base rates are such that the levels of prediction (all under 50%) can be seriously challenged for making recommendations and predictions about individual defendants.

The application of complexity theory to law and, specifically, to the prediction of dangerousness has been made (Williams and Arrigo, 2002). These authors have applied chaos theory processes of iteration, bifurcation, and sensitive dependence on initial conditions to risk estimation. In an interesting analysis, they pointed out that the Supreme Court took the position that a lower measure of standard of proof was appropriate when making decisions that would deprive a person of liberty. The issue that they presented involved contrasting probabilities. They argued that it is not possible beyond a 50% level to predict violence with respect to an individual. To meet the civil standard for commitment, clear and convincing, a 75% level of certainty is necessary. The Supreme Court, in *Addington v. Texas* (1979), articulated the clear and convincing standard for civil commitment cases rather than the lesser standard of more likely than not, to protect people from unjust deprivation of liberty. With respect to criminal defendants, where the standard of proof is at least 90%, they argued that there is no way that current predictions, which are essentially based on linear systems, can ever reach necessary levels to be acceptable evidence against an individual. It was noted that individuals are themselves extremely complex systems, with sensitive dependence on the conditions that occur at different times. Further, the changes and evolution of individual functioning are themselves complexly determined. Therefore, there cannot be prediction of individual dangerousness that meets either legal or scientific adequacy in the context of a process by which life and liberty are both at issue.

Furthermore, not only are the data of questionable adequacy for courtroom presentation but how testimony proceeds also becomes part of determining impact. Thus, in a discussion of the PCL-R and its use as a predictor of violence, DeMatteo and Edens (2006) made the following interesting comments:

> Our case law survey is not a useful means of addressing this question {probative versus prejudicial impact} directly as the potentially prejudicial effects of psychopathy, by the fact finder in each case, likely depend on the content of the proffered testimony and the types of opinions expressed by the examiner. For example, in criminal cases, descriptions of psychopaths as being similar to "fake fruit" might be considerably less biasing than describing them as being similar to Ted Bundy. Similarly, the statement that psychopathy is the single best correlate of violence among released psychiatric patients might have a stronger impact on legal decision makers than an equally correct statement indicating that psychopathy explains only 7% of the variance in violent behavior among these same patients. (p. 232)

The above quote from the work of DeMatteo and Edens (2006), which supported the use of the PCL-R in assessing and giving testimony regarding dangerousness in the court system, indicates that the indeterminacy aspects are amply present. The authors indicated that the effects on fact finders "likely depend on" or "might be considerably less biasing" or "might have a stronger impact" depending on the context. All of these phrases clearly reflect that the vicissitudes of wording and the particular ways in which concepts are put forward can make a difference to the impact of the testimony.

The above concepts and concerns have been addressed by Hart (2003), who detailed an approach to assessment that lends itself to understanding and explaining individuals in the context of crime events. He does not eliminate the importance of actuarials in his "anchored narrative approach," but he is clear that statistics based on group outcomes cannot either adequately account for a complex set of variables in a unique pattern or be reasonably used to predict the behavior of an individual. He advocates for the development of carefully grounded information that tells the story using various perspectives and varying sources. His discussion included details from a homicide case and nicely parallels the work that is characteristic for mitigation in death penalty work. Consistent with the position of the present author, his theoretical posture included principles of uncertainty and reiterated the rather fundamental principle that scientific theory is about explanation, whereas prediction has to do with correlations.

Treatment Considerations

Generally, assessment work in mitigation does not extend to an involvement in treatment. However, it is not uncommon for treatment recommendations to be made. Treatment recommendations need to be realistic in terms of available resources when they are included. A strict understanding of the forensic task in NGRI would not include a treatment recommendation, but it is not impossible to make conditional suggestions for certain kinds of treatment where these seem to be in the interest of the entire case situation. In mitigation to sentencing, treatment recommendations are properly part of the task. Also, as already discussed, death penalty work can involve consultation of a type that includes some interventions of limited scope.

Writing Forensic Reports and Acting as an Expert Witness

Forensic reports should be written to facilitate both examination and cross-examination as part of the legal process. Although many graduate school programs emphasize creating a document that explains an individual and integrates psychological test findings, forensic reports should provide test-by-test information as well as an integration and contextualization of that data.

Borum and Grisso (1996), on the basis of survey research into report writing for the court, made specific recommendations in writing criminal responsibility-related reports as follows:

1. Essential identifying material: basic personal information, identification of referral source, description of charges, purpose of evaluation, date of evaluation and date of report, place of evaluation, list of sources of data, statement of confidentiality, and indication of information given to defendant for purpose of evaluation.
2. Essential clinical content: mental health history, current mental status, formal mental status examination (MSE), and current psychotropic medication (the present author would note that although the MSE is generally expected in many evaluations, its reliability and validity have never been established and for all of its points, better sources of information exist; it does have the value of structuring inquiry to cover across a number of areas).
3. Often necessary: records and reports of behavior, such as police reports and other ancillary information along with mental health records.
4. Sometimes needed: psychological testing—in the survey, there was more tendency to use tests among psychologists than among psychiatrists, whereas the latter felt medical history was essential (the present author would note that the basis for information gathering should relate to the forensic goal and not to the practitioner's area of expertise).

Finally, these authors noted the importance of applying professional judgment to the assessment process, specifically recognizing that a hard and fast blueprint is not likely to serve well in the real-life situations which will be presented in criminal responsibility work. In any situation where test results or other data suggest potentials for malingering of responses, specific strategies must be designed, including use of standardized procedures such as the SIRS (Rogers et al., 1992), to evaluate potentials for sabotaging of the process. It is often very appropriate to videotape or audiotape interviews, both for later presentation to the court and for accuracy of review of behavior and verbal responding. Recording in most jails cannot be accomplished without obtaining a court order.

There are cases of record where discrepancies between narratives of defendants and victims have been "tested" by the use of polygraph. However, the admissibility of a polygraph is limited. In many respects, it is a tool not unlike psychological tests and other aspects of psychological assessment. It provides physiological correlates that have a probability of association with dissimulation. Three major questioning techniques exist whose selection may depend on the circumstances. Defendants have a right to not be compelled to self-incrimination (The Fifth Amendment to the U.S. Constitution), and it is only under relatively special circumstances that defense counsel will permit their clients to undergo such examinations. In some cases, attorneys will obtain private polygraph evaluations from experts they trust; depending on the outcome, they will then advise their clients to take a police-administered examination. For the most part, it is unlikely that polygraphy will be an option in cases of equivocal malingering (for contrasting opinions, see http://www.SkepDic.com and http://www.polygraph.org).

Of perhaps even more concern from the standpoint of "junk science" in the courtroom is the endorsement of many law enforcement groups of voice stress analysis. This technology has proven far less supportable than the polygraph, but in many U.S. law enforcement settings it has been favored because it takes much less expertise to manage (Virginia Department of Professional and Occupational Regulation, 2003).

There are many sources for expert witness behavior and guidelines, notably Melton et al. (1997). However, the fundamental principle is that one answers the questions on the basis of the information collected and with the proper caveats. It is incumbent on any forensic practitioner to know the rules of examination and cross-examination, as well as to know some of the techniques for presenting information that respond to courtroom strategies.

Direct and cross-examination can be conceptualized as an inverted triangle in which the scope of questioning continually narrows. The expert is brought forward and questioned in nonleading fashion for what was done, what were the results, and how those results relate to the issues at hand. Any attempts on the part of counsel conducting a direct examination to incorporate the desired answer into the question constitute leading and will generally be eliminated by objection from opposing counsel. At the same time, and presumably on the basis of pretrial preparation, the particular areas of interest will be amply developed through the acceptable nonleading general questions that are selected to serve that purpose—which, of course, is a prompt to experts to do pretrial preparation with counsel.

Cross-examination is limited to the scope of direct examination; however, the doors that are opened under direct are often construed relatively broadly by the court in the interest of giving cross-examination a full range. Cross-examination can often involve a requirement that the expert answer yes or no. However, where a question contains within it elements that are not supportable from the expert's opinion, there is the option of indicating that the question cannot be answered because either a positive or negative response would not be the whole truth. In some cases where a question ostensibly calling for a positive response is flawed with respect to its wording, a negative response will create the opening for an informed answer. Such a response either causes the cross-examiner to open the door wider for more discourse or cues the other lawyer for redirect. However, such a relatively active strategy on the part of an expert needs to be employed rarely and judiciously. The most important point is that the expert is not conducting the examinations. The attorneys have as their own expertise and duty the job of determining when and if any further questioning is necessary. It is however extremely important that experts not get into arguments and not become emotionally engaged because questions are not viewed as entirely legitimate.

Experts on the witness stand should develop extremely good ability to listen to the exact wording of questions given to them and respond consistent with that wording. It is rarely appropriate to make jokes or other frivolous comments and it is never appropriate to assume an air of arrogance or superiority. Such behavior on the part of experts will reduce the impact of even well-conceived responses to questions and make their work unpalatable to jurors. It is extremely important to use clear language that conveys to a reasonable audience the information. The ability to clarify and simplify abstruse concepts is one of the more important ones that a good witness brings to the courtroom.

Good cross-examination often makes of the opposing counsel's expert witness an ally. When that occurs, it is not the job of the expert to attempt in some way to counter the impact. Even in death penalty work where the expert may be identified as a part of the defense team, the duty is to present the data and answer the questions in a truthful and straightforward fashion regardless of the impact on the outcome of the case. Thus, in concluding a recent cross-examination of the present author, prosecution asked, after securing that my findings revealed no mental illness or deficiency, the following question: "Dr. McPherson, in any of the testimony you have offered here today, were there any mitigating factors directly bearing on the commission of the crime?" My answer was negative since all of the mitigating factors pointed to his history and the presence of negative role models. That answer allowed the prosecution an argument based on my data, but the duty of honesty to the court and the process was served. (In the end, the jury offered a life without parole recommendation.)

Other issues about which the expert must be knowledgeable are those regarding hearsay and ultimate issue testimony. In many jurisdictions and under many circumstances, testimony about the issue before the court is not permitted to an expert. Exceptions exist for NGRI where an opinion regarding sanity may be expected in many state courts but is expressly prohibited in the federal courts. Similarly, some of the diminished capacity approaches that have been in existence will ask that experts speak to the presence or absence of certain conditions. However, the expert is enjoined in either his or her report, or on the stand, from actually concluding on the basis of the data collected, whether the individual meets the specific legal category.

Hearsay is another area that has given some problems in all aspects of forensic work. Psychological data involve interviewing defendants and others and thereby hearing information about what people think as well as what they express that they have been told; additionally, there is a review of records (see the section "Empirically Based Methods and Applications" on third-party information) that contain all kinds of uncontrolled and unverifiable information from third parties. There have been objections raised regarding the overall admissibility of psychological or psychiatric expertise on the basis that it "back doors" otherwise inadmissible hearsay. In general, the decisions that are made in the courts have favored the testimony by the mental health professional that references both evaluation of defendants and collateral data so long as it is clear that the information collected is not being treated as factual but rather as indicative of the mental state or other psychological aspect of the subject(s) of the assessment. However, that distinction can be troublesome to judges and periodically can lead to limitations on the expert's presentation. At times, experts will be instructed either before or during testimony that certain areas or statements have been ruled inadmissible. Since a mistrial can result in some of these situations, it is incumbent on the expert to follow these instructions.

In the special case of death penalty mitigation, many persons, but not all, working in mitigation have been publicly identified as being in opposition to the death penalty. That is certainly the case of the present author. In preparation for anticipated questions about opposition to the death penalty, the purpose of which is to imply to the jury that the entire testimony is somehow biased, it is recommended that experts in this category speak with the attorneys who bring them to the court. It is often effective for the direct examination or redirect examination to include explorations of this area in which it can be asked whether the opposition to the death penalty has affected the presentation of expertise. The answer is to the effect that whenever the psychologist appears in court, there is a duty to reflect honestly and truthfully on the implications of the data. The expert can also state, if it is so, that in cases where results of assessments have been deemed unhelpful to defendants, attorneys have decided not to present the psychological expertise. (On one such occasion, I was asked for specific case examples; I refused to provide the same on the ethical and legal basis of confidentiality and privileged communication.)

Wellman's *Art of Cross-Examination* was first published in 1903 with the last edition in 1936. Wellman worked as both a corporate counsel and assistant district attorney at the end of the nineteenth century and he was widely known for his expert use of the art about which he wrote. In a foreword to the fourth edition, John W. Davis wrote:

> Undoubtedly, cross-examination is among the most difficult of all the arts of the advocate ... only experience can give the advocate that sixth sense, which tells him when he has reached dangerous ground, when he may advance, when he must retreat, and when he can risk his case upon a single throw. There are, as Mr. Wellman points out, no set rules that will fit all situations, unless indeed it be the one which he reinforces with his quotation from Josh Billings: 'When you strike Ile,' stop boring; many a man has bored clean through and let the 'Ile' run out of the bottom. (p. 15)

In his volume and based on his experience, Wellman put forth models for the proper use as well as misuse of cross-examination. Thus, "questions which throw no light upon the real issues ... nor upon the integrity or credit of the witness under examination, but which expose misdeeds ... for the sole purpose of causing humiliation and disgrace ..." (p. 196) represent an abuse of the art. Wellman considered that winning on such bases was a discredit to the profession. At another point, it is noted that cross-examination is subject to two significant errors, the first of which is unnecessary cross-examination and the other the overdoing of the procedure. Clearly, there are multiple variables that cannot be necessarily anticipated and that reflect constellations of experience and talent of individual litigators.

A special note may be made regarding hypothetical questions. There are procedural rules regarding such questions that play out sometimes in the form of objections being raised when such a question is presented to a witness. (A basic rule for witnesses is to avoid any responding when objections are made until rulings occur from the bench.) One of the duties of the questioning attorney is to fashion such questions with elements that can all be substantiated by evidence either already presented or to be presented. At times, witnesses are allowed to respond but whether those particular opinions will be included in the later decision-making will be dependent on the attorney actually coming forth with the evidence referenced. (In a jury trial, the impact of information that is made available but then ruled not acceptable becomes one of the unknown variables.) For the witness, however, evaluation of the question is NOT one of the duties: the witness must answer the question on the basis of the suppositions it includes and not on the basis of what the witness may know or believe about the case.

The forensic practitioner has a duty to his or her data and to expressing accurately the implications of that data. On such a basis he or she is likely to survive well either poor or good cross-examinations. Nonetheless, it is true that how a jury will perceive the information that is made available to it through the process of testifying is, in part, dependent upon the strategy of the attorney conducting the cross-examination.

An example of an approach that backfired occurred in the context of a death penalty mitigation trial. In this case, the present author had been able to develop little in the way of mitigatory factors for the jury to balance against the aggravating specifications that were a part of the offense for which the defendant had been found guilty. Therefore, it was decided in consultation with counsel to rest on simple pleas made by the defendant's mother, his family pastor, and the basic facts of the psychological assessment: that he was not mentally ill, that he was not impaired with respect to intelligence, and that he would be able to function in the prison system. In effect, the psychologist and attorney agreed to present but de-emphasize psychological data.

The unexpected occurred. The prosecutor, sensing a victory, decided to vigorously cross-examine the pastor on the biblical endorsement of the death penalty ("an eye for an eye …"). The pastor, however, was well versed in the Bible, and responded with chapter and verse to point out that that passage does not, in fact, endorse the ultimate penalty but rather illustrates the advance of the concept of justice to incorporate proportionality. Immediately upon given this pronouncement, the foreperson in the jury suffered a major epileptic seizure. The trial came to a halt. The jury person was removed on a gurney.

The judge allowed defense counsel to either go forward or move to defer to the following day. Counsel asked for advice about the strategy that would be the best. The present author responded that there was no psychological or scientific basis for advising one way or the other except that the attorney's experience and "gut feeling" might serve best. (There is good anecdotal evidence that experienced people, acting on their conscious and unconscious processing of a known arena, can best arrive at successful strategies. This situation thus also nicely illustrated the importance and ethicality of not advising when there is no basis for doing so.)

A decision was made to go forward, rather than defer until the next day, the completion of the mitigation hearing and the jury's verdict, perhaps at that point predictably, was a life sentence. It can be speculated that the jurors may have wished to avoid incurring the wrath of God as it had apparently already been displayed.

Novel Applications of Forensic Evidence and Knowledge

In presentations at the June 2006 meetings of the European Association of Psychology and Law in Liverpool, Michael Perlin and Eric Drogin combined forces to look at implications of therapeutic jurisprudence (TJ) for criminal law. The primary thrust of TJ originated in connection with civil law with the work of Wexler and Winick and has been extended to criminal arenas (Stolle, Wexler, and Winick, 2000). TJ looks at how workings of the legal system can facilitate therapeutic goals rather than interfere with the same. One example of research done in this vein involved inquiry into the procedures of involuntary hospitalization. To the extent that family members had to become adversaries of the patient, a source of therapeutic strength (family alliance) was weakened (Kennedy, 2001). In a similar vein, Drogin applied a TJ perspective to decisions with respect to competency and sanity with the suggestion that criminal defense counsel can become agents for enhancement of therapeutic results. As is seen in Table 11.2, his suggestions imply areas of work for forensic psychologists primarily working from a consulting role.

Finally, it was his opinion that by increasing the psychological mindedness and mental health knowledge of attorneys, a force would be developed that could lobby for institutional treatment options to make a difference in the lives of mentally ill defendants who are found guilty and held criminally responsible.

Table 11.2   Consultation from a TJ Perspective in the Criminal Justice Context

Drogin Suggestion	Contribution of Psychologist
1. Lawyers could become competent consumers of psychological products using the information in self-reflective ways for decision making with their clients.	1. Information provider.
2. Lawyers could help clients understand the connection between their psychological condition and their arrival in the criminal justice system, thus acting as prevention agents for recurrence.	2. Recommendations for approach based on mental health knowledge.
3. Lawyers could be trained in motivational interviewing and other psychological intervention techniques that will assist them in working with their clients to make the right connections and explore the issues that are relevant not only for the legal situation but also in the larger context. The attorney is in a unique position in terms of relationship to the client and the client's dependence on him or her to act as therapeutic agents.	3. Consultant, trainer, identifier of limits for safe applications.
4. Attorneys could be assisted to coordinate between family and other relationship-based resources on behalf of the client.	4. Provider of resource information.
5. In the more traditional role as litigators, attorneys could present motions for rehabilitation-oriented components available in the legal system such as the use of drug or mental health courts, and treatment *in lieu* of incarceration.	5. Possible expert witness regarding treatment needs and likely responding.

In a similar vein, Perlin also supported the idea of criminal defense lawyers as change agents and implementers of TJ in the criminal court. He noted that insanity defendants who are found guilty are often incarcerated without adequate access to treatment. Beyond the issue of treatment needs, however, was the more subtle concept of sanism—the notion that a diagnosis of mental illness places an individual in a category of people for which there is significant prejudice (Perlin, 2003). In the 2006 presentation, Perlin noted that lawyers unwittingly collaborate in what he called "sanist-based processing" of their clients. Similarly, the psychologist who is called upon to provide consultation in criminal cases where degrees of responsibility are present may also support sanist injury. It is not unknown for persons who are obviously and seriously mentally ill to reject their diagnoses and to want to continue a "normal" active involvement in their cases without any mental health pleas being presented. Overriding that client posture needs to be taken seriously for both the pros and cons involved. It is the duty of courts as well as counsel not to victimize persons who are ill and it is the duty of the attorney to provide the best possible defense available. Clearly, exculpation by way of a sanity pleading may be, in fact, the best possible defense as well as one that is warranted. However, it will come, in some cases, at the cost of publicly shaming the defendant, at least in the defendant's eyes, and may in fact place the defendant in a negative social category. The work of the psychologist who identifies the condition and who may be retained by defense for the opinion might well be extended to include some efforts to moderate the impacts of such a decision.

In this context, mention can be made of alternative sentencing programs. Drug and mental health courts have been established, notably in the United States, the United Kingdom, and Australia. In some versions, these courts may involve opportunities to ultimately expunge a record of criminal wrongdoing if the remedial (drug/alcohol or mental health) program is completed and the individual is functioning adequately. Some programs are available *in lieu* of jail time; some involve reduction of sentences. All would require that the individual acknowledge the problem domain and his or her membership in the same. Most, if not all, are limited to less serious and usually nonviolent offenses. Issues have been raised regarding how defendant rights and due process may be negatively impacted even though treatment needs are addressed. (For a discussion of pros and cons and some of the evaluative efforts that have been made of such alternatives, see Winick and Stefan, 2005.) Such programs essentially recognize substance abuse/dependency and mental illness as significant factors that may reduce criminal responsibility and can qualify the individual for specialized treatment in the legal system.

Another area of novel contribution comes about as a function of legal decisions with implications for psychological research. However, while there has been significant research in the area of jury functioning that has relevance for mitigation, a certain curious anomaly can present. Thus, Weiner (2006) suggested that the *Oregon v. Guzek* (2006) decision, in which residual doubt was reaffirmed as not proper evidence in mitigation, created an arena wherein psychological research could explore through mock jury and other approaches the impact of making or not making such an argument. However, the suggestion may ignore some complicating features. A review of the history of post–*Furman* decisions indicates an initial phase in which the Supreme Court decisions opened doors for defendants followed by a period continuing to date in which restrictive legislation and decisions were characteristic. Elimination of residual doubt has a certain logical respectability in that the phase for arguments regarding any aspects of guilt is completed prior to mitigation where the only question goes to sentencing. Research findings would either support that residual doubt does reraise the issue of guilt and therefore would likely be excluded in any testimony in mitigation or satisfy that there is no demonstrated impact, in which case testimony about the same would be irrelevant.

Conclusions

In this chapter, it was argued that mitigation as a concept, the legal system itself, and the application of psychology to the forensic issues involved, all in intersection, can be better understood from the standpoint of the so-called chaos or complexity theory. The notion is that emergent patterns have order, but specific events and outcomes are more often than not unpredictable in the linear sense, especially where it is not possible to view those patterns or to process the multiple factors at work. Within that mindset, the individual forensic practitioner proceeds at some hazard, but nonetheless with contributory potential, thus illustrating the wisdom inherent in the Chinese character for "chaos," which includes the concept of "opportunity."

References

American Law Institute. (1962). *Model Penal Code*. Philadelphia: American Law Institute.
American Psychiatric Association. (2000). *Diagnostic and Statistical Manual of Mental Disorders, Fourth Edition, Text Revision (DSM-IV-TR)*. Washington, DC: American Psychiatric Association.

American Psychological Association. (2002). *Ethical Principles of Psychologists and Code of Conduct.* Washington, DC: American Psychological Association.

Boettcher, B. (2006). Is diminished responsibility relevant? www.priory.com/psych/dimishe.htm (Accessed 7/21/06).

Borum, R. (1996). Improving the clinical practice of violence risk assessment: Technology, guidelines, and training. *American Psychologist, 51*(9), 945–956.

Borum, R., and Grisso, T. (1996). Establishing standards for criminal forensic reports: *Bulletin of the American Academy of Psychiatry and the Law, 24,* 297–317.

Brown, D., Scheflin, A., and Hammond, D. (1998). *Memory, Trauma Treatment, and the Law.* New York: W.W. Norton and Company.

Bruening, C. C., Wagner, W. G., and Johnson, J. T. (1997). Impact of rater knowledge on sexually abused and non-abused girls' scores on the Draw-A-Person; S screening, P procedure, E emotional, D disturbance (DAP:SPED). *Journal of Personality Assessment, 68*(3), 665–677.

Buchanan, G. (1992). *Biblical and Theological Insights from Ancient and Modern Civil Law.* Lewiston, NY: Edwin Mellen Press.

Bűtz, M. R. (1997). *Chaos and Complexity: Implications for Psychological Theory and Practice.* Washington, DC: Taylor & Francis.

California Penal Code. (2002). Available on-line at http://www.leginfo.ca.gov/calaw.html.

Chitra, M., Rao, S., Gangadhar, B., and Hezck, A. (1989). Neuropsychological functioning in postconcussive syndrome. *Institute of Mental Health Journal, 7*(1), 37–41.

Danesh-Khoshdoo, (1991). *The Civilization of Law: A Commentary on the Laws of Hammurabi and Magna Carta.* Berrien Springs, MI: Vandevere.

DeMatteo, D., and Edens, J. F. (2006). The role and relevance of the Psychopathy Checklist—Revised, in court: A case law survey of U.S. Courts (1991–2004). *Psychology, Public Policy, & Law, 12*(2), 214–241.

Drogin, E. (2006). The criminal lawyer as 'counselor': Ethical obligations and transforming opportunities from a therapeutic jurisprudence perspective. Presentation at the European Association of Psychology and Law Conference, Liverpool, UK.

Elkins, J. K. (Fall, 2005). Dimished capacity. College of Law, West Virginia University. http://myweb.wvnet.wvnet.edu/~jelkins/crimlaw/note/dimishedcapacity.html.

Flynn, J. R. (2006). Tethering the elephant: capital cases, IQ, and the Flynn effect. *Psychology, Public Policy, & Law, 12*(2), 170–189.

Gacono, C. B., Evans, F. B., and Viglione, D. J. (2002). The Rorschach in forensic practice. *Journal of Forensic Psychology Practice, 2,* 33–54.

Garb, H. N. (1999). Call for a moratorium on the use of the Rorschach Inkblot Test in clinical and forensic settings. *Assessment, 6,* 313–317.

Gayford, J. J. (1975). Battered wives: Research on battered wives. *Research on Social Health Journal, 90*(6), 288–289.

Gerber, R. J. (1984). *The Insanity Defense.* Port Washington, NY: Associated Faculty Press.

Grove, W. M. and Barden, R. C. (1999). Protecting the integrity of the legal system: The admissibility of testimony from mental health experts under *Daubert/Kumho* analyses. *Psychology, Public Policy, & Law, 5,* 224–242.

Grove, W. M., Barden, R. C., Garb, H. N., and Lilienfeld, S. O. (2002). Failure of Rorschach-Comprehensive-System-based testimony to be admissible under the *Daubert-Joiner-Kumho* standard. *Psychology, Public Policy, & Law, 8,* 216–234.

Gudjonsson, G. (2003). *The Psychology of Interrogation and Confessions: A Handbook.* Hoboken, NJ: Wiley.

Hart, S. D. (2003). Violence risk assessment: An anchored narrative approach. In: M. Vanderhallen, G. Vervaeke, P. J. Van Koppen, and J. Goethals (Eds.), *Much Ado about Crime: Chapters on Psychology and Law.* Brussels, Belgium: Uitgeverij Politeia NV.

Hiday, V. A. (2006). Putting community risk in perspective: A look at correlations, causes and controls. *International Journal of Law and Psychiatry, 29*(4), 316–331.

Hilsenroth, M. J., and Stricker, G. (2004). A consideration of challenges to psychological assessment instruments used in forensic settings: Rorschach as exemplar. *Journal of Personality Assessment, 83,* 141–152.

Huckabee, H. M. (2006). Dodging the insanity defense with diminished capacity. http://www.diminishedcapacity.com (Accessed 7/21/06).

Kennedy, C. (2001). The perception and role of the involuntary civil commitment hearing through the eyes of the petitioner: Procedural vs. distributive justice. Dissertation submitted to Fielding Graduate University. UMI #3028770.

Keyes, D. (1981). *The Minds of Bill Milligan.* New York: Bantam.

Lanius, R. A., Williamson, P. C., Boksman, C., Dersome, M., Gupta, M., Nerfeld, R., Gate, J. S., and Menon, R. S. (2002). Brain activation during script driven imagery induced dissociative responses in PTSD: A functional magnetic resonance imaging investigation. *Biological Psychiatry, 52*(4), 305–311.

McCann, J. T. (1998). Defending the Rorschach in court: An analysis of admissibility using legal and professional standards. *Journal of Personality Assessment, 70,* 125–144.

McMillan, T., and Glucksman, E. (1987). The neuropsychology of moderate head injury. *Journal of Neurology, Neurosurgery and Psychiatry, 50*(4), 393–397.

McPherson, S. B. (1998). Capital punishment: Implications for institutional violence vs. individual rights. In: H. V. Hall and L. C. Whitaker (Eds.), *Collective Violence: Effective Strategies for Assessing and Interviewing in Fatal Group and Institutional Aggression.* Boca Raton, FL: CRC Press.

Meloy, J. R. (2005). Some personal and professional reflections upon *What's Wrong with the Rorschach?* Unpublished manuscript.

Melton, G. B., Petrila, J., Poythress, N. A., and Slobogan, C. (1997). *Psychological Evaluations for the Courts,* 2nd edition. New York: Guilford Press.

Perlin, M. (2003). "You have discussed lepers and crooks": Sanism in clinical teaching. *9 Clinical Law Review 683.* Westlaw 2004.

Perlin, M. (2006). Representing criminal defendants in incompetency and sanity cases: Some therapeutic jurisprudence dilemmas. Presentation at the European Association of Psychology and Law Conference, Liverpool, UK.

Ritzler, B., Erard, R., and Pettigrew, G. (2002a). A final reply to Grove and Barden: The relevance of the Rorschach Comprehensive System for expert testimony. *Psychology, Public Policy, & Law, 8,* 235–246.

Ritzler, B., Erard, R., and Pettigrew, G. (2002b). Protecting the integrity of Rorschach expert witnesses: A reply to Grove and Barden (1999): The admissibility of testimony under *Daubert/Kumho* analyses. *Psychology, Public Policy, & Law, 8,* 201–215.

Roberts, C. F., and Golding, S. L. (1991). The social construction of criminal responsibility and insanity. *Law and Human Behavior, 15*(4), 349–374.

Rogers, R. (1997). *Clinical Assessment of Malingering and Deception.* New York: Guilford Press.

Rogers, R., Bagby, R. M., and Dickens, S. E. (1992). *Structured Interview of Reported Symptoms (SIRS).* Psychological Assessment Resources.

Rogers, R., and Ewing, C. P. (1992). The measurement of insanity: Debating the merits of the R-CRAS and its alternatives. *International Journal of Law and Psychiatry, 15,* 113–123.

Savitz, D. B. (1990). The legal defense of persons with the diagnosis of multiple personality disorder. *Dissociation, 3*(4), 195–203.

Sjostedt, G. (2002). *Violent Recidivism among Sexual Offenders: Risk Factors and Assessment Procedures.* Stockholm, Sweden: Karolinska Institutet, NEUROTEC, Division of Forensic Psychiatry.

Slovenko, R. (1993). The multiple personality and the criminal law. *Medicine and Law 12,* 329–340.

Spanos, N. P. (1994). Multiple identity enactments and multiple personality disorder: A sociocognitive perspective. *Psychological Bulletin, 116*(1), 143–165.

Spanos, N. P. (1996). *Multiple Identities and False Memories: A Sociocognitive Perspective.* Washington, DC: American Psychological Association.

Stolle, D. P., Wexler, D. B., and Winick, B. J. (2000). *Practicing Therapeutic Jurisprudence: Law as a Helping Profession.* Durham, NC: Carolina Academic Press.

Strut, R. L., and Black, F. W. (1988). *Neurobehavioral Disorders.* Philadelphia: F. A. Davis Co.

Uma, H., and Shobhini, L. (1987). Information processing in patients with closed head injury. *Journal of Psychological Researches, 3*(2), 70–76.

U. S. Department of Justice. (2003). Four measures of serious violent crime. http://www.ojp.usdoj.gov/bjs/glance/cv2.htm (retrieved 07/04/06).

Waldrop, M. N. (1992). *Complexity: The Emerging Science at the Edge of Order and Chaos.* New York: Simon and Schuster.

Walsh, T., and Walsh, Z. (2006). The evidentiary introduction of Psychopathy Checklist-Revised Assessed Psychopathy in U. S. Courts: Extent and appropriateness. *Law and Human Behavior, 30*(4), 493–507.

Weiner, R. L. (2006). Residual doubt in death penalty cases. *Monitor on Psychology, 37*(6), 41.

Westen, D., and Weinberger, J. (2004). When clinical description becomes statistical prediction. *American Psychologist, 59*(7), 595–613.

Wellman, F. L. (1936). *The Art of Cross-Examination*, 4th edition. New York: Macmillan.

Williams, C. R., and Arrigo, B. A. (2002). *Law, Psychology, and Justice: Chaos Theory and the New (Dis)order.* Albany, NY: State University of New York Press.

Winick, B. J., and Stefan, S. (2005). Mental health courts. *Psychology, Public Policy & Law, 11*(4).

Legal References

Addington v. Texas. 441 U.S. 418 (1979).
Adkins v. Virginia. 536 U.S. 304 (2002).
Ake v. Oklahoma. 470 U.S. 68 (1985).
Barefoot v. Estelle. 463 U.S. 880 (1983).
Daubert v. Merrell Dow Pharmaceuticals. 509 U.S. 579 (1993).
Durham v. United States. 214 F.2d 862. (D.C. Circ. 1954).
Furman v. Georgia. 408 U.S. 153 (1972).
Gregg v. Georgia. 428 U. S. 153 (1976).
Ibn-Tamas v. United States. 407 A. 2d 626 (D.C. 1979).
Insanity Defense Reform Act of 1984. Pub. L., No. 98-473 (1984).
Jackson v. The State of Texas, Fifth Court of Appeals, Dallas County, No. PD-1655-03, FindLaw for Legal Professionals—Case law, Federal and State Resources. April 13, 2005.
Johnson v. State. 42 Md L. Rev. 522 (1983).
Jurek v. Texas. 428 U.S. 262 (1976).
Lockett v. Ohio. 438 U.S. 586 (1978).
M'Naghten's Case. 8 Eng. Rep. 718. (1843).
Oregon v. Guzek. 126S.Ct. 1226 (2006).
Parsons v. State. 2 So.854, 866-67 (Ala. 1887).
Payne v. Tennessee. 501 U.S. 808 (1991).
People v. Mendez. New York Court of Appeals. Case no. 2, no. 118. October 23, 2003.
People v. Moore. California Appellate District. C036773. March 17, 2002.
Simmons v. Roper. 112 SW 3d 397 (2003).

State v. Bishop. 753 P.2d 439 (Utah 1988).

State v. Hall. 958 S.W.2d 679, 688-89 (Tenn 1997).

State v. Milligan, 77-CR-11-2908 (Franklin County, Ohio, December 4, 1978).

State v. Staten. 18 Ohio St. 2d (1969); 25 Ohio St 2d 107 (1971).

State v. Wilcox. 70 Ohio St. 2d 182 (1982).

State of New Jersey v. Moore. 122 NJ 420, 585 A. 2d 864 (1991).

Wagner v. State 687 S.W. 2d 303 (Tex. Crim. App. 1985).

Mental Retardation and the Criminal Justice System: Forensic Issues

12

RONALD S. EBERT

Psychological Services, Inc., Braintree, Massachusetts

JEFFERY S. LONG

Psychological Services, Inc., Braintree, Massachusetts

Contents

Mary was charged with being a "habitual offender," having been before the court on 25 different charges over her 40 years. Usually charged with prostitution, she was now charged with possessing vast quantities of cocaine, found in a dropped ceiling in her filthy apartment. Her attorney requested an assessment of her competency, complaining that Mary said "yes" to every question, but seemed not to fully understand his questions or even appreciate the seriousness of the charges. Additionally, she was unable to recall the slightest information provided to her. Assessment revealed that Mary had been in special classes throughout her education, that she had been sexually abused by two of her brothers and an uncle, and that she currently functioned in the mentally retarded range. The drugs appeared to belong to her "boyfriend" who kept her in prostitution and paid her meager rent. He doled out her disability income to pay for her food and clothing, while the rest went to him. She had no idea how much she received or paid out. Not only was she currently incompetent to stand trial, it was likely that she had never been competent in her previous trials, nor had she been competent to plead, as she had done on numerous occasions.

Mentally retarded and developmentally disabled individuals present a complex and costly dilemma for the courts and correctional facilities. It is estimated that although the prevalence of mental retardation is less than 1–2% of the population at large, mentally retarded individuals represent 4–10% of those in the criminal justice system (Petersilia, 1997; Sundram, 1990). Unlike individuals with physical or emotional disabilities, the deficits of mentally retarded individuals are not always readily apparent to the forensic clinician, much less to attorneys or criminal justice personnel.

Many intellectually impaired men and women move through the criminal justice system without adequate attention to their unique needs, resulting in inequity and victimization by the system. At every stage, mentally retarded individuals are at a distinct disadvantage. In comparison to other defendants, mentally retarded individuals are more likely to waive essential rights, to confess (often falsely), to go to trial, to plead guilty, to serve lengthier sentences, and to serve their full sentence without parole review (The Arc, 2002; Goldman, 2001; Petersilia, 1997; Santamour, 1986). While incarcerated, they are subject to victimization and brutality, not only by other inmates but also by a system that does not understand their particular needs and fails to offer protection, treatment, and direction.

These are people whose disabilities are commonly missed by the police, attorneys, courts, and the correctional system. These are also people who typically are compliant, may try to hide their disabilities, are acquiescent to authority, and offer little resistance or complaint in the face of incompetent counsel, unfair practices, or blatant mistreatment. Thus, vital questions regarding competence and criminal responsibility are rarely raised, particularly with those individuals who have mild retardation. The purpose of this chapter is to review major issues as they pertain to mental retardation in the criminal justice system, to identify pitfalls and perils in the legal system, to explore the nature of these inequities, and to provide a roadmap for forensic practitioners who deal with mentally retarded persons.

Definition of Mental Retardation

The American Association of Mental Retardation (AAMR, 2002a) defines mental retardation as being characterized by subaverage intellectual functioning as indicated by an IQ that is at least two standard deviations below the mean of a given measure of intelligence, which typically translates into a cutoff IQ score of approximately 70 on most intellectual measures. The AAMR cautions that the standard error of measurement for the specific assessment should be addressed to denote that the individual's true IQ score likely falls within a range of potential scores (i.e., "This individual obtained a full-scale IQ score of 69. At the 95th confidence level, this individual's true IQ score likely falls within a range of 64 to 74"). Intellectual deficits alone are not sufficient for diagnosis but must also be accompanied by limitations in adaptive skills such as deficits in the areas of social functioning, conceptual skills, communication, and practical daily living skills, as indicated by performance on measures of adaptive functioning that are two standard deviations below the mean (AAMR, 2002a). The onset of mental retardation must occur before age 18 and excludes individuals whose neurocognitive deficits developed or were acquired during adulthood. The American Psychiatric Association's definition of mental retardation is similar, requiring a three-pronged criterion of (1) an IQ less than 70; (2) deficits in adaptive functioning, and (3) onset before age 18 (American Psychiatric Association [APA], 2000).

On the surface, this definition appears relatively straightforward; however, for the forensic psychologist, there are a number of potential concerns embedded in these criteria. Commonly, an IQ score is viewed as the primary determinant of mental retardation, whereas the importance of adaptive functioning is ignored or downplayed, despite the requirement that impairment in both areas be present (Kanaya, Scullin, Ceci, 2003). Further, IQ scores are frequently misinterpreted as magical, permanent markers of functioning rather than an estimate or snapshot in time. Unfortunately, when IQ scores are used in the absence of other information, the results can be highly misleading and potentially harmful. In fact, the variation of an IQ point or two in capital crimes can mean the difference between life imprisonment and death (Atkins v. Virginia, 2002). This is particularly alarming given that IQ scores can vary over time and across situations and carry with them a degree of testing error (Kanaya et al., 2003).

The etiology of mental retardation is multifactorial and can involve any one of numerous risk factors. The AAMR identifies four categories of risk for development of mental retardation (biomedical, social, behavioral, and educational) that can occur across three time dimensions (prenatal, perinatal, and postnatal) (AAMR, 2002a). To illustrate, poor education regarding medical issues during pregnancy might result in a lack of appropriate diet or in continued use of substances during the prenatal period, which might, in turn, cause neurological compromise in the fetus. Similarly, traumatic brain injury might represent a biomedical risk factor that if occurring before age 22 and if resulting in global deficits might result in a diagnosis of mental retardation in an individual who had previously functioned adequately.

Most mentally retarded individuals are in the mild range of mental retardation, roughly corresponding to IQ estimates between 55 and 75. Individuals with mild mental retardation often do not have an outward sign of disability and may appear to the casual observer as "normal." Certain forms of mental retardation, notably Down syndrome, do carry obvious stigmata, making diagnosis easier. Defendants with more severe forms of mental retardation are frequently, but not always, screened out because their intellectual deficits tend to be more obvious, as there may be noticeable communication difficulties, profound confusion, and concomitant physical problems that are readily evident to the casual observer. In contrast, individuals with mild mental retardation may not be recognized until well into the legal process, sometimes not until postconviction and occasionally not at all.

Starting with a comprehensive definition of mental retardation provides direction for the clinician to make deeper statements and comparisons regarding functioning. Additionally, although it is important to understand what mental retardation is, it is equally important to understand what it is not. Frequently, mental retardation is viewed as an arrested state of development, such that a mentally retarded individual might be seen as frozen at a certain developmental stage or age level. In the past, it was not uncommon to hear of a mentally retarded person described as functioning "at a 7-year-old level." Upon first hearing, such a characterization appears to provide a colorful and easily understood point of comparison. However, upon deeper thought, such descriptions do more to cloud than to clarify matters. From a developmental perspective, such a global description fails to explain specific aspects of functioning that need to be reviewed by involved parties. Global descriptors such as this do little to describe the average 7-year-old child, let alone an adult who happens to function at a developmentally equivalent level to a 7-year-old child. Mentally retarded adults and children, even though sharing some similarity in skill sets, differ radically in terms of physical development, experiences, and societal expectations and protections. The forensic clinician should avoid using such descriptors and, if it is necessary to do so, should clearly explain what is meant by such a comparative description.

By the same token, traumatic brain injury and other forms of severe cognitive deterioration are occasionally viewed as similar or even synonymous with mental retardation. However, it is important to distinguish between acquired neurocognitive deficits and those deficits typically associated with mental retardation. Beyond the age cutoff embedded in the definition, mental retardation connotes global delays or deficits that affect most or all areas of functioning (although exceptions occur in certain cases) and that are viewed as persistent. In contrast, severe traumatic brain injury may result in global deficits or alternately might result in focalized deficits with other areas of functioning remaining intact. Further, functional deficits may not be permanent but may improve over time and with treatment (Lezak, 1995). That being said, in certain cases involving mentally retarded individuals, it may be advisable to pursue a comprehensive neuropsychological evaluation in addition to assessment of intellectual and adaptive functioning for the purpose of deeply exploring specific functional areas (i.e., receptive language skills, executive functioning, and so forth) that might be relevant to a particular forensic issue.

Although diagnostic labels connoting the severity of mental retardation (i.e., "mild," "moderate," "severe," and "profound") may be beneficial to convey the level of functioning to other clinicians, such qualifiers might be inadequate and misleading when used in forensic settings, particularly with audiences who may not know what these terms mean. For example, when the term "mild mental retardation" is used, the layperson may misinterpret this statement as suggesting that the observed deficits are "only mild" and "not that bad," not realizing that this qualifier indicates a comparison to other mentally retarded individuals and not to the population at large. As with many other areas of forensic practice, definitions, labels, and qualifiers should be adequately explained and simplified such that the audience's understanding is accurate. If this is not possible, ambiguous terms should be avoided altogether.

Characteristics of the Mentally Retarded Offender

Beyond definitional issues regarding intelligence and adaptive functioning, mentally retarded defendants typically demonstrate specific deficits in social functioning and reasoning that can greatly affect the judicial process. These difficulties include the following:

- Acquiescence: Individuals with mental retardation might be unusually accommodating and eager to please, particularly to those who are in positions of authority (Kebbell and Hatton, 1999). For example, such individuals might smile inappropriately and indiscriminately, which others might inaccurately interpret as lack of remorse, or they may answer affirmatively to questions, regardless of the content. They will, for example, talk readily to the police, often without appreciation of their Miranda rights.
- Deference to authority: Related to acquiescence, mentally retarded individuals have learned to depend on authority figures and "protectors" as a way to remain safe and

to get needs met. Such individuals may misinterpret the actions of the police and prosecutors as being unfailingly protective, not understanding that obliging their requests for information (e.g., confessing) may not be in their best interests. Put simply, they say what they think others want to hear, often at their own expense. Forensic examiners need to recognize that they, too, may be seen as authority figures by such individuals and may also encounter such self-defeating deference.

- Masking their disability: Individuals with mild mental retardation often pretend to have greater understanding than they actually hold. Rather than asking questions that would reveal their limited understanding, many simply assent in the hopes of passing as "normal" (Appelbaum, 1994) and avoiding pejorative labeling. Importantly, most mildly disabled people resist the label "mental retardation" because of the negative connotations—forensic examiners are advised to avoid such labels when meeting with these clients. Instead, the terms "learning problems" or "educational difficulties" might be used in such circumstances.

- Mimicking: Mentally retarded persons often try to fit in and to determine what is the "right thing to do" by copying the actions of others (Lustig, 1996). In doing so, their mimicry can mask the extent of their deficits and can help to explain their association with antisocial people who manipulate and use them.

- Concrete thinking: Because of significant cognitive deficits, individuals with mental retardation think concretely, rather than abstractly. Thus, they frequently have difficulty understanding complex legal issues such as plea bargaining, waiving rights, and trial process in general. Most are unable to engage in the strategic planning required to navigate the criminal justice system (Smith, 1993).

- Language difficulties: Mentally retarded persons often have limited vocabularies and may not fully understand key legal concepts and lengthy explanations (Finlay and Lyons, 2001). Their "yes" to questions (or to Miranda warnings, for example) may merely mask a lack of understanding. Probing for comprehension becomes a critical tool for the forensic examiner.

- Impaired attention and memory: Individuals with mental retardation may have difficulty recalling events and details of conversations, particularly when they see no immediate purpose for doing so. Sometimes time concepts are impaired, leading to confusing histories and recall.

Collectively, these characteristics often undermine the mentally retarded individual's ability to participate fairly in his or her defense at all stages. Yet many individuals are considered competent to confess, to stand trial, or to make knowing and intelligent decisions and are quietly convicted, all the while failing to understand their rights, confused by the process, and agreeing with statements and decisions that are both unfair and not in their best interests. It is vital for forensic clinicians to keep each of these points in mind when conducting assessments and when assisting involved parties to understand how to accurately assess an individual's functioning. It is also imperative for the forensic professional to be mindful that his or her experience during the interview process may parallel evaluations by other parties and thus may not be fully indicative of the defendant's true functioning or understanding. Therefore, collateral sources of information will be necessary to provide additional information about the individual's typical functioning.

Types of Crimes Committed by Mentally Retarded Individuals

Individuals with mental retardation may be susceptible to particular types of crimes because of the nature of their deficits. The same poor impulse control, limited planning ability, and impaired coping skills that cause difficulty in day-to-day functioning can, in certain circumstances, provide the backdrop to criminal behavior (Kinsler, Saxman, and Fishman, 2004). Myths abound concerning the violent, out-of-control mentally retarded offender; the research, however, is mixed concerning the "typical" mentally retarded defendant. Although felony crimes by their nature are high profile and get wide press coverage, most mentally retarded defendants are actually charged with committing misdemeanors and less serious crimes (White and Wood, 1986). Further, many commit crimes in concert with others, having been talked into or manipulated into engaging in criminal behavior that they do not fully understand. Often, when a crime has been committed, they are the last to run away and the first to be caught.

> George, a 37-year-old who lives with his mother, was rearrested for the 12th time for auto theft—he was again found asleep in the back seat of a stolen car, his "friends" having run away when the police chased them down. George is mute, has an estimated intelligence in the moderately retarded range (40 to 55), and is seen by the local police as a chronic offender who is frequently left behind at crime scenes by people he thinks are his buddies.

Many crimes committed by mentally retarded offenders represent difficulties with impulse control and inhibitory behaviors. Assaultive behavior was frequently seen among institutionalized individuals with mental retardation, with estimates of aggressive behavior causing injury to others as high as 36.9% (Hill and Bruinink, 1984). Among individuals who had been forensically hospitalized for aggression, the rates of postadmission aggression indicate a higher prevalence of 46.5% (Novaco and Taylor, 2004). Further, studies have suggested that as intellectual functioning declines, there is a rise in the rate of aggression (Hill and Bruinink, 1984; Novaco and Taylor, 2004). Violent crimes such as assault and battery and homicide are typically unplanned responses to intense feelings of fear, anger, or panic, occasionally resulting when another crime goes wrong (Human Rights Watch, 2001). Sexual offenses are also common in the forensic population with mental retardation. Estimates suggest that mentally retarded individuals commit approximately 10–15% of all sexual offenses (Murphy, Coleman, and Haynes, 1983), the most common being indecent exposure, sexual touching, and other minor offenses (Day, 1997). Retrospective analysis demonstrates that many of these individuals are lacking in adequate training concerning appropriate expressions of sexuality, and instead are offered a list of "do not's" that they fail to fully understand. Many of the sexual "crimes" turn out to be naïve exploration of sexual interests, absent appropriate understanding of social rules. Choice of children or adolescents for sexual exploration is often based on choice of an intellectual peer, rather than deviant sexual interest.

Comorbidity/Dual Diagnoses

Although psychiatric and legal definitions attempt to establish a clear demarcation between mental retardation and mental illness, comorbidity represents an additional diagnostic dilemma. The prevalence of psychiatric disorder in individuals with mental retardation has been estimated as being four to six times greater than observed with the general population (Matson and Barrett, 1982; McLean, 1993). Further, the symptoms of psychiatric disorders might present differently in mentally retarded individuals, further complicating diagnostic accuracy. For example, Glick and Zigler (1995) noted that psychiatric inpatients with mental retardation demonstrated a significantly higher rate of expressing their symptoms actively, outwardly, and aggressively in comparison to inpatients without mental retardation whose aggressive impulses appeared more self-directed and ruminative. As such, individuals presenting with both mental retardation and psychiatric disorder are much more likely to incur diagnoses that reflect aggressive and seemingly antisocial behavior than psychiatric patients of normal intelligence (Charlot, Doucette, and Mezzacappa, 1993; Reiss and Rojahn, 1993). Thus, in the aftermath of a crime when the focus is likely to be more on illegal behavior rather than the disability, mentally retarded individuals may be inaccurately regarded as "antisocial" rather than impaired. This problem underscores the necessity of a prompt and thorough diagnostic evaluation in legal situations where there is any suspicion of mental retardation (Hewitt, 1986; Kinsler et al., 2004).

Specific Issues: Competence and Criminal Responsibility

As noted, individuals with mental retardation suffer at every stage in the criminal process. From the moment of arrest through the trial process and into incarceration, these individuals are at a disadvantage because of the cognitive and social deficits associated with their disability. Despite the recent Supreme Court ruling that all competencies involved in the legal process (i.e., competency to stand trial, competency to waive rights, competency to represent oneself, and so forth) should be deemed equivalent (*Godinez v. Moran*, 1993), mentally retarded defendants must possess a number of key and unique capacities central to competence at each stage of the legal process. Forensic evaluators should be mindful of how specific deficits might affect each type of competency.

Competency to Confess

Earl Washington Jr. was accused of the 1982 rape and murder of Rebecca Lynn Williams. Washington, who had an estimated IQ of 69, was unable of his own accord to give any details of the crime, including the race of the woman. Yet, he was convinced by the police to admit committing the crime, and this admission of guilt was enough to send him to death row. After eighteen years in prison, Washington was given a full pardon after DNA evidence showed that he did not commit the crime. (See *Washington v. Commonwealth*, 1984; Freedman, 2001.)

In general, mentally retarded defendants are more likely to waive their rights and to confess (often erroneously) to please authority figures and to hide their disability (Davis, 2000). At the outset, when first accused or arrested, individuals with mental retardation may not fully realize the gravity of the charges against them. They may simply know that they have disappointed authority figures and are in trouble. Afraid, such individuals may blurt out confessions, believing that by saying they are sorry they will no longer be in trouble. By the same token, they may acquiesce to police questioning (and occasionally manipulation), giving answers, both factual and fictional, that they feel will satisfy their accusers and stop them from being in trouble. Friedman (2001) notes that maliciousness may not be the motivation for such "forced" confessions; "sloppiness will do." Believing that individuals are intentionally withholding facts, the police might generate an account that roughly fits the facts and then pressure the individual to "admit" his or her guilt. The mentally retarded individual may not be aware of, request, or even understand the need for legal counsel. When informed of their Miranda rights, individuals may feign understanding, responding "Yes" to each "Do you understand?" and even sign forms indicating such. However, it is not uncommon to find cases in which illiterate mentally retarded defendants have signed waivers and confessions that they are completely unable to read. Studies also suggest that in the general population, individuals who are truly innocent are significantly more likely to sign a waiver than those who are guilty, believing that their innocence will translate into freedom (Kassin and Norwick, 2004). Not realizing the subtleties and hazards of doing so, mentally retarded individuals who are inaccurately accused of crimes may be even more susceptible to waiving their Miranda rights out of a naïve belief that innocence alone is sufficient to be set free. The police are increasingly using the "Reid technique" in interrogations, a nonscientific strategy that is supposed to increase detection of lying by analyzing body language, facial expression, and other pseudoscientific measures of behavior (Perske, 2000). Such strategies, unfortunately, often result in false confessions and waiver of rights, especially in easily manipulated, naïve populations. Taken together, because such individuals are often quietly compliant and secretly confused, their lack of competence to waive constitutional rights and to produce confessions may not be adequately assessed, significantly compromising due process rights. Two suggested ways of combating inappropriate Miranda confessions would be to request the individual to restate each aspect of the Miranda rights in his or her own words and to record the administration of Miranda rights for later review by trained professionals.

> After six hours of interrogation by the police, Henry signed a confession describing his digital rape of an infant. When later questioned he appeared not to be aware of the details of his statement and seemed unaware that he had signed a confession. He reported that he had signed "the paper" because the police promised he could go home if he did so. Examination of his language skills revealed that he did not possess an understanding of many of the critical terms in the confession such as "digit," "penetration" and "index finger." The confession was not admissible after relevant testimony was given.

Competence to Stand Trial

> Limmie Arthur, who had an IQ of 66, was convicted of murdering a neighbor after stealing his social security check. Mr. Arthur's mental retardation was not recognized until after he was convicted. His appeals attorney noted, "Retarded people who function at [Arthur's] level are good at one thing and one thing only and that is covering up their disability ... A lawyer or prosecutor or judge talking to him is not going to realize that he is talking to a retarded person." At a resentencing hearing, evidence of Mr. Arthur's mental retardation was presented based on a review of school records, testimony from his teachers, and psychological testing. One evaluator noted that Mr. Arthur tried diligently to conceal his deficits by pretending to read and perform other tasks. However, when asked to recite the alphabet, he was able to sing only part of the nursery rhyme of the ABCs, failing to remember all the letters. When asked, he believed he could be sentenced to death because he could not read. (*State v. Arthur*, 1988; Human Rights Watch, 2001)

Competence to stand trial represents another complicated issue with regard to mentally retarded defendants. To review, the Dusky standard requires that a defendant have "sufficient present ability to consult with his lawyer with a reasonable degree of rational understanding, and whether he has a rational as well as factual understanding of the proceedings against him" (*Dusky v. United States*, 1960). All states have competency to stand trial standards that either adopt the Dusky standard verbatim or represent some variation of the standard. Some jurisdictions such as Florida state that in addition to the Dusky standard, forensic practitioners can consider "any other factors deemed relevant" (Melton, Petrila, Poythress, and Slobogin, 1997). Frequently, mentally retarded individuals who are new to the judicial process may not possess a "factual understanding" of the trial process. In other words, when questioned, they may not understand the nature or severity of their crimes, the roles of the various participants, or the various types of defenses that might be used. Yet, with some education and rehearsal, some individuals may be able to acquire a basic working knowledge of the legal process. However, although a factual knowledge may give the impression of competence, many mentally retarded individuals fail to meet the "rational" portion of the Dusky standard, which implies that the individuals are able to utilize their knowledge to assist their lawyers and thus participate in their defense. When asked to apply their knowledge to their individual cases, many mentally retarded defendants are unable to weigh options and make reasoned decisions regarding how their cases will be handled. As in other situations, to mask their disability, these individuals in essence "borrow" competency from others, pretending to have a deeper grasp of the legal process than they actually possess. Although their acquiescence in other situations may have been incredibly adaptive, in the legal arena, mentally retarded defendants are at risk for serving time with only a dim idea of how they got there. Fortunately, the U.S. Supreme Court has recognized the unfairness of indefinite commitment of defendants solely on account of incompetency to stand trial (*Jackson v. Indiana*, 1972), which offers some protection for mentally retarded defendants who in the past may have suffered prolonged, even lifelong commitments awaiting a "restoration of competence" that would not and could not occur.

As in all areas requiring evaluation of functioning, the forensic clinician is advised to conduct a thorough, thoughtful assessment that not only moves beyond asking questions to evoke mere recitation of facts but also assesses a defendant's rational understanding by asking him or her questions regarding practical application of this information. Thus, the assessment might ask the defendant to talk through scenarios or to apply legal facts to his or her specific case, or alternately, it may involve *in vivo* observation about how the defendant actually interacts and collaborates with his or her attorney.

Competency to Enter a Plea

Because the majority of criminal prosecutions end with a guilty plea (U.S. Sentencing Commission [USSC], 1998–2002), competence to tender a guilty plea also deserves consideration. Like inappropriate confessions made out of fear or deference to authority, mentally retarded defendants may prematurely or inaccurately plead guilty to crimes without adequate exploration of the alternatives. Rather than revealing their deficits and incurring criticism, these individuals may plead guilty as a way to circumvent a trial. Further, concepts such as plea bargaining may be confusing. As a result, they may focus concretely on the possibility of spending less time incarcerated and agree hastily to a plea bargain without weighing other alternatives and without fully understanding that doing so is an admission of guilt.

Competency to be Executed

> Doil Lane, who remains on death row in Texas, confessed to the murder of a young girl, when he climbed into the lap of a police officer. During his trial, he asked for crayons so he could draw pictures. In a letter to prison officials, he wrote, "I like to clore [color] in my clorel [coloring] book but you all tuck [took] away my clores when you can not hurt no one with a box 24 clores, just in my book." (Bonner and Rimer, 2000)

Until recently, a mentally retarded individual could be executed (and many were) for capital offenses. However, in 2002, the U.S. Supreme Court ruled that it was unconstitutional to execute a mentally retarded individual (*Atkins v. Virginia*, 2002), reversing previous rulings that indicated that the constitutionality should be determined on a case-by-case basis (*Penry v. Lynaugh*, 1989). In the *Atkins* case, which ruled that executions of mentally retarded offenders represent "cruel and unusual punishment," Justice Stevens stated, "Because of their disabilities in areas of reasoning, judgment, and control of their impulses ... they do not act with the level of moral culpability that characterizes the most serious adult criminal conduct. Moreover, their impairments can jeopardize the reliability and fairness of capital proceedings against mentally retarded defendants" (*Atkins v. Virginia*, 2002). This change underscores the importance of accurately diagnosing mental retardation, as only a few IQ points could determine the difference between life in prison and death (Kanaya et al., 2003). Notably, each state is currently allowed to develop its own procedure concerning restrictions on executions (*Atkins v. Virginia*, 2002), which has been refined to include case-by-case adjudication of mental retardation claims as they pertain to capital sentences (*Schriro v. Smith*, 2005).

Criminal Responsibility

> Oliver Cruz was convicted of raping and murdering a woman in 1988. Mr. Cruz had a history of mental retardation, as established by school testing. As an adult, testing estimated his IQ at 64. He was functionally illiterate, reading and writing below a third grade level. Further, he had difficulties with substance abuse and was intoxicated at the time of the crime. Mr. Cruz's co-defendant, who was not mentally retarded, pled guilty and received a 65-year sentence in return for testifying against him. Mr. Cruz waived his Miranda rights and gave a confession, although testimony at trial indicated that the concept of waiving rights was beyond his comprehension. The prosecution, which did not contest Mr. Cruz's mental retardation, argued that the fact that he was mentally retarded made him more dangerous and less apt to change. On August 9, 2000, the Supreme Court refused to grant a writ of certiorari or to stay the execution. Mr. Cruz was executed that evening. (Human Rights Watch, 2001)

The way in which the courts view mental retardation varies from one state to another. Often, there is little distinction between mental illness and mental retardation, as both are viewed as potentially reducing a defendant's blameworthiness for a crime (Stavis, 1994). Although both mental illness and mental retardation (or defect, according to some legal definitions) can affect an individual's criminal responsibility, it is important to note that unlike mental illness, mental retardation represents a static, lifelong condition for which there is no cure or "restoration" of functioning.

In some jurisdictions, mental retardation can be viewed as a mitigating factor, reducing but not excusing the culpability of the offender. In other states, mental retardation can be used as a foundation for a criminal responsibility defense. Although states vary with regard to the specific standard (e.g., ALI Model Penal Code or M'Naughten's case, 1984) used to determine lack of criminal responsibility, most definitions involve some variation of a person's inability to "appreciate" the wrongfulness of his or her behavior (Rolf, 2006). Though this "appreciation" prong is multifaceted, it conveys in part that an individual must have the cognitive awareness to understand or "appreciate" that his or her behavior is contrary to the law. In certain cases, when an individual is readily seen as impaired, minor "nuisance" crimes such as inappropriate touching, shoplifting, and so forth may be resolved by release on probation, to a treatment program, or to a guardian (Stavis, 1994). Further, it should be noted that federal and state courts also differ with regard to the opinion that can be ventured by a forensic clinician. Federal courts are more restrictive, requesting that the clinician speak solely to whether an individual is mentally retarded or mentally ill, whereas state courts may allow the clinician to speak to the ultimate issue of criminal responsibility (Rolf, 2006). The forensic clinician is advised to be aware of the legal standard within his or her jurisdiction regarding criminal responsibility and to tailor the evaluation and any associated opinion to reflect that specified standard.

Criminal responsibility is ultimately determined by the court; however, forensic evaluators may offer clinical opinions regarding the extent to which mental retardation might affect a defendant's ability to appreciate the wrongfulness of his or her behavior. For example, a mentally retarded individual may fail to understand the inappropriateness and illegality of sexual contact with a minor (Davis, 2002). At times, such behavior can be due to poorly developed self-control and lack of social education regarding sexuality, as the mentally retarded offender might view a minor victim as an emotional equal and coparticipant. This is not to say that sexual offenses or any other criminal offense committed by a mentally retarded person should be dismissed on the basis of mental retardation alone, as mental retardation in and of itself is not an adequate defense against a criminal act. Yet, forensic evaluators can play a vital role by documenting specific deficits as they pertain to criminal offenses committed by mentally retarded defendants.

As previously noted, mental retardation often co-occurs with mental illness, substance abuse, or both. The forensic examiner needs to parse out the effects of each of these conditions on the criminal behavior and then speak on their individual and combined effects.

> Jerry, age 21, was arrested for exposing himself to his 7-year-old next-door neighbor with whom he frequently played. Jerry, whose IQ was estimated at around 45, shared many interests with this neighbor boy, including playing with cars and trucks and watching children's television programming. When asked why he exposed himself, Jerry said simply that he and the boy were talking about different body parts, which prompted him to show his genitals. While Jerry had learned that certain body parts were considered "private," upon questioning he did not understand why it was wrong for him to show his body to his friend.

Writing Forensic Reports and Acting as an Expert Witness

The Written Report

The standard format for forensic reports may be utilized when evaluating mentally retarded individuals. However, if mental retardation is of central concern, a key portion of the report should involve a thorough review of the individual's developmental history and may involve additional testing. Data gathering should include an exploration of school records including special education services, previous psychological evaluations, employment records, and a review of any interventions or services provided by social and governmental agencies. If an individual has qualified for and is a client of any agency providing mental retardation services, the qualification information and services should be described in detail. If mental retardation has been adequately documented and recent psychological testing is available, a summary of testing should be incorporated into the report. Conversely, if testing is unavailable, dated, or seems inaccurate, a reassessment might be required.

In addressing the diagnostic criteria for mental retardation, a forensic report should address three main issues. First, as mentioned, a thorough review of the individual's history is required with special attention paid to any signs of cognitive deficits or developmental delays noted prior to age 18. Second, an intelligence test should be referenced (or performed) to document current intellectual deficits. Psychologists routinely perform intelligence testing across a wide range of clinical circumstances, and a variety of intelligence tests are available and utilized for the purpose of documenting subaverage intelligence. In a recent survey of forensic experts conducted by Lally (2003), the Wechsler Adult Intelligence Scales—Third Edition (WAIS-III) was rated as a "recommended" or "acceptable" instrument to evaluate issues of competency and mental state at the time of offense. Third, the evaluation should include a measure of adaptive functioning, of which several are routinely used (e.g., Vineland Adaptive Behavior Scales). Such instruments are typically completed by interviewing caregivers or relatives who have enough day-to-day experience with the individual, which enables them to rate the individual on a variety of functional domains. Such ratings typically include some assessment of social functioning, communication skills, and daily living/self-care tasks.

Taken together, these issues serve an added function to provide behavioral data regarding both generalized impairment and more specific deficits in information processing as they pertain to an individual's overall ability to navigate the legal process. Once mental retardation has been documented either historically or through current evaluation, the evaluator must then move beyond diagnostic issues to explore specific deficits as they relate to the legal question at hand. For example, if an individual meeting the criteria for a diagnosis of mental retardation also demonstrates deficits in his "factual" and "rational" understanding of the proceedings against him, a clear and supported clinical opinion can be ventured regarding how mental retardation might affect the individual's competency to stand trial.

Expert Testimony

The role of the expert witness in these cases is often focused on educating the judge and jury about two basic issues. First, the expert might speak generally to the nature of mental retardation as it pertains to deficits pertinent to the legal issue at hand. The expert might clarify the distinction between mental retardation and mental illness, note the lifelong nature of mental retardation, and address the nature of treatment. When testifying about competencies, the focus will need to be on the difficulties in understanding abstract and complex legal concepts, as well as any deficits in language that might be present. When testifying about criminal responsibility, the focus shifts to the impact of the disability on the ability to control and understand the criminality of his or her behavior. Second, the expert should speak specifically about a defendant's unique deficits. If relevant, the expert might review the individual's history and current functioning, tailoring the information as necessary to attend to the legal matter in question (i.e., competency, criminal responsibility, dispositional issues, and so forth). On the whole, the expert serves a primary role as educator about intellectual disabilities, constructing a framework on which legal decisions by all parties can be based.

Ethical Considerations

Forensic practitioners serve a distinct role as educators at all levels of the legal process. Lawyers and police officers are rarely trained in such areas and will frequently need assistance to identify whether mental retardation may be present and to understand the specific care that a defendant with mental retardation might require. For all involved parties, questions and issues that might serve as a preliminary "screen" might include inability to read, write, tell time, or make change. Individuals suspected of having mental retardation might be slow to respond to questions, inordinately quiet or acquiescent, or unable to explain their actions in any detail. Historical indicators might include special education placement, failure to hold a steady job, or lack of independent living.

Because mental retardation is a condition requiring cognitive and behavioral assessment, it is important that forensic evaluators conducting such assessments have adequate training about both the clinical and the legal aspects of mental retardation. Because many clinical training programs do not offer specific courses in this area, clinicians should avail themselves of postdoctoral training to gain experience with diagnosis, assessment, intervention, and treatment of mental retardation. Individuals without such training should defer to those who are experienced in forensic evaluations of mentally retarded defendants. In those circumstances where alternative evaluators are not available, it is incumbent upon the forensic professional to consult with persons who are expert in the field, to review contemporary literature, to be conservative in offering clinical opinions, and to be forthright about professional limitations. Further, inexperienced evaluators should inform attorneys of their limitations early on, so alternatives can be discussed. State and private agencies that offer services to this population frequently maintain listings of experienced clinicians.

Ethical conduct requires forensic evaluators to be cautious and mindful of the limitations of psychological tests. Many popular and widely used forensic instruments are completely inappropriate for use with mentally retarded defendants, often portraying true and documented deficiencies as malingering (Hurley and Deal, 2006). Relatively few instruments have been specifically developed for evaluating competency issues with mentally retarded defendants. However, the CAST-MR (Competence Assessment for Standing Trial for Defendants with Mental Retardation) attempts to sidestep traditional problems inherent in evaluating mentally retarded defendants, which include language limitations, a focus on symptoms rather than concrete legal understanding, and an open-ended format that often yields inaccurate results (Everington, 1990).

Forensic practitioners also have an ethical obligation to dispel the myths that are often inherent with mentally retarded offenders. These misconceptions include notions of a mentally retarded individual as being dangerous, violent, "out of control," or "oversexed" (Davis, 2002) or alternately, that a mentally retarded individual is never capable or culpable, but is merely "angelic." The expert may also need to sensitize involved parties to the universal impact of mental retardation on all levels of behavior. Disparaging and derogatory terms such as "retard," "idiot," and "imbecile" that may arise over the course of legal proceedings must be directly tackled and dismantled to create a more sensitive and fair legal environment.

Additional ethical concerns might involve maintaining a clear demarcation between the role of evaluator and other potentially competing roles. Often, an ethical and caring clinician might be inappropriately pulled into the role of advocate as well as evaluator, which might obscure and weaken his role. Yet, it is important to keep in mind that the act of evaluating, summarizing, and bringing to light a defendant's history and deficits can serve a dual function of addressing a specific legal issue and of highlighting a need for services. In many cases, the forensic expert might be invited to comment directly on the dispositional matters, which might include revising existing services or providing new services. While clearly a dual role, advocating for a defendant in need might be a moral stance required by the situation.

Dispositional/Treatment Considerations

As mentioned, mental retardation is often seen concomitantly with other medical and psychiatric issues. Physical disabilities such as seizure disorder and other organic conditions are not uncommon in some forms of mental retardation, and correctional settings may require assistance and direction in dealing with these special needs. Additionally, psychiatric disorders, especially depression, are highly prevalent in mentally retarded individuals (Matson and Barrett, 1982; McLean, 1993), but they may present a different symptom pattern than in the general psychiatric population. Mentally retarded individuals may be less capable of expressing themselves and in turn might be more prone to acting out behaviors that can be misinterpreted superficially as mere behavior problems. Frequently, a diagnosis of mental retardation overshadows other psychiatric issues that may be equally or even more contributory to criminal behavior (Jopp and Keys, 2001). Thus, it is absolutely imperative that all aspects of a mentally retarded defendant's functioning be addressed to make solid and effective treatment recommendations.

If an individual is not receiving services but is eligible for them, this issue should be discussed together with a strategy for obtaining them. If there is a likelihood that a defendant will be incarcerated, the impact of the individual's disability on incarceration should be discussed, along with recommendations for appropriate supervision, protective custody, and other pertinent issues. The court may need to be educated that mentally retarded people no longer are sent to institutions but rather are housed in community settings such as group homes or staffed apartments.

These services may require a multifactorial approach, as many mentally retarded individuals grapple with concurrent homelessness, abuse, mental illness, and substance abuse. The number of mentally retarded individuals living in institutional settings has dropped by over half in the past 50 years (Levine and Perkins, 1997). In an ideal world, these individuals should be absorbed into families and communities that understand their particular needs and are willing and able to provide them. Unfortunately, limited funding and services force many of these individuals to remain with elderly parents, or homeless and without services until they resort to criminal behavior and end up in the court or jails, which represent "institutions of last resort" (Kinsler et al., 2004). Further, in many jurisdictions, individuals suffering from both mental retardation and mental illness often bounce between two delivery systems, being adequately serviced by neither and falling between the proverbial cracks.

Treatment of persons with mental retardation has become increasingly professionalized, particularly with regard to utilization of behavior management strategies for acting-out behaviors (i.e., aggression and inappropriate sexual behavior). Doctoral-level psychologists are often utilized to plan and direct treatment programs that are in turn carried out by direct care staff who may have limited formal training. Many treatment programs offer specialized and more restrictive interventions for persons who present a risk to the community, such as sex offenders. Although designing and implementing such treatment programs is typically outside the role of the forensic expert, forensic psychologists or psychiatrists might be asked to give dispositional recommendations regarding treatment, which might take place in a variety of settings including correctional situations or, alternatively, in psychiatric or community-based settings. Further, dispositional statements might require a risk assessment to explore the level of structure and security an individual might require.

Future Implications

In trying to develop intervention strategies with such handicapped individuals, correctional and treatment systems will have to evolve beyond traditional, existing modes of intervention. Alternate models of intervention have been proposed for underserved mentally retarded individuals. One such example is the Vermont Defendant Accommodation Project, which identifies individuals with multiple problems (creatively labeled as "horrible life disorder") and provides broad-based services to assist individuals in navigating the legal process and in obtaining services beyond the need to address immediate legal woes (Kinsler et al., 2004). This approach recommends appointment of an evaluation team and subsequently a "cognitive facilitator" to aid defendants and to recommend accommodations as needed (i.e., through simplification of forms, slowing the pace of court proceedings, simplifying courtroom discussion, and so forth). The team report accompanies the individual to the correctional facility, where it helps augment programming. On a smaller scale, the AAMR recommends the appointment of an advocate, in addition to its attorney, who has expertise in the field of mental retardation and who can assist the defendant and his or her lawyer as needed (AAMR, 2002b).

At a macrolevel, there remains a continuing need for focused teaching and experiential training so that experts have a solid, seasoned basis for making statements and recommendations regarding mentally retarded defendants. This need for specialized training is true at all levels, including clinicians who may have only a smattering of training in this area. Surprisingly few clinicians have focused training in the area of mental retardation and instead try to adapt their limited clinical training to address forensic issues, harkening back to longstanding warnings regarding ignorance, irrelevance, and insufficiency as they pertain to trying to bend clinical knowledge to address forensic needs (Grisso, 1986). This serves to underscore the continuing need for focused training in mental retardation for forensic clinicians (and clinicians in general) to address the unique needs of this population and to intervene effectively and accurately. Training of the police, defense, and prosecutors serves to sensitize these professionals to the need for prompt and careful assessments.

Training might include expeditious assessments of language, reasoning, functioning, and history that alert the police and legal professionals that deficits potentially exist with a given individual. Broader interventions might involve policymaking and development of specific standards and guidelines for dealing with defendants suspected as being or known to be mentally retarded. Continued integrative research is also required to offer practitioners a blueprint for structuring their work. Such research might include development of psychological instruments designed to address a particular forensic issue (such as competency to confess), as opposed to trying to bend existing psychological instruments to meet a forensic need for which they were never intended. Existing instruments might benefit from refinement or the development of specialized norms to make them applicable to mentally retarded defendants. Integrative research might also involve collaboration with other disciplines (e.g., medical, legal, social work) both to expand general understanding of mental retardation and to adapt this understanding to address practical issues within the forensic arena, moving beyond conjecture and myth.

Mary, described at the opening of this chapter, was found not competent to stand trial, was placed on probation, and was helped to obtain services from the local mental retardation agency. She now lives in a staffed apartment with two other women, works at a supervised workshop, and has severed her relationship with her "boyfriend," who was imprisoned for his major drug dealing. For the first time in her adult life, she is safe, healthy, and secure; she reports that she is "happy just to be alive."

References

American Association of Mental Retardation. (2002a). *Mental Retardation: Definition, Classification, and Systems of Supports.* 10th ed. Annapolis, MD: Author.

American Association of Mental Retardation. (2002b). *AAMR/ARC Position Statements: Criminal Justice.* Retrieved September 18, 2006, from http://www.aamr.org/Policies/pos_criminal_justice.shtml.

American Psychiatric Association. (2000). *Diagnostic and Statistic Manual of Mental Disorders IV-TR Fourth Edition (Text Revision).* Washington, DC: Author.

Appelbaum, K. L. (1994). Assessment of criminal-justice-related competencies in defendants with mental retardation. *Journal of Psychiatry and Law, 22(3),* 311–327.

Bonner, R. and Rimer, S. (2000, August 7). Executing the Mentally Retarded Even as Laws Begin to Shift. *New York Times,* A1.

Charlot, L. R., Doucette, A. C., and Mezzacappa, E. (1993). Affective symptoms of institutionalized adults with mental retardation. *American Journal on Mental Retardation, 98,* 408–416.

Davis, L. A. (2000). People with mental retardation in the criminal justice system. *The Arc,* Arlington, TX: Author. Retrieved July 31, 2006, from http://www.thearc.org/faqs/crimjustice.doc.

Davis, L. A. (2002). People with cognitive, intellectual and developmental disabilities and sexual offenses. *The Arc,* Arlington, TX: Author. Retrieved July 31, 2006, from http://www.thearc.org/posits/crimjusticepos.doc.

Day, K. (1997). Clinical features and offense behavior of mentally retarded sex offenders: A review of research. *The NADD Newsletter, 14,* 86–89.

Everington, C. T. (1990). The competence for standing trial for defendants with mental retardation. *Criminal Justice and Behavior, 17,* 147–148.

Finlay, W. M. L. and Lyons, E. (2001). Methodological issues in interviewing and using self-report questionnaires with people with mental retardation. *Psychological Assessment, 13(3),* 319–335.

Freedman, E. (2001). Earl Washington's ordeal. *Hofstra Law Review, 29(1089)*, 1089–1112.

Glick, M. and Zigler, E. (1995). Developmental differences in the symptomatology of psychiatric inpatients with and without mild mental retardation. *American Journal on Mental Retardation, 99(4)*, 407–417.

Goldman, M. (2001). Systematic treatment of criminal offenders having developmental delay. *The NADD Bulletin, 4(3)*, 56–57.

Grisso, T. (1986). *Evaluating Competencies: Forensic Assessments and Instruments.* New York: Plenum Press.

Hewitt, S. E. K. (1986). Mentally retarded persons and the criminal justice system. *Medicine and Law, 5*, 265–272.

Hill, B. K. and Bruinink, R. H. (1984). Maladaptive behavior of mentally retarded individuals in residential facilities. *American Journal of Mental Deficiency, 88*, 380–387.

Human Rights Watch. (2001). *Beyond Reason: Mental Retardation: An Overview.* Retrieved June 15, 2006, from http://www.hrw.org/reports/2001/ustat/ustat0301-01.htm.

Hurley, K. E. and Deal, W. P. (2006). Assessment instruments measuring malingering used with individuals who have mental retardation: Potential problems and issues. *Mental Retardation, 44(2)*, 112–119.

Jopp, D. and Keys, C. (2001). Diagnostic overshadowing reviewed and reconsidered. *American Journal on Mental Retardation, 106(5)*, 416–433.

Kanaya, T., Scullin, M. H., and Ceci, S. J. (2003). The Flynn Effect and U.S. policies. *American Psychologist, 58(10)*, 778–790.

Kassin, S. M. and Norwick, R. J. (2004). Why people waive their *Miranda* rights: The power of innocence. *Law and Human Behavior, 28(2)*, 211–221.

Kebbell, M. R. and Hatton, C. (1999). People with mental retardation as witnesses in court: A review. *Mental Retardation, 37*, 179–187.

Kinsler, P. J., Saxman, A., and Fishman, D. B. (2004). The Vermont Defendant Accommodation Project: A case study. *Psychology, Public Policy, and Law, 10(1/2)*, 134–161.

Lally, S. J. (2003). What tests are acceptable for use in forensic evaluations? A survey of experts. *Professional Psychology: Research and Practice, 34(5)*, 491–498.

Levine, M. and Perkins, D. V. (1997). *Principles of Community Psychology: Perspectives and Applications.* 2nd ed. New York: Oxford University Press.

Lezak, M. D. (1995). *Neuropsychological Assessment.* 3rd ed. New York: Oxford University Press.

Lustig, S. (1996). *Defendants with Mental Retardation: A Guide for Attorneys* [Brochure]. The Developmentally Disabled Offenders Program and the New Jersey Bar Foundation. Retrieved June 15, 2006, from http://www.njsbf.com/njsbf/publications/mental.cfm.

Matson, J. L. and Barrett, R. P. (1982). *Psychopathology in the Mentally Retarded.* New York: Grune and Stratton.

McLean, W. E. (1993). Overview. In J. L. Matson and R. P. Barrett (Eds.), *Psychopathology in the Mentally Retarded* (2nd ed., pp. 1–16.). Needham Heights, MA: Allyn and Bacon.

Melton, G. B., Petrila, J., Poythress, N. G., and Slobogin, C. (1997). *Psychological Evaluations for the Courts.* 2nd ed. New York: Guilford Press.

Mittenberg, W., Patton, C., Canyock, E. M., and Condit, D. C. (2002). Base rates of malingering and symptom exaggeration. *Journal of Clinical and Experimental Neuropsychology, 24(8)*, 1094–1102.

Murphy, W., Coleman, E., and Haynes, M. (1983). Treatment and evaluation issues with the mentally retarded sex offender. In J. G. Greer and I. R. Stuart (Eds.), *The Sexual Aggressor: Current Perspectives on Treatment* (pp. 22–41). New York: Van Nostrand Reinhold.

Novaco, R. W. and Taylor, J. L. (2004). Assessment of anger and aggression in male offenders with developmental disabilities. *Psychological Assessment, 16(1)*, 42–50.

Perske, R. (2000). Deception in the interrogation room: Sometimes tragic for persons with mental retardation and other developmental disabilities. *Mental Retardation, 38(6)*, 532–537.

Petersilia, J. (1997). Justice for All? Offenders with Mental Retardation and the California Corrections System. *The Prison Journal, 77(4)*, 358.

Reiss, S. and Rojahn, J. (1993). Joint occurrence of depression and aggression in children and adults with mental retardation. *Journal of Intellectual Disability Research, 37*, 287–294.

Rolf, C. A. (2006). From M'Naghten to Yates: Transformation of the insanity defense in the United States—Is it still viable? *Rivier College Online Academic Journal, 2(1)*, 1–18. Retrieved September 13, 2006, from http://www.rivier.edu/journal/ROAJ-2006-Spring/J41-ROLF.pdf.

Santamour, M. (1986, Spring-Summer). The offender with mental retardation. *The Prison Journal, 66(7)*, 3–18.

Smith, S. A. (1993). Confusing the terms "guilty" and "not guilty": Implications for alleged offenders with mental retardation. *Psychological Reports, 73*, 675–678.

Stavis, P. (1994, March-April). Treatment of persons with mental retardation in the criminal justice system. *Quality of Care Newsletter: NY's Commission on Quality of Care, 59*. Retrieved September 13, 2006, from http://cqc.state.ny.us/counsels_corner/cc59.htm.

Sundram, C. (1991, March). *Inmates with Developmental Disabilities in New York Correctional Facilities.* Albany: New York State Commission of Quality Care for the Mentally Disabled. Retrieved July 31, 2006, from http://www.cqcapd.state.ny.us/publications/pubinmat.htm.

The Arc. (2002). *Position Statements of The Arc: Criminal Justice.* Arlington, TX: Author. Retrieved July 31, 2006, from http://www.thearc.org/posits/crimjusticepos.doc.

U.S. Sentencing Commission. (1998–2002). Datafiles, USSCFY98–USSCFY02.

White, D. and Wood, H. (1986). The Lancaster County, Pennsylvania, Mentally Retarded Offenders Program. *The Prison Journal, 65(1)*, 77–84.

Legal References

Atkins v. Virginia, 122 S. Ct. 2242 (2002).

Dusky v. United States, 362 U.S. 402, 80 S. Ct. 788 (1960).

Godinez v. Moran, 61 U.S.L.W. 4749, 113 S. Ct. 2680 (1993).

Jackson v. Indiana, 406 U.S. 715, 92 S. Ct. 1845 (1972).

M'Naughten's Case, 8 Eng. Rep. 718, 8 Eng. Rep. 722 (1843).

Penry v. Lynaugh, 492 U.S. 302 (1989).

Schriro v. Smith, 546 U.S. (2005).

State v. Arthur, 374 S.E. 2d. 291, 293-294. (S.C. 1988).

Washington v. Commonwealth, 323 S.E.2d 577, 589 (Va. 1984).

MMPI-Based Forensic Psychological Assessment of Lethal Violence

13

ROBERT J. CRAIG

Roosevelt University, Chicago, Illinois

Contents

Synopsis

This chapter presents findings from objective psychological tests (i.e., MMPI/MMPI-2) in the assessment of lethal violence. It discusses the legal basis for using the MMPI-2 in court, and then presents (a) a review of the empirical literature in the use of the MMPI/MMPI-2 with murderers, (b) an MMPI-derived criminal offender classification system and its applicability with murderers, and (c) the assessment of a particular kind of murderer, referred to as the "overcontrolled" type. Cases presented throughout the chapter illustrate the use and utility of the concepts presented in the chapter.

This work is an expanded version of a chapter that originally appeared in H. Hall (Ed.). (1996). MMPI-based psychological assessment of lethal violence. *Lethal Violence 2000.* Boca Raton, FL: CRC Press. With permission.

Introduction

This chapter deals with a specific type of assessment—psychometric assessment using objective personality tests. Although a comprehensive psychological evaluation of an individual defendant recognizes and utilizes all sources of data (e.g., clinical interviews, collateral sources, patient records, forensic, and police reports), this chapter only discusses assessment using objective personality tests. Hence, it is more limited than in actual clinical practice, where psychological test findings are integrated with other sources of information.

Objective psychological tests are standardized instruments or inventories that present the respondent with structured stimuli and with a limited number of response options. The test taker answers either "true" or "false," "yes" or "no," "a," "b," or "c." Hence, these tests are easily scored because one is only required to sum the responses in these few categories. Objective psychological tests tend to be more reliable than personality tests using subjective stimuli (i.e., the Rorschach, etc.). Because of the standardized material, limited response options, and better reliability, objective tests of personality lend themselves to more objective interpretation. Hence, they usually have more evidence of validity than other types of assessment tools or methodologies.

The most frequently used objective tests for the assessment of personality include the Minnesota Multiphasic Personality Inventory (MMPI: Hathaway and McKinley, 1940), and its revision, the MMPI-2 (Butcher, Dahlstrom, Graham, Tellegen, and Keammer, 1989), the Millon Clinical Multiaxial Inventory—III (MCMI-III: Millon, 1994), the California Psychological Inventory—Revised (CPI-R: Gough, and Heilbrun, 1987), and the 16 personality factors questionnaire (16PF: Cattell, 1989). These tests have been used in a number of forensic issues (see Craig, 2005a), but the MMPI/MMPI-2 has been the most frequently used psychological test with murderers.

Recent surveys of psychological test usage among forensic psychologists reflect the preeminent role that the MMPI-2 continues to play in a variety of assessment questions. These include mental state at the time of the offense, violence and sexual risk evaluations, competency to stand trial, competency to waive Miranda rights evaluations, assessment of malingering, and parental competency evaluations (Archer, Buffington-Vollum, Stredny, and Handel, 2006; Lally, 2003; Stredny, Archer, and Mason, 2006).

Because there is a substantial literature base with perpetrators of lethal violence, and because there have been some assessment refinements, particularly in the area of developing homogeneous patient profiles and in developing special scales from the MMPI item pool, this chapter presents only MMPI/MMPI-derived studies that have assessed murderers.

The MMPI as a Measuring Instrument

The MMPI was originally developed around 1940 to measure the major psychopathologies that were then of interest to psychiatrists. It was used for both diagnostic and descriptive purposes. The test's developers (Starke Hathaway and J. Charnley McKinley) advanced measurement in this area by selecting items from the original test item pool that statistically differentiated members in the clinical (criterion) group from members in the nonclinical, standardization sample—people who were considered to be normal. This is a standard practice today but was an innovation at that time.

The scales that appeared in the original MMPI scales measured eight clinical syndromes: hypocondriasis (Hs), depression (Dep), hysteria (Hy), psychopathic deviance (Pd), paranoia (Pa), psychasthenia (Pt) (an older psychiatric term no longer in use and now referred to as neurotic anxiety), schizophrenia (Sc), and hypomania (Ma). They then tried to develop a scale that would distinguish between normal males and homosexual males without other psychopathology. This was done because, at that time, homosexuality was considered a psychopathology, whereas today, it has been removed from psychiatric diagnostic nomenclature. Because they were unable to devise a scale that successfully differentiated a heterosexual from a homosexual male, they created a scale that measured stereotypic masculine and feminine interests (MF Scale). The MMPI-2 retained the MF Scale, but keyed the items to endorsement rates of men and women that were tied to the 1980 national census. This provides the user with more contemporary norms for male and female interests. Validity scales were added to detect lying, exaggerating, or underreporting of actual problems and the test was published. Shortly thereafter, a special scale called the Social Introversion (Si) Scale was developed by an independent researcher and became attached to the clinical scales of the test, thereby creating a test of 3 validity scales and 10 clinical scales.

The test became immediately popular, largely because of its clinical utility. The test generated a substantial amount of research and, after a while, it became clear that the test was not working in the way it was expected to work. The original idea was that only a patient who was depressed would get elevated scores on the Depression Scale. Similarly, a psychopath was expected to score in the clinically elevated ranges on the Pd scale, but non-psychopaths would not. However, patients who were not clinically depressed and patients who were not psychopathic were obtaining elevated scores on those respective scales. Consequently, researchers began to determine which extra-test traits, symptoms, and characteristics were associated with each of the clinical scale elevations. Furthermore, certain traits and symptoms were associated with a given scale at one range, but a different set of traits and characteristics were associated at another range of scores. Hence, clinicians who use the MMPI or, now, the MMPI-2, rarely refer to a scale by its original name. Rather, numbers have been assigned to the clinical scales as follows: hypocondriasis (1), depression (2), hysteria (3), psychopathic deviance (4), masculinity/femininity (5), paranoia (6), psychasthenia (7), schizophrenia (8), hypomania (9), and social introversion (0).

Despite the immense popularity of the test, over the years there developed a number of problems. Some of the test items were outdated, some of the language was sexist, some items were considered offensive, and there was a debate about whether the test was racially biased because no minorities had been included in the original standardization sample. Also, in attempting to adapt the MMPI to other cultures, some items were lost in translation and had no equivalence in other cultures.

As a result, a committee of prominent MMPI researchers and clinicians was formed to revise the test. The committee went to great lengths to ensure that research knowledge from the original MMPI was applicable to revision, and the current evidence suggests that it was quite successful in this regard. Thus, much of our knowledge about murderers that was derived from the MMPI is applicable to using the MMPI-2.

Pertinent Legal Cases Applied Ethics and Moral Considerations

Ogloff (1995) has presented the legal basis for using the MMPI-2 in court. He cited 22 different types of cases in which the MMPI/MMPI-2 has been used at the state level and 13 different types of cases where the MMPI/MMPI-2 has been used at the federal level. These include cases involving murder, death penalty, wrongful death, dangerousness, criminal responsibility, and both risk assessments and insanity evaluations pertaining to these issues (see also Ben-Porath, Graham, Hall, Hirschman, and Zaragoda, 1995; Heilbrun and Heilbrun, 1995; Hess and Weiner, 1999; Litwack and Schlesinger, 1999). Additionally, various sources provide suggestions regarding how to best present MMPI-2-derived evidence and testimony in court (Pope, Butcher, and Seelen, 1993). Furthermore, the MMPI/MMPI-2 meets the Daubert standard for admissible evidence. This body of evidence is so compelling that the MMPI-2 is essentially unchallenged as admissible evidence in court. However, the interpretation of the test and other factors associated with administration and degree of expertise can be challenged.

Overview and Epidemiology

There are several issues that need to be understood prior to discussing research findings using the MMPI/MMPI-2:

1. All of the research has assessed the individual being tested and presented empirical group data after the commission of the crime and after the perpetrator has been apprehended. The defendant's psychological state prior to the commission of the crime or at the time the crime was committed is a matter of conjecture, extrapolation, and judgment. The offender's psychological state at the time of the assessment is what is actually being measured. The psychological effects of imprisonment itself might also be reflected in test findings (Westermeyer, 1974).

2. Timing of the assessment may affect test results. An offender who is tested in conjunction with a hearing to determine competency to stand trial or while addressing other pretrial evaluation issues in association with an insanity plea might show different test results than an offender who is tested as part of a research protocol after sentencing or one who has been confined in prison for a determined length of time (Finney, Skeeters, Auvenshine, and Smith, 1973; Holcolm, Adams, Nicholas, Ponder, and Anderson, 1984; Panton, 1976).

3. Perpetrators of lethal acting out are a heterogeneous population. Intuitively, one would believe that the political assassin or gangland hit man would have different personality traits and motivations than an armed robber who, based on circumstances, goes too far and kills a store employee. The fired employee who returns to the scene of his former employment with a shotgun, killing those in his path, is certainly driven by different psychological forces than the chronically abused housewife who, after sustaining years of physical abuse, engages in a violent and lethal act out of desperation. The drug dealer who was "burned" by a street addict and arranges for a substantial increase in the heroin content of a "bag" which, when ingested, results in a lethal overdose, is operating from a different psychological framework than the man who murders while drunk. The point is that these differences must be addressed methodically and understood psychologically in order for us to have a full accounting of the personality and motives of those who commit murder.

4. Moderator variables are variables that, in themselves, have the capacity to alter scores on tests. The moderator variables that have been most researched are race, gender, and educational level (and its correlates IQ, social status, and occupational status) (Holcolm and Adams, 1982; Holcolm, Adams, and Ponder, 1984). For example, McDonald and

Paitich (1981) found that variables that differentiated murderers from nonmurderous felons disappeared when they were compared to people who were unemployed. Researchers and the individual psychologist evaluating an individual patient must consider these variables and how they may have affected scores on the test (Sutker and Moan, 1973).

5. Finally, there are problems with self-report methodology as a method of psychological assessment. First, the patient has to have some self-understanding and self-awareness. Second, the defendant must be willing to report the knowledge in an unbiased and truthful manner. However, in forensic settings, there are myriad motivations that might compel an offender to lie, exaggerate, fake illness, or underreport certain key problems that could be detrimental to the defendant at trial. Malingering, defined as the voluntary production of false or grossly exaggerated physical or psychological symptoms for purposes of secondary gain, may be common among murderers. In fact, a significant number of patients awaiting trial claim amnesia and attribute it to alcohol, drug use, or some emotional block related to the facts of the crime (Parwatikar, Holcolm, and Menninger, 1985). While the MMPI has scales that screen for such tendencies, the psychologists, clinicians, or researchers must take such factors into consideration when writing a report or when publishing test findings.

Empirically Based Methods and Applications

There are three types of studies that have used the MMPI on murderers. The first type of study compares MMPI profiles of murderers to some other control group. An offshoot of this type of research is to use multivariate statistics and cluster analysis to discern meaningful subgroups within the larger group. The second type of study utilizes this subgroup methodology in an attempt to find distinct cluster or group profile types, and then determine external characteristics associated with each group profile. The Megargee classification system is the most elegant and differentiated study of this type and will also be discussed in depth later in this chapter. Finally, special scales have been derived from the MMPI item pool that pertains to the question of lethally aggressive behavior. The scale that has been given the most attention by researchers is the Overcontrolled Hostility (OH) Scale, which will be discussed later in this chapter.

MMPI Group Profiles of Murderers

Tables 13.1 and 13.2 present an overview of studies that have reported MMPI scores for male, female, and adolescent murderers. For males, there were 14 studies, totaling 1114 MMPIs on murderers in the published literature. Inspection of the data reveals a number of facts: (a) The Pd scale is clinically elevated in almost all profiles. However, this sign is not pathognomonic of murderers. Most people with elevated Pd scores do not commit murder. (b) Among the 30 datasets, Pd (4) combined with Sc (8) scales was clinically elevated in 11 studies. (c) Pa (6) was elevated in 17 studies. The modal code type was characterized by clinically significant elevations in the psychopathic deviate (4) and the schizophrenic (8) scales. Also, a "within normal limits" code type, suggesting no psychopathology, appeared in five datasets.

The aggregated median profile of male murderers is a 468 three-point code reflecting a severe emotional disorder. It is graphically portrayed in Figure 13.1.* Consulted interpreted

---

* Jeffrey Dahmer, the homosexual, cannibalistic murderer from Wisconsin, produced a similar MMPI code type, though his elevations on the scales were substantially higher than those found here.

Table 13.1 MMPI T-Scores of Perpetrators of Lethal Violence

	Study 1		Study 2	Study 3	Study 4	Study 5	Study 6		Study 7 Adult Murderers—Cluster Analysis					Study 8	Study 9	
Scale	White Murderers	Black Murderers	Male Murderers	Death Row	Male/Female Murderers	Male Psych	Sane Murderers	Insane Murderers	Type I	Type II	Type III	Type IV	Type V	Males	White	Black
N	51	51	44	34	61	53	40	12	17	26	21	25	21	137	111	49
L	63	64	53	52	50	50	52	51	46	53	53	50	64	50	50	53
F	52	51	60	58	68	68	71	74	96	120	53	68	80	83	85	86
K	55	56	59	53	50	54	51	53	40	45	60	49	56	50	52	53
Hs	60	65	59	61	47	78	69	62	72	90	52	54	77	54	53	49
Dep	57	56	63	64	76	63	72	67	80	95	58	65	80	75	74	68
Hy	57	56	63	60	68	61	69	64	65	82	56	55	73	66	67	65
Pd	76	74	71	72	63	78	79	77	78	90	67	74	81	68	68	65
Mf	57	57	57	54	68	68	57	65	61	68	51	59	61	61	60	62
Pa	59	64	59	59	69	70	73	68	94	105	55	70	83	83	83	80
Pt	60	64	60	61	50	86	75	77	85	97	52	66	77	50	53	45
Sc	64	70	65	61	55	92	83	81	101	130	55	75	88	67	69	67
Ma	65	70	58	60	59	68	69	70	70	85	58	69	63	63	60	65
Si	53	52	50	54	55	58	58	58	67	72	47	54	63	62	63	55
Code	4'	489'	4'	4'	2'	8741'	8476+	847'	8672+	8672+	WNL	8469	8647	6243	62'	6'

Scale	Study 10 Cluster Analysis					Study 11 Violent		Study 12		Study 13 Male Murderers				Study 14 Male Murderers	Study 15[a] Male Murderers	Mean T-Scores
	Type I	Type II	Type III	Type IV	Type V	Sober	Drunk	Domestic Murder	Stranger Murder	Type I	Type II	Type III	Type IV			
N	20	13	18	14	15	48	41	20	19	45	26	31	16	35	135	37
L	45	53	56	50	60	53	53	57	56	56	51	58	62	55	56	54
F	100	115	58	66	76	78	78	55	54	50	58	56	61	67	76	71
K	40	46	62	48	55	49	53	60	58	55	52	65	61	54	45	53
Hs	58	80	31	39	52	49	49	56	52	46	50	55	68	59	46	58
Dep	77	96	64	65	75	70	72	57	53	52	55	56	72	66	67	68
Hy	64	86	60	56	69	64	65	58	53	53	50	61	67	63	62	63
Pd	79	80	50	60	67	61	62	59	67	59	70	72	76	76	55	71
Mf	61	71	60	57	61	62	59	55	53	55	55	55	58	62	48	60
Pa	100	108	59	70	85	76	76	55	55	51	54	56	60	69	75	70
Pt	71	79	21	40	44	43	46	56	55	48	56	55	68	70	42	60
Sc	96	117	23	50	55	61	57	56	57	49	62	56	70	75	53	70
Ma	75	75	50	58	58	63	58	57	65	56	68	58	60	66	49	64
Si	66	71	48	54	62	56	60	53	47	47	50	49	58	57	60	58
Code	6842	8623	WNL	6'	62's	62'	62'	WNL	WNL	WNL	4'	4'	48'	48'	6'	468'

Studies: (1) Sutker and Moan (1973); (2) Deiker (1974); (3) Panton (1976); (4) McDonald and Paitich (1981); (5) Langevin, Paitich, Orchard, Handy, and Russon (1982); (6) Rogers and Seman (1983); (7) Holcolm and Anderson (1983); (8) Holcolm and Adams (1983); (9) Holcolm, Adams and Ponder (1985); (10) Holcolm, Adams, Nicholas, and Ponder (1985); (11) Holcolm and Adams (1985); (12) Kalichman, 1988a; (13) Kalichman, 1988b; (14) Fraboni, Cooper, Reed, and Salstone (1990).

[a] Shea and McKee (1996) (MMPI-2).

Table 13.2 MMPI T-Scores for Female and Adolescent Murderers

| | Study 1 | Study 2 | | | Study 3 |
| | Female | Female[a] | | | Adolescents |
Scale		Filicide	Matricide	Homicide	
N	16	24	15	14	18
L	51	57	60	60	47
F	56	66	72	68	86
K	53	50	47	52	46
Hs	56	62	64	61	74
Dep	53	66	73	64	68
Hy	56	59	64	59	68
Pd	65	62	68	70	75
Mf	43	52	52	60	59
Pa	63	71	71	68	76
Pt	53	65	68	64	70
Sc	56	66	69	69	77
Ma	57	50	55	52	68
Si	55	59	59	53	60
Code	WNL	6287	2687	486	8641

Studies: (1) Kalichman (1988a); (2) McKee et al. (2001); (3) Cornell, Miller, and Benedek (1988).
[a] McKee et al. (2001) (MMPI-2).

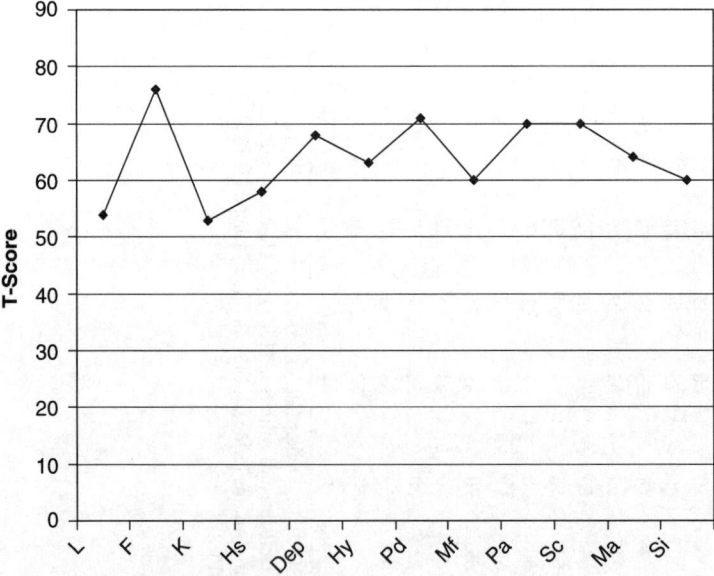

Figure 13.1 MMPI mean profile of male murderers averaged among 30 samples from 1114 inmates.

MMPI/MMPI-2 references indicate that patients with this code type tend to get easily upset over acute situational crises. They tend to show a variety of paranoid symptoms, ruminating about perceived past injustices. They have poor judgment, are overly sensitive, bitter, resentful, argumentative, irritable, quite angry, overly suspicious, and quickly rationalize their behavior with self-justifications. In addition to rationalization, their primary defenses are projection, externalization, and acting out. They tend to have thought disturbances, fragmented thinking, and poor contact with reality. They are unpredictable, brooding, hostile, nonconforming, and impulsive. They tend to make excessive demands on others for attention although they resist demands being placed on them. Their histories tend to reflect adjustment difficulties, especially with authority, problematic interpersonal relationships, irresponsibility, and criminal behavior. Their crimes are often senseless, brutal, savage, and involve sexual or homicidal attacks (Craig, 1999; Friedman, Lewak, Nichols, and Webb, 2001). This personality description is considered characterological rather than situational and reflects the person's basic personality prior to the act of murder. Keep in mind that an individual murderer may or may not have this prototype MMPI profile.

There has been a relative lack of research on females who murder, with only two published reports in the literature (see Table 13.2). The most recent study (McKee, Shea, Mogy, and Holden, 2001) used the MMPI-2 and studied three groups of female murderers: (a) a group of those who killed their child, (b) a group who killed their spouse, and (c) the third group who killed a nonrelative. All three groups had elevated scores on Pa (6) and Sc (8) suggesting elevated paranoid sensitivity, feelings of alienation and estrangement, and unusual thought processes and behavior. Two of the three groups were also elevated on Pd (4). These authors also presented MMPI-2 Content Scales, which are the scales of the main homogeneous content items on the test. These groups were elevated on items pertaining to depression and endorsed items that contained negative treatment attitudes, suggesting that psychological treatment interventions for the psychopathology would likely be unsuccessful. Their Anger (ANG) and Antisocial Practices (ASP) Content Scales were in the normal ranges, suggesting that, as a rule, these women were not angry or antisocial. They did have mild elevations in the Bizarre Mentation (BIZ) Content Scale, suggesting a possible thought disorder.

It is important to keep in mind that there are a number of variables that can affect test scores. Studies that have addressed these variables are reviewed briefly below:

Race. Holcolm and Adams (1982) reported that Black murderers scored higher than White murderers on Ma (9) and lower on Si (0). However, when IQ was controlled, earlier differences between Black and White murderers disappeared (Holcolm et al., 1984).

Relationship to the victim. There is some evidence that MMPI scores differ based on the relationship of the murderer to the victim. Research shows marked differences in the psychology and personality of stranger-to-stranger murderers as compared to spousal murders or parent-child murderers. For example, women who murdered their domestic partner scored higher on Pa (6) and Si (0) compared to men who murdered either their partner or a stranger. These results suggest that women had more sensitivity and social withdrawal, perhaps as a result of physical abuse. In fact, their MMPI was normal, referred to as a "within normal limits" profile. In contrast, men who murdered strangers, compared to men who murdered their domestic partners, had higher levels of social extraversion and impulsivity (low Si). They also had more evidence of sociopathy (Pd) (0) compared to female murderers (Kalichman, 1988a)

Substance abuse. Holcolm and Adams (1985) compared four groups of murderers and the role of substance abuse in relation to the crime. Group 1 consisted of 41 men who murdered while intoxicated, Group 2 was made up of 48 men who murdered while sober, Group 3 consisted of 130 male psychiatric patients without histories of substance abuse or violence, and Group 4 consisted of 40 nonviolent patients in a detoxification program. The violent groups scored higher on Pa (6) and lower on Ma (9), reflecting more suspiciousness and irritability. Men who murdered while sober scored lower on Mf, suggesting lower sensitivity but more psychopathology (Pd) (4) compared to those who murdered while drunk. The latter group had higher lie (L) scores suggesting psychological naïveté.

Amnesia. Inmates undergoing pretrial evaluation were divided into three groups: (a) those who had confessed to the crime ($N = 50$), (b) those who denied the crime ($N = 31$), and (c) those who claimed amnesia ($N = 24$). Inmates claiming amnesia scored higher on scales Hs (1), Dep (2), and Hy (3). These claims of more physical problems and depression were interpreted as signs of malingering (Parwatikar et al., 1985).

Death row status. Inmates on death row had higher elevations on Pd (4) and Sc (8). The elevation of scores suggested hopelessness, frustration, alienation, and resentment, rather than psychotic processes, and were most certainly attributed to the effects of possible death by execution rather than to preexisting personality characteristics (Dahlstrom, Panton, Bain, and Dahlstrom, 1986).

The literature reviewed here suggests that there is no single MMPI profile code type specific to people who murder. There are certain code types that appear more frequently within groups of murderers, but they also appear in those who do not murder. However, any individual patient who has an MMPI profile similar to that of modal types should receive a more thorough scrutiny and evaluation regarding violent tendencies, assaultive behavior, and probability estimates for being at risk for lethal violence.

MMPI Group Classification of Murderers

Edwin Megargee (1977) sought to develop a prisoner taxonomic system that was reliable, economical, valid, and dynamic, and which would have treatment implications. His classification system based on his taxonomy now meets the Standards of the American Correctional Association and satisfies federal court mandates. Using cluster analysis techniques, 10 MMPI "types" were found in a sample of 1344 males, age range 18–27, incarcerated at a Tallahasse federal medium security prison (Megargee and Dorhout, 1977a, 1977b; Meyer and Megargee, 1977). In addition to the MMPI, these prisoners were given other psychological tests. These included the California Psychological Inventory, State-Trait Anxiety Inventory, Adjective Checklist, Personal Opinion Study, Interpersonal Sensitivity Inventory, an Attitudes-Towards-Parents Scale, and a prisonization scale. This battery of tests was given along with a structured clinical interview that was tape-recorded and scored on 250 items by independent raters. Additional data included prison investigation reports and Bureau of Prisons demographic sheets.

Megargee's analysis indicated that these 10 MMPI-based types differed substantially in their family and social history, lifestyle and personality patterns, prison adjustment, and recidivism. In fact, they differed on 140 of 164 variables tested. Modal characteristics of a typical member of the group were then established (Megargee, 1984a, 1984b; Megargee and Bohn, 1977). By 1983, 30,000 federal prisoners have been typed using the Megargee typology (Kennedy, 1986). When the Tallahasse Federal Correctional Institution assigned inmates to living arrangements based on the Megargee classification system, serious assaults dropped by 46% (Megargee, 1984a). Thus, the classification system provides us with a means of distinguishing between potentially violent and no-violent prisoners.

Megargee chose nondescriptive names for these 10 types in an alphabetized format as follows: Able, Baker, Charlie, Delta, Easy, Foxtrot, George, How, Item, and Jupiter, and the system has been ordered on a continuum from most benign to most pathological (Types I, E, B, A, G, D, J, F, C, and H) (Motiuk, Bonta, and Andrews, 1986). The types along with their basic characteristics are presented in Table 13.3.

The reliability of the Megargee typology has been established by (a) studying the inter-rater reliability in terms of classifying individual MMPI profiles, (b) using test–retest methodology, and (c) determining the typology's replicability in other populations (Zager, 1988). Research has provided strong support for the validity of the original 10 types. These types have appeared in federal penitentiaries (Bohn, 1979; Edinger, 1979; Edinger and Auerbach, 1978; Edinger, Reuterfors, and Logue, 1982; Hanson, Moss, Hosford, and Johnson, 1983; Johnson, Simmons, and Gordon, 1983; Louscher, Hosford, and Moss, 1983; Megargee, 1986; Megargee and Bohn, 1977; Mrad, Kabacoff, and Cuckro, 1983; Simmons, Johnson, Gouvier, and Muzyczka, 1981; Van Voorhis, 1988; Walters, Mann, Miller, and Chlumsky, 1988), state penitentiary samples (Booth and Howell, 1980; Carey, Garski, and Ginsberg, 1986; Edinger, 1979; Wright, 1988), medium security facilities (Carey et al., 1986; Johnson et al., 1983), high medium security facilities (Van Voorhis, 1988; Wrobel, Wrobel, and McIntosh, 1988), high security facilities (Louscher et al., 1983; Simmons et al., 1981), and maximum security settings (Louscher et al., 1983; Motiuk et al., 1986; Walters, 1986; Walters et al., 1988). They also appear in death row inmates (Dahlstrom et al., 1986), prison halfway house participants (Motiuk et al., 1986; Mrad et al., 1983), military prisoners (Walters, 1986; Walters, Scrapansky, and Marlow, 1986; Walters et al., 1988), forensic populations (DiFrancesca and Meloy, 1989; Hutton, Miner, and Langfeldt, 1993; Wrobel et al., 1988), presentencing psychiatric samples (Wrobel, Calovini, and Martin, 1991), and presidential threateners (Megargee, 1986).

The typology has been documented across a variety of geographic settings and states, including Alabama (Edinger, 1979), California (DiFrancesca and Meloy, 1989; Hanson et al., 1983; Hutton, Miner, and Langfeldt, 1993; Louscher et al., 1983), Kansas (Walters, 1986), Indiana (Van Voorhis, 1988), Kentucky (Johnson et al., 1983), Louisiana (Schaffer, Pettigrew, Blouin, and Edwards, 1983), Missouri (Anderson and Holcolm, 1983; Megargee, 1986; Mrad et al., 1983), North Carolina (Dahlstrom et al., 1986; Edinger, 1979; Edinger et al., 1982; Megargee, 1986), Ohio (Carey et al., 1986; Van Voorhis, 1988; Wrobel et al., 1991), Tennessee (Simmons et al., 1981; Veneziano and Veneziano, 1986), and Utah (Booth and Howell, 1980), as well as in Canada (Motiuk et al., 1986).

While the system has been used with female prisoners (Edinger, 1979; Schaffer et al., 1983; Wrobel et al., 1991), and with adolescent incarcerates (Doren, Megargee, and Schreiber, 1980; Veneziano and Veneziano, 1986), research has not yet established the utility of the Megargee classification with these groups. Use of adolescents may be particularly prob-lematic because their personalities may not have solidified into their adult forms. Megargee has applied his typology for criminal offenders to adolescent offenders using the adolescent version of the MMPI (i.e., MMPI-A). This work continues under development. However, many adolescents may not have the requisite sixth-grade reading level to take the test. To date, there has been relatively little interest in Megargee's treatment recommendations asso-ciated with the typology (Kennedy, 1986; Pena, and Megargee, 1997).

Although not designated specifically as a classification system for murderers, Megargee reported that the types Charlie, Foxtrot, and How, the more pathological types, were more prone toward violent behavior. Edinger (1979) independently replicated the typology and

Table 13.3   Capsule Characteristics of the 10 Types

Name (Proportion)	MMPI Characteristics		Observed Modal Characteristics
	Elevation	Pattern	
Able (17%)	Moderate, peak score c70 or less	Bimodal with peaks on 4 and 9	Charming, popular, impulsive, and manipulative. Middle class, achievement oriented, do well in institutions but emerge relatively unaffected.
Baker (4%)	Moderate; Pd c70 D c65	Peaks on 4 and 2 slopes down to right	Inadequate, anxious, defensive, constricted, and dogmatic; tends to abuse alcohol but not other drugs.
Charlie (9%)	High; peak scale >80; several >70	Peaks on 8, 6, and 4 slopes up to right	Hostile, misanthropic, suspicious with extensive history of maladjustment, crime, and drug and alcohol abuse. Alienated, aggressive, antagonistic, and antisocial.
Delta (10%)	Moderate to high Pd at least 70, often 80 or 90	Unimodal; prominent Pd spike others below 70	Amoral, hedonistic, egocentric, bright, and manipulative. Poor relations with peers and authorities. Impulsive, sensation-seeking. Leads to frequent infractions.
Easy (7%)	Low, top scales below 80, often below 70	43 profile; slopes down to right	Bright, stable, well-educated middle class, with good adjustment and resources. Under-achievers who take easy path, but have good interpersonal relationships.
Foxtrot (8%)	Top scale(s) over 80 and others over 70	Slopes up to right 8, 9, and 4 top scales	Tough, street-wise, cynical, anti-social. Deprivation and deviance lead to extensive criminal histories, poor prison adjustment. Defiant in all areas.
George (7%)	Moderate; D and Pd c70 more elevated	Like Baker but scales 1, 2, and 3; learned criminal values	Hardworking, submissive, anxious, from deviant families. Do their own time and take advantage of educational and vocational opportunities.
How (13%)	Very high top scales >80 or 90	Elevated multimodal profile; no particular code pattern	Unstable, agitated, disturbed, "mental health" cases. Function ineffectively in all areas and have extensive needs.
Item (19%)	Very low; scales usually under 70	No particular code pattern	Stable, effectively functioning well-adjusted group with minimal problems, few authority conflicts.
Jupiter (3%)	Moderate to high peak scales over 70	Slopes up to right with top scores on 8, 9, and 7	Overcoming deprived background fairly well but have conflicts with staff and other inmates. Work hard and do better than expected after release.

Table 13.3 (*continued*)

Name (Proportion)	Management and Treatment Recommendations
Able (17%)	Need change agent with sense of humor and structured setting to deal with their manipulative games and confront them with outcomes of their behavior
Baker (4%)	Initial anxiety requires supportive help; later many will benefit from alcohol treatment and educational programming; need counseling to stop self-defeating patterns
Charlie (9%)	Require secure setting and extensive programming; consistency, fairness, and perseverance needed to avoid further need of drugs and acting out when stressed
Delta (10%)	Often have extensive records requiring incarceration; separate from weaker, more easily exploited inmates; challenging and confronting needed but prognosis poor
Easy (7%)	Minimal needs for structure or treatment; challenge them to take advantage of assets; respond well to educational programming
Foxtrot (8%)	Require structure and strong change agent; extensive changes needed; peer counseling program with obvious contingencies required to make behavior more socialized
George (7%)	Need to learn alternatives to crime as livelihood; supportive treatment at outset, followed by rational-cooperative approach and education and vocational programming
How (13%)	Require further diagnosis and program aimed at overcoming mental-health problems; warm but structured therapeutic environment with mental health resources needed
Item (19%)	Basically normal group with minimal needs for structure, support, or treatment beyond that dictated by legal situation
Jupiter (3%)	Change agent supportive of efforts to overcome deficits via educational and/or vocational programming; counseling and tolerance for setbacks that occur

Source: Megargee, E., *Medicine and Law*, 3, 109–118. With permission from Springer-Verlag.

found that the types Charlie and Jupitor had committed more violent crimes, including murder, and showed more aggressive behavior in prison compared to the other groups. Because the Charlie type has been particularly implicated in violence and murder (Anderson and Holcom, 1983; Edinger, 1979; Hanson et al., 1983; Motiuk et al., 1986), a more detailed discussion of this MMPI code type is presented.

MMPI profile of Charlie type is characterized by elevations on the scales of schizophrenia (8), paranoia (6), and psychopathic deviance (4)—referred to as an 864 code type. It is an acting-out aggressive type and suggests a personality style that is sensitive to perceived threats and insults, a hostile and bitter demeanor ready to strike at the slightest provocation, and antisocial traits. Individuals with this profile tend to have authority problems, considerable anxiety, a deviant value system, and poor ego strength. They lack empathy, are cognitively and emotionally constricted, and feel alienated, resentful, bitter, and hostile. Charlie types show poor adjustment histories and tend to have many criminal convictions. On the Adjective Checklist, these men endorsed adjectives that indicated negative effect and described themselves as less stable and irresponsible (Megargee, 1977, 1986). They also tend to have a formal thought disorder, substantial energy, and much anger, and are quite defensive (DiFrancesca and Meloy, 1989). Table 13.4 presents an overview of studies that have published T-score information on Charlie type.

With the revision of the MMPI-2, Megargee studied the impact of the restandardization of his classification system. He has determined that new rules were needed for classification (Megargee, 1993, 1994; Megargee, Mercer, and Carbonell, 1999) and has subsequently done so. He found that these new rules were able to successfully classify 97% with both the MMPI and the MMPI-2, and that 87% of the cases were classified identically among 400 female offenders (Megargee, 1997). Megargee is presently conducting research to determine if the empirical correlates established for the MMPI will be similar to those found with

Table 13.4   MMPI T-Scores on Type "Charlie" Profiles in Published Studies

Scale	Study 1	Study 2 Total	Men	Women	Study 3 A	B	Study 4	Study 5
L	50	51	50	48	52	47	49	52
F	80	79	76	76	77	76	79	79
K	46	48	44	49	50	48	46	49
Hs	60	60	60	57	60	59	57	59
Dep	65	65	65	61	64	65	63	68
Hy	59	59	58	52	61	58	53	59
Pd	77	77	75	74	79	78	70	76
Mf	61	61	61	51	61	64	62	67
Pa	81	79	78	80	79	75	73	78
Pt	72	73	75	74	70	71	70	73
Sc	84	90	89	88	84	84	96	88
Ma	75	75	74	68	75	70	74	69
Si	57	56	60	62	53	61	58	59

Studies: (1) Megargee (1977); (2) Edinger (1979); (3) Edinger et al. (1982); (4) Mrad et al. (1983) (5) Hutton et al. (1993).

the MMPI-2 (Megargee, 1993, 1994). Pearson Assessment Systems, the publisher of the MMPI-2, has a computer program that scores and classifies MMPI-2 profiles according to the Megargee classification types.

In summary, research on the Megargee classification system has found the following: (a) An individual in the group may not show all of the characteristics of the group itself and may show variability around the prototype characteristics. (b) The system is dynamic and an individual may change group membership over the course of his or her sentence. (c) The 10 types have appeared in multiple prison settings, although the prevalence of each type within each setting shows considerable variability. Types Able, Charlie, Foxtrot, and How show exceptional validity. (d) It is possible that different sorting rules may be required for Black and White inmates, and there is little justification for using the system with females or adolescents due to a paucity of research with these populations; however, early research in this area is promising. (e) While the types have been replicated across many settings, there is less research verifying the correlates associated with each type. (f) The Charlie type is particularly associated with poor adjustment and violent behavior, but this type is not specific to murderers.

MMPI Special Scales (Overcontrolled Hostility Scale)

Early research sought to develop scales derived from the MMPI item pool that might be able to detect meaningful differences between criminal classification groups. Results were mixed. For example, Panton (1958), using the Prison Adjustment Scale (PAS), reported that the PAS was unable to distinguish among six crime classification groups, while Christensen and LeUnes (1974) found that the PAS, along with the Lie and Psychopathic Deviant (4) scales, did differentiate among crime classification groups. Upon the restandardization of the MMPI, these scales lost too many items and are no longer used.

One scale that has been retained, however, is Megargee's OH Scale. This scale was an outgrowth of previous attempts to measure differences on hostility and impulse control between assaultive and nonassaultive criminals (Megargee, 1966; Megargee, Cook, and Mendelsohn, 1967). Megargee and his colleagues reasoned that there may be at least two distinct personality types among assaultive individuals, which were labeled "chronically overcontrolled" and "undercontrolled" aggressive types. The former type is characterized by excessive inhibitions against the expression of aggression in any form. Individuals of this type are extremely frustrated, and because of their anger and hostility, build up over time, until suddenly, they commit an aggressive act of homicidal intensity.

Megargee conducted an item analysis of MMPI test responses of four groups consisting of extremely assaultive, moderately assaultive, nonassaultive, and normal, and found that 31 MMPI items were able to differentiate successfully among these four groups. This scale was cross-validated using independent samples. Surprisingly, the kinds of items that successfully differentiated between overcontrolled and undercontrolled types were passive and nonaggressive in quality (e.g., answered True to the item "I do not mind being made fun of"). The scale correlated positively with MMPI scales L, K, and Hy (3), suggesting rigidity, repression of conflicts, and a self-presentation of positive adjustment; it correlated negatively with Pt (7), Pd (4), Sc (8), and Ma (9) scales, suggesting inhibition of acting out rebelliousness and authority conflicts. Megargee suggested that the OH Scale is measuring impulse control and hostile alienation. Megargee set a raw score of >18 (T 70) on the OH Scale as indicating people who are highly overcontrolled, and a raw score of <11 (T 40) as reflecting undercontrolled hostility. Scores in the midrange could reflect either hostility or control.

A substantial amount of research has been conducted on the OH Scale. Much of this research has studied the scale's construct validity and its ability to distinguish between highly, moderately, and infrequently or nonassaultive inmates. Research has supported the construct validity of the OH Scale (du Toit and Duckitt, 1990; Gudjonsson, Petursson, and Siguardottir, 1991; Quinsey, Maguire, and Varney, 1983; White, 1975; White, McAdoo, and Megargee, 1973). These studies demonstrated that patients with high OH scores, when given other tests, have personality dimensions reflecting greater degrees of control, inhibition of aggression, and social adjustment.

In general, most of the studies have generally validated the OH Scale, with high scores on the scale reflecting rigid control of aggression (Deiker, 1974; Henderson, 1983; Lane and Kling, 1979; Quinsey et al., 1983; Walters, Solomon, and Greene, 1982). Studies that failed to support the Megargee typology have typically administered it apart from the MMPI—removing the 31 items from the MMPI and then giving the scale as a single test (Hoppe and Singer, 1976; Rawlings, 1973).

Only three published studies, which are discussed below, have reported on OH scores with a criterion group of exclusively murderers. Many other studies have used inmate populations in which murderers were included in the assaultive group and that also included nonlethal violent inmates. These studies will not be reviewed because inclusion of nonlethal violent assaulters contaminates the groups for our purposes.

Deiker (1974) studied a sample of 44 homicidal males in Massachusetts. These inmates had an average OH score of 14.5. They would have been rated as "moderately overcontrolled." Quinsey, Arnold, and Pruesse (1980) reported that 25 murderers of family members had a mean score of 13.5 on the OH Scale, while nonfamily murderers had a mean score of 14.0. Once again, these scores were in the moderate range. Finally, Quinsey et al. (1983) found that inmates who were classified as overcontrolled murderers attained a mean score of 18.5 on the OH Scale, while inmates classified as undercontrolled inmates had a mean score of 12.5. Thus, two studies were viewed as not supporting the scale's ability to differentiate violent from nonviolent murderers, while the last study supported the typology of overcontrolled and undercontrolled hostile personalities.

Research has largely supported the validity of the Megargee typology of the overcontrolled and undercontrolled hostility personality types. However, Megargee never asserted that these are the only two types who commit murder and never developed the scale to distinguish murderers from nonviolent inmates. The OH Scale was designed to detect one type of murderer—the overcontrolled type—and the scale seems to function well in this area. There are certainly many other types of murderers and motivations for the murders, such that the OH Scale would not be appropriate for these types. For example, some murderers have been socialized into a deviant subculture with norms that approve and reward aggression and violence in certain circumstances because of their instrumental value to the subgroup (du Toit and Duckitt, 1990). Researchers have sought to extend the OH Scale beyond its original intent and we now know some of its limitations (Hutton, Miner, Blades, and Langfeldt, 1992; White, 1987).

Case Presentation and Analysis Integrating Megargee Typology and OH Scale

Case Illustration

The inmate is a 45-year-old Black male who was admitted to the medical clinic of a correctional facility for treatment of recurrent depression. He had an extensive psychiatric history since his early teens and had 40 psychiatric admissions to public and private psychiatric hospitals. He had a history of self-mutilation and had made five suicide attempts since the age of 18. At age 7, he began swallowing marbles and rocks whenever he became angry at his parents.

In his most recent attempt, he tried to kill himself by swallowing wire and bedsprings. During his incarceration, he swallowed broken glass, wire, and bedsprings to cope with his anger. The precipitant to his most recent attempt was a threat from a correctional officer to transfer him from the psychiatric residential wing to the general population.

His diagnoses at the time of evaluation were major depression, recurrent; opiate and cocaine dependence by history; and antisocial and borderline personality disorders. Psychiatric medications included lithium and Prozac. He had a period of opiate addiction and was treated with methadone maintenance. He was also HIV positive and was taking AZT.

The inmate's mother had died when he was a young child and his father had died of a gunshot wound when the inmate was in his teens. He had never married, but had fathered two children from two different females. Both his current girlfriend and their infant were HIV positive. He contracted the disease from a former girlfriend who later committed suicide.

This inmate had a long history of violence and was convicted of murder and armed robbery on five separate occasions. He was awaiting trial for charges of arson and murder. He became involved with gangs early in life and started selling drugs at age 14. He reported difficulty in controlling his anger since age 8, when he stabbed his grammar school teacher in the back with a pair of scissors. He admitted to having a nasty temper and problems with authority. His temper emerges whenever he believes that someone is trying to control him. During the elementary grades, he was placed in behavior disordered programs. He did not go to high school and supported himself by selling drugs and by pimping. His IQ is in the average range.

Figure 13.2 presents the inmate's MMPI-2 profile. The Megargee classification of this profile is type "Charlie."

The profile suggests exaggeration in which the inmate reported more symptoms than would be established by an objective review. This response is understandable, given his motivation to remain in the psychiatric wing and his desire not to return to the general population. This circumstance nicely illustrates the effects of the context of testing

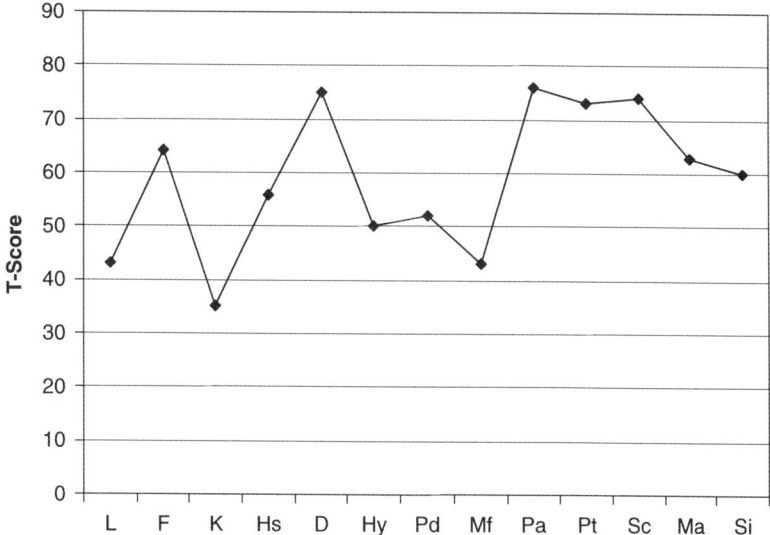

Figure 13.2 MMPI-2 type "Charlie" for a 20-year-old, Black male murderer.

discussed earlier in this chapter. However, by scrutinizing his current situation and with his extensive psychiatric history, we can interpret a "scaled-down" version of this profile.

The profile suggests the presence of delusions, and possible hallucinations (Pa and Sc), hyperactivity (Ma), and antisocial behavior and traits (Pd). His content scales were not systematically elevated, as would be the case in a random response set, but were specifically elevated, consistent with his history. He reported family problems (FAM), ASP, ANG, and BIZ.

Interestingly, both Clinical Scale and Content Scale, suggesting depression, were not significantly elevated. This may reflect a positive treatment response to the antidepressant drug Prozac.

This inmate has problems controlling his anger, is hyperactive, tends to act out, has a low frustration tolerance, is emotionally labile, shows evidence of a thought disorder, is narcissistic, and is prone toward sexual acting out, lying, stealing, aggressive outbursts, and assaultive behaviors. His OH Scale has a T-score of 55 and suggests that he is not an OH type. He has a number of persecutory ideas, lacks control, has problems with authority, and has a defensive structure characterized by projection and acting out. He is at extremely high risk for continued adjustment problems within the correctional facility. If this inmate is to receive psychological treatment, goals need to be directed at anger management. It seems that this person would not be able to function in society at the time of the evaluation and that long-term prognosis is poor. Confinement with humane care seemed to be the appropriate treatment plan for him. While the medication appears to have effectively treated his depression, psychotic symptoms remain. Thus, he might be started on a trial of an appropriate atypical antipsychotic.

Group Differences and Individual Prediction

Until recently, the psychological literature has focused on group differences and has ignored the predictability of the criterion for any individual member of the group. This issue pertains to actuarial versus clinical prediction. Actuarial predictions tend to be accurate for the group, but are unable to successfully predict which member of the group will demonstrate the criterion behavior—in this case, lethal violence. Clinical prediction from psychological tests relies on the test properties of sensitivity and specificity. Test sensitivity is defined as the probability that the person has the trait in question, given a test score that suggests the presence of the trait. Test specificity is the probability that a person does not have the trait if the test score suggests that he or she does not have it.

In order for psychologists to make individual predictions from psychological tests, information must be available on the test's sensitivity and specificity. However, base rates also affect the accuracy of our predictions. By base rates, we mean the rate of occurrence of the criterion in the general population. For example, if the rate of lethal violence in the general population is 1%, then we know that 99% of the people we evaluate, in general, for lethal violence will not become violent. Of course the rate of violence in a forensic population is higher than 1%. Individual prediction is most reliable when the base rate of the predicted behavior is 50%, but it becomes inordinately difficult when the base rate is less than 5%. There is no published information to date on the sensitivity and specificity of any scale in the prediction of lethal violence. Megargee has presented preliminary data on the rate of violence for his MMPI prototype codes, and the Megargee OH has research to support its concurrent but not its predictive validity. This means that we have to rely on clinical prediction rather than on actuarial prediction of lethal violence.

Avoiding Evaluation and Consultation Errors

Objective personality tests have their highest validity when used to determine present symptoms, problems, traits, and disorders. Various degrees of inference are required to postdict psychological states retrospectively.

1. Consider the possible effects of the context of testing on test scores. Also, evaluate whether certain moderator variables have affected test scores.
2. Use both objective and projective psychological tests in the evaluation and integrate test results with other sources of information, such as arrest records and collateral information, to produce a comprehensive report. Never use psychological tests alone to make final recommendations.
3. When selecting an objective psychological test, the MMPI/MMPI-2 has been the most frequently used and most frequently researched personality test with perpetrators of lethal violence and should be the instrument of choice.
4. Maintain an adequate level of knowledge of the professional literature regarding how murderers tend to score on the MMPI and on other instruments used in the evaluation. Also, consider local base rates, on how particular patients tend to score on an instrument, such as the MMPI-2, in your particular setting.
5. Understand and appreciate the limitations of your assessment instruments, as well as the limitations of other sources of data.
6. Render a professional evaluation based on all known sources of information, adhering to data, rather than speculation, hunches, intuition, guesses, and theoretical proclamations.
7. Make affirmative statements (either positive or negative) and do not be afraid to say "I don't know." Others will afford you greater respect.

Treatment Considerations

There is a growing consensus that mental health treatment should be made available to inmates for humane care. Medications for major psychiatric syndromes, which would include anxiolyics, antidepressants, and antipsychotics, can be useful in helping an individual as well as having institutional benefits. Psychosocial interventions, especially substance abuse education and treatment, could help reduce recidivism. These interventions are more likely to be rendered in cases of verdicts including "not guilty by reason of insanity" (NGRI) and in cases where the defendant has been judged incompetent to stand trial. However, it must also be realized that a substantial amount of research suggests that treatment for violent offenders is not necessarily helpful in reducing recidivism. However, it is helpful to promote institutional adjustment (Weiner, 1999).

Writing Forensic Reports and Acting as an Expert Witness

Ackerman (2006) has published some recent suggestions on writing forensic reports.

Forensic evaluations are considered "high stakes" testing. As a consequence of the evaluation, a person may collect damages, gain a desired job, or get remedial help. On the contrary, they may lose benefits, become imprisoned, or lose custody of a child. It is incumbent for us to use the highest standards when conducting forensic evaluations and writing forensic report.

Forensic evaluations are conducted to address a specific referral question and the report must address and answer those questions. While doing so, it is important to keep in mind who is the recipient of the report. A report written to a mental health professional will likely contain more technical jargon and terminology compared to a report written to someone untrained in mental health. When more esoteric psychological terms are included in the report, they should be clearly defined.

The format of the report can be written on a test-by-test basis and then integrated at the end or it can be presented as a holistic report, which generally is shorter and more readable. There should be nothing in the report that cannot be supported by research or by the professional literature (Ackerman, 2006).

Forensic reports are generally briefer than traditional psychological reports. However, psychologists may be cross-examined on not only what is in the report but also what may be left out of the report. This compels the writer of the report to be both brief and comprehensive, and provide information about the essence of the referral issue (with substantiation). Since forensic evaluations are generally not protected by standards of confidentiality, it should be assumed that a variety of people would eventually gain access to this report. Therefore, the content of the report should only contain material relevant to the issue at hand.

American Psychological Association (APA) ethical standards (2002) specify the conditions under which the release of test data is permitted (Section 9.04) and further require the maintenance of test security (Section 9.11). Forensic reports should not include test data or test material as that could be considered a violation of ethics or copyright laws.

Computer-generated narrative interpretive reports should be avoided in forensic cases. It is preferable to have test data computer scored as much as possible because that eliminates scoring errors. However, if a computer narrative report has been used, then it must be so indicated in the forensic report, even though the examiner did not use it in making final determinations. This leaves the expert witness vulnerable to cross-examination about what material was excluded. Also, if the psychologist disagrees with the computer narrative report, you are placed in the position of having to disagree with a nationally recognized expert who wrote the computer report.

Ackerman (2006) recommends the following outline of a forensic report: (a) report heading, which includes basic demographic information and tests administered; (b) reason for referral; (c) background information; (d) interview and collateral contacts; (e) test findings and results; (f) conclusions regarding the "ultimate issue" before the court; and (g) signature with credentials. I prefer to begin the report with a one-paragraph summary indicating the reason for the psychological evaluation and my ultimate findings, and then proceed with a more detailed explanation of my findings.

Final Comments

The knowledge based on the use of the MMPI/MMPI-2, the Megargee classification system, and the OH Scale has not advanced much in the past 10 years. Research seems to be lagging in this area. Similar findings have been reported elsewhere on the use of the MCMI-III (Craig, 2005b). However, the assessment, evaluation, and prediction of lethal violence require the highest degree of professional acumen and are one of society's most important functions. Patients have the right to the most competent assessment with validated measures and reliable and empirically determined predictors. This is our science and this is our mission.

References

Ackerman, M. J. (2006). Forensic report writing. *Journal of Clinical Psychology*, 62, 59–72.
American Psychological Association (2002). *Ethical Principles of Psychologists and Code of Conduct*. Washington, DC: American Psychological Association.
Anderson, W., and Holcolm, W. R. (1983). Accused murderers: Five personality types. *Journal of Clinical Psychology*, 39, 761–768.
Archer, R. P., Buffington-Vollum, J. K., Stredny, R. V., and Handel, R. W. (2006). A survey of psychological test use patterns among forensic psychologists. *Journal of Personality Assessment*, 87, 84–94.
Ben-Porath, Y. S., Graham, J. R., Hall, G. C., Hirschman, R. D., and Zaragoda, M. S. (1995). *Forensic Application of the MMPI-2*. Thousand Oaks, CA: Sage Publications.
Bohn, M. J. (1979). Management classification for young adult inmates. *Federal Probation*, 43, 53–59.
Booth, R. J., and Howell, R. J. (1980). Classification of prison inmates with the MMPI: An extension and validation of the Megargee typology. *Criminal Justice and Behavior*, 7, 407–422.
Buthcer, J. N., Dahlstrom, W. G., Graham, J. R., Tellegen, A., and Kaemmer, B. (1989). *Minnesota Miltiphasic Personality Inventory-2: Manual for Administration and Scoring*. Minneapolis, MN: University of Minnesota Press.
Carey, R. J., Garske, J. P., and Ginsberg, J. (1986). The prediction of adjustment to prison by means of an MMPI-based classification. *Criminal Justice and Behavior*, 13, 347–365.
Cattell, R. B. (1989). *The 16 PF: Personality in Depth*. Champaign, IL: Institute for Personality and Ability Testing.
Christensen, L., and LeUnes, A. (1974). Discriminating criminal types and recidivism by means of the MMPI. *Journal of Clinical Psychology*, 30, 192–193.
Cornell, D. G., Miller, C., and Benedek, E. P. (1988). MMPI profiles of adolescents charged with homicide. *Behavioral Sciences and the Law*, 6, 401–407.

Craig, R. J. (1996). MMPI-based psychological assessment of murderers. In H. V. Hall (Ed.), *Lethal Violence: 2000: Fatal Domestic, Criminal, and Institutional Aggression* (pp. 505–526). Boca Raton, FL: CRC Press.

Craig, R. J. (1999). *Interpreting Personality Tests: A Clinical Manual for the MMPI-2, MCMI-III, CPI-R, and 16 PF*. New York: Wiley.

Craig, R. J. (2005a). *Personality-Guided Forensic Psychology*. Washington, DC: American Psychological Association.

Craig, R. J. (2005b). On the decline of MCMI-based research. In R. J. Craig (Ed.), *New Directions in Interpreting the Millon Clinical Multiaxial Inventory-III* (pp. 284–289). New York: Wiley.

Dahlstrom, W. G., Panton, J. H., Bain, K. P., and Dahlstrom, L. E. (1986). Utility of the Megargee-Bohn MMPI typological assignments: Study with a sample of death row inmates. *Criminal Justice and Behavior*, 13, 5–17.

Deiker, T. E. (1974). A cross-validation of MMPI scales of aggression on male criminal criterion groups. *Journal of Consulting and Clinical Psychology*, 42, 196–202.

DiFrancesca, K. R., and Meloy, J. R. (1989). A comparative investigation of the "How" and "Charlie" MMPI subtypes. *Journal of Personality Assessment*, 53, 396–403.

Doren, D. M., Megargee, E. I., and Schreiber, H. A. (1980). The MMPI criinal classifications applicability to a juvenile population. *The Differential View: A Publication of the International Differential Treatment Association*, 9, 42–47.

du Toit, L., and Duckitt, J. (1990). Psychological characteristics of over-and undercontrolled violent offenders. *Journal of Psychology*, 124, 125–141.

Edinger, J. D. (1979). Cross validation of the Megargee MMPI topology for prisoners. *Journal of Consulting and Clinical Psychology*, 47, 234–242.

Edinger, J. D., and Auerbach, S. M. (1978). Development and validation of a multidimensional multivariate model for accounting for infractionary behavior in a correctional setting. *Journal of Personality and Social Psychology*, 36, 1472–1489.

Edinger, J. D., Reuterfors, D., and Logue, P. (1982). Cross validation of the Megargee MMPI typology. *Criminal Justice and Behavior*, 9, 184–203.

Finney, J. C., Skeeters, D. E., Auvenshine, C. D., and Smith, D. F. (1973). Phases of psychopathology after assassination. *American Journal of Psychiatry*, 130, 1379–1380.

Fraboni, M., Cooper, D., Reed, T. L., and Salstone, R. (1990). Offense type and two-point MMPI code profiles: Discriminating between violent and nonviolent offenders. *Journal of Clinical Psychology*, 46, 774–777.

Friedman, A. F., Lewak, R., Nichols, D. S., and Webb, J. T. (2001). *Psychological Assessment with the MMPI-2*. Mahwah, NJ: Lawrence Earlbaum Associates.

Gough, G. H., and Heilbrun, A.B. (1983). *The Adjective Check List Manual (1983 edition)*. Palo Alto, CA: Consulting Psychologists Press.

Gudjonsson, G. H., Petursson, H., and Sigurdardottir, H. (1991). Overcontrolled hostility among prisoners and its relationship with denial and personality scores. *Personality and Individual Differences*, 12, 17–20.

Hanson, R. W., Moss, C. S., Hosford, R. E., and Johnson, M. E. (1983). Predicting inmate penitentiary adjustment: An assessment of four classificatory methods. *Criminal Justice and Behavior*, 10, 293–309.

Hathaway, S. R., and McKinley, J. C. (1940). *Minnesota Multi-Phasic Personality Inventory*. Minneapolis, MN: University of Minnesota Press.

Heilbrun, K., and Heilbrun, A. B. (1995). Risk assessment with the MMPI-2. In Y. S. Ben-Porath, J. R. Graham, G. C. Hall, R. D. Hirschman, and M. S. Zaragoda (Eds.), *Forensic Application of the MMPI-2* (pp. 160–178). Thousand Oaks, CA: Sage Publications.

Henderson, M. (1983). Self-reported assertion and aggression among violent offenders with high or low levels of over-controlled hostility. *Personality and Individual Differences*, 4, 113–115.

Hess, A. K., and Weiner, I. B. (Eds.). (1999). *The Handbook of Forensic Psychology*. 2nd ed. New York: Wiley.

Holcolm, W. R., and Adams, N. A. (1982). Racial influences on intelligence and personality of people who commit murder. *Journal of Clinical Psychology*, 38, 793–796.

Holcolm, W. R., and Adams, N. A. (1983). The inner-domain among personality and cognition variables in people who commit murder. *Journal of Personality Assessment*, 47, 524–530.

Holcolm, W. R., and Adams, N. A. (1985). Personality mechanisms of alcohol-related violence. *Journal of Clinical Psychology*, 41, 714–722.

Holcolm, W. R., Adams, N. A., Nicholas, A., Ponder, H. M., and Anderson, W. (1984). Cognitive and behavioral predictors of MMPI scores in pretrial psychological evaluations of murderers. *Journal of Clinical Psychology*, 40, 592–597.

Holcolm, W. R., Adams, N. A., Nicholas, A., and Ponder, H. M. (1985). The development and cross-validation of an MMPI typology of murderers. *Journal of Personality Assessment*, 49, 240–244.

Holcolm, W. R., Adams, N. A., and Ponder, H. M. (1984). Are separate black and white norms needed? An IQ-controlled comparison of accused murderers. *Journal of Clinical Psychology*, 40, 189–193.

Hoppe, C. M., and Singer, R. D. (1976). Overcontrolled hostility, empathy, and egocentric balance in violent and non-violent psychiatric offenders. *Psychological Reports*, 39, 1301–1308.

Hutton, H. E., Miner, M. H., Blades, J. R., and Langfeldt, V. C. (1992). Ethnic differences on the MMPI overcontrolled-hostility scale. *Journal of Personality Assessment*, 58, 260–268.

Hutton, H. E., Miner, M. H., and Langfeldt, C. C. (1993). The utility of the Megargee-Bohn typology in a forensic psychiatric hospital. *Journal of Personality Assessment*, 60, 572–587.

Johnson, D. A., Simmons, J. D., and Gordon, D. C. (1983). Temporal consistency of the Meyer-Megargee inmate typology. *Criminal Justice and Behavior*, 10, 263–268.

Kalichman, S. C. (1988a). MMPI profiles of women and men convicted of domestic homicide. *Journal of Clinical Psychology*, 44, 847–853.

Kalichman, S. C. (1988b). Empirically derived MMPI profile subgroups of incarcerated homicide offenders. *Journal of Clinical Psychology*, 44, 733–738.

Kennedy, T. D. (1986). Trends in inmate classification: A status report on two computerized psychometric approaches. *Criminal Justice and Behavior*, 13, 165–184.

Lally, S. J. (2003). What tests are acceptable for use in forensic evaluations? A survey of experts. *Professional Psychology: Research and Practice*, 34, 491–498.

Lane, P. J., and Kling, J. S. (1979). Construct validation of the overcontrolled hostility scale of the MMPI. *Journal of Consulting and Clinical Psychology*, 47, 781–782.

Langevin, R., Paitich, D., Orchard, B., Handy, L., and Russon, A. (1982). Diagnosis of killers seen for psychiatric assessment: A controlled study. *Acta Psychiatrica Scandinavica*, 66, 216–228.

Litwack, T. R., and Schlesinger, L. B. (1999). Dangerous risk assessment: Research, legal, and clinical considerations. In A. K. Hess and I. B. Weiner (Eds.), *The Handbook of Forensic Psychology* (2nd ed., pp. 171–217). New York: Wiley.

Louscher, P. K., Hosford, R. E., and Moss, C. S. (1983). Predicting dangerous behavior in a penitentiary using the Megargee typology. *Criminal Justice and Behavior*, 10, 269–184.

McDonald, A., and Paitich, D. (1981). A study of homicide: The validity of predictive test factors. *Canadian Journal of Psychiatry*, 26, 549–554.

McKee, G. R., Shea, S. J., Mogy, B., and Holden, C. E. (2001). MMPI-2 profiles of filicidal, matricidal, and homicidal women. *Journal of Clinical Psychology*, 57, 367–374.

Megargee, E. I. (1966). Undercontrolled and over-controlled personality types in extreme antisocial aggression. *Psychological Monographs*, 80 (Whole No. 611).

Megargee, E. I. (1977). A new classification system for criminal offenders. I: The need for a new classification system. *Criminal Justice and Behavior*, 4, 107–114.

Megargee, E. I. (1984a). Derivation, validation and application of an MMPI-based system for classifying criminal offenders. *Medicine and Law*, 3, 109–118.

Megargee, E. I. (1984b). A new classification system for criminal offenders: VI. Differences among the types on the Adjective Checklist. *Criminal Justice and Behavior*, 11, 349–376.

Megargee, E. I. (1986). A psychometric study of incarcerated presidential threateners. *Criminal Justice and Behavior*, 13, 243–260.

Megargee, E. I. (1993). Using the MMPI-2 with criminal offenders: A progress report. *MMPI-2 & MMPI-A News & Profiles*, 4, 2–3.

Megargee, E. I. (1994). Using the Megargee MMPI-based classification system with MMPI-2s of male prison inmates. *Psychological Assessment*, 6, 337–344.

Megargee, E. I. (1997). Using the Megargee MMPI-based classification system with the MMPI-2s of female prison inmates. *Psychological Assessment*, 9, 75–82.

Megargee, E. I., and Bohn, M. J., Jr. (1977). A new classification system for criminal offenders, IV: Empirically determined characteristics of the ten types. *Criminal Justice and Behavior*, 4, 149–210.

Megargee, E. I., Cook, P. E., and Mendelsohn, G. A. (1967). Development and validation of an MMPI scale of assaultiveness in overcontrolled individuals. *Journal of Abnormal Psychology*, 72, 519–528.

Megargee, E. I., and Dorhout, B. (1977a). A new classification system for criminal offenders, III: Revision and refinement of the classification rules. *Criminal Justice and Behavior*, 4, 125–148.

Megargee, E. I., and Dorhout, B. (1977b). A new classification system for criminal offenders, II: Initial development of the system. *Criminal Justice and Behavior*, 4, 115–124.

Megargee, E. I., Mercer, S. J., and Carbonell, J. L. (1999). MMPI-2 with male and female state and federal prison inmates. *Psychological Assessment*, 11, 177–185.

Meyer, J., Jr., and Megargee, E. I. (1977). A new classification system for criminal offenders. II: Initial development of the system. *Criminal Justice and Behavior*, 4, 115–124.

Millon, T. (1994). *Millon Clinical Multiphasic Personality Inventory-III*. Minneapolis, MN: Pearson Assessments.

Motiuk, L. L., Bonta, J., and Andrews, D. A. (1986). Classification in correctional half-way houses: The relative and incremental predictive criterion validities of the Megargee-MMPI and LSI systems. *Criminal Justice and Behavior*, 13, 33–46.

Mrad, D. F., Kabacoff, R. A., and Cuckro, P. (1983). Validation of the Megargee typology in a half-way house setting. *Criminal Justice and Behavior*, 10, 252–262.

Ogloff, J. R. (1995). The legal bases of forensic application of the MMPI-2. In Y. S. Ben-Porath, J. R. Graham, G. C. Hall, R. D. Hirschman, and M. S. Zaragoda (Eds.), *Forensic Application of the MMPI-2* (pp. 18–47). Thousand Oaks, CA: Sage Publications.

Panton, J. H. (1958). MMPI profile configurations among crime classification groups. *Journal of Clinical Psychology*, 14, 308–312.

Panton, J. H. (1976). Personality characteristics of death-row inmates. *Journal of Clinical Psychology*, 32, 306–309.

Parwatikar, S. D., Holcolm, W. R., and Menninger, K. A. (1985). The detection of malingered amnesia in accused murderers. *Bulletin of the American Academy of Psychiatry and the Law*, 13, 97–103.

Pena, L., and Megargee, E. I. (1997). *Application of the Megargee typology for criminal offenders to adolescents with the MMPI-A*. Paper presented at the 32nd Annual Symposium on Recent Developments in the Use of the MMPI-2 and MMPI-A. Minneapolis, MN: June 8, 1997.

Pope, K. S., Butler, J. N., and Seelen, J. (1993). *The MMPI, MMPI-2, & MMPI-A in Court*. Washington, DC: American Psychological Association.

Quinsey, V. L., Arnold, L. S., and Pruesse, M. G. (1980). MMPI profiles of men referred for a pretrial psychiatric assessment as a function of offense type. *Journal of Clinical Psychology*, 36, 410–417.

Quinsey, V. L., Maguire, A., and Varney, G. W. (1983). Assertion and overcontrolled hostility among mentally disordered murderers. *Journal of Consulting and Clinical Psychology*, 51, 550–556.

Rawlins, M. D. (1973). Self-control and interpersonal violence. *Criminology*, 11, 23–48.

Rogers, R., and Seman, W. (1983). Murder and criminal responsibility: An examination of MMPI profiles. *Behavioral Sciences and the Law*, 1, 89–95.

416   Forensic Psychology and Neuropsychology for Criminal and Civil Cases

Schaffer, C. E., Pettigrew, C. G., Blouin, D., and Edwards, D. W. (1983). Multivariate classification of female offender MMPI profiles. *Journal of Crime and Justice*, 6, 57–66.

Shea, S. J., and McKee, G. R. (1996). MMPI-2 profiles of men charged with murder or other offenses. *Psychological Reports*, 78, 1039–1042.

Simmons, J. G., Johnson, J. L., Gouvier, W. R., and Muzyczka, M. J. (1981). They Meyer-Megargee inmate typology: Dynamic or unstable? *Criminal Justice and Behavior*, 15, 49–55.

Stredny, R. V., Archer, R. P., and Mason, J. A. (2006). MMPI-2 and MCMI-III characteristics of parental competency examinees. *Journal of Personality Assessment*, 87, 113–115.

Sutker, P., and Moan, C. E. (1973). A psychosocial description of penitentiary inmates. *Archives of General Psychiatry*, 29, 663–667.

Van Voorhis, P. (1988). A cross classification of five offender typologies: Issues of construct and predictive validity. *Criminal Justice and Behavior*, 15, 109–124.

Veneziano, C. A., and Veneziano, L. (1986). Classification of adolescent offenders with the MMPI: An extension and cross-validation of the Megargee typology. *International Journal of Offender Therapy and Comparative Criminology*, 30, 11–23.

Walters, G. D. (1986). Correlates of the Megargee criminal classification system: A military correctional setting. *Criminal Justice and Behavior*, 13, 19–32.

Walters, G. D., Mann, M. F., Miller, M. P., Hemphill, L., and Chlumsky, M. L. (1988). Emotional disorder among offenders: Inter- and intrasetting comparisons. *Criminal Justice and Behavior*, 15, 433–453.

Walters, G. D., Scrapansky, T. A., and Marlow, G. A. (1986). The emotionally disturbed military offender: Identification, background and institutional adjustment. *Criminal Justice and Behavior*, 13, 261–285.

Walters, G. D., Solomon, G. S., and Greene, R. J. (1982). The relationship between the overcontrolled hostility scale and the MMPI 4-3 high point pair. *Journal of Clinical Psychology*, 38, 613–615.

Weiner, I. B. (1999). Writing forensic reports. In A. K. Hess, and I. B. Weiner (Eds.), *The Handbook of Forensic Psychology* (2nd ed., pp. 501–520). New York: Wiley.

Westermeyer, J. (1974). Caveats on diagnosing assassins. *American Journal of Psychiatry*, 131, 722–723.

White, A. (1987). The overcontrolled-undercontrolled typology and the overcontrolled-hostility scale of the MMPI: A review of the literature. Unpublished paper. Florida State University.

White, W. C. (1975). Validity of the Overcontrolled-Hostility scale: A brief report. *Journal of Personality Assessment*, 39, 587–590.

White, W. C., McAdoom, W. G., and Megargee, E. I. (1973). Personality factors associated with over-and undercontrolled offenders. *Journal of Personality Assessment*, 37, 473–478.

Wright, K. N. (1988). The relationship of risk, needs, and personality classification systems and prison adjustment. *Criminal Justice and Behavior*, 15, 454–471.

Wrobel, T. A., Calovini, P. K., and Martin, T. O. (1991). Application of the Megargee MMPI typology to a population of defendants referred for psychiatric evaluation. *Criminal Justice and Behavior*, 18, 397–405.

Wrobel, N. H., Wribel, T. A., and McIntosh, J. W. (1988). Application of the Megargee typology to a forensic psychiatric population. *Criminal Justice and Behavior*, 15, 247–254.

Zager, L. D. (1988). The MMPI-based criminal classification system: A review, current status, and future directions. *Criminal Justice and Behavior*, 15, 39–57.

Legal Reference

Daubert v. Merrell Dow Pharmaceuticals, 2786 L.Ed. 2nd (U.S. 113 S. Ct. 1993).

The Juvenile Sex Offender

JOSEPH G. POIRIER

Independent Practice, Rockville, Maryland

14

Contents

Synopsis of Case

A juvenile court found 17-year-old Peggy involved* in a matter of child sexual abuse. Peggy was Caucasian, and repeating her junior year of high school. Peggy resided with her family in an upper-middle-class, suburban residential area. The victim was an 11-year-old Hispanic girl named Maria who lived in a low-income housing area with her maternal grandmother and two younger cousins who were in the grandmother's care. The neighbor-hoods where the two girls lived were adjoining. Peggy befriended Maria and the two girls spent more and more time together usually at Peggy's home when no one else was at home. Occasionally, Maria's grandmother would give Peggy a few dollars for babysitting Maria. Following a school presentation conducted by police officers about child abuse, Maria con-fided in a school counselor about inappropriate sexual activity with Peggy. The counselor notified Child Protective Service and there was an investigation. Because of her status in the babysitting/caretaking role, Peggy was charged with child sexual abuse. The alleged abuse had begun with Peggy and Maria playing house and role-playing husband and wife. The role-playing eventually led to disrobing, then digital, oral, and genital contact. Accord-ing to Maria's account, Peggy had orchestrated the inappropriate fondling activity all the while insisting to Maria that nothing was wrong. The juvenile court ordered an evaluation of Peggy to address risk of reoffending and to generate dispositional recommendations.

---

* A finding of "involved" in a Maryland Juvenile Court is the juvenile court equivalent of a finding of "guilty" in the adult court.

Introduction

This chapter focuses on the problem of juveniles who perpetrate sexual offenses. The effort to address the problem of sexual offenses by juveniles continues as a vexing and costly problem in contemporary society (Andrade, Vincent, and Saleh, 2006; Barbaree, Blanchard, and Langton, 2003; Barbaree and Marshall, 2006; Broxholme and Lindsay, 2003; Gerardin and Thibaut, 2004; Murphy, DiLillo, Haynes, and Steere, 2001; Poirier, 1999b, 2005; Ryan, 1997a; Seager, Jellicoe, and Dhaliwal, 2004). Ongoing research has made it increasingly clear that the problem is complex and will require a multimodal effort that in most cases will be long term (i.e., approximately 36 months) and costly. For comprehensive bibliographies relating to the problem of juvenile sex offending see Craig, Smith, Hayler, and Pardie (1999) and Smith, Craig, Loose, Brodus, and Kimmelman (2002).

The problem of juvenile sex offending is *severe* as reflected in the number of victims; these data are presented below. The *extent* of the problem is reflected in the totality of trauma imposed by victimizations (Hunter, 2000; Barbaree and Marshall, 2006). The actual number of juvenile sex offenders (JSOs) is unknown because so many crimes go unreported; the data for reported cases are described below.

The term "juvenile sex offender" is a legal concept and not an inherently clinical notion. The history of the clinical body of knowledge regarding sexual paraphilias is fraught with definitional issues, cultural taboos, and legal precedents. The last 20 years has brought increased legal scrutiny of both adult sexual offenders and JSOs. The judicial system has also imposed progressively harsher legal sanctions and penalties for offenders (Letourneau and Miner, 2005). The history of the legal/mental health interface regarding sexual predator legislation is lengthy and complex (for a review, see American Psychiatric Association, 1999).

Sexual abuse of children by any age perpetrator transects with nearly universal, moral, and social taboos. These taboos impose a pervasive impact on how child sexual abuse is approached by both the judicial and the mental health systems (Poirier, 1999c). Through the early 1990s, the criminal justice/mental health interface made scattered strides in addressing the JSO population. Societal demand and expectations for meaningful treatment interventions, however, far outpaced the advances that research was able to produce (Davis and Leitenberg, 1987).

A recent and important meta-analysis study by Hanson and Morton-Bourgon (2005) summarized findings regarding predictors of adult sexual offender recidivism. The meta-analysis findings (described see Risk Assessment section in this chapter) reflected a number of significant advances in our understanding of treatment-relevant risk factors. The findings also identified a number of treatment considerations, historically considered essential in working with sex offender treatment, but not found to be particularly effective in the meta-analysis. Finally, the study addressed the all-important question of whether predictors of sexual recidivism differ from those of nonsexual crime recidivism.

Data from law enforcement agencies and correctional facilities collected by the FBI and maintained by the Bureau of Justice provide the most comprehensive and up-to-date information regarding crime, but these data are not exhaustive or nationally representative because of high failure to report rates and also differences across jurisdictional crime definitions and differences in reporting methodology.

Among other sources, the Bureau of Justice utilizes data from the Uniform Crime Reporting Program (UCR) to generate crime statistics. Historically, the UCR only reported forcible rape and sexual assault incidents (FBI, 1997, 2005). The UCR has now incorporated the National Incident-Based Reporting System (NIBRS), which has the potential to yield detailed descriptions of sexual assaults reported by participating law enforcement agencies (Snyder, 2000).

There is some overlap of demographic, etiological, and classification data between adult and juvenile sexual offenders, but there are also important distinctions (Caldwell, 2002; Pithers, Becker, Kafka, Morenz, Schlank, and Leombruno, 1995). A high percentage of victims of rape and sexual assault crimes are children and adolescents. Table 14.1 presents highlights of recent Bureau of Justice demographics regarding sex offenses by adult and juvenile offenders (Greenfield, 1997). The most recent law enforcement data regarding sexual assault of young children and offender characteristics were compiled by the Bureau of Justice for the years 1991–1996 (Snyder, 2000). These data were compiled from the NIBRS. There were two databases in the study: the first included approximately 61,000 victims, and the second consisted of approximately 58,000 offenders. The data are based on reports of sexual assault of young children to law enforcement resources as provided by 12 states from 1991 through 1996. These data provided a wealth of data regarding victim and offense characteristics that will be useful to the interested reader, but we will focus here primarily on the data regarding offenders.

Table 14.2 highlights the data that are specific to the juvenile sexual offender.

Table 14.3 presents sample probability statements about victim/offender profile data on the basis of NIBRS statistical data. These are the types of data that researchers utilize to develop risk factors associated with likelihood of reoffending.

The Honorable Judge Luis Perez is a judge at the Worcester Juvenile Court in Worcester, Massachusetts. Judge Perez recently pointed out that the courts alone would not be

Table 14.1   Highlights of Recent Bureau of Justice Demographics Regarding Sex Offenses and Sex Offenders[a]

- A high percentage of victims in all rape and sexual assault crimes were children.
- 67% of all sexual assault victims reported to law enforcement were children and adolescents.
- Juvenile offenders perpetrated 23.2% of these cases (3.6% aged 7–11; and 19.5% aged 12–17).
- Self-reports of convicted rape and sexual assault offenders serving time in state prisons indicated that two-thirds had victims under the age of 18.
- 44% of rape victims were under age 18.
- 58% of imprisoned violent sex offenders cited their victims were age 12 and younger.
- The majority of violent sex offending involves males assaulting female victims.
- Females account for a small percentage of violent sex offenders.
- Victims and offenders are of the same sex in only a small fraction of violent sex offenses.
- Victims reported that in three out of four rape and sexual assault incidents, the offender was not a stranger.
- In 90% of rape incidents involving child victims under the age of 12, the child knew the offender.
- JSOs account for 10% of sexual assault murders since 1976.
- Of 485,290 rape and sexual assault crimes in 1993, 10.9% were committed by juvenile offenders.
- One in eight rapists were under age 18. In nine out of ten rapes in which the offender was under 18 so was the victim.
- Of approximately 33,800 rape offenders in state prison, 0.6% were juveniles and of 54,300 sexual assault offenders 1.1% were juveniles.
- Arrests were made more often with juvenile victims (29%) compared to adult victims (20%).

[a] These data include adult and juvenile offenders. See Table 14.2 for data of JSO only.

Source: Adapted from Greenfield, L.A. in *Sex Offenses and Offenders: An Analysis of Data on Rape and Sexual Assault* (NCJ-163392), Bureau of Justice Statistics, Washington, DC, 1997; Snyder, H.N. in *Sexual Assault of Young Children as Reported to Law Enforcement: Victim, Incident, and Offender Characteristics* (NCJ 182990), Bureau of Justice, Washington, DC, 2000.

Table 14.2   Highlights of Recent Bureau of Justice Demographics Regarding Juvenile Sex Offenders

- Younger victims were the least likely to have strangers as perpetrators.
- Female victims younger than age 12 were more likely to have a family member as the perpetrator (47%) compared to same age male victims (40%).
- 23% of all sexual assault offenders were under age 18.
- JSOs were responsible for 17% of rape crimes, 23% of sexual assaults with an object, and 27% of forcible sodomies.
- JSOs relationships to juvenile victims were 34.2% family members, 58.7% acquaintances, and 7.0% strangers.
- 16% of juvenile offenders were under age 12. These very young offenders were seldom involved in forcible rape (7% of all juvenile offenders), but made up the greater proportion of juvenile offenders in forcible fondling (19%), sexual assault with an object (17%), and forcible sodomies (23%).
- Younger juvenile victims (40%) tended to have a greater proportion of juvenile offenders than did older juvenile victims (27%).
- Arrests occurred in only 27% of the reported cases.
- In 7% of the cases, victims refused to cooperate as witnesses, and another 6% of the cases were declined by prosecutors typically because of insufficient evidence.

Source: Adapted from Greenfield, L.A. in *Sex Offenses and Offenders: An Analysis of Data on Rape and Sexual Assault* (NCJ-163392), Bureau of Justice Statistics, Washington, DC, 1997; Snyder, H.N. in *Sexual Assault of Young Children as Reported to Law Enforcement: Victim, Incident, and Offender Characteristics* (NCJ 182990), Bureau of Justice, Washington, DC, 2000.

Table 14.3   Juvenile Sex Offender Victim/Offender Risk Factor Data from NIBRS Statistical Data[a]

- If a victim under 6 is assaulted in a residence then most likely offender was a juvenile acquaintance age 12 through 17 (probability 15.2%), or a family member age 25 through 34 (probability 15.0%).
- When a very young victim (6 and younger) was assaulted other than in a residence, the probability that the offender was an adult family member declines, while the probability that the offender was a juvenile acquaintance increases substantially.
- With somewhat older victims (ages 6 through 11) and assaults in some place other than a residence, the likelihood that the offender was a juvenile acquaintance increases even more (probability 41.0%).
- The single age with the greatest number of JSOs was 14 years.

[a]   The Uniform Crime Reporting System (UCR) now incorporates a National Incident-Based Reporting System (NIBRS), which unlike earlier reporting systems captures a wide range of information on each incident of sexual assault reported to law enforcement.

Source: Offender probability statements adapted from Snyder, H.N. in *Sexual Assault of Young Children as Reported to Law Enforcement: Victim, Incident, and Offender Characteristics* (NCJ 182990), Bureau of Justice, Washington, DC, 2000.

able to solve pressing social problems like juvenile crime. Judge Perez made the following sobering comments:

> Since 1984, there has been a 68 percent increase in juvenile court filings nationwide. Since 1987, juveniles detained and committed to state institutions have risen from approximately 90,000 to 400,000 in 2002. The system is plagued by overcrowding, and understaffing in courtrooms, treatment programs, and detention facilities. Failure to invest in children now—and at the earliest point of intervention possible—may entail high costs later in increased crime and social decay. It costs each state approximately $6000 per year to educate a child. Yet it costs a state over $30,000 per year to detain a child in a residential facility (including prison). It appears cost-effective to invest in early intervention to prevent children from reaching the point where the state must detain them away from their families. (Perez, 2003, p. 5)

The attainment of an integrated etiological model of juvenile sex offending continues to be an elusive quest (Bischof and Rosen, 1997; Marshall, 1996; Marshall, 2000; Marshall and Marshall, 2000; Quinsey and Harris, 1998; Ryan, 1997b). On the basis of extensive work with sexual offenders, Marshall and his colleagues hypothesized that prospective offenders have poor quality relationships with parenting figures during childhood (Barbaree, Marshall, and McCormick, 1998; Marshall, 2000). The authors postulate that histories of poor parenting increase the risk of sexual victimization for children. These child victims are then at risk of becoming potential offenders.

During adolescence, this background of dynamics combines with usual sexual fantasies associated with passage into puberty. Marshall has observed that the JSO sexual histories are characterized by high rates of masturbation as a preferred means of coping with stress. Heightened masturbatory practice increases the likelihood that sexual fantasies will gradually incorporate elements of power and control. Poor self-esteem is a related risk factor in JSO histories. These dynamics serve as the triggering backdrop for deviant sex arousal patterns for the JSOs (Hunter and Becker, 1994; Kaermingk, Morales, Becker, and Kaplan, 1995).

According to Marshall's etiological model, over time, the offender's fantasies become progressively deviant. When the offender's sense of values and acquired social constraints are inhibited for some reason (e.g., peer pressure, substance abuse, gang activity, availability of opportune child victim, etc.), the likelihood of sexual offense becomes more urgent. Early developmental exposure to abusive family circumstances by potential offenders induces a syndrome of "social disability" (Barbaree et al., 1998). The authors described that comorbid risk factors for JSOs include lack of healthy adult attachments, low self-esteem, and participation in varying degrees of antisocial behavior. Because of impaired ability to experience empathy, the prospective JSO has difficulty in initiating, and then nurturing, intimate and mature relationships (Curwen, 2003; Garlick, Marshall, and Thornton, 1996).

Pertinent Legal Cases

Case law regarding juvenile offenders in general is diverse and portrays the struggles of the judiciary attempting to balance different interests, for example, the rights of children and parents with the provisions of the Constitution. The courts have recognized that different strategies are necessary to address the problem of juvenile sex offending. That is, the problem of juvenile sex offending goes well beyond specific instances of a sex offense perpetrated by a juvenile. The problem extends from parental values to societal attitudes. One example of the social influences bearing juvenile sexual behavior is laws regarding pornography that utilize child actors or child portrayals.

Case law often follows and reflects the evolution of sociological thinking, as well as the changes in cultural mores. In some instances, case law contributes to the definition of the evolutionary process. A case in point is the well-known, and still controversial, 1973 Supreme Court *Roe v. Wade* decision regarding abortion. As the public has increasingly become concerned about the JSO, the courts have progressively become more involved in addressing the problem. Table 14.4 summarizes landmark court decisions regarding juvenile offenders in general; we have included these data because they serve as a historical backdrop to the data in Table 14.5, which summarizes case law specifically regarding JSO issues.

Applied Ethics and Moral Consideration

Clinical work with children and adolescents imposes ethical considerations that are unique to the age group. In turn, there are special clinical, ethical, and legal complexities for clinicians working with the subpopulation of JSOs (Hunter and Lexier, 1998). As a preliminary point, we note that, as with all areas of the mental health/legal interface, it behooves practitioners to be familiar with statutory requirements in their local jurisdiction. Statutory requirements regarding juvenile offenders can have considerable variation from one jurisdiction to another. Ignorance of the specific statutory requirements in a given jurisdiction is a first step to incurring malpractice and ethical complaints.

A fundamental ethical requirement of all clinical works is the expectation that the clinician will function within the limits of his or her competence. Given the still germinal nature of clinical efforts with the JSO population, the issue of clinician competence is of compelling importance. Continuing education offerings regarding JSOs, formal training programs, or opportunities for structured supervision with the JSO population are still

Table 14.4   Summary of Case Law Decisions Relevant to Regarding Juvenile Offenders in General

Case Citation	Case Synopsis
Kent v. United States, 1966	The Supreme Court wrote, "There is much evidence that some juvenile courts lack the personnel, facilities, and techniques to perform adequately as representatives of the state in parens patriae capacity, at least with respect to children charged with law violations."
In re Gerald Gault, 1967	Supreme Court determined that juvenile hearings must measure up to the essentials of due process. This includes questioning juveniles in a safe place after notifying parents. Juveniles have the same rights as adults except trial by jury.
In re Winship, 1970	Determination of criminal action in juvenile cases "must be based on a preponderance of the evidence." The standard in adult criminal actions is that the prosecution must prove "beyond a reasonable doubt."
Juvenile Justice and Delinquency Prevention Act of 1974	Congress has clear preference for release of delinquents as opposed to detention (§ 504).
Mullaney v. Wilbur, 1975	Extended the protection of Winship to determinations that went not to a juvenile defendant's guilt or innocence, but simply to the length of sentence.
Parham v. J. R., 1979	Regarding voluntary admission of children to state mental hospitals, there is a presumption that fit parents act in their children's best interests.
New Jersey v. T. L. O., 1985	T. L. O. was a 14-year-old girl discovered smoking in school bathroom. A search of her purse yielded marijuana and paraphernalia. Supreme Court found no violation of 4th and 14th amendment rights. There was a reasonable suspicion by the school principal of criminal activity.

Table 14.5   Case Law Decisions Regarding Juvenile Sex Offenders and Related Issues

Case Citation	Synopsis of Case Impact
Ashcroft v. Free Speech Coalition, 2002	The Free Speech Coalition, an adult-entertainment trade association, petitioned that the CPPA (see the entry below) abridged freedom of speech that is neither obscene under Miller v. California (see below), nor child pornography under New York v. Ferber (see below), Supreme Court concurred that the two prohibitions above were overbroad and unconstitutional.

Table 14.5 (*continued*)

Case Citation	Synopsis of Case Impact
Child Pornography Prevention Act of 1996 (CPPA)	The Act expanded federal prohibitions on child pornography. The Law banned a range of techniques, including computer-generated images and use of youthful-looking adults who were designed to convey the impression of minors engaging in sexually explicit conduct.
Children's Safety Act, 2005	Federal measure currently pending before Congress. The bill seeks to improve the current sex offender registration program by increasing penalties for failure to comply with registration requirements. It also expands types of offenders to include juveniles who victimize children and increases the minimum and maximum sentences on specified sexual offenses against children and authorizes civil commitment at the federal level.
Globe Newspaper Co. v. Superior Court, 1982	Massachusetts statute excluding members of the press and public from certain cases involving sexual offenses and testimony of victims less than 18 years old violated the first amendment. Protecting the psychological well-being of a child does not justify a mandatory closure rule. That is closure of hearings permitted to protect juvenile defendants, but not juvenile victims.
Jacob Wetterling Crimes Against Children and Sexually Violent Offender Act, 1994	Requires state implementation of a sex-offender registration program, or a 10% forfeiture of federal funds for state and local law enforcement under the Byrne Grant Program of the U.S. Department of Justice.
Kansas v. Hendricks, 1997	Supreme Court upheld Kansas version of sexual violent predator law whereby adult offenders deemed likely to recidivate can be civilly committed at expiration of any prison term. Not yet adopted by all states, and it is unclear whether Hendricks will have any impact on JSOs.
Lawrence v. Texas, 2003	U.S. Supreme Court holds that punishment of unlawful voluntary sexual conduct between members of the same sex cannot constitutionally carry greater penalty than unlawful voluntary sex between members of the opposite sex.
Miller v. California, 1973	Court held that obscene materials did not enjoy first amendment protection. The basic guidelines for the trier of fact must be (a) whether the "average person, applying contemporary standards" would find that work, taken as a whole, appeals to prurient interest; (b) whether the work depicts or describes, in a patently offensive way, sexual conduct specifically defined by the applicable state law; and (c) whether the work, taken as a whole, lacks serious literary, artistic, political, or scientific value.
New York v. Ferber, 1982	A New York child pornography law prohibited persons from knowingly promoting sexual performances by children under the age of 16 by distributing material that depicts such performances. Supreme Court ruled 1st and 14th amendments not violated. The statute intent was to target against child pornography.
People v. Michael Jackson, 2004	The Act expanded prohibitions in California, evidence of prior acts of abuse against a minor may be admitted at a trial where there are current charges of sexual abuse against a minor (Cal. Evid. Code §1108; West, 2001). Critics have charged that these laws will result in juries convicting based on past behavior alone. The Jackson case outcome suggests that juries can follow the law and be fair.
State v. Limon, 2004	Extended the application of *Lawrence v. Texas* to juveniles.

limited. Accordingly, the burden is on the individual clinician to demonstrate appropriate training and experience as the basis for claimed competence in working with JSOs.

Clinical work with children and adolescents also imposes layers of boundary concerns beyond what is conventional in work with adults. Most children and adolescents are involved with a multitude of caretakers and providers (parents and other family members, educators, pediatricians, etc.). To be effective, the assessing/treating clinician must be prepared to interface effectively with all of these collaterally involved figures. When we add the additional dimension of sexual offending, the case management challenges become exponentially more involved (police, child protective services, juvenile court, attorneys, juvenile justice, probation officers, collaterally involved clinicians, etc.). The ethical concerns and constraints of clinicians working with the JSO population are considerable. This is particularly true when JSOs are involved in litigation. Clinicians must be mindful of cultural and ethnic issues when working with children and families (American Psychological Association, 2003; Hansen, Randazzo, Schwartz, Marshall, Kalis, Frazier, Burke, Kershner-Rice, and Norvirg, 2006; Smith, Constantine, Dunn, Dinehart, and Montoya, 2006). These issues can have a bearing on how a JSO or family members view what is appropriate and what is inappropriate in terms of juvenile sexual behavior. From the legal perspective, however, it is the established statutory requirements that define what is lawful and what is unlawful.

One glaring gap in the support matrix for JSOs is the universal lack of community-based support systems. For virtually every other problem area encountered by children and adolescents, there are community-based services to address the problem. In contrast, for JSOs most communities are content to provide limited funding for treatment programs as a means of "keeping our children safe."

A common ethical quandary in working with children and perhaps more importantly with adolescents revolves around issues such as confidentiality (i.e., ethical) and privilege (i.e., legal). Especially in working with older adolescents, there is always the problem of establishing and maintaining the therapeutic alliance with the adolescent while at the same time respecting the rights of the parents/guardians/family members to have access to information regarding their sons and daughters. This can be especially complicated in a case where there is already poor parent to child/adolescent communication. The topics of sexuality, child victimization, and sexual offending render parent to child/adolescent communication still more delicate and sensitive. Clinicians must be careful about not imparting knowledge about sexuality or values about sexuality to JSOs that will only exacerbate existing problems. Related to this is the consideration that parents have the primary responsibility to teach their children about sexuality, and clinicians must tread carefully with respecting this parental responsibility.

In every collaboration effort, clinicians must be cautious about what information regarding juvenile sexual offenders is appropriate for disclosure, to whom, and for what purpose. Practitioners must also make a special effort to ensure that offenders and responsible guardians have unambiguous "informed consent" regarding any dissemination of clinical information, and this consent should be in writing utilizing acceptable written forms.

Statutory provisions regarding juvenile sexual offenses and the rights of victims and perpetrators continue in an evolving status. Sensitive areas of legal/ethical issues, peculiar to the juvenile sexual offender population, include legal mandates for the reporting of suspected abuse and neglect. Other still emerging issues of concern for working with the JSO population include the following:

a. Requirements for community registration of adjudicated sexual offenders including JSOs (Zevitz and Farkas, 2000a, 2000b, 2000c)
b. Procedures for preadjudication evaluations and for involuntary treatment (Roberts, Doren, and Thornton 2002)
c. Procedures for use of cognitive-behavioral techniques
d. Procedures for the use of psychopharmacological interventions (Galli, Raute, McConville, and McElroy, 1998; Hunter and Lexier, 1998)
e. Procedural guidelines for the use of phallometric and polygraph techniques

A controversial area of research and practice with JSOs is the use of psychoactive substances to reduce or control JSO risk. Although the use of medications with JSOs is an area of potential promise, more research is necessary to identify which medications and what doses have efficacy in lowering JSO risk for recidivism. Perhaps the primary usefulness of psychotropics with JSOs will be to ameliorate comorbid forms of psychopathology that can exacerbate JSO risk.

Another controversial biologically based approach with JSOs is chemical castration of offenders as a condition of probation or parole (Miller, 1998). Chemical castration is a contemporary alternative to surgical castration. The use of castration techniques with adult sex offenders has a long and complicated legal history (for a review see Miller, 1998). There have been pharmacological castration attempts with the JSO population also.

The use of phallometric (Hunter and Becker, 1994) and polygraph techniques (Emerick and Dutton, 1993) with JSOs is ethically questionable for a number of reasons. These reasons include the cognitive abilities of JSOs to understand the legal implications of their circumstances and the related issue of informed consent (Ilgen and Bell, 2001). Phallometric techniques are expensive and invasive. Phallometry requires use of explicit sexual stimuli, raising concerns about teaching awareness of sexual stimulation especially with younger offenders. Nevertheless, there has been phallometric research with adolescents (Becker, Kaplan, and Tenke, 1992; Becker, Stein, Kaplan, and Cunningham-Rathner, 1992; Hunter, Becker, and Kaplan, 1995; Hunter, Goodwin, and Becker, 1994). Phallometry has been demonstrated to discriminate specific pedophilic interests among adolescent sex offenders compared to nonoffenders (Seto, Lalumière, and Blanchard, 2000). The inference is that phallometric findings could be useful as one aspect of a comprehensive evaluation effort (for a review see Marshall and Fernandez, 2001). There is consensus, however, that phallometric techniques alone are not empirically sufficient for determination of whether or not an offender has committed a sexual offense, in part because phallometric responses can be falsified (Harris, Rice, Chaplin, and Quinsey, 1998). Phallometry continues as a questionable tool in forensic-related assessments much in the same way as polygraphy is of questionable validity in forensic matters.

The misuse of psychological and actuarial instruments is another area of potential ethical difficulty (Edens, 2001). There are no currently available psychological instruments that have validity for definitively predicting degree of JSO reoffending risk. There are, however, a number of instruments that show initial promise. Any use of these instruments must be judicious, and forensic reports should incorporate cautionary statements acknowledging the limitations of these instruments. However, there are a number of standardized psychological instruments that can and should be utilized with juvenile offenders with respect to general psychological functioning as well as evaluation for the possibility of comorbid psychopathology (Kafka and Hennen, 2002; Lalumière, Harris, Quinsey, and Rice, 2005b; Poirier, 2002).

All use and development of psychological instruments for assessment of sex offenders must adhere to the standards espoused by the American Educational Research Association (AERA) (1955, 1999), the American Psychological Association (APA), (1954, 1966, 1974, 1985, 2002), and the National Council on Measurement in Education (1995). The potential outcomes for both offenders and victims are simply too consequential if test instruments are misused.

Most professional mental health disciplines have established ethical guidelines for practitioners. As examples, psychologists must adhere to the ethical standards of the American Psychological Association (2002) and forensic psychologists to the ethical standards of the Committee on Ethical Guidelines for Forensic Psychologists (1991).

Aspiring toward Empirically Based Methods and Applications[*]

The typical identification of JSOs usually occurs when a first offense takes place. It is at or after that point that clinicians will typically become involved with JSOs. In this chapter, we identify a number of statistical and research-established risk factors that empirically appear to be associated with juvenile sex offending. None of these characteristics, however, singly, or in any yet determined group or pattern, has been demonstrated to be necessarily predictive of juvenile sex offending. We will summarize the state of the effort to develop actuarial approaches to assess risk with JSOs in the section "Risk Assessment."

Diagnostic Assessment

A variety of approaches have been described for the assessment of JSOs (Bonner, Marx, Thompson, and Michaelson, 1998; Bourke and Donahue, 1996; Quinsey and Lalumière, 2001; Ross and Loss, 1991; Stickrod, Gray, and Wallace, 1992; Zussman, 1989). These approaches include taxonomic systems (Butler and Seto, 2002; Gray, Pithers, Busconi, and Houchens, 1997; O'Halloran et al., 2002) and continuum classifications (Johnson and Feldmeth, 1993). They also include classification schemas for placement of JSOs in multi-disciplinary or multifacility treatment models (McGrath, Cumming, and Holt, 2002).

A number of early efforts attempted to establish discernable patterns or types among juvenile sexual offenders (Gray et al., 1997; Johnson and Feldmeth, 1993; Knight and Prentky, 1993; Simourd, Hoge, Andrews, and Leschied, 1994). There were proposals of classification schemas (MacHovec and Wieckowski, 1992; O'Brien and Bera, 1986). Over time, these attempts were not determined to be particularly helpful; JSOs are a

[*] The concept of "empirically based" is arguably broader than the concept of "evidence-based practice" (EBP) as recently adopted by the APA Council of Representatives (APA, 2005). The intent of the EBP concept is to capture the notion that "... doctoral psychologists should be trained as both scientists and practitioners ..." (p. 1). The task force adopted the following definition: "Evidence-based practice in psychology (EBPP) is the integration of the best available research with clinical expertise in the context of patient characteristics, culture, and preferences" (p. 5). This chapter espouses this definition of EBP.

too heterogeneous population to be categorized in a simplistic manner. Other studies proposed retrospective profiles of youngsters who may be at risk of being victimized by JSOs (Berliner and Conte, 1990; Faller, 1989a; Green, Ramelli, and Mizumoto, 2001; Rice, Harris, and Quinsey, 2002).

The application of standard psychological testing instruments to assist with the assessment of JSOs is amply documented (Curnoe and Langevin, 2002; Dalton, Ruddy, and Simon-Roper, 2003; Hunter et al., 1995; Hunter, Becker, Kaplan, and Goodwin, 1991; Hughes, DeVille, Chalhoub, and Romboletti, 1992; Kraerner, Spielman, and Salisbury, 1997; Losada Paisley, 1998). Available standardized tests, however, do not directly address basic issues of psychosexuality status or risk for recidivism.

The assessment of JSO offenses must take into consideration contextual and situational factors. For example, contexts that would mean one thing for an adult offender, soliciting relationships with adolescents over the Internet, may have an entirely different meaning for an adolescent (Lalumière, Harris, Quinsey, and Rice, 2005a).

Several researchers have emphasized the importance of being mindful of developmental issues in the assessment and treatment of JSOs (Harnett and Misch, 1993; Pithers et al., 1995; Prescott, 2004; Quinsey and Rice, 1993). That is, cognitive abilities, social-emotional maturity, and understandings of morality vary substantially at different developmental levels. Additionally, developmental levels determine physical readiness and psychological sexual awareness in the child/adolescent. One study found that adult incest offenders with younger victims (<6 years old) generally showed more psychopathology compared to those whose victims were older (>12 years old). (Firestone, Dixon, Nunes, and Bradford, 2005). A number of authors have noted the importance of clinicians staying updated on the ongoing evolution of legal standards regarding JSOs (Doren, 2002; Winick and La Fond, 2003; Witt, DelRusso, and Ferguson, 1996).

Lanyon proposed a concise and useful six-part scheme for organizing areas of clinical inquiry when assessing sex offenders (2001, p. 254). These assessment questions are summarized as follows:

1. Identify the *general psychological characteristics* of the offender with an emphasis on any comorbid psychopathology. Essential to any assessment is a database of comprehensive biographical information regarding the offender to include data from collateral resources. Lanyon also suggests that standardized psychological tests such as the Minnesota Multiphasic Personality Inventory, the Millon personality instruments, and others may be useful in assessing offender comorbid psychopathology. He noted that biographical data help in checking the validity of test findings.

2. An assessment of the offender's *deviant sexual interests*. The clinician must determine how compelling the deviant interests are, and how they compare with the offender's nondeviant sexual interests. A number of instruments are available to assist with this assessment. These instruments include structured interviews, sexual behavior inventories, specific adaptations of standardized tests, and penile plethysmography.

3. *Risk assessment* involves the prediction of the likelihood of reoffense. Once again, a number of instruments have been proposed. Most of these instruments, however, have been developed with incarcerated adult sexual offenders and thus far have limited application to the child/adolescent sexual offender population. Presently, there are a number of promising actuarial instruments in early development for use with the JSO population (see Table 14.9).

4. An assessment of the JSO's amenability *to treatment*. A number of factors have been identified that appear to correlate favorable prognosis with JSOs. These factors include the offender's willingness to accept responsibility for offense behavior, and being appropriately motivated to participate in the rehabilitation process. Other positive prognostic factors include age-appropriate heterosexual interests and experiences, available family support system, and lack of comorbid psychopathology to especially include substance abuse and impulsive-aggressive behavior.

5. A common dynamic with all sexual offenders is *self-serving misrepresentation*. The potential for offenders engaging in deception is inherent in every forensic-related evaluation (Hall and Poirier, 2001). Hall and Poirier described techniques for assessing deception in a variety of forensic matters, but in the end, accurate and reliable evaluation of deception is an effort fraught with pitfalls for the clinician. Prudence in forming and rendering opinions regarding deception is imperative. With sexual offenders, the inclination to engage in deception is heightened by cultural taboos, the potential of severe legal penalties, and practiced asocial behavior that becomes integral to many offenders' personalities.

6. An assessment of the offenders' inappropriate sexual behavior(s) as comprising a fit with specific formal criteria. These criteria may be of a legal, or clinical nature, or some other criteria category as required by the specific context of the evaluation effort.

Risk Assessment

A relatively recent area of research effort with the JSO population has been risk assessment. Clinicians who work with JSOs will inevitably be called upon to render estimates of likelihood of sexual reoffending. The violence literature has described three essential models of risk assessment. These three models are (1) unstructured clinical decision-making, (2) actuarial decision-making, and (3) structured professional judgment (Kropp et al., 2004).

Although *unstructured clinical decision-making* is probably the most widely applied method in violence risk assessment, it is the most empirically unsound approach (Quinsey and Harris, 2006a). Unstructured clinical decision-making is little more than the best intuitive guess on the part of the clinician (Monahan, 1996). The approach relies on a review of the offender's prior history and current levels of JSO functioning as judged by the clinician. The approach is laden with problems of clinician bias and potentially erroneous clinician interpretation. Because of the foregoing risks, this approach should be utilized with appropriate constraint in forensic matters (Harris and Rice, 2003; Quinsey, V. L., Lalumière, M. L., Rice, M. E., and Harris, G. T., 1995). Kropp, Hart, and Belfrage (2004) commented on the unstructured clinical decision-making approach as follows: "Recommendations for management strategies—if they are made at all—might be based more on the training preferences, and biases of the evaluator rather than on (1) well-reasoned consideration of dynamic and criminogenic (i.e., crime relevant) risk factors, and (2) intervention strategies that are either empirically valid or well accepted in the field" (p. 35).

Practicing clinicians are confronted with the reality that many specific areas of risk assessment for aggressive or violent behavior do not have formally developed assessment instruments. In these circumstances, clinicians essentially have no other options but to utilize unstructured clinical decision-making in an effort to assist with risk assessment and contribute to management plans. Such assessment findings, however, should clearly outline the limitations of the clinical effort and be frugal in rendering findings.

The purpose of the *actuarial assessment* model is to provide an approach that improves the lack of reliability and validity of the unstructured clinical approach (Quinsey and Harris, 2006b). Actuarial assessment compares the risk of violence of an individual to that of a reference group of known offenders. Offender risk factors are "totaled" and then compared to established norms for the reference group. One limitation of actuarial assessment is its fixed temporality. That is, the estimated risk factors are for fixed time interval and therefore have predictive value for limited intervals.

Heilbrun (1997) noted the practical utility of pursuing "management"-oriented models of risk assessment over "prediction" models. A management model of risk assessment strives to match offender needs with available resources as opposed to attempting to "predict" offender risk in some quantified way. The latter quest is probably more elusive.

The defining aspect of an actuarial risk scale is "… that items are weighted and combined according to a fixed and explicit algorithm" (Kropp, Hart, and Belfrage, 2004, p. 103). Thus, with an actuarial risk scale, it is unimportant whether the content of the scale was empirically derived or derived based on clinical intuition. When using the actuarial approach, the clinician considers a fixed set of risk factors, and not other parameters. The latter characteristic is the actuarial approach's strength, and at the same times its essential limitation.

The *structured professional judgment* approach is an attempt to combine the relative strengths of unstructured clinical assessment and actuarial assessment (Douglas and Kropp, 2002; Harris, Rice, and Quinsey, 1998). Kropp et al. (2004) characterized the structured professional judgment approach as follows:

> Here, the evaluator must conduct the assessment according to guidelines that reflect current theoretical, professional, and empirical knowledge about violence. Such guidelines provide the minimum set of risk factors that should be considered in every case. The guidelines will also typically include recommendations for information gathering (e.g., the use of multiple sources and multiple methods), communicating opinions, and implementing violence prevention strategies. (p. 36)

The structured professional judgment approach does not eliminate the intuition of the clinician, but augments it with consideration of multiple sourced, actuarially based, risk factor data. According to Douglas and Kropp (2002), the primary objective of the structured professional judgment is the prevention of violence. *Structured professional judgment* attempts to prevent violence by systematic identification of static and dynamic risk factors (Kropp et al., 2004). Because of its reliance on actuarial assessment, the approach is considered to be empirically grounded.

Requests for psychological assessment of JSOs can occur at a number of points in the juvenile justice system adjudication process (Prentky, Harris, Frizell, and Righthand, 2000). In most instances, the judiciary will be more interested in risk estimates as opposed to more conventional clinical assessments. Risk assessments coupled with strategies designed to prevent recidivism are areas that have received considerable attention from researchers (McCarthy, 2001; Pecker, Harris, and Sales, 1993; Smith and Monastersky, 1986; Vizard, Monck, and Minsch, 1995; West, 2001). Risk assessment needs to be comprehensive, well documented, and mindful of risk management issues. Risk assessment studies have incorporated a combination of actuarial and traditional clinical methods.

Beech, Fisher, and Thornton (2002) summarized four broad risk factor categories that have been identified in the risk assessment literature for sexual offenders. The four categories are as follows:

a. *Dispositional* factors, including psychopathic, antisocial, or other prominent personality disorder features
b. *Historical* factors, including developmental traumas, prior history of criminal activity or violence, prior psychiatric history, and history regarding treatment compliance
c. *Contextual* antecedents to violence, including risk factors for criminal behavior, involvement in deviant social networks, and lack of positive social supports
d. *Clinical* factors, including psychiatric diagnosis, poor levels of functioning, and substance abuse (p. 339)

We note that examples of most of these factors are identified in the data cited in Tables 14.1 through 14.3. There has been considerable debate within the evolution of risk assessment research about the need to go beyond consideration of *static* risk factors, which essentially do not change over time and placement of more emphasis on *dynamic* risk factors (Craig, Browne, Stringer, and Beech, 2005; Dvoskin and Heilbrun, 2001; Douglas and Skeem, 2005; Quist and Matshazi, 2000). Quinsy and Lalumière (2001) suggested that in addition to static and dynamic risk factors, *proximal* (i.e., to the offense) risk factors are also important.

Skeem and Mulvey (2002) described "risk state" as a concept encompassing static and dynamic risk factors. Dynamic risk factors (e.g., substance abuse, recent acquisition of a weapon, emergence of a vulnerable victim, etc.) are those that are changeable from one point in time to another. Dynamic risk factors are therefore more likely to be more imminently predictive of the likelihood of violent behavior. Heilbrun (1997) suggested that dynamic risk factors were most directly related to the effort to achieve violence reduction (and violence management) as opposed to violence prediction.

Beech et al. (2002) described a framework for integrating actuarial and clinically based assessments. They suggested combining three main assessment strategies: (1) functional analyses, (2) actuarial risk assessments, and (3) dynamic risk assessments. Table 14.6 outlines the essential components of these three assessment strategies.

Canadian researchers have described a number of actuarial methods for predicting adult offender risk (Harris and Rice, 2003). Table 14.7 cites these adult sexual offender actuarial instruments. The utility of each of these instruments is limited by the specificity of each of their validation samples (e.g., incarcerated adult offenders, contact versus noncontact recidivists, violent versus nonviolent sexual offenders, etc.). We emphasize that

Table 14.6 Main Assessment Strategies of Comprehensive Risk Assessment[a]

1. *Functional analyses:* A clinical tool that attempts to document and understand the offense circumstances. The functional analysis should be detailed and comprehensive in exploring the *antecedents*, *behaviors*, and *consequences* (ABC model) of the offense.

2. *Actuarial risk prediction:* Recent actuarial scales (e.g., ERASOR) have incorporated dynamic/changeable risk factors as opposed to earlier scales that comprised primarily static/historical factors.

3. *Measurement of dynamic risk factors:* In an effort to overcome the limitations of purely static risk factors, researchers have incorporated dynamic (i.e., subject to change) risk factors.

[a] Strategies proposed by Beech et al. (2002); see text.

Table 14.7   Adult Sex Offender Actuarial Measures of Risk Potential

1. HCR-20 (Webster, Hart, Kropp, and Webster, 1997)
2. Minnesota Sex Offender Screening Tool—Revised (MnSOST-R; Epperson et al., 1995)
3. Multifactorial Assessment of Sex Offender Risk for Recidivism (Barbaree et al., 2001)
4. Rapid Risk Assessment for Sexual Offense Recidivism (RRASOR; Hanson, 1997)
4. Sex Offender Needs Assessment Rating (SONAR; Hanson and Harris, 2001)
5. Sex Offender Risk Appraisal Guide (SORAG; Quinsey et al., 1998)
6. Sexual Violence Risk—20 (SVR-20; Boar Hart, Kropp, and Webster, 1997)
7. Static-99 (Hanson and Thornton, 2000)

the use of the adult actuarial instruments cited in Table 14.7 with JSOs is inappropriate because, to date, there are no cross-validation studies justifying such application.

Hanson and Morton-Bourgon (2005) recently updated the Hanson and Bussière (1998) meta-analysis of sexual offender's recidivism studies. The authors noted that the 1998 study was based on static (i.e., historical) risk factors. The updated study added dynamic risk factors. On the basis of 82 recidivism studies (1,620 findings from 29,450 sexual offenders) the authors identified deviant sexual preferences and antisocial orientation as the major predictors of sexual recidivism for both adult and adolescent sexual offenders. The major risk predictor of violent recidivism was antisocial orientation. This was also the major predictor of general (any) recidivism. The authors identified dynamic risk factors that have the potential of being useful targets of treatment. These included sexual preoccupation and general self-regulation problems. In contrast, a number of variables commonly addressed in JSO treatment programs had no relationship with sexually violent recidivism. These included psychological distress, denial of sex crime, victim empathy, and stated motivation for treatment.

Actuarial measures are dependent on base rates of violent behavior and the selection ratio, or both. Base rates essentially reflect the *prevalence* of the type of violence, and the selection ratio is the proportion of people predicted to evidence the violence (Rice and Harris, 1995; Quinsey, Harris, Rice, and Cormier, 1998). The problem arises when predictive instruments generate false negative and false positive estimates. A recent advance in violence prediction was the application of a measure derived from receiver operating characteristics (ROC) (Beech et al., 2002; Harris and Rice, 2003; Hilton, Rice, and Harris, 2006) The ROC concept was originally developed to assist with (radar) signal detection years ago. ROC is the best index of the predictive accuracy of an assessment method. ROCs can also compare the predictive performance of different instruments (Rice and Harris, 1995). It has the advantage of not being distorted by variations in the base rates of recidivism. "In general, it can be interpreted as the probability that a randomly selected recidivist would have a more deviant score than a randomly selected nonrecidivist. This varies from .5 (no predictive accuracy) to 1.0 (perfect predictive accuracy)" (Beech et al., 2002, p. 341).

Research has demonstrated that the frequency of violent crime including sexual crimes diminishes with age (Barbaree et al., 2003). Wollert (2006) observed that ROC curves for actuarial tests for sexual recidivism do not consider the effects of the magnitude of base rates (e.g., different base rates for different age groups) on instrument performance. As a result, the information provided by sexual abuse recidivism instruments is insufficient with reference to the instrument efficiency for any specific critical test range. According to the MacArthur Study of Mental Disorder and Violence (Monahan, Steadman, Silver, Applebaum, Robbins, Mulvey, Roth, Grisso, and Banks, 2001), clumps of different risk factors may be relevant for different age groups. As a correction, Wollert recommended the application of Baye's theorem, which extends the range of ROC analysis. "When applied to sexual recidivism, Baye's theorem enables an evaluator to determine an average estimate (E) of the rate with which a class of offenders with high actuarial scores—in particular, those classified as likely recidivists—will reoffend" (p. 63). The author states that Baye's theorem is simple to calculate. It requires three pieces of information. The first is P (i.e., base rate) or Q (i.e., the sample-wise nonrecidivism rate, which is equal to 1 minus P) in the parent population that covers the age interval (A) into which the defendant falls. The other informations are T (i.e., the proportion of recidivists the test identifies) and F (i.e., the proportion of nonrecidivists) for scores covered by C (i.e., values in the critical range). A statistical formula is applied to these values. Generally, recidivism instruments are reasonably accurate with the youngest age groups because they have the largest base rates. The Bayesian method helps extend this accuracy to older age groups. Actuarial measures hold promise for establishing relationships between risk factors and patterns of offending (Macpherson, 2003; Doren, 2004).

While a number of risk assessment actuarial instruments have been developed for adult sexual offenders, the comparable process for juvenile sexual offenders, with one or two exceptions, lags significantly behind (Hunter, Hazelwood, and Slesinger, 2000; Langstrom and Grann, 1999). JSO researchers have attempted to capitalize on the accomplishments of risk assessment with adult offenders, but such extrapolation has limits because of the significant developmental differences between the adult and juvenile populations. Table 14.8 presents the several assessment instruments described in the JSO literature. The use of any of these instruments should be discreet. Likewise, use of the instruments should involve the clinicians becoming thoroughly familiar with the instruments, the specific limitations of each instrument, and their intended clinical application. The JSO literature includes a number of proposed checklists for use with JSOs (Bremer, 2001; Christodoulides, Richardson, Graham, Kennedy, and Kelly, 2005; Epps, 1997; Perry and Orchard, 1992a; Ross and Loss, 1991). None of these items, however, has established reliability or validity data. We have included Bremer's Protective Factors Scale (PFS) and Christodoulides et al.'s "Proposed" risk assessment tool in Table 14.8 as examples of these checklists.

Of the instruments described in Table 14.8, only two have gained a semblance of acceptance as empirically based actuarial risk assessment scales (Beech et al., 2002). These two scales are the Juvenile Sex Offender Protocol (J-SOAP; Prentky et al., 2000; Righthand, Prentky, Knight, Carpenter, Hecker, and Nangle, 2005), and the Estimate of Risk of Adolescent Sexual Offender Recidivism (ERASOR; Worling and Curwen, 2000). We note that most risk assessment researchers advocate use of numerous risk assessment instruments in the assumption that "more is better." Seto (2005), however, has challenged this assumption. Seto utilized four validated adult actuarial risk instruments (i.e., VRAG, SORAG, RRASOR, and Static-99) with a sample of 215 adult male sex offenders. Seto concluded, "no combination method provided a statistically significant or consistent advantage over the predictive accuracy of the single best actuarial scale" (p. 156). The author acknowledges a number of limitations to his study beginning with the similarity in derivation and content of the four instruments. Nevertheless, the findings raise questions as to the inefficiency of the practice of administering multiple risk assessment instruments.

The J-SOAP comprises four factors as outlined in Table 14.9. According to Worling (2004), the J-SOAP was designed so that coding could be achieved from archived data, and as a result, the majority of its items are static, that is, historical in nature. Because of this, the J-SOAP is not sensitive to changes due to offense-specific treatment and we note that neither was this the intended purpose of the J-SOAP. Prentky et al. (2000) stated that the

Table 14.8   Instruments for Assessing Juvenile Offender/Juvenile Sex Offender Risk

Instrument/Source	Measure	Validity
Child and Adolescent Functional Assessment Scale (CAFAS; Hodges and Wong, 1996; Hodges, 1996)	Juveniles at risk for future offending	According to the authors, CAFAS was positively correlated with a number of constructs to include juveniles with a history of difficulties with the law. Actuarial instrument made up of a number of subscales: role performance (with the following subscales: School/Work Roles and Community Roles), Behavior Toward Others, Moods/Self-Harm (with the following subscales: Moods/Emotion and Self-Harmful Behavior), Substance Use, and Thinking.
Quist and Matshazi (2000)	Replication study that applied CAFAS to a small sample	Study found a significant relationship between CAFAS scoring and juvenile recidivism.
Four-Factor Risk Index (Langstrom and Grann, 1999)	Risk for sexual recidivism	Small Swedish study. Instrument has not received any follow-up attention. Utilized four factors: (1) previous sex offending behavior, (2) poor social skills, (3) any male victim, and (4) two or more victims in the offense.
Juvenile Sex Offender Assessment Protocol (J-SOAP; Prentky et al., 2000; Righthand et al., 2005)	JSO risk	Actuarial scale that has fixed and explicit scoring and item weighting rules. Most scale items were chosen based on risk factors identified in the literature. The protocol has now been updated to version II (J-SOAP-II).
"Proposed" risk assessment tool (Christodoulides et al., 2005)	Adolescent sex offender risk	Small study of male offenders designated recidivists and nonrecidivists on the basis of clinician judgment and Home Office records for reconvictions. Tool did not distinguish the two groups.
Structured Assessment of Violence Risk in Children (SAVRY; Borum, Bartel, and Forth, 2005)	Violence risk in youth	Structured, empirically guided clinical judgment approach. The instrument incorporates *dynamic* (changeable) risk factors and *protective* factors (e.g., social connectedness, problem-solving confidence, etc.).
The Protective Factors Scale (PFS; Bremer, 2001)	Prediction of level of placement for successful intervention with JSOs of both genders	Scale emphasizes factors in three areas: (1) sexuality, (2) personal development, and (3) environmental support. The scale focuses on factors that will help are reduce risk as opposed to offering an estimate of risk. No validity data are available for the scale. The author describes the PFS as an empirically based checklist.
Estimate of Risk of Adolescent Sex Offender Recidivism (ERASOR; Worling and Curwen, 2000; Worling, 2004)	Risk of sex offender recidivism	Empirically grounded structured risk assessment method; scale includes both static and dynamic risk factors.
Youth Level of Service Inventory (YLSI; Hoge and Andrews, 1994)	Youth offender level of risk	Instrument characterized youth offender's types into five clusters: low risk, generalized high risk/need, difficulties in the community, family and personal distress, and economically distressed.
Simourd et al. (1994)		This follow-up study of YLSI utilized 256 male juvenile offenders (ages 12–18). YLSI capably classified youth offenders into five predefined clusters.
Ilacqua, Coulson, Lombardo, and Nutbrown (1999)		A study of the YLSI's predictive validity. Found the instrument useful with male and female offenders.

Table 14.9   The Four Factors and Factor Items of the Juvenile Sex Offender Assessment Protocol (J-SOAP-II)

Factor 1—Sexual Drive/Preoccupation Scale
• Prior charges for sexual offenses
• Number of sexual abuse victims
• Duration of sexual offense history
• Sexual drive and preoccupation
• Degree of planning in sexual offense(s)
• Sexualized aggression
• Sexual victimization history

Factor 2—Impulsive/Antisocial Behavior Scale
• Caregiver consistency
• Pervasive anger
• School behavior problems
• History of conduct disorder
• Juvenile antisocial behavior
• Ever charged or arrested before age 16
• Multiple types of offenses

Factor 3—Intervention Scale
• Accepting of responsibility for offense(s)
• Internal motivation for change
• Empathy
• Remorse and guilt
• Cognitive distortions
• Quality of peer relationships

Factor 4—Community Stability/Adjustment Scale
• Management of sexual urges and desires
• Management of anger
• Stability of current living situation
• Stability of school
• Evidence of positive support systems

Source: Adapted from Righthand, S., Prentky, R., Knight, R., Carpenter, E., Hecker, J., and Nangle, D., *Sex Abuse*, 17, 13, 2005.

J-SOAP was an initial contribution to risk assessment with JSOs and that additional work would be necessary to produce a valid instrument. The authors have since updated the protocol to version II (J-SOAP-II; Righthand et al., 2005). The first step in utilizing a protocol is a determination of the offender's level of cognitive development. J-SOAP is useful with youngsters as young as age 10 in terms of cognitive ability. Thus, there may be teenagers whose cognitive ability is less than age 10 and use of the J-SOAP would not be appropriate.

The ERASOR was developed to be sensitive to offender risk-factor changes secondary to treatment impact. ERASOR was developed in a manner similar to the Adult instrument SVR-20; both are *empirically guided clinical judgment* risk assessment approaches. In characterizing the ERASOR, Worling (2004) stated, "Furthermore our aim was to produce a tool that could assist clinicians to assess dynamic, or potentially alterable, variables that would be targeted in specialized treatment for adolescents and their families" (p. 238). The ERASOR was designed for use with 12- to 18-year-old males and females. Because the examiner does the ratings, the ERASOR may be useful with offenders who are developmentally younger than 12 years. Of the 25 ERASOR risk factors, 16 are dynamic; the dynamic risk factors require reassessment following passage of time or marked behavior change.

Table 14.10 Items from the Estimate of Risk of Adolescent Sex Offender Recidivism Scale (ERASOR)

Sexual interests, attitudes, and behaviors
- Deviant sexual interest (younger children, violence, or both)
- "Obsessive" sexual interests/preoccupation with sexual thoughts
- Attitudes supportive of sexual offending
- Unwillingness to alter deviant sexual interests/attitudes

Historical sexual assaults
- Ever sexually assaulted two or more victims
- Ever sexually assaulted same victim two or more times
- Prior adult sanctions for sexual assault(s)
- Threats of, or use of, violence/weapons during sexual offense
- Ever sexually assaulted a child
- Ever sexually assaulted a stranger
- Indiscriminate choice of victims
- Ever sexually assaulted a male victim (male adolescent only)
- Diverse sexual assault behaviors

Psychosocial functioning
- Antisocial interpersonal orientation
- Lack of intimate peer relationships/social isolation
- Negative peer associations and influences
- Interpersonal aggression
- Recent escalation in anger or negative affect
- Poor self-regulation of affect or behavior

Family/environmental functioning
- High-stress family environment
- Problematic parent-offender relationship/parental rejection
- Parent(s) not supporting sexual-offense-specific assessment/treatment
- Environment supporting opportunities to reoffend sexually

Treatment
- No development or practice of realistic prevention plans/strategies
- Incomplete sexual-offense-specific treatment

Source: Adapted from Worling, J.R., *Sex. Abuse*, 16, 235, 2004.

Table 14.10 presents an outline of the ERASOR items. We emphasize that the data in Tables 14.9 and 14.10 only provide the reader with a cursory outline of the J-SOAP and ERASOR scales. Actual use of the scales should entail a careful reading and understanding of the respective author's original definitions and explicit scoring criteria. The authors note that deriving a final estimate of risk (i.e., "low," "moderate," or "high") with the ERASOR is a matter of clinical judgment. This is because, presently, there is no specific algorithm for summing the identified risk factors. Clinical judgment with the ERASOR should be based on a review of the combination of risk factors as opposed to the mere number of risk factors. In order to be considered empirically valid, a risk assessment instrument should be actuarially based and have demonstrated internal and external validity. Additionally, the instrument should have reliability across users and across administrations over longitudinal replication.

Empirically Based Juvenile Sex Offender Characteristics

Table 14.11 provides an overview of a recent evidence-based research with JSOs. Table 14.12 provides an overview of characteristics of judicial processing of JSOs.

Table 14.11 Evidence-Based Research with Juvenile Sex Offenders

Study	Findings
Breer (1996), Broadhurst and Loh (2003), Waite, Keller, McGarvey, Wieckowski, Pinkerton, and Brown (2005)	Adolescent sex offenders tend to have criminal records that include non-sex-related offense cases.
Bischof, Stith, and Whitney (1995)	The study compared the family environments of adolescent sex offenders, and violent and nonviolent juvenile delinquents, and a normative sample of adolescents utilizing the Family Environment Scale Form—R (FES). Family environments characterized by emotional disengagement, a lack of perceived cohesion among family members, and a strong reliance on parental control and rules correlate with adolescent violence.
Butler and Seto (2002)	Adolescent sex offenders were similar to nonsex offenders in their childhood conduct problems, current behavioral adjustment, and antisocial attitudes and beliefs, but they had a lower risk for future delinquency. The typological distinction between the two groups has implications for assigning juvenile offenders to appropriate interventions.
Efta-Breitbach and Freeman (2004a, 2004b)	The majority of JSO research is dominated by the study of risk factors associated with recidivism. The majority of existing treatments with JSOs is guided by research that attempts to identify what makes offenders reoffend. Absent in the research is an examination of strengths and positive characteristics that may prove useful in increasing positive outcomes. One such characteristic may be forms of resilience.
Frick, Cornell, Barry, Bodin, and, Dane; Frick, Stickle, Dandreaux, Farrell, and Komonis (2005), Frick (2006)	Studied the presence of callous-unemotional traits (CU) as traits distinguishing children with conduct problems who evidence an especially severe and chronic pattern of conduct problems and delinquency.
Caputo, Frick, and Broadsky (1999)	The study compared incarcerated male juvenile offenders: 23 sex offenders, 17 violent offenders, and 30 noncontact offenders. A history of witnessing severe domestic violence was related not only to juvenile sex offending, but related to contact offending in general. There were no group differences on measures of impulse control or sexist attitudes toward women. Sex offenders had more callous and unemotional traits. These traits do not mediate the effects of witnessing family violence; they do seem to be important in distinguishing juvenile sex offenders from other juvenile offenders.
Hagan, Gust-Brey, Cho, and Dow (2001)	Longitudinal study of 150 adolescents released to the community from a secure juvenile facility. Fifty of the youths were adolescent rapists with victims being same-aged peers or older. Another 50 of the perpetrators had sexually victimized children, and the other 50 were adjudicated or nonsexual incidents. The findings reflected that the JSOs were more likely to reoffend over an 8-year period as compared to the delinquent (nonsexual offenses) control group from the same facility. Additionally, the nonsexual offenders, the child sex offenders, and the adolescent rapists were at higher risk for sexually reoffending compared to a general male adolescent population sample in the U.S.
Hanson and Morton-Bourgon (2005)	Meta-analysis study of recidivism studies that updated an earlier meta-analysis study (Hanson and Bussière, 1998). Update study included dynamic risk factors. The new study identified deviant sexual preferences and antisocial orientation as the major predictors of sexual recidivism for adolescent sex offenders.
Lalumière, Harrish, Quinsey, and Rice (1998)	Having older brothers but not sisters positively correlates with a history of sexual deviance.

Table 14.11 (continued)

Study	Findings
McMackin et al. (2002)	Trauma exposure correlates positively with sex offending behavior among male juvenile sex offenders.
Schmidt and Pierce (2004)	The authors compiled research data regarding female adolescent sex offenders (ASOs). Female ASOs account for 1% of forcible rapes committed by juveniles and 7% of juvenile arrests for sex offenses. Prospective analysis of sample of 300 registered male sex offenders who were juveniles at time of original arrest. Typical juvenile offender is a 15-year-old Caucasian male who was arrested for sexual assault or indecency with a child. Majority of victims were female with average age of 8. Most female ASOs do not meet the criteria for pedophilia. The most common sexual offenses committed by female ASOs are nonaggressive acts such as mutual fondling. As adults, 13 of the sample were rearrested for a sexual offense, and more than half the sample arrested for a nonsexual offense. There is no evidence justifying inclusion or exclusion of female ASOs in traditional male ASOs treatment methods. Some female ASOs have histories of being sex-abuse victims; their treatment plans should include empirically validated abuse-focused intervention if these ASOs exhibit PTSD symptoms.
Spataro, Moss, and Wells (2001)	Australian study reporting that 90% of JSOs were male and the majority of their victims were female. The authors found that male victims were underreported for a variety of reasons including male personality factors of self-reliance, machismo-oriented values, and fear of homosexuality. The authors also reported that male victims more often reported violent, aggressive sexual abuse (e.g., penetration) whereas female victims more often reported abuse in the form of exhibitionism and fondling.
Vandiver (2006)	Prospective analysis of sample of 300 registered male sex offenders who were juveniles at time of original arrest. Typical juvenile offender is a 15-year-old Caucasian male who was arrested for sexual assault or indecency with a child. Majority of victims were female with average age of 8 years. As adults, 13 of the sample were rearrested for a sexual offense, and more than half the sample arrested for a nonsexual offense.
Zankman and Bonomo (2004)	Since the family environment is a potential risk factor for adolescent sex offenders, integration of relapse prevention into daily family life may be a significant part of these youths' success or failure in the community.

Table 14.12 Characteristics of Judicial Processing/Follow-Up of Juvenile Sex Offenders

Source	Characteristic
Craissati and McClurg (1997)	Untreated sex offender recidivism base rate is between 15 and 35%.
Hall (1995)	Overall JSO recidivism rate at 19% after treatment based on a meta-analysis of studies.
Kenny and Press (2006)	Violence classifications of JSOs have an impact on the significance of other key factors in the management and processing of JSOs.
Vandiver and Teske (2006)	For similar offenses, male juvenile offenders receive longer sentences compared to female JSOs.
Waite et al. (2005)	Rearrest is most likely to be for a nonsexual offense (<5%). Juveniles who indicate high levels of impulsive/antisocial behaviors are significantly more likely to recidivate than offenders without these characteristics.

Basic Points to Consider in Clinical/Forensic Assessment

The consequences of clinical/forensic evaluation of JSOs can be life changing in either a positive or a negative way. Clinicians must be vigilant in recognizing the significance of the potential impact on the future life of JSOs balanced with the paramount need to protect the community. Other basic points to keep in mind when working with JSOs are as follows:

1. As with any specialized clinical work, clinicians must have competence in the area of proficiency by virtue of training, supervision, research, or a combination of the above. The burden of responsibility to demonstrate competence is on the clinician. With JSOs, in particular, clinicians should have expertise in the assessment of adolescents and their families. Clinicians should also have training and expertise regarding the assessment and management of sexual aggression.

2. When doing forensic work it is very important for the clinicians to know their precise role and make a concerted effort to maintain the boundaries of that role. The clinician must also communicate as thoroughly as possible, and as frequently as necessary, what that role is to the juvenile offender and to his or her parents. When doing forensic work there are so many points of interest and competing players that clinicians can be easily seduced to compromise roles or boundary issues. For example, a clinician can complete a court-ordered assessment of a juvenile offender. All parties concerned can be pleased with the clinician's work. Later, as part of disposition, there are invitations for the forensic evaluator to become involved in a treating role with the offender. This is not professionally or ethically appropriate because the clinician has previously been in the role of an objective, impartial evaluator, and the boundaries of that primary role should not be compromised assuming a new role. The basic concern is that a change in clinician's role may be confusing to the JSO and his or her family members in a way that the effectiveness of the treatment could be compromised.

3. As a follow-up to the above point, if the clinician is conducting a court-ordered evaluation of a JSO, the clinician must explicitly indicate that they are not serving in a treating capacity; the clinician is not, and will not be, the juvenile's therapist.

4. We have stressed throughout the body of the chapter that proper assessment of juvenile sex defendants must include accessing as many domains of functioning as possible. In addition to usual clinical and developmental history information, the assessment of JSOs should include review of physical health history, psychosexual history, familial, intrapersonal, and interpersonal domains.

5. Data collection with JSOs should also include data from as many assessment sources as deemed relevant. At a minimum this would include clinical interviews, psychological tests and instruments, behavioral observation (in multiple settings if possible), and thorough review of all referral information including prior reports and case records.

6. Obtain information from as many collateral sources as deemed relevant. These would include but not be limited to the offender, offender family members, the police, juvenile intake workers, probation officers, child welfare caseworkers, and other collaterally involved professionals. Finally, we would emphasize the values of interviewing the victims and their family members. Unfortunately, this is not always possible for a number of reasons not the least of which is victims' attorneys objecting to the practice. One of the best approaches is to try to educate juvenile judges as to the clinical/forensic value of having access to victims. Once the need

is understood, in appropriate situations, judges can ask victims if they are willing to be part of an evaluation. Victims can often provide valuable insight into a risk assessment effort.

7. Clinicians need to remain up to date with ongoing risk estimation research with JSOs. The author notes that, presently, most of the risk estimation research continues to be with adult sex offenders. Clinicians should be familiar with this research also, but be mindful of its qualified application with JSOs.

8. It is important to be aware of reliability and validity coefficients with risk assessment instruments as well as with applicable longitudinal research. At the current time, these data regarding JSOs are sparse and this state of affairs should be acknowledged in written reports and expert testimony.

9. One part of every risk assessment should be consideration of data from empirically validated actuarial risk instruments.

10. Clinicians should acknowledge that risk assessment instruments particularly those utilizing dynamic factors are time limited with respect to the period of application. A given risk assessment may be rendered obsolete with change in risk factors; other instruments or other risk factors may be more robust.

Avoiding Evaluation and Consultation Errors

Most of these considerations are embodied in the foregoing discussion regarding "basic points." The essential issue here is to avoid errors that will diminish or negate the clinician's findings and opinions. As we have attempted to illustrate, this is rather easy to accomplish with forethought and a careful approach. Part of every attorney's training is learning how to cope with expert witnesses. The primary trial strategy of many attorneys is to challenge expert testimony in an effort to minimize its impact on the trier of fact. In turn, the utilization of expert witnesses has become a major, national, financial enterprise. For most clinicians, however, involvement in the adversarial process regarding JSOs is a relatively more commonplace undertaking.

The beginning point of professional practice is to practice within one's area of competence. Areas of limited professional competence should be acknowledged in a forthright and before-the-fact manner. This is a much-preferred strategy to allowing a crafty attorney to bring out inadequacies when the expert is on the witness stand. If this happens, the attorney will posture the expert as attempting to hide issues and thereby suggesting that the experts' credibility is suspect. Another precaution would be to suggest accessing additional consultation expertise as early as possible to the major players in the case. Except in high-profile cases, such recommendations will usually go unheeded because of the cost, but the clinician can always point out that limitations were recognized and the expert made a remedial recommendation during the early stages of the assessment effort.

The clinician's database must be comprehensive and well conceived by the clinician. Often the ideal database will not be obtainable because of the cost or inaccessibility of key individuals. Once again, acknowledgment of this state of affairs and the limitations imposed on the expert's findings should be cited. Our discussion in the preceding section regarding accessing information directly from victims is a good example of a source of data that may not always be accessible. Nevertheless, the clinician wants to be able to state that this would have been a desired part of the database and then cite the reasons why it was not possible.

Use of psychological tests and instruments should be prudent and justified, and the clinician should carefully explain how these data were incorporated into the findings and recommendations and what limitations may exist. The usual expectation by the bench is that the forensic expert will assist the bench in arriving at a meaningful finding regarding JSO involvement in an offense circumstance and then assist with dispositional considerations. A recommended management plan needs to be realistic in terms of the JSO's clinical needs and with respect to available and accessible resources. With children and adolescents, this always means taking into consideration the interests of the parents and the family constellation. Frequently in these situations, the family perceptions will be at variance from what is indicated clinically. Nevertheless, most families will appreciate an effort to at least recognize their involvement as well as their interests on behalf of the JSO. It is also important to balance presentation of the recommended dispositional plan with any assets or strengths the JSO may have. The expert's written report/testimony should convey sensitivity to the fact that the offender is a child/adolescent who may have committed a serious act of sexual misconduct, but that in the offender's youth there remains the hope of rehabilitation and a wholesome future.

Treatment Considerations

It is often difficult to engage JSOs in treatment particularly when victims are much younger (Dolan and Fullam, 2005; Efta-Breitbach and Freeman, 2004b; Perry and Orchard, 1992b; Seager et al., 2004). There are a number of reasons for this, but the principal one is the cultural taboo dynamic associated with the sexual offending of young children. Some clinicians are rankled by the thought of utilizing court stipulation to engage offenders in treatment. With JSOs, however, this is usually an effective and necessary tactic and clinicians should welcome the collateral assistance of the court with this population.

There has been research attempting to identify issues that make it conducive for JSOs to acknowledge complicity in sexual offenses, but most JSOs will engage in denial or only partial acknowledgment of wrongdoing (Faller et al., 2001). Another common early treatment issue with JSOs is claims of amnesia about offense circumstances. Treatment interventions to address this issue have been described (Marshall, Serran, Marshall, and Fernandez, 2005; Serran and Marshall, 2005). The foremost treatment objective with JSOs is preventing recidivism (Marshall and Serran, 2000). JSO treatment begins with the proper identification of deviant sexual arousal patterns and the diagnosis of any comorbid psychopathology in JSOs (Firestone, Bradford, Greenberg, and Serran, 2000).

Historically, wide arrays of treatment approaches have been described for JSOs (Becker, Harris, and Sales, 1993; Camp and Thyer, 1993; Erti and McNamara, 1997; Flora, 2001; Freeman-Longo, Bird, Stevenson, and Fiske, 1995; Kaplan, Morales, and Becker, 1995; Morenz and Becker, 1995; Pecker, 1990; Pithers and Gray, 1998; Schwartz, 2003; Seabloom et al., 2003; Weinrott, Riggan, and Frothingham, 1997). Treatment approaches for victims of sexual assault have also been described (Pharris and Nafstad, 2002).

The initially proposed treatment modalities for JSOs were adaptations of treatment approaches in vogue years ago for other clinical problems felt to be pertinent to JSOs, for example, treatment approaches for addictions and aggressive behavior, as well as established treatment approaches for adult sexual offenders. Other proposed vogue modalities were group therapy, encounter groups, multiple family groups, art therapy, Pavlovian conditioning, and cognitive restructuring. Today, most of these treatment applications have been discarded as not being effective with the JSO population.

The majority of contemporary treatment programs for JSOs report using cognitive behavioral approaches (Kolko, Noel, Thomas, and Torres, 2004; Winick and La Fond, 2003). For historical reviews of cognitive and behavioral approaches as utilized with sexual offenders, see Laws and Marshall (2003) and Marshall and Laws (2003).

Nearly 20 years ago, Davis and Leitenberg (1987, p. 424) described primary treatment goals for working with JSOs. Although outdated in some respects, the thrust of these goals still remains relevant today; the following is a summary:

a. Reducing denial and increasing acceptance of responsibility and accountability for the sexual offense, including the use of peer group confrontation techniques
b. Increasing youths' understanding of the impact of the assault on the victim
c. Providing insight into the specific motives and antecedent events that precipitated the sexual offense
d. As applicable, focusing in counseling on the adolescent offender's own sexual victimization experiences
e. Education about human sexuality, sexual values, and sex roles
f. Using techniques for eliminating deviant arousal patterns and fantasies, including various masturbatory-reconditioning procedures and aversive-conditioning procedures
g. Cognitive restructuring around a host of destructive beliefs and myths pertaining to rape and sexual abuse of children
h. Training in interpersonal, dating, and social skills
i. Training in anger management and assertion
j. Using family therapy to promote positive parenting behaviors and to reintegrate the offender into the family (i.e., where appropriate in incest cases) (p. 424)

Bunston (2000) described that many juvenile sexual offenders have distorted notions they employ to justify their inappropriate behaviors. These distortions include belief systems whereby offenders magically attribute their behavior to some fault or indiscretion on the part of the victim (Ward, Hudson, Johnston, and Marshall, 1997). One method of identifying and monitoring these distortions is tracking JSO sexual fantasies (Aylwin, Reddon, and Burke, 2005). Treatment strategies must incorporate restructuring these distortions. Treatment must also facilitate the JSO's ability to experience remorse and to experience empathy for the victim's plight (Marshall, O'Sullivan, and Fernandez, 1996).

JSOs usually require many collateral services in addition to the core, sexual-offense-specific treatment. These services can include a variety of psychotherapy, educational, and recreational modalities. Additionally, collateral therapies can include substance abuse treatment, anger management, family therapy, and psychopharmacologic treatment. Many JSOs evidence problems with anger expression, anger control, and sadistic impulses and will require treatment specific to these issues (Myers and Monaco, 2000; Poirier, 1984, 1999a).

Work with the JSO population also typically involves an immense case management effort with innumerable collateral resources. Not the least of collaborative resources for the clinician involves probation and parole officers (POs). There is, however, controversy as to the extent of actual participation POs can and should have in treatment modalities, for example, sitting in on peer group therapy sessions or other treatment modalities (McGrath et al., 2002).

Critical to effective treatment process with JSOs is a meaningful therapeutic alliance between the offender and therapist. Effective therapy with JSOs is enhanced by collaborative interface of the therapist's style and the offender's perceptions of the therapist (Marshall et al., 2003, 2005). Cognitive-behavioral techniques are effective in addressing the issues of JSO cognitive distortions, enabling JSOs to achieve feelings of empathy toward victims, and enhancing offender motivation to adopt mature expressions of sexuality (Serran, Fernandez, Marshall, and Mann, 2003).

Marshall and his colleagues explored the issue of therapist qualities determined to be effective in treatment with JSOs. The usual therapist features of empathy, warmth, and being directive were identified as effecting desired change (Serran et al., 2003). Although aggressive confrontation was once considered essential in working with adult sexual offenders, it was not effective with JSOs (Marshall et al., 2003). Family therapy is another essential component of JSO treatment although not always from the beginning (Kolko et al., 2004). One issue that is imperative to address during family treatment is the presence of any intergenerational family history of JSO behavior (Faller, 1989b; Janus and Walbek, 2000). We comment finally that treatment of JSOs in community settings (e.g., as opposed to placement in correctional or residential facilities) carries the expectation that safeguards for public safety will be in place (Douglas and Skeem, 2005; *Tarasoff v. Regents of California*, 1976).

Writing Forensic Reports and Acting as an Expert Witness

The writing of forensic reports and offering expert testimony are acquired skills. Expert testimony must follow applicable ethical proscriptions; must be based on a sound, empirically based database; and must be creative and persuasive. This is a hefty mix of expectations. Achieving the mix can be a challenge for the forensic clinician to master consistently.

Clinicians must remember that ultimate legal issues (e.g., guilt, custodial fitness, dangerousness, etc.) are the final prerogative of the bench. The law has a long history of what constitutes decorum in the courtroom and what the roles of courtroom players should be (Heilbrun, 2001). The author has encountered situations where experts attempt to circumvent this legal authority. The clarification is that an expert rendering opinions is not the same as making a final legal determination. From the legal perspective, the primary purpose of expert testimony is to educate triers of fact about information not commonly available to the average layperson. Experts who attempt to upend this history neither assist the court nor represent their professional discipline well. The expert's contribution must from start to finish respect these longstanding traditions of the legal/mental health interface; the content and tone of forensic reports and testimony should always be mindful of these areas of sensitivity. Once the expert is on the witness stand, it is too late to undo what may have been a moment of intemperance or arrogance when writing a report.

There is perhaps no better example of attempting to proffer an unswerving opinion, while at the same time maintaining an appropriate balance of constraint, than with the estimation of risk. In this chapter, we have attempted to underscore the empirically tentative nature of risk assessment in general and with specific instruments regarding JSOs. Risk assessment research has enjoyed immense and rapid development, but remains far from having accuracy even approximating 90% (i.e., approaching the legal "beyond a reasonable doubt" level of proof).

Forensic clinicians need to bear in mind that the degrees of freedom embodied in field research of risk assessment tools are fundamentally different from taking risk assessment data into the courtroom. The language in forensic reports must have precision and ideally stem from a schema embraced by the scientific community. Today, the best risk assessment findings can only be described using qualitative terms, which avoid implied logarithmic precision (e.g., "minimal risk," "moderate risk," etc.). Another option is to document the array of empirically based risk factors evidenced by a JSO, which research has recognized as indicators of JSO risk.

Novel Applications of Forensic Evidence and Knowledge

There is a growing body of neuropsychological research with adult criminal offenders. The data suggest that a significant number of this population evidence neuropsychological deficits. A common finding is that of frontal-lobe executive dysfunctions. Veneziano, LeGrand, and Richards (2004) reported similar findings with subsets of groups of juvenile delinquent offenders and JSOs. The findings have the potential of profound implications for working with this population. There is also a growing body of research on the neurobiology of aggressive behavior (de Almeida, Ferrari, Parmigiani, and Miczek, 2005; Gollan, Lee and Coccaro, 2005; Goodman, New, and Siever, 2004; Turecki, 2005). Baumbach (2002) suggested that JSOs who have histories of prenatal alcohol exposure might require modified treatment strategies. Future neurobiological studies with JSOs will likely shed further light on Baumbach's hypothesis particularly with respect to the prevalence and impact of fetal alcohol exposure with JSOs. The author anticipates that future neuropsychological research will have a significant impact on assessment and intervention strategies with JSOs.

We have already commented on the particular problem of distortion and deception when working with assessment effort with JSOs (Hall and Poirier, 2001). Psychological researchers have encountered the effects of distortion (both deliberate and nondeliberate) when attempting to assess socially stigmatic beliefs (e.g., chauvinism, homophobia, racial prejudice, and sexual offending). Subjects overrespond or underrespond to research addressing such topics, thereby causing distortion of the findings. In an effort to address the problem, techniques of measuring beliefs by indirect or implicit means have been developed. Gray, Bravn, MacCulloch, Smith, and Snowden (2005) described a preliminary attempt to use an implicit model with adult pedophiles. The subjects viewed control and target stimulus words. Stimulus words were presented as attribute pairs on a computer screen, and subjects were asked to classify the attribute words as "sex" or "not-sex" as quickly as possible. Reaction times and errors were statistically analyzed. The findings indicated that pedophile subjects demonstrated an association between children and sex compared to nonpedophilic offenders who demonstrated an association between adults and sex. The approach may hold promise for application (i.e., nonforensic) with JSOs in an effort to address the problem of falsehood by subjects, which always impedes both evaluation and treatment efforts.

Prescott (2004) noted the importance of clinicians and researchers maintaining a focus on the developmental fluidity of adolescence. An important example of this is the nonlinearity of neurobiological growth. In the future, neuropsychological research may shed more light on these developmental idiosyncrasies. In the meantime, the effort to understand JSOs within collective frameworks may not mirror actual developmental events by individual JSOs.

Risk assessment with the JSO population is in the very early stages of development. We expect the future to bring an increasing number of advances as research strategies continue to be improved. For example, risk assessment instruments will be developed specifically for the different juvenile age groups. Instruments specifically for female JSO population will also be forthcoming. It is conceivable that current instruments for male JSOs will be applicable to, or adaptable for, female JSOs; it may be that entirely new instruments will be needed. This problem exists in part because according to available data, male JSOs significantly outnumber female JSOs (Greenfield, 1997; Snyder, 2000; Stroud, Martens, and Baker, 2000). Additionally, there are gender differences in the expression of aggression (Archer, 2004). Still another factor is that the judiciary in general is reluctant to incarcerate female offenders of any age as compared to practice with male offenders. This reality has an obvious suppressing effect on the number of female JSOs who are identified (Schwartz and Cellini, 1995). We also anticipate that the future will lead to the development of risk assessment instruments for other special populations such as mentally retarded, physically challenged, and mentally ill JSOs (Broxholme and Lindsay, 2003).

Unlike all other forms of juvenile offending, there are virtually no community-based support programs for integrating JSOs back into normalized life in the community (Faller and Henry, 2000; Poirier, 1998). Although this situation is historically and culturally understandable, it serves as a considerable impediment for JSOs and their families who attempt to take responsible advantage of available treatment. The problem is even greater for adult pedophiles who have to contend with offender reporting registries and web site lists. Because of the thrust of recent legal decisions, certain JSOs will also have to cope with registry listings. Our point here is, of course, not to suggest that communities adopt other than a cautious approach with adult or juvenile sexual offenders. Rather, we are attempting to suggest that especially with JSOs part of the ultimate solution rests at the community level, which is where the problem begins. Perhaps the future will bring reasoned and prudent acceptance by communities when this is justified.

References

American Educational Research Association and National Council on Measurements Used in Education. (1955). *Technical Recommendations for Achievement Tests*. Washington, DC: National Education Association.

American Educational Research Association, American Psychological Association, and National Council on Measurement in Education. (1999). *Standards for Educational and Psychological Testing*. Washington, DC: American Educational Research Association.

American Psychiatric Association. (1999). *Dangerous Sex Offenders*. A Task Force Report of the American Psychiatric Association. Arlington, VA: Author.

American Psychological Association. (1954). *Technical Recommendations for Psychological Tests and Diagnostic Techniques*. Washington, DC: Author.

American Psychological Association. (1993). Guidelines for providers of psychological services to ethnic, linguistic, and culturally diverse populations. *American Psychologist, 58*, 45–48.

American Psychological Association. (2002). Ethical principles of psychologists and code of conduct. *American Psychologist, 57*, 1060–1073.

American Psychological Association. (2003). Guidelines on multicultural education, training, research, practice, and organizational change for psychologists. *American Psychologist, 58*, 377–404.

American Psychological Association, American Educational Research Association, and National Council on Measurement in Education. (1966). *Standards for Educational and Psychological Tests and Manuals.* Washington, DC: Author.

American Psychological Association, American Educational Research Association, and National Council on Measurement in Education. (1974). *Standards for Educational and Psychological Tests.* Washington, DC: American Psychological Association.

American Psychological Association, American Educational Research Association, and National Council on Measurement in Education. (1985). *Standards for Educational and Psychological Testing.* Washington, DC: American Psychological Association.

American Psychological Association Task Force on Evidence-Based Practice. (2005, 1 July). Retrieved from www.apa.org/practice/ebpreport.pdf.

Andrade, J., Vincent, G., and Saleh, F. (2006). Juvenile sex offenders: A complex population. *Journal of Forensic Sciences, 51*(1), 163–167.

Archer, J. (2004). Sex differences in aggression in real-world settings: A meta-analytic review. *Review of General Psychology, 8*(4), 291–322.

Aylwin, A., Reddon, J., and Burke, A. (2005). Sexual fantasies of adolescent male sex offenders in residential treatment: A descriptive study. *Archives of Sexual Behavior, 34*(2), 231–239.

Barbaree, H., Blanchard, R., and Langton, C. (2003). The development of sexual aggression through the life span: The effect of age on sexual arousal and recidivism among sex offenders. *Annals of the New York Academy of Science, 989,* 59–71; discussion 144–153.

Barbaree, H. E., and Marshall, W. L. (Eds.) (2006). *The Juvenile Sex Offender* (2nd ed.). New York: Guilford Press.

Barbaree, H. E., Marshall, W. L., and McCormick, J. (1998). The development of deviant behavior among adolescents and its implications for prevention and treatment. *Irish Journal of Psychology, 19*(1), 1–31.

Barbaree, H. E., Seto, M. C., Langton, C. M., and Peacock, E. J. (2001). Evaluating the predictive accuracy of six risk assessment instruments for adult sex offenders. *Criminal Justice and Behavior, 28,* 490–521.

Baumbach, J. (2002). Some implications of prenatal alcohol exposure for the treatment of adolescents with sexual offending behaviors. *Sex Abuse, 14*(4), 313–327.

Becker, J. V., Harris, C. D., and Sales, B. D. (1993). Juveniles who commit sexual offenses: A critical review of research. In: G. C. Nagayama-Hall, R. Hirschman, J. R. Graham, and M. S. Zaragoza (Eds.), *Sexual Aggression: Issues in Etiology, Assessment, and Treatment* (pp. 215–228). Washington, DC: Taylor & Francis.

Becker, J. V., Kaplan, M. S., and Tenke, C. E. (1992). The relationship of abuse history, denial, and erectile response of profiles of adolescent sexual perpetrators. *Behavior Therapy, 23,* 87–97.

Becker, J. V., Stein, R. M., Kaplan, M. S., and Cunningham-Rathner, J. (1992). Errection response characteristics of adolescent sex offenders. *Annals of Sex Research, 5*(2), 81–86.

Beech, A. R., Fisher, D. D., and Thornton, D. (2002). Risk assessment of sex offenders. *Professional Psychology: Research and Practice, 34*(4), 339–352.

Berliner, L., and Conte, J. R. (1990). The process of victimization: The victims' perspective. *Child Abuse & Neglect, 14,* 29–40.

Bischof, G. P., and Rosen, K. H. (1997). An ecological perspective on adolescent sexual offending. *Journal of Offender Rehabilitation, 26*(1/2), 67–88.

Bischof, G. P., Stith, L. S., and Whitney, L. M. (1995). Family environments of adolescent sex offenders and other juvenile delinquents. *Adolescence, 30*(117), 157–170.

Boar, D., Hart, S., Kropp, P., and Webster, C. (1997). *Manual for Sexual Risk—20.* Burnaby, British Columbia: Mental Health, Law and Policy Institute, Simon Fraser University.

Bonner, B. L., Marx, B. P., Thompson, T. J., and Michaelson, P. (1998). Assessment of adolescent sexual offenders. *Child Maltreatment, 3*(4), 374–383.

Bourke, M. L., and Donohue, B. (1996). Assessment and treatment of Juvenile sex offenders: An empirical review. *Journal of Child Sexual Abuse, 5*(1), 47–70.

Borum, R., Bartel, P. A., and Forth, A. E. (2005). Structured assessment of violence risk in youth. In: T. Grisso, G. Vincent, and D. Seagrave (Eds.), *Mental Health Screening and Assessment in Juvenile Justice* (pp. 311–323). New York: Guilford Press.

Breer, W. (1996). *The Adolescent Molester* (2nd edn.). Springfield, IL: Charles C Thomas.

Bremer, J. F. (2001). *The Protective Factors Scale: Assessing Youth with Sexual Concerns.* Presented at the plenary address presented at the 16th annual conference of the National Adolescent Perpetration Network, Kansas City, MO.

Broadhurst, R., and Loh, N. (2003). The probabilities of sex offender re-arrest. *Criminal Behavior and Mental Health, 13*(2), 121–139.

Broxholme, S., and Lindsay, W. (2003). Development and preliminary evaluation of a questionnaire on cognitions related to sex offending for use with individuals who have mild intellectual disabilities. *Journal of Intellectual Disabilities, 47*(6), 472–482.

Bunston, W. (2000). Working with adolescent and children who have committed sex offences (sic). *Australian and New Zealand Journal of Family Therapy, 21*(1), 1–7.

Butler, S., and Seto, M. (2002). Distinguishing two types of adolescent sex offenders. *Journal of the American Academy of Child and Adolescent Psychiatry, 41*(1), 83–90.

Caldwell, M. (2002). What we do not know about juvenile sexual reoffense risk. *Child Maltreatment, 7*(4), 291–302.

Camp, B. H., and Thyer, B. A. (1993). Treatment of adolescent sex offenders: A review of empirical research. *Journal of Applied Social Sciences, 17*(2), 191–206.

Caputo, A. A., Frick, P. J., and Brodsky, S. L. (1999). Family violence and juvenile sex offending: The potential mediating role of psychopathic traits and negative attitudes toward women. *Criminal Justice and Behavior, 26*, 338–356.

Child Pornography Prevention Act of 1996 (CPPA) P. L. 104–208, H.R. 3610 (H. Rept. 104–863).

Christodoulides, T. E., Richardson, G., Graham, F., Kennedy, P. J., and Kelly, T. P. (2005). Risk assessment with adolescent sex offenders. *Journal of Sexual Aggression, 11*, 37–48.

Committee on Ethical Guidelines for Forensic Psychologists. (1991). Specialty guidelines for forensic psychologists. *Law and Human Behavior, 15*, 655–666.

Craig, L., Browne, K., and Stringer, I. (2004). Comparing sex offender risk assessment measures on a UK sample. *International Journal of Offender Therapy and Comparative Criminology, 48*(1), 7–27.

Craig, L.A., Browne, K. D., Stringer, I., and Beech, A. (2005). Sexual recidivism: A review of static, dynamic and actuarial predictors. *Journal of Sexual Aggression, 11*(1), 65–84.

Craig, K. S., Smith, C. J., Hayler, B., and Pardie, P. L, (1999). *Juvenile Sex Offender Research Bibliography.* Office of Juvenile Justice and Delinquency Prevention. Retrieved on 19 December 2004, from http://odjp.ncjrs.org/juvsexoff/sexbibtopic.html.

Craissati, J., and McClurg, G. (1997). The challenge project: A treatment program evaluation for perpetrators of child sexual abuse. *Child Abuse and Neglect, 21*, 637–648.

Curnoe, S., and Langevin, R. (2002). Personality and deviant sexual fantasies: An examination of the MMPIs of sex offenders. *Journal of Clinical Psychology, 58*(7), 803–815.

Curwen, T. (2003). The importance of offense characteristics, victimization history, hostility, and social desirability in assessing empathy of male adolescent sex offenders. *Sex Abuse, 15*(4), 347–364.

Dalton, J., Ruddy, J., and Simon-Roper, L. (2003). Adolescent sex offenders' mean profile on the BASC Self-report of Personality. *Psychological Reports, 92*(3), 883–888.

Davis, G. E., and Leitenberg, H. (1987). Adolescent sex offenders. *Psychological Bulletin, 101*(3), 417–427.

de Almeida, R. M., Ferrari, P. F., Parmigiani, S., and Miczek, K. A. (2005). Escalated aggressive behavior: dopamine, serotonin, and GABA. *European Journal of Pharmacology, 5*; *526*(1–3), 51–64.

Dolan, M., and Fullam, R. (2005). Factors influencing treatment entry in sex offenders against children. *Medical Science and the Law, 45*(4), 303–310.

Doren, D. M. (2002). *Evaluating Sex Offenders: A Manual for Civil Commitments and Beyond.* Thousand Oaks, CA: Sage Publications.

Doren, D. M. (2004). Toward a multidimensional model for sexual recidivism risk. *Journal of Interpersonal Violence, 19,* 835–856.

Douglas, K., and Kropp, P. R. (2002). A prevention-based paradigm for violence risk assessment: Clinical and research applications. *Criminal Justice and Behavior, 21,* 617–658.

Douglas, K. S., and Skeem, J. L. (2005). Violence risk assessment: Getting specific about being dynamic. *Psychology, Public Policy, and Law, 11,* 347–383.

Dvoskin, J. A., and Heilbrun, K. (2001). Risk assessment and release decision-making: Toward resolving the great debate. *Journal of the American Academy of Psychiatry and the Law, 29,* 6–10.

Edens, J. F. (2001). Misuses of the Hare Psychopathy Checklist-Revised in court: Two case examples. *Journal of Interpersonal Violence, 16,* 1082–1093.

Efta-Breitbach, J., and Freeman, K. A. (2004a). Treatment of juveniles who sexually offend: An overview. *Journal of Child Sexual Abuse, 13,* 125–138.

Efta-Breitbach, J., and Freeman, K. A. (2004b). Recidivism and resilience in juvenile sexual offenders: An analysis of the literature. *Journal of Child Sexual Abuse, 13,* 257–279.

Emerick, R. L., and Dutton, W. A. (1993). The effect of polygraphy on the self-report of adolescent sex offenders: Implications for risk assessment. *Annals of Sex Research, 6*(2), 83–103.

Epperson, D. L., Kaul, J. D., and Huot, S. J. (1995, October). *Predicting Risk for Recidivism for Incarcerated Sex Offenders: Updated Development on the Sex Offender Screening Tool (SOST).* Poster session presented at the Annual Conference of the Association for the Treatment of Sexual Abusers, New Orleans, Louisiana.

Epps, K. J. (1997). Managing risk. In: M. S. Hoghughi, S. R. Bhate, and F. Graham (Eds.), *Working with Sexually Abusive Adolescents* (pp. 35–51). Thousand Oaks, CA: Sage Publications.

Erti, M. A., and McNamara, J. R. (1997). Treatment of juvenile sex offenders: A review of the literature. *Child and Adolescent Social Work Journal, 14*(3), 199–221.

Faller, K. C. (1989a). The role relationship between victim and perpetrator as a predictor of characteristics of intrafamilial sexual abuse. *Child & Adolescent Social Work Journal, 6,* 217–229.

Faller, K. C. (1989b). Why sexual abuse? An exploration of the intergenerational hypothesis. *Child Abuse & Neglect, 13,* 543–548. Faller, K., Birdsall, W., Henry, J., Vandervort, F., and Silverschanz, P. (2001). What makes sex offenders confess? An exploratory study. *Journal of Child Sexual Abuse, 10*(4), 31–49.

Faller, K., and Henry, J. (2000). Child sexual abuse: A case study in community collaboration. *Child Abuse and Neglect, 24*(9), 1215–1225.

Federal Bureau of Investigation. (1997). *Uniform Crime Reports for the United States.* Washington, DC: Author.

Federal Bureau of Investigation. (2005). *Uniform Crime Reports for the United States (preliminary).* Washington, DC: Author.

Firestone, P., Bradford, J., Greenberg, D., and Serran, G. (2000). The relationship of deviant sexual arousal and psychopathy in incest offenders, extrafamilial child molesters, and rapists. *Journal of the American Academy of Psychiatry and the Law, 28*(3), 303–308.

Firestone, P., Dixon, K., Nunes, K., and Bradford, J. (2005). A comparison of incest offenders based on victim age. *Journal of the American Academy of Psychiatry and the Law, 33*(2), 223–232.

Flora, R. (2001). *How to Work With Sex Offenders: A Handbook for Criminal Justice, Human Services, and Mental Health Professionals.* New York: Haworth Clinical Practice Press.

Freeman-Longo, R. E., Bird, S., Stevenson, W. F., and Fiske, J. A. (1995). *1994 Nationwide Survey of Treatment Programs & Models Serving Abuse-Reactive Children and Adolescent and Adult Sex Offenders.* Brandon, VT: Safer Society Program.

Frick, P. J. (2006). Developmental pathways to conduct disorder. *Child and Adolescent Psychiatric Clinics of North America, 15,* 311–331.

Frick, P. J., Cornell, A. H., Barry, C. T., Bodin, S. D., and Dane, H. E. (2003). Callous-unemotional traits and conduct problems in the prediction of conduct problem severity, aggression, and self-report of delinquency. *Journal of Abnormal Child Psychology, 31*, 457–470.

Frick, P. J., Stickle, T. R., Dandreaux, D. M., Farrell, J. M., and Kimonis, E. R. (2005). Callous-unemotional traits in predicting the severity and stability of conduct problems and delinquency. *Journal of Abnormal Child Psychology, 33*, 471–487.

Galli, V., Raute, N., McConville, B., and McElroy, S. (1998). An adolescent male with multiple paraphilias successfully treated with fluoxetine. *Journal of Child and Adolescent Psychopharmacology, 8*(3), 195–197.

Garlick, Y., Marshall, W. L., and Thornton, D. (1996). Intimacy deficits and attribution of blame among sexual offenders. *Legal and Criminal Psychology, 1*(Part 2), 251–258.

Gerardin, P., and Thibaut, F. (2004). Epidemiology and treatment of juvenile sexual offending. *Pediatric Drugs, 6*(2), 79–91.

Gollan, J. K., Lee, R., and Coccaro, E. F. (2005). Developmental psychopathology and neurobiology of aggression. *Developmental Psychopathology, 17*(4), 1151–1171.

Goodman, M., New, A., and Siever, L. (2004). Trauma, genes, and the neurobiology of personality disorders. In: R. Yehuda and B. McEwen (Eds.), *Biobehavioral Stress Response: Protective and Damaging Effects* (pp. 104–116). New York, NY: Academy of Sciences.

Gray, A., Pithers, W. D., Busconi, A., and Houchens, P. (1997). Children with sexual behavior problems and their caregivers: Demographics, functioning, and clinical patterns. *Sexual Abuse: A Journal of Research and Treatment, 9*, 267–290.

Gray, N. S., Brown, A. S., MacCulloch, M. J., Smith, J., and Snowden, R. J. (2005). An implicit test of the associations between children and sex in pedophiles. *Journal of Abnormal Psychology, 114*(2), 304–308.

Green, T., Ramelli, A., and Mizumoto, M. (2001). Patterns among sexual assault victims seeking treatment services. *Journal of Child Sexual Abuse, 10*(1), 89–108.

Greenfield, L. A. (1997). *Sex Offenses and Offenders: An Analysis of Data on Rape and Sexual Assault* (NCJ-163392). Washington, DC: Bureau of Justice Statistics.

Hagan, M. P., Gust-Brey, K. L., Cho, M. E., and Dow, E. (2001). Eight-year comparative analyses of adolescent rapists, adolescent child molesters, other adolescent delinquents, and the general population. *International Journal of Offender Therapy and Comparative Criminology, 45*, 314–324.

Hall, G. C. N. (1995). Sexual offender recidivism revisited: A meta-analysis of recent treatment studies. *Journal of Consulting and Clinical Psychology, 63*, 802–809.

Hall, H. V., and Poirier, J. G. (2001). *Detecting Malingering and Deception: Forensic Distortion Analysis* (2nd ed.). Boca Raton, FL: CRC Press.

Hanson, N. D., Randazzo, K. V., Schwartz, A., Marshall, M., Kalis, D., Frazier, R., Burke, C., Kershner-Rice, K., and Norvig, G. (2006). Do we practice what we preach? An exploratory survey of multicultural psychotherapy competencies. *Professional Psychology: Research and Practice, 37*, 66–74.

Hanson, R. K. (1997). *The Development of a Brief Actuarial Risk Scale for Sexual Offense Recidivism* (User Report 97-04). Ottawa, Ontario: Department of the Solicitor General of Canada.

Hanson, R. K., and Bussière, M. T. (1998). Predicting relapse: A meta-analysis of sexual offender recidivism studies. *Journal of Consulting and Clinical Psychology, 66*, 348–362.

Hanson, R. K., and Harris, A. J. R. (2001). A structured approach to evaluating change among sexual offenders. *Sexual Abuse: A Journal of Research and Treatment, 13*, 105–122.

Hanson, R. K., and Morton-Bourgon, K. E. (2005). The characteristics of persistent sexual offenders: A meta-analysis of recidivism studies. *Journal of Consulting and Clinical Psychology, 73*(6), 1154–1163.

Hanson, R. K., and Thornton, D. (2000). Improving risk assessments for sex offenders: A comparison of three actuarial scales. *Law and Human Behavior, 24*, 119–136.

Harris, G. T., Rice, M. E., and Quinsey, V. L. (1998). Appraisal and management of risk in sexual aggressors: Implications for criminal justice policy. *Psychology, Public Policy, and Law.* 4(1–2), 73–115.

Harris, G. T., and Rice, M. E. (2003). Actuarial assessment of risk among sex offenders. *Annals of the New York Academy of Sciences, 989,* 198–210.

Harris, G. T., Rice, M. E., Chaplin, T. C., and Quinsey, V. L. (1998). Dissimulation in phallometric testing of rapists. *Psychology, Public Policy, and Law,* 4(1–2), 73–115.

Harris, G. T., Rice, M. E., Quinsey, V. L., Lalumière, M. L., Harris, G. T., Quinsey, V. L., and Rice, M. E. (2003). A multisite comparison of actuarial risk instruments for sex offenders. *Psychological Assessment, 159,* 413–425.

Harnett, P., and Misch, P. (1993). Developmental issues in the assessment and treatment of adolescent perpetrators of sexual abuse. *Journal of Adolescence, 16,* 397–405.

Heilbrun, K. (1997). Prediction versus management models relevant to risk assessment: The importance of legal decision-making context. *Law and Human Behavior, 21,* 347–359.

Heilbrun, K. (2001). *Principles of Forensic Mental Health Assessment. Perspectives in Law and Psychology,* Vol. 12. New York: Kluwer Academic/Plenum Publishers.

Hilton, N. Z., Harris, G. T., and Rice, M. E. (2006). Sixty-six years of research on the clinical versus actuarial prediction of violence. *Counseling Psychologist, 34,* 400–409.

Hodges, K., and Wong, M. M. (1996). Psychometric characteristics of a multidimensional measure to assess impairment: The Child and Adolescent Functional Assessment Scale. *Journal of Child and Family Studies, 5,* 445–467.

Hoge, R. D., and Andrews, D. A. (1994). *The Youth Level of Service/Case Management Inventory and Manual.* Ottawa, Ontario: Department of Psychology, Carleton University.

Hughes, S. A., DeVille, C., Chalhoub, M., and Romboletti, R. (1992). The Rorschach human anatomy response: Predicting sexual offending behavior in juveniles. *Journal of Psychiatry and the Law, 20*(3), 313–333.

Hunter, J. A. (2000). *Understanding JSOs: Research findings and guidelines for effective treatment and management* (Juvenile Justice Fact Sheet.). Charlottesville, VA: Institute of Law, Psychiatry, and Public Policy.

Hunter, J. A., and Becker, J. V. (1994). The role of deviant sex arousal in juvenile sexual offending. *Criminal Justice and Behavior, 21*(1), 139–149.

Hunter, J. A., Becker, J. V., and Kaplan, M. S. (1995). The Adolescent Sexual Interest Card Sort: Test-retest reliability and concurrent validly in relation to phallometric assessment. *Archives of Sexual Behavior, 24*(5), 555–562.

Hunter, J. A., Becker, J. V., Kaplan, M., and Goodwin, D. W. (1991). Reliability and discriminative utility of the Adolescent Cognitions Scale for juvenile sexual offenders. *Annals of Sex Research, 4,* 281–286.

Hunter, J. A., Goodwin, D. W., and Becker, J. V. (1994). The relationship between phallometrically measured deviant sexual arousal and clinical characteristics in juvenile sexual offenders. *Behavioral Research and Therapy, 32*(5), 533–538.

Hunter, J. A., Hazelwood, R. R., and Slesinger, D. (2000). Juvenile-perpetrated sex crimes: Patterns of offending and predictors of violence. *Journal of Family Violence, 15*(1), 81–93.

Hunter, J. A., and Lexier, L. J. (1998). Ethical and legal issues in the assessment and treatment of juvenile sexual offenders. *Child Maltreatment, 3*(4), 219–228.

Ilacqua, G., Coulson, G., Lombardo, D., and Nutbrown, V. (1999). Predictive validity of the Young Offender Level of Service Inventory for criminal recidivism of male and female young offenders. *Psychological Reports, 84*(3), 1214–1218.

Ilgen, D. R., and Bell, B. S. (2001). Informed consent and dual purpose research. *American Psychologist,* 56, 1177.

Janus, E., and Walbek, N. (2000). Sex offender commitments in Minnesota: A descriptive study of second-generation commitments. *Behavioral Science and the Law, 18*(2), 343–374.

Johnson, T. C., and Feldmeth, J. R. (1993). Sexual behaviors: A continuum. In: E. Gill and T. C. Johnson (Eds.), *Sexualized Children: Assessment and Treatment of Sexualized Children and Children Who Molest* (pp. 39–52). Rockville, MD: Launch Press.

Kafka, M., and Hennen, J. (2002). A DSM-IV Axis I comorbidity study of males (n = 120) with paraphilias and paraphilia-related disorders. *Sex Abuse, 14*(4), 349–366.

Kaplan, M. S., Morales, M., and Becker, J. V. (1993). The impact of verbal satiation on adolescent sex offenders: A preliminary report. *Journal of Child Sexual Abuse, 2*(3), 81–88.

Kaermingk, K. L., Koselka, M., Becker, J. B., and Kaplan, M. S. (1995). Age and adolescent sexual offender arousal. *Sexual Abuse: A Journal of Research and Treatment, 7*(4), 249–257.

Kenny, D. T., and Press, A. L. (2006). Violence classifications and their impact on observed relationships with key factors in young offenders. *Psychology, Public Policy, and Law, 12*(1), 86–105.

Knight, R. A., and Prentky, R. (1993). Exploring characteristics for classifying juvenile sex offenders. In: H. E. Barbaree, W. L. Marshall, and S. M. Hudson (Eds.), *The Juvenile Sex Offender* (pp. 45–79). New York: Guilford Press.

Kolko, D., Noel, C., Thomas, G., and Torres, E. (2004). Cognitive-behavioral treatment for adolescents who sexually offend and their families: Individual and family applications in a collaborative outpatient program. *Journal of Child Sexual Abuse, 13*(3), 157–192.

Kraerner, B. D., Spielman, C. R., and Salisbury, S. B. (1997). In: B. K. Schwartz and H. R. Cellini (Eds.), *Juvenile Sex Offender Psychometric Assessment* (Vol. II, pp. 11–13). Kingston, NJ: Civic Research Institute.

Kropp, P. R., Hart, S. D., and Belfrage, H. (2004). *The development of the Brief Spousal Assault Form for the evaluation of risk (B-SAFER): A tool for criminal justice professionals* (Research and Statistics Division/Family Violence Initiative No. rr05fv-le). Ottawa, Canada: Department of Justice.

Kubik, E., and Hecker, J. (2005). Cognitive distortions about sex and sexual offending: A comparison of sex offending girls, delinquent girls, and girls from the community. *Journal of Child Sexual Abuse, 14*(4), 43–69.

Lalumière, M. L., Harris, G. T., Quinsey, V. L., and Rice, M. E. (1998). Sexual deviance and number of older brothers among sexual offenders. *Sexual Abuse: A Journal of Research and Treatment, 10,* 5–15.

Lalumière, M. L., Harris, G. T., Quinsey, V. L., and Rice, M. E. (2005a). Contextual and situational factors. In: M. L. Lalumière, G. T. Harris, V. L. Quinsey, and M. E. Rice (Eds.), *The Causes of Rape: Understanding Individual Differences in Male Propensity for Sexual Aggression* (pp. 143–157). Washington, DC: American Psychological Association.

Lalumière, M. L., Harris, G. T., Quinsey, V. L., and Rice, M. E. (2005b). Psychopathology. In: M. L. Lalumière, G. T. Harris, V. L. Quinsey, and M. E. Rice (Eds.), *The Causes of Rape: Understanding Individual Differences in Male Propensity for Sexual Aggression* (pp. 129–141). Washington, DC: American Psychological Association.

Langstrom, N., and Grann, M. (1999). The medico-legal status of young sex offenders: Forensic psychiatric evaluations in Sweden 1988–1995. *Behavioral Science and the Law, 17*(2), 219–225.

Lanyon, R. I. (2001). Psychological assessment procedures in sex offending. *Professional Psychology: Research and Practice, 32,* 253–260.

Laws, D. R., and Marshall, W. L. (2003). A brief history of behavioral and cognitive behavioral approaches to sexual offenders: Part 1. Early developments. *Sexual Abuse: A Journal of Research and Treatment, 15,* 275–292.

Letourneau, E., and Miner, M. (2005). Juvenile sex offenders: A case against the legal and clinical status quo. *Sex Abuse, 17*(3), 293–312.

Losada-Paisey, G. (1998). Use of the MMPI-A to assess personality of juvenile male delinquents who are sex offenders and nonsex offenders. *Psychological Reports, 83*(1), 115–122.

MacHovec, F., and Wieckowski, E. (1992). The 10FC Ten-Factor Continua of classification and treatment criteria for male and female sex offenders. *Medical Psychotherapy, 5,* 53–63.

Macpherson, G. J. D. (2003). Predicting escalation in sexually violent recidivism: Use of the SVR-20 and PCL: SV to predict outcome with non-contact recidivists and contact recidivists. *Journal of Forensic Psychiatry and Psychology, 14,* 615–627.

Marshall, W. L. (1996). Assessment, treatment, and theorizing about sex offenders: Developments during past twenty years and future directions. *Criminal Justice and Behavior, 23*(1), 162–199.

Marshall, W. L. (2000). The origins of sexual offending. *Trauma, Violence and Abuse, 1*(3), 250–263.

Marshall, W. L., and Fernandez, Y. M. (2001). Phallometry in forensic practice. *Journal of Forensic Psychology Practice, 1,* 77–87.

Marshall, W. L., Fernandez, Y. M., Serran, G. A., Mulloy, R., Thornton, D., Mann, R. E., and Anderson, D. (2003). Process variables in the treatment of sexual offenders: A review of the relevant literature. *Aggression and Violent Behavior, 8,* 205–234.

Marshall, W. L., and Laws, D. R. (2003). A brief history of behavioral and cognitive behavioral approaches to sexual offender treatment: Part 2 The modern era. *Sexual Abuse: A Journal of Research and Treatment, 15*(2), 93–120.

Marshall, W. L., and Marshall, L. E. (2000). The origins of sexual offending. *Trauma Violence and Abuse, 1*(3), 250–263.

Marshall, W. L., O'Sullivan, C., and Fernandez, Y. M. (1996). The enhancement of victim empathy among incarcerated child molesters. *Legal and Criminal Psychology, 1*(Part 1), 95–102.

Marshall, W. L., and Serran, G. A. (2000). Improving the effectiveness of sexual offender treatment. *Trauma Violence and Abuse, 1*(3), 203–222.

Marshall, W. L., Serran, G. A., Fernandez, Y. M., Mulloy, R., Mann, R. E., and Thornton, D. (2003). Therapist characteristics in the treatment of sexual offenders: Tentative data on their relationship with indices of behavior change. *Journal of Sexual Aggression, 9*(1), 25–30.

Marshall, W. L., Serran, G. A., Marshall, L. E., and Fernandez, Y. M. (2005). Recovering memories of the offense in "amnesic" sexual offenders. *Sexual Abuse: A Journal of Research and Treatment, 17,* 31–38.

Marshall, W. L., Ward, T., Mann, R. E., Moulden, H., Fernandez, Y. M., Serran, G., and Marshall, L. E. (2005). Working positively with sexual offenders: Maximizing the effectiveness of treatment. *Journal of Interpersonal Violence, 20,* 1096–1114.

McCarthy, J. (2001). Risk assessment of sexual offenders. *Psychiatry, Psychology and Law, 8,* 56–64.

McGrath, R. J., Cumming, G., and Holt, J. (2002). Collaboration among sex offender treatment providers and probation and parole officers: The beliefs and behaviors of treatment providers. *Sexual Abuse: A Journal of Research and Treatment, 14,* 49–65.

McMackin, R., Leisen, M., Cusack, J., LaFratta, J., and Litwin, P. (2002). The relationship of trauma exposure to sex offending behavior among male juvenile offenders. *Journal of Child Sexual Abuse, 11*(2), 25–40.

Miller, R. D. (1998). Forced administration of sex-drive reducing medications to sex offenders: Treatment or punishment. *Psychology, Public Policy, and Law, 4,* 175–199.

Monahan, J. (1996). The past twenty and the next twenty years. *Criminal Justice and Behavior, 23,* 107–120.

Monahan, J., Steadman, H., Silver, E., Applebaum, P., Robbins, P. C., Mulvey, E. P., Roth, L., Grisso, T., and Banks, S. (2001). *Rethinking Risk Assessment: The MacArthur Study of Mental Disorder and Violence.* New York: Oxford University Press.

Morenz, B., and Becker, J. (1995). The treatment of youthful sexual offenders. *Applied and Preventive Psychology, 4*(4), 247–257.

Murphy, W., DiLillo, D., Haynes, M., and Steere, E. (2001). An exploration of factors related to deviant sexual arousal among juvenile sex offenders. *Sex Abuse: A Journal of Research and Treatment, 13*(2), 91–103.

Myers, W., and Monaco, L. (2000). Anger experience, styles of anger expression, sadistic personality disorder, and psychopathy in juvenile sexual homicide offenders. *Journal of Forensic Science, 45*(3), 698–701.

National Council on Measurement in Education Ad Hoc Committee in the Development of a Code of Ethics. (1995). *Code of Professional Responsibilities in Educational Measurement.* Madison, WI: Author.

O'Brien, M., and Bera, W. W. (1986). *Adolescent sexual offenders: A descriptive typology.* Preventing sexual abuse: A newsletter of the National Family Life Education Network, pp. 1–4.

O'Halloran, M., Carr, A., O'Reilly, G., Sheerin, D., Cherry, J., Turner, R., Beckett, R., and Brown, S. (2002) Psychological profiles of sexually abusive adolescents in Ireland. *Child Abuse & Neglect.* 26(4), 349–370.

Pecker, J. V. (1990). Treating adolescent sexual offenders. *Professional Psychology: Research and Practice, 21*(5), 362–365.

Pecker, J. V., Harris, C. D., and Sales, B. D. (1993). Juveniles who commit sexual offenses: A critical review of research. In: G. C. Nagayam Hall, R. R. Hirschman, J. R. Graham, and M. S. Zaragoza (Eds.), *Sexual Aggression: Issues in Etiology, Assessment, and Treatment* (pp. 215–228). Washington, DC: Taylor & Francis.

Perez, L. G. (2003). Juvenile Courts in the United States. *Issues in Democracy.* Retrieved 10 April 2006 from http://usinfo.state.gov/journals/itdhr/0503/ijdf/frperez.htm.

Perry, G. P., and Orchard, J. (1992a). *Assessment and Treatment of Adolescent Sex Offenders.* Sarasota, FL: Professional Resource Press/Professional Resource Exchange.

Perry, G. P., and Orchard, J. (1992b). Sexual abuse prevention in a correctional center. In: L. VandeCreek, S. Knapp, and T. L. Jackson (Eds.), *Innovations in Clinical Practice: A Source Book* (Vol. 11, pp. 413–423). Sarasota, FL: Professional Resource Press.

Pharris, M., and Nafstad, S. (2002). Nursing care of adolescents who have been sexually assaulted. *Nursing Clinics of North America, 37*(3), 475–497.

Pithers, W., Becker, J. V., Kafka, M., Morenz, B., Schlank, A., and Leombruno, T. (1995). Children with sexual behavior problems, adolescent sexual abusers, and adult sex offenders: Assessment and treatment. *Review of Psychiatry, 14,* 779–818.

Pithers, W., and Gray, A. (1998). The science of sex offenders: Risk assessment, treatment, and prevention: The other half of the story: Children with sexual behavior problems. *Psychology, Public Policy, and Law, 4,* 200.

Poirier, J. G. (1984). *Assumptions in the Assessment and Management of the Dangerous Juvenile Offender.* Paper presented at the American Psychological Association, Divisions 29 and 42 Mid-Winter Convention, San Diego, CA.

Poirier, J. G. (1998). *Mobilizing Community Resources for the Identification and Treatment of Juvenile Sex Offenders.* Paper presented at the American Psychological Association, Divisions 29, 42, and 43 Mid-Winter Convention, San Diego, CA.

Poirier, J. G. (1999a). Violent juvenile crime. In: H. V. Hall and L. C. Whitaker (Eds.), *Collective Violence: Effective Strategies for Assessing and Interviewing in Fatal Group and Institutional Aggression* (pp. 183–212). Boca Raton, FL: CRC Press.

Poirier, J. G. (1999b). *Evaluation and Treatment of the Juvenile Sex Offender.* American Psychological Association, Division 42, Practice Information Clearinghouse of Knowledge, Niche Guide. Order information available at http://www.division42.org/MembersArea/PractDevelop/PICK42main.html.

Poirier, J. G. (1999c, August). The mental health/judicial interface: Taboo dynamics and collaboration strategies with the juvenile sex offender. In: T. R. Saunders (Chair), *Professional Collaboration in Independent Practice.* Symposium presented at the Annual Meeting of the American Psychological Association, Boston, MA.

Poirier, J. G. (2002). *Mentally Ill Offenders: An Imperative for Interdisciplinary Collaboration.* Paper presented at a symposium at the National Academies of Practice and Interdisciplinary Health Care Team Conference, Arlington, VA.

Poirier, J. G. (2005). *Evaluation and Treatment of the Juvenile Sex Offender.* American Psychological Association, Division 42, Practice Information Clearinghouse of Knowledge, Niche Guide.

Order information available at http://www.division42.org/MembersArea/PractDevelop/PICK42main.html.

Prentky, R. A., Harris, B., Frizzell, K., and Righthand, S. (2000). An actuarial procedure for assessing risk with juvenile sex offenders. *Sexual Abuse: A Journal for Research and Treatment, 12,* 71–93.

Prescott, D. (2004). Emerging strategies for risk assessment of sexually abusive youth: Theory, controversy and practice. *Journal of Child Sexual Abuse, 13*(3), 83–105.

Quinsey, V. L., Lalumière, M. L., Rice, M. E., and Harris, G. T. (1995). Predicting sexual offenses. In: J. C. Campbell (Ed.), *Assessing Dangerousness: Violence by Sexual Offenders, Batterers, and Child Abusers* (pp. 114–137). Thousand Oaks, CA: Sage Publications.

Quinsey, V. L., Harris, G. T., Rice, M. E., and Cormier, C. A. (1998). Fifteen arguments against actuarial risk appraisal. In: V. L. Quinsey, G. T. Harris, M. E. Rice, and C. A. Cormier (Eds.), *Violent Offenders: Appraising and Managing Risk* (pp. 171–190). Washington, DC: American Psychological Association.

Quinsey, V. L., and Harris, G. T. (1998). Sex offenders. In: V. L. Quinsey, G. T. Harris, M. E. Rice, and C. A. Cormier (Eds.), *Violent Offenders: Appraising and Managing Risk* (pp. 119–137). Washington, DC: American Psychological Association.

Quinsey, V. L., and Harris, G. T. (2006a). Clinical judgment. In: V. L. Quinsey, G. T. Harris, M. E. Rice, and C. A. Cormier (Eds.), *Violent Offenders: Appraising and Managing Risk* (2nd ed., pp. 61–81). Washington, DC: American Psychological Association.

Quinsey, V. L. and Harris, G. T. (2006b). Criticisms of actuarial risk assessment. In: V. L. Quinsey, G. T. Harris, M. E. Rice, and C. A. Cormier (Eds.), *Violent Offenders: Appraising and Managing Risk* (2nd ed., pp. 267–278). Washington, DC: American Psychological Association.

Quinsey, V. L., Harris, G. T., Rice, M. E., and Cormier, C. A. (1998). *Violent Offenders: Appraising and Managing Risk*. Washington, DC: American Psychological Association.

Quinsey, V. L., and Rice, M. E. (1993). The phylogenetic and ontogenetic development of sexual age preferences in males: Conceptual and measurement issues. In: H. E. Barbaree, W. L. Marshall, and S. M. Hudson (Eds.), *The Juvenile Sex Offender* (pp. 143–163). New York: Guilford Press.

Quinsey, V. L., Rice, M. E., and Harris, G. T. (1995). Actuarial prediction of sexual recidivism. *Journal of Interpersonal Violence, 10,* 85–105.

Quinsy, V. L., and Lalumière, M. (2001). *Assessment of Sexual Offenders against Children* (2nd ed.). Thousand Oaks, CA: Sage Publications.

Quist, R. M., and Matshazi, D. G. M. (2000). The child and Adolescent Functional Assessment Scale (CAFAS): A dynamic predictor of juvenile recidivism. *Adolescence, 35*(137), 181–192.

Rice, M. E., and Harris, G. T. (1995). Violent recidivism: Assessing predictive validity. *Journal of Consulting and Clinical Psychology, 63,* 737–748.

Rice, M. E., Harris, G. T., and Quinsey, V. L. (2002). The appraisal of violence risk. *Current Opinion in Psychiatry, 15,* 589–593.

Righthand, S., Prentky, R., Knight, R., Carpenter, E., Hecker, J., and Nangle, D. (2005). Factor structure and validation of the Juvenile Sex Offenders Assessment Protocol (J-SOAP). *Sex Abuse, 17*(1), 13–30.

Roberts, C. F., Doren, D. M., and Thornton, D. (2002). Dimensions associated with assessments of sex offender recidivism risk. *Criminal Justice and Behavior, 29,* 569–589.

Ross, J., and Loss, P. (1991). Assessment of the juvenile sex offender. In: G. D. Ryan and S. L. Lane (Eds.), *Juvenile Sexual Offending* (pp. 195–251). Lexington, MA: Lexington Books.

Ryan, G. (1997a). Sexually abusive youth. In: G. Ryan and S. Lane (Eds.), *Juvenile Sexual Offending: Causes, Consequences and Correction* (new and revised ed., pp. 3–9). San Francisco: Jossey-Bass.

Ryan, G. (1997b). Theories of etiology. In: G. Ryan and S. Lane (Eds.), *Juvenile Sexual Offending: Causes, consequences and correction* (new and revised ed., pp. 19–35). San Francisco: Jossey-Bass.

Schmidt S., and Pierce, K. (2004). What research shows about female adolescent sex offenders. National Center on Sexual Behavior of Youth Fact Sheet, No. 5, University of Oklahoma Health Sciences Center, Norman.

Schwartz, B. (2003). Overview of rehabilitative efforts in understanding and managing sexually coercive behaviors. *Annals of the New York Academy of Science, 989,* 360–383; discussion 441–445.

Schwartz, B. K., and Cellini, H. R. (1995). Female sex offenders. In: B. K. Schwartz and H. R. Cellini (Eds.), *The Sex Offender: Corrections, Treatment and Legal Practice* (pp. 5–1, 5–22). Kingston, NJ: Civic Research Institute.

Seabloom, W., Seabloom, M., Seabloom, E., Barron, R., and Hendrickson, S. (2003). A 14- to 24-year longitudinal study of a comprehensive sexual health model treatment program for adolescent sex offenders: Predictors of successful completion and subsequent criminal recidivism. *International Journal of Offender Therapy and Comparative Criminology, 47*(4), 468–481.

Seager, J., Jellicoe, D., and Dhaliwal, G. (2004). Refusers, dropouts, and completers: Measuring sex offender treatment efficacy. *International Journal of Offender Therapy and Comparative Criminology, 48*(5), 600–612.

Serran, G., Fernandez, Y., Marshall, W. L., and Mann, R. E. (2003). Process issues in treatment: Application to sexual offender programs. *Professional Psychology: Research and Practice, 34,* 368–375.

Serran, G. A., and Marshall, W. L. (2005). The "Memory Recovery Technique": A strategy to improve recall of offense-related details in men who commit sexual assaults. *Clinical Case Studies, 4,* 3–12.

Seto, M. C. (2005). Is more better? Combining actuarial risk scales to predict recidivism among adult sex offenders. *Psychological Assessment, 17*(2), 156–167.

Seto, M. C., Lalumière, M. L., and Blanchard, R. (2000). The discriminative validity of a phallometric test for pedophilic interests among adolescent sex offenders against children. *Psychological Assessment, 12,* 319–327.

Simourd, D. J., Hoge, R. D., Andrews, D. A., and Leschied, A. W. (1994). An empirically-based typology of male young offenders. *Canadian Journal of Criminology, 36*(4), 447–461.

Skeem, J., and Mulvey, E. (2002). Monitoring the violence potential of mentally disordered offenders being treated in the community. In: A. Buchanan (Ed.), *Care of the Mentally Disordered Offender in the Community* (pp. 111–142). New York: Oxford Press.

Smith, W. R., and Monastersky, C. (1986). Assessing juvenile sex offenders for risk for reoffending. *Criminal Justice and Behavior, 13*(2), 115–140.

Smith, T. B., Constantine, M. G., Dunn, T. W., Dinehart, J. M., and Montoya, J. A. (2006). Multicultural education in the mental health professions: A meta-analytic review. *Journal of Consulting Psychology, 53*(12), 132–145.

Smith, C. J., Craig, K. S., Loose, P., Brodus, S. M., and Kimmelman, C. (2002). *Juvenile Sex Offender Research Bibliography* (Office of Juvenile Delinquency and Prevention, Ed.). Retrieved 3/3/06, from http://ojjdp.ncjrs.gov/juvsexoff/JSOBib_2003.htm.

Snyder, H. N. (2000). Sexual Assault of Young Children as Reported to Law Enforcement: Victim, Incident, and Offender Characteristics (NCJ 182990). Washington, DC: Bureau of Justice.

Spataro, J., Moss, S. A., and Wells, D. L. (2001). Child sexual abuse: A reality for both sexes. *Australian Psychologist, 36,* 177–183.

Stickrod Gray, A., and Wallace, R. (1992). *Adolescent Sexual Offender Assessment Packet.* Brandon, VT: Safer Society Press.

Stroud, D., Martens, S., and Barker, J. (2000). Criminal investigation of child sexual abuse: A comparison of cases referred to the prosecutor to those not referred. *Child Abuse and Neglect, 24*(5), 689–700.

Turecki, G. (2005). Dissecting the suicide phenotype: The role of impulsive-aggressive behaviors. *Journal of Neuropsychiatry and Neurosciences, 30*(6), 398–408.

Vandiver, D. M. (2006). A prospective analysis of juvenile male sex offenders: Characteristics and recidivism rates as adults. *Journal of Interpersonal Violence, 21*(5), 673–688.

Vandiver, D. M., and Teske, R. J. (2006). Juvenile female and male sex offenders: A comparison of offender, victim, and judicial proceedings. *International Juvenile Offender Therapy and Comparative Criminology, 50*(2), 148–165.

Veneziano, C., Veneziano, L., LeGrand, S., and Richards, L. (2004). Neuropsychological executive functions of adolescent sex offenders and nonsex offenders. *Perceptual and Motor Skills. 98*(2), 661–674.

Vizard, E., Monck, E., and Misch, P. (1995). Child and adolescent sex abuse perpetrators: A review of the research literature. *Journal of Child Psychology and Psychiatry, 36*, 731–756.

Waite, D., Keller, A., McGarvey, E., Wieckowski, E., Pinkerton, R., and Brown, G. (2005). Juvenile sex offenders re-arrest rates for sexual, violent nonsexual and property crimes: A 10-year follow-up. *Sexual Abuse: A Journal of Research and Treatment, 17*(3), 313–331.

Ward, T., Hudson, S. M., Johnston, L., and Marshall. W. L. (1997). Cognitive distortions in sex offenders: An integrative review. *Clinical Psychology Review, 17*(5), 479–507.

Webster, C. D., Douglas, K. S., Eaves, D., and Hart, S. D. (1997). *HCR-20: Assessing Risk for Violence.* Burnbry, British Columbia: The Mental Health, Law, and Policy Institute of Simon Fraser University.

Weinrott, M. R., Riggan, M., and Frothingham, S. (1997). Reducing deviant arousal in juvenile sex offenders using vicarious sensitization. *Journal of Interpersonal Violence, 12*(5), 704–728.

West, A. G. (2001). Current approaches to sex-offender risk assessment: A critical review. *British Journal of Forensic Practice, 3*, 31–41.

Winick, B., and La Fond, J. Q. (2003). *Protecting Society from Sexually Dangerous Offenders: Law, Justice, and Therapy.* Washington, DC: American Psychological Association.

Witt, P. H., DelRusso, J., and Ferguson, G. (1996). Sex offender risk assessment and the law. *Journal of Psychiatry and the Law, 24*(3), 343–377.

Wollert, R. (2006). Low base rates limit expert certainty when current actuarials are used to identify sexually violent predators: An application of Bayes' theorem. *Psychology, Public Policy, and Law, 12*(1), 56–85.

Worling, J. R. (2004). The Estimate of Risk of Adolescent Sexual Offense Recidivism (ERASOR): Preliminary psychometric data. *Sexual Abuse: A Journal of Research and Treatment, 16*(3), 235–254.

Worling, J. R., and Curwen, T. (2000). Adolescent sexual offender recidivism: Success of specialized treatment and implications for risk prediction. *Child Abuse and Neglect, 24*(7), 965–982.

Zankman, S., and Bonomo, J. (2004). Working with parents to reduce juvenile sex offender recidivism. *Journal of Child Sexual Abuse, 13*(3), 139–156.

Zevitz, R. G., and Farkas, M. A. (2000a). Sex offender community notification: Managing high risk criminals or exacting further vengeance? *Behavioral Sciences and the Law*, 18, 375–391.

Zevitz, R. G., and Farkas, M. A. (2000b). Sex offender community notification: Examining the importance of neighborhood meetings? *Behavioral Sciences & the Law*, 18, 393–408.

Zevitz, R. G., and Farkas, M. A. (2000c). The impact of sex-offender community notification on probation/parole in Wisconsin. *International Journal of Offender Therapy and Comparative Criminology*, 44, 8–21.

Zussman, R. (1989). Forensic evaluation of the adolescent sex offender. *Forensic Reports, 2*, 25–45.

Legal References

Ashcroft v. Free Speech Coalition (00-795) 535 U.S. 234 (2002) 198 F.3d 1083, affirmed.

Children's Safety Act § 3132 109th Congress (2005).

Globe Newspaper Co. v. Superior Court 457 U.S. 596 (1982).

In re Gerald Gault, 387 U.S. (US Supreme Court AZ 1967).

In re Winship, 397 U.S. 358 (1970).

Jacob Wetterling Crimes Against Children and Sexually Violent Offender Act, 42 U.S.C. §§14071, et seq. (1994).

Juvenile Justice and Delinquency Prevention Act of 1974 (42 U.S.C. 5611 et seq.).

Kansas v. Hendricks, 117 S. Ct. 2072 (1997).

Kent v. United States, 383 U.S. 541 (1966).

Lawrence v. Texas (02-102) 539 U.S. 558 (2003) 41 S.

Miller v. California, 413 U.S. 15 (1973) 413 U.S. 15.

Mullaney v. Wilbur, 421 U.S. 684 (1975).

New Jersey v. T. L. O., 469 U.S. 325 (1985).

New York v. Ferber, 458 U.S. 747 (1982).

Parham v. J. R., 442 U.S. 584(1979).

People v. Michael Jackson, No. 1133603 (Superior Court of the State of California 2004).

State v. Limon, 32 Kan. App. 2d 369, 373, 83 P.3d 229 (2004).

Tarasoff v. Regents of the University of California, 551 p.2d 334 (1976).

Part III

Civil-Forensic Evaluation

Evaluation of Effort in Independent Neuropsychological Evaluations for Workers' Compensation Cases

15

LYLE E. BAADE

University of Kansas School of Medicine, Wichita, Kansas

ROBIN J. HEINRICHS

University of Kansas School of Medicine, Wichita, Kansas

DANA K. SOETAERT

University of Kansas School of Medicine, Wichita, Kansas

Contents

Synopsis of Cases

Tom, a supervising engineer for a manufacturing company, was driving between job sites when his car was struck by another vehicle. He sustained a serious head injury that caused posttraumatic amnesia for 5 days after the accident. Tom was referred for an independent neuropsychological evaluation (INE) as part of his workers' compensation case. A clinical interview, neuropsychological test battery, and behavioral observations revealed that Tom had residual cognitive and emotional deficits secondary to the injury. Tom returned to work where he reported struggling to meet the demands of his previous position. Tom received the recommended treatment. The report was later used in a successful civil suit against the driver of the other vehicle.

Lisa, a nurse in a juvenile detention center, was escorting one detainee to his room when a second detainee of the facility struck her in the face and shoulders. She sustained, at most, a mild head injury with no posttraumatic amnesia. Lisa was referred for an INE as part of her workers' compensation case. Her evaluation included a review of records, clinical interview, neuropsychological testing, and behavioral observations. Inadequate effort during testing resulted in invalid test scores on most elements of the neuropsychological test battery. This and other factors led to the conclusion that she was feigning neurocognitive deficits. Lisa did not return to work. The evaluation led to termination of her workers' compensation benefits.

Introduction

In this chapter, we will illustrate the use of multiple sources of information to evaluate patient effort in the context of claims covered under workers' compensation law. A combination of record review, behavioral presentation, specific tests of effort, and embedded effort indices from routinely administered tests such as the Wechsler Adult Intelligence Scale—III (WAIS-III) is recommended to identify inadequate patient effort. This approach to the identification of effort is demonstrated through two sharply contrasting clinical cases.

The first is an individual with a serious unequivocally established brain injury who put forth good effort during neuropsychological testing. His scores demonstrate mild-to-moderate neurocognitive deficits in current functioning compared to his premorbid ability. The second case involves an individual with an injury of questionable severity whose effort was poor and who produced test scores, which if accepted as valid, would be commensurate with neurocognitive impairment far more severe than that in the first case. The premorbid ability and educational level in the two cases are similar. The claim of impairment by the patient with poor effort was supported by the reports of psychologists and psychiatrists who conducted earlier evaluations, but it was not supported by our evaluation.

Workers' Compensation

Workers' compensation laws are designed to provide employees with medical benefits and fixed monetary awards when they have been injured or disabled in an accident on-the-job or as the result of occupational disease. If a worker dies as the result of a work-related accident or illness, there are provisions within the law to provide benefits to the worker's dependents. Another function of workers' compensation laws is to protect employers by limiting the amount that an injured employee can recover from the employer. Protection is also provided to fellow workers for whom liability, in most cases, is eliminated. In essence, the worker forfeits the common law right to sue in exchange for a fixed benefit. In exchange for ensuring these benefits, the employer receives immunity from further liability. For most workers, their state workers' compensation statutes establish the rules and regulations that cover the process and their benefits. However, for federal employees and those employed in some aspects of interstate commerce, federal statutes apply.

An important goal of workers' compensation laws is elimination of the need for and expense of unregulated litigation. This goal leads to distinct features that make providing services for parties in a workers' compensation case different from other types of litigation. Although specifics differ from state to state and between state and federal programs, there are some common themes. First, workers' compensation is a "no fault" system; questions of negligence or fault are not an issue. Second, a worker cannot recover pain and suffering as a result of a workers' compensation injury. In spite of these conditions, disputes may arise during negotiation of a workers' compensation incident, some of which lead to requests for INEs.

A request for a neuropsychological evaluation usually involves evaluation of the severity of the injury and recommendations for treatment or evaluation of the severity of residual impairment from the injury. The independent neuropsychological examination is performed to assist the parties in determining diagnosis and prognosis. Diagnosis amounts to establishing whether the worker sustained neurocognitive or psychological impairment. However, the question of prognosis involves additional statements of what the injured worker may or may not be capable of doing currently, and how that differs from what the worker was or was not able to do prior to the injury or illness.

The end toward which the workers' compensation system works is to make the worker whole; thus, treatment is a primary focus of the system. Workers' compensation regulations may include limitations in the worker's choice of treatment providers and associated limitations in the type of treatment that can be provided. This can be a cause for dispute during a workers' compensation negotiation, and the issue of appropriate medical treatment may lead to a request for an INE.

An important difference between workers' compensation cases and common lawsuits is the manner in which they are adjudicated. In workers' compensation cases, disputes are heard by an administrative law judge or by a workers' compensation board. During these hearings, medical care providers, including psychologists who have conducted independent neuropsychological examinations, are often asked to provide testimony regarding injuries and necessary treatment. Testimony may be given either in court or through a deposition. Most often, testimony from medical care providers is provided through depositions taken prior to the hearing and read by the administrative judge or hearing officer.

Payment for an INE is often different from payment for other forensic work. In workers' compensation cases, state statute may dictate the amount of fee an independent evaluator may collect for evaluations, depositions, and testimony. Because of this, the neuropsychologist providing services in the area of workers' compensation must be knowledgeable of the state or federal system that provides coverage for the referred worker. Prior to accepting the case, the neuropsychologist should obtain a letter of agreement stipulating the compensation rate, the amount of time authorized for the evaluation, and any anticipated depositions or testimony.

The Independent Neuropsychological Evaluation

An INE in a workers' compensation case will include a review of records, a clinical interview, and the administration, scoring, and interpretation of neuropsychological tests.

Review of Records

The review of records is an important aspect of this process; however, the records provided to the neuropsychologist in a workers' compensation case are often limited. Typically, these include only reports of the accident, reports of any medical and psychological evaluations conducted since the accident, and reports of any treatment provided as a result of the accident. It is helpful to review education and employment records as they can be used in establishing the individual's level of premorbid functioning. The insurance company or the attorneys in the case, however, seldom provide these records, so the neuropsychologist will have to request these. The parties may or may not comply with such requests. In case the request is refused, the report should reflect this fact and any limitations it posed for the examiner in forming his opinion.

It is also valuable to obtain psychological records from preinjury assessments or treatments. Like the education and employment records, these records are often not provided unless specifically requested by the evaluator. When requesting such records, it is important to ask specifically that the raw test data be provided in addition to any reports that were written. Raw data provide an opportunity to score unreported scales or indices of relevance including the embedded indices of effort discussed in the section "Validity." The raw data also give the examiner the opportunity to inspect for the occasional error in scoring or in reporting of scores from which erroneous conclusions might have been drawn. Additionally, examination of raw data can help identify blatantly slanted or biased reporting by other evaluators.

Preinjury test scores can serve as a baseline of premorbid functioning for the worker, thus providing the independent evaluator the opportunity to judge the extent to which the data collected in current testing support the findings of injury, the severity of injury, or both. Baseline scores also allow the examiner to assess whether the individual's performances have been consistent within and across tests, and consistent within and across neurocognitive domains (Lezak, Howieson, Loring, Hannay, and Fischer, 2004; Strauss, Sherman, and Spreen, 2006).

In a similar fashion, data from postinjury evaluations provide an opportunity to examine change in and consistency of performance since the injury. When found, dramatic negative changes in performance may be explainable by changes in effort. For example, in a recent case, the claimant earned a general memory score of 118 (Wechsler Memory Scale—Third Edition [WMS-III]) when tested shortly after her injury, but on an evaluation a year later, she earned a general memory score of 84. There had been no interim injuries, and medical evaluations revealed no neurological damage associated with her injury. Therefore, this drop in scores is likely due to a lack of effort during the second evaluation.

When requesting records, it is helpful to ask for records of any premorbid medical treatments and evaluations. These records may be reviewed to establish a baseline of the individual's medical condition prior to the injury. Evidence of preexisting medical conditions that might affect test performances or provide alternative explanations for test performances may be found. In the absence of this evidence, the performance deficits might be attributed to the claimed injury.

Clinical Interview

The clinical interview in an INE for workmen's compensation is much like the standard clinical evaluation interview. The goal is not to form a therapeutic alliance but to obtain diagnostic information. Early in the interview, one should obtain the worker's report of the facts of the accident or toxic exposure and the extent of the injury, a description of diagnostic and treatment procedures received, and the worker's perception of the course of his or her recovery. It is helpful to begin with open-ended questions that permit the worker to talk about the accident and to outline the extent and severity of related neurocognitive and emotional problems. Attitudes toward work, coworkers, and employers may become obvious in this process. Specific questions should be used later to assess for the presence or absence of any neurological or psychological symptoms that might be reasonably expected from the injury. Additional questions should address neurocognitive domains in which no residuals are to be expected on the basis of the known facts. Some worker feigning deficits may endorse unexpected and nonexistent injuries in this process. This process can be extended to inquiries about outlandish imaginary symptoms that would point to feigning if endorsed.

The interviewer should obtain a history including relevant aspects of each of the following areas: (1) general medical, (2) psychosocial, (3) educational, (4) employment, (5) military, and (6) legal. In addition, a personal and family history of psychiatric treatment and neurological disease and a personal history of head injury should be obtained. Behavioral observations of the worker during the interview are important, and any discrepancies between behavior and known patterns of brain functioning should be noted. A mental status examination is also a part of the interview process. On the basis of observation of the worker during the interview and answers given to questions during the interview, the examiner can form a preliminary idea of the patient's current neurocognitive and emotional well-being.

The INE differs from the standard clinical evaluation in some important ways. Because the psychologist is typically hired by one of the two parties in the dispute, or by the trier of fact, the worker is not the psychologist's client or patient and does not have the same rights to confidentiality as other nonforensic clients have. This means that the worker will not be informed by the psychologist of results of the assessment and will not receive treatment from the evaluating psychologist. Instead, the content of the interview, the results of the neuropsychological tests, and the psychologist's opinion of the records will all be reported to the hiring attorney. The report is usually then shared with the opposing counsel and the trier of fact. All notes and records of the evaluation are subject to being subpoenaed and to disclosure through the proceedings. Either side in the dispute may choose to depose the expert or to call the expert to testify before the trier of fact. Because of the unique nature of this relationship, it is prudent to have the worker sign an informed consent that covers the above points. We obtain such consent at the beginning of the initial interview.

Behavioral Presentation

Just as behavior during the interview is an important variable to note, the worker's behavior during neuropsychological testing reveals much about the worker's deficits and effort. At present, there is no established schema of the interpretation of behavioral observations or established reliability or validity. Unusual behavior alone should not be used to invalidate a testing session but can alert a clinician to look more closely at symptom validity indices and personality testing such as the Minnesota Multiphasic personality inventory—Second Edition (MMPI-2). It is important to have good notes detailing the worker's behavior during the evaluation process. We have observed that patients in our clinic with poor effort may present with a slower rate of progress through testing, a more dramatic demeanor, inconsistencies in behavior, less effort exerted in recovery, and less observable effort during testing. In addition, they require more energy from the examiner in the process of eliciting optimal performance. The following are descriptions of behavioral patterns that can be used as cautionary measures, which, when present, direct the clinician to look closely at other indices of effort.

Rate of Progress

One behavior that we have seen in patients who provide inadequate effort in testing is slowed progression through testing. Patients with poor effort may take twice as long as the average patient to complete the same amount of testing. Although seriously impaired patients also take longer than average, the patients with poor effort take more time than do neurocognitively deficient patients with adequate effort.

Dramatic Demeanor

Another type of behavior that has been demonstrated in our clinic by patients with poor effort is a dramatic demeanor. Patients will make angry or tearful statements such as "I can't take it anymore" or "This is terrible" in the middle of a test. We have also had patients who made dramatic attempts to behave like a child. They often demonstrate incongruent and odd body posturing and movements such as sitting in odd positions, holding their limbs in unusual postures, and moving in stilted or awkward ways. These postures and movements may be inconsistently present. Observation of the patient during entry and exit to the clinic and when on break may reveal this inconsistency. One patient who was dramatic in his expressive language impairments in the testing room conversed fluently with the examiner about a football game while walking down the hall on break. The language impairment returned when they reentered the testing room.

Effort in Activities of Living

Some patients incur an injury and continue to function as best as they can, even if in a simpler way, whereas other patients simply quit trying after an accident. Patients' reports of the effort they exert in their daily life can be a cue to the effort they deliver during testing. After a head injury, some individuals work hard to regain functional capacity and others do not. Individuals who do not put much effort into their rehabilitation are likely to approach neurocognitive testing in a similar manner and provide insufficient effort.

Observable Effort

To some extent, an examiner can observe how hard a patient is trying during testing. In some cases, it is clear that a patient is not providing much effort at all, whereas in other cases, a patient will give as much effort as is possible, whether it elicits a good or a bad performance. In yet others, we see dramatic, exaggerated expressions of effort that are ultimately not productive and actually represent poor effort.

Examiner Effort

The effort required from the examiner to elicit the best testing performance is an important factor in evaluating patient effort. When a patient is not providing adequate effort, it is necessary for the examiner to provide additional effort. This may take the form of a greater frequency of positive reinforcement or reassurance. When a client is providing inadequate effort, an examiner is likely to find it necessary to be more vigilant regarding the patient's mood state and task focus. In general, the examiner works harder and expends more energy eliciting patient performance.

The Neuropsychological Test Battery

The heart of an INE is the administration, scoring, and interpretation of the neuropsychological test battery. Tests are selected to address each of the major neuropsychological domains, and only tests with established reliability and validity are used. It is helpful to utilize a standard battery and adjust it according to the characteristics of the worker, the known facts of the injury or illness, and the need to replicate portions of previous evaluations. The principal elements in the battery used in our clinic are as follows:

> WAIS-III
> WMS-III
> Halstead–Reitan Neuropsychological Test Battery (HRNB)
> Delis–Kaplan Executive Function System (D-KEFS): selected subtests
> Wechsler Test of Adult Reading (WTAR)
> MMPI-2
> Two-symptom validity indicators or other freestanding tests of effort such as
>> Victoria Symptom Validity Test (VSVT)
>> Green's Word Memory Test (WMT)
>> Test of Memory Malingering (TOMM)

This group of tests assesses the neurocognitive domains of fund of knowledge, attention, memory, problem solving, executive functions, visual spatial abilities, sensory and motor functions, and emotion. It also includes specific tests and embedded indices of effort or response bias.

The Report

The INE report for a workers' compensation case differs little from a well-formulated civil litigation report. The basic elements include clear identification of the worker, the referral source, the reason for referral, and the data sources used in forming the opinion. The report also has segments that discuss the presenting problem, mental status, neuropsychological test results, personality test results, and a summary and conclusion. Within the INE report, diagnoses, prognoses, and treatment recommendations should be clearly stated. In many cases, there is an expectation that the worker's disability will be rated according to the American Medical Association's *Guides to the Evaluation of Permanent Impairment* (AMA, 2001), which is in its fifth edition. However, other guides to impairment exist and regulations may set forth which of these disability-rating systems must be used. In Kansas, for example, the law specifies that disability ratings will be performed according to an earlier edition of the AMA guides. The quantitative description of disability should include the clearest possible statement of how the patient's neurocognitive or emotional disorders are likely to impact that worker's ability to perform his or her old job and beyond that his or her general employability. Statements should clarify whether the impairment is continuously present, how it interacts with other neurocognitive variables, how it interacts with environmental variables, and how the combination affects the worker's ability to perform his or her work.

Some neuropsychologists routinely append raw data to INE reports, whereas others do so only in certain cases (Freides, 1993; Naugle and McSweeny, 1995; Freides, 1995; Matarazzo, 1995). For evaluators who choose not to include raw data in the report, the concern is often one of ensuring that only a trained and qualified neuropsychologist reviews it. Neuropsychologists who append raw data do so with the understanding that within a workers' compensation case, the opposing counsel will routinely retain a neuropsychologist who will review such data. It is our practice to append a summary of major test scores to forensic reports. Discussion of the issue of the release of raw data to the courts is available in the studies by Lees-Haley and Courtney (2000a, 2000b), Shapiro (2000), Tranel (2000), Barth (2000), and Lees-Haley, Courtney, and Dinkins (2005).

Validity

Test validity is central to the neuropsychological evaluation. The first step to establishing valid testing is choosing valid tests to administer. Valid tests in this sense are those meeting traditional standards of test reliability and validity, both of which are reported in test manuals and the literature. Beyond the simple fact of responsible professional practice, clinicians practicing in the forensic arena should be familiar with the literature supporting the reliability and validity of the tests they use because attorneys often ask questions in this area.

After selecting valid tests to administer to the worker, the evaluator must ensure that the test scores produced are valid in terms of the worker's effort. If a patient has sensory impairment, is illiterate, is experiencing fatigue, or experiences a medical event such as a seizure during testing, the scores are likely invalid. Aside from these types of situations, valid test scores are obtainable only when the worker answers questions and performs tasks to the best of his or her ability. If the individual fails to provide his or her best effort, the test results will not accurately reflect his or her abilities.

Patients can invalidate testing in a variety of ways and for a variety of reasons. They may answer questions in a careless manner, marking answers without first thinking about them. Careless responding can produce challenges in interpretation as it may reflect a lack of interest in the outcome, a long-standing personality style, or an apathy secondary to frontal lobe damage. If haphazard responding is detected, the evaluator should ascertain why the patient has not given careful thought to his or her answers.

Other patients attempt to present themselves in the most favorable light and answer questions accordingly. During neurocognitive testing, attempts to present oneself in a positive light are of little consequence because patients can only perform as well as their abilities allow. However, "faking good" does impact assessment of personality or emotional disturbance. Tests that function as our primary measures such as the MMPI-2 are self-report measures. Fortunately, the MMPI-2 provides validity scales to detect this response bias.

Patients attempting to portray themselves as more impaired than they really are present the most frequently encountered response bias seen in neurocognitive testing. Like the other types of response biases, "faking bad" also impacts assessment of personality and emotional disturbance.

Psychologists have a responsibility to examine each test performance as to its accuracy as a measure for the individual who has taken the test. When a test is invalid, the reason for the invalidity should be stated clearly and the scores should not be reported in a manner that would lead anyone to assume they reflect the worker's true ability. Invalid results should not be excused and nor should a report contain a full discussion of the invalid scores. The evaluator's opinion should be limited to statements such as "the tests are invalid due to a lack of effort on the part of worker," and the evaluator should clearly state that he or she is unable to provide a diagnosis based on test performance. If all or most of the test data are invalid, it is likely that much of the information given by the patient during the interview and statements attributed to the patient in the medical records are less than truthful and at best unreliable. Consequently, the evaluator should also report that information and conclusions drawn from the interview are based primarily on worker report and are, at best, questionable.

Psychologists who perform INEs should become familiar with and follow the growing body of literature on patient effort. Writings regarding insufficient patient effort are found under the terms "motivation," "response bias," and "malingering." Symptom validity testing (SVT) is an important subset of insufficient effort measures (Pankratz, 1979; Millis, 2004). SVTs involve a forced-choice format (Pankratz, 1998) that allows for the computation of the probability that the patient is performing below chance. Within this format, if the individual has a 50% probability of choosing a correct answer by chance alone, they should get 50% of the test items correct without any knowledge or ability in the area being assessed. If the worker scores significantly below 50% correct, it is likely that he or she knew the correct answers and purposely chose to answer incorrectly (Bianchini, Mathias, and Greve, 2001). Putting it another way, it takes as much knowledge to score at the 10% level as it does to earn a score at 90%.

This methodology is sound, and a positive finding on an SVT is accepted as a definitive indication of malingering (Slick, Sherman, and Iverson, 1999). However, most SVT tasks are simple and studies show that many individuals who provide insufficient effort score above chance (Hiscock, Branham, and Hiscock, 1994; Greiffenstein, Baker, and Gola, 1994;

Guilmette, Hart, and Guiliano, 1993). Insufficient effort can be effectively detected with cutoffs on the SVT set above 50%. The use of such cutoffs has also been applied to other stand-alone tests of effort such as the WMT (Green, 2003; Green, Iverson, and Allen, 1999) and the TOMM (Tombaugh, 1996; Rees, Tombaugh, Gansler, and Moczynski, 1998).

Although we encourage the use of SVTs and other stand-alone tests, it is also advisable to examine effort on tests like the WAIS-III. To this end, "embedded indices" of effort have been devised for a number of commonly used psychological tests. These indices allow the evaluator to evaluate whether the worker was providing his or her best effort on a test designed to measure problems in other domains. Embedded indices are helpful in determining whether the individual's effort was consistent within and across testing sessions. Embedded indices, such as some SVTs, use cutoff scores to classify effort as insufficient (see Appendix P for a listing of stand-alone validity tests and embedded validity indices).

To ensure the diagnostic utility of a cutoff score, the sensitivity and specificity of the cutoff must be considered. Sensitivity is the proportion of persons with poor effort who score below the cutoff (Larrabee, 2005). If sensitivity is low, it is not possible to identify a large number of people who are providing insufficient effort. Specificity is the proportion of persons with good effort who score above the cutoff. If specificity is low, honest responders are erroneously labeled as having poor effort. Since we want to avoid this misclassification of honest test takers, the goal in setting a cutoff is to attain the highest degree of sensitivity while keeping the specificity as close to 100% as possible. Although the higher the specificity, the better, tests with specificity above 90% are generally considered adequate for clinical application (Boone and Lu, 2003; Greve and Bianchini, 2004).

Another way to assess a cutoff score is to evaluate the positive predictive power (PPP) of the cutoff. The PPP is the probability that a person with insufficient effort will be identified by the cutoff (Larrabee, 2005), with an ideal PPP = 1.00. When researching and choosing a test of effort to be used in an evaluation, the psychologist should examine the literature documenting the specificity, sensitivity, and PPP of each index being considered and choose tests according to their performance. For more information on this type of measurement, readers may refer to *Compendium of Neuropsychological Tests: Administration, Norms and Commentary* (Strauss et al., 2006).

At present, there is an impressive array of stand-alone and embedded measures of effort. To apply all of them is time consuming and unnecessary and leads to the impression of fishing expedition. We recommend administering at least one stand-alone effort measure during each test administration session as an aid in evaluating the effort the patient provided that day. Additionally, an embedded effort measure should be calculated for each major test administered, such as the WAIS-III, WMS-III, Wisconsin Card Sort Test (WCST), or California Verbal Learning Test—Second Edition (CVLT-II). In our clinic, embedded indices are chosen for a patient on the basis of neurocognitive tests to be administered, research on sensitivity and specificity, and characteristics of the patient such as the level of sophistication (lack of effort by very bright patients is unlikely to be detected by simplistic measures).

When conducting an INE, the neuropsychologist should use effort indices to answer two distinct questions. The first question is whether the patient is malingering. This use of effort tests has been the primary focus in the literature. The second question is whether a specific test score is valid and should be accepted as a true (valid) reflection of the patient's neurocognitive or emotional status. Short of diagnosing a patient as a malingerer, there are times when a test score is clearly invalid and should not be reported in any manner where it might be mistakenly used as an accurate measure of neurocognitive or emotional status.

Lack of effort can be caused by a number of situations including apathy from a frontal lobe injury, a desire for attention, or an intention to deceive. The *Diagnostic and Statistical Manual of Psychiatric Disorders* (DSMIV-TR) provides diagnoses that differ according to the motivation behind the lack of effort or feigning of symptoms. If the feigned performance is associated with the wish to claim the sick role, the appropriate diagnosis is a factitious disorder. But if the feigned performance is associated with an attempt to obtain monetary or other concrete rewards, the diagnosis is malingering. In assigning a diagnosis of malingering, the evaluator should become familiar not only with the DSMIV-TR criteria but also with the proposed guidelines for diagnosing malingering set forth by Slick et al. (1999).

In these guidelines, Slick et al. present criteria for possible, probable, and definite malingered neurocognitive dysfunction (MND). The criteria are organized under the following lettered items: (a) presence of a substantial external incentive, (b) evidence from neuropsychological tests, (c) evidence from self-report, and (d) behaviors meeting necessary criteria from (b) or (c) that are not fully accounted for by psychiatric, neurological, or developmental factors.

The diagnosis of *definite MND* can only be made if evidence of a definite negative response bias exists. A definite negative response bias is defined as a below-chance performance on one or more forced-choice format tests (SVTs) (see Slick et al., 1999 for criteria).

The diagnosis of *probable MND* can be made if at least two pieces of neuropsychological testing evidence such as that provided by embedded indices are present or if at least one type of evidence from the patient's self-report is present (see Slick et al., 1999 for criteria).

The diagnosis of *possible MND* can be made if evidence of feigning is present in the patient's self-report. It can also be made if the criteria for definite or probable MND are failed because there is evidence of neurological or psychiatric conditions that might explain the finding (see Slick et al., 1999 for criteria).

Two Contrasting Case Studies

The Referral Incidents

Tom. Tom is a 45-year-old Caucasian male born and raised in the Midwest. He earned a master's degree in business administration while working full-time as an engineer. In his capacity as the supervising engineer of a multiproject team for a local manufacturing company, Tom was driving between job sites when his car was struck by another vehicle traveling at high speed on an unpaved road. The accident was a driver's side impact collision during which Tom was restrained by a seat belt. Tom was hospitalized for 7 days following the accident and then transferred to a rehabilitation hospital.

Tom was able to return to work after several months. Although he returned to work in his former capacity, at the time of referral he had received no review of his work performance since his accident. His personal evaluation was that he was performing below his previous level. Following his stay at the rehabilitation hospital, he had not received any psychological or psychiatric follow-up. His primary care physician and his neurosurgeon made the referral supported by his workers' compensation attorney on the basis of appropriateness of treatment. An attorney representing Tom in a lawsuit against the driver of the vehicle that struck him, later joined in the referral.

Lisa. Lisa is a 46-year-old Caucasian female with a master's degree in nursing. She was raised and currently lives in the Midwest. At the time of her injury, Lisa was working for a local health care system with an assignment to a juvenile detention center. The injury occurred as Lisa was escorting back to his room a patient whom she had treated following a conflict with another resident. As she was leaving the room, another resident of the detention facility assailed her. The individual struck her several times about the face and shoulders with his fists before other employees intervened. Lisa was taken to an immediate care clinic the same day and seen by a physician who treated and released her. She attempted to return to work a few days later but found this to be too traumatic.

During the 3 years following the incident, two psychiatrists, four psychotherapists, a chiropractor, a massage therapist, and Lisa's family physician have treated her. In addition to superficial injury to her face, she claims posttraumatic stress disorder (PTSD) and a closed head injury. She claims that the head injury resulted in severe memory loss and loss of previously acquired educational skills including her reading, math, and writing skills. An attorney for her employer referred Lisa with a question of the appropriateness of treatment.

Review of Medical Records

Tom's Records
Immediate Action
Tom was extricated from his vehicle by an emergency response team. He was stabilized in a cervical collar on a spine board and transported by ambulance to a trauma center and classified as a level 1 trauma patient. Upon arrival at the trauma center, he was moving all extremities, but not following commands. Because of his agitation and decreased oxygen saturation levels, Tom was intubated shortly after his arrival. His Glasgow Coma Scale on arrival at the hospital was 5. He received a computed tomography (CT) scan of the head and was diagnosed with a basilar skull fracture and bilateral frontal parenchymal hemorrhages.

The patient sustained several collateral injuries including a laceration to the spleen, which required intervention. He was found to have a rib fracture and lacerations to the face, head, and forearm, all of which required suturing.

Initial Treatment
Tom was hospitalized in the surgical intensive care unit for 7 days. He initially experienced a great deal of confusion, but this improved rapidly. At discharge to a rehabilitative hospital, he was awake and alert, but still disoriented. He was able to follow commands and his neurological examination was otherwise normal. He remained at the rehabilitative hospital for 25 days.

Length of Posttraumatic Amnesia
Tom had no recollection of details surrounding his accident or the 5 days after the incident. His last recall before the accident was leaving the parking lot.

Additional Information
Approximately 2 months postinjury, the patient fell during what was believed to be a seizure and experienced a nondisplaced orbital fracture. The CT scans at this time showed the basilar skull fracture to be healing.

Lisa's Records

Immediate Action

Lisa initially experienced a mild nosebleed but did not lose consciousness. As dictated by her employer's emergency preparedness plan, her coworkers drove her to an immediate care clinic within 3 hours of her attack. The clinic record states that she was alert, oriented times three, and in no acute distress. She was able to respond to commands and she demonstrated no difficulties with verbal or other cognitive tasks. A Glasgow Coma Scale was not computed. The medical record specifically stated that there was no abrasion, although edema was noted on the left side of the face. A full examination was conducted and no other injuries were noted. Her neurological examination was unremarkable. Lisa was released and in no acute distress. Assessment at discharge: "contusion, left face."

Imaging

Lisa had a complete set of facial x-rays, which were unremarkable. Additionally, CT scans with and without contrast of the head and maxillofacial areas were obtained and read as negative for any fracture, brain abnormalities, or bleeding abnormalities.

Initial Treatment

Lisa was advised to ice her face and to take acetaminophen and ibuprofen as needed for the pain. As a precaution, she was given standard head injury instructions. She was released and advised to return to the clinic for follow-up in 3–4 days for a re-examination and a release to return to work.

Length of Posttraumatic Amnesia

Lisa did not experience any posttraumatic amnesia and was able to relay pertinent details of the assault to the initial treating physician. However, in subsequent interviews, Lisa's subjective description of the attack included increasing periods of loss of consciousness and difficulty recalling details of the attack, other than "the look on his (her attacker's) face."

Follow-Up

Four days after assault (at the risk management department), Lisa was described as "oriented times three, ambulating without disparity, some tenderness over the left superior and inferior orbit, but no swelling or ecchymosis is noted; and left temporal and parietal area discomfort where she states she was hit." She was released to return to work.

At 1 week, imaging studies were repeated and again reported as negative. A neurologist was consulted for the continuing headaches. Additional assessments included electroencephalogram (EEG), a third set of CT images of the head, an magnetic resonance imaging (MRI) of the head, and a positron emission tomography (PET) scan, all of which were negative.

Further Treatments

Lisa continued to complain of headaches, dizziness, fatigue, depression, and flashbacks of the incident and never returned to work. The consulting neurologist suggested an underlying psychiatric diagnosis such as depression or PTSD as the cause of the headaches and recommended that Lisa see a psychiatrist or psychologist, indicating that inpatient psychiatric treatment might be necessary.

The following treatments were provided:

Language therapy
Individual psychotherapy

Eye movement desensitization reprocessing (EMDR) therapy
Massage therapy (myofascial release techniques and deep tissue massage)
Narcotic pain medications for "severe head pain"
A psychiatrist-recommended 3-month trip to visit her family to help her heal from the
   assault, approved and paid for by her employer

A review of treatment notes indicated that the claimant was cooperative and responsive to her various therapists so long as sessions consisted primarily of listening to recitations of claimant's problems, deep relaxation training, or other techniques that might be viewed as comfortable or comforting. However, when the patient was pushed to "work" in therapy sessions, she became resistant and requested a new therapist. After an initial session, she refused the EMDR recommended by two of her therapists.

Review of Psychological Records

Tom. Prior to referral to our clinic, Tom had received no psychological testing or treatment.

Lisa. Lisa's psychological assessment and treatment records were extensive. Her first evaluation was performed by a neuropsychologist and included the MMPI-2, WAIS-III, Wide Range Achievement Test, Third Edition (WRAT-III), Trail Making Test, Memory Assessment Scales (MAS), and the Halstead Category Test. In addition, two specific tests of effort, the TOMM and the validity indicator profile (VIP), were administered.

The report indicated that the MMPI-2 was invalidated due to an L scale elevation (T = 81). VRIN, TRIN, F, F(B), Fp, and K were all within normal limits. Upon receiving the raw data, our clinic scored the FBS and found it to be 30.

No formal estimate of premorbid intelligence was provided within the report. Our clinic computed a Barona formula and obtained an estimated full-scale IQ score of 107. On the WAIS-III, Lisa earned a full-scale IQ score of 75, a score significantly below her estimated premorbid IQ. Results from memory testing were a MAS global memory index of 68. Achievement testing showed WRAT-III scores of 88, 81, and 98, respectively, for reading, spelling, and math. Lisa made 127 errors on the category test including one error on the first subtest, and her trail-making-test scores were both below the fifth percentile.

No embedded indices of effort were computed, but Lisa failed the TOMM with scores of 28, 35, and 34, respectively, on the first, second, and retention trials. Similarly, both the verbal and nonverbal subtests of the VIP were reported as invalid and the neuropsychologist offered the opinion that Lisa was malingering.

We had no specific criticisms of this evaluation but point out that calculation of embedded indices may have strengthened the neuropsychologist's argument. Although we requested raw data from the evaluation, we were provided with only a data summary that contained insufficient information to compute major embedded indices on such tests as the WAIS-III, WMS-III, or category test. It is of note that a 32-point drop in IQ as a result of a mild (at most) head injury is highly improbable. Her academic achievement scores, ranging from the 10th to the 45th percentile, are also improbable given her master's degree in nursing.

At the request of her attorney, Lisa received a new evaluation 3 months later from a clinical psychologist. This psychologist administered the MMPI-2, the TOMM, and the structured interview of reported symptoms (SIRS). The raw data from the MMPI-2 show the F(B), Fp, and L scales to be elevated with T scores of 97, 73, and 81, respectively. In his report, the psychologist indicated that the MMPI-2 was invalid and could not be interpreted further and suggested that Lisa "may be attempting to present herself as more impaired than she actually is." As with the first evaluation, the evaluator did not score the FBS; however, with the raw data, our clinic scored the FBS and found it to be 31. Lisa's TOMM scores for this second administration were within normal limits, a change from the first-time administration. But the second SVT, the SIRS (a test designed to measure malingering of psychotic and other psychiatric symptoms; Rogers, Bagby, and Dickens, 1992) showed three primary scores in the "probable feigning" range, representing a 97.9% likelihood of feigning.

The patient also completed the Millon Clinical Multiaxial Inventory—3rd Edition (MCMI-III) for the first two evaluations. This test lacks the full range of validity scales available on the MMPI-2, and Lally (2003), on the basis of a survey of forensic psychology diplomats, found scant support for its use in forensic evaluations including evaluations of malingering. The test is in our opinion unacceptable in terms of our ability to assess the validity of a patient's responses. We take the position that in the presence of an invalid MMPI-2, the MCMI-III should also be considered invalid. It is noteworthy, however, that on the two MCMI-III administrations, the patient presented herself in contrastingly different ways. In the first administration, she presented herself as a virtuous individual with relatively few problems of any type, and on the second evaluation as an individual with significant impairment. This inconsistency in responding also brings into question the validity of the MCMI-III tests taken by her.

Unfortunately, the second evaluating psychologist, having reviewed the evidence of malingering from the first evaluation and the similar evidence from his own evaluation, stated, "Lest we too quickly believe that Lisa's complaints are untrue, the overall data from this evaluation substantiate a diagnosis of PTSD." This evaluation formed the primary basis for treatment of Lisa over the next 2 years. During this 2-year period, two psychiatrists, two clinical social workers, and two clinical psychologists treated Lisa for her PTSD. No progress was made during any of these treatments, and each practitioner, with the exception of her second psychiatrist, eventually terminated the client due to her resistance to follow their treatment recommendations.

An educational evaluation of the patient was requested by one of the psychiatrists because he viewed the patient's failure to make gains in psychotherapy as secondary to her traumatic head injury. The educational psychologist administered the Woodcock–Johnson—III (WJ-III), CVLT-II, and several lesser known tests. As a result of this evaluation, Lisa was diagnosed not only with PTSD but also with an acquired attention deficit hyperactivity disorder (ADHD) (moderate to severe), acquired dyslexia (severe), acquired severe auditory memory disorder, and acquired learning disorders in the areas of reading, writing, and math. The educational evaluator reported that these problems "stem from the physical trauma of her assault and the resulting damage to her brain."

No tests of effort or symptom validity were administered during this educational evaluation, and embedded indices for the CVLT-II were not computed. In his report, the evaluator described the patient's limited responses on the CVLT-II as reflecting a recency and primacy pattern that "is the active strategy of a person trying hard to remember." With the raw data from the CVLT-II, our clinic calculated embedded indices of effort and found her performance on the CVLT-II to be invalid. In contrast to the evaluator's opinion of Lisa's effort as a "pounding of words into memory and making them stick using high-level thinking," a more appropriate assessment of Lisa's effort would be inadequate effort.

The INE completed for Lisa by our clinic was requested at the behest of the same concerned psychiatrist who remained convinced that the patient had incurred a traumatic brain injury. Because he believed that this injury was responsible for her lack of progress in treatment and because the goal of workmen's compensation law is to restore the worker to "whole(ness)," this psychiatrist requested an INE expecting that it would document her brain injury and allow for continued treatment and compensation of the patient.

Behavioral Presentation

During the current INE, the behavior during testing of each worker was documented. Anomalies in behavior can serve to alert the evaluator to closely examine the effort given by the worker throughout the evaluation.

Rate of Progress

Tom was observed during testing sessions to have impaired processing speed. On many tests, the latency to response time was longer than the norm as he focused on the material. Even with this slowed processing, Tom completed a full neuropsychological assessment battery in 9 hours spread over 3 days. Although some patients seen in our clinic complete the same amount of testing in 8 hours spread over 2 days, Tom's total testing time is within the usual range of completion times among patients administered this battery in our clinic. Breaks are a necessary part of testing, but they add time to the length of the testing sessions. Tom requested no breaks during testing, but was accepting of examiner-initiated breaks in testing. During a break, he walked around the clinic and had some water before returning to the testing room.

Lisa's progress through a similar neurocognitive battery was slow. She completed the battery in 15 hours spread over 4 days. Lisa took longer to complete each individual test and requested breaks, frequently saying that she felt too ill to continue. To get Lisa through testing, the examiner refused to give breaks as often as requested, but gave at least one break every hour. During these breaks, Lisa remained in the testing room and laid her head on the table.

Dramatic Demeanor

Tom incurred a severe head injury involving a loss of consciousness and a 7-day stay in the hospital, but his description of the incident and of his losses was not particularly dramatic. He described the details of the accident only but talked a little more frequently about the changes since the accident. Tom demonstrated no dramatic verbalizations and no dramatic or incongruent behaviors during testing. Although Tom perseverated in talking about the changes in his ability to function, he spoke about specific changes. For example, he found he could not drive with minor distraction such as the radio, a fact that impacted his relationship with his adolescent children. This type of perseveration on specific deficits is something we often see in patients who have sustained brain damage.

Lisa wept frequently, spoke out loud, "God, please help me" and "It is so horrible," frequently complained that the room and the situation were making her ill, and lay her head and upper body down on the table. Lisa also asked the examiner questions like "Why is this happening to me?" and "Don't you know that this is making me more depressed?" Throughout testing, Lisa spoke about the injury that had occurred 2 years earlier with great emotion. In an effort to move forward with testing, the examiner acknowledged the patient's feelings but did not encourage elaboration. In many patients, this will decrease the focus on and verbalizations about a topic, but with Lisa, this elicited increased dramatization. The patient seemed to try harder to involve the examiner in her behavior.

Effort in Activities of Living

Tom returned to work at his old position where he said he was experiencing cognitive changes including memory deficits, decreased processing speed, expressive and receptive language problems, problems multitasking, and problems shifting set. In spite of this, Tom continued to go to work and struggled throughout the day to perform his job and not let anyone know that he was having problems. He developed compensatory behaviors to help him function.

Lisa made a single brief attempt to return to work. When her employer offered to move her to a clinic or hospital and a service of her choice, she reported that she was unable to return to work. Lisa states that she does not leave her house very often and does not do things for herself anymore. If her husband cooks, she will eat, but she has little energy for activities in which she formerly engaged. According to her report and that of her husband, Lisa exerts little effort in her daily life at home, provides little effort toward improving her functioning, and has developed no compensatory behaviors.

Observable Effort

Tom worked hard throughout testing. Deficits were apparent, but he compensated in these areas as best he could and, if anything, increased his effort during these tasks. His behavior was commensurate with his descriptions of how he has functioned at work since the injury.

Lisa was confronted by the examiner regarding her slow performance and directed to try her hardest. The admonishment extended to the fact that not doing so would be detected and would reflect poorly on her and make identification of problems impossible. This prompted tears and a request for a break, but no change in performance. Later in testing, she was again confronted and told that she would have to keep coming back to our office until she completed all of the tests that were outlined at the beginning of the evaluation. Lisa became angry and insisted that testing resume immediately so that she could "get it done." From this point on, her dramatic verbalizations decreased and she proceeded through testing at a quicker pace. Her effort did not, however, improve. Her demeanor remained angry for the time required to complete testing.

Inconsistencies in Behavior

Tom was very consistent in his presentation during the three testing sessions.

Lisa reported during intake that she had problems of dizziness and imbalance. When the examiner was in the room with her, she would stand up, laboriously grab her head and comment on her dizziness. She also exhibited an unsteady gait. When Lisa was unaware of the examiner's presence, her gait and balance were unremarkable.

Examiner Effort

Tom was easy to work with. Although he perseverated on thoughts and had to be redirected periodically, he was self-motivated and responded readily to encouragement and support.

Lisa's dramatic verbalizations, continuous requests for breaks, and crying necessitated greater than normal examiner effort. In addition to several direct confrontations in which Lisa was encouraged to work harder, the examiner frequently had to prompt Lisa to go on to the next item. After Lisa was found to be asleep during self-administered portions of the examination, the examiner monitored subsequent self-administered tests, and frequent prompts to complete the task were provided. Lisa was given some positive reinforcement; however, this decreased her effort, so the examiner remained more guarded or distant than would ordinarily be expected.

Test Battery and Results

The discussion of test results that follows is focused exclusively on the topic of effort. In preparing this discussion, we calculated, for illustrative purposes, many of the possible embedded indices that could be applied in these cases. Not all of these embedded indices were calculated when these cases were evaluated in our clinic. In practice, we select and calculate a limited number of effort indices such that for each domain of assessment, an embedded indicator evaluates the patient's effort. The evaluator should use caution when calculating increasing numbers of embedded indices as this may not increase the specificity of diagnosis, and with each added indicator comes increased measurement error (Millis and Volinsky, 2001).

Estimated Premorbid Ability

The Barona formula (Baron, Reynolds, and Chastain, 1984), the WTAR (2001), and ACT scores (Baade and Schoenberg, 2004) were used to estimate Tom's premorbid abilities, and the Barona formula and WTAR were used to estimate Lisa's premorbid abilities.

Tom. In Tom's case, the Barona returned an estimated full-scale IQ of 118, the WTAR combining demographic and WTAR ability estimate was 121, and the ACT-based estimate was 116. When assessing patients with injuries as severe as Tom's head injury, there is always a possibility that language skills have been impacted by the injury. Since the WTAR uses language skills to provide an estimate, this estimate may be suppressed by the patient's language deficits and may not adequately capture the patient's premorbid abilities. In Tom's case, however, the three estimates are close to one another and the WTAR was actually the highest estimate.

Lisa. For Lisa, the Barona provided an estimated full-scale IQ of 117. Our request for educational records was denied; therefore, an ACT-based estimate could not be calculated. Additionally, a WTAR score could not be calculated because her performance on the WTAR was too poor. The WTAR manual indicates that if the WTAR score earned by the patient is more than 20 points below the WTAR score predicted on the basis of the patient's education, a valid IQ prediction cannot be made (WTAR, 2001). When this discrepancy occurs in an individual with known language impairment, a discrepancy of this size is likely due to the language deficit. In the absence of a language deficit, this type of discrepancy is suggestive of inadequate effort on the WTAR. At present, no research has been published regarding this hypothesis; thus, such discrepancies without language impairment should not be used as forensic evidence of incomplete effort. On the contrary, this type of a discrepancy should be noted and is a reason to closely examine other indices of effort.

General Cognitive Ability

The WAIS-III was administered to both patients as the primary measure of current general cognitive ability.

Tom. Tom earned verbal, performance, and full-scale IQ scores of 118, 113, and 117, respectively. These are commensurate with his estimated premorbid functioning. Further examination of the WAIS-III revealed interpretable discrepancies among the four factor scores with processing speed being below the other three. Computation of embedded indices for the WAIS-III (Greiffenstein et al., 1994; Greve, Bianchini, Mathias, Houston, and Crouch, 2003; Iverson and Tulsky, 2003) revealed no problems with test validity.

Lisa. On the WAIS-III, Lisa earned verbal, performance, and full-scale IQ scores of 83, 74, and 77, respectively. The full-scale IQ score is thus 40 points below her estimated premorbid ability. Although some drop in IQ is associated with head injury, a drop of this magnitude in the absence of obviously observable neurological sequelae is improbable (Jones and Rizzo, 2004; Donders, Tulsky, and Zhu, 2001). There are studies that support emotional conditions such as depression, anxiety, and PTSD with a drop in IQ; however, such drops are in general rather small (Mittenberg, DiGuilio, Perrin, and Bass, 1992; Binder, 1997). Again it is clear that Lisa's effort was likely inadequate. Likewise, her reliable digit span (Greiffenstein et al., 1994) score of 6 falls below the recommended cutoff of 7, adding further evidence of invalid effort during the WAIS-III. The reliable digit span is especially interesting because it has been demonstrated to be unaffected by pain (Etherton, Bianchini, Ciota, and Greve, 2005). Other embedded indices based on digit span such as those proposed by Iverson and Tulsky (2003) also raise questions regarding the validity of Lisa's WAIS-III. One effort indicator for the WAIS, the discriminant function approach (Mittenberg, Theroux-Fichera, Zielinski, and Heilbronner, 1995; Greve et al., 2003), does not classify this test protocol as invalid. This fact notwithstanding, the invalid reliable digit span, disparity from premorbid levels, and disparity relative to injury form the weight of the evidence and strongly indicate that the scores on the WAIS-III should be classified as invalid.

When a patient presents during the clinical interview with complaints of serious problems in language abilities, as did Lisa, we often administer the Raven Standard Progressive Matrices (RSPM) as means of measuring ability while minimizing the demands for language comprehension and expression. The RSPM contains five sets of problems of increasing difficulty, but the sets overlap each other in terms of difficulty. This provides opportunities for validity assessment in ways unavailable in other neuropsychological tests (Raven, Court, and Raven, 1992). On the five sets, Lisa correctly answered eight, three, three, six, and one of the problems, respectively, earning a total score of 21, which fell below the norms. Although she correctly answered six of the problems in the relatively difficult fourth set, she answered only three items correctly in the much easier second set, raising logical questions about her effort on the test. Additional comparison of item difficulty can be made within sets with the expectation that a patient will answer the easiest items and miss the most difficult ones. This is not the case with Lisa, who missed the easiest items and answered correctly six of the difficult items in the fourth set. This analysis is based on a simple logic, but can be used to support observations of gross lack of effort. However, a formula to detect malingering on the RSPM has been developed and cross-validated (Gudjonsson and Shackleton, 1986; McKinzey, Podd, Krehbiel, and Raven, 1999). This approach compares performance on the first 24 items to performance on the last 24 items and provides cutoffs for each total score. The formula results in a score of 3 for Lisha and this is well below the cutoff value of 10 established for a total score of 21. Lisa's performance is invalid, and with the specificity of this index at .95, there is only a 5% chance that this index would wrongly accuse her of invalid effort. The sensitivity of the index is .74.

Executive Functioning

Tom and Lisa were given the category test and the following selected subtests from the D-KEFS: trails, verbal fluency, design fluency, sorting, and tower. Additionally, Lisa was given the WCST.

Tom. Tom had 27 errors on the category test, only slightly higher than the 22 errors predicted by his IQ (Strauss et al., 2006). His scaled scores on the primary measures from the administered D-KEFS subtests ranged from 8 to 15 with only 4 out of 16 scores being at the mean or below.

Lisa. Lisa had 74 errors on the category test. This score, if valid, would suggest significant brain impairment. Effort indices proposed by Tenhula and Sweet (1996) were computed and all but the difficult item index were passed. Although the difficult item index was failed, it has poor specificity at .81, and by itself should serve only as a caution. Her scaled scores on the primary measures from the administered D-KEFS subtests ranged from 1 to 6, and the tower had to be discontinued due to Lisa's reports of fatigue. We are unaware of any available effort indices that have been developed for the D-KEFS, but there is research establishing a score at or below the fifth percentile as indicative of possible malingering on the Halstead Reitan trail-making test (Iverson, Lange, Green, and Franzen, 2002; Ruffulo, Guilmette, and Willis, 2000; Binder, Kelly, Villanueva, and Winslow, 2003). The trail-making test is similar to the D-KEFS trails subtest, but overgeneralization should be avoided. This caution notwithstanding, Lisa's scaled scores of 1 on the D-KEFS trails warrant concern. Lisa's D-KEFS scores are less than what would be expected, given her educational attainments and estimated premorbid abilities, and her performance is worse than what would be expected, given the degree of her reported head injury.

On the WCST, Lisa was able to come up with only one category, took 34 trials to complete that one category, and made surprisingly few perseverative errors. Although she had no "failures to maintain set," this reflects the fact that she never had enough sequentially correct answers to establish set, except once when she completed a category solution. In short, her responses were random. Among embedded indices developed for the WCST, those by King, Sweet, Sherer, Curtiss, and Vanderploeg (2002) and Suhr and Boyer (1999) look for failure to maintain set as an indicator of insufficient effort. Because Lisa never established set, these indices did not invalidate her performance. The embedded indicator developed by Bernard, McGrath, and Houston (1996) did, however, find her test performance to be invalid; it utilizes the number of categories and number of preservative errors produced.

Memory

The primary memory test administered to both Tom and Lisa was the WMS-III.

Tom. The WMS-III articulates some of Tom's deficits. Although his index scores on each of the basic WMS-III scales are within the average range, they are close to 25 points below his WAIS-III full-scale IQ score. Given the severity of his injury, this is not an unusual finding. Use of the embedded indicators (Langeluddecke and Lucas, 2003; Glassmire, Bierley, Wisniewski, Greene, Kennedy, and Date, 2003) produced acceptable results.

Lisa. By contrast, Lisa earned a general memory index score of 83, a score consistent with her invalid WAIS-III IQ score, but inconsistent with the known facts of her injury and with her premorbid ability. Indices developed to detect malingering on the WMS depend in large part on failures on recognition memory (Langeluddecke and Lucas, 2003; Glassmire et al., 2003), and Lisa's performances in these areas, while poor, were not poor enough to register as invalid. Taken alone, the WMS-III scores would be accepted as valid. It is noted, however, that if they were found to be valid within the battery, they indicate impairment that is grossly disproportionate relative to Lisa's known injury. This alone should cause the evaluator to examine the rest of her testing for signs of invalid effort.

Motor and Sensory Performance

In assessing the somatosensory and motor areas, scores were obtained for each patient on grip strength, finger-tapping speed, grooved pegboard, finger agnosia, fingertip number writing, tactile form recognition, and the Tactual Performance Test (TPT).

Tom. In accordance with the *Revised Comprehensive Norms for an Expanded Halstead–Reitan Battery* (Heaton et al., 2004), all of Tom's scores were within normal limits. There was, however, a clear pattern wherein his right (dominant)-hand performances were mildly impaired relative to those with his left. This pattern held true for grip strength, finger tapping, grooved pegboard, and tactile form recognition. On the TPT, this pattern of impairment was not reflected, and on finger agnosia and fingertip number writing, there were no errors. This overall pattern of motor and sensory performances is consistent with the presence of mild deficits from a closed head injury.

Lisa. Lisa earned scores at or below the second percentile in her performances on fingertip number writing, tactile form recognition, tapping, grip strength, and grooved pegboard. She made only one error on finger agnosia, but the TPT was discontinued due to her escalating reports of fatigue and distress. With respect to right/left comparisons, the data were mixed, with the right (dominant) hand superior to the left on fingertip number writing, grip strength, and grooved pegboard, but the left hand superior to the right on tactual form recognition and finger tapping. In terms of embedded indices of effort, Strauss et al. (2006) summarize attempts to establish indices of malingering for the motor and sensory tests. Although studies of these motor and sensory tests have established that malingerers often suppress their performances on individual tests, there are no established indices that are acceptable for forensic work. Thus, very poor performances on these tests such as those seen by Lisa should be a signal for the evaluator to examine the rest of the test protocol carefully for evidence of poor effort or malingering. With Lisa, we found it improbable that her scores reflected her abilities on these simple tasks.

Halstead–Reitan Battery

The Halstead–Reitan Battery was included in the evaluation of each patient. Individual tests from this battery have been discussed in other sections, but the entire Halstead–Reitan Battery can be assessed for effort using an embedded index developed by Mittenberg et al. (1996). When the Mittenberg index was computed for Tom's performances on the Halstead–Reitan Battery, it showed him to be providing adequate effort and the test deemed valid. The same index could not be computed for Lisa because of her failure to complete the TPT.

Adjustment and Personality

Both patients completed the MMPI-2 as a measure of personality and psychopathology.

Tom. The validity scales on Tom's MMPI-2 profile were all within normal limits and suggest that he answered the questions on this test in a straightforward and honest manner.

The clinical profile primarily indicates that Tom was depressed and that this depression was accompanied by a lack of energy and social isolation. This interpretation is consistent with the reports of Tom and his wife during the interview. In addition to the MMPI-2, Tom and his wife were asked to complete the appropriate versions of the Frontal Systems Behavior Scale (FrSBe). Both the patient and his wife indicated on the FrSBe that Tom is much more apathetic and demonstrates less executive functioning ability now compared with his behavior prior to the accident. His wife reports greater changes than does Tom.

Lisa. Because Lisa complained of reading difficulties, she was provided with an audio version of the MMPI-2 as well as the print version. Her MMPI-2 clinical profile was invalid because of elevations on scales L, S, and FBS. In spite of the fact that the MMPI-2 profile is invalid, it is important to review all validity scales to assess response style. The variable response indicator (VRIN) scale was within normal limits, demonstrating that the patient read and comprehended the test items well enough to answer different questions with similar content in a consistent manner. This means that her answers to the test questions were made with understanding, and thus, elevations on other validity scales may be considered the result of purposeful responding. The L scale on Lisa's profile was high enough to indicate that she was being dishonest in her responses by claiming unrealistically positive attributes. The elevation on scale S adds weight to the position that the patient attempted to present herself as virtuous and responsible, and having few or no moral flaws. On the contrary, the elevation on the FBS scale indicates that the patient was also endorsing numerous problems. In the case of the FBS scale, the endorsement of problems is that which would be expected from someone attempting to fake or exaggerate problems related to a head injury.

Stand-Alone Effort Tests

As indicated earlier, there are two types of tests specifically designed to assess effort and possible malingering. The first type utilizes symptom validity test forced-choice formats and relies on the probability to classify patient performances. The second relies on cutoffs established by research in which the cutoffs have been shown to correctly identify patients with poor effort. In our clinic, we include at least two stand-alone effort tests in all of our forensic assessments, one to be given during each testing session. Tom and Lisa both completed the TOMM and the WMT.

Tom. Tom scored a perfect 50 out of 50 on each of the three trials on the TOMM and scored 100% correct on each of the three primary effort measures on the WMT. These scores affirm that he provided adequate effort during testing.

Lisa. Lisa had taken the TOMM in a previous testing session and fallen well below the cutoffs to indicate inadequate effort. It has been our experience that some litigants who fail an SVT in a prior evaluation pass SVTs in subsequent evaluations. Lisa fell into this group, scoring in the passing range on the TOMM and also passing the WMT during our test battery. Although it would have been helpful in establishing lack of effort if the patient had failed both of these measures, it is important to remember that though a failure on an SVT is a strong indication of lack of effort and possibly of malingering, a passing score is not an indication of good effort or an honest approach to the tests.

Discussion

After reading the reviews of medical and psychological records, the descriptions of behavior during testing, and the discussion of effort tests and indices, one might conclude that the nature and severity of injury in each of the sample cases is indisputable. In reality, though Tom's case was settled easily, our involvement in Lisa's case began when the mental health professionals and the attorneys were unsure of why Lisa was not responding to the treatments offered for her psychiatric diagnoses. Two psychiatrists, two clinical psychologists, one psychoeducational psychologist, and two clinical social workers treated Lisa for PTSD, and some of them considered her to have severe neurocognitive deficits secondary to head injury. It was our opinion in the report submitted following our INE that Lisa was feigning her deficits. Before the report was completed, the most recent clinical social worker treating Lisa came to the same conclusion, and shortly after our report was submitted, we received information confirming this opinion.

Reports

Reports for Tom and Lisa are included in the appendices. They follow the approach outlined earlier. There is no data summary appended to Lisa's report because the data from testing are not valid. Disability ratings are not included in either report. Lisa's data do not support a disability and Tom's attorney preferred that such ratings occur later in the process.

Conclusion

In this chapter, we have discussed the use of record review, behavioral observations, symptom validity tests, and embedded validity tests to evaluate patient effort in the context of claims covered under workers' compensation law. This approach to the identification of effort was illustrated through two sharply contrasting clinical cases. Although Lisa's case appears to be extreme in nature, our clinic sees no less than five similar cases every year. The principles used in this case allow for the detection of less obvious cases of insufficient effort and are applied routinely to INEs in our clinic.

References

Allen, L. M., Iverson, G. L., and Green, P. (2002). Computerized assessment of response bias in forensic neuropsychology. *Journal of Forensic Neuropsychology*, 3, 205–225.

American Medical Association. (2001). *American Medical Association Guides to the Evaluation of permanent impairment*. 5th ed. Chicago, IL: American Medical Association.

Baade, L. E. and Schoenberg, M. R. (2004). A Proposed method to estimate premorbid intelligence utilizing group achievement measures from school records. *Archives of Clinical Neuropsychology*, 19, 227–243.

Barona, A., Reynolds, C. R., and Chastain, R. (1984). A demographically based index of premorbid intelligence for the WAIS–R. *Journal of Consulting and Clinical Psychology*, 52, 885–887.

Barth, J. T. (2000). Commentary on "disclosure of tests and raw test data to the courts" by Paul Lees-Haley and John Courtney. *Neuropsychology Review*, 10, 179–176.

Beetar, J. and Williams, J. (1995). Malingering response styles on the memory assessment scales and symptom validity tests. *Archives of Clinical Neuropsychology*, 10, 57–72.

Bernard, L. C., McGrath, M. J., and Houston, W. (1996). The differential effects of simulating malingering, closed head injury, and other CNS pathology on the Wisconsin card sort test: Support for the "pattern of performance" hypothesis. *Archives of Clinical Neuropsychology*, 11, 231–245.

Bianchini, K. J., Mathias, C. W., and Greve, K. W. (2001). Symptom validity testing: A critical review. *The Clinical Neuropsychologist*, 15, 19–45.

Binder, L. M. (1997). A review of mild head trauma. Part II: Clinical implications. *Journal of Clinical and Experimental Neuropsychology*, 19, 432–457.

Binder, L. M., Kelly, M. P., Villanueva, M. R., and Winslow, M. W. (2003). Motivation and neuropsychological test performance following mild head injury. *Journal of Clinical and Experimental Neuropsychology*, 25, 420–430.

Binder, L. M. and Willis, S. C. (1991). Assessment of motivation after financially compensable minor head trauma. *The Clinical Neuropsychologist*, 3, 175–181.

Bolter, J. F., Picano, J. J., and Zych, K. (1985). *Item Error Frequencies on the Halstead Category Test: An Index of Performance Validity*. Paper presented at the annual meeting of the National Academy of Neuropsychology, Philadelphia, PA.

Boone, K. B. and Lu, P. H. (2003). Noncredible cognitive performance in the context of severe brain injury. *The Clinical Neuropsychologist*, 17, 244–245.

Boone, K. B. and Lu, P. H. (1999). Noncredible cognitive performance in the context of severe brain injury. *The Clinical Neuropsychologist*, 13, 414–419.

Boone, K., Lu, P., and Herzberg, D. S. (2002a). *The b Test*. Los Angeles: Western Psychological Services.

Boone, K., Lu, P., and Herzberg, D. S. (2002b). *The Dot Counting Test*. Los Angeles: Western Psychological Services.

Chouinard, J. and Rouleau, I. (1997). The 48-pictures test: A two-alternative forced-choice recognition test for the detection of malingering. *Journal of the International Neuropsychological Society*, 3, 545–552.

Curtis, K. L., Greve, K. W., Bianchini, K. J., and Brennan, A. (2006). California verbal learning test indicators of malingered neurocognitive dysfunction: Sensitivity and specificity in traumatic brain injury. *Assessment*, 13, 46–61.

Curtis, K. L., Greve, K. W., Bianchini, K. J., and Heinly, M. (October 2005). *Sensitivity and Specificity of WAIS Indicators to Malingered Neurocognitive Dysfunction in Traumatic Brain Injury*. Poster presented at the 25th annual meeting of the National Academy of Neuropsychology, Tampa, FL.

Donders, J., Tulsky, D. S., and Zhu, J. (2001). Criterion validity of new WAIS-III subtest scores after traumatic brain injury. *Journal of the International Neuropsychological Society*, 7, 892–898.

Etherton, J. L., Bianchini, K. J., Ciota, M. A., and Greve, K. W. (2005). Reliable Digit Span is unaffected by laboratory-induced pain: Implications for clinical use. *Assessment*, 12, 101–106.

Frederick, R. I. (2002a). A review of Rey's strategies for detecting malingered neuropsychological impairment. *Journal of Forensic Neuropsychology*, 2, 1–25.

Frederick, R. I. (2002b). *Introduction to the Development and Interpretation of the VIP Test: VIP Validity Indicator Profile*. National Computer Systems, Minneapolis.

Fredrick, R. I. and Foster, H. G. (1991). Multiple measures of malingering on a forced-choice test of cognitive ability. *Psychological Assessment*, 3, 596–602.

Freides, D. (1993). Proposed standard of professional practice: Neuropsychological reports display all quantitative data. *The Clinical Neuropsychologist*, 7, 234–235.

Freides, D. (1995). Interpretations are more benign than data? *The Clinical Neuropsychologist*, 9, 248.

Glassmire, D. M., Bierley, R. A., Wisniewski, A. M., Greene, R. L., Kennedy, J. E., and Date, E. (2003). Using the WMS-III faces subtest to detect malingered memory impairment. *Journal of Clinical and Experimental Neuropsychology*, 25, 465–481.

Green, P. (2003). *Green's Word Memory Test for Microsoft Windows*. Edmonton, Alberta: Green's Publishing.

Green, P., Iverson, G. L., and Allen, L. M. (1999). Detecting malingering in head injury litigation with the word memory test. *Brain Injury*, 13, 813–819.

Greiffenstein, M. F., Baker, W. J., and Gola, T. (1994). Validation of malingered amnesia measures with a large clinical sample. *Psychological Assessment*, 6, 218–224.

Greiffenstein, M. F., Baker, W. J., and Gola, T. (1996). Motor dysfunction profiles in traumatic brain injury and postconcussion syndrome. *Journal of the International Neuropsychological Society*, 2, 477–485.

Greve, K. W. and Bianchini, K. J. (2004). Setting empirical cut-offs on psychometric indicators of negative response bias: A methodological commentary with recommendations. *Archives of Clinical Neuropsychology*, 19, 533–541.

Greve, K. W., Bianchini, K. J., Mathias, C. W., Houston, R. J., and Crouch, J. A. (2002). Detecting malingered performance with the Wisconsin card sorting test: A preliminary investigation in traumatic brain injury. *The Clinical Neuropsychologist*, 16, 179–191.

Greve, K. W., Bianchini, K. J., Mathias, C. W., Houston, R. J., and Crouch, J. A. (2003). Detecting malingered performance on the Wechsler adult intelligence scale: Validation of Mittenberg's approach in traumatic brain injury. *Archives of Clinical Neuropsychology*, 18, 245–260.

Greve, K. W., Bianchini, K. J., and Roberson, T. (2007). The booklet category test and malingering in traumatic brain injury: Classification accuracy in known groups. *The Clinical Neuropsychologist*, 21, 318–337.

Gudjonsson, G. and Shackleton, H. (1986). The pattern of scores on Raven's matrices during "faking bad" and "non-faking" performance. *British Journal of Clinical Psychology*, 25, 35–41.

Guilmette, T. J., Hart, K. J., and Guiliano, A. J. (1993). Malingering detection: The use of forced-choice method in identifying organic versus simulated memory impairment. *The Clinical Neuropsychologist*, 7, 59–69.

Heaton, R. K., Miller, W., Taylor, M. J., and Grant, I. (2004). *Revised Comprehensive Norms for an Expanded Halstead–Reitan Battery: Demographically Adjusted Neuropsychological Norms for African American and Caucasian Adults. Professional Manual*, Lutz, FL: Psychological Assessment Resources.

Heaton, R. K., Grant, I., and Matthews, C. G. (1991). *Comprehensive Norms for an Expanded Halstead–Reitan Battery: Demographic Corrections, Research Findings, and Clinical Applications*. Odessa, FL: Psychological Assessment Resources.

Heinly, M. T., Greve, K. W., Bianchini, K. J., Love, J. L., and Brennan, A. (2005). WAIS digit span-based indicators of malingered neurocognitive dysfunction: Classification accuracy in traumatic brain injury. *Assessment*, 12, 429–444.

Hiscock, C. K., Branham, J. D., and Hiscock, M. (1994). Detection of feigned cognitive impairment: The two-alternative forced-choice method compared with selected conventional tests. *Journal of Psychopathological Behavior*, 16, 95–110.

Hiscock, M. and Hiscock, C. K. (1989). Refining the forced-choice method for the detection of malingering. *Journal of Clinical and Experimental Neuropsychology*, 11, 967–974.

Iverson, G. L. (2000). Detecting malingering on the WAIS-III and WMS-III. *American Psychological Association Annual Conference*. Washington, DC.

Iverson, G. L. and Franzen, M. (1994). The recognition memory test, digit span, and Knox cube test as markers of malingered memory impairment. *Assessment*, 1, 323–334.

Iverson, G. L., Franzen, M. D., and McCracken, L. M. (1991). Evaluation of an objective assessment technique for the detection of malingered memory deficits. *Law and Human Behavior*, 15, 667–676.

Iverson, G. L., Lange, R. T., Green, P., and Franzen, M. D. (2002). Detecting exaggeration and malingering with the trail making test. *The Clinical Neuropsychologist*, 16, 398–406.

Iverson, G. L. and Tulsky, D. S. (2003). Detecting malingering on the WAIS-III. Unusual digit span performance patterns in the normal population and in clinical groups. *Archives of Clinical Neuropsychology*, 18, 1–9.

Jones, R. D. and Rizzo, M. (2004). Head trauma and traumatic brain injury. In M. Rizzo and P. J. Eslinger (Eds.), *Principles and Practice of Behavioral Neurology and Neuropsychology* (pp. 615–634). Philadelphia, PA: W. B. Saunders.

Killgore, W. D. S. and DellaPietra, L. (2000). Using the WMS-III to detect malingering: Empirical validation of the rarely missed index (RMI). *Journal of Clinical and Experimental Neuropsychology*, 22, 761–771.

King, J. H., Sweet, J. J., Sherer, M., Curtiss, G., and Vanderploeg, R. D. (2002). Validity indicators within the Wisconsin card sorting test: Application of new and previously researched multivariate procedures in multiple traumatic brain injury samples. *The Clinical Neuropsychologist* 16, 506–523.

Lally, S. J. (2003). What tests are acceptable for use in forensic evaluations? A survey of experts. *Professional Psychology: Research and Practice*, 34, 491–498.

Lang, R. T., Iverson, G. L., Sullivan, K., and Anderson, D. (2006). Suppressed working memory on the WMS-III as a marker for poor effort. *Journal of Clinical and Experimental Neuropsychology*, 28, 294–305.

Langeluddecke, P. M. and Lucas, S. K. (2003). Quantitative measures of memory malingering on the Wechsler Memory Scale—Third Edition in mild head injury litigants. *Archives of Clinical Neuropsychology*, 18, 181–197.

Larrabee, G. J. (2003). Detection of malingering using atypical performance patterns on standard neuropsychological tests. *The Clinical Neuropsychologist*, 17, 410–425.

Larrabee, G. J. (October 2005). Improving the Slick et al. criteria. In D. Slick (Chair), *Diagnostic Approaches to Malingered Neurocognitive Dysfunction: Expert Perspectives on the State of the Art, Current Controversies and Future Directions*. Symposium conducted at the meeting of the National Academy of Neuropsychology, Tampa, FL.

Lees-Haley, P. R. and Courtney, J. C. (2000a). Disclosure of tests and raw test data to the courts: A need for reform. *Neuropsychology Review*, 10, 169–174.

Lees-Haley, P. R. and Courtney, J. C. (2000b). Reply to the commentary on "disclosure of tests and raw test data to the courts." *Neuropsychology Review*, 10, 181–182.

Lees-Haley, P. R., Courtney, J. C., and Dinkins, J. P. (2005). Revisiting the need for reform in the disclosure of tests and raw test data to the courts: The 2002 APA ethics code has not solved our dilemma. *Journal of Forensic Psychology Practice*, 5, 71–81.

Lezak, M. D., Howieson, D. B., Loring, D. W., Hannay, H. J., and Fischer, J. S. (2004). *Neuropsychological Assessment*. 4th ed. New York, NY: Oxford University Press.

Matarazzo, R. G. (1995). Psychological report standards in neuropsychology. *The Clinical Neuropsychologist*, 9, 249.

McKinzey, R. M., Podd, M. H., Krehbiel, M. A., and Raven, J. (1999). Detection of malingering on the Raven's standard progressive matrices: A cross-validation. *British Journal of Clinical Psychology*, 38, 435–439.

Miller, L. J., Ryan, J. J., Carruthers, C. A., and Cluff, R. B. (2004). Brief screening indexes for malingering: A confirmation of vocabulary minus digit span from the WAIS-III and the rarely missed index from the WMS-III. *The Clinical Neuropsychologist*, 18, 327–333.

Millis, S. R. (2004). Evaluation of malingered neurocognitive disorders. In M. Rizzo and P. J. Eslinger (Eds.), *Principles and Practice of Behavioral Neurology and Neuropsychology* (pp. 1077–1089). Philadelphia, PA: W. B. Saunders.

Millis, S. R., Putnam, S. H., Adams, K. M., and Ricker, J. H. (1995). The California verbal learning test in the detection of incomplete effort in neuropsychological evaluation. *Psychological Assessment*, 7, 463–471.

Millis, S. R., Ross, S. R., and Ricker, J. H. (1998). Detection of incomplete effort on the Wechsler Adult Intelligence Scale—Revised: A cross-validation. *Journal of Clinical and Experimental Neuropsychology*, 20, 167–173.

Millis, S. R. and Volinsky, C. T. (2001). Assessment of response bias in mild head injury: Beyond malingering tests. *Journal of Clinical and Experimental Psychology*, 23, 809–828.

Mittenberg, W., DiGuilion, D. V., Perrin, S., and Bass, A. E. (1992). Symptoms following mild head injury: Expectation as etiology. *Journal of Neurology, Neurosurgery, and Psychiatry*, 55, 200–204.

Mittenberg, W., Rotholc, A., Russell, E., and Heilbronner, R. (1996). Identification of malingered head injury on the Halstead–Reitan battery. *Archives of Clinical Neuropsychology*, 11, 271–281.

Mittenberg, W., Theroux-Fichera, S., Aguila-Puentes, G., Bianchini, K., Greve, K., and Rayls, K. (2001). Identification of malingered head injury on the Wechsler Adult Intelligence Scale—Third Edition. *The Clinical Neuropsychologist*, 15, 440–445.

Mittenberg, W., Theroux-Fichera, S., Rayls, K., Aguila-Puentes, G., Bianchini, K., Greve, K., and Rayls, K. Identification of malingered head injury on the Wechsler Adult Intelligence Scale. *The Clinical Neuropsychologist*, in press.

Mittenberg, W., Theroux-Fichera, S., Zielinski, R. E., and Heilbronner, R. L. (1995). Identification of malingered head injury on the Wechsler Adult Intelligence Scale—Revised. *Professional Psychology: Research and Practice*, 26, 491–498.

Naugle, R. I. and McSweeny, A. J. (1995). On the practice of routinely appending neuropsychological data to reports. *The Clinical Neuropsychologist*, 9, 245–247.

Pankratz, L. (1979). Symptom validity testing and symptom retraining: Procedures for the assessment and treatment of functional sensory deficits. *Journal of Consulting and Clinical Psychology*, 47, 409–410.

Pankratz, L. (1998). *Patients Who Deceive*. Springfield, IL: Charles C Thomas.

Raven, J. C., Court, J. H., and Raven, J. (1992). Standard Progressive Matrices. Oxford: Oxford Psychologists Press Ltd.

Rees, L. M., Tombaugh, T. N., Gansler, D., and Moczynski, N. (1998). Five validation experiments of the test of memory malingering (TOMM). *Psychological Assessment*, 10, 10–20.

Reitan, R. M. and Wolfson, D. (2002). Detection of malingering and invalid test results using the Halstead–Reitan battery. *Journal of Forensic Neuropsychology*, 3, 275–314.

Rogers, R., Bagby, R. M., and Dickens, S. E. (1992). *Structured Interview of Reported Symptoms (SIRS): A Professional Manual*. Odessa, FL: Psychological Assessment Resources.

Ruffulo, L. F., Guilmette, T. J., and Willis, W. G. (2000). Comparison of time and error analysis on the trail making test among patients with head injuries, experimental malingerers, patients with suspect effort on testing and normal controls. *Clinical Neuropsychology*, 9, 518–528.

Schagen, S., Schmand, B., de Sterke, S., and Lindeboom, J. (1997). Amsterdam Short-Term Memory Test: A new procedure for the detection of feigned memory deficits. *Journal of Clinical and Experimental Neuropsychology*, 19, 43–51.

Shapiro, D. L. (2000). Commentary: Disclosure of tests and raw test data to the courts: A need for reform. *Neuropsychology Review*, 10, 175–176.

Shimoyama, I., Ninchoji, T., and Uemura, K. (1990). The finger tapping test: A quantitative analysis. *Archives of Neurology*, 47, 681–684.

Slick, D. J., Hoop, G., and Strauss, E. (1995). *The Victoria Symptom Validity Test*. Odessa, FL: Psychological Assessment Resources.

Slick, D. J., Sherman, E. M. S., and Iverson, G. L. (1999). Diagnostic criteria for malingered neurocognitive dysfunction: Proposed standards for clinical practice and research. *The Clinical Neuropsychologist*, 13, 545–561.

Strauss, E., Sherman, E. M. S., and Spreen, O. (2006). *A Compendium of Neuropsychological Tests: Administration, Norms, and Commentary*. 3rd ed. New York: Oxford University Press.

Suhr, J. A. and Boyer, D. (1999). Use of the Wisconsin Card Sorting Test in the detection of malingering in student simulator and patient samples. *Journal of Clinical and Experimental Neuropsychology*, 21, 701–708.

Sweet, J. J. and King, J. H. (2002). Category test validity indicators: Overview and practice recommendations. *Journal of Forensic Neuropsychology*, 3, 241–272.

The Psychological Corporation. (2001). Wechsler Test of Adult Reading: Manual, San Antonio.

Tenhula, W. N. and Sweet, J. J. (1996). Double cross-validation of the booklet category test in detecting malingered traumatic brain injury. *The Clinical Neuropsychologist*, 10, 104–116.

Tombaugh, T. N. (1996). *Test of Memory Malingering (TOMM)*. New York: Multi Health Systems.

Tranel, D. (2000). Commentary on Lees-Haley and Courtney: There is a need for reform. *Neuropsychology Review*, 10, 177–178.

Warrington, E. K. (1984). *Recognition Memory Test: Manual*. Berkshire, UK: NFER-Nelson.

Malingered Pain and Memory Deficits in Civil-Forensic Contexts

16

HAROLD V. HALL

Pacific Institute for the Study of Conflict and Aggression, Kamuela, Hawaii

JOSEPH G. POIRIER

Independent Practice, Rockville, Maryland

JANE THOMPSON

University of Hawaii, Hilo, Hawaii

Contents

Case

Greg Lance is a 32-year-old single Caucasian construction worker who was a passenger in a vehicle involved in a serious accident as it rear-ended a luxury car on the freeway. Although the driver of Greg's vehicle claimed the car ahead of him caused the accident by abruptly stopping, police noted that he had an extensive record of fraud and theft convictions including two for falsely claiming injuries from other auto accidents for insurance compensation. Greg's injuries consisted of an alleged stress response with suicidal tendencies and a cervico-cephalic syndrome unverified by various examinations at the emergency room and the hospital.

Notes during hospitalization contain examples of serious prevarication in order to leave the hospital grounds, have sex with a disabled patient, and "con" money from the staff. When questioned about previous alleged suicide gestures, he finally admitted that the only instance occurred while in custody several years earlier as a ruse to change cells. A substantial history of incarceration for property crimes was uncovered. During the forensic hospital stay, a worker noted: "... he has been observed in animated interaction and activity with some patients, but when speaking to staff, assumes a 'depressive' and suicidal attitude." On a neurological test referral, Dr Smith observed that "his MMPI findings would strongly indicate that the patient is faking the symptoms of isolation, depression, pain, and impoverishment of emotional experience. This evidence is supported by the fact that in unguarded moments, the patient exhibits the full range of affective state as well as the pain-free state."

Other suggestions of malingering included: (a) obtaining significantly worse scores on some intellectual tests, for example, on the Wechsler Adult Intelligence Test, than on highly correlated tests, for example, on the Shipley Institute of Living Scale; (b) during administration of different neuropsychological tests, he showed the ability to perform multiplication and other complex mathematical manipulations on one test while exhibiting the inability to do simple addition problems on another test; (c) correctly identifying words such as "kayak," "descend," "bereavement," "appraising," and "amphibian" while showing the inability to define simpler words such as "winter," "slice," and "conceal"; and (d) exhibiting inconsistent memory skills (digits forward and digits backward) instead of a consistently poor performance. Greg left the hospital against medical advice on his own accord, showing no problems in ambulation, when he was informed of the results of the testing. He was not arrested for fraud but was turned down in his application for health insurance benefits.

Introduction

Civil claims of mental injury, trauma, or defect may be broadly categorized into tort claims and eligibility claims. Tort claims allege that a personal injury was caused to the plaintiff (personal tort) or to the plaintiff's property (property tort) by the negligence or intentional act of the defendant. The defendant would be another person or business, although in cases where there are claims and counterclaims, the distinction between plaintiff and defendant can become blurred. Injuries are compensable through awards for the actual damages sustained and, sometimes, for punitive damages as well. Theoretically, tort claims cover all losses, and there are no limits to the financial awards. In recent years, however, the courts have become concerned about frivolous claims and extravagant damage awards. Accordingly, in many jurisdictions, maximum limits for tort claims have been established.

Eligibility claims allege that the claimant satisfies current criteria for special assistance from a government program. The eligibility claims systems evolved, historically, because of the complex, adversarial, fault-oriented tort system. Examples of disability assistance programs include social security supplemental income (SSI) program for disabled persons, workers' compensation programs, and veterans administration (VA) program. These disability programs are alternatives to the tort claim system; they are no-fault in application and based on functional loss, that is, loss of earning capacity.

Tort claims are originally tried in state and federal inferior courts and are decided based on a judicial decision process. Eligibility claims are originally heard before administrative boards or tribunals, and outcomes are the result of an administrative process as compared with the judicial process of tort actions. The threshold legal questions, rules of evidence, rules of procedures, and burdens of proof differ between these two types of forums, as do the types of outcomes. Frequently, cases that begin as eligibility matters can evolve into tort actions.

The following discussion outlines the features of these two classes of claims. Special attention is given to issues involving claims of psychological injury or disability (Hall, 1990; Hall and Hall, 1991; Lees-Haley, 1985). For illustration purposes, our particular area of interest is (1) faked pain and loss of sensation, and (2) malingered amnesia. In all of these types of claims, distortion and outright malingering of complaints is a significant probability. Our primary interest in civil actions is the meaningful assessment of any contributory elements of distortion or malingering (Lees-Haley, Williams, and English, 1996; Weissman, 1990).

In an article showing the high incidence of malingering, from a survey of the members of the American Board of Clinical Neuropsychology (ABCN), Mittenberg, Patton, Canyock, and Condit (2002) determined the base rate for faking bad based on over 33,500 cases involving personal injury, disability, criminal, and medical matters. Base rates for malingering did not change for geographic location or type of setting but were affected by type of referral (plaintiff vs. defense). The following rates for probable malingering were reported: personal injury 29%, disability 30%, criminal 19%, medical cases 8%, mild head injury 39%, fibromyalgia/chronic fatigue 35%, chronic pain 31%, neurotoxic 27%, and electrical injury 22%. Mittenberg et al. (2002) stated, "Diagnosis was supported by multiple sources of evidence, including severity (65% of cases) or pattern (64% of cases) of cognitive impairment that was inconsistent with the condition, scores below empirical cut-offs on forced-choice tests (57% of cases), discrepancies among records, self-report, and observed behavior (56%), implausible self-reported symptoms in interview (46%), implausible changes in test scores across repeated examinations (45%), and validity scales on objective personality tests (38% of cases)."

Pertinent Legal Cases

Under the law, all persons owe a duty of care to one another that can logically be expected from ordinary, reasonable, and prudent persons. A tort is simply an injury to one's person, interests, reputation, or property that is caused by a breach of that duty. The primary goal of tort law is to compensate injured parties for damages caused by breach of certain commonly recognized duties. The successful prosecution of a tort claim requires proof: (1) that a personal injury occurred, (2) that the injury was the result of the defendant's negligence or intentional act, or (3) that the injury should have been foreseen by the defendant. The distinction between negligent torts and intentional torts is important, because the former allow awards only for actual damages suffered, while the latter also permit punitive damages.

The issue of deception in tort claims speaks to the question of the existence or severity of the alleged injury. If the defendant can show that no injury was actually suffered, then the claim has been successfully defended. If the defendant can show that the actual injury suffered is less severe than claimed, then the size of any damage may be reduced accordingly.

Civil courts have shown a combination of reluctance and fear in accepting opinions that a plaintiff is malingering. In *Miller v. United States Fidelity and Guaranty Co.* (1957), the court stated:

> The principle that courts will stigmatize a claimant as a malingerer only upon positive and convincing evidence justifying such a conclusion is so well embedded in our jurisprudence as to preclude the necessity for specifications.

The damage done to the plaintiff's reputation is one reason for this reluctance to accept opinions of malingering. Another is the logic of the economic situation. In both *King Mining Co. v. Mullins* (1952) and *Sutcliffe v. E. I. Dupont De Nemours & Co.* (1948), the courts found it difficult to believe that the plaintiffs would sacrifice relatively well-paying jobs in order to fake an injury for a mere fraction of the amount of their pay. The courts want neither to label one as a malingerer nor to allow recovery for malingering to take place. As Shuman (1986) said, "The common law has long been wary of permitting recovery for mental or emotional injuries because of the fear that an absence of demonstrably verifiable injuries posed a risk of fraud to which the courts could not effectively respond."

Juries appear to become very rigid, however, when they feel the plaintiff may have attempted to dupe them. In *Freeman v. Bandlow* (1962), an old plaintiff bus passenger was hit by the defendant's auto. The jury awarded the plaintiff only $280—the amount of a doctor's bill. The court noted as follows (pp. 548–549):

> The plaintiff alleged that he was severely injured in the area of the neck and back, suffered great physical and mental pain, which will continue in the future, and sustained temporary and permanent diminution of income and earning capacity. There was little doubt as to defendant's negligence, but the record reflects considerable doubt as to the cause, nature and extent of plaintiff's pathological condition during the two-year interim between the collision and the trial of the case early in 1961. [and] Thus there was substantial expert opinion testimony tending to show that plaintiff's injuries were grossly exaggerated and that he was largely a malingerer and was not, in fact, appreciably disabled as a result of his mishap.

Controversy over the latitude of the courts in allowing either direct or indirect testimony regarding malingering has continued to the present day. There is an entire area of disability law dealing with the admissibility of collateral sources of income for plaintiffs. The collateral source rule essentially holds that a plaintiff's recovery need not be offset by other sources of income. In cases where malingering is an issue, collateral source evidence can be very prejudicial to the plaintiff's case. In a landmark case addressing the discretion of courts to permit testimony regarding malingering, the U.S. Supreme Court ruled against a lower court allowing such testimony (*Eichel v. New York Cent. R. R. Co.*, 1963). In Eichel, the court opined, "[i]nsofar as the evidence bears on the issue of malingering, there will generally be other evidence having more probative value and involving less likelihood of prejudice than the receipt of a disability pension."

Eichel was decided before the current Federal Rules of Evidence were enacted. Rule 403 of the Federal Rules conferred, "… broad discretion upon the district court to weigh unfair prejudice against probative value" (709 F.2nd at 741). In *Savoie v. Otto Candies, Inc.* (1982), the court found that the adjudicatory analysis in Eichel was consistent with Rule 403. More recently in *McGrath v. Consolidated Rail Corporation* (1998), the Federal Court ruled that the lower court did not abuse its discretion by permitting testimony regarding malingering. The court found:

> As its motion in limine to admit the collateral source evidence argues, Conrail offered the evidence of McGrath's disability payments on the issue of McGrath's credibility. Specifically, Conrail presented collateral source evidence to show McGrath's lack of motivation for returning to work. In allowing Conrail to question McGrath about collateral source evidence, the district court, on several occasions, issued cautionary instructions to the jury, advising it to consider the evidence only on the issue of malingering.

The courts have made clear that, absent evidence of malingering, awards can be made under many conditions for psychological trauma in the absence of physical injury. "Loss of consortium" as one application of psychic harm has been consistently recognized as compensable (*Metropolitan Dade County v. Orlando Reyes et al.*, 1996; *Byerley and Byerley v. Citrus Publishing, Inc.*, 1999). The courts have also recognized delayed-onset symptoms, for example, symptoms appearing in adulthood that stem from childhood trauma. In *Teater v. State of Nebraska* (1997), the appeals court overturned a lower court decision that a claim was time barred because it was made well after a 2-year statute of limitations had been exceeded. The claimant was an adult who had been placed as a child by the Department of Social Services in a foster home. As a child, her foster father continually subjected Ms Teater to sexual assaults from the age of 6 to the age of 14. The plaintiff's claim was not made until 22 years after the first reported abuse. The claim was that Ms Teater suffered permanent psychological injury and that the State of Nebraska had been negligent in providing adequate safeguards. Expert witnesses differed as to whether the alleged sexual abuse had ever occurred, and as to any injuries (i.e., damages).

The experts in *Teater* were opining from having reconstructed psychological events over 20 years earlier. This is an imposing task even under ideal circumstances. It could legitimately be argued that the state of the art of the mental health profession is not even close to being able to do what was called for in this case. At the optimum, only a very qualified best "guess" could be reasonably offered. The adversarial process has little patience, however, with other than "reasonable degree of certainty" opinions that are expressed with apparent certitude.

A relatively recent area of emphasis in personal injury claims is the introduction of claims of sexual harassment in both tort and eligibility claim actions. Sexual harassment claims have appeared with increasing frequency as stand-alone claims or as simultaneous actions in tort and eligibility claims (see *Underwood v. NCUA*, 1995; *Neal v. Director, D.C. Department of Corrections*, 1996; *Nichols v. American Nat'l. Ins.*, 1999).

The *Underwood* matter in particular demonstrates the potential judicial complexities of a civil claim and serves to alert the forensic clinician of how convoluted such matters can be in terms of deception. A litigant, for example, may begin with a *bona fide*, work-related physical health problem, but end up malingering the severity of those symptoms, and also be induced to malinger or exaggerate psychological symptoms, as well as claim sexual harassment, or any combination thereof.

Numerous tort cases have emerged, reflecting the court's dependence on testimony from mental health experts regarding claims of psychological damage/trauma, but then being overwhelmed and confused by apparently divergent and contradictory expert opinions (see *Lowery v. Miller, Van Rybroek, Maier, & Roach*, 1990). One working factor in this situation may not so much be the disparate views of mental health experts, as opposed to attorneys using the adversarial process to polarize what in an actual clinical setting may be working opinions regarding diagnosis, personality dynamics, and treatment needs. Yet another major change in civil litigation was introduced by *Daubert v. Merrell Dow Pharmaceuticals* (1993). In *Daubert*, the U.S. Supreme Court gave trial judges a "gate keeping" function to decide whether or not scientific expert testimony was sufficiently reliable to be admissible. The trial judges are empowered with wide discretion to make this determination. In *Nichols v. American Nat'l. Ins.* (1999), the appeals court cited *Daubert* and ruled inadmissible the testimony of an expert witness psychiatrist. The court stated that the psychiatrist's testimony regarding the claimant's "psychiatric credibility" based on "theories" of recall bias, secondary gain, and malingering did not meet the *Daubert* criteria for having a scientific basis. The court also noted that, moreover, the issue of the claimant's credibility was exclusively the purview of the jury.

Eligibility Claims

Eligibility claims require evidence that the claimant satisfies current criteria for admission to special government programs developed to assist eligible persons. These programs differ from entitlement programs, since the applicant must prove that special eligibility criteria are satisfied. There does not have to be a total disability for compensation to be awarded. The largest eligibility programs include the SSI program, the social security disability insurance program (SSDI), workers' compensation programs, and VA disability assistance programs.

The social security disability insurance program (SSDI) provides cash assistance to currently disabled workers and their dependents that have contributed to social security taxes according to a statutorily set minimum work period. The SSI program provides a minimum income to the needy disabled (regardless of whether or not they paid social security taxes in the past). Both programs require proof that the applicant has a medically determinable impairment which interferes with the ability to engage in substantial gainful work and which can be expected to last for at least 12 months. Each state's Disability Determination Service makes original decisions regarding eligibility. Adverse decisions are appealable to the federal court system.

Some, but not all, mental disorders are considered impairments for purposes of determining eligibility for these SS programs. Organic mental disorders, schizophrenic, paranoid and other psychotic disorders, affective disorders, mental retardation and autism, anxiety-related disorders, somatoform disorders, personality disorders, and substance addiction disorders are eligible disorders in adults. However, the criteria used to define these categories are not necessarily the same as those in related categories of the Diagnostic and Statistical Manual-IV (DSM-IV). Griffin, Normington, May, and Glassmire (1996) estimated one-fifth of social security disability claims to be compromised by malingering.

Workers' compensation programs provide compensation or insurance for injuries arising in the course and scope of employment, regardless of whether the injury was due to the negligence or intentional fault of the employer. The amount of compensation is set by a fixed schedule according to the degree of loss. Youngjohn (1991) estimated as many as one-half of all workers' compensation cases may be compromised by malingering.

Federal employees are covered under the Federal Employees Compensation Act; seamen are covered by the federal Jones Act; and longshoremen are covered by the federal Longshoremen's and Harbour Workers' Compensation Act. In addition, each state has its own employee compensation program with varying coverage, rules, and compensation schedules. These local Acts should be consulted for specific information on the operation of workers' compensation programs in each locale. Adverse decisions are appealable to either the federal or state court systems.

The VA offers programs of medical and mental health treatment to honorably discharged veterans on *a priority* basis (Campbell and Tueth, 1997). The availability of these services depends on current VA resources; eligibility depends on one's status at the time of discharge, and whether or not the disorder is "service-connected." In addition, the VA administers a program of monetary payments to veterans (and their dependents) who are totally or partially disabled by a service-connected disability. Regional Offices of Jurisdiction, whose decisions are appealable to the Board of Veterans Appeals (BVA), determine eligibility for disability payments and the degree of disability. Decisions of the BVA are appealable to the U.S. Court of Veterans Appeals.

All of these types of eligibility claims are vexed with problems of malingering (Beal, 1989; Braverman, 1978; Hall, 1990; Hall and Hall, 1991; Lipman, 1962; Rickarby, 1979; Wasyliw and Cavanaugh, 1989; Williams, Lees-Haley, and Djanogly, 1999). For example, the U.S. Department of Veterans Affairs, *Physician's Guide for Disability Evaluations*, 1985 Ch. 1, Sec. II, Para. 1.14, 1.16 and 13.6(f), 13.6(g) (1985), 1B11-56, states as follows:

> Physicians encounter some veterans or other claimants who are not capable of reliably participating in examinations because they are too ill physically or mentally to provide an accurate report of current symptoms or current level of functioning. Some veterans may exaggerate their disabilities, while others, particularly older veterans, may deny or be unrealistic in reporting the extent of their disablement.

Generally, the claimant in administrative hearings is given much leeway in demonstrating disability. Although malingering per se is not grounds for denial of eligibility, it may likely be a contentious element in many claims. In *Board of Trustees of Fire and Police Employees Retirement System of City of Baltimore v. Ches* (1982), a police officer claimant was held to be disabled from an August 1, 1977, rear-end accident in his police car despite medical testimony of his malingering (pretending to be ill or injured to avoid work). In *Transit Authority of River City v. Vinson* (1985), collateral evidence of social security, disability, and insurance benefits paid to a plaintiff after an accident was excluded where the court felt that the jury would be misled by evidence of malingering. In *Cockrell v. U.S.* (1934), the plaintiff's deliberate failure to obtain work to avoid discontinuance of a VA disability was admissible as evidence of malingering and in Board of Veterans Appeals Decision of March 17, 1978, Docket No. 77-36-991, feigned reactive depression was admissible evidence in a

VA case. The essential feature of most eligibility programs is the adversarial nature of the disability determination evaluation. Claimants are presumed to be ineligible for services unless they can prove that their injury/disability satisfies current eligibility criteria.

Current Methods and Applications

Paul Lees-Haley (1988, p. 196) described nondeliberate factors in civil claims in terms of the following progression: (1) a physical or psychological trauma occurs, (2) this trauma causes genuine transient effects such as pain, anxiety, and depression, and (3) the patient develops a combination of reactions during treatment, including (a) hysterical reactions to real and imagined problems, (b) hypochondriacal reactions to real and imagined problems, (c) genuine side effects of prescribed medications, (d) hysterical and hypochondriacal reactions to the side effects, and (e) secondary gain. Throughout this process, the patient learns the "language" of stress disorder claims through interactions with attorneys, relatives, friends, health care providers, and others, including popular magazines. This knowledge influences the patient's view of symptoms and interpretations of other, irrelevant experiences.

Thus, fakers who are wholly conscious of their deception and who target specific symptoms for deception may be in the minority. Malingering associated with real conditions, representing an exaggeration rather than a fabrication, may represent the norm. Furthermore, it must be remembered that disability may be represented for different periods of time (e.g., for the time of an evaluation, for the past, or for the future), adding to the difficulty of assessing disability claims.

Response Styles

In a typology of deceivers within an industrial injury context, Braverman (1978) described several styles of malingering:

1. *"True," deliberate, or fraudulent malingerer.* This category comprised less than 1% of Braverman's 2500 clients. Detection was simple as they were all persons with (a) gross psychopathology, (b) no binding ties within a migratory pattern, (c) all men between the ages of 25–37 years, (d) intolerance for long diagnostic testing, and (e) a quick termination of the case once confronted with the possibility of malingering.
2. *Cover-up or decoy malingerer.* Here the faker experienced real trauma (most likely to the head). The compensable disease, such as cancer, is misattributed to the genuine injury. Fear of death and a family history of the disease emerged as central dynamics. About 3% of Braverman's sample is accounted for by this type of deception.
3. *The hysterical malingerer.* Comprising about 31% of the patients and the largest proportion of the sample, malingering in this type stems from a hysteric process culminating in loss of hope and victim distress. Braverman stated (1978, p. 38):

   > By "hysteric malingering" reference is made to a condition which emerges following objective or threatened injury after the affected person (a) loses all hope of recovery to preinjury status; (b) begins to perceive himself with a new identification, namely, as "the injured," in which development of the "part" (injured) becomes more important than the "whole" (the intact residual). Reaction to the injured "part" may pervade the "intact residual"; and (c) becomes aware that his very sustenance is to be determined no

longer by his previous capacity to work (now lost), but by the obligation the effects of his injury and incapacity impose upon society.

4. *The psychotic malingerer.* Comprising about 2% of the sample, this type usually has paranoid and bizarre features to his or her disability.
5. *The organic malingerer.* Comprised largely of Korsakoff patients and consisting of 2% of the sample, this type invents pathology due to the organic condition. Associated features included hypersuggestibility, shifting of symptoms, and uncertainty about the symptoms.

Braverman makes the valid point that work-related malingering is seldom planned in advance and is usually concocted after genuine injury and attendant loss of face occur. In anticipation of fluctuating response styles, he stated that malingering, like most other defenses to loss of face, waxes and wanes in accordance with environmental stimuli. Overall, as the above percentages suggest, he found that about one-third of his 2500 clients engaged in psychotraumatic malingering.

Four types of response styles have been described by Lipman (1962, p. 143):

1. Invention—the patient has no symptoms, but fraudulently represents that he has
2. Perseveration—genuine symptoms formerly present have ceased, but are fraudulently alleged to continue
3. Exaggeration—genuine symptoms are present, but the patient fraudulently makes these out to be worse than they are
4. Transference—genuine symptoms are fraudulently attributed to a cause other than the actual cause in fact

In general, the response styles delineated by investigators describe one or more of the classic types propounded in this chapter. Applied to civil situations, these are as follows:

1. Honesty. Attempts to be accurate within one's perceptions. Here, deficits are portrayed as they are seen, even though nonintentional distortion, such as caused by stress, may be operative to a considerable degree.
2. Faking bad. Exaggeration or fabrication of symptoms and behaviors, or denial/minimization takes place in order to look worse than one is. Exaggerated back injuries, common and difficult to disprove, are placed into this category.
3. Faking good. Minimization or denial of symptoms and behaviors, or exaggeration/fabrication of symptoms in order to look good. The claimant may try to hide the fact that illicit substances contributed to an auto accident or that safety equipment was not operative.
4. Invalidation. Attempts to render the evaluation meaningless (e.g., irrelevant, random responding). The claimant may feign cooperation with the retained expert but may not report for appointments with the opposition expert.
5. Mixed responding. Combination of above within same evaluation period. The claimant may exaggerate back injury but deny alcohol problems.
6. Fluctuating. Change of response styles between or within evaluation periods. The claimant may start off honestly in order to become familiar with testing procedures, then switch to mixed responding, then to random responding as tiredness sets in.

Detection Methods

Lees-Haley (1990a, 1991a, 1991b) has proposed several existing (ego strength) or new (fake bad, credibility) scales from the Minnesota Multiphasic Personality Inventory (MMPI) item pool for use with civil litigants. However, these scales have not been widely used or cross-validated.

In another study, Lees-Haley (1997) assessed the accuracy of MMPI-2 base-rate variables for distinguishing malingering with personal injury plaintiffs. Drawing upon a large sample of 492 Ss, possible malingering was indicated in 20–30% of the sample based on the studied MMPI-2 validity measures (L, F, K, F minus K, Ds-r, fake bad, ego strength, back F, total obvious minus subtle, VRIN, and TRIN). The author described contaminating variables of coaching by attorneys and congruence between personality styles and the expected demands by plaintiffs of personal injury litigation.

Boccaccini and Brodsky (1999) reported a survey among 80 concurrent members of American Psychological Association Divisions 12 and 41. The psychologists were asked to describe psychodiagnostic instruments used in emotional injury assessments. The study found that test selection and the reasons for test selection were highly variable. The authors concluded that psychological experts need to select tests more carefully and need to keep the *Daubert* criteria (i.e., *Daubert v. Merrell Dow Pharmaceuticals*, 1993) in mind.

In general, a large database is suggested for the detection of both intentional and unintentional distortion among civil litigants. One important database source is base-rate information regarding specific complaints. Lees-Haley and Brown (1993), for example, described base-rate data for neuropsychological complaints. The database should include information regarding the pretrauma psychological status of the plaintiff(s). It is also important to consider pretrauma risk factors known to predispose, or exacerbate, post-trauma events. The forensic distortion analysis (FDA) model suggests that any combination of methods—interviewing, testing, observation, base-rate comparison—can be utilized.

Applied Ethics

Previous chapters, including those on deception, discuss in detail how the practitioner may apply the ethics code as well as the forensic guidelines. Nothing is different in civil matters. A glaring exception is the focus on money. In the senior author's opinion, deliberate distortion in the form on unintentional bias and error, as well as deliberate deception by involved attorneys and experts, is especially rampant in civil matters. It is highly recommended that the APA ethics code and forensic guidelines be regularly reviewed and that at the outset the retaining attorney be apprised of any incipient or expected issues that may impact the case.

Investigations Involving Faked Pain and Loss of Sensation

The forensic assessment of malingered pain continues to be an elusive quest. It is not yet possible to differentiate in any reliable manner malingered representations of pain from actual pain. As a result, empirical approaches to detection of feigned pain remain reliant on intuitive measures (Craig, Hill, and McMurtry, 1999). The costs of fraudulent injury claims based on pain symptoms are enormous (James, 1998). The problem of fraudulent claims has resulted in a maze of recovery processes pitting claimants against insurers, with both sides ultimately being penalized.

Psychological variables are fundamental, causative factors in pain perception. Presently, we are primarily interested in the experience of physical pain, but this is not to ignore the reality that psychologically based pain can also be an excruciating human experience. Miller (1992) described patient dishonesty in psychotherapy as the "Pinocchio syndrome" and suggested that lies in therapy were often motivated by the patient's need to camouflage painful psychological realities. The Pinocchio syndrome is often motivated by the patient's efforts to cope with feelings of guilt and anxiety. References throughout this chapter will document the efforts of Lees-Haley and his colleagues to champion the need for evaluators to exercise caution with the self-reports of personal injury claimants (Williams et al., 1999).

One area of pain research has been assessing the ability of judges to subjectively detect pain deception. A common paradigm has been for judges to assess dissimulated pain manifested in nonverbal facial expressions (for a review see Poole and Craig, 1992). In one laboratory study, judges were asked to differentiate facial expressions that displayed genuine pain, no pain, masked pain, and exaggerated pain (Hadjistavropoulos, Craig, Hadjistavropoulos, and Poole, 1996a). The findings indicated that the judges' classification decisions were better than chance, but the error rate was still high. The level of the judges' confidence was consistent with their level of accuracy. The researchers suggested that systematic training regarding specific facial cues that were, and were not, reliable would probably improve the judges' accuracy. Galin and Thorn (1993) found that judges provided with facial action training and enhanced feedback did improve ability to distinguish between genuine and distorted facial pain displays.

Judgments made by observers of displayed facial pain in experimental designs are tainted by a number of factors. Advanced warning of pain deception did not improve judges' accuracy but did result in more conservative or nonempathic judging styles (Poole and Craig, 1992). In another study, observer judgments were significantly biased by the S's gender and physical attractiveness (Hadjistavropoulos, McMurtry, and Craig, 1996b). Male patients and physically attractive patients were judged to be functioning better than female and physically unattractive patients.

Undergraduate nursing students were asked to judge pain experience based on videotapes of preterm and full-term infants being exposed to heel incisions for blood sampling procedures (Hadjistavropoulos, Craig, Grunau, and Whitfield, 1997). The findings indicated that viewing the incision procedure contributed uniformly to judgments of pain experience. Judgments based on infant facial expression produced the most variance followed by bodily activity and gestational age.

The self-report of experienced pain by persons with intellectual disabilities is predictably not very reliable. LaChapelle, Hadjistavropoulos, and Craig (1999) described an attempt to objectively rate the pain experience of an intellectually disabled population who experienced intramuscular injections. The facial reactions of the subjects were recorded and subjected to observer judgments. The findings supported the validity of both objectively coded and observer-rated facial expressions as research tools in assessing pain levels with this disabled population.

Mere self-attention to somatic symptoms can significantly influence experience of neuropsychological symptoms. Participants in one study were told to attend to physical and psychological symptoms (Williams, Lees-Haley, and Price, 1998). Those instructed subjects evidenced more complaints of physical symptoms and reports of anxiety and depression, compared to controls that were not instructed. The findings support careful consideration of self-reported symptoms by assessors.

Two other factors significantly affecting the assessment of malingered pain are litigation and compensation. Studies have demonstrated that legal definitions and compensation criteria can and do influence pain syndrome presentation (Hadjistavropoulos, 1999; Lees-Haley, 1989, 1990b; Lees-Haley and Fox, 1990). Researchers have found, for example, that patients in litigation consistently reported more favorable preinjury status compared to controls (Lees-Haley et al., 1996, Lees-Haley, Williams, Zasler, Marguilies, English, and Stevens, 1997). Such a response style by plaintiffs underscores the need for caution in approaching personal injury cases involved in litigation. Self-reported symptoms by plaintiffs are subject to response bias that must be considered in the assessment process. The biased response set does not necessarily implicate deceit over a reliable report.

One of the most important aids to neuropsychological assessment is awareness by the clinician of base-rate data for given categories of symptoms (Dunn, Brown, Less-Haley, and English, 1993). Base-rate studies of self-reported symptoms by personal injury claimants reflect spuriously high rates of reported symptoms (Lees-Haley, 1992; Lees-Haley et al., 1996). These high rates of reported symptoms by personal injury claimants have led to some investigators labeling the phenomenon as the "Barnum" effect (Lees-Haley, Williams, and Brown, 1993). The effect refers to ambiguous interpretations (nondeliberate distortion) of circumstances and symptom effects based on individual personality differences. Another consideration is the relative ease involved with even naive, untrained individuals to accurately mimic a variety of psychiatric and neuropsychological symptoms, for example, mild brain injury, posttraumatic stress disorder (PTSD), major depression, and anxiety disorders (Lees-Haley and Dunn, 1994). According to Stein (1972), professionals should be cautious in concluding that feigned pain indicates malingering. In *Boyd v. General Industries* (1987), the court held that a 47-year-old assembly line worker who injured her back on the job in 1980 could recover for increased or prolonged disability due to subjective pain in view of the testimony of doctors that her experience of pain was real to her. Furthermore, plaintiffs may recover damages even if they engaged in willful deception, based on the principle that genuine deficits such as psychological pain can be accompanied by unrelated lying and distortion. The court stated as follows (p. 755):

We have also said, however, that the Commission may not refuse compensation to a claimant simply because he is untruthful (*Guidry v. J. & R. Eads Const. Co.*, 1984). In the case at bar, Boyd's credibility is only relevant on the issue of whether she is malingering, and the Commission's decision carries with it an implicit finding that she is malingering.

Here, there is no substantial evidence to support a finding of malingering. Dr. Hutt, upon whose testimony the Commission particularly relied, said that Boyd's perceptions of pain are 'very real to her,' and that there was no evidence of malingering or intentional distortion of perceived severity of pain. Dr. Bevilacqua stated that Boyd appeared "very sincere and reliable" and that "she has absolutely no insight into her obvious emotional conflicts."

Dr. Kaczenski said Boyd was not malingering. None of the many doctors who have seen Boyd have so much as suggested that she might be malingering. Although compensation claims predicated upon mental disorders must be carefully scrutinized in order to protect the employer against unwarranted claims, the danger of denying recovery to a deserving claimant must be guarded against with equal enthusiasm. *Royer v. Cantrelle*, 267 So.2d 601 (La.Ct. App. 3rd 1972), writ denied, 263 La. 626, 268 So.2d 680 (1972).

In contrast, in *Yager v. Labor and Industry Review Commission, Sentry Insurance Company and Lands' End* (1999), the appeals court upheld the earlier finding of the Labor and Industry Review Commission (LIRC) of malingering by the plaintiff. The court cited the LIRC opinion:

> The inconsistencies in the applicant's testimony as compared to her medical records undercuts her credibility. In addition the evidence indicated that the applicant had a history of preexisting neck, shoulder, and back problems which required treatment and were bothering her up until the day before the alleged incident on January 25, 1996. Given the medical evidence in the record, including the reports from Dr. Goodman and Dr. Marsh ... the evidence was sufficient to raise a legitimate doubt that the applicant sustained a shoulder, neck, or back injury arising out of her employment ... on January 25, 1996.

Defining pain and its possible deception is difficult. The standard definition suggests that pain is a response to noxious stimuli—those which produce or threaten to produce tissue damage. Yet, psychic pain produced by psychological stimuli may be just as distressing as purely physical pain to affected individuals. In many cases, there may be no difference between physical and psychological pain in reported intensity, frequency, or duration. Both intertwine to a considerable extent, with depression, anxiety, and frustration increasing experienced pain, and vice versa.

The most common types of chronic pain syndromes include: (a) headaches—tension, migraine, vascular, and posttraumatic; (b) back pains—disc disease, spondylitis, osteoporosis, and fractures; (c) psychologically induced pain—trauma, PTSD, etc.; and (d) others—myofascial pain, muscle spasm, and sympathetic dystrophies. These, of course, are types of disorders in which pain is the primary complaint.

In addition, headaches around the eyes can be also due to glaucoma, around the back of the neck to meningitis, and in the face to trigeminal neuralgia. Psychological pain is a common correlate of many DSM-IV (1994) conditions. These include the depressive and anxiety disorders, hypochondriasis and hysteria, and the organic mental disorders. The International Classification of Diseases (ICD, 1989) describes many pain-related diseases, including musculoskeletal disorders (e.g., osteoarthritis and Paget's disease), ischemic disorders (angina pectoris and claudication), neurological disorders (e.g., causalgia, coccydynia, and scar pain), and miscellaneous categories such as chronic pancreatitis and temporomandibular joint syndrome.

In sum, pain may be either the defining or an associated feature of a disorder and may be due to either physical or psychological causes. It may be exaggerated or distorted without being totally fabricated. It may be genuine even when there is evidence of outright lying.

Recent court findings have focused on dispositional concerns with pain claimants, as compared with earlier cases that attempted to define and refine conditions under which pain claims met legal criteria. In *Keever v. Middletown* (1998), the plaintiff Keever was a disabled police officer who claimed that his alleged forced retirement amounted to a constructive discharge from duty and thereby violated disability statutes. The appeals court found that reasonable accommodations had been offered to the plaintiff. The count found invalid Mr Keever's perception that his being offered a "desk job" was punitive. In another personal injury case that stems from on-the-job injuries, the employer argued that the plaintiff had not submitted to actual physical assessments of her incapacities to definitively determine whether the claimed injuries were factual (*Quint v. A. E. Staley*, 1999). The court ruled that no court precedent existed to require ADA plaintiffs to submit to such physical assessment. Instead, the court ruled that the plaintiff might rely on competent medical testimony to justify a personal decision to refrain from a life activity that could result in imminent risk of further injury.

The issue of plaintiffs' "subjective testimony" regarding claims of personal injury was addressed in *Smolen v. Chater* (1998). The court described that the administrative law judge (ALJ) must perform two stages of analysis in making a determination to accept or reject a claimant's subjective testimony regarding claimed symptoms. The two stages of analysis are:

1. The Cotton test (*Cotton v. Bowen*, 1986). The standard of this test requires that claimants who allege disability based on subjective symptoms must produce objective medical evidence of an underlying impairment that "could reasonably be expected to produce" the claimed symptoms. The evidence must also support a causal relationship between the impairments and symptoms.
2. Credibility analysis. The standard of this test is the ALJ finding no "affirmative evidence" that the plaintiff is malingering.

These two analyses outline a process for judges in personal injury cases to assess and try claims based on subjective pain symptoms. Nonetheless, the door remains open for malingering. Another obvious problem is the process of the ALJ making a subjective determination about a subjective symptom.

Neuropsychological Factors

The brain has few pain endings, and cerebral lesions rarely cause pain. The exception is the (rare) thalamic pain syndrome, which may cause vague, difficult-to-localize pain. Strokes and surgery involving the thalamus create a burning sensation, contralateral from the lesioned site (Kaufman, 1985).

Both physical and psychic pain pathways involve the limbic system, thus associating sensory with affective information. Parker (1990) notes some psychological features of pain:

1. At low levels of arousal, pain may serve an informative function.
2. At high levels of arousal and stress, pain is accentuated.
3. Elevated tension and anger are associated with increased acute pain; chronic anxiety (e.g., "anxiety proneness") and depression are also associated with an increased perception of pain, as well as the presence of collateral physical impairment.
4. Increased pain is associated with inability to express one's feelings.

The usual psychological consequences of chronic pain include deteriorating self-esteem, irritation, sexual dysfunction, anger, and guilt. Depression may be a key psychological correlate of chronic pain (Griffith, 1990).

Social/Cultural Factors

Pain often functions as a signal to others for help or attention. Flor, Kerns, and Turk (1987) reported that the best predictor of self-reported pain was the person's perception of spousal reinforcement. Patients who viewed their spouses as solicitous reported higher levels of pain and lower levels of activity. Increased dependency on others as a response to pain is common. A progressive withdrawal and isolation from others is seen in some cases. This process is exacerbated by a noted tendency for family, friends, and acquaintances to avoid people in pain. One reason for this avoidance is to reduce exposure to the unpleasant displays of the affected party. Loss of work may further reduce self-esteem and increase depression, as well as destroy the financial basis for the future of the individual.

Culturally, some persons are not encouraged to show pain responses (e.g., some Oriental groups, Northern Europeans). Other groups are much more expressive (e.g., Mediterranean people, Polynesians). The evaluator needs to consider communication styles when assessing an individual's complaints of pain. In some individuals, apparently exaggerated complaints of pain may represent personal (e.g., histrionic) or subcultural (e.g., Mediterranean) styles of communication rather than evidence of intentional distortion.

Targets of Deception

Both pain and loss of sensation may be compensable losses. All chronic pain and sensation-loss syndromes can be targeted for deception. Although pain complaints are overrepresented in the lower back area (where nerves are in abundance) (Griffith, 1990), reported pain can be widely distributed over the body. Lifestyle should be adversely affected with genuine pain. Thus, the evaluator needs to be alert to many targets of deception and to assess the entire lifestyle of the assessee.

Examples of potentially malingered pain include:

Behavior	Discrete motor behaviors associated with low back pain were shown by a 25-year-old male who engaged in vigorous exercise when not posturing weakness and immobility
Somatic/psychosomatic	Pseudo-seizures following an alleged painful aura-like experience were presented by a 32-year-old brick mason in an attempt to collect workers' compensation
Sensation	Extreme reactivity to touch and pressure was shown on two-point threshold tests by an 18-year-old burn patient 4 years after suffering minor (first-degree) burns
Imagery	Painful images (flashbacks) of war were experienced by a 35-year-old male veteran even though it was determined that he had not been stationed in a combat area
Affect	Anxiety lowered, rather than raised, perceived pain in a 45-year-old female seeking compensation for an accident involving a slight fall while disembarking from a marine craft
Cognition	"Suicide" ideation and gestures of an unrealistic nature (hitting self with fists, trying to strangle himself) were shown by a 27-year-old in an alleged attempt to escape from a painful love relationship
Interpersonal	Interpersonal manipulation was suggested by a 59-year-old when he required family members to wait on him after making up a history of painful heart attacks

It is important to note genuine symptoms of pain, or signs associated with pain, which cannot be faked. These include (Goldberg, 1987): (a) muscle atrophy and fasciculation, the latter consisting of a sometimes painful contraction of skeletal muscles in which groups of muscle fibers innervated by the same neuron contract together and (b) visual disturbances such as the pupillary light reflex, abnormal retinal appearance, ocular divergence, and nystagmus. All the above should be considered involuntary in nature.

Evaluators should not confuse complainers with fakers. False-positives are frequent in this (primitive) stage of pain analysis as the following case demonstrates:

> Lt. Arnold walked into the army mental health clinic stating that he had been referred by the internist to rule out psychological factors to a reported injury. This young officer explained that no medical cause had been found for a sharp, excruciating but episodic pain in his lower back, first experienced when leading his platoon in calisthenics, and that he did not feel the examining physician believed him. Psychometric tests revealed many traits associated with hysteria including a substantial conversion "V" on the MMPI.
>
> Subsequently, the lieutenant reported that the military physician, upon receiving the psychological test results, had accused the officer of malingering and ordered him back to the field. The psychologist referred the client to an osteopath who cleared up the problem in less than 15 minutes with spinal manipulation.

Response Styles

Like targets, the kinds of behaviors associated with faking some aspect of pain include any response that may yield a successful outcome for the faker. Honesty is common when there is no reason to fake or when cross-validating data are readily available to the evaluator. Faking good sometimes occurs when the client wishes to minimize or deny a more negatively perceived problem such as sexual dysfunction. This denial covaries with cultural upbringing and with contexts where the expression of pain may be disapproved (e.g., military and sports).

Malingering pain and faking sensory numbness may be linked to a payoff for the deceiver. Mixed and fluctuating responding can be exhibited, such as when one type of pain is exaggerated (e.g., backache) and another denied (e.g., headache), with both changing in the reported level of severity over time.

Help-seeking behaviors associated with pain and injury are instructive to study. Peck, Fordyce, and Black (1978) studied a wide range of pain behavior in tort claim litigants. Only two conditions identified the possible fakers—they consulted fewer physicians and utilized more supportive devices (i.e., crutches and prosthetics) that cost more than $200. As part of this study, Peck et al. found that claimants used less prescribed pain-relieving drugs than nonlitigants for the first month of postinjury. By the sixth month, drug ingestion had dropped off sharply for both groups. In sum, the Peck et al. (1978) study suggests there are few differences between claimants and nonlitigants in help-seeking behaviors. If anything, those who had reason to fake seemed to avoid evaluators and treatment personnel. None of the following categories considered by these investigators should be regarded as indicative of faking: (a) number of hospital admissions, (b) length of stay in the hospital, (c) number of diagnostic procedures in the hospital, (d) help-seeking in regard to rehabilitative centers, (e) days lost from work, and (f) number of patient–physician contacts or specialists consulted.

In a study exploring a relationship between personality disorder diagnosis and malingering response style, a significant relationship was found between personality test validity scales and faking bad (Grillo, Brown, Hilsabeck, Price, and Less-Haley, 1994). The investigators administered the MCMI-II and the MMPI-2 (F, K, L, F-K, O-S, Es, and FBS) to personal injury claimants. There was a positive relationship between histrionic, compulsive, schizoid, schizotypal, paranoid, borderline, antisocial, avoidant, and passive-aggressive personality disorders and fake bad elevations on validity indices. There was no such relationship between dependent and narcissistic personality disorders. The authors concluded that psychopathologic variables, and specifically personality disorders, as opposed to malingering, could account for symptom exaggeration in forensic settings. The next question is whether or not there is a comorbid relationship between certain personality disorders and malingering.

Detection Strategies

Most evaluators of pain use a consistency model in determining faked pain. Yet, pain may be inconstant due to habituation, change in context, psychological modification, and other factors. This argues for a multifaceted approach to evaluation, hopefully with the results pointing in the same direction.

A few methods for detecting faked pain are as follows:

1. Anatomical inconsistencies.
    a. Pain versus temperature: These sensations tend to coincide because they are located in the same nerve bundles. When the temperature sensation is preserved while there is a loss of pain sensation, the deficit is not considered organic in etiology. Kaufman (1985) reports that a lesion of the pain–temperature pathway (spinothalamic tract) will result in loss of pain–temperature sensation contralateral to and below the level of the lesion. This holds true whether the lesion is in the brain or in the spinal cord. Additionally, the loss of pain–temperature sensation in the right leg and loss of proprioception in the left leg suggest a single lesion on the spinal cord.
    b. Faked hemiparesis is clinically more common in the left limb than the right, perhaps because of the more frequent right-limb dominance. Often, there will be a short period of normal activity prior to the limbs "giving away" and the patient reassuming the paretic position.
    c. Fakers often have an incorrect belief about laterality of symptoms. This is exhibited when the faker describes right- or left-sided headaches in conjunction with other anomalies (e.g., hearing, sight, smell, and motor deficits) on the right side. The faker is not aware that contralateral and not ipsilateral deficits are expected from the suggested injury. Multiple lesions, causing unilateral symptoms, are required in order to account for the reported effects.
    d. Self-inflicted pain is usually avoided when there is voluntary control. In this sense, a person will not strike himself or herself when pretending to be in a coma or paretic. Neurologists will often use a "face-hand" test assessing alleged motor impairment, pulling the hand away from the face and suddenly letting it go.
    e. Motor inconstancies are suggested when impairments disappear under hypnosis, sodium amytal, or when the faker believes he or she is unobserved. Findings from hypnosis and drug interviews, however, should be considered weak evidence unless corroborated by independent data.
    f. Alleged pain imperception or loss of sensation is difficult to fake upon repeated bilateral stimulation. This is because fakers are relying on a subjective strategy rather than responding to the strength of the stimulus. Von Frey hairs, for example, can be used to bilaterally test a faked sensory imperception.

2. Drug response discrepancies. Some drugs have differing chemical composition, yet are similar in terms of effect on reducing pain. Thus, two tablets of aspirin (600 mg) are reported to have the same effect as a standard dose of Darvon, codeine, or Demerol (Kaufman, 1985). Suspected faking is associated with widely divergent pain relief from the two. This is a weak hypothesis until confirmed by cross-validating data suggesting malingering.

3. Clinical interview behavior. Data are lacking on interview behavior associated with faked pain. However, systems looking at faked pain and loss of sensation are beginning to be developed. Barkemeyer, Callon, and Jones (1989) have developed a malingering test for pain, loss of sensation, and other complaints.

4. Presence of psychometric signs.

    a. Although the "conversion V" on the MMPI and MMPI-2 may or may not reflect a conversion based on a psychological conflict, it does suggest the clients' (a) perception of their pain, (b) their perception of affect related to their disability, and (c) degree of functional impairment (Tapp, 1990). This pattern is associated with a poorer prognosis for recovery and with the experience of acute, high-intensity pain. A hysterical overlay to exhibited pain may be present. The hysteria may not be subject to control by the assessee and should not be considered deception by the evaluator.

       Validity indices on the MMPI and other objective tests may be used to determine general response style. Indications of faking bad on the MMPI, for example, may suggest (but do not prove) that reported pain may also be exaggerated. Furthermore, pain is seldom experienced in the absence of other affective and psychological problems. These other problems should also be apparent in psychological test scores and profiles. In a study designed to determine the various MMPI-2 indicators of exaggeration, the profiles of 289 claimants from worker compensation and personal injury cases were examined (Fox, Gerson, and Lees-Haley, 1995). The test indices that were reviewed included the intercorrelations of the F, F-K, the MMPI-2 dissimulation scale-revised, the total of obvious minus subtle scales, the fake bad Scale, VRIN, and TRIN. The relative sensitivity of the different scores was estimated according to various cut-offs. Factor analysis indicated that malingering could be evidenced as inconsistent responding and as symptom exaggeration. Not surprisingly, the study also found that patients evaluated at the request of plaintiff attorneys appeared to show a greater degree of symptom exaggeration and inconsistent responding compared to those referred by defense counsel.

    b. An illness questionnaire developed in Australia by Clayer, Bookless, and Ross (1984) appears promising for the global assessment of distress. Validated on 164 male and female public utility workers, half of whom were instructed to fake a serious injury, and 82 male and female clients at a pain clinic, the questionnaire appeared effective in differentiating fakers from those experiencing distress which was neurotically determined.

       Base rates for normals and neurotics generally revealed an increasing percentage of item endorsement by the latter group. Fakers were very clearly differentiated from nonfakers (i.e., normals and neurotics) on 7 of the 62 total questions. Recalculating the data, the majority of fakers (64.2%) endorsed all the following questions compared to 27% of the nonfakers, with a 25–50% point spread between the two groups (mean difference = 36.8%) on each question:

    i. Do you care whether or not people realize you are sick?

    ii. Do you find that you get jealous of other people's good health?

    iii. Do you ever have silly thoughts about your health which you cannot get out of your mind, no matter how hard you try?

    iv. Are you upset by the way people take your illness?

    v. Do you often worry about the possibility that you have a serious illness?

    vi. Do you often think that you might suddenly fall ill?

    vii. Do you get the feeling that people are not taking your illness seriously enough?

c. The Millon Behavioral Health Inventory (MBHI; Millon, Green, and Meagher, 1979) attempts to measure responsivity to pain treatment as well as a host of basic coping and prognostic signs. The MBHI illustrates the great difficulty of measuring variables associated with distress. The 150-item true-false questionnaire yields 20 scores and a three-item validity scale. Test construction, reliability, and validity of the measure have been vigorously challenged (Allen, 1985; Lanyon, 1985).

d. Chronic pain self-report inventories. A number of self-report measures for chronic pain have been described. All these measures must be used with caution because of the potential for deliberate as well as nondeliberate distortion. Accordingly, none of these inventories should be considered to be specific tests for faking pain as no such reliable and valid measure exists. These checklist inventories may be useful in developing a broad database before arriving at conclusions.

    The pain survey checklist (PSCL) (see Appendix Q) is one example of a self-report inventory. The PSCL is comprehensive, covering most known parameters of the pain experience. Significant others may be asked to independently fill out the checklist in regard to the patient, thereby providing information where follow-up assessment may be needed.

    In a comparative study, Mikail, DuBreuil, and D'Eon (1993) reviewed the following nine commonly used self-report measures:

    i. Oswestry Back Pain Disability Questionnaire

    ii. Pain Behavior Questionnaire

    iii. Beck Depression Inventory

    iv. State-Trait Anxiety Inventory

    v. Coping Strategies Questionnaire

    vi. Pain Beliefs Questionnaire

    vii. McGill Pain Questionnaire

    viii. West Haven-Yale Multidimensional Pain Inventory

    ix. Life Impact Scale

Factor analysis identified five factors across the battery of inventories. The factors were general affective distress, coping, support, pain description, and functional capacity. The investigators reported that the combination of the multidimensional pain inventory, the Beck depression inventory, and the McGill pain questionnaire best captured the pain experience with minimal overlap across instruments. The investigators also recommended that if anxiety was an issue with a specific pain case, the trait anxiety inventory should be administered.

The Chronic Pain Coping Inventory (CHIP) (Jensen, Turner, Romano, and Strom, 1995) is another self-report checklist instrument. The CHIP is designed to provide measures of emotion-focused and task-oriented responses to injury (Hadjistavropoulos, Asmundson, and Norton, 1999). In terms of deception, all of these instruments are subject to the pitfalls of any self-reported data. The judicious use of such inventories may provide, however, records of the patient's postinjury status. These data could also provide indirect measures of the patient's ongoing experience with pain and genuine commitment to rehabilitation.

e. Other methods. Previously discussed methods for detecting malingering (e.g., analysis of learning curves, regression equations, parallel testing, and Explicit Alternative Testing (EAT)) may be used in pain deception analysis, if those methods measure an associated feature of reported pain (e.g., loss of sensation).

5. Inconsistency in community versus evaluation behavior. A detailed analysis of pain reportedly experienced outside the evaluation context is necessary for sound conclusions. This is based on two assumptions: (a) reduced motor activity level accompanies genuine pain, and (b) the activity level shown during evaluation should be similar to that shown outside the evaluation session. Some impairment in work and in central love relationships should be reported with chronic pain. Is the claimant willing to have you speak with significant others? A refusal is suspicious. A list of specific questions that can be asked is provided in Appendix Q. The same list can be given to different relatives and acquaintances to fill out independently of one another. Inconsistencies can be evaluated. A statement by significant others, for example, that nothing the claimant does changes reports of pain needs to be explored. The claimant needs to be asked what he or she does to reduce pain. The evaluator should explore statements of changes in pain in the absence of events which would explain them.

Malingered pain is suggested when behavior in the community is inconsistent with complaints of pain.

> A 32-year-old mail carrier was routinely administered psychological and medical exams as part of on-going evaluation and treatment for an alleged neck injury reportedly caused by a fall due to an attacking dog on his route several years previously. Claimed discomfort in the neck area persisted in spite of normal MMPIs and physical/neurological exams over the years. Complaints abruptly ended when a full (and permanent) medical retirement was awarded. After retirement, the party was seen frequently on the golf driving range, engaging in strenuous exercise that only a few months previously had been reported impossible to perform.

6. Lack of response to common interventions. Almost all clients should show some pain relief with (a) biofeedback, (b) hypnosis, (c) mild analgesics, (d) psychotherapy for anger and arousal management, (e) relaxation exercises, (f) heat and ice, and (g) mild exercise. The client should show pain relief in his limbs or lower back with transcutaneous electrical nerve stimulation (TENS). TENS involves an electric stimulus being applied near the painful site, which has the effect of creating analgesia. Why a person with chronic pain would not show some improvement with these methods needs to be answered and integrated into evaluation findings.

Indications of Faked Pain and Loss of Sensation

1. a. Pain. Pain-free behaviors observed in community are absent or denied during evaluation, or
   b. Loss of sensation. Behavior in community implies sensitivity that is absent or denied during evaluation.
2. Admission of exaggeration or fabrication.
3. Violation of anatomical laws involving dermatomes, pain versus temperature loss, paresis, cerebral laterality, and motor functioning.
4. a. Malingering on psychometric measures of psychopathology.
   b. Failing tests specifically designed to assess faking.
5. Failure to show improvement when treated with typically effective interventions.

Research investigating the nature of pain syndromes continues to be a very challenging area of clinical practice. The experience of pain is an inevitable and ubiquitous aspect of human existence. The evaluation, treatment, and management of pain is a very costly expense in the ongoing effort to achieve productive and functional life styles for all cross-sections of socioeconomic strata (Block, Kremer, and Fernandez, 1999).

Perhaps an indication of the frustration with the challenge of forensic evaluations, some authors (e.g., Johnson and Lesniak-Karpiak, 1997) have suggested warning patients that simulation of symptoms may be detected. Such a warning is an ethically questionable assertion, given the current limitations in detecting pain deception. An additional consideration is that others (Youngjohn, Lees-Haley, and Binder, 1999) have noted that such warnings only serve to prevent detection of deception. When warned, malingers feign symptoms with less exaggeration and generally offer more believable presentation. Although still far from a refined art, the clinical differentiation of actual and falsified pain continues to be an area of active research. Craig et al. (1999) summarized that the most recent research regarding malingered pain provides evidence that:

1. Genuine presentations of pain differ from deceptive presentations; the research challenges are to develop procedural methodologies that reliably distinguish these differences across various types of pain presentations and in real-life clinical situations.
2. Informed and careful clinicians, as well as others, can discriminate genuine and deceptive presentations.
3. Empirically informed assessment approaches can be developed.

Faked Amnesia and Recall Skills

Memory deficits are found in everyday life and in pathological conditions. They span chronological ages from childhood to old age. They are transient and permanent, specific and global, functional and organic, and normal and pathognomic. Moreover, of course, because they are largely private events, they are fake-able and highly subject to distortion. Memory problems can arise from dysfunctions at any stage of information processing: registration, short-term storage, consolidation, long-term storage, or retrieval (McCarthy and Warrington, 1990). Failure of registration, for example, may be due to limits in the span of apprehension (e.g., children may apprehend three items of information, while adults may apprehend seven items) or to deficits in "chunking" or categorizing information. Problems in short-term storage may be due to deficits in the durability of the memory trace or to attentional deficits. Problems in retrieval may be due to a heightened sensitivity to interference or to a failure of consolidation.

These various deficits may have diverse origins. Impaired memory performance per se has no value for differential diagnosis of pathological conditions.

Forensic Issues

Claimed memory problems are frequent in civil cases involving both tort claims and eligibility claims. Motor vehicle accidents, assaults, industrial accidents, and sporting accidents are leading causes of head injuries that frequently find their way into civil suits for negligence, into social security disability claims and into workman's compensation claims. Mnestic deficits are the most prevalent residual symptoms of head injuries and therefore figure prominently in civil claims. "In extreme cases, the injured person is forever bound to an extended present, with recollections of the past and anticipation of the future only fleetingly within awareness. In milder cases, where performance on experimental psychometric memory tasks falls within premorbid expectations, attention and memory difficulties may show as periodic absent-mindedness, especially when dealing with tasks that place a strain on these functions and that rarely can be simulated by conventional assessment procedures" (Grimm and Bleiberg, 1986, p. 500).

Memory problems in cases of closed head injury involve both anterograde and retrograde amnesia. Anterograde amnesia (sometimes called posttraumatic amnesia) refers to memory deficits during the period after a head injury and includes the time of any coma, the time of any confusional period after consciousness is regained, and, in severe cases, a time of varying length thereafter. Retrograde amnesia refers to deficits in the retrieval of memories already consolidated prior to the head injury. In the natural course of recovery from head injury, "anterograde posttraumatic amnesia gradually improves, after which the duration of the retrograde amnesia commonly shows a progressive shrinking to within a few minutes or seconds of the accident" (Cummings and Benson, 1983). This process of salvaging old memories and consolidating new memories is quite variable, depending on the severity of the injury and age of the patient, and may range from a few seconds to years.

Even in cases of mild closed head injury, with no loss of consciousness and normal radiological and neurological tests, memory deficits may be apparent in everyday functioning. As Corthell and Tooman (1985) stated:

> After even the mildest of injuries, *incidental* memory, i.e., the ability to recall information not specifically attended to, may be severely impaired. For example, misplaced keys, charge cards, packages, and shoes are common; appointments and commitments are instantly forgotten if not written down, despite every good intention and motivation to carry through. Standard intellectual examinations tend to test familiar, previously learned information and skills.
>
> Very little new learning or extended memory may be required on standard psychological examination. Head trauma clients often score in the "average" range or above on standard mental ability (IQ) tests, and yet can be severely impaired in their capacities for new learning and memory. (p. 15)

In general, there is a positive correlation between the severity of a head injury (as measured, for example, by length of coma) and the severity and duration of both anterograde and retrograde amnesia. There is also a positive correlation between the severity/duration of anterograde amnesia and the severity/duration of retrograde amnesia, although retrograde amnesias tend to be brief. Furthermore, there is a positive correlation between the duration of anterograde amnesia and everyday functioning. "Within broad limits it may be predicted that a patient with a[n anterograde amnesia] of less than an hour will usually return to work within a month, with a[n anterograde amnesia] of less than a day within two months, and with a[n anterograde amnesia] of less than a week within four months. [Anterograde amnesias] exceeding a week will often be followed by invalidism extending over the greater part of a year" (Lishman, 1987, p. 145).

Therefore, the severity of a closed head injury and the duration of anterograde amnesia can provide a rough clue as to the genuineness of claimed memory deficits. If a head injury was mild, residual memory deficits should be mild and should be more apparent in incidental memory than in psychometric memory. A patient presenting with a history of mild head injury and complaints of severe mnestic deficits would appear suspicious. If the closed head injury was severe, longer lasting and more severe anterograde amnesia can be expected. A patient presenting with a history of severe head injury and complaints of mnestic difficulties even years after the injury is more plausible.

When the head injury is caused by penetrating or crushing forces (e.g., a gunshot wound), the duration of anterograde amnesia is a less reliable guide to severity and prognosis. "With penetrating injuries due to missiles or with depressed skull fractures … Concussion and amnesia may then be brief or absent, yet focal cognitive deficits can be severe especially if haemorrhage or infection have occurred" (Lishman, 1987, p. 157). These focal deficits include specific amnesias, such as auditory-verbal or visual-mnestic deficits, rather than global amnesia. Depending on the severity of the specific deficits, the degree of everyday impairment may vary from mild to incapacitating. In such clinical cases, there is no "natural course" of recovery against which to assess the genuineness of a patient's complaints.

Similarly, the residual effects of anoxia or exposure to neurochemicals (including prescription medications) is highly variable, depending on such factors as the extent and duration of the anoxia and the toxicity and dosage of the neurochemical, and on patient variables such as age and sensitivity. In drowning cases, the extent of central nervous system damage, for example, is mediated by the victim's core body temperature during the period of anoxia. In cases of heavy metal, poisoning (e.g., lead, mercury, and manganese), and solvent inhalation (e.g., "glue sniffing"), the cumulative dosage level is determinative of any residual effects of exposure. Dosage, individual sensitivity, and length of exposure to phenothiazines (e.g., "Haldol") are all critical in producing Parkinsonism, akathisia, and tardive dyskinesia. Global and specific, mild and severe forms of amnesia may be found among survivors of anoxia or neurotoxicity.

In a review article, Schacter (1986) suggested that genuine versus faked recall can be distinguished by examining the behavior of the accused in general. For example, was the offense well prepared or impulsive? The amnesia claim itself may help identify malingered amnesia. Limited recall during the crime with a sharply defined onset and termination is suggestive of faked or exaggerated amnesia. A suspect's "feeling of knowing" may also be used as a detection method. A "feeling of knowing" is a "subjective conviction that one could retrieve or recognize an unrecalled item, event, or fact if one were given some useful hints or cues." The examiner asks possible fakers to rate their feeling of knowing that they could recall or recognize crime events if given assistance. Fakers tend to discount the chance that their recall would improve. Thus, feigning memory problems is a fundamental concern for forensic professionals in both civil and criminal cases. The essentially private nature of the complaint of amnesia and the possible motive to malinger in legal situations encourage some persons to hide their intentional deception behind the variability and complexity of genuine amnesia. Distinguishing genuine from faked memory problems calls upon the best of psychological, neuropsychological, and forensic skills.

Everyday Assumptions about Memory

Faked recall almost always involves assumptions about the way memory normally functions. These assumptions may conform to a common sense or layman's view of memory, but rarely encompass empirical facts about memory processes. The typical person is unlikely to distinguish recognition and recall processes, primacy and recency effects, learning curves and forgetting curves (e.g., Wiggins and Brandt, 1988).

The evaluation of erroneous assumptions made by deceivers should be studied for clues to deception. Herrmann (1982) noted that:

1. People know their memory only to a moderate degree. Fakers may wrongly think, for example, that they can recall their answers to a particular test, yet are unable to repeat their performance when retested.
2. Some types of memory are more stable over time than others; for example, visual experiences involving places (visual memory) are generally recalled more reliably than conversations (auditory-verbal memory). The faker may not know this and perform differentially on various sensory tasks. Information that even true amnesiacs generally don't forget over time also includes word completion. Graf, Squire, and Mandler (1984) found that word completion (cued recall) in amnesic patients declined at a normal rate when subjects were presented with the first three letters of each word presented earlier. They also cite literature that shows that amnesic patients perform normally when (1) given degraded versions of previously presented words, (2) reading words from a mirror-reversed display, and (3) completing puzzles.
3. In most people, recognition appears better than free recall. This is true in normals, those experiencing posthypnotic amnesia, and the brain damaged (Brandt, Rubinsky, and Lassen, 1985; Iverson, Franzen, and McCracken, 1991). In this latter study, subjects feigning amnesia ($n = 10$) performed worse on free recall compared to normals ($n = 12$), those with Huntington's disease ($n = 14$), and those with head trauma ($n = 5$). Recognition performance was above chance levels for both normals and head trauma subjects. Of the 14 subjects with Huntington's disease, eight performed better than chance and the rest at chance levels. All of the malingerers performed at chance ($n = 7$) or below chance ($n = 3$).

   Wiggins and Brandt (1988) presented critical questions for which the probability of obtaining wrong answers by both nonsimulating controls and amnesiacs with bona fide organic conditions approaches zero. Incorrect answers to these questions should be expected only among those with clinically severe retrograde amnesia and, even in those cases, performance might be improved by cueing, prompting or presenting choices (McCarthy and Warrington, 1990, pp. 307–313).

Any mnestic deficit can be faked. This includes immediate, short-term, and long-term recall problems. Any event that occurred in a person's life can be denied; recollection can be patchy and variable as memory returns.

Fakers tend to distort signs relevant to intended symptoms only on certain tests. Further, mild-to-moderate deficits appear to be faked more often than severe memory problems (e.g., dementia and global amnesia). Most likely, these types of deficits are selected because of their difficulty in detection. Faking recall should be suspected if (a) there is a loss of crystallized knowledge of skills, which almost never happens; (b) recognition is worse than recall, for example, for lists of words; (c) the person is exhibiting inconsistent organic or psychiatric signs (e.g., DSM-IV conditions).

Response Styles

Most fakers show longer latencies in responding to recall questions (Resnick, 1984). This may be because they are simultaneously performing two mental operations—stopping a correct response and presenting another. Many of the faking-bad response styles that depend on memory tasks may be utilized by the malingerer. Faking partial deficits may include the following strategies: (a) fractional effort, (b) approximate answers, (c) distributing errors among correct answers, and (d) overall attempt to control error percentage. Fakers often make intentional mistakes early in the evaluation and may change style. (Hall and Shooter, 1989; Pankratz, 1988, 1998)

Lande (1993) described an interesting case study depicting a rather unusual and complex malingering response style. The case involved a senior enlisted soldier who worked as a recruiter and made $18,000 worth of unauthorized 900 phone calls on a government telephone. Subsequent clinical assessment based on the phone abuse generated an array of initial differential diagnoses including the following: malingering, dissociative disorder (psychogenic amnesia), depression, obsessive-compulsive disorder, an unusual paraphilia (telephone scatologia), a seizure disorder, and an adult antisocial disorder. In the end, the clinical data did not persuasively suggest the presence of a significant mental disorder. The soldier was found guilty by a military court martial.

Detection Strategies

The development of popular episodic memory tests was the result of traditional neuropsychological measures not satisfactorily discriminating between cerebral brain impairment and malingered impairment (Greiffenstein, Baker, and Gola, 1994). For a review of traditional memory instruments and batteries see Lezak (1995). Over the years, the efficacy of different instruments to detect malingered memory deficits has received mixed reviews across empirical studies. One problem has been studies using different instruments or different clinical populations and then suggesting that the findings generalize to all types of brain injury where malingering may be an issue. Another problem has been validation studies based solely on the performance of normal dissimulators, usually undergraduates. It has become apparent that the detection of malingering from actual brain trauma must involve careful and selective use of assessment instruments, collaborative use of assessment instruments, and selective use of cut-off scores adjusted to brain injury type.

Herrmann (1982, pp. 438–439), in his review, discusses a wide variety of commonly used memory questionnaires. Yet, these tests correlate only moderately with actual recall abilities. A further problem is they have no built-in deception scales and are predicated on the notion that the subject will give his or her best performance. At best, they can be used in parallel fashion if test–retest improvement is taken into consideration. The faker may have difficulty repeating his or her own first (inferior) performance.

Rey (1964) devised a 15-item visual memory test specifically designed to detect feigned memory difficulties. The task consists of five rows of patterned stimuli (e.g., ABC, 123, and abc) which give the impression of task complexity (15 items) but which are easily "clustered" into just five memory units. Lezak (1983) and Goldberg and Miller (1986) suggested a cut-off score of nine recalled items was optimal for detecting suspicious mnestic performances. Bernard and Fowler (1990) suggested a cut-off score of 8 and Lee, Loring, and Martin (1992) suggested a cut-off score of 7. Clearly, the optimal cut-off score for detecting malingering will vary from population to population (e.g., demented patients, retarded patients, and naive Ss) (Flowers, Sheridan, and Shadbolt, 1996; Schretlen, Brandt, Kraft, and Van Gorp, 1991). Greiffenstein, Baker, and Gola (1996) observed that Rey's measures appeared to be valid for assessment of cognitive malingering in situations where litigated disability claims were out of proportion to injury characteristics. They cautioned that Rey's measures were not appropriate for globally and severely impaired patients in clinical settings.

The Wechsler Memory Scale-Revised (WMS-R) (Wechsler, 1987) and the Memory Assessment Scale (Williams, 1991) are multifaceted measures of memory functioning. They can be used for adolescents and adults and include tests for verbal and figural stimuli, meaningful and abstract material, and delayed as well as immediate recall. Olfactory and tactile recall, autobiographical memory, and recall of learned skills (such as operating a machine) are not tested with these measures.

> Deception on the WMS-R can be assessed by (a) comparing test scores between retests; (b) comparing WMS-R subscale scores with those of other tests with the same task (e.g., digit span on WMS-R with WAIS-R; visual reproduction scores with performance on Bender Gestalt); (c) comparing test performance with cross-validating sources (e.g., significant others); (d) comparing the Wiggins and Brandt (1988) list to responses on the information and orientation questions since there is considerable overlap; (e) comparing easy versus difficult item scores on the verbal paired associates tasks; and (f) observing behavior during testing (see p. 12 of WMS-R manual) and noting attitude toward testing, motivation, reaction to success or failure, and work habits.

One investigation compared a number of traditional memory instruments with traumatic brain injury (TBI) Ss and probable malingerers (Greiffenstein et al., 1994). All the Ss were actual clinical cases. The probable malingerers were determined by at least two of four criteria: (1) two or more severe impairment ratings on neuropsychological tests in comparison with expected performance based on age and education, (2) improbable symptom history, (3) disability of 1 year or more, and (4) remote memory loss claims. The findings reflected that the popular auditory verbal learning test (AVLT), the WMS, and the WMS-R did not differentiate the TBIs from the malingerers. In contrast, the probable malingerer group performed poorly on the Rey 15-Item, Rey Word Recognition List, Reliable Digit Span, Portland Digital Recognition Test, and the Rey's Auditory Verbal Learning Test (RAVLT) Recognition Trial. The probable malingerer group was comprised primarily of patients with histories of chronic complaints of mild head injury. The authors concluded that the latter group might have a much higher incidence of malingering than previously recognized because of their adequate performance on instruments erroneously assumed to rule out malingering.

Neurobehavioral Techniques and Amnesia

The neurological substrates of memory continue to be an area of considerable study and controversy (for a review see Lezak, 1995). New technologies are enhancing our understanding of neurobehavioral functions in general and of memory functioning in particular. One such technology is functional neuroimaging using positron emission tomography (PET). Costello, Fletcher, Dolan, Frith, and Shallice (1998) described the case study of a man in his 40s who suffered a stroke and presented with a dense isolated retrograde amnesia for the 19 years preceding the stroke. The stroke was caused by a left superior dorsolateral prefrontal hemorrhage. The case history reflected that the man's forgotten personal life contained many highly stressful situations such that malingering was at least a suspicion. Functional neuroimaging was used while the man attempted to recall life events using family photos as stimuli. The findings reflected distinctly different areas of cortical activation depending on whether the man had been present for the stimulus event, had not been present, or if the stimulus presented an analogous event outside the period of amnesia. With the present-for-stimuli condition, compared to the other two conditions, activation was greater in part of the precuneus, and less both in the right posterior ventrolateral frontal cortex and in a region close to the lesion. The authors concluded that the man's amnesia was not the result of malingering, but due to the lesion preventing recursive self-cueing of memory traces that were characteristic of the autobiographical retrieval with the not-present-for stimuli conditions.

Another recent area of psychophysiological detection of malingering involves EEG event-related brain potential (ERP) studies. The preliminary research findings have been encouraging. In one study of a series (Rosenfeld, Ellwanger, and Sweet, 1995), thirteen undergraduate Ss were instructed to simulate autobiographical amnesia related to head injury. The ERP amplitudes were significant for the main effect of stimulus type. That is, the Ss simulated amnesia, but the ERP findings indicated recognition of the stimuli. A second study using a similar paradigm but measuring intactness of recognition memory with Ss simulating amnesia produced similar findings (Ellwanger, Rosenfeld, Sweet, and Bhatt, 1996). In a third ERP study, the investigators used a forced-choice, matching-to-sample task (Rosenfeld, Reinhart, Bhatt, Ellwanger, Gora, Sekera, and Sweet, 1998). "Priming" of Ss to achieve (i.e., manipulate) different behavioral hit rates did not adversely affect the ERP amplitudes of simulators, which were essentially comparable to the control group (truth-tellers). The authors described that additional analysis of the data preliminarily suggested evidence for a deception-related amplitude tomography across different paradigms and conditions. A final study in the series attempted to establish a mode of ERP patterns that actual amnestic patients might demonstrate (Ellwanger, Rosenfeld, Hankin, and sweet, 1999). Undergraduate Ss were exposed to a range of relatively easy recognition memory tests graduated to increasingly difficult match-to-sample recognition memory tests. All of the Ss in the modeled amnesia sample maintained intact recognition memory as measured by ERP tracings. These are findings with obvious potential for eventually providing definitive discrimination of malingered amnesia. These laboratory-based findings can only be considered as preliminary data. The findings may eventually prove useful in actual forensic matters. The EEG ERP test is not very portable and at the current time is a rather labor intensive, costly procedure. With continued research and validation, it is conceivable that it may eventually be worthwhile to conduct ERP examinations of high profile cases of suspected malingered amnesia. As with any technique or methodology, the ultimate forensic test will be refinement of ERP technology so that it meets scientific standards warranting acceptance of such findings in the courtroom.

Forced-Choice Testing

EAT is a promising forensic neuropsychological tool that attempts to measure faked sensory and recall deficits (Grosz and Zimmerman, 1965; Pankratz, 1979, 1983, 1988; Pankratz, Fausti, and Peed, 1975; Theodor and Mandelcorn, 1973). Also known as forced-choice, two-alternative, or symptom-validity testing, EAT involves the presentation of stimuli, which the client denies or affirms that he or she can perceive/remember. Almost no one should miss presented items unless a genuine impairment exists, in which case one's performance should approximate chance responding (one-half of the items in two-choice formats). Deviation from chance is defined as a total-%-correct, which falls significantly below 50% as defined by the binomial probability distribution (e.g., 1.96 standard deviations below 50% correct). For example, the (one-tailed) probability of obtaining fewer than 40 correct responses in 100 trials of a two-choice task is less than 2%. Obtaining less than 36 correct answers in the 100 trials would occur by chance less than two times in 1000. Subjects intent on faking typically make an initial assumption that they must respond correctly less than 50% of the time in order to demonstrate mnestic difficulties (Haughton, Lewsley, Wilson, and Williams, 1979; Pankratz, 1988). One advantage of the forced-choice format is avoiding the problem of conventional memory instruments not being useful with malingerers who claim no recollection of previously presented stimuli. As discussed later, the EAT paradigm sets the stage for a generation of new instruments, now generically referred to as indirect memory tests (Baker, Hanley, Jackson, Kimmance, and Slade, 1993; Hanley, Baker, and Ledson, 1999; Horton, Smith, Barghout, and Connolly, 1992).

Hall and Shooter (1989) achieved a positive hit rate of 84.6% in identifying 52 subjects instructed to "fake bad" on a forced-choice memory recognition task. Shooter and Hall (1990) boosted the positive hit rate to almost 95% ($n = 19$) on the same task. A third study addressed the question of whether 50 or 100 trials are required for successful detection of faking in EAT. Thirty-five subjects (males = 16, females = 19; mean age = 29.37, SD = 10.46; mixed ethnicity; mixed occupations) were randomly assigned to one of two groups: (1) those administered 100 trials ($n = 10$) or (2) those administered 50 trials ($n = 25$). There were two (20%) successful fakers in the 100-item group and six (24%) in the 50-item group. Chi-square analysis comparing the successful and unsuccessful fakers for the 100- versus 50-trial group showed no significant differences.

As one would suspect, deception strategies differed between the successful versus unsuccessful fakers. The most popular strategy used by the unsuccessful fakers was consistently choosing the incorrect response, accounting for 41% of the strategies named. The second-most common strategy used by the unsuccessful fakers was giving occasional correct or incorrect responses (accounting for 20% of the strategies used), with attempting to forget being the third-most common strategy. It was common for those employing a shift in strategy to switch from consistently choosing the incorrect answer to giving an occasional correct response.

The successful group employed random responding most frequently (accounting for 28%). The second-most frequent strategy was consistently using the same response (19%), which necessarily resulted in a total-%-correct of 50%. The third-most frequent strategy was consistently choosing the incorrect response (16%), which necessarily involved a strategy shift at some point in order to produce a total-%-correct greater than 40%. Among those subjects who identified a shift in strategy during the test, 29% named adhering to one response as their first strategy, while 21% reported using random responding as their first strategy. Random responding was 40% of the time used as the second strategy.

   Pritchard (1992) has developed a computerized version of EAT, which employs a 72-trial memory recognition task divided into three subsets of 24 trials each. The subject is presented on each trial with a 5-digit number ("target") for 5 s, followed by a 3- to -5-s delay and then a pair of 5-digit numbers from which to select the "target" previously shown. A %-correct score is calculated for each subset of 24 trials and for the total 72 trials. Pritchard and Moses (1992) demonstrated that this task was 100% accurate (negative hit rate) in identifying a sample of severely impaired psychiatric and brain-injured patients and was 66% accurate (positive hit rate) in identifying a sample of subjects instructed to "fake bad" without being detected.

   Results from EAT studies suggest that:

1. Forced-choice methodology is indeed promising. The hit rates of EAT studies far exceed other deception-detecting strategies, even when distinguishing "fakers" from severely impaired patients. Individuals with a high stake in faking—such as defendants facing prison terms or plaintiffs standing to gain monetary compensation for damages—may be even more strongly motivated than volunteer subjects to fake successfully. This would then increase the power of the EAT technique when applied to clinical cases. Indeed, anecdotal examples from the authors' experiences confirm the success of EAT with actual clinical cases.

   > Case: A Caucasian, right-handed, 23-year-old ex-stripper at a go-go club was stabbed in the neck by her boyfriend, creating through-and-through puncture wound of the jugular vein and carotid artery. Residual signs included the Brown-Sequard syndrome, a right Horner's pupil and an ataxic gait favoring the left. Neuropsychological testing several months after the trauma revealed normal functioning except on tasks requiring motor speed, coordination of upper extremities, manual dexterity, and sensitivity to stimulation. Recall abilities were above average for both short- and long-term memory. The victim later sued the nightclub for failure to protect her, claiming pervasive mental deficits stemming from the stabbing. Neuropsychological testing on the same battery two years afterwards revealed uniformly poor scores with an impairment index of 1.0, meaning 100% of her scores were in the impaired range. This was in striking contrast to her normal clinical appearance and lack of any event since the stabbing which would explain this deterioration. MMPI testing revealed a pronounced tendency to fake bad. On the EAT, 15% of her responses were accurate, strongly suggesting that she was feigning a visual memory deficit. She did not admit to faking, but was eventually awarded a reduced settlement upon negotiation with the (civil) defendant.

2. Results suggest that as few as three sets of 24 trials or even 50 total trials of EAT can be utilized with no loss of detection accuracy. Thus, EAT can be designed to be both accurate and economical.

3. The use of successive sets of EAT trials, rather than just a total accuracy score based on all trials, appears to make EAT sensitive to fluctuating deception strategies. Fakers may perform poorly in the beginning of EAT testing and switch to honest responding after it is too late to hide their deception. Or subjects may attempt to fake bad after they have adapted to the test and decided on a strategy for deception.

4. EAT may be uniquely adapted to detect deception in individual cases. For criminal cases, this might involve information about an offense that only a perpetrator would know. As suggested by Hall and Shooter (1989), data bits—such as type of weapon utilized, injuries sustained by the victim, and clothing characteristics—could be presented to the suspect with instructions to affirm or deny recognition of them.

A suspect with no knowledge of the instant crime should perform at approximately chance levels, while the perpetrator may be (statistically) placed at the scene of the crime. In a practical application of this suggestion, two-alternative, forced-choice memory questions were used to assess suspicious complaints of amnesia in three actual cases (Frederick, Carter, and Powel, 1995). Of the three cases, two involved competency to stand trial and the third an insurance medical examination. In each case, the Ss claimed forgotten critical knowledge. Symptom validity testing (SVT) was adapted to questions tapping the "forgotten" knowledge in the forced-choice format. The number of correctly answered questions was then compared to the expected number of questions to be correctly answered if no knowledge actually existed. In each of the three cases, the response patterns generated the conclusion that the knowledge claimed to be forgotten was in fact remembered. The clinical circumstances were complex, however, and malingering was not the conclusion in each case.

Contemporary Research of Malingered Amnesia

RAVLT was administered to 28 Ss twice using a different version of the test on each trial (Flowers et al., 1996). During the second trial, the Ss were instructed to simulate a mild-to-moderate memory impairment. The patterns of scores in the two conditions reflected that the malingered Ss differed from the typical performance of genuine amnesiacs in three respects: they showed a primacy effect in free recall, they overperformed on the delayed recall trial, and they underperformed on the recognition task. The authors suggested that this pattern of findings may be useful in the AVLT distinguishing between genuine and faked amnesia, at least with naive Ss.

A case study described by Pachana, Boone, and Ganzell (1998) highlights the problems encountered by extrapolating from malingering instruments that work well with laboratory populations, but present with problems when used in actual clinical applications. A 32-year-old woman with Wernicke-Korsakoff syndrome was administered a series of select neuropsychological tests designed to detect malingering. There was no clinical evidence to suggest that the woman was presenting with exaggeration or feigning of performance. Her performance exhibited mixed results across the instruments indicative of different sensitivity to actual memory impairment. The findings on several measures were contaminated by the presence of organic amnesia and produced false-positive findings of malingering. These measures included the Rey 15-Item and the Rey 15-Word Recognition Test. By comparison, other instruments (e.g., Dot Counting and Portland Digit Recognition) were unaffected by true memory impairment.

In a variety of studies, approaches involving structured indirect measures of malingered amnesia have been introduced. These studies offer creative paradigms wherein the Ss are not cued at the outset what specific behavior is under scrutiny, or they are distracted from a task explicitly involving memory. Many of the traditional techniques were rather transparent in presentation such that Ss were cued to attempt to engage in more sophisticated deception. Indirect presentation was one of the features of EAT.

In one indirect memory test, Ss were asked to study a list of words and subsequently performed either a word completion or a fragment completion task (Horton et al., 1992). Genuine amnesics' performance on indirect tests was comparable to normals. When the Ss in the study were motivated to simulate amnesia, target completion rates were reliably below baseline rates. Baker et al. (1993) compared simulators to genuine amnesiacs under distraction and no-distraction conditions. The genuine amnesiacs performed significantly worse than controls under distraction conditions. The simulators performed worse than controls under both distraction and no-distraction conditions. Simulators also exaggerated overall memory deficits relative to the genuine amnesiacs.

Kapur (1994) described a nifty and effective "bedside" test for the detection of patients suspected of malingering memory disorders called the Coin-in-Hand Test (CHT). The clinician instructs the patient to observe and recall which hand holds a coin. The test is a simple series of 10 trials in which the coin is alternated consecutively right to left. After exposing the coin for 2 s, the patient is instructed to close their eyes and count backwards for 10 s. The patient is instructed that no trickery will be employed. In a laboratory study with control Ss, instructed simulators, and patients with amnestic disorders, Baker et al. (1993) found that over the 10 trials, controls averaged a score of 9.95 of a maximum score of 10. Amnesic Ss had average scores of 9.65, compared to averages of 4.10 for simulators. A more recent assessment of the CHT concludes that the technique is practical, brief, and can easily be used across settings, symptoms, and different characteristics of clients (Colwell and Sjerven, 2005).

Another investigation utilized the forced-choice model to compare instructed simulators to amnestic patients (Davis, King, Bloodworth, Spring, and Klebe, 1997). A category classification test was used to differentiate between a control group of student Ss, a group of student Ss instructed to simulate amnesia, and a group of amnestic patients. The simulators were instructed to fake a memory deficit for academic credit and possible financial compensation. The Ss studied a list of highly distorted dot patterns and then were asked to choose if a new set of dot patterns belonged to the original category of dot patterns. The simulating (malingerers) Ss performed significantly worse than the controls or the amnesic patients. A discriminant function analysis indicated that the classification test could differentiate the three groups of Ss at an above-chance level. The investigators suggested that the category classification test could be used to supplement standard forced-choice tests in the detection of malingering.

In a recent study using the SVT, although the SVT was only able to detect 7% of the simulating participants, the simulators displayed memory-undermining effects such as poor free recall, commission errors, and lower SVT scores relative to the honestly responding controls (van Oorsouw and Merckelbach, 2006). Other recent studies have provided support for the Victoria SVT's ability to confirm the validity of patients' cognitive impairments (Grote, Kooker, Garron, Nyenhuis, Smith, and Mattingly, 2000; Slick, Tan, Strauss, Mateer, Harnadek, and Sherman, 2003; Thompson, 2002).

By way of leading into the next area of discussion, we comment that one unique aspect of the category classification test is that while it involves a memory component, the classification task is the focal instruction. Accordingly, malingerers may not be cued to defensiveness from the outset. In one study, Baker et al. (1993) compared the performance of genuine amnesiacs to a group of simulators. One condition involved Ss being distracted by having to count backward between presentation and recall. A second condition involved no-distraction in that the retention interval was unfilled. The findings reflected that the genuine amnesiacs performed significantly worse compared to nonsimulating controls under no-distraction. The simulators performed significantly worse than controls under no-distraction as well as under distraction conditions. The simulators also exaggerated the memory deficit overall relative to genuine amnesiacs. The distraction/nondistraction (D/ND) paradigm offers a unique *in vivo* approach to the detection of malingered amnesia.

Greiffenstein, Gola, and Baker (1995) divided 177 Ss referred for neuropsychological assessment into three groups: TBIs, probable malingering, and persistent postconcussions.

Comprehensive neuropsychological test batteries (i.e., MMPI-2, AVLT Recognition Word List, Reliable Digit Span, and Rey's 15-Item Memory Test) were administered to all Ss. The findings showed that domain-specific compliance measures were generally more sensitive to noncompliance than were the MMPI-2 measures. Only the Sc scale of the MMPI-2 improved on base-rate predictions of probable malingering. The Pd scale had no relationship to malingered amnesia.

Chouinard and Rouleau (1997) described the 48-Pictures Test, a two-alternative forced-choice recognition test designed to detect exaggerated memory impairments. They compared the test to the RAVLT and the Rey's Complex Figure Test (RCFT). Three groups of Ss were utilized: 17 suspected malingerers, 39 patients with memory impairments (6 amnesic, 15 frontal lobe dysfunctions, and 18 other etiologies), and 17 volunteers instructed to act as simulators. On the 48-Pictures Test, the clinical group showed good recognition performance averaging above 90%. The two simulator groups showed poor performance: suspected malingerers 62% correct; volunteer simulators 68%. The RAVLT and RCFT did not adequately discriminate among the S groups except on two measures. Both simulator groups tended to show a performance decrement from the last recall trial to immediate recognition of the RALVT and also performed better on the immediate recall of the RCFT. A discriminant analysis utilizing the last two measures and the 48-Pictures Test correctly classified 94% of the Ss.

Three of the indirect memory tests that we have reviewed were empirically cross-compared by Hanley et al. (1999). The findings reflected inherent problems with all three. The tests were the D/ND test (Baker et al., 1993), the CHT (Kapur, 1994), and Word Fragment Completion (WFC) (Horton et al., 1992). The D/ND and the CHT were both effective at distinguishing amnestic patients from simulators. The CHT was noted to be particularly effective at reflecting excellent performance by the amnestic patients compared to chance or below-chance performance by the simulators. The WFC effectively discriminated simulators from controls, but was ineffective at discriminating the amnestic patients from simulators. It remains to be seen in future research if these findings can be replicated with Ss who have sophisticated knowledge of performance levels associated with actual memory deficits. As cautioned by Rogers (1988), it also remains to be seen what effect incentives (e.g., financial compensation) will have on simulators' ability to avoid detection. Most of all, it remains to be seen how the use of indirect memory tests will fare in actual forensic application.

Qualitative Aspects of Malingered Memory Deficits

Iverson (1995) investigated qualitative aspects of malingered memory deficits based on interviews generating self-reported strategies of 160 Ss. The Ss were from a variety of backgrounds including adult community volunteers, psychiatric inpatients, Federal inmates who participated in analog malingering studies, and undergraduates.

Summary and Conclusions

Feigned memory deficits are essentially private events, which require sensitive psychological and neuropsychological skill to detect. The current state of the art in detecting faked memory problems includes the following:

1. The empirical ability to differentiate malingered amnesia from actual amnesia and a thousand gradations of possibilities between these two poles has become increasingly

sophisticated. Empirical assessment, however, is still not a definitive science. Lewis, Yeager, Swica, Pincus, and Lewis (1997) described a retrospective case study review of 12 murderers who the authors concluded had "child abuse-based dissociative identity disorder." The investigators concluded that "once and for all" their analysis established a linkage between early severe childhood abuse and dissociative identity disorder; they concluded further that their data demonstrated that the disorder could be distinguished from other disorders to include malingering. In forensic-related matters, it is axiomatic for clinicians to avoid making sweeping conclusory generalizations, and to avoid couching findings in superlatives or absolutes. Klein (1999) soundly rejected the conclusions of the foregoing study citing the inability to determine (1) what data had actually come from the records preceding legal involvement, (2) what prior data clearly pertained to the issues of abuse, and (3) what prior data supported the diagnoses of dissociative identity disorder.

2. In conducting forensic evaluations, clinicians must always be mindful of clinical presentations that mask another problem. Sundheim and Ryan (1999) described a sobering case example of an emergency room evaluation of a frequently visiting patient who was initially diagnosed as malingering an unusual amnestic syndrome. Further investigation eventually revealed that the patient actually was developmentally disabled (mild mental retardation).

3. Another caution comes from the literature regarding domestic violence, a phenomenon of increasing occurrence in our society. It has been observed that domestic violence perpetrators do not always remember assaulting family members. Following the violence, the perpetrators have no recollection of their violent behavior but accept full responsibility for it. Swihart, Yuille, and Porter (1999) described that these domestic incidents constitute "red outs" in which there is amnesia for a violent crime carried out in a state of rage. Unlike stranger-to-stranger crime circumstances, domestic violent crime occurs in a context of powerful feelings between the perpetrator and victim. Malingering alone, alcohol intoxication/blackouts, or organic dysfunction cannot explain amnesia in these domestic situations. In the clinical/forensic arena, things may not always be what they initially appear to be.

References

Allen, M. (1985). Review of Millon Behavioral Health Inventory. In J. V. Mitchell (Ed.), *The Ninth Mental Measurements Yearbook*. Lincoln, NE: University of Nebraska Press.

Baker, G. A., Hanley, J. R., Jackson, H. F., Kimmance, S., and Slade, P. (1993). Detecting the faking of amnesia: Performance differences between simulators and patients with memory impairment. *Journal of Clinical & Experimental Neuropsychology*, 15(5), 668–684.

Barkemeyer, C., Callon, E., and Jones, G. (1989). *Malingering Detection Scale Manual*. Baton Rouge, LA: North Street Publishing Company.

Beal, D. (1989). Assessment of malingering in personal injury cases. *American Journal of Forensic Psychology*, 7(4), 59–65.

Bernard, L., and Fowler, W. (1990). Assessing the validity of memory complaints: performance of brain-damaged and normal individuals on Rey's task to detect malingering. *Journal of Clinical Psychology*, 46, 432–436.

Block, A. R., Kremer, E. F., and Fernandez, E. (1999). *Handbook of Pain Syndromes: Biopsychosocial Perspectives*. Mahwah, NJ: Lawrence Erlbaum Associates.

Boccaccini, M. T., and Brodsky, S. L. (1999). Diagnostic test usage by forensic psychologist in emotional injury cases. *Professional Psychology, 30,* 253–259.

Brandt, J., Rubinsky, E., and Lassen, G. (1985) Uncovering malingered amnesia. *Annals of the New York Academy of Sciences, 44,* 502–503.

Braverman, M. (1978). Post injury malingering is seldom a calculated ploy. *Occupational Health and Safety, 47*(2), 36–48.

Campbell, W., and Tueth, M. J. (1997). Misplaced rewards: Veterans Administration System and symptom magnification. *Clinical Orthopaedics and Related Research, 336,* 42–46.

Chouinard, M., and Rouleau, I. (1997). The 48-Pictures Test: A two-alternative forced-choice recognition test for the detection of malingering. *Journal of the International Neuropsychological Society, 3*(6), 545–552.

Clayer, J., Bookless, C., and Ross, M. (1984). Neurosis and conscious symptom exaggeration: Its differentiation by the illness behavior questionnaire. *Journal of Psychosomatic Research, 28,* 237–241.

Colwell, K., and Sjerven, E. R. (2005). The "coin-in-hand" stratagem for the forensic assessment of malingering. *American Journal of Forensic Psychology, 23*(1), 83–89.

Corthell, D., and Tooman, M. (1985). *Rehabilitation of TBI (Traumatic Brain Injury).* Menomonie, WI: Stout Vocational Rehabilitation Institute.

Costello, A., Fletcher, P. C., Dolan, R. J., Frith, C. D., and Shallice, T. (1998). The origins of forgetting in a case of isolated retrograde amnesia following a haemorrhage: Evidence from functional imaging. *Neurocase: Case Studies in Neuropsychology, Neuropsychiatry, & Behavioral Neurology, 4*(6), 437–446.

Craig, K. D., Hill, M. L., and McMurtry, B. W. (1999). Detecting deception and malingering. In A. R. Block, E. F. Kremer, and E. Fernadez (Eds.), *Handbook of Pain Syndromes: Biopsychosocial Perspectives* (pp. 41–58). Mahwah, NJ: Laurence Erlbaum Associates.

Cummings, J., and Benson, D. (1983). *Dementia: A Clinical Approach.* Boston: Butterworths.

Davis, H. P., King, J. H., Bloodworth, M. R., Spring, A., and Klebe, K. J. (1997). The detection of simulated malingering using a computerized category classification test. *Archives of Clinical Neuropsychology, 12*(3), 191–198.

Dunn, J. T., Brown, P. R., Lees-Haley, P. R., and English, L. T. (1993). *Neurotoxic and Neuropsychologic Symptom Base Rates: A Comparison of Three Groups.* Presented at the 13th Annual Conference of the National Academy of Neuropsychology, Phoenix, AZ.

Ellwanger, J., Rosenfeld, J. P., Hankin, B. L., and Sweet, J. J. (1999). P300 as an index of recognition in a standard and difficult match-to-sample test: A model of amnesia in normal adults. *Clinical Neuropsychogist, 13*(1), 100–108.

Ellwanger, J., Rosenfeld, J. P., Sweet, J. J., and Bhatt, M. (1996). Detecting simulated amnesia from autobiographical and recently learned information using the P300. *International Journal of Psychophysiology, 23*(1–2), 9–23.

Flor, H., Kerns, R., and Turk, D. (1987). The role of spouse reinforcement, perceived pain, and activity levels of chronic pain patients. *Journal of Psychosomatic Research, 31,* 251–259.

Flowers, K. A., Sheridan, M. R., and Shadbolt, H. (1996). Simulation of amnesia by normals on Rey's auditory verbal learning test. *Journal of Neurolinguistics, 9*(2), 147–156.

Fox, D. D., Gerson, A., and Lees-Haley, P. R. (1995). Interrelationship of MMPI-2 validity scales in personal injury claims. *Journal of Clinical Psychology, 51*(1), 42–47.

Frederick, R. I., Carter, M., and Powel, J. (1995). Adapting symptom validity testing to evaluate suspicious complaints of amnesia in medicolegal evaluations. *Bulletin of the American Academy of Psychiatry and the Law, 23*(2), 231–237.

Galin, K. E., and Thorn, B. E. (1993). Unmasking pain: Detection of deception in facial expressions. *Journal of Social and Clinical Psychology, 12*(2), 182–197.

Goldberg, S. (1987). *The 4-Minute Neurologic Exam.* Miami, FL: MedMaster.

Goldberg, J., and Miller, H. (1986). Performance of psychiatric inpatients and intellectually deficient individuals on a task that assesses the validity of memory complaints. *Journal of Clinical Psychology, 42,* 792–795.

Graf, P., Squire, L. R., and Mandler, G. (1984). The information that amnesic patients do not forget. *Journal of Experimental Psychology: Learning, Memory, and Cognition,* 10, 164–178.

Greiffenstein, M., Baker, W. J., and Gola, T. (1994). Validation of malingered amnesia measures with a large clinical sample. *Psychological Assessment,* 6(3), 218–224.

Greiffenstein, M. F., Baker, W. J., and Gola, T. (1996). Comparison of multiple scoring methods for Rey's malingered amnesia measures. *Archives of Clinical Neuropsychology,* 11(4), 283–293.

Greiffenstein, M. F., Gola, T., and Baker, W. J. (1995). MMPI-2 validity scales versus domain specific measures in detection of factitious brain injury. *Clinical Neuropsychologist,* 9(3), 230–240.

Griffin, G. A. E., Normington, J., May, R., and Glassmire, D. (1996). Assessing dissimulation among social security disability income claimants. *Journal of Consulting and Clinical Psychology,* 64, 1425–1430.

Griffith, J. (1990). *Pain Management: Learning to Live with On-going Pain and Disability.* Presented at Hickam Air Force Base, Honolulu.

Grillo, J., Brown, R. S., Hilsabeck, R., Price, J. R., and Lees-Haley, P. R. (1994). Raising doubts about claims of malingering: Implications of relationships between MCMI-II and MMPI-2 performances. *Journal of Clinical Psychology,* 50(4), 651–655.

Grimm, B., and Bleiberg, J. (1986). Psychological rehabilitation in traumatic brain injury. In Filskov, S., and Boll, T. (Eds.), *Handbook of Clinical Neuropsychology: Volume 2.* New York: John Wiley & Sons.

Grosz, H., and Zimmerman, J. (1965). Experimental analysis of hysterical blindness: A follow-up report and new experiment data. *Archives of General Psychiatry,* 13, 255–260.

Grote, C. L., Kooker, E. K., Garron, D. C., Nyenhuis, D. L., Smith, C. A., and Mattingly, M. L. (2000). Performance of compensation seeking and non-compensation seeking samples on the Victoria Symptom Validity Test: Cross-validation and extension of a standardization study. *Journal of Clinical and Experimental Neuropsychology,* 22(6), 709–719.

Hadjistavropoulos, T. (1999). Chronic pain on trial: The influence of litigation and compensation on chronic pain syndromes. In A. R. Block, E. F. Kremer, and E. Fernandez (Eds.), *Handbook of Pain Syndromes: Biopsychosocial Perspectives* (pp. 59–76). Mahwah, NJ: Lawrence Erlbaum Associates.

Hadjistavropoulos, H. D., Asmundson, G. J. G., and Norton, G. R. (1999). Validation of the coping with health, injuries, and problems scale in a chronic pain sample. *Clinical Journal of Pain,* 15(1), 41–49.

Hadjistavropoulos, H. D., Craig, K. D., Grunau, R. E., and Whitfield, M. F. (1997) Judging pain in infants: Behavioural, contextual and developmental determinants. *Pain,* 73(3), 319–324.

Hadjistavropoulos, H. D., Craig, K. D., Hadjistavropoulos, T., and Poole, G. D. (1996a). Subjective judgments of deception in pain expression: Accuracy and errors. *Pain,* 65(2–3), 251–258.

Hadjistavropoulos, T., McMurtry, B., and Craig, K. D. (1996b) Beautiful faces in pain: Biases and accuracy in the perception of pain. *Psychology and Health,* 11(3), 411–420.

Hall, F. L., III. (1990). *Materials on Law of Malingering.* Unpublished manuscript.

Hall, F. L., III, and Hall, H. V. (1991). *The Law and Psychology of Malingering.* Unpublished manuscript.

Hall, H. V., and Shooter, E. (1989). Explicit alternative testing for feigned memory deficits. *Forensic Reports,* 2, 277–286.

Hanley, J. R., Baker, G. A., and Ledson, S. (1999). Detecting the faking of amnesia: A comparison of the effectiveness of three different techniques for distinguishing simulators from patients with amnesia. *Journal of Clinical and Experimental Psychology,* 21(1), 59–69.

Haughton, P. M., Lewsley, A., Wilson, M., and Williams, R. G. (1979). A forced-choice procedure to detect feigned or exaggerated hearing loss. *British Journal of Audiology,* 13, 135–138.

Herrmann, D. (1982). Know thy memory: The use of questionnaires to assess and study memory. *Psychological Bulletin,* 92, 434–452.

Horton, K. D., Smith, S. A., Barghout, N. K., and Connolly, D. A. (1992). The use of indirect memory tests to assess malingered amnesia: A study of metamemory. *Journal of Experimental Psychology: General*, 121(3), 326–351.

Iverson, G. L. (1995). Qualitative aspects of malingered memory deficits. *Brain Injury*, 9(1), 35–40.

Iverson, G. L., Franzen, M., and McCracken, L. (1991). Evaluation of an objective assessment technique for the detection of malingered memory deficits. *Law and Human Behavior*, 15(6), 667–676.

James, S. (1998). Malingering: Maze of recovery, money, and law confronts insurers. *Issues of Injury*, 12(3), 1–5.

Jensen, M. P., Turner, J. A., Romano, J. M., and Strom, S. E. (1995). The chronic pain inventory: Development and preliminary validation. *Pain*, 60(2), 203–216.

Johnson, J. L., and Lesniak-Karpiak, K. (1997). The effects of warning on malingering on memory tasks in college samples. *Archives of Clinical Neuropsychology*, 12(3), 231–238.

Kapur, N. (1994). The coin-in-hand test: A new "bedside" test for the detection of malingering in patients with suspected memory disorder. *Journal of Neurology, Neurosurgery & Psychiatry*, 57(3), 385–386.

Kaufman, D. (1985). *Clinical Neurology for Psychiatrists* (2nd ed.). Orlando, FL: Grune and Stratton.

Klein, D. T. (1999). Multiples: no amnesia for childhood. *American Journal of Psychiatry*, 156(6), 976–977.

LaChapelle, D. L., Hadjistavropoulos, T., and Craig, K. D. (1999). Pain measurement in persons with intellectual disabilities. *Clinical Journal of Pain*, 15(1), 13–23.

Lande, R. (1993). Mental responsibility and 900 phone abuse. *Journal of Psychiatry & Law*, 21(1), 109–121.

Lanyon, R. I. (1985). Review of Millon Behavioral Health Inventory. In J. V. Mitchell (Ed.), *The Ninth Mental Measurements Yearbook*. Lincoln, NE: University of Nebraska Press.

Lee, G., Loring, D., and Martin, R. (1992). Rey's 15-Item Visual Memory Test for the detection of malingering: Normative observations on patients with neurological disorders. *Psychological Assessment*, 4(1), 43–46.

Lees-Haley, P. R. (1985). Psychological malingerers: How to detect them. *Trial*, 21, 68.

Lees-Haley, P. R. (1988). Unintentionally fraudulent claims for stress disorders. *Defense Counsel Journal*, 2, 194–197.

Lees-Haley, P. (1989). Litigation response syndrome: How the stress of litigation confuses the issues in personal injury, family and criminal litigation. *Defense Counsel Journal*, 56(1), 110–114.

Lees-Haley, P. R. (1990a). Provisional normative data for a credibility scale for assessing personal injury claimants. *Psychological Reports*, 66(3), 1355–1360.

Lees-Haley, P. R. (1990b). Contamination of neuropsychological testing by litigation. *Forensic Reports*, 3(4), 421–426.

Lees-Haley, P. R. (1991a). A fake bad scale on the MMPI-2 for personal injury claimants. *Psychological Reports*, 68(1), 203–210.

Lees-Haley, P. R. (1991b). Ego strength denial on the MMPI-2 as a clue to simulation of personal injury in vocational neuropsychological and emotional distress. *Perceptual and Motor Skills*, 72(3), 815–819.

Lees-Haley, P. (1992). Neuropsychological complaint base rates of personal injury claimants. *Forensic Reports*, 5(5), 385–391.

Lees-Haley, P. R. (1997). MMPI-2 base rates for 492 personal injury plaintiffs: Implications and challenges for forensic assessment. *Journal of Clinical Psychology*, 53(7), 745–755.

Lees-Haley, P. R., and Brown, R. S. (1993). Neuropsychological complaint base rates of 170 personal injury claimants. *Archives of Clinical Neuropsychology*, 8, 203–209.

Lees-Haley, P., and Dunn, J. T. (1994). The ability of naive subjects to report symptoms of mild brain injury, post-traumatic stress disorder, major depression, and generalized stress disorder. *Journal of Clinical Psychology*, 50(2), 252–256.

Lees-Haley, P., and Fox, D. (1990). Neurological false positives in litigation: Trail making test findings. *Perceptual and Motor Skills*, 70, 1379–1382.

Lees-Haley, P. R., Williams, C. W., and Brown, R. S. (1993). The Barnum effect and personal injury litigation. *American Journal of Forensic Psychology*, 11(2), 21–28.

Lees-Haley, P. R., Williams, C. W., and English, L. T. (1996). Response bias in self-reported history of plaintiffs compared with nonlitigating patients. *Psychological Reports*, 79(3), 811–818.

Lees-Haley, P. R., Williams, C. W., Zasler, N. D., Marguilies, S., English, L. T., and Stevens, K. B. (1997). Response bias in plaintiffs' histories. *Brain Injury*, 11(11), 791–799.

Lewis, D. O., Yeager, C. A., Swica, Y., Pincus, J. H., and Lewis, M. (1997). Objective documentation of child abuse and dissociation in twelve murders with dissociative identity disorder. *American Journal of Psychiatry*, 154(12), 1703–1710.

Lezak, M. (1983). *Neuropsychological Assessment* (2nd ed.). NY: Oxford University Press.

Lezak, M. (1995). *Neuropsychological Assessment* (3rd ed.). NY; Oxford University Press.

Lipman, F. D. (1962). Malingering in personal injury cases. *Temple Law Quarterly*, 35(2), 141–162.

Lishman, W. (1987). *Organic Psychiatry*. London: Blackwell Scientific Publications.

McCarthy, R., and Warrington, E. (1990). *Cognitive Neuropsychology: A Clinical Introduction*. New York: Academic Press.

Mikail, S. A., DuBreuil, S., and D'Eon, J. L. (1993). A comparative analysis of measures used in the assessment of chronic pain patients. *Psychological Assessment*, 5(1), 117–120.

Miller, M. J. (1992). The Pinocchio syndrome: Lying and its impact on the counseling process. *Counseling and Values*, 37(1), 25–31.

Millon, T., Green, C. J., and Meagher, R. B. (1979). The MBHI: A new inventory for the psychodiagnostician in medical settings. *Professional Psychology*, 10, 529–539.

Mittenberg, W., Patton, C., Canyock, E. M., and Condit, D. C. (2002). Base rates of malingering and symptom exaggeration. *Journal of Clinical and Experimental Neuropsychology*, 24(8), 1094–11020.

Pachana, N. A., Boone, K. B., and Ganzell, S. L. (1998). False positive errors on selected tests of malingering. *American Journal of Forensic Psychology*, 16(2), 17–25.

Pankratz, L. (1979). Symptom validity testing and symptom retraining: Procedures for the assessment and treatment of functional sensory deficits. *Journal of Consulting and Clinical Psychology*, 47, 409–410.

Pankratz, L. (1983). A new technique for the assessment and modification of feigned memory deficit. *Perceptual and Motor Skills*, 57, 367–372.

Pankratz, L. (1988). Malingering on intellectual and neuropsychological measures. In R. Rogers (Ed.), *Clinical Assessment of Malingering and Deception*. New York: Guilford Press.

Pankratz, L. (1998). *Patients Who Deceive: Assessment and Management of Risk in Providing Health Care and Financial Benefits*. Springfield, IL: Charles C Thomas.

Pankratz, L., Fausti, S., and Peed, S. (1975). A forced-choice technique to evaluate deafness in the hysterical or malingering patient. *Journal of Consulting and Clinical Psychology*, 43, 421–422.

Parker, R. (1990). *Traumatic Brain Injury and Neuropsychological Impairment*. New York: Springer-Verlag.

Peck, C., Fordyce, W., and Black, R. (1978). The effect of the pendency of claims for compensation upon behavior indicative of pain. *Washington Law Review*, 53, 251–264.

Poole, G. D., and Craig, K. D. (1992). Judgments of genuine, suppressed, and faked facial expressions of pain. *Journal of Personality and Social Psychology*, 63(5), 797–805.

Pritchard, D. A. (1992). *Tests of Neuropsychological Malingering*. Orlando, FL: Paul M. Deutsch Press.

Pritchard, D. A., and Moses, J. (1992). Tests of neuropsychological malingering. *Forensic Reports*, 5, 287–290.

Resnick, P. J. (1984). The detection of malingered mental illness. *Behavioral Sciences and the Law*, 2(1), 21–38.

Rey, A. (1964). *L'examen clinique en psychologie* (The Clinical Examination in Psychology). Paris: Presses Universitaires de France.

Rickarby, G. A. (1979). Compensation neurosis and the psychosocial requirements of the family. *British Journal of Medical Psychology*, 52, 333–338.

Rogers, R. (1988). Researching dissimulation. In R. Rogers (Ed.), *Clinical Assessment of Malingering and Deception* (pp. 309–327). New York: Guilford.

Rosenfeld, J. P., Ellwanger, J., and Sweet, J. (1995). Detecting simulated amnesia with event-related brain potentials. *International Journal of Psychophysiology*, 19(1), 1–11.

Rosenfeld, J. P., Reinhart, A. M., Bhatt, M., Ellwanger, J., Gora, K., Sekera, M., and Sweet, J. (1998). P300 correlates of simulated malingered amnesia in a matching-to-sample task: Topographic analyses of deception versus truthtelling responses. *International Journal of Psychophysiology*, 28(3), 233–247.

Schacter, D. L. (1986). Amnesia and crime: How much do we really know? *American Psychologist*, 41(3), 286–295.

Schretlen, D., Brandt, J., Kraft, L., and Van Gorp, W. (1991). Some caveats in using the Rey 15-Item Memory Test to detect malingered amnesia. *Psychological Assessment*, 3(4), 667–672.

Shooter, E., and Hall, H. V. (1990). Explicit alternative testing for deliberate distortion: Toward an abbreviated format. *Forensic Reports*, 3(2), 115–119.

Shuman, D. W. (1986). *Psychiatric and Psychological Evidence* (Trial Practice Series). Colorado Springs: Shepard's/McGraw-Hill.

Slick, D. J., Tan, J. E., Strauss, E., Mateer, C. A., Harnadek, M., and Sherman, E. M. S. (2003). Victoria symptom validity test scores of patients with profound memory impairment: Non-litigant case studies. *Clinical Neuropsychologist*, 17(3), 390–394.

Stein, J. A. (1972). *Damages and Recovery-Personal Injury and Death Actions* (Sec. 22, pp. 38–39). San Francisco, CA: Bancroft Whitney Co.

Sundheim, S. T., and Ryan, R. M. (1999). Amnestic syndrome presenting as malingering in a man with developmental disability. *Psychiatric Services*, 50(7), 966–968.

Swihart, G., Yuille, J., and Porter, S. (1999). The role of state-dependent memory in "red-outs." *International Journal of Law & Psychiatry*, 22(3–4), 199–212.

Tapp, J. (1990). A multisystems perspective on chronic pain. *Psychotherapy in Private Practice*, 7, 1–16.

Theodor, L. H., and Mandelcorn, M. S. (1973). Hysterical blindness: A case report and study using a modern psychophysical technique. *Journal of Abnormal Psychology*, 82(3), 552–553.

Thompson, G. B. III (2002). The Victoria symptom validity test: An enhanced test of symptom validity. *Journal of Forensic Neuropsychology. Special Issue: Detection of Response Bias in Forensic Neuropsychology: Part I*, 2(3–4), 43–67.

U.S. Department of Veterans Affairs. (1985). *Physician's Guide for Disability Evaluations* (1B11 56).

van Oorsouw, K., and Merckelbach, H. (2006). Simulating amnesia and memories of a mock crime. *Psychology, Crime & Law*, 12(3), 261–271.

Wasyliw, O. E., and Cavanaugh, Jr., J. L. (1989). Simulation of brain damage: Assessment and decision rules. *Bulletin of the American Academy of Psychiatry & the Law*, 17(4), 373–386.

Wechsler, D. (1987). *Wechsler Memory Scale-Revised Manual*. New York: Psychological Corporation.

Weissman, H. (1990). Distortions and deceptions in self-presentation: Effects of protracted litigation on personal injury cases. *Behavioral Sciences and the Law*, 8, 67–74.

Wiggins, E., and Brandt, J. (1988). The detection of simulated amnesia. *Law and Human Behavior*, 12, 57–78.

Williams, J. (1991). *Memory Assessment Scales Professional Manual*. Odessa FL: Psychological Assessment Resources.

Williams, C. W., Lees-Haley, P. R., and Djanogly, S. E. (1999). Clinical scrutiny of litigants' self-reports. *Professional Psychology: Research & Practice*, 30(4), 361–367.

Williams, C. W., Lees-Haley, P. R., and Price, J. R. (1998). Self-attention and reported symptoms: Implications for forensic assessment. *Professional Psychology: Research & Practice, 29*(2), 125–129.

Youngjohn, J. R. (1991). Malingering of neuropsychological impairment: An assessment strategy. *Journal for the Expert Witness, the Trial Attorney, and the Trial Judge,* 4, 29–32.

Youngjohn, J. R., Lees-Haley, P. R., and Binder, L. M. (1999). Comment: Warning malingerers produces more sophisticated malingering. *Archives of Clinical Neuropsychology,* 14(6), 511–515.

Legal References

Board of Trustees of Fire and Police Employees Retirement System of City of Baltimore v. Ches, 294 Md. 668, 452 A.2d 422 (Md. 1982).

Board of Veterans Appeals Decision March 17, 1978, Docket No. 77 991.

Boyd v. General Industries, 11 Ark. 103, 733 S.W.2d 750 (Ark.Ct.App. 1987), 244 Ark. 141, 424 S.W.2d.

Byerley and Byerley v. Citrus Publishing, Inc., 24 FLW D262 (1999).

Cockrell v. U.S., 74 F.2d 151 (8th Cir. 1934).

Cotton v. Bowen, 799 F.2d 1403 (9th Cir. 1986).

Daubert v. Merrell Dow Pharmaceuticals, 125 L. Ed.2d 469, 113 (S. Ct. 2786, 1993).

Eichel v. New York Cent. R. R. Co., 375 U.S. 253 (U.S. Supreme Court 1963) (per curium).

Freeman v. Bandlow, 143 So.2d 547 (2d DCA Fla. 1962).

Guidry v. J & Eads Const. Co., 11 Ark.App. 219, 669 S.W.2d 48 (1984).

Keever v. Middletown, 1998 FED App. 0167 (6th Cir. 1998) (No. 95-00716).

King Mining Co. v. Mullins, 252 S.W.2d 871 (Ky. App. 1952).

Lowery v. Miller, Van Rybroek, Maier, & Roach, LEXIS 677 (Court of Appeals, District Four 26 Jul, 1990).

McGrath v. Consolidated Rail Corporation, 943 F. Supp. 95.97 (D. Mass. 1996), No. 97-1063, 1998 http://www.Law.Emory.Edu/Pub-Cgi/p (District of New Hampshire/Eleventh Circuit aff'd (1996/1998).

Metropolitan Dade County v. Orlando Reyes et al., 21 FLW (Florida/Florida Supreme Court 19/ December, 1996).

Miller v. United States Fidelity and Guaranty Co., 99 So.2d 511, 516 (La. App. 1957).

Neal v. Director, D. C. Department of Corrections, U.S. Dist. LEXIS 8874, *(1996).

Nichols v. American Nat'l. Ins., 154 F3d. 875 8th Cir. (1999).

Quint v. A. E. Staley, 172 F.3d 1, *1999 U.S. LEXIS 4145 (1999).

Royer v. Cantrelle, 267 So.2d 601 (La.Ct.App. 3rd 1972), writ denied, 263 La. 626, 268 So.2d 680 (1972).

Savoie v. Otto Candies, Inc., 692 F.2nd 363,371 (5th Cir. 1982).

Smolen v. Chater, 80 F.3rd 1273 (1998) (No. 94-35056).

Sutcliffe v. E. I. Dupont De Nemours & Co., 36 So.2d 874, 877 (La. App. 1948).

Teater v. State of Nebraska, 559 N.W.2nd 758 LEXIS 70 (Neb./Supreme Court of Nebraska 1997).

Transit Authority of River City v. Vinson, 703 S.W.2d 482 (Ky. App. 1985).

Underwood v. NCUA, 665 A.2nd 621 (District of Columbia Court of Appeals 31 August, 1995) (No. 92-CV-840, No. 92-CV-936).

Yager v. Labor and Industry Review Commission, Sentry Insurance Company and Land's End, 599 N.W.2d 666 (1999) (Wisc. App. LEXIS 631) (No. 98-2378).

Evaluating the Evaluators in Custodial Placement Disputes

17

DAVID A. MARTINDALE

Child Custody Consultants, Morristown, New Jersey

JONATHAN W. GOULD

Child Custody Consultants, Charlotte, North Carolina

Contents

Introduction

Since the publication of the American Psychological Association's (APA) *Guidelines for Child Custody Evaluations in Divorce Proceedings* (1994), much has changed in the world of custody evaluation. More professionals, at all educational levels, are performing child custody evaluations without having obtained formal training; many practitioners are performing evaluations that do not meet the needs of the courts that have appointed them; with increasing frequency, judges have expressed concern over the poor quality of the reports being submitted to them by evaluators; and problems with the custody evaluation process have become the subject of front page articles in newspapers as prestigious as *The New York Times* (Eaton, 2004).

In New York State, in response to much publicly expressed discontent, in June 2004, Chief Judge Judith S. Kaye appointed a Matrimonial Commission "to review all aspects of matrimonial litigation and make recommendations for improving how the courts handle such litigation in both Family Court and Supreme Court" [source: announcement posted by the New York State Office of Court Administration at the court's web site: www.nycourts.gov]. In the last decade, complaints against evaluators have increased dramatically (Kirkland and Kirkland, 2001), as have malpractice actions (Marine and Bogie, 2004).

For a variety of reasons, many mental health professionals with backgrounds in health care have entered the forensic arena without first having undertaken the study that is needed to appreciate the important differences between treatment-related and forensic roles and responsibilities (Greenberg and Shuman, 1997). The APA has designated forensic psychology as a specialty area (Otto and Heilbrun, 2002). This action by the APA makes it clear that psychologists wishing to offer their services as custody evaluators have a responsibility to acquire the specialized skills, training, and knowledge associated with the specialty.

The Association of Family and Conciliation Courts' *Model Standards of Practice for Child Custody Evaluation* (AFCC, 2006) declares, in model standard 1.1, "evaluators shall gain specialized knowledge and training in a wide range of topics...." The list of topics is extensive. It is also pointed out that "[s]ince research and laws pertaining to the field of divorce or separation and child custody are continually changing and advancing, child custody evaluators shall secure ongoing specialized training."

As dissatisfaction with the work of custody evaluators has grown, more and more attorneys have begun requesting that the reports with which they are displeased be reviewed by retained experts. Experts retained to review the work product of an evaluator can provide the retaining attorney with candid input concerning the strengths and deficiencies of the evaluator's work. In particular, a reviewer can offer commentary on the methodology employed, the assessment devices utilized, the interpretation of assessment data, and the nexus between information gathered and opinions expressed.

The scope of a reviewer's task is limited and should not be confused with the work of a practitioner conducting a second evaluation. If a reviewer identifies deficiencies in an evaluator's work, the reviewer's task is to articulate those deficiencies and explain why they may have had a significant impact on the process of formulating the opinions that have been communicated to the court by the evaluator in his or her advisory report. Although it is appropriate that reviewers identify missing information and opine concerning the likely consequences of formulating an opinion without the identified information, they should not attempt to address the identified deficiencies.

The formulation of opinions on the basis of data that are insufficient, skewed, or inappropriately analyzed is a serious error, whether it is made by an evaluator or by a reviewer. For example, reviewers who meet with litigants obtain information that is, by its very nature, insufficient and skewed, and it cannot be appropriately analyzed.

In 2001, a Pennsylvania psychologist functioning as a case reviewer was disciplined by the Commonwealth's Bureau of Professional Affairs for what mental health professionals would describe as a failure to maintain appropriate role boundaries (*Grossman v. State Board*, No. 3023 C. D. 2001). The state's expert testified that Dr. Grossman had "moved from evaluating existing data to creating his own data" and explained that meeting participants in an evaluation transforms the review process into an evaluative process in which reviewers are formulating their own opinions concerning the issues in dispute.

Reviewers cannot second-guess evaluators and cannot opine responsibly on the issues before the court. Reviewers can call attention to methodological errors, flawed data analyses, and opinions that are not linked to the reported data. They can also point out that sound methodology increases the probability of formulating a supportable opinion and deficient methodology increases the probability of formulating a questionable opinion. No responsible reviewer would deny, however, that in all fields of endeavor, satisfactory solutions to simple and complex problems have been stumbled upon by individuals who were utilizing substandard methods and unproven problem-solving strategies.

Legal Basis

Experts who are retained by attorneys for the purpose of conducting a work product review are functioning as agents of the retaining attorneys. Unless the retained experts are called to testify, materials prepared by them are protected from disclosure by the attorneys' work product privilege. This privilege is derived from the attorney–client privilege. Epstein (2001) has explained that communication with a professional such as a retained reviewer "is deemed necessary to assist the attorney to understand better the facts and give a legal opinion to the client. The principle that extends the privilege to certain categories of experts, defined as agents of the attorney for the purpose of rendering legal advice, is often referred to as the Kovel doctrine, after the case that set forth the concept of derivative privilege attaching to experts necessary for the rendering of legal advice" (p. 152) (refer to *United States v. Kovel*, 296 F.2d 918, 921 [2d Cir. 1961]).

When a retained expert assists an attorney in preparing for anticipated litigation by communicating to the attorney mental impressions, conclusions, opinions, or theories, the communication between the expert and the attorney is ordinarily deemed to be privileged. Epstein (2001) points out that reviewers are more likely to be "cloaked with the derivative privilege" (p. 153) if they are retained by attorneys rather than by litigants. In particular, Epstein opines that "if the expert was retained to assist the lawyer in understanding data that is either actually or technically in another language so that the attorney can render legal advice, the information exchanged will be protected" (p. 154).

Methods and Applications

Work product reviews conducted by psychologists in litigation that relates to disputes concerning custody and access should be written in a manner that focuses on the science that is the foundation of psychology.

A reviewer can examine three broad areas and, within each of these, several specific elements. Reviewers examine (1) methodology, (2) formulation of opinions, and (3) communication of findings and opinions to the court.

Methodology

In examining an evaluator's methodology, a reviewer formulates opinions concerning the elements that follow:

1. The use (or lack thereof) of appropriate procedural safeguards. Issues in this category include ascertaining whether the purpose of the evaluation, the scope of the evaluation, those to whom the report is to be disseminated, the manner in which the report is to be disseminated, and those to whom the file will be made available have all been specified in writing in advance of the evaluation. Additionally, such issues as the sequence in which evaluative sessions have been conducted should be examined.
2. The techniques employed in interviewing the parents. The reviewer seeks to ascertain whether systematic procedures were employed that would increase the probability that the evaluator will obtain pertinent historical information and current

information bearing on functional abilities related to parenting and will not be distracted by information that is not pertinent to the evaluative task.

3. The manner in which information has been obtained from children. The reviewer examines the techniques that were employed, to see whether they were tailored to the cognitive development and expressive and receptive language abilities of the child. Additionally, the reviewer considers the reliability and validity of any special techniques employed.

4. The methods employed in conducting observational sessions between the two parents and between each parent and the children. In order to be maximally useful, observations should be conducted in some systematic manner, evaluators should know in advance what types of information they wish to gather, and whatever data are gathered should be gathered in a structured manner.

5. The extent to which pertinent documents were utilized by the evaluator. Evaluators must take great care not to view certain types of documents as constituting verification of oral reports from litigants. Some documents presented to evaluators are no more than written records of oral reports made earlier to different people.

6. The manner in which the evaluator selected collateral sources of information, obtained information from those sources, and assessed the reliability of the information obtained. Austin and Kirkpatrick (2004), for example, have called attention to the fact that as psychological distance from the custody dispute increases, so, too, does objectivity. School personnel are likely to provide more objective information than neighbors. Evaluators who limit their collateral source inquiries to those who are deemed to be objective are likely to overlook information that, despite its delivery by subjective sources, is nevertheless potentially enlightening.

7. The methods employed by the evaluator to corroborate information that he or she relied upon. Despite overwhelming evidence that psychologists are not particularly impressive as human lie detectors (DePaulo, Charlton, Cooper, Lindsay, and Muhlenbruck, 1997; Ekman and O'Sullivan, 1991; Feeley and Young, 1998; Frank and Feeley, 2003), far too many evaluators trust their clinical intuition to tell who is being forthright and who is being disingenuous.

8. The criteria employed in the selection of assessment instruments. Although in some jurisdictions the criteria to be employed in assessing custodial suitability are statutorily defined, in many jurisdictions evaluators must decide for themselves what constitutes effective parenting and what observable indices can be utilized.

9. The manner in which assessment instruments were administered. Evaluators should administer assessment instruments in accordance with the instructions in the manuals that accompany the instruments and should be responsive to the admonitions that appear in the *Standards for Educational and Psychological Testing* (APA, 1985, 1999).

10. The accuracy of the evaluator's interpretation of assessment data. Many evaluators have become dependent upon computer-generated interpretive reports, despite the clarity of Ethical Standard 9.09(c), which reminds psychologists that they "retain responsibility for the appropriate application, interpretation, and use of assessment instruments, whether they score and interpret such tests themselves or use automated or other services." (p. 1072) Millon, Davis, and Millon (1997) have called attention to the unfortunate reality that computer-generated interpretive reports have certain "intrinsic difficulties, most notably a lack of substantial empirical data to validate

their configural interpretations" (p. 134). They also point out that "[t]he logic by which the computer generates its report leads to a product that is inadequately individualized, or 'canned'" (p. 134).

11. The degree to which the evaluator maintained appropriate role boundaries. Model standard 8.1 of the AFCC's *Model Standards of Practice for Child Custody Evaluation* (AFCC, 2006) calls attention to the fact that "[t]he responsible performance of a child custody evaluation requires that evaluators be able to maintain reasonable skepticism, distance, and objectivity." Evaluators are reminded that "their objectivity may be impaired when they currently have, have had, or anticipate having a relationship with those being evaluated, with attorneys for the parties or the children, or with the judges." When role boundaries have not been respected, reviewers can call attention to the ways in which evaluator objectivity may have been impaired as a result.

12. The evaluator's compliance with ethical standards, laws, and regulations governing the creation, maintenance, and production of appropriate records. Although it is not the task of a reviewer to pass judgment on the ethical propriety of an evaluator's actions, a knowledgeable reviewer can cite sections of ethics codes and similar documents and explain their pertinence to actions (or failures to act) on the part of the evaluator.

Formulation of Opinions

It goes without saying that the formulation of an opinion (personal or professional) is an internal mental process the dynamics of which are not perceptible to even the keenest observer. It is precisely for this reason that experts bear an obligation to articulate the manner in which their opinions have been developed. Readers of reports submitted by evaluators in custody disputes can reasonably expect that they will not be required to speculate concerning the manner in which the reported data are linked to the expressed opinions. Reviewers offer commentary not on the opinions expressed by evaluators but rather on the procedures that the evaluators appear to have employed in formulating their opinions.

Reviewers look for indicators of (1) the degree to which evaluators have explored competing hypotheses and have sought data that would either confirm or disconfirm those hypotheses, (2) the degree to which consideration appears to have been given to data that are not supportive of the opinions expressed, (3) the degree to which pertinent case law and statutes appear to have been considered, and (4) possible examiner bias. Although bias is not directly observable, its role in opinion formation can often be inferred when evaluators apply different standards in examining and commenting on the actions of the two parents; use insulting terminology in describing the nonfavored parent; use glowing terminology in describing the favored parent; assign minimal importance to possible parenting deficiencies in the favored parent; assign much importance to reported flaws in the nonfavored parent; appear to unquestioningly accept the favored parent's perspective; and appear to reflexively reject the nonfavored parent's perspective.

Communication of Findings

Evaluators continue to debate among themselves concerning the optimal length of reports prepared for the court. Not surprisingly, most have taken the very pragmatic approach of giving the consumer what the consumer seems to want. In a culture in which bigger is often deemed better, judges often express a preference for short reports. In their desire to avoid burdening judges with more information than the judges wish to have, some evaluators neglect to include basic information reasonably needed by the court.

Readers of reports from custody evaluators should be informed of the criteria that were employed in examining the best interests standard, should be informed of the procedures that were employed in gathering data pertinent to those criteria, should be informed of the manner in which the data shed light on one or more of the stated criteria, and should be informed of the manner in which any decisions were made concerning the weight to be assigned to different criteria.

The AFCC's *Model Standards* addresses the issue of "articulation of the bases for opinions expressed." Model standard 12.2 reads, in its entirety: "Evaluators shall only provide opinions and testimony that are a) sufficiently based upon facts or data; b) the product of reliable principles and methods; and c) based on principles and methods that have been applied reliably to the facts of the case. In their reports and in their testimony, evaluators shall be careful to differentiate among information gathered, observations made, data collected, inferences made, and opinions formulated. Evaluators shall explain the relationship between information gathered, their data interpretations, and opinions expressed concerning the issues in dispute. There shall be a clear correspondence between the opinions offered and the data contained in both the forensic report and the case file."

Knowledgeable reviewers are aware of the peer-reviewed published literature and are better able than litigants, attorneys, or judges to identify personal perspectives that have been included in evaluators' reports in the guise of professional opinions. Similarly, reviewers are aware of the limitations inherent in our data gathering procedures and in our assessment instruments and can comment on the degree to which evaluators have acknowledged the known limitations of their data. Where formal psychological testing has been conducted, reviewers can comment on the manner in which the data have been presented and, in particular, can opine on whether pertinent, nonsupporting data have been reported.

Model standard 4.6 of the AFCC's *Model Standards* offers fairly detailed information concerning the manner in which findings and opinions should be communicated by evaluators in their reports and in their testimony. Evaluators are admonished not to "present data in a manner that might mislead the triers of fact or others likely to rely upon the information and/or data reported." Evaluators are also "strongly encouraged to utilize and make reference to pertinent peer-reviewed published research in the preparation of their reports." Evaluators are urged to "recognize that the use of diagnostic labels can divert attention from the focus of the evaluation (namely, the functional abilities of the litigants whose disputes are before the court) and that such labels are often more prejudicial than probative." Finally, evaluators are reminded that "information not bearing directly upon the issues before the court may cause harm when disclosed and may have a prejudicial effect."

Applied Ethics and Moral Considerations

Just as incompetent evaluators leave damage in their wake, so, too, do incompetent reviewers. In the portion of the psychologists' ethics code that addresses the issue of competence, psychologists are reminded that they should provide services "only within the boundaries of their competence, based on their education, training, supervised experience, consultation, study, or professional experience" [Ethical Standard 2.01 (a)]; that "[w]hen assuming forensic roles, psychologists are or become reasonably familiar with the judicial or administrative rules governing their roles" [Ethical Standard 2.01 (f)]; that they must "undertake ongoing efforts to develop and maintain their competence" (Ethical Standard 2.03); and that their work must be "based upon established scientific and professional knowledge of the discipline" (Ethical Standard 2.04).

The performance of custody evaluations requires specialized knowledge, so, too, does the performance of review work. It cannot be presumed that any psychologist who is competent to conduct a custody evaluation is therefore competent to review the work of other custody evaluators. Reviewers should have intimate knowledge of the guidelines and standards that are pertinent to custody work. These include the APA's *Ethical Principles of Psychologists and Code of Conduct* (APA, 2002), *Guidelines for Child Custody Evaluations in Divorce Proceedings* (APA, 1994), *Standards for Educational and Psychological Testing* (APA, 1985, 1999), and *Record-Keeping Guidelines* (APA, 1993); *The Specialty Guidelines for Forensic Psychologists* (Committee on Specialty Guidelines for Forensic Psychologists, 1991); and the AFCC's *Model Standards of Practice for Child Custody Evaluation* (AFCC, 2006).

Experts who have been retained by one side are often disparagingly referred to as "hired guns." Those who view themselves as dedicated educators often find that they must contend with the hurdle that is created by the negative stereotype. The phrase *ethical review work* is not an oxymoron. Ethical reviewers provide feedback that addresses both the strengths and the deficiencies of the work that has been reviewed. Retaining attorneys then get to decide how, if at all, the expert can be of additional assistance. In preparing their reports, ethical reviewers work independently of the attorneys who have retained them. The reviewers do not collaborate with the attorneys in order to produce a document that will more effectively advance the attorneys' goals.

Good reviewers are perpetual students. They follow developments in the field, as reported in peer-reviewed professional literature, and they draw upon the knowledge base of the field of psychology. They do not simply compare the work under review with their own favorite way of conducting evaluations. Skilled and ethical reviewers are knowledgeable and familiar with applicable research, able to discern the difference between sound methodology and flawed methodology, and able to interpret test data without computer-generated interpretive reports. Not surprisingly, knowledge and an active mind lead to the formulation of opinions. Inevitably, there will be times when an opinion formulated by a reviewer concerning the methodology employed by an evaluator will turn out to be the opinion that a particular attorney wants a judge to hear. When the ethical reviewer is paid to come to court and explain that opinion to the judge, the reviewer is being paid for time expended and nothing more. The ethical reviewer takes seriously the most basic obligation of an expert witness—the obligation to assist the trier of fact.

Although the evidence is only anecdotal, there is good reason to believe that many of the ethical pits into which psychologists fall have been inadvertently dug by the psychologists themselves. In particular, when providers of a service lead those who are utilizing those services to develop unrealistic expectations, the pit-digging has begun.

It is understandable that attorneys retaining reviewers will view them as allies. When testifying reviewers have become enmeshed in a team mentality, they may find themselves tailoring their testimony to meet the perceived needs of the team and neglect their obligation to the court. Prudent reviewers make it abundantly clear in writing that, in their testimony, they will focus on procedure and methodology and will not opine on matters of custodial suitability, professional ethics, standards of care, or law. They also make clear that they are obligated to respond in a forthright manner to all questions posed and that, in doing so, information, opinions, or both may be expressed that will not be helpful to the position of the retaining attorney's client.

Avoiding Evaluation and Consultation Errors

Retaining reviewers to examine the work of evaluators and possibly to testify concerning deficiencies in the evaluators' methodology only makes tactical and economic sense if the reviewers have the necessary expertise and, if called upon to testify, will be perceived by the court as credible in spite of the fact that they have been retained by one side in inherently adversarial proceedings.

In the initial stage of a reviewer's work, the task is to educate the retaining attorney. After having conducted a preliminary review, the reviewer communicates with the retaining attorney and candidly shares impressions of the work that has been reviewed. Once this has been done, the retaining attorney must decide whether further services are needed and, if so, what services are likely to be most beneficial.

An attorney may decide that the reviewer can be of most assistance functioning as a trial consultant. In this role, the reviewer can prepare questions for cross-examination, assist at trial, or provide some other type of consultative service. If, however, an attorney decides that he or she wishes a reviewer to testify at trial, the reviewer's objective changes and the reviewer implicitly accepts the ethical obligation to function as an educator to the court.

Calloway (1997), in comments on review work, opined that "[c]ourtesy and wisdom obviously dictate that we first inform the court-appointed or consent-ordered psychologist whose work we are requested to review. By speaking with our colleague, we may discover facts about the conflictual situation and encourage collaboration, to help us prevent the misuse of our services" (p. 10). We disagree.

Not all professionally desirable professional behaviors can be neatly enumerated on a list of prescribed acts and not all professionally undesirable behaviors can be compiled and incorporated into that section of an ethics code that delineates proscribed behaviors. Sometimes, people with doctoral degrees must be trusted to extrapolate based upon what is contained in our ethics codes and similar documents. Standard 1.05 of the psychologists' ethics code addresses the topic of reporting ethical violations. The standard "does not apply when an intervention would violate confidentiality rights or when psychologists have been retained to review the work of another psychologist whose professional conduct is in question."

Under ordinary circumstances the professional interactions between a psychologist and patient are protected from disclosure by privilege. The privilege is held by the patient, not by the psychologist. Similarly, the professional interactions between an attorney and a retained consultant are protected from disclosure until such time as the consultant is proffered as a testifying expert. In this professional relationship, the privilege is held by the attorney, not by the retained consultant. A treating psychologist may feel that it would be helpful to speak to a patient's spouse, but the psychologist cannot do so without the consent of the patient. Similarly, even when a retained consultant feels that it would be courteous and wise to collaborate with the evaluator whose work is being reviewed, the decision rests with the retaining attorney and not with the consulting psychologist.

Although no survey data are available, it is our impression that far more often than not, reviewers do not communicate directly with those whose work is under review. Discussions between reviewers and evaluators bring to the process information that is not part of the record and, in our view, such a procedure leads to problems that cannot be ignored. Explanations offered by evaluators concerning the bases for their expressed opinions are explanations that should appear in their reports, not offered orally in discussions with reviewers. Decisions concerning the adequacy of such explanations must be made by the parties during pretrial settlement endeavors and by the court if the case proceeds to trial. An explanation offered orally to a reviewer is not a suitable substitute for an explanation incorporated into an evaluator's written discussion of the bases for opinions expressed.

Writing Reports

Reports are most useful when they address the issues of methodology, formulation of opinions, and the communication of findings and opinions to the court. Reviewers should describe the manner in which they were retained, the nature of their assigned task, and the items examined in formulating their opinions. In discussing the limitations inherent in the review process, reviewers should make it clear that they have had no significant contact with the litigants or with others involved in the evaluative process (aside from attorneys). Reviewers are educators to the attorneys who retain them and, if they testify, to the judges who hear their testimony. For this reason, reviews should contain citations to current peer-reviewed published literature and should provide clear explanations of any criticisms registered.

Although reviews focus on the work done by evaluators *as described by the evaluators in their reports,* when information concerning the professional background of the evaluator is available, it is often useful for reviewers to offer commentary on the education, training, and supervised experience obtained by evaluators in preparation for their work. Where deficiencies are noted, the relevance of the identified deficiencies should be explained.

Acting as an Expert Witness

It must be stressed at the outset that reviewers often do not testify. After having conducted a review, the reviewer may often function as an unidentified consultant to the retaining attorney. The case material that accompanies this chapter is a compilation of cross-examination questions prepared for attorneys in custody cases.

Ordinarily, in order for reviewers to assist attorneys who have retained them as consultants or to assist triers of fact if the reviewers ultimately offer testimony, reviewers must be familiar with the contents of evaluators' files. In most review work, though a reviewer's preliminary impressions may appropriately be formulated based upon a reading of the report submitted by the evaluator, going forward necessitates having access to the file. Appointment orders, pleadings, evaluators' statements of understanding, contemporaneously taken notes, documents reviewed, and test data are all important.

When a full review is performed, reviewers should not limit their examination of the file to those items identified by evaluators as having played a role in the formulation of their opinions. Particularly when retaining attorneys assert that information provided to the evaluator appears not to have been utilized, that information should be examined with care.

In some situations, full file reviews are not necessary. Triers of fact can often benefit from educational testimony offered by forensic psychologists whose expertise in methodology enables them to offer useful commentary on the evaluative methodology described by experts in their reports. In such situations, reviewers focus their attention on the information provided by the evaluators in their reports and the reviewers formulate their opinions based upon the evaluators' own information.

In discussing different review methods, we should not overlook the role of the *case-blind didactic expert* (Martindale, 2006). A case-blind educator provides information concerning some well-researched dynamic and leaves it to the court to decide how (if at all) the dynamic that has been explained is applicable to the issues in dispute. The concept is not a new one; other writers (for example, Vidmar and Schuller, 1989) have used the term "social framework testimony." Our preference for the term "case-blind didactic testimony" lies in the fact that the words "case-blind" emphasize the importance of diligently maintaining constructive ignorance of the facts of the case.

Often, when framework testimony is offered, the expert is familiar with many (but never all) of the facts of the case. In offering testimony, the expert is at least implying (if not directly opining) that the framework being described is applicable to the facts of the case. The case-blind didactic expert, in contrast, makes clear that he or she knows nothing about the case and has simply been retained to explain some psychological dynamic to the court. In such cases, it is obvious to all that the parties who retain such experts believe that the psychological dynamics being explained are applicable to the case being adjudicated, but the experts do not opine on the issue of applicability and make it clear that they are unable to do so.

Innovations and Advances

It might be said that a review is a review is a review. Just as reviewers of books, plays, movies, and TV shows have done their work in essentially the same manner for many decades, so, too, have reviewers of child custody reports been consistent in the manner in which they approach the task. Changes occurring in the custody evaluation field over the past decade have, however, made it easier for reviewers to *document* the existence of broad consensus with regard to methodology and related matters. More and more documents are outlining generally accepted procedures and criteria to be employed in considering the usefulness of assessment data.

Even the issue of evaluator credentials, an issue concerning which reviewers may offer commentary, has been addressed by oversight groups such as New York's Matrimonial Commission. In its 2006 report, the Commission noted that "certain credentials may be misleading"; urged those reviewing Curriculum Vitae (CVs) to "be informed about the accreditations included therein"; and called attention to the importance of establishing the "validity of such credentials" (www.nycourts.gov/reports/matrimonialcommissionreport.pdf, p. 48).

Over the past 10 years, the field of child custody has witnessed the development of professional practice guidelines (AACAP, 1997; APA, 1994; CEGFP, 1991) and professional practice standards (AFCC, 2006) that guide the field. There has been an increasing consensus expressed in the peer-reviewed literature about a common set of methods and procedures to be used in crafting a scientifically informed, reliable, and relevant child custody evaluation (Austin, 2002; Kirkpatrick and Austin, 2005; Amundson, Duda, and Gill, 2000; Baerger, Galatzar-Levy, Gould, and Nye, 2002; Galatzer-Levy, Baerger, Gould, and Nye, 2002; Gould and Bell, 2000; Gould and Lehrmann, 2002; Gould and Stahl, 2000; Kirkland, 2002; Kirkpatrick, 2004; Martindale and Gould, 2004).

We have witnessed the growth of several important journals that focus attention on issues related to child custody, such as *Family Court Review*, *The Journal of Child Custody*, *The Journal of Forensic Psychological Practice*, and *The American Journal of Forensic Psychology*. Historically, the field of child custody has often been viewed as the stepsister to more traditional forensic psychological endeavors such as those in the area of criminal competency, criminal responsibility, or personal injury. We believe that the work of child custody evaluators is gaining greater status among more traditional forensic psychologists as witnessed by child custody articles appearing in mainstream forensic psychology journals such as *Psychology, Public Policy and Law*; *Law and Human Behavior*; and *Behavioral Science and the Law*. Journals that publish articles about psychological tests and measures, such as *Psychological Assessment*, have also begun to accept and publish research on normative data for child custody litigants on different tests and measures.

There has been a proliferation of mental health journals that address areas of special interest to child custody evaluators such as *Child Maltreatment*; *Child Abuse and Neglect*; *Violence Against Women*; *Trauma, Violence and Abuse*; *The Journal of Interpersonal Violence*; and *The Journal of Child Sexual Abuse* to name just a few.

With increasing frequency, legal journals have also begun to publish articles about child custody, such as those found in the *Family Law Quarterly* and *The Journal of the American Association of Matrimonial Lawyers*. Judges' journals also have shown an increasing interest in child custody works, such as those found in the *Juvenile and Family Court Journal* and *The Court Journal*.

Professional organizations from a variety of disciplines offer workshops on many areas of child custody, from basic courses in forensic methods and procedures applied to child custody evaluations to more advanced courses on cross-examining an expert witness and factors to consider in relocation cases.

Through use of the Internet, several custody-related list-serve and bulletin boards have emerged. Among them is the child custody list-serve to which we both belong and to which we both actively contribute. The American Bar Association's list-serve focusing on child custody and domestic violence issues is also an important contributor to professional exchange.

The following sources can be referred to by reviewers as they formulate their opinions and can serve to document opinions expressed:

1. Abduction of children by parents: Johnston and Girdner (2001).
2. Attachment theory and research: Ainsworth (1979); Bowlby (1969); Main (1996); Cassidy and Shaver (1999); Kelly and Lamb (2000).
3. Child adjustment and custodial arrangements: Bauserman (2002); Amato and Booth (2001); Hetherington, Bridges, and Insabella (1998).

4. Child custody evaluation (CCE) approaches, general methods and procedures: Gould (1998, in press); Gould and Martindale (2005, in press); Martindale and Gould (2004); Gould and Stahl (2000); Gould and Bell (2000); Gould and Lehrmann (2002); Stahl (1994, 1999); Galatzer-Levy and Kraus (1999); Kirkpatrick (2004); Schutz, Dixon, Lindenberger, and Ruther (1989); Weissman (1991a).

5. Child maltreatment evaluations: Kuehnle, Coulter, and Firestone (2000).

6. Child development research: Kelly and Lamb (2000); Solomon and Biringen (2001); Whiteside (1998); Lamb and Kelly (2001); Gould and Stahl (2001); Lamb (2002).

7. Child resiliency and mastery: Masten and Coatsworth (1998).

8. Child sexual abuse evaluations and testimony: Ceci and Hembrooke (1998); Kuehnle (1996); Friedrich (2002).

9. Child sexual abuse interviewing and suggestibility: Ceci and Bruck (1995); Ceci and Hembrooke (1998); Lyon (1999); Poole and Lamb (1998).

10. Collateral sources in CCEs: Austin (2002); Kirkpatrick and Austin (2005); Heilbrun (2001); Heilbrun, Warren and Picarello (2003).

11. Confirmatory bias in CCEs: Martindale (2005).

12. Cultural differences: American Psychological Association (1990).

13. Custody arrangements: Lamb, Sternberg, and Thompson (1997); Fabricius and Hall (2000); Bauserman (2002); Maccoby and Mnookin (1992); Lamb (2002).

14. Divorce effects research: Amato and Keith (1991); Emery (1999); Hetherington and Kelly (2002); Hetherington et al. (1998); Wallerstein and Kelly (1980); Amato and Sobolewski (2001); Kelly and Emery (2003).

15. Domestic and partner violence: Holden, Geffner, and Jouriles (1998); Graham-Bermann and Edleson (2001); Austin (2000c, 2001); Johnston and Campbell (1993); Jaffe and Geffner (1998); Bancroft and Silverman (2002); Jaffe, Lemon, and Poisson (2003); Mullender, Hague, Imam, Kelly, Malos, and Regan (2002); Dutton (2005); Johnson (2005).

16. Expert testimony issues: Shuman (1997); Shuman and Sales (1999); Krauss and Sales (1999); Goldstein (2003); Ewing (2003); Gross and Mnookin (2003).

17. Family systems and divorce: Ahrons (1994); Amato and Gilbreth (1999).

18. Fatherhood research: Braver and O'Connell (1998); Lamb (1997); Rohner and Venezio (2001).

19. Forensic evaluations, generally: Melton, Petrila, Pythress, and Slobogin (1997); Heilbrun (2001); Goldstein (2003).

20. Forensic role issues: Greenberg and Shuman (1997); Greenberg and Gould (2001).

21. Gender issues in custody: Warshak (1996); Cuthbert, Slote, Driggers, Mesh, Bancroft, and Silverman (2002); Dutton (2005); Johnson (2005).

22. High-conflict families: Johnston and Roseby (1997); Warshak (2001); Baris, Coates, Duvall, Garrity, Johnson, and LaCrosse (2001); Garrity and Baris (1994); Johnston and Campbell (1988); Lamb (2002).

23. Interview and observational techniques: Hynan (1998); Poole and Lamb (1998); Gould and Martindale (in press).

24. Overnight parenting time: Warshak (2000a); Biringen, Greve-Spees, Howard, Leith, Tanner, Moore, Sakoguchi, and Williams (2002); Kelly and Lamb (2000); Pruett, Ebling, and Insabella (2004).

25. Nonresidential parenting: Depner and Bray (1993); Amato and Gilbreth (1999); Lamb (2000).

26. Parental alienation/rejection: Clawar and Rivlin (1991); Kelly and Johnston (2001); Lee and Olesen (2001); Sullivan and Kelly (2001); Stoltz and Ney (2002); Bruch (2001); Gardner (2002); Warshak (2001).

27. Parenting: Bornstein's (2002) multivolume *The Handbook of Parenting* (second edition).

28. Parenting time: Kelly and Lamb (2000); Lamb and Kelly (2001); Lamb (2002).

29. Psychological maltreatment of children: Binggeli, Hart, and Brassard (2001); Briere, Berliner, Bulkley, Jenny, and Reid (2001); Faller (1999); Gould and Martindale (in press).

30. Psychological testing in CCEs, generally: Flens and Drozd (2005); Heilbrun (1995); Otto, Edens, and Barcus (2000); Roseby (1995); Medoff (1999, 2003); Shuman (2002); Heinze and Grisso (1996).

31. Psychological testing with the Minnesota Multiphasic Personality Inventory-2 (MMPI-2): Bathurst, Gottfriew and Gottfried (1997); Bagby, Nicholson, Buis, Radovanovic, and Fidler (1999).

32. Psychological testing with other personality inventories: McCann, Flens, Campagna, Collman, Lazarro, and Conner (2001).

33. Psychological testing with the Rorschach: Weiner (2001); Rosenthal, Hiller, Bornstein, Berry, and Brunell-Neuleib (2001); Garb, Wood, Nezworski, Grove, and Stejskal (2001).

34. Relocation cases: Austin (2000a, 2000b); Weissman (1994); Warshak (2000b); Kelly and Lamb (2003); Braver, Ellman, and Fabricius (2007); Wallerstein and Tanke (1996); Austin and Gould (2006); Stahl and Drozd (2006).

35. Sexual orientation and issues in custody and parenting time: Stacey and Biblarz (2001).

36. Standards of evidence and admissibility: Krauss and Sales (1999); Shuman and Sales (1998, 1999, 2001).

37. Third party and grandparent parenting time: Lussier, Deater-Deckard, Dunn, and Davies (2002).

References

Ahrons, C. (1994). *The Good Divorce: Keeping Your Family Together When Your Marriage Comes Apart*. New York: Harper Perennial.

Ainsworth, M. D. (1979). Infant-mother attachment. *American Psychologist*, 34, 932–937.

Amato, P. R., and Booth, A. (2001). The legacy of parents' marital discord: Consequences for children's marital quality. *Journal of Personality and Social Psychology*, 81(4), 627–638.

Amato, P. R., and Gilbreth, J. G. (1999). Nonresident fathers and children's well-being: A meta-analysis. *Journal of Marriage and the Family*, 61, 557–573.

Amato, P. R., and Keith, B. (1991). Parental divorce and the well-being of children: A meta analysis. *Psychological Bulletin*, 110, 26–46.

Amato, P. R., and Sobolewski, J. M. (2001). The effects of divorce and marital discord on adult children's psychological well being. *American Sociological Review*, 66, 900–921.

American Academy of Child and Adolescent Psychiatry (AACAP). (1997). Practice parameters for child custody evaluation. *Journal of the American Academy of Child and Adolescent Psychiatry*, 36(10 Suppl.), 57S–68S.

American Psychological Association. (1985). *Standards for Educational and Psychological Testing*. Washington, DC: Author.

American Psychological Association. (1993). *Record Keeping Guidelines*. Washington, DC: Author.

American Psychological Association. (1994). Guidelines for Child Custody Evaluations in Divorce Proceedings. *American Psychologist*, 49, 677–680.

American Psychological Association. (1999). *Standards for Educational and Psychological Testing*. Washington, DC: Author.

American Psychological Association. (2002). Ethical principles of psychologists and code of conduct. *American Psychologist*, 57, 1060–1073.

American Psychological Association, Office of Ethnic and Minority Affairs. (1990). Guidelines for providing services to ethnic, linguistic, and culturally diverse populations. *American Psychologist*, 48, 45–48.

Amundson, J. K., Duda, R., and Gill, E. (2000). A minimalist approach to child custody evaluations. *American Journal of Forensic Psychology*, 18(3), 63–87.

Association of Family and Conciliation Courts (2006). *Model Standards of Practice for Child Custody Evaluation*. Madison, WI: Author.

Austin, W. G. (2000a). A forensic psychology model of risk assessment for child custody relocation law. *Family and Conciliation Courts Review*, 38, 186–201.

Austin, W. G. (2000b). Assessing credibility in allegations of martial violence in the high-conflict child custody case. *Family and Conciliation Courts Review*, 38, 462–477.

Austin, W. G. (2000c). Relocation law and the threshold of harm: Integrating legal and behavioral perspectives. *Family Law Quarterly*, 34, 63–82.

Austin, W. G. (2001). Partner violence and risk assessment in child custody evaluations. *Family Court Review*, 39, 483–496.

Austin, W. G. (2002). Guidelines for utilizing collateral sources of information in child custody evaluations. *Family Court Review*, 40, 177–184.

Austin, W.G., and Gould, J.W. (2006). Exploring three functions in child custody evaluation for the relocation case: Prediction, investigation, and making recommendations for a long-distance parenting plan. *Journal of Child Custody*, 3/4, 63–108.

Austin, W. G., and Kirkpatrick, H. D. (2004). The investigation component in forensic mental health evaluations: Considerations for parenting time assessments. *Journal of Child Custody*, 1, 23–43.

Baerger, D. R., Galatzer-Levy, R., Gould, J. W., and Nye, S. (2002). A methodology for reviewing the reliability and relevance of child custody evaluations. *Journal of the American Academy of Matrimonial Lawyers*, 18 (1), 35–73.

Bagby, R. M., Nicholson, R. A., Buis, T., Radovanovic, H., and Fidler, B. J. (1999). Defensive responding in the MMPI-2 in family custody and access evaluations. *Psychological Assessment*, 11(1), 24–28.

Bancroft, L., and Silverman, J. G. (2002). *The Batterer as Parent: Addressing the Impact of Domestic Violence on Family Dynamics*. Thousand Oaks, CA: Sage.

Baris, M. A., Coates, C. A., Duvall, B. B. Garrity, C. B., Johnson, E. T., and LaCrosse, E. R. (2001). *Working with High-Conflict Families of Divorce: A Guide for Professionals*. Northvale, NJ: Jason Aronson.

Bathurst, K., Gottfried, A. W., and Gottfried, A. E. (1997). Normative data for the MMPI-2 in child custody litigation. *Professional Psychology: Research and Practice*, 9, 205–211.

Bauserman, R. (2002). Child adjustment in joint-custody versus sole-custody arrangements: A meta-analytic review. *Journal of Family Psychology*, 16, 91–102.

Binggeli, N. J., Hart, S. N., and Brassard, M. R. (2001). *Psychological Maltreatment of Children*. APSAC Study Guides 4. Thousand Oaks, CA: Sage Publishers.

Biringen, Z., Greve-Spees, J., Howard, W., Leith, D., Tanner, L., Moore, S., Sakoguchi, S., and Williams, L. (2002). *Family Court Review*, 40, 204–207.

Bornstein, M. H. (Ed.). (2002). *The Handbook of Parenting* (2nd ed., Vols. 1–4). Hillsdale, NJ: Erlbaum.

Bowlby, J. (1969). *Attachment and Loss: Vol. 1. Attachment*. New York: Basic Books.

Braver, S. L., Ellman, I. M., and Fabricius, W. V. (2007). Relocation of children after divorce and children's best interests: New evidence and legal considerations. *Journal of Family Psychology*, 17(2), 206–219.

Braver, S. L., and O'Connell, E. (1998). *Divorced Dads: Shattering the Myths*. New York: Tarcher/Putnam.

Briere, J., Berliner, L., Bulkley, J. A., Jenny, C., and Reid, T. (Eds.) (2001). *The APSAC Handbook on Child Maltreatment* (2nd ed.). Thousand Oaks, CA: Sage Publishers.

Bruch, C. S. (2001). Parental alienation syndrome and parental alienation: Getting it wrong in child custody cases. *Family Law Quarterly*, 35, 527–552.

Calloway, G. C. (1997). Ethical issues in the professional role of critiquing child custody evaluations. *The North Carolina Psychologist*, November–December, 10–11.

Cassidy, J., and Shaver, P. R. (Eds.) (1999). *Handbook of Attachment*. New York: Guilford.

Ceci, S. J., and Bruck, M. (1995). *Jeopardy in the Courtroom*. Washington, DC: American Psychological Association.

Ceci, S. J., and Hembrooke, H. (1998). *Expert Witnesses in Child Abuse Cases: What Can and Should Be Said in Court*. Washington, DC: American Psychological Association.

Clawar, S. S., and Rivlin, B. (1991). *Children Held Hostage: Dealing with Programmed and Brainwashed Children*. Chicago: American Bar Association Family Law Section.

Committee on Ethical Guidelines for Forensic Psychologists (CEGFP). (1991). Specialty guidelines for forensic psychologists. *Law and Human Behavior*, 15, 336–345.

Committee on Specialty Guidelines for Forensic Psychologists. (1991). Specialty guidelines for forensic psychologists. *Law and Human Behavior*, 15(6), 655–665.

Cuthbert, C., Slote, K., Driggers, M. G., Mesh, C. J., Bancroft, L., and Silverman, J. (2002). *Battered Mothers Speak Out: A Human Rights Report on Domestic Violence and Child Custody in the Massachusetts Family Courts*. Wellesley, MA: Wellesley Center of Women.

DePaulo, B. M., Charlton, K., Cooper, H., Lindsay, J. J., and Muhlenbruck, L. (1997). The accuracy-confidence correlation in the detection of deception. *Personality and Social Psychology Review*, 1, 346–357.

Depner, C. E., and Bray, J. H. (Eds.) (1993). *Nonresidential Parenting: New Vistas in Family Living*. Newbury Park, CA: Sage.

Dutton, D. G. (2005). Domestic abuse assessment in child custody disputes: Beware the domestic violence research paradigm. *Journal of Child Custody*, 2(4), 23–42.

Eaton, L. (2004). For arbiters in custody battles: Wide power and little scrutiny. *The New York Times*, May 23, 2004, p. 1.

Ekman, P., and O'Sullivan, M. (1991). Who can catch a liar? *American Psychologist*, 46, 913–920.

Emery, R. E. (1999). *Marriage, Divorce, and Children's Adjustment* (2nd ed.). Thousand Oaks, CA: Sage.

Epstein, E. S. (2001). *The Attorney-Client Privilege and the Work-Product Doctrine* (4th ed.). New York: National Book Network.

Ewing, C. P. (2003). Expert testimony: Law and practice. In A. M. Goldstein (Ed.), *Handbook of Psychology, Forensic Psychology* (Vol. 11, pp. 55–66). New York: Wiley.

Fabricius, W. V., and Hall, J. A. (2000). Young adults' perspectives on divorce: Living arrangements. *Family and Conciliation Courts Review*, 38, 446–461.

Faller, K. C. (1999). *Maltreatment in Early Childhood: Tools for Research Based Intervention*. Binghamton, NY: Haworth Press.

Feeley, T. H., and Young, M. J. (1998). Humans as lie detectors: Some more second thoughts. *Communication Quarterly*, 46(2), 109–126.

Flens, J., and Drozd, L. (Eds.) (2005). *Psychological Testing in Child Custody Evaluations*. Binghamton, NY: Haworth Press.

Frank, M. G., and Feeley, T. H. (2003). To catch a liar: Challenges for research in lie detection training. *Journal of Applied Communication Research*, 21(3), 58–75.

Friedrich, W. N. (2002). *Psychological Assessment of Sexually Abused Children and Their Families.* Thousand Oaks, CA: Sage Publishers.

Galatzer-Levy, R., Baerger, D. R., Gould, J. W., and Nye, S. (2002). Evaluating the evaluation: How to understand and critique custody evaluations. In R. Brown and L. Morgan (Eds.), *2003 Family Law Update* (pp. 139–211). Gaithersburg, MD: Aspen Publishers.

Galatzer-Levy, R. M., and Kraus, L. (Eds.) (1999). *The Scientific Basis of Child Custody Decisions.* New York: John Wiley & Sons.

Garb, H. N., Wood, J. M., Nezworski, M. T., Grove, W. M., and Stejskal, W. J. (2001). Toward a resolution of the Rorschach controversy. *Psychological Assessment,* 14, 433–448.

Gardner, R. A. (2002). Parental alienation syndrome vs. parental alienation: Which diagnosis should evaluators use in child-custody disputes? *American Journal of Family Therapy,* 30, 93–115.

Garrity, C. B., and Baris, M. A. (1994). *Caught in the Middle: Protecting the Children of High-Conflict Divorce.* San Francisco: Jossey-Bass.

Goldstein, A. M. (Ed.). (2003). *Handbook of Psychology: Forensic Psychology* (Vol. 11). New York: Wiley.

Gould, J. W. (1998). *Conducting Scientifically Crafted Child Custody Evaluations.* Thousand Oaks, CA: Sage.

Gould, J. W. (2006). *Conducting Scientifically Crafted Child Custody Evaluations,* 2nd Edition. Sarasota, FL: Professional Resource Press.

Gould, J. W., and Bell, L. C. (2000). Forensic methods and procedures applied to child custody evaluations: What judges need to know in determining a competent forensic work product. *Juvenile and Family Court Journal,* 38(2), 21–27.

Gould, J. W., and Lehrmann, D. (2002). Evaluating the probative value of child custody evaluations. *Juvenile and Family Court Journal,* 53(2), 17–30.

Gould, J. W., and Martindale, D. A. (in press). *The Art and Science of Child Custody Evaluations.* New York: Guilford.

Gould, J. W., and Martindale, D. A. (2005). A second call for clinical humility and judicial vigilance: Comments on Tippins and Wittmann (2005). *Family Court Review,* 43(2), 253–259.

Gould, J. W., and Stahl, P. (2000). The art and science of child custody evaluations: Integrating clinical and forensic mental health models. *Family and Conciliation Courts Review,* 38, 392–414.

Gould, J. W., and Stahl, P. (2001). Never paint by the numbers: A response to Kelly and Lamb (2000), Solomon and Biringen (2000), and Lamb and Kelly (2001). *Family Court Review,* 39, 372–376.

Gould, J. W., Kirkpatrick, H. D., Austin, W., and Martindale, D. A. (2004). Critiquing a colleague's forensic work product: A suggested protocol for application to child custody evaluations. *Journal of Child Custody,* 1(3), 37–64.

Graham-Berman, S. A., and Edleson, J. L. (Eds.) (2001). *Domestic Violence in the Lives of Children: The Future of Research, Intervention, and Social Policy.* Washington, DC: American Psychological Association.

Greenberg, L., and Gould, J. W. (2001). The treating expert: A hybrid role with firm boundaries. *Professional Psychology: Research and Practice,* 32, 469–478.

Greenberg, S. A., and Shuman, D. W. (1997). Irreconcilable conflict between therapeutic and forensic roles. *Professional Psychology: Research and Practice,* 28(1), 50–57.

Gross, S. R., and Mnookin, J. L. (2003). Expert information and expert evidence: A preliminary taxonomy. *Seton Hall Law Review,* 34, 139–185.

Heilbrun, K. (1995). Child custody evaluation: Critically assessing mental health experts and psychological tests. *Family Law Quarterly,* 29, 63–78.

Heilbrun, K. (2001). *Principles of Forensic Mental Health Assessment.* New York: Kluwer Academic/ Plenum Publishers.

Heilbrun, K., Warren, J., and Picarello, K. (2003). Third party information in forensic assessment. In A. Goldstein (Ed.), *Handbook of Psychology: Forensic Psychology* (Vol. 11). Hoboken, NJ: Wiley.

Heinze, M. C., and Grisso, T. (1996). Review of instruments assessing parenting competencies used in child custody evaluations. *Behavioral Sciences and the Law*, 14, 293–313.

Hetherington, E. M., Bridges, M., and Insabella, G. M. (1998). What matters? What does not? Five perspectives on the association between marital transitions and children's adjustment. *American Psychologist*, 53, 167–184.

Hetherington, E. M., and Kelly, J. (2002). *For Better or for Worse: Divorce Reconsidered*. New York: Norton.

Holden, G. W., Geffner, R. A., and Jouriles, E. N. (1998). *Children Exposed to Marital Violence: Theory, Research, and Applied Issues* (pp. 371–408). Washington, DC: American Psychological Association.

Hynan, D. J. (1998). Interviewing children in custody evaluations. *Family and Conciliation Courts Review*, 36, 466–478.

Jaffe, P. G., and Geffner, R. (1998). Child custody disputes and domestic violence: Critical issues for mental health, social service, and legal professionals. In G. W. Holden, R. A. Geffner, and E. N. Jouriles (Eds.), *Children Exposed to Marital Violence: Theory, Research and Applied Issues*. Washington, DC: American Psychological Association.

Jaffe, P. G., Lemon, N. K. D., and Poisson, S. E. (2003). *Child Custody and Domestic Violence: A Call for Safety and Accountability*. Thousand Oaks, CA: Sage Publishers.

Johnston, J., and Roseby, V. E. (1997). *In the Name of the Child: A Developmental Approach to Understanding and Helping Children of Conflicted and Violent Divorce*. New York: The Free Press.

Johnston, J. R., and Campbell, L. E. G. (1993). A Clinical Typology of Interparental Violence in Disputed Custody Divorces. *American Journal of Orthopsychiatry*, 63, 190–199.

Johnston, J. R., and Campbell, L. E. G. (1988). *Impasses of Divorce: The Dynamics and Resolution of Family Conflict*. New York: Free Press.

Johnston, J. R., and Girdner, L. K. (2001). *Family Abductors: Descriptive Profiles and Family Interventions*. Washington, DC: Office of Juvenile Justice Prevention.

Johnson, M. (2005). Apples and oranges in child custody disputes: Intimate terrorism vs. situational couple violence. *Journal of Child Custody*, 2(4), 43–52.

Kelly, J. B., and Emery, R. E. (2003). Children's adjustment following divorce: Risk and resilience perspectives. *Family Relations*, 52, 352–362.

Kelly, J. B., and Johnston, J. R. (2001). The alienated child: A reformulation of parental alienation syndrome. *Family Court Review*, 39, 249–266.

Kelly, J. B., and Lamb, M. E. (2000). Using child development research to make appropriate custody and access decisions for young children. *Family and Conciliation Courts Review*, 38, 297–311.

Kelly, J. B., and Lamb, M. E. (2003). Developmental issues in relocation cases involving young children: When, whether, and how? *Journal of Family Psychology*, 17, 193–205.

Kirkland, K. (2002). The epistemology of child custody evaluations. *Family Court Review*, 40(2), 185–189.

Kirkland, K., and Kirkland, K. L. (2001). Frequency of child custody evaluation complaints and related disciplinary action: A survey of the Association of State and Provincial Psychology Boards. *Professional Psychology: Research and Practice*, 32(2), 171–174.

Kirkpatrick, H. D. (2004). A floor, not a ceiling: Beyond guidelines—An argument for minimum standards of practice in conducting child custody and visitation evaluations. *Journal of Child Custody*, 1(1), 61–75.

Kirkpatrick, H. D., and Austin, W. G. (2005). Response to Amundson, Lux, and Hindmarch: Critique of Investigative Practices Article. *Journal of Child Custody*, 2(4), 85–94.

Krauss, D. A., and Sales, B. D. (1999). The problem of "helpfulness' in applying Daubert to expert testimony: Child custody determination in family law as an exemplar. *Psychology, Public Policy, & Law*, 5(1), 78–99.

Kuehnle, K. (1996). *Assessing Allegations of Child Sexual Abuse*. Sarasota, FL: Professional Resources Press.

Kuehnle, K., Coulter, M., and Firestone, G. (2000). Child protection evaluations: The forensic step-child. *Family and Conciliation Courts Review*, 38, 368–391.

Lamb, M. E. (1997). Fathers in child development: An introductory overview and guide. In M. E. Lamb (Ed.), *The Role of the Father in Child Development* (pp. 1–18). New York: Wiley.

Lamb, M. E. (2000). The history of research on father involvement: An overview. *Marriage and Family Review*, 29(2–3), 23–42.

Lamb, M. E. (2002). Placing children's interests first: Developmentally appropriate parenting plans. *Virginia Journal of Social Policy and the Law*, 10(1), 98–119.

Lamb, M. E., and Kelly, J. B. (2001). Using empirical literature to guide the development of parenting plans for young children: A rejoinder to Solomon and Biringen. *Family Court Review*, 39, 365–371.

Lamb, M. E., Sternberg, K. J., and Thompson, R. A. (1997). The effects of divorce and custody arrangements on children's behavior, development, and adjustment. *Family and Conciliation Courts Review*, 35, 393–404.

Lee, S. M., and Olesen, N. W. (2001). Assessing alienation in child custody and access evaluations. *Family Court Review*, 39, 282–298.

Lussier, G., Deater-Deckard, K., Dunn, J., and Davies, L. (2002). Support across generations: Children's closeness to grandparents following divorce and remarriage. *Journal of Family Psychology*, 16, 363–376.

Lyon, T. D. (1999). The new wave in children's suggestibility research: A critique. *Cornell Law Review*, 84, 1004–1105.

Maccoby, E. E., and Mnookin, R. H. (1992). *Dividing the Child: Social and Legal Dilemmas of Custody*. Cambridge, MA: Harvard University Press.

Main, M. (1996). Introduction to the special section on attachment and psychopathology: 2. Overview of the field of attachment. *Journal of Consulting and Clinical Psychology*, 64(2), 237–243.

Marine, E. C., and Bogie, M. A. (2004). Professional liability claims: Processes and outcomes. www.athealth.com (on-line CE course).

Martindale, D. A. (2005). Confirmatory bias and confirmatory distortion. *Journal of Child Custody*, 2(1/2), 31–48.

Martindale, D. A. (2006). Consultants and role delineation. *The Matrimonial Strategist*, 24(4), 4 ff.

Martindale, D. A., and Gould, J. W. (2004). The forensic model: Ethics and scientific methodology applied to child custody evaluations. *Journal of Child Custody*, 1(1), 1–22.

Masten, A. S., and Coatsworth, J. D. (1998). The development of competence in favorable and unfavorable environments. *American Psychologist*, 53, 205–220.

McCann, J. T., Flens, J. R., Campagna, V., Callman, Lazzaro, T., and Connor, E. (2001). The MCMI-III in child custody evaluations: A normative study. *Journal of Forensic Psychology Practice*, 1, 27–44.

Medoff, D. (1999). MMPI-2 validity scales in child custody evaluations: Clinical versus statistical significance, *Behavioral Sciences and the Law*, 17(4), 409–411.

Medoff, D. (2003). The scientific basis of psychological testing: Considerations following *Daubert, Kumho* and *Joiner*. *Family Court Review*, 41(2), 199–213.

Melton, G. B., Petrila, J., Pythress, N. G., and Slobogin, C. (1997). *Psychological Evaluations for the Courts: A Handbook for Mental Health Professionals and Lawyers* (2nd ed.) New York: Guilford.

Millon, T., Davis, R., and Millon, C. (1997). *MCMI-III Manual* (2nd ed.) Minneapolis, MN: NCS Pearson.

Mullender, A., Hague, G., Imam, U., Kelly, L., Malos, E., and Regan, L. (2002). *Children's Perspectives on Domestic Violence*. Thousand Oaks, CA: Sage Publishers.

Otto, R. K., Edens, J. F., and Barcus, E. H. (2000). The use of psychological testing in child custody evaluations. *Family and Conciliation Courts Review*, 38, 312–340.

Otto, R. K., and Helibrun, K. (2002). The practice of forensic psychology: A look toward the future in light of the past. *American Psychologist*, 57(1), 5–18.

Poole, D. A., and Lamb, M. E. (1998). *Investigative Interviews of Children*. Washington, DC: American Psychological Association.

Pruett, M. K., Ebling, R., and Insabella, G. (2004). Critical aspects of parenting plans for young children: Interjecting data into the debate about overnights. *Family Court Review*, 42(1), 39–59.

Rohner, R. P., and Veneziano, R. A. (2001). The importance of father love: History and contemporary evidence. *Review of General Psychology*, 5(4), 382–405.

Roseby, V. (1995). Uses of psychological testing in a child-focused approach to child custody evaluations. *Family Law Quarterly*, 29, 97–110.

Rosenthal, R., Hiller, J. B., Bornstein, R. F., Berry, D. T. R., and Brunell-Neuleib, S. (2001). Meta-analytic methods, the Rorschach, and the MMPI. *Psychological Assessment*, 14, 449–451.

Schutz, B. M., Dixon, E. B., Lindenberger, J. C., and Ruther, N. J. (1989). *Solomon's Sword*. San Francisco: Josey-Bass.

Shuman, D. W. (1993). The use of empathy in forensic examinations. *Ethics and Behavior*, 3, 223–302.

Shuman, D. W. (2002). The role of mental health experts in custody decisions: Science, psychological tests, and clinical judgment. *Family Law Quarterly*, 36, 135–162.

Shuman, D. W., and Sales, B. D. (1998). The admissibility of expert testimony based upon clinical judgment and scientific research. *Psychology, Public Policy and Law*, 4(4), 1226–1252.

Shuman, D. W., and Sales, B. D. (1999). The impact of *Daubert* and its progeny on the admissibility of behavioral and social science evidence. *Psychology, Public Policy, and Law*, 5(1), 3–15.

Shuman, D. W., and Sales, B. D. (2001). *Daubert*'s wager. *Journal of Forensic Psychology Practice*, 1(3), 69–78.

Solomon, J., and Biringen, Z. (2001). Another look at the developmental research. *Family Court Review*, 39, 355–364.

Stacey, J., and Biblarz, T. J. (2001). (How) Does the sexual orientation of parents matter? *American Sociological Review*, 66, 159–183.

Stahl, P. M. (1994). *Conducting Child Custody Evaluations: A Comprehensive Guide*. Thousand Oaks, CA.: Sage.

Stahl, P. M. (1999). *Complex Issues in Custody Evaluations*. Thousand Oaks, Ca.: Sage.

Stahl, P. M., and Drozd, L.M. (2006). *Relocation Issues in Child Custody Evaluations*. New York: Haworth Press.

Stoltz, J. M., and Ney, T. (2002). Resistance to visitation: Rethinking child and parental alienation. *Family Court Review*, 40, 220–231.

Sullivan, M. J., and Kelly, J. B. (2001). Legal and psychological management of cases with an alienated child. *Family Court Review*, 39, 299–315.

Vidmar, N., and Schuller, R. A. (1989). Juries and expert evidence: Social framework testimony. *Law and Contemporary Problems*, 52, 133–177.

Wallerstein, J. S., and Kelly, J. B. (1980). *Surviving the Breakup: How Children and Parents Cope with Divorce*. New York: Basic Books.

Wallerstein, J. S., and Tanke, T. J. (1996). To move or not to move: Psychological and legal considerations in the relocation of children following divorce. *Family Law Quarterly*, 30, 305–332.

Warshak, J. W. (2000a). Blanket restrictions: Overnight contact between parents and young children. *Family and Conciliation Courts Review*, 38, 422–445.

Warshak, J. W. (2000b). Social science and children's best interests in relocation cases: Burgess revisited. *Family Law Quarterly*, 34, 83–113.

Warshak, R. A. (1996). Gender bias in child custody decisions. *Family and Conciliation Courts Review*, 34, 396–409.

Warshak, R. A. (2001). *Divorce Poison*. New York: Regan.

Weiner, I. B. (2001). Advancing the science of psychological assessment: The Rorschach inkblot method as exemplar. *Psychological Assessment*, 13, 423–432.

Weissman, H. N. (1991). Child custody evaluations: Fair and unfair professional practices. *Behavioral Sciences and the Law*, 9, 469–476.

Weissman, H. N. (1994). Psychotherapeutic and psycholegal considerations: When a custodial parent seeks to move away. *The American Journal of Family Therapy*, 22(2), 176–181.

Whiteside, M. F. (1998). Custody for children: Age 5 and younger. *Family and Conciliation Courts Review*, 36, 479–502.

Employment and Discrimination Litigation: The Dysfunctional Side of Workplace Diversity

18

JAY M. FINKELMAN

Alliant International University, Alhambra, California

Contents

Introduction and Overview

Much of the forensic research that is conducted—and most of the public's attention—is directed toward high-profile criminal cases. Many universities devote disproportionate time in their forensic programs to addressing criminal issues and their legal agendas. But the reality is that noncriminal business–related litigation involves several billions of dollars each year and often determines the fate of companies and their employees.

This chapter addresses an important special business litigation practice focusing on issues of employer misconduct, specifically charges of discrimination, harassment, retaliation, and wrongful termination. All these categories fall within the science and the practice of human resources management that will be more fully described in the following section. They are typically addressed by line human resource management professionals, internal and external consultants, and experts specializing in employment and human resource practices.

For most companies, people are their most important asset and their most critical resource. Caring for and protecting that asset—and protecting the organization from unreasonable employment-related claims originating from that human resource—is the responsibility of human resource management. This task is difficult and poses special problems and risks.

This chapter discusses key issues in civil employment litigation, starting with a brief description of the role of human resource management in the process and the rationale for the initiation of litigation. It provides a more detailed consideration of juror perception of employment litigation, including how jurors deal with uncertainty, how they process case information, what they understand about employment cases, and how they make decisions and render verdicts. This is followed by a discussion on the importance and utility of a professionally conducted investigation of all allegations of employer misconduct. Next, the chapter provides guidance for risk management professionals who need to present their defense to a jury, including the value of keeping presentations simple and straightforward, mounting an aggressive case, and never underestimating the wisdom of a jury. Psychological anchors are defined and explained. Expert testimony in employment litigation is analyzed with respect to both admissibility and value. A heuristic California employment litigation case is introduced as an example. The Supreme Court–mandated *Daubert* test discussion provides perspective as well as precedent with respect to expert testimony in employment cases. The chapter concludes with a brief discussion of fundamental employment discrimination regulations and representative case law in the domains of sexual discrimination and harassment, age discrimination, and disability discrimination, emphasizing key Supreme Court decisions.

The Role of Human Resource Management

Human resource management is a subdiscipline of industrial/organizational psychology. Over the years, a pattern of policies and practices that are consistent with good human resource management policies and practice has evolved. Although there is typically more than one acceptable way to accomplish human resource objectives, there are absolute prohibitions on discriminatory practices or consequences that adversely impact employees on the basis of gender, age, race, and physical disability, as well as retaliation against employees reporting the same. In essence, good human resource management practices are primarily designed to preclude opportunities for discrimination, harassment, and retaliation. Thus, human resource policies and practices that are considered to be consistent with generally accepted human resource management policies and practices are those that protect against unlawful discrimination, harassment, and retaliation.

Human resource management has a dual constituency and dual responsibilities within organizations. It must safeguard the rights of employees and protect them from unlawful practices (discrimination, harassment, and retaliation) while also protecting the organizations from the liability associated with improper policies and practices. Typically, the best way to accomplish both objectives is to ensure that good human resource management policies and practices are in place—namely, ones that protect employees from discrimination, harassment, and retaliation.

Generally accepted human resource management practices allow for a variety of approaches to accomplish these objectives. These include such techniques as preventive training, vigilant monitoring, management coaching, proper postings of employee rights and complaint channels, effective employee and management manuals, prompt and effective investigations of allegations of improper conduct, user-friendly complaint procedures and mechanisms, appropriate disciplinary procedures, and mechanisms to preclude retaliation, among others.

It is these human resource management practices—and the alleged failure to observe them—that typically become the basis of employment discrimination, harassment, or retaliation lawsuits. Good and consistently applied human resource management policies and practices are often the key elements in an effective defense.

When Litigation Cannot Be Avoided

Finkelman (2006) notes that

> While it is said that no one wins in litigation, it is not always true. Litigation sometimes is necessary from an employer's perspective in order to discourage frivolous claims in the future. Plaintiffs may use the threat of litigation to exact "settlements" from defendants who wish to avoid the cost and risk of litigation. Moreover, defendants sometimes elect to settle in order to avoid embarrassing disclosures in public court.

Regardless of who is litigating or why, it is instructive to understand how jurors are likely to perceive employment litigation (Kassin and Garfield, 1992). To do that, it is necessary to know how jurors interpret information and make decisions so that consultants can help litigants make good decisions. Our system of jurisprudence actually depends upon this knowledge and getting the process to operate properly.

Manipulations of the system are usually easy to detect. An expert or consultant who supports fairness and equity in the litigation process is making a significant contribution in the service of justice. Smart attorneys want this to happen—even as they battle to support their client's position in litigation or settlement negotiations.

Juror Perception of Employment Litigation

According to Finkelman (2005), most jurors approach employment-related litigation with the sincere desire to facilitate justice and to do the right thing. The exceptions are jurors who have had related experiences on either the employee or the employer side, who cannot separate themselves from those experiences, and who do not candidly disclose those issues during *voir dire* (Dexter, Cutler and Moran, 1992; Kassin and Garfield, 1992; Narby, Cutler and Moran, 1993). Sometimes a juror may sincerely believe that he or she is uninfluenced by such experiences. However, these issues can operate below the surface and influence perceptions and ultimately decisions (Lecci, 2002; Myers and Lecci, 1998; Shestowsky and Horowitz, 2004).

Jurors typically use their common sense and basic instincts when assessing and interpreting the facts presented by both sides in employment litigation. Arguments that do not make sense or that are contrary to conventional wisdom with respect to employment issues are quickly dismissed to the detriment of the attorneys who proposed them. Without doubt, jurors incorporate their own work-related experiences into judgments about the parties and events in employment litigation.

Jurors are not lawyers and may not always understand the fine points of the law, even after they are explained by a judge. Jurors have even privately admitted (in posttrial interviews) that they did not always feel compelled to follow the law, but rather chose to interpret it to fit the circumstances as they viewed them. It is pointless to debate the wisdom or ethics of this situation. Suffice it to say that it is usually done in good faith and it is a reality that may often result in the correct decision from a societal perspective.

Jurors are just as uncomfortable with uncertainty as the rest of us and attempt to minimize it as quickly as possible. Thus, they tend to make rapid credibility assessments of all the players in the courtroom, especially the plaintiff, the defendants, the fact witnesses, and the expert witnesses (Cooper, Bennett, and Sukel, 1996; Cutler, Penrod, and Dexter, 1990; Finkelman, 2002; Hemsley and Doob, 1978; Hosman and Wright, 1987; Lind, Erickson, Conley, and O'Barr, 1978; Penrod, and Cutler, 1995). In many ways, jurors react as though they were on a blind date, meeting potential matches for the first time. They make initial assessments of the integrity and the character of the various parties in the courtroom. Often the first impressions are very rapid, similar to superficially sizing up prospects in a singles bar before making a decision to approach them. After the initial credibility assessment, jurors spend the remainder of the trial confirming or refuting their first impressions. Social psychologists have observed that people engage in selective attention and perception of events after they form their initial impression (Hastorf and Cantril, 1954; Festinger, 1957). Similar processes are at work in the courtroom. Jurors are not equally attentive to every element in a trial. People are more likely to perceive and accept new information that is consistent with their earlier assessments. It is not that it is impossible to change preconceived notions, but rather that it gets more difficult to do so with the passage of time and the process of selective attention and perception.

Juror Comprehension and Decision Making in Employment Litigation

Jurors, and most people for that matter, make decisions on the basis of their understanding of the relevant facts and issues and how they relate to the way the world is viewed. This means that verdict decisions are not made in isolation, even after allowing for specific facts and issues in employment cases, but rather in response to the very specific way that individual jurors view the world of work in all of its manifestations. Jurors process trial information as a function of how they view the world in applicable situations.

In essence, discrimination, harassment, and retaliation trials can be viewed within the context of a familiar and heuristic information processing and information overload model (as applied in a different context by Finkelman, Zeitlin, Filippi, and Friend, 1977), in which jurors perceive, retain, and process the facts and issues in the case as a function of their prior experiences and preconceptions. The implication is that basic trial understanding, memory, and interpretation of key facts and issues by jurors will be shaped by influences that are apart from the actual trial experience. Smart attorneys know that they need this juror-related information in advance to ensure a fair trial, minimize potential bias, and favor their clients' interests.

It should not be surprising that jurors would view alleged job discrimination, harassment, and retaliation as a function of their own experiences with such employment misconduct. Jurors also make use of their own experiences with individuals similar to the plaintiffs who initiated the claims. What is intriguing is that jurors have been found to rely on "psychological anchors" (Vinson, 1986, p. 173) to help them understand and interpret the facts and issues. Effective litigators make use of these anchors to help jurors see key elements of a lawsuit from their clients' perspective. This might either create a competitive advantage or simply establish a level playing field in which there is equity for both sides in employment litigation (Finkelman, 2005).

Angeletti (2006) observes that some of the published analysis of the effects of individual differences on juror verdicts claims that personality and background variables are reliable indicators of juror propensity to favor plaintiff or defendant. Other authors argue that the evidence alone determines the verdict and that juror differences are irrelevant. Although these authors may maintain that demographics such as race, gender, and occupation are not reliable predictors of the final verdict, it has been noted that juries are rarely unanimous on the first ballot. Something must account for the difference. The evidence presented is exactly the same for all jurors, but the perception and interpretation are obviously not. Ellseworth (1993) concluded logically that the individual difference must make a difference.

The Importance of Employment Misconduct Investigations to Jurors

Having right on your side is possibly the best guarantee of prevailing in a discrimination, harassment, or retaliation lawsuit as a defendant. But a professionally conducted misconduct investigation may be just as important. In fact, innocent corporate defendants who do not promptly initiate investigations in response to complaints of misconduct are at a severe disadvantage in protecting themselves against bogus lawsuits. Even if misconduct has occurred, a thorough investigation may still serve to mitigate damages. Jurors understand that employers cannot always preclude improper and discriminatory behavior by other employees. They do, however, expect the management to control such behavior by supervision, and strict liability legal guidelines may prevail as well. An effective investigation is usually interpreted as a good faith effort to control improper conduct, especially when it results in a determination of fault and when an appropriate punishment is imposed. A problem is that most investigations are inconclusive meaning that there is insufficient evidence to find fault or to definitively clear the alleged perpetrator. Or the evidence may be contradictory such that an equitable determination is not possible. Although this is rarely satisfying to the accuser, it is a reality. And innocence must, in fairness, be presumed.

But a series of inconclusive determinations after investigations of claims by multiple accusers, especially if directed at the same individual, needs to be taken as a potentially significant warning sign.

All things being equal, external investigations are more persuasive than internal investigations because they suggest a greater level of neutrality. However, that is not always the case. For example, if outside investigators (or firms) almost always find for the side that hired them, their neutrality may be subject to challenge. In fact, no one is entirely neutral in most investigations, and investigators tend to get paid by someone. But this should not be used to discredit findings absent in specific impeaching evidence. Professional ethics and integrity still count and must be respected.

Guidance for Risk Management Professionals in Employment Discrimination

Once a discrimination, harassment, or retaliation complaint has been filed and a lawsuit initiated, it is too late to rely upon traditional prophylactic measures in order to protect a workforce. However, there is a lot that can be done to facilitate a fair employment misconduct trial for both plaintiffs and defendants. Much of it flows from the principles described earlier in this chapter:

1. Never underestimate the jury.
2. Focus on effective opening and closing statements.
3. Avoid presenting overly complex cases.
4. Provide credible explanations for unclear behavior.
5. Suggest coherent psychological anchors to help the jury understand case theory.
6. Mount an aggressive prosecution or defense.

Jurors try to do what they think is correct (Van Detta and Gallipeau, 2000), and their ability to get at the core issues of an employment case should never be underestimated. Although they do not always grasp all the subtle points and arcane legal details of a civil trial, they generally do get it and, in my opinion, they generally get it right when it comes to matters of discrimination, retaliation, and harassment. Attorneys and risk management professionals who underestimate the wisdom of juries do so at their peril.

Employment litigation is generally more complex than many people think, and cohesive opening and closing remarks certainly help focus and orient a jury. Research suggests that the jury's decision making is heavily influenced by these statements, initially to provide an explanatory overview during opening remarks and then to summarize positions during closing (Pyszczynski, Greenberg, Mack, and Wrightsman, 1981; Pyszczynski and Wrightsman, 1981). It is probably true that many employment cases are won and lost on the basis of the persuasiveness of opening and closing remarks.

Overly complex cases may appeal to those who make them, but rarely to those who hear them. Although it is understandable that certain technical points may have to be included for the legal record, it is preferable to minimize the degree to which they may intrude on a clear presentation of the real facts and issues in a case (Horowitz, 2001). It is sometimes surprising how often this obvious point gets lost in the heat of presenting a technically perfect argument.

Jurors are, of course, only humans and want to understand why things are the way they are—and why they happened the way they did. The most effective attorneys provide clear and compelling explanations early in the trial, often in opening arguments, and continue to reinforce them throughout the trial. Then they summarize them in closing arguments. These explanations, if credible, fill a psychological void for many jurors and may serve to "inoculate" them against opposing arguments and evidence.

Psychological anchors are compelling explanatory concepts that jurors remember as a way to understand and bring order to events and circumstances that might not otherwise make sense. Sometimes the anchors develop on their own as jurors process the facts and issues in a case, whereas at other times, they are suggested by counsel or witnesses. The most effective psychological anchors take on significance that is disproportionate to the underlying events that they help explain (Vinson, 1986). It is difficult to envision their impact until jurors are actually interviewed after a trial.

It almost seems too obvious to emphasize, but it is essential for both plaintiffs and defendants to mount an aggressive case in support of their positions. Jurors expect and are entitled to no less than that. It is fascinating that though most plaintiffs aggressively pursue their employment cases before a jury, some large corporations are reluctant to appear excessively aggressive in their own defense. The fear is that they might offend jurors by using their size and clout to unfairly overwhelm a much smaller and less capable plaintiff. However, the reality is that jurors expect large organizations to mount substantial defenses—precisely because they are large organizations. To do less is disappointing and perhaps even suspicious.

Human Resources Management Comes of Age in the Courtroom

Nielsen* (2005) wrote a classic article regarding employment litigation that has been adopted for this section of the chapter. In the article, he noted that

> A milestone in the study of human resources management practices was reached, recently, but few so far have taken notice. On January 28, 2004, the days of industrial psychology or human resources management being characterized as 'junk science' in courtrooms abruptly ended with the California Court of Appeal's opinion, *Dee Kotla v. Regents of the University of California.*† Now persons with such expertise formally join the ranks of recognized experts who may testify in litigation. (p. 157)

The events in the case that Nielsen describes are instructive for us as a case study. On December 16, 1996, Lawrence Livermore Laboratory employee, Dee Kotla, was giving testimony in a deposition in support of a sexual harassment plaintiff, and former coworker, and against the laboratory. During the deposition, the laboratory's attorney demanded that Kotla reveal her work computer's password so that the laboratory could search it. The attorney called her supervisor and described Kotla to him as a "hostile witness." A "bathroom" break was called. While Kotla occupied a stall in the women's restroom, she heard her employer's attorneys come in and talk out loud. According to her, the laboratory's counsel said, "*If Kotla*

---

* Jan C. Nielsen is an attorney at law and experienced trial lawyer with the law firm of Gwilliam, Ivary, Chiosso, Cavalli & Brewer in Oakland, CA. He was one of the attorneys representing Dee Kotla.
† 2004 Cal.App.Lexis 109.

knows what's good for her, she'll shut up." That very day, the laboratory's counsel accessed Kotla's computer, found some personal information, and initiated a criminal investigation of Kotla for purportedly using her employer's computer to help out a friend's business. In the past, discipline for computer misuse had been fairly minimal, mostly 5-day suspensions. But in Kotla's case, although the investigation found little evidence to support the charges (barely $4.30 in personal telephone calls and "insignificant" use of her computer to help her friend), she was fired. The termination occurred barely 1 month after Kotla had completed her deposition testimony against the laboratory. According to Nielsen, Kotla's psychological makeup was such that she suffered an extreme reaction to her employer's abrupt, unjust, and "pretextual" termination. That evening, February 20, 1997, she fell into a deep and severe depression. Kotla attempted suicide and nearly died.

Nielsen reports that after a 2-month trial in which a substantial body of evidence was introduced, including testimony of the plaintiff's human resources expert, Jay Finkelman, on March 11, 2002, in the Alameda County, CA, Superior Court, a majority of jurors found for Kotla under her complaint alleging retaliation and awarded her $1 million in total damages. The Lab appealed. On January 28, 2004, in *Dee Kotla v. Regents of the University of California,* the Court of Appeals, First Appellate District, Division One reversed the award and ordered a new trial, contending Kotla's human resources expert's testimony was "improper and prejudicial." According to Nielsen, the Court of Appeals gave some as well as took away. In *Kotla*, the court enshrined the legitimacy of the testimony of human resources experts in California courtrooms.

Human Resources as Junk Science

The laboratory's attorney claimed in his brief to the California Court of Appeals that "when junk science masquerades as 'expert' testimony—injustice is certain …" (Nielsen, 2005, p. 161). Nielsen notes that the junk science that purportedly did in his client was the plaintiff expert's testimony in the well-established field of industrial psychology, or human resources management. Human resources expertise never was junk and could hardly be considered unjust given a balanced look at employment litigation. Industrial psychology provides the scientific and empirical basis for human resources management. It is a specialty taught in colleges and universities and may lead to a master's or a doctoral degree, as it does in a number of the programs at the Marshall Goldsmith School of Management at Alliant International University.

Human resources has evolved its own standards of policy and practice. Consultants regularly evaluate cases for employers, advise and assist in developing proper procedures and policies, and conduct investigations, and experts regularly testify in employment cases. Actually, it would be unjust not to allow them to testify. Sometimes human resources departments have drafted policies and procedures that assured employees of fair and equitable treatment but do not follow them. Or they fail to follow generally accepted practices in the human resources field in disciplining or terminating employees.

According to Nielsen, without testimony from a person with specialized knowledge in human resources, employment litigation plaintiffs are usually at a huge disadvantage in counteracting the testimony of the employers' human resources personnel about the propriety of a termination. However, for year after year in numerous pretrial motions, defense

* The Regents manage the laboratory under a contract with the U. S. Department of Energy.

attorneys fought to exclude or limit human resources experts from testifying on behalf of plaintiffs in employment litigation. Often times, especially given the hostile demeanor of some courts to expert testimony in general, such testimony was excluded, or at least substantially limited. Employers might then have witnesses from their own human resources departments available to testify that everything was done according to their personnel policies and procedures. From a defense perspective, human resources expert testimony is also valuable as a way to objectively explain human resource management policies and practices to a jury and perhaps counter emotional plaintiff claims that are not grounded in the science and practice of industrial–organizational psychology.

Human Resources Experts Clearly May Testify

Nielsen notes that on January 28, 2004, human resources expert testimony became enshrined in law, no longer to be derogatorily labeled "junk science." In *Kotla,* the Court of Appeals ruled, "Expert testimony on predicate issues within the expertise of a human resources expert is clearly permissible" (115 Cal.App.4th at 294). The court cited specific examples of predicate issues that human resources could appropriately testify about, including the assessment of disproportionate punishment and whether an employer significantly deviated from ordinary personnel procedures in taking retaliatory adverse employment action *vis-à-vis* the employee—as legitimate for expert testimony.

Initially, the Appellate Court favored the laboratory's position, felt that the plaintiff's expert (the author of this chapter) had ventured too far with his opinions, and found error in the trial court's allowance of the expert's specific testimony relative to indicators of retaliatory motive.* It granted a new trial. But, according to Nielsen (2005), the laboratory's "worse than junk science" (p. 162) argument went too far, and the court responded unfavorably. It implied that trial courts cannot limit or exclude human resources expert testimony in litigation as junk or argue that it is not science at all as they had done in the past. The *Kotla* court enshrined human resources management as permissible expert testimony. As a postscript, Nielsen notes that *Kotla v. Regents of the University of California* was retried in 2005, again using this author as plaintiff's expert witness, and Kotla won again. The jury doubled her award to a judgment of $5.9 million, including attorneys' fees.

Supreme Court Precedent: The *Daubert* Test Rules

The decision as to whether expert testimony is admissible in federal and state courts is a function of whether the opinion is proper for an expert to render at all and whether the expert in question is qualified to render an opinion in that area. As it was alluded to in "Human Resources as Junk Science," many trials start with pretrial motions filed by both sides, although more typically by the defense, to bar the opposing expert from testifying because of one or both of these factors. Technically, these are referred to as motions *in limine.*

In ruling on these motions, the court must first determine whether the expert testimony in question will improperly address a question of law that is not, of course, subject to

---

* The Court of Appeals explained that "in the context of employment litigation, motive must be inferred from a unique constellation of facts that are subject to conflicting interpretations." As such, a human resources expert would not be able to infer motive unless the expert "previously encountered circumstances duplicating those that gave rise to this litigation."

expert testimony. Then the court will determine whether the opinion is based on specula-tion or conjecture or matters that are not properly relied upon. Finally, the court will con-sider the reasonableness of the methodology that the expert used to render an opinion.

This review process was formalized by the U. S. Supreme Court in 1993 when it advanced the *Daubert* test (*Daubert v. Merrell Dow Pharmaceuticals, Inc.*, 1993). The trial court was required to assure that an expert would be testifying to scientific knowledge that would assist the jury in understanding issues that would permit them to render a fair verdict. The Supreme Court explained that the reasoning and methodology of testifying experts needed to be scientifically valid and properly applied to the facts and issues in the case.

The standards were to include consideration of whether the conclusions of the expert could be tested and subjected to peer review by other qualified professionals. The trial court was also tasked with determining whether there was a known or potential rate of error as well as whether there is widespread acceptance of the knowledge and methodol-ogy used by the testifying expert. More recent Supreme Court decisions have clarified that the *Daubert* test applies to all expert testimony, not only to scientific testimony (*General Electric Co. v. Joiner*, 1997; *Kumho Tire Co. v. Carmichael*, 1999).

Prior to the Daubert decision, the standards for expert testimony were identified in a 1923 Supreme Court decision that became known as the Frye standard (*Frye v. United States*, 1923). That decision required that for expert testimony to be admissible, it only had to be generally accepted by the relevant scientific community. The *Daubert* decision changed everything. It tasked the trial judge with the responsibility to make certain that the testimony of the expert was scientifically valid, reliable, and relevant. The trial judge became the gatekeeper.

Employment Law and Litigation

The most significant legislation pertaining to employment opportunity and employment discrimination is the Civil Rights Act of 1964, as amended by the Equal Employment Opportunity Act of 1972. Specifically, Title VII of the Civil Rights Act was enacted by the Congress to guarantee all workers in the United States equal job opportunities regardless of race, sex, religion, color, or national origin. Title VII specifically prohibits discrimina-tion with respect to all aspects of employment, including recruitment, selection, evalua-tion, training, placement, promotion, retention, termination, and compensation, among other functions. The Equal Employment Opportunity Commission (EEOC) is charged with the responsibility to enforce the requirements of Title VII.

Sexual Discrimination and Harassment

Morris (2005), reports that the current flood of sex discrimination cases, including sexual harassment, is sobering. For most management jobs, pay and promotional opportunities are not even close between men and women. Therefore, women are suing and in some cases winning large awards. Changes in civil rights legislation that took place in 1991 now permit jury trials and punitive and compensatory damage awards to be enforced against organizations that engage in gender discrimination. Morris notes that over a lifetime, earning potential can be significantly affected by even small pay discrepancies between men and women. She references the $72.5 million that Boeing agreed to pay to settle a class action lawsuit brought by female employees who claimed that they were paid less than men for the same work and that they were also not promoted as rapidly.

The following month a court ruled that the lawsuit charging Wal-Mart with discriminatory pay and promotion practices could move forward as a class action. The next month, Morgan Stanley announced a $54 million settlement to a similar class action suit just as the case was going to trial. The month after that, an assistant store manager for Costco sued for denial of promotion. Her lawyers have asked that the case also proceed as a class action. The pattern is obvious.

Price Waterhouse v. Hopkins

The Price Waterhouse litigation, which rose to the Supreme Court, is considered a classic sex discrimination and a groundbreaking sex stereotyping case. Wexler and Davis (2005) note that "sex" was eventually added to the Civil Rights Act of 1964 as a one-word amendment after "religion" (p. 44). They conclude that it transformed the landscape of Title VII law pertaining to sex stereotyping. Hopkins was a female, senior manager who was proposed for partnership at Price Waterhouse. Although some partners praised her performance, others were concerned that she lacked interpersonal skills. When she was denied partnership, she sued under Title VII, claiming sex discrimination. Partners had described her as macho and overcompensating for being a woman and needing to talk and dress more femininely and wear makeup and jewelry!

The district court concluded that it was impossible to label any particular negative reaction to Hopkins as being motivated by intentional sex stereotyping, but still found in her favor. The Court of Appeals supported the district court because Price Waterhouse could not convince them that it would have made the same decision not to promote her in the absence of discrimination. The Supreme Court agreed and reaffirmed the importance of objective standards in performance appraisal and promotion.

Burlington Northern & Santa Fe Railway Co. v. White

Savage (2006) reports that this case began in June 1997 when Sheila White was hired to operate a forklift on a track maintenance crew at Burlington's Tennessee Yard in Memphis. The only woman on the crew, she claims her foreman uttered sexist comments involving bathroom breaks and monthly periods. The foreman also allegedly repeated his view that women should not be working on the track crews. Three months later, White filed an internal complaint of sexual harassment. The next day, the yard supervisor took her off the forklift and said she would work as a track laborer. In December, a week after she filed a formal complaint with the EEOC alleging sex discrimination, her supervisor dismissed her, claiming that she had been insubordinate.

White grieved through her union, and 37 days after her suspension, she was reinstated with full back pay. Savage notes that the question for the court was whether a temporary suspension and transfer to somewhat different responsibilities was retaliatory. The jury said it was because her supervisor intended to punish her for filing a discrimination complaint and awarded $43,000 in damages. A panel of the Sixth U.S. Circuit Court of Appeals in Cincinnati reversed the verdict saying that the plaintiff had not suffered an adverse employment action because she retained her job title and was not deprived of pay or benefits. But the full Sixth Circuit reversed the reversal and ruled that the plaintiff had effectively been demoted and then (temporarily) dismissed for filing a complaint.

Weeks v. Baker & McKenzie

This is probably the best-known and most infamous sexual harassment case because it was filed against one of the country's largest and well-known law firms. A secretary at Baker & McKenzie filed an employment discrimination lawsuit against Martin Greenstein, a partner, and against the firm. It alleged that she was sexually harassed along with other employees since approximately 1991. Suggestive remarks, physical gestures, and inappropriate personal questions were part of the complaint. Some women testified that they felt so uncomfortable that they quit.

In 1994, a California Superior Court jury awarded the plaintiff $6.9 million in punitive damages against Baker & McKenzie and $225,000 in punitive damages against Greenstein. Compensatory damages, in contrast, were only $50,000—not an atypical scenario. The trial court reduced the punitive damages against the firm by about half—to $3.5 million. This judgment was affirmed by the Appeals Court.

The outcome sent a dramatic message to law firms throughout the country, especially the fact that the partner was hit with damages personally and not just as part of the firm. However, some legal observers such as Gillette (2006) question whether the jury's decision really made a difference in the conduct of legal professionals: "I think there is much more awareness than there ever was before, and I think there's more concern that this could be a liability … I don't know that this translates to a change in behavior."

Retaliation

From a human resource management perspective, retaliation against an employee, especially for engaging in some type of protected activity such as filing an administrative complaint, is often more serious than the alleged conduct that is the subject of the complaint. Retaliation is considered a special form of disparate treatment. Employers are absolutely prohibited from retaliating against employees who have filed discrimination or harassment charges, among other activities. Retaliation may take the form of punishment, demotion, harassment, firing, or any inequitable treatment in response to an employee engaging in a proper activity.

Casucci v. Faughnan

Casucci was an officer in the Clinton Connecticut Police Department who claimed that a supervisor grabbed him in a headlock and threw him against a wall during what was referred to as violent workplace roughhousing. Casucci resigned from the department and sued his former supervisor. The case settled in 1990. Almost a decade later, Casucci applied to another police department, listing his former employer as a reference. The Clinton Police Department's response to an inquiry was that the applicant likes to sue everybody and is divisive. Casucci sued for retaliation because of the negative references.

The trial court granted summary judgment and threw the case out prior to trial. Casucci appealed. The Court of Appeals ruled against him noting that his original lawsuit was not a matter of public concern because it only involved one employee's act of battery that did not rise to a level of abusive police behavior as Casucci claimed. Had his original claim involved corruption, or an unconstitutional policy within the department, the outcome might have been different.

Robinson v. Shell Oil Company

Robinson worked for Shell Oil for over 11 years before being fired in 1991. He charged Shell with race discrimination and filed charges with the EEOC. Robinson applied for another job with a company that contacted Shell for a reference. He claimed that Shell gave a negative reference in retaliation for having filed the EEOC claim. Robinson again complained to the EEOC claiming that Shell violated Title VII of the Civil Rights Act because he experienced retaliation for having engaged in a protected activity under the act. Robinson was given permission to file suit in District Court.

Shell asked the Court to dismiss the retaliation claim because the alleged conduct occurred after Robinson had already been fired. The District Court agreed with Shell and dismissed the case. Robinson appealed to the Fourth Circuit Court of Appeals. The Appellate Court sided with Robinson and reversed the dismissal while interpreting the act more broadly to include any entity that might affect an employment relationship—including Shell as a former employer. Shell appealed to the U.S. Supreme Court.

Age Discrimination

Age Discrimination lawsuits have become the fastest growing category of complaints filed with the EEOC. Carnahan (2002) takes the position that these rapidly growing lawsuits are also the most expensive—and have the capacity to backfire against applicants over 40 who are looking for jobs. The median court award in successful age discrimination lawsuits is $269,000, compared to $121,000 in race discrimination cases and $100,000 in sex discrimination lawsuits. So why take a chance of being sued by hiring an older worker? Instead, Carnahan suggests that the Congress help older job seekers by giving them the option to waive their right to sue for age discrimination if they are subsequently dismissed. This is a somewhat self-serving solution for business and hardly satisfying to antidiscrimination advocates. However, there is little question but that some (unknown) of the age discrimination lawsuits are frivolous and initiated in response to performance deficiencies that are unrelated to age.

It is interesting that the Age Discrimination in Employment Act (ADEA) that was passed by the Congress in 1967 was to protect older workers from discrimination in hiring. But today most claims under that act are for wrongful or constructive discharge, whereas only 10% relate to hiring practices. In general, hiring cases are tougher to prove and yield lesser awards to plaintiffs than wrongful termination cases. This makes hiring cases less attractive to plaintiff lawyers working on a contingency basis.

Snyder v. City of Romulus

The Romulus Michigan Police Department reorganized in 2002 in response to a decrease in its budget, which allowed an increase for the fire department. Officers with 25 or more years of service were offered an enhanced early retirement package. Some senior command officers claimed that although they had no immediate plans to retire, they were forced to take the package because their work environment had become so intolerable in an effort to force them out. They sued for age discrimination, retaliation, and conspiracy. But the trial court granted the city summary judgment. The senior command officers appealed. The Michigan Court of Appeals sided with the city because they ruled that the officers did not present sufficient evidence of the claimed discrimination, retaliation, or conspiracy.

Uber v. Slippery Rock University of Pennsylvania of the State System of Higher Education

Uber worked for Slippery Rock University since 1981 as a police officer #1. When a vacant police officer #2 position was announced in 1998, Uber and four younger officers applied. Uber was interviewed but not selected. He claimed that a younger and less qualified officer was selected. Uber initially grieved to the university's director of social equity, but an investigator found no evidence of age discrimination and observed that the selected candidate was over 40 years old. Uber filed a state discrimination claim, but the state agency also found insufficient evidence in his favor. Uber alleged that after filing his claim, the university retaliated against him and harassed him by excluding him from certain meetings, interfering with his requests for vacation and leave and issuing an unfair performance review. He filed a federal discrimination complaint and sued for age discrimination and retaliation.

The court granted summary judgment to the university on the age discrimination complaint because of a late filing. It also granted summary judgment for all issues except the unfair performance review on the retaliation complaint. The trial court found against Uber on the performance review issue because he could not prove that the university had taken an adverse action against him with the one performance review that had an overall rating of good—the same as he had received in the previous year. Uber appealed to the Commonwealth Court of Pennsylvania, which found insufficient evidence of age discrimination and retaliation to support his claim. And because he did not apply for another promotion after the review, it could not have resulted in an adverse job action.

Smith v. City of Jackson, Mississippi

In this case, the Supreme Court ruled on a question of whether the ADEA allowed plaintiffs to sue on the basis of indirect discrimination, typically known as disparate impact, rather than only on the basis of disparate treatment. Police and public safety officers claimed that when Jackson revised a pay plan to make salaries competitive with other municipalities by providing greater increases to less senior officers, it had a discriminatory impact on the officers older than 40 years, in violation of the ADEA. The Fifth Circuit Court of Appeals said no, after determining that disparate impact claims are not available under the ADEA. But the Supreme Court disagreed and held that the ADEA had to be consistent with Title VII of the Civil Rights Act and permit consideration of disparate impact claims, although its scope was restricted. Nonetheless, the Supreme Court ruled that plaintiffs had not identified the specific practice that had disparate impact, and thus failed to prove their case.

Disability Discrimination

In response to a concern that disabled Americans were subject to neglect and discrimination, the Congress passed the Rehabilitation Act of 1973. It protected the disabled from discrimination in federally funded programs. A 1978 amendment extended the act's protection to private causes of action. The resulting litigation led to many inconsistencies in enforcement. The situation was compounded as 41 states passed a variety of antidiscrimination laws with very different levels of interpretation and enforcement. Finally, the Congress attempted to remedy the situation by passing a comprehensive act designed to prohibit discrimination against individuals with disabilities—the Americans with Disabilities Act of 1990 (ADA). It was designed to ensure that Americans with disabilities would enjoy equal opportunity and would not be subject to purposeful unequal treatment.

In 1999, the Supreme Court rendered three key rulings that changed the face of disability litigation throughout the United States, predominantly in favor of the defendants, as the following case summaries will illustrate.

Sutton v. United Airlines, Inc.

This was a case about twin sisters with severe myopia who wanted to become commercial airline pilots with United Airlines. They both met all preliminary requirements with respect to their education, experience, age and Federal Aviation Administration (FAA) certification. However, they did not meet United Airlines minimum vision requirement, although they were mistakenly invited for interviews and flight simulator tests. They sued under the ADA for disability discrimination.

The U.S. District Court in Colorado dismissed the suit because it determined that plaintiffs were not substantially limited in a major life activity because their vision was correctable to 20/20. The 10th Circuit Court agreed with the District Court after the decision was appealed. Ultimately, the Supreme Court upheld the dismissal, reasoning that the plaintiffs were not actually disabled under the ADA, because the evaluation needed to be made in consideration of corrective measures, such as corrective lenses. The Supreme Court also dismissed a related ADA claim that plaintiffs were disabled, merely because they were perceived as having an impairment that substantially limits a major life activity, because they were only precluded by United Airlines from becoming a global airline pilot. The court noted that many other viable positions were still available, including regional pilots and flight instructors.

Murphy v. United Parcel Service, Inc.

This was a case about a mechanic with high blood pressure, who was hired as a mechanic by United Parcel Service. The position required that he occasionally drive commercial vehicles and meet Department of Transportation (DOT) requirements to do so. When hired, Murphy's blood pressure was so high that he could not meet these requirements, but he was granted certification in error. He was fired after United Parcel Service discovered the error. In a case similar to the prior *Sutton* matter, plaintiff raised the question as to whether mitigating medication should be considered and whether high blood pressure qualified as a disability under the ADA. Both questions were decided against the plaintiff, as they were in *Sutton*. The Supreme Court also determined that Murphy was not substantially limited in the major life activity of working because many other mechanic type jobs were still available to them.

Albertsons, Inc. v. Kirkingburg

This was another similar case in which Albertsons hired Kirkingburg as a truck driver, but required that he meet the DOT vision standards for such drivers. He was incorrectly certified as meeting basic vision standards and hired, despite the fact that he was afflicted with an uncorrectable condition that resulted in monocular vision. After plaintiff was injured on the job, placed on a leave of absence, and required to take a physical examination before returning to work, he was informed that he did not meet DOT vision standards, but that he might qualify for a waiver. Kirkingburg was fired for not meeting DOT standards, although he applied for and ultimately received the waiver.

In the lawsuit that followed, Albertsons was initially granted summary judgment by the district court, which was reversed by the Ninth Circuit Court of Appeals. For the third ADA case in a row, the Supreme Court ruled against the plaintiff, reasoning that his unusual monocular vision was not a qualifying disability because it did not impose a substantial limitation on his ability to perform a major life activity. The court also determined, consistent with its prior decisions, that lower courts failed to consider specific mechanisms that Kirkingburg had developed to cope with his visual impairment and compensate for his disability.

Concluding Thoughts and Admonitions

Diverse workforces are desirable for myriad reasons but do have the potential of triggering adverse actions that may or may not be justified. Of course, the failure to hire diverse workforces may also give rise to unpleasant consequences. This chapter addressed the dysfunctional side of diversity, in the form of discrimination, harassment, and retaliation litigation and claims.

The challenge is to differentiate legitimate misconduct in employment practices claims from bogus claims that are initiated to obfuscate real performance deficiencies or perhaps simply fraudulent money scams. In our society, the court system is often relied upon to make the determination and juries are tasked with the responsibility to evaluate the facts and issues in each case that does not settle before trial. This explains the importance of understanding how the legal system works and how juries render decisions in these matters.

The good news is that most jurors try to ensure that justice is done, as they view it. And in my opinion, they usually get it right. They do not always understand arcane legal issues, nor do they feel obligated to follow the letter of the law, but they do use common sense and good judgment. They also make frequent and rapid assessments of the credibility of the parties to litigation and selectively attend to information that is presented at trial. Therefore, it is important that litigants understand how juries make decisions in response to employment litigation, to ensure a fair trial and equitable consideration for all parties.

Proper and professional investigation of any alleged employment-related misconduct is essential to defend a cause of action and perhaps to mitigate damages. There are no absolute guidelines for conducting these investigations, but there are minimal professional standards that should be followed. Many investigations are inconclusive, and this is a reality that must be understood and shared. It does not mean that it was not a good investigation. However, the absence of an investigation is difficult to defend if one was required by circumstances.

Finally, litigants are advised never to underestimate the wisdom of a jury and to ensure that their opening and closing statements are persuasive, to keep their presentations clear and straightforward, to explain ambiguous behavior, to use psychological anchors where appropriate, and to present an aggressive prosecution or defense. Justice is best served under these circumstances.

Acknowledgment

The author wishes to gratefully acknowledge the research assistance and manuscript support provided by Shawn Peacock, a Doctoral Student in the Organizational Psychology Division of the Marshall Goldsmith School of Management of Alliant International University.

References

Angeletti, D. L. (2006). Toward Improving the Methodology for Determining the Effects of Juror Demographics and Attitudes on Civil Verdicts. Unpublished doctoral dissertation, Alliant International University, Los Angeles, manuscript in preparation.

Carnahan, I. (2002). Removing the scarlet A. *Forbes. 170*(3), 78.

Cooper, J., Bennett, E. A., and Sukel, H. L. (1996). Complex scientific testimony: How do jurors make decisions? *Law & Human Behavior,* 20, 379–394.

Cutler, B. L., Penrod, S. D., and Dexter, H. R. (1990). Juror sensitivity to eyewitness identification evidence. *Law & Human Behavior, 14,* 185–191.

Devine, D. J., Clayton, L. D., Dunford, B. B., Seying, R, and Pryce, J. (2001). Jury decision-making: 45 years of empirical research on deliberating groups. *Psychology, Public Policy and Law, 9,* 622–727.

Dexter, H. R., Cutler, B. L., and Moran, G. (1992). A test of voir dire as a remedy for the prejudicial effects of pretrial publicity. *Journal of Applied Social Psychology, 22,* 819–832.

Ellseworth, P. C. (1993). Some steps between attitudes and verdicts. In R. Hastie (Ed.), *Inside the Juror.* New York: Cambridge University Press.

Festinger, L. (1957). *A Theory of Cognitive Dissonance.* New York: Harper & Row.

Finkelman, J. M. (2002). 2002 expert witness update new developments in personal injury litigation. In J. M. Purver (Ed.), *The Expert Witness in Employment Litigation* (pp. 153–169). New York: Aspen Law & Business.

Finkelman, J. M. (2005). Juror perception of employment litigation. *The Psychologist-Manager Journal,* 8(1), 45–54.

Finkelman, J. M. (March, 2006). *Coaching and Consulting in Multicultural Contexts.* Presentation at the Annual Conference of the California Psychological Association, San Francisco, CA.

Finkelman, J. M., Zeitlin, L. R., Filippi, J. A., and Friend, M. A. (1977). Noise and driver performance. *Journal of Applied Psychology, 62,* 713–718.

Gillette, P. K. in M. Neil. (2006). Hidden harassment. *ABA Journal, 92,* 42.

Hastorf, A. H. and Cantril, H. (1954). They saw a game: A case study. *Journal of Abnormal and Social Psychology, 49,* 129–234.

Hemsley, G. D., and Doob, A. N. (1978). The effect of looking behavior on perceptions of a communicator's credibility. *Journal of Applied Social Psychology, 8,* 136–144.

Horowitz, I. A. (2001). The effects of complexity on jurors' verdicts and construction of evidence. *Journal of Applied Psychology, 86,* 641–652.

Hosman, L. A. and Wright, J. W. (1987). The effects of hedges and hesitations on impression formation in a simulated courtroom context. *Western Journal of Speech Communication, 51,* 173–188.

Kassin, S. M. and Garfield, D. A. (1992). Blood and guts: General and trial-specific effects of videotaped crime scenes on mock jurors. *Journal of Applied Social Psychology, 21,* 1459–1472.

Lecci, L. (2002). Examining the construct validity of the original and revised JBS: A cross-validation of sample and method. *Law & Human Behavior, 26,* 455–463.

Lind, E. A., Erickson, B. E., Conley, J., and O'Barr, W. M. (1978). Social attributions and conversation style in trial testimony. *Journal of Personality and Social Psychology, 36*, 1558–1567.

Morris, B. (2005). How corporate America is betraying women. *Fortune, 151*(1), 64.

Myers, B. and Lecci, L. (1998). Revising the factor structure of the Juror Bias Scale: A method for the empirical validation of theoretical constructs. *Law & Human Behavior, 22*, 239–256.

Narby, D. J., Cutler, B. L., and Moran, G. (1993). A meta-analysis of the association between authoritarianism and jurors' perceptions of defendant culpability. *Journal of Applied Psychology, 78*, 34–42.

Nielsen, J. (2005). Human resources management comes of age in the courtroom. *The Psychologist-Manager Journal, 8*(2), 157–164.

Overland, S. G. (2003). *Re-examining the Links Between Juror Characteristics and Civil Court Verdicts: NEW Data, Improved Models and Their Implications for American Politics*, Department of Political Science, UCLA.

Penrod, S. D. and Cutler, B. (1995). Witness confidence and witness accuracy: Assessing their forensic relation. *Psychology, Public Policy, and Law, 1*, 817–845.

Pyszczynski, T., Greenberg, J., Mack, D., and Wrightsman, L. S. (1981). Opening statements in a jury trial: The effect of promising more than the evidence can show. *Journal of Applied Social Psychology, 11*, 434–444.

Pyszczynski, T. and Wrightsman, L. S. (1981). The effects of opening statements on mock jurors' verdicts in a simulated criminal trial. *Journal of Applied Social Psychology, 11*, 301–313.

Saks, M. J. (1997). *Jury Verdicts*. Lexington, MA: Heath.

Savage, D. (2006). Open for business. *ABA Journal, 92*, 18.

Shestowsky, D. and Horowitz, L. M. (2004). How the need for cognition scale predicts behavior in mock jury deliberations. *Law and Human Behavior, 28*, 305–337.

Vinson, D. E. (1986). *Jury Trials*. Charlottesville, VA: Michie.

Visher, C. (1987). Juror decision-making : The importance of evidence. *Law and Human Behavior, 11*, 1–17.

Wexler, M. and Davis, A. (2005). Transsexualism, sex stereotyping, and *Price Waterhouse v. Hopkins*: A staircase to paradise or a slippery slope? *The University of Memphis Law Review, 36*(1), 41–65.

Legal References

Albertsons, Inc. v. Kirkingburg, 119 S. Ct. 2162 (1999).

Burlington Northern & Santa Fe Railway Co. v. White, 548 U.S._(2006).

Casucci v. Faughnan, 2nd U.S. Circuit Court of Appeals, No. 02-7861 (2004).

Civil Rights Act of 1964, 42 U.S.C. 2000a *et seq.*

Civil Rights Act of 1964, Title VII, 42 U.S.C. 2000e *et seq.*

Daubert v. Merrell Dow Pharmaceuticals, Inc., 509 U.S. 579 (1993).

Equal Employment Opportunity Act of 1972, Pub. L. No. 92-261, 86 Stat. 103 (1972).

Frye v. United States, 1923 U.S. App. Lexis 1712 (1923).

General Electric Co. v. Joiner, 522 U.S. 136 (1997).

Kumho Tire Co. v. Carmichael, 526 U.S. 137 (1999).

Murphy v. United Parcel Service, Inc., 119 S. Ct. 2133, 2137-39 (1999).

Price Waterhouse v. Hopkins, 490 U.S. 228 (1989).

Robinson v. Shell Oil Company, 4th U.S. Circuit Court of Appeals, No. 93-1562 (1995).

Smith v. City of Jackson, Mississippi, 125 S. Ct. 1536 (2005)

Snyder v. City of Romulus, Court of Appeals of Michigan, Nos. 264545 & 264546 (2006).

Sutton v. United Airlines, Inc., 119 S. Ct. 2143 (1999).

Uber v. Slippery Rock University of Pennsylvania of the State System of Higher Education, Commonwealth Court of Pennsylvania, No. 269 CD (2005).

Weeks v. Baker & McKenzie, 63 Cal. App. 4th 1128 (1998).

Forensic Neuropsychological Examination with Emphasis upon the Postconcussive Syndrome

19

ROLLAND S. PARKER

New York University School of Medicine, New York, New York

Contents

This chapter discusses the preparation of a forensic neuropsychological evaluation after an accident when there is a claim of traumatic brain injury (TBI), most specifically the postconcussive syndrome (PCS). When there is polytrauma (multiple injuries), a wide range of disorders should be explored: neurological, somatic, mental, and social. To reduce errors of diagnosis, and avoid not recognizing trauma-related neurobehavioral conditions, the examiner should consider the condition known as polytrauma. Polytrauma is defined as multiple injuries in various sections of the body that are comorbid with TBI (Moore, Feliciano and Mattox 2004). Thus, the forensic examiner of any profession needs a wide database to include the neurobehavioral and other adaptive consequences of noncentral nervous system trauma. TBI in children differs significantly in pathology and outcome (Broman and Michel, 1995; Semrud-Clikeman, 2001). It will be demonstrated that after an accident, the range of dysfunctions far exceeds those attributable primarily to the brain. An approach to comorbid injury brain and somatic injury will be offered. This contrasts with one widely accepted approach to the neuropsychological examination that emphasizes the study of cognition in numerous conditions and aspects of behavior. Here, it will be emphasized that reasonably complete assessment includes the neurobehavioral effects of both nervous system and somatic injuries over an extended range of neurobehavioral disorders. The medical examinations used for the accident victim (neurological, SPECT, MRI, CT, EEG, and X-ray) document different domains of trauma from the complex neurobehavioral functions studied by the neuropsychologist. The latter are more sensitive to TBI dysfunctions at the nonsurgical level of brain injury, and the complex systemic consequences of chronic injuries.

TBI is officially referred to by the (U.S.) National Center for Injury Prevention and Control as "the Silent Epidemic" since "the actual number of TBIs that occur in the U.S. is not known and much of the public is unaware of the impact of TBI ... and many of the people who are seen in outpatient clinics or doctors' offices and who do not receive medical are not included" (Langlois, Rutland-Brown and Thomas, 2004; Langlois, Marr, Mitchko and Johnson, 2005). While the term *minor* traumatic brain injury (mTBI) will be mentioned in citing published studies, the writer discourages its forensic use. First, as generally used, it erroneously combines the issues of brain trauma and traumatically impaired behavior. Second, many individuals who are categorized with "mTBI" experience significant and long-lasting neurobehavioral conditions. Use of the term PCS makes no statement concerning the extent of behavioral disturbance and is factually correct since an accident may create both cerebral and widespread somatic injuries.

A variety of considerations in claims of personal injury will be considered: (1) physical forces and the environment of the accident that create bodily injury; (2) trauma, or personal injury from an accident, and the phases that brain and somatic tissue go through into a chronic condition; (3) the wide range of potential neurobehavioral disorders caused by an accident that the examiner should sample; (4) biomechanics, i.e., the interaction between environmental objects, physical forces, and tissue, which result in brain and somatic injury; (5) polytrauma, i.e., the condition of multiple somatic injuries that are comorbid with head injuries; (6) the neurobehavioral outcome of chronic unhealed injuries, i.e., chronic post-traumatic stress with adverse effects upon behavior, health, and stamina; (7) professional considerations in performing a forensic neuropsychological examination to assess claims of personal injury after an accident.

Professional Considerations of Forensic Neuropsychology

A large proportion of accidents causing head injuries lead to lawsuits and claims of disability (impairment, loss of wages, and suffering), involving numerous administrative and legal domains. Forensic neuropsychology is a very complex professional application. I recommend board certification in neuropsychology as a standard of qualification. Further, the examiner requires clinical skills to relate to adults and children who are injured, anxious or suspicious, and their collaterals. Essential capacities include empathy and intuition permitting the translation of observational data into clinical entities.

The examiner addresses this question: Has the patient suffered dysfunction, deficits, or discomforts due to an accident? This is supported by direct examination or review of records. The examination and report is performed under the restraints of various laws and regulations. Since the economic stakes are large, the examiner must assess the credibility of the injury and its effects. This requires both a wide-range examination and an attempt to reconstruct the physical characteristics of the accident. High-quality forensic work requires extensive examination, thought, written documentation and an extensive technical database (see below) to draw conclusions about diagnosis, performance, and outcome. Yet, should a case proceed to trial, since the stakes are high, the examiner can expect critical and sometimes abusive attack far beyond the usual clinical presentation.

Training and Database for Injury

Training should include neuroscience, introduction to chemistry (inorganic, organic, and aspects of biochemistry), life sciences (physiology, anatomy, and medical trauma), stress response, personality issues (mood, identity, defenses, and developmental patterns), neuropsychological principles (ability, cognition, concentration, sensorimotor, and communication), and training in counseling. The personal injury database includes: (1) behavioral dysfunctions, (2) medical and emotional trauma, (3) life sciences (physiology, gross anatomy, and neuroanatomy), (4) trauma physiology (hormonal, immune, and inflammatory systems), (5) how somatic injury can contribute to impairment and psychological disturbance in order to increase diagnostic efficiency, (6) potential behavioral and health disorders after trauma, (7) measuring impairment, (8) recommending rehabilitation, (9) psychological reactions to injury and rejection, and (10) personality reactions to being frightened and injured.

Patients' Credibility

It is often asserted that claimants who engage in litigation are to be regarded suspiciously, since it is commonly believed that all except 15% of concussion victims' problems "resolve." I know of no research offering such an estimate that is based on thorough study with a wide-range examination, deviation measured from an estimated preinjury baseline, and verification of high proportion of complaint "resolution" after an extended interval. The appellation is sometimes used to describe the patient with chronic complaints as "the miserable minority." This is not objective. It implies that most chronic complaints after injury are subjective or faked and not related to an accident. In some research studies to validate procedures intended to identify symptom exaggerators, to be engaged in litigation is considered to be a marker of suspicious motivation. One wonders whether this is a violation of the civil rights of a plaintiff seeking damages for personal injury.

An objective examiner avoids either easy credulousness for complaints or a premature assumption of exaggeration. Please note that in addition to deliberate faking and unconscious motivation for secondary gain, some patients cannot or will not present to the examiner honest statements concerning the difficulties of their postaccident condition (see Expressive Deficits, below). To the extent possible, the examiner should seek extensive range of study (see Neurobehavioral Taxonomy), and independent information from schools, collaterals, employers, and so on. The writer believes that overcoming a false claim for damages requires a standard of proof as strong as is needed to convict a thief. Offering a reduced standard of proof that a person is malingering lacks objectivity. It raises the possibility of depriving an injured person of compensation.

Adaptation

Adaptation is a powerful biological concept that helps the neurobehavioral examiner to organize and assess current status. The neuropsychological examination studies the effects of an accident or medical problem upon the patient's adaptation to the daily requirements of life. Adaptation is the way in which a person's copes with one's environment and its demands and rewards, and which includes the psychological changes and moods that develop. It describes the person's physiological, functional, and subjective style of coping with circumstances, or surviving in stressful conditions. It is composed of genetic, physiological, and learned ways of solving problems of daily living and dealing with difficult or changing circumstances. Successful adaptation is contingent upon the ability to be independent, and also the lack of impairment and symptoms detailed in the Taxonomy of Neurobehavioral Symptoms (see below). Unimpaired adaptability leads to productivity, pleasant moods, and adequate self-esteem. Injury may impair adaptive capacity. Affiliation and social attachment ("bonding") arise in infancy. Since this behavior is a complex brain function (Panksepp, Nelson and Bekkedal, 1997), it is vulnerable to polytrauma. Complex social behavior has been attributed to the increased size of the neocortex compared with the rest of the forebrain, and to the influence of the mother, including neural and hormonal mechanisms of care (Keverne, Nevison, and Martel, 1997).

Polytrauma: Comorbid Somatic Injury and TBI

Conclusions will be incomplete and perhaps significantly inaccurate when the examiner (of any profession) does not consider the multiple effects of trauma that often accompanies a "head injury." For example, fibrosis and brachial plexus damage cause lateralized reduced strength directly due to tissue damage and pain, resembling contralateral brain injury. A survey of definitions of *head injury* included these potential traumatic components: trauma to the brain or spinal cord; altered or loss of consciousness (LOC); scalp or forehead laceration; skull fracture or injury; unconsciousness; amnesia; neurological deficit; seizure; physical damage to the cranial contents; posttraumatic amnesia (PTA); skull swelling, abrasion, contusion, laceration; blow to the head; fracture at the base of the skull (Fearnside and Simpson, 2005).

The National Center for Injury Prevention and Control (2003) classifies brain injuries as follows: no medical care, nonhospital-based care, hospital emergency department (ED) care, inpatient hospital care of more than 24 hours that is classified as more severe than "minor" TBI (mTBI). Impairment for persons with a history of mTBI utilizes the following list for mTBI symptoms not present before injury or those that made worse in severity or frequency the mTBI: problems with memory, concentration, emotional control, headaches, fatigue, irritability, dizziness, blurred vision, and seizures. Current limitations in reported mTBI functional status are: basic activities of daily living (e.g., personal care, ambulation, and travel), major activities (e.g., work, school, and homemaking), leisure and recreation, social integration, and financial independence.

Epidemiology

Adults

In the U.S., an estimated average of 1.4 million TBIs are reported each year, yet this underestimates the real extent. This figure includes ED visits, hospitalizations, and deaths (Langlois, Rutland-Brown and Wald, 2006). It does not include persons treated for TBI in other settings, those who do not seek immediate treatment, or persons treated after an accident for other injuries, with no record of the condition of the head being studied. Average numbers for the years 1995–2002 were 50,000 diagnosed TBI persons, 235,000 hospitalizations, 1,111,000 ED visits, and an unknown number receiving other medical care or no care (Langlois et al., 2004). The leading cause of TBI (ED visits, hospitalization, and deaths) is falls (28%), followed by motor vehicle traffic (20%), assault (11%), other causes (32%), and unknown (9%) (Langlois et al., 2004).

Children

The majority of pediatric head injuries are "minor," but the incidence is underestimated as the victims often do not present to the ED or require hospital admission. The trauma pattern differs from adults (ages 0–14 years): falls (39%), motor vehicle traffic (11%), assault (4%), other (41%), and unknown (5%) (Langlois et al., 2004). The overall rates for TBI per 100,000 are age 0–4, 1,121; 5–9, 659; and 10–14, 629. Overall, falls are the most common cause of head injury in the age group 0–15 years. Rates of falling are highest for children aged 0–4 years and for adults aged 75 years and older. Note the rapid rise in deaths as childhood develops into adolescence (calculated per 100,000 individuals): 0–4, 5.7; 5–9, 3.1; 10–14, 4.8; 15–19, 24.2. For serious injuries, pedestrian injuries from motor vehicle accidents were most common, followed by falls, bicyclists, and then occupants of motor vehicles (Fearnside and Simpson, 2005).

mTBI

The writer emphasizes that the common nomenclature mTBI is frequently factually incorrect. This nomenclature is faulty since it does not differentiate between these disparate conditions: neurobehavioral disorders, and, brain trauma that cannot be documented with current medical procedures after an impact or hyperextension/hypoflexion injury. To use this term as a guide for professional practice could contribute to a reduced quality of professional service. mTBI's neurobehavioral consequences can be disabling. It appears to the writer that mTBI is more accurately characterized as the PCS (Parker, 2001), which is often impairing or disabling and is a major public health problem. A review of symptoms, criteria for return to sports and for ordering imaging studies, symptomatic treatment, and controversies is available (Ropper and Gorson, 2007). Prompt resolution of litigation is encouraged. This is a controversial point. On the one hand, delay of settlement of cases and unreasonable denial of treatment and diagnostic assessment frequently worsens outcome and damages the mental condition of the accident victim. However, the possibility of delayed expression of symptoms (see Phases of Brain Injury 3–5) should be reported by the examiner. These authors also state that there is a return to baseline cognitive function within several weeks. A study of more severe concussion than experienced by athletes (Parker, 1990, pp. 161–162), during an interval after a TBI of 1 month to 10 years, indicates that on the average there is absolutely no cognitive improvement [Wechsler Adult Intelligence Scale-Revised (WAIS-R)] provided that individual measurements are used, i.e., there is no practice effect. The mean deviation from the estimated preinjury baseline (Matarazzo and Herman, 1984) was –9.1 points of full-scale IQ.

A substantial, yet unknown proportion, of concussive accident victims experience significant chronic posttraumatic impairment and disturbed quality of life (Parker, 2001). The preface to a National Center for Injury Prevention and Control (2003) report to Congress stated that "the consequences of mTBI may not, in fact, be mild …." Clinical experience has provided evidence that these injuries can cause serious lasting problems.

A particular definition of mTBI was the basis for a comparison of accident victims with and without head injury (Kraus, Schaffer, Ayers, Stenejem, Shen and Afifi, 2005). An uncomplicated head injury is generally characterized as a concussion. In such injuries, there is evidence of head impact or acceleration/deceleration. This may resulting in one or more of the following symptoms or signs: confusion or disorientation; observed or reported LOC for less than 30 min; PTA for less than 24 h; a Glasgow Coma Scale (GCS) of 13–15 on arrival at the ED. A comparison of this study and the next illustrates the complexity of head injury outcome, the lack of agreement between different reports of mTBI, and the significance of the extent of trauma upon outcome. Prognosis is a significant forensic consideration. After 6 months, the mTBI cohort were more likely to report headaches, double vision, memory or learning problems, and lower tolerance for alcohol. Yet they were less likely to report a change of employment or falling, they were less likely to be taking prescribed medication, and they exhibited no difference in use of medical service. From a forensic viewpoint, such patients require diagnostically directed postinjury medical management. In contrast, concerning outcome, Selassie, McCarthy, Ferguson, Tian and Langlois (2005) offer evidence that greater TBI creates a shortened life expectancy, which is a major factor in issues of compensation. In their study of patients who underwent hospitalization for TBI, comorbid conditions significantly influenced the likelihood of death within the first year after injury, particularly cardiac conditions, fluid and electrolyte imbalance, anemia, diabetes, chronic obstructive pulmonary disease, and psychiatric conditions. Severe TBI led to death postdischarge 1.8 times more frequently than mild TBI. Socioeconomic conditions influence morbidity and treatment as indicated by the fact that those insured by Medicare were 1.6 times more likely to die than those covered by commercial insurance.

The PCS

The PCS is a group of disparate dysfunctions consequent to injuries of various components of the nervous system, the soma, and the physiological and psychological consequences of chronic unhealed injuries. It is composed of symptoms expressing widely different etiologies: those reasonably attributed to TBI; those inaccurately attributed to TBI but are in actuality a consequence of somatic injury and dysfunction; and symptoms consequent to the somatic injury that have neurobehavioral consequences, but are ignored as not trauma related in the usual neuropsychological or neurological examination.

Accidents are complex events whose pathological consequences include the entire range of human performance and experience. Attention to the effects of somatic trauma (physical impairment, posttraumatic physiological disorders such as chronic dysregulation, health disorders, and fatigability) avoids misattribution of symptoms and complaints, identifies conditions that would respond to appropriate treatment, and reduces false-negative findings (Parker, 2005b).

The Taxonomy of Neurobehavioral Disorders: An Organization of PCS Symptoms

Organizing examination findings by this taxonomy offers these advantages: (1) By specifying the range of potential dysfunctions, the examiner can select procedures that reduce the likelihood that significant impairment will be ignored; (2) Information elicited by the examination can be presented in an orderly way; (3) It helps summarize the findings, i.e., findings relevant to a particular taxon elicited from multiple procedures are presented together. Results of specific test findings can be presented separately.

    I. **Neurological:** arousal, sensorimotor, cerebral personality disorder:
        Dysfunctions directly attributable to diffuse brain injury, and to injuries of definable centers and circuits of the central nervous system (CNS) (cerebrum, basal ganglia, cerebellum, and brain stem), sensory organs (Tomsak, 2004), cranial and peripheral nerves, plexuses in the torso, and integrated sensorimotor pathways (Saper, Woertgen and Brawanski, 2000). Arousal symptoms include seizures, altered consciousness, dissociation, problems of focused attention, and sleep. Cerebral personality disorders

include "frontal lobe syndrome," loss of motivation, reduced or increased libido, disinhibition and impulsivity, temper and violence outbursts, poor judgment, inability to plan for the future, inability to learn from experience, and apathy. Reduced libido may result from cerebral damage, medical illness, and stress-related conditions as anxiety. Sensorimotor: sensation, coordination, balance, gait, and stance. Body schema disorder (neurologically based) is a result of loss of proprioceptive and somesthetic input, in complex circuits involving the hippocampus, sensorimotor, and parietal cortices (Diamond, Harris and Petersen, 2002). Depersonalization is due to disturbed body schema of the parietal lobes, cerebellum. Motor vocalization disorders (neurological and somatic injury): dysarthria; dysprosodia; vocalization apparatus. Aphasic disorders (non-motor disorders of communications, expressive and receptive, including clinically significant reduction of verbal ability): Broca's, Wernicke's, conduction, anomic, transcortical, etc. (Kirshner, 1996).

II. **Somatic:** Performance and health disorders consequent to soft-tissue damage, bone injury, disturbed internal milieu (physiologically based symptoms), pain, and developmental disorders of children.

Developmental disorders of children; (Prematured and delayed or absent puberty, growth disturbance, etc.); performance reduction due to damaged tissue; systemic dysregulation caused by chronic stress; unhealed tissue; disturbance of health and stamina due to exhaustion; behavioral and systemic disturbances consequent to the exchange of chemical signals between the body and CNS. TBI poses a significant risk of hypothalamic and pituitary injury; motion disorders consequent to skeletal and soft-tissue injuries, pain, and scar tissue: weakness, reduced range of motion, pain and headaches: result of injury to tissue, radiculopathy (spinal disc injury), headaches from direct trauma and referred pain from neck and torso, other headaches (migraine, tension, and vascular); disorders of brain perfusion due to vascular trauma and stress-related spasm of arteries of the neck and skull base—dizzy spells, hypoperfusion of the brain parenchyma, basal ganglia and thalamus; physiological dysregulation of systems (hypopituitarism and stress reactions), mood disorder consequent to hormonal dysfunctioning.

III. **Mental control:** information processing, executive functioning, concentration, error monitoring, mental speed.

Executive function (cognitive autoregulation) describes processes that control and support mental tasks of high complexity: foresight, judgment and error monitoring. Information processing converts stimuli into meaningful units that are applied to more complex cognitive phenomena.

Symptoms: disorders of focused attention; concentration (defined as continuing performance for a useful interval); multitasking; flexibility; organizing future activity; interference with recent memory; inappropriate emotional reactions; and lack of originality (Damasio and Anderson, 1993).

IV. **General intelligence:** The level of mental ability that supports comprehension, problem solving, and learning.

Although a general measure can be obtained, e.g., full-scale intelligence quotient, the individual's ability may vary according to the task and the performance environment: structured and unstructured, crystallized and fluid; verbal and visual. The patient's performance efficiency and cognitive maturity for general intelligence and level of learned material are assessed relative to his/her estimated preinjury baseline: demographic characteristics (age, occupation, and education), personality and social qualities (family and social relationships and use of leisure time).

V. **Learning and memory:** The ability to retrieve a previously experienced mental content, on a voluntary basis, after an interval that may be immediate, or extending into the far past. The contents may be formally learned, episodic in the sense of being an event of living, or implicit (the person is not directly aware of the event being preserved in memory). Intrusive memories and sleep-related disturbances, such as nightmares, which are stress related, probably have a different neurological and physiological origin. PTA (anterograde and retrograde) are considered here.

VI. **Personality:** The subjective quality of life—style: psychodynamics, motivation, moods, and defenses.

   Affect or mood (anger, depression, and anxiety); whether there is personality regression and personality change; action autoregulation (impulse control); and psychological defenses.

VII. **Identity, insight, morale, Weltanschauung (world view):** The patient's reaction to being an injured person. Concern with the event and reaction to a world that may be experienced as depriving, rejecting, harsh, and frightening. The stressed and injured person has a disturbed identity characterized by low self-esteem: frequently unattractive, damaged, victimized, and vulnerable to further injury. The accident victim is frequently socially withdrawn for lack of money to participate, and experiences social rejection for impairment. Inability to cope with need for further assessment and treatment creates frustration.

VIII. **Empathy and social life:**
   The quality of social relations usually deteriorates after an accident, creating head injury. Withdrawal and detachment are common, even within one's family; loss of interest in human relations, and reduced capacity for empathy and to experience love. Social withdrawal may be consequent to low esteem due to loss of attractiveness, reduced funds, impaired mobility; fear of seizures; anxiety, loss of social skills; reduced libido and sexual dysfunction. Lack of social activity is noted by the patient, perhaps without experiencing distress. Poor social support interferes with the patient's quality of life. The patient's disturbed or dysfunctional behavior (cerebral personality disorder) can create rejection.

IX. **Stress reactions: Acute/chronic; psychological; physiological:**
   Stress may be defined as a condition, momentary or extended, psychologically or physically injurious, which creates physical or mental trauma, which is not self-healing after a brief interval. Mental symptoms include dissociation and depersonalization (Steinberg, 2000a, b). Acute stress refers to a momentary event such as an accident or assault. Chronic stress refers to a continuous condition, such as combat, imprisonment, harassment, pain, impairment, or the persistent secondary effects of an unhealed physical or mental injury. Stress symptoms vary from time to time. They overlap the PCS (Parker, 2002). "Distracting symptoms" are often consequent to an unhealed wound and interfere with work and other activities of daily living (Parker, 1995), e.g., headaches, pain, balance and vertigo, reduced range of motion, etc.

X. **Adaptive capacity:** community functioning and communications:
   Are there any preexisting coping difficulties? Pragmatic communication (verbal and nonverbal comprehension and expression; written and oral communications;

capacity for self-report). Productive efforts, e.g., school, work, family and social life, and community activities. Motivation for useful or pleasurable activities. Can the person lead life safely or is some kind of supervision needed? How does the person cope with, or improve, current condition? Is presentation to the provider motivated by occult need for financial or secondary gain? What are the retained or dysfunctional strengths? Can the person utilize or have access to social and community resources? The accident victim may be unable or unwilling to describe legitimate discomforts and dysfunction resulting in an assessment that does not take into consideration the true range of accident-related impairment. (See Expressive Deficits, below.)

Comorbidity of PTSD and PCS

There is a controversy whether the PCS and PTSD can coexist. PCS is associated with PTA, clouded consciousness, or brief (less than 1 hour) LOC around the time of the accident. In contrast, the PTSD definition specifies retention of the memory of the trauma (American Psychiatric Association, 2000, pp. 46–468). The accident initiates the *complex physiological acute stress reaction, altered cerebral arousal*, and a *traumatic affective state*. Clinical experience suggests that indeed they can coexist (Parker and Rosenblum, 1995). Of 33 consecutive victims of a motor vehicle accident, 16 were comorbid for PCS and PTSD. We can accept the PTSD definition as including memory of a traumatic event, but the perceived traumatic event can be after the actual accident, e.g., waking up confused and in pain in a hospital, with physicians around and tubes coming out of one's body, or waking up on a road after a car crash.

Cognitive Activities

Environmentally produced alteration of physiological responsiveness to stressors is an interface between cognitive regulation of behavior and more basic response regulation that may be genetic (Kraemer, 1997). Non-event alteration of ongoing mental and physiological activities can create and imprint false imagery or pseudomemories that initiate the syndrome.

1. Information offered by family or friends (which may not be correct).
2. *Implicit memory* of events or bodily trauma that occurred during a period of altered consciousness creates images or memories creating anxiety even though the identified trauma seems unrecorded (Krikorian and Layton, 1998).
3. *Priming* (sensitization for ongoing stimuli) makes unnecessary the retrieval of explicit or total memory for the traumatic episode. Later, a cue facilitates the identification of the previously unsalient stimuli that occurred after the initial trauma (Schachter, Chiu and Ochsner, 1993).
4. *Conditioning* can trigger stimuli that arouse a complex fear network leading to intrusive reexperiencing of the trauma (Joseph and Masterson, 1999).

Physiological Background

The physiological dysregulation caused by severe trauma may be accompanied by sufficient external and internal sensations to create an imprint, even if an integrated image of the actual moment of impact is not created (Parker, 2002). A clear event memory may not have been imprinted due to dissociation, altered consciousness, confusion and fugue-like states, in the context of circulation in the brain's internal milieu of neuroactive substances such as the cortisol-releasing hormone (CRH) and cortisol, and the neurotransmitters epinephrine and norepinephrine. These may contribute to the imprinting of salient but disorganized images.

The current diagnostic criteria for PCS (Parker, 2001, Chapters 2 and 3) and PTSD overlap greatly (Parker, 2002) in terms of symptoms. A contributor to this ambiguity is comorbid stress-related hyperarousal. The examiner of a highly anxious victim of an accident should also be alert to common subjective disturbances that have varied etiologies, including reaction to the event, cerebral trauma, and reaction to chronic and significant impairment (e.g., reduced motivation, mood changes, and poor morale). Cytokine release during response to injury and chronic stress creates responses frequently observed in TBI. The specific etiology may be described as the behavioral sequelae of the physiological reaction to primarily noncerebral injury: sickness behavior (malaise, social withdrawal, somnolence, and hyperesthesia) and depression (somnolence, anorexia, diminished libido, malaise, fatigue, slow-wave sleep, apathy, and irritability) (Kop and Cohen, 2001; Marshall and Rossio, 2000). A subjective reaction to the impairment incurred in both PTSD and TBI elicits the experience of incapacity, reduced self-confidence, and can lead to the belief that one is socially unattractive. The sense of foreshortened future of PTSD victims resembles the discouragement from persistent impairment and discomfort of the TBI victim. Depression is common in both TBI and PTSD. Organic mood disorder (depressed type consequent to TBI) or organic anxiety disorder (Van Reekum, Cohen and Wong, 2000) can be confused with the dysphoric moods of PTSD. Head injury predicts the experience of depression more than does the severity of PTSD (Vasterling, Constans and Hanna-Pladdy, 2000).

Special Issues of Children

A substantially different knowledge database is needed for children's claims than for adults. The child's undeveloped muscles, skull, and brain (Parker, 2001, p. 101) and smaller body size and stiffer brain tissue (Levchakov, Linder-Ganz, Raghupathi, Margulies and Gefen, 2006) contribute to different patterns of concussive alterations of consciousness and outcome (Semrud-Clikeman, 2001). The examiner's estimate of prognosis considers both current functioning and predicted performance during the sequence of development. Focusing momentarily upon academic achievement, I have observed that standard scores obtained shortly after an accident, in some children, may approximate the preinjury level. Sometimes 3 years may go by before standardized achievement scores manifest a significant deficit. My hypothesis is that the children perform according to prior learning, and achievement test standards vary little over a period of years.

The forensic examiner must consider brain development. Development may be impaired by medical illness (considered as a preexisting condition) or by TBI. The brain grows and specializes according to a precise genetic program. At birth, a newborn's brain is a fifth of its adult volume; at 6 it is 90% of its final adult volume. The 12% greater boys' than girls brain volume is accounted for by height with large intersubject variability. Disordered or delayed brain development can be caused by malnutrition, maternal drug abuse, and viral infection (Thompson et al., 2005). From age 4 to 20, there are linear decreases in gray matter and increases in white matter. The patterns vary between different cortical regions (Giedd, Blumenthal, Jeffries, Castellanos, Liu, Zijdenbos, et al., 1999; Thompson, Sowell, Goglay, Giedd, Vidal, Hayashi, et al., 2005). After trauma, this would have implications both for localization of trauma and for development of particular brain functions that either are localized or participate in distributed circuits.

Nonrecognition of Children TBI

The forensic neuropsychologist's need for external documentation of a claim of TBI for a child is less likely to be satisfied than for an adult. Difficulties in assessing concussion add to nonrecognition of children's TBI (see LOC in Children; nonrecognition of Childrens TBI; nonrecognition TBI). The child's lesser cognitive development at the time of injury is a contributing factor; a description of an injurious event may not be elicited. The child may not be considered to be badly injured and therefore not brought to an emergency room or admitted to a hospital. Children's brain trauma is less likely to be associated with LOC than adults (see below). At the emergency room (ER), there is nonrecognition of TBI due to lack of inquiry concerning the details of the injury, and to proper examination of the head and mental condition of the child. Thus, after a relatively severe accident that would cause LOC in an adult, the child appears to be shaken up but not severely injured. This is followed by inadequate examination subsequently for TBI by health care providers. Therefore, symptoms are not attributed to a head injury since the possibility of an accident is ignored.

The accident may be occult. The child may not reveal an accident due to fear of punishment; the child may have retrograde amnesia; the child may be too young to remember the event; the accident is out of memory because it occurred many years previously; the parent or caretaker may conceal injury due to child abuse or neglect. Since the child does not have support systems available to the adult, revelation is less probable. Late development of symptoms also hampers attribution to an accident. Correct assessment for the purposes of litigation is rendered difficult. Overall children's dysfunctions can be easily attributed to incorrect causes. Careful personality study is required to overcome statements from the school or previous examiners, that the child is considered to be a troublemaker, a faker, or lazy. It may be determined that unpleasant behavior evolves from feeling rejected.

Nonrecognition of TBI causes the educational, social, and medical needs of the child to be ignored. The social costs of the injury are higher than with adults since the period of survival is longer than with adults. Children with TBI exhibit long-term behavior problems in spite of cognitive recovery. What is often termed "good recovery" by clinicians, based on incomplete examination or premature conclusions, might not be correct when assessed by a wide-range examination after several years.

LOC in Children

Since it is not easy to assess the level of consciousness in infants and children, mistakes are often made. An injured infant cries or whimpers and is thought to be fully "conscious"; further examination to assess possible TBI is not performed. Preverbal infants are too undeveloped to offer motor and verbal responses of the GCS. Lethargy may be a sign of altered consciousness (DeLorenzo, 1991). Garvey, Gaillard, Rusin, Ochsenschlager, Weinstein,

Conry, Winkfield, Renee and Vezina, (1998) offer a case of a 6-year-old who had a generalized seizure within 1 h of a minor head trauma not associated with LOC. Takahashi and Nakazawa (1980) describe a pattern in which children under 10 years of age had no LOC after a "trivial" head injury, and then, after a latent period, manifested transient neurological disorders, with or without convulsion, with recovery. Convulsions were not associated with hematoma. The pattern included no initial LOC or skull fracture, headache, nausea or vomiting, pale complexion, disturbance of consciousness, hemiparesis or hemiplegia, motor aphasia, convulsion or no convulsion, with complete recovery within 6–48 h. Fearnside and Simpson (2005, citing Brookes et al., 1990) report that children's brain trauma is less likely to be associated with LOC than adults (1 versus 5% but is followed by lethargy, irritability, and vomiting, attributed to brain-stem torsion) (Rosman, 1989). Older children who are frightened but fully conscious may withhold speech or cooperation (Simpson, 2005).

Cognitive and Other Deficiencies

The following are characteristic dysfunctions in children: reduced IQ; development of language; deficient behavioral adjustment and social competence that may cause rejection by peers and teachers; reduced school performance or educational lag, with increased likelihood of enrollment in special education; motor skills; increased likelihood of unemployment; troubled family relationships; poor health; and neuropsychological dysfunctioning.

One criterion of traumatic dysfunction is progressively decreased academic and IQ standard scores, reflecting inability to keep up with one's age cohort. This may require years to be observed because school grades may reflect small demands and credit for long-term memory rather than expecting much new learning each year. Intellectual deficiencies are more apparent in the older child, upon whom more demands are made, although the child's outward appearance may appear "recovered," or subsequent developmental disorders (e.g., frontal lobes) may not have been manifested (Berg, 1986). Cognitive loss or reduced potential for learning and problem solving may be compensated for by the uninjured hemisphere. Only close observation or careful neuropsychological examination may reveal an occult deficiency. Late expression of developmental symptoms causes lack of attribution of the disorder to an earlier accident. The results may not show up until years later in lack of mental development or lack of physiological development (e.g., inability to attain puberty). Moreover, the connection between immaturity due to lack of endocrine development and the brain injury may not be recognized.

The number of symptoms is related to the intensity of the head injury as measured by the GCS at hospital admission, computerized tomography (CT), neurological examination, or skull fracture. Intensity of anxiety seems not to be a reflection of the extent of neurological injury. Anxious children had a higher incidence of other symptoms after controlling for injury severity. After mild head trauma, adults reported a significantly larger number of symptoms (only one), but in the moderate-to-severe head trauma range, there was no difference in the reported number of symptoms. Ongoing stressors enhance symptom maintenance (Mittenberg, Wittner and Miller, 1997).

Pituitary Gland Injury and Disorders of Sexual Development

The issue of deviant sexual development merits special attention. The examiner's observations are crucial since developmental deviations may be ignored by parents and by physicians. Neural pathways inhibit secretion of sexual development hormones until puberty. Later, sexual development is controlled by releasing hormones under some neural control, created in the hypothalamus, and transported by blood vessels of the pituitary stalk to the secretory cells of the anterior pituitary gland. There, hormones vital for development and normal physiological functioning are released: Adrenocorticotrophic hormone (ACTH), growth hormone (GH), thyroid-stimulating hormone (TSH), luteinizing hormone (LH), follicle-stimulating hormone (FSH), and prolactin (PRL). Since these are entrained (linked in time) to the sleep–wake cycle, with maximum rate of secretion occurring at specific times after sleep onset (Molitch, 2001), the examiner may consider possible endocrine disturbance accompanying *sleep disorders*. Feedback mechanisms operate within the hypothalamo-pituitary-target gland axes to ensure fine control of endocrine function (Pocock and Richards, 2004, pp. 216–220).

Since the pituitary gland is fixed in place in a cavity of the base of the skull (the sella turcica), and attached to the hypothalamus by the pituitary stalk, the secretory structure is vulnerable to trauma. A head impact, usually followed by movement of the brain in all directions (caused by its acceleration and deceleration), may stretch the pituitary stalk emerging from the hypothalamus with its end fixed to the enclosed pituitary gland. The hypothalamus or pituitary stalk may be stretched or torn. This is the etiology of traumatic hypopituitarism in the adult and developmental disorders in the child. Trauma may create neural injury removing the inhibition of maturational secretion, resulting in premature puberty. Since this causes bone maturation before growth reaches its intended limit, there is a growth deficiency. An alternate consequence occurs when trauma injures various secretory cells in the hypothalamus or anterior pituitary, or blood vessels conveying hypothalamic releasing hormones for the anterior pituitary's hormonal system. This delays or prevents puberty.

Delayed Puberty

Sexual development and growth disorders (MacGillivray, 1995) are commonly neglected as a consequence of a TBI. The writer has seen several late adolescents with undeveloped beards that were not considered to be clinically significant and therefore were not attributed to juvenile head injuries. Yet, disturbed sexual development can have a variety of nontraumatic causes so that referrals should be made for further study. Since it is traditional for the examiner who is retained by a defendant (independent medical examination, i.e., IME) to be instructed to refrain from making clinical recommendations, in this writer's opinion it is unethical to conceal this information if observation indicates a developmental or other medical disorder that is not already known to the parent or noted in a medical record. Since the retaining attorney has the right not to utilize the examiner's report, it cannot be assumed that information concerning a child's status will ultimately be conveyed to the claimant's attorney, and then to a parent. In any event, years might be go by. Since the mother's status during pregnancy may be a forensic issue, prenatal stress (exogenous and internal) is associated with adverse pregnancy outcomes, i.e., fetal growth and maturation, and parturition (Wadhwa, Sandman, Chicz-DeMet, and Porto, 1997).

Delayed adolescence may be associated with lesions of the hypothalamus and pituitary gland, causing varied hormonal deficiencies. Radiation therapy may be followed by delayed puberty or precocious puberty. Trauma can result in gonadal failure with loss of libido, impotence, amenorrhea, and sexual infantilism consequent to hypothalamic insufficiency (Cytowic, Smith, and Stump, 1986; Grossman and Sanfield, 1994).

Hypogonadotropic hypogonadism, i.e., absent or decreased ability of the hypothalamus to secrete gonadotrophin-releasing hormone (GnRH) or the pituitary gland to secrete LH and follicle-stimulating hormone (FSH), denotes an irreversible condition requiring replacement therapy. A rare cause is trauma (Styne, 2004).

Growth Deficiency

Growth outcome can be an interaction between factors that accelerate or decelerate growth (Styne, 2004), i.e., between the results of injuries that reduce normal inhibition of puberty, i.e., prematurely permitting it, and those that prevent normal development of puberty. GH and sex steroids contribute to the pubertal growth spurt. Acquired GH deficiency can result from perinatal disturbances, child abuse, accidental trauma, and perhaps glucocorticoid excess (MacGillivary, 2001). Juvenile hypothyroidism causes severe reduction of linear growth, with delayed puberty (sexual maturation). The child appears much younger than the chronological age. Precocious puberty may occur in the absence of imaging findings. It is considered rare, but may be associated with galactorrhea, an inappropriate secretion of milk (Grumbach and Styne, 2003).

Precocious Puberty

Trauma can prematurely remove hypothalamic inhibition of pituitary gonadotrophin production, resulting in premature puberty with short adult stature due to precocious sexual maturation. *Epilepsy* and *developmental delay* are associated with central precocious puberty.

Outcome of Children TBI

There are several patterns of outcome: (1) immediate, permanent deficit without recovery; (2) improvement through the use of compensatory mechanisms; (3) early arrest of development, or reduced rate of progress; (4) delayed onset of a disorder after apparent normal functioning. Outcome is determined by the interaction of many elements: maturation of the brain and the patient's age at the time of injury; the spatial extent, location, intensity of the injury, whether it is focal, diffuse, develops secondary trauma, etc.; its progress through various phases (Eslinger, Grattan, Damasio and Damasio, 1992; Parker, 1994); and the appearance of late expressed symptoms (see Tertiary, Quaternary, and Pentary Phases, below). Outcome will be negatively affected by noncerebral "distracting" symptoms (see Stress, above). Persistent insomnia can lead to impaired daytime function, injury due to accidents, depression, and variability of circadian rhythm associated with cardiac diseases and stroke (Creisler, Winkelman and Richardson, 2005). Poor sleep has been proposed as a risk factor for depression (Kupfer and Frank, 1997). Disturbed sleep patterns (altered circadian rhythms) are common after head injuries, contributing to hormonal dysfunctions. Posttraumatic outcome may be worse due to health disorders consequent to disturbance of hormonal secretion.

Biomechanics

A key issue in many claims of TBI is the credibility of the accident: were the forces (e.g., of vehicular impact) sufficient to create injury (see *Trauma*, below) (Parker, 2001, Chapter 5; Parker, 2005a)? Biomechanics (Anderson and McLean, 2005) describes the interaction of physical forces (including movement, direction, and speed) and impacting objects with the structure of the torso, neck, head, and the brain tethered to the spinal cord. The physical concept of shearing explains many kinds of TBI. Within the context of brain injury, it may be defined as displacement, or sliding, i.e., one layer separates from an adjacent one because it moves at a different speed, or the brain slides against the slower moving inner surface of the skull. To determine the credibility of an injury, the examiner collects data concerning the physical characteristics of the impact: The surface struck or striking (stiff, soft, flexible); head motion (hyperflexion, hypoflexion; rotation in various planes ("whiplash"); the pattern of impact and energy transfer between the patient, and the surrounding area (stationary or moving); the total number of head impacts in the accident (detailed interview is needed); was the patient ejected from a vehicle, or struck by it, and the pattern of impacts and bodily injury; what was the shape and structure of any enclosure (e.g., car and its passengers); speed and nature of a projectile or moving vehicles; place of head impact, and are there residual tender areas, scars, indentations, etc.

Injury is determined by the characteristics of the impacting surface: hardness (whether it is firm or yielding) and shape (sharp/dull). These affect the deformation of the skull and enclosed brain, whether it is penetrated or pushed. The shape of the impacting surface may apply force narrowly, or disperse the surface area to which energy is applied. A vital physical concept determining the location and extent of TBI is shearing. The speed of the body interacts with the type of the impacting surface to affect the rate of deceleration or acceleration of the skull, creating the degree of brain shearing of layers and massive nuclei, or tensile strain in which one part of the brain pulls away from adjoining tissue. The examiner will seek to determine the number of head impacts, the hardness of the head-impacting surface, distance of falling objects, and the speed of single or multiple crash of vehicles.

Dynamics is the study of the forces and the changes in motion they cause (the laws of Newton). Mechanics is the study of the motion of material objects. Kinematics (Hunt, Weintraub, Yang and Buechter, 2004) and kinetics refer to the interaction of force (impact) and mass (body structure and weight), momentum (the total energy of a physical accident), and the description of motion of bodies (acceleration, velocity, and vectors that combine the motion due to forces applied in different directions). Force is defined as that which causes the acceleration of a material body. It has direction and duration. The direction of the force contributes to the location of TBI (see Biological Issues). Motion of the body may be described as velocity, direction, acceleration, and deceleration. Momentum is defined as the mass of an object multiplied by its velocity. It is conserved, which means that when two objects collide, the loss of momentum of one is transmitted to the second. Thus, a small object, e.g., a smaller car, having a smaller mass, will rebound at a higher speed than the change in the speed of the larger car. An object falling on a head will transmit momentum to the head, with greater speed of motion created with increasing speed at the moment of impact (related to distance of the fall). Momentum transmitted to the head determines the coup (impact) effect upon the brain inside the skull. Loading is energy transmitted to the tissue (duration and amount of force). It causes strain deformations (impact, pressure waves, and cavitation) that damage the brain. Cavitation refers to the vacuum when the brain's momentum causes it to rebound from the contrecoup impact with the skull. Acceleration and deceleration forces create movement, stretching, and shearing of the brain against the skull and between different brain layers. They are involved in the subdural hematomas that have been observed after roller coaster rides that were exceptionally high and fast. The ride's design created up-and-down, to-and-fro, and rotary acceleration that produced tensile and shearing stress that apparently caused tearing of bridging veins that leave the brain for the surrounding dura and skull, resulting in subdural hemorrhage (Fukutake, Mine, Yamakami, Yamaura and Hattori, 2000).

Biological Issues

The pattern of brain injuries will vary considerably, from diffuse axonal injury (DAI) to contusions, mass effects, and gross and petechial hemorrhages (Margoles, 1999). In fact, complex molecular and cellular changes (synaptic) occur during a period of hours after the trauma that do not offer evidence of structural damage but have been demonstrated experimentally to persist for weeks or months (Reilly and Bullock, 2005). Sufficiently intense mechanical forces (Valadka, 2004) cause tissue changes that may result in TBI directly or because of acceleration/deceleration movements of the head. These cause impact, rotation, stretching, and shearing of the brain. After head movement and impact, and acceleration or deceleration, the brain, which is enclosed in the skull, moves against the skull's surfaces and compartments. These support the brain when all is well, but scrape, cut, and impact the brain when movement and momentum brings the skull or body into contact with surfaces. The location of the TBI is consequent to the irregular shape of the brain and the skull, the brain's inhomogeneity of content, and the firm structures that impact the brain when it is accelerated or decelerated (the surfaces and ledges of the skull that support the brain, the meninges, and the penetrating blood vessels whose course is anatomically fixed and tears tissue moving past it). The characteristics of tissue influence the nature of the injury: Strain (deformation) overcoming the brain tissue's elasticity (capacity to return to original shape. Surfaces may be described as flexible (padded headrest surface) or stiff (not yielding under the load of the impacting head). Among the injuring forces are momentum, rotation of the brain within the skull tethered to the neck or inside the skull, and forces transmitted within the skull and brain that push it, stretch it, and cause it to be cut by tissues between the compartments (meninges) and surfaces of the brain. A physical accident causes direct and indirect transmission of energy, momentum, acceleration, or deceleration of the brain, that results in injury to the surface and interior of the brain confined inside the skull whose movement, direction, and speed are affected by the fact that it is tethered to the neck, causing first hyperflexion then hyperextension ("whiplash"). It is frequently asserted that the *cerebrospinal fluid (CSF)* serves as a "cushion." While it keeps the weight of the brain in small gravity-induced movements from putting strain on pain-sensitive structures (Ransom, 2005), it seems likely that CSF is insufficient to prevent the brain from impacting the skull beyond a minor range of head impact or acceleration/deceleration.

The Brain

The direction of the body/impacting object determines the planes of brain movement and rotation. It may rotate laterally, radially along with the neck or move directly forward (translational), or its planes may rotate at different radii and speeds around an origin low in the skull (shear). The concept of DAI derives from the compression wave that is propagated through molecules within a medium whenever a solid object is struck (e.g., head impact). The medium is cell walls, extracellular fluid, connective tissue, cell membranes and contents, or blood vessels and contents. Impact causes compression wave strain injuries of the brain's internal structure without skull fracture or much contusion underneath the point of impact. Displacement parallel to the direction of motion of a pulse is called longitudinal. Transverse displacement at right angles to the direction of the pulse is one mechanism by which waves radiate from the point of impact. The brain's viscoelastic qualities (resistance to flow when there are adjacent shearing forces while simultaneously being elastic) make it vulnerable to pressure waves that can induce shearing damage as different planes separate from each other. Volume or bulk distortion stems from application of pressure (external compression of the head and internal pressure caused by brain swelling). Since the brain is quite incompressible, when external forces are applied, it can only move, rather than be distorted inwardly. Cerebral damage can occur through stress wave concentration after impact, or acceleration-induced brain damage resulting in tissue-tear hemorrhages (Gennarelli and Graham, 1998). Compression-rarefaction is characterized by a change in volume without a change of internal shape. Since the brain is virtually incompressible, it has a lower tolerance to shear strains, which separate tissues, than to compression strains (Adams, Graham and Gennarelli, 1982).

Phases of TBI

Trauma refers to anatomical and emotional damage. The neuropsychological examiner's duty is to explain to the Court the process of TBI, and its potentially complex pathology and neurobehavioral outcome in the context of a particular claim of injury. Review of the records, interview of the patient, and reconstruction of the accident and alleged injuries, using the physical and physiological principles explicated here, may lead to the conclusion that no significant injury has occurred. The examiner explains that the ultimate brain injury is not always described by the initial (primary injury). Further injury can occur subsequently, some injury is not detected by current procedures, impairment may be expressed or develop years later, and comorbid injuries both react with the CNS and create documentable disorders that should be considered by the clinician. TBI does not remain static. Physiological dysregulation caused by unhealed chronic injuries in other parts of the body affects later brain functioning. Chronic conditions develop characteristic disorders of physiological dysregulation and health disorders.

The Baseline

Examination posttrauma commences with the developmental and pathological condition of the person when injured: constitutional and hereditary illness; acquired disease; prior accidents; educational, work, and family history; personality and social functioning. Premorbid traits interact with pathology to contribute to capacity for coping or vulnerability to trauma (see Estimating the Baseline).

Primary Phase: The Immediate Mechanical Tissue Damage

This refers to the event creating initial damage, i.e., impact and change of direction and speed. Impact creates brain movement and impact against other structures, pressure waves, skull fractures, and brain indentation. In concussion, characteristic brain injury includes diffuse axon injury, and cortical lacerations and contusions. It also causes contusions due to brain rebounding after hitting another area of the skull after acceleration or impact, resulting in a lower pressure area (cavitation) into which brain tissue expands. Stretching and tearing of axons results in disturbed association between brain centers. Blood vessels and brain tissue may be damaged by shearing forces as inertia and internal pressure waves move brain tissue against blood vessels tethered in place. Mechanical forces damage nerve cell bodies and axons, blood vessels, the meninges, soft tissues including muscle, tendons, ligaments, and organs, and fracture the skull and other bones. There are cellular and molecular changes creating further cell damage and necrosis, which are part of the second phase.

Secondary Phase: Tissue Pathology Following the Initial Trauma

Continuing pathological effects after the primary tissue damage initiates further brain injury that could have far worse effects than the initial physical damage: gross (e.g., hemorrhage and swelling), physiological (loss of cerebral autoregulation of pressure, oxygen, etc.), cellular, microvascular, and molecular responses that are either autodestructive or neuroprotective (Bullock and Nathoo, 2005). There may be prolonged posttraumatic impairment of brain energy metabolism (Geeraerts et al., 2006). These processes cause neurotoxic effects upon membranes and cellular messenger systems. Secondary trauma interferes with communication between centers by functional axons, or by posttraumatic injury to axons. Very young and older adults' brains are more vulnerable to vascular damage (hemorrhage) created by shearing forces (Bullock and Nathoo, 2005; Reilly and Bullock, 2005).

Tertiary Phase: Late Developing Physiological Disorders

This represents the direct physiological consequences of damage to the neurological input and endocrine feedback of the hypothalamo-pituitary-target endocrine axes, direct damage to these structures, and consequent disorders of the posterior pituitary, thyroid, gonads, the adrenal cortex and medulla, and other glands. Late developing physiological disorders can be caused both by the injury creating TBI and due to the persistent stress consequent to the unhealed wound and problems of adaptation. The effectors are the hormonal axes, immune and inflammatory systems, autonomic and enteric nervous systems, and also hypothalamic integration and output. Chemical signaling systems through the blood, vagus nerve, and cerebrospinal fluid parallel the nervous system.

Disorders include physiological developmental disorders of children, posterior pituitary disorders (diabetes insipidus, syndrome of inappropriate antidiuretic hormone [SIADH]) from head trauma, and anterior pituitary hormonal disorders such as hypothyroidism, hypopituitarism, and GH deficiency (for hormonal stress effects see Pentary Phase).

Quaternary Phase: Late Developing Neurological Conditions

Late developing neurological conditions include stress-related hippocampal damage, premature cerebral atrophy, enhanced incidence of Alzheimer's disease with a genetic predisposition (Blumbergs, 2005), posttraumatic epilepsy, movement disorders, and cochlear and vestibular dysfunctions. Late-appearing movement disorders may occur after numerous neurological changes and inflammatory changes (Goetz and Pappert, 1996).

The age of trauma may determine the interval before onset. Hemidystonia associated with brain damage has a longer latency in children injured before age 7 than in adults (Krauss and Jankovic, 2002).

Pentary Phase: Chronic Stress Effects upon Personality and Health

Chronic stress reactions are consequent to persistent emotional distress such as anxiety and depression, the psychological results of injury such as impairment, destruction of the quality of life, and unhealed injuries (what I refer to as "*The Unhealed Wound*"). The trauma may persist so long that its obscure origin is not recognized or considered. The patient is considered to be a malingerer or exaggerator, or treatment is based on an incorrect diagnosis (see Credible Evidence).

Several mechanisms are involved in the chronic stress reaction; note that the neurobehavioral effects of stress overlap those of TBI.

1. Overactivity of the hypothalamic-pituitary-adrenal axis (Hellhammer, Schlotz, Stone, Pirke and Hellhammer, 2004). Elevations in the stress hormones cortisol, norepinephrine, and epinephrine may be accompanied by decrements in immune function. Altered immune functioning is associated with depression, suppression of affectivity, perceived helplessness, and intrusive thoughts associated with the trauma. High stress level is also associated with increased depressive symptoms, dissatisfaction with social support, and limited uses of adaptive coping strategies (Fletcher, Ironson, Goodkin, Antoni, Schneiderman and Klimas, 1998).
2. Trauma and stress may damage or exhaust tissue required for functioning of a system, or create demands that exceed the body's capacity to function indefinitely at this level. Exhaustion of various physiological systems is due to persistent dysregulation after chronic injury: scars, fibrous and otherwise injured tissue, skeletal damage, peripheral nerve damage, internal injuries, limited range of motion, pain and headaches, concern with seizures, imbalance, vertigo, and so on. The dysregulated systems are circadian, hormonal, inflammatory, and immune. The consequences of chronic dysregulation may be summarized by the concept of *allostatic load* which signifies systemic exhaustion or "burnout" (Dhabar and McEwen 2001; McEwen, 2000, 2004). Its neurobehavioral consequences are stress-related health disorders; chronic PTSD symptoms; illness behavior (malaise, fatigue, loss of appetite, apathy, social withdrawal, and inactivity), reduced stamina (fatigability), vulnerability to infectious disease, tissue exhaustion, organ damage, and sexual dysfunction (Curle and Williams, 1996; Lombardi, Savastano, Valentino, Selleri, Tommaselli, Rossi, Gigante and Covelli, 1994; Schnurr et al., 2004). This constellation is consistent with the frequent complaints of patients concerning loss of energy resulting in inability to fulfill the responsibilities of domestic life and employment.

Chemical Signals and Multisystem Integration

Physiological disorders characteristic of the polytrauma (brain plus somatic injuries) that may be comorbid with TBI, create the PCS affect that significantly impairs the outcome of head injuries. The body's *systematic reactions* (physiology) and the *internal milieu* (the liquid environment providing nutrients and toxins) are part of the database of trauma and stress (acute and chronic). *Toxins* are any substance interfering with the brain's stability and functioning.

The Internal Milieu

The brain is merely a portion of a entire-body network functioning through multiple pathways, influencing healing and disease processes, somatic efficiency, moods, and cognitive efficiency. Chemical signals are exchanged between the nervous and other physiological systems through the blood, vagus nerve, and cerebrospinal fluid. Entry of substances into the brain is partially restricted by the blood–brain and other barriers (De Vries and Prat, 2005; Laterra and Goldstein, 2000). Their function is to provide a stable environment for neurons to function effectively. However, trauma restricts the barrier's effectiveness in preventing entry of disorganizing toxins and neuroactive substances (norepinephrine and glutamate). Thus, some neurobehavioral disorders are the result of dysregulation of the *internal milieu* after injury.

The brain's performance is maintained by an internal milieu consisting of the vascular system and cerebrospinal fluid within the ventricles that surrounds the brain. By internal milieu is meant the liquid environment of the CNS (the cerebrospinal fluid), which is lined with blood vessels and supplies the brain with oxygen, nutrients, and neuroactive substances. Survival requires that physiological supplies support neurobehavioral functions. For these systems to be coordinated with each other, and so that components of a system operate in sequence, each system generates chemical signals. Some of the physiological and neural signals are common to both. Exchange of chemical signals occurs between the brain and the circadian, inflammatory, immune, and hormonal systems. System disorders reduce neural efficiency leading to observable disturbances of performance and health. In the event of an accident, or disease process, there is a reciprocal relationship between the immune, inflammatory, and hormonal systems and the brain. Their chemical signals affect tissues and infiltrate the brain.

Signal Molecules

The nervous system, immune system (IS), and neuroendocrine system share common signal molecules and receptors with each other, presumably having neurobehavioral effect. The immune-related chemicals involved in brain function affect behavior, neuroendocrine activity, sleep, neurodegeneration, fever, and depression. *Psychoimmunology* is the study of the bidirectional communication between the CNS and the IS, specifically anatomical, physiological, and psychological (Kemeny, Solomon, Morley, and Herbert, 1992; Vedhara and Irwin, 2005; Vedhara and Irwin, 2005). The neural and neuroendocrine cooperation modulating the immunological reaction, i.e., the system of vessels, circulating hormones, and nerve fibers linking the brain with all viscera, has been termed *the hard-wired neuroimmune network* (Downing and Miyan, 2000). A particular hormone, neurotransmitter, or other chemical can be created in various tissues. It causes different tissues to respond if they carry the same receptor. The changed function in the organ depends upon the particular receptor. Thus, one neurochemical can affect multiple somatic organs and brain centers. The first are *stress response signals* (1) the outflow from the hypothalamic-pituitary-adrenal axis, utilizing hormones carried by the blood to activate the adrenal cortex (adrenocorticotropic hormone, or, ACTH), and (2) sympathetic nervous system activation of the adrenal medulla and catecholamines released systemically into the blood from nerve endings.

Response to Trauma

After a head injury, one may expect, in various combinations, injury to any portion of the CNS; fright; slow-to-heal tissue injuries; long-lasting endocrine and other physiological dysfunctions consequent to continued stress and inflammatory system activity; and secondary stress from adaptive problems such as impairment, pain, dysphoria, loss of social support, etc. The psychological, nervous, endocrine, immune, cerebrovascular, and somatic systems interact to modulate adaptive and defense responses. Traumatic dysregulation of various systems impairs outcome significantly.

Polytrauma: The Noncerebral Contribution to Impairment

Impairment is not necessarily attributable only to cerebral trauma. Accidents are complex events whose pathological consequences include the entire range of human performance and experience. *The PCS is actually an incomplete summary of a disparate group of dysfunctions consequent to injuries to the brain, spinal cord and column, peripheral nerves, autonomic nervous system, cranial nerves, nerves, neck, limbs, musculoskeletal system, and soft tissue (ligaments, tendons, connective tissue, internal organs, and skin).* The site of noncerebral trauma has been described by the abbreviated injury scale (AIS) (Fearnside and Simson, 2005) as head or neck, face, chest, abdomen or pelvic contents, extremities or pelvic girdle, external. Additional specifiers in summarizing records are spinal column and other bones, muscles, fascia, and viscera. One sample of 8-year-old children manifested 26% multiple injuries (Klonoff, Clark and Klonoff, 1995). Somatic trauma may cause cerebral-like symptoms: fibrosis and brachial plexus damage may cause lateralized reduced strength directly and through pain that could be confused with cerebral damage to motor cortex or somesthetic area, or motor pathways. Extracranial injuries result in reduced return to work, limitations in physical functioning, and contribute to a period of recovery exceeding 6 months. However, these patients do not report more severe PCSs (Stulemeijer et al., 2006a).

Dysregulation is a significant contributor to the common posttraumatic symptoms of fatigability ("burnout") and reduced health. Unhealed tissue causes continued abnormal levels of the hormonal, immune, and inflammatory systems, which ordinarily perform within lower limits, except for activity demands, minor injuries, or medical illness. Dysregulation of body systems is due to continued effects of unhealed injuries after trauma, including the hormonal, immune, and inflammatory systems, creating chemical signals to the brain and other structures. After trauma, considerable dysregulation can occur.

The stress reaction to an accident causing bodily injury is far more extensive than the familiar PTSD. Late endocrine-related dysfunctions are related to persistent demands upon the hypothalamic-pituitary-endocrine axes, and stress-related health disorders, including immunosuppression, dysfunctions of various systems, and endocrine exhaustion. Common symptoms are accounted for by this model: fatigue, exhaustion, and burnout, illness behavior, loss of appetite, apathy, social withdrawal, inactivity, and sleepiness, sexual dysfunction, and dysfunction of pediatric sexual development. These persistent symptoms may be misattributed to symptom exaggeration, or emotional factors (e.g., cytokines). This secretion can be reflected in mood disorders, cognitive dysfunctions, and presumably other disrupted neural patterns causing impairment. Persistent unhealed injuries cause continued functioning of regulatory systems that integrate and control the internal milieu and would ordinarily keep it within a satisfactory physiological range (allostasis) and cease after a period. Characteristically, sleep disorders (disruptions of the circadian rhythm) may be considered as interfering with the pattern of daily hormonal secretion. Since the neuroactive chemicals enter the brain, and interact with nearby organs and tissues, there are systemic effects of trauma upon health, mood, cognition, metabolism, and so on.

Allostatic load: In chronic stress, what is disrupted is the regulatory system known as allostasis. This functions during greater physiological demands than maintenance within narrow limits of specified functions needed for life (*homeostasis*), e.g., oxygen level, blood pressure, salt level in the blood, and so on. In contrast, after a period of chronic stress (with the requirement of coordinating many different systems), allostasis undergoes system exhaustion and is replaced by allostatic load. This can be the cause of fatigability leading to reduced ability to work, and to maintain interests, household responsibilities, and so on. This impairment can be somatic trauma related, and not a direct result of TBI. It is a persistent stress reaction from exhausted physiological systems requiring sophisticated medical treatment and psychological support. A study compared two groups, mTBI and minor injury. Severe fatigue was associated with other symptoms, e.g., nausea and headache (Stulemeijer, van der Werf, Jacobs, Biert, van Vugt, Brauer and Vos, 2006a; 2006b). This is consistent with the concept of chronic symptoms leading to allostatic load (see Pentary Phase).

Immune reaction—Wound healing and neurobehavioral effects: Injuries activate the immune reaction, whose function is wound identification, dead tissue removal, enhancement of healing, and prevention of damage from dying cells. The IS is involved in behavioral interactions between the psychosocial and biological environments (Bohus and Koolhaas, 1996). The brain and IS form a bidirectional communication network. CNS regulates many aspects of immune function via the sympathetic nervous system and neuroendocrine pathways to organs and cells of the IS. There are bidirectional interactions between the immune and nervous systems at all levels, including the brain, pituitary, peripheral nervous system, neuroendocrine mechanisms, and the autonomic nervous system. After trauma, the IS interacts with the nervous, stress, inflammatory, autonomic, and other systems. Its messengers create neuropsychological effects. The IS participates in a regulatory feedback loop with the hypothalamo-pituitary axis (HPA), with immune and inflammatory mediators stimulating HPA hormone synthesis and secretion (Crofford, 2002). The IS's products communicate with the CNS, altering neural activity that influences behavior, hormone release, and autonomic function. Thus, the immune cells function as a *diffuse sense organ*, informing the CNS about events in the periphery relating to infection and injury (Maier, Watkins, and Nance, 1994).

Inflammatory reaction: Damaged or stimulated structures activate the inflammatory system that brings inflammatory cells to the wound site, accomplishing wound healing (Yang and Glaser, 2005). Inflammatory products, e.g., cytokines, have numerous effects upon mood and cognition. Chronic inflammation, which may occur in unhealed injuries, plays a role in Alzheimer's and other neurodegenerative diseases. A high level of serum markers of inflammation (IL-6; CRP) was associated with poor cognitive performance and greater risk of cognitive decline over 2 years of follow-up. The effects were cumulative. It is hypothesized that inflammation contributes to cognitive decline in the elderly. However, nonsteroid anti-inflammatory drug use (NSAID) did not change the association between inflammation and cognitive decline (Yaffe, Lindquist, Penninx, Simonsick, Pahor, Kritchevsky, et al., 2003).

Hormonal response—Chronic stress and neurobehavioral effects: A stress disorder may be extremely long-lasting. The hormonal stress response is complex, i.e., multiple chemical responses at each phase from acute to chronic (De Kloet and Deruk, 2004). The gross outflow of various neurotransmitters, internally manufactured opiates (endorphins), and other neuroactive substances cause permanent or long-lasting changes in neural circuits that account for the long-lasting effects (Southwick, Bremner, Krystal and Charney, 1994; Southwick, Yehuda and Morgan, 1995). Prolonged and increased production of CRH (a hypothalamic hormone that stimulates release of ACTH) from the anterior pituitary, a vital component of the stress response. CRH coordinates behavioral, neuroendocrine, autonomic, and immunologic adaptation, which could explain the pathogenesis and manifestations of chronic stress syndrome: psychiatric, circulatory, metabolic, and immune. There are numerous mood and endocrine disorders associated with enhanced (hyperarousal) and decreased (hypoarousal) functioning of the HPA axis (Tsigos and Chrousos, 1996). Chronic stress elicits a *vigilance reaction* involving activation of the HPA (Benarroch, 1997). Increased response seen in chronic stress is associated with melancholic depression, panic disorder, diabetes mellitus, central obesity, Cushing's syndrome, elevated excretion of cortisol, and immunosuppression. Decreased activity occurs after prolonged exposure to stress and is associated with adrenal insufficiency, atypical depression, chronic fatigue syndrome, fibromyalgia, decreased free cortisol secretion, and increased activation of inflammation.

Hypopituitarism creates deficits and symptoms commonly observed in TBI, which may be ignored by health care practitioners or misattributed: reduced strength, aerobic capacity, fatigue, erectile dysfunction, cold intolerance, weight gain, cognitive impairment, sense of well-being, general health, vitality, and mental health, with commonly experienced depression and anxiety. A survey of eight cases indicates that the average delay in diagnosis was 12.4 years with a range of 0–44 years (D'Angelica, Barba, Morgan, Dobkin and Pepe, 1995). These symptoms (anterior hypopituitarism) may be overlooked or attributed to other causes. Hypopituitarism can exacerbate existing impairments of physical, cognitive, and psychosocial functioning caused by a TBI and may be the major impediment to successful rehabilitation. The examiner should consider endocrinological referral to assess ACTH, GH, gonadotroph, thyroid study (TSH, free T_4), and basal morning cortisol. In women, cognitive function and memory appear to be impaired by low estrogen levels (Kelly, Gonzalo, Cohan, Berman, Swerdloff and Wang, 2000; Lieberman, Oberoi, Gilkison, Masel and Urban, 2001; Schneider, Schneider and Stalla, 2005).

Some Neuropsychological Examination Considerations

In a claim of personal injury or disability, the forensic neuropsychologist offers documentation concerning deficits, dysfunctions, and discomforts. To meet forensic objectives (e.g., disorders of daily living), I recommend a multidimensional approach exploring a range of disorders as categorized in the *Taxonomy*. A wide-range examination and referral to other specialists is required to minimize the possibility that significant impairment is ignored (false-negative).

The neuropsychological examiner's task is complex. In order to address the referral issue, it may be necessary to conduct an examination that samples the wide range of disorders that may occur after physical accidents, obtain other information (record review and collateral's interviews), and report the patient's current status.

An overview of commonly used neuropsychological procedures is provided by Lezak, Howieson and Loring, 2004; Mitrushina, Boone, Razani and D'Elia, 2005; and Strauss, Sherman and Spreen, 2006. I recommend the flexible battery approach, which implies that the examiner may choose procedures: (1) It permits selection of procedures that assess those functions at issue in a case; (2) It increases the precision of assessment of patients or others whose demographic characteristics do not match the norms of people raised in the country where assessment occurs or do not match the norms of procedures preferred by the examiner. Examples of unusual demographic characteristics include persons illiterate in English; special occupational history needing documentation; educational history at an extreme of achievement; sensory or orthopedic deficits rendering examination difficult or requiring assessment for safety, educational, or occupational reasons, and so on.

Some Questions to Address

What are the patient's adaptive problems and their prognosis, considering (1) the patient's age, (2) the interval since the accident, and (3) preexisting conditions?

Can new conditions or losses be credibly attributed to a particular accident or event? The examiner attempts to describe in detail the physical event (Parker, 1995). An attempt should be made to determine whether reduced performance and regressed style are consequent to TBI, faking, or a psychodynamic reaction to being injured and scared.

What are the contributions and interactions of comorbid somatic injury and physiological disorders to neurobehavioral performance disorders?

What is the patient's adaptive functioning in his usual environment? Does the patient's condition create safety concerns? Are adaptive functions mature or regressed? How much support does he receive from the family, community, and administrative organizations responsible for providing diagnosis and treatment?

What are the deleterious effects upon performance and motivation of "distracting symptoms," e.g., pain, headaches, fear of falling, stress-related anxiety, fatigue, sensory phenomena consequent to partial seizures, and so on?

What is the patient's restitutive capacity (ability to compensate for, or recover from, difficulties)? Do preexisting coping difficulties add to difficulties? Does impairment suffice to interfere with the usual or other employment? Are there disturbances in relationships with family and community?

Is the patient's performance level altered by motivation for financial or secondary gain? Is the patient motivated to restore preinjury capacity?

Is the patient able to give a complete self-report (see Expressive Deficits)?

What is the prognosis and likely permanency? What are the patient's coping mechanisms? Will the patient have permanent inefficiency in school and work? Consider such issues involving employment and education as pragmatic communication.

Are there safety concerns (poor alertness, judgment, memory, and physical competence)? Will a chronic condition affect quality of life?

Preinjury Baseline and Robust Conclusions about Outcome

What is the estimated preinjury baseline performance and style? If there is a credible accident or other event, disturbances of adaptive ability or of a range of performance are evidence for a pathological process, particularly if the current findings appear to be significantly below the baseline. This is true even if particular procedures such as the neurological examination, EEG, and most radiological procedures are negative, since they are insensitive to microscopic, cellular, and biochemical disorders.

Estimating the preinjury baseline is a strategy to assess whether posttraumatic impairment has occurred. While prior psychometric evaluations are usually not available, functional descriptions from collaterals (family, friends, and employers) are useful. The examiner is concerned with the developmental and pathological condition of the person when injured. The assessment of the baseline involves information that may or may not be obtained at the time of the formal examination. Numerous topics are listed, but the examiner will explore those issues determined by the nature of the referral and information that can reasonably be obtained. Sections in the Examination section below will vary significantly in utility for current or preinjury functioning.

Outcome will be affected by reduced motivation and the availability and utilization of social and community resources, inefficiency in school and work, reduced motivation to participate in treatment and to assume family and work responsibilities, and poor morale interfering with activities needed for improvement or creating pessimism about the future. The examiner will consider the following possibilities: brain damage is associated with possible posttraumatic seizures, increased vulnerability to further head injuries, and greater incidence of premature senility. Chronic stress increases vulnerability to a variety of diseases. High levels of anxiety and depression, or PTSD, predict the development of hypertension or other medical disorders.

"Resolution" and the Baseline

The frequently expressed statement that most cases "resolve" in 3 months has no firm support in this writer's opinion. Reliance upon published research concerning the benign outcome of concussive brain injury should be performed with the following caveat in mind: Not estimating a preinjury baseline reduces the possibility of accurate determination of benign resolution, recovery, or outcome of this condition. Two other sources of imprecision invite the examiner's caution in using some published research as a guideline for determining outcome of the patient's credibility. First, study of the trauma sample utilizing only narrow range of samples of performance may be inadequate. Second, use of the concept of results in the "Average" range as evidence of no loss or recovery may be incorrect. Consider a person with high-level intelligence or other measurement of achievement. "Average" would actually be evidence for significant loss of ability! Basing conclusions on these kinds of data to estimate the effect of a given event upon the patient's condition is dubious. The neuropsychological examiner will be on firmer ground concerning the attribution of injury and predicted outcome, by observational and procedural data available in the particular case, and understanding how the physical conditions of an accident contributed (or were not consequential) to the injury to brain and soma. One guiding principle is that clinically significant changes after a credible accident (see Credible Evidence of TBI) are attributable to that event if no other reliable possible causes for dysfunctioning can be determined.

Credible Evidence of TBI

The examiner must be alert to contrasting possibilities of error: a claimant's deliberate invention or exaggeration of symptoms versus the opposite, i.e., the characterological trait of minimizing or not presenting complaints and difficulties. I term this "Expressive Deficits"; this is presented in detail below (Parker, 1972, 1981). It is possible for the examiner to be incredulous of the validity of a patient's complaints when there are paradoxical components to the presentation as will be detailed below. Thus, observation during the interview and formal examination requires sensitivity to a variety of nonverbal cues and awareness of how certain kinds of lesions create dysfunctions that may be misinterpreted.

With chronic complaints, it is necessary to establish whether these are associated with the claimed traumatic event ("Unhealed Wounds"). Have there been other accidents or illnesses, before or after the accident that is the purported cause of the impairment or other dysfunctioning? Until recently, there has usually been no laboratory evidence of TBI. The neuropsychologist may wish to seek further information about new procedures that offer scanning and physiological evidence of neuronal trauma that may be more sensitive to lesser levels of TBI, including the following:

1. Single-photon emitting computerized tomography (SPECT) (Abu-Judeh, Parker, Singh, El-Zeftaway, Atay, Kumar, Naddaf, Aleksic and Abdel-Dayen, 2000) has detected small lesions in the basal ganglia and thalamus in patients with negative CT and MRI.
2. Varied new forms of imaging (Levine, 2006).
3. Biochemical markers: Several biochemical substances are considered to be sensitive to neurotrauma and to damage to the nonneuronal glial cells that comprise more than 50% of the total population of the brain. These have multiple roles in development, neuronal processes, and reaction to brain trauma (Kandel, 2000; Messam, Hou, Janabi, Monaco, Gravell and Major, 2002): neuron-specific enolase (NSE); S-100A and B (de Kruijk et al., 2002; Otto et al., 2000; Stigbrand et al., 2000; Biberthaler et al., 2000; Zingler and Pohlmann-Eden, 2005). They also seem to predict outcome (Lomas and Dunning, 2005; Rothoerl, Woertgen, and Brawanski, 2000).

Much of the neurobehavioral research concerning asserting the identification and outcome of the PCS is not conclusive. The range of domains studied is very narrow when compared with the range of potential posttraumatic behavioral disorders (see Taxonomy). By not sampling many functions that are vulnerable to cerebral and emotional trauma, these studies create false-negatives. Accident victims may be described as "normal" without comparing data to an estimated preinjury baseline (see pp. 29–35). The emergency physicians may not be trained in TBI and therefore will not make appropriate observations and examination of systems. The statement that there was "no LOC" may be unsubstantiated. The physician was not at the accident scene. The patient cannot differentiate between being unconscious, comatose, or experiencing PTA. The record reviewer should take into consideration whether there was a careful study of the head and torso. There may have been no attempt to determine whether at some time after the accident there was continued alterations of consciousness.

Predicting Outcome or Permanency

The precision of the examiner's inference should be made clear. Thus, one differentiates between evidence for TBI, estimated deficits assuming the accuracy of the estimated baseline, and attribution of cause for the deficits. Are they due to a preexisting condition, direct brain damage, or a disorder of *supporting functions* of more complex tasks (executive functioning)? Examples of the latter include slow reaction time and deficient processing of information; inability to delay actions causing impulsive responses to test items; poor performance after delay may represent a kind of memory loss; poor judgment (defective accuracy of the perceptions of the internal and external environment leading to false conclusions and inappropriate actions) creates a high proportion of obviously bad responses; poor error monitoring causes accepting erroneous responses as correct; imprecise or overly general thinking produces responses that are poorer than those that would be offered after higher preference for precise responding.

Thoughts about Some Neuropsychological Domains

This section reflects procedures utilized by the writer. Its content is relevant to estimating the preinjury baseline (predominantly using nonexamination data) and establishing an approach to the examiner's findings in the formal examination.

Educational History

What is the highest grade or college year completed? Obtain a description of any college or associate's degree obtained. Did the patient undergo technical or military training? How long was the training? What were the chief skills learned?

Medical History

The examiner will ask about birth, genetic, and developmental disorders. Then information is elicited about "serious" medical conditions, which I describe as those that were "life threatening, lasted for a long time, brought you to the hospital, or interfered with work or study, required surgery, seizures, etc." Caution is needed since the patient's statements about prior diagnoses may not be supported by the medical records. A definite assertion about having a given condition may come from an unreliable source.

Accident History

To avoid false attribution of findings, the patient is asked about the occurrence of other accidents and their after-effects. Clarification avoids errors of attribution since a prior accident may cause a current one to have paradoxically grave consequences. Levin (1985) observes that each injury destroys neurons, thus diminishing the reserve available for performance. Later injury can result in a demand for a performance that is now above the patient's lowered mental level. The patient's capacity to function is now below the *ecological demand*.

Head injury: Inaccurate denials of injury are common. Statements made by patients or collaterals concerning lack of preinjury TBI must be approached with the love for precision of a tax examiner. Precise and persistent interviewing can bring out information about a credible injury that was never previously considered to be important by the patient, not carefully assessed by a clinician, or forgotten.

Different samples of college students offered a positive response when asked about TBI: 23–34% of males and 12–16% of females. The proportion of people having a prior head injury increases with age. Consequently, there is a larger proportion of older people who experience an unexpectedly grave level of impairment after apparently minor head injury (Crovitz, Diaco, and Apter, 1992).

Neurotoxic exposures: These include farm work employment using pesticides, exposure to chemicals in a factory, or working in confined quarters with art supplies (Derelanko and Hollinger, 2002).

Electrical injuries: These include domestic, industrial, and other civil accidents (Chen et al., 1999).

Anoxic and carbon monoxide: Events include fire, defective ventilation and heating units, and stoves not burning while the gas is still emitted.

Preexisting Emotional or Personality Patterns

The clinician should inquire into previous psychiatric illness, including hospitalization, psychotherapeutic or psychopharmacological treatment, drug use, psychosocial difficulties (domestic, financial, and occupational), and constitutional characteristics (genetic vulnerability, personality and prone to accidents) (Lishman, 1988). Independent verification may be needed through record review and interviewing collaterals. While it has been stated that the symptoms of the PCS are found in both patients and noninjured persons, patients report significantly more severe symptoms compared with control persons (Bohnen, Wijnen, Twijnstra, van Zutphen and Jolles, 1995).

Caution is recommended concerning attribution of current personality dysfunctions (anxiety, psychodynamics, personality disorders, and so on) to a preexisting condition. Using intense interviews as a criterion, associations of the accident to prior experiences seem extremely rare. The overwhelming event, accompanied by fright, injuries, and reduced adaptability, and the meaning of the event to the victim, is usually a separate contributing factor to posttraumatic emotional reactions, i.e., of more importance than a preexisting personality disorder. A separate issue concerns coping and stress resistance. In the author's experience (intensive interviewing, projective testing, and so on), clinical personality studies of accident victims rarely offer any evidence that a preexisting neurosis shaped characteristic PCS symptoms. Rather, current impairment, depression, and anxiety contribute to regression. Symbolic interpretation of Rorschach responses frequently indicates the existence of intrusive anxiety, and changes of identity (injury, victimization, and vulnerable to further injury) that are reasonably related to the accident and its consequences. Preinjury depression did not seem to increase the incidence of postconcussive symptoms (Cicerone and Kalmar, 1997). Impulsive personalities and young males have a higher incidence of accidents causing TBI.

Employment History/Level

Employment history is a significant component of the adult patient's baseline and is a reference point in determining whether current functioning permits return to work. Preinjury IQ and academic functioning can be estimated on the basis of vocational group characteristics (Hartlage 1990, pp. 8–10); Wonderlic personnel test manual using percentiles of numerous vocational groups, 1992) and clinical experience with individuals with varying employment history.

Components useful for an estimate of preinjury functioning include: the age of first employment; when full-time employment began; the most skilled position ever held; whether or not the patient was employed at the time of injury; and employment characteristics (the number of people supervised, amount of training required, job requirements for planning, concentration, writing, calculations, personality, specific skills, and so on). Prior employment status seems not to predict stress susceptibility (Rimel et al., 1981). The examiner should obtain work samples, employment reviews, the formal job description, training history, job stability, promotions, temperament, and personality qualities (Guilford, 1985).

Military History

This extreme environment demands sensorimotor capacity, physical strength and stamina, social ability, intelligence, stress-resistance and health, leadership, responsibility, absorption and application of complex training demands, learning verbal and nonverbal skills and concepts, and administrative ability. The examiner should inquire about training, length of service, highest rank, duties and military occupational specialty, combat experience, and so on. Military records may reveal conduct problems, psychiatric history, and medical disorders. Using weapons and maintaining vehicles requires nonverbal intelligence. Record maintenance and personnel actions involves sequencing, precise work habits, and verbal ability. A command position implies integrating considerable information (episodic, written, graphic, and oral), planning a sequence of events, error monitoring as the operation proceeds, anticipation of consequences, and a bit of tolerance for ambiguity.

Hobbies and Optional Time Activities

These reflect skills, interests, social capacity, conceptual and learning abilities, level of independence, social interests, available energy, initiative, and range of interests. Samples of writing, graphics, and handicrafts are useful as baseline representatives. Deviations may be conspicuous, e.g., between preinjury artwork and impaired house and figure drawings, or formerly planning activities for friends and regression to a solitary life style. Sports reflect stamina, coordination, motor speed, strength, and a preference for solitary activities, or teamwork and such social skills as coaching.

Interview with Collaterals

This may be the only source of description of preinjury functioning, particularly with children, or with an unresponsive or uninsightful patient. The examiner should seek preinjury behavior, personality, preferred activities, comprehension, employment or educational functioning, health and personal hygiene, social interest, walking and use of transportation, domestic duties, interests, and community participation. Family, friends, and work associates can offer information about work, independence, responsibility, personality and temperament, social interest, frustration tolerance, and use of leisure time. Information about integrated and qualitative community functioning is useful. Pre- and posttraumatic status should be compared.

I begin an interview (or telephone conversation) with collaterals by asking the person to describe the patient before the injury, then asking about any changes that have occurred. I direct the conversation toward social participation; moods; sexuality; frustration tolerance; lifestyle changes (use of free time and interests); health, strength and stamina; coordination; work habits; and household participation.

Caution is indicated since veracity and memory may be inadequate. Response biases by patient and collaterals may create some inaccuracy in comparison of current and preinjury status. These include problems of memory, assigning meaning to current conditions, and expectations as to what is expected (Putnam et al., 1999). For children, such data as parent ratings, family demographics, and concurrent word-reading skills obtained soon after an injury are not sufficiently accurate to be desirable for use for individual assessment. Yet, children with TBI were five to ten times more likely to show a large discrepancy between estimates and performance, although the question was raised whether this information after a longer interval would remain useful (Yeates and Taylor, 1997).

Clinical Observation

The observation of the patient during interview may offer insight into preinjury style: appearance (e.g., cleanliness, neatness, and clothing); height and weight as baselines for sensorimotor study; complexion); verbal expression (vocabulary usage); aphasic indicators; education; indicators of personality development); affective expression (mood, range and intensity of affect, aprosodia). The patient's style and emotional reactions while offering information and solving problems lead to inferences about level of education and vocational experience, and whether there has been regression from the baseline; nonverbal aspects of behavior such as demeanor and frustration at difficulty or failure in performing particular activities; and social functioning, e.g., reaction to the examiner in a friendly, withdrawn, or hostile manner. Problem-solving style can be observed with Wechsler performance-type tasks such as block design and object assembly: observing whether problem-solving style is mature (preplanning) or immature or regressive (trial-and-error).

The Record Review

Data sought include preexisting conditions; posttraumatic changes in behavior, personality, and performance observed by collaterals, employers, and so on; description of the accident, with head and somatic injuries; radiological and other laboratory studies; and response to treatment. The records frequently are unreliable concerning actual cerebral trauma. Injuries to the head are frequently ignored. Potentially relevant symptoms may be ignored, misdiagnosed, or misattributed. Statements concerning "no LOC" are unreliable since the informant was usually not present at the moment of impact, and may not have inquired of the patient at all. The writer may be a poor observer concerning altered consciousness when the patient was observed (scene of accident, hospital, and so on). The statement "no LOC" may have no foundation, or be offered by a patient in a confused state of awareness and not a high level of competence of use of the English language.

Educational records are particularly significant for children because they have no other performance data. If possible, the report should not be prepared until they are available. They may offer a numerical and observational baseline. The examiner notes immediate and subsequent posttraumatic changes in achievement status and personality relative to peers since the accident. Sometimes, reduction in child's rank (percentile) may take years to be expressed (Parker, 1994) since school achievement seems to rely considerably upon long-term memory of earlier study.

The reviewer should judge whether conclusions offered by an earlier examiner are based on good professional knowledge and practice. Are they in accord with the examiner's own observations and findings, and with the reports of others?

Comprehensive, but Structured, Interview

The comprehensive interview is essential, although time consuming (I use 2½ to 3½ hours when possible). Information sought includes:

Development and health history: date and location of birth; family structure; early and later health history; mother's health and pregnancy if known; congenital and postnatal diseases; later health history, particularly for serious disease.

Demographic: Emigration age, age when English was learned, and current usage of media (newspapers, TV, and radio); preferred oral language; marriage and children, siblings, and military history (see above).

Current status: Domicile and with whom; need for assistance in daily living and community mobility; leisure-time activities; and social contacts.

Employment: Training; usual occupation and skills; occupation at the time of injury. Has the person returned to work? Was there any interval for returning to work? Was there any difficulty upon resuming employment?

Accident history (see baseline study): accidents prior to and postevent under study (head injury, neurotoxic exposure, electrical injury, anoxia/carbon monoxide i.e., smoke, fire, lack of air).

Emotional history: Problems; treatment; and hospitalization.

Reconstructing the accident (see above for principles that may guide the obtaining of information): How did the person become injured? The goal is to obtain information in order to assess the credibility of the accident as a cause for alleged trauma. Caution: Certain patient's statement do not belong in the report. Generally speaking, only what the patient has observed or experienced. Any statement in a report might be presented or cross-examined in court. Therefore, the examiner should not state something that might be controverted by a witness unless it is asserted as an observed fact or direct observation by the patient. The patient should be guided to refer particularly to how he or she was injured, not statements about outside events that might have been seen differently by an eye-witness or interpreted differently by an expert (e.g., speed, distance, and liability for the accident).

Physical injury: Details of the injury in sequence and description of blows to head and body, bruises and cuts on the head, pain, the number of head impacts and where it struck (e.g., once or more within a car), then being ejected and striking the pavement; as a pedestrian being struck by a car, being hurled onto the hood or windshield striking the head, then being thrown off and a second impact by striking the head or body on the roadway; movement of the head when seat belted and then impacting the door frame, head rest, or another passenger. Environmental details include the hardness of the head-impacting surface (e.g., the head rest); approximate speed of vehicles; and the immediate experience of headache, dizziness, and nausea.

Consciousness and memory: Memory for events before (anterograde) and after the accident (retrograde); memory for the moment of injury; alteration of consciousness (confusion, feeling "spacy," or "cloudy"); duration of the alteration of consciousness.

Current somatic concerns: Headache, pain elsewhere, sleep problems, seizures at any time in the patient's life, dizziness, balance, walking, strength, visual, hearing, movement (tics, tremors); autonomic (sweating, nausea); frequent urination (drinks too much but not thirsty) alert for diabetes insipidus due to posterior pituitary or stalk damage is an alert change; bowels, appetite change, weight change, activity level change), easily tired; women's conditions (menstrual problems and unusual secretion of milk); changes of health, body function, medical and psychological treatment; sickness and fatigability; sensitivity to heat, cold, bright light, and loud sounds; Posttraumatic stress disorder (PTSD) screen: intrusive anxiety and hyperarousal; somatic arousal symptoms (heart, breathing, startle); nightmares; flashbacks; numbness.

Social: Lack of awareness of social criticism; changes in quality and amount of social contact.

Partial seizures screen (Moore, 1997): A simple partial seizure arises from a localized area of epileptic activity with consciousness and awareness maintained. Strange experiences, including visual sensations attracting attention then head turning, but there is nothing there; auditory sensations, similar to the previously described visual response; feeling something move on the skin; tasting something others do not taste; smelling something others do not smell; thinking somebody is standing behind (Arzy, Seeck, Ortigue, Spinelli and Blanke, 2006); sudden mood change for no reason; "absence" screen: losing time, not knowing what happens for a period; getting to a place and not knowing how you got there.

Mood screen: Change in level and control of anxiety, anger, depression (dull and empty OR sad OR both); sexual changes in interest, frequency, and capacity.

Dissociative experiences: Does the outside world ever feel unreal? Does your body feel changed or unreal? Déjà vu: Do you ever feel that something has happened that you know never happened before?

Outcome: Is there a change in what you like to do since the accident? Do you get tired more easily? What makes you tired? Any change in your social life? Worst effect of the accident? Will your condition get better, get worse, or remain the same? Are you able to handle your problems, or they are too much for you? What do you do to make yourself feel better? Is there anything else you want to tell me?

Current Achievement Testing: Toward an Estimated Baseline

Current academic achievement scores can be compared with earlier achievement records. These are more objective than grades because they offer percentiles from nationally standardized achievement tests that correlate well with IQ (Anastasi, 1988) and current psychometric findings. Caution is needed in interpretation of early low scores and few years of education. These can be caused by lack of motivation, disinterest, leaving school because of poverty, change of residence, and so on. The number of years of education is also imprecise, since advancement can occur due to social promotion, parental pressure, low educational standards, and so on. Where possible, the completed years of education should be verified by collaterals, due to memory deficits and sometimes exaggeration on the patient's part. The General Educational Diploma (GED) certificate is a 12-year educational equivalent (Dalton, 1990), although some clinicians consider it to represent a lesser academic achievement.

Demographic formulae for predicting preinjury level (race, education, geographic region, and occupation) are imprecise due to restricted range of scores that underestimate a bright person's ability, and also specifying for demographic category vague occupational or demographic categories. It may be more useful to estimate single capacities rather than composite scores such as IQ (Larrabee et al., 1985; Phay et al., 1986; Putnam et al., 1999). Although educational year achievement has an imprecise meaning, WAIS-R scales, tables by age and education, offer an estimated mean of preinjury IQ (Matarazzo and Herman, 1984; Sattler, 1988), or can be obtained through percentile ranks (Ryan, Paolo, and Findley, 1991). Current WAIS-III educational equivalents are available in the manual of the Wechsler Test of Adult Reading (WTAR) (The Psychological Corporation, 2001). Norms are available by WTAR scores, sex, age, and ethnicity for full-scale IQ and several indices, for the U.S. and United Kingdom. The lower means for African Americans should be considered in the use of these tables, noting that they tell us more about social structure than phenotype.

Estimation of preinjury capacity through use of scores believed to be stable (most commonly utilized is vocabulary) is often referred to as "hold" versus "nonhold." This seems no longer accepted as a measure of before-injury ability, perhaps due to the unreliability of scores for individual cases. A specific measurement can be reduced by traumatic lateralization effects. Subtests influenced by preinjury achievement might be low for noncognitive reasons, e.g., poor education or motivation, sensory processing deficits, or any other source of unreliability that can reduce a subtest score and offer distorted information concerning pretraumatic ability. A score might be reduced because of a short-term or long-term memory disorder. Aphasic disorder might lower a verbal score, or as is frequently observed, the wording of the items may require a high educational level inappropriate to the person tested.

The Sensorimotor Examination

Study of this domain comes closest to measuring brain status directly, as well as practical functioning required for work, home, and play. In contrast to highly verbal occupations (the learned professions and office work), the sensorimotor examination assesses occupational functioning of skilled craftsmen, e.g., operators of power tools, pilots and drivers, and craftsmen (jewelers, watch repairers, chefs, and so on). The neuropsychological examiner may directly explore certain cranial nerve functions, e.g., olfaction (various procedures produced by Sensonics, Inc.), extraocular muscles (visual tracking radially into all quadrants, and rotation around the center of the visual field); tongue, facial, and shoulder movements; and the torso (station), gait (limbs), finger movement, and sensation. Lateralized disorders can be measured by comparison for each arm of grip strength (Smedley Dynamometer, Lafayette Instrument Co.) and fine motor coordination (Grooved Pegboard, Lafayette); children's fine motor coordination (wide-range assessment of visual and motor abilities pegboard, now PAR is distributor). One must be cautious in interpretation. Lateralized differences can be due to chronic peripheral and neural injuries (muscles, nerve trunks, ligaments, neural plexi, and pain), which have to be differentiated from brain injuries (cerebral motor or somesthetic areas), cerebellum, or descending pathways.

Visual observation: Broadly integrated sensorimotor functions include station (posture), gait, and balance. Proprioceptive contribution to upper and lower limb control is observed through gait and complex arm motions with and without visual input. When a patient walks, does he/she point the head down to watch his or her feet? Observe whether there are uneven shoulders when the patient stands erect (perhaps shoulder injury during an accident). Broad-based walking suggests cerebellar disorder. Is tremor observed when drawing, or when the hands are observed or held?

Motor vocalization disorders: Aprosodic speech so that anxiety, anger, and depression are not expressed as nonverbal vocal cues; poor enunciation suggesting dysarthria, and so on.

Palpation (by patient, collateral, or examiner when appropriate): To determine whether tender spots (trigger points) indicate soft-tissue injury of trapezius, pectoral, or paraspinal muscles, which may be unilaterally referred to the head as an apparent (though probably false) source of unilateral headaches (Travell and Simons, 1996).

General Mental Ability in Structured Situations

Standard scores of mental ability and academic achievement are not the only source of data for present functioning. The use of pragmatic language may be compared to subjective estimates of preinjury performance. Scores reflect both the educability of children and young adults, and their long-term memory. Deviations from the estimated baseline, e.g., expected level of certain professions and office occupations, may be a sign of impairment. While the writer prefers full-length mental ability tests such as the Wechsler scales, he has found the following scales to be useful: Kaufman Brief Intelligence Test, 2nd Ed. (AGS Publishing) and Wide Range Intelligence Test (Riverside Publishing Co.). With persons illiterate in the English language, I use the Comprehensive Test of Nonverbal Intelligence (AGS Publishing), the 12-min Wonderlic Personnel Test correlated to Wechsler scales, with similar items (in English or a foreign language translation, e.g., Chinese and Spanish), and Wide Range Intelligence Test (Riverside Publishing). For academic achievement, I suggest Wide Range Achievement Test, 4th Ed.; the Gray Oral Reading Test, 4th Edition (children: AGS Publishing); subtests from the Woodcock–Johnson Tests of Cognitive Ability and Achievement, 3rd Ed. (writing samples, academic knowledge, and delayed memory, 3–8 days; Riverside Publishing); for verbal and visual memory, Wide Range Assessment of Memory and Learning, 2nd Ed. (Riverside Publishing).

Cognitive Functioning in Unstructured Situations

Projective procedures offer information concerning current cognitive performance in an unstructured situation, e.g., reduction in expressive language ability, inability to organize ideas, regressed imagery suggesting unproductive and idiosyncratic ideas that do not reflect either a constructive use of images for either internal use or interpersonal communication, indications of poor error monitoring (reduced accuracy of perceived forms), increased reaction time (average time of the first response to the 10 inkblots), and reduced constructive original thinking and imagination. The experienced examiner can infer deviation from an estimated preinjury Rorschch baseline from expectations based upon IQ (current and former), and the estimated preinjury baseline. However, paradoxical findings occur in which the performance in an unstructured situation exceeds that expected on the basis of current measured IQ. The Thematic Apperception Test (TAT) is used to offer information about stressful and interpersonal experiences, but useful observations can be made concerning current verbal ability. The Rorschach inkblot procedure often offers a different assessment of cognitive findings in an unfamiliar situation without known ground rules than the structured environment performance of the familiar IQ. The brain-damaged person frequently presents a sparse protocol by the expected standards of demographic status and measured IQ. The images are subject to standards of acceptance by norms based on sizable groups for children and adults (Exner, 1993). Thus, the Form +% offers a useful measure of reality testing (error monitoring). Occasionally, TBI victims offer a paradoxically rich record by these standards, whose meaning is obscure. Responses available for consideration include the organization of the images, the balance between precise and impressionistic or inaccurate responses that organize the entire inkblot (Whole), and the balance between percepts that are frequently perceived (Popular) and rare responses (scored as accurate or inaccurate). Images that reflect the anxieties and pleasant anticipations of the patient contribute to our understanding of the person's daily experience.

Cognitive efficiency and executive functioning: These are functions that are vulnerable to TBI. Thus, some cognitive losses may be due to incurred inefficiency in underlying activities that process information and responses, or loss of skills, memory, and ability for specific procedures. It is necessary to detect the basic cause contributing to reduced performance in broader functions. Mental speed is vulnerable to cerebral trauma and is also reflective of temperamental differences between individuals. Useful procedures include various clusters of the Woodcock–Johnson Tests of Cognitive Ability and Achievement-3 (Riverside Publishing Co.), average initial reaction time to the 10 Rorschach inkblots, and Wechsler Adult Intelligence Scale-III, processing speed.

Graphomotor (Visuoconstructive) Representation

Procedures used by the writer are the Bender Gestalt (original edition) House-Man-Woman Clock Drawings and the Wide-Range Assessment of Visual and Motor Abilities, 2nd Ed. (WRAML-2). Information is elicited concerning cognitive development of children, possible regressive reaction to stress, and visuoconstructive ability. Significant dysfunction invites consideration of particular disorders—visuoconstructive apraxia and distortions of neurological body schema.

Personality

The emotional life of the accident victim is often greatly disturbed by an accident causing TBI. The result occurs both directly as a cerebral personality disorder and as an emotional reaction to being an injured person (Parker, 2001, chapters 12 and 13). Issues include identity, defined as the way we label our own qualities (Parker, 1983); affect; regression; mood; and personality (motivation, impulse control, reality testing, and peculiar thinking). These qualities reflect the experience of daily living, social acceptability, and adaptability. Assessment of subjective qualities of life is performed by neuropsychologists in primarily these essentially different ways: (1) clinical procedures, e.g., interviewing and observation; (2) psychometric procedures, e.g., self-rating scales for depression and symptom scales; and (3) projective tools of the clinical psychologist. These permit observation of the idiosyncratic, personal responses of the patient more closely than psychometric instruments. The goal is to determine how personality experiences and moods shape behavior. The procedures I use are the Rorschach Inkblot Procedure (PAR), the TAT (PAR), House-Man-Woman Drawings, and the clinical interview.

The Rorschach is the most complex procedure in this examiner's repertory and obtains potentially the widest range of personality and nonverbal cognitive data. It requires more training and supervised experience than any other assessment procedure I am aware of. It is very time consuming to administer, score, and interpret. Among the data sought from the Rorschach are the *subjective experiences* of the injured person: images suggesting intrusive anxiety (a marker of the PTSD), symbolic representations of a sense of self (identity), mood disorders (anxiety, depression, and anger), and symbolic representations of stress and being an injured, vulnerable, unattractive, and victimized person.

The question has been asked whether these procedures will pass standards for admission as evidence (e.g., *Daubert*). They are not used for evidence in support of particular diagnoses, e.g., the PCS. They are established procedures with decades of professional acceptance by specialists who are concerned with the emotional reactions of distressed people.

Expressive Deficits: Patients' Inability to Self-Describe

"Expressive deficits" is a term the author has proposed to describe brain-damaged patients' inability or unwillingness to describe their personal experience of TBI. Expressive deficits may conceal symptoms in every area of the neuropsychological taxonomy. When the patient cannot offer reasonably correct and complete information concerning difficulties, significant conditions may be ignored. There are numerous reasons why a patient may be unable or unwilling to communicate to the examiner or other party legitimate deficiencies consequent to an accident or other circumstance.

The problem is compounded by the fact that as TBI is more severe, there is likely to be enhanced difficulties of communication. Certain types of information come directly from the patient so that loss of self-description may cause specific problems to be ignored, such as (1) sensory complaints: (A) primarily based on neurological damage; and (2) partial seizures (see above) in which sensory phenomena may reflect not environmental stimuli but activity of the related cortex; (B) mood and personality disorders; (3) intrusive anxiety; and (4) identity as an injured and impaired person with poor morale and feeling vulnerable to more injury.

The Examiner's Contribution to Inaccurate Information Gathering

The clinician requires care in the assessment of moods, since various cerebral and personality traits create inaccurate impressions or similar appearing affects despite disparate etiologies.

Reduced distress misleads the clinician: Cerebral damage, leading to reduced intensity of affect, perhaps prevents the patient from discomfort, and so is not motivated to relate problems to others. A *gross absence of complaints* in a seemingly highly impaired person may be a sign of brain damage per se. One differentiates between verbal explicit denial of illness (*anosognosia*) and indifference (*anosodiapheria*) (Heilman, 1991). Subtypes include anosognosia (indifference to or unawareness of a neurological deficit), indifference toward failure or events concerning the family, minimization of hemiplegia through attributing it to some less anxiety-provoking cause, or emotional indifference and unthinking resignation (Bisiach and Geminiani, 1991). Inability to reveal concerns may be due to avoidance of anxiety-related repression of particular experiences. Reduced expression or experience of anxiety prevents the patient from revealing problems to the examiner. Capacity to report any condition depends on the integrity of the language apparatus. Cultural differences between examiner and patient can also affect communication, e.g., the described intensity of a complaint may vary according to background ("keep a stiff upper lip" or "let it all hang out"). Neurological impairment (e.g., commissurotomy) may render the contents of awareness inaccessible to the language expressive system (Rugg, 1992). This might be a "split brain" effect in which interference between the two hemispheres is attributable to injury of the corpus callosum. This has been described as two independent conscious selves. Lateralization would cause some information to be available primarily to one hemisphere (Dronkers, Pinker and Damasio, 2000). After a high-velocity, rapid acceleration/deceleration head injury, the edge of the dura mater extending down to the corpus callosum can create lacerations of the corpus callosum as the brain moves vertically and laterally (Rosenblum, 1989) and thus interferes with integration of the two cerebral hemispheres.

Flat affect also misleads the examiner: The brain-damaged person often expresses himself with a flat affect. This can be due to *aprosodia*, a motor disorder of vocalization, which causes the voice to appear flat or uninflected. The patient offers a misleading impression of lack of concern, even when describing the most painful kind of impairment, despair, or damage to life-style. Seeming emotional blandness and cerebral personality depression conceals from the observer the deep distress experienced because of impairment, disorganization of life, and hopelessness. The pseudo dull mood can be misunderstood as indifference, and the patient may not be taken seriously. Thus, a disorder can remain unrecognized because of the lack of overtly expressed distress. Depression, anxiety, and anger when described, although deeply experienced, may appear to the examiner as false because of approsodic non-expression of feelings. Alternatively, endogenous depression, perhaps consequent to a high-secretion posttrauma of CRH, or a thyroid deficiency, can be misperceived by the examiner as psychodynamic depression rather than a medical disorder.

Alexythymia may create misinterpretation of affective state. It is a condition, not necessarily caused by brain damage, in which the person does not identify or label feelings, fantasies, or physiological reactions (Acklin and Bernat, 1987; Taylor, 1984). The patient is unable to formulate and express affect and psychological conflicts verbally (Yager and Gitlin, 1995), i.e., does not verbally describe feeling states, impoverished fantasy life, reduced dreaming, and so on. It may not be a single personality characteristic (Norton, 1989). Rather, the patient expresses affective distress through somatic language. Alexythymics are prone to develop somatoform disorders and psychosomatic illnesses. It is claimed that they are seen in the ranks of patients with persistent PCS, chronic pain, and other traumatic disability.

Examiner's Data Gathering Is Affected by Prior Clinicians

The examiner's responsibility, when it is reasonable to form conclusions, is to enable the patient to understand his present condition and then to convey information to later clinicians. Benvenga, Campenni, Ruggeri, and Trimarchi (2000) note that an examiner's too sophisticated language used with a poorly educated man would not facilitate recollection of the details of a trauma suffered years previously. Thus, obtaining information concerning prior injuries is partially dependent upon the efficiency of prior examiners' conveying of findings to the patient. When I inquire whether this is the first time a patient has been queried concerning prior injuries, the reply is usually "Yes." Preexisting accident-related conditions are frequently ignored by health care providers. Thus, the patient is not alerted that some conditions experienced for some time may be attributed to a known accident. Therefore, the patient may not associate injury with the symptom. The event causing TBI, when not properly diagnosed at the time of trauma, may be forgotten, and therefore not associated with subsequent problems of personality and cognitive effectiveness. Pain that is caused by a trigger point in the torso or neck, and then referred (usually unilaterally) to the head, can be misunderstood if not discussed by a clinician, as being caused directly by pain in the head. Temporomandibular joint syndrome can also cause headaches that are not associated with a blow. If brain damage or concussion is not diagnosed at the time of trauma, then the potential nonskull origin of such symptoms may not be suspected, and thus can be misattributed to personality problems. Should the examiner become aware of the possible attribution of the pain paradoxically attributed to a body area away from the headache, a possible explanation may be offered to the patient, and a referral made for further examination by a physician.

Reduced Comprehension, Awareness, and Insight of the Patient

To offer an accurate self-report requires complex cognitive functioning—indeed, an intact brain. Both preexisting low intelligence and postinjury impaired intelligence or comprehension contribute to inability to understand the deficit and its effects, and would hamper the patient's effort to communicate the circumstances and result of an injury. The unintelligent or illiterate subject would have particular difficulty in judging and then providing a correct self-description (Lecours et al., 1987). Reduced performance, foresight, and planning ability may not be recognized by the patient. They may not understand the true requirements or standards for a given situation and thus may not know why job performance or fulfillment of domestic responsibilities is considered poor. Poor memory for events reduces the details of the patient's self-description. In a long interview, more material may be spontaneously offered later. It may be necessary for the examiner to probe, although this leads to possible confabulation.

Reduced comprehension does interfere with a useful report to the examiner. Lack of self-awareness interferes with self-reporting of problems of everyday memory (Garcia, Godoy Garcia, Guerro, Laserna Triguero and Puente, 1998). Error monitoring leading to correction of inappropriate behaviors or erroneous responses has been attributed to the frontal limbic area (Stuss, 1991). With certain kinds of injury (e.g., dementia, or the *frontal lobe syndrome*); (Parker, 2001, pp. 233–234 for cases), poor adaptation is not recognized by the patient. Poor judgment permits repetitive maladaptive behavior, which seems unmodifiable by social criticism or repetitive unsatisfactory experiences. This can give the impression of indifference. The patient appears *psychopathic* since behavior that is socially rejected is expressed as if it were actually satisfactory. Apparent indifference as to the self-destructive consequences of one's behavior is misunderstood; the basis is actually poor foresight and judgment.

Poor error monitoring and inability to learn from experience gives the observer the impression of indifference or immaturity (frontal lobe syndrome).

In an interview, the patient may be slow to realize that a certain dysfunction exists. Self-understanding can come later in the interview, some time after the question was initially raised. Lack of awareness of illness itself is called anosognosia (Bisiach et al., 1986). Right hemisphere-damaged patients may state that they are now "okay" or "much better"—even with physical disability—when, in fact, they may behave childishly or without expression. Without awareness or recollection that a change has taken place, the patient cannot offer a report of a problem. Patients tend to overrate their abilities compared to estimates by their families, and to report more physical than nonphysical impairment. Family members and the clinician are more likely to agree in their ratings than with patient self-ratings (Sherer, Boake, Levin, Silver, Ringholz and High, 1998). Reduced patient insight (self-awareness) is associated with lower verbal IQ and reduced temporal orientation, but association with the extent of lesion is not definitely known. A lack of foresight or judgment will cause patients not to realize that they have created acts damaging to themselves, or they are likely to do so in the future.

One patient's forehead struck his car's windshield. He, a physician, described his condition: "I didn't see the change in myself. I didn't know that was wrong." His psychotherapist (this writer) pointed out that he was once better able to concentrate. "I thought that's the way it's always been. How else could it have been? I was unaware that my symptoms were related to the accident. I denied I was ill and acted as if nothing was wrong. I went to a conference, received 35 hours of credit, and I don't remember anything. I thought everybody else was strange. I was seeing them differently. I thought that you (this writer) were asking strange questions."

Various kinds of agnosia and neglect imply lack of awareness of the nature of the injury. When there is lack of insight, patients may not realize the extent of their intellectual impairment. Professional level individuals return to work unaware of IQ deficiencies of 20–30 points that produce gross deficits of ability. If compensation for deficits is utilized, the client may not be completely aware of his deficits. Successful use of coping strategies also conceals dysfunctioning from the examiner. Examples include memory problems that are solved through the use of lists, and someone with a poor sense of direction always using a compass and map. Sometimes a patient is unaware of visual loss due to a combination of occipital and parietal injury (Anton's syndrome), which can lead to incorrect identification of patient behavior as an inappropriate emotional reaction to injury, i.e., denial of the visual defect and confabulation (Selhorst, 1989).

Aphasic Problems

Concealment in an aphasic patient has varied origins. A minimum verbal capacity is needed to alert the examiner. Aphasic communication deficits imply an inability to understand others, find appropriate self-descriptive words, or express otherwise understood thoughts coherently. Aphasia contributes to voluntary concealment. There may be a combination of actual inability to express oneself correctly and clearly and embarrassment concerning this difficulty (see Embarrassment, below). Embarrassment that conceals information is consequent to aphasic difficulties that are observable in talking, e.g., word-finding difficulties, or other receptive and expressive problems. The patient may remain silent, evasive, or stay away from any topic requiring detailed use of language. The patient may state that everything is fine, use nonverbal communication, express generalities, refuse to talk, or remain isolated.

Lack of Social Feedback

We are all dependent on feedback from family, friends, and employers to inform us whether our behavior is appropriate and satisfactory. Nonverbal and indirect expressions of dissatisfaction are common. Noncomprehension of cues of dissatisfaction, or withdrawal of comment by family and friends, eliminates social and emotional cues. Inability to monitor behavior, to learn from experience, and therefore to be aware of and report a problem, may be examples of the frontal lobe syndrome.

Concealment of Symptoms: Anxiety, Embarrassment, Consequences

There can be deliberate concealment of legitimate symptoms to the examiner due to embarrassment. One possibility is reluctance to describe a specific environmental or emotional condition. The patient does not want to discuss a situation in which he is unable to succeed, or that will create anxiety. The following are some clinical examples:

Reluctance to relive the trauma: The individual may be reluctant to express a complaint in order to avoid reexperiencing the pain. Perhaps crying would make the patient feel conspicuous when discussing the trauma and its after-effects. Moreover, repetitive or intrusive memories and reminders of impairment, pain, and loss of the quality of life lead to active attempts to avoid discussion of the experience. One woman who was knocked down by a car said that she "pretended that there was no accident."

Employment: Inability to work may be concealed by an injured worker due to fear of loss of employment. Perhaps impairment may cause one to take a less-demanding job or avoid challenging situations. The employee is afraid that if the employer knew the extent of the inability to function due to headaches, loss of concentration, problem-solving ability, and memory, then employment could be terminated (Parker, 1987). He or she may succeed temporarily in concealing reduced effectiveness since other workers cover up deficiencies. Unless the examiner asks about reduced effort or achievement, the individual may appear to be stable and uncomplaining.

Embarrassment: People fear loss of friendship due to reduced social acceptability should their limitations be known. For example, one man did not want to discuss his loss of sexual capacity with his friends, because bragging about sex with their wives was a source of prestige. In a psychometric test (true/false responses), one boy would not acknowledge any significant degree of anxiety. On the Rorschach procedure, which makes it more difficult to conceal basic feelings, he revealed a gross level of anxiety and feelings of bodily damage.

One woman's seizures were concealed because she was reluctant to tell her neurologist that she lost bladder control. A child did not tell his parents of a serious fall resulting in unconsciousness.

The defenses of denial and avoidance: Denial is a psychological defense against admitting to oneself the existence of a condition that reduces the person's value in his own self-esteem or in the opinion of others. To admit to a weakness is a blow to one's self-esteem. The loss of a better condition of life or higher capacity to achieve is so painful that self-concealment is common. This is to be distinguished from "agnosias" and inability to express emotional pain (Parker, 1972). Individuals avoid facing situations in which they are unable to succeed, or will create anxiety.

Social Inhibitions against Revelation of Difficulties

One woman was reluctant to discuss the difficulties caused by an accident because of *religious beliefs*. She engaged in litigation only because of her husband's insistence. Since she believed that God had visited this affliction on her for His own reasons, there was no purpose in offering complaints. Some families offer *social training* to their children not to complain but to accept their lot (a "Spartan mentality"). *Pride* can create a wish to overcome affliction by oneself, leading to concealment of the extent of impairment. This attitude is expressed by some people who are trained not to express emotional pain. They give themselves reasons not to ask for what is coming to them, or to assert their rights (Parker, 1972, 1981).

Organization of the Comprehensive Neuropsychological Examination

Formulation

Demographic/Identifying Information
Name of patient; date of examination; date of injury; present age; referral source; age at injury; elapsed time; type of injury; reason for referral; and procedures and CPT codes.

Summary and Formulation
Background, baseline, and preexisting conditions (details from a comprehensive interview).

Summary of the accident (obtained from patient, police report, and records).

Summary of the records: This does not include dates or specific sources, but sufficient data to describe the injury, and to lend credibility to the examiner's conclusions concerning diagnosis, attribution, and adaptability.

Summary of current status: Employment and school attendance or withdrawal; participation in family and community; and access to treatment.

Patient's complaints (differentiated from examination data): They are presented in groups, i.e., mental, potentially neurological, health and stamina, stress, and "distracting" or uncomfortable (interfere with performance independent of the direct effects of the injury: headaches, pain, mood disorders, seizure phenomena, orthopedic difficulties, and fatigability).

Symptom categories: Psychological; somatic, health and stamina (consequent to bodily injuries comorbid to cerebral injury); potentially neurological; stress related—acute and chronic stress disorders, including PTSD and chronic stress disorders (fatigability, allostatic load due to dysregulation of physiological systems, and poor morale due to constant impairment or pain).

Abstract of the examiner's observations.

Assessment of the representativeness of the examination: It is stated that the examination took place in a protected environment, but may not be typical of job or home. This is followed by the examiner's inference that there was or was not evidence for exaggerating difficulties.

     Summary of findings organized by the Taxonomy:

    I. *Neurological*: Arousal, sensorimotor, cerebral personality disorder.
   II. *Somatic*: Performance and health disorders consequent to tissue damage, physiologically based symptoms, pain, fatigability, and developmental disorders.
  III. *Mental control*: Information processing, executive functioning, concentration.
  IV. *General intelligence*: Cognitive performance in different stimulus situations.

     An estimate is offered of preinjury estimated mental ability (structured situations) in standard score points, then the current findings, and the clinical significance of any measured difference. A separate mental ability estimate for performance in an unstructured environment (e.g., Rorschach) is made if data are available.

    V. *Memory*: Short-term/working memory; long-term memory (academic achievement scores, autobiographical).
  VI. *Personality*: Psychodynamics, motivation, moods, defenses.
  VII. Identity, Insight, morale, Weltanschauung (world view).
VIII. Empathy, social life, and social role
  IX. *Stress reactions*: Acute/chronic; psychological; physiological; dissociative. These reflect both diagnostic and statistical manual-text revision (DSM-4-TR) PTSD characteristics, and chronic stress reactions as outlined in this chapter.
   X. *Adaptive capacity*: Community functioning and communications, assessment of restitutive capacity.

Diagnoses:

Attribution of dysfunctions to particular events or conditions:

Injuries: Focused upon those with current neurobehavioral relevance. Include both neural and somatic that cause impairment, pain, and physiological dysregulation.

Recommendations: Review of medications; review when further records are obtained; vocational and domestic retraining; consideration for safety and support at home; medical care and further examination, e.g., internal medicine (immune, inflammatory, and hormonal systems); psychotherapy; psychotherapy, counseling, further study to explore altered consciousness, i.e., possible "absence" or dissociation; personal counseling; family counseling.

Review of Records

I offer a summary of each record, organized by the source (psychological, medical, and educational). All materials from a provider are listed together, with selected notes presented chronologically. Each practitioner is listed in chronological order.

Neuropsychological Examination Data

Interviews (patient and collaterals)
Clinical observations
Organized presentation of data. Include numerical findings, e.g., subtest standard scores, percentiles, and test results evolving from the examiner's preferred test battery

Selected Ethical Issues

Different Code of Ethics

The neuropsychological forensic examiner experiences significant professional and ethical stress. The legal profession follows a different ethics code from the health care provider. Maintaining the best interests of a client (whether a defendant or an accident victim) need not be identical with professional standards of clinical practice. Presenting a forensic report to an attorney occurs in a nonclinical context. The defendant may have to take action (offering or denying treatment or further assessment, accepting or rejecting a claim for compensation). The plaintiff may have to accept the examiner's findings that extensive "damages" have not been documented. The attorney may then decide to drop the case (it will be best if you are paid in full at that point).

Clinical practitioners are mandated by law and ethical principles to maintain high competence and to avoid a conflict of interest. Such a code of ethics does not permit misrepresentation of examination findings. It has sometimes occurred to the writer that the analogous requirement for both a legal representative and retained professional consultants is less rigorous. Considering the professional practitioner, in the writer's jurisdiction (New York), I have seen both psychologists and medical examiners offer service that was obviously inadequate, or reports that were warped or obviously in error or perhaps false.

How is this possible? Practitioners retained by the defendant to perform IME have what is considered to be a "contractual" relationship with the attorney, i.e., not a "professional" relationship. Thus, unethical practitioners may, in the writer's experience, offer examinations that are short and incomplete, make statements ignoring the trauma and the research database, and offer largely false conclusions. Complaints to licensing boards inform the naive communicant that this is a civil matter, take it to court if you do not like it, but the governmental office is in no position to act.

Financial Conflict of Interest

It is true for examiners retained by either side that there is an unstated conflict of interest. It is hoped that the report will support the interests of the party expending funds. Consequently, the forensic neuropsychologist may be judged not by neuroscientific brilliance but by whether the findings influence who wins or loses money and how much. There is an associated problem for the examiner of an alleged accident victim. Attorneys and insurance company employees are frequently technically unable to understand the implications of an examination, regardless of laws covering compensation for personal injury or the terms of insurance policies. The outcome can be difficulty in obtaining payment for examination or treatment services ("not medically necessary"). The recommendations for recommending expensive diagnostic study or treatment may not be received in a professional manner. In this writer's opinion, whether one is retained by plaintiff or defendant, it is important for the examiner to educate the recipient of the report concerning the significance of the findings in the context of the claim of damages.

Examination Hours Authorized

Insurance companies attempt to place restrictions on the number of hours authorized for an examination (medicare, medicaid, workers compensation, and no fault). The thorough examiner will be denied a full fee for exceeding hours above "generally accepted standards" for examination (which do not exist). In other claims of personal injury, the possibility of the accident victim obtaining thorough examinations and treatment (neuropsychological and medical) is bleak. An undercapitalized or thrifty attorney may not wish to pay for a comprehensive examination; the injured person may have been impoverished even before the injury. Thus, when asked to perform an examination where the fee is not reasonable by the examiner's standards, what is the examiner to do? Offer a limited examination, or a complete one with considerable unpaid service? This is an ethical problem.

There are numerous circumstances that require additional time for accurate and thorough examination: (1) the foreign-born person whose English is poor, or who has to be examined through an interpreter (requires two to three times the examination length); (2) slow performance associated with trauma, psychopathology, or the resistant child who is hard to examine; (3) reviewing voluminous records which may have crucial information, summarizing them, offering inferences, and integrating these with the report.

Standard of Service

There are examiners who spend a few minutes or a quarter of an hour with the patient and then write detailed observations and definitive conclusions. The writer has often been told by patients, whose reports denied TBI, that the examinations were brief, and the reports offered inaccurate statements ascribed to the patient. As observed above, any conclusion that there is no after-effect of an accident based on a brief examination is irresponsible.

Liens

This is a difficult ethical issue. A lien is an agreement to be paid if the plaintiff wins a settlement. There is merit to the usual admonition not to accept a lien since this will be perceived as a conflict of interest, i.e., the examiner will alter conclusions in order to gain a self-serving verdict. To the knowledge of this writer, there is a definite, alternative ethical problem that has never been raised. Most injury victims do not have the funds to pay for a neuropsychological examination. Many plaintiffs' attorneys are unwilling to invest the capital and may even withdraw from the case should a report suggest that the settlement may be small. Thus, the impoverished accident victim may be unable to obtain documentation of the condition. To accept the politically correct pressure to avoid liens (which has merit) disregards injustice within our present compensation system in which the injured person who is unemployed and without substantial savings cannot adequately document the effects of an injury or afford treatment which may not be authorized or paid for in a timely way by an appropriate settlement. Further, since such a patient may not have private insurance, treatment can be lacking, inadequate, or too late for maximum benefit.

Translators

For foreign-born patients, there is a controversy concerning the use of untrained translators who are friends or family members. Some practitioners claim that only "certified" or trained translators should be used. This is unethical in my opinion. It would prevent collection of vital data for poor people with undercapitalized attorneys. This writer affirms the utility of using an intelligent but untrained translator. There is some imprecision in obtaining information. However, knowledgeable foreign-speaking persons have told me that due to dialect differences, mistakes are made even by professional translators.

Clinical Recommendations

When retained by the plaintiff's attorney, a recommendation is made for further study or treatment. However, it is customary (in this writer's jurisdiction) that when practitioners are retained by the defendant that instructions are given that recommendations are inappropriate. If the examiner makes important statements favoring the other side (plaintiff or defendant), the attorney may decide not to forward the report to the adversary during the "discovery" process. The practitioner will consider carefully and ethically how to proceed if in the course of the examination it is concluded that there are disorders meriting further examination and treatment. It may be ethically necessary to forward a report findings that supports the claim of injury details.

Using Symptom Validity Tests (SVT)

This is a complex controversial topic. Many practitioners consider these to be mature procedures that are useful in determining the validity of neuropsychological data. Others, this writer included, use them while being aware of their limitations.

The procedures represent an extremely narrow range of domains (e.g., memory) compared to that of potential neurobehavioral disorders.

There are a variety of meanings if a score is outside that considered to be representative of honest responses. One example is a plea for help. The writer examined one woman whose husband insisted in the examiner's presence that she was faking her impairment; the writer believed that there was a credible brain injury. The possibility of secondary gain or factitious disorder should be considered. Data concerning the accident and its reported consequences and others' assessments of the patient's condition always merit consideration concerning outcome.

The user of SVT procedures must consider the lack of validity studies in which known malingerers are used as a criterion group. Instead, other groups are used as markers for assessing malingering: (1) "simulators" whose performance is supposed to be the equivalent of cheaters, and (2) "litigators," i.e., accident victims who are suing to obtain compensation. The latter is, in my opinion, prejudicial against accident victims and is an important psychometric error. May we please assume that some "litigators" in fact are not fakers but indeed have incurred injuries for which they have not been properly compensated? Perhaps the mere fact of entering into the difficult pathway of litigation may be a consequence of a relatively high level of impairment? Thus suing for personal injury is an inappropriate marker for placement within a malingering criterion group.

In balance, SVTs offer some observational information that may be useful for judging performance motivation within a narrow context of the neuropsychological examination. A firm statement that a patient is malingering would not be acceptable in court since the issue of *credibility* belongs to the jury and not to the examiner. If the examiner concludes (privately) that there is reason to suspect dishonest responding, a cautious statement is appropriate.

Summary and Clinical Implications

The issues of diagnosis, attribution of injuries, and damages are complex and intertwined. Assessment of these issues requires consideration of a wide range of data. The examiner should study whether TBI is comorbid with bodily injury, i.e., polytrauma. A thorough examination is concerned with a wide range of disorders: neurological, somatic, mental, and social. Important forensic issues include the range of neurobehavioral disorders, diagnostic inferences from deviations from an estimated preinjury baseline, unique aspects of children's TBI, capacity to adapt to the new condition or resume former activities, prognosis, and recommendations for further examination and treatment. The examiner should attempt to determine performance loss due to "distracting symptoms," e.g., pain, headaches, fear of falling, stress-related anxiety, fatigue, sensory phenomena consequent to partial seizures, and so on. Their effects should be differentiated from TBI.

It is misleading to draw conclusions as to etiology and prognosis without considering the age and condition of the person at the time of injury, the interval since the injury, and the usual outcome of particular conditions in the context of a wide-range examination and review of records. The course of TBI does not remain static. Late-developing symptoms are neurological, physiological, and disturbed maturation of children. The symptoms of the PCS overlap those of the PTSD, while chronic stress disorder differs significantly from acute PTSD. Estimation of the credibility of claims is a complex task. In addition to cautious utilization of SVT procedures, the examiner is guided by the significance of neurological and physical injury, the range of potential neurobehavioral disorders studied, the expected outcome of particular disturbances, and deviation from the estimated preinjury baseline.

Should the examiner restrict information gathering and conceptualization only to cerebral and other strictly neurological trauma, there will be errors of commission and omission. In patients with chronic complaints, it is necessary to establish whether these are due to comorbid body injuries. Neck, torso, limb, and peripheral and spinal neurological trauma may result in cerebral-like symptoms. Chronic unhealed injury can cause physiological dysregulation. This can reduce neural efficiency, with or without direct TBI. Chronic injuries ("unhealed wounds") have acute and chronic physiological effects of significant neurobehavioral consequence, i.e., dysregulation of systems that are neuroactive and also affect health and stamina (circadian, immune, inflammatory, and hormonal). Somatic chemical signals can act as neurotransmitters in the CNS. Posttraumatic neurobehavioral disorders partially stem from disturbance of the exchange of chemical signals between brain and somatic structures (psychoneuroimmunology). Trauma and disease reduces the efficiency of the blood–brain (and other) barriers that ordinarily reduce the entry of neuroactive substances into brain cells. The consequence is a degradation of the normal pattern of neuronal functioning.

During good health, the body responds to demands and minor stress by coordinating bodily systems, thus maintaining biological adaptation to life's necessities (allostasis). This represents a far greater range of control than homeostasis. After an extended period (the chronic stress reaction), the physiological systems are exhausted (allostatic load). The effects are commonly observed effects of head injury: fatigue, loss of stamina, and stress-related health conditions.

References

Abu-Judeh, H. H., Parker, R., Singh, M., El-Zeftaway, H., Atay, S., Kumar, M., Naddaf, S., Aleksic, S., and Abdel-Dayem, H. M. (1999). SPET brain perfusion imaging in mild traumatic brain injury without loss of consciousness and normal computed tomography. *Nuclear Medicine Communications*, 20, 505–510.

Adams, J. H., Graham, D. I., and Gennarelli, T. A. (1982). Neuropathology of acceleration-induced head injury in the subhuman primate. In R. G. Grossman and P. L. Goldenberg (Eds.), *Head injury* (pp. 141–149). New York: Raven Press.

Anderson, R., and McLean, R. (2005). Biomechanics of closed head injury. (2005). In P. L. Reilly and R. Bullock (Eds.), *Head injury, 2nd Ed.* (pp. 26–40). Hodder Arnold-New York: Oxford University Press.

Acklin, M. W., and Bernat, E. (1987). Depression, alexithymia, and pain proneness disorder. Rorschach study. *Journal of Personality Assessment*, 51(3), 462–479.

American Psychiatric Association. (2000). *Diagnostic and statistical manual of mental disorders, 4th Ed.-TR (Text revision)*. Washington, DC: Author.

Anastasi, A. (1988). *Psychological testing, 6th Ed.* New York: Macmillan.

Arzy, S., Seeck, M., Ortigue, S., Spinelli, L., and Blanke, O. (2006). Induction of an illusory shadowy person. *Nature*, 443, p. 287.

Benarroch, E. E. (1997). The central autonomic network. In P. A. Low (Ed.), *Clinical autonomic disorders: Evaluation and management, 2nd Ed.* (pp. 17–23). Philadelphia, PA: Lippincott-Raven.

Benvenga, S., Campenni, A., Ruggeri, R. M., and Trimarchi, F. (2000). Hypopituitarism secondary to head trauma. *The Journal of Clinical Endocrinology and Metabolism*, 85, 1353–1361.

Berg, R. (1986). Neuropsychological effects of closed-head injury in children. In J. E. Obrzut and G. W. Hynd (Eds.), *Child neuropsychology, II* (pp. 113–135). New York: Academic Press.

Biberthaler, P., et al. (2000). Influence of alcohol exposure on S1000B serum levels. *Acta Neurochirurgica-Supplement*, 76, 177–179.

Bisiach, D. E. (1992). Understanding consciousness: Clues from unilateral neglect and related disorders. In A. S. Milner and M. D. Rugg (Eds.), *The neuropsychology of consciousness* (pp. 114–137). San Diego: Academic Press.

Bisiach, E., and Geminiani, G. (1991). Anosognosia related to hemiplegia and hemianopia. In G. P. Prigatano and D. L. Schachter (Eds.), *Awareness of deficit after brain injury* (pp. 17–39). New York: Oxford University Press.

Bisiach, E., Vallar, G., Pirani, D., Pagagno, D., and Berti, A. (1986). Unawareness of disease following lesions of the right hemisphere: Anosognosia for hemiplegia and anosognosia for hemianopia. *Neuropsychologia*, 24, 471–482.

Blumbergs, P. C. (2005). Pathology. In P. L. Reilly and R. Bullock (Eds.), *Head injury, 2nd Ed.* (pp. 41–72). New York: Hodder Arnold (Oxford University Press).

Bohnen, N. J., Wijnen, G., Twijnstra, A., van Zutphen, W., and Jolles, J. U. (1995). The constellation of late post-traumatic symptoms of mild head injury patients. *Journal of NeuroRehabilitation*, 9, 33–39.

Bohus, B., and Koolhaas, J. M. (1996). Psychoimmunology and psychobiology of parasitic infestation. In H. Friedman, T. W. Klein, and A. L. Friedman (Eds.), *Psychoimmununology, stress, and infection* (pp. 263–272). Boca Raton, FL: CRC Press.

Broman, S. H., and Michel, M. E. (Eds.) (1995). *Traumatic head injury in children*. New York: Oxford University Press.

Bullock, R., and Nathoo, H. (2005). Injury and cell function. In P. L. Reilly and R. Bullock (Eds.), *Head injury, 2nd Ed.* (pp. 113–139). Hodder Arnold-New York: Oxford University Press.

Chen, C.-T., Lee, R. C., Shih, J.-X., and Zhong, M.-H. (1999). Occupational electrical injury: An international symposium. *Annals of the New York Academy of Sciences*, vol. 888.

Cicerone, K. D., and Kalmar, K. (1997). Does premorbid depression influence post-concussive symptoms and neuropsychological functioning? *Brain Injury*, 11, 643–648.

Creisler, C. A., Winkelman, J. W., and Richardson, G. S. (2005). In *Harrison's principles of internal medicine, 16th Ed.* (Vol. I, pp. 153–162). New York: McGraw-Hill.

Crofford, L. J. (2002). The hypothalamic–pituitary–adrenal axis in the pathogenesis of rheumatic diseases. *Endocrinology and Metabolism Clinics of North America*, 31, 1–13.

Crovitz, H. F., Diaco, D. S., and Apter, A. (1992). Consistency in recalling features of former head injuries: Retrospective questionnaire vs. interview retest. *Cortex*, 28, 509–512.

Curle, C. E., and Williams, (1996). Post-traumatic stress reactions in children: Gender differences in the incidence of trauma reactions at two years and examination of factors influencing adjustment. *British Journal of Clinical Psychology*, 35(2), 297–309.

Cytowic, R. E., Smith, A., and Stump, D. (1986). Transient amenorrhea after closed head trauma (letter). *New England Journal of Medicine*, 314, 715.

Dalton, J. E. (1990). Neuropsychological equivalence of the G.E.D. *International Journal of Clinical Neuropsychology*, 12, 138–139.

D'Angelica, M., Barba, C. A., Morgan, A. S., Dobkin, E. C., and Pepe, J. L. (1995). Hypopituitarism secondary to transfacial gunshot wound. *The Journal of Trauma: Injury, Infection, and Critical Care*, 39, 768–771.

Damasio, A. R., and Anderson, S. W. (1993). The frontal lobes. In K. M. Heilman and E. Valenstein (Eds.), *Clinical neuropsychology, 3rd Ed.* (pp. 409–460). New York: Oxford University Press.

De Krujik, J. R., et al. (2002). Prediction of post-traumatic complaints after mild traumatic brain injury: Early symptoms and biochemical markers. *Journal of Neurology, Neurosurgery and Psychiatry*, 73, 727–732.

De Kloet, E. R., and Deruk, R. (2004). Signaling pathways in brain involved in predisposition and pathogenesis of stress-related disease: Genetic and kinetic factors affecting the MR/GR balance. *Annals of The New York Academy of Sciences*, 1032, 14–34.

DeLorenzo, R. J. (1991). The epilepsies. In W. G. Bradley, R. B. Daroff, G. M. Fenichel, and C. D. Marsden (Eds.), *Neurology in clinical practice, II.* (pp. 1443–1447). Boston: Butterworth-Heinemann.

Derelanko, M. J., and Hollinger, M. A. (Eds.) (2002). *Handbook of toxicology, 2nd Ed.* Boca Raton: CRC Press.

De Vries, E., and Prat, A. (Eds.) (2005). *The blood–brain barrier and its microenvironment*. New York: Taylor & Francis.

Dhabar, F. S., and McEwen, B. S. (2001). Bidirectional effects of stress and glucocorticoid hormones on immune function: Possible explanations for paradoxical observations. In R. Ader, et al. *Psychoimmunology, 3rd Ed., Vol. 1.* (pp. 301–338). San Diego: Academic Press.

Diamond, M. E., Harris, J. A., and Petersen, R. S. (2002). Sensory learning and the brain's body map. In R. J. Nelson (Ed.), *The somatosensory system: Deciphering the brain's own body image* (pp. 183–195). Boca Raton, FL: CRC Press.

Dronkers, N. F., Pinker, S., and Damasio, A. (2000). Language and the aphasias. In E. R. Kandel, et al. (Eds.), *Principles of neural science, 4th Ed.* (pp. 1169–1187). New York: McGraw Hill.

Downing, J. E., and Miyan, J. A. (2000). Neural immunoregulation: emerging roles for nerves in immune homeostasis and disease. *Immunology Today,* 21, 281–289.

Eslinger, P. J., Grattan, L. M., Damasio, H., and Damasio, A. R. (1992). Developmental consequences of childhood frontal lobe damage. *Archives of Neurology,* 49, 764–769.

Exner, J. (1993). *Rorschach: A comprehensive system. Vol. I, 3rd Ed.* New York: Wiley.

Fearnside, M. R., and Simson, D. A. (2005). Epidemiology. In P. L. Reilly and R. Bullock (Eds.), *Head injury, 2nd Ed.* (pp. 3–25). Hodder Arnold-New York: Oxford University Press.

Fletcher, M. A., Ironson, G., Goodkin, K., Antoni, M. H., Schneiderman, N., and Klimas, N. G. (1998). In J. R. Hubbard and E. A. Workman (Eds.), *Handbook of stress medicine: An organ system approach* (pp. 69–85). Boca Raton, FL: CRC Press.

Fukutake, T., Mine, S., Yamakami, I., Yamaura, I., and Hattori, T. (2000). Roller coaster headache and subdural hematoma. *Neurology,* 54, 264.

Garcia, M. P., Godoy Garcia, J. F., Guerro, N. V., Laserna Triguero, J. A., and Puente, A. E. (1998). Neuropsychological evaluation of everyday memory. *Neuropsychology Review,* 8, 203–227.

Garvey, M. A., Gaillard, W. D., Rusin, J. A., Ochsenschlager, D., Weinstein, S., Conry, J. A., Winkfield, D., Renee, and Vezina, L. G. (1998). Emergency brain computed tomotgraphy in children with seizures: Who is most likely to benefit? *The Journal of Pediatrics,* 133, 664–669.

Geeraerts, T., et al. (2006). Changes in cerebral energy metabolites induced by impact-acceleration brain trauma and hypoxic-hypotensive injury in rats. *Journal of Neurotrauma,* 23, 1059–1071.

Giedd, J. N., Blumenthal J., Jeffries, N. O., Castellanos, F. X., Liu, H., Zijdenbos, A., et al. (1999). Brain development during childhood and adolescence: A longitudinal MRI study. *Nature Neuroscience,* 2(10), 861–863.

Gennarelli, T. A., and Graham, D. I. (1998). Neuropathology of head injuries. *Seminars in neuro-psychiatry,* 3, 160–175.

Goetz, C. G., and Pappert, E. J. (1996). In R. W. Evans (Ed.), Movement disorders: Post-traumatic syndromes. *Neurology and trauma* (pp. 569–580). Philadelphia, PA: W. B. Saunders.

Grossman, W. F., and Sanfield, J. A. (1994). Hypothalamic atrophy presenting as amenorrhea and sexual infantilism in a female adolescent: A case report. *Journal of Reproductive Medicine,* 39, 738–740.

Grumbach, M. M., and Styne, D. M. (1998). Puberty: Ontogeny, neuroendocrinology, physiology, and disorders. In J. D. Wilson, et al., *Williams textbook of endocrinology, 9th Ed.* (pp. 1509–1625). Philadelphia: Saunders.

Guilford, J. P. (1985). Structure-intellect model. In B. B. Wolman (Ed.), *Handbook of Intelligence* (pp. 225–266). New York: Wiley.

Hartlage, L.G. (1990). *Neuropsychological evaluation of head injury.* Sarasota, FL: Professional Resource Exchange.

Hellhammer, J., Schlotz, W., Stone, A. A., Pirke, K. M., and Hellhammer, D. (2004). Allostatic load, perceived stress, and health. *Annals of The New York Academy of Sciences,* 1032, 8–13.

Heilman, K. M. (1991). Anosognosia: Possible neuropsychological mechanisms. In G. P. Prigatano and D. L. Schachter (Eds.), *Awareness of deficit after brain injury* (pp. 53–62). New York: Oxford.

Hunt, J. P., Weintraub, S. L., Yang, Y. Z., and Buechter, K. J. (2004). Kinematics of trauma. In E. E. Moore, D. V., Feliciano, and K. L. Mattox (Eds.), *Trauma, 5th Ed.* (pp. 159–174). New York: McGraw Hill.

Indefrey, P., and Develt, W. J. M. (2000). The neural correlates of language production. In M. S. Gazzaniga (Ed.), *The new cognitive neurosciences, 2nd Ed.* (pp. 845–865). Cambridge, MA: MIT Press.

Joseph, S., and Masterson, J. (1999). Posttraumatic stress disorder and traumatic brain injury: Are they mutually exclusive? *Journal of Traumatic Stress,* 12, 437–454.

Kandel, E. R. (2000). Nerve cells and behavior. In E. R. Kandel, et al., *Principles of neural science, 4th Ed.* (pp. 19–35). New York: McGraw Hill.

Kelly, D. F., Gonzalo, I. T., Cohan, P., Berman, N., Swerdloff, R., and Wang, C. (2000). Hypopituitarism following traumatic brain injury and aneurysmal subarachnoid hemorrhage: A preliminary report. *Journal of Neurosurgery,* 93, 743–752.

Kemeny, J. E., Solomon, G. F., Morley, J. E., and Herbert, T. L. (1992). Psychoneuroimmunology. In C. B. Nemeroff (Ed.), *Neuroendocrinology* (pp. 563–591). Boca Raton, FL: CRC Press.

Keverne, E. B., Nevison, C. M., and Martel, F. L. (1997). Early learning and the social bond. In S. C. Carter, I. I. Lederhendler, and B. Kirkpatrick (Eds.), *The integrative neurobiology of affiliation* (pp. 329–339). Annals of the New York Academy of Sciences, vol. 807.

Kirshner, H. H. (1996). Speech and language disorders. In M. S. Samuels and S. Feske (Eds.), *Office practice of neurology* (pp. 718–722). New York: Churchill Livingstone.

Kop, W. J., and Cohen, N. (2001). Psychological risk factors and immune system involvement in cardiovascular disease. In R. Ader, D. L. Felten, and N. Cohen. *Psychoneuroimmunology, Vol. 2, 3rd Ed.* (pp. 525–544). San Diego: Academic Press.

Klonoff, H., Clark, C., and Klonoff, P. S. (1995). Outcome of head injuries from childhood to adulthood: A twenty-three year follow-up study. In S. H. Broman and M. E. Michel (Eds.), *Traumatic head injury in children* (pp. 219–234). New York: Oxford University Press.

Kraemer, G. W. (1997). Psychobiology of early social attachment in rhesus monkeys. In S. C. Carter, I. I. Lederhendler and B. Kirkpatrick (Eds.). *The integrative neurobiology of affiliation* (pp. 401–418). Annals of the New York Academy of Sciences, vol. 807.

Kraus, J., Schaffer, K., Ayers, K., Stenejem, J., Shen, H., and Afifi. (2005). Physical complaints, medical service use, and social and employment changes following mild traumatic brain injury: A 6-month longitudinal study. *Journal of Head Trauma Rehabilitation,* 20, 239–256.

Krauss, J. K., and Jankovic, J. (2002). Head injury and posttraumatic movement disorders. *Neurosurgery,* 50, 927–940.

Krikorian, R., and Layton, B. S. (1998). Implicit memory in posttraumatic stress disorder with amnesia for the traumatic event. *Journal of Neuropsychiatry and Clinical Neurosciences,* 10, 359–362.

Kupfer, D. J., and Frank, E. (1997). Role of psychosocial factors in the onset of major depression. In S. C. Carter, I. I. Lederhendler and B. Kirkpatrick (Eds.), *The integrative neurobiology of affiliation* (pp. 429–439). Annals of the New York Academy of Sciences, vol. 807.

Langlois, J. A., Rutland-Brown, W., and Wald, M. M. (2006). The epidemiology and impact of traumatic brain injury. *Journal of Head Trauma Rehabilitation,* 5, 375–378.

Langlois, J. A., Rutland-Brown, W., and Thomas, K. E. (2004). Emergency department visits, hospitalizations, and deaths. Atlanta (GA) Centers for Disease Control and Prevention, National Center for Injury Prevention and Control.

Langlois, J. A., Marr, A., Mitchko, J., and Johnson, R. L. (2005). Tracking the silent epidemic and educating the public: CDC's traumatic brain injury's associated activities under the TBI Act of 1996 and the Children's Health Act of 2000. *Journal of Head Trauma Rehabilitation,* 20, 196–204.

Larrabee, G. J., Largen, J. W., and Levin, H. S. (1985). Sensitivity age-decline resistant ("hold") WAIS subtests to Alzheimer's disease. *Journal of Clinical and Experimental Neuropsychology,* 497–504.

Laterra, J., and Goldstein, G. W. (2000). Ventricular organization of cerebrospinal fluid: Blood-brain barrier, brain edema and hydrocephalus. In E. R. Kandel, et al. (Eds.), *Principles of neural science, 4th Ed.* (pp. 1288–1300). New York: McGraw Hill.

Lecours, A. R., Mehler, J., et al. (1987). Illiteracy and brain damage-I: Aphasia testing in culturally contrasted populations (control subjects). *Neuropsychologia,* 25, 231–245.

Levchakov, A., Linder-Ganz, E., Raghupathi, R., Margulies, S. S., and Gefen. A. (2006). Computational studies of strain exposures in neonate and mature rat brains during closed head impact. *Journal of Neurotrauma,* 23, 1570–1580.

Levin, H. S. (1985). Outcome after head injury: Part II. Neurobehavioral Recovery. In Becker, D. P., and Povlishock, J. T. (Eds.), *Central nervous system status report—1985* (pp. 281–299). National Institute of Neurological and Communicative Disorders and Stroke, National Institutes of Health.

Levine, B. (2006). Introduction to neuroimaging in traumatic brain injury. *Journal of Neurotrauma*, 23, 1394–1395.

Lezak, M. D., Howieson, D. B., and Loring, D. W. (2004). *Neuropsychological assessment, 4th Ed.* New York: Oxford University Press.

Lieberman, S. A., Oberoi, A. L., Gilkison, C. R., Masel, B. E., and Urban, R. J. (2001). Prevalence of neuroendocrine dysfunction in patients recovering from traumatic brain injury. *Journal of Clinical Endocrinology and Metabolism*, 86, 2752–2756.

Lishman, W. A. (1988). Physiogenesis and psychogenesis in the 'post-concussional syndrome'. *British Journal of Psychiatry*, 153, 460–469.

Lomas, J. P., and Dunning, J. (2005). Best evidence topic report. S100B protein levels as a predictor of long-term disability after head injury. *Emergency Medicine Journal*, 22, 889–891.

Lombardi, G., Savastano, S., Valentino, R., Selleri, A., Tommaselli, A. P., Rossi, R., Gigante, M., and Covelli, V. (1994). Neuroendocrine axis and behavioral stress. In N. A. Fabris et al., (Eds.), *Immunomodulation: the state of the art* (pp. 216–222). Annals of the New York Academy of Sciences, vol. 741.

MacGillivary, M. H. (2001). Disorders of growth and development. In P. Felig and L. A. Frohman (Eds.), *Endocrinology and metabolism, 4th Ed.* (pp. 1265–1316). New York: McGraw-Hill.

Maier, S. F., Watkins, L. R., and Fleshner, M. (1994). Psychoimmunology: The interface between behavior, brain, and immunity. *American Psychologist*, 49, 1004–1007.

Margoles, M. S. (1999). Soft tissue pain problems: Introduction. In M. S. Margoles and R. Weiner (Eds.), *Chronic pain: assessment, diagnosis, and management* (pp. 91–92). Boca Raton, FL: CRC Press.

Marshall, G. D., and Rossio, J. L. (2000). Cytokines. In G. Fink (Ed.), *Encyclopedia of stress, Vol. 1* (pp. 626–633). San Diego: Academic Press.

McEwen, B. S. (2000). The neurobiology of stress: from serendipity to clinical relevance. *Brain Research*, 886, 172–189.

McEwen, B. (2004). Protection and damage from acute and chronic stress: Allostasis and allostatic overload and relevance to the pathophysiology of psychiatric disorders. *Annals of The New York Academy of Sciences*, 1032, pp. 1–7.

Mitrushina, M., Boone, K., B., Razani, J., and D'Elia, L. F. D. (2005). *Handbook of normative data for neuropsychological assessment, 2nd Ed.* New York: Oxford University Press.

Moore, D. P. (1997). *Partial seizures and interictal disorders: The neuropsychiatric elements.* Boston: Butterworth-Heinemann.

Moore, E. E., Feliciano, D. V., and Mattox, K. L. (Eds.) (2004). *Trauma, 5th Ed.* New York: McGraw Hill.

Matarazzo, J. D., and Herman, D. O. (1984). Relationship of education and IQ in WAIS-R standardization sample. *Journal of Consulting and Clinical Psychology*, 52, 631–634.

Messam, C. A., Hou, J., Janabi, N., Monaco, M. C., Gravell, M., and Major, E. O. (2002). Glial cell types. In V. S. Ramachandran (Ed.), *Encyclopedia of the human brain, Vol. II* (pp. 369–387). Boston: Academic Press.

Mittenberg, W., Wittner, M. S., and Miller, L. J. (1997). Postconcussion syndrome occurs in children. *Neuropsychology*, 11, 447–452.

Molitch, M. E. (2001). Neuroendocrinology. In P. Felig and L. A. Frohman (Eds.), *Endocrinology and metabolism, 4th Ed.* (pp. 111–171). New York: McGraw-Hill.

National Center for Injury Prevention and Control. (2003). *Report to Congress on Mild Traumatic Brain Injury in the United States: Steps to Prevent a Serious Public Health Problem.* Atlanta, GA.

Norton, N. C. (1989). Three scales of alexythymia: Do they measure the same thing? *Journal of Personality Assessment*, 53, 621–637.

Otto, M., et al. (2000). Boxing and running lead to a rise in serum levels of S-100B protein. *International Journal of Sports Medicine*, 21, 551–555.

Panksepp, J., Nelson, E., and Bekkedal, M. (1997). Brain systems for the mediation of social separation-distress and social-reward. In S. C. Carter, I. I. Lederhendler, and B. Kirkpatrick (Eds.), *The integrative neurobiology of affiliation* (pp. 78–100). Annals of the New York Academy of Sciences, vol. 807.

Parker, R. S. (1972). The patient who cannot express pain. In R. S. Parker (Ed.), *The emotional stress of war, violence and peace* (pp. 71–85). Pittsburgh: Stanwix House.

Parker, R. S. (1981). *Emotional common sense, 2nd Ed*. New York: Harper & Row.

Parker, R. S. (1983). *Self-image psychodynamics: Rewriting your life script*. Englewood Cliffs, NJ: Prentice Hall.

Parker, R. S. (1987). Recognizing employees who have suffered brain damage. *EAP Digest* (Employees Assistance Program), 7, March/April, pp. 55–60.

Parker, R. S. (1990). *Traumatic brain injury and neuropsychological impairment*. New York: Springer-Verlag.

Parker, R. S. (1994). Neurobehavioral outcome of minor head injury in children. *Seminars in Neurology*, 14(1), 67–73.

Parker, R. S. (1995). Distracting effects pain, headaches, and hyper-arousal upon employment after "minor" head injury. *Journal of Cognitive Rehabilitation*, 13(3):14–23.

Parker, R. S. (2001). *Concussive brain trauma*. Boca Raton, FL: CRC Press.

Parker, R. (2002). Recommendations for the revision of DSM-IV diagnostic categories for co-morbid posttraumatic stress disorder and traumatic brain injury. *NeuroRehabilitation*, 17, 131–143.

Parker, R. S. (2005a). Traumatic brain injury. In D. S. Younger (Ed.), *Motor disorders, 2nd Ed*. (pp. 707–710). Philadelphia: Lippincott Williams and Wilkins.

Parker, R. S. (2005b). Dysregulation of the internal milieu after an accident causing head injury. In T. Corales (Ed.), *Trends in posttraumatic stress disorder research* (pp. 67–101). Hauppage, NY: Nova Science Publishers.

Parker, R. S., and Rosenblum, A. (1995). Intelligence and emotional dysfunctions after mild head injury incurred in a car accident. *Journal of Clinical Psychology*, 52, 32–43.

Phay, A., Gainer, C., and Goldstein, G. (1986). Clinical interviewing of the patient and history in neuropsychological assessment. In Incagnoli, T., Goldstein, G., and Golden, C. J. (Eds.), *Clinical application of neuropsychological test batteries* (pp. 45–73). New York: Plenum.

Pocock, G., and Richards, C. D. (2004). *Human physiology, 2nd Ed*. New York: Oxford.

The Psychological Corporation. (2001). *Wechsler test of adult reading*. San Antonio, TX.

Putnam, S. H., Ricker, J. H., Ross, S. R., and Kurtz, J. E. (1999). Considering premorbid functioning: Beyond cognition to a conceptualization of personality in postinjury functioning. In J. J. Sweet (Ed.), *Forensic neuropsychology* (pp. 39–81). Exton, PA: Swets and Zeitlinger.

Ransom, B. R. (2005). The neuronal microenvironment. In W. F. Boron and E. L. Boulpaep (Eds.), *Medical physiology, up-dated edition* (pp. 399–419). Philadelphia, PA: W. B. Saunders.

Reilly, P. L., and Bullock, R. (Eds.) (2005). *Head injury*. London: Hodder Arnold.

Rimel, R. W., Giordani, B., Barth, J. T., Boll, T. J., and Jane, M. A. (1981). Disability caused by minor head injury. *Neurosurgery*, 9, 221–228.

Ropper, A. H., and Korson, K. C. (2007). Concussion. *New England Journal of Medicine*, 356, 166–172.

Rosenblum, W. I. (1989). Pathology of human head injury. In D. P. Becker and S. K. Gudeman. *Textbook of head injury* (pp. 525–537). Philadelphia: Saunders.

Rosman, N. P. (1989). Acute brain injury. In K. Swaiman (Ed.), *Pediatric neurology, Vol. II. Principles and Practice* (pp. 715–734). St. Louis: C. V. Mosby.

Rothoerl, R. D., Woertgen, C., and Brawanski, A. (2000). S-100 serum levels and outcome after severe head injury. *Acta Neurochirurgica-Supplement*, 76, 97–100.

Rugg, M. D. (1992). Conscious and unconscious processes in language and memory-Commentary. In A. S. Milner and M. D. Rugg (Eds.), *The neuropsychology of consciousness* (pp. 263–278). San Diego: Academic Press.

Ryan, J. R., Paolo, A. M., and Findley, P. G. (1991). Percentile rank conversion tables for WAIS-R IQs at six educational levels. *Journal of Clinical Psychology*, 47, 104–107.

Saper, C. B., Iverson, S., and Frackowiak, R. (2000). Integration of sensory and motor function: The association of the association areas of the cerebral cortex and the cognitive capabilities of the brain. In E. R. Kandel, et al., *Principles of neural science, 4th Ed.* (pp. 349–380). New York: McGraw Hill.

Sattler, J. M. (1988). *Assessment of children*. San Diego: Jerome M. Sattler.

Schachter, D. L., Chiu, P. C., and Ochsner, K. N. (1993). Implicit memory: A selective review. *Annual Review of Neuroscience, 16* (pp. 159–182). Palo Alto, CA: Annual Reviews.

Schneider, J., Schneider, M. J., and Stalla, G. K. (2005). Anterior pituitary hormone abnormalities following traumatic brain injury. *Journal of Neurotrauma*, 22, 937–946.

Schnurr, P. P., Friedman, M. J., Engel, C. C., Foa, E. H., Shea, M. T., Chow, B. K. et al. (2004). Cognitive behavioral therapy for posttraumatic stress disorder in woman. *Journal of the American Medical Association*, 27(8), 820–830.

Selassie, A. W., McCarthy, M. L., Ferguson, P. L., Tian, J., and Langlois, J. (2005). Risk of posthospitalization mortality among persons with traumatic brain injury, South Carolina 1991–2001. *Journal of Head Trauma Rehabilitation*, 20, 257–269.

Selhorst, J. B. (1989). Neurological examination of head-injured patients. In D. P. Becker and S. K. Gudeman. *Textbook of head injury* (pp. 82–101). Philadelphia: Saunders.

Semrud-Clikeman, M. (2001). Traumatic brain injury in children and adolescents.

Sherer, M., Boake, C., Levin, E., Silver, B. V., Ringholz, G., and High, Jr., W. (1998). Characteristics of impaired awareness after traumatic brain injury. *Journal of the International Neuropsychological Society*, 4, 380–387.

Simpson, D. A. (2005). Clinical examination and grading. In P. L. Reilly and R. Bullock (Eds.), *Head injury, 2nd Ed.* (pp. 143–163). Hodder Arnold-New York: Oxford University Press.

Southwick, S. M., Bremner, D., Krystal, J. H., and Charney, D. S. (1994). Psychobiologic research in post-traumatic stress disorder. *Psychiatric Clinics of North America*, 17(2), 251–264.

Southwick, S. M., Yehuda, R., and Morgan, C. A. III. (1995). Clinical studies of neurotransmitter alterations in post-traumatic stress disorder. In M. J. Friedman, D. S. Charney, and A. Y. Deutch (Eds.), *Neurobiological and clinical consequences of stress: From normal adaptation to PTSD* (pp. 345–349). Philadelphia: Lippincott-Raven.

Steinberg, M. (2000a). Dissociative disorders. In B. J. Sadock and V. A. Sadock (Eds.), *Comprehensive textbook of psychiatry, 7th Ed.* (pp. 1544–1564). Lippincott Williams and Wilkins: Philadelphia, PA.

Steinberg, M. (2000b). Depersonalization disorders. In B. J. Sadock and V. A. Sadock (Eds.), *Comprehensive textbook of psychiatry, 7th Ed.* (pp. 1564–1570). Lippincott Williams and Wilkins: Philadelphia, PA.

Stulemeijer M., van der Werf, S.P., Jacobs B., Biert J., van Vugt, A. B., Brauer, J. M., and Vos, P. E. (2006a). Impact of additional extracranial injuries on outcome after mild traumatic brain injury. *Journal of Neurotrauma*, 23, 1561–1569.

Stulemeijer, M., Van Der Werf, S., Bleijenberg, G., Biertg, J., Brauer, J., and Vos, P. E. (2006b). Recovery from mild traumatic brain injury: a focus on fatigue. [Journal Article. Research Support, Non-U.S. Gov't] *Journal of Neurology*, 253, 1041–1047.

Strauss, E., Sherman, E. M. S., and Spreen, O. (2006). *A compendium of neuropsychological tests. Administration, norms, and commentary*. New York: Oxford University Press.

Stuss, D. T. (1991). Disturbance of self-awareness after frontal system damage. In G. P. Prigatano and D. L. Schachter (Eds.), *Awareness of deficit after brain injury* (pp. 63–83). Oxford: New York.

Styne, E. (2004). Puberty. In F. S. Greenspan and D. G. Gardner (Eds.), *Basic and clinical endocrinology, 7th Ed.* (pp. 608–636). New York: Lange Medical Books.

Takahashi, H., and Nakazawa, S. (1980). Specific type of head injury in children. *Child's Brain*, 7, 124–131.

Taylor, J. G. (1984). Alexythymia: Concept, measurement, and implications for treatment. *American Journal of Psychiatry*, 145, 725–732.

Thompson, P. M., Sowell, E. R., Goglay, N., Giedd, J. N., Vidal, C. N., Hayashi, K. M., et al. (2005). Structural MRI and brain development. *International Review of Neurobiology*, 67, 285–323.

Tomsak, R. L. (2004). Vision loss. In W. G. Bradley et al. (Eds.), *Neurology in clinical practice, 4th Ed. Vol. 1* (pp. 177–183). Boston: Butterworth-Heinemann.

Travell, J. G. (1996). *Travell & Simons' trigger point flip charts.* Baltimore: Lippincott Williams and Wilkins.

Tsigos, C., and Chrousos, G. P. (1996). Stress, endocrine manifestations, and diseases. In C. L. Cooper (Ed.), *Handbook of stress, medicine, and health* (pp. 61–85). Boca Raton, FL: CRC Press.

Valadka, A. B. (2004). Injuries to the cranium. In E. E. Moore, D. V. Feliciano, and K. L. Mattox (Eds.), *Trauma 5th Ed.* (pp. 385–406). New York: McGraw Hill.

Van Reekum, R., Cohen, T., and Wong, J. (2000). Can traumatic brain injury cause psychiatric disorders? *Journal of Neuropsychiatry and Clinical Neurosciences*, 12, 316–327.

Vasterling, J. J., Constans, J. I., and Hanna-Pladdy, B. (2000). Head injury as a predictor of psychological outcome in combat veterans. *Journal of Traumatic Stress*, 13, 441–451.

Vedhara, K., and Irwin, M. (Eds.), *Human psychoimmunology.* New York: Oxford University Press.

Wadhwa, P. D., Sandman, C. A., Chicz-DeMet, and Porto, M. (1997). Placental CRH modulates maternal pituitary-adrenal function in human pregnancy. In *Neuropeptides in development and aging* (pp. 276–281). Annals of the NY Academy of Sciences, vol. 814.

Yaffe, K., Lindquist, K., Penninx, B. W, Simonsick, E. M., Pahor, M., Kritchevsky, S., et al. (2003). Inflammatory markers and cognition in well-functioning African-American and white elders. *Neurology*, 61, 76–80.

Yager, J., and Gitlin, M. J. (1995). Clinical manifestations of psychiatric disorders. In H. I. Kaplan and B. J. Sadock (Eds.), *Comprehensive textbook of psychiatry, 6th Ed. Vol. I* (pp. 637–669). Baltimore: Williams and Wilkins.

Yang, E. V., and Glaser, R. (2005). Wound healing and psychoneuroimmunology. In K. Vedhara and M. R. Irwin (Eds.), *Human psychoimmunoimmunology* (pp. 264–204). New York: Oxford University Press.

Yeates, K. O., and Taylor, H. (1997). Predicting premorbid neuropsychological functioning following pediatric traumatic brain injury. *Journal of Clinical and Experimental Neuropsychology*, 19, 825–837.

Zingler, V. C., and Pohlmann-Eden, B. (2005). Diagnostic pitfalls in patients with hypoxic brain damage: three case reports. *Resuscitation*, 65, 107–110.

Child Maltreatment Parental Assessments

JAMES MANLEY

Independent Practice, Kailua-Kona, Hawaii

DEBORAH CHAVEZ

Independent Practice, Kailua-Kona, Hawaii

20

Contents

Synopsis

Assessing parents who maltreat their children is an important subspecialty of forensic psychology. A Child Maltreatment Parental Assessment (CMPA) formulates data compiled from collateral and interview information, assisting state courts and social services in arriving at a disposition toward family reunification or parental right termination. The chapter discusses child maltreatment and the relationship with methamphetamine use and domestic violence. The basic components of a CMPA will be outlined as well as the differences between forensic assessments and clinical assessments. Key points of expert witness testimony in court proceedings will be offered. Ethical considerations specific to CMPA will be discussed. A work sample of a CMPA has been attached in Appendix S to illustrate the forensic work product.

Child Maltreatment Parental Assessment

This chapter examines the forensic assessment of parents who have been involved with state social services due to the maltreatment of a child. There are three sections in the chapter. The first section offers a definition of child maltreatment and reviews two correlates of child abuse—methamphetamine use and domestic violence. The second section examines the inherent difference between a clinical assessment and forensic assessment. In addition, the basic components of a CMPA are reviewed including the forensic referral question, the clinical interview, collateral information, third-party interviews, psychological testing, and treatment recommendations. The final section discusses expert witness testimony and ethical considerations related to a CMPA.

Child Maltreatment Parental Assessment: Construct

The term child maltreatment incorporates all forms of child abuse and neglect, as defined by federal and state regulations (National Clearinghouse on Child Abuse and Neglect Information and National Adoption Information Clearinghouse, 2005). While states' definitions of child abuse and neglect may differ, the term typically includes the threat or harm of physical abuse, physical neglect, emotional abuse, emotional neglect, and sexual abuse (Choy, 1993; National Clearinghouse on Child Abuse and Neglect Information and National Adoption Information Clearinghouse; Trocmé et al., 2001; World Health Organization, 1999). For purposes of this chapter, child maltreatment is defined as harm or threat of harm of physical abuse, physical neglect, and sexual abuse. In addition, the term child maltreatment includes inadequacies in the following areas: (a) food, clothing, or shelter; (b) psychological care; (c) medical care; (d) supervision; (e) psychological injury; and (f) provision of harmful drugs (State of Hawaii, 2000, 2004).

Reported instances of child maltreatment cases within the United States have exceeded 3 million per year (Daro, 1995). Child maltreatment cases within the state of Hawaii have also escalated. As an example, on the island of Hawaii, a 41% increase of confirmed reports of child abuse and neglect occurred between 1999 and 2003 (State of Hawaii, 2003). Historically, simple child neglect has not warranted similar attention as physical and sexual child abuse. Over the past few years, this perspective has changed. Research has indicated victims of neglect are also at significant risk for criminal behavior during adolescence and adulthood (Hall, 1996).

Children's welfare services are rooted in the assumption that state and juvenile interests coexist. According to Feld (1995), the state has a duty to protect the child thereby acting on the child's behalf and providing socialization. However, state intervention in child maltreatment cases represents a direct conflict with family privacy and parental liberty (Melton, Petrila, Poythress, and Slobogin, 1997). For example, the state has an interest in the socialization of the child to be a responsible citizen, but the state also has an interest in the preservation of the family as an intact unit. These conflicts are reflected when constructing a finite definition of child abuse, child neglect, and child maltreatment. Defining adult behaviors and the types of parenting that are dangerous or socially unacceptable have been challenging.

Within most state's social services systems, child protection agencies are the referral source for CMPA in child maltreatment cases. State agency interventions include protective custody of the child or family supervision of the case. Subsequent referrals for forensic evaluations are requested to assist the fact finder in understanding parental fitness. The ability to provide a safe and appropriate home environment for possible family reunification is primary in the disposition of the case. The quality of the parents' mental status and ability to safely parent is the focus of such evaluations. Research related to parental fitness suggests a causal link between child maltreatment, methamphetamine or other substance abuse, and domestic violence (Choy, 1993). Child maltreatment is often entrenched within the family system. Psychological assessments attempt to investigate the underlying causalities of the abuse and neglect, with the goal of reduction of risks related to future harm of the child.

Melton et al. (1997) addressed two important areas of state intervention. First, upon receipt of a child maltreatment intake, child protection agency representatives must investigate the allegations. Second, if maltreatment is confirmed, child protection services evaluate the situation and develop a plan to best alleviate future maltreatment toward the child. The outcome of this process often takes the form of a family service plan and referrals to follow-up services for the indicated problem areas. A CMPA is a valuable tool that provides insight into the parents' psychological functioning and assessment of the parents' motivation to comply with the service plan.

Child Maltreatment Parental Assessment: Evaluative Process

The CMPA assists public agencies in determining (a) the parents' psychological functioning, (b) their behaviors or attitudes that may affect the safety of the child, (c) whether psychological harm may exist upon reunification between the child and parent, and (d) recommendations of social, psychological, and medical services to prevent future harm toward the child (American Psychological Association Committee on Professional Practice and Standards, 1998). Assessments regularly include an analysis of personality traits, coping strategies, and psychosocial barriers (Poirier, 2000). Identifying these psychological factors is instrumental toward mitigating future abusive and neglectful behaviors. Competency in the psychological dynamics of child maltreatment is necessary for an accurate assessment and treatment recommendations.

In addition to the specific forensic training components required for an effective evaluation, clinical experience with similar populations can be helpful. For example, a background in substance abuse assessment and treatment would assist the evaluator when estimating a client's ability or commitment to remain abstinent. Accordingly, diagnostic experience with clients assigned with personality disorders and clients with interpersonal violence histories would allow precise analysis and individualized prescriptive recommendations. This expertise is highly recommended as parents, when being evaluated, can be manipulative, avoidant, and at times untruthful.

Parents often present with resistance and defensiveness against the intrusion of state agency representatives. The untrained professional may experience difficulties discerning the differences between parental resistance, failure to accept responsibility for their abusive actions, and the existence of a serious underlying mental health condition. Parents suffering from mental health illnesses often decompensate upon initial contact with child protection agencies due to the intensified pressure of external stressors (Faller and Bellamy, 2000). Research findings (Dinwiddie and Bucholz, 1993; Famularo, Kinscherff, and Fenton, 1992) indicated a greater occurrence of personality disorders and mood disorders among parents who were abusive toward their children. Yanagida and Ching's (1993) study suggested that abusive parents maintained personality characteristics of impulsivity, suspiciousness, and immaturity. Without a thorough CMPA, parents suffering from personality disorders may be mistakenly interpreted as uncooperative or oppositional.

Assessing the parent–child relationship is significant to the welfare of the child, including analysis of parenting styles that may increase the likelihood of abuse and neglect (American Psychological Association Committee on Professional Practice and Standards, 1998). Critical components to the forensic analysis encompass inquiry into the parent–child relationship, including how parental decisions influence maltreatment, attachment, and bonding toward the child (Groth-Marnat, 2003). In addition, the evaluation must address the parent's future caretaking abilities in the child's physical, emotional, and psychological needs.

Examination of personality characteristics (Choy, 1993), cognitive processing, and learning deficits that may have contributed toward child maltreatment will assist the evaluator in accurate diagnosis and treatment recommendations. Assessment of current and historical status of substance abuse and domestic violence will offer additional analysis of the parent–child relationship and future risks of harm toward the child. The complexities of child maltreatment increase when methamphetamine and domestic violence enter the family system. Methamphetamine and its more potent version, crystal methamphetamine, have severely influenced the incidence of child maltreatment, causing increased assessment and treatment needs among those families involved in child protection agencies.

Child maltreatment commonly refers to the threat of harm, physical abuse, and sexual abuse. Each state varies in the definition of these areas, but often includes physical neglect, medical neglect, and psychological abuse. Evaluation of child maltreatment is complex and requires specialization in domestic violence, substance abuse, and mental illness. Accurate diagnosis and treatment recommendations are dependent upon the integration of these specialties, to analyze and evaluate the parent's ability for caregiving and protection of the child from future harm.

Correlates of Child Maltreatment

Establishing statistical evidence among any given adult population of child maltreaters in conjunction with substance abuse has proved difficult. Research conducted with state child welfare agencies indicated that the majority of state data systems did not track information related to the parent's substance abuse (Child Welfare League of America, 1997). The relationship between substance abuse and child maltreatment has garnered limited research (United States Department of Health and Human Services and Gaugin, 1993). The sparse research (Kelleher, Chaffin, Hollenberg, and Fischer, 1994) on this topic proposes a strong relationship between substance abuse disorders and child maltreatment (National Clearinghouse on Family Violence, 2000). In 1999, substance abuse, cognitive deficiencies, and psychiatric disorders were designated as risk factors for child abuse and neglect (Kelleher et al.; World Health Organization, 1999). Substances, such as methamphetamine and crystal methamphetamine, were correlated with increased aggressive behaviors (Pamenter, 2002). Additional risk factors, including low socioeconomic status, poor academic functioning, and mental illness, were common among families involved with child protection agencies.

Methamphetamine Use

There is an abundance of evidence linking familial aggression with methamphetamine use. Methamphetamine has been described as the first illegal substance to bisect gender and socioeconomic levels through its effortless availability in both urban and rural communities of the United States (Pamenter, 2002). Between 1992 and 2002, methamphetamine treatment admissions in the United States increased between 12 and 50% (United States Department of Health and Human Services, 2004). Similar to other states, Hawaii has attempted to address the damage resulting from methamphetamine abuse. Between 1992 and 2002, methamphetamine treatment admissions in this state increased from 92 to 97% (United States Department of Health and Human Services).

Methamphetamine's impact on children has been devastating. In 2002, 90% of confirmed child protection service cases were related to methamphetamine abuse (Goodwin, 2004). Austin's (2004) study of Native Hawaiians found that methamphetamine abuse had negatively affected the Hawaiian racial ethnic group. The study further showed that using the crystallized form of methamphetamine was positively correlated with a younger age at first use, age of first violent act against an individual, age of onset of chronic methamphetamine use, and frequency of crystal methamphetamine use.

Methamphetamine is commonly used throughout the United States (Jefferson et al., 2005) and is either inhaled or injected into the bloodstream (Alberta Alcohol and Drug Abuse Commission, 2001; National Institute on Drug Abuse, 2002). The drug releases excessive levels of dopamine into the brain's limbic and nucleus accumbens. Increased dopamine levels trigger erratic behaviors hallmarked by agitation, paranoia, and hallucinations. Stimulation of the nucleus accumben affects movement, cognition, and motivation (Rawson, 1999). The crystallized form of methamphetamine oversimulates the brain's reward system, heightening the user's sensory experiences, including appetite, sexual pleasure, and the effects of other substances, such as alcohol or marijuana. In sum, methamphetamine severely undermines the user's ability to be present and interact appropriately within the family system.

Methamphetamine is a highly physically and socially destructive drug that severely debilitates drug users, their children, and families. Research findings (Haight, Jacobsen, Black, Kingery, Sheridan, and Mulder, 2005) suggest that the methamphetamine user's familial environment is detrimental to the children and increases the risk of child maltreatment. Research studies investigating the relationship between child maltreatment, methamphetamine use, and domestic violence within the Hawaiian population are limited. Zweben et al.'s (2004) randomized controlled study was conducted with outpatient methamphetamine users in California, Montana, and Hawaii. Symptoms of paranoid ideation, psychoticism, and anxiety were found to be elevated in the sample population. Research participants reported that high levels of interpersonal violence were commonplace in the methamphetamine user's lifestyle. Recurring features of a methamphetamine drug user's home environment included physical and sexual abuse, neglect, poor parental bonding, and exposure to environmental toxins (Haight et al.). Children of methamphetamine users frequently displayed violent behavior, deceitfulness, theft, and other developmental precursors of an antisocial personality. The same children exhibited poor academic performance, concentration difficulties, poor socialization skills, and a general mistrust toward adults (Haight et al.).

Methamphetamine use has a predictable pattern of cognitive deterioration. The abuser's binge often includes food and sleep deprivation commonly lasting between 3 and 15 days. The most dangerous period is the final stage of extended use. The drug user frequently experiences dysphoria, intense feelings of detachment (Hall, 1996), and psychotic delusions. Hallucinations and paranoia are not uncommon, including occurrences of restricted speech and unprovoked violent outbursts (Pamenter, 2002). The methamphetamine user typically uses other illegal substances in an effort to minimize withdrawal symptoms, thus exacerbating the substance abuse syndrome. Concurrent with the drug user's methamphetamine intoxication, their children are frequently left unprotected and ignored, with exposure to dangerous environments. The severity of the maltreatment triggers extrafamilial intervention, often through mandated reporting to child protection agencies. The children are frequently removed from parental custody and placed into the protective custody of the state.

In summary, methamphetamine's physiological and psychological damages to the drug user are extensive. The drug user is unable to adequately parent his or her child. The child maltreatment is profound and frequently warrants intervention by child protective services. Clinical interviewing often reveals that the drug user's home environment includes domestic violence, exposure to the illicit substance abuse, and toxic chemical exposure. Anecdotal evidence of clinicians treating children of methamphetamine users suggest commonalities among the children, including frequent academic truancies, homelessness, inadequate health treatment, and poor social development.

Domestic Violence

Domestic violence is a form of violence toward a significant other, spouse, or family member. Domestic violence has also been identified as intimate partner violence (Geffner, Geis, and Aranda, 2006), battering, spousal abuse, and domestic abuse (Houry et al., 2004). Numerous research studies (Hartley, 2002; Straus and Gelles, 1990) have identified a strong link between child maltreatment and domestic violence. When drug-using parents were arrested, the correlation between substance use and child maltreatment was substantial (Phillips, Barth, Burns, and Wagner, 2004). Children exposed to domestic violence risk serious harm and placed at higher risk for physical abuse and neglect (Stover, 2005; Straus and Gelles). Children of these families often risked injury when attempting to intervene between their parents, or they have been used as intermediaries between the perpetrator and victim

(Office on Child Abuse and Neglect, 2003). Researchers Beeman, Hagemeister, and Edleson (2001) and Stover reported that over 60% of child protection referrals have included child maltreatment and domestic violence. Many states have identified domestic violence as a risk factor for child maltreatment. Once families have been identified, child protection agency representatives regularly request a CMPA.

Clinical Assessment Evaluations and Forensic Assessment Evaluations

There are several differences between writing a clinical assessment and a forensic assessment. Melton et al. (1997) described seven dimensions distinguishing clinical assessment from forensic assessment. The first difference addresses the scope of the assessment. Generally, the focus of most clinical assessments is broad in nature and includes various areas of psychological functioning. Typical inquiry includes areas of enduring and acute problems of mental functioning, characterlogical conditions, intellectual functioning, social functioning, and often psychological testing. The forthcoming information is analyzed to formulate a working hypothesis, diagnosis, and treatment plan recommendations. The focus of a forensic assessment addresses a specific event or interaction of a nonclinical nature. The legal components of the forensic case are directly referenced to the referral question, and peripheral clinical data are not critical. As an example, forensic evaluators are frequently asked legal questions involving the client's mental status during a specific time or during a sequence of behaviors.

The second difference between a clinical assessment and a forensic assessment is the utilization of the client's perspective. The clinical assessment requires the evaluator to focus on understanding the client's insight into the presenting problem. A clinical assessment often focuses on the individual's optimal level of functioning and is considered a helpful document to aid clinical intervention and can assist mitigating identified problematic behaviors, increasing coping skills, and enhancing client well-being. A clinical assessment accepts the client's input with high validity. While accurate information from the client is important in both settings, the forensic assessment is primarily concerned with an objective and accurate formulation of an individual's mentation during specific events. A forensic evaluator may be questioned concerning a client's legal and psychological competency while conducting an aggressive act. Forensic assessments regularly examine supplemental data sources such as police reports, insurance records, and medical records to address the legal question. In these cases, the client's opinion and recount are equally weighed with other collateral information.

An additional difference between the assessment styles is the voluntary versus mandated nature of the referral. Clients voluntarily participate in clinical assessments as part of the therapeutic process. The assessment becomes a therapeutic tool in the development of treatment recommendations. In contrast, court representatives or public agencies generally request forensic assessments and the relevant statutes that define the legal dispute to determine the assessment's objective. The forensic client has very little to do with the course of the assessment. The information is not confidential and may be used in future legal proceedings.

Although unconscious distortion of information is a threat to validity in both types of assessments, clinical evaluators consider their client's treatment needs. The clinical assessment is designed to assist the client within a confidential setting. This setting promotes frank discussion about problematic clinical issues. Because of the nature of forensic assessments, lack of confidentiality, and legal involvement, clients would be less likely to divulge similar information to the evaluator.

Clinical assessments are regularly conducted within a trusting therapeutic relationship fueled with empathic dynamics. The clinical assessment builds upon these interactions and the resulting formulation is gleaned over a period of several sessions. The forensic assessment does not foster a perception of a nurturing or "helping" environment. Detachment is maintained between the forensic evaluator and the client. Forensic assessments are time-limited and affected by numerous factors, including court schedules and limited resources.

The inherent differences between writing a clinical assessment and a forensic assessment require several adjustments in the evaluator's attitude and approach. The forensic assessment is driven by a legal query, and therapeutic considerations are secondary. The client is likely an unwilling participant during a CMPA. The forensic evaluator is advised to be clear about the specific legal questions involved in the assessment. The next section addresses the fundamental points of a CMPA.

Essential Components of a Child Maltreatment Parental Assessment

Similar to general psychological evaluations, CMPAs are conducted through a clinical interview, mental status examination, behavioral observations, intellectual testing, psychological testing, collateral information gathering, interpretation of findings, and treatment recommendations (Groth-Marnat, 2003). The controversies between parental and children's rights, child maltreatment, and substance abuse lay cause for numerous and complicated situations. Mental illness, childhood history of child abuse, or other converging data deepen the color and texture of the family crisis. When formulating an opinion, these data points are organized into a document that addresses a particular forensic question.

The CMPA follows a predictable organizational pattern. The initial contact with the referral source should outline the forensic question necessary to complete the assessment. Parental interviews and collateral sources of information, including third-party interviews, are mainstays of the data collection. In addition, psychometric testing can supplement the available data. Once completed, the CMPA typically offers useful treatment recommendations to guide service providers. Frequently, the evaluator is called upon to offer opinion and court testimony for additional clarification of the CMPA analysis. The following discussion guides future evaluators in the production of a thorough CMPA.

The Forensic Referral Question

A CMPA must answer specific questions related to the problems or issues raised by the referral source. All too often, the cases are referred via a harried attorney or child protection agency case manager who may be unclear about the underlying forensic issues. In turn, the evaluator may receive generalized information and rote instructions. The evaluator must clearly understand the referral question and the reason for the report. Upon clarification of the referral question, the evaluator organizes the available information into a cogent document. The referral source should submit background information including legal documents and comprehensive treatment reports related to the case history.

To avoid confusion, the evaluator must clearly understand the essence of the forensic question prior to the interview. Common referral topics include the following:

- Does the parent have the required life skills needed for appropriate parenting?
- Has the parent adopted an abstinent lifestyle?
- What are the strengths and weaknesses of the parent in the context of avoiding future maladaptive parenting responses?

The Clinical Interview

As the referral is often initiated due to problematic parental behaviors, the evaluator must review the available file material prior to the interview appointment. The parents will frequently have "their side of the story" to tell and may present complex clinical profiles. They may be fearful of revealing characteristics about themselves that would be used against them in their quest for regaining custody of their child. Parents may conceal information from their caseworkers and treatment providers. For example, parents who are abusing methamphetamine may unwittingly describe their most recent use to the evaluator, while neglecting to report the use to their substance abuse treatment providers.

The use of Open-Ended questioning is a common interviewing tactic used in a CMPA interview allowing the interviewee a chance to respond in a variety of forms. The evaluator is then able to observe the individual's response content and assess his or her comprehension, organization, and self-expression within a minimally structured framework (Groth-Marnat, 2003). Conducting a CMPA interview differs from general psychological evaluations. In the forensic setting, the parent may intentionally communicate a plethora of detailed, tangential, or vague information that is irrelevant to the assessment in an attempt to circumvent the interview's direction. Requesting the parent to provide concrete examples of vague statements may eliminate the intentional ruse of misinformation.

According to Carkhuff (Groth-Marnat, 2003), inconsistencies occur when individuals attempt to distort or conceal information about them. Parents required to participate with child protection agencies may attempt to portray themselves in a positive light. Parent's behaviors may not be consistent with their self-reports. While parents may not always intentionally misrepresent themselves, their self-perceptions may be distorted, inconsistent, and unrealistic. As an example, an active crystal methamphetamine user may describe maintaining a drug-free lifestyle.

There will be instances when the discovery information or third-party information does not support parental statements. The evaluator is advised to question the parent's inconsistencies in an effort to obtain more comprehensive information (Groth-Marnat, 2003). For example, there have been cases where court documents did not elaborate on details that the parent found important and wanted to clarify during a clinical interview. In other instances, the parent wanted to correct an allegedly erroneous report regarding their specific behaviors toward their child.

Collateral Information Review

Reviewing collateral file information often adds to the information offered by the parent. Ancillary information can confirm the parent's statements or reveal differing perspectives of the parent's performance in other settings, such as within a therapeutic relationship, parental education groups, and substance abuse treatment groups. Multiple data sources contribute to the emerging analysis and working hypotheses to guide the finding of the assessment. Typical collateral resources include:

1. Child welfare reports outlining parental behavioral patterns and custodial history.
2. Substance abuse facility treatment reports.
3. Supervised visitation summaries.
4. Previous psychological reports of the parent or child.
5. Police reports related to domestic abuse, court appearances, incarceration, and probation requirements.

Considering additional documentation from multiple sources assists the evaluator in the development of a comprehensive document. A CMPA is frequently used as a critical legal document in contested court hearings. Consideration of multiple data points in the formulation of a forensic opinion supports the evaluator's findings during testimony.

Third-Party Interviews

Third-party interviews are an additional source of information for a CMPA and offer further insight into the family dynamics. For example, foster parents may discuss how the child has responded to their care or offer information about the child's reaction during parental visitations. In addition, a child may report to a foster parent details regarding the family's history that may help the evaluator understand the family's relationships. The evaluator must be mindful of possible biases when interviewing foster parents. Particular hazards include financial gain by the foster parents and a desire to adopt their foster child. Substance abuse treatment providers will likely have updates regarding the parent's treatment progress and commitment to abstinence. Child protection agency case managers may have additional information not detailed in the submitted documentation.

The evaluator's objectivity is paramount while considering information offered from collateral sources. Providers often have their own opinions about the disposition of the case and may attempt to sway the evaluator toward their own perspective. To illustrate, a treating therapist may offer a clinical interpretation in reaction to a personal bias instead of offering an impartial perspective of the parent's progress.

Psychological Testing

Psychological testing is an important component of a CMPA. Testing instruments offer additional sources of information to support or refute a working hypothesis or treatment recommendation. In addition, psychological testing offers insight into the parent's motivation for changes conducive to the reunification of the child. For example, was the test taker open to the testing administration, or were the answers determined to be unrealistically virtuous? Parents who refuse to participate or complete psychological testing may be demonstrating resistance or lack the commitment necessary to identify possible risk factors for child maltreatment. The evaluator must also be cognizant of adults with limited education or mental illness. These adults may not have the capacity to participate in a written test administration. These cases require oral administration of the testing instruments.

Minnesota Multiphasic Personality Inventory-2 (MPPI-2) (Hathaway and McKinley, 1989). The MMPI-2 is commonly used for a CMPA due to the complexity of child maltreatment cases. Researchers (Otto, Buffington-Vollum, and Edens, 2003) noted that the MMPI-2 was an effective assessment for psychopathology and analysis of the emotional stability of parents in relationship to their childrearing style. The MMPI-2 has consistently proven strong validity and reliability with the standardized norms of the general population. The evaluator must analyze the resulting test data and determine whether the parent was unconsciously providing inaccurate responses to the test protocol. The MMPI-2 provides specific validity scales to measure this type of item response.

Computer-based test interpretative (CBTI) reports of intellectual and personality testing instruments, including the MMPI-2, are common and efficient. Software programs' interpretative output is based on actuarial assessment and expertise of the developers of the software programs (Cohen and Swerdlik, 2002). *Standards for Educational and Psychological Testing* (American Educational Research Association, American Psychological Association, and National Council on Measurement in Education, 1999) advised that CBTIs must be used with caution, as the interpretation does not factor information such as gender, education, occupation, ethnic race, and medical history. Norming samples and inappropriate application were based on nonforensic populations. If evaluators choose to utilize CBTI services, these computer reports must be used only as a working hypothesis tool, used in conjunction with the clinical interview, collateral data, and additional testing instruments. In addition, Standard 5.11 in the *Standards for Educational and Psychological Testing* (American Educational Research Association, American Psychological Association, and National Council on Measurement in Education) cites that the evaluator must make available the CBTI source, rationale for use, limitations, and empirical basis when utilizing CBTI reports.

Specialized Psychometric Instruments

There are few standardized assessment instruments designed to assess a parent's ability to be reunified with the child. Specialized instruments have been developed for the assessment of parental competence, parental attitudes, and family relations. However, Melton et al. (1997) advised these instruments were not validated for use in child maltreatment cases. Grisso (2003) reported that although some assessment instruments were normed with families involved in social services programs, these instruments analyzed perceptions of the parent–child relationship, parental awareness, and parental stress level. Evaluators are cautioned in interpreting findings based on instruments with weak psychometrics for the parents who were identified as child maltreaters.

Child Abuse Potential Inventory (CAPI) (Milner, 1986, 1994). The CAPI is a potentially useful instrument that assesses parents at risk for physical child abuse. The instrument was used as a screening tool by child protection agencies to assess parental risk for physical child abuse. The CAPI developers operationalized "child abusers" as those parents defined by social service workers as having committed abuse, based on the North Carolina child abuse reporting law. All cases were not necessarily adjudicated.

The CAPI has 160 test items that employs a forced-choice approach with either "agree" or "disagree" responses (Milner, 1986). Items typically refer to a specific attitude or feeling (e.g., "I am lonely inside," "Children should never be bad") (Grisso, 2003). Seventy-seven test items constitute a physical abuse scale producing six factor scores: distress, rigidity, unhappiness, problems between the child and parent, problems with the family, and problems with others (Milner, 1994). The CAPI has three validity scales: (a) a lie scale, (b) a random response scale, and (c) an inconsistency scale. These scales are used in various combinations to form three validity indices: Faking Good, Faking Bad, and Random Response. In addition, two specialized scales evaluate ego strength and loneliness (Grisso, 2003). Grisso also cautioned that the CAPI was not intended for diagnoses or conclusions.

Melton et al. (1997) indicated the CAPI showed a strong correlation in the identification of known abusers within highly selected samples. However, he does not recommend the instrument for clinical screening use in child maltreatment cases. Further, the CAPI's strong ability to identify past abusers is related to the validation sample in which half of the participants had previously physically abused their children. The higher-than-normal base rate, compared to the general population, may cause misinterpretation of the instrument's findings when assessing parents without a history of physical child abuse (Melton et al.).

Parent Awareness Skills Survey (PASS) (Bricklin, 1990) and *Parent Perception of Child Profile (PPCP) (Bricklin and Elliot, 1991)*. The PASS is a clinical tool designed to highlight the strengths and weaknesses of parental awareness. The survey gathers parental reactions toward typical childcare situations with children up to 12 years of age. It is composed of 18 childcare scenarios and designed to sample relevant parenting behaviors that might be used with children. The PPCP was designed to assess parental understanding and awareness of a child's development and needs across eight areas: interpersonal relationship, daily routine, health history, developmental history, school history, fears, personal hygiene, and communication style.

Grisso (2003) reviewed the PASS and PPCP and indicated that these testing instruments generally assessed the domains relevant to parenting. The measure is grounded in the notion that parental skills can be measured through self-report. Additional content validation was suggested to determine the appropriateness and comprehensiveness of the PASS and PPCP measurements.

Parenting Stress Index (PSI) (Abidin, 1995). The PSI is a 120-item self-report questionnaire designed to assess stressors between parent and child, their interrelationship, and life event stressors. Three subscales in the "parent domain" assess depression, competence, and attachment. Additional parent subscales include spouse, health, role restriction, and isolation. Subscales within the "child domain" scale include adaptability, demandingness, mood, and distractibility–hyperactivity. These three subscales are combined to produce a total stress score.

The PSI is a testing instrument that provides information relevant to legal decision-making (Grisso, 1993). The PSI is described as useful in decision-making in parental custody disputes. PSI testing scores were also correlated with several outcome measures of interest to forensic psychologists. Acton and During (1992) reported decreased parent and child PSI testing scores after completion of an aggression management intervention program. Mash, Johnston, and Kovitz (1983) noted consistent correlation of elevated PSI testing scores among abusive and neglectful mothers and their children.

Psychological Testing and Ethnic Racial Groups

While psychological testing plays an important role in a CMPA, over-reliance on testing outcomes is cautioned. The use of intelligence testing and personality testing with nonnormed racial ethnic groups is controversial (Groth-Marnat, 2003). Evaluators using intellectual and psychological testing instruments with ethnic racial groups must consider possible testing bias when administering and interpreting testing results.

The clinical interview offers the opportunity to inquire about the parent's level of identification with their cultural and racial ethnic group and level of participation in their ethnic racial heritage. The parent's degree of ethnic assimilation, acculturation, and cultural norms must be considered during interpretation of testing results. Within the state of Hawaii, there are multiple racial ethnic groups including Hawaiian, Micronesians, Marshallese, Filipino, and other Pacific-Rim ethnicities. Standardized testing instruments were not normed for these diverse ethnic populations. Groth-Marnat recommended evaluators understand different racial ethnic subgroup norms, including the levels of accuracy, when making predictions based on intellectual and personality testing scores.

Personality inventory research compares test score performance between racial ethnic populations and the norming sample. Findings have consistently shown differences between the normative group and racial ethnic groups (Groth-Marnat, 2003). Numerous research studies have investigated the MMPI test scoring patterns between African American, Asian American, Hispanic, and American Indian populations, and were unable to discern a consistent pattern of skill differences between any two ethnic groups (Green, 1987; Butcher and Williams, 2000). Research suggested that socioeconomic status, intelligence, and education were moderate variables affecting MMPI profiles.

Racial ethnic groups may experience stress factors that affect personality inventory performance (Graham, 2000). When MMPI scores are deviant, the clinical interview plays a critical role in the analysis of the parent's life situation, environmental stressors, and adjustment levels. The evaluator is advised to maintain knowledge of current research regarding validity and reliability of the psychological tests used with racial ethnic groups. Resources such as the *Mental Measurements Yearbook* (Buros Institute of Mental Measurements, 2006), which is updated every six months, are valuable sources for the determination of the appropriateness of specific psychological tests with racial ethnic groups.

Child Maltreatment Parental Assessment: Recommendations Section

The recommendations section is the final section of the assessment and offers practical and specific ways to address any residual parental requirements necessary for family reunification. Regularly, a family service plan is developed by the child protection agency. The CMPA recommendation section can offer more specific or directive methods of addressing parental needs. As an example, the family service plan may notate "sobriety" while the recommendations section might outline a specific type of substance abuse treatment (e.g., inpatient services, sober support group meetings).

Service providers frequently refer to the recommendations section rather than reading the lengthy assessment report. Therefore, the treatment recommendations must be prescriptive and concise and must address interventions and further assessments. Lichtenberger, Mather, Kaufman, and Kaufman (2004) noted that unimplemented recommendations were frequently vague, complicated, or impossible to carry out within the community. Recommendations should be targeted as opportunities for parents to develop or enhance their parenting abilities, thus reducing the risks of harm toward their child. Recommendations may include interventions that address modifications of the parent's behavior and personality functioning. Maintenance of accomplished behavioral changes, such as substance abuse recovery, is also included in the recommendations section.

For example, the island of Hawaii does not have an inpatient substance abuse treatment facility. During the evaluation process, the evaluator determines that inpatient methamphetamine substance abuse treatment is the best intervention for the parent. Should the evaluator recommend inpatient substance abuse treatment regardless of whether the treatment was readily accessible? In this case, the substance abuser was eventually referred to an off-island treatment facility. Treatment recommendations for services that are not assessable within the community oftentimes serve to demonstrate an unmet service need within the community. Eventually, inpatient treatment facilities were initiated on-island as a result of successful demonstration of unmet societal needs by community members. Concurrently, the recommendations, while noting the ideal, should offer backup methods of intervention.

Substance Abuse Treatment Recommendations

It is well established that a parent who is abusing methamphetamine or other substances impairs the development and socialization of the child (Otto et al., 2003). Unfortunately, the intoxicated substance user is likely unaware of the impact of harm upon his or her child. Inquiry about the parent's perception of the child's medical problems, academic performance, and socialization skills may provoke a defensive stance, intense sadness, or an emotional breakdown from the parent, altering the clinical interview. Parents in early substance abuse recovery may be suffering from depressive symptoms, or realize that their behaviors have negatively affected their children. The evaluator must gauge the parent's emotional resilience with the time constraints of the clinical interview, noting potential recommendations for treatment services. Treatment recommendations should address abstinence (with or without random urinalysis testing), short-term therapy needs, and the examination of possible underlying conditions supportive of substance abuse. For instance, the drug user's social environment, maintenance of abstinence, and prevention methods for triggers of potential substance abuse relapse should be integrated within the treatment recommendations.

Mental Disorders and Treatment Recommendations

Empirical evidence suggests that parenting abilities are diminished when mental disorders remain untreated (Otto et al., 2003). Depression is likely to influence the quality and effectiveness of caregiving abilities. Research findings reveal that children of parents diagnosed with major affective disorders are up to five times more likely to develop psychopathology compared to children of nondepressed parents (Otto et al.). Affective disorders do not cause poor parenting; however, parents may display unsupportiveness, inattentiveness, and criticalness toward their children.

Studies suggest a relationship between parents diagnosed with antisocial personality traits and dysfunctions occurring during their childhood (Otto et al., 2003). Children living with parents who consistently violate social codes often display adjustment problems related to aggression and peer socialization, often with externalized behaviors. In a longitudinal study conducted by Farrington (2000), 411 high-risk males were followed up from the ages of 8–10 years through middle adulthood. Sixty percent of the males met the personality measurements for antisocial personality disorder by the time they reached

32 years of age. High risk factors included criminal convictions, low intelligence scores, poor child rearing, and disruption within the familial environment. Zuckerman (1999) reported that child abuse and child neglect doubled the risk of being diagnosed with antisocial personality disorder. Genetics and inadequate familial socialization may contribute toward the relationship between adult antisocial personalities and the subsequent effect upon their children (Otto et al.; Zuckerman).

Domestic Violence and Treatment Recommendations

Domestic violence is a critical area that must be investigated during the assessment. Research on intrafamilial aggression reveals children witnessing domestic violence are at high risk for child abuse (Bow and Boxer, 2003). In addition, researcher Austin (2000) reported that parents in domestic violent relationships were uncooperative when compared to nonviolent parents. It is conceivable that a parent may admit to domestic violence, as either a perpetrator or victim, during the clinical interview without a prior report of the violence to their child protection case manager or other service treatment providers. Understanding the dynamics of domestic violence is essential when performing a CMPA. The forensic evaluator must investigate male-instigated domestic violence, female-instigated domestic violence, and bidirectional domestic violence. Research findings on child custody evaluations of domestic violence allegations suggested that 51% were male initiated, 11% were female initiated, and 38% consisted of combined bidirectional violence (Bow and Boxer). Other researchers suggested (Geffner et al., 2006) mutual abuse, or bidirectional violence, was less common than male-initiated violence.

Recommendations for active domestic violence include psychoeducational and behavioral treatment models for the perpetrator and victim (Almeida and Durkin, 1999). Individual therapy may be warranted depending on contextual factors, such as mental illness and affective disorders. Family therapy and mediation services are not appropriate recommendations for couples who are actively violent and involved in child maltreatment cases. Victims frequently feel unsafe during couples' therapy and are unable to disclose incidents of domestic violence when the perpetrators are present. Parents who previously engaged in domestic violence may have unresolved issues surrounding their role as perpetrator or victim. Recommendations should include interventions specifically targeted to increase parental skills in anger management, communication, and understanding the impact upon the children of previous violent behaviors.

Child–Parent Visitation Recommendations

Children removed from the family home experience a unique type of trauma that may go unnoticed by service providers involved in the case. Nocturnal enuresis, aggression, depression, anxiety, and poor academic performance are common behaviors when a child is initially placed in foster care. The evaluator must assess all facets of the visitation arrangement between the child and parent, including collateral contact with the child's service providers, when available. Parental visitation is complex, with intertwining dynamics between parent, child, foster parent, and service providers.

The evaluator should be cautious when considering parental visitations. Confusion and secondary (e.g., logistical) issues frequently surround visitation. Children may become angry toward the parents after remaining in foster care for a significant period. The child may attempt to run away before a parental visit occurs, react negatively during a visit, or display destructive behaviors after a visit. Alternatively, a child may display depressive symptoms due to the separation. Children's behaviors often deteriorate upon return from their parental visit. In addition, substance-abusing parents often discuss their frustration around visitation schedules, including the infrequency of visitation with their children.

There are numerous types of visitation, including supervised visitation, unsupervised visitation at a public site for a limited time span, and unsupervised overnight visitation. Supervised visitation is often initiated when parents are active substance users, there is a threat of child abduction, or the child's safety is placed at risk if alone with a parent. Unsupervised overnight visitation often occurs when the parent has displayed satisfactory progress toward change and risks of future maltreatment have diminished.

The CMPA recommendation section represents the final summation of the report. An effective recommendations section offers practical directives of interventions, services, and referral evaluations that are designed to assist the parent in diminishing the risk factors that brought the family to the crisis point of child protection involvement. Ideally, recommendations are written in understandable language allowing service providers and parents direction without misinterpretation.

Professional Insight

Given the multitude of data points considered while evaluating a parent's readiness for reunification, the clinician must remain objective. The forensic evaluator is required to absorb the available information and effectively report findings regarding parental fitness. Personal bias can become a barrier as the interpretation of test data, clinical interview, collateral data sources, and historical information must be filtered through the evaluator's personal perspectives, biases, and experiences. At first, this process may seem obvious as the CMPA hinges on objective opinion, but evaluators must know themselves to identify their own human biases.

For example, the parent might trigger a recollection of an abusive client that the evaluator had previously discharged from treatment services. Alternatively, the facts of the case (e.g., domestic violence, child sexual abuse) might cause a visceral reaction by the evaluator. The parent may have similar characteristics of a friend or family member. In addition, the parent's socioeconomic status, lifestyle, or cultural background may also influence the evaluator's objectivity. Forensic evaluators have human reactions, and knowledge of their biases will help sustain the quest for a neutral mindset. It is far better to acknowledge personal biases rather than to deny the existence. When a parent or the facts of the case elicit a significant reaction from the evaluator, a consultation with a colleague or a referral to another evaluator is recommended.

In summary, when writing a CMPA, the evaluator has several fundamental points to consider. A clear understanding of the referral question will establish the crux of the assessment. Collateral information is a rich source of supporting information. Third-party interviews assist the evaluator's understanding the different facets of the case's complexity. Psychometric testing adds to the evaluation's database, and important ethnic racial differences must be considered while interpreting test protocols. Finally, the evaluator is advised to develop personal awareness toward his or her own human biases to circumvent possible compromise in the objectivity of the report. The CMPA is a forensic document that expresses an opinion; the findings are frequently referenced in legal proceedings. The next section offers practical guidelines for expert court testimony.

Expert Witness Testimony

Child maltreatment cases are usually civil cases and typically heard in a specialized court, such as family court. The evaluator's expert testimony is requested when the court or attorney seeks additional information from the evaluator. The expert may testify on clarification points on the CMPA or expand on the assessment's scope. The content of expert testimony is required to rest on facts or data in the particular case in which the expert bases an opinion (Federal Rules of Evidence for United States Courts and Magistrates, 1987). The expert witness should (a) remain unbiased prior to the development of the assessment, (b) synthesize and formulate an opinion based on all facets of available data, rather than reporting individual findings, and (c) speak clearly and concisely (Heilbrun, 2001).

Expert testimony in these cases must also be based on the findings of the CMPA. The testifying expert must be able to explain the etiology of the child maltreatment and have an understanding of the circumstances leading to the maltreatment. The expert must be knowledgeable in the psychological treatment of child maltreatment and the interventions designed to mitigate inappropriate parental behaviors. Factors such as mental illness, mental retardation, substance abuse, and criminogenic factors may complicate the CMPA.

Stern (1997) explained that the quality of the decisions made by judges and jurors are largely influenced by the expert witnesses. Thus, it is the job of the expert witness to educate and convince the fact finders to adopt his or her position. When considering the art of testifying, there is no "best" way, as each case is unique. Facts of the case, attorney style, and opposing experts produce certain conditional settings for testimony. Brief responses, such as "yes" or "no" may be an appropriate strategy in some settings, while similar responses may not be suitable in other situations. The following are general guidelines for expert witness testimony.

An effective expert witness must listen closely to the questions asked and avoid common mistakes (Stern, 1997). One common error is an attempt to answer a question that the evaluator did not completely understand. If an attorney asks a question that is not understood, the evaluator should request either clarification or rephrasing of the question. This technique is also effective when an attorney asks a question that is actually several questions rolled into one inquiry. Another common mistake is to allow the attorney to disorient, fluster, or disrupt the evaluator's concentration. This can be done by using physical ploys or tactics such as standing too close, speaking rapidly, and misquoting the expert's prior testimony. The evaluator may request that the attorney reword the question, slow his or her speech, or move away from the evaluator.

During cross-examination, the opposing council will attempt to control the witness. One common strategy is rapid-fire questioning in an attempt to elicit yes or no responses thereby limiting the content of the testimony. Brief responses permit the attorney to educate the fact finders, lessening the credibility of the evaluator. Stern (1997) suggested that the evaluator respond in full statements, not with simple "yes" and "no" answers. A complete answer allows the evaluator to educate the fact finder, rather than offering the opportunity to the opposing counsel. Alternatively, if the opposing counsel is hostile toward the evaluator, less informative answers may be a more fitting response.

Heilbrun (2001) recognized two fundamental aspects of legal communication. The first aspect is similar to psychological evaluation report writing: testimony must be substantively strong and stylistically effective. Accordingly, substantively weak, yet stylistically strong testimony may represent (a) inadequate information about forensic assessment principles, (b) testimony that is an "opinion for hire," or (c) a predetermined opinion of the expert regarding the case before gathering information. In contrast, testimony that is substantively strong but presented ineffectively will be unpersuasive regardless of whether the data were accurate. Finally, testimony that is neither substantively strong nor stylistically effective will likely be viewed as ineffectual testimony.

Brodsky (1991) described 62 maxims for the expert witness and discussed common problems of expert testifying. These constructive resolutions assist evaluators in presenting expert opinions within an adversarial setting. Brodsky suggested that an expert witness would increase the effectiveness of their testimony if the answers are personalized, the format is varied, and narratives are used during testimony. Brodsky's substantive principles describe how to strengthen the relationship between the experts' findings and testimony. Stylistic guidelines included approaches designed to enhance the speaker's credibility, persuasiveness, and perceived professionalism. When considering testimony designed to assist a persuasive situation, Brodsky noted that witnesses talk neither too much nor too little. Further, the witness should remain calm, poised, and offer modulated answers that are neither too quick nor too slow. Ideally, the witness' flowing statements will increase the testifier's believability. Researchers (Melton et al., 1997; Stern, 1997) agreed that the testifier's speech patterns should be controlled and include pausing before answering questions, limiting responses to a specific question, and using clear, evenly modulated speech.

Brodsky (1991) discussed stylistic errors that increase ineffective testimony. The witness' style in answering the opposing attorney's questions will influence the trier of fact. For example, ineffective witnesses are frequently overly talkative, adopt an angry or antagonistic presentation toward the opposing attorney, or become overly dramatic. Certain answer patterns also negatively affect the testifier, including over qualifying the response, responding in an overly slow manner, and using words unfamiliar to the trier of fact. The expert's rhythm of speech is also important. O'Barr (1978) found that speech qualifiers such as "uh," "er," or "maybe" and speech intensifiers such as "most certainly" are less persuasive than direct responses. To minimize ineffective testimony, the evaluator should speak directly to the jury in a fluid conversational tone, and be confident in their presentation (Heilbrun, 2001; Stern, 1997).

In some cases, the trier of fact will ask the evaluator to answer the legal question at hand. An example of this tact would be the question, "Doctor, was the defendant insane at the time of his offense?" This query asks the evaluator to answer a legal question: "Was the person insane?" Although there may be much evidence to suggest a mental status consistent of the legal definition of insane, the evaluator is put on the spot. Directly answering a legal question should be avoided (Heilbrun, 2001). Instead, the evaluator could take the opportunity to describe pertinent psychological data or capacities that would help the trier of fact make a legal decision. However, many courts regularly request this information as part of the evaluator's findings.

The Ethical Principles of Psychologists and Code of Conduct (American Psychological Association, 2002) offers no specific guidance on the issue. In addition, *The Specialty Guidelines for Forensic Psychologists* (Committee on Ethical Guidelines for Forensic Psychologists, 1991) does not clarify the issue but instead suggests that the forensic psychologist be prepared to explain the distinction between the differences between the facts of the case and their opinions and conclusions:

> Forensic psychologists are aware that their essential role as expert to the court is to assist the trier of fact to understand the evidence or to determine a fact in issue. In offering expert evidence, they are aware that their own professional observations, inferences, and conclusions must be distinguished from legal facts, opinions, and conclusion. Forensic psychologists are prepared to explain the relationship between their expert testimony and the legal issue and facts of an instant case. (Committee on Ethical Guidelines for Forensic Psychologists, 1991)

The expert could assist the trier of fact by describing the pertinent psychological data related to the case, rather than answer a direct legal question (Heilbrun, 2001).

Ethical Guidelines for a Child Maltreatment Parental Assessment

The following section reviews applied ethics within the specific context of forensic evaluation of CMPA and returning the child to their parent's custody or initiation of visitation. Prior to addressing the specifics in parental maltreatment and child custodial matters, the evaluator must be first trained in forensic psychology. The evaluator is required to be knowledgeable with the interface between the legal and psychological domains (American Psychological Association, 2002; Goldstein and Weiner, 2003; Melton et. al., 1997). The evaluator is advised to be expert in the following areas: (a) training in forensic reports and interviewing; (b) basic understanding of diagnostic principles; and (c) clinical training in substance abuse, domestic violence, and child maltreatment. This knowledge is then applied to psychological evaluations with the specific population (American Psychological Association Committee on Professional Practice and Standards, 1998) and the guidelines for forensic psychologists (Committee on Ethical Guidelines for Forensic Psychologists, 1991). Further, evaluators must have comprehensive mastery of the ethical principles and conduct codes of the psychological field (American Psychological Association), guidelines and standards for psychological testing (American Educational Research Association, American Psychological Association, and National Council on Measurement in Education, 1999), and the guidelines for computer-based test interpretations (American Psychological Association, 1986). The following sections have been identified as common ethical situations that arise when conducting a CMPA.

Dual Relationships

The evaluator may experience conflicts between overlapping professional roles. As an example, rural community psychologists in private practice serve multifaceted roles and often consider performing forensic evaluations as a supplement to their services. Balancing these dual roles requires the psychologist to clearly understand the differences between therapeutic and forensic perspectives. Confusion or uncertainty with these distinctions can lead the psychologist onto the slippery slope toward unethical practice. Because of the low population of psychologists in rural areas, the likelihood of dual relationships increases because the psychologist serves multiple roles, such as therapist, clinical supervisor, and evaluator. In addition, the presenting forensic population could be later referred for psychological treatment.

Privacy

The evaluator must be aware of the legal proceedings in which the CMPA is used. Frequently, the assessment is read by the parents, child protection case managers, prosecutors, defense attorneys, and the family court judge. Child maltreatment cases have specific confidentiality issues involving invasion of privacy issues (Groth-Marnat, 2003) such as the release of the CMPA to third parties or treatment providers who are not involved in the case, or court subpoenas for family court hearings, such as termination of parental rights.

Informed consent from the parent prior to the onset of a CMPA is mandatory. The parent must clearly understand the limits of confidentiality in a forensic evaluation, that the assessment will not be held in confidence, and that the evaluation meeting is not a therapy session. The parent is to be informed that the clinical interview may focus on areas that the parent may not want to discuss.

Misconceptions of the Child Maltreatment Parental Assessment

The clinical interview allows the evaluator to clarify any misconceptions the parent may have about the CMPA. Common misconceptions include fears that the evaluator will recommend that the child be permanently removed from the parental home, or apprehension that their answers will be used to discredit or misrepresent their parenting abilities. Parents sometimes enter the clinical interview with suspiciousness, nervousness, and resistance. Parents may be fearful that the evaluator will judge them as "bad parents." An ethical approach requires clear explanation of the intent and purpose of the assessment. It is the evaluator's responsibility to explain to the parent that the CMPA will become a legal document, will be added to the case file, and may likely be submitted as a legal document for subsequent court hearings.

Referral Agencies and Ethical Dilemmas

The referral question and the motivation behind the referral request may differ. The forensic evaluator is advised to clearly understand the motivation behind the referral request. Otherwise, the evaluator may be drawn into areas beyond the scope of the assessment. As an example, the referral source may request a CMPA with consideration of the parental fitness of a nonreferred parent.

Child protection agencies use CMPAs in two ways. First, the assessment is used to ascertain a comprehensive psychological construct of the parent. Second, the assessment is used to help establish what is in the best interest of the child. This duality forces the assessment to incorporate both clinical and forensic assessment techniques. Clinical assessments include measurement of emotional states, personality traits, and intelligence, whereas forensic assessments include the investigation of the parent–child relationship and analysis of state and trait behaviors (Weissman and DeBow, 2003).

Other psychologists may have previously evaluated parents involved with a child protection agency over several years. Child protection case managers often submit copies of these evaluations to the evaluator prior to the parental clinical interview. Situations may occur when the case manager intentionally limits the evaluator's access to previous psychological reports. Reasons may include possible contamination of the current psychological assessment or disagreements over the previous assessment's findings. The evaluator must determine whether the restricted access is detrimental to the analysis and interpretation of the current assessment.

CMPAs may have grave effects on the parent, immediate family, and extended family members. Termination of parental rights is a life-altering decision that will permanently affect the child and family. Maintaining objectivity is paramount in conducting an ethical CMPA (American Psychological Association Committee on Professional Practice and Standards, 1998). *The Guidelines in Child Protection Matters* (American Psychological Association Committee on Professional Practice and Standards) addresses the seriousness of objectivity in the psychological findings of the CMPAs.

The evaluation must be written clearly in a language understandable to all readers. The *APA Ethics Code* prescribes that psychologists explain their reports using understandable language and written at the level of the intended audience (American Psychological Association, 2002). Therefore, accuracy, honesty, and candidness are the basis of the formulation of ethical expert opinions in child maltreatment cases. Evaluators must communicate their findings in a writing style that promotes understanding and avoids deception, given the particular characteristics, roles, and abilities of various recipients of the work product.

Future Directions

Although the results of a CMPA are disbursed to the family court, social agencies, and parents, there is limited inquiry regarding the effectiveness of the assessment or recommendations within the treatment section. The authors recommend future research investigating the factors that indicate successful reunification, as well as evaluate the efficacy of treatments that assist in reaching reunification between parent and child.

On a local level, treatment outcomes are unknown and a clearer understanding of what helps children and families overcome child abuse or neglect is necessary to evaluate the effectiveness of CMPAs. The first step identifies coordination of a comprehensive database, including documentation of the clientele who received social services, treatment services, and the antecedent behaviors (e.g., drug abuse, domestic disputes) that triggered state intervention with the family. The second step is to understand the typology of (a) families who were reunified and (b) families whose children were placed in permanent foster placement. The third step is to identify successful treatment modalities.

On a state level, information about the outcomes of placement data among child protection agencies should be part of a collective database to assist in a statewide and national case tracking system. State child protection agencies and outside contract social service agencies would benefit from sharing the information gathered through an interstate database. The question "What works?" is a very provocative notion, and improved interagency and intraagency data sharing could assist in exploring answers that would assist child maltreatment and the families.

The CMPA is a document of particular information gathered from multiple domains, and used by clinicians and court representatives to understand the particular parental dynamics leading to the child maltreatment in a case. Because of the unique nature of each family intervention, the assessing professional is challenged to provide a systematic approach to the assessment. A structured assessment protocol is required, due to the multidimensional nature of a comprehensive parental assessment and the amount of collateral information gathering data. A structure can assist the evaluator in organizing various clinical interview strategies and minimize forgotten areas discovered only after the one-time interview. In addition, the guidelines for forensic psychologists (Committee on Ethical Guidelines for Forensic Psychologists, 1991) is currently under revision and may offer additional guidance regarding the issue of discussing psychological data to assist the court with legal decisions.

Conclusion

Development of a comprehensive CMPA is a complex undertaking. Legal statutes involve child, parent, and state interests. Individual and familial interactions are impacted by family member presence and living situation. Parental behaviors have brought on the attention of social service providers and the court system. Social agencies minister to the families and present gathered evidence to the family court to assist in the custodial decision. Experts often testify to explain their work, or to offer information to the court. Conducting, administering, and formulating a competent and ethical document requires the forensic evaluator address the following: (a) specific training in forensics, (b) knowledge of the population being evaluated, (c) understanding of the scope of this specialty's work, (d) and the ability to effectively communicate, in written and verbal context, the assessment's findings. Privacy issues, including informed consent, are to be clearly explained during the initial contact with the parent. The evaluator must ensure the parent understands the evaluation's purpose and who may eventually read the document.

Specific components of a CMPA include a clinical interview, review of collateral material, third-party interviews, and psychological testing. As psychological testing is an important component of the CMPA, the evaluator is advised to analyze the psychometric data of the instruments used, including the validity, reliability, and standardized norms for racial and cultural relevance. A cohesive CMPA will include integrating the data sources to offer comprehensive and practical case recommendations.

References

Abidin, R. (1995). *Parenting Stress Index: Professional Manual* (3rd ed.). Lutz, FL: Psychological Assessment Resources.

Acton, R., and During, S. (1992). Preliminary results of aggression management training for aggressive parents. *Journal of Interpersonal Violence*, 7, pp. 410–417.

Alberta Alcohol and Drug Abuse Commission. (2001). Frequently asked questions. *AADAC information on amphetamines and methamphetamines*. Retrieved May 26, 2003, from http://www.crystalrecovery.com/Pages/AADACinfoMA.html.

Almeida, R., and Durkin, T. (1999). The cultural context model: Therapy for couples with domestic violence. *Journal of Marriage and Family Therapy*, 25, pp. 33–324.

American Educational Research Association, American Psychological Association, and National Council on Measurement in Education. (1999). *Standards for Educational and Psychological Testing*. Washington, DC: Author.

American Psychological Association (1986). *American Psychological Association Guidelines for Computer-Based Tests and Interpretations*. Washington, DC: Author.

American Psychological Association. (2002). *Ethical Principles of Psychologists and Code of Conduct.* Washington, DC: Author. Retrieved June 22, 2006, from http://www.apa.org/ethics/code2002.html.

American Psychological Association Committee on Professional Practice and Standards. (1998). *Guidelines for Psychological Evaluations in Child Protection Matters.* Washington, DC: American Psychological Association. Retrieved June 22, 2006, from http://www.apa.org/practice/childprotection.html.

Austin, A. (2004). Alcohol, tobacco, other drug use, and violent behavior among Native Hawaiians; ethnic pride and resilience. *Substance Use and Misuse,* 39(5), pp. 721–746.

Austin, W. G. (2000). Assessing credibility in allegations of marital violence and the high conflict, child custody case. *Family and Conciliation Courts Review,* 38, pp. 462–477.

Beeman, S., Hagemeister, A., and Edleson, J. (2001). Case assessment and service receipt in families experiencing both child maltreatment and woman battering. *Journal of Interpersonal Violence,* 16(5), pp. 437–458.

Bow, J. N., and Boxer, P. (2003). Assessing allegations of domestic violence and child custody evaluations. *Journal of Interpersonal Violence,* 18(12), pp. 1394–1410.

Bricklin, B. (1990). *Parent Awareness Skills Survey Manual.* Philadelphia, PA: Village Publishing Company.

Bricklin, B., and Elliot, G. (1991). *Parent Perception of Child Profile Manual.* Philadelphia, PA: Village Publishing Company.

Brodsky, S. L. (1991). *Testifying in Court: Guidelines and Maxims for the Expert Witness.* Washington, DC: American Psychological Association.

Buros Institute of Mental Measurements. (2006). *Mental Measurements Yearbook.* Lincoln, NE: Author.

Butcher, J. N., and Williams, C. L. (2000). *Essentials of MMPI-2 and MMPI-A Interpretation* (2nd ed.). Minneapolis, MN: University of Minnesota Press.

Child Welfare League of America. (1997). *Alcohol and other drug survey of child welfare agencies.* Retrieved August 7, 2005, from http://www.cwla.org/programs/chemical/1997stateaodsurvey.html.

Choy, S. (1993). The psychological perspective. In F. F. Untalan and C. S. Mills (Eds.), *Interdisciplinary Perspectives in Child Abuse and Neglect* (p. 57). New York: Praeger.

Cohen, R. J., and Swerdlik, M. E. (2002). Psychological testing and assessment: An introduction to test and measurement (5th ed.). MA: McGraw-Hill Companies.

Committee on Ethical Guidelines for Forensic Psychologists. (1991). Specialty guidelines for forensic psychologists. *Law and Human Behavior,* 15(6), pp. 655–665.

Daro, D. G. (1995). *Current Trends in Child Abuse Reporting and Fatalities: NCPCA's 1995 Annual Fifty-State Survey.* New York: American Professional Society on the Abuse of Children.

Dinwiddie, S., and Bucholz, K. (1993). Psychiatric diagnoses of self-reported child abusers. *Child Abuse and Neglect,* 17(4), pp. 465–476.

Faller, K. C., and Bellamy, C. D. (2000). *Mental health problems and child maltreatment.* Retrieved June 6, 2006 from www.ssw.umich.edu/icwtp/mentalHealth/d-mhpar.pdf.

Famularo, R., Kinscherff, R., and Fenton, T. (1992). Psychiatric diagnoses of abusive mothers: A preliminary report. *Journal of Nervous and Mental Disorders,* 180(10), pp. 658–661. Retrieved August 18, 2005, from http://www.ncbi.nlm.nih.gov/entrez/query.fcgi?cmd=Retrieve&db=PubMed&list_uids=1.

Farrington, D. P. (2000). Psychosocial predictors of adult antisocial personality and adult convictions. *Behavioral Sciences and the Law,* 18(5), pp. 605–622. Retrieved June 24, 2006 from http://www.ncbi.nlm.nih.gov/entrez/query.fcgi?cmd=Retrieve&db=PubMed&list_.

Federal Rules of Evidence for United States Courts and Magistrates. (1987). *Federal rules of evidence for United States Courts and Magistrates effective July 1, 1975 as amended to March 2, 1987.* St. Paul, MN: West Publishing Company.

Feld, B. C. (1995). Violent youth and public policy: A case study of juvenile justice law reform. *Minnesota Law Review*, 79, pp. 965–1099.

Geffner, R., Geis, K., and Aranda, B. (2006). Family violence allegations in child custody evaluations: The overlap of family and forensic psychology. *The Family Psychologist, Bulletin of the Division of Family Psychology*, 22(2), pp. 9–13. Retrieved September 29, 2006, from www.apa.org/divisions/div43/news/NewsArchives/Spr06TFP.pdf.

Goldstein A. M., and Weiner, I. B. (2003). *Handbook of Psychology: Volume II, Forensic Psychology.* Hoboken, NJ: John Wiley & Sons.

Goodwin, C. L. (2004). Statement of Charles L. Goodwin, Special Agent in Charge—Honolulu Division; Before the House Government Reform Subcommittee on Criminal Justice, Drug Policy, and Human Resources. August 2, 2004. Retrieved June 16, 2006, from http://www.fbi.gov/congress/congress04/goodwin080204.htm.

Graham, J. R. (2000). *MMPI-2: Assessing Personality and Psychopathology* (3rd ed.). New York: Oxford University Press.

Green, R. L. (1987). Ethnicity and MMPI performance: A review. *Journal of Consulting and Clinical Psychology*, 55, pp. 497–512.

Grisso, T. (2003). *Evaluating Competences: Forensic Assessments and Instruments* (2nd ed.) New York: Kluwer Academic Plenum Publishers.

Groth-Marnat, G. (2003). *Handbook of Psychological Assessment* (4th ed.). Hoboken, NJ: John Wiley & Sons.

Haight, W., Jacobsen, T., Black, J., Kingery, L., Sheridan, K., and Mulder, C. (2005). "In these bleak days": Parent methamphetamine abuse and child welfare in the rural Midwest. *Children and Youth Services Review*, 27(8), pp. 949–971.

Hall, H. V. (1996). Overview of lethal violence. In H. V. Hall (Ed.), *Lethal Violence 2000: A Sourcebook on Fatal Domestic, Acquaintance and Stranger Aggression* (pp. 1–52). Kamuela, HI: Pacific Institute for the Study of Conflict and Aggression.

Hartley, C. (2002). The co-occurrence of child maltreatment and domestic violence: Examining both neglect and physical abuse. *Child Maltreatment*, 7(4), pp. 349–358.

Hathaway, S. R., and McKinley, J. C. (1989). *Minnesota Multiphasic Personality Inventory-2.* Minneapolis, MN: University of Minnesota Press.

Heilbrun, K. (2001) *Principles of Forensic Mental Health Assessment.* New York: Kluwer Academic Plenum Publishers.

Houry, D., Feldhaus, K., Perry, B., Abbott, J., Lowenstein, S., Al-Bataa-De-Montero, S. et al. (2004). A positive domestic violence screen predicts future domestic violence. *Journal of Interpersonal Violence*, 19(9), pp. 955–966.

Jefferson, D. J., Shenfeld, H., Murr, A., Campo-Flores, A., Childress, S., Skipp, C. et al. (2005). America's most dangerous drug. *Newsweek*, 146(6), pp. 40–48.

Kelleher, K., Chaffin, M., Hollenberg, E., and Fischer, E. (1994). Alcohol and drug disorders among physically abusive and neglectful parents in a community-based sample. *American Journal of Public Health*, 84(10), pp. 1586–1590.

Lichtenberger, E. O., Mather, N., Kaufman, N. L., and Kaufman, A. S. (2004). *Essentials of Assessment Report Writing.* NJ: John Wiley & Sons.

Mash, E., Johnston, C., and Kovitz, K. (1983). A comparison of the mother-child interactions of physically abused and non-abused children during play and task situations. *Journal of Clinical Child Psychology*, 12, pp. 337–346.

Melton, G., Petrila, J., Poythress, N., and Slobogin, C. (1997). *Psychological Evaluations for the Courts: A Handbook for Mental Health Professionals and Lawyers* (2nd ed.). New York: Guilford Press.

Milner, J. (1986). *The Child Abuse Potential Inventory: Manual* (2nd ed.). Webster, NC: Psytec Corporation.

Milner, J. (1994). Assessing physical child abuse risk: The Child Abuse Potential Inventory. *Clinical Psychology Review,* 14, pp. 547–583.

National Clearinghouse on Child Abuse and Neglect Information and National Adoption Information Clearinghouse. (2005). *State statutes series 2005: Definitions of child abuse and neglect.* Retrieved August 17, 2005, from http://nccanch.acf.hhs.gov/general/legal/statutes/define.pdf.

National Clearinghouse on Family Violence. (2000). *Child neglect: Current definitions and models—A review of research 1993–1998.* Retrieved August 15, 2005, from http://www.phac-aspc. gc.ca/ncfv-cnivf/familyviolence/html/nfntsnegldefmod_e.html.

National Institute on Drug Abuse. (2002). *Research Report Series: Methamphetamine Abuse and Addiction* [Brochure]. Washington, DC: Author.

O'Barr, W. M. (1978). Legal assumptions about language. In L. N. Massery II (Ed.), *Psychology and Persuasion in Advocacy.* Washington, DC: The Association of Trial Lawyers of America.

Office on Child Abuse and Neglect. (2003). *Child protection in families experiencing domestic violence.* Retrieved August 14, 2005, from http://nccanch.acf.hhs.gov/pubs/usermanuals/domesticviolence /domesticabuse.

Otto, R. K., Buffington-Wollum, J. K., and Edens, J. F. (2003). Child custody evaluation. In A. M. Goldstein and I. B. Weiner (Eds.), *Handbook of Psychology: Volume 11 Forensic Psychology* (pp. 179–208). Hoboken, NJ: John Wiley & Sons.

Pamenter, D. (2002). *Crystal Meth: Frequently asked questions on treatment.* Retrieved May 3, 2003, from http://www.crystalrecovery.com/FAQ/FAQ2l.html.

Phillips, S., Barth, R., Burns, B., and Wagner, R. H. (2004). Parental arrest and children involved with child welfare services agencies. *American Journal of Orthopsychiatry,* 74(2), pp. 174–186.

Poirier, J. (2000). Violence in the family. In H. V. Hall (Ed.), *Lethal Violence 2000: A Sourcebook on Fatal Domestic, Acquaintance and Stranger Aggression* (pp. 259–292). Kamuela, HI: Pacific Institute for the Study of Conflict and Aggression.

Rawson, R. A. (1999). *Methamphetamine and Cocaine.* Beverly Hills, CA: The Matrix Center Incorporated.

State of Hawaii. (2000). Hawaii revised statutes (Chapter 587). *Child Protective Act.* Retrieved August 16, 2005, from http://www.capitol.hawaii.gov/hrscurrent/Vol12_Ch0501-0588/HRS0587/HRS_0587-.htm.

State of Hawaii. (2003). *A statistical report on child abuse and neglect in Hawaii.* Retrieved August 14, 2005, from http://ehawaii.gov.

State of Hawaii. (2004). *Guide to Child Welfare Services* [Brochure]. Oahu, Hawaii: State of Hawaii Department of Human Services. Retrieved August 17, 2005, from http://www.hawaii.gov/dhs/A%20Guide%20To%20Child%20Welfare%20Services/A%20GUIDE%20TO%20CHILD%20WELFARE%20SERVICES%20-%20BIG%20ISLAND.pdf.

Stern, P. (1997) *Preparing and Presenting Expert Testimony in Child Abuse Litigation.* Thousand Oaks, CA: Sage Publications.

Stover, C. S. (2005). Domestic violence research: What have we learned and where do we go from here? *Journal of Interpersonal Violence,* 20, pp. 448–454.

Straus, M., and Gelles, R. (1990). How violent are American families? Estimates from the national family violence resurvey and other studies. *Physical Violence in American Families.* New Brunswick, NJ: Transaction.

Trocmé, N., MacLaurin, B., Fallon, B., Daciuk, J., Bilingsley, D., Tourigny, M., Mayer, M., Wright, J., Barter, K., Burford, G., Hornick, J., Sullivan, R., and McKenzie, B. (2001). *Canadian Incidence Study of Reported Child Abuse and Neglect: Final Report.* Ottawa, ON: Minister of Public Works and Government Services Canada.

United States Department of Health and Human Services, and Gaudin, J. (1993). *Child neglect: A guide for intervention* [User manual series]. Retrieved August 17, 2005, from http://nccanch. acf.hhs.gov/pubs/usermanuals/neglect/neglectc.cfm.

United States Department of Health and Human Services. (2004). *The drug and alcohol services information (DASIS) report: Smoked methamphetamine/amphetamines 1992–2002* [Brochure]. Arlington, VA: Substance Abuse and Mental Health Service Administration.

Weissman, H. N., and DeBow, D. M. (2003). Ethical principles and professional competencies. In A. M. Goldstein and I. B. Weiner (Eds.), *Handbook of Psychology: Volume 11 Forensic Psychology* (pp. 33–53). Hoboken, NJ: John Wiley & Sons, Inc.

World Health Organization. (1999). *Child abuse and neglect.* Retrieved August 17, 2005, from http://www.who.int/violence_injury_prevention/violence/neglect/en/print.html.

Yanagida, E., and Ching, J. (1993). MMPI profiles of child abusers. *Journal of Clinical Psychology*, 49(4), pp. 569–576.

Zuckerman, M. (1999). *Vulnerability to Psychopathology: Psycho-Social Model.* Washington, DC: American Psychological Association.

Zweben, J., Cohen, J., Christian, D., Galloway, G., Salinardi, M., Parent, D., and Iguchi M. (2004). Psychiatric symptoms in methamphetamine users. *The American Journal on Addiction*, 13(2), pp. 181–190.

Glossary

A

A posteriori: "From the effect to the cause"; from what comes after. Denotes an argument based on experience or observation.

A priori: "From the cause to the effect"; from what goes before. Denotes an argument that posits a general principle or admitted truth as a cause and deduces from it the effect that must necessarily follow.

Ab initio: "From the first act"; from the beginning, referring to the validity of statutes and so forth. In contrast to *ex post facto.*

Abnormal: Maladaptive behavior detrimental to the individual and/or the group.

Abrogate: To cancel annul or destroy; to repeal a former law by a legislative act or by usage.

Absence seizures: Petit mal seizures in children, shown by brief altered states of consciousness.

Absolute refractory phase: A period of complete unresponsiveness.

Acalculia: Impaired calculation abilities, more often associated with left parietal or occipital lesions.

Acapnia: A marked diminution in the amount of carbon dioxide in the blood.

Acceptance: An agreement to the act or proposal of another person.

Acetone bodies: Acetoacetic acid, β-hydroxybutyric acid, and acetone; found in blood and urine in increased amounts whenever too much fat in proportion to carbohydrate is being oxidized. Also called ketone bodies.

Acetylcholine (ACh): One of the best-known synaptic transmitters. Acetylcholine acts as an excitatory transmitter at synapses between motor nerves and skeletal muscles but as an inhibitory transmitter between vagus nerve and heart muscle.

Acetylcholinesterase (AChE): An enzyme that inactivates the neurotransmitter acetylcholine, thus halting its effects.

Achromatopsia: Impaired perception of colors due to cerebral dysfunction. Can be hemianopic or involve both visual fields.

Acidosis: Diminution in the reserve supply of fixed bases (especially sodium) in the blood.

Acquit: To set free or release from an obligation, burden, or accusation; to certify legally the innocence of a person charged with a crime.

Action: A formal proceeding or complaint brought within the jurisdiction of a court to enforce any right.

Action potential: Nerve impulse that flows along the membrane of the neuron. The membrane is receptive to potassium ions in the resting state and sodium ions when excited. The reversal in permeability causes the impulse.

Actuarial approach: Application of probability statistics to human behavior, as in insurance.

Actus reus: "Guilty act"; a wrongful act. As opposed to guilty, *mens rea*.

Acute alcohol hallucinosis: State of alcoholic intoxication characterized by hallucinations.

Acute paranoid disorder: Psychoses characterized by transient and changeable paranoid delusions, usually related to an identifiable stressor and transient in nature.

Acute post-traumatic stress disorder: Disorder in which symptoms develop within 6 months of an extremely traumatic experience instead of entering the recovery state.

Ad hoc: "For this"; for a special purpose or particular action.

Adaptation: Adjustment to a stimulus; also used to denote changes in the retina on exposure to different intensities of light. A progressive loss of receptor sensitivity as stimulation is maintained.

Adenohypophysis: *See* Anterior pituitary.

Adequate stimulus: The type of stimulus for which a given sense organ is particularly adapted (e.g., light energy for photoreceptors).

Adhesion: Abnormal union of two surfaces as a result of inflammation.

Adipsia: A condition in which an individual refuses to drink.

Adjustment disorder with depressed mood: Moderately severe affective disorder behaviorally identical to a dysthymic disorder or depressed phase of a cyclothymic disorder but having an identifiable, though not severe, psychosocial stressor occurring within 3 months prior to the onset of depression.

Admissible evidence: Evidence that can be received by the court or judge.

Adventitia: The outermost covering of a structure that does not form an integral part of it.

Adversarial system: A legal system in which opposing parties contend against each other by presenting arguments and information in the interest of their clients. The judge acts as a decision maker. In contrast to the inquisitorial system.

Adversary process: Having two opposing parties. In contrast to an *ex parte* proceeding.

Adverse party: A person whose interests are opposed to the interests of another party to an action.

Adverse witness: A witness who gives evidence that is prejudicial to the party examining the witness at the time. Commonly refers to a witness whose testimony is prejudicial to the party that called the witness.

Afferent fibers/traits: Data going toward the brain through neuronal pathways from the peripheral area of the central nervous system.

Affidavit: A written or printed statement of fact, made voluntarily, and signed and sworn before a person having the authority to administer such an oath (e.g., a notary public).

After potentials: Positive and negative changes of membrane potential that may follow a nerve impulse.

Aggregation theory: Proposed by Halstead, this theory holds that discrete sensory areas within the cortex are joined by a multitude of cortical connections. The aggregation produces an integration of cortical function.

Aggression: Behavior aimed at hurting or destroying someone or something.

Agitation: Marked restlessness and psychomotor excitement.

Agnosia: Defect in object recognition not due to primary sensory system dysfunction.

Agrammatism: Speech deficits characterized by language abbreviation such as omission of articles, prepositions, and inflectional forms. Language is essentially reduced to substantives.

Agraphia: Disturbances in writing skills (not motor execution). Usually seen with aphasia.

Akathisia: A general motor restlessness together with elevated inner tension, subjectively reported by the patient.

Akinesia: Inability to move due to brain dysfunction.

Alarm and mobilization reaction: First stage of the general adaptation syndrome, characterized by the mobilization of defenses to cope with a stressful situation.

Albuminuria: Presence of albumin in the urine.

Alcoholic intoxication: State reached when alcohol content of the blood reaches or exceeds a legally prescribed level (0.08 to 0.1% or above in many jurisdictions).

Alcoholism: Dependence on alcohol to the extent that it seriously interferes with life adjustment.

Aldosterone: A mineralocorticoid hormone that helps maintain homeostasis in the concentrations of ions in blood and extracellular fluid.

Alexia: Inability to read due to brain dysfunction. Refers to total loss of ability to read due to a brain lesion, typically located in the posterior cerebral cortex.

Alexia without agraphia: Inability to read in the absence of other language deficit.

Alien hand syndrome: Also termed the "Dr. Strangelove effect," intermanual conflict between the two hands is seen, with patients learning to use their "obedient" hand to control the alien hand. Contralateral supplementary motor area (SMA) and corpus collosum lesions have been implicated.

Alkalosis: Increased bicarbonate content of the blood; may be the result of ingesting large amounts of sodium bicarbonate, prolonged vomiting with loss of hydrochloric acid, or hyperventilation.

All-or-none: Refers to the fact that the amplitude of the nerve impulse is independent of stimulus magnitude. Stimuli above a certain threshold produce nerve impulses of identical magnitude (although they may vary in frequency); stimuli below this threshold do not produce nerve impulses.

Allesthesia: Sensation of being touched on the side ipsilateral to a lesion when contralateral stimulation was, in fact, presented.

Alpha motoneurons: Motoneurons that control the main contractile fibers (extrafusal fibers) of a muscle.

Alpha rhythm: A brain potential that occurs during relaxed wakefulness, especially at the back of the head; frequency 8 to 12 Hz.

Alzheimer's disease (AD):   A degenerative disease characterized by the presence of neurofibrillary tangles and senile plaques. The disease is progressive in that it starts with memory and affect problems, then goes on to speech and motor problems, and eventually to an immobile and confused bedridden status. The disease lasts from 1 to 15 years.

Amblyopia: Reduced visual acuity not caused by optical or retinal impairment.

Amenorrhea: The absence of the menses.

*Amicus curiae***:**   "Friend of the court." A person who petitions the court for permission to provide information to the court on a matter of law that is in doubt, or one who is not a party to a lawsuit but who is allowed to introduce evidence, argument, or authority to protect his or her interests.

Amnestic syndrome: Inability to remember events more than a few minutes after they have occurred coupled with the ability to recall the recent and remote past.

Amoeboid movement: Movement of a cell by extending from its surface processes of protoplasm (pseudopodia) toward which the rest of the cell flows.

Amorphosynthesis: Loss of ability to synthesize more than a few properties of a stimulus. Multiple sensory stimuli cannot be simultaneously processed. Ascribed to parietal lobe dysfunction. Damage to part of one sensory system causing an inequality in the overall cerebral system. The hemisphere receiving the decreased stimulation due to damage now needs increased input to balance the level of awareness.

Amorphous: Without definite shape or visible differentiation in structure; not crystalline.

Ampulla: A saccular dilation of a canal. An enlarged region of each semicircular canal that contains the receptor cells (hair cells) of the vestibular system.

Amusia: A temporal lobe deficit associated with inability or reduced skill in perception of tonal patterns, individual tones, singing or humming to a rhythmical pattern, or even enjoying music.

Amygdala: A structure of a limbic system associated with flight/fight and other primitive responses. Located at the base of the temporal lobe. A group of nuclei in the medial anterior part of the temporal lobe.

Analgesia: Loss of sensitivity to pain.

Anaphylactic: Increasing the susceptibility to the action of any foreign protein introduced into the body; decreasing immunity.

Anarithmetria: Impaired primary calculation skills due to brain damage. Left hemisphere lesions are implicated.

Anastomose: To open one into the other; used in connection with blood vessels, lymphatics, and nerves.

Anergia: Decreased or absent motivation or drive.

Anesthesia: Loss of sensation.

Aneurysm: A dilation or bulging of a blood vessel that fills with blood. A sac formed by the dilation of the walls of an artery and filled with blood.

Angiogram: A technique for examining brain structure in intact humans by taking radiographic images after special dyes are injected into cerebral blood vessels. Inferences about adjacent tissue can be made by examining the outline of the principal blood vessels.

Angiography: Radiography of the head subsequent to injection of a radiopaque contrast medium into a major artery. Designed to enhance images of the cerebral vasculature.

Angiotensin II: A substance produced in the blood by the action of renin; may be involved in control of thirst.

Angular gyros: A cortical convolution on the parietal lobe, associated with speech functions.

Anions: Negatively charged ions, such as protein and chloride ions.

Anomia: Inability to name objects due to brain dysfunction.

Anomic aphasia: A fluent aphasia characterized by difficulty in naming objects or words. Comprehension and articulation may be unimpaired.

Anorexic: Lacking in appetite for food.

Anosmia: Absence of the sense of smell.

Anosodiaphoria: Unconcern over, but admission of an actual neurological impairment. *See also* Anton's syndrome.

Anosognosia: Denial of those affected with neglect syndrome that their paretic extremity belongs to them. Total ignorance with denial of obvious disability. Examples include Anton's syndrome with denial of blindness, and denial of amputation, amnesia, and hemiplegia. Usually accompanied by confusion or clouding of awareness.

Anterior aphasias: Primarily indicating a left frontal lesion, these include Broca's aphasia, transcortical motor aphasia, and supplementary motor area (SMA) disturbance.

Anterior cerebral artery (ACA): One of the two major vascular networks of the frontal lobes, the ACA and its branches feed the medial aspects of the anterior portion of the brain.

Anterior pituitary: The front lobe of the pituitary gland, which secretes tropic hormones; also called adenohypophysis.

Anterograde amnesia: Inability to recall life events from the time of a previous trauma or condition. Inability to learn and poor short-term memory are associated features.

Anterograde degeneration: Loss of the distal portion of the axon resulting from injury to the axon; also called Wallerian degeneration.

Antidiuretic hormone (ADH): A hormone from the posterior pituitary that controls the removal of water from blood by the kidneys; also called vasopressin.

Antigen: Any substance that, when introduced into the blood or the tissues, incites the formation of antibodies, or reacts with them.

Anton's syndrome: *See also* Anosognosia. Adamant denial of blindness, often associated with bilateral posterior cerebral vascular accident (CVA).

Antrom: A cavity, or chamber, especially one within a bone, such as a sinus; the pyloric end of the stomach.

Apathetico-akinetico-abulic behavior: Produced by massive damage to the prefrontal areas, among others. This syndrome is characterized by low drive and reduced motor output. Ongoing behavior may be disorganized. The effector aspect of action seems to be impaired in what has been termed the "pathological inertia of existing stereotypes."

Aperture: An opening or orifice.

Aphagia: Refusal to eat, often related to damage to the lateral hypothalamus.

Aphasia: Impairment in language understanding and/or production due to brain injury.

Aphemia: A poorly articulated, slow, hypophonic, breathy speech with no syntax deficits. Usually follows initial mutism and is associated with Broca's area lesions or a subcortical undercutting of Area 44.

Apoplexy: A sudden loss of consciousness, followed by paralysis resulting from cerebral hemorrhage or blocking of an artery of the brain by an embolus or a thrombus.

Appellant: The party who appeals a decision from one court or jurisdiction to another.

Appellate court: A court having jurisdiction of appeal and review.

Appellee: The party against whom an appeal is taken in a cause; the party who has an interest opposed to the setting aside or reversing of a judgment.

Apperceptive visual agnosia: The inability to synthesize or integrate visual input. Awareness of discrete parts may be intact. Inability to perceive meaning in or visually recognize objects, due to cerebral dysfunction, most likely in posterior areas. Patients act blind but can avoid obstacles, indicating preserved ability to see.

Apraxia: Refers to impaired goal-directed motor behavior in individuals with unimpaired comprehension and primary motor skills (e.g., coordination, strength).

Apraxia of speech: Known also as verbal apraxia or Broca's aphasia. Speech movement/articulation problems may include (1) articulation errors; (2) phoneme substitution; (3) greater latency of response; (4) greater trouble with initial than subsequent phonemes; (5) no major vocal musculature problems; (6) sparse output; (7) poor melody; and (8) articulation with much effort.

Apraxic agraphia: Deficit in forming graphemes when writing to dictation or spontaneously. Lesions are in the parietal lobe contralateral to the dominant (writing) hand.

Apraxic agraphia without apraxia: Preserved oral spelling with illegible graphemes in spontaneous and dictated writing. Normal praxis is apparent, including the ability to hold and use a writing instrument. Associated with parietal lobe lesions.

Aprosodias: Deficits in the comprehension and expression of affect and emotion, traditionally associated with right hemisphere dysfunction.

Aqueduct: A canal for the conduction of a liquid; the cerebral aqueduct of Sylvius connects the third and fourth ventricles of the brain.

Arachnoid space: Allows for cerebrospinal fluid to move about the cerebrum. Filled with fibroid matter and considered one of the three layers of the meninges.

Arbitration: A method of resolving a dispute by using an impartial third party by whose decision both parties agree in advance to abide.

Arteriovenous malformation (AVM): Involving the frontal lobe preferentially and focally, AVMs are usually unrecognized until one or more episodes have occurred. Subsequent attacks by AVM hemorrhage widens the area of deficit.

Articulate: To join together so as to permit motion between parts; enunciation in words and sentences. Divided into joints.

Asphyxia: Unconsciousness owing to interference with the oxygenation of the blood.

Assertiveness training: A behavior therapy technique for helping individuals become more self-assertive in interpersonal relationships.

Association areas: Part of the cortex next to the motor or sensory cortex, involving an overlap of functions. Allows for integration of data; damage causes patterned rather than specific deficits.

Associative visual agnosia: Inability to recognize objects visually with intact ability to copy, draw, or match to sample.

Astereognosis: Inability to identify objects placed by touch in spite of intact appreciation of tactile sensation. Also called tactile agnosia.

Asthenia: Weakness.

Astrocyte: A star-shaped glial cell with numerous processes or extensions that run in all directions. Their extensions provide structural support for the brain and may isolate receptive surfaces.

Astrocytoma: Neoplastic disease arising from the astrocyte cells. Usually unencapsulated, intracerebral, and fatal.

Ataxia: Muscular coordination and balance problems due to brain dysfunction. A loss of the power of muscular coordination. Impairment in the direction, extent, and rate of muscular movement; often due to cerebellar pathology.

Athetosis: Slow, involuntary, twisting movements of the arms and legs. May occur either during movement or when at rest. Associated with lesions of the cortex and subcortex (especially globus pallidus and thalamus).

Atresia: Congenital absence, or pathologic closure, of a normal opening or passage.

Atrophy: A wasting, or diminution, in the size of a part of the body or brain.

Atropine: An alkaloid obtained from atropa belladonna; it inhibits the action of the parasympathetic division of the autonomic system.

Attention deficit disorder: Maladaptive behavior in children characterized by impulsivity, excessive motor activity, and inability to focus attention for appropriate periods of time; also called hyperactive syndrome or hyperkinetic reaction.

Attest: To bear witness to; to affirm as true or genuine.

Attribution theory: The theory of social psychology in which people explain causes of the behavior of others based on unseen or unrecognized qualities in themselves.

Auditory affective agnosia: Impaired ability to recognize or comprehend affectively intoned speech due to a cerebral disorder.

Auditory agnosia: Impaired hearing due to cerebral dysfunction with intact receptive abilities, as measured by audiometry or other means.

Auditory cortex: A region of the temporal lobe that receives input from the medial geniculate nucleus.

Auditory sound agnosia: Impaired ability to recognize nonspeech sounds due to cerebral dysfunction.

Auscultation: The act of listening for sounds within the body; employed as a diagnostic method.

Automated assessment: Psychological test interpretation by electronic or mechanical means.

Automatism: Producing without effort or delay material learned by rote in childhood for a given temporal period (e.g., alphabet, number series). Errors reflect attention, disturbances; nonacute condition–related errors may indicate significant memory dysfunction.

Autonomic nervous system: Part of the peripheral nervous system that supplies neural connections to glands and to smooth muscles of internal organs. Composed of two divisions (sympathetic and parasympathetic) that act in opposite fashions.

Autosome: Any ordinary paired chromosome as distinguished from a sex chromosome.

Autotopagnosia: Disorientation of personal space. Associated with left frontal aphasic signs. The subject is typically assessed for ability to touch, name, or imitate the examiner in touching body parts. Associated with parietal lobe damage.

Axon hillock: A cone-shaped area from which the axon originates out of the cell body Depolarization must reach a critical threshold here for the neuron to transmit a nerve impulse.

Axoplasmic streaming: The process that transports materials synthesized in the cell body to distant regions in the dendrites and axons.

Azygos: An unpaired anatomic structure; the azygos vein arises from the right ascending lumbar vein and empties into the superior vena cava.

B

Bailiff: An officer or attendant of the court who has charge of a court session in matters such as keeping order and having custody of the jury and of prisoners while in court.

Balint's syndrome: A syndrome consisting of (l) occulomotor apraxia, of focus from a near to a distant stimulus; (2) optic ataxia, shown by impaired visually guided movements; and (3) impaired visual attention in the absence of general attentional deficits, with initial random gaze until a stimulus is fixated upon.

Ballism: Uncontrollable violent tossing of the limbs due to basal ganglia dysfunction.

Ballistic: Classes of rapid muscular movements thought to be organized or programmed by the cerebellum. Contrast to ramp.

Bar: The entire body of attorneys, or the collective members of the legal profession.

Basal ganglia: Forebrain nuclei including those in the amygdala, caudate nucleus, claustrum, globus pallidus, and putamen. A group of forebrain nuclei found deep within the cerebral hemispheres.

Bases: Components of a DNA or RNA molecule. DNA contains four bases (adenine, thymine, cytosine, and guanine), a pair of which forms each rung of the molecule. The order of these bases determines the genetic information of a DNA molecule.

Basic neuroglial compartment: A level of brain organization that includes a single nerve cell with all its synaptic endings, associated glial cells surrounding extracellular space, and vascular elements.

Basilar artery: An artery formed by the fusion of the vertebral arteries; its branches supply blood to the brain stem and to posterior portions of the cerebral hemispheres.

Basilar membrane: A membrane in the cochlea containing the principal structures involved in auditory transduction.

Behavioral teratology: Impairments in behavior produced by early exposure to toxic substances.

Bench: A seat of judgment for the administration of justice; the seat occupied by the judge in court; the aggregate of the judges that comprise the court.

Berry aneurysm: A small sac formed by the dilation of the wall of a cerebral artery. The anterior portion of the circle of Willis is the site of about 90% of berry aneurysms.

Bifurcated trial: A two-phase trial in which issues are tried separately, e.g., guilt is determined in the first phase and punishment in the second, or in sanity cases, guilt is determined in the first phase and sanity in the second.

Bill of particulars: A written statement setting forth the demands for which a legal action is brought. Designed to inform the defendant of the specific information regarding the cause of action stated in the complaint.

Binocular disparity: The slight difference between the views from the two eyes, important in depth perception.

Bipolar neurons: Nerve cells with a single dendrite at one end of the nerve cell and a single axon at the other end. Found in some vertebrate sensory systems.

Bitemporal hemianopsia: Optic chiasm damage resulting in visual field loss in both temporal (as opposed to nasal) areas.

Blind spot: A place through which blood vessels enter the retina. Because there are no receptors in this region, light striking it cannot be seen.

Blindsight: Denial of recognition in the face of previous correct recognition and stimulus responses.

Blood–brain barrier: The mechanisms that make the movement of substances from capillaries into brain cells more difficult than exchanges in other body organs, thus affording the brain a greater protection from exposure to some substances found in the blood.

Body schema: Body image.

Bolus: A rounded mass of soft consistency.

***Bona*:**   Good or virtuous.

Bradycardia: Abnormal slowness of the heart or pulse.

Bradykinesia: Motor slowing.

Brain stem: Thalamus, hypothalamus, ganglia, midbrain, hindbrain, and associated structures.

Brain stem reticular formation: Part of the brain stem involved in arousal.

Brandeis brief: A form of appellate brief that includes social science principles along with legal arguments. Takes its name from late Supreme Court Associate Justice Louis D. Brandeis, who used such briefs.

Brief: A written statement prepared by the attorney arguing a case in court, including a table of relevant cases, a summary of issues and facts, and an argument of law as it supports a litigant's position.

Broca's aphasia: An expressive speech disorder with relatively intact auditory comprehension. A nonfluent speech is noticed that is slow, labored, dysarthric, incomplete, and concrete. Agrammatism consists of missing grammatical words and inflectional endings. Considered an anterior aphasia.

Broca's area: An area in the frontal region of the left hemisphere involved in the production of speech.

Brown–Peterson distractor technique: Counting backward by twos or threes upon presentation of a verbal or nonverbal stimulus. Rehearsal is prevented by the counting.

Bruit: A sound or murmur heard in auscultation, especially an abnormal one.

Buccolinguofacial apraxia: An oral apraxia affecting voluntary movements of the larynx, pharynx, tongue, lips, and related suborgans in which simple, automatic movements are intact. Commanded tasks may yield deficits (e.g., no swallowing, laughing) in the presence of noncommanded, contextual responses (e.g., swallowing food after eating, smiling). Deficit in performing voluntary buccofacial motor activities (e.g., chewing, swallowing, raising eyebrows) with intact ability to perform reflexive movements with the same muscle groups.

Buffer: Any substance that tends to lessen the change in hydrogen ion concentration, which otherwise would be produced by adding acids or bases.

Burden of proof: In the law of evidence, the duty of a party to affirmatively prove a fact in dispute. The obligation of a party to convince the trier of fact as to the truth of a claim by establishing by evidence a required degree of belief concerning a fact. In civil cases, proof must be by a preponderance of the evidence. In criminal cases, all crime elements must be proved by the government beyond a reasonable doubt. In some equity issues and more recent decisions of the Supreme Court, the standard of proof is clear and convincing evidence.

C

Calcitonin: A hormone released by the thyroid gland.

Calculus: A stone formed in any portion of the body.

Calorie: A unit of heat. A small calorie (cal.) is the standard unit and is the amount of heat required to raise 1 g of water from 15 to 16°C. The large calorie (Cal.) is used in metabolism and is the amount of heat required to raise 1 kg of water from 15 to 16°C.

Canaliculus: A small canal or channel; in bone, minute channels connect with each lacuna.

Capgras syndrome: Involves the reduplication of relatives, friends, possessions, and the like, and is often viewed as a psychiatric, as opposed to neurological, problem. The target person, almost always a close relative, is considered an imposter.

Carcinoma: A malignant tumor or cancer; a new growth made up of epithelial cells, tending to infiltrate and give rise to metastases.

Case law: The sum of reported cases forming a body of law. The law of a certain subject as evidenced or formed by the adjudged case, as opposed to statutes or other sources of law.

Catabolism: Reactions in a plant or animal that result in the degradation, or exudation, of molecules.

Catalysis: Change in the speed of a reaction produced by the presence of a substance that does not form part of the final product.

Catalyst: Any substance that brings about catalysis.

Cataract: A loss of transparency of the crystalline lens of the eye or of its capsule.

Catastrophic reaction: Intensely negative but temporary emotional reaction, associated with left hemisphere lesions. Often occurs when subjects are informed of their limitations or shortcomings, in response to task demands. A heightened sensitivity to one's limitations.

Caudal: An anatomical term meaning toward the tail end. Opposed to rostral.

Caudate nucleus: One of the basal ganglia with a long extension or tail.

Cell differentiation: The prenatal stage in which neuroblasts acquire the distinctive appearance of cells characteristic of a region of the nervous system.

Cell proliferation: The production of nerve cells.

Cellular fluid: *See* Intercellular fluid.

Central deafness: Hearing impairments related to lesions in auditory pathways or centers, including sites in the brain stem, thalamus, or cortex.

Central nervous system (CNS): The portion of the nervous system that includes the brain and the spinal cord.

Central sulcus: Known also as the fissure of Rolando, this sulcus divides the anterior from the posterior areas of the brain (frontal from parietal).

Cephalic: An anatomical term referring to the head end. Also called rostral.

Cerebellar cortex: The outer surface of the cerebellum.

Cerebellar fits: Not really seizures, these movements consist of periods of decerebrate rigidity. Associated with large midline cerebellar lesions.

Cerebellar syndrome: Due to a lesion in the cerebellum, ambulation is unsteady with side-to-side swaying. Equilibrium is adversely affected.

Cerebellum: A structure located at the back of the brain, dorsal to the pons; it is involved in the central regulation of movement.

Cerebral contusion: A brain bruise. Refers to superficial damage to gyri or other crests of the cortical convolutions.

Cerebral cortex: The outer bark or cortex of the cerebral hemispheres, which consists largely of nerve cell bodies and their branches.

Cerebral hemispheres: The right and left halves of the forebrain.

Cerebrospinal fluid: The fluid filling the cerebral ventricles.

Certiorari: "To be informed of." An action or writ issued by a superior court requiring an inferior court to produce a certified record of a particular case tried by the latter. The purpose of this action is to enable the higher court to inspect the proceedings to determine whether or not there were any irregularities. Most commonly used by the U.S. Supreme Court as a discretionary device to choose the cases it wishes to hear.

Cerveau isole: An animal with the nervous system transected at the upper level of the midbrain (between the inferior and superior colliculus). Contrast with the encephale isole.

Cervical: Pertaining to the neck region.

Chalazion: A small tumor of the eyelid; formed by the distention of a meibomian gland with secretion.

Character Disorder: *See* Personality disorder.

Cheiro-oral: Refers to the simultaneous twitching of the thumb and same-sided corner of the mouth. Occurs in epilepsy due to close proximity of motor execution zones for these body parts (i.e., the motor homonculus has its thumb in its mouth).

Chiasma: A crossing; specifically, the crossing of the optic nerve fibers from the medial halves of the retinae.

Child abuse: The infliction of physical damage upon a child by parents or other adults.

Child advocacy: A movement concerned with protecting the rights and ensuring the well-being of children.

Chlorpromazine: An antipsychotic drug, one of the class of phenothiazines.

Cholinergic: Refers to cells that use acetylcholine as their synaptic transmitter.

Chorda tympani: A portion of the facial nerve that serves as taste receptor in the anterior two thirds of the tongue.

Choreic movements: Uncontrollable, brief, and forceful muscular movements related to basal ganglia dysfunction.

Chromidial substance: Pertaining to granules of extranuclear chromatin seen in the cytoplasm of a cell.

Chromosome: A body of chromatin in the cell nucleus that splits longitudinally as the cell divides, one half going to the nucleus of each of the daughter cells; the chromosomes transmit the hereditary characters.

Ciliary: Relating to (1) any hairlike process, (2) the eyelashes, or (3) certain of the structures of the eyeball.

Cingulate bodies: Limbic system tissue above or superior to the corpus callosum.

Cingulum: A region of medial cerebral cortex lying dorsal to the corpus callosum. Also called cingulate cortex.

Circadian rhythms: Behavioral, biochemical, and physiological fluctuations during a 24-hour period.

Circle of Willis: A structure at the base of the brain formed by the joining of the carotid and basilar arteries.

Circumlocution: Often seen in fluent aphasia, the substitution of an incorrect word for another word. The substitution may itself demand a specific but unobtainable word, thus producing a convoluted output.

Circumventricular organs: Organs lying in the walls of the cerebral ventricles. These organs contain receptor sites that can be affected by substances in the cerebrospinal fluid.

Cistern: A closed space serving as a reservoir for fluid.

Civil: Of or pertaining to the state of the citizenry. Relates to an individual's private rights and remedies sought through civil action, in contrast to criminal proceedings.

Civil commitment: Procedure whereby an individual certified as mentally disordered can be hospitalized, either voluntarily or against the person's will.

Civil law: The body of law, concerned with civil or private rights and remedies, established by every particular municipality for itself; as opposed to the "law of nature."

Civil rights: The body of law pertaining to personal, natural rights that are guaranteed and protected by the Constitution, such as freedom of speech and press, freedom from discrimination.

Clarendon jury: In a procedure established by Henry II of England, at least 12 "good and lawful" men, reporting to the king's representative, were summoned as jurors to determine if a trial should be held and to decide actual innocence or guilt.

Clear and convincing: A standard of proof greater than preponderance but less rigorous than reasonable doubt. Proof that should leave the trier of fact with no reasonable doubt about the truth of the matters in issue.

Clear and present danger: A standard used to determine when one's First Amendment rights to freedom of speech and press may be curtailed. Pursuant to a doctrine in constitutional law, if necessary, government restrictions will be upheld to prevent grave and immediate danger to interests which government may lawfully protect.

Clinical neuropsychology: That which deals with the psychometric or other objective psychological methods in the assessment of higher cortical functions in humans.

Coactivation: A central nervous system control program that activates or inhibits the skeletal motoneurons at the same time as it alters the sensitivity of the muscle spindles.

Cochlea: A snail-shaped structure in the inner ear that contains the primary receptors for hearing.

Cochlear duct: One of the three principal canals running along the length of the cochlea.

Cochlear microphonic potential: An electrical potential produced by hair cells that accurately copies the acoustic wave form of the stimulus.

Cochlear nuclei: Brain stem nuclei that receive input from auditory hair cells and send output to the superior olivary complex.

Coenzyme: A nonprotein substance that is required for activity of an enzyme.

Cognitive dissonance: Condition existing when new information is contradictory to one's assumptions.

Collateral: Accompanying; running by the side of; not direct; secondary or accessory; a small side branch of an axon.

Colliculus: One of two pairs of structures on the dorsal midbrain. *See* Inferior colliculus, Superior colliculus.

Colloid: A state of subdivision of matter in which the individual particles are of submicroscopic size and consist either of large molecules, such as proteins, or aggregates of smaller molecules; the particles are not large enough to settle out under the influence of gravity.

Collusion: The making of an agreement between two or more persons with the purpose of defrauding another of his or her rights by the forms of law, or to obtain an object forbidden by law.

Coma: A state of profound unconsciousness from which one cannot be roused.

Coma vigil: Immobility and unresponsiveness with eyes open and moving, associated with posteromedial-inferior frontal and/or hypothalamic damage.

Common carotid arteries: Arteries that ascend the left and right sides of the neck. The branch that enters the brain is called the internal carotid artery.

Common law: The body of legal principles and rules of action that derives its authority from customs and general usage and rules of conduct existing among the people. In contrast to civil law. Originated in England.

Complaint: The original or initial charge by which a legal action is begun, naming a person by whom the offense was committed. In criminal law, a written statement containing the essential facts and legal theory on which the charge is based.

Complex cortical cells: Cells in the visual cortex that respond best to a bar of a particular width and direction anywhere within a particular area of the visual field.

Complex partial seizures: Epileptic seizures in which consciousness is altered (complex) and which are restricted or at least arise from a circumscribed area of the brain (partial).

Compos mentis: Being sound of mind; mentally competent.

Compulsion: An irrational and repetitive impulse to perform some act.

Compulsive gambling: *See* Pathological gambling.

Compulsive personality: A personality disorder characterized by excessive concern with rules, order, efficiency, and work.

Computer assessment: Use of computers to obtain or interpret assessment data.

Computer axial tomography: A technique for examining brain structure in intact humans through a computer analysis of x-ray absorption at several positions around the head. This technique affords a virtual direct view of the brain.

Computer model: Use of computers to simulate psychological functioning.

Conciliation: The mode of adjusting and resolving a dispute through voluntary and unantagonistic settlement of the issues between opposing parties with a view toward avoiding litigation.

Concordance rates: Rates at which a diagnosis or a trait of one person is predictive of the same diagnosis or trait in relatives.

Conduct disorders: Childhood disorders marked by persistent acts of aggressive or anti-social behavior that may or may not be against the law.

Conduction aphasia: A constellation of behaviors produced by a lesion in the white matter fibers connecting the posterior/anterior portions of the brain (near the arcuate fasciculus). A severe repetition deficit is apparent relative to good auditory comprehension and expression of speech. A language disorder, involving intact comprehension but poor repetition of spoken language, related to damage of the pathways connecting Wernicke's area and Broca's area.

Cones: Receptor cells in the retina that are responsible for color vision. The three types of cones have somewhat different sensitivities to light of different wavelengths.

Confabulation: Production of bizarre, false, or unverifiable verbal/written responses, usually in association with amnesia. A close correlation exists between confabulatory tendencies and impairment in self-correction.

Congenital: Born with a person; existing at or before birth.

Consideration: The cause, price, or motivating factor that induces a party to enter into a contract.

Consolidation: A state of memory formation in which information in short-term or intermediate-term memory is transferred to long-term memory.

Conspiracy: A combination of two or more persons who propose to commit an unlawful or criminal act, or to commit a lawful act by criminal means.

Constructional disorders: Deficits in constructional tasks (e.g., drawing, assembling) in which the spatial form of the target object may be lost. Associated with pathology of the nondominant (nonspeech) hemisphere.

Contempt of court: An act or an omission that is calculated to obstruct or interfere with the orderly administration of justice or that is calculated to lessen the authority or dignity of the court.

Contingent negative variation (CNV):   A slow event-related potential recorded from the scalp. It arises in the interval between a warning signal and a signal that directs action.

Contract: A binding agreement between two or more competent parties, based on mutual assent and made for a lawful purpose, which creates an obligation to do or not to do a specified thing.

Contralateral: Situated on, or pertaining to, the opposite side.

Contrast sensitivity function (CSF): A psychophysical function determined by finding the contrast necessary for perceiving different spacings of dark and light bars. Used to measure spatial acuity of the visual system.

Contrecoup: Refers to the contusion (bruise) in the area opposite the point of impact (coup).

Conversion disorders: Neurotic condition in which symptoms of organic illness appear in the absence of any related organic pathology; previously called hysteria.

Coronal (plane): The plane dividing the body or brain into front and back parts. Also called frontal or transverse. The band of axons that connects the two cerebral hemispheres.

Corpus callosum: Intracerebral white matter connecting the right and left cerebral hemispheres.

***Corpus delecti*:** The body or material substance of a crime that provides objective proof that a crime has been committed.

***Corpus juris*:** A body of law. A term signifying a comprehensive book of several collections of law.

Cortical deafness: *See also* Cortical auditory disorder. Difficulty recognizing both verbal and nonverbal stimuli due to cerebral dysfunction. Most often associated with cardiovascular accident.

Corticotropin-releasing hormone (CRH): A releasing hormone from the hypothalamus that controls the daily rhythm of ACTH release.

Cortisol: A glucocorticoid hormone of the adrenal cortex.

Court martial: An *ad hoc* military court that is convened under the authority of government and the Uniform Code of Military Justice, that has penal and disciplinary jurisdiction in trying and punishing offenses committed by members of the armed forces. The type (e.g., general, summary, special) and composition vary according to the seriousness of offenses.

Cranial nerves: Originating from the brain, these are 12 pairs of nerves that transmit motor and/or sensory impulses to and from peripheral central nervous system sites. One of the three main subdivisions of the peripheral nervous system, composed of a set of pathways mainly concerned with sensory and motor systems associated with the head.

Cretinism: Reduced stature and mental retardation caused by thyroid deficiency.

Creutzfeldt–Jakob disease: A rare, transmittable (i.e., through a virus that has a 2-year incubation) dementia with a relatively short clinical course (9-month average). Similar to "mad cow" disease. Of cases, 10% may be inherited. Anxiety and memory loss first appear. Myoclonic jerking appears in conjunction with motor neurocerebellar, basal ganglion, or pyramidal tract lesions. Dementia with progressive rigidity and mutism are end-stage symptoms.

Criminal responsibility: Legal question of whether an individual should be permitted to use insanity as a defense after having committed some criminal act.

Cross-examination: The questioning of a witness during a trial, hearing, or deposition by the party opposing that which originally produced the witness to testify. Generally, the scope of cross-examination is limited to matters addressed in direct examination.

Crossed aphasia: Aphasic symptoms occurring, usually temporarily, in a right-handed person with a right hemisphere lesion.

Cruel and unusual punishment: Punishment found to be unfair, shocking, or offensive to the ordinary person's reasonable sensitivity. The Eighth Amendment states that "excessive bail shall not be required nor excessive fines imposed nor cruel and unusual punishment inflicted."

Crystalloid: A body that, in solution, can pass through an animal membrane, as distinguished from a colloid, which does not have this property.

Culpable: Blame worthy; deserving of moral blame. Addresses fault rather than guilt.

Curare: A highly toxic extract that paralyzes muscle; it acts on the motor end plates.

Custody: The caring for, keeping, guarding, preserving of a thing or person. Implies responsibility for the protection and preservation of the thing or person in custody. When applied to a person, may mean lawfully authorized detention by means of restraint and physical control.

Cutaneous: Pertaining to the skin.

Cyanosis: A dark, purplish coloration of the skin and the mucous membrane caused by deficient oxygenation of the blood.

Cyclic adenosine monophosphate (cyclic AMP or cAMP): A second messenger involved in the synaptic activities of dopamine, norepinephrine, and serotonin.

Cyclothymic disorder: Mild affective disorder characterized by extreme mood swings of nonpsychotic intensity.

Cytoarchitectonics: The study of anatomical divisions of the brain based on the kinds of spacing of cells and distribution of axons.

D

Dacrystic epilepsy: Seizures where crying is the predominant ictal event.

Damages: A monetary compensation that may be recovered in court by any party who has suffered a loss or injury to person, property, or rights as the result of an unlawful act or negligence.

Damages, actual: The amount awarded in compensation for a complainant's actual and real losses or injury that can readily be proved to have been sustained.

Damages, compensatory: A monetary award to the injured party strictly for the loss of injury sustained.

Damages, double (or treble): An award for certain statutorily authorized kinds of injuries in an amount two to three times the damages normally awarded by a court or jury.

Damages, nominal: A trivial sum awarded to a plaintiff in an action where there is no substantial loss or injury for which to be compensated. Or, in a case where there has been real injury, but the plaintiff's evidence fails to show its amount.

Damages, punitive (exemplary):   Compensation in an amount greater than actual damages in cases where the wrong done to a plaintiff was aggravated by malice, violence, or fraud on the part of the defendant.

Damages, special (consequential):   An award not arising directly or immediately from the act of a party, but only from the consequences or results of such an act.

***De bene esse*:**   Conditionally or provisionally; in anticipation of future need. Applies to proceedings taken provisionally and allowed to stand for the present but which may be subject to future challenges.

***De facto*:**   In fact, actually, in reality. Characterizes an officer, government, past action, or state of affairs that is illegal or illegitimate, but for all practical purposes, must be accepted.

***De novo* hearing:**   A new hearing or a hearing for the second time in which the judgment of the trial court is usually suspended, with the reviewing court determining the case as though it originated in the latter court.

Decerebrate (rigidity):   Extension and rigidity of the limbs caused by brain stem or cerebellar injury.

Deep dyslexia: Deletion of grammatical morphemes with the presence of semantic paralexias, due to cerebral dysfunction. The loss of grapheme-to-phoneme processing is seen during reading.

Default judgment: A decision of the court against a defendant because of his or her failure to respond to a plaintiff's action.

Defendant: The person from whom relief or recovery is sought in an action or suit. In a criminal case, the accused.

Defense: That which is offered and alleged by the party against whom an action or suit is taken, such as the lawful or factual reasons against the plaintiff recovering or establishing that which he seeks.

Delirium: State of mental confusion characterized by clouding of consciousness, disorientation, restlessness, excitement, and often hallucinations.

Delirium tremens: Acute delirium associated with prolonged alcoholism; characterized by intense anxiety, tremors, and hallucinations.

Delusion: Firm belief opposed to reality but maintained in spite of strong evidence to the contrary.

Delusion of persecution: False belief that one is being mistreated or interfered with by one's enemies. Often found in schizophrenia.

Delusion system: An internally coherent, systematized pattern of delusions.

Dementia pugilistica: The "punch drunk" syndrome. Symptoms associated with repeated head trauma include dysarthria, tremor, seizures, and frontal signs. Memory and concentration problems are marked.

Dendrites: Receptor structures of a neuron that project out in branchlike fashion. Extensions of the cell body that are the receptive surfaces of the neuron.

Dendritic branching: The pattern and quantity of branching of dendrites.

Dendritic spines: Outgrowths along the dendrites of neurons.

Dendritic tree: The full arrangement of a single cell's dendrites.

Deoxyribonucleic acid (DNA): A nucleic acid present in the chromosomes of cells containing hereditary information.

Dependent personality: A personality disorder marked by lack of self-confidence and feelings of acute panic or discomfort at having to be alone.

Dependent variable: In an experiment, the behavior that is measured to determine whether changes in the independent variable affect the behavior being studied.

Depersonalization disorder: A dissociative neurotic disorder, usually occurring in adolescence, in which individuals lose their sense of self and feel unreal or displaced to a different location.

Depolarization: A reduction in membrane potential (the inner membrane surface becomes less negative in relation to the outer surface); this is caused by excitatory neural messages.

Deponent: One who testifies to the truth of certain facts; one who gives a written state deposition; a witness.

Deposition: A witness's testimony taken under oath outside of the courtroom in question-and-answer form, reduced to writing and authenticated. Intended to be used at a civil or criminal trial.

Depressive disorder: Neurotic reaction characterized by persistent dejection and discouragement.

Depressive neurosis: Depression of intermediate severity with little or no evidence of personality breakdown or loss of contact with reality.

Depressive stupor: Extreme degree of depression characterized by marked psychomotor underactivity.

Derepression: The mechanism through which regions of the DNA molecule that are repressed from transcription become unblocked. This process allows for the selection of genetic information that will be utilized by a particular cell.

Dermatome: A strip of skin innervated by a particular spinal root.

Desensitization: Therapeutic process by means of which reactions to traumatic experiences are reduced in intensity by repeatedly exposing the individual to them in mild form, either in reality or in fantasy.

Deterrence: The premise that punishment for criminal offenses will deter that criminal and others from future criminal acts.

Dexedrine: An amphetamine drug; a stimulant used to curb appetite or elevate mood.

Dextral: Refers to right-handedness. Opposed to sinistral, or left-handedness.

Dialysis dementia: Chronic, degenerative intellectual problems (aphasia, memory difficulties), seizures, and motor signs (e.g., facial grimacing) seen occasionally as the result of long-term dialysis. The pathogenesis is unknown although the accumulation of aluminum in the brain has been implicated.

Dialysis disequilibrium syndrome: A consequence of the dialysis procedure itself, encephalopathy characterized by development of intermittent slowing speech, stuttering, and word-finding problems. Progression of dyspraxia, memory loss, concentration problems, and (occasionally) psychosis. Shifts in sodium and potassium are associated with the disorder.

Diapedesis: The passage of blood cells through the unruptured walls of the blood vessels.

Diaschisis: Reduction of neuronal activity in brain sites outside the immediate perimeter of the lesion. Associated with acute, focal conditions.

Diastole: The rhythmic period of relaxation and dilatation of the heart, during which it fills with blood.

Diathesis: A predisposition or vulnerability toward developing a given disorder.

Diathesis-stress model: View of abnormal behavior as the result of stress operating on an individual with a biological, psychosocial, or sociocultural predisposition toward developing a specific disorder.

Dichotic: Refers to studies where different stimuli are simultaneously presented to both ears and eyes, or tactilely to the subject.

Dictum (pl. dicta):   A statement, remark, or observation of the law made by the court, not necessarily relevant or essential to the outcome of a case.

Diencephalon: The central core of the brain, which, together with the telencephalon, forms the cerebrum. Consists of the thalamus, subthalamus, hypothalamus, and epithalamus. The posterior part of the forebrain; it includes the thalamus and hypothalamus.

Differential reinforcement of other behavior (DOR):   Behavior modification technique for extinguishing undesirable behavior by reinforcing incompatible behaviors.

Digitalis: The dried leaves of purple foxglove; used in the treatment of certain cardiac disorders.

Dilantin: An anticonvulsant medication often used in controlling epileptic seizures.

Diopter: The unit of refracting power of a lens; denoting a lens whose principal focus is at a distance of 1 m.

Diploid: Having two sets of chromosomes, as normally found in the somatic cells of higher organisms.

Diplopia: Double vision, due to eye muscle imbalance, metabolic disturbances, or other causes.

Direct examination: The initial questioning or examination of a witness by the party who originally called the witness to testify.

Directed verdict: A verdict ordered by the judge when, as a matter of law, the judge rules that the party with the burden of proof has failed to present a prima facie case. The judge orders the jury to return a verdict for the opposing party.

Disconnection syndromes: Disrupted neuronal transmission through the white matter that cuts cortical pathways, thus disconnecting a cortical area from the rest of the brain. Corpus callosum disconnections are the most dramatic.

Discovery: A pretrial procedure by which one party can obtain vital facts and information material to the case to assist in preparation for the trial. The purpose of discovery is to make for a fair trial and to allow each party to know what documents and information the opponent possesses.

Disinhibition syndrome: Inability to stop actions or impulses once initiated. Often attributed to frontal system deficits in exerting an inhibitory effect on ongoing mental or behavioral processes.

Disintegration: Loss of organization or integration in any organized system.

Disorganized schizophrenia: Subtype representing most severe disintegration of personality and poor prognosis for recovery; characterized by marked incoherence, silly or inappropriate responses.

Dissociation: Separation or "isolation" of mental processes in such a way that they become split off from the main personality or lose their normal thought–affect relationships.

Dissociative disorder: Psychoneurotic disorder characterized by amnesia, fugue, somnambulism, or multiple personality.

Distal: An anatomical term meaning toward the periphery or toward the end of a limb.

Diural: Daily.

Divergence: A system of neural connections that allows one cell to send signals to many other cells.

DNA: *See* Deoxyribonucleic acid.

Docket sounding: A meeting between the judges and attorneys for the purpose of determining the schedule of cases for a specific period of time.

Dopamine (DA):   A neurotransmitter produced mainly in the basal forebrain and diencephalon that is active in the basal ganglia, the olfactory system, and limited parts of the cerebral cortex. For location of dopaminergic fibers.

Dopaminergic: Refers to cells that use dopamine as their synaptic transmitter.

Dorsal: An anatomical term meaning toward the back of the body or the top of the brain; opposite of ventral.

Dorsal root: Root at the back of the spinal cord.

Double-dissociation: Differential effects of lesions, allowing for comparison of both independent and dependent variables. Lesion x causes x but not y, whereas lesion y causes y but not x.

Double tracking: The simultaneous operation of two mental operations. Digits backward on the Wechsler Adult Intelligence Scale (WAIS), for example, calls for memory and reversing operations at the same time.

Down syndrome: A form of mental retardation associated with an extra chromosome.

Due process of law: The regular course of law as administered through courts of justice. In each particular case, refers to the legal proceedings in accordance with the rules and principles established in our legal system to enforce and protect private rights.

Duplex theory: A theory of pitch perception combining the place theory and volley theory. Volley theory operates for sounds from about 20 to 1000 Hz, and place theory operates for sounds above 1000 Hz.

Duplication of DNA: A process through which a cell duplicates (or replicates) its genetic information during mitosis.

Dura: First or outermost layer of the three layers of the meninges.

Durham rule: The "irresistible impulse" test of criminal responsibility deriving from a 1954 decision of the U.S. Court of Appeals. States that a defendant is not criminally responsible if he suffered from a mental disease or defect at the time the unlawful act was committed if it is determined beyond a reasonable doubt that the act was a product of the mental disease or defect.

Duty: A legal or moral obligation or responsibility to perform an act or service.

Dyad: A two-person group.

Dynamic formation: An integrated evaluation of a patient's traits, attitudes, conflicts, and symptoms that attempts to explain the individual's problem.

Dysarthia: Refers to speech disorders based on peripheral motor deficits. The quality of speech is affected, as in hypenasality, breathy phonation, and stridor (flaccid paretic dysarthria), slow, low pitch, harsh and difficult phonation (spastic paretic dysarthria), or explosive speech (ataxic or cerebellar dysarthria).

Dysfluency: Difficulty in generating words.

Dysmetropia: Defects in the visual appreciation of object size discrimination. Also called "past-pointing phenomenon" (i.e., in finger-to-nose examination). Associated with cerebellar lesions.

Dysnomia: Word-finding disability. Shown by failure to correctly name objects or by choosing words that are "off center." Associated with temporal lobe dysfunction.

Dysphagia: Difficulty in swallowing.

Dysthymic disorder: Moderately severe affective disorder characterized by extended periods of nonpsychotic depression and brief periods of normal moods.

Dystonia: Prolonged abnormal posture as a consequence of involuntary muscle tension. Often a side effect of neuroleptic medication.

E

Echopraxia: The mimicking of another's motor movements. Indicates that extant motor problems are not due to lack of inactivity.

Ectoderm: The outer cellular layer of the developing fetus; this layer gives rise to the skin and to the nervous system.

Ectopic: Out of the normal place.

Edema: An abnormal accumulation of clear, watery fluid in the lymph spaces of the tissues. The swelling of tissue, especially in the brain, in response to brain injury.

Effusion: The escape of fluid from the blood vessels or the lymphatics into the tissues or a cavity.

Ego-dystonic homosexuality: Category of "mental disorder" in which the individual wishes to change his or her homosexual orientation.

Ejaculatory incompetence: A male's inability to ejaculate.

Electric synapse: Junctional region where the presynaptic and postsynaptic membranes approach so closely that the nerve impulse can jump to the postsynaptic membrane without being translated into a chemical message.

Electroencephalography (EEG):   The recording and study of gross electrical activity of the brain recorded from large electrodes placed on the scalp.

Electrolyte: Any substance that, in solution, conducts an electric current.

Embolism: Obstruction, or occlusion, of a vessel by a transported clot, a mass of bacteria, or other foreign material.

Emotional inoculation: Therapeutic procedures designed to prepare persons who face stressful situations, such as surgery, by providing the person with adaptive techniques.

Empiricism: The philosophical view based on the belief that knowledge is acquired through experience and observation.

Empyema: The presence of pus in any cavity.

Encephale isole: An animal in which the brain stem is separated from the spinal cord by a cut below the medulla. Contrast with cerveau isole.

Encephalitis: A generalized viral infection of the brain's neurons or glial cell bodies.

Encephalomalacia: Cerebral tissue softening.

Encephalopathy: Brain degeneration.

Encoding: A process of memory formation in which the information entering sensory channels is passed into short-term memory.

Endocrine: Refers to glands that secrete products into the bloodstream to act on distant targets; opposite of exocrine.

Endorphins: Neurotransmitters that have been called the body's own narcotics.

Endothelial cells: The tightly fitting cells that make up the walls of the capillaries in the brain.

Enhancement: Independent of behavior, the increase in activity of some posterior parietal neurons by motivationally important visual stimuli. Responses to those stimuli are enhanced.

Enjoin: To command or require that a person perform or desist from a certain act.

Enuresis: Involuntary passage of urine after the age of 3 years.

Enzyme: A protein that catalyzes a biochemical reaction.

Epicritic: Sensory experiences that can be located on the body of the organism and are of brief duration (e.g., a sharp pain in the foot). Opposed to protocritic.

Epinephrine: A compound that acts both as a hormone (secreted by the adrenal medulla) and as a neurotransmitter; also called adrenaline.

Episodic dyscontrol syndrome: Totally unprovoked violence associated with an aura, consisting of rising anxiety, headaches, illusions, numbness, drowsiness, and hyperacusis. The attack lasts 15 minutes to 2 hours and is very violent, often directed toward property or persons. May be due to temporal-limbic structure dysfunction. Associated features include hypersensitivity to alcohol, multiple traffic accidents, and sexual impulsiveness, the last rising to the level of forensic concern.

Episodic memory: Recall for events in one's life and experiences. It is therefore unique and anchored to distinct points in time and space.

Equilibrium potential: The state in which the tendency of ions to flow from regions of high concentration is exactly balanced by the opposing potential differences across the membrane.

Equipotentiality: Notion that a lesion anywhere on the cortex will produce equivalent deficits. This holistic approach was espoused by Lashley.

Equity: A system of law and courts administered according to fairness and justness. Based on a system that originated in England as an alternative to common law.

Estrogen: A hormone produced by female gonads.

Estrus: The period during which female animals are sexually receptive.

Eustress: Positive stress.

Evagination: A protrusion of some part of an organ.

Event-related potentials: Gross electrical potential changes in the brain that are elicited by discrete sensory or motor events.

Excitatory postsynaptic potentials (EPSPs):   Depolarizing potentials in the postsynaptic neuron caused by excitatory presynaptic impulses. These potentials may summate to trigger a nerve impulse in the postsynaptic cell.

Exclusionary rule: The rule that defines whether evidence is admissible in a trial. In cases where evidence has been illegally obtained, it must be removed from consideration by the fact finders.

Exculpatory: Clearing or excusing a party from alleged fault or guilt.

Exemplary damages: A monetary award in an amount over and above what is required to compensate a plaintiff for a loss in a case where the wrong was aggravated by violence, malice, or fraud on the part of the defendant.

Exhaustion and disintegration: The third and final phase in the general adaptation syndrome, in which the organism is no longer able to resist continuing stress; at the biological level, may result in death.

Exner's area: Formally seen as a "frontal writing center," located at the base of the second frontal convolution. Lesions in this area produce agraphia.

Exocrine: Refers to glands that secrete their products through ducts to the site of action; opposite of endocrine.

Exophthalmos: A protrusion, or prominence, of the eyeball.

Experimental research: A research approach in which the experimenter manipulates the independent variable, controls outside conditions, and determines the effect on a dependent variable to test for causal linkages.

Expert witness: A witness who has special knowledge in a field, obtained from education or personal experience.

External validity: The degree to which experimental findings can reasonably be generalized to nonlaboratory situations.

Extinction: One of a stimulus pair simultaneously presented to different parts of the body visual fields, etc., is not perceived.

Extinction to double simultaneous stimulation: Failure to report the stimulus presented to the contralateral side of a lesion upon bilateral simultaneous stimulation.

Extracerebral: Extrinsic to or outside of the brain hemispheres, for example, between the skull and the brain on one of the three layers of meninges.

Extrapunitive: Characterized by a tendency to evaluate the source of frustrations as external and to direct hostility outward.

Extrapyramidal system: A motor system that includes the basal ganglia and some related brain stem structures.

Extravasation: The act of escaping from a vessel into the tissues; said of blood, lymph, or serum.

Extrinsic: Originating outside of the part where it is found or upon which it acts.

F

5HT: *See* Serotonin.

Fabrication: Relating imaginary events as if they were true without intent to deceive; confabulation.

Face–hand test: Touching the face simultaneously with another body part, particularly same-sided. Suppression or displacement of the more peripheral stimulus indicates possible parietal lobe dysfunction.

Facial nerve: A cranial nerve that innervates facial musculature and some sensory receptors.

Fasciculation: Localized contraction of muscle fibers, or an incoordinated contraction of skeletal muscle in which the fibers of one motor unit contract.

Feature detector model: A model of visual pattern analysis in terms of linear and angular components of the stimulus array. Contrast with spatial frequency filter model.

Felony: A crime of a more serious or harmful nature than a misdemeanor. Under federal law and many state statutes, any offense punishable by imprisonment for a term of more than 1 year or by death.

Fetal alcohol syndrome: Observed pattern in infants of alcoholic mothers in which there is a characteristic facial or limb irregularity, low body weight, and behavioral abnormality.

Fiduciary: A person having the duty to act in a relationship of high trust and confidence for another's benefit in the capacity of trustee, executor, or administrator.

Field properties: Characteristics of the environment surrounding a living system.

Finger agnosia: Inability to identify the fingers of one's own hand, or those of another person, due to brain damage.

Fistula: A pathologic, or abnormal, passage leading from an abscess cavity or a hollow organ to the surface, or from one organ to another.

Fixed action patterns: Complex preprogrammed species-specific behaviors triggered by particular stimuli and carried out without sensory feedback.

Flaccid: Relaxed, flabby, soft.

Flashback: The recurrence of a drug experience, usually in a negative manner, without further ingestion of the drug.

Flatus: Gas or air in the stomach or the intestine; commonly used to denote passage of gas by rectum.

Flexion reflex: Abrupt withdrawal of a limb in response to intense stimulation of the foot.

Flooding: Anxiety-eliciting technique involving placing the client in a real-life, anxiety-arousing situation.

Fluent aphasia: Speech difficulty with incomprehension, jargon speech, and other signs such as lack of awareness. Often associated with posterior lesions. Nonfluent aphasia is associated with anterior lesions and almost always involves expressive speech deficits.

Folia: Folds or convolutions of the cerebellar cortex.

Folie à deux: A psychotic interpersonal relationship involving two people; e.g., husband and wife both become psychotic with similar or complementary symptomatology.

Follicle-stimulating hormone (FSH):   A tropic hormone released by the anterior pituitary that controls the production of estrogen and progesterone.

Forcible rape: An act of violence in which sexual relations are forced upon an unwilling partner who is over the age of 18.

Forebrain: The frontal division of the neural tube that contains the cerebral hemispheres, the thalamus, and the hypothalamus. Also called the prosencephalon.

Forensic psychiatry: Branch of psychiatry dealing with legal problems relating to mental disorders.

Fornix: A fiber tract that runs from the hippocampus to the mammillary body.

Fovea: A cup-shaped depression or pit.

Fovea centralis: Small central pit in the retina, packed with cones, where vision is sharpest and color accuracy most developed.

Frontal amnesia: Difficulty in switching from one set of memory traces to another in the face of intact operating memory. "Forgetting to recall," as in disregarding instructions, is an illustration.

Frontal gait disturbance: *See* Magnetic apraxia and Utilization behavior.

Frontal inattention: A contralateral visual field defect caused by damage to particular frontal sites (arcuate sulcus in monkeys). Associated features may include conjugate deviation of the eyes and forced circling, the latter in the direction of the lesion.

Frontal psychosurgery: Includes leukotomies aimed at severing frontal-thalamic connections, orbital undercutting, for example, by placement of radioactive yttrium pellets in the orbital tissues, cingulomotomy, stereotactic destruction of focal sites, and topectomy, ablation of selected frontal areas.

Frontal "release" signs: These are primitive reflexes that long have been considered frontal signs. The grasp reflex is associated with midline frontal pathology. Frontal system problems are indicated by rooting, sucking, and snout reflexes indicating a brain stem diencephalic lesion.

Frye test: A test emphasizing the subject of an expert witness's testimony must conform to a generally accepted explanatory theory. Named after the case in which the determination was made.

Fugue: A neurotic dissociative disorder that entails a loss of memory accompanied by actual physical flight from one's present life situation to a new environment or less-threatening former one.

Functional psychoses: Severe mental disorders attributed primarily to psychological stress.

Fundus: The bottom of a sac or hollow organ; the farthest removed from the opening.

Future shock: A condition brought about when social change proceeds so rapidly that the individual cannot cope with it adequately.

G

Gambling: Wagering on games or events in which chance largely determines the outcome.

Gamma efferents: Motor neurons by means of which the central nervous system controls muscle spindle sensitivity.

Ganglion: A collection of nerve cell bodies. Also called a nucleus.

Ganglion cells: Cells in the retina whose axons form the optic nerve.

Gangrene: A form of necrosis combined with putrefaction; death of the tissue.

Gel: A colloidal system consisting of a solid and a liquid phase that exists as a solid or semisolid mass; a jelly or solid or semisolid phase.

Gelastic epilepsy: Seizures where laughter is the predominant ictal behavior.

Gene: An ultimate, ultramicroscopic, biologic unit of heredity; self-reproducing; located in a definite position on a particular chromosome.

General adaptation syndrome: Reaction of the individual to excessive stress; consists of the alarm reaction, the stage of resistance, and the stage of exhaustion.

General paresis: A progressive mental deterioration due to syphilitic invasion of the central nervous system.

Gerstmann's syndrome: The symptom cluster of ocalculia, agraphia, left-right disorientation, and finger agnosia. Traditionally considered to involve the parietoccipital region of the brain.

Glabellar tap sign: The subject is tapped lightly just above and between the eyebrows to see whether blinking will normally and quickly habituate. Patients with Parkinson's disease will continue to blink with each tap.

Glial cells: Nonneural brain cells that provide structural, nutritional, and other support to the brain. Also called glia or neuroglia.

Glioblastoma (multiforma): A neoplasm arising from the glial cells, characterized by a high degree of lethality and malignancy.

Gliomas: Brain tumors resulting from the aberrant production of glial cells.

Global alexia: Inability to read letters or words.

Global aphasia: Severe comprehension and articulation deficits associated with a large lesion of the entire perisylvian area of the frontal, temporal, and parietal lobes. Prognosis is grim.

Global stereopsis: Depth perception in the presence of ambiguous stimulus forms. Presumed to be mediated by right hemisphere and is differentiated from a stereoacuity.

Glossopharyngeal nerve: A cranial nerve that serves taste receptors in the tongue.

Glucocorticoids: Hormones released by the adrenal cortex that affect carbohydrate metabolism.

Golgi tendon organs: Receptors located in tendons that send impulses to the central nervous system when a muscle contracts.

Gonadotropin-releasing hormone (GnRH):   A hypothalamic hormone that controls release of luteinizing hormone (or interstitial-cell-stimulating hormone). Also called luteinizing-hormone-releasing hormone.

Graded potentials: Potentials that can vary continuously in size; also called local potentials; contrast with all-or-none potentials.

Gradient: An ascending or descending slope. In the body, gradients are determined by the difference in concentration or electric charges across a semipermeable membrane.

Grand mal seizures: A type of generalized epileptic seizure that involves nerve cells firing in high-frequency bursts. These seizures cause loss of consciousness and sudden muscle contraction.

Grandfather clause: Certain legal provisions permitting those engaged in a business or profession before the passage of an act regulating them to receive a license, power, or privilege without meeting the criteria established for those new to the field.

Grievance: A denial of legal right or an injury, injustice, or wrong that is grounds for a complaint due to being unjust, discriminatory, and oppressive.

Growth hormone: A tropic hormone secreted by the anterior pituitary that influences the growth of cells and tissues. Also called somatotropic hormone (STH).

Guardian *ad litem*:   A person appointed by the court to represent the interests of a minor or an incompetent person in a litigation and to act on the person's behalf until the conclusion of the case.

Guilt: Feelings of culpability arising from behavior or desires contrary to one's ethical self-devaluation and apprehension growing out of fears of punishment.

Gyri: The ridged or raised portions of a convoluted brain surface. Contrast with sulci.

H

Habeas corpus: "You have the body." A writ or order commanding the authority that is detaining an individual to produce the body of the detainee before the court to determine whether the detainment is lawful.

Health psychology: Subspecialty within the behavioral medicine approach that deals with psychology's contributions to diagnosis, treatment, and prevention of behaviorally caused physical illnesses.

Hearsay: A statement made during a trial or hearing that is not based on the personal, firsthand knowledge of the witness.

Hearsay rule: The regulation making a witness's statement inadmissible if it is not based on the witness's personal knowledge.

Heat of vaporization: The heat energy required to convert 1 g of liquid into a vapor without a change in temperature of the substance being vaporized.

Hebephrenic schizophrenia: Type of schizophrenia characterized by severe personality decompensation or disintegration.

Hematoma: An accumulation of blood within the meninges of the brain. Most often caused by head trauma.

Hematosis: The arrest of bleeding; the checking of the flow of blood through any part of a vessel.

Hematuria: The presence of blood in the urine.

Hemiparesis: Weakness on one side of the body.

Hemiplegia: Weakness or paralysis of one side of the body.

Hemispatial neglect: Neglect of the hemisphere contralateral to a lesion. Also termed visuospatial agnosia or neglect, unilateral spatial neglect, or hemispatial agnosia.

High-risk: Individuals showing great vulnerability to physical or mental disorders.

Hilus: A depression or pit at that part of an organ where the vessels and nerves enter or leave.

Hippocampus: Actively concerned with memory consolidation functions, located at the anterior temporal lobe.

Histrionic personality: Personality pattern characterized by excitability, emotional instability, and self-dramatization.

Holistic: A systematic approach to science involving the study of the whole or total configuration; the view of human beings as unified psychobiological organisms inextricably immersed in a physical and sociocultural environment.

Homeostasis: Tendency of organisms to maintain conditions making possible a constant level of physiological functioning.

Homologous: Corresponding; having similar relations.

Homonymous field cuts: Loss of vision in the same part of both visual fields.

Homonymous hemianopsia: Loss of one half of the visual field in each eye, right or left sided (e.g., right temporal/left nasal; right nasal/left temporal).

Huntington's disease: A progressive, hereditary, dementing condition that affects the basal ganglia with atrophy of the frontal lobes and corpus callosum. Involuntary and spasmodic movements are associated features, along with declining cognitive and personality/social skills.

Hyaluronidase: An enzyme causing breakdown of hyaluronic acid in protective polysaccharide barriers, promoting invasion of cells and tissues by the invading agent; it is a spreading factor.

Hyperacusis: The perception of sounds as abnormally loud.

Hypergraphia: Overwriting, as when too many words are written in response to task demands.

Hyperplasia: The abnormal multiplication, or increase, in the number of normal cells in normal arrangement in a tissue.

Hypertrophy: The morbid enlargement, or overgrowth, of an organ or part, resulting from an increase in size of its constituent cells.

Hypnosis: Trancelike mental state induced in a cooperative subject by suggestion.

Hypnotherapy: Use of hypnosis in psychotherapy.

Hypnotic regression: Process by which a subject is brought to relive, under hypnosis, early forgotten or repressed experiences.

Hypochondriacal delusions: Delusions concerning various horrible disease conditions, such as the belief that one's brain is turning to dust.

Hypochondriasis: Condition dominated by preoccupation with bodily processes and fear of presumed diseases.

Hypophonia: Lowered voice volume. Contrasted to aphonia, or total lack of voice. The most common cause of both disorders is laryngitis.

Hypothalamus: Involved in homeostatic, motivational activities such as sexual activity, eating, drinking, and emotions, this structure is located in the limbic system, dorsal to the thalamus.

Hypothermia: Low temperature; especially a state of low body temperature induced for the purpose of decreasing metabolic activities and need for oxygen.

Hypotonia: The state of muscles tiring easily. Associated with cerebellar lesions.

Hypoxia: Refers to insufficient blood oxygen to the brain. Contrasted to anoxia, which refers to a total lack of blood oxygen to brain structures.

Hysterical amnesia: Loss of memory for emotional/psychological reasons without a known organic basis.

Hysterical disorder: Disorder characterized by involuntary psychogenic dysfunction of motor, sensory, or visceral processes.

I

Iconic memory: A very brief type of memory that stores the sensory impression of a scene.

Ideographic methodology: A method of study emphasizing the individual case and the uniqueness of each personality.

Ideomotor apraxia: Simple execution of motor responses (e.g., hitchhiking sign, salute, whistling) is impaired or absent in the presence of intact comprehension. Implies deficits in planning and initiation. Associated with left hemisphere lesions.

Idiopathic epilepsy: A seizure disorder of unknown origin. Opposed to symptomatic epilepsy whose cause is known.

Illusion: Misinterpretation of sensory data; false perception.

Impeachment: A criminal proceeding against a public official before a quasi-political court. In regard to the testimony of a witness, to question the veracity of the evidence offered.

In bank (*en banc*):   "In the bench." Refers to a court session in which the entire membership of the court participates in making a decision instead of the regular quorum or one judge and jury.

In camera: In chambers; in private. The hearing of a case before a judge in his private chambers, when all spectators are excluded from the courtroom, or when the judge performs a judicial act while the court is not in session.

***In loco parentis*:**   In place of a parent. A party charged to legally act in behalf of the parents.

***In re*:**   In the matter of; concerning or regarding. The usual method of assigning a title to a case in which there are no adversary parties.

***In situ* research:**   Research in which real-1ife social situations are the emphasis of study.

***In vivo*:**   Taking place in a real-life situation as opposed to the therapeutic or laboratory setting.

Inattention: Decreased/absent awareness of events occurring on the side of the body contralateral to the hemispheric lesion.

Incompetency: Lacking the physical, intellectual, or moral capacity or qualification to perform a required duty.

Independent variable: The variable in an experiment that is controlled or manipulated by the experimenter.

Indifference reaction: Denial, unawareness, or minimizing psychological/neuropsychological deficits, traditionally associated with right hemisphere lesions. Inappropriate elevated affect may be present.

Infarct: Impoverished or dead brain tissue associated with vascular occlusions.

Inferior colliculus: The auditory center in the midbrain; it receives input from the brain stem auditory nuclei and sends output to the medial geniculate nucleus.

Inflammation: A series of reactions produced in the tissues by an irritant; marked by an afflux of blood with exudation of plasma and leukocytes.

Informed consent: A person's agreement to the occurrence of a specified event based on a full disclosure of facts needed to make an intelligent decision.

*Infra***:**   Below, under, following; the opposite of *supra*.

Infundibulum: A funnel-shaped structure or passage. The stalk of the pituitary gland.

Inhibitory postsynaptic potentials (IPSPs):   Hyperpolarizing potentials in the postsynaptic neuron caused by inhibitory connections. These potentials decrease the probability that the postsynaptic neuron will fire a nerve impulse.

Innervation ratio: The ratio expressing the number of muscle fibers innervated by a single motor axon. The fewer muscle fibers an axon innervates (the lower the ratio) the finer the control of movement.

Inquisitorial system: A system in which the judge, as the primary figure in a trial, conducts his or her own investigation. The judge generally maintains more control over the proceedings than in the adversarial system.

Insanity: A social or legal term indicating a condition in which a person is unfit and lacks legal responsibility or capacity due to mental illness. As stated in the American Law Institute Penal Code, "A person is not responsible for criminal conduct if at the time of such conduct as a result of mental disease or defect he lacks substantial capacity either to appreciate the criminality or wrongfulness of his conduct or to conform his conduct to the requirements of the law."

Insanity defense: "Innocent by reason of insanity" plea used as a legal defense in criminal trials.

Instrumental use of empirical data: The application of concrete social science information of concepts to a case.

Integration: Organization of parts (psychological, biological functions) to make a functional whole.

Intent: A state of mind (inferred from the facts or from a person's actions) showing purpose, design, or resolve to act in a certain manner.

Intention tremor: Also called kinetic tremor, this anomaly occurs at the end of a movement. Contrasted to "rest" tremor, which occurs when no movement is present. A tremor that occurs only during a voluntary movement, e.g., when the person reaches out to grasp an object.

Interictal: Refers to behaviors/events between the time seizures occur. Adversive personality traits (e.g., irritability, obsessional traits) are associated features.

Intermediate coup lesions: Scattered areas of focal tissue damage in line with the point of trauma impact (coup) and possible terminal point of the damage (contrecoup).

Intermediate-term memory: A form of memory lasting longer than short-term memory, and requiring no rehearsal, but not lasting as long as long-term memory.

Internal carotid artery: *See* Common carotid artery.

Internal validity: A measure of the lack of confounding variables.

Interstitial policy making: Laws that may be "made" by judges when the issues in a case fall "between the gaps"—interstices—of previous decisions.

Intracerebral: Intrinsic to or inside of the brain hemispheres, usually referring to brain dysfunction caused by neoplasms or cardiovascular accidents.

Intracranial steal: Complicating the finding of an arteriovenous malformation (AVM) location, here blood is shunted away from normal brain tissue to the AVM site. Thus, the unaffected area may show evidences of neuropsychological deficit.

Intravascular: Within a vessel or vessels.

Intropunitive: Responding to frustration by tending to blame oneself.

Invagination: The pushing of the wall of a cavity into the cavity.

Involution: The return of an enlarged organ to normal size; retrograde changes.

Ion: An electrically charged atom or group of atoms formed by the loss or gain of electrons.

Ipsilateral: Same side; homolateral; opposed to contralateral (opposite side), bilateral (both sides), unilateral (one side).

Ischemia: Cutoff of blood flow to an area of the brain or body organ.

Ischemic infarction: A disruption of blood flow (infarction) creating dead or damaged tissue (infarct), resulting more from impaired or absent blood flow rather than from insufficient nutrients in the blood.

Isotope: An element that has the same atomic number as another but a different atomic weight. Radioactive isotopes, used clinically, usually refer to elements rendered radioactive by artificial means.

J

Jargon aphasia: A form of paraphasias that has no meaning to those who hear the sounds.

Judicial notice: The act by which a court, during a trial or while framing its decision, recognizes the existence and truth of certain facts that judges and jurors may take into consideration and act upon without proof because the facts are already known to them.

Jurisdiction: The authority and power by which courts and judicial officers hear and decide cases; the geographic area in which a court has authority.

Just-world hypothesis: The hypothesis stating that the world is fair and that victims deserve what happened to them and, therefore, do not deserve help.

Juvenile courts: A court system, established in the late 19th century, having special jurisdiction over delinquent, dependent, and neglected minors. Set up to treat youthful offenders separately from adults. The court acts in a parental, protective role.

Juvenile delinquency: Legally prohibited behavior, such as disobedient, indecent, or immoral conduct, committed by minors.

K

Ketosis: The condition marked by excessive production of ketone bodies in the body.

Kinesthetic: Pertaining to muscle sense, or to the sense by which muscular movement, weight, and position are perceived.

Kinesthetic afferentiation: Gathering data concerning one's own current muscle tone, body position, oral status, etc. Considered a function of the posterior association areas.

Kinetic afferentiation: Integration of input from parietal–occipital tertiary zones, basal ganglia, and premotor areas producing sequential and integrated actions. Depends initially on kinesthetic afferentiation.

Kinetic apraxia: Disorganized transition of single movements (*see also* Apraxia, Echopraxia, Apraxia of speech). Associated with lesions in basal ganglia-premotor areas. Subordination of movements to intentions is impaired.

Kluver–Bucy syndrome: A condition manifested by hyperorality, hypersexuality, labile emotions, and inability to form new memories. Associated with temporal lobe or limbic system lesions.

Korsakoff's psychosis: A progressive dementia considered subcortical in focus and associated with a nutritional deficiency of vitamin B_1 (thiamine). The condition is considered secondary to alcohol abuse. Memory impairments are paramount with associated confabulation, blandness, and passivity. Hippocampus lesions have been associated with this condition. A memory disorder, related to a thiamine deficiency, generally associated with chronic alcoholism.

Kuru: A slow virus of the brain, which produces trembling and, eventually, paralysis of the limbs.

L

Labeled lines: A view of stimulus coding stating that particular nerve cells are intrinsically labeled for particular sensory experiences such as cold, touch, pain, and so forth.

Labile memory: An early state of memory formation during which formation of a memory can be easily disrupted by conditions that influence brain activity.

Lacunar state: Multiple but small infarctions in the subcortical regions leaving lacunae. One of the end stages of hypertensive cerebrovascular conditions.

Laminar (form of organization):   The horizontal layering of cells found in some brain regions.

Lateral: An anatomical term meaning toward the side; opposite of medial.

Lateral geniculate nucleus: Part of the thalamus that receives information from the optic tract and sends it to visual areas in the occipital cortex.

Lateral hypothalamus (LH): A hypothalamic region involved in facilitating eating.

Lateral inhibition: A phenomenon produced by interconnected neurons that inhibit their neighbors, producing contrast at the edges of the stimulus.

Law of effect: Principle that responses that have rewarding consequences are strengthened and those that have aversive consequences are weakened or eliminated.

Leading question: A question posed by a trial lawyer that is improper because it suggests the desired answer to a witness.

Lecithin: A monoaminomonophosphatide found in animal tissues, especially nerve tissue, semen, egg yolk, and in smaller amounts in bile and blood.

Legal fiction: An assumption of fact or a situation contrived by the law to decide a legal question.

Lethality scale: Criteria used to assess the likelihood of an individual's committing suicide.

Leukemia: A disease of the blood marked by persistent leukocytosis, associated with changes in the spleen and the bone marrow, or in the lymphatic nodes.

Level of aspiration: Standard by which the individual judges success or failure of his behavior.

Lexical agraphia: Impaired ability to spell irregular or unknown works with an intact ability to spell regular words. Associated with lesions in the parieto-occipital lobule.

Limb-kinetic apraxia: Complex/serial movement impairment in the presence of intact simple, repetitive movement. Brodman areas 4 and 6 are implicated in almost all cases.

Limbic system: Interconnected and primarily subcortial structures that are involved in emotional responses and memory.

Literal paraphasia: Production of off-target sounds with effortless articulation. Associated with postrolandic lesions.

Litigant: One who is party to a lawsuit.

Local circuit neurons: Small neurons that make contact only with neurons that are within the same functional unit.

Localization of function: The concept that specific brain regions are responsible for various types of experience, behavior, and psychological processes.

Locked-in syndrome: Also known as deefferentiation; due to bilateral pontine lesions and characterized by aphonia and quadriplegia. The patient is aware of his or her surroundings.

Logical positivism: A philosophy that emphasizes the creation of knowledge and its verification through observation and experiment.

Long-term memory: An enduring form of memory lasting for weeks, months, or years.

Lumbar: Referring to the lower part of the spinal cord or back.

Lumen: The space in the interior of a tubular structure such as an artery or the intestine.

Luteinizing hormone (LH):   A tropic hormone released by the anterior pituitary that influences the hormonal activities of the gonads. In males, this hormone is called interstitial-cell-stimulating hormone (ICSH).

Luteinizing hormone-releasing hormone: *See* Gonadotropin-releasing hormone.

M

M'Naughten rule: In most jurisdictions, the test applied for the defense of insanity. Under this test, an accused is not criminally responsible if he or she was suffering from a mental disease or defect at the time of committing the act and does not understand the nature and quality of the act or that what he or she was doing was wrong. To be considered "sane" and therefore legally responsible for the act committed, the defendant must know and understand the nature and quality of the act and have been able to distinguish between right and wrong at the time the offense was committed.

Macula: A spot.

Magnetic apraxia: Compulsive exploration of the immediate environment in the usual presence of intact comprehension skills. Forced hand grasping with difficulty "letting go" is an example. Prefrontal, mesial, and contralateral lesions are implicated.

Major affective disorders: Category of affective disorders in which a biological defect or other aberration renders a person liable to experience episodes of a more or less severe affective disorder.

Major depression (unipolar disorder):   A severe affective disorder in which only depressive episodes occur.

Malaise: A feeling of general discomfort or uneasiness; an out-of-sorts feeling, often the first indication of an infection.

Malfeasance: The commission of an unlawful, wrongful act; any wrongful conduct that affects, interrupts, or interferes with the performance of official duties.

***Malleus Malleficarum*:**   Infamous handbook prepared by two monks dealing with the "diagnosis" and "treatment" of witches and witchcraft.

Mammillary bodies: Paired nuclei at the base of the brain slightly posterior to the pituitary stalk.

Mandamus: A writ or order issued from a superior court to a lower court or to a private or municipal corporation commanding that a specified act be performed. Used when other judicial remedies have failed.

Manic–depressive psychoses: Older term denoting a group of psychotic disorders characterized by prolonged periods of excitement and overactivity (mania) or by periods of depression and underactivity (depression) or by alternation of the two.

Masked fascies: An unblinking, bland, expressionless stare.

Masochism: Sexual variant in which an individual obtains sexual gratification through being subjected to pain.

Mass action: Proposed by Lashley, this notion stated that the degree of deficit shown by a lesion was a function of how much cortical tissue was destroyed.

Meatus: A passage, or channel, especially the external opening of a canal.

Medial: An anatomical term meaning toward the middle; opposite of lateral.

Medial geniculate nucleus: A nucleus in the thalamus that receives input from the inferior colliculus and sends output to the auditory cortex.

Mediation: A way of resolving disputes by using a third party to intervene between contending parties to bring them to a satisfactory settlement without resorting to litigation.

Medulla: The lowest part of the brain, also called myelencephalon.

Melokinetic apraxia: Deficit in speech, skill, and coordination of movement, usually confined to a small muscle group. Unilateral and contralateral to lesion in premotor area.

Memory traces: Persistent changes in the brain that reflect the storage of memory.

Meninges: Thin membranes on the brain dura mater, pia mater, and arachnoid, which provide a venous drainage system.

Meningioma: Neoplastic growth arising from the meninges.

Meningitis: Inflammatory disease of the meninges with associated signs of fever, headache, and stiff neck.

***Mens rea*:**   A guilty mind; having a guilty or wrongful purpose or criminal intent.

Mental anguish: A compensable injury including all forms of mental, as opposed to physical, injury. In connection with a physical injury, includes the mental sensation of pain and accompanying feelings of distress, grief, anxiety, or fright.

Mesencephalon: The midbrain.

Mesmerism: Theories of "animal magnetism" (hypnosis) formulated by Anton Mesmer.

Messenger RNA (mRNA):   A strand of RNA that carries the code of a section of a strand of DNA to the cytoplasm.

Metabolism: The sum of the chemical changes whereby the function of nutrition is affected; consists of anabolism, or the constructive and assimilative changes, and catabolism, or the destructive and retrograde changes.

Metamorphosias: Visual illusions where objects are distorted in size, shape, distance, and color. May occur with lesions anywhere in visual system, with substance intoxication, or in conjunction with psychological disorder.

Metencephalon: A subdivision of the hindbrain that includes the cerebellum and the pons.

Meter: A measure of length, 100 cm, the equivalent of 39.371 inches.

Methadone: An orally administered narcotic that replaces the craving for heroin and weans the individual from heroin addiction.

Microglia: Extremely small glial cells that remove cellular debris from injured or dead cells.

Microgram: One one-millionth of a gram, or 1/1000 of a milligram.

Micron: One one-millionth of a meter or 1/1000 of a millimeter.

Microtubules: Hollow cylindrical structures in axons that are involved in exoplasmic streaming.

Midbrain: The middle division of the brain. Also called mesencephalon.

Middle cerebral artery (MCA):   The MCA and its branches are one of the two major vascular networks of the frontal lobes. The lateral convexity is fed by anterior branches of the MCA.

Milieu: The immediate environment, physical or social or both; sometimes used to include the internal state of an organism.

Millimeter: One one-thousandth of a meter; about 1/25 inch.

Misdemeanor: An offense less serious than a felony, typically punishable by a fine or short-term incarceration.

Misfeasance: The improper performance of an act a person has the right or duty to perform.

Misoplegia: A type of unilateral inattention where the lesioned individual, usually hemiplegic, exhibits a strong dislike for the affected limbs or portions of the body. Intense hatred resulting in self-mutilation may be expressed.

Mistrial: A trial that is terminated before its normal conclusion and declared invalid prior to the returning of a verdict. A judge may declare a mistrial due to an extraordinary event (e.g., death of a juror), for a fundamental, prejudicial error that cannot be corrected by instructions to the jury, or because of the jury's inability to reach a verdict (hung jury). In a criminal case, may prevent a retrial under the doctrine of double jeopardy.

Mitochondria: Organelles in the cytoplasm of cells; contain enzymes that make possible the reactions whereby energy is liberated from food and stored temporarily in the chemical bonds of ATP.

Mitosis: The process of division of somatic cells that involves duplication of DNA.

Model psychoses: Psychotic-like states produced by various hallucinogenic drugs such as LSD.

Modulation of formation of memory: Facilitation or inhibition of memory formation by factors other than those directly involved in memory formation. Also called modulation of memory storage processes.

Modus operandi: Manner or mode of behavior; a criminal's typical pattern of performing crimes.

Monopolar neurons: Nerve cells with a single branch leaving the cell body, which then extends in two directions—one end is the receptive pole, the other end the output zone.

Moot: A subject for debate; unsettled; undecided. A case is "moot" when a determination of a matter is sought that, when rendered, has no practical effect on the matter under dispute.

Moral nihilism: Doctrine that denies any objective or real ground for moral beliefs, and holds that the individual is not bound by obligation to others or society.

Moral therapy: Therapy based on provision of kindness, understanding, and favorable environment; prevalent during the early part of the 19th century.

Motion: An application made to a court or judge, orally or in writing, requesting that a rule or order be given in favor of the applicant.

Motivational selectivity: Influence of motives on perception and other cognitive processes.

Motive pattern: Relatively consistent cluster of motives centered around particular strivings and goals.

Motoneurons: Nerve cells in the spinal cord that transmit motor messages from the spinal cord to muscles.

Motor aprosody: Inability to sing or to change pitch or voice tempo with intact ability to recognize melodies.

Motor cortex: A region of cerebral cortex that sends impulses to motoneurons.

Motor extinction: Increased contralateral limb akinesia when simultaneously using ipsilateral extremities, due to cerebral dysfunction.

Motor impersistence: Inability to maintain an initiated, voluntary (motor) behavior chain. Implies distraction due to interference factors. Common impersistences include lack of tongue protrusion, eyelid closure, mouth opening, breath holding, hand-grip pressure, and central gaze.

Motor neuron: Spinal cord neurons involved in movement that extend to effector muscle sites.

Motor unit: A single motor axon and all the muscle fibers it innervates.

Multi-infarct dementia: A vascular disease that has a progressive, stepwise course caused by multiple strokes and arteriosclerosis. Cognitive symptoms usually precede personality problems. Motor anomalies are distinctive of this condition and reflect subcortical involvement.

Multiple personality: Type of dissociative disorder characterized by the development of two or more relatively independent personality systems in the same individual.

Multiple sclerosis (MS):   A degenerative condition involving deterioration of the myelin sheath on nerve fibers. This disease therefore affects primarily the white matter. Multiple cognitive and emotional deficits are noted. The rate of progression of MS is extremely variable.

Multipolar neurons: Nerve cells with many dendrites and a single axon.

Muscarinic: A cholinergic receptor (one responsive to acetylcholine) that mediates chiefly the inhibitory activities of acetylcholine.

Myasthenia gravis: A neurological disease characterized by easy fatigability and weakness of muscles.

Myelencephalon: A subdivision of the hindbrain; the medulla.

Myelin: The fatty insulation around an axon, formed by accessory cells; this improves the speed of conduction of nerve impulses.

Myelin sheath: A thin cover on the axons of many neurons.

Myelinization: The process of formation of myelin.

N

Narcolepsy: A disorder involving frequent, intense episodes of sleep, which last from 5 to 30 minutes, and can occur anytime during the usual waking hours.

Narcosis: Stupor, or unconsciousness, produced by some narcotic drug.

Narcotherapy (narcoanalysis, narcosynthesis): Psychotherapy carried on while the patient is in a sleeplike state of relaxation induced by a drug such as sodium pentothal.

Narcotic drug: Drug such as morphine, which leads to physiological dependence and increased tolerance.

Natural law: A philosophy that refers to a system of rules and principles for the guidance of human behavior; the system arises from the rational intelligence of humans. These rules are apart from enacted laws and stem from and conform to the entire human mental, moral, and physical constitution.

Necker cube: An optical illusion using "rate of apparent change (RAC)" to differentiate normal from brain-injured individuals. Fewer and slower reversals are reported by brain-injured individuals, with damage associated with right hemisphere or frontal lobe lesions.

Necrosis: Local death of tissue.

Negative feedback system: A regulatory system in which output is used to reduce the effect of input signals.

Negativism: Form of aggressive withdrawal that involves refusing to cooperate or obey commands, or doing the exact opposite of what has been requested.

Negligence: The failure to exercise the degree of care that a reasonable person, guided by ordinary considerations under similar circumstances, would exercise.

Neocortex: The relatively recently evolved portions of the cerebral cortex.

Nerve growth factor: A substance that controls the growth of neurons of the spinal ganglia and the ganglia of the sympathetic nervous system.

Nerve impulses: The propagated electrical messages of a neuron that travel down from the axon to adjacent neurons. Also called action potentials.

Neural tube: A prenatal structure with subdivisions that correspond to the future forebrain, midbrain, and hindbrain. The cavity of this tube contains the cerebral ventricles and the passages that connect them.

Neurasthenic neurosis: Neurotic disorder characterized by complaints of chronic weakness, easy fatigability, and lack of enthusiasm.

Neuroblasts: Early forms of cells during the stage of cell migration.

Neurofibrillary tangles: Abnormal whorls of neurofilaments within nerve cells that are especially apparent in people suffering from dementia.

Neurofilaments: Small rodlike structures in axons that are involved in transport materials.

Neuroglia: "Nerve glue" or glia, these cells make up about half the volume of the central nervous system and provide structural and metabolic support to neurons. *See* Glial cells.

Neurohypophysis: *See* Posterior pituitary.

Neurological examination: Examination to determine presence and extent of organ damage to the nervous system.

Neuromodulators: Substances that influence the activity of synaptic transmitters.

Neuron: The basic unit of the nervous system, composed of a cell body (also known as soma or perikaryon), receptive extensions, and a transmitting extension (axon). A cell of the brain or spinal cord composed of a cell body, axon, and dendrites.

Neuron doctrine: A hypothesis that states that the brain is composed of separate cells that are distinct structurally, metabolically, and functionally.

Neuropathies: Peripheral nerve destruction.

Neurosecretory cells: Neurons that manufacture and secrete hormones.

Neurospecificity: A theory of nervous system development that states that each axon grows to a particular site.

Neurotic nucleus: Basic personality characteristics underlying neurotic disorders.

Neurotic paradox: Failure of neurotic patterns to extinguish despite their self-defeating nature.

Neurotic style: A general personality disposition toward inhibiting certain anxiety-causing behaviors; distinguishable from anxiety, somatoform, and dissociative disorders in that neurotic styles do not manifest themselves in specific, disabling neurotic symptoms.

Neurotransmitter: Biochemical substances that transmit information between neurons: *See* Synaptic transmitter.

Nicotinic: A cholingergic receptor that mediates chiefly the excitatory activities of acetylcholine.

Night hospital: Mental hospital in which an individual may receive treatment during the night while carrying on his usual occupation in the daytime.

Nigrostriatal bundle (NSB): A dopaminergic tract that runs from the substantia nigra of the midbrain to the lateral hypothalamus, the globus pallidus, and the caudate putamen.

Nihilistic delusion: Fixed belief that everything is unreal.

Nociceptors: Receptors that respond to stimuli that produce tissue damage or pose the threat of damage.

Node of Ranvier: A gap between successive segments of the myelin sheath where the axonal membrane is exposed.

Nomadism: Withdrawal reaction in which the individual continually attempts to escape frustration by moving from place to place or job to job.

Nomothetic methodology: An approach in which the discovery of relationships between variables by studying large numbers of cases or events is emphasized.

Non compos mentis: Insane; not sound of mind. A very general term including all varieties of mental derangement.

Norepinephrine (NE): A neurotransmitter produced mainly in brain stem nuclei, also called noradrenalin.

Normal pressure hydrocephalus (NPH): A reversible condition involving obstruction of cerebral spinal fluid (CSF). Increased pressure leads to ventricle enlargement with the primary lesion in the midbrain reticular formation.

Nosology: The classification of diseases, including mental diseases.

NSB: *See* Nigrostriatal bundle.

Nucleotide: A portion of a DNA molecule composed of a single base and the adjoining sugar-phosphate unit of the strand.

Nucleus: An anatomical collection of neurons, e.g., caudate nucleus.

Nystagmus: Abnormal to and fro movements of the eye during attempts to fixate. Rhythmic oscillation of the eyeballs, horizontal, rotary, or vertical.

O

Occipital cortex: The cortex of the occipital (posterior) lobe of the brain.

Ocular-dominance histogram: A graph that shows the strength of a neuron's response stimuli presented to either the left or right eye. Used to determine the effects of depriving one eye of visual experience.

Ondine curse: A type of sleep apnea where automatic breathing during sleep is disrupted. Lesions of the reticulospinal tract have been implicated in this condition.

Oneirism: Prolonged dream state despite wakefulness.

Optic aphasia: Inability to name visually presented objects with intact recognition. Spared recognition is shown by demonstration of use or matching (pointing) to the object when named.

Optic ataxia: Inability to localize objects in space by visual guidance. Difficulty in shifting (stimulus boundedness) is an associated feature.

Optic chiasm: The site where optic neurons from the eye separate and cross over to the contralateral hemisphere. Located near the pituitary gland.

Optic radiation: Axons of the lateral geniculate nucleus that terminate in the primary visual areas of the occipital cortex.

Optic tract: The axons of the retinal ganglion cells after they have passed the optic chiasm.

Optokinetic system: A closed-loop system controlling eye movement and keeping the gaze on target.

Organ of Corti: A structure in the inner ear that lies on the basilar membrane; contains the hair cells and the terminations of the auditory nerve.

Orifice: Any aperture or opening.

Osmoreceptors: Cells in the hypothalamus that were thought to respond to changes in osmotic pressure.

Osmotic thirst: The response to increased osmotic pressure in brain cells. Contrast with hypovolemic thirst.

Ostium: A small opening, especially one that forms an entrance into a hollow organ or canal.

Overutilization anoxia: Occurring during epileptic seizures, a lack of sufficient oxygen secondary to the abnormal electrical discharges. Seen as due to the high metabolic rates during seizures.

Oxidation: The combining of food and oxygen in the tissues; chemically, the increase in valence of an element.

Oximeter: An instrument for measuring the oxygen saturation of hemoglobin in the circulating blood.

Oxytocin: A hormone released by the posterior pituitary that triggers milk let-down in the nursing female.

P

Pacchionian bodies: Small projections of the arachnoid tissue, chiefly into the venous sinuses of the dura mater.

Pain asymbolia: Loss of appreciation for pain, associated with left parietal lesions.

Pain cocktail: A concoction of all the medication a pain patient is taking in a single liquid, which can be systematically controlled and reduced in strength.

Paleocortex: Evolutionary old cortex, e.g., the hippocampus.

Palilalia: Progressively more rapid and softer speech productions, ending in an indistinguishable mutter. Associated with bilateral frontal lesions or with subcortical structures.

Palpitation: Forcible pulsation of the heart perceptible to the individual.

Papilledema: Edema of the optic disk, associated with increased intracranial pressure.

Paradigmatic change: A new way of viewing the world.

Paradoxical sleep: *See* Rapid-eye-movement sleep (REM).

Parallel processing: Using several different circuits at the same time to process the same stimuli.

Paralysis: A loss of power of voluntary movement in a muscle through injury or disease of its nerve supply.

Paranoia: Psychosis characterized by a systematized delusional system.

Paranoid personality: Individual showing behavior characterized by projection (as a defense mechanism), suspiciousness, envy, extreme jealousy, and stubbornness.

Paranoid schizophrenia: Subtype of schizophrenic disorder characterized by absurd, illogical, and changeable ideas and hallucinations of grandeur and persecution.

Paranoid state: Transient psychotic disorder in which the main element is a delusion, usually persecutory or grandiose in nature.

Paraphasias: Errors in word usage associated with aphasia. Substitutions for a correct word may occur (e.g., "I ate night") or substitution for syllables (e.g., "I ate rupper"). Neologisms may occur (e.g., "I ate ronks").

Parasympathetic division: One of the two systems that compose the autonomic nervous system. The parasympathetic division arises from both the cranial and sacral parts of the spinal cord.

Paraventricular nucleus: A nucleus of the hypothalamus.

Parenchyma: The essential elements of an organ; the functional elements of an organ, as distinguished from its framework or stroma.

Parens patriae: Literally, "parent of the country." Refers to the role of the state as sovereign or guardian of such persons as minors and insane and incompetent persons.

Parkinson's disease: A degenerative neurological disorder involving dopaminergic neurons of the substantia nigra. A subcortical, progressive dementia that is primarily caused by neuronal degeneration of the basal ganglia, particularly the substantia nigra. There may also be cortical impairment. The three primary symptoms are tremor, rigidity, and bradykinesia. Egocentricity, irritability, and suspiciousness are common.

Partial seizures: Epileptic seizures arising from pathological foci that do not have widespread distribution. These include focal repetitive motor spasms and do not involve loss of consciousness.

Parturition: Giving birth to young.

Path analysis: Statistical technique that takes into account how variables are related to one another through time and how they predict one another.

Pathological gambling: Addictive disorder in which gambling behavior disrupts the individual's life.

Pederasty: Sexual intercourse between males via the anus.

Perceptual defense: A process in which threatening stimuli are filtered out and not perceived by the organism.

Perceptual filtering: Processes involved in selective attention to aspects of the great mass of incoming stimuli that continually impinge on the organism.

Perimeter: An instrument delimiting the field of vision.

Peripheral nerves: Neurons that lie outside the central nervous system.

Peripheral nervous system: The portion of the nervous system that includes all the nerves outside the brain and spinal cord.

Permanent planning: Placing children who are drifting through foster homes back into their original families.

Perseveration: Persistent continuation of a line of thought or activity once it is under way. Clinically inappropriate repetition.

Perseveration–consolidation hypothesis: A hypothesis stating that information passes through two stages in memory formation. During the first stage the memory is held by perseveration of neural activity and is easily disrupted. During the second stage the memory becomes fixed, or consolidated, and is no longer easily disrupted.

Personality disorder: A group of maladaptive behavioral syndromes originating in the developmental years and not characterized by neurotic or psychotic symptoms.

Perversion: Deviation from normal.

Petit mal seizures: A type of generalized epileptic seizure characterized by a spike-and-wave electrical pattern. During these seizures the person is unaware of the environment and later cannot recall what happened.

pH: The symbol commonly used in expressing hydrogen ion concentration; signifies the logarithm of the reciprocal of the hydrogen ion concentration expressed as a power of 10.

Phantom limb: The experience of sensory messages attributed to an amputated limb.

Phasic receptors: Receptors that show a rapid fall in nerve impulse discharge as stimulation is maintained.

Phlebothrombosis: Thrombosis of a vein without inflammation of its walls.

Phonological agraphia: Impaired ability to spell nonwords with intact ability for familiar words. Associated with lesions of the supermarginal gyrus or associated areas.

Phosphemes: Flashes of light caused by dysfunction of the auditory-visual association area. Visual hallucinations may also be produced, related or not to past experiences.

Photopic system: A system in the retina that operates at high levels of light, shows sensitivity to color, and involves the cones; contrast with scotopic system.

Phrenology: The belief that bumps on the skull reflect enlargements of brain regions responsible for certain behavioral faculties.

Pick's disease: Similar to Alzheimer's disease, here neuronic damage is typically confined to the frontal and temporal lobes. Personality changes usually precede memory loss. Affects twice as many women as men.

Pilocarpine: An alkaloid that stimulates the parasympathetic division of the autonomic nervous system.

Pitch: A dimension of auditory experience in which sounds vary from low to high.

Pituitary gland: A small complex endocrine gland located in a socket at the base of the skull. The anterior pituitary and posterior pituitary are separate in function.

Place theory: A theory of frequency discrimination according to which pitch perception depends on the place of maximal displacement of the basilar membrane produced by a sound. Contrast with volley theory.

Plaintiff: A person who initiates an action or legal suit. In a civil suit, the party who complains or sues.

Planum temporale: A region of superior temporal cortex adjacent to the primary auditory area.

Plea: In a legal action, the defendant's answer to the plaintiff's declaration.

Plea bargaining: In a criminal case, the process in which the accused and the prosecutor negotiate a mutually satisfactory disposition of the case subject to the approval of the court. Usually involves the defendant pleading guilty to a reduced punishment or offense or to a lesser number of counts in a multicount indictment.

Pleading: The formal allegations made by the opposing parties of their respective claims and defenses.

Pleasure principle: In psychoanalysis, the demand that an instinctual need be immediately gratified regardless of reality.

Plexus: A network, or tangle, of interweaving nerves, veins, or lymphatic vessels.

Pneumoencephalogram: A technique for examining brain structure in intact humans by taking radiographic images after a gas is injected into the ventricles.

Pons: A portion of the metencephalon.

Positive law: A system of rules and laws enacted or adopted by the government of an organized political community for the purpose of controlling the conduct of its people.

Positron emission tomography (PET) scan: A technique for examining brain structure and function in intact humans by combining tomography with injections of radioactive substances used by the brain. An analysis of metabolism of these substances reflects regional differences in brain activity. Computer-assisted radiographic procedure designed to analyze and track glucose utilization in the brain.

Postcentral gyrus: Involved in sensory mediation, this cortical convolution is located just posterior to the fissure of Rolando.

Posterior pituitary: The rear division of the pituitary gland. Also called neurohypophysis.

Posthypnotic amnesia: The subject's lack of memory for the period during which he or she was hypnotized.

Posthypnotic suggestion: Suggestion given during hypnosis to be carried out by the subject after he or she is brought out of hypnosis.

Postpartum disturbances: Emotional disturbance of the mother associated with childbirth.

Postsynaptic potentials: *See* Graded potentials.

Post-traumatic amnesia (PTA): A form of anterograde amnesia seen as a postconcussional effect of head trauma. Correlates well with coma length and severity. Some retrograde amnesia may accompany PTA.

Post-traumatic stress disorder: Category of disorder in which the stressor is severe and residual symptoms occur following the traumatic experience.

Postural tremor: A tremor that occurs when a person attempts to maintain a posture such as holding an arm or leg extended, resulting from pathology of the basal ganglia or cerebellum.

Precedent: A previous judgment or decision of a court considered as an authority for deciding later identical or similar cases. Under the doctrine of stare decisis, case: which establish that a rule of law are authoritative and must be adhered to.

Precentral gyrus: Involved in the mediation of motor activity, this cortical convolution is located just anterior to the fissure of Rolando.

Precipitating cause: The particular stress that triggers a disorder.

Predisposing cause: The factor that lowers the individual's stress tolerance and paves the way for the appearance of a disorder.

Predisposition: Likelihood that an individual will develop certain symptoms under given stress conditions.

Pressor: Excited vasoconstrictor activity, producing increased blood pressure; denoting afferent nerves that, when stimulated, excite the vasoconstrictor center.

Presumption: An inference resulting from a rule of law or the proven existence of a fact that requires such rule(s) or action(s) be established in the action. Presumption can be irrefutable, such as the presumption of incapacity in a person under 7 years of age to act, or rebuttable, in which case it can be disproved by evidence.

Presumption of innocence: A principle of criminal law in which the government carries the burden of proof beyond a reasonable doubt for every element of a crime, with the defendant having no burden of proof to prove his or her innocence.

Prima facie **case:**   A case in which there is sufficient evidence for the matter to proceed beyond a motion for a directed verdict in a jury case or a motion to dismiss in nonjury trial; requires that the defendant proceed with his or her case.

Prima facie **evidence:**   Evidence that, in the judgment of the law, is good and sufficient to establish a given fact or a chain of facts making up the party's claim or defense. If such evidence is unexplained or uncontradicted, it is sufficient to sustain favorable judgment for the issue it supports; may be contradicted by other evidence.

Primary reaction tendencies: Constitutional tendencies apparent in infancy, such as sensitivity and activity level.

Privilege: A particular benefit or exemption enjoyed by a person, company, or class beyond the common ones held by other citizens.

Privileged communication: Statements that are made in a setting of legal or other professional confidentiality. Applies to certain persons within a protected relationship, such as husband–wife and attorney–client, who are legally protected from forced disclosure on the witness stand at the option of the witness.

Pro bono publico: For the welfare or good of the public, such as when an attorney or other professional handles a case without compensation to advance a social cause or represents a party who cannot afford to pay.

Problem drinker: Behavioral term referring to one who has serious problems associated with drinking alcohol. Term is currently preferable to alcoholic.

Process (poor premorbid, chronic) schizophrenia: Schizophrenia pattern that develops gradually and tends to be long-lasting.

Prodrome: Behavioral/mood change preceding onset of a seizure. Prodromal signs may be apparent for several days before the seizure.

Progressive supranuclear palsy: An uncommon Parkinson-like condition that usually begins in the 50s with emotional liability, imbalance, and problems with downward gaze. A dementia develops with relative sparing of language and constructional abilities.

Projection neuron: Large neurons that transmit messages to widely separated parts of the brain.

Prosecution: A criminal proceeding to determine the guilt or innocence of a person charged with a crime. Refers to the state or federal government as the party proceeding in a criminal action.

Prosencephalon: *See* Forebrain.

Prosody: Rhythm, pitch, tempo, and similar characteristics of speech. Important in communication of affective content. Typically seen as a right hemisphere activity.

Prosopagnosia: Inability to recognize faces of those with whom one was previously familiar. Loss of ability to recognize unfamiliar faces is a variant of this disorder. Usually associated with right lesions.

Protocritic: A diffuse type of sensory experience (e.g., temperature) that is common to all homeostatic internal mechanisms. Cognitive processing does not lead to identifying a discrete place or duration for the sensation. Opposed to epicritic.

Proximal: An anatomical directional term meaning near the trunk or center; opposite of distal.

Proximate cause: An occurrence that, in a natural and unbroken chain of events, results in an injury and without which the injury would not have occurred. The event that is closest in the causal relationship to the effect.

Pseudo-community: Delusional social environment developed by a paranoid person.

Pseudobulbar state: Strong affective expressions to include laughing and crying, often simultaneously, but also incongruous to the stated feeling of the person. Associated with lesions of connecting pathways between the frontal lobes and lower brain structures.

Pseudodementia: A pattern of deficit behavior resembling organically produced dementia. Depression is the primary factor causing the intellectual suppression.

Pseudodepression: The major pathology involves the dorsal-lateral frontal convexity, severe bilateral frontal pathology, or severing of frontal-thalamic pathways. This is a pathology of reduced/absent motor responses (e.g., mutism, inactivity, helpless unconcern). The subject may be aware of his or her deficit.

Pseudohemianopsia: Lack of attention to visual stimulation from the contralateral side despite intact visual fields.

Pseudopsychopathy: The major pathology involves the orbital frontal areas and reflects motor excess (e.g., puerile acts, restlessness, bursting into motion, impulsive antisocial acts). The subject knows but cannot control the motor behavior.

Psychic cortex: Anterior portion of the temporal lobe that when stimulated produces recollection of previous experience (e.g., music, visual scenes). Temporal lobe tumors may produce hallucinations involving previous experiences.

Psychomotor epilepsy: State of disturbed consciousness in which the individual may perform various actions, sometimes of a homicidal nature, for which he or she is later amnesic.

Psychosexual dysfunction: Inability or impaired ability to experience or give sexual gratification.

Psychotogens: Substances that generate psychotic behavior.

Psychotropic drugs: Drugs whose main effects are mental or behavioral in nature.

Pterygoid: Shaped like a wing.

Ptosis: Drooping eyelid caused by a lesion to the oculomotor cranial nerve.

Pure agraphia: Writing deficits caused by brain damage in the absence of other significant language disturbance.

Pure word deafness: Inability to understand spoken words with an intact ability to read, write, and speak. Usually does not occur in isolation of other defects and is associated with cardiovascular accidents.

Purkinje cell: A type of large nerve cell in the cerebellar cortex.

Putative: Reputed or supposed.

Pyramidal cell: A type of large nerve cell in the cerebral cortex.

Pyramidal system: A motor system including neurons within the cerebral cortex and the axons that form the pyramidal tract.

Q

Quasi-experimental design: A research study in which the experimenter has partial experimental control over the setting and variables.

R

Ramp movements: Slow, sustained motions thought to be generated in the basal ganglia. Also called smooth movements. Contrast with ballistic.

Ramus: A branch; one of the primary divisions of a nerve or a blood vessel; a part of an irregularly shaped bone that forms an angle with the main body.

Random assignment: An experimental method that ensures that every subject has an equal chance of being selected for the experimental or control group.

Range fractionation: A hypothesis of stimulus intensity perception stating that a wide range of intensity values can be encoded by a group of cells, each of which is a specialist for a particular range of an intensity scale.

Rape: An act of violence in which sexual relations are forced upon another person.

Raphe nucleus: A group of neurons in the midline of the brain stem that contains serotonin, involved in sleep mechanisms.

Rapid-eye-movement (REM) sleep: A state of sleep characterized by small-amplitude, fast electroencephalographic (EEG) waves, no postural tension, and rapid eye movements. Also called paradoxical sleep.

Ratio decidendi: The principal ground or reason for a court's written decision. The point in a case that is essential to determining the court's judgment.

Reaction formation: Ego-defense mechanism in which the individual's conscious attitudes and overt behavior are opposite to repressed unconscious wishes.

Readiness potential: An electrical potential that occurs over widespread posterior regions of the scalp prior to the onset of a voluntary movement.

Reality assumptions: Assumptions that relate to the gratification of needs in the light of environmental possibilities, limitations, and dangers.

Reality principle: Awareness of the demands of the environment and adjustment of behavior to meet these demands.

Reasonable doubt: The degree of doubt required to justify an acquittal of a criminal defendant, based on reason and arising from evidence or lack of evidence.

Reasonable doubt standard: A standard beyond which guilt must be shown.

Receptive field: The stimulus region and features that cause the maximal responses of a cell in a sensory system.

Receptor: Nerve ending that receives a stimulus. The initial element in sensory systems, responsible for stimulus transduction, e.g., hair cells in the cochlea or rods and cones in the retina.

Receptor proteins: Substances at synaptic receptor sites whose reaction to certain transmitters causes a change in the postsynaptic membrane potential.

Receptor sites: Regions of specialized membrane containing receptor proteins located on the postsynaptic surface of a synapse; these sites receive and react with the chemical transmitter.

Recess: A short interval during a trial or hearing when the court suspends business without adjournment.

Reduplicative paramnesia: Associated with right parietal and/or frontal damage of a coarse nature. Involves relocating a place (e.g., hospital) to another place (e.g., one's home town).

Reflex: A simple, highly stereotyped, and unlearned response to a particular stimuli (i.e., an eyeblink in response to a puff of air).

Refractory: A period during and after a nerve impulse in which the axon membrane's responsiveness is reduced. A brief period of complete insensitivity to stimuli (absolute refractory phase) is followed by a longer period of reduced sensitivity (relative refractory phase) during which only strong stimulation produces a nerve impulse.

Regression: Ego-defense mechanism in which the individual retreats to the use of mature responses in attempting to cope with stress and maintain ego integrity.

Remand: To send a case back to the court from which it came to have further action taken on it there.

Remedy: The means by which a right is enforced or the violation of a right is prevented or compensated for.

Repression: Ego-defense mechanism by means of which dangerous desires and intolerable memories are kept out of consciousness.

Residual schizophrenia: Category used for persons regarded as recovered from schizophrenia but still manifesting some symptoms.

Resistance: Tendency to maintain symptoms and resist treatment or uncovering repressed material.

Resistance to extinction: Tendency of a conditioned response to persist despite lack of reinforcement.

Resorption: The loss of substance through physiologic or pathologic means.

Respondent: The party answering a charge or the party contending against an appeal.

Resting potential: Potential differences across the membrane of nerve cells during inactive period. Also called membrane potential.

Retainer: A contract between an attorney and a client stating the nature of the service to be rendered and the cost of such services. By employing an attorney to act on their behalf, clients prevent the attorney from acting for their adversary.

Rete mirabile: A network of fine blood vessels located at the base of the brain in which blood coming from the periphery reduces the temperature of arterial blood before it enters the brain.

Reticular: Netlike.

Reticular activating system: Brain stem area that mediates level of arousal.

Reticular formation: A region of the brain stem (extending from the medulla through the thalamus) that is involved in arousal.

Retinaculum: A special fascial thickening that holds back an organ or part; helps retain an organ or tissue in its place.

Retrieval: A process in memory during which a stored memory is utilized by an organism.

Retroactive amnesia: A type of memory loss in which events just before a head injury are not recalled.

Retrograde amnesia: Inability to recall events previous to the onset of a trauma; recovery of remote events usually occurs first.

Retrograde degeneration: Destruction of the nerve cell body following injury.

Reuptake: A mechanism by which a synaptic transmitter released at a synapse is taken back into the presynaptic terminal, thus stopping synaptic activity.

Reverse tolerance: Situation in which a decreased amount of some psychoactive drug brings about the effects formerly achieved by a larger dose.

Rh antigen or factor: An agglutinogen, or antigen, first found in the erythrocytes of rhesus monkey, hence the Rh. Rh positive and Rh negative terms denote presence or absence, respectively, of this antigen.

Rhodopsin: The photopigment in rods that responds to light.

Ribosomes: Organelles that appear as dots lining the endoplasmic reticulum; they are the protein factories of cells.

Right: A power or privilege, enforced legally, giving a person control over the actions of others.

Rigid control: Coping patterns involving reliance upon inner restraints, such as inhibition, suppression, repression, and reaction formation.

Role obsolescence: Condition occurring when the ascribed social role of a given individual is no longer important to the social group.

Roots: The two distinct branches of a spinal nerve, each of which serves a separate function. The dorsal root carries sensory information from the peripheral nervous system to the spinal cord. The ventral root carries motor messages from the spinal cord to the peripheral nervous system.

Rostral: An anatomical term meaning toward the head end; opposite of caudal.

S

Saccades: Rapid movements of the eyes that occur regularly during normal viewing.

Saccadic suppression: The suppression of vision during saccades, which provides the viewer with perception free of these abrupt movements.

Sacral: Refers to the lower part of the back or spinal cord.

Sadism: Sexual variant in which sexual gratification is obtained by the infliction of pain upon others.

Sagittal plane: The plane that bisects the body or brain into right and left halves.

Saltatory conduction: The form of conduction seen in myelinated axons in which the nerve impulse jumps from one node of Ranvier to the next.

Schizo-affective psychosis: Disorder characterized by schizophrenic symptoms in conjunction with pronounced depression or elation.

Schizoid personality: Personality pattern characterized by shyness, oversensitivity, seclusiveness, and eccentricity.

Schizophrenia: Psychosis characterized by the breakdown of integrated personality functioning, withdrawal from reality, emotional blunting and distortion, and disturbances in thought and behavior.

Schizophreniform disorder: Category of schizophrenic psychosis, usually in an undifferentiated form, with a duration of less than 6 months.

Schizophrenogenic: Qualities in parents that appear to be associated with the development of schizophrenia in offspring; often applied to rejecting, cold, domineering, overprotective mothers or passive, uninvolved fathers.

Schwann cell: The kind of accessory cell that forms myelin in the peripheral nervous system.

Scotoma: A region of blindness caused by injury to the visual pathway.

Scotopic system: A system in the retina that responds to low levels of light.

Second messenger: A relatively slow acting substance in the postsynaptic cell that amplifies the effects of nerve impulses and can initiate processes that lead to changes in electrical potentials at the membrane.

Selective vigilance: A tuning of attentional and perceptual processes toward stimuli relevant or central to goal-directed behavior, with decreased sensitivity to stimuli irrelevant or peripheral to this purpose.

Sella turcica: A saddlelike depression on the upper surface of the sphenoid bone, in which the hypophysis lies.

Semantic agraphia: Deficit or loss of ability to spell or write with meaning, produced by brain damage to various sites.

Semantic memory: Memory for what is learned as knowledge. This recall therefore is considered "timeless and spaceless" (e.g., a number system, a foreign language).

Senile dementia: A neurological disorder of the aged involving progressive behavioral deterioration including personality change and profound intellectual decline.

Senile plaques: Neuroanatomical changes correlated with senile dementia due to the build-up of beta amyloid.

Sensorineural deafness: A hearing impairment originating from cochlear or auditory nerve lesions.

Sepsis: A morbid condition resulting from the presence of pathogenic bacteria. From septic.

Septo-hypothalamo-mesencephalic (SHM) continuum: One of three limbic mechanisms, the SHM continuum has distinct circuitry connecting the hypothalamus, the limbic midbrain area, and other sites. Only the prefrontal lobe has direct connections with the SHM continuum, out of the entire isocortex.

Serial lesion effect: The lessened severity of cerebral symptoms (e.g., due to diaschisis) when lesions are introduced in stages as opposed to all at once.

Serotonergic: Refers to neurons that use serotonin as their synaptic transmitter.

Serotonin (5HT):   A neurotransmitter produced in the raphe nuclei and active in structures throughout the cerebral hemispheres; plays a role in the systems that control memory, emotion, and perception. A compound (5-hydroxytryptamine) found in the bloodstream that has vasoconstrictive properties.

Short-term memory: Memory that usually lasts only for seconds or as long as rehearsal continues.

Significant others: In interpersonal theory, parents or others on whom an infant is dependent for meeting all physical and psychological needs.

Simple cortical cells: Cells in the visual cortex that respond best to an edge or a bar of a particular width and with a particular direction and location in the visual field.

Simulation: An intentional imitation of the basic processes and outcomes of a real-life situation, carried out to better understand the basic mechanisms of the situation. In civil law, misrepresenting or concealing the truth, as when parties pretend to perform an act different from that in which they really are engaged.

Simultagnosia: The perception of one stimulus when two objects are presented. Often associated with inertia of gaze.

Sinus: A channel for the passage of blood; hollow in a bone or other tissue; antrum; one of the cavities connecting with the nose; a suppurating cavity.

Sinusoid: A blood space in certain organs, as the brain.

Situational stress reaction (acute): Superficial maladjustment to newly experienced life situations that are especially difficult or trying.

Sleep apnea: A sleep disorder that involves slowing or cessation of respiration during sleep, which wakens the patient. Excessive daytime somnolence results from frequent nocturnal awakening.

Slow-wave sleep: Stages of sleep including stages 1 through 4, defined by presence of slow electroencephalographic (EEG) activity.

Socialized-aggressive disorder: Pattern of childhood maladaptive behaviors involving social maladaption, such as stealing, truancy, gang membership.

Sodium pentothal: Barbiturate drug sometimes used in psychotherapy to produce a state of relaxation and suggestibility.

Sodomy: Sexual intercourse via the anus.

Somatosensory agnosia: Loss of tactile recognition due to cerebral dysfunction in the presence of intact somatosensory receptive functions.

Somatosensory modalities: Refers to different types of body sensation (e.g., touch, pain, pressure). Distinguished from auditory and visual senses.

Somesthetic: Pertaining to somatesthesia, or the consciousness of having a body.

Somnolent mutism: Immobility and unresponsiveness with eyes closed, associated with mesencephalic–diencephalic lesions. Intense stimulation yields minimal responses.

Spasm: An involuntary, convulsive, muscular contraction.

Spatial acalculia: Spatial misarrangement of the numbers during arithmetic calculation with intact knowledge of correct principle. Associated with right hemisphere lesions.

Spatial agraphia: Deficits in spatial motor aspects of writing due to brain damage located in the nondominant parietal lobe. Frequently associated with the neglect syndrome.

Spatial summation: The summation of the axon hillock of postsynaptic potentials from across the cell body. If this summation reaches threshold, a nerve impulse will be triggered.

Special vulnerability: Low tolerance for specific types of stress.

Specific heat: The heat energy required to raise the temperature of 1 g of a substance by 1°C.

Spectrally opponent cell: A visual receptor cell with opposite firing responses to different regions of the spectrum.

Spinal nerves: The 31 pairs of nerves that emerge from the spinal cord.

Split-brain: Individuals who have had the corpus callosum severed, halting communication between the right and left hemispheres.

Squamous: Scalelike.

Stage 1 sleep: The initial stage of slow-wave sleep involving small-amplitude electroencephalographic (EEG) waves of irregular frequency, slow heart rate, and a reduction of muscle tension.

Stage 2 sleep: A stage of slow-wave sleep defined by bursts of regular 14 to 18 Hz electroencephalographic (EEG) waves that progressively increase and then decrease in amplitude (called spindles).

Stage 3 sleep: A stage of slow-wave sleep defined by the spindles seen in stage 2 sleep mixed with larger amplitude slow waves.

Stage 4 sleep: A stage of slow-wave sleep defined by the presence of high amplitude slow waves of 1 to 4 Hz.

Star chamber: An ancient court of England that originally had jurisdiction in cases in which the ordinary course of justice was obstructed by one party to the extent that no inferior court would find its process obeyed. Abolished in modern jurisprudence.

***Stare decisis*:**   The legal policy of courts stating that once a principle of law is laid down, it will be adhered to and applied to all future cases in which the facts are substantially the same. Serves to ensure security and certainty of legal principles.

Static phase of weight gain: A later period following destruction of the ventromedial hypothalamus during which the animal's weight stabilizes at an obese level and food intake is not much above normal.

Statistical test of significance: A standard of probability stating that an experimental finding is significant if, by chance alone, it could have occurred fewer than 1 or 5 times in 100 occurrences. In the field of psychology, 5 times in 100 is usually the standard of acceptability for statistical significance.

Statute: An act of legislation by which a law is created, as opposed to unwritten or common law.

Statutory law: The body of law created by the legislature.

Statutory rape: Sexual intercourse with a minor.

Stellate cell: A kind of small nerve cell with many branches.

Stenosis: Narrowing or contraction of a body passage or opening.

Stereoacuity: The ability to discriminate small differences in visual depth by point-by-point matching in the retinas.

Stereopsis: The ability to perceive depth, utilizing the slight difference in visual information from the two eyes.

Stimulus enhancement: The second stimulus in a pair adds rather than masks the neural effects of the first stimulus. Studies include those that present letters of one half of a word (first stimulus) and then letters of the remaining portion of the word (second stimulus).

Stimulus masking: A second stimulus leads into or masks a first stimulus if the trace of the initial stimulus is longlasting or otherwise sufficient. The target stimulus (e.g., letters of the alphabet) is interfered with by the masking stimulus (e.g., patterned line segments).

Stimulus persistence: Effects of external stimulation are lasting in the central nervous system, dependent on many factors. Stimulus persistence acting as an interference to new stimuli has been advanced to account for deficient perception in the older person.

Stipulation: An agreement made between opposing parties that certain facts or principles of law are true and applicable and will not be contested.

Stress-decompensation model: View of abnormal behavior that emphasizes progressive disorganization of behavior under excessive stress.

Striate cortex: A portion of the visual cortex with input from the lateral geniculate nucleus.

Strict liability: Liability without a showing of fault, as when a person, who engages in a hazardous activity, is totally liable for injuries caused by the activity even without negligence being shown.

Stricture: A circumscribed narrowing of a tubular structure.

Stroma: The tissue that forms the ground substance, framework, or matrix of an organ, as distinguished from that constituting its functional element, or parenchyma.

***Sub nom*:**   Under the name. In the name of. Often used when the original name of a case must be changed due to a change in parties.

Subpoena: A command for a witness to appear at a certain time and place to testify in court on a certain matter.

Subpoena duces tecum: A command that a witness produce a specified document or record.

Substance-abuse disorders: Pathological use of a substance for at least a month, resulting in self-injurious behavior and biological dependence on the substance.

Substance-induced organic disorder: Category of disorders based on organic impairment resulting from toxicity or physiologic changes in the brain.

Substance-use disorder: Patterns of maladaptive behavior centered around regular use of substance involved.

Sulci: The furrows of convoluted brain surface. Contrast with gyri.

Superior colliculus: A structure in the midbrain that receives information from the optic tract.

Superior olivary complex: A brain stem structure that receives input from the left cochlear nuclei, providing the first binaural analysis of auditory information.

Supplementary motor area (SMA) location: Area 6 and partially area 7, anterior to paracentral lobule. Function: volitional (self-initiated) movements; perineal and leg movements are found in the medial extension of the motor homunculus. Considered also a secondary speech area.

Supra: Above, upon.

Supraoptic nucleus: A nucleus of the hypothalamus.

Synapse: An area composed of the presynaptic (axonal) terminal, the postsynaptic (usually dendritic) membrane, and the space (or cleft) between them. This is the site at which neural messages travel from one neuron to another. Also called the synaptic region.

Synaptic assembly: A level of brain organization that includes the total collection of all synapses on a single cell.

Synaptic bouton: The presynaptic swelling of the axon terminal from which neural messages travel across the synaptic cleft to other neurons.

Synaptic cleft: The space between the presynaptic and postsynaptic membranes.

Synaptic region: *See* Synapse.

Synaptic transmitter: The chemical in the presynaptic bouton that serves as the basis for neural communication. It travels across the synaptic cleft and reacts with the postsynaptic membrane when triggered by a nerve impulse. Also called neurotransmitter.

Synaptic vesicles: The small, spherically shaped structures that contain molecules of synaptic transmitter.

T

Tactile: Pertaining to the sense of touch.

Tactual hallucinations: Hallucinations involving the sense of touch, such as feeling cockroaches crawling over one's body.

Tardive dyskinesia: Abnormal involuntary movements involving the extremities or facial area (e.g., tongue, jaw, facial surface). Results as a late side effect of neuroleptic drug treatment and, in many cases, is irreversible. Involuntary movements—especially those involving the face, mouth, lips, and tongue—that are related to prolonged use of antipsychotic drugs, such as chlorpromazine.

Telecephalon: Consists of the cerebral cortex, corpus striatum, and medullary center. The frontal subdivision of the forebrain that includes the cerebral hemispheres when fully developed.

Temporal summation: The summation of postsynaptic potentials that reach the axon hillock at different times. The closer together they are, the more complete the summation.

Testosterone: A hormone produced by male gonads that controls a variety of bodily changes that become visible at puberty.

Tetany: Intermittent tonic muscular contractions of the extremities.

Thalamic syndrome: Disturbance of the senses with initial hemianesthesia, followed by a raised threshold to touch, pain, heat, and cold on the side opposite the lesion. The sensations may be extremely adversive when reached. Due primarily to a thalamic infarct.

Thalamus: The brain regions that surround the third ventricle.

Third-party beneficiary: A person who has enforceable rights created by a contract to which he is not party and for which he gives no consideration.

Thrombophlebitis: The condition in which inflammation of the vein wall has preceded the formation of a thrombus, or intravascular clot.

Thrombosis: The formation of a clot within a vessel during life.

Thrombotic stroke: Results from blockage or occlusion by blood or tissue particles or overgrowth. Forms most often where blood vessels branch.

Thrombus: A clot of blood formed within the heart or the blood vessels, usually caused by slowing of the circulation of the blood or by alteration of the blood itself or the vessel walls.

Thyroid-stimulating hormone (TSH):   A tropic hormone released by the anterior pituitary gland that increases the release of thyroxin and the uptake of iodine by the thyroid gland.

Thyrotropin-releasing hormone (TRH):   A hypothalamic hormone that regulates the release of thyroid-stimulating hormone.

Thyroxin: A hormone released by the thyroid gland.

Tinnitus: A ringing or singing sound in the ears.

Tolerance: Physiological condition in which increased dosage of an addictive drug is needed to obtain effects previously produced by smaller doses.

Tomogram: *See* Computer axial tomogram.

Tonic receptors: Receptors in which the frequency of nerve impulse discharge declines slowly or not at all as stimulation is maintained.

Tort: A private or civil wrong or injury, excluding a breach of contract, for which the court will provide a remedy in the form of an action for damages.

Toxicity: The poisonous nature of a substance.

Trabecula: A septum that extends from an envelope into the enclosed substance, forming an essential part of the stroma of the organ.

Transcortical motor (TCM) aphasia: Separation of general conceptual functions (posterior) from Broca motor output area (anterior). Lesions in the supplementary motor area (SMA) or in Broca's area. The patient can repeat words but has difficulty with comprehension and/or speech.

Transient global amnesia: A relatively brief (several hours to several days) amnestic condition with few neurological sequelae. Associated features include (1) a major symptom of anterograde amnesia, (2) some retrograde amnesia, (3) confusion and time/place disorientation, and (4) speech and orientation to person are unimpaired. There is usually a sudden onset and cessation with no prodromal symptoms or known cause.

Transient ischemic attacks (TIAs): Neurological deficits of sudden onset; less intense and temporary strokes that may precede thrombotic strokes. Last less than 24 hours by definition. About half of those who experience TIAs will have a major stroke.

Transient situational disorder: Temporary mental disorder developing under conditions of overwhelming stress, as in military combat or civilian catastrophes.

Transmethylation hypothesis: A hypothesized explanation of schizophrenia suggesting that the addition of a methyl group to some naturally occurring brain compounds can convert some substances to hallucinogenic agents, or psychotogens.

Transverse: *See* Coronal.

Tremor at rest: A tremor that occurs when the affected region, such as a limb, is fully supported.

Tremors: Rhythmic repetitive movements caused by brain pathology.

Trial: A judicial examination or determination, either civil or criminal, of issues between parties to an action.

Trigeminal neuralgia: Intense and sudden pain in area of a trigeminal nerve lesion. The episodic pain may be set off by light stimulation such as touching the skin.

Tropic hormones: Anterior pituitary hormones that affect the secretion of other endocrine glands.

U

Unconscious motivation: Motivation for an individual's behavior of which he or she is unaware.

Undifferentiated schizophrenia: Subtype in which the patient either has mixed symptoms or moves rapidly from one type to another.

Undue influence: Any wrongful or improper persuasion whereby the person's will is overpowered, thereby causing the person to act in a way he or she would normally not have acted.

Uniform laws: A body of written laws, in various subject areas, approved by the commissioners on uniform state laws, which are often adopted by individual states.

Unilateral apraxia: Apraxia affecting one side of the body. Sympathetic and callosal types have been postulated. The sympathetic aspect occurs when other functions are likewise impaired (e.g., right hemiparesis, left-hand apraxia) and Broca aphasia produced by left motor association destruction of callosal fibers.

Unipolar disorder: A severe affective disorder in which only depressive episodes occur, as opposed to bipolar disorders in which both manic and depressive processes are assumed to occur.

Unmyelinated: Refers to fine-diameter axons that lack a myelin sheath.

Unsocialized disturbance of conduct: Childhood disorder in which the child is disobedient, hostile, and highly aggressive.

Urticaria: Nettle rash; hives; elevated, itching, white patches.

Utilization behavior: Considered a type of magnetic apraxia, where the afflicted individual pursues a stimulus to grasp within a set of actively exploring the environment. Considered a strong frontal sign. Gegenhalten occurs when contact is made. Walking is then impaired when attempted, with leg stiffening and no movement.

V

Vaginismus: An involuntary muscle spasm at the entrance to the vagina that prevents penetration and sexual intercourse.

Vagus nerve: One of the cranial nerves.

Variant sexual behavior: Behavior in which satisfaction is dependent on something other than a mutually desired sexual engagement with a sexually mature member of the opposite sex.

Ventral: An anatomical term meaning toward the belly or front of the body or the bottom of the brain; opposite of dorsal.

Ventricles: Cavities in the brain that contain cerebrospinal fluid. The four cavities in the brain that contain cerebrospinal fluid. The choroid plexus produces the cerebrospinal fluid. Spaces within the brain, filled with cerebrospinal fluid, which provide support and cushioning for the brain.

Ventricular layer: A layer of homogeneous cells in the neural tube of the developing organism that is the source of all neural and glial cells in the mature organism. Also called the ependymal layer.

Ventromedial hypothalamus (VMH):   A hypothalamic region involved in inhibiting eating, among other functions.

Venue: The particular geographic area in which a court with jurisdiction may hear and determine a case.

Verbal adynamia: Diminished speech spontaneity. There is slow speech initiation and/or reluctance to continue verbal output. Usually accompanies general apathy.

Verdict: The formal decision or finding made by a judge or jury on the matters or questions submitted for their deliberation and determination.

Vertigo: Dizziness, giddiness.

Vesicle: A small bladder, or sac, containing liquid.

Vesicles (synaptic):   Small structures located at the end point (terminus) of the axon that are filled with neurotransmitter substances.

Vestibular: Pertaining to a vestibule; such as the inner ear, larynx, mouth, nose, vagina.

Vestibuloocular reflex: A rapid response that adjusts the eye to a change in head position.

Viscosity: A condition of more or less adhesion of the molecules of a fluid to each other so that the fluid flows with difficulty. A behavioral pattern characterized by stickiness in interactional contexts. Associated with frontal system damage.

Visual anosognosia: Denial of blindness caused by brain lesions. The subject attempts to behave as if the deficit were not present. *See* Anton's syndrome.

***Voir dire*:**   To speak the truth. The preliminary examination made by the court or by attorneys of one presented as a prospective juror to determine his or her competence.

W

Wada technique: Designed to assess which hemisphere is language dominant. Here, sodium amytal is injected into one carotid artery to deactivate an entire hemisphere. Changes in counting behaviors while the injection is in process indicate which hemisphere is dominant for speech and language.

Waive: To abandon or give up a claim or right.

Waiver: An intentional and voluntary surrendering or giving up of a known right.

Warrant: A document directing a public official to perform a particular act.

Weight of the evidence: The relative value of the credible evidence presented by one side balanced against the evidence presented by the other side. Indicates to the jury that the party having the burden of proof will be entitled to the verdict if the greater amount of evidence supports the issue.

Wernicke's aphasia: A fluent disorder with severe auditory comprehension and processing deficits. Empty speech, press for speech, and a moderate to substantial naming deficit are apparent. Considered a posterior aphasia.

Wernicke's area: A region of the left hemisphere involved in language comprehension.

White matter: Consists of densely packed conduction fibers that transmit neural messages between the cortex and lower centers (projection fibers), between the hemispheres (commissural fibers), or within a hemisphere (association fibers). A shiny layer underneath the cortex consisting largely of axons with white myelin sheaths.

Witness: One who testifies, under oath, to what he or she has seen, heard, or otherwise observed.

Word deafness: Also called pure word deafness. Here, nonspeech sounds are recognized but not spoken words. Usually produced by subcortical lesion disconnecting auditory input from auditory processing.

Work product: Work done by an attorney while representing a client, such as writings, statements, or testimony in regard to the attorney's legal impressions, tactics, strategies, and opinions, which are ordinarily not subject to discovery. Discovery may be obtained only when the party seeking it has a substantial need for the material to prepare his or her case and is unable to obtain the substantial equivalent of the material by other means without undue hardship.

Writ: An order issued by a court mandating the performance of a specified act, or giving authority to have it done.

X

X cells: Retinal ganglion cells that continue to respond to maintained visual stimuli.

Xanthrochromia: Blood cells in the cerebrospinal fluid with discoloration due to an abnormal somatic condition.

Y

Y cells: Retinal ganglion cells that respond strongly initially but rapidly decrease the frequency of response to a visual stimulus.

Part IV

Appendices

Ethical Principles of Psychologists and Code of Conduct 2002

History and Effective Date Footnote

CONTENTS

INTRODUCTION AND APPLICABILITY

The American Psychological Association's (APA's) Ethical Principles of Psychologists and Code of Conduct (hereinafter referred to as the Ethics Code) consists of an Introduction, a Preamble, five General Principles (A – E), and specific Ethical Standards. The Introduction discusses the intent, organization, procedural considerations, and scope of application of the Ethics Code. The Preamble and General Principles are aspirational goals to guide psychologists toward the highest ideals of psychology. Although the Preamble and General Principles are not themselves enforceable rules, they should be considered by psychologists in arriving at an ethical course of action. The Ethical Standards set forth enforceable rules for conduct as psychologists. Most of the Ethical Standards are written broadly, in order to apply to psychologists in varied roles, although the application of an Ethical Standard may vary depending on the context. The Ethical Standards are not exhaustive. The fact that a given conduct is not specifically addressed by an Ethical Standard does not mean that it is necessarily either ethical or unethical.

This Ethics Code applies only to psychologists' activities that are part of their scientific, educational, or professional roles as psychologists. Areas covered include but are not limited to the clinical, counseling, and school practice of psychology; research; teaching; supervision of trainees; public service; policy development; social intervention; development of assessment instruments; conducting assessments; educational counseling; organizational consulting; forensic activities; program design and evaluation; and administration. This Ethics Code applies to these activities across a variety of contexts, such as in person, postal, telephone, internet, and other electronic transmissions. These activities shall be distinguished from the purely private conduct of psychologists, which is not within the purview of the Ethics Code.

Membership in the APA commits members and student affiliates to comply with the standards of the APA Ethics Code and to the rules and procedures used to enforce them. Lack of awareness or misunderstanding of an Ethical Standard is not itself a defense to a charge of unethical conduct.

The procedures for filing, investigating, and resolving complaints of unethical conduct are described in the current Rules and Procedures of the APA Ethics Committee. APA may impose sanctions on its members for violations of the standards of the Ethics Code, including termination of APA membership, and may notify other bodies and individuals of its actions. Actions that violate the standards of the Ethics Code may also lead to the imposition of sanctions on psychologists or students whether or not they are APA members by bodies other than APA, including state psychological associations, other professional groups, psychology boards, other state or federal agencies, and payors for health services. In addition, APA may take action against a member after his or her conviction of a felony, expulsion or suspension from an affiliated state psychological association, or suspension or loss of licensure. When the sanction to be imposed by APA is less than expulsion, the 2001 Rules and Procedures do not guarantee an opportunity for an in-person hearing, but generally provide that complaints will be resolved only on the basis of a submitted record.

The Ethics Code is intended to provide guidance for psychologists and standards of professional conduct that can be applied by the APA and by other bodies that choose to adopt them. The Ethics Code is not intended to be a basis of civil liability. Whether a psychologist has violated the Ethics Code standards does not by itself determine whether the psychologist is legally liable in a court action, whether a contract is enforceable, or whether other legal consequences occur.

The modifiers used in some of the standards of this Ethics Code (e.g., *reasonably, appropriate, potentially*) are included in the standards when they would (1) allow professional judgment on the part of psychologists, (2) eliminate injustice or inequality that would occur without the modifier, (3) ensure applicability across the broad range of activities conducted by psychologists, or (4) guard against a set of rigid rules that might be quickly outdated. As used in this Ethics Code, the term *reasonable* means the prevailing professional judgment of psychologists engaged in similar activities in similar circumstances, given the knowledge the psychologist had or should have had at the time.

In the process of making decisions regarding their professional behavior, psychologists must consider this Ethics Code in addition to applicable laws and psychology board regulations. In applying the Ethics Code to their professional work, psychologists may consider other materials and guidelines that have been adopted or endorsed by scientific and professional psychological organizations and the dictates of their own conscience, as well as consult with others within the field. If this Ethics Code establishes a higher standard of conduct than is required by law, psychologists must meet the higher ethical standard. If psychologists' ethical responsibilities conflict with law, regulations, or other governing legal authority, psychologists make known their commitment to this Ethics Code and take steps to resolve the conflict in a responsible manner. If the conflict is unresolvable via such means, psychologists may adhere to the requirements of the law, regulations, or other governing authority in keeping with basic principles of human rights.

PREAMBLE

Psychologists are committed to increasing scientific and professional knowledge of behavior and people's understanding of themselves and others and to the use of such knowledge to improve the condition of individuals, organizations, and society. Psychologists respect and protect civil and human rights and the central importance of freedom of inquiry and expression in research, teaching, and publication. They strive to help the public in developing informed judgments and choices concerning human behavior. In doing so, they perform many roles, such as researcher, educator, diagnostician, therapist, supervisor, consultant, administrator, social interventionist, and expert witness. This Ethics Code provides a common set of principles and standards upon which psychologists build their professional and scientific work.

This Ethics Code is intended to provide specific standards to cover most situations encountered by psychologists. It has as its goals the welfare and protection of the individuals and groups with whom psychologists work and the education of members, students, and the public regarding ethical standards of the discipline.

The development of a dynamic set of ethical standards for psychologists' work-related conduct requires a personal commitment and lifelong effort to act ethically; to encourage ethical behavior by students, supervisees, employees, and colleagues; and to consult with others concerning ethical problems.

GENERAL PRINCIPLES

This section consists of General Principles. General Principles, as opposed to Ethical Standards, are aspirational in nature. Their intent is to guide and inspire psychologists toward the very highest ethical ideals of the profession. General Principles, in contrast to Ethical Standards, do not represent obligations and should not form the basis for imposing sanctions. Relying upon General Principles for either of these reasons distorts both their meaning and purpose.

Principle A: Beneficence and Nonmaleficence

Psychologists strive to benefit those with whom they work and take care to do no harm. In their professional actions, psychologists seek to safeguard the welfare and rights of those with whom they interact professionally and other affected persons, and the welfare of animal subjects of research. When conflicts occur among psychologists' obligations or concerns, they attempt to resolve these conflicts in a responsible fashion that avoids or minimizes harm. Because psychologists' scientific and professional judgments and actions may affect the lives of others, they are alert to and guard against personal, financial, social, organizational, or political factors that might lead to misuse of their influence. Psychologists strive to be aware of the possible effect of their own physical and mental health on their ability to help those with whom they work.

Principle B: Fidelity and Responsibility

Psychologists establish relationships of trust with those with whom they work. They are aware of their professional and scientific responsibilities to society and to the specific communities in which they work. Psychologists uphold professional standards of conduct, clarify their professional roles and obligations, accept appropriate responsibility for their behavior, and seek to manage conflicts of interest that could lead to exploitation or harm. Psychologists consult with, refer to, or cooperate with other professionals and institutions to the extent needed to serve the best interests of those with whom they work. They are concerned about the ethical compliance of their colleagues' scientific and professional conduct. Psychologists strive to contribute a portion of their professional time for little or no compensation or personal advantage.

Principle C: Integrity

Psychologists seek to promote accuracy, honesty, and truthfulness in the science, teaching, and practice of psychology. In these activities psychologists do not steal, cheat, or engage in fraud, subterfuge, or intentional misrepresentation of fact. Psychologists strive to keep their promises and to avoid unwise or unclear commitments. In situations in which deception may be ethically justifiable to maximize benefits and minimize harm, psychologists have a serious obligation to consider the need for, the possible consequences of, and their responsibility to correct any resulting mistrust or other harmful effects that arise from the use of such techniques.

Principle D: Justice

Psychologists recognize that fairness and justice entitle all persons to access to and benefit from the contributions of psychology and to equal quality in the processes, procedures, and services being conducted by psychologists. Psychologists exercise reasonable judgment and take precautions to ensure that their potential biases, the boundaries of their competence, and the limitations of their expertise do not lead to or condone unjust practices.

Principle E: Respect for People's Rights and Dignity

Psychologists respect the dignity and worth of all people, and the rights of individuals to privacy, confidentiality, and self-determination. Psychologists are aware that special safeguards may be necessary to protect the rights and welfare of persons or communities whose vulnerabilities impair autonomous decision making. Psychologists are aware of and respect cultural, individual, and role differences, including those based on age, gender, gender identity, race, ethnicity, culture, national origin, religion, sexual orientation, disability, language, and socioeconomic status and consider these factors when working with members of such groups. Psychologists try to eliminate the effect on their work of biases based on those factors, and they do not knowingly participate in or condone activities of others based upon such prejudices.

ETHICAL STANDARDS

1. Resolving Ethical Issues

1.01 Misuse of Psychologists' Work
If psychologists learn of misuse or misrepresentation of their work, they take reasonable steps to correct or minimize the misuse or misrepresentation.

1.02 Conflicts Between Ethics and Law, Regulations, or Other Governing Legal Authority
If psychologists' ethical responsibilities conflict with law, regulations, or other governing legal authority, psychologists make known their commitment to the Ethics Code and take steps to resolve the conflict. If the conflict is unresolvable via such means, psychologists may adhere to the requirements of the law, regulations, or other governing legal authority.

1.03 Conflicts Between Ethics and Organizational Demands
If the demands of an organization with which psychologists are affiliated or for whom they are working conflict with this Ethics Code, psychologists clarify the nature of the conflict, make known their commitment to the Ethics Code, and to the extent feasible, resolve the conflict in a way that permits adherence to the Ethics Code.

1.04 Informal Resolution of Ethical Violations
When psychologists believe that there may have been an ethical violation by another psychologist, they attempt to resolve the issue by bringing it to the attention of that individual, if an informal resolution appears appropriate and the intervention does not violate any confidentiality rights that may be involved. (See also Standards 1.02, Conflicts Between Ethics and Law, Regulations, or Other Governing Legal Authority, and 1.03, Conflicts Between Ethics and Organizational Demands.)

1.05 Reporting Ethical Violations
If an apparent ethical violation has substantially harmed or is likely to substantially harm a person or organization and is not appropriate for informal resolution under Standard 1.04, Informal Resolution of Ethical Violations, or is not resolved properly in that fashion, psychologists take further action appropriate to the situation. Such action might include referral to state or national committees on professional ethics, to state licensing boards, or to the appropriate institutional authorities. This standard does not apply when an intervention would violate confidentiality rights or when psychologists have been retained to review the work of another psychologist whose professional conduct is in question. (See also Standard 1.02, Conflicts Between Ethics and Law, Regulations, or Other Governing Legal Authority.)

1.06 Cooperating With Ethics Committees
Psychologists cooperate in ethics investigations, proceedings, and resulting requirements of the APA or any affiliated state psychological association to which they belong. In doing so, they address any confidentiality issues. Failure to cooperate is itself an ethics violation. However, making a request for deferment of adjudication of an ethics complaint pending the outcome of litigation does not alone constitute noncooperation.

1.07 Improper Complaints
Psychologists do not file or encourage the filing of ethics complaints that are made with reckless disregard for or willful ignorance of facts that would disprove the allegation.

1.08 Unfair Discrimination Against Complainants and Respondents
Psychologists do not deny persons employment, advancement, admissions to academic or other programs, tenure, or promotion, based solely upon their having made or their being the subject of an ethics complaint. This does not preclude taking action based upon the outcome of such proceedings or considering other appropriate information.

2. Competence

2.01 Boundaries of Competence
(a) Psychologists provide services, teach, and conduct research with populations and in areas only within the boundaries of their competence, based on their education, training, supervised experience, consultation, study, or professional experience.

(b) Where scientific or professional knowledge in the discipline of psychology establishes that an understanding of factors associated with age, gender, gender identity, race, ethnicity, culture, national origin, religion, sexual orientation, disability, language, or socioeconomic status is essential for effective implementation of their services or research, psychologists have or obtain the training, experience, consultation, or supervision necessary to ensure the competence of their services, or they make appropriate referrals, except as provided in Standard 2.02, Providing Services in Emergencies.

(c) Psychologists planning to provide services, teach, or conduct research involving populations, areas, techniques, or technologies new to them undertake relevant education, training, supervised experience, consultation, or study.

(d) When psychologists are asked to provide services to individuals for whom appropriate mental health services are not available and for which psychologists have not obtained the competence necessary, psychologists with closely related prior training or experience may provide such services in order to ensure that services are not denied if they make a reasonable effort to obtain the competence required by using relevant research, training, consultation, or study.

(e) In those emerging areas in which generally recognized standards for preparatory training do not yet exist, psychologists nevertheless take reasonable steps to ensure the competence of their work and to protect clients/patients, students, supervisees, research participants, organizational clients, and others from harm.

(f) When assuming forensic roles, psychologists are or become reasonably familiar with the judicial or administrative rules governing their roles.

2.02 Providing Services in Emergencies
In emergencies, when psychologists provide services to individuals for whom other mental health services are not available and for which psychologists have not obtained the necessary training, psychologists may provide such services in order to ensure that services are not denied. The services are discontinued as soon as the emergency has ended or appropriate services are available.

2.03 Maintaining Competence
Psychologists undertake ongoing efforts to develop and maintain their competence.

2.04 Bases for Scientific and Professional Judgments
Psychologists' work is based upon established scientific and professional knowledge of the discipline. (See also Standards 2.01e, Boundaries of Competence, and 10.01b, Informed Consent to Therapy.)

2.05 Delegation of Work to Others
Psychologists who delegate work to employees, supervisees, or research or teaching assistants or who use the services of others, such as interpreters, take reasonable steps to (1) avoid delegating such work to persons who have a multiple relationship with those being served that would likely lead to exploitation or loss of objectivity; (2) authorize only those responsibilities that such persons can be expected to perform competently on the basis of their education, training, or experience, either independently or with the level of supervision being provided; and (3) see that such persons perform these services competently. (See also Standards 2.02, Providing Services in Emergencies; 3.05, Multiple Relationships; 4.01, Maintaining Confidentiality; 9.01, Bases for Assessments; 9.02, Use of Assessments; 9.03, Informed Consent in Assessments; and 9.07, Assessment by Unqualified Persons.)

2.06 Personal Problems and Conflicts
(a) Psychologists refrain from initiating an activity when they know or should know that there is a substantial likelihood that their personal problems will prevent them from performing their work-related activities in a competent manner.

(b) When psychologists become aware of personal problems that may interfere with their performing work-related duties adequately, they take appropriate measures, such as obtaining professional consultation or assistance, and determine whether they should limit, suspend, or terminate their work-related duties. (See also Standard 10.10, Terminating Therapy.)

3.   Human Relations

3.01 Unfair Discrimination
In their work-related activities, psychologists do not engage in unfair discrimination based on age, gender, gender identity, race, ethnicity, culture, national origin, religion, sexual orientation, disability, socioeconomic status, or any basis proscribed by law.

3.02 Sexual Harassment
Psychologists do not engage in sexual harassment. Sexual harassment is sexual solicitation, physical advances, or verbal or nonverbal conduct that is sexual in nature, that occurs in connection with the psychologist's activities or roles as a psychologist, and that either (1) is unwelcome, is offensive, or creates a hostile workplace or educational environment, and the psychologist knows or is told this or (2) is sufficiently severe or intense to be abusive to a reasonable person in

the context. Sexual harassment can consist of a single intense or severe act or of multiple persistent or pervasive acts. (See also Standard 1.08, Unfair Discrimination Against Complainants and Respondents.)

3.03 Other Harassment
Psychologists do not knowingly engage in behavior that is harassing or demeaning to persons with whom they interact in their work based on factors such as those persons' age, gender, gender identity, race, ethnicity, culture, national origin, religion, sexual orientation, disability, language, or socioeconomic status.

3.04 Avoiding Harm
Psychologists take reasonable steps to avoid harming their clients/patients, students, supervisees, research participants, organizational clients, and others with whom they work, and to minimize harm where it is foreseeable and unavoidable.

3.05 Multiple Relationships
(a) A multiple relationship occurs when a psychologist is in a professional role with a person and (1) at the same time is in another role with the same person, (2) at the same time is in a relationship with a person closely associated with or related to the person with whom the psychologist has the professional relationship, or (3) promises to enter into another relationship in the future with the person or a person closely associated with or related to the person.

A psychologist refrains from entering into a multiple relationship if the multiple relationship could reasonably be expected to impair the psychologist's objectivity, competence, or effectiveness in performing his or her functions as a psychologist, or otherwise risks exploitation or harm to the person with whom the professional relationship exists.

Multiple relationships that would not reasonably be expected to cause impairment or risk exploitation or harm are not unethical.

(b) If a psychologist finds that, due to unforeseen factors, a potentially harmful multiple relationship has arisen, the psychologist takes reasonable steps to resolve it with due regard for the best interests of the affected person and maximal compliance with the Ethics Code.

(c) When psychologists are required by law, institutional policy, or extraordinary circumstances to serve in more than one role in judicial or administrative proceedings, at the outset they clarify role expectations and the extent of confidentiality and thereafter as changes occur. (See also Standards 3.04, Avoiding Harm, and 3.07, Third-Party Requests for Services.)

3.06 Conflict of Interest
Psychologists refrain from taking on a professional role when personal, scientific, professional, legal, financial, or other interests or relationships could reasonably be expected to (1) impair their objectivity, competence, or effectiveness in performing their functions as psychologists or (2) expose the person or organization with whom the professional relationship exists to harm or exploitation.

3.07 Third-Party Requests for Services
When psychologists agree to provide services to a person or entity at the request of a third party, psychologists attempt to clarify at the outset of the service the nature of the relationship with all individuals or organizations involved. This clarification includes the role of the psychologist (e.g., therapist, consultant, diagnostician, or expert witness), an identification of who is the client, the probable uses of the services provided or the information obtained, and the fact that there may be limits to confidentiality. (See also Standards 3.05, Multiple Relationships, and 4.02, Discussing the Limits of Confidentiality.)

3.08 Exploitative Relationships
Psychologists do not exploit persons over whom they have supervisory, evaluative, or other authority such as clients/patients, students, supervisees, research participants, and employees. (See also Standards 3.05, Multiple Relationships; 6.04, Fees and Financial Arrangements; 6.05, Barter With Clients/Patients; 7.07, Sexual Relationships With Students and Supervisees; 10.05, Sexual Intimacies With Current Therapy Clients/Patients; 10.06, Sexual Intimacies With Relatives or Significant Others of Current Therapy Clients/Patients; 10.07, Therapy With Former Sexual Partners; and 10.08, Sexual Intimacies With Former Therapy Clients/Patients.)

3.09 Cooperation With Other Professionals
When indicated and professionally appropriate, psychologists cooperate with other professionals in order to serve their clients/patients effectively and appropriately. (See also Standard 4.05, Disclosures.)

3.10 Informed Consent
(a) When psychologists conduct research or provide assessment, therapy, counseling, or consulting services in person or via electronic transmission or other forms of communication, they obtain the informed consent of the individual or individuals using language that is reasonably understandable to that person or persons except when conducting such activities without consent is mandated by law or governmental regulation or as otherwise provided in this Ethics Code.

(See also Standards 8.02, Informed Consent to Research; 9.03, Informed Consent in Assessments; and 10.01, Informed Consent to Therapy.)

(b) For persons who are legally incapable of giving informed consent, psychologists nevertheless (1) provide an appropriate explanation, (2) seek the individual's assent, (3) consider such persons' preferences and best interests, and (4) obtain appropriate permission from a legally authorized person, if such substitute consent is permitted or required by law. When consent by a legally authorized person is not permitted or required by law, psychologists take reasonable steps to protect the individual's rights and welfare.

(c) When psychological services are court ordered or otherwise mandated, psychologists inform the individual of the nature of the anticipated services, including whether the services are court ordered or mandated and any limits of confidentiality, before proceeding.

(d) Psychologists appropriately document written or oral consent, permission, and assent. (See also Standards 8.02, Informed Consent to Research; 9.03, Informed Consent in Assessments; and 10.01, Informed Consent to Therapy.)

3.11 Psychological Services Delivered To or Through Organizations
(a) Psychologists delivering services to or through organizations provide information beforehand to clients and when appropriate those directly affected by the services about (1) the nature and objectives of the services, (2) the intended recipients, (3) which of the individuals are clients, (4) the relationship the psychologist will have with each person and the organization, (5) the probable uses of services provided and information obtained, (6) who will have access to the information, and (7) limits of confidentiality. As soon as feasible, they provide information about the results and conclusions of such services to appropriate persons.

(b) If psychologists will be precluded by law or by organizational roles from providing such information to particular individuals or groups, they so inform those individuals or groups at the outset of the service.

3.12 Interruption of Psychological Services
Unless otherwise covered by contract, psychologists make reasonable efforts to plan for facilitating services in the event that psychological services are interrupted by factors such as the psychologist's illness, death, unavailability, relocation, or retirement or by the client's/patient's relocation or financial limitations. (See also Standard 6.02c, Maintenance, Dissemination, and Disposal of Confidential Records of Professional and Scientific Work.)

4. Privacy And Confidentiality

4.01 Maintaining Confidentiality
Psychologists have a primary obligation and take reasonable precautions to protect confidential information obtained through or stored in any medium, recognizing that the extent and limits of confidentiality may be regulated by law or established by institutional rules or professional or scientific relationship. (See also Standard 2.05, Delegation of Work to Others.)

4.02 Discussing the Limits of Confidentiality
(a) Psychologists discuss with persons (including, to the extent feasible, persons who are legally incapable of giving informed consent and their legal representatives) and organizations with whom they establish a scientific or professional relationship (1) the relevant limits of confidentiality and (2) the foreseeable uses of the information generated through the psychological activities. (See also Standard 3.10, Informed Consent.)

(b) Unless it is not feasible or is contraindicated, the discussion of confidentiality occurs at the outset of the relationship and thereafter as new circumstances may warrant.

(c) Psychologists who offer services, products, or information via electronic transmission inform clients/patients of the risks to privacy and limits of confidentiality.

4.03 Recording
Before recording the voices or images of individuals to whom they provide services, psychologists obtain permission from all such persons or their legal representatives. (See also Standards 8.03, Informed Consent for Recording Voices and Images in Research; 8.05, Dispensing With Informed Consent for Research; and 8.07, Deception in Research.)

4.04 Minimizing Intrusions on Privacy
(a) Psychologists include in written and oral reports and consultations, only information germane to the purpose for which the communication is made.

(b) Psychologists discuss confidential information obtained in their work only for appropriate scientific or professional purposes and only with persons clearly concerned with such matters.

4.05 Disclosures
(a) Psychologists may disclose confidential information with the appropriate consent of the organizational client, the individual client/patient, or another legally authorized person on behalf of the client/patient unless prohibited by law.

(b) Psychologists disclose confidential information without the consent of the individual only as mandated by law, or where permitted by law for a valid purpose such as to (1) provide needed professional services; (2) obtain appropriate professional consultations; (3) protect the client/patient, psychologist, or others from harm; or (4) obtain payment for services from a client/patient, in which instance disclosure is limited to the minimum that is necessary to achieve the purpose. (See also Standard 6.04e, Fees and Financial Arrangements.)

4.06 Consultations
When consulting with colleagues, (1) psychologists do not disclose confidential information that reasonably could lead to the identification of a client/patient, research participant, or other person or organization with whom they have a confidential relationship unless they have obtained the prior consent of the person or organization or the disclosure cannot be avoided, and (2) they disclose information only to the extent necessary to achieve the purposes of the consultation. (See also Standard 4.01, Maintaining Confidentiality.)

4.07 Use of Confidential Information for Didactic or Other Purposes
Psychologists do not disclose in their writings, lectures, or other public media, confidential, personally identifiable information concerning their clients/patients, students, research participants, organizational clients, or other recipients of their services that they obtained during the course of their work, unless (1) they take reasonable steps to disguise the person or organization, (2) the person or organization has consented in writing, or (3) there is legal authorization for doing so.

5. Advertising and Other Public Statements

5.01 Avoidance of False or Deceptive Statements
(a) Public statements include but are not limited to paid or unpaid advertising, product endorsements, grant applications, licensing applications, other credentialing applications, brochures, printed matter, directory listings, personal resumes or curricula vitae, or comments for use in media such as print or electronic transmission, statements in legal proceedings, lectures and public oral presentations, and published materials. Psychologists do not knowingly make public statements that are false, deceptive, or fraudulent concerning their research, practice, or other work activities or those of persons or organizations with which they are affiliated.

(b) Psychologists do not make false, deceptive, or fraudulent statements concerning (1) their training, experience, or competence; (2) their academic degrees; (3) their credentials; (4) their institutional or association affiliations; (5) their services; (6) the scientific or clinical basis for, or results or degree of success of, their services; (7) their fees; or (8) their publications or research findings.

(c) Psychologists claim degrees as credentials for their health services only if those degrees (1) were earned from a regionally accredited educational institution or (2) were the basis for psychology licensure by the state in which they practice.

5.02 Statements by Others
(a) Psychologists who engage others to create or place public statements that promote their professional practice, products, or activities retain professional responsibility for such statements.

(b) Psychologists do not compensate employees of press, radio, television, or other communication media in return for publicity in a news item. (See also Standard 1.01, Misuse of Psychologists' Work.)

(c) A paid advertisement relating to psychologists' activities must be identified or clearly recognizable as such.

5.03 Descriptions of Workshops and Non-Degree-Granting Educational Programs
To the degree to which they exercise control, psychologists responsible for announcements, catalogs, brochures, or advertisements describing workshops, seminars, or other non-degree-granting educational programs ensure that they accurately describe the audience for which the program is intended, the educational objectives, the presenters, and the fees involved.

5.04 Media Presentations
When psychologists provide public advice or comment via print, internet, or other electronic transmission, they take precautions to ensure that statements (1) are based on their professional knowledge, training, or experience in accord with appropriate psychological literature and practice; (2) are otherwise consistent with this Ethics Code; and (3) do not indicate that a professional relationship has been established with the recipient. (See also Standard 2.04, Bases for Scientific and Professional Judgments.)

5.05 Testimonials
Psychologists do not solicit testimonials from current therapy clients/patients or other persons who because of their particular circumstances are vulnerable to undue influence.

5.06 In-Person Solicitation
Psychologists do not engage, directly or through agents, in uninvited in-person solicitation of business from actual or potential therapy clients/patients or other persons who because of their particular circumstances are vulnerable to undue influence. However, this prohibition does not preclude (1) attempting to implement appropriate collateral contacts for the purpose of benefiting an already engaged therapy client/patient or (2) providing disaster or community outreach services.

6. Record Keeping and Fees

6.01 Documentation of Professional and Scientific Work and Maintenance of Records
Psychologists create, and to the extent the records are under their control, maintain, disseminate, store, retain, and dispose of records and data relating to their professional and scientific work in order to (1) facilitate provision of services later by them or by other professionals, (2) allow for replication of research design and analyses, (3) meet institutional requirements, (4) ensure accuracy of billing and payments, and (5) ensure compliance with law. (See also Standard 4.01, Maintaining Confidentiality.)

6.02 Maintenance, Dissemination, and Disposal of Confidential Records of Professional and Scientific Work
(a) Psychologists maintain confidentiality in creating, storing, accessing, transferring, and disposing of records under their control, whether these are written, automated, or in any other medium. (See also Standards 4.01, Maintaining Confidentiality, and 6.01, Documentation of Professional and Scientific Work and Maintenance of Records.)

(b) If confidential information concerning recipients of psychological services is entered into databases or systems of records available to persons whose access has not been consented to by the recipient, psychologists use coding or other techniques to avoid the inclusion of personal identifiers.

(c) Psychologists make plans in advance to facilitate the appropriate transfer and to protect the confidentiality of records and data in the event of psychologists' withdrawal from positions or practice. (See also Standards 3.12, Interruption of Psychological Services, and 10.09, Interruption of Therapy.)

6.03 Withholding Records for Nonpayment
Psychologists may not withhold records under their control that are requested and needed for a client's/patient's emergency treatment solely because payment has not been received.

6.04 Fees and Financial Arrangements
(a) As early as is feasible in a professional or scientific relationship, psychologists and recipients of psychological services reach an agreement specifying compensation and billing arrangements.

(b) Psychologists' fee practices are consistent with law.

(c) Psychologists do not misrepresent their fees.

(d) If limitations to services can be anticipated because of limitations in financing, this is discussed with the recipient of services as early as is feasible. (See also Standards 10.09, Interruption of Therapy, and 10.10, Terminating Therapy.)

(e) If the recipient of services does not pay for services as agreed, and if psychologists intend to use collection agencies or legal measures to collect the fees, psychologists first inform the person that such measures will be taken and provide that person an opportunity to make prompt payment. (See also Standards 4.05, Disclosures; 6.03, Withholding Records for Nonpayment; and 10.01, Informed Consent to Therapy.)

6.05 Barter With Clients/Patients
Barter is the acceptance of goods, services, or other nonmonetary remuneration from clients/patients in return for psychological services. Psychologists may barter only if (1) it is not clinically contraindicated, and (2) the resulting arrangement is not exploitative. (See also Standards 3.05, Multiple Relationships, and 6.04, Fees and Financial Arrangements.)

6.06 Accuracy in Reports to Payors and Funding Sources
In their reports to payors for services or sources of research funding, psychologists take reasonable steps to ensure the accurate reporting of the nature of the service provided or research conducted, the fees, charges, or payments, and where applicable, the identity of the provider, the findings, and the diagnosis. (See also Standards 4.01, Maintaining Confidentiality; 4.04, Minimizing Intrusions on Privacy; and 4.05, Disclosures.)

6.07 Referrals and Fees
When psychologists pay, receive payment from, or divide fees with another professional, other than in an employer-employee relationship, the payment to each is based on the services provided (clinical, consultative, administrative, or other) and is not based on the referral itself. (See also Standard 3.09, Cooperation With Other Professionals.)

7. Education and Training

7.01 Design of Education and Training Programs
Psychologists responsible for education and training programs take reasonable steps to ensure that the programs are designed to provide the appropriate knowledge and proper experiences, and to meet the requirements for licensure, certification, or other goals for which claims are made by the program. (See also Standard 5.03, Descriptions of Workshops and Non-Degree-Granting Educational Programs.)

7.02 Descriptions of Education and Training Programs
Psychologists responsible for education and training programs take reasonable steps to ensure that there is a current and accurate description of the program content (including participation in required course- or program-related counseling, psychotherapy, experiential groups, consulting projects, or community service), training goals and objectives, stipends and benefits, and requirements that must be met for satisfactory completion of the program. This information must be made readily available to all interested parties.

7.03 Accuracy in Teaching
(a) Psychologists take reasonable steps to ensure that course syllabi are accurate regarding the subject matter to be covered, bases for evaluating progress, and the nature of course experiences. This standard does not preclude an instructor from modifying course content or requirements when the instructor considers it pedagogically necessary or desirable, so long as students are made aware of these modifications in a manner that enables them to fulfill course requirements. (See also Standard 5.01, Avoidance of False or Deceptive Statements.)

(b) When engaged in teaching or training, psychologists present psychological information accurately. (See also Standard 2.03, Maintaining Competence.)

7.04 Student Disclosure of Personal Information
Psychologists do not require students or supervisees to disclose personal information in course- or program-related activities, either orally or in writing, regarding sexual history, history of abuse and neglect, psychological treatment, and relationships with parents, peers, and spouses or significant others except if (1) the program or training facility has clearly identified this requirement in its admissions and program materials or (2) the information is necessary to evaluate or obtain assistance for students whose personal problems could reasonably be judged to be preventing them from performing their training- or professionally related activities in a competent manner or posing a threat to the students or others.

7.05 Mandatory Individual or Group Therapy
(a) When individual or group therapy is a program or course requirement, psychologists responsible for that program allow students in undergraduate and graduate programs the option of selecting such therapy from practitioners unaffiliated with the program. (See also Standard 7.02, Descriptions of Education and Training Programs.)

(b) Faculty who are or are likely to be responsible for evaluating students' academic performance do not themselves provide that therapy. (See also Standard 3.05, Multiple Relationships.)

7.06 Assessing Student and Supervisee Performance
(a) In academic and supervisory relationships, psychologists establish a timely and specific process for providing feedback to students and supervisees. Information regarding the process is provided to the student at the beginning of supervision.

(b) Psychologists evaluate students and supervisees on the basis of their actual performance on relevant and established program requirements.

7.07 Sexual Relationships With Students and Supervisees
Psychologists do not engage in sexual relationships with students or supervisees who are in their department, agency, or training center or over whom psychologists have or are likely to have evaluative authority. (See also Standard 3.05, Multiple Relationships.)

8.   Research and Publication

8.01 Institutional Approval
When institutional approval is required, psychologists provide accurate information about their research proposals and obtain approval prior to conducting the research. They conduct the research in accordance with the approved research protocol.

8.02 Informed Consent to Research
(a) When obtaining informed consent as required in Standard 3.10, Informed Consent, psychologists inform participants about (1) the purpose of the research, expected duration, and procedures; (2) their right to decline to participate and to withdraw from the research once participation has begun; (3) the foreseeable consequences of declining or withdrawing; (4) reasonably foreseeable factors that may be expected to influence their willingness to participate such as potential risks, discomfort, or adverse effects; (5) any prospective research benefits; (6) limits of confidentiality; (7) incentives for participation; and (8) whom to contact for questions about the research and research participants' rights. They provide opportunity for the prospective participants to ask questions and receive answers. (See also Standards 8.03, Informed Consent for Recording Voices and Images in Research; 8.05, Dispensing With Informed Consent for Research; and 8.07, Deception in Research.)

(b) Psychologists conducting intervention research involving the use of experimental treatments clarify to participants at the outset of the research (1) the experimental nature of the treatment; (2) the services that will or will not be available to the control group(s) if appropriate; (3) the means by which assignment to treatment and control groups will be made; (4) available treatment alternatives if an individual does not wish to participate in the research or wishes to withdraw once a study has begun; and (5) compensation for or monetary costs of participating including, if appropriate, whether reimbursement from the participant or a third-party payor will be sought. (See also Standard 8.02a, Informed Consent to Research.)

8.03 Informed Consent for Recording Voices and Images in Research
Psychologists obtain informed consent from research participants prior to recording their voices or images for data collection unless (1) the research consists solely of naturalistic observations in public places, and it is not anticipated that the recording will be used in a manner that could cause personal identification or harm, or (2) the research design includes deception, and consent for the use of the recording is obtained during debriefing. (See also Standard 8.07, Deception in Research.)

8.04 Client/Patient, Student, and Subordinate Research Participants
(a) When psychologists conduct research with clients/patients, students, or subordinates as participants, psychologists take steps to protect the prospective participants from adverse consequences of declining or withdrawing from participation.

(b) When research participation is a course requirement or an opportunity for extra credit, the prospective participant is given the choice of equitable alternative activities.

8.05 Dispensing With Informed Consent for Research
Psychologists may dispense with informed consent only (1) where research would not reasonably be assumed to create distress or harm and involves (a) the study of normal educational practices, curricula, or classroom management methods conducted in educational settings; (b) only anonymous questionnaires, naturalistic observations, or archival research for which disclosure of responses would not place participants at risk of criminal or civil liability or damage their financial standing, employability, or reputation, and confidentiality is protected; or (c) the study of factors related to job or organization effectiveness conducted in organizational settings for which there is no risk to participants' employability, and confidentiality is protected or (2) where otherwise permitted by law or federal or institutional regulations.

8.06 Offering Inducements for Research Participation
(a) Psychologists make reasonable efforts to avoid offering excessive or inappropriate financial or other inducements for research participation when such inducements are likely to coerce participation.

(b) When offering professional services as an inducement for research participation, psychologists clarify the nature of the services, as well as the risks, obligations, and limitations. (See also Standard 6.05, Barter With Clients/Patients.)

8.07 Deception in Research
(a) Psychologists do not conduct a study involving deception unless they have determined that the use of deceptive techniques is justified by the study's significant prospective scientific, educational, or applied value and that effective nondeceptive alternative procedures are not feasible.

(b) Psychologists do not deceive prospective participants about research that is reasonably expected to cause physical pain or severe emotional distress.

(c) Psychologists explain any deception that is an integral feature of the design and conduct of an experiment to participants as early as is feasible, preferably at the conclusion of their participation, but no later than at the conclusion of the data collection, and permit participants to withdraw their data. (See also Standard 8.08, Debriefing.)

8.08 Debriefing

(a) Psychologists provide a prompt opportunity for participants to obtain appropriate information about the nature, results, and conclusions of the research, and they take reasonable steps to correct any misconceptions that participants may have of which the psychologists are aware.

(b) If scientific or humane values justify delaying or withholding this information, psychologists take reasonable measures to reduce the risk of harm.

(c) When psychologists become aware that research procedures have harmed a participant, they take reasonable steps to minimize the harm.

8.09 Humane Care and Use of Animals in Research

(a) Psychologists acquire, care for, use, and dispose of animals in compliance with current federal, state, and local laws and regulations, and with professional standards.

(b) Psychologists trained in research methods and experienced in the care of laboratory animals supervise all procedures involving animals and are responsible for ensuring appropriate consideration of their comfort, health, and humane treatment.

(c) Psychologists ensure that all individuals under their supervision who are using animals have received instruction in research methods and in the care, maintenance, and handling of the species being used, to the extent appropriate to their role. (See also Standard 2.05, Delegation of Work to Others.)

(d) Psychologists make reasonable efforts to minimize the discomfort, infection, illness, and pain of animal subjects.

(e) Psychologists use a procedure subjecting animals to pain, stress, or privation only when an alternative procedure is unavailable and the goal is justified by its prospective scientific, educational, or applied value.

(f) Psychologists perform surgical procedures under appropriate anesthesia and follow techniques to avoid infection and minimize pain during and after surgery.

(g) When it is appropriate that an animal's life be terminated, psychologists proceed rapidly, with an effort to minimize pain and in accordance with accepted procedures.

8.10 Reporting Research Results

(a) Psychologists do not fabricate data. (See also Standard 5.01a, Avoidance of False or Deceptive Statements.)

(b) If psychologists discover significant errors in their published data, they take reasonable steps to correct such errors in a correction, retraction, erratum, or other appropriate publication means.

8.11 Plagiarism

Psychologists do not present portions of another's work or data as their own, even if the other work or data source is cited occasionally.

8.12 Publication Credit

(a) Psychologists take responsibility and credit, including authorship credit, only for work they have actually performed or to which they have substantially contributed. (See also Standard 8.12b, Publication Credit.)

(b) Principal authorship and other publication credits accurately reflect the relative scientific or professional contributions of the individuals involved, regardless of their relative status. Mere possession of an institutional position, such as department chair, does not justify authorship credit. Minor contributions to the research or to the writing for publications are acknowledged appropriately, such as in footnotes or in an introductory statement.

(c) Except under exceptional circumstances, a student is listed as principal author on any multiple-authored article that is substantially based on the student's doctoral dissertation. Faculty advisors discuss publication credit with students as early as feasible and throughout the research and publication process as appropriate. (See also Standard 8.12b, Publication Credit.)

8.13 Duplicate Publication of Data

Psychologists do not publish, as original data, data that have been previously published. This does not preclude republishing data when they are accompanied by proper acknowledgment.

8.14 Sharing Research Data for Verification
(a) After research results are published, psychologists do not withhold the data on which their conclusions are based from other competent professionals who seek to verify the substantive claims through reanalysis and who intend to use such data only for that purpose, provided that the confidentiality of the participants can be protected and unless legal rights concerning proprietary data preclude their release. This does not preclude psychologists from requiring that such individuals or groups be responsible for costs associated with the provision of such information.

(b) Psychologists who request data from other psychologists to verify the substantive claims through reanalysis may use shared data only for the declared purpose. Requesting psychologists obtain prior written agreement for all other uses of the data.

8.15 Reviewers
Psychologists who review material submitted for presentation, publication, grant, or research proposal review respect the confidentiality of and the proprietary rights in such information of those who submitted it.

9.   Assessment

9.01 Bases for Assessments
(a) Psychologists base the opinions contained in their recommendations, reports, and diagnostic or evaluative statements, including forensic testimony, on information and techniques sufficient to substantiate their findings. (See also Standard 2.04, Bases for Scientific and Professional Judgments.)

(b) Except as noted in 9.01c, psychologists provide opinions of the psychological characteristics of individuals only after they have conducted an examination of the individuals adequate to support their statements or conclusions. When, despite reasonable efforts, such an examination is not practical, psychologists document the efforts they made and the result of those efforts, clarify the probable impact of their limited information on the reliability and validity of their opinions, and appropriately limit the nature and extent of their conclusions or recommendations. (See also Standards 2.01, Boundaries of Competence, and 9.06, Interpreting Assessment Results.)

(c) When psychologists conduct a record review or provide consultation or supervision and an individual examination is not warranted or necessary for the opinion, psychologists explain this and the sources of information on which they based their conclusions and recommendations.

9.02 Use of Assessments
(a) Psychologists administer, adapt, score, interpret, or use assessment techniques, interviews, tests, or instruments in a manner and for purposes that are appropriate in light of the research on or evidence of the usefulness and proper application of the techniques.

(b) Psychologists use assessment instruments whose validity and reliability have been established for use with members of the population tested. When such validity or reliability has not been established, psychologists describe the strengths and limitations of test results and interpretation.

(c) Psychologists use assessment methods that are appropriate to an individual's language preference and competence, unless the use of an alternative language is relevant to the assessment issues.

9.03 Informed Consent in Assessments
(a) Psychologists obtain informed consent for assessments, evaluations, or diagnostic services, as described in Standard 3.10, Informed Consent, except when (1) testing is mandated by law or governmental regulations; (2) informed consent is implied because testing is conducted as a routine educational, institutional, or organizational activity (e.g., when participants voluntarily agree to assessment when applying for a job); or (3) one purpose of the testing is to evaluate decisional capacity. Informed consent includes an explanation of the nature and purpose of the assessment, fees, involvement of third parties, and limits of confidentiality and sufficient opportunity for the client/patient to ask questions and receive answers.

(b) Psychologists inform persons with questionable capacity to consent or for whom testing is mandated by law or governmental regulations about the nature and purpose of the proposed assessment services, using language that is reasonably understandable to the person being assessed.

(c) Psychologists using the services of an interpreter obtain informed consent from the client/patient to use that interpreter, ensure that confidentiality of test results and test security are maintained, and include in their recommendations, reports, and diagnostic or evaluative statements, including forensic testimony, discussion of any limitations on the data obtained. (See also Standards 2.05, Delegation of Work to Others; 4.01, Maintaining Confidentiality; 9.01, Bases for Assessments; 9.06, Interpreting Assessment Results; and 9.07, Assessment by Unqualified Persons.)

9.04 Release of Test Data

(a) The term *test data* refers to raw and scaled scores, client/patient responses to test questions or stimuli, and psychologists' notes and recordings concerning client/patient statements and behavior during an examination. Those portions of test materials that include client/patient responses are included in the definition of *test data*. Pursuant to a client/patient release, psychologists provide test data to the client/patient or other persons identified in the release. Psychologists may refrain from releasing test data to protect a client/patient or others from substantial harm or misuse or misrepresentation of the data or the test, recognizing that in many instances release of confidential information under these circumstances is regulated by law. (See also Standard 9.11, Maintaining Test Security.)

(b) In the absence of a client/patient release, psychologists provide test data only as required by law or court order.

9.05 Test Construction

Psychologists who develop tests and other assessment techniques use appropriate psychometric procedures and current scientific or professional knowledge for test design, standardization, validation, reduction or elimination of bias, and recommendations for use.

9.06 Interpreting Assessment Results

When interpreting assessment results, including automated interpretations, psychologists take into account the purpose of the assessment as well as the various test factors, test-taking abilities, and other characteristics of the person being assessed, such as situational, personal, linguistic, and cultural differences, that might affect psychologists' judgments or reduce the accuracy of their interpretations. They indicate any significant limitations of their interpretations. (See also Standards 2.01b and c, Boundaries of Competence, and 3.01, Unfair Discrimination.)

9.07 Assessment by Unqualified Persons

Psychologists do not promote the use of psychological assessment techniques by unqualified persons, except when such use is conducted for training purposes with appropriate supervision. (See also Standard 2.05, Delegation of Work to Others.)

9.08 Obsolete Tests and Outdated Test Results

(a) Psychologists do not base their assessment or intervention decisions or recommendations on data or test results that are outdated for the current purpose.

(b) Psychologists do not base such decisions or recommendations on tests and measures that are obsolete and not useful for the current purpose.

9.09 Test Scoring and Interpretation Services

(a) Psychologists who offer assessment or scoring services to other professionals accurately describe the purpose, norms, validity, reliability, and applications of the procedures and any special qualifications applicable to their use.

(b) Psychologists select scoring and interpretation services (including automated services) on the basis of evidence of the validity of the program and procedures as well as on other appropriate considerations. (See also Standard 2.01b and c, Boundaries of Competence.)

(c) Psychologists retain responsibility for the appropriate application, interpretation, and use of assessment instruments, whether they score and interpret such tests themselves or use automated or other services.

9.10 Explaining Assessment Results

Regardless of whether the scoring and interpretation are done by psychologists, by employees or assistants, or by automated or other outside services, psychologists take reasonable steps to ensure that explanations of results are given to the individual or designated representative unless the nature of the relationship precludes provision of an explanation of results (such as in some organizational consulting, preemployment or security screenings, and forensic evaluations), and this fact has been clearly explained to the person being assessed in advance.

9.11. Maintaining Test Security

The term *test materials* refers to manuals, instruments, protocols, and test questions or stimuli and does not include *test data* as defined in Standard 9.04, Release of Test Data. Psychologists make reasonable efforts to maintain the integrity and security of test materials and other assessment techniques consistent with law and contractual obligations, and in a manner that permits adherence to this Ethics Code.

10.   Therapy

10.01 Informed Consent to Therapy

(a) When obtaining informed consent to therapy as required in Standard 3.10, Informed Consent, psychologists inform clients/patients as early as is feasible in the therapeutic relationship about the nature and anticipated course of therapy, fees, involvement of third parties, and limits of confidentiality and provide sufficient opportunity for the client/patient to ask questions and receive answers. (See also Standards 4.02, Discussing the Limits of Confidentiality, and 6.04, Fees and Financial Arrangements.)

(b) When obtaining informed consent for treatment for which generally recognized techniques and procedures have not been established, psychologists inform their clients/patients of the developing nature of the treatment, the potential risks involved, alternative treatments that may be available, and the voluntary nature of their participation. (See also Standards 2.01e, Boundaries of Competence, and 3.10, Informed Consent.)

(c) When the therapist is a trainee and the legal responsibility for the treatment provided resides with the supervisor, the client/patient, as part of the informed consent procedure, is informed that the therapist is in training and is being supervised and is given the name of the supervisor.

10.02 Therapy Involving Couples or Families

(a) When psychologists agree to provide services to several persons who have a relationship (such as spouses, significant others, or parents and children), they take reasonable steps to clarify at the outset (1) which of the individuals are clients/patients and (2) the relationship the psychologist will have with each person. This clarification includes the psychologist's role and the probable uses of the services provided or the information obtained. (See also Standard 4.02, Discussing the Limits of Confidentiality.)

(b) If it becomes apparent that psychologists may be called on to perform potentially conflicting roles (such as family therapist and then witness for one party in divorce proceedings), psychologists take reasonable steps to clarify and modify, or withdraw from, roles appropriately. (See also Standard 3.05c, Multiple Relationships.)

10.03 Group Therapy

When psychologists provide services to several persons in a group setting, they describe at the outset the roles and responsibilities of all parties and the limits of confidentiality.

10.04 Providing Therapy to Those Served by Others

In deciding whether to offer or provide services to those already receiving mental health services elsewhere, psychologists carefully consider the treatment issues and the potential client's/patient's welfare. Psychologists discuss these issues with the client/patient or another legally authorized person on behalf of the client/patient in order to minimize the risk of confusion and conflict, consult with the other service providers when appropriate, and proceed with caution and sensitivity to the therapeutic issues.

10.05 Sexual Intimacies With Current Therapy Clients/Patients

Psychologists do not engage in sexual intimacies with current therapy clients/patients.

10.06 Sexual Intimacies With Relatives or Significant Others of Current Therapy Clients/Patients

Psychologists do not engage in sexual intimacies with individuals they know to be close relatives, guardians, or significant others of current clients/patients. Psychologists do not terminate therapy to circumvent this standard.

10.07 Therapy With Former Sexual Partners

Psychologists do not accept as therapy clients/patients persons with whom they have engaged in sexual intimacies.

10.08 Sexual Intimacies With Former Therapy Clients/Patients

(a) Psychologists do not engage in sexual intimacies with former clients/patients for at least two years after cessation or termination of therapy.

(b) Psychologists do not engage in sexual intimacies with former clients/patients even after a two-year interval except in the most unusual circumstances. Psychologists who engage in such activity after the two years following cessation or termination of therapy and of having no sexual contact with the former client/patient bear the burden of demonstrating that there has been no exploitation, in light of all relevant factors, including (1) the amount of time that has passed since therapy terminated; (2) the nature, duration, and intensity of the therapy; (3) the circumstances of termination; (4) the client's/patient's personal history; (5) the client's/patient's current mental status; (6) the likelihood of adverse impact on the client/patient; and (7) any statements or actions made by the therapist during the course of therapy suggesting or inviting the possibility of a posttermination sexual or romantic relationship with the client/patient. (See also Standard 3.05, Multiple Relationships.)

10.09 Interruption of Therapy

When entering into employment or contractual relationships, psychologists make reasonable efforts to provide for orderly and appropriate resolution of responsibility for client/patient care in the event that the employment or contractual relationship ends, with paramount consideration given to the welfare of the client/patient. (See also Standard 3.12, Interruption of Psychological Services.)

10.10 Terminating Therapy

(a) Psychologists terminate therapy when it becomes reasonably clear that the client/patient no longer needs the service, is not likely to benefit, or is being harmed by continued service.

(b) Psychologists may terminate therapy when threatened or otherwise endangered by the client/patient or another person with whom the client/patient has a relationship.

(c) Except where precluded by the actions of clients/patients or third-party payors, prior to termination psychologists provide pretermination counseling and suggest alternative service providers as appropriate.

History and Effective Date Footnote

This version of the APA Ethics Code was adopted by the American Psychological Association's Council of Representatives during its meeting, August 21, 2002, and is effective beginning June 1, 2003. Inquiries concerning the substance or interpretation of the APA Ethics Code should be addressed to the Director, Office of Ethics, American Psychological Association, 750 First Street, NE, Washington, DC 20002-4242. The Ethics Code and information regarding the Code can be found on the APA web site, http://www.apa.org/ethics. The standards in this Ethics Code will be used to adjudicate complaints brought concerning alleged conduct occurring on or after the effective date. Complaints regarding conduct occurring prior to the effective date will be adjudicated on the basis of the version of the Ethics Code that was in effect at the time the conduct occurred.

The APA has previously published its Ethics Code as follows:

American Psychological Association. (1953). Ethical standards of psychologists. Washington, DC: Author.

American Psychological Association. (1959). Ethical standards of psychologists. American Psychologist, 14, 279-282.

American Psychological Association. (1963). Ethical standards of psychologists. American Psychologist, 18, 56-60.

American Psychological Association. (1968). Ethical standards of psychologists. American Psychologist, 23, 357-361.

American Psychological Association. (1977, March). Ethical standards of psychologists. APA Monitor, 22-23.

American Psychological Association. (1979). Ethical standards of psychologists. Washington, DC: Author.

American Psychological Association. (1981). Ethical principles of psychologists. American Psychologist, 36, 633-638.

American Psychological Association. (1990). Ethical principles of psychologists (Amended June 2, 1989). American Psychologist, 45, 390-395.

American Psychological Association. (1992). Ethical principles of psychologists and code of conduct. American Psychologist, 47, 1597-1611.

Request copies of the APA's Ethical Principles of Psychologists and Code of Conduct from the APA Order Department, 750 First Street, NE, Washington, DC 20002-4242, or phone (202) 336-5510.

Ethics Code 2002.doc 10/8/02

Specialty Guidelines for Forensic Psychology

Prepared by: Committee on the Revision of the Specialty Guidelines for Forensic Psychology, Division 41 American Psychological Association and American Board of Forensic Psychology

SECOND OFFICIAL DRAFT - RELEASED JANUARY 11, 2006

OUTLINE

1. INTRODUCTION

1.01 History of the *Specialty Guidelines for Forensic Psychology*

This document replaces the 1991 *Specialty Guidelines for Forensic Psychologists* which was approved by the American Psychology-Law Society, Division 41 of the American Psychological Association (APA) and the American Board of Forensic Psychology. The current revision has also been approved by the Council of Representatives of the American Psychological Association. Appendix I includes a discussion of the revision process, enactment, and current status of these *Guidelines*.

1.02 Definitions and Terminology

Appendix II includes definitions and terminology as used for the purposes of these *Guidelines*.

1.03 Nature of Forensic Psychology

For the purposes of these *Guidelines*, forensic psychology refers to all professional practice by any psychologist working within any sub-discipline of psychology (e.g., clinical, developmental, social, cognitive) when the intended purpose of the service is to apply the scientific, technical, or specialized knowledge of psychology to the law and to use that knowledge to assist in solving legal, contractual, and administrative problems. Application of the *Guidelines* does not depend on the practitioner's typical areas of practice or expertise, but rather on the services provided in the case at hand. These *Guidelines* apply all matters in which practitioners provide forensic psychological expertise to judicial, administrative, and educational systems including, but not limited to examining persons in anticipation of legal, contractual, administrative, or disability determination proceedings; offering expert opinion about psychological issues in the form of amicus briefs or testimony to a judicial, legislative or administrative body acting in an adjudicative capacity; serving as a trial consultant or otherwise offering expertise to attorneys, the courts, or others; conducting research for the purpose of, or in the anticipation of, litigation; or involvement in educational activities to forensic practitioners and the legal system.

Professional psychological conduct is not considered forensic practice solely because the conduct takes place in, or the product is presented in, a tribunal or other judicial, legislative, or administrative forum. Similarly, when a party (such as a civilly or criminally detained individual) or another individual (such as a child whose parents are involved in divorce proceedings) is ordered into treatment with a practitioner, that treatment is not necessarily the practice of forensic psychology. Psychological testimony that is solely, reasonably, and reliably based on the provision of psychotherapy would not ordinarily be considered forensic practice.

For the purposes of these *Guidelines*, "forensic practitioner" refers to a psychologist when engaged in the practice of forensic psychology as described above. Such professional conduct is considered forensic from the time the practitioner reasonably anticipates or agrees to, or is legally mandated to, provide expertise on an explicitly psycholegal issue.

1.04 Services and Functions

Forensic practitioners recognize that a) the nature of forensic services and functions may be unfamiliar to many clients and service recipients, b) the substantial rights, liberties, and properties may be at risk in forensic matters, and c) attorneys and their clients may incorrectly believe that forensic practitioners are retained to provide partisan advocacy.

The provision of forensic services and functions may appropriately include a wide variety of psycholegal roles and functions. As researchers, forensic practitioners may participate in the collection and dissemination of empirical and scientific data that is intended to be relevant to the answering of various legal questions. As advisors, forensic practitioners may provide an attorney with an informed understanding of the role that psychology can play in the attorney's case. As consultants, forensic practitioners may explain the practical implications of relevant research, examination findings, and the opinions of other psycholegal experts. As forensic examiners, forensic practitioners may examine a party's functioning and report findings to the attorney, to a legal tribunal, or to others. As mediators or negotiators, forensic practitioners may serve in a third-party neutral role and may assist parties in resolving a dispute. As arbiters, special masters, or case managers with decision-making authority, forensic practitioners may, by agreement or court order, serve the parties, the attorneys, and the court in a decision-making role.

2. NATURE AND SCOPE OF THE *GUIDELINES*

2.01 Intended Users

These *Guidelines* are intended for use by members of the APA, members of the American Psychology-Law Society, and Diplomates of the American Board of Forensic Psychology when they are engaged in the practice of forensic psychology as described above (1.02, 1.03, and 1.04). The *Guidelines* may also provide guidance on professional conduct to the legal system, other organizations and professions, and independent professionals. Other organizations, disciplines, professionals, entities, and individuals are encouraged to consider these *Guidelines* as guiding principles for the provision of forensic services and other work products.

2.02 Aspirational Model

The *Guidelines* are an advisory statement that recommend professional behavior, endeavors, and conduct for forensic practitioners. The *Guidelines* are intended to educate, not mandate. They are not intended to override the judgment of forensic practitioners, but rather to inform their judgment. In the process of making decisions regarding their professional behavior in forensic contexts, forensic practitioners consider the *Guidelines*, all appropriate sources of professional authority, applicable codes of ethics, and applicable laws, rules, and regulations operating in the relevant jurisdiction.

2.03 Goals

The goals of the *Guidelines* are to improve the quality of forensic psychological services; enhance the practice and facilitate the systematic development of forensic psychology; encourage a high level of quality in professional practice; and encourage forensic practitioners to acknowledge and respect the rights of those whom they serve.

2.04 Professional Discretion and Judgment

Guidelines differ from practice standards and other required codes of conduct. Standards are mandatory and may be accompanied by an enforcement mechanism; guidelines reflect aspirations for accomplishment and are not accompanied by an enforcement mechanism.

For forensic practitioners who are members of the APA, the Ethical Principles of Psychologists and Code of Conduct (EPPCC), and not the *Guidelines*, contain rules of conduct enforceable by the APA. Such rules of the EPPCC define the proper conduct of psychologists, including forensic practitioners, for purposes of professional discipline. In contrast to the EPPCC, the *Guidelines* are advisory and are to be understood only as providing further guidance for forensic practitioners, their clients, parties, the judiciary, and the general public.

The *Guidelines* are not mandatory or exhaustive and may not be applicable to every forensic situation or jurisdiction. As such, and regardless of the specific language used, the *Guidelines* are to be understood as advisory, permissive, and facilitative in areas in which the forensic practitioner has discretion to exercise professional judgment that is not prohibited or mandated by the EPPCC or by law. The *Guidelines* neither add obligations to nor eliminate obligations from the EPPCC, but provide additional guidance for psychologists subject to compliance with the EPPCC. To the extent that the *Guidelines* make statements similar to those in the EPPCC, members of APA should consider those statements as discretionary with regard to the *Guidelines*, even if they are mandatory with regard to the APA and the EPPCC.

The modifiers used in the *Guidelines* (e.g., reasonably, appropriate, potentially) are included in order to allow professional judgment on the part of forensic practitioners; eliminate injustice or inequality that would occur without the modifier; ensure applicability across the broad range of activities conducted by forensic practitioners; and reduce the likelihood of enacting an inflexible set of *Guidelines* that would be unable to evolve as conceptualizations of generally accepted and desirable practices evolve.

The use of these modifiers, and the recognition of the role of professional discretion and judgment, also reflects that forensic practitioners are likely to encounter facts and circumstances not anticipated by the *Guidelines* and they may have to act upon uncertain or incomplete evidence in an immediate situation. The *Guidelines* may provide general or conceptual guidance in such circumstances. The *Guidelines* do not, however, exhaust the legal, professional, moral, and ethical considerations that inform forensic practitioners, for no complex activity can be completely defined by legal rules, codes of conduct, and aspirational guidelines.

2.05 Limitations

The *Guidelines* are not intended to serve as a basis for disciplinary action or civil liability. The standard of care is established by the competent authority in a legal tribunal, not by the *Guidelines*. The *Guidelines* may assist in establishing standards of care in their attempt to identify the best possible practice, but they do not, in and of themselves, identify what other conduct may also be competent practice and what may be the standard of care in a particular case. No ethical, licensure, or other administrative action or remedy, nor any other cause of action, should be taken *solely* on the basis of a forensic practitioner acting or not acting in a manner advised by these *Guidelines*. Whether a forensic practitioner has acted in a manner contrary to that advised in these *Guidelines* should not, in and of itself, determine whether the forensic practitioner is liable in a legal action, whether an agreement or contract is enforceable, or whether other legal or administrative consequences should occur.

The *Guidelines* do recognize that a competent authority may reference the *Guidelines* when formulating standards. In that context, the *Guidelines* advise that the authority consider that a) the *Guidelines* attempt to identify a high level of quality in practice in common forensic contexts; b) competent practice is defined as the conduct of a reasonably prudent forensic practitioner engaged in similar activities in similar circumstances; c) professional conduct evolves and may be viewed along a continuum of adequacy, and d) "minimally competent" and "best possible" are usually different points along that continuum.

The *Guidelines* are designed to be national in scope and are intended to be consistent with state and federal law. Although their scope may be more limited outside of the United States, they nonetheless may provide some direction that informs forensic practitioners in other countries and jurisdictions.

To the extent that the *Guidelines* may be construed as being applicable to the advertisement of services or the solicitation of clients, they are intended to prevent false or deceptive advertisement or solicitation, and should be construed in a manner consistent with that intent.

3. RESPONSIBILITIES

3.01 Integrity

Forensic practitioners seek to promote accuracy, honesty, and truthfulness in the science, teaching, and practice of forensic psychology and they resist partisan pressures to provide services in any ways that might tend to be misleading or inaccurate.

3.01.01 Impartiality and Fairness

When offering expert opinion to be relied upon by a decision maker, or when teaching or conducting research, forensic practitioners demonstrate commitment to the goals of accuracy, objectivity, fairness, and independence. Forensic practitioners treat all participants and weigh all data, opinions, and rival hypotheses impartially.

When conducting forensic examinations, forensic practitioners are unbiased and nonpartisan, and they eschew partisan presentation of unrepresentative, incomplete, or inaccurate evidence that might mislead finders of fact. This principle does not preclude forceful representation of the data and reasoning upon which a conclusion or professional product is based. When assisting the finder of fact, forensic practitioners offer facts and opinions impartially and irrespectively of who retains, compensates, or calls them to present the evidence to the judicial process.

When providing forensic educational services, forensic practitioners represent alternative perspectives in an accurate, fair and professional manner and demonstrate a willingness to weigh and present all views, facts, or opinions impartially.

When conducting research, forensic practitioners represent results in a fair and objective manner. Forensic practitioners utilize research designs and scientific methods that adequately and fairly test the questions at hand, and they resist partisan pressures to develop designs or report results in ways that might be misleading.

3.01.02 Respect

Forensic practitioners do not use their knowledge of psychology and the legal system inappropriately to harass, intimidate, or mislead others. Forensic practitioners demonstrate respect for the legal system and all its participants. When challenging the accuracy and validity of the claims of others, forensic practitioners do so with respect for the individual and the legal process, and in a responsible manner.

3.01.03 Avoidance of Conflicts of Interest

Forensic practitioners refrain from taking on a professional role when personal, scientific, professional, legal, financial, or other interests or relationships could reasonably be expected to impair their objectivity, competence, or effectiveness in providing forensic services.

Forensic practitioners identify and address real or apparent conflicts of interest in an attempt to maintain the public confidence and trust, discharge professional obligations, and maintain responsibility, objectivity, and accountability. Forensic practitioners recognize that harm caused by the appearance of a conflict may be as damaging as that caused by a real conflict, and they consider this when deciding whether to proceed in a matter. Forensic practitioners consider whether a prudent and competent forensic practitioner engaged in similar circumstances would determine that the ability to make a proper decision is likely to become impaired under the immediate circumstances.

When a conflict of interest is determined to be manageable, continuing services are provided in an even more stringent and fully documented manner to help ensure that conflicts are managed appropriately, that accountability is maintained, and that the trust of all relevant persons is preserved.

3.02 Community and Professional Service

Forensic practitioners seek to improve the field of forensic psychology, the quality of services rendered, and the public's understanding of and confidence in forensic practice. Forensic practitioners aid in pursuing these objectives, assist the profession of psychology in general, assist in the regulation of forensic psychology in the public interest, and exemplify the profession's ideal of public and professional service.

Because of the value of educating the public about forensic psychology practice, forensic practitioners make available the *Guidelines* on request.

3.03 Pro Bono Activities

Forensic practitioners are encouraged to devote professional time and resources to allow greater access to forensic services for those whose ability to pay customary fees is limited. Forensic practitioners who derive substantial income from the delivery of forensic services are encouraged to offer some portion of their professional services on a pro bono or reduced fee basis where the public interest or the welfare of parties may be constrained by insufficient financial resources.

4. COMPETENCE

4.01 Scope of Competence

Forensic practitioners provide competent services to clients and other recipients of forensic services in a manner consistent with the standards of their profession. Competent provision of services includes the psychological and legal knowledge, skill, thoroughness, and preparation reasonably necessary for the provision of those services.

In determining whether to proceed in a particular matter, forensic practitioners consider factors including the relative complexity and specialized nature of the service required, their general training and experience, their training and experience in the specialty area in question, the preparation and study they are able to devote to the matter, and the opportunities for consultation with a professional of established competence in the subject matter in question. Even with regard to subjects in which they are competent, forensic practitioners are encouraged to consult with other experts in particularly complex or contentious matters.

4.02 Gaining and Maintaining Competence

Forensic practitioners provide services only within the boundaries of their competence. Competence can be acquired through various combinations of education, training, supervised experience, consultation, study, and professional experience. Competent services can also be provided through consultation with, and as appropriate, supervision by, another professional of established competence in the subject matter in question. Forensic practitioners planning to provide services, teach, or conduct research involving populations, areas, techniques, or technologies that are new to them undertake relevant education, training, supervised experience, consultation, or study.

Forensic practitioners undertake ongoing efforts to develop and maintain their competencies. To maintain the requisite knowledge and skill, forensic practitioners keep abreast of developments in the fields of psychology and the law, engage in continuing study and education, and comply with any continuing education requirements to which they may be subject.

4.03 Representation of Competencies

Forensic practitioners adequately inform clients, examinees, judges, attorneys, parties, triers of fact, and other recipients of their services about relevant aspects of the nature and extent of their experience, training, credentials, and qualifications. The amount and type of information provided will vary according to the service involved and the context in which it is provided. Forensic practitioners do not, by either commission or omission, participate in misrepresentation of their abilities, training, credentials, or qualifications or the manner in which they were obtained.

4.04 Knowledge of the Legal System and the Legal Rights of Individuals

Forensic practitioners are responsible for a fundamental and reasonable level of knowledge and understanding of the legal and professional standards, laws, rules, and precedents that govern their participation in legal proceedings and that guide the impact of their services on service recipients. Forensic practitioners manage their professional conduct in a manner that does not threaten or impair the rights of effected individuals. They consult with, and refer others to, qualified legal counsel on matters of law and legal process.

In their role as forensic practitioners, forensic practitioners do not provide formal legal advice or formal legal opinion. When forensic practitioners provide legal information to examinees or other parties, they explain to parties that legal information is not the same as legal advice or legal opinion. The legal information provided by forensic practitioners may be based on their knowledge and experience in forensic practice. Forensic practitioners encourage parties to consult with an attorney for guidance regarding relevant legal issues and applicability of any legal information provided regarding the most advisable course of action for the person's particular situation.

4.05 Knowledge of the Scientific Foundation for Testimony and Other Sworn Statements

Through reports, written statements, and testimony, forensic practitioners provide scientific, technical and other specialized knowledge to the court that may assist the trier of fact to understand evidence or to determine a fact in issue. Forensic practitioners only offer opinions to the court in those areas for which they are competent to do so, based on adequate knowledge, skill, experience, and education. When providing opinions and testimony that are based on novel or emerging principles and methods, forensic practitioners make clear the known limitations of these principles and methods. Forensic practitioners typically provide opinions and testimony that are a) sufficiently based upon facts or data and on adequate scientific foundation; b) the product of reliable principles and methods; and c) based on principles and methods that have been applied reliably to the facts of the case.

4.06 Knowledge of the Scientific Foundation for Teaching and Research

Forensic practitioners engage in teaching and research activities in which they have adequate knowledge, experience, and education. They adhere to recognized and accepted principles of research design and scientific method, and acknowledge substantial relevant limitations and caveats inherent in their procedures and conclusions.

4.07 Considering Impact of Personal Beliefs and Experience

Forensic practitioners recognize that their own attitudes, values, beliefs, opinions, or biases may have the effect of diminishing their ability to practice in a competent and impartial manner. Under such circumstances, forensic practitioners take steps to correct or limit such effects; decline participation in the matter; or limit their participation in a manner that is consistent with professional obligations.

4.08 Appreciation of Individual Differences

When scientific or professional knowledge in the discipline of psychology establishes that an understanding of factors associated with age, gender, gender identity, race, ethnicity, culture, national origin, religion, sexual orientation, disability, language, socioeconomic status, or other relevant individual differences affects implementation or use of their services or research, forensic practitioners gain the training, experience, consultation, or supervision necessary.

Forensic practitioners are aware of and respect cultural, individual, and role differences, including those based on age, gender, gender identity, race, ethnicity, culture, national origin, religion, sexual orientation, disability, language, and socioeconomic status and consider these factors when working with members of such groups. They do not engage in unfair discrimination based on such factors or on any basis proscribed by law. They take steps to correct or limit the effects of such factors on their work; decline participation in the matter; or limit their participation in a manner that is consistent with professional obligations. They also avoid participating in or condoning prejudicial activities of others based upon such factors.

4.09 Competence of Supervisees and Trainees

Forensic practitioners are responsible for the conduct of those individuals whom they employ or directly supervise. When delegating work to employees, supervisees, students, or research or teaching assistants, or using the services of others, such as interpreters, forensic practitioners avoid using persons who have multiple relationships with those being served that would be likely to result in diminished or impaired performance, exploitation, or loss of objectivity; authorize only those responsibilities that such persons can be expected to perform competently on the basis of their education, training, or experience, either independently or with the level of supervision that is provided; and take reasonable steps to ensure that such persons perform these services competently and diligently.

4.10 Appropriate Use of Services and Products

Forensic practitioners make a reasonable effort to ensure that their services and the products of their services are used in a competent and responsible manner, balancing this consideration with the need not to threaten or impair the legal rights of parties or to interfere with the ability of their attorneys to adequately represent them. Forensic practitioners are not bound to correct all possible misuses of their services but to exercise professional discretion in determining the extent and means by which misuses may be addressed.

When asked to engage in conduct or provide a product that they believe is unethical, unprofessional, or falls below the standard of care, forensic practitioners decline to provide the service or product and, if appropriate, inform the person making the request of the reason for doing so.

5. DILIGENCE

5.01 Provision of Services

Forensic practitioners act with reasonable diligence and promptness in providing agreed-upon and reasonably anticipated services subject to their agreement with their clients. Forensic practitioners are not bound, however, to provide services not reasonably anticipated when retained, nor to provide every possible aspect or variation of service. Instead, forensic practitioners exercise professional discretion in determining the extent and means by which services are provided and agreements are fulfilled.

5.02 Responsiveness

Forensic practitioners manage their workload so that services can be provided thoroughly, competently, and promptly. Acting with reasonable promptness, however, does not require acquiescing to service demands that could not have been reasonably anticipated to occur at the time the service was requested, nor does it include the provision of services if the client has not acted in a manner consistent with existing agreements, including with regard to the payment of fees. Explicit agreements between forensic practitioners and their clients will help define the scope and timeliness of the services for which forensic practitioners are responsible.

5.03 Communication

Forensic practitioners keep their clients reasonably informed about the status of their services, comply with their clients' reasonable requests for information, and consult with their clients about any substantial limitation on their conduct or performance that may arise when they reasonably believe that their clients anticipate a service that may not be consistent with the *Guidelines*. Forensic practitioners attempt to keep their clients reasonably informed regarding new facts, opinions, or other potential evidence that may be salient, whether that information is helpful to their clients' desired outcomes of their matters or not.

Forensic practitioners may withhold information from a party, but ordinarily would not withhold information from the retaining attorney or entity. When forensic practitioners reasonably believe that disclosing information to a party would likely result in substantial and otherwise avoidable harm to that party or to others, the retaining attorney or entity is so informed.

5.04 Availability

When being retained, forensic practitioners and their clients agree on the terms of compensation and the scope of the services that are to be provided. Unless the forensic practitioner-client relationship is terminated pursuant to the retainer agreement, the forensic practitioner carries through to conclusion all matters undertaken for a client. When a forensic practitioner's employment is limited to a specific matter, the relationship terminates when the matter has been resolved, when anticipated services have been provided, or when the retainer agreement has been violated. Doubts about whether a valid and binding client-forensic practitioner relationship still exist are clarified by the forensic practitioner so that the client will not mistakenly assume that the previously existing agreement remains in effect.

6. RELATIONSHIPS

Whether a forensic practitioner-client relationship exists for any specific purpose depends on the circumstances and is determined by a number of factors which may include the information exchanged between the potential client by the forensic practitioner prior to, or at the initiation of any contact or service, the nature of the interaction, and the purpose of the interaction.

6.01 Common Forensic Relationships

6.01.01 Attorney-Client Relationships

The relationship between the attorney and the legal party is usually the relationship referred to as the attorney-client relationship. The legal party retains the attorney whose duty it is to defend and protect the party's legal rights and to zealously assert and pursue the party's interests and positions under the rules of the adversary system.

6.01.02 Attorney-Forensic Practitioner Relationships

The attorney-forensic practitioner relationship refers to the relationship between the party's attorney and the forensic practitioner who the attorney has retained on behalf of the attorney's client in the matter. Typically, the attorney retains the forensic practitioner on behalf of the attorney's client and is to be considered the client of the forensic practitioner.

The forensic practitioner may also be retained by a *pro se* litigant or other party. The forensic practitioner encourages a *pro se* litigant or other party to consult with an attorney before entering into a retainer agreement.

6.01.03 Party-Forensic Practitioner Relationships

The party is typically the client of the attorney and not the client of the forensic practitioner. At the request of the retaining attorney or by order of the court, forensic practitioners provide services to the party or to others who impact the party. Forensic practitioners relate to represented parties knowing that the duties of the attorney are to be distinguished from the duties of the forensic practitioner.

6.02 Responsibilities

Most of the responsibilities flowing from the forensic practitioner-client relationship attach only after a) the client has requested the forensic practitioner to render professional services, b) the forensic practitioner has agreed to do so, and c) an agreement regarding compensation has been reached. Forensic practitioners are aware that there are some responsibilities, such as privacy, confidentiality, and privilege that may attach when the forensic practitioner agrees to consider whether a forensic practitioner-client relationship shall be established.

At the initiation of any contact with an individual for whom they might provide services, forensic practitioners clarify the nature of the relationship and the services to be provided including the role of the forensic practitioner (e.g., trial consultant, forensic examiner, expert witness); which person or entity is the client; the probable uses of the services provided or information obtained; and any limitations to privacy, confidentiality, or privilege.

6.03 Multiple Relationships

A multiple relationship occurs when a forensic practitioner is in a professional role with a person and at the same time or at a subsequent time is in a conflicting role with the same person; is involved in a personal, fiscal, or other relationship with an adverse party; at the same time is in a relationship with a person closely associated with or related to the person with whom the forensic practitioner has the professional relationship; or offers or agrees to enter into another relationship in the future with the person or a person closely associated with or related to the person.

Forensic practitioners are vigilant in recognizing the potential conflicts of interest and threats to objectivity inherent in multiple relationships with attorneys, judges, parties, examinees, patients, and other participants to a legal proceeding. Forensic practitioners recognize that some personal and professional relationships may interfere with their ability to practice in a competent and objective manner and they seek to minimize any detrimental effects by avoiding involvement in such matters whenever feasible or limiting their assistance in a manner that is consistent with professional obligations.

6.03.01 Therapeutic-Forensic Role Conflicts

Forensic practitioners recognize that providing both forensic and therapeutic services with regard to the same individual, or with closely related individuals, is likely to create a role conflict and an apparent conflict of interest. Because forensic and therapeutic roles are fundamentally different and conflicting, forensic practitioners ordinarily avoid engaging in both activities with the same person either concurrently or sequentially. Nevertheless, it is sometimes necessary to provide both forensic and therapeutic services, such as when another reasonably skilled and competent provider is otherwise unavailable to provide either service or when providing both services is mandated by court, law, contract, statute, or job requirements. When requested or ordered by a court to provide either concurrent or sequential forensic and therapeutic services, forensic practitioners avoid providing both services when another reasonably skilled and competent provider of either service is available and they advise the requestor of the reasons that such provision of services is ill-advised.

Upon determining that it is reasonable, appropriate, or required to provide both types of service either concurrently or sequentially, forensic practitioners take reasonable steps to minimize the potential negative effects of these circumstances on the rights of the party; on privacy, confidentiality, and privilege; and on the processes of treatment and evaluation. In determining whether the provision of such multiple services is reasonable and appropriate, forensic practitioners consider risks and benefits to all parties and to the legal system or entity likely to be impacted, the availability of alternative providers, the possibility of separating each service widely in time, seeking judicial review and direction, and consulting with knowledgeable colleagues.

6.03.02 Expert Testimony by Practitioners Providing Therapeutic Services

Providing expert testimony about a patient who is a participant in a legal matter does not necessarily involve the practice of forensic psychology even when that testimony explicitly embraces a psycholegal issue that is before the decision-maker. For example, providing testimony on matters such as a patient's reported history or other statements, mental status, diagnosis, and treatment provided, as well as expert opinion regarding the patient's response to treatment, prognosis, and likelihood of relapse or remission would not ordinarily be considered forensic practice even when the testimony is related to a psycholegal issue before the decision-maker. Rendering opinions and providing testimony about a person on psycholegal issues (e.g., criminal responsibility, legal causation, proximate cause, trial competence, testamentary capacity, the relative merits of parenting arrangements) would ordinarily be considered the practice of forensic psychology.

Forensic practitioners provide testimony only on those issues for which they have adequate foundation and only when a reasonable forensic practitioner engaged in similar circumstances would determine that the ability to make a proper decision is unlikely to be impaired. As with testimony regarding forensic examinees, the testimony identifies any substantial lack of corroboration or other substantive limitation that may affect the reliability and validity of the fact or opinion offered and communicates these to the decision maker.

6.05 Provision of Emergency Mental Health Services

In an emergency and in an attempt to avoid imminent harm, forensic practitioners may provide advice, service, or other assistance in a matter in which they do not have the skill ordinarily required, where referral to or consultation with another forensic practitioner would be impractical. Forensic practitioners limit such assistance to that reasonably necessary in the circumstances and limit disclosures of information to that which is consistent with applicable law, code, statute, and order of the court. When providing such services, forensic practitioners inform the retaining attorney, legal representative, or the court (if court-retained) in a manner consistent with the requirements of the emergency situation.

Upon providing emergency treatment services, forensic practitioners determine whether forensic examination services can be provided after considering whether doing so is likely to impair their objectivity, competence, or effectiveness, or otherwise risk exploitation or harm to the individual or the legal system.

7. FEES

7.01 Determining Fees

When determining the reasonableness of a fee, forensic practitioners may consider salient factors such as the experience and ability of the forensic practitioner performing the services; the time and labor required, the novelty and difficulty of the questions involved, and the skill requisite to perform the service properly; the fee customarily charged in the locality, regionally, or nationally for similar forensic services; the likelihood that the acceptance of the particular employment will preclude other employment by the forensic practitioner; the time limitations imposed by the client or by the circumstances; and the nature and length of the professional relationship with the client.

7.02 Fee Arrangements

As part of the retention process, forensic practitioners and recipients of their services reach an agreement specifying the scope and timing of the service to be provided, the compensation to be paid for the study and testimony, and all billing and service arrangements. If limitations to forensic services can be anticipated because of limitations in financing, this is discussed with the recipient of the services as early as is feasible.

Forensic practitioners avoid undue influence upon their methods, procedures and products that might result from financial compensation or other gains. Because of the threat to objectivity presented by the acceptance of contingent fees, forensic practitioners avoid providing professional services on the basis of contingent fees when those services involve the offering of evidence to a court or administrative body, or when called upon to make sworn statements or other affirmations to be relied upon directly by a court or tribunal.

Letters of protection, financial guarantees, and other security for payment of fees in the future are not considered contingent fees unless payment is promised to originate from future proceeds or settlement benefits from the matter. Future payment that is guaranteed in a manner not dependent on the outcome of the matter does not constitute a contingent fee. Such letters and other fee agreements are to be considered part of the forensic practitioner's billing and financial records.

7.03 Representation of Fees

Billing statements from forensic practitioners accurately reflect the forensic nature, extent, and purpose of the service provided and the context in which the service was provided.

8. NOTIFICATION, ASSENT, CONSENT, AND INFORMED CONSENT

Because substantial rights, liberties, and properties are frequently, immediately, and irrevocably at risk in forensic matters and because the methods and procedures of forensic practitioners are complex and may not be accurately anticipated by the recipients of forensic services, forensic practitioners inform service recipients about the nature and parameters of the services to be provided.

8.01 Timing and Substance

Forensic practitioners notify clients, examinees, and others who are the recipients of forensic services as soon as is feasible regarding the provision of all reasonably anticipated forensic services and all relevant professional conduct.

In determining whether the information and subsequent explanation provided as the basis for consent are reasonably adequate, relevant factors include whether the person is experienced or trained in psychological and legal matters of the type involved and whether the person is represented by counsel when providing the consent. Normally, more experienced persons need less information to provide adequate informed consent than would others. When questions or uncertainties remain after the forensic practitioner has made the effort to communicate the necessary information, forensic practitioners recommend the person seek legal advice regarding the possible consequences of the forensic services.

8.02 Communication with Legal Representatives Seeking to Retain a Forensic Practitioner

Forensic practitioners seek to insure that attorneys and others considering to contract with them for services are knowledgeable about factors that might reasonably affect the decision to retain them.

As part of the initial process of being retained, or as soon thereafter as previously unknown information becomes available, forensic practitioners disclose to the client all information that would reasonably be anticipated to affect a decision to retain or continue the services of the forensic practitioner. This disclosure includes all information that the reasonably prudent recipient of service would desire to know. The factors to disclose may include a) the fee structure for anticipated services; b) prior and current personal or professional activities, obligations and relationships that would reasonably lead to the fact or the appearance of a conflict of interest; c) the forensic practitioner's knowledge, skill, experience, and education relevant to forensic services in the matter being considered, including any significant limitations; d) the substantial scientific bases and limitations of the methods and procedures which are expected to be employed, including any limitations; and e) any other factor that might reasonably be anticipated to substantially limit the forensic practitioner's ability or qualification to testify or that might substantially limit the weight accorded to the forensic practitioner's opinions.

8.03 Communication with Forensic Examinees

Forensic practitioners disclose to the examinee who is the identified client; the purpose, nature, and anticipated use of the examination; any factor reasonably expected to substantially impair the objectivity, competence, or effectiveness of the forensic practitioner; who will have access to the information; associated limits on privacy, confidentiality, and privilege including who is authorized to release or access the information contained in the forensic practitioner's records; the voluntary or involuntary nature of participation, including potential consequences of non-participation, if known; and if the cost of the service is the responsibility of the examinee, the anticipated cost of the service, the means by which the cost will be calculated, and the billing arrangements.

8.03.01 Persons Not Ordered or Mandated to Undergo Examination

If the examinee is not ordered by the court to participate in a forensic examination, the forensic practitioner obtains the informed consent of the examinee, or the examinee's attorney, before proceeding with examinations and procedures. If the examinee declines to proceed after receiving a notification of the purposes, general methods, and intended uses of the forensic examination, the forensic practitioner postpones the examination, advises the examinee to contact his or her attorney, and notifies the retaining attorney about the examinee's unwillingness to proceed.

After advising an examinee about the intended uses of the examination and its work product, the forensic practitioner avoids using information gained from the examination or work product for other purposes unless the examinee or organization has consented to such use or there is legal authorization to do so.

8.03.02 Persons Ordered or Mandated to Undergo Examination

If the examinee is ordered by the court to participate, the forensic practitioner may engage in the professional activity over the objection, and without the consent, of the examinee. If the examinee declines to proceed after receiving a notification of the purposes, general methods, and intended uses of the forensic examination, the forensic practitioner may attempt to conduct the examination, postpone the examination, advise the examinee to contact his or her attorney, or notify the retaining attorney about the examinee's unwillingness to proceed.

Forensic practitioners attempt to secure assent when consent and informed consent can not be obtained because of the examinee's unwillingness or limited capacity.

When, due to law, court order, contract, mandate, or organizational rule, the product of the service is not to be provided to an examinee or other party by the forensic practitioner, the forensic practitioner makes this known to the recipient of services at the time of attempting to acquire initial informed consent or as soon thereafter as is practical.

8.03.03 Persons Lacking Capacity to Provide Informed Consent

For examinees adjudicated or presumed by law to lack the capacity to provide informed consent for the anticipated forensic service, the forensic practitioner nevertheless provides an appropriate explanation (as indicated above); seeks the examinee's assent; considers the examinee's preferences and best interests; and obtains appropriate permission from a legally authorized person or attorney, if such substitute consent is permitted or required by law.

For examinees whom the forensic practitioner has concluded lack capacity to provide informed consent to a proposed, non-court-ordered service, but who nonetheless have not been adjudicated as lacking such capacity, the forensic practitioner takes reasonable steps to protect their rights and welfare. This may be accomplished by suspending the proposed service, notifying the examinee's attorney or the referral source.

8.04 Communication with Other Direct Recipients of Forensic Services Such As Collaterals and Non-Party Examinees

Forensic practitioners disclose to all service recipients who is the identified client; who has retained or the entity who has employed the forensic practitioner; the nature, purpose, and intended use of the forensic examination or other procedure; associated limits on privacy, confidentiality, and privilege; and whether participation is voluntary.

8.05 Communication in Research Contexts

When engaging in research or scholarly activities conducted as a service to a client in a legal proceeding, forensic practitioners clarify any anticipated further use of such research or scholarly product, disclose their role in the resulting research or scholarly products, and obtain whatever consent or agreement is required. This applies whether forensic practitioners are conducting research in the laboratory or in a field setting and whether the research is being conducted for general educational purposes or in connection with specific legal proceedings.

9. CONFLICTS IN PRACTICE

In forensic psychology practice, conflicting responsibilities and demands may be encountered. When conflicts occur, forensic practitioners maintain a disciplined, fair, and professional attitude toward all persons involved in the matter. In resolving conflicts, forensic practitioners are guided by the law, any applicable codes of ethics, these *Guidelines*, and their understanding of their relationship to the profession and to the legal system.

9.01 Conflicts with Legal Authority

When their responsibilities conflict with law, regulations, or other governing legal authority, forensic practitioners make known their commitment to the *Guidelines* and take steps to resolve the conflict. When the conflict cannot be resolved via such means, forensic practitioners may adhere to the requirements of the law, regulations, or other governing legal authority. In situations where the *Guidelines* may be in conflict with the requirements of law, attempts to resolve the conflict are made in accordance with the procedures set forth below.

9.02 Conflicts with Organizational Demands

When the demands of an organization with which they are affiliated or for whom they are working conflict with the *Guidelines*, forensic practitioners clarify the nature of the conflict, make known the recommendations of the *Guidelines*, and to the extent feasible, resolve the conflict in a way consistent with the *Guidelines*.

9.03 Conflicts with Fellow Professionals

When an apparent or potential ethical or practice standards violation has substantially harmed or is likely to substantially harm a person or organization, forensic practitioners take further action appropriate to the situation. When considering appropriate actions to take and the timing of such actions, forensic practitioners consider a number of factors including the nature and the immediacy of the potential harm; applicable privacy, confidentiality, and legal privileges; how the rights of the relevant parties may be affected by various courses of action; and the legal obligations imposed on forensic practitioners.

When retained by fellow professionals in consultative or supervisory capacities, or attorneys representing fellow professionals, forensic practitioners incur no obligation to bring perceived ethical violations to the attention of third parties. When retained in any other capacity, forensic practitioners take further action appropriate to the situation, including consideration of making a report to third parties of the perceived ethical violation.

When forensic practitioners believe that there may have been an ethical violation by another professional, an attempt is made to resolve the issue by bringing it to the attention of that individual, if that attempt at resolution does not violate any rights or privileges that may be involved and if an informal resolution appears appropriate. In most instances, in order to minimize unforeseen risks to the party's rights in the legal matter, forensic practitioners will consult with the retaining attorney before attempting to resolve a perceived ethical violation with another professional in such a circumstance.

Steps to resolve perceived ethical conflicts may include, but are not limited to, obtaining the consultation of knowledgeable colleagues, obtaining the advice of independent counsel, and conferring directly with the attorneys involved.

10. PRIVACY, CONFIDENTIALITY, AND PRIVILEGE

Forensic practitioners keep private and in confidence information relating to a client or party except so far as disclosure is consented to by the client or required or allowed by law.

10.01 Knowledge of Legal Standards

Forensic practitioners are reasonably aware of the legal standards that may affect or limit the privacy, confidentiality, or privilege that may attach to their services or their products, and they conduct their professional activities in a manner that respects those rights and privileges.

10.02 Release of Information

Forensic practitioners comply with properly noticed and served subpoenas or court orders directing release of records, or other legally proper consent from duly authorized persons, unless there is a compelling reason not to do so. Reasons to offer an objection to complying include, but are not limited to, contractual obligations, or federal or state privacy, confidentiality, or privilege regulations, or notice by another counsel of counsel's intent to quash or otherwise petition the court to amend or void the subpoena or order for the records. Absent compelling reason otherwise, forensic practitioners make available all records specified in the consent, subpoena, or order. Their decision-making regarding access to and release of information in the record is informed by the relevant jurisdiction(s) of the matter. When in doubt about an appropriate response or course of action, forensic practitioners seek assistance from the attorney, agency or court that has retained them, retain and seek legal advice from their own attorney, or formally notify the drafter of the subpoena of their uncertainty.

10.03 Access to Information

If requested, forensic practitioners provide their clients access to, and a meaningful explanation of, all information that is in their records for the matter at hand, consistent with existing federal and state statutes, applicable codes of ethics and professional standards, and institutional rules and regulations. Unless the party is the client, the party typically is not provided access to the forensic practitioner's records without the consent of the client. Non-client access to records is governed by legal process, usually subpoena or court order, or by explicit consent of the client. Forensic practitioners may charge a reasonable fee for the costs associated with the storage, reproduction, review, and provision of records.

10.04 Acquiring Third Party Information

When forensic practitioners request information or records from collateral sources, they do so with the consent of the relevant attorney, the relevant party, or as a consequence of an order of a court to conduct the forensic examination or to access the information being requested.

10.05 Use of Case Materials in Teaching, Continuing Education, and Other Scholarly Activities

Forensic practitioners using case materials for purposes of teaching, training, or research, present such information in a fair, balanced, and respectful manner. They attempt to protect the privacy of persons by disguising the confidential, personally identifiable information of all persons and entities who would reasonably claim a privacy interest; using only those aspects of the case information available in the public domain; obtaining consent from the relevant clients, parties, participants, and organizations to use the materials for such purposes and in ways that might serve to identify them.

11 METHODS AND PROCEDURES

11.01 Use of Appropriate Methods

Forensic practitioners practice in a competent manner, consistent with accepted forensic and scientific standards. They utilize forensically appropriate data collection methods and procedures when providing examinations, consultation, educational activities or scholarly investigations.

11.02 Avoiding Bias

When providing examinations, consultation, educational activities or scholarly investigations, forensic practitioners maintain integrity by examining the issue at hand from all reasonable perspectives and actively seeking information that will differentially test plausible rival hypotheses.

11.03 Use of and Reliance on Second Hand Information and Data

When considering accounts, observations, records, or sworn statements provided by others, forensic practitioners disclose the source of, and minimize sole reliance upon, such information. Forensic practitioners attempt to corroborate data that form a substantial basis of their professional product. Corroboration may include interviewing or reviewing the original source of secondhand information, or seeking related information in other reasonable ways. When relying upon data that have not been corroborated, forensic practitioners identify the origin and acknowledge the uncorroborated status of that data, any associated strengths and limitations, and the reasons for relying upon it. When seeking corroboration, forensic practitioners distinguish corroboration that something was said from corroboration of the truth of what was said.

11.04 Opinions Regarding Persons Not Examined

Forensic practitioners only provide written or oral evidence about the psychological characteristics of particular individuals when they have sufficient information or data to form an adequate foundation for those opinions or to substantiate their findings. Forensic practitioners make reasonable effort to obtain such information or data, and they document their efforts to obtain it. When it is not possible or feasible to examine individuals about whom they are offering an opinion, forensic practitioners make clear the impact of such limitations on the reliability and validity of their professional products, evidence or testimony.

When conducting record reviews or providing consultation or supervision, and an individual examination is not warranted or necessary for the opinion, forensic practitioners explain this and the sources of information on which they are basing their opinions and recommendations, including the substantial caveats and limitations to their opinions and recommendations.

12. ASSESSMENT

12.01 Focus on Legally Relevant Factors

12.01.01 Assessment of Functional Abilities

Forensic examiners assist the trier of fact to understand evidence or to determine a fact in issue. They provide information that are most relevant to the psycholegal issue. In reports and testimony forensic practitioners typically provide information about examinees' functional abilities, capacities, knowledge, and beliefs, depending on the psycholegal issue in question and address their opinions and recommendations to the factors identified in the court order, law, rule, or contract relevant to the matter.

12.01.02 Use of Diagnostic Classification Procedures

Forensic practitioners consider the strengths and weaknesses of utilizing diagnostic categorization procedures in forensic assessment tasks, including the limits of category validation studies in forensic contexts; that impairments, abilities, and disabilities vary widely within each diagnostic category; and that being diagnosed may result in unfair prejudice and may carry unwarranted implications beyond the intended meaning of the actual diagnosis.

12.02 Appropriate Use of Assessment Procedures

Forensic practitioners use assessment procedures in the manner and for the purposes that are appropriate in light of the research on or evidence of their usefulness and proper application. This includes assessment techniques, interviews, tests, instruments, and other procedures and their administration, adaptation, scoring, interpreting, and employing computerized scoring and interpretation systems.

Forensic practitioners ordinarily use assessment instruments whose validity and reliability have been established for use with members of the population tested or other representative populations. When such validity or reliability has not been adequately established in the forensic context or with this population, forensic practitioners describe the strengths and limitations of any test results and interpretation and explain the extrapolation of this data to the forensic context. Forensic practitioners explain the strengths and limitations of extrapolating such data and interpretation to forensic contexts.

12.03 Appreciation of Individual Differences

When interpreting assessment results, including automated interpretations, forensic practitioners take into account the purpose of the assessment as well as the various test factors, test-taking abilities, and other characteristics of the person being assessed, such as situational, personal, linguistic, and cultural differences, that might affect their judgments or reduce the accuracy of their interpretations. Forensic practitioners identify any significant strengths and limitations of their procedures and interpretations.

12.04 Appreciation of Contextual Differences

Assessment in forensic contexts differs from assessment in therapeutic contexts in important ways that forensic practitioners take into account when conducting forensic examinations. Forensic practitioners consider the strengths and limitations of employing traditional assessment procedures in forensic examinations and are mindful of the cautions and risks inherent in this process. They take into account and make known potential effects of the context and of demand characteristics on the examinee's presentation and performance. Forensic practitioners consider and make known that forensic examination results can be affected by factors unique to, or differentially present in, forensic contexts including response style; voluntariness of participation; and situational stress associated with involvement in the forensic or legal matters.

Because of the many differences between forensic and therapeutic contexts, forensic practitioners are aware and make known that some examination results may warrant substantially different interpretation when administered in forensic and therapeutic contexts.

12.05 Providing Assessment Feedback

Forensic practitioners conducting examinations take reasonable steps to explain assessment results to the individual being assessed or to a designated representative, unless the nature of the relationship or circumstances precludes provision of an explanation of results, and this fact has been clearly explained to the examinee in advance.

Forensic practitioners provide information about professional work to clients and other parties in a manner consistent with professional and legal standards for the disclosure of test results, interpretation of data, and the factual bases for conclusions. A full explanation of the test results and the bases for conclusions is provided in language that the intended recipient can understand.

13. DOCUMENTATION

13.01 Documentation and Compilation of Data Considered

From the moment they reasonably know that the data and potential evidence derived from their services may be subject to discovery or relied upon by a trier of fact or other decision maker, forensic practitioners document all data they consider with enough detail and quality to allow for reasonable judicial scrutiny and adequate discovery by all parties. This documentation includes, but is not limited to, letters and consultations; notes, recordings, and transcriptions; assessment and test data, scoring reports, and interpretations; and all other records in any form or medium that were created or exchanged in connection with a matter.

13.02 Provision of Documentation

Pursuant to proper subpoenas or court orders, or other legally proper consent from duly authorized persons, forensic practitioners make available all documentation described in 13.01, all financial records related to the matter, and any other records, including reports, that might reasonably be related to the opinions to be expressed. Forensic practitioners are not obligated to include draft reports not yet considered final, unless such has previously been provided to a party, attorney, or other entity for review.

13.03 Record Keeping and Retention

Forensic practitioners establish and maintain a system of record-keeping and professional communication that is consistent with law, rules, and regulations, and that safeguards applicable privacy, confidentiality, and legal privileges. Forensic practitioners maintain all records, notes, and data that they have generated for the full length of time that is proper for the jurisdiction in which the matter was heard or the jurisdiction of the forensic practitioner's practice, whichever is longer. When indicated by the extent of the rights, liberties, and properties that may be at risk, the complexity of the case, the amount and legal significance of unique evidence in the care and control of the forensic practitioner, and the likelihood of future appeal, forensic psychologists inform the retaining attorney or entity of the limits of record-keeping times. If requested to do so, forensic practitioners either maintain such records until notified that all appeals in the matter have been exhausted or they send a copy of any unique components/aspects of the record that are in their care and control to the requesting attorney before destruction of the record.

13.04 Knowledge of Applicable Rules

Documentation of data reviewed and relied upon is subject to the applicable rules of discovery, disclosure, privacy, confidentiality, and privilege. Forensic practitioners have a reasonable understanding and awareness of those rules, and regulate their conduct in accordance with them.

14. PROFESSIONAL AND OTHER PUBLIC COMMUNICATIONS

14.01 Accuracy, Fairness, and Avoidance of Deception

Forensic practitioners make reasonable efforts to ensure that the products of their services, as well as their own public statements and professional reports and testimony, are communicated in ways that promote understanding and avoid deception.

Regardless of who is the client, forensic practitioners are aware that, when in their role as expert to the court or other tribunals, their task is to facilitate understanding of the evidence or dispute of fact. Forensic practitioners do not distort or withhold relevant evidence or opinion in reports or testimony because this is potentially misleading, and is incompatible with their role as experts to the court or other tribunals. When responding to discovery requests and when providing sworn testimony, forensic practitioners have readily available for inspection all data which they considered during the course of providing professional services, subject to and consistent with court order, relevant rules of evidence, test security issues, and professional standards.

When providing professional reports and other sworn statements or testimony in any form, forensic practitioners present their conclusions, evidence, opinions, or other professional products in a fair manner. This principle does not preclude forceful representation of the data and reasoning upon which a conclusion or professional product is based. It does, however, preclude an attempt, whether active or passive, to engage in partisan distortion or misrepresentation.

Forensic practitioners do not, by either commission or omission, participate in a misrepresentation of their evidence, nor do they participate in partisan attempts to avoid, deny or subvert the presentation of evidence contrary to their own position or opinion. Forensic practitioners recognize that, to the extent consistent with the rules of the adversary system, a retaining attorney's opposing counsel and opposing party are as fully entitled to all the benefit that might reasonably be implied or concluded from their products and opinions as are the retaining attorney and client.

14.02 Differentiating Observations, Inferences, and Conclusions

In their communications, forensic practitioners are careful to differentiate among their observations, inferences, and conclusions. Forensic practitioners are prepared to explain the relationship between their expert reports or testimony and the legal issues and facts of an instant case.

14.03 Disclosing Sources of Information and Bases of Opinions

Forensic practitioners affirmatively disclose all sources of information obtained in the course of their professional services. Forensic practitioners affirmatively disclose which information from which source was considered and relied upon in formulating a particular conclusion, evidence, opinion, or other professional product.

14.04 Comprehensive and Accurate Presentation of Opinions in Reports and Testimony

Consistent with relevant law and rules of evidence, when providing professional reports and other sworn statements or testimony in any form, forensic practitioners offer a complete statement of all relevant opinions that they formed within the scope of their retention, the basis and reasoning underlying the opinions, the salient data or other information that was considered in forming the opinions, and an indication of any additional evidence that may be used in support for the opinions to be offered. The specific areas to be included in forensic reports are determined by the type of psycholegal issue and any relevant laws or rules in the jurisdiction in which the work is completed.

Forensic practitioners limit discussion of background information that does not bear directly upon the legal purpose of the examination or consultation. With respect to evidence of any type, forensic practitioners avoid offering information from investigations or examinations that is irrelevant to the legal purpose of the services and that does not provide a substantial basis of support for their product, evidence, or testimony, except where such disclosure is required by law.

Forensic practitioners organize and communicate their opinions, the data upon which such opinions are based, and the rationale that connects their data and opinions in a manner that is consistent with the psycholegal issue raised by the nature of the referral and in conformity with the rules, regulations, statutes and case law of the jurisdiction in which the opinion is offered. Reports, evidence, and testimony are organized and communicated for the purpose of informing and not misleading the intended recipient. Schemas that serve partisan attempts to avoid impartial, equitable, and representative presentation of reports, opinions, or other evidence are to be avoided.

14.05 Commenting Upon Other Professionals and Participants

When evaluating or commenting upon the work product or qualifications of other professionals involved in a legal proceeding, or otherwise when acting as a rebuttal expert, forensic practitioners represent their disagreements in a professional and respectful tone, and base them on a fair examination of the data, theories, standards and opinions of the other expert or party.

When describing or commenting upon examinees or other participants in a legal proceeding, forensic practitioners do so in a fair and objective manner. Forensic practitioners also report the representations, opinions, and statements of forensic examinees or other participants in the legal proceedings in a fair and objective manner. When they are retained to provide limited services, such as rebuttal testimony or a critique in anticipation of cross-examination of another professional's work product, forensic practitioners make the limited scope of their task clear to the trier of fact [see also 14.01].

14.06 Out of Court Statements

Ordinarily, forensic practitioners avoid making detailed public (out-of-court) statements about particular legal proceedings in which they have been involved. When adequate justification for such public statements exists, forensic practitioners refrain from releasing private, confidential, or privileged information and attempt to protect persons from harm, misuse, or misrepresentation as a result of their statements.

When making public statements, forensic practitioners' primary goals are to educate the public about the role of forensic practitioners in the legal system, the appropriate practice of forensic psychology, and clinical and forensic issues that are relevant to the matter at hand. Forensic practitioners refrain from making self-serving and self-aggrandizing public statements. Forensic practitioners address particular legal proceedings in publications or communications only to the extent that the information relied upon is part of a public record or when consent for that use has been properly obtained from the party holding any privilege.

When offering public statements about specific cases in which they have not been involved, forensic practitioners offer opinions for which there is sufficient information or data and make clear the limitations of their statements and opinions resulting from having had no direct knowledge of or involvement with the case.

APPENDIX I: BACKGROUND OF THE *GUIDELINES* AND THE REVISION PROCESS

A. History of the *Guidelines*

The previous version of the *Specialty Guidelines for Forensic Psychologists* (Committee on Ethical Guidelines for Forensic Psychologists, 1991) was approved by the American Psychology-Law Society, Division 41 of the American Psychological Association, and the American Board of Forensic Psychology in 1991. The current revision, now called the *Specialty Guidelines for Forensic Psychology* (referred to as *Guidelines* throughout this document), replace the 1991 *Specialty Guidelines for Forensic Psychologists.*

B. Revision Process

This revision of the *Guidelines* was coordinated by the Committee for the Revision of the Specialty Guidelines for Forensic practitioners, which was established by the American Board of Forensic Psychology and the American Psychology-Law Society/Division 41 of the American Psychological Association in 2002 and operated through 200x. This Committee consisted of two representatives [1] of each organization and a Chairperson [2].

This document was revised in accordance with American Psychological Association Rule 30.08 and the APA policy document *Criteria for the development and evaluation of practice guidelines* (APA, 2001). The Committee posted announcements regarding the revision process to relevant electronic discussion lists and professional publications [insert footnote to all list servers and publications here]. In addition, an electronic discussion list devoted solely to issues concerning revision of the *Guidelines* was established in December 2002, and all interested individuals were invited to subscribe to the list. Individuals could provide input and commentary on the existing *Guidelines* or proposed revisions via the list. Any messages posted to the list were automatically distributed to all subscribers. In addition, [insert number] public meetings were held throughout the revision process at conferences sponsored by the American Psychological Association and the American Psychology-Law Society.

Upon development of a draft that the Revisions Committee deemed suitable, the revised *Guidelines* were submitted for review to the Executive Committee of the American Psychology-Law Society and Division 41 of the American Psychological Association, and to the American Board of Forensic Psychology. Once the revised *Guidelines* were approved by these two organizations, they were submitted to the American Psychological Association for review, commentary, and acceptance, consistent with the American Psychological Association's Criteria for Practice Guideline Development and Evaluation (Committee on Professional Practice and Standards, 2001) and Rule 30-8. The *Guidelines* were adopted by the American Psychological Association Council of Representatives on [insert date here].

C. Need for the Guidelines

Professional standards for the ethical practice of psychology as a discipline are addressed in the Ethical Principles of Psychologists and Code of Conduct (American Psychological Association, 2002, hereinafter EPPCC). As such, codes of ethics are intended to describe standards for competent and adequate professional conduct. In contrast to applicable codes of ethics, these *Guidelines* are intended to describe the most desirable and highest level professional conduct for psychologists when engaged in the practice of forensic psychology.

---

[1] Drs. Solomon Fulero, Stephen Golding, Stuart A. Greenberg, vice-chair, and Christina Studebaker
[2] Dr. Randy K. Otto, chair

The *Guidelines*, although informed by applicable codes of ethics and meant to be consistent with them, are designed to be educative and to provide more specific and thorough guidance to psychologists who are determining their professional forensic conduct.

The 1991 *Specialty Guidelines for Forensic practitioners* needed revision due to advancements in the field that have taken place since the framing of the original guidelines and due to the need for a broader and more thorough document that addresses the wide variety of professional forensic practice areas that have developed and expanded since the adoption of the original guidelines.

D. Developers and Support

The *Specialty Guidelines for Forensic Psychology* were developed by the American Psychology-Law Society, Division 41 of the American Psychological Association, and the American Board of Forensic Psychology.

E. Background Literature

Resources reviewed in the development of the *Guidelines* include:

American Academy of Child & Adolescent Psychiatry: Code of Ethics; American Board of Forensic Psychology: Specialty Guidelines for Forensic Psychologists; American Academy of Psychiatry & Law: Ethical Guidelines for the Practice of Forensic Psychiatry; American Bar Association: Model Rules of Professional Conduct; American Board of Examiners in Clinical Social Work: Code of Ethics; American Psychiatric Association: The Principles of Medical Ethics With Annotations Especially Applicable to Psychiatry; American Psychological Association: Ethical Principles of Psychologists and Code of Conduct; American Psychological Association: Guidelines for Child Custody Evaluations in Divorce Proceedings; American Psychological Association: Guidelines for Psychological Evaluations in Child Protection Matters; American Psychological Association: Guidelines for Psychotherapy with Lesbian, Gay, & Bisexual Clients; American Psychological Association: Guidelines on Multicultural Education, Training, Research, Practice, and Organizational Change for Psychologists; American Psychological Association: Professional, Ethical, and Legal Issues Concerning Interpersonal Violence, Maltreatment, and Related Trauma; American Psychological Association: Record Keeping Guidelines; American Psychological Association: Rights and Responsibilities of Test Takers: Guidelines and Expectations; Association for the Treatment of Sexual Abusers: Professional Code of Ethics; Association of State & Provincial Psychology Boards: Supervision Guidelines; Joint Committee on Testing Practices: Code of Fair Testing Practices in Education; Mental Health Patient's Bill of Rights; National Association of Social Workers: Code of Ethics; Guidelines for Dealing with Faculty Conflicts of Commitment and Conflicts of Interest in Research, the Association of American Medical Colleges, 1990.

F. Current Status

These *Guidelines* are scheduled to expire [insert date here]. After this date, users are encouraged to contact the American Psychological Association Practice Directorate to confirm that this document remains in effect.

APPENDIX II: DEFINITIONS AND TERMINOLOGY

For the purposes of these *Guidelines*:

Appropriate, when used in relation to conduct by a forensic practitioner means that, according to the prevailing professional judgment of competent forensic practitioners, the conduct is apt and pertinent and is considered befitting, suitable and proper for a particular person, place, condition, or function. "Inappropriate" means that, according to the prevailing professional judgment of competent forensic practitioners, the conduct is not suitable, desirable, or properly timed for a particular person, occasion, or purpose; and may also denote improper conduct, improprieties, or conduct that is discrepant for the circumstances.

Agreement refers to the objective and mutual understanding between the forensic and the person or persons seeking the professional service and/or agreeing to participate in the service. See also Assent, Consent, and Informed Consent.

> *Assent* refers to the agreement, approval, or permission, especially regarding verbal or nonverbal conduct, that is reasonably intended and interpreted as expressing willingness, even in the absence of unmistakable consent. Forensic practitioners attempt to secure assent when consent and informed consent can not be obtained or when, because of mental state, the examinee may not be able to consent.

> *Consent* refers to agreement, approval, or permission as to some act or purpose.

> *Informed Consent* denotes the knowledgeable, voluntary, and competent agreement by a person to a proposed course of conduct after the forensic practitioner has communicated adequate information and explanation about the material risks and benefits of, and reasonably available alternatives to, the proposed course of conduct.

Client refers to the attorney, law firm, court, agency, entity, party, or other person who has retained, and who has a contractual relationship with, the forensic practitioner to provide services.

Conflict of Interest refers to a situation or circumstance in which the forensic practitioner's objectivity, impartiality, or judgment may be jeopardized due to a relationship, financial, or any other interest that would reasonably be expected to substantially affect a forensic practitioner's professional judgment, impartiality, or decision-making.

Decision-maker refers to the person or entity with the authority to make a judicial decision, agency determination, arbitration award, or other contractual determination after consideration of the facts and the law.

Examinee refers to a person who is the subject of a forensic examination for the purpose of informing a decision maker or attorney regarding the psychological condition of that examinee.

Forensic Examiner refers to a forensic practitioner who examines the psychological condition of a person whose psychological condition is in controversy or at issue.

Forensic Practice refers to the application of the scientific, technical, or specialized knowledge of psychology to the law and the use that knowledge to assist in resolving legal, contractual, and administrative disputes.

Forensic Practitioner refers to a psychologist when engaged in forensic practice.

Forensic Psychology refers to all forensic practice by any psychologist working within any sub-discipline of psychology (e.g., clinical, developmental, social, cognitive).

Party person or entity named in litigation, or who is involved in, or is witness to, an activity or relationship that may be reasonably anticipated to result in litigation.

Reasonable or *Reasonably*, when used in relation to conduct by a forensic practitioner, denotes the conduct of a prudent and competent forensic practitioner who is engaged in similar activities in similar circumstances.

Record or *Written Record* refers to all notes, records, documents, memorializations, and recordings of considerations and communications, be they in any form or on any media, tangible, electronic, hand-written, or mechanical, that are contained in, or are specifically related to, the forensic matter in question or the forensic service provided.

Legal Representative refers to a person who has the legal authority to act on behalf of another.

Tribunal denotes a court or an arbitrator in an arbitration proceeding, or a legislative body, administrative agency, or other body acting in an adjudicative capacity. A legislative body, administrative agency or other body acts in an adjudicative capacity when a neutral official, after the presentation of legal argument or evidence by a party or parties, renders a judgment directly affecting a party's interests in a particular matter.

E:\SGFP\SGFP version 3.6 of 1-11-06.wpd; printed on January 11, 2006

Forensic Neuropsychological Evaluation from Chapter 1 (Hall)

February 4, 2004

NAME: Paul Smith
DOB: November 3, 1963
POB: Santa Barbara, California
SSN: 123-45-6789

RE: *State of California v. John Paul Smith*
     Criminal Case No. 03-474

Count One:	First-degree murder
Count Two:	First-degree murder
Count Three:	First-degree murder
Count Four:	First-degree murder
Count Five:	First-degree murder
Count Six:	First-degree murder
Count Seven:	Second-degree murder
Count Eight:	Second-degree murder
Count Nine:	Second-degree murder
Count Ten:	(Attempt) First-degree murder
Count Eleven:	(Attempt) First-degree murder
Count Twelve:	Kidnapping
Count Thirteen:	Burglary
Count Fourteen:	Indecent assault
Count Fifteen:	Indecent assault
Count Sixteen:	(Attempt) Rape
Count Seventeen:	Rape
Count Eighteen:	Sodomy
Count Nineteen:	Child abuse
Count Twenty:	Child sexual abuse

Evaluation Dates: March 10 (twice), March 11, and March 13, 2004.

Referral: John Paul Smith is a 38-year-old, right-handed, single male who was referred on November 3, 2003, for forensic evaluation by [his court-appointed attorneys]. Authorization to obtain my services as an expert on state of mind issues relating to the defendant's declared intent to rely on the insanity defense was obtained on November 20, 2003, the order signed by [the judge]. The evaluation was to assess the defendant's cognitive strengths and weaknesses in a neuropsychological evaluation as well as to examine methamphetamine-related issues in this case. No previous neuropsychological or psychological evaluations were available or on record.

Forensic Database: Relevant documents reviewed include the following:

1. Police and investigation reports, including witnesses' statements
2. Federal Bureau of Investigation criminal history information
3. Criminal history report including a 1995 conviction for first-degree criminal sexual assault in Oregon
4. Autopsy reports (regarding decedents)

The following individuals were interviewed:

1. [his mother]
2. [his maternal aunt]
3. [his maternal uncle]
4. [a friend of the victim family]
5. [his work supervisor]
6. [his previous probation officer]
7. [the girlfriend of the accused]
8. [his sister]

In addition to inspecting the defendant's residence on November 25, 2003, with the defense team, prosecution, police, and landlord, I evaluated the defendant four times with the following measures for a total of approximately 15 h of direct contact over the three evaluation dates:

1. Clinical interviews and mental status evaluation
2. Minnesota Multiphasic Personality Inventory-2 (MMPI-2)
3. Millon's Clinical Multiaxial Inventory-III (MCMI-III)
4. Multiphasic Sex Inventory
5. Stroop Color and Word Test
6. Standard Progressive Matrices (Ravens)
7. California Memory Test
8. Clock Draw
9. CEP Aphasia Screening
10. Wahler Physical Symptoms Inventory (twice for present and 1 week before the alleged offenses)
11. Sensory perceptual examination (vision and audition)
12. Wechsler Memory Test-Revised (Digit Span, Mental Control, Logical Memory I and II, and Recognition Testing)
13. Incomplete Sentence Blank (Rotter)
14. Boston-Rochester Neuropsychological Screening Test (Metaphors and Proverbs, Orientation, Repetition, Word List Generation, Praxis, Presidents, Visual Immediate Delayed and Recognition Recall, and Copy and Narrative Writing)
15. Tactile Performance Test (TPT)
16. Cancellation Test
17. Psychopathy Checklist-Revised (PCL-R)
18. Shipley Institute of Living Scale

19. Suicide Probability Scale
20. Visual Organization Test (Hooper)
21. Wechsler Adult Intelligence Scale-Revised (Digit symbol, Comprehension, Information, and Similarities)
22. California Verbal Learning Test (CVLT)
23. Cognitive Estimation Test
24. Stress audit (completed as homework on March 12, 2004)
25. Mooney Problem Checklist (completed as homework on March 12, 2004)
26. Personal Problems Checklist for Adults (completed as homework on March 12, 2004)
27. HCL-20 (Historical, Clinical, and Risk Management)
28. Violence Risk Appraisal Guide (VRAG)
29. Hare PCL-R

The Rogers' Criminal Assessment Scales (R-CRAS) were used to retrospectively analyze the American Law Institute (ALI) decision tree to reach legal conclusions regarding the defendant's criminal responsibility.

Background Information: Except as otherwise indicated, the following history is as reported by the defendant and his significant others. He was born after an uneventful pregnancy and did not have any problems in reaching the usual developmental milestones. He remained in Santa Barbara until the age of 2, and his mother reported that he did not have any adjustment difficulties at that age. He moved to Oklahoma with his mother and his siblings and remained there until he was about 20 years old. He claimed that he first began hearing voices before he started kindergarten. They consisted of laughing, derisive sounds when he made a mistake, occurring approximately two or three times weekly. Others thought that he was talking to himself. The voices were more or less continuous and increased in frequency when he was excited or fatigued. He learned to ignore the voices over the years by doing something physically active. He occasionally heard negatively toned words, such as the voices saying "See, I told you" when he makes a mistake. Retrospectively, he believes that he created the voices himself. He claimed that he has been hiding from others that he has been hearing the voices all these years.

The defendant has a history of loss of consciousness. During childhood, he fell out of a tree and, as a separate incident, was attacked and bitten on the head by a dog. He claimed that his mother beat him to the point of his losing consciousness (between 1965 and 1968). Between 1969 and 1971, he was in a motor vehicle accident with his mother. He lost consciousness and was hospitalized at [a hospital in Oklahoma]. On at least one occasion during the same time period, he was beaten and knocked out by a neighbor. From 1972 to 1975, he engaged in many fights with his brother and peers, and he lost consciousness at least once.

The defendant has an extensive history of drug use. From 1972 to 1975, influenced by his brother and his gang involvement, he began smoking marijuana and inhaling glue and gasoline. Starting in 1978, he inhaled gasoline approximately 30 times. Starting at the age of 8, he began smoking marijuana and estimates that, over his lifetime, he has smoked marijuana approximately 4000 times. He started drinking alcohol at the age of 12 and has been drinking alcohol regularly since he was 14 years old. He drank at least a couple of beers a day and, more typically, drank a six-pack of beer in combination with drugs when given the opportunity. Over the years, he has passed out several times from drinking alcohol (particularly vodka). He typically drinks alcohol until he "drops"; alternatively, he imbibes alcohol to assist him in coming down from methamphetamine usage. In 1976, he lost consciousness from a motorcycle accident. During that year, he started abusing heroin by first inhaling and in later years by injecting the drug. He overdosed on heroin in 1980, almost died, and gave it up. He estimated that he used heroin approximately 50 times before stopping its use.

From 1977 to 1979, while in junior high school, he was involved in frequent schoolyard fights. On one occasion, his coach attacked him and wrestled him to the ground, yelled in his face, and had to be restrained by police officers. He said he was falsely accused of spraying the coach with Mace™ and that the coach subsequently apologized to him. During the seventh through the ninth grades, he fought frequently on weekends, primarily at the local skating rink. He described these altercations as "territorial fights" between his group and youths from another village. He took pride in the fact that although weapons were not involved, his group won most of the fights. Several times, however, he was admitted to [a hospital] for bruises and other nonserious injuries. During this period, he fell out of a moving truck but was not injured. He started smoking opium during the mid-1970s for an estimated 100 times over the next 10 years. In 1980 or 1981, he was involved in yet another motor vehicle accident but was not hospitalized. He was involved in a major gang fight in which some individuals were hurt. This impelled him to move to Oregon to live with relatives.

While in Oregon, he lived with [an uncle]. He attended [college] in an attempt to redirect his life, but quickly became involved with the "wrong crowd." He stated injecting methamphetamine and dropped out of school. He was arrested once for driving under the influence (DUI) and was convicted of that offense.

His methamphetamine use started in 1984 and continued until 1996 for 1800+ times, calculating the number of times he typically used this drug during the week and multiplying it by the number of years. Except when the drug was unavailable, he recalled injecting, smoking, snorting, or drinking methamphetamine with coffee almost every day when given the opportunity. He twice overdosed on methamphetamine and lost consciousness. According to the defendant's mother, his uncle reported that the defendant left Oregon because he was wanted by the police for drug-related activities.

In 1984, he started also started using lysergic acid diethylamide (LSD) and estimated that he used LSD approximately 100 times between 1984 and 1996. From 1984 to 1985, he used cocaine and mushrooms. Between 1984 and 1986, he used barbiturates about 10 times and also got high on whipped cream by inhaling the gas to give him a giddy feeling about 10 times.

The defendant reported that over the years, the voices got worse when he drank alcohol or ingested any kind of drug. He hastened to add that he also hears the voices when he is not high on any substance.

From 1986 to 1994, he resided in California, largely in the San Diego area. He was in a motorcycle accident in 1991. During that he year, he spent 3 months in jail for a traffic ticket. While in California, he worked regularly. He estimated that during most years, he worked between 20 and 30 h per week in construction or culinary businesses. During some years, he worked 60 h per week. He provided references to verify portions of his work history to include [names and addresses of supervisors].

According to the defendant's mother, when he returned to Oklahoma in approximately 1994, he lived at her house and worked occasionally as a mechanic. Due to her fear of the defendant, she lost weight and became severely depressed. She reported several instances where the defendant threw objects at the wall (he once threw the telephone when she was talking to a friend), but stated that the defendant would never hurt her. She reported that the defendant once punched his sister in the face.

In 1995, the defendant began serving six and a half years in prison for raping his "niece." According to his mother, the physician who examined the victim incorrectly stated that there had been only "touching," with no sexual intercourse. His mother reported that the defendant had threatened the victim's life if she told anyone of the sexual assault. When questioned about this incident by this examiner, the defendant stated that he was smoking "ice" with the victim (his adopted sister) and that he had indeed threatened her, stating, "Be quiet, or I'll kill you." The victim as a result became withdrawn and depressed, largely confining herself to her bedroom, which then alerted the defendant's mother that something was wrong.

The defendant's mother also reported that she called the police on occasion. She stated the defendant's ongoing substance abuse was a contributory factor to his going to prison. According to the defendant, while in prison, he was involved in two "big" fights. During one of the fights, he was knocked unconscious and was repeatedly choked almost to the point of suffocation. The defendant stated that during his 6 years in [an Oklahoma prison], he was attacked numerous other times by inmates. Once, he was attacked in the bathroom by two inmates. On another occasion, he was hit on the head a couple times by [dominant] inmates and did not fight back. He stated that he saw a "shrink" while in prison. He denied hearing the voices because such an admission would result in limited privileges and being administered psychotropic medication. He reported being seen by a "Dr. [Brown]" on a regular basis for individual and group treatment, including anger management and drug rehabilitation. He stated that while in prison, drugs were readily available, but that he avoided them and therefore his therapy was successful.

In 2002, upon him being released from prison and returning to Santa Barbara, he stayed with his sister, [Jane Smith], and her family. He remained in a small room in the residence until the time of the alleged offenses.

Defendant's Reconstruction of the Incident: The following version of events stems from written statements by the defendant and the multiple interviews. He affirmed the truthfulness of his statements to police after reading it for the first time in my presence.

For the 6 months before the incident, the defendant was working regularly and was not abusing methamphetamine. He affirmed the following stressors for the 6 months prior to the incident (see items on stress audit):

1. Holidays, family celebrations, and get-together which were stressful for the defendant and marked by conflict.
2. Serious illness in the family (unspecified).
3. Insufficient time to get things done for himself outside of work. He stated that the traffic in Santa Barbara was a stressor to him in addition to long work hours. He said that he was once promoted at work and that the new position, which involved the coordination of work activities, was stressful to him. Additional stress at work included changes in work hours and conditions, irregular work hours, and the lack of real benefits. For the 6 months prior to the incident, he reported stress-related tightness of muscles. He had migraine headaches and frequently felt restless. He did not have any real intimate or social relationships to satisfy his social needs. He saw himself during this period as unable to organize his time effectively. He felt that he was unable to limit himself to fewer than three cups of coffee or cola drinks a day. He did not take quiet time for himself during work.

For the week before the incident, the defendant continued to work a heavy load, resided with his sister, and continued to abstain from methamphetamine use. He reported the following symptoms occurring nearly every day or at least twice weekly (see Wahler physical symptoms inventory): (1) trouble with ears or hearing; (2) arm or leg aches or pains; (3) shakiness; (4) stuttering or stammering; (5) backaches; (6) aches or pains in the hands or feet; (7) excessive perspiration; (8) burning, tingling, or crawling feelings in the skin; (9) feeling tired; and (10) excessive gas. Interestingly, he did not report hearing voices or seeing visions, which he had stated was an almost daily occurrence previously.

Concerning the time before, during, and after the alleged offenses, the defendant's version of the alleged offenses as written by Sergeant Tad York, in a verbatim statement, was as follows:

1. Stated that on Sunday December 21, 2003, he got off from work at around 5:00 p.m. from the job site on Elm Street. He stated that he drove [a] truck (4 ton) to [a] store and bought 4 ea Regular Budweiser. He stated he drove the truck home (sister's house) and started drinking his beers for about an hour when his friend arrived. He stated that him and his friend then smoked the "Ice Methamphetamine." He stated that this "Ice" that they smoked was a gift to him for Christmas from his friend. He stated that the Ice they smoked was over 1 g. He stated when he smoked the "Ice," his friend would take a puff while he takes 3 puff until they finished the entire "Ice." He stated that as soon as they finished the "Ice" his friend asked him if he was willing to sell Ice, but he refused and only wanted to smoke whenever he has money to purchase the Ice from him. He stated that he was only thinking in his own mind where would he find anything valuable so that he can sell and buy some more "Ice." He stated while thinking, he though[t] about [the victim's] house that when he drives to his job site he would never see anybody around at this particular house. He further stated the occupants of this particular house must have gone for a vacation, and that would be an ideal place to rob. He thought about many places to rob like bank, store, or business, but he decided to check out this particular house. He stated after much though[t] he decided to go to this house, so he drove his sister's car that was parked outside with the keys in the ignition. He stated that he did not really look at the time when he left, but he knew it was after midnight. He described his sister's car as dark blue Toyota Camry with California plate No., but he does not know the license No. He stated that he drove straight to [victim's house] and parked his sister's car outside the gate to the residence. He stated that after parking he walked straight to this house. He described the house as whi[t]e in color, and concrete house and it's the first house on the right side as you enter the gate. He stated that as soon as he reached the house he went to the back of the house and looked for a window that he will enter. He stated that he removed a mosquito screen to the kitchen window and used a hallow block that was in the walkway in the back, and pushed it as step in order to enter the kitchen window. He stated t[h]at as soon as he removed the security screen with his pocketknife, he slide the window that was unlocked. He stated that he climbed through the window to the kitchen area and that he could see the living room area that was turned on. He further stated he saw a video player and TV sitting next to the piano, so he walked to the living room and continued walking toward the hallway. He stated that as he reached the hallway he saw a room on the right side and saw what appeared to be computer and as soon as he

entered the room someone turned on the lights and when he looked back he saw both man and a lady trying to corner him or trap him in the computer room.

2. He stated that when he first walked to the house, he walked past the house toward eastside of the house by the lawn and walked on the rear side (Southside) to the kitchen window on the far southwest side of the house. He stated that he walked back and forth on the same route probably three times just to make sure nobody was in the house. He stated that the second time he walked around he tripped on a big log, but it was dark, so he just felt the ground to grab something to use just in case a dog appeared. He stated when he saw the computer room he left the wooden stick by the bathroom door and went inside the computer room. He stated that when he was cornered in the computer room, he fought his way and escaped thinking toward the living room, but instead it was the hallway to another bedroom. He stated that as he entered another bedroom he realized that it was the wrong way, but [t]he man and woman were right behind him, and that's when he fought both the man and woman inside the bedroom just by the bedroom door.

3. He stated that he whacked the man by face and fought both of them thinking of knocking them out by punching and elbowing to ran [sic] out of the bedroom. He further stated that he took some wild swing just hitting both man and woman and ran out the bedroom to the hallway and grabbed the stick that he placed earlier on the bathroom door. He stated that as soon as he grabbed the stick he saw the young man standing in the hallway in front of his bedroom and so he swung the stick and struck the young boy in the head. He stated that he struck the young boy about five times, with some misses and that is when the young boy knocked out. He stated on the second time he swung at the boy both man and woman were behind him so he swung the wooden stick back and hit both of them. He stated that he did not know where he hit them, but he was aiming high (meaning the head). He stated that at that point he could not control himself and kept on hitting all of them, man, woman, and the young boy until they all fell to the floor on the hallway in front of bathroom and unconscious. He stated that after they all fell to the floor he walked again to the master bedroom and opened some drawers trying to look for anything valuable and at the same time he grabbed some bed sheets, comforter, blankets, and pillow to cover the body and the bloods on the floor. He stated that as he came out of the master bedroom with all the bed sheets, comforter, blankets, and pillows, the lady lying on her back facing toward him with her eyes opened and freaked him out. He stated that he used what he had in his hand and covered the lady, the man, and the young boy and tried to cover the blood. He stated that he turned the lady on her left side toward the eastern part of the house and removed her short pant and underwear thinking of raping the lady, but changed his mind. He stated that he walked into the computer room thinking of stealing the computer, but as he entered the computer he heard the man moaning, so he turned around and saw the man who was removing the cover from his face and holding his right hand up, so he hit on the head with both hands on the stick with a force. He stated that as he hit him he was sitting in a slumping position and he fell to the floor. He stated at that time, he grabbed the man's both feet and pulled him into a bedroom across from computer room. He stated that as he was pulling the man he tripped over the young boy, so he left (sic) go the man's feet and then grabbed the young boy both arms while facing down and pulled him into the same bedroom that is across from the computer room.

4. He stated as he was pulling the young boy he was still moving and moaning as if he was mad. He stated that he came out and then grabbed the man's feet again and pulled him to the same bedroom, as the young boy. He also said that the man also was moving by kicking and moaning. He stated he walked to computer room thinking of getting the computer but was undecided of what to do, but when he looked around he saw the young girl standing in the hallway to the living room staring at him. He stated that, he ordered the young girl to her bedroom and sit and wait for him. He stated that he walked to the living room and looked at the TV and the VCR and also at the same time he checked outside by peeking through the sliding door in the back to see if anybody saw or heard anything. He stated that young girl was wearing a white short and a white shirt. He stated that he took a rope from the laundry room and tied it around the young girl's neck and decided to bring the young girl to finish her off somewhere. He stated that they left through the rear sliding door while he was holding the young girl's left hand along with rope tied to her neck. He stated that they walked toward parked car outside of gate and the young girl started complaining about her feet, so he carried her close to the car. He stated that he carried her on his back and put her down and placed her in the front door (driver) to the front passenger. He stated that he drove up the dirt road toward the airport, and just about closer to the paved road. He stated the car and ordered her in the trunk of the car because he was paranoid that someone might see her in the car. He stated that he drove down the road from the airport and made a right turn toward the nearest town. He drove to the Shell Gas Station made a right turn to the dirt road toward [another town]. He stated that he drove a couple miles on the dirt road thinking of finding a place where he could find that is steep and just pushed her to her dead and go home. He stated that he decided to go back toward the Shell Gas Station and he continued driving until he returned to the paved highway and drove toward [another town]. He stated that he drove to the intersection to the airport and decided to go back again, so he drove back again to the dirt road to [another town], and drove a couple more miles further thinking of what to do with the young girl. He was thinking of killing her, leaving her on the dark road or pushing her on a steep cliff to her dead, but he was undecided and also he was in a hurry because the daylight is approaching and he has to go to [the nearest town]. He stated that he decides to go back and he drove until he reached the paved road in front of shell Gas Station. He further stated that he drove toward [another town] until he reached a cliff just before [local] store and then made turn and drove back toward Shell Gas Station and made a turn toward the dirt road, but decided and made a u-turn and drove toward [same town] again and drove straight to his house. As he reached his house he parked and opened the trunk and used a mat to wrap the girl and carried her to his room. He stated that, inside his bedroom she sat in the bed and he looked at her she was wet from the rain so he told to remove her clothes and dried them. He stated that as she removed her clothing he started caressing her boobs and body and started masturbating. He stated that he was masturbating, but he was already late for work and he ejaculated on her back.

5. He stated he put his clothes on, a short black and a red [work] uniform, and instructed her not to make noise and wait for him until he returned, or he would kill her. He stated that he asked her if she was hungry and she told him that she was hungry and she is a vegetarian, and he was supposed to find some vegetarian food, but it slipped his mind. He stated he left on the company truck and drove to the job site pick up

point by the warehouse to pick up some workers (3) and then drove them to the job site itself and dropped off two of the workers. He stated he drove the other one worker to a shop and drops the worker, and upon his return toward [a town] he stopped by a theater and picked up another worker and dropped him at batch plant next to the warehouse in [another town]. He stated that he drove back to [main town] to [a] hardware store to get some materials, such as nails, lumber, carpentry glue, and varnish. He stated he dropped the varnish at the job site. He stated that it was lunchtime, he returned to his house and the young girl was still there. He stated that upon returning he was surprised to see the young girl was still in his bedroom and he was hoping that she would leave by now because she has the opportunity. He stated that the young girl was sleeping in the bed naked but covered with bed sheet. He stated when he first left the house that early Monday morning, he placed the mat that he was using to wrap to shield the door to his bedroom. He stated when he first entered the room the young girl woke up and the bed sheet fell and he saw her naked body and not [sic] aroused so he started touching her breast and vagina. He stated that he instructed her lay on her stomach, and he started touching her buttock while masturbating. He stated that as he was masturbating he inserted his middle finger on this right hand in her anus and that is when he ejaculates on her back then he wiped his penis, put on his clothes, and went back to work. [He stated that he first tried to get her to give him a "blow job" and then settled for touching her buttocks and masturbating because he did not want to look at her face. He said he thought of killing her and then changed his mind but the sun was coming up and he could not think of a place to kill her. Importantly, he stated that he felt he was coming down from ice and "tweaking real bad". He was beginning to feel the fear and paranoia of coming down. He felt that he went into the tweaking stage right after he knocked the victims down with the stick at the house. He stated that he "went down" on the young girl when he came home for lunch from work, meaning that he [performed cunnilingus on] her. He stated that he was waiting for his sister and brother-in-law to go to sleep to take her out in order to kill her and thus get rid of a witness.] He stated before left to work he felt bad, so he told the young girl that when it was dark enough I drop you off, and the young girl asked if it will be today and he replied saying yes. He stated he went to work and returned back to the house around 5:10 p.m. [H]e stated that at the house they sat inside his bedroom waiting for the people in the house to go to sleep before leaving with the young girl. He stated that during that time the young girl asked on three occasions if its time or not. But as he walked to the house people were still awake so he told her not. He stated that he fell asleep and when he woke up the young girl also fell asleep so he woke her up and by that time the television was off and everyone asleep. He stated that he went to the car to check on the keys and it was there, so he went back inside and walked her outside and to car and put her on the back seat of the car and they drove toward [main town]. He made up his mind and prepared his black pouch with a piece of rope[,] a bottle of vodka and wanted to drive the young girl [main town] to a church and dropped her off. He further stated that after dropping her off he would drive back toward [another town], find a secluded area and plan his suicide by having his rope tied around his neck, finish the bottle of vodka, and then jumped to hang himself.

6. He stated that as he neared the Shell Gas Station he kept thinking to himself that this girl is a witness, so get on the dirt road and kill the young girl because she is a witness, then he suddenly turn on dirt road to [town] and drove toward [another town].

He stated that he drove to the intersection at [two streets] and made a turn drove back maybe half a mile and stopped the car on the right side[,] got out[,] took the young girl out of the car and then started choking her, but the young girl was looking at him in the eyes, so he turned his head away and he also felt the young girl weakening, so he finally let go of her neck and held his head and suddenly dropped her because she was still alive and she rolled down the small cliff about three times and he got in the car and drove off. He stated that as he was driving away he kept thinking to himself to go back and finish her off because she is a witness, but he kept driving toward the Shell Gas Station until he reached the paved road in front of the gas station and then drove to this house as he reached the house it was around 1:00 a.m. Tuesday morning. He stated that he took the same black pouch with rope and bottle of vodka and went to [a] baseball field trying to look for a nice tree to hang himself, but he could not find any so he went back home again and stayed until morning without going to sleep. He stated on Tuesday morning at around 6:15 am. he left his house to go to the batch plant at his job site to pick up the workers. He stated he picked up the two Bangladesh workers and drove to the project, but when he goes there, the Officers at the gate let him pass the gate to job site, but the police turn him back, so he drove the workers the 2 Bangladesh workers back to the batch plant at the job site and dropped them off. He stated that after dropping them off he drove to Masons Hardware and took 4 gallons of paint and returned to the batch plant and dropped off the paint. He stated that when he left the batch plant to [another location] it was around 10:30 a.m. and he drove straight to [same location] to see his boss. He stated that when he arrived in [same location] it was around 12:15 p.m. because they were finished work. He stated as soon as he arrived he spoke to his supervisor Jimmy Peters if he could dropped him off in [a town] because there is an emergency. He stated that as they went to the supervisor vehicle his boss asked him if he is involved in the horrible murder in [victims' area] and he said "No." He stated that as soon as they were in the vehicle he told his supervisor that he only went there to find some electronics stuff to sell, and all hell broke loose, and there is only one way to finish this. He states that his supervisor dropped him at the house, he kind of knew that his supervisor would make a report to the police, so he asked him i[f] he would give him 4 hours, and his supervisor said, yes and left. He stated that he fed the dog[,] took his black pouch with the stuff in it (rope, bottle of vodka), and left toward the highway toward [a location]. He stated that in front of [a gas station], the police stopped him and arrested him and brought him to the police station.

Additional information provided by the defendant to me was as follows:

1. He had a few beers with his boss after work, not alone. He and his friend smoked in the driveway in his friend's car and then later, because of the heat, inside the defendant's truck. His friend left after the defendant stated he wanted to go inside to take a shower.
2. While inside, he looked for a syringe that he had previously taken away from his nephew. He found the syringe and shot up the rest of the methamphetamine in his left arm. (He then showed me scars in the crook of his left elbow where he typically injects methamphetamine.) He then lay down in his room, thinking that he needed some fast money. He wanted to find something valuable that he could sell and buy more ice. He had $400 in his wallet at the time, and the next day was payday. However,

he had earmarked those funds for home improvements and automobile repairs. He then remembered a house that would be a likely prospect to burglarize. This was a house in [victims' area] which he passed on the way to his job site. He recalled that he had never seen anyone at that house. He remembered thinking that the occupants of the house must have gone on vacation and that it would be an ideal place to burglarize. He systematically thought about several places to rob, like a bank, store or business, but decided to burglarize this particular house because it overall presented a low risk for apprehension. He stated that he thought it was a teacher's house and had no idea that it was the residence of a missionary family.

3. After much thought, the defendant got into his sister's car parked outside the residence. He described it as a dark blue Toyota Camry. Shortly after midnight, he drove straight to the residence in [victims' area] and parked outside the gate to the residence. (He estimated that the gate was 20 yards from the house, when in reality it is closer to 10 times that distance, as I measured during the crime scene inspection.) After parking, he walked to the house, walked around the residence about three times to make sure that no one was around or in the house. On the second go around, he tripped on a "big log." He felt the ground and picked up a stick in case a dog appeared. The stick, which he broke off from a larger piece, was approximately 3 feet long. The house was white, concrete, and the first on the right side as you enter the gate. He used his Phillips screwdriver to remove the four screws in the frame of the window screen.

4. He then lost control and started swinging wildly, hitting the man, the woman, and the boy until they all were on the floor in front of him, unconscious. He then walked to the master bedroom and opened drawers looking for anything valuable to steal. He grabbed bed sheets, a comforter, blankets, and a pillow to cover the bodies and the blood on the floor. He stated that he wished to cover the blood because it was "making [him] sick." He stated that as he came out of the master bedroom with all the bed sheets, comforter, blankets, and pillows, the woman lying on her back facing him opened her eyes. This "freaked [him] out." He stated that he turned the woman on her left side (toward the eastern part of the house) and removed her short pants, thinking of raping her, but then changed his mind.

5. The defendant then returned to the computer room, thinking of getting the computer. He then saw a young girl standing in the hallway, staring at him. He tried to swing the bat but could not because of the eye contact.

6. He amplified the following portion of the statement as follows: He stated that as he was masturbating, he inserted his middle finger on his right hand in her anus. He ejaculated on her back, then wiped his penis, put on his clothes, and returned to work. During the interview, he stated that he first tried to get her to give him a "blow job" and then settled for touching her buttocks and masturbating because he did not want to look at her face. He added that he thought of killing her and then changed his mind but the sun was coming up and he could not think of a place to kill her. Importantly, he stated that he felt he was coming down from ice and "tweaking real bad." He was beginning to feel the fear and paranoia of coming down. He felt that he went into the tweaking stage right after he knocked the victims down with the stick at the house.

Current Medications: None

CT/EEG/MRI/SPECT: None

Appearance and Test Behavior: Oriented to time, place, person, and circumstance, the defendant exhibited a logical and coherent stream of thought during the four examination periods. He was focused and persistent on all tasks. Affect was appropriate, but during the last session, he was somewhat anxious and tense because he had not slept the previous night, stating that there was a disturbance near his cell at the police station as another inmate was brought in. He affirmed the following problems on the Wahler Physical Symptoms Inventory for the time of the evaluation, these problems occurring nearly every day, or at least twice weekly: (1) nausea; (2) headaches; (3) neck aches and pains; (4) arm or leg aches and pains; (5) insomnia; (6) losing weight; (7) backaches; (8) stomach trouble; (9) numbness or lack of feeling in a part of his body; (10) aches and pains in his feet and hands; (11) excessive perspiration; (12) inability to move various parts of his body; (13) visual trouble; (14) burning, tingling, or crawling feelings in the skin; (15) skin trouble; (16) fatigue; (17) muscular weakness; (18) dizzy spells; (19) muscular tensions (unspecified); (20) trouble with taste or smell; (21) twitching muscles; (22) poor health in general; (23) excessive gas; (24) bowel trouble; (25) chest pains; and (26) hay fever or other allergies. Despite these problems, there was no indication of any substantial interference with evaluation procedures. On the various deception scales, he showed mixed responding. On the Wahler, he was in the extreme high percentile of individuals affirming problems, suggesting that there may have been some embellishment of symptoms for secondary gain. There was no indication of malingering memory problems on the California Memory Test. On the Multiphasic Sex Inventory, he showed substantial deception in the areas of child molestation, rape, and exhibitionism, denying all problems in these areas sufficient to be statistically labeled "frankly dishonest." On the MMPI-2 validity indicia, his score was suggestive of faking bad. On the MCMI-III validity indicia, he scored in a similar manner, essentially endorsing items reflecting psychopathology that could not possibly be true (e.g., endorsed "I hear voices 24 hours a day, even when I am asleep"; "I can run a mile in less than 3 minutes").

The clinical information he presented on the voices may have been fabricated. If not, he did not present psychotic signs for the time of the alleged offenses.

Overall, it was felt that an accurate measure of his psychological and neuropsychological abilities and deficiencies was obtained, taking into account response set, history, psychological traits, and other factors.

On the Mooney Problem Checklist, he endorsed the following problems as being of most concern to him currently: (1) poor living conditions (i.e., his cramped, dirty, noisy, and hot jail cell); (2) having a member of his family in poor health; (3) death in his family; (4) worried about members of his family working too hard; (5) disliking financial dependence on others; (6) not having a home; (7) science conflicting with his religion; (8) not having a systematic savings plan; (9) parents having a hard time of it and sacrificing too much for him; (10) worrying about security and old age; (11) bothered by thoughts of suicide; (12) giving in to temptation; (13) having unusual sex desires; and (14) afraid of losing his job. Other problems affirmed on the Mooney that are of clinical interest include indicia of deterioration under stressful conditions, fear of the future due to the legal proceedings, thinking that others disapprove of him, and feeling many feelings of self-blame and fear of losing control such as being bothered by thoughts running through his head and a fear of going insane. He admitted that he is sometimes dishonest, and the reader should keep in mind that there may be some embellishment to these items because the Mooney has no built-in validity scale. He wrote that his additional problems included losing self-control in terms of blacking out and waking up in the morning, making a fool out of himself which he attributes to a combination of alcohol and drugs in the past. He did not specifically relate this to the incident. His second additional problem was arguing with himself in the sense of indecisiveness and frequently changing his mind. He related this to the incident, stating that he changed his mind a number of times in regard to whether he should kill the young girl or not.

On the Mooney, he wrote a brief summary of his chief problems as follows: "Over doing the drugs and Boose to the point of doing something unexpected and dum. like making an ass of my self." He stated that he would like to talk to someone, like a counselor or psychologist, about these problems.

On the Personal Problems Checklist for Adults, which also does not have validity scales, he may have embellished his problems. The following problems were offered for the present: (1) being criticized by others; (2) being let down by others; (3) not having a job; (4) working in unsafe conditions in the past; (5) working too many hours; (6) job having no future; (7) needing more education to succeed ; (8) his current residence (i.e., jail cell) being too small, needing repairs, and being dirty and unsanitary; (9) problems in budgeting money, not earning enough, not having any savings, depending on others for financial support, and not being able to pay for his financial obligations; (10) in the area of religion, feeling confused about his religious beliefs, and that his prior work interfered with religious practices; (11) in the area of emotions, trouble concentrating, memory difficulties, feeling guilty, worrying about diseases and illnesses, feeling as if things are unreal, worrying a lot, anxiety, having no joy in life, being influenced by others, and behaving in strange ways; (12) in the area of sex, being afraid of sexual diseases, has an absent sexual relationship with anyone, and thinks about sex too often; (13) legally, feeling as if he experiences much stress from the current criminal charges; and (14) in terms of health, being fearful of being physically hurt or abused, losing his temper and hurting someone else, smoking too many cigarettes, using drugs or alcohol, which he maintains are available in any correctional setting, not getting enough exercise, and having poor sleeping habits. In general, he does not feel good about himself or the world.

Test Results

Intelligence and General Neuropsychological Status: On the WAIS III, the defendant obtained a full-scale IQ of 100 with a slightly but not significantly worse verbal IQ of 97 and a performance IQ of 103. He obtained borderline intelligence on the nonverbal, cross-culturally derived Ravens test which presents different visual patterns of increasing difficulty (37R, 7th percentile). The Ravens is generally a good measure of intellectual "g" as well as a measure of visual organization. On the Shipley Institute of Living Scale, which correlates quite closely with overall WAIS-R results, he obtained an Estimated Full-Scale WAIS-R IQ of 103. His abstraction score was above average (60T, 84th percentile), but his vocabulary score on this test was substantially lower (46T, 30–35th percentile).

On the Halstead-Reitan Neuropsychological Test Battery (HRNTB), he received an impairment index of .6, meaning that approximately 60% of the test results were in the brain-damaged range. The premorbid indicators on the WAIS-III and other tests showed some scatter but were overall in the average or above-average range. Together with his impairment index, a mild, static, probably diffuse brain injury in a person who has a significant history of cerebral insult was suggested.

Attention and Concentration: During this evaluation, the defendant did not show distractibility or other suggestions that his cognitive focus was impaired. He estimated that his attentional skills are "90% of what they should be, cuz I lost a lot of brain cells from all the drugs I took." On examination, attention and concentration were largely intact, with no overt lapses during the testing procedures themselves. His recitation of overlearned sequences such as counting backward from 20 to 1 and reciting the alphabet was flawless. He received full credit on a more difficult measure of attention (adding 3s in serial fashion). Attention to auditory stimuli on a simple task of repeating numbers spoken to him was average (Digits Forward = 7, 44th percentile). His performance on a more difficult task of concentration on auditory stimuli was poor (Digits Backward = 3, 4th percentile). On the Speech-Sounds Perception Test, he had nine errors, which is in the mildly brain-damaged area. On the Seashore Rhythm Test, which calls for the assessee to discriminate between simple tapping patterns, he performed poorly, committing 11 errors and a rank of 10, which is in the mildly to moderately impaired range. He did fine on a Cancellation Test which required him to X-out certain letters within a large stimulus field. Overall, his attentional skills were intact but tended to degrade under complexity.

Sensory/Perceptual and Motor Skills: The defendant believes that he has some deficiencies in these areas. During this evaluation, this right-handed (right-handed signature = 6 s; left-handed signature = 11 s), right-footed, left-eyed male showed intact right-left discrimination skills. Visual copy skills for simple geometric designs were within expectation. Performance on a task of attempting to uncover an object from cut up portions of the object was within normal limits (29/30). Color naming was below average (44T; 30th percentile). Asteriognosis was not suggested for being able to identify coins of different denominations—penny, nickel, and dime—placed in each hand separately with his eyes closed. Auditory acuity was within normal limits for hearing the thumb and forefinger being rubbed together by each ear separately and together while his eyes were closed. No imperceptions or suppressions were suggested. His visual fields were full upon confrontation, with no indication of field cuts. Visual organization skills were borderline (7th percentile). On the TPT, he performed in the very mildly impaired range in terms of total time for all the procedures (total time = 17 min, 22 s). Right-hand performance on the TPT was average (8 min, 48 s). On the left hand, however, his performance fell to mildly impaired (6.33 min). Overall, skills in this domain were adequate with some mild impairment in select areas.

Speech/Language: The defendant's ability to read simple sentences was adequate (e.g., "down to earth," "The lawyer's closing argument convinced him"). His ability to read simple words on the Stroop was below average (41T, 20th percentile). Writing skills were good (flawless on "The quick brown fox jumps over the lazy dog"). Arithmetic skills were marginal, with him answering two out of four questions correctly with near-misses on the incorrect answers. His repetition skills were fine except for "Methodist Episcopal," which he self-corrected on a second attempt. Response to ideomotor practic commands was good. His auditory comprehension in responding to commands and to simple questions was within normal limits. On the Shipley, his vocabulary skills in regard to recognizing the correct meaning of words was toward the lower end of the average range (46T, 30–35th percentile). The WAIS-R Similarity Test, which taps creativity, verbal flexibility, and association skills yielded a superior performance (Age-Corrected Score = 15, where 10 is average). His information skills on a test of items testing fund of knowledge on a graduated type of scale were toward the lower end of the average range (Age-Corrected Score = 8). His comprehension skills on the WAIS-R were average (Age-Corrected Score = 10).

Memory: The defendant estimated that his memory skills are overall 70% normal because of previous extensive substance abuse. His crystallized memory for naming presidents since 1950 was adequate. On the Logical Memory Test of the Wechsler Memory Scale, which includes simple passages being read to him with instructions to remember the passages, he achieved a score of 38T, which places him in the borderline range (less than 15th percentile). On a test of delayed memory 30 min later, his score was 42T (43rd percentile). Recognition skills on this test were adequate (18/20). On the CVLT, he had overall above-average performance (Trial 1 = 1 standard deviation above the mean, Trial 5 = 2 standard deviations above the mean). Short-delay free recall was 2 standard deviations above the mean. Short-delay cued responding was 1 standard deviation above the mean. Long-term free recall was 2 standard deviations above the mean, with long-delayed cued recall equaling 1 standard deviation above the mean. His recognition skills were overall slightly above average (1 standard deviation above the mean).

The sole exception to these above-average scores on the CVLT was in his List B performance, which measures response to an introjected list of unrelated words. It also gives an indication of one's ability to perform adequately with prior exposure to a similar task. The defendant achieved a minus 1 standard deviation which compared to his above-average scores on other measures suggests that he has a clinically significant vulnerability to proactive interference.

His performance on the TPT for incidental memory for shapes of blocks in the form board was good. His placement of the blocks in their correct locations when asked to draw the blocks in their proper place was above average. His nonverbal memory for geometric figures was at least average. Recognition skills on this same test of nonverbal geometric figures were adequate.

Executive Skills: Current testing revealed that the defendant's ability to formulate goals, plan behavior, initiate action, maintain set, competently execute task behavior, and monitor his performance was intact for basic tasks but below expectation given his overall intelligence. Verbal fluency was below expectation and showed mild impersistence. His abstract skills for proverbs and metaphors were borderline/low average. Performance on the Stroop Color-Word Test, which requires one to name the color in which a word is printed, rather than the reading the word itself, was above average with several self-corrections (62T, about 90th percentile). His Color-Word score was clearly above average, with the predicted Color-Word score being 35. His interference showed a +22. He thus performed well on the Stroop task that measures susceptibility to interference. Performance on this test also suggests that a progressive brain disorder is unlikely. His strong score shows high cognitive flexibility and creativity.

On the Shipley Abstraction Subtest, he obtained a score of 60T (84th percentile). His score on Digit Symbol was below average (age-corrected score = 7). On the Wonderlic Personnel Test, he scored in the lower portion of the average range (R = 18, 31.3rd percentile). His Wonderlic score suggests that he could successfully complete high-school courses, but would probably do better on the less academic track, which actually conforms to his background. The scores suggests that he would be successful in elementary settings but would benefit from programmed or mastery learning approaches. Conforming to his vocational history, his score shows that he must be allowed enough time and "hands-on" (on-the-job) experience to do well. At most, he could perform well running simple equipment. Given enough time, he could learn and perform jobs with lengthy, routinized steps, perform simple operations with lists of names and numbers, and avoid the kinds of mistakes that he showed on this examination. He was mildly impersistent on word list generation tasks (F, A, S, foods). The first letter (F) yielded an average response, but the last category (naming foods) was 2 standard deviations below the mean, a borderline performance. On the Trail Making Test, Part A, his executive skills were within expectation (TMT A = 33 s, 0 errors). On a more difficult measure of sequencing and cognitive ability, he was mildly impaired (TMT B = 92 s, 1 error). His ability to abstract the meaning of proverbs and metaphors was borderline/low average. His ability to draw a clock and set the hands at the correct position was adequate. His performance was low average on a digit symbol coding task, possibly the most sensitive measure of cerebral damage on the WAIS-R (Age-Corrected Score = 7). On a Cognitive Estimate Test, requiring him to make numerical judgments on questions to which there is no precise answer, he was mildly impaired (exceeded $R = 7$, cut-off for impairment). On the CVLT, as stated, he did show proactive interference which is considered a frontal impairment (List B performance was 1 standard deviation below the mean).

Social/Emotional Functioning: The defendant showed significant maladjustment on the psychological tests employed. On the MMPI-2, an excellent measure of diagnostic and statistical manual (DSM) Axis I disorders and the most commonly used psychological objective test in the world, he showed the following:

On the Incomplete Sentence Blank, much regret and remorse over his past maladaptive behavior was expressed, including and especially abusing substances and becoming involved in the alleged offenses. Currently, he is ashamed of what he did, and his self-esteem is at a low point.

His judgment is poor. He would yell "fire" if he were the first person to see smoke and fire while in a movie theater, rather than notify someone in authority, the proper answer. Suicide potential is moderate. The Suicide Probability Scale indicates a 45% chance that the defendant belongs to a group of lethal suicide attempters and, because of his previous threats and self-destructive behaviors, is high risk. He has, therefore, in my judgment, moderate suicide potential, which should be the target of intervention to ensure that he does not kill himself while in custody. Appropriate interventions would include the consideration of antidepressant medication from a physician and counseling from a psychologist or other mental health professional for his current distress and stressors.

His denial and minimization on the Multiphasic Sex Inventory suggest that he was dishonest and may have a problem in the area of sexual aggression. His history, in addition to the incident itself, suggests that this issue needs to be explored to determine whether he is a pedophile or has some other paraphilia.

On the MCMI-III, an excellent measure of DSM Axis II disorders, he showed the following:

On the Hare PCL-R, he showed historical and behavioral tendencies for the following: (1) need for stimulation/proneness to boredom (likes risky activities, may discontinue routine tasks); (2) poor behavioral controls, short temperedness, hypersensitivity; (3) early behavior problems as a child or young adolescent; (4) lack of realistic long-term goals (in the past, not overly concerned about the future, and living day-by-day); (5) impulsivity, acting before thinking because he feels like it, unreflecting; (6) irresponsibility (fails to honor obligations, commitments, problems with loyalty); (7) criminal versatility (applies to entire life pattern of law-breaking); (8) promiscuous sexual behavior, part and parcel of his previous lifestyle, along with several short-term relationships; (9) glibness, superficial charm along with low anxiety for this trait in mild amounts; (10) lying and prevarication, with minimal embarrassment when caught; (11) conning/manipulative behavior in many areas—drugs, sex, money, etc.; (12) some indications of lack of guilt or remorse. He experiences remorse but he has a tendency to project blame; (13) callous/lack of empathy for others, including victims, disregarding the feelings, thoughts, or welfare of others; and (14) failure to accept true responsibility for his own actions. He uses excuses or denies or minimizes faults.

Impressions: Findings from the psychological and neuropsychological evaluation included: (1) overall average verbal intelligence but borderline nonverbal intelligence; (2) adequate attention and concentration but with deterioration under increased complexity; (3) adequate and in fact above-average verbal memory skills with particular problem in proactive inhibition; (4) nonverbal memory was average for both simple and complex designs; (5) some deficiencies in his sensory-perceptual and motor abilities, for example, on the TPT, his total time in placing blocks in a form board and his left-handed performance, the mild impairment in this latter test suggesting right hemisphere involvement; (6) his speech and language skills were essentially spared, but his fund of information and knowledge of word meaning, probably a function of his impoverished education, were below expectation given his overall average intelligence. Verbal memory and nonverbal memory skills were also spared; mild impersistence in verbal fluency (i.e., word list generation), along with difficulty alternating between numbers and letters on a visual-spatial sequencing task; (7) borderline/low-average abstraction skills. His cognitive estimation ability for numbers was mildly impaired. His Digit Symbol score was low average; and (8) maladjusted personality disorder along with current depression and stress. He is considered a moderate suicide risk, and antidepressant medication and supportive counseling are recommended.

The above pattern of strengths and deficiencies is consistent with the long-term effects of cerebral insults due to fighting and accidents, as well as from severe and chronic polysubstance abuse. Given these historical factors, it would be surprising if he had shown no cognitive deficiencies during current testing. Indeed, the defendant's performance on current testing was the best that I have seen in methamphetamine abusers with his severity and high frequency of use. Overall, his brain impairment can be considered to be mild on a scale of negligible, minimal, mild, moderate, and severe, but is at least moderately deficient in terms of judgment and adaptive level of functioning. The defendant has chronic personality and character trait disturbances.

He is not a full-blown psychopath but does have tendencies in that direction, achieving a moderately high score on the PCL-R. Secondary to the effects of incarceration and his overall compromised physical health, cumulatively experienced over the years from substance abuse and his lifestyle, he experiences a variety of Axis I disorders which are at least moderate in severity.

Overall, prognosis for improvement in neuropsychological functioning is fair, assuming that he stays off substances and does not compromise his brain further by closed-head trauma or other types of cerebral insult. There was no indication from testing that his condition was progressive. The prognosis for removal of his personality disorders is negligible to minimal. Personality disorders are typically ingrained and stubbornly resistant to change. Mental health solutions have not worked in this particular area. The prognosis for change for his Axis I psychological problems is fair, assuming that he receives adequate intervention, to include proper psychotropic medication and supportive counseling during this time of stress.

Diagnostic Formulation: The following mental conditions from the Diagnostic and Statistical Manual, Fourth Edition, Text Revision (DSM-IV-TR, 2000) were operative at the time of the evaluation:

Axis I	Cognitive disorder NOS
	(Rule out) Pedophilia
	Depressive disorder NOS
Axis II	Personality disorder NOS, with psychopathic traits
Axis III	Status postcerebral injuries over the years from severe polysubstance abuse and closed-head trauma from fighting/accidents
Axis IV	Severity of stressors: extreme problems in general ability to function, financial, legal, and social problems
Axis VI	Current Global Assessment Functioning (GAF) = 20 (danger of hurting himself inadvertently through accident proneness or deliberate injury) Highest GAF level over past year = 20

The diagnoses for the time of the alleged offenses are the same. In addition, the defendant was methamphetamine intoxicated, having smoked a considerable amount of ice for a prolonged period of time. He may have entered the "tweaking" or crashing stage of methamphetamine use during the course of the alleged crimes. Tweaking is considered to be a direct effect of the methamphetamine use and a sign that the defendant as operating under its influence. At the time of the alleged offenses, he may have been mildly alcohol intoxicated.

Instant Offense Self-Regulation: The defendant presented a full account of the incident and therefore there is no question of amnesia or loss of memory for the alleged crimes. Overall, indicia of choice, self-control, and awareness were present for the times before, during, and after the alleged offenses.

The defendant showed a considerable amount of self-control, choice, and awareness for the time prior to the alleged violence against the victims. He generally planned the alleged burglary and showed other kinds of preparation for this event.

During the commission of the alleged killings of the three victims at their house, the defendant showed choice, self-control, and awareness by retrieving the stick or club and aiming high, meaning for the victims' heads. Although the defendant claimed that he lost control just before this moment when the victims attacked and cornered him, his goal of striking them in the head with the stick is inconsistent with blind fear or emotion associated with simply trying to get out of the situation. He continued to strike the victims after they stopped resisting. The choice, awareness, and self-control for the time during the alleged sexual assault, kidnapping, and other behaviors on the daughter were exceptionally strong and varied and continued over a prolonged period of time, thus removing any doubt as to whether the defendant was aware of what he was doing or his ability to control his behavior. Moreover, in the alleged offenses toward the daughter, he embedded those events within the context of routine activities, such as going to work, eating, dressing, driving his vehicle, and so forth.

For the time after the alleged offenses, he again showed considerable self-control. He told his work supervisor what he had done in considerable detail, thus displaying memory for the events. The remorse and guilt which he expresses are predicated on awareness and his memory of what transpired. The detailed description of the alleged offenses he gave to police stands unchallenged.

In sum, it is my opinion that considerable choice, self-control, and awareness were shown at the times before, during, and after the alleged offenses. Although indicia of deception and malingering did occur, as discussed previously, the defendant did not claim a psychosis for the time of the alleged offenses. He did offer stress and intoxication from methamphetamine to explain his behaviors.

The alleged offenses can now be analyzed for the defendant's abilities and deficits in areas relevant to behavioral self-regulation. Using the R-CRAS variables, the following parameters are considered. The reader should be aware that there is a 90% agreement with judges and judicial outcome measures when the R-CRAS variables and decision trees are utilized.

1. *Reliability of defendant's self-report under his voluntary control.* This was rated a reliable self-report; the defendant reported information in a factual, sincere manner. He also volunteered potentially self-damaging information but did gloss over a few details.

2. *Involuntary interference with defendant's self-report.* This was rated between 2 and 3, from minimal involuntary interference, slight, or suspected organic interference of doubtful clinical significance to mild involuntary interference in terms of clear evidence of peripheral impairment. Even here, the defendant answered most questions with a fair degree of accuracy. There was difficulty with details, with times and dates especially, and there was distortion in a few specific areas.

3. *Level of intoxication at the time of the alleged crimes.* This was rated severe, in that there was a major impairment in reasoning and actions due to methamphetamine intoxication.

4. *Evidence of brain damage or disease.* This was rated between suspected brain damage where there is fairly reliable evidence based on observation or marginal evidence from neuropsychological testing to definite brain damage of a mild degree, based on the neuropsychological test findings, history, and clinical presentation in its entirety.

5. *Relationship of brain damage to the commission of the alleged crimes.* The mild brain damage, if cross-validated, was not seen as having a relationship to the commission of the alleged offenses.

6. *Mental retardation.* No mental retardation.

7. *Relationship of mental retardation to the commission of the alleged crimes.* No mental retardation.

8. *Observable bizarre behavior of the time of the alleged crimes.* No bizarre behavior other than the alleged crimes themselves.

9. *General level of anxiety of the time of the alleged crimes.* Mild-to-moderate anxiety secondary to the effects of methamphetamine as well as the circumstances of the alleged offenses was suggested.

10. *Amnesia for the alleged crimes.* None. The defendant recalls the entire incident in considerable detail.

11. *Delusions at the time of the alleged crimes.* Absent.

12. *Hallucinations at the time of the alleged crimes.* Absent.

13. *Depressed mood at the time of the alleged crimes.* Not at all. He was intoxicated, not depressed.

14. *Elevated or expansive mood at the time of the alleged crimes.* Not al all.

15. *Defendant's level of verbal coherence at the time of the alleged crimes.* No impairment in speech.

16. *Intensity and appropriateness of affect during the commission of the alleged crimes.* Strong-to-extreme expression of emotion, appropriate to the effects of methamphetamine.

17. *Evidence of formal thought disorder at the time of the alleged crimes.* None.

18. *Planning and preparation for the alleged crimes.* Some planning which lacked specific details and time tables, little or no preparation.

19. *Awareness of criminality during the commission of the alleged crimes.* Relatively complete awareness of the criminality of the alleged offenses with a general understanding of the possible penalties. The defendant made concerted efforts to avoid discovery and showed other indicia of awareness.

20. *Focus of the alleged crimes in terms of how intentional the defendant was in choosing and selecting the purpose and situation of the alleged crimes.* Markedly specific; the defendant's actions were highly focused toward time, persons, and situation.

21. *Level of activity in commission of the alleged crime.* Moderate to marked. Required a concerted and high sustained level of activity.

22. *Responsible social behavior during the week prior to the commission of the alleged crime.* Average functioning at work and with friends, but with some physical problems and stresses as discussed above, was suggested.

23. *Defendant's report self-control over the alleged criminal behaviors.* Severe impairment; the defendant reported himself as having lost control of his behavior when he was attacked by the victims in this case after choosing to initiate behavior with criminal intent.

24. *Examiner's assessment of defendant's self-control over criminal behavior.* This concerns the deliberateness and self-control of the defendant, regardless of the presence of other factors, such as stress. The defendant was mildly impaired. He chose to commit the alleged offenses, although they were committed in an impulsive manner.

25. *Was loss of control the result of a psychosis?* Psychotic signs such as hearing voices or seeing visions, although affirmed in his history, were not presented or discussed at any time by the defendant as he went through his version of the alleged offenses.

Linkage of Alleged Crime Behaviors with Decision Models: In my opinion, in spite of the above-diagnosed mental conditions, there was no substantial impairment in the defendant's (cognitive) capacity to appreciate the wrongfulness of his acts or in his (volitional) capacity to conform his conduct to the requirements of the law.

The R-CRAS decision model for the ALI standard can be presented as follows:

Psycholegal Criteria	My Opinion
A-1 Does the defendant have definite malingering, in terms of intentionally fabricating symptomotology?	No (for time of incident)
A-2 Does the defendant have definite organicity?	Yes (mild impairment)
A-3 Does the defendant meet DSM criteria for a major psychiatric disorder?	Yes
A-4 Was there definite loss of cognitive control? Did the defendant lack substantially the ability to comprehend the criminality of his behavior?	No
A-5 Was there definite loss of behavioral control? The defendant must have been unable to substantially change, monitor, or control his criminal behavior	No
A-6 If yes on A-4 or A-5, was the loss of cognitive and behavioral control over the criminal behavior directly resulting from a mental defect or a major psychiatric disorder?	N/A

The defendant fails to meet the ALI standard for the insanity defense under the R-CRAS decision model because although he scored "no" on malingering and he has neuropsychological and other impairments, there was no loss of cognitive or behavioral control. Therefore, there was no direct relationship or linkage between the diagnosed mental disorders and the cognitive or volitional control.

Conclusions

1. The forensic database was sufficient to draw relevant conclusions to a reasonable degree of psychological and neuropsychological probability. All conclusions were rendered independently of other investigators and evaluators in this case.
2. The forensic distortion analysis of nondeliberate and deliberate data sources suggests that the evaluation is an accurate representation of the defendant at the time of the alleged offenses. The mental conditions of the defendant for the time of the evaluation were cognitive disorder, Not Otherwise Specified (NOS); rule out pedophilia; depressive disorder, NOS; and personality disorder, NOS. The mental conditions of the defendant for the time of the alleged offenses in addition include methamphetamine intoxication. He has a number of Axis III physical problems secondary to multiple previous injuries and prolonged and continuous polysubstance abuse. The severity of psychosocial stressors (Axis IV) for the year before the alleged offenses is seen as moderate, using DSM criteria as manifested by his readjustment efforts upon returning to California, his lack of a social life, his poor living conditions with his sister, and other factors. The highest level of adaptive functioning (Axis V) is 20, meaning that he was at risk for acting out currently and in the past.
3. The defendant is competent to legally proceed. He understands the nature and quality of the legal proceedings, the possible consequences to himself, and can cooperate with his attorneys in his own defense. Although he claims to hear voices daily, he has stated that he has learned to ignore them. I am not sure whether he is, in any case,

reporting genuine auditory hallucinations. He is currently moderately suicidal, scoring like 45% of the lethal responders group. Recommendations include evaluation for antidepressant medication and supportive counseling. Competency to proceed may even improve somewhat as he remains in institutional remission from all substances and prepares for the coming legal proceedings. His adjustment may also improve if he is placed in a cell that is less stressful. His ability to rationally consult with his attorney is unimpaired. He has a clear understanding of the roles of the court officers. He sees no condition that would interfere with his ability to stand trial.

4. In my opinion, the extent to which the above-diagnosed conditions impaired the defendant's cognitive ability to appreciate the wrongfulness of his acts was mild on a scale of negligible, minimal, mild, moderate, considerable, and substantial. He knew that he was doing wrong at the time of the alleged offenses and full recall for events.

5. In my opinion, the extent to which the above-diagnosed conditions impaired the defendant's volitional capacity to conform his conduct to the requirements of the law was mild. This rating was based on the interactive effects of demonstrated and intact choice and self-control for the times before, during, and after the alleged offenses.

It may be questioned whether methamphetamine intoxication by itself substantially impaired the defendant in terms of his choice and self-control. The defendant showed ample choice and self-control for the times before, during, and after the alleged offenses, despite claiming to have ingested a considerable amount of methamphetamine. He even decided not to kill the daughter just a few moments after the alleged violence against the other family members. Such an ability to stop and decide not to kill suggests that he could have decided similarly a few moments earlier.

6. Risk of danger to self, others, and property and proposed intervention, are usually offered only if an exculpating mental condition is proffered. In this case, the defense attorneys agreed to present the results of the violence risk analysis in this report. Violence potential for the defendant toward himself is seen as moderate due to a high level of depression, suicidal ideation, and a past history of reckless and self-injurious behavior. Appropriate antidepressant medication and counseling interventions were proposed. The violence potential of the defendant toward others, as shown on the VRAG, is a mild-moderate .58 over a 10-year period. This score is founded on the base rate for dangerousness for the sample which is approximately 33%. His score on the Historical, Clinical, Risk Management (HCR) also suggested a moderate risk of dangerousness toward others in the future.

Report prepared by
Harold V. Hall, PhD, ABPP

Capital Mitigation Case from Chapter 2 (Marczyk, Knauss, Kutinsky, DeMatteo, and Heilbrun)

Re: John Doe
P.P. #123456

Referral

John Doe is a 24-year-old Hispanic male who is currently charged with murder (two counts), weapons offenses (two counts [6801]), criminal conspiracy (two counts), theft (two counts), rape (one count), indecent assault (one count), weapons offense (two counts [6103]), robbery (two counts), P.S.P. (two counts), sexual assault (one count), and unlawful restraint (two counts). A request for a mental health evaluation to provide the defense with information relevant to sentencing, pursuant to 42 Pa. C.S.A. section 9711(e), was made by Mr Doe's attorney.

Procedures

Mr Doe was evaluated for approximately 6 h on 30 September, 1998, at the Correctional Facility, where he is currently incarcerated. In addition to a clinical interview, Mr Doe was administered a standard screening instrument for currently experienced symptoms of mental and emotional disorder (the Brief Symptom Inventory, or BSI), a standard test of current functioning in relevant academic areas (the Wide Range Achievement Test, 3rd Edition, or WRAT-3), a measure of personality functioning relevant to recidivism risk and rehabilitation potential (the Psychopathy Checklist-Revised, or PCL-R), a test of current cognitive and intellectual functioning (the Wechsler Adult Intelligence Scale-3rd Edition, or WAIS-III), a measure of response style related to cognitive tasks (the Validity Indicator Profile, or VIP), and a standard objective test of mental and emotional functioning (the Minnesota Multiphasic Personality Inventory, 2nd Edition, or MMPI-2). In addition, Mr Doe's mother, Ms Jane Doe, was interviewed by phone regarding Mr Doe's past and current functioning. Mr Doe's neighbor, Ms Sally Jones, was also interviewed by phone regarding Mr Doe's past and current functioning. The following documents, obtained from Mr Doe's attorney, were reviewed as part of the evaluation:

1. *Miranda* rights waiver form
2. Philadelphia Police Department Investigation interview record of John Doe
3. Memorandum from Mr Doe's attorney

Prior to the evaluation, Mr Doe was notified about the purpose of the evaluation and the associated limits on confidentiality. He appeared to understand the basic purpose of the evaluation, reporting back his understanding that he would be evaluated and that a written report would be submitted to his attorney. He further understood that the report could be used in his sentencing hearing and, if it were, copies would be provided to the prosecution and the court.

Relevant History

Historical information was obtained from the collateral sources described above as well as from Mr Doe himself. Whenever possible, the consistency of the factual information provided by Mr Doe was assessed through the use of multiple sources. If additional collateral information is obtained prior to Mr Doe's court date, a supplemental report will be filed.

John Doe was born to Jane Doe and John Doe, Sr. Mr Doe reported that he has three half-siblings on his mother's side and two half-siblings on his father's side. Mr Doe reported that his parents divorced when he was between one and one-and-a-half years old. He stated that his father, who was reportedly an alcoholic, physically abused his mother during their marriage. He also reported, however, that his parents "got along" after the divorce. Mr Doe's mother, Ms Jane Doe, reported that the divorce occurred when Mr Doe was about 5 months old. She reported that the marriage ended because her husband was "very abusive" toward her. She also reported, however, that her husband never abused Mr Doe. Ms Doe reported that she remained "friends" with Mr Doe's father following the divorce. She also reported that Mr Doe was "always mad that his father wasn't around." Mr Doe's neighbor, Ms Sally Jones, also reported that Mr Doe had "anger inside him" that may have been the result of not having his father around. Mr Doe stated that his father died about 5 years ago. Mr Doe reported that he was raised entirely by his mother. He reported that he never lived with his father and that he only spent time with him on the weekends. Mr Doe and his mother both reported that he helped raise his younger brothers and sisters while he was growing up. Mr Doe also reported that he lived with his maternal aunt for about 1 year when he was about 16 years old. He reported that he moved in with his aunt because "my 'so-called' friends kept breaking into my mom's house and I didn't want her to go through it anymore."

Mr Doe reported that he had a "fine relationship" with his mother while he was growing up because she was "always there for me." Similarly, Ms Doe reported that she and Mr Doe had a good relationship. She reported that they "talked about everything" while he was growing up. Mr Doe also reported, however, that he would occasionally "do things that made her disappointed." When questioned further, Mr Doe reported that he stole money from his mother and lied to her as well. Mr Doe reported that his mother was affectionate toward him while he was growing up. When Mr Doe was asked about his current relationship with his mother, he reported that it is "the same." Mr Doe reported that his mother has been employed at a local grocery store for the past couple of months. He also reported that he speaks to his mother on a daily basis. When Mr Doe was asked about his relationship with his father, he reported that he only saw his father on the weekends while he was growing up. According to Ms Doe, however, Mr Doe only saw his father on the weekends for about 1 month when he was 7 years old. She reported that Mr Doe's father was "in and out" of Mr Doe's life and that he would often "disappear" from Mr Doe's life for long periods of time. Mr Doe reported that his father showed that he cared for him by "spending time with me … treat[ing] me like a son." He also reported, however, that his father "never showed emotional feelings" toward him. Mr Doe reported that he has always had a good relationship with his siblings. Mr Doe reported that there were not many rules in his house, but that he was punished if he did something wrong. When Mr Doe was asked if he was physically abused while growing up, he replied, "not really … I call it punishment." When questioned further, Mr Doe reported that his mother "put my hands over the stove" when he got caught stealing. He also reported that his mother occasionally hit him when he did something wrong. Ms Doe denied that Mr Doe was ever physically abused while he was growing up. Mr Doe denied being sexually or emotionally abused.

Mr Doe reported that he has two children, is currently separated from his wife, and is in the process of getting a divorce. He reported that although the divorce was originally his wife's idea, he wants to get a divorce because "our marriage is broken." Mr Doe reported that he and his wife did not have a good relationship because they would "fight and argue." He also reported that they occasionally were physically abusive toward each other. Specifically, he reported that his wife would hit him and that he would "smack or push her" when they argued. Ms Jones reported that she saw Mr Doe hit his wife on one occasion. Specifically, Ms Jones reported that she witnessed Mr Doe "slap his wife and then cry." Mr Doe reported that he has only seen his children on four or five occasions during this past year and that he would like to see them more often.

When Mr Doe was asked about his educational background, he reported that he stopped attending school in 9th grade and subsequently obtained his general equivalency diploma (GED). Mr Doe reported that he attended the following schools: Elementary School One (kindergarten to 4th grade), Middle School One (5th to 8th grade), High School One (9th grade), and Special Needs High School. Mr Doe reported that he was transferred to High School Two after he stopped attending High School One, but that he never attended High School Two. He reported that he was subsequently sent to Special Needs High School, where he spent 14 to 16 months. Mr Doe reported that he started taking GED classes while at Special Needs High School and subsequently obtained his GED. Mr Doe reported that his attendance was "perfect" until 8th grade. When Mr Doe was asked about his academic performance, he reported that he usually received "As, Bs, and Cs." He also reported that he occasionally received failing grades, but that he would "bring them up before the year ended." Mr Doe also reported that he received good grades while at Special Needs High School. Specifically, he reported that he was "on the honor roll and got straight As" while at Special Needs High School. Similarly, Ms Doe reported that Mr Doe received "first honors almost every month" while at Special Needs High School. Mr Doe reported that he was required to repeat "6th or 7th grade" as a result of not paying attention, talking in class, and not doing his homework. Mr Doe reported that he did not get in trouble for behavior problems while in school, adding that he "was a good little kid." Specifically, he reported that he was not rowdy and never fought with the other students. He did report, however, that he occasionally received detention for talking in class. Ms Jones reported that Mr Doe started getting into trouble when he was in 2nd or 3rd grade, noting that he got into some "scrapes" at that time. Ms Jones also noted, however, that Mr Doe "never displayed hostility … with any adult … or with his own peers." Ms Doe reported that Mr Doe occasionally had difficulties in school because of his "problem with stuttering." Specifically, she reported that "teachers got on him" because he was reluctant to read out loud due to his stuttering. Ms Doe noted that Mr Doe began receiving speech therapy when he was 7 or 8 years old. Mr Doe reported that he was suspended on one occasion for cutting class in 7th grade. Mr Doe reported that he was never expelled from any school. Official academic records were not available at the time this report was written.

Mr Doe reported that he does not currently suffer from any serious medical problems and that he has never had any serious illnesses or injuries. Mr Doe and his mother both reported that he has never been prescribed medication for mental, emotional, or behavioral problems. Mr Doe described a limited history of contact with mental health professionals. Specifically, he reported that his only contact with mental health professionals has been in the Correctional Facility. Mr Doe reported that he has almost completed a 6-week program for "anger and stress management" that is offered in the Correctional Facility. He reported that a social worker at the Correctional Facility recommended that he enter the program, which he attends on a weekly basis. Mr Doe reported that the program has been helpful because it has helped him to handle arguments in a more productive manner. When Ms Doe was asked about Mr Doe's mental health history, she reported that Mr Doe attended weekly therapy sessions for a couple of months when he was 14 years old. She reported that he voluntarily sought therapy when he came out of the Special Needs High School because "he didn't feel like he was himself." Mr Doe's medical and psychiatric records were not available at the time this report was written.

Mr Doe reported a fairly significant history of substance abuse. He reported that he has used marijuana, cocaine (powder), PCP, and alcohol. Mr Doe reported that he started using marijuana and alcohol when he was 15 years old. He reported that he smoked marijuana "about every other day" from age 15 until age 22. Mr Doe reported that he smoked "two to three blunts a day" with his friends. He also reported that he often smoked marijuana "two or three times a day." Mr Doe reported that he started using cocaine in 1994. He reported that he used cocaine every day for one and a half years because he needed to "stay up for a night job." Mr Doe reported that he only used PCP "once in a while." Mr Doe stated that he used drugs because of "peer pressure … to be like everybody else." Mr Doe reported that he stopped all drug use after being arrested in 1996. Mr Doe stated that he will "only drink on special occasions" because he is concerned about the history of alcoholism in his family, adding that he does "not want to turn out like my father." Mr Doe denied that he currently has a substance-abuse problem. Mr Doe also reported that he has engaged in the sale of drugs. Specifically, he reported that he sold drugs "off and on" for about 2 years. He reported that he usually sold drugs during periods of unemployment. Ms Jones also reported that Mr Doe sold drugs when he was unable to find a job. Mr Doe reported that he made between $300 and $400 per night from the sale of "crack cocaine, heroin, marijuana, and any other drugs I could get my hands on."

Mr Doe reported that he has had about seven or eight jobs since he began working. Specifically, Mr Doe reported that he has been employed as a sales representative, disk jockey, carpet installer, and automobile alarm installer. In addition, Mr Doe reported that he worked in the horticulture department at the Special Needs High School. He reported that his longest job was 2 years and his shortest job was 3 or 4 months. Mr Doe reported that his most recent job was as an automobile alarm installer, where he reportedly worked full time for approximately 1 year. Mr Doe gave conflicting information regarding the length of his employment as an automobile alarm installer. Specifically, when Mr Doe was first asked about his employment as an automobile alarm installer, he reported that he worked there for about 3 or 4 months. When questioned later, however, he reported that he worked as an automobile alarm installer for about 9 months. Mr Doe reported that his job duties as an automobile alarm installer included changing tires, installing car alarms and radios, and ordering parts. He reported that he enjoyed this job, but was released from employment after a previous employee came back to work. Mr Doe reported that he has only been fired from one job. Specifically, he reported that he was fired from his position as a carpet installer because "they claimed I didn't know how to take orders." Official employment records were not available at the time this report was written. Mr Doe reported that he has never received any form of social assistance (i.e., welfare, unemployment insurance, etc.), but that his wife received social assistance while they were living together. Mr Doe reported that he supported himself through periods of unemployment by "selling drugs and mechanics jobs." He also reported that his mother has always provided support for him.

According to Mr Doe, prior to his arrest for the current charges, he had been arrested on three other occasions. He reported that his first arrest, which occurred in "late 1994 or 95," was for drug-related offenses ("two bundles of heroin"). Mr Doe reported that a bench warrant was issued, but that the charges were eventually dropped. Mr Doe reported that his second arrest occurred in 1995, when he was charged with a weapons violation. He similarly reported that a bench warrant was issued, but that the charges were eventually dropped. Finally, Mr Doe reported that his third arrest occurred in 1996, when he was charged with drug-related offenses after being caught with "a bundle of crack cocaine." Mr Doe reported that he pleaded guilty to the charges and received a sentence of 6 to 23 months (time served) and was placed on probation and parole. He reported that he will be released from probation and parole in April of 2000. An official arrest history was not available at the time this report was written.

Mr Doe also reported that he was arrested three times as a juvenile. He reported that his first arrest occurred when he was 14 years old. He reported that he was charged with "raping a boy," but that the charges were eventually dropped. Ms Doe reported that Mr Doe was incarcerated for 1 month in the Youth Detention Facility before the charges were eventually dropped. Ms Doe also reported that Mr Doe "came back different [from the Youth Detention Facility]." Specifically, she reported that Mr Doe's experience of being incarcerated "changed him." When questioned further, Ms Doe reported that Mr Doe "wouldn't sleep and cut school" after being released from the Youth Detention Facility. Ms Doe was unable to explain the reason for Mr Doe's behavior change. Mr Doe reported that his second arrest as a juvenile was for robbery when he was 15 years old. He reported that the charges were eventually dropped. Finally, Mr Doe reported that his third arrest as a juvenile occurred when he was 15 or 16 years old. Although he was unable to remember the exact charge, he reported that it may have been "truancy." According to Mr Doe, he was placed on after-care probation as a result of this offense.

Current Clinical Condition

Mr Doe presented as a Hispanic male with a large, muscular build who appeared his stated age. He was dressed in prison garb and well groomed when seen for the evaluation at the Correctional Facility, where he is currently incarcerated. Initially, he was cooperative and polite, although somewhat reserved. He remained cooperative and polite throughout the entire evaluation. His speech was clear, coherent, and relevant, although he occasionally spoke with a slight stammer. He appeared to give reasonable effort to the tasks involved. His capacity for attention and concentration appeared adequate, and he was able to focus reasonably well on a series of tasks during the 6-h evaluation without becoming visibly distracted. Therefore, it would appear that this evaluation provides a reasonably good estimate of Mr Doe's current functioning.

Mr Doe's mood throughout the evaluation was largely subdued and neutral. He did, however, become visibly upset when he spoke about the death of his father. He was correctly oriented to time, place, and person. Overall level of intellectual functioning was formally measured with the Wechsler Adult Intelligence Scale-III (WAIS-III) and was found to be within the borderline range (verbal IQ = 76, performance IQ = 85, full-scale IQ = 78). Individuals with such scores are below the 7th percentile, relative to the adult population (in other words, functioning at a lower level than over 93% of adults). Mr Doe's verbal IQ score suggests that his functioning in verbal areas is less well developed than in visual-motor areas. Mr Doe performed below average on all but one of the verbal subtests (digit span, average range). Conversely, Mr Doe performed in the average range on all but one of the performance subtests (object assembly, below average). The results of VIP suggest that Mr Doe's performance on other tests of cognitive capacity, such as the WAIS-III and WRAT-3, should be considered a valid representation of his abilities (overall subtest validity, valid; subtest response style, compliant). Mr Doe appears to have exhibited good effort and intended to respond correctly on the both the verbal and nonverbal subtests, producing a valid profile. Therefore, tests that cover similar content areas (e.g., word knowledge, reading ability, general language skills, abstract reasoning, perceptual accuracy, and attention to detail) that were administered concurrently with the VIP can probably be interpreted with confidence.

Mr Doe's basic academic skills, as measured by the WRAT-3, showed deficits in all three areas measured: reading (grade 7 equivalent), spelling (grade 4 equivalent), and arithmetic (grade 8 equivalent). Each of these areas should be considered in need of remediation.

Mr Doe did not report experiencing any perceptual disturbances (auditory or visual hallucinations), and his train of thought was clear and logical. Mr Doe also did not report experiencing delusions (bizarre ideas with no possible basis in reality). On a structured inventory of symptoms of mental and emotional disorders (the BSI), Mr Doe reported being "moderately," "quite," or "extremely" bothered by various symptoms. Some of the symptoms reported by Mr Doe involved nervousness or shakiness inside; feeling easily annoyed or irritated; trouble falling asleep; having to check and double-check what he does; difficulty making decisions; having to avoid certain things, places, or activities because they frighten him; the idea that he should be punished for his sins; feeling hopeless about the future; thoughts of death or dying; feeling very self-conscious with others; and feeling that people will take advantage of him if he lets them.

Mr Doe reported that he has been bothered by feelings of nervousness "ever since this [incident] happened." Mr Doe reported that he gets easily annoyed or irritated when people talk to him when he does not "want to be bothered." He also reported that he gets annoyed when "somebody [is] being a pain." Mr Doe reported that he has difficulty falling asleep "mainly because of this situation and my toothache." Mr Doe reported that he often has to check and double-check what he does because "I forget I did it and have to check if it's done." Mr Doe reported that he has difficulty making decisions regarding "whether to do the right thing or not." Mr Doe reported that he often avoids certain places because they frighten him. When questioned further, he reported that he will occasionally "walk in the wrong place … or at the wrong time" and, as a result, he prefers to "take somebody with me because anything can happen." Mr Doe reported that he believes that he should be punished for his sins because "sinners should be punished if they don't repent." Mr Doe reported that he occasionally feels hopeless about the future because "if I don't do the right things, I won't have a life for myself." Mr Doe reported that he occasionally thinks about death or dying because "anything can happen … an enemy might kill me." He also reported, however, that he does not have thoughts of suicide. Mr Doe reported that he feels self-conscious when he is with others and, as a result, he prefers to have people with him when he goes out. Finally, Mr Doe reported that he believes that people will take advantage of him if he lets them.

Mr Doe responded to the items on the MMPI-2 in a cooperative manner. It appears, however, that Mr Doe may have exaggerated some of his symptoms. Nevertheless, Mr Doe's MMPI-2 profile is valid and probably provides a reasonably good basis for describing his current functioning. Individuals with this profile (Welsh code: 67"8'90+2-415/3: F/L:K) are often described as intense, anxious, and distressed. These individuals tend to ruminate a great deal, and they may manifest obsessive or compulsive behavior. These individuals may overreact to environmental situations with intense anxiety, suspicion, and concern. Individuals with this profile are often described as feeling insecure and inadequate when they are dealing with their problems. Additionally, these individuals often have problems controlling and directing their anger and, consequently, they may often behave in inappropriate and occasionally violent ways. These individuals often view the world as a threatening place, and they see themselves as having been unjustly blamed for the problems of other people. Mr Doe endorsed a number of items that suggest that he is experiencing low morale and a depressed mood.

Individuals with this profile tend to be experiencing some interpersonal distress. They are often described as being inflexible in social situations. These individuals are often described as having hostile interpersonal relationships, and they may brood over what they think others have done to them. In addition, these individuals often have unstable interpersonal relationships, with marital breakups being relatively common. These individuals are often quite shy and inhibited in social situations, and they may avoid other people out of fear of being hurt. In addition, individuals with this profile often feel emotionally alienated from others and they are likely to have very few friends. These individuals often view relationships with other people as threatening and harmful. In addition, individuals with this profile are often described as being quiet and submissive, and they often lack self-confidence in dealing with other people. Moreover, these individuals are often unable to assert themselves appropriately and are frequently taken advantage of by other people.

Individuals with this profile often exhibit excessive anxiety and obsessive behavior. The possibility of a paranoid disorder or paranoid personality should also be considered. In addition, Mr Doe's self-reported tendency of experiencing depressed mood should also be considered in any diagnostic formulation. Individuals with this profile often have difficulty forming a therapeutic relationship. These individuals often feel vulnerable to outside threats, and they may have suspicious or paranoid ideas that must be considered when a treatment plan is being formulated and implemented. Treatment programs for these individuals often require a great deal of structure, with explicit and consistent rules that are openly, firmly, and fairly administered to cope with their extreme sensitivity to insults and perceived injustice.

Individuals with such a classification (Megargee Classification [Rev.] Charlie, medium) are often viewed as distrustful, cold, irresponsible, and unstable. These individuals often have anti-social, aggressive, and hostile attitudes toward other people. Other people often view individuals with this classification as alienated, bitter, rigid, and dogmatic. These individuals tend to have unstable interpersonal relationships, and their suspicious attitudes and hostility toward others may make rehabilitation more difficult. In a correctional setting, individuals with this classification often have difficulty adjusting to prison life. It may often be necessary to separate them from weaker and more vulnerable inmates during incarceration. In addition, incarceration may often increase their hostility and resentment. These individuals often exhibit major deficits in most areas of functioning. Specifically, these individuals often experience academic difficulties, vocational problems, and poor interpersonal relationships. In addition, these individuals often have significant substance-abuse problems. Individuals with this classification have been described as manifesting the most authority conflict, the most social/emotional constriction, the least sociability, and the least adaptability to the environment. They have also been characterized as loners who are socially withdrawn and aggressive.

The results of the PCL-R indicate that Mr Doe would not be classified as a psychopath, which would have put him at a higher risk for reoffending, both for crime in general and for violent crime against people. Mr Doe's overall PCL-R score (21) would place him at the 37th percentile relative to other male prison inmates. The cut-off score for a classification of psychopathy is 30. Mr Doe's score on factor 1 (5), which measures features often associated with narcissistic personality disorder, would place him at the 22nd percentile relative to other male prison inmates. Mr Doe's score on factor 2 (10), which measures features often associated with antisocial personality disorder, would place him at the 34th percentile relative to other male prison inmates. These results suggest that, relative to psychopathic inmates, Mr Doe's risk for reoffending is lower, and his capacity to respond favorably to treatment or other rehabilitation interventions is higher.

Treatment Needs and Amenability

There are four areas in which Mr Doe has treatment/rehabilitation needs which, if addressed, should serve to reduce his risk for future antisocial behavior. These areas include treatment for substance abuse; continued education/training; training in anger control, impulse control, and decision-making/problem-solving skills; and development of a more positive social support network.

First, Mr Doe has treatment/rehabilitation needs in the area of substance abuse. Mr Doe reported a significant history of substance abuse beginning when he was 15 years old. In addition, Mr Doe reported that he has been arrested for drug-related offenses on two occasions. Furthermore, individuals with Mr Doe's MMPI-2 classification often manifest significant substance-abuse problems. Mr Doe also reported that he has engaged in the sale of drugs. Specifically, Mr Doe reported that he sold drugs "off and on" for about 2 years. Therefore, treatment for substance abuse would probably have the biggest risk reduction value as far as Mr Doe's risk for engaging in future antisocial behavior. Treatment in this area may be especially important because it does not appear that Mr Doe has ever received treatment for his substance-abuse problem. In addition, Mr Doe reported that he does not believe that he needs treatment for his substance-abuse problem. Given the length and severity of Mr Doe's substance-abuse problem, he would particularly benefit from a treatment plan that includes relapse prevention strategies.

Second, Mr Doe would benefit from continued education/training. Given Mr Doe's age, educational level, and current situation, he would particularly benefit from training in both specific job skills and functional academic areas related to his areas of interest. This area may be especially important because Mr Doe displayed severe deficits on all three areas measured by the WRAT-3. This area is indirectly relevant to public safety and Mr Doe's risk for future antisocial behavior to the extent that it enhances Mr Doe's ability to obtain and keep a job, thereby providing him with an income from a legitimate source that may serve to lessen any financial incentive he might have for committing future criminal acts. This is an important consideration in light of Mr Doe's self-reported history of engaging in antisocial behavior (i.e., selling drugs and robbery) to obtain money and other items. Continued education/training and subsequent employment may also be particularly important because Mr Doe reported that he usually sold drugs during periods of unemployment and when he was "in between jobs." Ms Jones reported that vocational training would be beneficial for Mr Doe because he sold drugs when he was unable to find a job. In addition, Ms Jones reported that vocational training would be helpful because it would "give him renewed hope [and he would] become a productive human being." In addition to providing Mr Doe with necessary work skills, continued education/training would also serve to take up free time, thereby lessening the likelihood that Mr Doe will collaborate with peers in criminal offending. When Mr Doe was asked about continued education and job training, he reported that continuing his education and receiving job training would help to keep him from committing future antisocial acts.

Third, Mr Doe is in need of training in the areas of anger control, impulse control, and decision-making/problem-solving skills. Mr Doe presents as an individual who can be polite, cooperative, and nonaggressive. Mr Doe reported, however, that he has a bad temper. He also reported that other people have told him that he has a bad temper. In addition, Mr Doe reported that he has physically abused his wife when he got angry during arguments. Furthermore, Mr Doe's MMPI-2 profile suggests that he may have problems controlling and directing his anger, which may often result in inappropriate and occasionally violent behavior. Moreover, individuals with such MMPI-2 profiles tend to have antisocial, aggressive, and hostile attitudes toward other people. It should be noted, however, that Ms Jones stated that Mr Doe "never displayed hostility ... with any adult ... or with his own peers." Mr Doe reported that he is currently participating in a 6-week "anger and stress management" program offered in the Correctional Facility. He reported that the program, which he entered at the suggestion of a social worker, has been helpful because he has always had some problems controlling his anger. In addition to training in the area of anger control, Mr Doe would benefit from impulse control training. Mr Doe reported that his antisocial behavior is "sometimes impulsive." He also reported that he did not always think about the consequences of his decisions when he was younger. He did report, however, that he currently thinks about the consequences of his decisions before he acts. Finally, Mr Doe would benefit from training in decision-making/problem-solving skills. Mr Doe reported that he has occasionally made decisions because he wanted to "be like everyone else." Specifically, he reported that he smoked marijuana because of "peer pressure," adding that he used drugs because he wanted to "try to be like everybody else." Additionally, Mr Doe reported that he has engaged in antisocial behavior because he "wanted to be in with the crowd." Ms Doe reported that Mr Doe is "more of a follower." She also reported that Mr Doe "ends up doing what others want him to do." Therefore, based on his current charges, some of his past offenses, his MMPI-2 profile, and his self-report, Mr Doe may need some skills training to help him control his behavior, improve his decision-making/problem-solving skills, and recognize and avoid "high-risk" situations that may make it more likely that he will become involved in future antisocial behavior. Training in this area is directly relevant to Mr Doe's risk for future antisocial behavior. If he responds favorably to such an intervention, it should serve to reduce his risk for future criminal offending.

Finally, Mr Doe is in need of a more positive social support network. Mr Doe reported that he "never had big brothers" and "never had a lot of friends." He also reported that he "hung out with an older crowd [and] they looked down on me." Furthermore, the description of the current alleged offense indicates that Mr Doe was with his friends, who were significantly older than him, when the alleged offense occurred. In addition, Mr Doe's description of some of his past offenses indicates that he was with his friends when some of those events occurred. Mr Doe also reported that his friends are involved with weapons and drugs, which may serve to increase his risk for continued substance abuse and anti-social behavior. Finally, Mr Doe stated that "if [my father] was there for me, I wouldn't have sold drugs. He would have taught me better ... right from wrong." Ms Doe noted that Mr Doe was "always mad that his father wasn't around." A positive social support network may be especially important because Mr Doe reported that he only has "two or three close friends." Mr Doe also reported that having a good relationship with his family would help to keep him from committing antisocial acts in the future. Specifically, Mr Doe stated that raising his family in a "righteous way" and "be[ing] there for my kids" would help to keep him from committing future acts of antisocial behavior. Similarly, Ms Doe reported that "spending more time with his kids" would help to keep Mr Doe from committing antiso-cial acts in the future. She also reported that Mr Doe's fiancé "keeps him out of trouble." Therefore, if Mr Doe develops a more positive social support network, particularly with respect to his family, his risk for future antisocial behavior should be reduced.

Sentencing Considerations

According to 42 Pa. C.S.A. section 9711(a)(2), any evidence relating to mitigating circum-stances can be presented as the sentencing hearing. The following factors, as enumerated in 42 Pa. C.S.A. section 9711(e), can be considered as mitigating factors:

1. The defendant has no significant history of prior criminal convictions.
2. The defendant was under the influence of extreme mental or emotional disturbance.
3. The capacity of the defendant to appreciate the criminality of his conduct or to con-form his conduct to the requirements of law was substantially impaired.
4. The age of the defendant at the time of the crime.
5. The defendant acted under extreme duress, although not such duress as to constitute a defense to prosecution ... or acted under the substantial domination of another person.
6. The victim was a participant in the defendant's homicidal conduct or consented to the homicidal acts.
7. The defendant's participation in the homicidal act was relatively minor.
8. Any other evidence of mitigation concerning the character and record of the defen-dant and the circumstances of his offense.

The mitigating factors that can be addressed through forensic mental health assessment (factors 2, 3, 5, and 8) will be discussed as they relate to Mr Doe and the circumstances surrounding the alleged offense.

Influence of Extreme Mental or Emotional Disturbance

Although Mr Doe's MMPI-2 profile suggests that he may be experiencing severe psycho-logical problems at the present time, it may be that such problems are situationally triggered (i.e., exacerbated by the conditions of prison incarceration). In addition, although he may be experiencing psychological problems at the present time, it is unclear whether he was experiencing psychological disturbances around the time of the alleged offense. Nonetheless, Mr Doe's MMPI-2 profile also suggests that he is socially withdrawn and experiencing unstable interpersonal relationships, and personality characteristics related to social introversion tend to be stable over time.

Capacity to Appreciate the Criminality of Conduct or to Conform Conduct to the Requirements of the Law

Despite borderline cognitive functioning, there is little to suggest that Mr Doe was unable to appreciate the criminality of acts such as robbery and homicide or to conform his conduct to the requirements of the law around the time of the alleged offense. Mr Doe did not report that he was delusional (experiencing beliefs with little or no possible basis in fact), experiencing perceptual disturbances (auditory or visual hallucinations), or grossly disturbed around the time of the alleged offense.

According to Mr Doe's version of the events, he was surprised by the actions taken by the other individuals involved in the alleged incident. Specifically, he reported that he was "shocked, stunned, [and] scared" during the alleged incident. In addition, Mr Doe reported that he was not aware that a robbery might have been contemplated by the individuals he was with. According to self-report, Mr Doe thought that they were going over to the victims' apartment to talk about jewelry that had exchanged hands a few weeks earlier. He also reported that he was not aware that one of the individuals he was with was carrying a gun. In addition, Mr Doe reported that the actions he took following the alleged incident were motivated by fear. Specifically, Mr Doe claims that he continually denied being involved in the alleged incident (or having any information about the alleged incident) because he feared for his life and the lives of his family members. He reported that one of the individuals involved in the alleged incident told him not to say anything about the alleged incident "or the same thing would happen to me and my family." When Ms Doe was asked about the events that occurred after the alleged incident took place, she reported that her house was "watched by [one of the other individual's] mother." She also reported that her house was broken into several times. Ms Jones also reported that the Does' house was broken into several times following the alleged incident. Ms Doe reported that she sent Mr Doe to live with his maternal aunt to protect him from the other individuals involved in the alleged incident. It should be noted that Ms Doe claims that she did not know about the alleged incident at the time these events occurred.

Action Under Extreme Duress or Under Substantial Domination of Another Person

It is difficult to describe Mr Doe's alleged actions in terms of being taken under extreme duress or under the substantial domination of another person because, as previously noted, Mr Doe claims that he was not aware that a robbery might have been contemplated by the other individuals he was with on the day the alleged incident took place. In addition, Mr Doe denies being involved in the planning or execution of the alleged acts. Mr Doe claims that he was a passive participant in the criminal actions of the other individuals he was with and, furthermore, that he was not aware that those actions would occur.

If, however, Mr Doe's version of the events is not fully accurate—if Mr Doe was involved in the planning or execution of the alleged offense—it is possible to describe his actions as being heavily influenced by the other individuals involved in the alleged incident. Mr Doe reported that he was the youngest of the four individuals involved in the alleged incident. Specifically, he reported that he was 16 years old and that the other individuals were in their late 20s and early 30s. He also reported that he "hung out with an older crowd [and] they looked down on me." In addition, Mr Doe's MMPI-2 profile suggests that he may lack self-confidence and be quiet and submissive when dealing with other people. Moreover, individuals with such profiles are often unable to assert themselves appropriately and are frequently taken advantage of by other people. Ms Doe reported that Mr Doe was always "more of a follower." She also reported that Mr Doe is easily influenced and "ends up doing what others want him to do." Similarly, Ms Jones reported that Mr Doe "was a follower." She also stated that Mr Doe "could be talked into anything." In addition, Ms Jones reported that Mr Doe was "intimidated" by one of the other individuals involved in the alleged incident. Therefore, based on Mr Doe's passive personality and his difficulty in asserting himself appropriately, it is possible to consider his actions as being heavily influenced by the other individuals involved in the alleged incident.

Other Mitigating Circumstances: Character, Record, or Offense Circumstances

There may also be other mitigating circumstances concerning Mr Doe's character, his criminal record, and the circumstances surrounding the alleged offense. First, Mr Doe apparently does not have a significant history of prior arrests and convictions. According to Mr Doe, prior to his arrest for the current charges, he was arrested three times as an adult. Specifically, Mr Doe reported that he was arrested twice for drug-related offenses and once for a weapons violation. He also noted, however, that the charges were subsequently dropped in one of the drug-related arrests and the arrest for the weapons violation. Of particular importance is the nature of his previous arrests. Mr Doe reported that he has never been charged with any violent offenses as an adult.

Second, although Mr Doe described his home life in generally positive terms, he also reported the presence of various problems that he experienced while he was growing up. Mr Doe reported that he never lived with his father because his parents divorced when he was less than 2 years old. Mr Doe reported that the absence of his father while growing up was the cause of many of the problems that he later experienced. He also reported that his father, who was reportedly an alcoholic, physically abused his mother during their marriage. In addition, although Mr Doe denied being physically abused while growing up, he reported that his mother inflicted severe "punishment" on him. Specifically, he reported that his mother would "put my hands over the stove" when he got caught stealing. He also reported that his mother occasionally hit him when he did something wrong. When Ms Jones was asked to describe Mr Doe's home life, she stated that his "home life was very dysfunctional." Furthermore, despite his current situation, Mr Doe has voluntarily and actively engaged in self-improvement behavior. Specifically, Mr Doe reported that he has almost completed a 6-week program for "anger and stress management" that is offered in the Correctional Facility.

Third, Mr Doe reported the presence of various psychological, behavioral, and emotional problems that have resulted from the alleged incident. Mr Doe reported that after the alleged incident took place, he feared for his life and the lives of his family members because of the death threats that were allegedly made by one of the individuals involved in the alleged incident. Ms Doe reported that Mr Doe was "on edge, jumpy" after the alleged incident took place. In addition, Ms Jones reported that Mr Doe was "withdrawn ... scared to death" because of the death threats that were allegedly made after the alleged incident took place. She also reported that Mr Doe often did not leave the house after the alleged incident took place.

Conclusion

In the opinion of the undersigned, based on all of the above, Mr Doe

1. May have been experiencing various interpersonal problems around the time of the alleged offense
2. May have taken actions during the alleged offense that were heavily influenced by the other individuals involved in the alleged offense
3. May have other mitigating factors concerning his character, his criminal record, and the circumstances surrounding the alleged offense
4. Has treatment/rehabilitation needs in the areas of substance abuse; continued education/training; anger control, impulse control, and decision-making/problem-solving skills; and development of a more positive social support network
5. Should be at a lower risk for future criminal offending if these recommendations, with appropriate monitoring to ensure compliance, can be implemented

Thank you for the opportunity to evaluate John Doe.

Interactional Report: A Case Illustration from Chapter 3 (Hall, Poirier, and Thompson)

Re: *State of Hawaii v. Anthony Barnes*
  Criminal Number 12-5555

  Count I: **Attempted Murder**
  Count II: **Assault in the First Degree**

Dear Ms. _____
  This is the report of the forensic psychologist requested by your office to examine and report on the instant case in regard to defendant–victim interaction and related behavior. A primary issue to be addressed in this report is to what extent self-control of the accused was adversely affected by extreme emotion at the time of the alleged offenses. A related issue is to what degree behavioral self-regulation was exhibited during the instant offenses, irrespective of operative emotion, stress, or other arousal factors.
  A secondary issue concerns the credibility and mental condition of the victim.
  The defendant, Anthony Barnes, DOB February 16, 1953, POB Waipahu, Hawaii, SSN 555-88-9876, is presently in pretrial detainment at the Hawaii Community Correctional Center (HCCC). The victim of the alleged attempted murder and assault is Carole Gordon, DOB October 18, 1962, POB Los Angeles, California, SSN 234-99-8778. The date of the alleged crimes was August 29, 1986, with the incident occurring at the Seaview Lounge on Montgomery Street in Honolulu.
  The following analysis sequentially focuses on (a) the forensic database utilized in terms of perpetrator, victim, and contextual stimuli; (b) an analysis of evaluation validity and victim/witness distortion. The mental condition of the victim is addressed here; (c) an analysis of emotional and self-control aspects of alleged crime behavior in terms of time flow; and (d) conclusions in regard to behavioral self-determination and emotion at the time of the alleged offenses. Some observations are based on the behavioral science literature such as from articles and sections regarding emotion and self-control from R. Corsini (Ed.), *Encyclopedia of Psychology*, John Wiley & Sons, New York, 1984; Kutash, Kutash and Schlesinger, *Violence: Perspectives on Murder and Aggression*, Jossey-Bass, San Francisco, 1978; and A. Montagu, *The Nature of Human Aggression*, Oxford University Press, New York, 1976. Clinical and experimental correlates of violence including emotional factors draw upon J. Monahan, *The Clinical Prediction of Violent Behavior*, National Institute of Mental Health, U.S. Department of Health and Human Services, 1981; H.V. Hall, A. Boissevain, E. Catlin, and J. Westgate, Dangerous myths about predicting dangerousness. *American Journal of Forensic Psychology*, 1984; and H.V. Hall, Predicting dangerousness of the courts. *American Journal of Forensic Psychology*, 1984.

Forensic Database: Relevant to the alleged perpetrator, the following materials were reviewed or individuals interviewed:

1. Central Medical Center records of hospitalization (August 29 to September 17, 1986)
2. Kamehameha Hospital records (September 3 to 5, 1986)
3. Records from T.E. Chang, M.D. (April 2, 1985, to April 10, 1986)
4. Records from the Williams Clinic, Inc., Kailua (May 24, 1984, to September 6, 1985)
5. Mililani Clinic and Hospital records of neurology examination; also containing an history of significant events, handwritten by the accused (September 18, 1986; September 29, 1986)
6. A letter from the Office of the Prosecuting Attorney to HCCC Intake Service Center recommending high bail status (Wayne S. Song, dated September 30, 1986)
7. Preliminary hearing transcript (October 9, 1986)
8. Honolulu Police Department (HPD) incident reports (K-11111 dated August 30, 1986; S-23232 dated December 10, 1986; P-38889 dated June 9, 1986; R-09876 dated June 12, 1986)
9. Ex parte petition for temporary restraining order for protection (FC-M, No. 86-0005 of July 30, 1986, for victim; FC-M No. 10029 of May 25, 1984, for wife, Tamara C. Barnes)
10. Letters and drawings by the defendant while at HCCC to the victim (all in 1986: September 6, September 29, October 5, October 15, November 19, November 28, December 8, December 16, and December 18)
11. Pretrial Bail Report by Samuel Kane of the Intake Service Center, HCCC (dated September 16, 1986)
12. A letter from the victim's current boyfriend to the defendant (dated November 6, 1986)
13. An interview of Samuel Taft, witness at the crime scene (April 13, 1987, by telephone)
14. An interview of Kevin Nielson, DOB February 5, 1952, witness and worker at the crime scene and acquaintance of the victim (April 17, 1987, by telephone)
15. An interview of Marcus Nishikawa, investigation officer of the instant offense (April 18, 1987, by telephone)
16. An interview of Keith D. Conley, DOB May 25, 1961, acquaintance of the accused and victim, and a witness to the instant offenses (April 18, 1987, by telephone, April 19, 1987, April 22, 1987)
17. Victim Assistance Program records in relationship to accused–victim interaction; also in regard to Tamara Barnes, the defendant's wife. Interview of Mary Jordan, victim assistance advocate (April 23, 1987)
18. An interview of Dennis King, Ph.D., treating psychologist at HCCC (April 24, 1987, twice by telephone)
19. An interview of Monica Johnson, M.S.W., former director of The Safe House (April 25, 1987, by telephone)
20. An interview of George Kam, employee at Hawaiian Photos, Waialae (April 27, 1987, by telephone)
21. An interview of Susan Fountaine, former employee of the Sky Lounge (April 27, 1987, by telephone)

22. An audio-visual film of the accused and others relating to the issue of family violence ("Abuse in the Family," a four-part series prepared for local television, dated February 2, 1983)

23. HCCC medical and dormitory adjustment records of the accused

24. An undated letter from the victim to the accused

25. HPD investigation reports of the instant offenses

26. State of Hawaii educational records reflecting the accused's academic progress, standardized test scores, and behavioral observations

27. Employment application forms for several previous jobs

28. U.S. Navy personnel records for the accused for the period from May 30, 1972, to October 7, 1975

29. Clinical neuropsychological report of Michael Parker, Ph.D. (August 15, 1986); also, test protocols and notes for second examination (February 2, 1987)

30. James Potter, Ph.D., Director of Psychology Workshops (April 23, 1987)

The undersigned's request to psychologically examine the defendant was denied by the defense attorney.

Relevant to the victim, the following materials were reviewed or individuals interviewed:

31. See 2, 3, 5, 6, 7, 8, 9, 10, 11, 12, 13, 14, 15, 16, 17, 18, 21, 24, and 25

32. Nimitz Medical Center (NMC) records reflecting July 23, 1986, to August 9, 1986, hospitalization of the victim at that facility. NMC outpatient clinic file contained some entries in regard to earlier medical intervention

33. Certificate of Live Birth of Carol Susan Carter, the victim, from Pennsylvania State Department of Health (certified as a true copy, March 30, 1980)

34. Decree of divorce regarding Mark T. and Carol S. Thompson (October 30, 1985, Case No. 85-P-999, District Court of King County, Montana)

35. Parkins Medical Center records reflecting August 1 to 9, 1986, hospitalization at that facility

36. Interview of Paul O. Lowrey, DOB May 29, 1964, who assisted the victim after the alleged stabbing (April 25, 1987)

37. Clinical interviews of the victim (May 10, 19, and 28, 1987, June 2, 1987)

38. Bipolar Psychological Inventory (BPI) Lie Scale (administered twice: May 28, 1987, June 2, 1987)

39. Sacks Sentence Completion Test (administered May 28, 1987)

40. Marital Precounseling Inventory for the relationship with her current boyfriend (Stuart, R.B., and R.S., 1973) (administered May 28, 1987); Marital Precounseling Inventory reconstructed for the time of the victim's relationship with the accused (administered June 2, 1987)

41. Fundamental Interpersonal Relationships [with] Others-Behavior (FIRO-B; administered June 2, 1987)

42. Bender Gestalt Visual-Motor Test (BGVMT, with recall and Koppitz system scoring; administered June 2, 1987)

43. Minnesota Multiphasic Personality Inventory (MMPI) critical items list (administered twice: May 28, 1987, June 2, 1987); MMPI, Form R (June 2, 1987)

44. Slosson Intelligence Test (SIT) for children and adults (administered May 28, 1987)

45. Booklet Categories Test (administered May 28, 1987)
46. Wechsler Adult Intelligence Scale-Revised (WAIS-R, administered June 2, 1987)
47. Tactual Performance Test (TPT) (administered June 2, 1987)
48. Seashore Rhythm Test (administered June 2, 1987)
49. Speech-Sounds Perception Test (administered June 2, 1987)
50. Finger Oscillation Test (administered June 2, 1987)
51. Wechsler Memory Test, Form I (administered June 2, 1987)
52. Trail Making Test, A and B (administered June 2, 1987)
53. Reitan–Klove Sensory Perceptual Exam (administered June 2, 1987)
54. Reitan-Indiana Aphasia Screening Test (administered June 2, 1987)
55. Consultation with Robert King, Ph.D., Head, Neuropsychological Department, Hawaii State Hospital (June 9, 1987)
56. Consultation with Ronald Miyake, M.D., neurologist, Central Clinic (June 10, 1987)
57. Writing tasks to include (a) year-by-year presentation of most significant events, from birth to present and (b) list of physical symptoms attributed to the instant offenses
58. Consultation with David Smith, Ph.D., neuropsychologist (June 10, 1987)

Relevant to the context of the crime, the following records were reviewed or procedures implemented:

59. See 14, 15, 16, 18, 21, and 25
60. Physical examination of the crime scene and escape route (May 29, 1987)
61. Examination of photos of the victim (March 23, 1987). Diagrams and photos of the crime scene were also examined (March 27, 1987; April 26, 1987)

Assessment Behavior and Database Validity: The victim was cooperative and of attractive appearance. This white, female, 24-year-old business school student exhibited a logical and coherent stream of thought. Affect was appropriate, with some emotional behaviors such as muscle twitches and eye reddening when discussing the present incident. A trend toward fear of the accused was observed. Orientation was apparent for time, place, person, and circumstance. Memory for immediate, short-term and long-term events was intact, as evidenced by performance on passages of words and sequences of numbers on standardized testing, and by accurate responses to inquiries by the examiner as to prior evaluation events. Episodic long-term memory involved recollection of independently verified historical events without a tendency to confabulate. Judgment was marginal, as shown by history and by some test responses. Abstraction ability was appropriate. Reading and writing skills seem normally developed but were low average in quality. Computationally, she had no difficulty counting backward from 20 or with basic adding, subtracting, and multiplication of math problems. Fund of information and vocabulary skills were marginal, possibly reflecting her eighth grade education and some cultural familial factors. Overall, her intelligence was measured as average on a screening test (SIT) and low average on a comprehensive intelligence test (WAIS-R). Overall, verbal abilities were low average and performance abilities were average.

Distortion analysis of the victim's evaluation responses revealed, for the time of the interview, an attempt to present herself in an accurate manner. This is based on (a) goodness of fit between test profile and clinical behavior, (b) performance on scales or test procedures specifically designed to assess attempts at misrepresentation, (c) little or no discrepancy between responses and established events, and (d) consistent performance on repeated measures. Distortion analysis for the time of the instant offenses revealed an attempt to present herself in an accurate manner, but was mitigated by loss of recall after the initial knife thrusts, shock effects of the stabbing, and subsequent posttraumatic stress disorder (PTSD) (discussed later). Further, she reported drinking several alcoholic beverages on the night of the instant offenses and affirmed cocaine ingestion on the previous evening (August 28, 1986).

The mental conditions of the victim at the time of the evaluation are as follows:

Axis I: PTSD, acute (DSM III Code 308.30)

A. Recognizable stressor that would evoke significant distress symptoms in almost anyone.

On August 29, 1986, at about 2 a.m., the victim was stabbed 12 times in the back and neck with another stab wound creating through and through puncture wounds of the jugular vein and carotid artery, penetrating three to four inches into the neck. She was unresponsive upon arrival at the emergency room. Deep tendon reflexes in her legs were unobtainable, toes were downgoing to bilateral plantar stimulation, and her blood pressure was 88/41, associated in part with a significant loss of blood. She received 4 l of crystalloid fluids followed by two units of transfused blood upon admission.

Secondary stressors include loss of work and position, financial problems, and subsequent medical interventions.

B. Reexperiencing the trauma.

Following the stabbing, the victim experienced the following: (a) nightmares of being trapped by the accused, (b) frequent flashbacks of the perpetrator dragging her out of the lounge while stabbing her, (c) suddenly acting or feeling as if the traumatic events were reoccurring because of an environmental or ideational stimulus. In regard to the last, unresponsiveness and memory for ongoing environmental events (e.g., someone talking) has been lost on occasion, with the victim exhibiting fear-related muscle tightening and escape responses (e.g., others noting her almost going off the edge of a chair or couch without realizing it when someone was discussing an unrelated stabbing), and (d) frequent ruminating about the stabbing event. Some of the above symptoms appear to be increasing in frequency and severity as a by-product of current involvement in the instant case.

C. Numbing of responsiveness to, or involvement with, the external world, beginning some time after the traumatic event.

The victim has shown a markedly diminished interest in or outright avoidance of several significant activities (e.g., eating, socializing, and drinking alcohol) and sites (lounges and cane fields) where violence involving the use or threatened use of a knife was experienced from the accused. Some constriction of affect is seen compared to descriptions of preinstant offenses behaviors. Level of distrust has increased, especially toward males.

D. Symptoms of autonomic arousal or suppression and related signs.

These include: (a) continual scanning of the environment with increased anxiety when by herself, (b) sleep pattern changes with a reduction of several hours in average total sleep time, (c) startle responses, (d) memory and concentration problems with no indication that these problems are of organic etiology, (e) guilt, to include occasional thoughts that she wished she had died during the knife assault, and (f) body image problems relating to scarring and disfigurement from the knife wounds.

Further, the victim exhibits the particular PTSD symptoms associated with assault (see Davis and Friedman, The emotional aftermath of crime and violence. In Figley, C. (Ed.), *Trauma and Its Wake: The Study and Treatment of Post-traumatic Stress Disorder*, Bruner Mazel, New York, 1985. See also H.V. Hall and F.L. Hall, Post-traumatic stress disorder as a legal defense in criminal trials. *American Journal of Forensic Psychology*, 5, 45–53, 1987.

Axis II: Mixed personality disorder, in remission (DSM III Code 310.89)

Presently, the victim is involved in training as a secretary, has a positive and satisfying central love relationship, and has substantially reduced her alcohol intake and eliminated drug abuse. Analysis of her history prior to the instant offenses, however, revealed frequent job changes and periods of unemployment. She showed an inability to maintain enduring attachments to her previous spouses and significant others in her life. There appeared to be a failure to plan ahead and some recklessness, especially when under the influence of alcohol or drugs. Previous abuse of alcohol appears to be significant and the substance of choice. Other personality features by history include occasional angry outbursts or tantrums, low frustration tolerance, a need to frequently receive assurance and support from others, and long-term family conflict and discord. Decision-making skills are poor.

Personality features revealed by psychological testing, exclusive of MMPI results, indicate a low-to-medium expression of affection toward others, with comparable (low to average) needs for involvement from others. This pattern is usually seen as a result of being "burned" in interpersonal relationships. In terms of expressed control, decision skills and perceived behavioral influence over others are low. Dependency needs are elevated. This is usually seen with individuals with low self-esteem. In terms of social interaction, social skills are intact. High anxiety is attached to many social situations where she does not feel accepted by others. Social selectivity is extremely high, meaning that she is "picky" when it comes to choosing others as (emotionally) close associates; this pattern is associated with close relationships that have turned out badly. Family relationships are poor, which is congruent with a reported developmental history of frequent corporal punishment, sexual abuse by extended family members, and gross behavioral problems on the part of parents and step-parents.

MMPI and MMPI Critical Items List: Her performance yielded the following MMPI profile (015′ 8246-739/:L/F′K#). Validity scale results and repeated testing on critical items over time suggested a valid profile with a high degree of consistency. This person admitted to personal and emotional difficulties, is asking for help, and is unsure of her own capabilities in dealing with perceived high current stress. Clinical scale elevations describe a person who is uncomfortable with herself and others, hypersensitive, distrustful of others, concerned about somatic functioning and physical appearance, withdrawn, and who engages in frequent ruminative behavior.

The type of profile elevation shown by the victim (high point pair 0–1) is rare and usually does not occur except when other scales are elevated, which then reflects possible additional psychopathological conditions (e.g., see Webb, 1971; Lachar, 1974; Green, 1980). The social style and interactive behavior of the victim prior to the instant offenses can be characterized as active, operating within an individual who knew how to respond interpersonally in an appropriate manner. This suggests that MMPI scales known to be elevated by PTSD symptomatology (see Axis I) contributed to the mild-to-moderate profile elevations and the overall configuration (see above Figley, 1985 cite, all MMPI scales elevated by

PTSD in some studies; others reflect elevations in F, 2, 3, 7, 8, 0). Removal of PTSD-related items would then reduce psychopathology to more normal levels. Some character features would undoubtedly remain, reflecting the chronic traits discussed in the first paragraph under Axis II considerations. No suggestions of a thought disorder or other psychotic process emerged upon testing.

Axis III: Physical disorders or conditions related to the instant case include (1) headaches, generalized or with a burning sensation toward the back of the head. Nerve sensations are occasionally experienced in the chest and arms when the head is learned forward, (2) surface numbness, from below the chin to below the knee on the right side of the body, and down the leg on the left side. Focal numbness is also experienced on the back in the area of the stab wounds. Leg stiffness is reported in the morning, (3) balance problems with falling if she is not concentrating on the synchrony required for ambulation. She loses her balance if she attempts to run, (4) occasional aphasic signs such as producing "blurred" words, or words switched around in sequence, when those verbal characteristics were not noticed prior to the stabbing.

The above signs appear to be residual symptoms from the sustained trauma. Earlier pathological signs included: (1) left hemiparesis (i.e., abnormal neurological; normal CT scan and C-spine at Kuakini); (2) residual central nervous system deficit corresponding to Brown-Sequard syndrome, resulting in loss of sensation and discrimination in certain body sites (i.e., spectrum analysis significant for turbulent flow of right carotid artery; CT scan, arch aortagram, and carotid arteriogram essentially normal; abnormal neurological); (3) right Horner's pupil; (4) equivocal Babinski on the left; (5) ataxic gait favoring the left; (6) relatively weaker left shoulder shrug; (7) weaker left compared to right arm; (8) adequate swallow reflexes with a right pull to uvula; downward left tongue protrusion; (9) positive bilateral Hoffman sign (clawing movement of fingers created by stimulating the index finger); (10) temporary blindness, accompanied by initial visual blurring and later pain on the top of her head (see October 2, 1986, medical note).

In order to further pinpoint possible neuropsychological impairment, a composite neuropsychological battery plus some focal tests were administered (see *Forensic Database*). Mild severity of cerebral processes were revealed (Halstead impairment index = .3) primarily on tasks requiring motor speed, coordination of upper extremities, manual dexterity, and sensitivity to stimulation (i.e., impaired performance on TPT, finger oscillation, and tactile finger recognition). Results suggested a primarily, not exclusively, right hemisphere involvement (i.e., left-handed finger oscillation, nondominant hand performance on TPT, left- versus right-handed TPT, and left-handed tactile finger recognition). The lesion appears static (with deficits improving) as opposed to progressive (i.e., little difference in verbal weighted scores (VWS) and performance weighted scores (PWS) on wechsler testing, no suppressions, intact scores for Seashore Rhythm Test and Speech-Sound Perception Test). The overall results are consistent with a cerebral circulatory dysfunction or insufficiency. In general, current neuropsychological deficits are mild and do not involve higher order cognitive processing, visual perception functioning, or long-term, short-term, or immediate recall skills.

In terms of input from significant/knowledgeable others, statements made during the present evaluation in regard to alleged crime events were generally, but not totally, consistent with earlier versions presented to various investigators; expected errors of omission occurred as a result of forgetting over time and other factors, but few errors of commission, as in fabrication, were presented. Several witnesses were reluctant to be interviewed and expressed fear of retaliation from the accused. The accounts of the offenses by significant/ knowledgeable others were concrete, clear, vivid, and contained much detailed description within the limitations of their involvement and the brief span during which the instant offenses occurred.

Accounts were original in terms of lack of stereotyping, internally consistent, and imbedded in the transpiring circumstances of the crime context and the reporting parties. The accounts contained behavioral chains of events and involved the reporting of subjective experiences and feelings. Unexpected complications and interruptions were mentioned as well as unfavorable behaviors on the part of witnesses. All of the above are fundamental or special semantic criteria which in combination are associated with truthfulness of crime accounts (see U. Undeutsch, 1956, 1957, 1959, 1967, 1983; also U. Undeutsch, Statement reality analysis in A. Trankell (Ed.), *Reconstructing the Past*, Kluver, Law and Taxation Publishers, 1982; see H.V. Hall, Dangerousness prediction and the maligned forensic professional: Suggestions for detecting distortion of true basal violence. *Criminal Justice and Behavior*, 9, 3–12, 1982; R. Rogers, *RCRAS: Rogers Criminal Responsibility Assessment Scales*, Psychological Assessment Resources, Inc., Odessa, FL: 1984; and H.V. Hall, The forensic distortion analysis: A proposed decision tree and report format. *American Journal of Forensic Psychology*, 4, 31–59, 1986).

The accused's account of the instant offenses is partially presented by spontaneous statements during and subsequent to the alleged crimes. Amnesia was claimed for the actual stabbing but not for immediately preceding events (discussed later), or for the suicidal behavior. Regaining memory for instant offense events was reported in Dr _____'s assessment records, dated _____.

Generally, evaluation results are considered an accurate portrayal of the temporal sequence of the instant offenses and related events, taking into consideration the mental status and condition of the victim, test-taking attitude, psychological, intellectual, and neuropsychological limitations and competencies, and witnesses' and investigators' input.

Sequential Assessment of Emotion and Behavioral Self-Regulation: Emotional level and behavioral self-regulation of the accused can be sequentially analyzed for the temporal flow of the instant offenses, based on knowledge of the victim, the accused, significant others, and the crime context. This will be in terms of database-reported events which suggest emotional and self-control impairments and abilities before, during, and after the instant offenses.

(a) Previous to the alleged offenses: The 6 to 7 months before and violence history.
During this period of time, the accused's marital relationship fell apart, with his three children being placed in foster care (March 1986), separation from his wife (April 1986), and his entering into an intimate but stormy relationship with the victim (March, 1986). His job of 1 year was lost, with several unsuccessful attempts to reintegrate into the working field. Substance ingestion during this period consisted of alcohol, tobacco (about one pack daily), and daily use of anabolic steroids as an adjunct to his body building. Social activities consisted in part of frequent dating and socializing with friends. Possession of weapons was observed during this period, to include carrying a knife on his person, keeping a samurai sword behind his truck seat, and ownership of lethal weapons, including an assortment of knives, "numchuks," "stars," and spears.

Violent or potentially violent activities toward self or others need to be examined as part of the accused's behavioral reaction to stress and placed within an historical perspective. It is important to note that violence in recent times represents a continual pattern, to include previous violence (1) as a victim of child abuse, (2) frequent fighting with peers (e.g., see school records), (3) animal cruelty, (4) a suicide attempt by drug overdose (1982), (5) physical assaults on his wife, Tamara Barnes, especially from 1981 to 1983. Victim assistance program files indicate kicking his wife's back, head, and shoulders with threats to kill her (March 2, 1984). Later, his wife was punched in the face and head, resulting in black, swollen eyes, lumps on her head, red marks and bruises by her temple, and severe pains in her head (July 3, 1984). During a conjoint counseling session, the accused threatened to hit her and police were called by the therapist (August 2, 1984). A temporary restraining order was obtained for the period from August 12, 1984, to February 10, 1985.

Violence toward others since 1983 is presented below:

Date	Event	Source
May 3, 1983	Spouse abuse with threats to kill	Victim assistance Program and family court records
June 8, 1983	Spouse abuse	Victim assistance Program and family court records
June 13, 1983	Spouse abuse	Victim assistance Program and family court records
May to June 1986	Threats to kill victim and self if victim tried to leave him	Victim
May to June 1986	Told acquaintance several times that if the victim left him, he would kill her	Witness
June 8, 1986	Multiple strikes with fists to victim's face/head	Temporary restraining order (TRO), victim, Honolulu Police Department (HPD) report
June 12, 1986	Kidnapping, assault with a weapon (knife) and attempt to do bodily harm complaints; grabbed victim by her hair, put knife to her throat in presence of coworkers, dragged victim into vehicle and left	HPD report
June 12, 1986	Assault on pregnant wife	Witness, wife, HPD report
June 27, 1986	Grabbed, yanked by hair, dragged, threw, and choked victim	TRO, victim
June 28, 1986	Grabbed, punched on head four or five times, restrained victim's head with foot	TRO, victim
June 29, 1986	Grabbed and swung victim by hair; placed loaded .45 caliber pistol to victim's head; later threatened to kill self	TRO, victim
July 18, 1986	Took victim to cane field, put knife to her throat, threatened to cut her throat if they did not have sex; victim complied; last contact with accused prior to the stabbing	Victim
July 21, 1986	Stabbing of the victim (instant offenses)	Witnesses

(b) Previous to the alleged stabbing: The week before.
In general, data suggest a period of high cumulative stress on Mr Barnes' part, to include (1) a disrupted relationship with the victim. Mr Barnes and Carol Gordon were living in separate quarters at this time; (2) the accused was sleeping in this truck and the victim was staying at a friend's apartment; (3) the defendant was not working; (4) he was in poor financial shape; (5) his pickup truck was in danger of being repossessed for nonpayment; and

(6) attempts on his part to reconcile with his wife were fruitless. Retrospective self-reported depression and hopelessness were evident. Self-regulation during this period included the ability to drive his vehicle, socialize with acquaintances, and go to recreational spots during the evening, engaging in a wide variety of lounge-appropriate behavior. The accused was aware of and was due to appear in court in connection with a temporary restraining order the victim had filed in an attempt to keep him away from her. A previous arrest for failure to appear at a TRO hearing should be noted.

(c) Previous to the alleged offenses: Before and after arrival at the crime scene.

For some hours prior to arrival at the Seaview Lounge, the accused allegedly consumed a large amount of hard liquor at various places with a friend or relative. Between 1:00 and 1:30 a.m. on August 29, 1986, he entered the bar with this individual and proceeded to the victim's table, where she was seated with three acquaintances. The accused introduced his companion as his brother and asked the victim if he could have his pet dog, a pit bull, back. He was polite, with no unusual behavior noted. The victim, allegedly fearing for her life, went to the lounge manager and told him of her fear. The manager then escorted the accused to the front entrance of the lounge to talk to him. At that point, the accused was observed to show signs of growing agitation and anger. He went to the bar counter area after the 5- to 10-min talk and had a beer with his "brother." He was observed to be staring at the table where the victim was seated, in what appeared to be an angry fashion, muscles tensed, eyes wide open, and head nodding up and down. The witnesses at the table commented that it was their belief that violence was imminent, but that they believed it would occur outside the bar. The victim left her table to prepare for her dance, stopped by the jukebox to play some songs, and proceeded back to her table. Upon the victim reaching her table, the accused moved toward her.

The accused's reported emotions during the portion of this time period when he was allegedly drinking with his companion were primarily depression and hopelessness. He reported that he did not mention his upset to his companion. Significant emotion, apparently anger, occurred (1) when he was talked to outside the lounge by the manager, and (2) when he was sitting at the bar subsequent to his return. Self-regulation shown during this period included: (1) gross motor, fine motor, and recall abilities in order to engage in man–machine interface, (2) ability to locate the bar, ambulate to the interior, scan the environment, spot the victim, leave the bar upon the manager's request, return to the bar, locate his acquaintance, go to him, and later walk to the victim, (3) verbal behaviors and social interactive skills as evidenced by the introduction of his "brother" and other prosocial behavior at that time, (4) ability to conceal the knife, (5) immediate, short-term, and long-term auditory and visual memory, which are necessary for successful execution, of the above behaviors. Immediate auditory recall, for example, is required when engaging in verbal conversation, as shown when he first entered the lounge. Long-term recall, as another example, is tapped when one remembers objects another party has in their possession, (6) the ability to delay the knife attack, if in fact there was such an intent when he was at the bar or at some prior time.

(d) During the instant offenses.

At approximately 2 a.m. on August 29, 1986, the accused approached the victim from his position at the bar, stating, "Get over here," or words to that effect. At that point, the victim had arrived at the table and lifted her glass about half way to her mouth. The accused then grabbed the victim by her hair with his left hand and pulled out a double-edged knife from his clothing with his right hand, blade upright (by thumb). He proceeded to stab her multiple times while dragging her toward the bar entrance. The victim collapsed and essentially lost recall after the assault commenced but witnesses recall her screaming, "No, no, no, don't do this," or words to that effect. The initial thrusts appeared to be in the upper back and neck areas. The final stab in the throat resulted in the carotid artery and jugular vein trauma. The victim was released at a point not far from the entrance and the accused ran off.

Emotion during the instant offenses appeared to be significant for all the preceding reasons regarding cumulative stress. Other events signifying some emotion concern (1) the perseverative nature of the stabbing, (2) no material gain was realized from the victim (e.g., money and possessions), and (3) it was unlikely that the accused could get away with the crime as it was perpetrated in the presence of 30 to 40 people.

Self-regulation shown during this period include: (1) the ability to verbalize, command, and follow through on statements, (2) simultaneous use of motor behaviors represented by holding, stabbing, and dragging the victim at the same time, all combined with (3) goal-direction, as represented by dragging the victim toward the door, irrespective of what he would do with her once there, (4) ability to multiply stab a relatively circumscribed section of the body, (5) specific focus of attack to a vital area, and (6) attempts to escape, as represented by running off, implying awareness of wrongdoing.

(e) After the alleged crimes until hospitalization.

Subsequent to releasing the victim, the accused ran outside the lounge (2:00 to 2:07 a.m.), then toward the mountain across Kapiolani Boulevard, then proceeded in the direction of Hawaii Community College (HCC). Bar patrons were in pursuit in both a vehicle and on foot. He climbed a 6-foot fence at the boundary of HCC and went into a side alley, attempting to conceal himself behind a vehicle. Police arrived shortly afterward and ordered him to come out with raised hands (2:09 a.m.). The accused emerged with his hands above his head, but then fell forward, saying, "Just let me die, I want to die," or words to that effect). While lying face down, the accused stated several times, "I love her," or words to that effect, 2:11 a.m.). He mentioned several times a "Jim Kalanaki" (phonetic). The police noticed lacerations on both of the accused's wrists. The knife was found several feet from his original hiding spot. He became semiconscious and was rendered first aid. He was arrested for attempted murder (2:12 a.m.) and shortly after was transported to the hospital (2:27 a.m.) At the hospital, he became less stuporous and offered that "They jumped my brother," or words to that effect. His wife, Tamara Barnes, came to the hospital and the accused told her that he loved the victim. He also stated that he attempted suicide because the children were out of the house and that he believed Mrs Barnes was not planning to reconcile with him (3:00 to 3:20 a.m.). The accused then went to sleep. He entered surgery a short time later for deep cuts to both wrists (4:55 a.m.) and was out later in the morning (6:35 a.m.). Later, he admitted to physically abusing the victim over the previous several weeks (see hospital consultation record). The next day, he was formally charged with attempted murder and assault in the first degree, with the accused declining to make a statement at that time.

Emotional distress during this period appeared to be the highest of all the time blocks. Panic, fear, and self-blame appear to be the type of emotion rather than the anger of the earlier stage. High emotion during this period is manifested by (1) running away from the bar, and under circumstances likely to result in apprehension, (2) attempting to escape in a disadvantaged manner when other means were available (e.g., he ran past his truck parked on the opposite side of the street; his companion was later seen by the truck with the driver's door open, (3) attempting to kill himself in what appears to be a genuine effort at suicide, (4) spontaneous and repetitious statements in regard to the victim and others, and (5) other behaviors.

Self-regulation during this period appeared to be at the lowest. Yet, running away and hiding behind the vehicle in the alley can be construed as a continuing awareness that he had done wrong, in addition to attempting to escape detection. He had the ability to scale a tall fence, to partially comply with police instructions, and to verbalize. The ability to prevaricate was intact, as evidenced by his false statement that his brother had been "jumped." Recent and remote memory was intact, as shown by a variety of behaviors and his statements to his wife.

(f) After initial medical treatment to the present.

The accused was transferred from the hospital to pretrial detainment at HCCC. Multiple psychiatric diagnoses during the hospitalization were given, to include DSM III adjustment reaction and borderline personality disorder. The suicide attempt was seen as genuine, but there were many apparent attempts to manipulate the social environment through the use of further suicide threats (see hospital records). Although the defendant denied recall of the instant offenses, he was repeatedly expressing remorse for his deeds. At other times, he stated that the victim laughed at him just prior to the attack. Self-regulation increased with hospitalization. Attempts to control the judicial process and the victim's behavior was shown by (1) multiple contacts by a family member to the victim in attempts to get her drop the charges against the accused; (2) a series of letters by the accused with the theme that the victim must share the blame due to her presumed traits of psychological insecurity, distrust, suspiciousness, short-temperedness, greed for money, and playing "mind games" with him (see letters in *Forensic Database*). He stated that he physically abused her when she made him tense, claimed no insight for the alleged offenses, and asked God to forgive both of them. He affirmed his love for the victim many times. He shared suicide ideation with the victim: "I mite as well hang myself with a strip of my sheet;" "[I'm] depressed;" "my body wants to die," "I honestly don't know what I mite [sic] do to myself right now." He later told the victim that he hopes she would leave for Alaska because he might then be able to rest his mind; (3) several pictures drawn by the accused, showing what appeared to be the accused with a large knife cutting through the air, labeled "The Edge," and signed by the accused. Other aggressive drawings were sent to the victim, including one labeled, "Gardenia Gardens Lounge," the scene of a previous knife wielding, assault, and dragging incident by the accused.

On _____, Judge James Meyer filed a report indicating that the accused had violated his TRO by contacting the victim through letters and his sister, Trudy King (HPD report # _____).

On _____, the accused complained of his transfer to a dormitory and wrote, "Been experiencing harassment because I am gay."

On _____, the accused admitted striking another inmate in the face with his fist. Mr Barnes stated that his wife was struck by a pimp in Waikiki and that he believed the victim-inmate was a pimp and therefore decided to take it out on him. The victim-inmate was transferred out of the HCCC dormitory and the accused was adjudged to have suffered an emotional break. He was placed on a suicide watch by HCCC officials.

On _____, the victim made a complaint to the HPD indicating that the accused was harassing her by issuing death threats to her and her roommate (HPD report #_____).

Summary of Self-Regulatory Behaviors: Characteristics or behaviors of the accused that indicate both knowledge of wrongdoing and self-regulation for the time of the alleged offenses, when taken in their entirety, are as follows:

1. As a predisposing variable relevant to basal violence, a significant violence history extended over years characterized by choice behaviors and reinforcing outcomes
2. As a predisposing variable relevant to intentional behaviors, multiple statements to significant others that he would kill the victim if she attempted to dissolve the relationship
3. As a predisposing variable relevant to opportunity factors, previous instances where the victim was assaulted by the accused where a knife was used as a threat stimulus
4. As a predisposing variable relevant to triggering stimuli and awareness of vulnerability, breakup in the central love relationship with both his wife and the victim
5. No indication of impaired intelligence or a major psychiatric disorder; examination after the instant offenses revealed logical thought processes, no delusions or hallucinations, and present suicidal ideation; history and recent diagnoses suggest a long-standing personality disorder
6. Suggestions that the accused may have prepared for or at least had foreknowledge of the alleged crimes
7. Intact orientation, scanning, and sensory skills during the crime time sequence
8. Intact memory skills for both recent and long-term events
9. Intact interpersonal skills before the attack
10. Ability to delay the attack for a significant period of time
11. The focus of the attempted homicide should be considered specific
12. At least three sets of motor behaviors were exhibited simultaneously during the attack
13. Knowledge of wrongdoing and attempting to escape from the crime scene
14. Prevarication subsequent to arrest in regard to crime events

Conclusions

1. The database is sufficient to draw some relevant conclusions with a reasonable degree of psychological certainty. Available data from other examiners were considered, but all conclusions rendered were derived independently of other psychological/medical examiners who are involved in this case.
2. Database sources were assessed for suggestions of deliberate and nondeliberate distortion. Conclusions rendered are considered an accurate representation of alleged crime events, taking into account report and witness limitations and competencies, the possible psychological disorders of the victim, biases of input sources, and other factors.

The victim emerged as a credible source of information, taking all factors into account. Deliberate distortion in terms of fabrication or lying was not suggested. Nondeliberate distortion created by the trauma of crime events and a subsequent PTSD was taken into consideration by comparison to both cross-validating information and to the victim's own input over time and across many test procedures.

The perpetrator's credibility for reporting some crime events could not be assessed as some data were not available for cross-validation. Distortion in regard to the manner in which the alleged crime events occurred is suggested by the accused's postarrest statements.

Distortion in regard to evaluation behavior, particularly faking bad (malingering), was
suggested by test procedures administered by evaluators in this case.

3. Level of emotion experienced by the accused appeared different as a function of temporal crime sequence. Mild emotion is suggested for the time he entered the crime
   scene until just before the stabbing. Behavioral self-regulation during this period
   was high and was characterized by (1) an ability to scan and orient himself to the
   crime scene, (2) an ability to conceal his knife, (3) normal speech patterns, (4) normal
   motor and other physical behaviors, (5) an ability to initiate and interact socially in
   an appropriate fashion, (6) an ability to delay the attack for a significant time span,
   and (7) adequate short- and long-term memory skills that were required to successfully execute the above.

Moderate emotion was suggested for the duration of the attack as demonstrated by
(1) demanding in an angry tone of voice that the victim come to him, (2) the potentially
lethal attack itself, and it occurring in the presence of others, and (3) the perseverative
nature of the multiple knife thrusts. Behavioral self-regulation during this period included
the (1) ability to verbalize, (2) the simultaneous multiplicity of motor behaviors shown
(grabbing and holding, dragging, and stabbing), (3) the goal-direction of the dragging,
(4) the near-lethal knife thrust in the front part of the victim's neck as a final killing thrust,
and (5) the decision to let the victim go and run from the crime scene.

Considerable to substantial emotion was suggested from the point of releasing the victim until his attempted suicide and was demonstrated by panic, escape, and self-destructive
behavior. Behavioral self-regulation during this period was lowest and included running
and climbing behaviors, an unsuccessful attempt to conceal himself, and partial compliance with police instructions.

In general, extreme emotion was not suggested for the time of the alleged offenses, as
shown by a substantial degree of self-control and self-regulation during and especially before
the attack. Further, momentary anger and long-standing resentment toward the victim,
shown by previous attacks and other relevant behaviors toward her, characterized his behaviors up to the final near-fatal knife thrust. Panic and self-destructive feelings characterized
his considerable to substantial level of emotion from the time he released the victim until his
arrest. Overall, data suggest that the accused could have refrained from the stabbing if he had
so chosen and that the highest level of emotion occurred subsequent to the attack.

4. At the conclusion of the multiple evaluations, a Tarasoff warning was issued to the
   victim in this case. This was based on (a) the violence history of the accused in general, (b) the preoccupation with the possession of multiple weapons, particularly
   lethal weapons, (c) preinstant offense violence toward women and the victim in particular, (d) the apparent homicidal intent of the attack in the instant case involving
   the use of a deadly weapon resulting in near-fatal injuries, and (e) postarrest intrusive
   and threatening behaviors toward the victim.

Sincerely,
CC: Presiding Judge
Defense Attorney
Prosecuting Attorney

Psychological Evaluation Involving Parents with Brain Impairment from Chapter 4 (Condie and Condie)

In re C&P Docket No. XXXX

Name	:	John Doe
Date of birth	:	Month XX, 19XX
Evaluation date	:	Month XX, 20XX
Examiner	:	Lois Oberlander Condie, Ph.D., ABPP

Reason for Evaluation

John Doe is a 4X-year-old man, referred for an evaluation to gather data relevant to the impact, if any, of chronic alcohol dependence on his neurobehavioral functioning and his parenting abilities. After the evaluation was delayed because of Mr. Doe's need for medical attention, a second question was added relevant to the impact of his recent stroke. The evaluation was requested in the context of an upcoming Care and Protection hearing. The state has petitioned for termination of parental rights.

Structure of the Evaluation

Prior to the evaluation, I informed Mr. Doe and all parties whom I interviewed that I was a psychologist retained by the court, by agreement of all parties to the case, to gather information relevant to Mr. Doe's neurobehavioral functioning and its relationship, if any, to his parenting abilities and his risk of harm to his children. I informed them that the evaluation was requested as a supplement to a previous evaluation by another psychologist concerning Mr. Doe's sexual offending risk, parenting abilities, and risk of harm to his children. I informed them that the content of the interview, assessment results, and my observations would not be confidential and would be shared with the court in an evaluation report. I informed them that the evaluation report would be made available to all attorneys who represented parties to the case. I informed Mr. Doe that the report contents would be made available to him through his attorney. I informed him that I might be asked to testify at his hearing as to the report contents. Because Mr. Doe's cognitive integrity was in question, consent for the evaluation was granted after a brief pretrial hearing on substituted judgment. At the hearing, his attorney stipulated to the recommendation of a special purpose guardian *ad litem* to proceed with the evaluation. Mr. Doe's attorney and the Court accepted the substituted judgment.

Assessment Methods

1. Interviews of Mr. Doe on <date>, <date>, <date>, and <date>
2. Observation of two visitation sessions on <date> and <date>
3. Mini Mental Status Examination
4. Mattis Dementia Rating Scale
5. Wechsler Adult Intelligence Scale, Third Edition (WAIS-III)
6. Wechsler Memory Scale, Third Edition (WMS-III)
7. Delis–Kaplan Executive Function System
8. Boston Diagnostic Aphasia Examination
9. Rey–Osterreith Complex Figure
10. Finger Tapping Test

Sources of Information

1. Report of Dr. Other-Evaluator, dated <date>
2. Educational records, Cityville Public School District
3. Educational assessment report dated <date> and cognitive assessment report dated <date>, by Jane School, M.Ed., Cityville Public School District
4. Educational records, Cityville Community College
5. Child protective service records
6. Consultation with Jane Casework, LICSW, child protective service agency
7. Treatment records, Agency Substance Abuse Rehabilitation Center
8. Telephone consultation with John Director, M.A., clinical director, Agency Substance Abuse Rehabilitation Center
9. Outpatient substance abuse treatment records from John Substance, M.A.
10. Telephone consultation with John Substance, M.A., outpatient substance abuse treatment provider
11. Outpatient sexual offending treatment records from John Prevention, Ph.D.
12. Telephone consultation with John Prevention, Ph.D., outpatient sexual offender group treatment provider
13. Treatment and discharge summary dated <date>, by Jane Neurology, M.D., Department of Neurology, Major Hospital
14. Rehabilitation center records (stroke rehabilitation)
15. Telephone consultation with Jane Neurology, M.D.
16. Interview of Mr. John Neighbor, friend of Mr. Doe
17. Interview of Mr. John Supervisor, former work supervisor of Mr. Doe

Relevant History

Historical data relevant to Mr. Doe's upbringing, relationship with Ms. Smith (children's mother), parenting skills, and history of alleged sex offending and substance abuse are found in the report of Dr. Other-Evaluator and in the child protective service records. The report of Dr. Other-Evaluator and the child protective service records have been made available to all parties to the case, and all parties stipulated to the information contained in the history section of Dr. Other-Evaluator's report, which was introduced into evidence. Both parties stipulated to Dr. Other-Evaluator's diagnosis of alcohol dependence. Mr. Doe's history is not repeated here, except to highlight factors of relevance to the integrity of his brain functioning, and to add information of relevance.

According to records, Mr. John Doe was investigated by the state child protective services agency because of allegations that he digitally fondled his 5- and 7-year-old daughters. The allegations were supported and he was referred for a sex offender evaluation and parenting assessment. He participated in the evaluation as a condition of pretrial probation for a parallel criminal charge. He confessed to the alleged conduct in the context of pretrial negotiations with the Office of the State Attorney, in the context of his sex offender evaluation, and later in treatment. In the evaluation report, Dr. Other-Evaluator opined that Mr. Doe was at moderate-to-high risk of reoffending. Mr. Doe agreed to move out of his home and was granted supervised visitation after the children's mother initially cooperated with the child protective services agency, allowing Mr. Doe to see the children only under supervised conditions specified by the agency. Mr. Doe was found to be in need of sex offender treatment and was diagnosed with alcohol dependence. He agreed to seek treatment as a condition of pretrial probation for his pending criminal matter. He entered and completed a 3-month residential substance abuse rehabilitation program. He then sought outpatient group sex offender treatment and group substance abuse relapse prevention treatment, two conditions of his child protective services intervention plan. He completed a 3-month cycle of treatment in both groups and his treatment providers wrote treatment summaries highlighting his progress, but expressing concern about possible mental confusion that was apparent in later sessions of his treatment.

Records indicated that in the 11th week of outpatient group treatment, providers became concerned about Mr. Doe's mental confusion. After my initial meeting with him, he was referred to a neurologist for an emergency appointment. He was briefly hospitalized after a determination that he had suffered a cerebrovascular accident in the middle cerebral artery that damaged the left anterior temporal and parietal lobes. He was transferred to a stroke rehabilitation facility for cognitive rehabilitation, speech and language therapy, and physical and occupational therapies. He was discharged to his home after 3 weeks, with residual motor and language impairment. Notes from the rehabilitation agency indicated that Mr. Doe told them about his dating partner who would check on him at least weekly. Mr. Doe later revealed that he misled the rehabilitation staff members because he was growing impatient for discharge. The discharge plan included weekly monitoring, follow-up appointments with his neurologist, and the use of his dating partner to help him to communicate when needed. Mr. Doe's driver's license had been revoked because of driving under the influence, but there was a note in the rehabilitation records that he could not drive for medical reasons until he was able to pass a reaction time and driving assessment in the rehabilitation agency's outpatient department. There was a note in the discharge summary that he would rely on his dating partner for transportation or for finding public transportation routes for appointments and shopping needs.

On the basis of child protection services agency records, during the interim, the children were removed from their mother's care on a supported neglect petition because she began cohabiting with a man who had a previous conviction of distributing child pornography. Her relationship with the man began prior to Mr. Doe's stroke, and there was verification that Mr. Doe was acquainted with the man and did not report his presence at home or the man's history of child pornography. The children's mother relocated shortly after the child protective services agency learned of her cohabiting relationship with the man. Her whereabouts were unknown for the remaining duration of Mr. Doe's involvement with the care and protection system. Because the children's mother could not be located, the agency delayed filing a termination of parental rights petition in favor of long-term foster placement and supervised paternal visitation. During paternal visitation, workers observed that Mr. Doe sometimes seemed confused. There was a report that he had showered with his younger daughter during an extended visit on <date> that was monitored by an unauthorized supervisor. The child protection agency lawyers eventually separated the state petitions against the parents and filed a separate petition for termination of the father's parental rights.

Records and Collateral Contacts

Educational records from the Cityville Public School District indicated that Mr. Doe was granted a high school diploma. His school transcript indicated he earned Bs, Cs, and Ds, with a 2.1 grade point average, or a "C average." He earned Bs in woodworking class, electrical repair, and business math. He earned Ds in history and social studies.

An educational assessment was completed when Mr. Doe attended 10th grade because of concern about his behavior. He was caught drinking alcohol on school grounds and disrupted class fairly frequently. His standard scores on an early version of the Woodcock–Johnson for measures of reading fundamentals, reading comprehension, oral expression, listening skills, mathematical calculations, and mathematical reasoning were within expectations, with standard scores ranging from 90 to 107 (mean of 100, standard deviation of 15). His reading fluency (93) and writing fluency (96) were within expectations, but math fluency (84) was below expectations. He was given in-class accommodations in the form of extra time for math assignments and lengthy assignments. He was placed on a behavior plan for classroom conduct. He was sanctioned with four 3-day in-school suspensions because of drinking on school grounds, returning from lunch appearing intoxicated, tipping over a locker during "boisterous play," and arriving at woodworking class smelling of alcohol.

Mr. Doe also was given a cognitive assessment in 10th grade. Results of the Wechsler Intelligence Scale for Children, Revised, indicated his overall intellect was within expectations, as were his verbal and nonverbal information-processing abilities. All subscale scores were within normal limits, according to the report, at a score of 8 or greater. His IQ scores were within expectations (mean of 100, standard deviation of 15). His full-scale IQ was 99, verbal IQ was 104, and performance IQ was 95.

Records from Cityville Community College confirmed that Mr. Doe successfully completed a 1-year program in carpentry and plumbing. He earned passing grades and received a certificate of completion.

Child Protection Services Agency Records

Mr. Doe's history of involvement with the child protection system is not repeated here except to highlight that he had no history of neurological care that predated his stroke. At the age of 23, he was involved in a physical fight outside a bar and was seen afterward in the emergency room for a sprained wrist. He did not suffer loss of consciousness, and no neurological services were recommended beyond a cursory examination. At the age of 31, he was charged with driving under the influence (of alcohol) after driving his car into a telephone pole. He was seat belted and the impact was insufficient to set off his air bags. He did not sustain injury to his head but he had neck pain for several days afterward. At age 37, he was charged again with driving under the influence (of alcohol) after being stopped for exceeding the speed limit. He had three charges of public drunkenness in his criminal records, one of which was related to the physical fight described above. The other charges resulted from loud verbal exchanges on the street in the nighttime.

The child protection service system records contained documentation of four incidents in which police officers were called to the residence because Mr. Doe was loud and intoxicated. He was allowed to remain at home at the time of the first incident, but he was removed by the police officers for the remaining three incidents. On the third occasion, he was taken to the emergency room for medical care secondary to intoxication that was described as reaching a "dangerous level." This entry appeared in the child protection service system records, but there was no original source documentation from emergency room records. Mr. Doe said in one of the interviews that he recalled the emergency room visit. He said he was told by the emergency room physician that he was "dangerously drunk" and if he did not stop drinking he "could die." When asked whether he recalled the incident clearly, in light of the fact that he was intoxicated, he said he recalled it vaguely, but his former partner reminded him of it repeatedly afterward. He said, "I took her word for it and I remembered it a little."

Child protective services substance abuse screening records indicated Mr. Doe had 7 random screens out of 20 in the past few months that were positive for alcohol. Mr. Doe said he thought some of the screens were inaccurate because, "I was eating food that might have been cooked with wine or something."

Ms. Jane Caseworker, LICSW, Child Protection Services Agency

Ms. Casework reported that she was visitation supervisor for the tenure of Mr. Doe's visitation with his children, except for some of his first 13 visits that were supervised by the children's mother. Ms. Caseworker said that for the first 3 months of his visitation, he attended all visitation appointments in his wife's apartment, arriving on time, following the rules of visitation, and ending visits appropriately. He sometimes had difficulty with parental maturity. For example, he had difficulty setting limits on behavior that was considered "silly" and "chaotic." He tended to "escalate" those interactions. He did not engage in touching of his daughters that was considered sexual or otherwise inappropriate. His older daughter shied away from him during the first four visits, preferring to retreat rather than greeting him. She gradually warmed up to the visits and expressed happiness to see him. She continued to "cringe" if he sat too close to her. During one visit, she angrily took a toy female doll and "pummeled" him with it, saying, "I don't want a daddy, no daddy." Mr. Doe did not set limits on the behavior, nor did he inquire into his daughter's reaction to him. Instead, "he laughed out loud and seemed to encourage it."

Ms. Caseworker reported that after 3 months, visitation was moved to a visitation center. Mr. Doe sometimes arrived up to an hour and a half late. The visitation sessions took place for 2 h, and his daughters became upset at his lateness. Mr. Doe began to "miss a session here and there." After another 2 months, his tardiness and absence increased in frequency. Ms. Caseworker said that during the month of <month>, he did not keep any of his visitation appointments. Ms. Caseworker said Mr. Doe seemed increasingly disorganized in his visitation sessions. He sometimes had difficulty listening to his children because "his mind was somewhere else." During one session, he arrived disheveled with the smell of alcohol on his breath. He was asked to go to the XXX clinic for a drug/alcohol screen as per his service plan. He said he would go to the XXX clinic immediately, which was within walking distance, but records from the clinic indicated he did not present himself for an appointment on that day. He reported to the clinic 3 days later, and his screen was negative for all substances. Mr. Doe said he attempted to obtain a screen on the day in question but he was turned away. Records from the clinic indicated it was a normal day of operation and no patients were turned away.

Ms. Caseworker said during one of Mr. Doe's visitation sessions in the month of <month> that he made inappropriate comments to his older daughter. He said she was "toying with him" and she "wanted something from him." He made a gesture toward his penis while making the statement. The session was terminated immediately, and Mr. Doe protested that he was gesturing toward some toys in his lap. Two weeks later, he told his older daughter she was "looking for more" and he squeezed her buttocks. The session was terminated, and Mr. Doe protested that his behavior was accidental and he was helping his daughter search for toys on the floor. The child protection agency petitioned for reduced visitation. The judge allowed a temporary 1-month termination of visitation, and visitation was reduced from once weekly to once semiweekly.

Ms. Caseworker said on <date> that there was noticeable deterioration in Mr. Doe's verbal comprehension and verbal expression. His speech was slurred, but it was "different from when he was drunk." He seemed to have difficulty finding the words that he needed. He referred to the door to the visitation room as a window, and he referred to the toy dollhouse as a schoolhouse. He "stuttered and stammered." When his children addressed him, he seemed to struggle to make conversation. He "sat staring at nothing." When his daughter spilled juice on a toy sink, he said, "clean up a stove, a slove, a stove." He added, "get a blanket" while gesturing to a rack of paper towels.

After Mr. Doe received rehabilitation for his stroke, visitation resumed and Mr. Doe's attendance remained variable due to "disorganization." The child protective service agency began providing him with a reminder call and a weekly taxi voucher for visitation. His attendance improved and the judge reinstated weekly visitation. The venue was changed to Mr. Doe's home rather than the department or the visitation center. Visitation remained supervised. Ms. Caseworker said Mr. Doe's communication with his children reportedly improved, but "It never returned to normal." He needed reminders to start a conversation with them. He misunderstood what they said to him. When they asked him questions, he sometimes "seemed to make things up because he couldn't remember." He "used the wrong words," he spoke in shorter sentences, and he sometimes gave a confused response to his children. His conversational flow was "stilted and halted." He "yelled at small things that would have made him laugh before." Ms. Caseworker said she had never known him to yell at the children prior to the stroke, except when he was intoxicated. She added, "He seemed irritable and sad." She said his daughter, who was practicing riddles in school, told him her riddles, but he did not seem to understand them or find them funny. Ms. Caseworker said Mr. Doe had a flat emotional reaction to the news that one of his children had an ear infection that included vomiting and a 24-h fever. He later told a story about his daughter's illness that bore little relationship to the original information that Ms. Caseworker provided to him.

Ms. Caseworker said the judge disallowed any further home visits after Mr. Doe showered with his older daughter during a home visit with an unauthorized supervisor.

A special visit had been allowed for 4 h rather than the usual 2 h to accommodate a special visit from an extended relative. It turned out that the extended relative was not a family member. The person arrived at Mr. Doe's residence and stayed for only 15 min until the caseworker departed the resident, and then Mr. Doe remained with his children under the supervision of his half-brother rather than the court-approved supervisor. The court-approved supervisor, a friend of the family who had been vetted by the child protective services agency, arrived before the caseworker vacated the premises. She had supervised other visits without incident. The children reported that she left shortly after the caseworker departed and she did not return to the premises until minutes before the caseworker arrived to collect the children. The children said she arrived out of breath and pleaded with the children to remain silent about her absence because "uncle was there to watch you." The supervisor, when interviewed about her absence, said she "ran out for a quick coffee" and was "gone only 5 min." The caseworker retraced the woman's steps and reported to the case manager that even if the visitation supervisor did only leave for coffee, the coffee shop trip would have taken 20 min by car and longer by foot. The visitation supervisor was released.

Substance Abuse Rehabilitation Center Records

Mr. Doe was admitted for 3 months to the substance abuse rehabilitation center. He had good attendance at relapse prevention group meetings and at self-help group meetings. His attendance at family meetings was variable. He attended the first four groups, refused to attend five groups, and then attended roughly every other family meeting until his discharge. Notes from the therapist indicated that he did not see a need for family therapy because his partner left him and he had no family. Mr. Doe was nearly terminated from the center halfway through his 3-month treatment cycle because of suspicion that he somehow gained access to a flask of vodka. His alcohol screen was negative, but staff members remained suspicious that a new resident, an acquaintance of Mr. Doe, had snuck the flask in for him.

John Director, M.A., Substance Abuse Rehabilitation Center

Mr. Director reported that Mr. Doe completed a full cycle of residential substance abuse treatment. He participated in daily group Alcoholics Anonymous meetings. He spoke at speaker meetings, "candidly describing his history of substance abuse." He provided support to group members. He avoided book meetings, but he did read several chapters of one book on the life of another individual with substance abuse problems who remained "clean and sober" for 15 years. Mr. Doe completed a relapse prevention plan for alcohol, using his sessions to modify the plan so that it included a broad variety of situations that might raise his risk of drinking in the future. Although "he swore he wouldn't drink no matter what," he seemed open to advice that most people struggle to refrain from drinking and that the struggle is more challenging in situations that raise the risk of drinking. He had difficulty independently identifying situations that might raise his risk, but he was "open to suggestions." He left the agency with a completed relapse prevention plan, "committed to paper and to memory." His attendance in family therapy was variable, and he tended to talk only about his partner. When he was asked to include his children in his family therapy discussions, he said, "That goes without saying," but he continued to place emphasis on his partner. Mr. Director said, "Mr. Doe refused to examine the relationship, if any, between his sex offending and his drinking." On the day before his discharge, Mr. Doe excitedly said to another resident, "I can't wait to you know what!" while making the motion of bringing a shot glass to his mouth. When asked what he meant, he insisted, "I'm going bowling. I was just talking about bowling." When asked where the alcohol-free bowling alley was located, he said, "I'll find one."

Outpatient Substance Abuse Treatment Agency Records

Records indicated Mr. Doe kept his outpatient appointments until the month of <month>, when he missed all appointments. He resumed his good attendance for 2 weeks, but then he missed 50% of his remaining appointments across the next 2 months. There was a note in Mr. Doe's records that said he attempted to initiate a verbal fight in the parking lot with another individual who sought treatment at the agency. The conflict was broken up by a staff member.

John Substance, M.A., Outpatient Substance Abuse Treatment Agency

Mr. Substance reported that Mr. Doe arrived at his first appointment promptly, carrying a self-help book about substance abuse prevention and a copy of his relapse prevention plan. Mr. Doe said he had read the entire book. Mr. Substance had read the book himself, and he could tell by Mr. Doe's description of the book's contents that Mr. Doe had not read the book. Mr. Substance suggested that they reread the book together, discussing one chapter per week. He "took it as an opportunity to get him interested in the book." On the basis of Mr. Doe's subsequent description of the book's contents, Mr. Substance estimated that he read the first three chapters of the eight-chapter book.

Mr. Substance said Mr. Doe's initial appointment attendance was consistent and his participation was "variable, but mostly good." Mr. Doe accepted advice about periodic updates of his relapse prevention plan, but he rarely initiated updates independently. He seemed "aware of his risk after it was pointed out," but "he had trouble identifying risk factors on his own." The outpatient agency periodically requested random alcohol screens from Mr. Doe. As described above, 7 out of 20 screens were positive. Mr. Substance pointed out that the screens were not truly random because they always took place on dates of Mr. Doe's appointments. He said during one appointment that there was concern that Mr. Doe came with an already prepared sample, but it was not possible to confirm the suspicion due to a break in protocol related to insufficient staffing on that particular day. All other screens were thought to be the product of reliable samples.

Mr. Substance said that after the stroke and cognitive rehabilitation, Mr. Doe signed up for a new 3-month cycle of weekly appointments. It was necessary to carefully tutor him to help him keep his relapse prevention plan updated. He sometimes quickly became angry in response to feedback from Mr. Substance that previously would have led to discussions rather than anger. Mr. Doe sometimes seemed indifferent. Mr. Substance and his colleagues began to provide services at a level reserved for patients with learning and memory weaknesses. They simplified questions, comments, and expectations. They provided step-by-step tutoring rather than expecting Mr. Doe to complete treatment assignments independently between sessions. Mr. Doe responded somewhat better to this approach. They altered their expectations that Mr. Doe would complete self-help reading assignments between sessions. They stopped asking for weekly updates of Mr. Doe's participation and progress in Alcoholics Anonymous meetings because they were not confident that he was sufficiently organized to attend or participate in the meetings. Mr. Substance said that the level of detail that Mr. Doe provided about the content of the meetings was significantly reduced. Mr. Doe sometimes was off-topic during relapse prevention and self-help meetings. On two occasions, he talked about his sexual interest in children. Mr. Substance said this was not something Mr. Doe did prior to his stroke.

Sexual Offender Treatment Agency Records

A complete review of the relevant records is found in the report of Dr. Other-Evaluator.

John Prevention, Ph.D., Sexual Offender Treatment Agency

Dr. Prevention's early sessions with Mr. Doe are summarized in the report of Dr. Other-Evaluator. They are not repeated here except to note that Mr. Doe's early treatment attendance and participation were good, with the exception of the month of <month> when his attendance also was poor at the substance abuse treatment agency and in his visitation sessions with his children. Dr. Prevention reported that Mr. Doe's treatment attendance was not optimal afterward. He missed an average of one group session per month. When he was in attendance, he continued to participate at an expected level, but there was ongoing concern about his tendency to blame his daughters for his sexual abuse of them.

After his stroke and cognitive rehabilitation, Mr. Doe was transferred to a group for men with limitations in their capacity for verbal expression. The group was more structured, and the group leader was more directive. Dr. Prevention said Mr. Doe sometimes made little sense when speaking to the group. Other times, he was able to verbally participate at an expected level. He said Mr. Doe's comprehension of what others said was variable and he sometimes made responses that were *non sequiturs* or that quickly moved the group off-topic. Although he made sexually inappropriate statements prior to his stroke, his poststroke statements about his daughters were "graphic." Dr. Prevention said Mr. Doe seemed to realize that his graphic statements would not serve him well in court, but he nonetheless seemed to have difficulty refraining from the statements. He made impulsive statements on other topics. For example, he yelled at the receptionist from the group room to shred his file and release him from his misery. Mr. Doe spent the rest of the group session opening the door imploring the receptionist to join him for dinner and a week-long sleepover. Dr. Prevention said the frequency of impulsive statements by Mr. Doe was much greater after the stroke than before the stroke.

Major Hospital Records

Records from Major Hospital indicated Mr. Doe suffered a cerebrovascular accident that damaged the left anterior temporal and parietal lobes. After a brief inpatient stay, he was discharged to the rehabilitation center for cognitive rehabilitation, speech and language therapy, and physical and occupational therapies.

Rehabilitation Center Records

Rehabilitation center records confirmed that Mr. Doe was admitted to the center for 3 weeks. He was then followed up in the outpatient department. During his rehabilitation, he gradually regained his ability to speak, his speech comprehension improved gradually, and he gradually regained functional motor skills such as ambulation, toileting, showering, toothbrushing, and using a writing instrument. He is right-hand dominant, and there was some discussion of whether to teach him compensatory strategies with the left hand. As his construction and handwriting skills improved, therapy focused on using the left hand for assistance of the right hand as needed. The physical therapist reported that he regained ambulation skills with a walker, but he no longer had equipment needs. She noted Mr. Doe had some mild balance problems because of residual right foot drag. She recommended outpatient therapy to help him reduce his foot drag. The occupational therapist cautioned that his handwriting speed and accuracy were not at premorbid levels but that they were functional. She recommended monitoring of him every quarter after discharge, along with a home program of fine motor exercises.

The speech and language pathologist noted significant concern about Mr. Doe's recovery of language comprehension and expression. She noted that he had word-finding problems, he had difficulty achieving premorbid levels of morphology and semantics, he engaged in confabulation when providing narratives due to difficulty with word finding, and he had difficulty following novel instructions of more than two steps. When instructions were given for highly familiar routine tasks, he sometimes completed three and four steps. He sometimes completed instructions out of sequence, even on familiar tasks. Mr. Doe had difficulty using full sentences during conversational speech, but his conversational skills were improving. He had a relatively flat vocal prosody and halting of his speech. Speech flow and prosody improved during the course of his rehabilitation.

Jane Neurology, M.D., Department of Neurology, Major Hospital

Dr. Neurology reported that Mr. Doe kept three of his six postrehabilitation outpatient appointments. She said Mr. Doe reported no change in his mental state from his prestroke condition. Dr. Neurology questioned Mr. Doe's ability to meaningfully track his improvements. She noted that Mr. Doe's speech productivity and comprehension improved gradually, but not to the presumed baseline for a man of his age and former occupation. Mr. Doe sometimes engaged in obvious confabulation when answering questions. She described Mr. Doe as "emotionally flat." He had residual right-sided weakness that nominally affected his ambulation. There was a significant change in Mr. Doe's handwriting, and he could write legibly with much effort. Dr. Neurology said that a friend accompanied Mr. Doe to the second visit and expressed concern about the cleanliness and organization of his home. She referred Mr. Doe to the department social worker for a determination of his eligibility for in-home living support, but Mr. Doe declined the appointment.

Interview of Mr. Neighbor

Mr. Neighbor was a high school friend of Mr. Doe, and they worked together in the construction business "off and on for 10 years." Mr. Neighbor said Mr. Doe began showing signs of the effects of heavy alcohol use in high school because he sometimes did not recall what he had done the night before when drinking. He said Mr. Doe finished high school and community college. Mr. Neighbor said Mr. Doe often had "hangovers" in college and he disliked getting up for class. After Mr. Doe completed his work for his 1-year certificate, both Mr. Neighbor and Mr. Doe worked in Mr. Neighbor's uncle's business. Mr. Neighbor said Mr. Doe's work was of good quality. After about 3 years of working together, Mr. Doe began getting into verbal arguments with other workers occasionally; he sometimes arrived late, and he was almost dismissed several times for not showing up at all. He said Mr. Doe was terminated from employment after he propositioned Mr. Neighbor's aunt.

Mr. Neighbor said Mr. Doe found work at another construction business but eventually moved from job to job because of verbal altercations with other workers or supervisors. He said Mr. Doe became increasingly forgetful at work and in his social life, forgetting social engagements, where he put tools, and where he left materials needed for work. He said Mr. Doe began purchasing lottery tickets with the hope of retiring. He spent most of his income on alcohol or lottery tickets. Mr. Neighbor said that after Mr. Doe's license was suspended because of driving under the influence, he continued to drive construction vehicles without a license. He said Mr. Doe became somewhat rigid in his political conversations. He made fewer jokes and he laughed at fewer jokes. He said, "It was like his mind was getting less lively and less functional." He said Mr. Doe began making mistakes at work.

Interview of Mr. John Supervisor

Mr. John Supervisor said he was Mr. Doe's construction supervisor for 2 years, from <year> to <year>. He said Mr. Doe was a good worker "when he wasn't hung over." He said he arrived on time and completed work in an expected manner for 4 or 5 months, and then he began to arrive late fairly frequently, talking about his nights "out on the town." Mr. Supervisor kept Mr. Doe in his employment because the quality of his work was good even though his punctuality was not. He said Mr. Doe had an animated and entertaining personality and he kept the other workers cheerful during the day. He said Mr. Doe's relationship with his coworkers usually was good, but he sometimes became embroiled in verbal conflict with them over political beliefs and "he would keep at it even when no one was listening." He said Mr. Doe usually had a gradual buildup of emotions. He did not recall rapid changes in mood, or emotions that occurred without apparent precipitating factors. Mr. Supervisor nearly terminated Mr. Doe when he had a loud argument with Mr. Supervisor about the quality of his work at 6:00 a.m., waking people who lived near the construction site. Mr. Supervisor said Mr. Doe did not notify him when his driver's license was suspended. He drove construction vehicles during the pendency of his suspended license. When Mr. Supervisor found out Mr. Doe had no license, he terminated his employment.

Assessment Results

Mental Status Examination

The first session of the evaluation took place just prior to Mr. Doe's diagnosis of a stroke. At that time, he demonstrated fairly significant right-sided weakness, mental confusion, and poor comprehension of speech. His gait was unsteady due to right foot drag, he had difficulty accurately paraphrasing my warning of the limits of confidentiality even when I broke it down into small parts, and he referred to his caseworker as his landlady. When I asked him to write his name on a piece of paper, he asked for a "stick" when he meant to ask for a writing instrument. He was right-handed, and his printing was slow, unsteady, and sometimes illegible. I had a sample of his premorbid handwriting in the records, and there was clear deterioration in the quality of his writing. The session was terminated, and I consulted with counsel.

The second through fourth sessions took place after Mr. Doe was released from rehabilitation. Mr. Doe arrived on time for each session. He arrived for the second session wearing a half-tucked shirt and unmatched and untied tennis shoes. When asked about his shoes, he said he did not realize they were different until I pointed it out. He said he had difficulty tying his shoes and he intended to purchase shoes that fastened another way. His right hand was sometimes fisted, but he was able to open it when the fisted posture was called to his attention. His gait was unsteady with mild right foot drag, but he kept his balance. He demonstrated less facial animation than expected.

Mr. Doe demonstrated reduced vocal prosody and mild apathy, but he sometimes became quickly emotionally aroused. During the third session, he yelled expletives when I asked him whether he thought the stroke had any impact on his capacity to refrain from inappropriate touching of his children. He answered the question after calming down. In the fourth session, he became quickly emotionally aroused and yelled expletives when I asked him if he wanted a cup of water or a soda during the break. He engaged in a 10-min loud diatribe about needing neither water nor soda. Members of the agency called security. A security officer monitored the situation, but he did not intervene except to observe Mr. Doe for safety. Later, in the fourth session, Mr. Doe again quickly went from an emotional demeanor of apathy and sadness to one of loud anger in response to a question about his address. His anger appeared to be related to his embarrassment that he was having difficulty recalling his address. He described himself as depressed.

Mr. Doe had difficulty comprehending interview questions. He demonstrated better comprehension of short and simple questions, but he occasionally answered fairly sophisticated questions. He was able to reason from hypothesized cause to effect when examining his behavior. He sometimes needed extra time to retrieve words. When he provided information that might be regarded as critical to his case, either favorably or unfavorably, I checked with him later to ensure that his quotes conveyed the information that he intended. His lawyer observed sessions two through four from behind a two-way mirror. The lawyer requested permission to clarify two of Mr. Doe's statements, one during the second session and the other during the fourth session. He did so after the sessions were completed. In both instances, Mr. Doe said his responses were as he intended.

Mr. Doe demonstrated difficulty with mental organization, but he made no odd or bizarre statements. When he made atypical statements, he usually found a better way to say what he meant. When I pointed out some atypical statements, he initially did not recognize their unusual nature. If I returned to those statements another day, he was able to clarify what he meant. The flow of his conversational speech often was halted and slow, and he had difficulty speaking at length on any topic.

I asked Mr. Doe some nonsense questions to gauge his level of understanding of reasonable versus nonsense questions. He recognized and laughed at simple nonsense questions, e.g., "Is your car in school today?" He had difficulty with more complex nonsense questions, sometimes engaging in mild confabulation in response to them. For example, when asked, "Did your hat buy a new subway ticket before you came here?" He said he bought a new subway ticket that morning (he had ridden the bus and not the subway). Mr. Doe sometimes engaged in confabulation in response to reasonable questions. Rather than saying, "I don't know," he provided information that was verifiably false.

On the Mini Mental Status Examination, Mr. Doe obtained a score of 26, a score that was within expectations for his age and level of education. The Mini Mental Status Examination is designed to detect orientation, attention, immediate and short-term recall, language, and the ability to follow verbal and written instructions. Mr. Doe struggled with the language items on the measure. He struggled with sentence repetition, following verbal directions of three steps, following a written direction of one step, object naming, serial 7s (subtracting by 7s from 100), and spelling a five-letter word backward. He refused to draw two intersecting shapes, stating he was "not in kindergarten."

On the Dementia Rating Scale, Mr. Doe's scores were within expectations for attention, construction, and memory. Scores were below expectations for task initiation and perseveration, and conceptualization. He did better on conceptualization tasks that were nonverbal compared to conceptual tasks that were verbal. His total score reflected difficulty on verbal tasks and on task initiation. His scores are contained in the table below and they have a mean of 50 and a standard deviation of 10, with scores of 40 or lower falling below expectations.

Dementia Rating Scale			
Scale	T-Score	Percentile	Description
Attention	44	27th	Within expectations
Initiation/perseveration	37	9th	Below expectations
Construction	53	61st	Within expectations
Conceptualization	36	8th	Below expectations
Memory	46	34th	Within expectations
Total score	39	13th	Below expectations

Cognitive Functioning and Information Processing

On the WAIS-III, Mr. Doe obtained a full-scale IQ score of 79 (error margin of 75–83, eighth percentile). Mr. Doe's full-scale score was in the range that is described as "borderline," but some of his cognitive abilities fell in the "low average" to "average" range. He demonstrated relative strength on the Perceptual Reasoning and Processing Speed Indices, and relative weakness on the Verbal Comprehension and Working Memory Indices. His IQ and Index scores are contained in the table below. IQ and Index scores have a mean of 100 and a standard deviation of 15. Scores between 85 and 115 fall within statistical expectations.

Wechsler Adult Intelligence Scale, Third Edition		
Index	Score	Percentile
Verbal comprehension index	80	9th
Perceptual reasoning index	93	32nd
Working memory index	78	7th
Processing speed	86	18th
Full-scale IQ	79	8th

Mr. Doe's WAIS-III subscale scores are contained in the table below. Subscale scores have a mean of 10 and a standard deviation of 3. Scores of 8–12 are within expectations. Scores of 7 or lower are statistically below expectations.

Wechsler Adult Intelligence Scale, Third Edition	
Verbal comprehension index	
Vocabulary	6
Similarities	7
Information	6
Comprehension	6
Working memory index	
Arithmetic	6
Digit span	7
Letter-number sequencing	6
Perceptual organization index	
Picture completion	10
Block design	9
Matrix reasoning	8
Picture arrangement	6
Processing speed index	
Digit symbol	6
Symbol search	7
Object assembly	5

Visual-Spatial and Visual-Motor Skills

On the Rey–Osterreith Complex Figure, Mr. Doe began with what is usually described as a "part" approach to his reproduction of the figure, piecing together the internal details and incidental elements without appreciating or first forming the structural elements. He gradually corrected it, adding structural elements. His overall approach fell in the range of an "intermediate" approach. He gradually pieced together the outer perimeters of the design, adding external details and including internal details. The internal details were not organized as expected, but most were included. He made errors of "misplacement" of the details, that is, drawing them in the incorrect quadrant of the internal portion of the design. When asked to reproduce the design in the immediate recall condition, his design again met criteria for the "intermediate" range of work. After a 20-min delay, he said he could not recall any of the design. With encouragement, he began the design and recalled its configuration, organization, and details in a manner consistent with an "intermediate" approach.

On the Finger Tapping Test, Mr. Doe's raw score for his right hand was 50 and his raw score for his left or nondominant hand was 55. Both scores were within expectations for his age. Usually there is a less than 10% difference between the dominant and the non-dominant hands, but the direction of the difference is in favor of the dominant hand. In Mr. Doe's case, the direction of the difference was in favor of the nondominant hand. The dominant or right side is the side presumably affected by the stroke.

On the Delis–Kaplan Design Fluency Test, Mr. Doe had no difficulty generating responses at an expected rate. His error rate was just below expectations for set-loss errors (not following the rules of the task at an expected level) and for repetition errors (repeating designs under conditions in which he is asked to draw a new design each time). His scores indicate he had adequate visual attention, motor speed, visual-perceptual skills, and constructional skills for the task. He had no difficulty with the switching condition, indicating adequate cognitive shifting skills for the task. Set-loss errors occur when the individual has difficulty processing the multiple demands of the task. Repetition errors occur when there are perseverative tendencies, memory problems, or both. Mr. Doe's errors tended to occur close together, which is associated with perseverative tendencies rather than memory weakness. He sometimes used his left hand to assist his right hand, commenting that he would not have done so prior to his stroke. Scores in the table below have a mean of 10 and a standard deviation of 3, and scores from 8 to 12 are within expectations. Scores of 7 or lower are below expectations.

Delis–Kaplan Design Fluency Test		
Scale	Scaled Score	Description
Filled dots	9	Within expectations
Empty dots	8	Within expectations
Switching	8	Within expectations
Composite score	9	Within expectations
Set-loss errors	7	Below expectations
Repetition errors	7	Below expectations
Total attempted designs	9	Within expectations

Phonological and Language Processing Skills

The Boston Diagnostic Aphasia Examination is a confrontational naming test that provides information on word retrieval skills. Individuals without brain impairment tend to name an average of 91% of the 60 items correctly. Mr. Doe made a few articulation errors as he completed the assessment. He gave no response to three items. He made no errors based on responding to the incorrect part of the pictured item or based on visual misperception. He made no errors of association. His errors consisted primarily of multiple naming responses without the correct response, and giving an incorrect single name for the item. His raw score of 47 was below expectations by two standard deviations below the mean score seen in a sample of adults without brain damage.

On the Delis–Kaplan Verbal Fluency Test, Mr. Doe had difficulty generating words based on a phonological cue while simultaneously observing several rules or restrictions. He had difficulty with rapid retrieval of words that began with the same letter or that shared the same category. The second scale, category fluency, is sensitive to left-hemisphere brain damage because it highlights difficulty with familiar and overlearned verbal tasks with a semantic component. Mr. Doe's struggle with dysnomia, or naming impairment, was apparent on this task. He demonstrated difficulty with the cognitive flexibility needed to switch between two semantic categories of object naming. He sometimes failed to shift categories. His difficulty with category switching and switching accuracy was not greater than his initial difficulty with word retrieval. An analysis of Mr. Doe's performance across the time intervals indicated he quickly exhausted his retrieval capacities and had difficulty sustaining verbal responses through the remaining time intervals. Scores in the table below have a mean of 10 and a standard deviation of 3, and scores from 8 to 12 are within expectations. Scores of 7 or lower are below expectations.

Delis–Kaplan Verbal Fluency Test		
Scale	Scaled Score	Description
Letter fluency	4	Below expectations
Category fluency	1	Below expectations
Category switching, total correct	3	Below expectations
Category switching accuracy	5	Below expectations
First interval	4	Within expectations
Second interval	2	Below expectations
Third interval	1	Below expectations
Fourth interval	1	Below expectations
Set-loss errors	7	Below expectations
Repetition errors	9	Within expectations

On the Delis–Kaplan Color-Word Interference Test, Mr. Doe obtained a significantly low score on a task of color naming. This task is associated with word-finding impairment and speed of mental processing. His word reading score was within expectations, but scores for scales requiring him to inhibit unwanted responses or to switch between competing demands were below expectations, as were his error rates. His difficulty with word initiation on the color-naming task was prevalent throughout the task. Although reading cues were helpful to him, he struggled with word finding and word confusion throughout the task. Most of his errors went uncorrected.

Delis–Kaplan Color-Word Interference Test		
Scale	Scaled Score	Description
Color naming	5	Below expectations
Word reading	8	Within expectations
Inhibition	6	Below expectations
Inhibition/switching	6	Below expectations
Inhibition errors	6	Below expectations
Inhibition/switching errors	6	Below expectations

Learning and Memory

On the WMS-III, Mr. Doe obtained a general memory index score of 72 (error margin of 66–83, third percentile), in the range that is described as "borderline." His index scores are found in the table below:

Wechsler Memory Scale, Third Edition		
Index	Score	Percentile
Auditory immediate	80	9th
Visual immediate	84	14th
Immediate memory	78	7th
Auditory delayed	74	4th
Visual delayed	84	14th
Auditory recognition delayed	85	16th
General memory	77	6th
Working memory	79	8th

Mr. Doe's WMS-III subscale scores are found in the table below. Subscale scores have a mean of 10 and a standard deviation of 3. Scores of 7 or lower are statistically below expectations.

Wechsler Memory Scale, Third Edition	
Auditory immediate	
Logical memory I	7
Verbal paired associates I	6
Auditory delayed	
Logical memory II	6
Verbal paired associates II	5
Working memory	
Letter-number sequencing	6
Spatial span	6
Visual immediate	
Faces I	8
Family pictures I	7
Visual delayed	
Faces II	8
Family pictures II	7
Auditory recognition delayed	
Auditory recognition	
Delayed	7

Executive Functions Attention, and Behavior Regulation

On the Delis–Kaplan Trail Making Test, Mr. Doe's scores were within expectations, except for the Number–Letter Switching Scale. On Number-Letter Switching, the individual is asked to switch back and forth between connecting numbers and letters in a pencil-paper sequence. The task requires cognitive flexibility and is associated with the ability to simultaneously process information using divided attention. Mr. Doe's Trail Making Test scores are summarized in the table below. Scores in the table below have a mean of 10 and a standard deviation of 3, and scores from 8 to 12 are within expectations. Scores of 7 or lower are below expectations.

Delis–Kaplan Trail Making Test		
Scale	Scaled Score	Description
Visual Scanning	8	Within expectations
Number Sequencing	8	Within expectations
Letter Sequencing	8	Within expectations
Number-Letter Switching	6	Below expectations
Motor Speed	8	Within expectations

On the Delis–Kaplan Tower Test, Mr. Doe's level of achievement, or correct completion of items, was within expectations. He used significantly more time to initiate his first response, sometimes associated with activation problems. He used more time between moves than is typical for his age, also associated with activation problems. His move accuracy was within expectations, as was the number of his rule violations.

Delis–Kaplan Tower Test		
Scale	Scaled Score	Description
Total achievement	8	Within expectations
Mean first-move time	6	Below expectations
Time per move ratio	6	Below expectations
Move accuracy ratio	8	Within expectations
Rule violations	10	Within expectations

On the Delis–Kaplan Proverbs Test, Mr. Doe tended to give accurate but literal interpretations of proverbs. He had difficulty providing abstract responses to uncommon proverbs, and sometimes to common proverbs. He had adequate verbal skills to understand the specific meanings of the words in the proverbs, but he had difficulty formulating interpretations beyond a literal level.

Delis–Kaplan Proverbs Test		
Scale	Scaled Score	Description
Total achievement: free inquiry	7	Below expectations
Common proverb achievement	8	Within expectations
Uncommon proverb achievement	7	Below expectations
Abstraction-only score	6	Below expectations

Neurobehavioral Abilities Related to Parenting Competence

When asked about his children's educational needs, Mr. Doe did not correctly state in what grade his children were. He knew the name of their school, and he knew they rode the bus to school. He did not know what time the school day started or ended, nor did he know whether his children attended the after-school program (they attended on Tuesdays and Thursdays). He did not know the names of their teachers even though part of his service plan was to call both teachers weekly for updates on his children's academic progress. He said his younger daughter had reading problems. School records indicated it was his older daughter who struggled with reading. She was given individual reading support two times weekly. Mr. Doe said his daughter was in special education. When asked whether there was a difference between special education and receiving individual reading support two times per week, he said there was not.

Mr. Doe did not know his children's medical histories. Even though he was at home when they both contracted croup, he did not recall that they had croup when they were younger. He said one of his daughters needed eyeglasses. The caseworker was unaware of any need for eyeglasses for either daughter. Mr. Doe did not know the name of the children's pediatrician, her address, or her phone number. When asked about his older daughter's recent trip to the school nurse after a minor playground accident, he said he knew nothing about it. (The caseworker had told him about it the previous day.)

When asked to describe a schedule for his children were he to regain custody of them, Mr. Doe said he would get them up at 7:00 (school started at 8:00 and involved a 20-min bus ride). He said he would walk them to the bus stop but would not wait with them because he "hated waiting." He would pick them up after school, and he would find out when school ended from the caseworker. He would get them dinner. When asked to describe some examples of nutritional meals, he said, "pizza," and "cheese sandwiches." When asked how to make a pizza, he said he would buy the frozen variety and cook it according to the instructions. When asked how to make a cheese sandwich, he said, "bread, cheese, mayo, microwave." He did not continue his description of a daily routine. When asked what time he would put the children to bed, he said, "at bedtime." When asked what time bedtime was, he said, "I don't know." When asked how much sleep children needed, he said, "Same as anyone else."

When asked about his level of energy and patience with the children, Mr. Doe said, "Not a problem." When asked to describe what he meant, he said his children had plenty of energy. When asked if he had sufficient energy to supervise them, he said, "Not a problem." When asked to describe how he would manage frustration in a variety of scenarios involving the need to remain patient with children, his options included "showing them who's boss," "sending them to their rooms," and "time out." When asked how he would set limits with the children, he said, "They know I'm boss." When I pointed out that child protective services records indicated his daughters sometimes ignored limits set by him and his former partner, he said, "They won't." When asked about developmental differences in his children's needs, he said they did not read at the same level. He offered no other examples. He said his younger daughter might be able to cook for him. When asked about children and safety issues in the kitchen, Mr. Doe shrugged. He said, "Too many cooks boil the kitchen."

When asked what methods he was using to remain sober, Mr. Doe said he kept his relapse prevention plan up-to-date, and he was in Alcoholics Anonymous. When asked about Alcoholics Anonymous, he said he attended book meetings and step meetings. When asked what step he was on, he said he was on step 4. When asked to describe step 4, he described steps 1 and 2. He said he could not recall step 4 because it temporarily slipped his mind. He appeared embarrassed and then he returned to his descriptions of steps 1 and 2. When asked to describe the book meetings, he said, "You read books." He then said he stopped attending book meetings after his stroke. He said he could not recall his relapse prevention plan, but he produced a copy of it. We examined it together, and it was incomplete and 3 months old. He said he did not have a mechanism for continual updates. When asked about his meetings with Mr. Substance, Mr. Doe said he did not like Mr. Substance because he was "no help at all." When asked if he thought the relapse prevention plan was useful, Mr. Doe said it was. When asked how it was useful, Mr. Doe said, "It helps." When asked how he intended to keep it updated, he said it was unnecessary because he would never drink again.

Mr. Doe described his history of drinking, and it was consistent with the information found in the report of Dr. Other-Evaluator and in his records. I asked him a sequence of questions involving scenarios similar to those in the past in which he used alcohol. In response to each scenario, he said he was 100% confident he would not drink at all if met with a similar situation in the future. When asked for his reasons, he said it was due to his involvement in the legal system, and because he was being monitored by a probation officer. When asked if he thought alcohol disinhibited his sexual behavior, he described how alcohol sometimes led to sex, but he did not think disinhibition was a problem for him. When asked a similar question about aggression, he said alcohol made him argue in the past, but he was "over that." He said because he would never drink again, he did not need to worry about disinhibition relevant to sex, aggression, or sexual abuse of his children. When asked about positive alcohol screens and a recent "slip" of alcohol use, he said it was irrelevant because it would not recur.

Mr. Doe had difficulty identifying factors that contributed to success in past periods of sobriety, or factors that hindered his sobriety. Mr. Doe described his level of participation in rehabilitation as "good." He said he was in his "final stage" of rehabilitation, having been discharged from an inpatient facility and having attended all outpatient appointments. He agreed he "missed a few appointments." When asked about urges to drink, Mr. Doe said he had an occasional urge when watching beer commercials during football games, but never at any other time.

When asked about the impact of his stroke on his parenting abilities, Mr. Doe said he was having difficulty "walking in a straight line," but he expected all would be well in a matter of weeks. When asked about his word-finding problems, he did not agree that he had word-finding problems. He said he did not have difficulty understanding others. He said he did not think there were any changes in his emotional control. When asked about the level of his organization at home, he said it was fine. When asked when he last organized or cleaned his kitchen, he said, "Just yesterday." When asked when he last did laundry, he said, "Just yesterday." He continued to give the same reply to all questions relevant to his organization within his household. When I asked him how often he had difficulty with route finding on the city bus, he said he never had difficulty. He said he felt optimistic he would have a full recovery from his stroke, and he added, "My kids didn't even notice." He named some support resources available for help if he needed it, but his caseworker later was unable to verify the existence of those support sources.

Observed Visitation Sessions

In the first visitation session that I observed, Mr. Doe arrived an hour and a half late, apologetic because he missed his bus stop. He entered the room and greeted his daughters. His younger daughter looked at him warily and then greeted him excitedly. His older daughter ignored him and played with a dollhouse. Mr. Doe centered his attention on his younger daughter, watching her throw a ball against the wall. He cautioned her that she might not be good at hockey, and then he said he meant basketball. He accidentally tripped her as she attempted to retrieve the ball. He left the room to ask the caseworker to calm her down. She cried for 10 min and turned to the caseworker for comfort. She repeatedly asked for her foster mother. Her older sister patted her on the back and attempted to comfort her, continuing to ignore her father.

At the suggestion of the caseworker, Mr. Doe introduced some puzzles and attempted to interest both girls in the activity. The older daughter said they were "baby puzzles," and the younger daughter, who had reached for one puzzle piece, pulled away and also declared they were "baby puzzles." Mr. Doe then told them to find a new toy and he began paging through a children's book. He did not ask the children if they would like him to read the book. He paged halfway through the book and then seemed to lapse into a vacant stare for about 5 min. The girls entertained themselves with a coloring activity. When Mr. Doe's younger daughter asked if he liked her drawing, he did not respond. When she asked a second time, patting his leg while doing so, he asked her if she wanted water. She asked a third time, and he said the drawing was not to his liking because she used only one color. She asked her sister if she liked the drawing, and her sister said it was nice. The older girl was working on a drawing of a house with smiling people that she later described as her foster home, foster parents, self, and sister. When the session ended, Mr. Doe left abruptly without saying goodbye to his daughters.

In the second observed session, Mr. Doe arrived 1 h late, complaining that no one could understand the bus schedule. He yelled at the caseworker and she cautioned him to quiet down. He calmed down, muttering about the bus schedule and using expletives to describe the individuals in charge of the bus schedule. Mr. Doe was allowed to enter the session after calming down. Both of his children began to cry when he entered the room because of their awareness that he was late. His older daughter used a paddle toy to hit the table. Mr. Doe did not intervene and the caseworker entered the room and asked her to play with a different toy. The girl gave the paddle to the caseworker and picked up a doll. When the caseworker left the room, Mr. Doe's daughter banged the doll on the table. The younger girl asked for the doll and then tried to take the doll. The older girl threatened to hit the younger girl with the doll. Mr. Doe did nothing to intervene. He began pacing the room and complaining about the bus schedule. He asked his youngest daughter if she rode the bus. She said she did, meaning the school bus. Mr. Doe thought she meant the city bus and he accused her of lying. She tried to explain, and he interrupted, saying, "No," and "no, you, you, no no." He then said, "Kids who lie are kids who die," and then repeated it six or seven times, gradually raising his voice, and sometimes tripping over his words or mixing up the sequence of words. The caseworker entered the room and ended the session. Mr. Doe swore at her and then yelled at his daughters for "messing my visit." After he left the agency, they both began to cry.

Interpretation

Neurobehavioral Impact of Chronic Alcohol Dependence

Mr. Doe demonstrated the following neurobehavioral features that are known to be associated with chronic alcohol dependence. He sometimes had lapses of attention, his problem-solving abilities gradually weakened, and he had memory problems. His memory problems, as illustrated by the assessment data, must be understood in light of his current language weaknesses, but people who knew Mr. Doe over time described gradually weakened attention and memory abilities that they observed prior to the stroke. Mr. Doe had increasing difficulty with organization. He sometimes had difficulty completing work tasks in the proper sequence. He had increased difficulty with planning, sequencing, and remaining organized. There was a gradual reduction in his emotional spontaneity, and he sometimes became verbally and emotionally intense about politics, a topic that held less interest for him in his young adulthood. He had gradually diminished awareness of the level of interest of others in the topics that he chose for conversation. He remained sociable, but he sometimes had conflicted interactions at work. Some of his social relationships were affected by his drinking behavior because of his decreased emotional spontaneity and growing rigidity in conversational style. He demonstrated lapses in judgment in the work environment.

There are competing explanations related to personality variables that might become more fixed over time, possible intoxication in the work environment, and changing interests in adulthood. But the overall pattern is suggestive of a process of gradual impairment that typifies the type of diminished abilities seen in individuals with heavy and chronic alcohol consumption with only brief periods of sobriety. Although there were some personality variables and drinking behavior apparent in adolescence that led to school behavior concerns and suspensions, Mr. Doe's premorbid behavior was sufficiently organized during the period when he remained in school, earned his high school diploma, and went on to complete 1 year of community college. He had friendships, he was described as gregarious and emotionally spontaneous, and he had an 8-year relationship with the children's mother. Deterioration took place gradually. He had some problems at work related to alcohol abuse, and he had some verbal altercations with other workers that were related to decreased emotional control, and increased intensity and perseveration on conversational topics that were of interest to him but not to others. He had verbal and physical altercations at home that led to police visits to his home and that sometimes led to his removal from the home. The police intervention was related to his active drinking. There is no record that the police were summoned to his home when he was sober. Some of his behavior reflects the social and behavioral outcome of intoxication, but there is evidence of gradual deterioration in functioning consistent with brain impairment associated with chronic heavy alcohol use. Family relationships deteriorated because of his sexual offending behavior, in addition to alcohol dependence.

Neurobehavioral Impact of Stroke

When Mr. Doe's cognitive assessment scores are compared to scores that he obtained in high school, they indicate significant deterioration in his verbal information and memory functioning, with the greatest impact seen in verbal cognition, verbal memory, working memory, and speed of information processing. Caution is in order in the interpretation of these changes in his intellectual abilities. Although it is likely that the changes are largely attributable to brain impairment related to chronic alcohol consumption and stroke, it should be noted that intellectual assessment and memory assessment scores tend to be less stable when there are large time gaps between assessments, changes sometimes take place when moving from one measure to another (in this case, from the children's scale to an adult intellectual scale), score changes sometimes occur when scales are updated because of a strengthening of the norms for the new version of the assessment, and some adults demonstrate normal deterioration of the strength of their intellectual and memory abilities because of factors associated with maturation and aging.

Even when these caveats are considered, however, the declines in Mr. Doe's verbal intellect and verbal memory are greater than expected, and therefore it is likely that they reflect the impact of the stroke, with some possible contributing effects related to chronic alcohol dependence. When the scores are viewed in the context of descriptions of his pre-morbid and poststroke language abilities, it is likely that the majority of the decline in verbal cognition and verbal memory functioning reflects the impact of the stroke.

Mr. Doe experienced significantly reduced poststroke speech fluency that gradually improved after the stroke, but not to baseline. He sometimes spoke in one- to two-word sentences. He suffered from dysnomia, or word retrieval problems. Word retrieval in the context of confrontational naming tends to return more gradually than speech fluency after strokes. Speech fluency returns across the course of about 1 month, if at all, but confrontational naming returns more gradually, across the course of about 6 months. It is possible that his word retrieval difficulties will lessen over time. Mr. Doe also demonstrated disinhibited speech, confused and disorganized speech, and impoverished speech. He sometimes engaged in confabulation of the type seen in individuals with combined memory and verbal expression difficulties. His speech comprehension was reduced. It often was necessary to simplify statements and questions, to avoid compound or complex statements and questions, and to ask him to paraphrase questions or statements to gauge his level of comprehension.

Mr. Doe experienced poststroke changes in his mood stability. Although he had difficulty with the management of emotions prior to the stroke, his poststroke emotional arousal occurred with a rapidity not seen prior to the stroke and with less apparent precipitating factors. Instead of slowly building intensity that centered on political beliefs, he demonstrated rapid emotional arousal, sometimes randomly and sometimes in response to innocuous stimuli. He engaged in impulsive actions and statements because of increased disinhibition. Prior to the stroke, he was described as animated and entertaining. After the stroke, observers saw him as indifferent, emotionally restricted, emotionally dysregulated, socially withdrawn, and intermittently apathetic.

Risk Factors

In this section, risk factors already identified in the report of Dr. Other-Evaluator are not repeated except when relevant. Because this evaluation is intended to serve as a supplement to that evaluation report, this section reviews only risk factors relevant to brain impairment. As cautioned prior to the commencement of this evaluation, it is not possible to definitively make a clear distinction between the effects of chronic alcohol dependence and the effects of Mr. Doe's stroke on the integrity of his brain functioning. There is some overlap in the expected impact of both conditions. One also must factor in the natural effect of aging on brain functioning.

Assessment data, interview data, and records illustrate the combined effects of chronic alcohol dependence and stroke on Mr. Doe's communication, his social and emotional functioning, his behavioral organization, and his intellect. Although some of the low memory scores are confounded by his low verbal scores, it is likely that memory also has deteriorated. The deterioration in Mr. Doe's functioning has had an impact on his risk of harm to his children and on his parental capacity. There is somewhat greater risk of harm to his children due to his increased disinhibition and reduced behavior organization, but it ironically might be easier to detect imminent risk because of his disinhibited speech. The impact does not significantly alter the already existing risk matrix described in the report of Dr. Other-Evaluator. The contribution of these risk factors is important, but they must be considered in the context of weightier existing risk factors specified in the report of Dr. Other-Evaluator. Of increasing concern is Mr. Doe's ability to function in the role of parent on a day-to-day basis.

Mr. Doe's history of chronic alcohol dependence and his stroke have contributed to parental incapacity in the form of increased disorganization, inadequate self-care, and difficulty identifying an organized schedule or daily routine for his children. He has shown decline in receptive and expressive language abilities. His behavioral intent sometimes might be different from his verbal capacity to discuss it. Although further recovery of functioning remains possible, he currently has difficulty communicating with his children because he misunderstands their statements, he sometimes speaks in one- and two-word utterances, he sometimes makes perseverative statement, he makes impulsive statements, and he has dysnomia or word-finding difficulties. The changes in his communication style have been confusing to his daughters, who already were wary of him. They are easily frightened by his verbal outbursts. Mr. Doe sometimes is despondent and apathetic, and his unresponsiveness confuses them. He vacillates between inactivity and emotional hyperarousal, often without clear precipitating factors that are apparent to observers.

Mr. Doe has reasoning and judgment problems related to his brain impairment and to other factors. Were he to regain custody of his daughters, he would have access to public assistance. His caseworker said she has had difficulty persuading him that it would be a good idea to take advantage of those resources. She noted that he had difficulty with follow-through of routine parenting tasks asked of him, such as weekly check-in telephone calls to his children's teachers. He is not fully aware or appreciative of the importance of supervision and safety concerns for his daughters. He has limited appreciation of child development, and how to understand his daughters' needs in light of their chronological ages or levels of development.

Mr. Doe's recovery from brain impairment depends on his neurological and rehabilitation follow-up and his dedication to remaining sober. His attendance at treatment and rehabilitation appointments has been inconsistent. He has difficulty sustaining his sobriety. Further drinking will lead to further brain deterioration. His gradual deterioration has lessened his behavior control, whether intoxicated or sober. Mr. Doe has experienced gradually increased disinhibition of his emotions and behavior over time. He has made disinhibited statements relevant to his sexual interest in his children, and he has made verbally confusing statements that have frightened his children.

Mr. Doe is not at an independent level in his recovery from alcohol dependence. He requires significant support from self-help group members and leaders and from treatment providers. Although he made some recent disparaging remarks toward his outpatient provider, their relationship typically has been positive. Mr. Doe's treatment attendance initially was good, but it has been inconsistent because of decreased interest in attending appointments prior to his stroke and because of mental disorganization and difficulty keeping a schedule subsequent to his stroke. Treatment approaches for substance abuse prevention and sex offending have needed modification to accommodate his deteriorated level of verbal intellect and behavioral functioning.

Mr. Doe needs close monitoring of his safety during visitation with his children, he will need close monitoring of his drinking urges and his capacity to update his alcohol and sexual abuse relapse prevention plans, and he will need continued encouragement and support to take advantage of self-help groups. He will need support to remain engaged in therapies. There is concern that Mr. Doe has recently shown reduced awareness of how and when to seek help. There was preexisting concern about his reasoning and logic with respect to the impact of his sexual fondling on his daughters. He has become less able to verbalize his understanding and appreciation of the impact of his previous actions on his children. His coping resources are less strong, and yelling and verbal altercations appear to be his main coping resources. He recently was seen consuming alcohol, and records described an incident in which he showered with his daughter during a visit. Both of these behavioral episodes raise further concern about his level of disinhibition and his difficulty taking preventive measures or using adaptive coping resources specified in his alcohol relapse prevention or sexual offending prevention plans.

Mediating Factors

Although his attendance is inconsistent, Mr. Doe has remained involved in treatment despite the new challenges of his poststroke condition. He has remained connected to his treatment providers even after finishing a 3-month cycle of outpatient treatment in both sex offender group treatment and outpatient substance abuse treatment. He has persistently expressed a desire to reunite with his children. He has had productive conversations with his caseworker about alternative arrangements for supervised and safe contact with them, should he fail to regain custody of them. He has met with his child protective services caseworker on a regular basis. He sometimes has taken advantage of resources designed to help him improve his consistency of visitation. He has alcohol and sex offender relapse prevention plans that he updates, but only with significant support from his outpatient treatment providers. He has made friends in self-help groups with individuals who support his sobriety.

Summary

To retain supervised visitation of his daughters, Mr. Doe will need significant emotional, communication, and parenting support. It is unlikely that he would be able to successfully parent them in appropriate manner were he to regain unsupervised visitation or custody of them. The primary concerns are his continued use of alcohol and his sexual statements toward and victim blame of his daughters. If he remains sober, there is a better prognosis for cognitive recovery from both chronic alcohol dependence and stroke. If he severely relapses, cognitive recovery from stroke will be significantly slow and some areas of brain recovery from alcohol dependence may be reversed. In a scenario of relapsing alcohol use and remitting sobriety, his likelihood of recovery would be variable. The state of the science does not permit specification of the length of time needed for recovery, but his best hope for recovery would be to refrain altogether from drinking, seek significant external support, seek follow-up physical rehabilitation as recommended, and agree to monitoring and supervision of his time with his children.

Lois Oberlander Condie, Ph.D., ABPP
Licensed Clinical Psychologist

Family Violence—Sample Case Report from Chapter 5 (Poirier)

[Date]
The Honorable Ralph Jones
[Address]

RE: *Maryland v. Roberta G. Brown*
   CR. No.: XX-XXXX
   Counts: Second-degree murder, assault with a deadly weapon

Dear Judge Jones,

This report responds to your [Date] Circuit Court order stipulating a psychological evaluation of the defendant Mrs Roberta Brown. The order requested an evaluation to address any mitigating psychiatric concerns and an assessment of recidivism risk for spousal abuse. Mrs Brown was evaluated at the [Name] Detention Center on [Dates]. The total evaluation time including completion of psychological testing was just over 11 h. For the most part, Mrs Brown was a motivated and cooperative defendant.

Forensic Database

The Assistant State's Attorney, the defendant's Public Defender, and the County Child Welfare Services (CWS) caseworker variously made the following records available:

1. District Court charging documents including the [Date] Application for Statement of Charges, and the [Date] Statement of Charges.
2. [Date] County Police Investigation Report, Addendums, and Attachments.
3. [Date] Grand Jury Indictment Statement citing seven charges in all.
4. [Dates] County Department of Social Services, CWS, case reports extending back to [Date] when CWS first followed-up on a neglect complaint regarding the Brown children. We note that there were five additional complaints, and CWS investigations [Dates] with varying findings of complicity by the parents. We also reviewed seven CWS follow-up reports [Dates]. All of the foregoing incidents occurred prior to the gunshot injuries of Mr Brown.
5. [Dates] State Forensic Services reports of findings regarding Mrs Brown's competency to stand trial and her criminal responsibility at the time of the offense.
6. [Date] Report regarding Mrs Brown's competency and criminal responsibility submitted by defense retained experts Drs [Name], [Name], and [Name].

There were no other prior psychological records regarding Mrs Brown. The children's caretakers, Mr and Mrs [Name] did provide us with copies of [Name] County Public

School records on each of the Brown children. The school records were accessed when the children went into care. The school records were remarkable for three of the children receiving special education support services because of suspected learning disabilities as identified by school psychologists. The records were also remarkable for staff concerns regarding the hygiene and shoddy, unclean attire of all four children. The Brown children had complained to school staff on numerous occasions of ridicule by peers. School staff had documented concerns about unusually precocious sexual interests and sexual references by the three younger children. Finally, the school records cited self-esteem concerns and identity problems with each of the Brown children.

Current Assessment

The following procedures were utilized in our assessment of Mrs Brown:

1. Developmental history
2. Familial history
3. Educational history
4. Physical health history
5. Employment history
6. Marital history
7. Mental status examination
8. Prior arrest history

The following instruments were utilized in our assessment of Mrs Brown:

1. Wechsler Adult Intelligence Scale-III (WAIS-III)
2. Minnesota Multiphasic Inventory-2 (MMPI-2)
3. Millon Multiaxial Clinical Inventory-III (MMCI-III)
4. Consideration of selected risk factors from the Spousal Assault Risk Assessment (SARA)*
5. Consideration of the Brief Spousal Assault Form for the Evaluation of Risk (B-SAFER)†

Pertinent Background Information

Mrs Brown was 42 years of age (DOB: [Date]). She was born in a hospital in a rural area of Maryland. Her parents were both 17 years old when Mrs Brown was conceived. Her father was a high-school dropout and a seasonal worker on the small rented dairy farm where Mrs Brown's parents attempted to eek out a living. Mrs Brown reported a mutually

---

* The SARA remains in early development and has not been normed with female spousal abusers. Our consideration of risk factors from SARA was judicious and served only as research-based, collaborative data regarding risk factors of domestic spousal abuse. The instrument was not the sole or primary basis of our findings.
† The B-SAFER remains in early development as an abbreviated (i.e., quicker to complete) form of the SARA. We employed the B-SAFER in the same manner characterized above for the SARA.

abusive relationship between her parents. When Mrs Brown realized she was pregnant, she dropped out of the 11th grade.

Mrs Brown was the youngest of three daughters. Mrs Brown's parents were both deceased; Mrs Brown characterized, "They both worked themselves to death." The older sisters were both married; they lived with their respective husbands and children in rural Maryland. Mrs Brown reported that she remained close to her older sister where the court temporarily placed the children.

Mrs Brown described her family and her early development with little emotion except for her feelings toward her next older sister. Mrs Brown stated that as a child she had grown up feeling isolated from her hardworking parents. She suggested that she and her next older sister were close in age, and their relationship had been fraught with rivalry and pettiness. When Mr Brown began working on her parents' farm, Mrs Brown acknowledged that she was immediately infatuated. She was drawn to Mr Brown's worldly ways. Even though they were both 17 years old, Mr Brown had been emancipated for several years. Mrs Brown stated that it was Mr Brown who introduced her to cannabis. Eventually, Mr Brown also introduced her to alcohol and other illicit substances. Within weeks of meeting each other, Mrs Brown stated her husband also introduced her to sexual intimacy.

When Mrs Brown became pregnant with her oldest child, the Browns married at the local courthouse. Mr Brown worked as a truck driver for a local grocery firm until approximately 1995 when he suffered a purported disabling on the job back injury. Around the same time, Mrs Brown discontinued her part-time employment as a school bus driver; she acknowledged that she was angry with Mr Brown because he did not return to work. Mrs Brown noted that her husband could spend hours every day in the garden, digging, weeding, and otherwise tending to an ever-increasing number of cannabis plants.

Mrs Brown related that especially when intoxicated, Mr Brown would be unbelievably humiliating and disparaging of her. Mr Brown appeared to delight in emotionally abusing Mrs Brown in front of the children. Mrs Brown also complained of sporadic victimizations by physical and sexual abuse, and she admitted that there were instances in which she took advantage of Mr Brown's intoxicated state and battered him. There were also instances of rage in which Mrs Brown had attempted to maim Mr Brown's genitals when he was "passed out." On several occasions, Mrs Brown had gone to different emergency rooms to have her injuries treated. In every instance, she had lied about how her injuries had occurred.

Mrs Brown described that as the years passed and the children grew older, Mr Brown was essentially intoxicated around the clock; Mr Brown's use of illicit substances would be especially heavy after he would make a large illicit drug sale to a growing number of adolescents and young adults who would come to the home to make purchases. Mrs Brown did not know exact numbers because Mr Brown would keep her uninformed, but she was aware that there had been days when the drug sales were in amounts of 2000$ to 3000$. The drug sales would always involve cash only, but there was also bartering of different substances. Mrs Brown stated that her husband would often brag about adulterating drugs to increase his profits.

Mrs Brown described her progressively increasing rage with Mr Brown; she was aware that she abused substances herself in an effort to cope with her anger. She described bitterly that Mr Brown would mete out illicit substances to her in moderation while indulging himself without limits. She stated that Mr Brown would taunt her over her substance of choice, which was crack-cocaine. Mrs Brown appeared oblivious to the impact on the children of the circumstances she was describing. Because of her own plight in the marital relationship, she felt entitled to her indulgences.

Test Results

1. WAIS-III. Mrs Brown's native intellectual ability was in the lower end of the average range of intelligence (WAIS, VIQ = 101; PIQ = 106; FSIQ = 102). Subtests sensitive to academic exposure were all notably lowered.

2. MMPI-2. Mrs Brown approached the MMPI-2 with mild defensiveness; this was not an atypical finding, given her pending status before the court. Otherwise, Ms Brown's validity scale findings were within limits. The resulting clinical profile was probably an adequate indication of her current personality functioning. Moderately high-profile definition characterized the MMPI-2 that included Scales Hy, Pd, Pa, and Ma. This not well-defined pattern was suggestive of a disorder of mixed features encompassing hyperemotionality, immaturity, suspiciousness, and unbounded but not well-directed energy. These features were suggestive of borderline personality disorder dynamics. Beyond this, the clinical scales did not reflect any major mental disorders, except for consistent elevations on scales reflecting psychological propensity for substance abuse as well as acknowledged actual substance abuse.

3. MMCI-III. According to the Millon Correction Scales, Mrs Brown approached the test with reasonable candor; she was not overly responsive to clinical items nor was she defensive or careless. The test results did not implicate any major psychiatric disorders (i.e., DSM-IV-TR, Axis I disorders) except for significant elevations on two scales addressing substance abuse. There were also a number of elevations on scales implicating personality disorder issues (i.e., DSM-IV-TR, Axis 2). The findings were consistent with a formal diagnosis of a mixed personality disorder (DSM-IV-TR: 301.9) with primarily borderline and antisocial features. This finding connotes a deeply engrained, maladaptive personality style encompassing a number of features. One prominent feature is a disregard for generally accepted social conventions. Additional personality characteristics included poor judgment, emotional unpredictability, volatility, and a likely pattern of stormy, unstable interpersonal relationships.

4. Consideration of the SARA. The SARA ratings were based on our interviews with Mrs Brown and a review of all relevant file information as recommended in the SARA manual. The 20 risk factors were coded on a 3-point scale (0 = absent, 1 = possibly or partially present, 2 = present). No items were omitted; we had sufficient information to code all items. The SARA has an override feature whereby evaluators can indicate when a risk factor is judged "critical," that is, present and strongly related to violence risk in the reference matter. Three summary scores are calculated from the item ratings: (1) total score is the sum of the individual item ratings, ranging from 0 to 40; (2) number of factors present which is an index of how many risk factors were rated as present in the index case ranging from 2 to 20; and (3) number of critical items, that is, the number of risk factors rated critical ranging from 0 to 20. A final rating is the evaluator rating of summary risk rating. This is an indication of evaluator judgment of the offenders risk for recidivistic spousal assault on a 3-point scale: 0 = low risk,

1 = moderate risk, and 2 = high risk. The SARA ratings for Mrs Brown are summarized below:

SARA Rating	Score	Total Possible Score
Total Score		
Part 1—(general violence risk factors)	13	20
Part 2—(spousal violence risk factors)	15	20
Factors Present		
Part 1—(general violence risk factors)	7	10
Part 2—(spousal violence risk factors)	8	10
Critical Items		
Part 1—(general violence risk factors)	5	10
Part 2—(spousal violence risk factors)	8	10
Summary Risk Rating	2 (high risk)	2

Mrs Brown's SARA ratings place her in a high-risk category for likelihood of recidivism as a perpetrator of spousal violence.

5. The B-SAFER. The B-SAFER was derived from the SARA in an effort to produce an instrument that could be completed more quickly (e.g., by police officers conducting initial, in-the-field investigations of domestic violence complaints). The expectation would be that the B-SAFER findings would be comparable to those of the SARA with the same offender. Compared to the SARA, which consists of 20 risk factor items, the B-SAFER has half as many items. The 10 B-SAFER items are rated: **O** = omit—insufficient information; **N** = not present; **P** = possibly or partially present. Each risk item is rated "currently" and "in the past." The ratings for Ms Brown on the B-SAFER are summarized below:

B-SAFER Risk Factors	Rating	
	Currently	In the Past
Part 1—Spousal Assault Risk Factors		
Serious physical/sexual violence	Yes	Yes
Serious violent threats, ideation, or intent	Yes	Yes
Escalation of physical/sexual violence or threats/ideation/intent	Yes	Yes
Violations of civil or criminal court orders	No	No
Negative attitudes about spousal assault	Yes	Yes
Part 2—Psychosocial Adjustment Currently		
Other serious criminality	Yes	P
Relationship problems	Yes	Yes
Employment or financial problems	Yes	Yes
Substance abuse	Yes	Yes
Mental disorder*	Yes	Yes

---

* The rating for this factor includes the presence of long-standing problems with anger, impulsivity, or instability.

Mrs Brown's B-SAFER ratings were consistent with the findings on the SARA. Both instrument ratings found Mrs Brown to present as a serious risk with respect to risk for recidivistic spousal abuse, imminently and in the future.

Summary: Mrs Brown's developmental background was remarkable for impoverishment and reported mutual abusiveness between her parents. Mr & Mrs Brown married young when Mrs Brown was pregnant for the first time. From the beginning, the Brown's marriage was suffused with substance abuse, immaturity, and acting out behavior by both parents. The Browns had four children, all of whom witnessed the most heinous behavior by the parents.

The circumstances culminated in the charge of attempted murder with Mrs Brown victimizing Mr Brown. Mr Brown had suffered life-threatening injuries but had since recovered. Mrs Brown was pending sentencing in the matter, and the bench requested the current evaluation. Current assessment reflected Mrs Brown to be a cognitively capable woman, although her weak academic background was apparent. She did not evidence any mitigating psychiatric illness (i.e., with respect to competency or criminal responsibility), but she was addicted to cocaine through the time of the offense circumstance. Additionally, current assessment indicates that Mrs Brown meets the criteria (DSM-IV-TR) for a diagnosis of mixed personality disorder that, among other concerns, compromises her judgment and connotes high risk for return to substance abuse. We note that the available data also suggested that Mr Brown was addicted to multiple substances.

Two instruments designed to assess risk for spousal abuse recidivism were utilized in our assessment effort. We have noted specific limitations with both instruments in that they are experimental, and neither has been explicitly normed with female offenders. Nevertheless, the instrument findings combined with psychological testing served as the basis of our estimate of Mrs Brown's risk potential. Additional considerations were our overall extensive review of Mrs Brown's history and current clinical presentation.

With specific reference to Mrs Brown's potential to engage again in spousal violence, our best estimate is that she poses a serious risk, and we recommend that the bench stipulate an appropriate dispositional plan that will be immediately and securely protective of Mr and Mrs Brown, as well as the children. Assuming Mrs Brown's adjudication would permit hospitalization, we are not aware of an available or accessible psychiatric facility that would adequately meet Mrs Brown's needs at this time. If adjudication results in incarceration, we would recommend consideration of the (name) Correctional Center for Women where an Addictions Treatment Track is available. Whatever final disposition determined by the bench, we would recommend a follow-up risk assessment in approximately 24 months.

Respectfully submitted,
Joseph G. Poirier, PhD, ABPP

Reports for Conditional Release from Chapter 6 (Hall)

February 4, 2005
The Honorable Jane Smith
The Judiciary, State of Hawaii Circuit Court of the Third Circuit Kaahumanu Hale
777 Punchbowl Street
Honolulu, HI 96813

RE: *State of Hawaii v. John Doe*
    CR. NO. 99-9999

    Count I: Terroristic threatening in the first degree
    Count II: Promoting dangerous drugs in the first degree
    Count III: Place to keep

Dear Judge Smith,

Pursuant to Hawaii Revised Statutes §§ 704-412 and 704-414 and the Court's Order dated January 14, 2003, the following report is presented. A previous evaluation report, dated March 13, 2002, regarding the same forensic issues was rendered to the Court wherein I recommended release from the Hawaii State Hospital (HSH).

Forensic Database: The defendant was clinically interviewed at HSH on January 31, 2003. The HSH files and staff members were interviewed regarding the defendant's adjustment at that facility. Findings from my 2002 evaluation, including psychometric test results and an interview of the alleged victim and a witness-observer, and the Adult Probation Department (APD) file were reviewed.

Tests administered included the MMPI-2, MCMI-III, VIP, HCR-20, Violence Risk Appraisal Guide (VRAG), NIJ Seriousness Scoring System, LSI-R, and the SARA. [A comprehensive database is essential in order to accurately gauge change over time.]

A deception analysis of the defendant's evaluation responses revealed, for the time of the interview, an attempt to:

- Present himself in an accurate manner fake good
- Fake bad
- Invalidate results
- Present a mixed style
- Present a fluctuating style

This was based on:

- Validity scale results from the psychometric testing
- Goodness of fit between test profile and clinical behavior

- Clinical behavior
- Performance on tests or procedures specifically designed to assess attempts to misrepresent
- Inconsistency in statements over time
- Discrepancy between representation of responses and established events

Mental Conditions: The Diagnostic and Statistical Manual, Fourth Edition, Text Revision (DSM-IV-TR, 2000) mental conditions of the defendant for the time of the evaluation were as follows:

Axis I	Bipolar II disorder versus amphetamine-induced psychotic disorder, in institutional remission
Axis II	Personality disorder NOS
Axis III	None
Axis IV	Chronic interactional, vocational, and psychological problems
Axis V	GAF = 50/50

The defendant was hospitalized at the Queen's Medical Center on two previous occasions, both followed by admissions to HSH (give dates of admission and discharge). On both occasions, he tested positive for methamphetamine. He affirmed smoking methamphetamine ("ice") on an infrequent basis, although significant others described him as a chronic methamphetamine user who ingests alcohol to "crash" from prolonged binges. At other times, when clearly not under the influence of methamphetamine, such as during his detainment at HSH, he showed bipolar symptoms with psychotic features. Medication compliance is questionable, as he has been caught disposing of his medication.

Dangerousness: Previous significant violence for the defendant includes the following [insert any of the following historical themes that apply to his basal history of violence as well as source of information]:

- Basal violence is isolated
- Violence is multiple and chronic
- Recent severe violence is suggested
- Victim injury has resulted from violence
- Direction of violence is (1) toward others, (2) toward property, (3) toward self, or (4) tandem or multiple directions
- Violence to others is associated with the presence of peers; bystanders have no suppressing effect on violence
- Violence to property is associated with theft
- Victim patterning is present
- Focus of attack is specific
- Assaults on others is more likely associated with methamphetamine intoxication (or when "tweaking")
- Sudden violence is more likely than delayed violence
- Mode of attack is more likely to involve fist strikes to head/face region
- Attacks are preceded by verbal abuse or attempts to control the victim
- Aggressive behavior continued despite pain cues or distress of victim
- Assaultive behavior is followed by attempts to avoid/escape aversive stimuli
- Other (explain)

Opportunity factors, which make the expression of violence possible or expand the possible degree of severity, such as the availability of firearms, include the following [tie into previous acts]. Triggering stimuli, such as intense stress and substance intoxication, which tended to set the defendant's violence into motion, have included the following [examiner inserts relevant events]. Inhibitions to violence, or those events or conditions, both internal and external (i.e., environmental, such as a "policeman at the elbow," or the presence of onlookers) have included [examiner inserts relevant events].

For the next year, the maximum duration of prediction proffered, if released into the community, it is my opinion that the defendant is dangerous to others to a minimal-mild degree (i.e., negligible, minimal, mild, moderate, and substantial). This is based on the assumption that the following factors in particular remain constant (specify factors, e.g., minimal availability of firearms, unresolved substance intoxication, continued high state of stress, and cognitive disorganization despite psychotropic medication). For the next year, it is my opinion that the defendant is minimally dangerous to self and property.

Recommendation: In my opinion, the defendant is ready for conditional release if he is first placed in a transition facility. He should be regularly tested for illicit drug use and should undergo frequent cognitive behavioral treatment for substance abuse and related psychological problems. He has reached the maximum benefit of treatment at HSH. His bipolar condition has stabilized on medication, and he is considered a high-functioning patient at HSH. He has successfully completed most intervention programs at HSH. The key to preventing a relapse is to ensure proper medication follow-up once he is placed in a community setting. He continues to deny aspects of his basal history of violence and (falsely) believes that he could most likely do well if he were to be phased off his medications. He eagerly informed me that he would comply with all instructions and recommendations if he is placed in the community.

Sincerely,
Harold V. Hall, PhD, ABPP

Sample Evaluation Report for Conditional Release

[Date]
The Honorable John Smith
[Address]

RE: *State of Hawaii v. [Defendant]*
    CR. NO. NNN

    Counts I–III: Sexual assault in the third degree

Dear Judge Smith,

Pursuant to your [Date] Order granting the State's motion for assessment of dangerousness of [Defendant], DOB _____, POB _____, SSN _____, this report is presented. The defendant is a _____ -year-old, single man, who is currently being detained at the _____ . No empirically based risk assessments were found in his records.

This same report has been submitted to the Honorable Jane White in the sentencing for the Kidnapping offense in Criminal Number _____ . The sole difference is that the index offense used as a basis for prediction corresponds to the separate charges for which the defendant was found guilty. The change in index offenses did not alter the risk probability as discussed below.

Forensic Database: Records supplied by the Department of the Prosecuting Attorney included police and Grand Jury audio and video tapes relevant to Criminal Numbers and _____ (original arrests for kidnapping, sexual assault in the third degree, and failure to register as a sex offender, and convicted of kidnapping and sexual assault in the third degree). Police report _____ for sexual assault and kidnapping was also reviewed. An Adult Probation Division criminal history list and background information and a Hawaii OBTS/CCH form were also reviewed.

Measures administered to the Defendant at _____ High Security Facility or later scored from data obtained from the defendant or from the _____ medical and the above records included the following:

1. Clinical interview and mental status evaluation
2. Shipley Institute of Living Scale (estimated WAIS-R full-scale IQ = 64–71)
3. Wechsler Memory Scale-Revised (mental control, 6/6 correct)
4. Wechsler Adult Intelligence Scale (digit span, digits forward = 6; digits backward = 4)
5. Violence Risk Appraisal Guide (VRAG): 82% (probability of violent recidivism over 10-year period)
6. Hare Psychopathy Checklist-Revised: 36 (severe psychopath)
7. Predictors of Violent Recidivism (meta-analysis): Positive for violent recidivism (see below)
8. HCR-20 (historical, clinical, risk management items: 28 (high risk for violent recidivism)
9. SVR-20 (sexual, violence, and risk): 13 indicators, high risk
10. Rapid Risk Assessment for Sexual Offense Recidivism: 4; 48.6% risk of sexual recidivism over 10-year period
11. Static Risk Assessment: 9; high-risk classification for recidivism
12. Minnesota Sex Offender Screening Tool-Revised (MnSORT-R): 8; percent correct high risk (70%)
13. National Severity Scoring System (increasing degrees of violence from 1970s, 1980s to 1990s)
14. Problem Identification Checklist (6-month period): negative for violence
15. Dangerousness Prediction Decision Tree (3-month period): negative for violence based on history, opportunity, and triggering stimuli
16. Dynamic Antisociality (1-month period): negative for violence based on traits and relevant behaviors

Test Results

1. The forensic database is sufficiently diverse and comprehensive to arrive at conclusions beyond a reasonable degree of psychological probability. Deception analysis revealed that, for the defendant's history and most recent convictions, he minimized and denied past violence and events/behaviors associated with violence.

2. The VRAG is considered the best validated extant measure of violence risk and generates a 10-year probability of recidivism as a function of risk scores (Quinsey et al., 1998). The percent probability for the defendant for the 10-year period was 82% (96th percentile, category 8).

    Predictive items typically considered but not weighted into the VRAG included:

   a. *Results of IQ Testing*

Results: <90 = high risk

Results of Shipley testing yielded a WAIS-R Estimated Full Scale IQ of 67 with impaired vocabulary ($T = 22$; <1st percentile) and abstraction skills ($T = 36$; <10th percentile). The standard error of measurement (SEM) for the Shipley is 8.6, which suggested that the defendant's true IQ ranges from defective to borderline. All test data considered, borderline intelligence is indicated.

    Attentional skills were overall low average to average (DF = 6; 24.6th percentile; mental control = 6/6); his ability to concentrate was low average (digits backward = 4; 17.6th percentile).

    Ability to abstract was poor (e.g., He said that "Strike while the iron is hot" means "iron clothes, cause it is hot"; he defined a "green thumb" as "your hand").

    Judgment was poor (e.g., he would "run" if he were the first person in a movie theater to see smoke and fire, then return and make sure everyone was out of the theater).

    Possible brain damage from years of sniffing paint thinner (see arrest history), which then, as with the above items, may increase his dangerousness beyond the obtained risk probability.

   b. *Attitudes Supportive of Crime:*

Yes = high risk

Includes for the defendant a criminal history from an early age with incarceration at the Hawaii Youth Correctional Facility, denial of responsibility for many offenses or projection of blame to others, and being critical of his victims.

   c. *Attitudes Toward Convention:*

Yes = high risk

Poor work history, chronic polysubstance abuse, limited responsibility for maintaining continual employment, and poor attachment and bonding with others.

    Since 1989, the defendant has been free in the community for only 1 year (1997 to 1998); he was imprisoned for the remainder of the time. His response to treatment has been poor.

3. The Hare Psychopathy Checklist-Revised is considered an excellent measure of violence by itself and is included in Quinsey et al.'s VRAG as well as some other tests discussed below. The defendant's score of 36 of a possible 40 reflects a severe psychopath with behaviors and attitudes in the two main factors: (1) selfish, callous, and remorseless use of others and (2) chronically unstable antisocial and socially deviant lifestyle.

4. Positive predictors of violent recidivism from a meta-analysis involving 52 studies and 16,191 persons by Bonta, Law, and Hanson (1998) included (a) adult criminal history, (b) juvenile delinquency, (c) antisocial personality, (d) nonviolent criminal history, (e) family problems, and (f) violent history. Only one negative predictor was found (age).

5. The HCR-20, Version II (Webster, Douglas, Eaves, and Hart, 1997) (history, clinical, and risk management items), score of 28 is considered high risk. Although the HCR-20 was designed as a guide to risk assessment and not a formal psychological test, empirical studies from a variety of settings and countries have validated the concept that increased risk occurs with increased scores. On this measure, the defendant revealed his problem with alcohol consumption (drinking cheap wine) despite Alcoholics Anonymous attendance. After the undersigned proceeded through the defendant's rap sheet, the defendant reluctantly admitted to an 8-year history of arrests for inhaling paint thinner with a rag (first arrest for promoting intoxicating compound on November 5, 1980, and last on September 3, 1988, with a total of seven arrests). He minimized his abuse of paint thinner by stating that it was infrequent, and that paint thinner is not really a drug since it was inhaled and only resulted in dizziness.

6. The SVR-20 (Boer, Hart, Kropp, and Webster, 1997), much like the HCR-20, is a guide to sexual risk evaluation. The defendant's sexual violence was rated high based on his scores. Relevant items which applied to the defendant included but were not limited to (a) high-density offenses (particularly with multiple victims in 1998); (b) multiple sex offense types (i.e., forced sex with adults to sexual overtures to children); (c) escalation in frequency/severity; (d) extreme minimization/denial of offenses; and (e) attitudes that support or condone violence (e.g., he alleged that the 1989 victim was a prostitute, which in part justified his behavior).

7. The Rapid Risk Assessment for Sexual Offense Recidivism (RRASOR) yielded a 48.6 chance of sexual recidivism over a 10-year period. The relatively low 48.6% change occurred because the measure loads heavily on male-on-male victims and only sexual violence. Nevertheless, the base rate for sexual offenses in the normal population is <1% and about 30% over 10 years among sexual offenders. Hence, the defendant's score is significantly higher than the base-rate group to which he belongs (sexual offenders).

8. The Static Risk Assessment indicated a high recidivism risk classification for the defendant. The static as opposed to dynamic items means that the high-risk classification will unlikely change in the future.

9. The Minnesota Sex Offender Screening Tool-Revised (MnSORT-R) score of 8 yields a percent correct high risk of 70%. This means that an evaluator would be correct 70% of the time if he predicted a high risk of sexual violence for an individual such as the defendant over a 6-year follow-up period.

10. The National Severity Scoring System, based on the survey of over 60,000 Americans by the National Institute of Justice (1985), allows for comparison and possible escalation of violence over time. Multiplying the scaled weights for the defendant shows an acceleration of violence for the 1970s to the 1990s, even though he spent much of the 1990s in prison. The resumption of sexual violence not long after he was released from prison is a very poor prognostic sign.

11. The Problem Identification Checklist, Dangerousness Prediction Decision Tree, and Dynamic Antisociality predict violence for periods of 1 month, 3 months, and 6 months, respectively. Together, they show that the defendant is not an imminent danger to others and comports with his overall good institutional adjustment. Further, risk is low because the defendant does not have the opportunity to aggress against others in the community. Overall, these low rates represent fine-tuning for short periods of time within an overall high risk (84%) on the VRAG over the 10-year period.

The above represent results from quantitatively derived, empirically based systems of prediction. Qualitatively, violence has been shown over the last century to fall into two types: affective (impulsive) and predatory (self-controlled aggression). A number of the defendant's violent acts and behaviors clearly fit the predatory type. For example, the 1989 kidnapping and sexual assault in the first degree yielded a statement from him that he was going to pay the victim ($100) for the sex but did not particularly enjoy the act itself. He neglected to discuss the proactive nature of the crime, the force that was employed, the threats to the victim, and the assault on the male party. He later admitted to assaulting the male party. For the 1998 offenses, he neglected to mention the planned, purposeful acts and denied that he sexually abused, molested, or raped anyone in his life.

When asked to state what he would say to the victims of the offenses if he had an opportunity, he disparaged and blamed the victims as well as their significant others (e.g., "Why do you do this to me?"; "I screw your mother every day; she is a dope addict.").

Summary: Testing on multiple scales of violence prediction revealed a 41-year-old sexual psychopath who has a high risk of violent recidivism for the next decade. Many strong signs of violent recidivism were apparent on these empirically derived scales. The defendant does not appear to be "burning out" in terms of his aggression toward others, a particularly disturbing finding. He is a low risk of violence while incarcerated because, among other factors, he does not have *ad lib* access to the victim pool in the community. The defendant has a significant history of dangerousness to others, resulting in criminally violent conduct, and such a history makes him a serious danger to others.

Sincerely,
Harold V. Hall, PhD, ABPP

Officer-Involved Shooting Case from Chapter 7 (Mohandie)

Kris Mohandie, Ph.D.
Licensed Psychologist
License# PSY12105
P.O. Box 88
Pasadena, CA 91102-008 8
666-6139

May 23, 2006
Eugene P. Ramirez
Manning & Marder, Kass, Ellrod, Ramirez
23rd Floor at Figueroa Tower
660 South Figueroa Street
Los Angeles, CA 90017

Re: *Hector Jones v. City of Los Angeles*, Case No. 1111.

Dear Mr. Ramirez,

Pursuant to your request, this is a preliminary report of my initial findings and opinions in the matter of *Hector Jones v. City of Los Angeles, US District Court Case No. 1111.*

It is noted that any information not available at the time of this report might alter the opinions included herein.

Expertise and Qualifications

I am a California licensed psychologist (PSY12105) trained in clinical, police, and forensic psychology. I have earned a Diplomate in Police Psychology issued by the Society for Police and Criminal Psychology. The following experience, training, and skills qualify me to offer testimony in this particular case (please see a copy of my curriculum vitae which has been attached):

a. Reviews of shooting incidents:
   - Dozens of pre- and postconviction interviews of individuals and witnesses to shooting and suicide by cop events in the context of barricade, hostage, and other police intervention situations.
b. Clinical work related to officer-involved shootings:
   - Counseling of hundreds of officer victims of shootings and other traumatic events, many of which involve suicide by cop.

c. Demonstrated crisis management expertise in consultation and training activities:
  - LAPD crisis/hostage negotiation and SWAT team from 1990 to 2003. On-site response to hostage and barricade incidents, profiling hostage taker/hostages/ victims, assessing for high risk, including violence and suicide by cop potential, interviewing witnesses to these crimes, and offering input to reduce risk and lead to safe apprehension/capture of suspects. In this capacity, I have responded to and reviewed dozens of suicide by cop situations and police shootings.
  - Hostage negotiation and SWAT teams nationwide since 1993. Training to police departments nationwide in the arena of crisis/hostage negotiation, teaching blocks of instruction on crisis negotiation theory and practice, communication skills, psychological aspects of negotiation, and suspect behavior in these situations, including suspect aggression, victim-precipitated aggression, and suicide by cop.
  - Contributed as expert on panel to 1999 Police Officer Standards and Training (POST) Suicide By Cop curriculum and law enforcement training video.
  - Editorial board of the *International Journal of Crisis Negotiations* since 1995 and the *Journal of Threat Assessment* since 1999.
  - Forensic consultation and review of many cases involving suicide by cop, victim precipitation, and victimology issues.
  - Professional presentations to the California Association of Hostage Negotiators annual conferences in 1993, 1994, 1996, 2001, 2002, 2003, 2005, and 2006.
  - Professional presentations to the Association of Threat Assessment Professionals annual conferences 1997–2006.
  - Professional presentations in the arena of suspect aggression, suicide by cop, hostage and barricade incidents, and victim-perpetrator dynamics throughout the United States.
d. Scholarly work related to suicide by cop and crisis management:
  - Primary researcher of an ongoing scientific study of suicide by cop and police shootings. Currently more than 500 shootings in the database, exploring prevalence, antecedents, indicators, and outcomes.
  - Primary author of an article published in 2000 issue of the *Journal of Forensic Sciences*, titled "Clinical and Forensic Indicators of 'Suicide by Cop,'" that reviews the dynamics of subject-precipitation incidents in which a suicidal, self-destructive, desperate, or aggressive individual attempts to get law enforcement to kill him.
e. Relevant training:
  - LAPD Crisis Negotiation Training in 1989.
  - FBI 2-week Crisis Negotiation Training in 1994.
  - Attendance at California Association of Hostage Negotiator's training conference in 1992–1999 and 2001.
f. Membership in relevant professional organizations:
  - California Association of Hostage Negotiators since 1992.
  - Member of Society of Police and Criminal Psychology since 1995.
  - Association of Threat Assessment Professionals since 1995.
  - National Tactical Officers Association since 1998.
  - International Criminal Investigative Analysis Fellowship Program since 2001.
  - International Association of Chiefs of Police since 1999.
g. Forensic consultation/testimony in other police use of force cases.

Reviewed articles:

Artwohl, A. (2003). No recall of weapon discharge. *Law Enforcement Executive Forum*, 3, 41–49.

Honig, A. and Sultan, S. (2005). Reactions and resilience under fire: What an officer can expect, *The Police Chief*.

Honig, A. and Roland, J. (1998). Shots fired: Officer involved, *The Police Chief*, 65, 116–120.

Lewinsky, W. (2002). Stress reactions related to lethal force encounters, *The Police Marksman*, May/June, 23–28.

Mohandie, K. and Meloy, J.R. (2000). Clinical and forensic indicators of "suicide by cop," *Journal of Forensic Sciences*, 45, 384–389.

Reviewed documents:

Federal civil rights complaint

Police report no.

Follow-up police reports

Decedent family interview reports

PD transcripts of interviews and tapes, including 911 tape

Autopsy report

Toxicology report

Dispatch event report

Criminal court sentencing transcript

Audiotapes

911 Tape

Tape

Tape

Transcripts of all tapes

Photographs

Walk-through

Findings and Opinions

1. Mr. Jones, the plaintiff, was actively suicidal when he encountered police officers on August 4, 2004.

   Foundation for opinion:
   a. Per the family, "the suspect had legal problems, was depressed and had previously talked about ending his life." On the Monday prior to the incident, he had met his friend at the park and said "to watch after his family and take care of them once he was gone." He stated that the suspect mentioned that he was tired of screwing things up and he was in a lot of pain and had mentioned that he just wanted "to end his life." Family interview, 16–17
   b. Officer Smith noted that "at one time the suspect put the handgun under his chin and walked around with it like that. The suspect continued similar actions with the handgun, putting it under his chin and yelling and screaming fuck you and continued walking in circles." PD report, 6
   c. Sgt. Gallegos "saw the suspect put the handgun to his mouth area or chin area. He said that the suspect's behavior was erratic and his movements were jagged and

inconsistent … they could never be quite sure what he was going to do next." PD
report, 8

2. The plaintiff, Mr. Jones, committed suicide by cop during the incident. This is a case
of a deliberate suicide by cop in which Mr. Jones encouraged the police to be called
so that he could use the police to commit suicide. Suicide by cop is the term for a
situation in which an individual poses an apparent or actual risk to others in order to
manipulate police into killing them.

Foundation for opinion:

a. Recent gun purchase:
   1. Chuck Jones told the investigator "his brother recently bought, in the last two
   to three months, a .38 caliber pistol." Family interview, 12

b. Verbal statements to third parties by decedent indicating preplanning.
   1. At 10:00 a.m., he told his ex-girlfriend that he would make the police kill him
   because she refused to talk any further about reuniting. He told her to make
   sure she watched the news. Luisa Donahue Interview, 10
   2. Mother, in deposition, denied that he had made suicidal statements to her.
   However, he can clearly be heard on the 911 tape making such a statement. 911
   transcript, 911 tape, and mother's depo, 22

c. Verbal statements to third parties by decedent of a suicide/suicide by cop nature:
   1. Sgt. Gallegos stated that "the requests for the subject to put the gun down were
   about twenty times and at times the suspect would acknowledge the officer talking to him with profanity—the suspect would respond back, "fuck you, shoot
   me, I don't care if you shoot me." PD report, 73
   2. Officer Smith could hear him yelling, "go ahead just shoot, just shoot me, why
   don't you just shoot me." PD report, 85
   3. 911 call, the subject could be heard yelling "go ahead call the police, I don't care,
   I'm going to make them kill me and it will be your fault!" 911 transcript

d. Behavior observed and attributed to Mr. Jones:
   Drew attention to himself:
   1. Engaged in behavior that mandated police attention and engaged the officers. Specifically, he went to a public location while armed with two weapons
   (handgun and knife) and engaged in behavior that would guarantee police
   response. Witness one stated that "guy walked around the apartment complex with police present with a gun in his hand … people were stuck in their
   apartments scared." Officers arrive during this call. Audiotape, 6:22, police
   report, 5
   2. Man armed with .38 handgun, walking around an apartment complex.
   3. Remained in the area as opposed to leaving while engaging in this behavior,
   assuring confrontation with police. My own expertise.
   Armed with two weapons, including a handgun:
   a. Was in possession of an actual firearm. "Pistol was examined and discovered
   to be cocked and loaded." PD report, 34, photographs of knife and handgun
   b. All the officers at scene saw these weapons as noted below.

Demonstrating on his body where he wanted to be shot—shooting motion to his head

1. "The subject looked towards Officer Smith's direction and pointed to his head while making a shooting motion with his hand and fingers. At one point, the subject put the gun in his waist band then pulled it out." PD report, 9
2. Officer Boston saw him turn to face him, "pointing at his head … could hear the individual yelling out, come on mother fucker right here, fucking right here!" PD report, 5

Created impression he was armed and posed a threat, ultimately escalating his conduct into an appearance of immediate threat:

1. Armed with a firearm and a knife, as noted above.
2. Officer Smith also heard him screaming and cussing, "I'm gonna take some of these cops with me!" PD report, 45
3. When the officer tried to talk him into putting the gun down, he continued his abusive language and "continued yelling fuck you! Fuck you!" Officer Smith said that the suspect would have the handgun in front of him at about waist level and would point it from side to side and forward. At one time the suspect spun completely around towards the officers who had surrounded him in the area." PD report, 46
4. Officer Taylor said "during this time the suspect would put the gun down then would bring it back up … he said he would bring up the gun and begin pointing it towards the officers but would bring it back down. He said he did this several times." PD report, 46
5. "After continual pleading with the suspect to put down his weapon, the suspect aggressively walked towards officers, reaching for his waistband and aimed what officers believed to be a firearm towards the group of Any City Police Officers. Officers felt they were in danger of injury or death. Two officers fired their department issued sidearm, for a total of three shots." PD report, 34
6. Sgt. Gallegos fired from his handgun after the suspect "grabbed quickly towards his waistband while turning quickly, and pointed what he believed to be a gun with his hands extended, clearly out in front of him, towards the officers. At this time, Sgt. Gallegos thought that the suspect was going to shoot at them and kill one of the officers or himself." He fired two rounds. PD report, 48
7. Officer Smith "then observed the suspect grab for the gun in his waistband with both his hands and raise his arms while turning quickly to face the officers." This was the moment at which he fired his weapon once. PD report, 63–64, transcript, 23

Minimal escape-oriented behavior

1. Ran and walked in direction of officers when he had multiple other options that would create distance as opposed to proximity.
2. Officer Smith heard officers talk to subject, "trying to convince him to drop the weapon so they could help him. The subject refused and failed to follow the commands, by yelling profanities and flipping his middle finger at the officers. The subject would walk away from the officers then come walking back towards them but would stop before entering the intersection." PD report, 44

3. For the duration of the incident there was no containment to the rear of the complex that led to an alleyway. From the plaintiff's vantage point, he should have seen that there were no officers in this vicinity. PD report, 32, My walk-through.

Attacking the officers:

1. Officer Smith said "one time the suspect spun completely around towards the officers who had surrounded him in the area." PD report, 46
2. Points noted above under "Created impression he was armed and posed a threat, ultimately escalating his conduct into an appearance of immediate threat."

Noncompliant to the officers' commands:

1. "Officers set up communications with the suspect to have him put down his weapon. The suspect failed to comply with all orders and continued exhibiting the firearm in a rude and threatening manner. Officers noticed a bladed weapon in suspect's hand. Suspect interchanges both weapons from hand to hand, as officers attempted to have him put down the weapon." 34, 35
2. Refusing to put gun down. Officer Smith "did recall the suspect tell him fuck you I ain't putting the gun down." PD report, 55, transcript, 58
3. Sgt. Gallegos heard officers talking to subject, "trying to convince him to drop the weapon so they could help him. The subject refused and failed to follow the commands, by yelling profanities and flipping the middle finger at the officers. The subject would walk away from the officers then come walking back towards them but would stop as if on some invisibly line, like just short of the point of no return." PD report, 44

Maintaining the continuous perception that he was armed, unpredictable, and dangerous:

1. Sgt. Gallegos would see the suspect pick up the knife and jab it in the air in a striking motion. He would alternate placing each in his waistband and pulling it out. PD report, 37
2. Officer Banuelos "saw the suspect put the handgun to his mouth area or chin area. He said that the suspect's behavior was erratic and his movements were jagged and inconsistent ... they could never be quite sure what he was going to do next." PD report, 4
3. Continued doing behaviors noted under "Created impression he was armed and posed a threat, ultimately escalating his conduct into an appearance of immediate threat" throughout the incident's duration. He was consistently threatening.

Intoxicated:

1. Toxicology indicates positive for amphetamines and marijuana. PD report, 436
2. Methamphetamine intoxication increases violence risk potential and lowers impulse control. My knowledge and experience.

Agitated, angry, and confrontational:

1. Officer Smith observed that "it was pretty apparent that he was using foul language like fuck you and could see him making gestures with his middle

finger, flipping them off. It appeared the individual was extremely angry." PD report, 49

2. Officer Bobbs observed the armed suspect as "very agitated." PD report, 65, transcript, 215

3. Officer Smith thought that "obviously this guy wants to shoot somebody … very agitated, I mean mad …. He was very agitated and he was very dangerous is what I thought." Transcript, 27

4. "Intense eye contact with officer as he reached for his waistband and turned rapidly." PD report, 25

e. Mental state and psychological issues:

1. Depressed. Chuck Jones, the plaintiff's brother, indicated that his brother "appeared to be very depressed" on the afternoon of the incident. Family interview, 110–111, 118

2. Final communications. Chuck Jones said "his brother made various statements to him, specifically saying that he told him everything was going to be alright, to take care of the house and make sure that his mother was taken care of." Family interview, 110

3. Poor life adaptation, impaired coping ability. My knowledge and experience.

4. Under the influence of mind-altering chemicals—methamphetamine. Charles Jones stated that "he and his brother had smoked two bowls of crank prior to the crisis between he and his mother." Family interview, 20; toxicology indicates positive for amphetamines. PD report, 36

f. Context and circumstances:

1. Relationship, legal, drug, and family problems. Family interview, 17; Criminal history, 5; ex-girlfriend interview, 23; point "e-4" above, and point "g-1" below

2. Told by judge he would be going to prison if he violated probation. Sentencing court transcript, p. 17

g. History:

a. Drug addiction and substance problems. Brother indicated the plaintiff regularly smoked meth. Family interview, 12

h. Empirical criteria for determining suicide (ECDS)

a. Mr. Jones's high scores of 13 on suicidal intent and 11 on self-infliction dimensions of ECDS was well over the score of 3 necessary on each to label his death and circumstances suicide. This measure is 92% accurate at categorizing cases as suicide versus other causes of death, and scientific studies have found it to have acceptable reliability.

3. At the time of the incident, the decedent aggressed upon the officers and appeared to pose a risk to innocent citizens. He actively aggressed, was noncompliant, and escalated the confrontation into a police use of deadly force. He posed a potential risk.

Foundation for opinion:
a. See point "2-d" above.

4. The decedent precipitated his own death—he is the proximate cause.

   Foundation for opinion:
   a. Subject-precipitated death describes those situations in which the injured party or decedent somehow initiates or contributes to the sequence of events that results in their injury or death. (Mohandie and Meloy, 2000)

5. The officers were confronted with a perceived life-threatening situation as presented by the decedent. Any other officers in their position would—and should—have perceived that threat. Yet their actions were consistent with contemporary crisis management practice.

   Foundation for opinion:
   a. See point "2-d" above.
   b. Officers set up a perimeter.
   c. Officers attempted to contain the subject.
   d. Officers attempted to establish dialogue.
       i. Officer Smith recalled saying "put the gun down, we don't want to hurt you, we just want to talk to you, put the gun down, and we can't hear you." PD report, 66, transcript, 16
   e. During the operation an emergency medical unit had been called to stand by. Immediately a paramedic was summoned to care for his injuries. Police report, 34
   f. They did not crowd him despite the fact that he was in an open-air environment. PD reports
   g. Lights and sirens were avoided.
   h. A negotiation team was contacted and consulted but the incident was over prior to their arrival.
   i. They offered to talk to him and tried to convince him verbally to put down his weapon for a substantial period of time.

6. Given several important psychophysiological factors, it is expected and consistent with critical incident dynamics that none of the officers perceived or was aware that Mr. Jones's loaded and operational firearm dropped and remained on the ground at some point after being fired.

   Foundation for opinion:
   1. Officer Smith never saw it on the ground. Smith depo, 47; police report, 7
   2. "I did not see a gun until the incident was over." Gallegos depo, 30, 36; police report, 7
   3. There are several important reasons that each officer would fail to see Mr. Jones's gun on the ground and continue to perceive that he is armed, dangerous, and posing an imminent threat.
       a. "I was locked onto his eyes as he moved about and was yelling obscenities at me." Smith depo, 25
       b. "Keep in mind, sir, that I actually have three different duties here. I have to establish the perimeter, try to evacuate, and keep my eyes on what was happening." Boston depo, 23
       c. "I was still behind the halo effect of the unit spotlights. And as they moved farther to the north, they were also in some shadows underneath the trees. So it

was dark where they were at and where I was at." "I did not see a gun until the incident was over." Boston depo, 30, 36

    d. Tunnel vision that occurs in these events and occurred with these officers. Point "7c" below; my knowledge and experience

    e. It is documented in the work of Dr. Bill Lewinsky that the radius of human eyesight and perception under normal conditions is five degrees beyond the focal point. This is further affected—diminished—by conditions of high stress and low light, which reduce this already limited zone even more due to tunnel vision of critical incidents and physiological changes to the eye that occur under conditions of stress and low light.

        i. "Lighting was not very good." Smith depo, 20; Boston transcript, 5; Gallegos depo, 35

        ii. All officers report a focus on the suspect or events that left them unable to see at what point the gun was not within Mr. Jones's grasp or potential control and separated from his person.

    f. Even if they had been able to perceive Mr. Jones was no longer armed with the loaded .38, there would be no reason for the officers to believe that he was not in possession of any additional weapons under the circumstances. "I asked Officer Smith if the guy had been searched to make sure he had no more weapons there because the paramedics were arriving on scene." Gallegos transcript, 9

  4. It is normal under the conditions described for officers to continue their gunfire. Officers are trained to continue to fire their weapons while they perceive a threat. In certain circumstances, this can result in officers failing to remember how many rounds they actually fired or firing more than they intended.

7. It is normal and expected for officers to forget portions of a traumatic incident due to perceptual distortions that occur during a highly stressful critical incident. Officer Smith demonstrates this phenomenon when he says "from the time that around when he advanced the final time and my gun went off to approximately two to three seconds after I could not tell you one thing that happened. I don't recall. I don't remember." Smith depo, 45

Foundation for opinion:

    a. Officer Smith has never fired his weapon other than at practice or training. Smith depo, 65

    b. Officer Smith believed that Mr. Jones intended to shoot him as he rapidly approached him while reaching for an apparent weapon. Smith depo, 50

    c. He had just been involved in a threatening event, a critical incident. Such incidents are known to cause officers perceptual distortions and memory problems for portions of the event itself. Scientific studies indicate that 90% of officers will report such perceptual distortions and 22–52% will forget portions of an event they are involved in which coincide with their perceptual focus (tunnel vision) versus what was in their peripheral vision. Tunnel vision is observed in 45–79% of officers involved in such events. My knowledge and experience; Honig and Roland (1998); Artwohl (2002, 2003)

    d. Has limited recall from that point on (Mr. Jones advancing the final time while reaching) about others' actions, for example, if anyone was saying anything to Mr. Jones. Smith depo, 48, 54

e. Does not remember himself yelling anything to Mr. Jones until he was on the ground. Others, however, recall him issuing commands. Smith depo, 58; Gallegos transcript, 5; Boston depo, 22

f. He reports the sound of the shots was less. Smith depo, 45–46

g. "I don't recall if I gave Mr. Jones a warning or not." Smith depo, 68

h. Reports "everything kind of, went like slower, like in slow motion…" Smith transcript, 16

i. Demanded a break during interview when describing. Others commented about his emotional level. Smith transcript, 13

j. Very specific recall for when and where his own hand was on the handle of his own gun, as well as the expressions on the suspect's face while he was advancing. That was where his focus was during that interval. "His mouth opened wide and his eyes seemed to change, they got bigger it seemed, and I just saw that his face seemed to get bigger too as he moved closer. I squeezed my gun tighter in my hands and looked at him over the front sight." Smith transcript, 12–14

k. The above point is important—officer's perception and recall for that which they were tunnel focused on will be highly specific. "As an officer's mind focuses on what is perceived to be the threat he gains volumes of information about what he's focusing on …. The price of focusing on something specific is the loss of a lot of other information." Lewinsky (2002); my knowledge and experience

Case Analysis

This is a clear-cut case of suicide by cop in which the plaintiff engaged in provocative, dramatic, and outrageous behavior designed to cause police to shoot him, with the explicit purpose of committing suicide. His handgun was operational and loaded. He clearly posed a potential threat to the officers and potentially citizens, and officers were restrained with his dangerous behavior, trying to buy time and obtain his peaceful surrender by not crowding him, seeking information, and engaging in dialogue to obtain a peaceful resolution. Unfortunately, Mr. Jones escalated the confrontation by advancing on the officers rapidly, while reaching for his waistband in a context of having on prior occasions produced this handgun. Often such subjects (as it appears Mr. Jones did) will test how far they have to push their threats in order to elicit lethal force, and engage in ambivalent behavior as they build up the psychological energy to pursue their suicidal agenda. The decedent had a history of depression, had been saying his goodbyes and getting his affairs in order, was under the influence of drugs associated with higher risk for violence and acting out, and made multiple threatening statements of a homicidal and suicidal nature during the confrontation with police. The officers' actions were consistent with current crisis management practice; however, Mr. Jones forcibly escalated the encounter into a deadly force incident.

Although it is noted that other information, not available to me at the time of this review, might modify my opinions, I believe there was sufficient information to arrive at my findings and opinions. Nonetheless, I would welcome any additional information if it were made available to me. If I can answer any questions please do not hesitate to telephone me.

Sincerely,
Kris Mohandie, Ph.D.
Licensed psychologist

Intelligence Data-Collection Guide

It is crucial for the negotiator to obtain relevant information regarding the perpetrator/hostage taker and the hostage/victim(s). Therefore, the intelligence team's role is vital. The following questions are provided to help guide investigators and the consulting forensic psychologist when questioning informational sources.

Perpetrator Basic Data

1. Has the perpetrator used other names? What were they?
2. What name does the perpetrator prefer?
3. What is the perpetrator's age, date of birth, race, height, weight, hair color, and eye color?
4. What is the perpetrator wearing?
5. Do you have a picture of the perpetrator? How has the perpetrator's appearance changed since this picture was taken?

Perpetrator's Education

1. What is the perpetrator's highest level of education?
2. If the perpetrator went to college what was his major?
3. What kind of grades did the perpetrator make?

Weapon Information

1. What kind of weapon does the perpetrator have?
2. Has the perpetrator ever used a weapon against a person before? Please describe.
3. Has the perpetrator served in the military? Please describe.
4. Has the perpetrator had weapon training? Please describe.

Perpetrator's History

1. *Past Aggression:* Does the perpetrator have a history of past aggression? Please describe.
2. *Past Aggression:* To your knowledge how often has the perpetrator acted out aggressively over the last 12 months? Please describe.
3. *Similar Incident:* Has the perpetrator ever done anything like this incident before? Please describe.
4. *Similar Incident:* What was the outcome of the previous incident?
5. *Abused Substances:* Does the perpetrator have a history of abusing substances? Please describe.
6. *Mental Health History:* To your knowledge has the perpetrator ever seen a mental health professional? When?

7. *Mental Health History:* What was the doctor's name?
8. *Mental Health History:* Why did the perpetrator seek mental health consultation?
9. *Mental Health History:* What was his diagnosis?
10. *Mental Health History:* What was the medication prescribed?
11. *Mental Health History:* Do you know if the perpetrator is still taking his medication?
12. *Mental Health History:* When talking to the perpetrator's treating mental health professional ask:
    a. Diagnosis
    b. Medications
    c. Has the perpetrator cooperated with treatment? Explain.
    d. Please describe perpetrator's substance abuse history.
    e. Does the perpetrator have any positive relationships in his life? With whom?
    f. Describe the current crisis situation and ask the treating mental health professional—What will the perpetrator likely do in this situation? Will he hurt himself? Will he hurt someone else?
13. *Early Family/Social Maladjustment:* Do you know anything about the perpetrator's early life or family? Please describe. Did the perpetrator have serious problems as a child? Did he or she get into trouble a lot? Please describe.
14. *Relationship Problems:* Can you describe the perpetrator's recent home life? Is he or she married or involved in a permanent relationship? What can you tell me about the relationships the perpetrator has had in the past?
15. *Employment Problems:* Is the perpetrator employed? What is his or her employment? How many jobs has he had during his life? How does the perpetrator get along with his co-workers?
16. *Legal Problems:* What can you tell me about the perpetrator's legal history? Has he or she been in trouble with the law before? Please describe.

Present Psychological Factors

1. *Insight Problem:* Why do you think the perpetrator is doing this? (precipitating the present crisis situation)
2. *Anger Problem:* How has the perpetrator been feeling lately? Has he or she been particularly angry? How do you know?
3. *Impulsivity Problem:* Would you describe the perpetrator as an impulsive person? Why?
4. *Impulsivity Problem:* Has the perpetrator complained of people making him angry? Do you know of any verbal or physical fights the perpetrator has been in? Please describe.
5. *Impulsivity Problem:* Does the perpetrator have a number of outstanding parking tickets? Speeding tickets?
6. *Empathy Problem:* Do you think that the perpetrator cares for anybody? Why? Who?
7. *Empathy Problem:* Does the perpetrator have any pets? What kind of pets? How does he or she care for them?
8. *Antisocial attitudes:* Does the perpetrator belong to any gangs? Describe.

9. *Antisocial Attitudes:* Does the perpetrator have a prison record? Describe.
10. *Current Mental State:* How does the perpetrator usually manage stress?
11. *Current Mental State:* What have you observed recently regarding how the perpetrator manages stress—any differences?
12. *Current Mental State:* Have you noticed the perpetrator doing anything recently that did not seem like him or her? Describe.
13. *Current Mental State:* How would you describe the perpetrator's recent mood and behavior?
14. *Current Mental State/Suicide:* Has the perpetrator said anything about committing suicide? What was said?
15. *Current Mental State/Suicide:* Has the perpetrator ever attempted suicide? Describe.
16. *Current Mental State/Suicide:* When was the last time he or she attempted suicide?
17. *Current Mental State/Suicide:* Has anyone in the perpetrator's family ever committed suicide? Describe the circumstances and when it occurred.
18. *Current Mental State/Suicide:* Has the perpetrator been losing weight?
19. *Current Mental State/Suicide:* Has the perpetrator been having trouble sleeping?
20. *Current Mental State/Suicide:* Has the perpetrator been giving away personal property?
21. *Current Mental State/Suicide:* Does today's date have any special significance for the perpetrator? If so what?
22. *Substance Abuse:* Do you think that the perpetrator is currently under the influence of drugs or alcohol?
23. *Substance Abuse:* When was the last time he or she used this drug or alcohol?
24. *Substance Abuse:* What is the perpetrator's usual behavior when using this drug or alcohol?
25. *Substance Abuse:* What is the perpetrator's usual behavior when he or she is withdrawing from this substance?
26. *Substance Abuse:* Is the perpetrator in Alcoholics Anonymous (AA) or Narcotics Anonymous (NA)? What is his or her AA or NA sponsor's name and telephone number?

Spouse/Partner/Victim Basic Data

1. What is the hostage/victim's age, date of birth, race, height, weight, hair color, eye color?
2. What is the hostage/victim wearing?
3. Do you have a picture of the hostage/victim? How has the hostage/victim's appearance changed since this picture was taken?

Spouse/Partner/Victim Factors

1. Do you know of any past relationship between the perpetrator and the hostage/victim? Please describe.
2. Describe the present relationship between the perpetrator and the hostage/victim.
3. Has the perpetrator ever abused the hostage/victim in the past? Please describe.
4. Has there ever been a victim protection order (VPO) placed on the perpetrator? Please describe.

5. Do you know of any past relationship between the hostage/victims, i.e., between hostage/victim A and hostage/victim B? Was the relationship positive or negative? Please describe.

6. Does the hostage/victim have a military or law enforcement background? Please describe.

7. Does the hostage/victim have any medical or psychological problems? Please describe.

8. Is the hostage/victim presently taking any medication? Please describe.

9. How do you think the hostage/victim is handling his or her current predicament? Please explain.

10. Do you think the hostage/victim will do anything to provoke the perpetrator during his or her captivity? Please explain.

Criminal-Forensic Deception Analysis from Chapter 9 (Hall, Poirier, and Thompson)

February 27, 2005
Hon. Craig Rosenquist
The Judiciary, State of Hawaii Circuit Court of the First Circuit
999 Maile Street
Pahoa, HI 96778

RE: *State of Hawaii v. Johnny Buck*
    NO. XX-XXXX
    Murder in the second degree
    Kidnapping
    Terroristic threatening in the first degree

Dear Judge Rosenquist,
    Pursuant to your January 20, 2005, Order to assess Mr Johnny J. Buck, DOB December 11, 1960, SSN XXX-XX-XXXX, on the issues of criminal responsibility and extreme mental or emotional disturbance (EMED), this report is presented. Please be aware that the undersigned as an expert for the State previously examined the defendant in January 2004 to determine whether he was malingering or engaging in other deceptive behavior to conceal his competency to stand trial, and to comment on fitness parameters. The undersigned was originally retained in this case to evaluate EMED issues by then-Deputy Prosecuting Attorney Marilyn Sugizaki on December 16, 1995, with services provided by the undersigned until January 17, 1996. No EMED conclusions were reached and the undersigned's involvement in the case ceased until he was again retained by Manfred Traphagen, Esq., Office of the Prosecuting Attorney, on January 14, 2004.

Forensic Database: Review of information gathered in 1995–1996 is as follows:

1. Police and investigation reports for the September 16, 1995, alleged offenses
2. Inspection of scene of alleged offenses (December 19, 1995)
3. Interview of victim's mother (December 22, 1995)
4. Photographs, news clippings, and other material supplied by victim's mother (December 22, 1995)
5. Interview of victim's boyfriend, P. Wellington (January 7, 1996, January 10, 1996, January 18, 1996, and January 23, 1996)
6. Interview of witness J. Spencer (January 5, 1996)
7. Interview of witness J. Miller (December 24, 1995)
8. Interview of S. Miller (January 7, 1996)
9. Interview of B. Scott (December 28, 1995)
10. Interview of L. Larson (January 7, 1996)

11. Interview of K. Remington (January 10, 1996)
12. Interview of B. Phillips (January 26, 1996)

Material gathered during January and February 2004 by the undersigned was reviewed and consisted of the following:

13. Psychiatric and psychological reports from Hawaii Revised Statutes (HRS) §704 examiners and Hawaii State Hospital (HSH) staff for the period subsequent to the defendant's psychiatric hospitalization
14. Test protocols, forms, and answer sheets, including objective personality and neuro-psychological tests, which allowed for scrutiny of individual items and in some cases rescoring to ensure accuracy of test results
15. An undated draft of a Memorandum in Support of Finding of Defendant Buck fit to Proceed to Trial, written by Senior Deputy Attorney Traphagen
16. CID closing report and summary of alleged murder
17. Copies of correspondence to attorneys and judges by the defendant (1996–1999) as well as correspondence to other parties
18. Copies of grievances made by the defendant while at HSH supplied by the law firm of Huey, Dewey, and Louie through Senior Deputy Attorney Traphagen
19. The eight volumes of HSH psychiatric notes, records, and other material, since 1997 (January 20, 2004 and January 21, 2004)
20. Oahu Community Correctional Center (OCCC) records, which were included as part of the HSH records but separately indexed. The complete set of OCCC records was later sent to the undersigned by Deputy Prosecuting Attorney Manfred Traphagen
21. Clinical interview and mental status evaluation of the defendant on January 21, 2004, initially at the ward nurse's office and then the ward conference room, followed by a brief discussion with and observation of the defendant subsequent to the interviews on January 21, 2004, and January 22, 2004, making a total of four brief contacts of about 1 h
22. Discussions with psychiatric staff at HSH from the evening and day shifts on January 21 and January 22, 2004 concerning the Defendant's adjustment at that facility. This included discussions with his treatment coordinator, Ms Leilani Peterson, who also witnessed the forensic orientation and initial portion of the clinical interview
23. Transcript of fitness proceedings supplied by Deputy Prosecuting Attorney Manfred Traphagen
24. Psychopathy Checklist-Revised (HARE, PCL-R), constructed from defendant's behavior and records

Materials collected subsequent to the above consisted of the following:

25. Interview of Peter Wellington in Kamuela (November 19, 2004, December 11, 2004)
26. Phone interview of Bradley Robins, PhD, previous 3-panel evaluator (January 23, 2005)
27. Clinical interview of the defendant at OCCC (January 31, 2005)
28. OCCC medical records (January 31, 2005)
29. Interview of Kalani Sutin, PhD, forensic psychologist at the Kole Mental Health Center (January 14, 2005)

30. Inspection of Dr Sutin's notes, tests protocols, and other materials relating to his evaluation of the defendant

The findings in this report stemmed from the above database and were arrived at independently of the other examiners in this case. The conclusions stated herein are rendered to a reasonable degree of psychological probability.

Mental Conditions: The Diagnostic and Statistical Manual, Fourth Edition, Text Revision (DSM-IV-TR) (American Psychiatric Association, 2000) mental conditions of the defendant at the time of the evaluation were as follows:

Axis I	Polysubstance abuse, in institutional remission malingering
Axis II	Antisocial personality disorder (psychopath)
Axis III	None
Axis IV	Chronic legal, psychosocial, and financial problems
Axis V	GAF = 50/50 (serious problems)

At the time of the alleged murder, the only mental condition is antisocial personality disorder.

Concerning the diagnosis of polysubstance abuse, held in check by his institutional confinement, there is a self-admitted history of abuse of lysergic acid diethylamide (LSD), phencyclidine (PCP), heroin, crystal methamphetamine, inhalants, and marijuana for the time prior to his arrest on the instant charges. During much of his HSH hospitalization, he met six/seven criteria from DSM-IV for substance abuse (see June 5, 2003, progress note). Records suggested as of the last evaluation that he still has attitudes supportive of substance abuse, despite intervention over the years, and would probably resort to substance abuse if released. It should be noted that on January 15, 2004, he again admitted to staff of prior substance abuse and also stated that he sold drugs to others.

Concerning the malingering diagnosis, he demonstrated deceptive behaviors for the time of the alleged offenses and the evaluation, as presented below. A strong and persistent history of malingering and other deceptive behavior has been demonstrated by the defendant and diagnosed by psychiatric staff over the years at OCCC, HSH, and by three-panel HRS §704 members, which is discussed in some detail to show the pervasiveness and persistence of deception by the defendant. He meets the DSM-IV-TR criteria for malingering, as well as criteria for malingering and other types of deception presented in the behavioral science literature.

Events and behavior suggesting that the defendant faked bad (i.e., malingered by creating or exaggerating deficiencies or downplaying his abilities) included, but are not limited to, the following:

1. During his first admission to HSH on April 14, 1997, to April 20, 1997, he obtained a Wechsler Adult Intelligence Scale-Revised (WAIS-R) IQ = 71, which is borderline in severity and two points above the range of mental retardation. Yet the defendant did not appear or act borderline or intellectually inferior at that time, as noted by examiners. On the WAIS-R information subtest, he missed simple items (e.g., Which direction does the sun rise? How many weeks in a year?) yet received full credit for more difficult items (e.g., What is the main theme in the Book of Genesis?, Which name is associated with the theory of relativity?, How far is it from New York to Paris?). Similar scatter was shown in vocabulary (e.g., not receiving full credit for defining a "penny" and "breakfast," but correctly defining more difficult words such

as "assume" and "assemble"). On other WAIS-R subtests, he showed a similar pattern of attempting to pretend he was less intelligent than he actually was.

2. On April 18, 1997, he pounded his head against the wall at HSH, later stating "I have an aneurysm in my head." He also claimed "hallucinations" consisting of seeing people and shadows that others do not see. Records from both OCCC and HSH suggested that he did not experience hallucinations or genuine symptoms of a thought disorder.

3. On April 19, 1997, on the Trail Making Test, Part A, which is a visual-motor sequencing test, he received a score which is in the brain-damaged range (114 s). On the same date, he obtained a score in the brain-damaged range on the Trail Making Test, Part B (212 s). Yet, his behavior outside of testing was not suggestive of the deficiencies shown on neuropsychological testing or of brain damage in general.

4. During his first admission to HSH in April 1997, he stated his wife was dead and that he was supposed to have killed himself as well. On September 10, 1999, he claimed he was informed by staff that his wife was dead. On December 5, 1999, he spoke of his wife in the present tense, saying that she was reincarnated. On January 8, 2002, he said he was not hungry because his wife was not eating with him. On January 12, 2002, he said he did not know if he killed his wife but admitted saying so in order to return to OCCC from HSH years before. In direct contradiction to everything else, on March 15, 2002, he said his wife visited him on the ward 10 months ago and they had sex together. He said his wife, at that time, supposedly encouraged him to seek help for his problems. On January 31, 2005, he stated to the undersigned that he knew his wife was dead.

5. On four different Minnesota Multiphasic Personality Inventory-2 (MMPI-2) Tests administered in 1999 and 2000, he faked bad by greatly exaggerating his psychopathology and attempting to place himself in a negative light. Importantly, he filled out the test in a systematic and consistent manner (see VRIN and TRIN scores, plus other indicia of consistency), which means that the results were not due to psychotic confusion, lack of reading ability, or other factors. The MMPI-2 results are strong evidence of malingering, as this test has been cross-validated in hundreds of studies involving thousands of subjects, patients, and forensic clients.

6. On the Neurobehavioral Cognitive Status Examination (NCSE), obtained on December 24, 1999, he attempted to appear brain damaged in his attention, language, memory, calculations, and reasoning skills, these scores all in the severely brain-damaged range. Again, these scores were markedly inconsistent with the skills in these domains he displays when not tested.

7. On October 20, 2001, he told staff that he could broadcast Hillary Clinton's thoughts and that he could read the mind of the evaluator, psychotic signs that he had never displayed before, and that were not associated with psychotic behavior and form of thought.

8. On January 14, 2002, he claimed voices were telling him to kill people and that people were reading his thoughts. Again, these behaviors were not associated with psychotic behavior and formal errors of thinking.

9. On January 29, 2002, he reversed himself on the above, denying that he had ever heard auditory hallucinations.

10. On March 9, 2002, in speaking of the instant killing, the defendant said he tried to shoot his ex-wife's boyfriend but "ended up shooting his girlfriend." For the first

time, he reported hearing voices to kill at the time of the shooting. On January 31, 2005, he denied hearing voices at the time of the killing, then changed his mind, saying a demon may have spoke to him (see 15).

11. On November 3, 2002, he was told by his treatment team that a letter would be written to the Court that he was psychologically fit to legally proceed. The HSH note reads: *"He began making bizarre statements immediately.* At the end of the month when I told him the psychiatrist had not written the letter, *he quit the 'crazy' act,'* though he is now focusing on two of the RNs, accusing them of voodoo to make them miserable. He and two patients, LC and JW, formed a 'mini gang.' They stayed up all night, most nights …" [emphasis added].

12. On January 21, 2004, the staff noted his previous "suicide attempts" were "feeble," with the patient, for example, supposedly preparing to jump off a low object a short distance to hang himself.

13. On January 21, 2004, he told this examiner that he had a microchip in his head and presented other bizarre themes, inconsistent with his previous history and behavior. Staff reported that he typically picks up bizarre statements and behaviors shown by other (genuinely) psychotic individuals on the unit. In other words, he copies behaviors suggestive of mental illness from others.

14. On January 21, 2004, the staff noted that the defendant typically puts up a "crazy act" in front of certain others that he wants to impress that he is severely mentally ill, including the undersigned, after the January 21, 2004, interview commenced.

15. On January 31, 2005, he repeatedly stated that just before the shooting he heard the laugh of a demon. He then demonstrated the laugh of the demon by making low, chuckling sounds. He later added that the demon's voice (not the victim's) said in a "crying" voice, "No, Jimmie, no." To explain his state of mind, he stated that he had a "serious mental breakdown" at the time of the shooting. The laugh of a demon, or the sound of one, is suspicious as it suddenly appeared after 8 years for the first time (no indication of a demon laughing in the voluminous records). The laughing demon appears to function as an entity to blame for the death of the victim. When asked to sum up why the instant offenses occurred, he responded with "Spirits controlling and manipulating me." In sum, Mr Buck presented with an obviously contrived mental event for the killing.

Indicia of faking good, or denial/minimizing of wrongdoing or problems, included the following:

1. On December 3, 1999, while at OCCC, he was observed trying to hide a plate of food and then lying about it by accusing staff of misconduct. The OCCC records contain entries related to violence and threats of violence shown by the defendant, associated with deception in attempting to get out of trouble.

2. For the time before the alleged offenses, the defendant shared that he used to lie on his job applications about his previous drug abuse (see December 23, 2001, HSH note).

3. On December 20, 2002, he distracted a staff member away from a patient. He came back and threw a container of urine on this patient, then walked to the restroom and calmly washed out the urinal.

4. On January 20, 2004, he denied malingering in the past to the undersigned, despite strong evidence that he did so. He also, on this date, denied to the undersigned that

he had ever lied to staff, in contradiction to his previous verbal behaviors. In other words, Mr Buck deceived about his deception.

5. On January 31, 2005, the defendant stated to the undersigned that he lied to OCCC staff when asked if he had ever been administered antipsychotic drugs. He claimed he was afraid of taking medication. The OCCC records indicated that after the most recent transfer to OCCC, the defendant did not complain of psychological or mental problems and was not placed on psychotropic medication.

6. On January 31, 2005, for the time of the alleged offenses, the defendant stated he thinks but is not sure that the victim may have said "kill me, I'm in pain," after she was shot the first time. This preposterous claim functions to place himself in the role of a compassionate individual attending to the needs of the victim he just shot.

7. On January 31, 2005, in contradiction to the database findings and other information, the defendant claimed he had the loaded shotgun in the back seat of the car to kill himself, and not anyone else. He claimed a witness (Peter Wellington) attacked and choked him. This party allegedly came over and kneeled over the victim after she was shot and on the ground, rifling through her fanny pack.

The defendant strongly denied that he ever admitted showing deceptive behaviors. Yet, in 1995, HSH notes indicated that he told Carl Pascoe, MD, the Director of a mental health clinic, that he had been malingering his symptoms and could not continue to lie to staff. On June 6, 1995, he told Dr Pascoe that he had malingered and that the behaviors or delusional beliefs were not real. Further, and most importantly, he stated that the agitation, pressure of speech, and other symptoms were intentional. He typically presents his fabrications in an agitated manner, speaking without interruption, as a means to control and dominate the situation.

A portion of an (undated) letter written by the defendant during this period is relevant in this regard:

Dear Dr. Carl Pascoe,
I am apologizing for lying to you, for wasting your time and the time of countless others. After reading the Honolulu magazine September 1999, and for a few other reasons I cannot go on feigning and malingering. It started back on May of 1999 … This is when I began to lie. I dislike dishonesty and always wanted the whole entire truth to come out. That is why I've insisted on truth serums.

The defendant in this letter goes on to say that his memory is severely damaged. He states also that it troubles him when he has to lie, especially when it concerns the victim in this case.

On June 6, 1998, the defendant admitted spitting out his medication when staff members were not observing him.

Events and behaviors suggesting that he chose to invalidate evaluation or results, a form of deception, included the following:

1. He declined to be evaluated by several three-panel and other evaluators in the past.
   For those sessions to which he was agreeable to be interviewed, he invalidated the sessions by various ploys, as discussed above. He showed the ability to meet with a defense expert, Dr Samuel Beers, for almost a dozen hours over several sessions.

2. On Friday, January 19, 2004, he left the evaluation room and did not return, evidently deciding to terminate that interview. When asked before the interview was terminated about legal issues, he answered irrelevantly, "I have bone cancer," and proceeded to dominate the interview by speaking incessantly about topics of his choice.

3. On Saturday, January 20, 2004, he refused to meet with the undersigned in the late morning, stating to a staff member that he was sleeping and was not to be bothered. Shortly after noon, he refused to meet again with the undersigned when the defendant came to the nurse's station for medication, stating that he was "... feeling sick and want to lie down; some other day." Both before and after this interaction, he was observed in the courtyard talking to staff and patients, and showing no inappropriate behavior.

4. On January 31, 2005, the defendant attempted to control and direct the interview by various behaviors—rapping on the glass, asking the evaluator if he was paying attention, showing him records from his past and wanting him to read and analyze them, and becoming circumstantial and evasive when asked about the alleged offenses.

The diagnosis of antisocial personality disorder overlaps with psychopathy. This defendant is a severe psychopath, as shown by persistent maladaptive behaviors and his score on the PCL-R, with a lifelong history of psychopathy. Information acquired during the last evaluation confirmed the presence of psychopathy. Psychopathic behavior at HSH includes the persistent and varied deceptions that the defendant has perpetrated on both staff and patients, as discussed above. On January 10, 2000, he grabbed a staff member by the right shoulder and physically turned him around to face him. He then grabbed his shirt at the collar. HSH notes indicated that the defendant held his ink pen in an upraised position with his right fist clenched. He then yanked the staff member's shirt down to his waist. It took several staff to wrestle the defendant to the ground. The defendant tried to bite staff in this process. On March 2, 2000, he told another psychiatric staff member, an RN, "I know your address. I'll take care of you," after he was confronted by her for inappropriate behavior. HSH notes suggest that the female staff are frightened of the defendant and suspect him on multiple occasions of making harassing phone calls to staff private residences, in addition to his purposeful disruptions and aggression on the unit.

The inappropriate aggression continued. Another example of psychopathic behavior is when he told yet another female staff member on March 15, 2000, that he would have smashed her head in with a can of juice if she had laughed at his leg injury. This is after he laid his hands on her shoulder, resulting in the staff member moving away from him to break contact. On April 4, 2000, he made slashing motions underneath a nursing staff's chin, touching her on the chin. The staff member told him not to touch her and the defendant became angry.

The defendant was diagnosed with an antisocial personality disorder (psychopath) because of relevant behaviors and attitudes. In addition to the above, a lengthy history of antisocial behavior was shown when he was a child. The January 28, 2000, HSH report by Dr Snodgrass indicated, for example, that the defendant started to get into trouble at age 11–12. He set fires and was involved in other acting-out behavior. He was prescribed Ritalin as a child. When in foster care, he threatened people and kept a knife under his pillow. Other DSM-IV-TR behavior of the adult personality disorder was suggested.

During the January 31, 2005, evaluation, the defendant showed the evaluator a January 16, 1980, Juvenile Court, Superior Court of California report that discussed a history of acting out, to include threats to kill his mother (the defendant does not recall whether he did this), hitting his mother (he again did not recall but if he did this violence, she did not get "all beat up" and he probably only hit her once), sleeping with a knife under his pillow, shoplifting, and running away. He stated that his mother was a prostitute and not a good person. The psychopathic, intense anger toward females was revealed as a finding synthesizing his juvenile history and behavior toward the victim and female HSH staff.

His PCL-R indicated elevated scores in the two primary factors: (a) aggressive narcissism or a ruthless exploitation of others for his own purposes, and (b) a disruptive, conflictual lifestyle. Specifically, this is shown by PCL-R items including, but not limited to (1) glibness/superficial charm when he wants something; (2) grandiose sense of self-worth; (3) a need for stimulation with a proneness to boredom; (4) pathological lying; (5) conning/manipulativeness; (6) lack of remorse or guilt; (7) shallow effect; (8) callous, lack of empathy; (9) poor behavioral controls; (10) early behavioral problems; (11) impulsivity; (12) irresponsibility; (13) failure to accept responsibility for his own actions; and (14) versatility of antisocial acts. The PCL-R score equals 34, which is the 94th percentile for male prison inmates and the 98th percentile for a separate sample of male forensic patients. Thus, Mr Buck is more psychopathic than most prison inmates and at the top in a forensic setting such as HSH. PCL-R scores also are the best predictor of violence, which comports with the defendant's violent behavior and frequent threats of violence.

Data did not suggest a thought disorder, other psychotic disorders, brain damage, or any other severe mental conditions, although the defendant has faked symptoms from a variety of mental conditions up to the time of the present evaluation. Abundant information suggested that he is a psychopath who has persistently deceived and distorted in the direction of his vested interests.

Competency to Stand Trial: In terms of general cognitive capabilities, displayed and revealed by his everyday behaviors, results of this evaluation indicate that the defendant continues to have intact intelligence and has adequate attentional, speech and language, memory, and executive skills to complete a wide variety of tasks and appropriately interact with others, if he chooses. In general, he can cooperate with his attorney, knows the nature and quality of the legal proceedings, but continually attempts to manipulate and control them, and knows the consequences if convicted of the offenses. He can rationally consult with his attorney if he decides to. No interfering (i.e., uncontrollable) condition was suggested that would prevent him from standing trial.

The defendant talked to HSH staff about the instant killing, which shows that he remembers it. Several weeks before the last evaluation, the defendant brought up that he did not mean to shoot his wife; he meant to shoot the man but he shot his wife by accident. He told the staff that he did not want her to suffer so he shot her again and later wanted to shoot himself. Thus, he recalled the alleged offenses.

Data suggested the defendant never lost recall of events of the alleged killing. The defendant told HSH staff when first admitted a remarkably similar story. This shows that over a span of years, the defendant maintained memory of the alleged crimes. During the January 31, 2005, evaluation, he recalled details of the incident to include bringing the loaded shotgun to the scene, the presence of the victim and her boyfriend, firing the shotgun five to seven times, the shotgun jamming, him being shot by a witness, laying on the ground, and other behaviors.

Criminal Responsibility: In spite of the above-diagnosed conditions, the defendant was not substantially impaired in his (cognitive) ability to appreciate the wrongfulness of his acts or in his volitional capacity to conform his conduct to the requirements of the law. His mental condition did not affect the highest mental capacity to have the state of mind required to establish an element of the offenses with which he is charged.

The basis for the above conclusions is that (1) no genuine and substantially incapacitating mental condition was present at the time of the shooting; (2) the instant offenses appear driven by anger toward the victim and a need for revenge, and (3) the presence of cognitive and volitional abilities at the time. These abilities include knowledge that the shooting was wrong and his orchestration of skills that culminated in the death of the victim.

EMED: EMED was not suggested for the time of the alleged offenses. Self-control and choice were strongly indicated for the times before and during the shooting. After killing and subsequently being shot himself, his mental capacity, as expected, diminished in response to the circumstances.

Please call the undersigned at (808) 885-9800 if clarification is needed. Thank you very much.

Sincerely,
Harold V, Hall, PhD, ABPP

Mitigation Case from Chapter 11 (McPherson)

A psychological report in death penalty work not only provides assessment results and their interpretation, but also may reference the connection of the individual's characteristics and history to the act committed—unless there is ongoing protestation of innocence. The report then can only describe general factors to be considered by the jury as mitigating while creating the opportunity for discussion of scientific findings relevant to understanding the defendant. The report and testimony, if given, then become one of the bases for the defense attorney's summation and argument for a life sentence. In the following example, the defendant continued to maintain innocence despite a finding of guilty.

Sandra B. McPherson, Ph.D., ABPP
12434 Cedar Road, Suite 15
Cleveland Heights, Ohio 44106
Phone: 216 721 1961; Fax: 216 721 1914
smcpher1@earthlink.net
Sensitive Material—Discretion is Necessary

Psychological Report

Date xx/xx/xx
SUBJECT: R.R.
dob: xx/xx/xx

Reason for Referral

At the request of defense counsel, Mr R was evaluated and other sources of information obtained as part of developing information relevant to the mitigation phase of his trial for aggravated murder with death penalty specifications.

Procedure

Interviews of Mr R, xx/xx/xx, xx/xx/xx
Meeting with mitigation specialist xx/xx/xx

Review of materials, including school records, juvenile, and prison records
Psychological testing, including Wechsler Adult Intelligence Test-III (WAIS-III) subtests, Minnesota Multiphasic Personality Inventory-2 (MMPI-2), Thematic Apperception Test (TAT), and Rorschach Inkblot Test
Contacts with counsel for defendant

Results

Interviews of Mr. R

Mr R was emotionally labile at the times that he was seen. He smiled a lot, but at times, the smiling was inappropriate with an ongoing tendency toward crying. The labile affect was acknowledged by the defendant who also indicated that he had been suicidal in the past and could not make a commitment for the immediate or long-term future insofar as keeping himself safe. However, he did agree to an evaluation process.

Formal mental status examination was not utilized. However, systematic inquiry and test data secured that he was fully oriented, did not have signs of active thought disorder, but did show ongoing emotional distress as already indicated.

He gave the following personal history. He was born on xx/xx/xx in YYY and lived in the ZZZ and WWW areas. He was involved with the juvenile court in connection with stealing, runaway, and truancy behaviors. He was referred for counseling to a psychologist located in his general geographic area. He indicated that he and his sister grew up with his mother. His father never invested in them and, in fact never really saw him. He said "I don't know him." His sister is married, has five children, and lives in MMM. He said there were also some step siblings in the family, but they were not there during the time that he was growing up and he did not have any significant contact with them. Asked about his health, he said something to the effect that it would be nice to have medication for the bad dreams but then renamed them good dreams because they reflected his wish for the family he did not have. The only physical problems that he thought he had involved the reconstructive work he had done on his left knee.

Asked about drug and alcohol use, he said that he rarely had anything to drink if ever and that he has not used drugs.

Educational background involved high-school attendance at various places. He did not graduate, but he did obtain his GED. He has had 2 years of instruction at HHH College in "liberal arts."

His legal history is fairly extensive. He was found guilty of receiving stolen property in xxxx and was given probation for 2 years. A year later, he was found guilty of aggravated burglary and went to the reformatory on a 5- to 25-year sentence. He was shocked out after 3 months. He was in prison in 1990 on a robbery charge and spent 8 years in that facility. He has had a few speeding tickets but no other serious legal history. (His reports were consistent with documentation obtained from records.)

Once out of prison, he was able to obtain employment. He held two jobs during the last year and a half. He held a full-time job as a shipping supervisor working about 48 h a week. He then worked 12 to 16 h on the weekend at a gas station. His girlfriend had become pregnant and needed maternity leave which was his reason for getting the second job. His child is now 1 year old.

He indicated he was extremely distraught by the situation. He stated that the prosecutors knew he was innocent but pursued him on unjust bases for their own purposes. He indicated that a police officer relative in law enforcement was negatively sanctioned because he had looked up the reports that were out on Mr R to help him. He also noted that his girlfriend was arrested as a co-defendant primarily to intimidate her (she was his alibi and was held for approximately a month as accessory after which charges were dropped and she was released). Mr R did not present himself when he was indicted, but he stated that the notification from the court did not reach him. Subsequently, he was picked up by the police and he gave statements when he was in custody.

Review of Records

School records: Early school records indicate some problems academically which appeared to remit between 4th, 5th, and 6th grades. In junior and senior high school, he was involved heavily in the juvenile system, and grades were poor. However, when he was tested, either in group or in individual assessments, he was at or even well above-average levels in terms of ability. Early on, he was identified as having serious behavior problems and was placed on an individualized educational plan to correct the problems. During this time, his mother reported that behavioral deficits had been present since the age of 2. By the time he reached age 12–15, she felt entirely overwhelmed and unable to control him or intervene effectively. At the same time, some positive behaviors were also noted. When he felt competent, he enjoyed being able to assist others. A lot of the details of his adjustment suggested underlying severe feelings of inadequacy and resulting overcompensation. Also of some interest, he was noted to have a fixed interested in electronic games. That preoccupation was also in evidence shortly before his arrest in the instant case and illustrates some lack of emotional maturation as well as what has been noted as an almost addictive-like responding that is characteristic of some people.

Juvenile records: Difficulties began at his age 12, when he was given a tour of the juvenile detention facilities in attempt to "scare him straight." His mother indicated that no other forms of discipline worked to correct behavior problems, but expressed that some of his reaction to that tour may have had an impact. To the degree that he was affected, it was short-lived. Juvenile problems continued and mounted throughout his minor years and included instances of "ungovernability," petty theft, receiving stolen property, violation of curfew, and truancy from home and school. He was committed to a youth facility in xxxx. In a later record, it was noted that he had escaped during some period of detention in the juvenile period. Interestingly, in one of the psychology reports made during these years, it was noted that he was a poor sleeper and that he seemed fearful throughout his childhood that his mother would abandon him.

Prison records: Adjustment in prison essentially mirrored the problems seen throughout his entire life. He had difficulty accepting authority and limits. He was apparently easily involved in altercations with others and was often cited for fighting. He also at one point was found with sheeting that he was making into rope. He was viewed as a suicide risk. There were references to past serious attempts. He acknowledged great difficulty controlling emotional reactivity.

Test Results

Cognitive assessment included administration of selected subtests of the WAIS-III (Digit Span, 8; Comprehension, 9; and Block Design, 14). Scores mirror the more complete intellectual assessments conducted earlier in his life and clearly indicate average-to-well-above capacity. He has always shown more adequate performance than verbal capacity, but no deficit in either area. His Bender was constricted, which can accompany insecurity as a personality trait. Organization was adequate, but he did not show much ability to engage in careful planning.

MMPI-2 was valid. His profile suggested adequate resources. He apparently feels pressured, has difficulty when it comes to relational issues, and is more reactive than proactive. He presents with stereotypic masculinity. He has the capacity to be socially outgoing albeit superficial. On the other hand, there is a sense of persecution, a lack of capacity to take responsibility for life, energy level at the current time is low, and suicidal thinking appears likely. While indicators of depressive affect are present, there are no indications of severe mental illness involving psychotic mentation or disruption of cognitive function.

TAT was consistent (and also quite consistent with analysis of the same test when he was in his mid-teens). He was able to produce well-developed stories, better than most in his situation. However, the themes of his stories suggest a desire to be indulged and immaturity of character formation. His enjoyment of games and adolescent pursuits was evident. Depression was present. His need to extricate himself and his desire to be seen as innocent was mirrored in his productions. Although a very emotional individual, he probably finds it difficult to share with others, to be vulnerable, and he uses passive aggressive and passive avoidant techniques to deal with problems.

Rorschach was consistent as well. Results were evaluated using the Exner method. His protocol was valid, albeit somewhat defensive (in this test, he was far less able to understand how results would be interpreted). In situations that are difficult, he acts to narrow his perception and therefore by simplification deals with what he wants to or feels able to handle. He tends toward some unconventionality of behavior, perhaps in part due to the fact that he does not really appreciate all aspects of complex and threatening situations. Distortion can also occur by virtue of degree of emotional arousal which can seriously interfere with his capacity to understand the world and respond to it rationally and effectively. Interestingly, in spite of the level of current stress, he presents as experiencing only limited input and having more than enough in the way of available resources for coping. There is underlying lack of self-esteem and lack of confidence. He can easily become emotionally driven.

Test summary: Cognitive assessment was not extensive, but screening as above detailed was consistent with background and current presentation. He is of average or better ability, and there are no indications of factors that would suggest any significant deficiencies, either formally or in how he dealt with the less structured aspects of personality testing. In the evaluation of his personality, the traits that accompany scores and patterns from both the MMPI-2 and the projectives all suggest an individual with some need to compensate over most of his lifetime with strategies that are at best inefficient.

Diagnosis

Axis I	Adjustment disorder with depression and anxiety; R/O dysthymic disorder
Axis II	Personality disorder with borderline, antisocial, and passive aggressive features
Axis III	No diagnosis
Axis IV	Problems with legal system, with primary support group
Axis V	GAF: 60 current

Summary

Mr R has been able to establish some relationships at different points in his life, but he has never been able to create the kind of long-term investments that would meet underlying emotional needs. His apparently lifelong concern about rejection may have been fed by the fact that his behavior was disrupted even before he developed adequate narrative speech to engage in communication of ideas. Aspects of his behavior and history suggest inherent defects such that only in a fully supported and high functioning family unit might he have had a chance of avoiding antisocial development. As things stood, efforts were made throughout his life, but none was effective in changing what was in part a "hard-wired" scripting for which only super-parenting and unusually benevolent life conditions could have intervened. His single mother, trying to manage on her own, clearly was not able to overcome the deficits. His concern about losing her, which now translates into concern about being left by others, was a testament to her efforts but also an indication of their failure. The lack of investment of a father would have contributed as well to his sense of inadequacy and lack of worth. His inability to learn from a variety of techniques of discipline throughout his young years is another indication that underlying biologically determined deficits were at work along with environmental inputs.

Sandra B. McPherson, Ph.D., ABPP
Clinical and Forensic Psychology

Competency to Stand Trial Evaluation from Chapter 12 (Ebert and Long)

November 14, 2006
RE: C.N.

Identifying Data

C.N. is a 39-year-old black female referred for this assessment of her competency to stand trial by her attorney, Joan. A. Ms. N. had previously been referred by Jennifer M., her prior attorney. Ms. N. is currently incarcerated, awaiting trial on charges of armed robbery and assault with a dangerous weapon (knife), and she is being charged as a habitual offender.

Following her arrest, Ms. N. was initially sent to the Lee Mental Health Center in Boston for an evaluation of her competency to stand trial. Following the evaluation, she was referred for Department of Mental Retardation (DMR) services where she was accepted as a client after a psychological assessment. While awaiting DMR services, she remained at the Lee Center and was granted visits into the community. She did not return from a visit to the community in August 2005. She was ultimately re-arrested and returned to the Lee Center in October 2005. She was subsequently transferred to the New Street Jail to await trial and has remained incarcerated ever since.

Structure of Evaluation

C.N. has been interviewed twice at the New Street jail by this examiner. The first interview occurred on 25 January and the second on July 9, 2006. During the second interview, she was interviewed in the presence of her attorney, Joan A.

Records reviewed for purposes of this evaluation include but are not limited to:

- Lee Mental Health Center records
- Competency evaluation by J.K., Ph.D., Boston Municipal Court (5/8/05)
- Neuropsychological assessment, W.E., Ph.D. (4/2/05)
- Competency and criminal responsibility reports by C.D., Ph.D. (5/31/05, 10/29/05)
- Boston Police Department files including investigations, criminal record, and report
- Boston Medical Center records
- New Street House of Correction records
- Arrest history, C.N.
- Letter by Dr. Q. to Court (8/15/05)
- Letter from Mr. P. to Court (8/24/05)

Informed Consent for Evaluation

Prior to my interviews, I informed Ms. N. that I am a licensed forensic psychologist retained by her attorney to conduct an evaluation of her mental state and of her competency to stand trial. I explained to Ms. N. that the information she provided would be shared with her attorney and placed in the form of a report to be given to the Court. I further explained that I might be requested to testify in Court. As a consequence of the limits of confidentiality, I explained to Ms. N. that she was not required to cooperate with the interview if she chose not to. I explained further that if she did agree to cooperate she was not required to answer specific questions.

Ms. N. appeared to listen with increasing concern to the above evaluation. When initially asked to paraphrase, she appeared puzzled and said, "Can you say it again?" The above warning was repeated, slowly and simply, and she said with hesitancy, "You said … you work for my lawyer … um … what you say you can tell my lawyer … um… I forgot." The warning was carefully explained a third time, and again she had very limited recall. When asked if the interview was private or not she stated that it *would* be private. This was corrected and she agreed to be interviewed. It was not clear that she understood the limits of confidentiality.

Of interest is that during the second interview, the same difficulty was present when she was asked, after repeated explanation, if the interview would or would not be private. She looked pleadingly at her attorney for help, and when told to answer on her own, she said that it would be private "between us three." Despite her apparent confusion, she agreed to be interviewed and was cooperative.

Standard for Competency to Stand Trial

The test for the defendant's competence to stand trial is whether she has sufficient present ability to consult with her lawyer with a reasonable degree of rational understanding and whether she has a rational as well as a factual understanding of the proceedings against her (*Dusky v. US*, 1960; accepted in *Commonwealth v. McHoul*, 1967).

Commonwealth v. Monzac (1997), in reliance upon *State v. Perry* (La. 1986), further expounded that the test for whether the defendant has sufficient present ability to consult with her lawyer involves: (a) whether (she) is able to recall and relate facts pertaining to (her) actions and whereabouts at certain times; (b) whether she is able to assist counsel in locating and examining relevant witnesses; (c) whether she is able to maintain a consistent defense; (d) whether she is able to listen to the testimony of witnesses and inform her lawyer of any distortions or misstatements; (e) whether she has the ability to make simple decisions in response to well-explained alternatives; (f) whether, if necessary to defense strategy, she is capable of testifying in her own defense; and (g) to what extent, if any, her mental condition is apt to deteriorate under the stress of trial.

Relevant to the determination of whether a defendant understands the nature of the proceedings, the following factors to be considered include: (a) whether she understands the nature of the charges and can appreciate their seriousness; (b) whether she understands what defenses are available; (c) whether she can distinguish a guilty plea from a not guilty plea and understand the consequences of each; (d) whether she has an awareness of her legal rights; and (e) whether she understands the range of possible verdicts and the consequences of conviction.

Current Mental Status Examination

C.N. is an obese woman (who has gained significant weight between the two interviews) who presents with a sad, puzzled expression throughout. The interviews are significant for limited language, frequent confusion, and repeated requests to the examiner—"Can you tell me?"—in response to questions. When interviewed in the presence of her attorney, she is clearly dependent upon her attorney and frequently turns to her for answers to questions, even those questions that are personal and would not necessarily be known by her attorney. Her mood appears significantly depressed, and there are frequent periods of tearfulness, especially when discussing her most recent child who was born while she was in prison.

When initially interviewed on January 25, 2005, she is asked the date, but does not know the answer. Asked if she knows the month, she is able to say that Christmas was last month, "My baby's birthday." However, she is not able to name either the present month or the previous month asking, "Can you tell me?" When pressed, she asserts the year is 2000. She knows her current location, and she knows that the interview is being done for her attorney. Thus, she is oriented to place and person, but not to time.

When asked to spell the word "world," she says she cannot spell. When asked to try, she sounds the word out and says only the letters "r" and "u." She is asked to make change from a dollar and cannot. When asked if she has ever been cheated when she gets change, she says, "I guess so. I take the change they give me." She knows that it takes four quarters to make a dollar. When asked how many dimes are in a dollar, she says, "I have to use a paper to try to count it." She demonstrates impaired social judgment in answers to specific questions. She acknowledges a head injury when she was younger, saying that she was in a car accident and "I was dead, they say. I was all broke up. I got hit by a car." Asked how she was affected, she says, "I was paralyzed. I can't walk." Asked what happened after that, she says simply, "I walked." Again asked if she was affected by the accident, she says she does not know. In this discussion, she appears to have a great deal of difficulty responding to abstract questions.

Ms. M. denies ever having had seizures or serious illnesses. She acknowledges that she has used cocaine and alcohol, but adds, "I don't drink daily." Asked if she thinks she is addicted to either alcohol or drugs, she says, "Do I have to take it? I don't know. No." She denies that she hears voices or experiences visual hallucinations. Asked if she is depressed, she initially says she does not know, but then states she feels sad because "I'm missing my family, yes." Asked if she has periods of crying, she first denies that she does and then says, "I can't remember." She denies she has ever attempted suicide. She says she has not been abused. However, she reports she has been beaten by her boyfriend. Asked why he beats her up, she says, "He tells me to do something and I take too long."

When asked why she continued to live with her boyfriend if he beat her, she appears puzzled, shrugs, and says softly, "He's my kid's father, but I guess he don't need me." As she says this, she appears increasingly sad and begins to speak softly and then mumbles to herself. She finally says, "He in trouble with me, too." Attempts by her attorney to question her about her boyfriend, the co-defendant, are equally ineffective, suggesting that she is able to participate in this aspect of her defense.

In order to test her reading ability, she is given a legal document that includes her name, and she is able to read only her last name. This is the only word she can read, but she brightens when she says that she does know other words such as "cat." She is unable to interpret proverbs and demonstrates concrete thinking in the process. She can only recall four numbers in order. She is unable to understand how to recite numbers in backward order. Yet, she perseveres in trying to solve this task, which is clearly too difficult for her. She is unable to subtract seven from 100 in her head, but attempts to solve this task by drawing groups of sevens on a sheet of paper. Having accomplished this task, she then attempts to respond to the examiner's question, but is unable to do so. She is asked to draw a picture of herself and draws a very childlike, primitive sketch. When asked to draw a clock, she is able to reproduce the clock face and numbers, but places the hands incorrectly on one side of the clock, seeming unable to render the requested time.

Asked to name the current president, she says, "Washington" and cannot name any other presidents. She has no idea what direction a person would go from Boston to Florida. Asked if she is able to take the bus or the subway, her answer is, "It depends. Sometimes I walk." When pressed, she says that if she has to take buses she will ask for help, but "I get lost, sometimes I get lost." She is asked if she knows what clothing to choose for the weather, and she says, "Sometimes, like when it's hot out, I have too many clothes on sometimes." Asked if she can cook, she says that she can cook some things such as spaghetti and pasta, but she is "still learning to cook." She does not have a regular doctor to go to for health problems, and when asked what she would do if she were sick she says, "City Hospital." Asked if she has health insurance, she says, "I just got some, but I forgot what it is (referring to Medicaid)."

Ms. N. is asked how she spends her days in prison and she says, "Sleep a lot." Asked if she is talking to other people while in prison, she says, "Sometimes, but peoples here, I don't talk to them. I don't know them. I never know them." As in other questions, it is not clear whether she fully understands what is being asked of her, despite her willingness to provide answers.

She is asked if she recently had a baby and her answer is, "Yes, a while ago." She does not know the date of the child's birth. She says the child's name is William and that he is with his aunt, J.S. When she is asked how old the child is, she looks at her attorney and says pleadingly, "Want to help me again?" When pressed to tell his age, she shrugs and says, "He's up there." She is then given options to choose from 1, 2, or 6 months, and she looks puzzled, tearfully stating, "I think, 10 months old? Help me … I can't remember the days."

The clinical impression is entirely consistent with the picture of a mentally retarded woman who has significant difficulty understanding and responding to the examiner's questions. Of importance is that her presentation is quite consistent over the course of the two interviews, which are approximately 6 months apart. There does not appear to be an attempt to exaggerate her symptoms or to present herself as more disabled than she is. In fact, rather than attempt to exaggerate her disability, she attempts to respond to questions she clearly does not understand, offers answers more often than not, and frequently asks for assistance from the examiner or her attorney.

Data Relevant to Competency to Stand Trial

When asked to name her charges, Ms. N. answers, "I forgot, but they said I did something. I don't remember." She then volunteers, "I'll know if I hear it." She is then asked what it is that they say she did and she says sadly, "I did a lot of stuff." Asked if she is said to have robbed anyone, she says, "Yep, that's it. I guess I rob somebody, a female." Asked what was taken, she says, "I know I was supposed to rob a person." Asked what it means to rob someone, she says, "You took something from somebody." Asked if this is considered to be a serious charge by the Court her answer is, "I think so." Asked if she knows the sentence if found guilty, she says, "I don't know 'cause, I always played [*sic*] guilty, said I did something. I went to jail."

Asked if she knows the legal term for being arrested a lot, she says, "I know the guy said that at the station. He said if I keep getting arrested, I go to jail for life. He arrested me for 'house invasioncy [*sic*].' He said if somebody is making you do this, you tell [and] you could go away for life." She is unable to come up with the term on her own, but when she is asked if the word is "habitual," she says, "Oh, I heard of it before. I don't know where I heard of it before. I can't remember that, but I heard of it."

Ms. N. initially knows that her attorney's name is Joan and her job is to "go to Court for me, help me." When she is interviewed with her new attorney (B.A.) she cannot remember this attorney's name and keeps calling her Joan. Asked how she is to work with her attorney, she says, "I don't know, sit there." Asked if there's anything she should tell her attorney, she says, "When she ask me a question."

Ms. N. is asked who is on her side in Court and her answer is, "My lawyer, Joan." Asked if she can describe the role of the district attorney, she says, "Who's that?" When asked if she understands the role of the prosecutor, she says, "No, I might have but I don't remember." Asked if there is anybody against her in Court, there is a long pause and she thinks and then says, "Not often." She is asked to describe the role of the judge, and she says, "He reads my record." Asked if there is anything else the judge does, she thinks and then says, "Tells us what to do, be quiet." Asked if the judge makes any decisions, her answer is, "I guess." Asked if the judge makes decisions about her, she thinks and says, "I don't know, court dates?" Despite further questioning, she does not appear to understand the role of the judge in determining her fate. She is asked if she can describe the role of a jury and she says that she cannot. Asked if she can describe a witness she says, "A person, on my side?" She cannot describe the terms "victim" or "defendant." Asked if she understands the word "guilty," she says, "I played [*sic*] guilty before. I said I did something." She is asked if she knows the meaning of the term "innocent," and her answer is, "I don't know. I never played [*sic*] that."

Ms. N. is asked why she has only pled guilty across time, and her answer is, "'Cause my lawyer said it's the best thing for me." Asked if she understood whether or not it was the best thing for her, she says, "Why would he lie to me?" She does not appear to understand the consequences of pleas and seems quite unable to weigh the defenses available. Her ability to make even simple decisions in this regard seems quite impaired. Asked how she usually behaves in Court, her answer is, "I just sit, like I'm doing now."

Ms. N. is asked if she can explain the process of a trial, and her answer is, "I never had one." She is asked to describe her Court experiences, and she says that the police take her and "you go in this room." Asked what she does, she says, "I laid down." Asked if there is a room where people talk, she says, "Yes, a lot of people in the room, a lot of people talking. I know that it be real loud. I don't know what they're saying." Asked if her name has ever been called in a Court, she says, "Might have." Asked what has happened at that point, she says, "I can't remember." Asked if her attorney was present she says, "Joan? I can't remember, might have." Asked if she can explain what goes on when she is in the courtroom and her name is called, she says with frustration, "I don't know! I told you, I just sit there!" In these responses, it appears she cannot assist her attorney in any meaningful defense of her case.

An opportunity to observe her attorney attempt to teach her client aspects of her case and relevant facts resulted in similar findings. Ms. N. was quite unable to learn, to retain, or to recall information necessary to assist her attorney. Despite careful and thorough explanations, she seemed unable to make simple decisions, understand her legal rights, or assist in forming a defense.

Additional Clinical Data

Attempts have been made by Ms. N.'s attorney to obtain school records, but as of this date such records have not become available. A review of a neuropsychological report by Dr. R. conducted in March 2005 is remarkable both for its thoroughness and for the consistency of his findings with these interviews. His tests document brain damage and performance in the mentally retarded range. He notes that Ms. N. "fails to comprehend much of what is said to her" and that her performance is "impaired" on nearly every test that he administered. He rates her overall degree of impairment as severe. He describes her as a woman who could easily become dependent and would be easy to exploit. Of significance is that he finds no compelling "indications that this patient has true psychopathic tendencies. She lacks the glib superficial charm of the true psychopath, as well as the typical grandiose sense of self-worth. Indeed she has strikingly low self-esteem." Dr. R. specifically assessed for malingering by testing for the "stroop effect." He notes that the results of this test and the pattern of her scores support evidence of a "true brain damage," rather than of malingering disability.

This evaluator has also reviewed records of the Lee hospitalizations and notes that staff alternately saw Ms. N. as a truly needy and helpless individual and as a manipulative and cunning person. These two views of this woman are not necessarily inconsistent in that mentally retarded persons certainly have the capacity to lie and manipulate. In my clinical observations, it is my professional opinion that Ms. N. was not deceptive in presentation. That is, her responses to questions, her psychological stance, and her testing are completely consistent with significant deficits due to mental retardation. It should also be noted that the Lee Center is a facility for persons with mental illness, run by the Department of Mental Health, and not for persons with mental retardation.

Records from the Boston Medical Center date back to 1975, when she was 10 years old—at that time she is described as unable to read or spell and functioning at the "low first grade level." Her later medical record is chilling for evidence of ongoing sexual abuse, truancy, battering, drug abuse, and the report of being raped by her own father at age 13.

The record serves to document a life of trauma, abuse, and depression, the latter of which has intensified since she gave birth in jail.

Summary and Conclusions

It is this forensic clinician's firm clinical opinion that C.N. is a person suffering with significant mental retardation, who also has the capacity to manipulate and deceive in part because of her lengthy history of surviving on the street. Her manipulative and streetwise behavior should not be misinterpreted as evidence that she is malingering her disability or exaggerating her impairments. Based on the historical record, recent neuropsychological testing, and my clinical interviews, there is no question in this examiner's opinion that she is a truly disabled and handicapped person who has lived a life in which she appears to have been chronically manipulated by others for their gain. Her "occupation" of prostitution and crime appears clearly to have been in the service of others who benefited from both her money and her willingness to accept responsibility by pleading guilty in a legal system that she simply does not and cannot comprehend. It is quite striking to see just how limited her understanding of the charges, of her possible defenses, of her rights, and of the judicial system remains, despite much experience in Court and recent attempts at training by this examiner and her attorney.

1. In my clinical opinion, C.N. suffers from significant mental retardation. Her retardation apparently stems from brain damage, which may be the result of a birth defect or of an automobile accident as a child. It should be noted that at age 10, before the car accident, she was functioning at the "low first grade level." She has a history of significant substance abuse involving cocaine and alcohol. She presents with a history and current signs of depressed mood as well.

2. In my clinical opinion, C.N. does not have sufficient present ability to consult with her attorney with a reasonable degree of rational understanding, and she does not have a factual understanding of the proceedings against her. Her understanding of the charges, their seriousness, the availability of defenses, the consequences of prior pleas, her legal rights, and the process and complexity of the judicial system is markedly impaired. Her passive and helpless stance puts her and her attorney at significant disadvantage in fashioning a defense.

3. It is my clinical opinion that attempts to remediate this woman's competence will be unsuccessful. Based on this examiner's attempts to train Ms. N. in areas of competency, as well as on observation of her attorney's extensive attempts, it is highly unlikely that this woman will ever be able to learn and retain sufficient material to become competent.

4. Should the court in its wisdom find Ms. N not competent to stand trial, it would be this clinician's recommendation that she be allowed to be transferred to a staffed residential setting run by the DMR where she can receive care and treatment. In such a setting, she will be assisted to care for her emotional, educational, and medical needs; will be assisted to obtain productive employment; and will be helped to remain drug free, safe, and away from others who would manipulate and use her.

Respectfully submitted
Ronald S. Ebert, Ph.D.

MMPI Case Report from Chapter 13 (Craig)

Case Report

Reason for Referral: Patient was to be placed on trial for murder. The court requested an independent psychological evaluation prior to trial.

Pertinent History. He is a 20-year-old, single, black male on trial for first-degree murder and attempted murder. He began drinking alcohol in substantial quantities around the eighth grade and drank to intoxication on special occasions on which he chose to celebrate. He denied using illicit drugs. He dropped out of high school in the tenth grade. Although he had no serious illness, he had received a gunshot wound to the head a few years ago, resulting in a 3-day hospitalization. Subsequent to this incident, he reported migraine headaches, jaw pain, and nonspecific memory problems, although he showed no apparent memory disorders.

The patient had argued with his eventual victims on a previous occasion and, upon seeing them on the street, left the area to find a means to kill them. He returned to the area, shot and killed one of the victims, and shot the other victim with the intent to kill him, but the victim recovered from his wounds. The patient would not provide any other details but stated that he was involved in gang-related activities, prior to his arrest.

Forensic Database. The patient was given the MMPI-2 as part of the evaluation. (Forensic database pertinent to this case is the Megargee Classification System discussed earlier in this chapter.)

Behavioral Observations and Test Behavior. The patient was cooperative with the evaluation. Although he had been told that the evaluation was not confidential and anything he said could be reported to the court, he was rather open about the extent of his many gang activities (although he would not discuss any further details related to the current charges). He spoke of the many people who had caused him harm in his life and how he would retaliate against them, if given the chance. He denied feeling any remorse toward his other victims, stating that they got what was coming to them. He was concerned about the upcoming trial and knew that they had enough evidence to convict him. His lawyer was looking into an insanity plea. His MMPI appears in Figure 13.3.

Information on Response Sets. The test results were valid. However, the MMPI-2 Validity Scale Configuration (i.e., L, F, and K) suggests severe maladjustment, deviant beliefs, and poor defenses.

Test Results. The profile suggests a person who is quite angry, depressed, and sullen. He gets upset with people who he believes have harmed him and blames others for his difficulties. These appear to be in the realm of malevolent projections. He appears tense, irritable, pessimistic, and preoccupied with his problems. Projection and acting out are

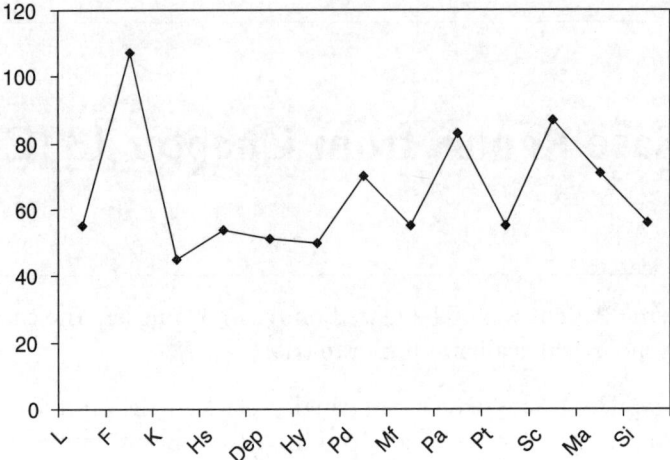

Figure 13.3 MMPI-2 profile of a 45-year-old incarcerated black male awaiting trial for murder.

his major defenses, and he seems prone to misunderstanding the motives of other people. Paranoid features to his personality are quite evident. He does report some somatic complaints with anxiety and ruminations. This is likely to be permeated by an obsessive quality. He views the world as a threatening place, feels he is getting a raw deal out of life, and sees little wrong in violating societal rules and conventions because of the perceived injustices that have been perpetuated upon him. Because these attitudes are ego-syntonic, he may have underreported the extent of actual psychopathic traits in his personality. He is high strung and reports bizarre perceptions, unusual thinking, a sense of alienation, and a lack of warm relationships, especially because he views others as potentially threatening and harmful. He reports suspicious attitudes and an ingrained hostility combined with malevolent projections.

Clinical Impression. This psychological state would put him at risk for lethal violence. Also, this profile meets the classification rules for Megargee's-type "Charlie" MMPI-2 code type, which also has been associated with violence and murder.

DSM-IV-TR

I.	Schizophrenia, paranoid type
	Alcohol abuse
II.	Antisocial personality disorder
III.	Migraines by patient self-report
IV.	Problems related to the interaction with the legal system
V.	GAF: 30

Treatment Considerations. There is a paucity of research associated with treatment recommendations for Megargee's-type "Charlie." Based on clinical considerations, it is likely that, if convicted, this patient will have adjustment problems in prison, will not get along with authority (i.e., prison guards), and may need a referral for medication evaluation with psychotropic drugs. While I believe he is competent to stand trial, if the rule is NGRI, then he will need both antipsychotic medication, social support services, and psychological interventions before he will be able to return to community living. It is anticipated that a lengthy incarceration (in a jail or in a prison mental hospital) will ensue.

Robert J. Craig Ph.D., ABPP
Licensed Clinical Psychologist

Postscript

The patient was deemed competent to stand trial, was convicted of both charges, and was sentenced to life in prison, where he continued to engage in antisocial and gang-related activities, refused to take psychotropic medication, as was advised, and remains a problem for prison authorities.

Juvenile Sex Offender—Sample Report from Chapter 14 (Poirier)

[Date]

The Honorable Ruth Jones
[Address]

RE: *State of Maryland v. Peggy A.*
    Juvenile Matter JC—05-XXXX
    Charge: Child Sexual Abuse

Respondent's DOB: [Date]
Respondent's SSN: _____-_____-_____

Dear Judge Jones,
    Pursuant to your [Date] Order granting the State's motion for a psychological evaluation of the above captioned juvenile respondent, we submit this report. The order specifically requested that the report address the juvenile's risk of reoffending and related to that, dispositional recommendations. The respondent is a 17-year-old female adolescent who was in detention at the _____ Children's Detention Center where we conducted our evaluation.

Forensic Database. We reviewed the following records and background materials as part of our evaluation effort. The Assistant State's Attorney provided copies of the charging documents, the police report including supplements, the Child Protective Services (CPS) report, and 10 Juvenile Services Intake Report. The respondent's Assistant Public Defender provided _____ County School System academic records for the last two school years including a school psychological evaluation report. The respondent's parents provided a summary statement from Ms. A.'s pediatrician.

(A)   Psychological measures
The following measures, tests, and assessment instruments were utilized in the evaluation:

1. Clinical interview including taking a developmental history and mental status examination
2. Clinical interviews with Ms. A.'s parents
3. Conjoint clinical interview with Ms. A. and her parents
4. Wechsler Intelligence Scale for Adults (WAIS-III)
5. Adolescent Anger Rating Scale (AARS)
6. Millon's Adolescent Clinical Inventory (MACI)
7. Minnesota Multiphasic Inventory for Adolescents (MMPI-A)

(B)   Juvenile sex-offender (JSO) recidivism risk measures
  8.   Estimate of Risk of Adolescent Sexual Offense Recidivism Version 2.0 (ERASOR)
  9.   JSO Assessment Protocol (J-SOAP-II)

Interview background information and findings. Mrs. A. described that her pregnancy with Ms. A. was normal coursed and uneventful. Likewise, Ms. A.'s delivery and postnatal status was without incident. Ms. A. was the only child, and her parents apologized that neither had very much prior experience with childrearing. Nevertheless, Ms. A. progressed through usual developmental milestones without any significant difficulties until her seventh year. At the age of 7 years, Ms. A. was in daycare because both parents worked outside the home. Ms. A. contracted meningitis apparently from another youngster who was in daycare.

There followed several months of hospitalization and difficult recovery. When it appeared Ms. A. was going to be released from the hospital, her parent arranged for a 17-year-old paternal niece to move into the family home to provide babysitting. The niece had dropped out of the 11th grade and had no intentions to return to academia. When it appeared that Ms. A. had essentially recovered from her illness, the parents reported noticing a decided change in their daughter's demeanor. Ms. A. became more sullen and moody; she was no longer affectionate with her parents, but appeared to have a close relationship with the niece. The parents expressed their concerns to the pediatrician who reassured them that a temporary change in a child's personality following a serious illness and hospitalization was to be expected.

The arrangement continued with occasional difficulties, but the parents were grateful for the niece's availability, and they compensated her well financially and by making her a part of all family activities. Approximately 4 years later and shortly after Ms. A.'s 11th birthday, Mrs. A. came home from work unexpectedly and discovered Ms. A. and the niece unclothed and in bed together. The niece was abruptly sent back to her family. The parents' efforts to discuss the situation with Ms. A. were not very productive because Ms. A. would refuse to engage, stating that she did not want to get the niece into further trouble. Ms. A. would tearfully beg her parents to have the niece return to the home. Several efforts with counseling also met with no success.

At the time of the incident, the parents did not make a report to the authorities. By the time of the current interview, the parents acknowledged that they had since become aware of the child-abuse reporting laws. After advising the parents that there was no statute of limitations in Maryland regarding reporting of suspected child abuse, the parents did contact CPS. CPS later advised the parents of that since Ms. A. was about to turn 18 (i.e., age of majority), they would not open an active case. CPS did indicate, however, that they would forward a report to out of state CPS authorities where the niece now resided.

Mr. and Mrs. A. related that since the foregoing circumstance Ms. A. had become a different child. Ms. A. became withdrawn from the family; she was quarrelsome and progressively defiant. The parents continued that Ms. A. had presented her relationship with the victim Maria as "my babysitting job." Mr. and Mrs. A. stated that they were pleased with what appeared to be Ms. A. assuming a responsible task for her. In the meantime, Ms. A.'s academic performance had deteriorated to the point where she failed three of six subjects. School officials had also complained of tardiness, truancy, and instances of Ms. A. instigating peers.

Mr. and Mrs. A. were appropriately distressed with their daughter being charged with child sex abuse, but in hindsight, they acknowledged that the turn of events did not come as a complete surprise given Ms. A.'s history with the niece. The parents also indicated that for the previous year and a half, they had been concerned about Ms. A.'s choice of friends.

The friends, Ms. A., and the niece talked openly about use of illicit substances and promiscuous behavior. Mr. and Mrs. A. felt helpless to deal with their daughter's obvious plight.

Our individual interview attempts with Ms. A. met with a resistant and not very cooperative adolescent. Ms. A. acknowledged that she remained in contact with her niece by telephone and e-mail. Ms A. stated that she and the niece intended to begin living together as soon as Ms. A. turned 18 which would happen in 4½ months. To routine mental status inquiries, Ms. A. stated that she had been smoking cannabis on essentially a daily basis with friends for the past year and a half or so. There was also occasional ingestion of alcohol, but she denied use of any other substances. She also laughed as she alluded to sexual experimentations when she and her peers were intoxicated on cannabis. Ms. A. asserted that she had not made up her mind whether she was bisexual or lesbian. She denied any florid symptoms associated with psychosis or mood disorder. Ms. A.'s primary aspiration was to leave her parents' home and suffice to say her planning was not realistic. She spoke without emotion about her parents; she perceived her parents to be respectfully absorbed with their jobs and she insisted that "It's been like that my whole life."

The conjoint interview with Ms. A. and her parents was not productive mostly because of Ms. A.'s belligerent attitude. Ms. A. exhibited no remorse for her inappropriate sex behavior and no empathy for the child victim. Ms. A. taunted her parents that they were "old fashioned" and that they should wake up to the new cultural values being pursued by Ms. A. The parents were overwhelmed and helpless in attempting to interact effectively with their daughter. We terminated the interview prematurely.

(A)   Psychological measures results
4. *WAIS-III.*   Ms. A. required persistent examiner prompting to stay on task during this testing. She complained repeatedly of being bored. It was apparent that Ms. A.'s performance on this test was not an optimal reflection of her native cognitive abilities. Ms. A. achieved a full-scale IQ of 112, placing her at the bottom end of the high average intelligence classification. Her performance was relatively even across the subscales except for her arithmetic subtest noticeably dipping below the other subtests. We would attribute the latter finding to a lack of effort and her likely disinterest during math classes in school. One of our primary concerns, short of finding any suggestion of learning disability or other issues, was a determination of cognitive ability above the 10-year-old level to justify use of the J-SOAP-II.

5. *AARS.*   Ms. A.'s scores on the AARS indicated significantly elevated levels of anger and poor anger control.

6. *MACI.*   On the Demographics portion of the test, Ms. A. identified "family" and "school" as the problem areas troubling her the most. Although it is not atypical of adolescents to exaggerate symptoms in an effort to be viewed with sympathy, Ms. A.'s style was exactly the opposite. Ms. A. was defensive and withholding, similar to her manner during interviewing. Ms. A. had uniformly low scores on the self-disclosure, social desirability, and self-effacing-modifying indices. These findings implicated a defensive, guarded demeanor, which was consistent with her presentation during interviewing.

On the Personality Patterns section of the test, Ms. A. had elevations on the doleful, oppositional, unruly, and forceful scales. In the *Expressed Concerns* category, Ms. A. evidenced elevations on the identity diffusion, body disapproval, sexual discomfort, peer insecurity, social insensitivity, and family discord scales. In the Clinical Syndromes category, Ms. A. had significantly high scores on the substance-abuse proneness, delinquent predisposition, and impulsive propensity scales. These latter findings suggest an adolescent prone to acting out problems marked by an indifference to desired social values and mores. Ms. A.'s predilection to acting out behavior would clearly only be exacerbated by her impulsivity and her involvement in substance abuse.

7. *MMPI-A.* Ms. A. had four unanswered items on the MMPI-A, even though she was urged to leave no items blank. Two of these items referenced substance abuse and the other two referenced sexual behavior. As already observed, Ms. A. was both guarded and careless in her completion of the MMPI-A. Her carelessness was evidenced in inconsistent responses to items at different points in the test that had similar content. That is, the expectation would be that these items would usually be answered in the same direction.

Three test scales measuring alcohol and drug problems were elevated, although two of the scales that reflect personality characteristics associated with substance abuse were more elevated than the third scale, which is associated with the extent of actual substance abuse.

Ms. A. complained that others frequently misunderstood her. Ms. A was prone to project blame onto others and she perceived that others were trying to control her. Overall, the MMPI-A profile was consistent with a DSM-IV-TR diagnosis of adolescent conduct disorder (312.82).

The MMPI-A also has a series of Content Scales intended to offer further insight into elevations on the foregoing Clinical Scales. As seen on an earlier test (i.e., AARS, 5 above), Ms. A. had a high score on a scale (A-ang) suggesting anger-control problems. Adolescents with this scale elevation typically have problems with being impatient and irritable with others. Anger-control issues are typically exacerbated with substance abuse. Another scale (A-lse) associated with adolescent-low self-esteem was elevated. This finding is associated with self-perceptions of being unattractive, lacking self-confidence, and often feeling useless. Adolescents with this finding are prone to peer influences and pressure. A scale measuring conduct problems (A-con) was moderately elevated, reflecting Ms. A.'s history of behavioral problems. Ms. A. also had an elevation on another scale (A-lse) which reflects adolescent-low self-esteem. Adolescents with this score elevated are typically disinterested in being successful, particularly academically. Their expectations of success are low. They are satisfied to allow other people to solve problems, and they believe others block their way to success.

Ms. A.'s profile also had moderate elevations on a scale (A-fam) addressing perceived family problems and another scale addressing perceived school problems (A-sch). A final Content Scale elevation (A-trt) reflected Ms. A. to have a number of attitudes and behaviors that are unlikely to make her amenable to psychotherapeutic intervention. High scores on the scale indicate a negative attitude toward mental health professionals. High scores on the A-trt scale are also associated with test takers' unwillingness to assume responsibility for negative events in their lives.

(B) JSO recidivism risk measures

The reader of this clinical report is cautioned that at the present time, there are no empirically validated, actuarial measures that can accurately estimate the risk of sexually reoffending by a JSO. Nevertheless, the research findings have identified a number of risk factors that are associated with reoffending. The following two measures incorporate these risk factor findings. The ERASOR and the J-SOAP-II data served as a partial basis for our estimate of the risk of sexual reoffending for Ms. A. More importantly, these data serve as a basis for opinion about the level of treatment care Ms. A. will require in the immediate future.

8. *ERASOR.*   The ERASOR data implicate a high degree of risk of a sexual reoffending by Ms. A. The following risk factors were identified: A preoccupation with sexual thoughts and an unwillingness to alter deviant sexual attitudes, acknowledgment of multiple sexual assaults and diverse sexual behaviors with the child victim. Additionally, Ms. A. evidenced a number of antisocial traits. Ms. A.'s primary peer associations were with peers who were similarly preoccupied with sexual behavior and impulsive promiscuity. Presently, Ms. A.'s relationship with her parents is highly stressed. Finally, Ms. A.'s attitude about the need for sexual offense-specific treatment was one of disinterest and lack of motivation.

9. *Juvenile Sex-Offenders Assessment Protocol (J-SOAP-II).*   Ms. A.'s level of cognitive development was well above the 10-year-old level, an initial requirement for application of this protocol. This instrument is *not* expressly normed for female JSOs; accordingly, we have utilized the instrument in this matter prudently. The protocol is a series of research-based risk factors that the clinician rates according to a precise scoring system. The protocol is comprised of two scales of static (historical) risk factors and two scales of dynamic (subject to change) risk factors. The scores on the respective scales are summed and converted to percentages. The percentages are indicators of relative proportion of risk. The following were Ms. A.'s percentage scores on the four factors:

Static scales scores	
Sexual drive/preoccupation scales score	38%
Impulsive/antisocial behavior scale score	44%
Dynamic scales scores	
Intervention scale score	93%
Community stability scale score	70%
Static score	41%
Dynamic score	83%
Total J-SOAP–II score	59%

It is important that the reader understand that the JSOAP-II percentage scores are numerical representations of clinician ratings on the risk factors. In addition, the J-SOAP-II risk factors are not intended to be exhaustive, nor do they reflect comparison to a normative sample. The JSOAP-II is an actuarial protocol designed to augment a comprehensive clinical assessment effort and to help refine overall clinical judgment of JSO risk for recidivism. In Ms. A.'s case, her static risk factors suggest minimal risk. The static risk factors are historical characteristics and have long-term predictive value. Ms. A.'s static risk factor findings offer long-term hope that with time she may prove amenable to intervention. According to Ms. A.'s parents, the onset of her difficulties began approximately 5 years ago and her static risk factors scores reflect her difficulties within that period. That is, prior to 5 years ago, there were no significant clinical concerns evidenced by Ms. A.; her difficulties have amassed in the last few years.

Ms. A.'s dynamic risk factors are in the moderate-to-severe risk range, reflecting her psychological turbulence over the past 5 years. Of significant concern was Ms. A.'s scoring of 93% on the intervention scale score. This finding implicates the need for an intensive, long-term treatment plan, most preferably a highly structured, residential program. The intervention scale score consists of risk factors reflecting the juvenile offender's ability to be to be truthful, candid, reasonable, and empathic, which are attributes known to affect treatment in a positive direction. Ms. A. scored low on all these factors, supporting that she is unlikely to be amenable to a community-based treatment plan.

Summary

The forensic database was sufficiently broad to justify being able to draw conclusions about Ms. A.'s risk for reoffending, her being able to respond to treatment, and the risk she may present if returned to the community at the present time. Our evaluation of Ms. A. included interviewing, psychological testing, and two actuarial instruments for measuring JSO recidivism risk. Across these multiple measures, there were rather consistent findings. At the age of 7, Ms. A. contracted meningitis. Following months of hospitalization and convalescence, Ms. A.'s parents arranged for an older niece to move into the home to assist with care of Ms. A. At some unknown point in time, the niece engaged Ms. A. in a lesbian relationship. Eventually, Ms. A.'s parents discovered the relationship and removed the niece from the home. A short time later, Ms. A. engaged a younger neighborhood girl in inappropriate sexual activity under the guise of babysitting for the younger girl.

The current evaluation was by juvenile court order to generate dispositional recommendations to include Ms. A.'s risk of sexually reoffending. Our findings reflected Ms. A. to be intellectually capable with her cognitive functioning at least into the bright normal range. In retrospect, it is clear that the bout with meningitis and then the relationship with the niece were sufficiently traumatizing to induce a number of developmental anomalies with A. One anomaly was the development of a severely troubled daughter/parent relationship brought on by Ms. A. allying herself with the attractions of the older niece over the bond with her conventionally minded parents. Another anomaly was Ms. A. becoming involved with a group of peers with shared common interests in pursuing substance abuse and sexual experimentation.

The upshot of these dynamics was Ms. A. sexually victimized a younger neighborhood girl. Our evaluation consistently found Ms. A. to have a negative attitude regarding any need for treatment involvement. Ms. A. made it apparent that she intended to pursue the relationship with the niece, once Ms. A. achieved the age of majority in a few months. Likewise, Ms. A. did not intend to redirect her involvements with untoward peers. These combined findings warrant stipulated placement of Ms. A. in a long-term residential treatment program offering sexual offense-specific treatment.

Finally, we comment that there are two considerations with respect to recommending reassessment of Ms. A.'s risk for recidivism in the future. First, the supporting research with JSO actuarial based risk assessment is based on follow-up data of less than 3 years in duration. Second, rapid developmental changes are characteristic of adolescence. It is essential then that a follow up risk estimate with Ms. A. should be completed after a period of no more than 2 years.

Thank you for the opportunity to provide this assessment input regarding Ms. A.'s clinical status and her needs.

Joseph G. Poirier, PhD, ABPP

Neuropsychological Workers' Compensation Case from Chapter 15 (Baade, Heinrichs, and Soetaert)

The *Journal of Forensic Neuropsychology* devoted all of volume 2 to a review and discussion of validity tests (*Journal of Forensic Neuropsychology*, 2002). For an excellent review of classification schemes and cutoffs for embedded indices, see Bianchini et al.'s (2001) review of SVTs. Strauss et al. (2006) have done a solid job of referencing embedded indices for various tests in the most recent edition of the *Compendium of Neuropsychological Tests*. Full citations for all items included in this appendix are provided in the references for Chapter 15.

Stand-Alone Symptom Validity Tests

Amsterdam Short-Term Memory Test (ASTM) (Schagen, Schmand, de Sterke, and Lindeboom, 1997)
Auditory Verbal Learning Test (AVLT) (Frederick, 2002a, 2002b)
b-test (Boone et al., 2000, 2002)
Computerized Assessment of Response Bias (CARB) (Allen, Iverson, and Green, 2002).
Dot Counting Test (Boone et al., 2002)
Forced Choice Test of Nonverbal Ability (FCTNV) (Fredrick and Foster, 1991)
48 Picture Test (48-PT) (Chouinard and Rouleau, 1997)
Green's Word Memory Test (WMT) (Green, 2003)
Hiscock Digit Memory Test (Hiscock and Hiscock, 1989)
Portland Digit Recognition Test (PDRT) (Binder and Willis, 1991)
Recognition Memory Test (RMT) (Warrington, 1984)
Rey 15-Item (Frederick, 2002a, 2002b)
Test of Memory Malingering (TOMM) (Tombaugh, 1996)
21-Item (Iverson et al., 1991)
Validity Indicator Profile (VIP) (Frederick, 2000)
Victoria Symptom Validity Test (VSVT) (Slick, Hoop, and Strauss, 1997)

Embedded Validity Indices

Booklet Category Test (Bolter, Picano, and Zych, 1985; Sweet and King, 2002; Tenhula and Sweet, 1996; Greve, Bianchini, and Roberson, accepted for publication)
California Verbal Learning Test (Curtis, Greve, Bianchini, and Brennan, 2006; Millis Putnam, Adams, and Ricker, 1995)

Halstead–Reitan Neuropsychological Test Battery (HRNB) (Greiffenstein, Baker, and Gola, 1996; Heaton, Grant, and Matthews, 1991; Larrabee, 2003; Mittenberg, Rotholc, Russell, and Heilbronner, 1996; Reitan and Wolfson, 2002; Shimoyama, Ninchoji, and Uemura, 1990)

Knox Cube Test (Iverson and Franzen, 1994)

Memory Assessment Scales (Beetar and Williams, 1995)

Raven's Standard Progressive Matrices (RSPM) (Gudjonsson and Shackleton, 1986)

Wechsler Adult Intelligence Scale-III (WAIS-III) (Greiffenstein, Baker, and Gola, 1994; Iverson and Tulsky, 2003; Miller, Ryan, Carruthers, and Cluff, 2004; Millis, Ross, and Ricker, 1998; Mittenberg, Theroux-Fichera, Zielinski, and Heilbronner, 1995; Mittenberg, Theroux, Aguila-Puentes, Bianchini, Greve, and Rayls, 2001; Mittenberg, Theroux-Fichera, Rayls, Aguila-Puentes, Bianchini, Greve, and Rayls, in press; Greve, Bianchini, Mathias, Houston, and Crouch, 2003; Heinly et al., 2005; Curtis, Greve, Bianchini, and Heinly, October, 2005)

Wechsler Memory Scale-III (WMS-III) (Glassmire, Bierley, Wisniewski, Greene, Kennedy, and Date, 2003; Iverson, 2000; Killgore and DellaPietra, 2000; Lang et al., 2006; Langeluddecke and Lucas, 2003)

Wisconsin Card Sorting Test (WCST) (Bernard, McGrath, and Houston, 1996; Greve et al., 2003; King, Sweet, Sherer, Curtiss, and Vanderploeg, 2002; Suhr and Boyer, 1999)

NEUROPSYCHOLOGICAL REPORTS

Patient	:	Tom
Age	:	45
Dates of evaluation	:	List all dates on which the patient was seen
Date of Report	:	Month/Day/Year

Referral

Tom was initially referred by his primary care physician and his neurosurgeon. However, additional referral sources were added before the first appointment including his workers' compensation attorney and an attorney representing him in a lawsuit against the driver of the other vehicle. The patient received a severe head injury with a basilar skull fracture in mm/yyyy. This was followed by several days of posttraumatic amnesia. This neurocognitive evaluation was requested to establish the patient's current level of neurocognitive functioning and to aid in treatment planning. The law firms provided the records listed below as reviewed.

Data Sources

Clinical interviews separately and together with the patient and his wife and administration of the following neuropsychological tests: WAIS-III, WMS-III, HRNB, Wechsler Test of Adult Reading (WTAR), selected subtests of the Delis–Kaplan Executive Function System (D-KEFS) (subtests administered were trails, verbal fluency, design fluency, sorting, and tower), reading comprehension subtest of the Peabody Individual Achievement Test—Revised (PIAT-R), spelling and arithmetic subtests of the Wide Range Achievement Test—Third Edition (WRAT-3), WMT, TOMM, Frontal Systems Behavior Scale (FrSBe) self-report form and family report form (the latter was completed by the patient's wife), Neurobehavioral Functioning Inventory (NFI) self-report form and family report form (the latter was completed by the patient's wife), Minnesota Multiphasic Personality Inventory—Second Edition (MMPI-2), and Millon Clinical Multiaxial Inventory—Third Edition (MCMI-III). Additionally, a review of the following records was conducted: educational records from grades kindergarten through high school graduation, educational records from the university from which he graduated, employment records, premorbid medical and dental records, EMS records from the accident, and hospitalization records from the surgical intensive care unit and the rehabilitation hospital. Additional records from the consulting neurosurgeon, general surgeon, dentist, neuropsychologist, and radiologist were also reviewed.

Presenting Problems

The patient reports a combination of cognitive, behavioral, emotional, and interpersonal changes following head trauma sustained in a motor vehicle accident on mm/dd/yyyy. The patient was hospitalized for about 1 week following the accident and then transferred to a rehabilitation hospital. The patient was able to return to work after several months. He currently complains of cognitive changes including memory problems, decreased processing speed, expressive and receptive language problems, and problems multitasking and shifting set. He also complains of personality changes including irritability, depression, apathy, lack of initiation, and anhedonia. He reports a loss of any desire to socialize. He also reports headaches that are less intense than in the recent past but still require use of prescription pain medication almost daily. The patient's work and his relationship with family members are adversely affected by these problems. He also describes a loss of libido that adversely affects his relationship with his wife. His speech, though clear most of the time, deteriorates and becomes slurred when tired or stressed. The patient states that he finds driving stressful, and though he finds it necessary to drive to work and some other places, he prefers to have his wife drive whenever possible. When he does drive, he turns off the radio because even this is more distraction than he can accept while driving. Both the patient and his wife indicate that the patient is less physically active and less socially active than before the accident. They also indicate that there has been significant negative impact on the sex life of the couple as the patient has had a tremendous decrease in libido.

History

The patient has been married for 22 years and the couple has two children studying in high school. He reports being in an accelerated/gifted program when he was in elementary school. He earned a bachelor's degree in mechanical engineering from a local university followed by a master's degree in business administration from the same school. Prior to the accident, the patient was an engineering supervisor with a manufacturing company and returned to the same position after the accident. He previously worked for a different manufacturing company for 13 years as a design engineer. He has not received an evaluation from his employer since his return to work but expresses the feeling that he is much less capable than he had been. Although he can find problems and engage in solving them, they are forgotten when something else demands his attention. It is difficult to shift back to the original problem without cues to recall what he was doing. Although he also reports previously having an exceptional memory for numbers before the accident, he now struggles in this area. He reports that his conversation and his thoughts ramble more now.

The patient was never in the military and has no record of criminal prosecution. His health was excellent prior to the accident. He denies any prior head injuries other than a mild concussion in high school. He denies any exposures to toxic chemicals or electric shock that have required medical attention. There is no personal or family history of psychiatric problems prior to the accident except for treatment of depression in one sibling. History of surgery prior to the accident was limited to a hernia repair as a child and the removal of a lipoma. In the accident, in addition to the head injury, he sustained rib fractures and an injury to his spleen. The spleen injury required surgical intervention at the time of the accident. He is scheduled for surgery to relieve pressure on nerves at the L4-L5 level, and this also is reported as secondary to the accident. He currently takes Zoloft for his depression and states that this has helped to some extent. Other current medications are Toprol, Tizanidine HCL, and Percocet.

Mental Status

The patient arrived on time for his appointment having been driven by his wife. He appeared to be his stated age and was well dressed and groomed. He was alert and oriented to person, place, time, and situation. His speech was fluent with normal rate and prosody. He had no obvious problems comprehending the interview questions. His responses, though appropriate in the main, tended to be quite long and rather redundant. When asked about this, his wife indicated that this was a change and the patient commented that since the accident he is concerned about people not understanding his points such that he feels a need to emphasize his point by making it in different ways. As indicated above, the patient has multiple concerns regarding his neurocognitive abilities. He states that it takes more effort to concentrate and that anything that requires multitasking is extremely difficult for him to do. He states that he used to be a "planner," but now he thinks of only getting through the day and does not think about the "next project." He denies suicidal or homicidal ideation.

Neuropsychological Test Results

The patient's premorbid intellectual ability was estimated using several different approaches. His premorbid full-scale IQ was estimated to be 118 using the Barona formula, 121 using the WTAR score plus demographic data, and 116 using the patient's ACT score from high school. There is reason to consider these estimates conservative for a combination of reasons: first, all three approaches regress toward the mean and thus would underestimate rather than overestimate individuals who functioned above the mean; second, the Barona formula tops out, and it is not possible to obtain a higher score; third, the WTAR is dependent on current language ability and may be lowered secondary to injury; and finally, the patient reports that he did not apply himself in high school, and he believes that his college performances are a better reflection of his ability than high school grades or tests administered during that time period. For admission to the master's degree program, the patient took the Graduate Management Admission Test (GMAT) and earned a score of 540, which places him in the upper half of individuals who have taken this test and are thus applying for graduate programs in management across the country. This test performance supports the above-average intellectual estimates derived from other sources and supports the conservative nature of those estimates. It is likely that premorbidly, the patient functioned somewhere in the top 10% of the population in his age group.

On the WAIS-III, the patient earned a full-scale IQ score of 117, which is commensurate with the various estimates of premorbid functioning. The patient's index scores on the four WAIS-III factors, however, vary by 35 points from the highest to the lowest. The verbal comprehension factor score was 112, the working memory score was 113, and the perceptual organizational score was 121. These scores are all commensurate with the earned full-scale IQ score and represent functioning in the top 20% of the population for the lower two scores and in the top 8% of the population for perceptual organizational skills. On the contrary, the processing speed index score was below average at 86 and represents functioning in the bottom 20% of the general population. It is noteworthy that the patient was observed to take longer to solve problems and complete the various test tasks than would be expected from someone with his educational and occupational background.

Academic achievement test scores were also disparate as the patient earned a score at the 82nd percentile on reading comprehension and at the 32nd percentile in arithmetic. This is more interesting, as the patient's math skill was reportedly a strength prior to the accident.

On the memory tests administered, the patient performed within the average range but well below the level that would be predicted on the basis of premorbid estimates and current IQ scores. With the exception of working memory, a measure of ability to focus and concentrate, all of the memory scores were below the mean and the general memory score of 92 was at the 30th percentile. The working memory score of 124 indicates that the patient can focus and maintain focus on information being presented. However, his ability to learn and to remember new information has fallen from an estimated premorbid level of functioning in the top 10% to current functioning in the bottom 30% of the general population.

As per the report of the patient on the FrSBe, executive functioning is significantly impaired, and the report of his wife indicates an even greater level of impairment. Test performances in the area of executive functioning range from below average to above average. Processing speed as indicated earlier is below average as per the WAIS-III, and this is also reflected by slow performances on the Trail Making Test and on the Tactual Performance Test. Both phonemic and semantic verbal fluency are low average compared to the general population and therefore impaired relative to expectations based on the patient's premorbid IQ. New problem solving as represented by the tower test is commensurate with expectations based on premorbid functioning, but the performance on the Category Test though average is below expectations.

In the area of sensory and motor skills, the patient's test scores are average to mildly impaired. Motor speed is average for the left hand but below average for the right hand. Strength is below average bilaterally. Fine motor coordination is mildly impaired on the right and below average on the left. Tactile form recognition is average for the right hand and above average for the left. None of the sensory and motor problems is severe enough to be noticed by the casual observer and even the patient is likely to be aware of deficits only during attempts to perform tasks requiring higher levels of psychomotor ability.

Patient effort and the validity of his test performances were assessed both through the administration of specific tests of effort/malingering and through various indices derived from tests administered to assess other functions. All performances on these tests and indices support accepting the patient's test performances as valid. Additionally, examiner observations suggest above-average effort during testing.

Personality Assessment

The patient completed the MMPI-2 and the MCMI-III, and both the patient and his wife completed the appropriate forms of the FrSBe and the NFI. Both the patient and his wife indicated on the FrSBe that he is much more apathetic and demonstrates less executive ability now compared with prior to the accident. His wife's report indicates larger changes in this direction than do the responses of the patient. The apathy is reflected in the patient's lack of initiative and spontaneity and the fact that he is more likely to sit around doing nothing, has lost interest in things, and shows little emotion. Changes in executive functioning are demonstrated by his inability to do more than one thing at a time, getting stuck on certain ideas, his inflexibility, and forgetting things only to remember when prompted or when it is too late. The patient agrees in large part with his wife's responses and indicates the possibility that maintaining his job now requires so much of him that by the time he gets home he lacks the energy to participate at home.

The patient's report and that of his wife were also somewhat different on the NFI. Both report mild depression in the patient. The wife observes a marked increase in somatic complaints and the patient appears relative unaware of making these complaints. Both view the patient's memory as impaired but the patient sees this as more severe than his wife. This likely reflects the greater demands on memory that the patient experiences at work as opposed to home observation. The patient also reports much greater difficulty in communication than his wife and again this may reflect work demands. Both report that the patient has some difficulty in word finding, auditory comprehension, carrying on a conversation, and reading speed. The patient views these items as more severely impaired than his wife.

The validity scales on the patient's MMPI-2 profile are all within normal limits and suggest that he answered the questions on this test in a straightforward and honest manner. The profile primarily indicates that the patient is depressed and that his depression is likely accompanied by a lack of energy and social isolation. This is consistent with the reports of the patient and his wife during interview and on the NFI but suggests a more severe depression than is evident from the NFI. The MCMI-III profile is consistent with that of the MMPI-2 in indicating depression and social avoidance. Although the MCMI-III suggests that some of the patient's avoidance might be longer term and characterological, this is not consistent with the report of the patient or his wife regarding the patient's premorbid behavior. Further, it is my experience with individuals with head injuries who have experienced significant cognitive changes that similar personality changes occur and are sometimes reflected in this manner on the MCMI-III.

Summary and Conclusions

The patient sustained a major head injury in a motor vehicle accident in mm/yyyy. Given the length of time since the injury, it is likely that residual cognitive problems revealed during this examination are permanent. It is clear that premorbidly, the patient's cognitive abilities were in the upper 10% of the population. Although the patient's current IQ score places him at the 87th percentile relative to others of his age, it should be understood that the IQ score reflects past learning more than current ability. The patient's current new learning ability as reflected by memory tests is in the average range but suggests that he learns as well as or better than 30% of the general population as opposed to the expectation that he be able to do so as well as or better than 90% of the population. As compared to new learning, the patient's ability to solve new and unique problems appears to be intact except that the speed with which he processes information and arrives at solutions is much slower than would be expected. Small distractions can disrupt the patient's thought process, and he has great difficulty doing more than one task at a time, even driving and listening to the radio. Sensory and motor problems are not observable in ordinary activities. However, the patient is aware of having lost a competitive edge in sports-type activities, and he is again slower than would be expected when motor activities also involve any cognitive analysis and judgment.

Emotionally the patient has also had tremendous negative changes. His MMPI-2 suggests a clinical depression despite the fact that the patient is being treated for depression. He also presents with avoidance of driving, which may be a symptom of posttraumatic stress disorder (PTSD) or may reflect the patient's difficulty with the cognitive demands of this task or both. There is also evidence of a frontal lobe syndrome with apathy and decreased executive ability.

Diagnostic Impressions

Axis I:	294.9	Cognitive deficits due to traumatic brain injury
	310.0	Frontal lobe syndrome
	293.83	Organic affective disorder; major depressive-like
Axis II:	None	
Axis III:	Posttraumatic brain injury with extended loss of consciousness	
Axis IV:	Difficulty maintaining job due to decreased cognitive ability; major changes in home and social life secondary to depression and brain injury with subsequent stress to these factors exacerbating the problems.	
Axis V:	60	

Recommendations

Feedback has been provided to the patient and his wife to assist them in recognizing the patient's current limitations and how these limitations relate to the injury. They have also been advised to pursue a review of current treatment for depression and to proceed with modifications as indicated.

Lyle E. Baade, Ph.D. ABPP

Neuropsychological Data Summary

Name: Tom
Date of birth: mm/dd/yyyy
Age: 45
Education: 18

Sex: male
Dom hand: right

Date of testing: mm/dd/yyyy
Occupation: supervising engineer
Location: UKSM-W Clinic

Wechsler Adult Intelligence Scale—III

Verbal	SS	Performance	SS
Vocabulary	11	Picture C.	11
Similarities	12	Digit symbol	7
Arithmetic	14	Block design	15
Digit Span	11	Matrix reas.	14
Information	14	Picture arrg.	13
Compreh.	16	Symbol srch.	8
Lt# seq.	12		

Factors	Index	%ile
Verbal comprehension	112	79
Perceptual organization	121	92
Working memory	113	81
Processing speed	86	18
Verbal IQ	118	88
Performance IQ	113	81
Full-scale IQ	117	87

Barona estimate	Index	S_{Em}
Est. VIQ	117	11.8
Est. PIQ	114	13.2
Est. FSIQ	118	12.1

Test				
Category Test			Errors	27
Trail Making Test	Part A	45″	Part B	72″
TPT	Memory	10	Location	1
Seashore rhythm			Correct	29
Spch sds perception			Errors	1
D-KEFS	SS			SS
Trails	Vis. scan	9	Motor	11
	Number	10	Letter	11
			Switching	11
V. fluency	Letter	8	Category	9
Design fl.	Switching	12	S. Accur.	13
Sorting	Correct	12	Composite	11
	Switching	12	Description	13
			Recognition	14
Tower			Total ach.	15
Proverbs			Free inqu.	14

Sensory-perceptual and motor tests

Fg. ag.	DH	0/20	NDH	0/20
FgT#W	DH	2/20	NDH	1/20
TFR	DH	11	NDH	8

Test	Dem	Index	S_Em
ACT estimate		Index	S_Em
Est. FSIQ		116	7.39
WTAR	Dem	WTAR	Com
Est. VIQ	118	114	122
Est. PIQ	114	111	115
Est. FSIQ	118	114	121
Academic achiev.		Index	%ile
PIAT-R Rd. comp.		114	82
WRAT-3 spelling		107	68
WRAT-3 arithmetic		93	32
WMS-III		Index	%ile
Basic scales			
Auditory immediate		94	34
Visual immediate		91	27
Immediate memory		91	27
Auditory delayed		94	34
Visual delayed		97	42
Auditory rec. delay		90	25
General memory		92	30
Working memory		124	95
Supplemental		SS	%ile
Visual reproduction I		16	98
Visual reproduction II		10	50
Visual reproduction		13	84

Test				
Tapping	DH	51	NDH	49
Hand dyn.	DH	46	NDH	44
G. pegbd	DH	78	NDH	73
TPT DH	Blks	10	Time	6.0
TPT NDH	Blks	10	Time	5.4
TPT BHD	Blks	10	Time	2.4
TPT total	Blks	30	Time	13.8

Word memory test			
Immediate recognition	100	Mlt. choice	100
Delayed recognition	100	Paired A	100
Consistency	100	Free recall	55
		LDFR	62

TOMM	Raw sc.
Trial 1	50
Trial 2	50
Retention	50

FrSBe self-report

T-scores	Apathy	Disinh.	Ex. fnc.	Total
Before	41	41	41	39
After	88	62	75	80

FrSBe family report

T-scores	Apathy	Disinh.	Ex. fnc.	Total
Before	60	32	48	46
After	117	76	119	123

Neuropsychological Report

Patient   :   Lisa
Dates of evaluation :   List all dates that the patient was seen
Date of Report   :   Month/Day/Year

Referral

The attorney for the health care system in the case of Lisa versus the health care system referred this patient for a neurocognitive evaluation. Patient is the claimant in a matter arising out of an incident in which she was injured while attempting to escort a patient who had been involved in a fight out of a treatment area within the juvenile detention center. Another detainee assaulted Lisa, resulting in claims of injury to her nose, left eye, and the back of her head. These injuries were evaluated and treated, as were additional claims of PTSD. Their current referral arises out of disputes of appropriateness of treatment and additional claims of neurocognitive dysfunction secondary to a closed head injury claimed as a result of the assault.

Data Sources

Clinical interview with the patient and administration of the following neuropsychological tests: WAIS-III, WMS-III, HRNB, WTAR, WCST, selected subtests of the D-KEFS (subtests administered were trails, verbal fluency, design fluency, and sorting), reading comprehension subtest of the PIAT-R, spelling and arithmetic subtests of the WRAT-3, RSPM, WMT, TOMM, and MMPI-2.

Background Information

Patient Report of the Events

Lisa reported that she was assaulted in the treatment area at the juvenile detention center on mm/dd/yyyy. She was working with a patient in the back of the examination area when two detainees in the front of the room began arguing. She was escorting one patient out of the room when "I remember the other kid was right there. He scared me so much. He looked like a monster he was so angry." She reported that this detainee hit her in the face and she then attempted to protect her face by holding her arms in front of her face. She states that this is the last thing that she recalls of the incident. From other sources, she knows that two other employees attempted to pull the assaulting juvenile away but that he broke free and punched her in the nose. Her first recall after the incident is of sitting at her desk with a coworker beside her and wondering where her patients were. She was taken to the immediate care clinic where she was treated and released with instructions for home observation over the next 72 hours.

Patient Report of the Problems

Lisa presents with complaints of memory problems, reading and writing problems, difficulty with speech articulation and fluency, decreased concentration, problems multitasking, slowed mental processing, fatigue, headaches, dizziness, seizures, weight gain, blackouts, weakness, problems with balance, nightmares, and depression. She denies any changes in her vision, hearing, and somatosensory functioning. She reported that she does not leave her house often, does not enjoy things she previously did, such as reading, and does not do things for herself anymore. If her husband cooks for her, she will eat. She does not feel that she can return to nursing, even at another facility. The patient's mother told her that she is not "making sense" in letters written to her. She also reports having difficulty comprehending what she is reading. She stated that she is a completely different person and that she angers easily, shouts at times, and withdraws. She cries frequently. She reports feeling sad and tired much of the time, and has little energy or interest for activities in which she formerly engaged.

Psychosocial History

Lisa was born in the Midwest and has lived here most of her life. She has a degree in biochemistry. She also has a master's degree in nursing. She is married and has two adult children who attend college out of the state. She was employed as a nurse by a local health care system until the time of the assault. Lisa has not driven a car since she had a motor vehicle accident 6 months after the assault. She lives at home with her husband.

Medical History

No additional medical history was provided other than that related to the presenting problems as reviewed above. Current medications include Lexapro, Oxycontin, Loratadine, Gabitril, and Lunesta. The patient denies use of alcohol or other substances.

Legal History

Patient denies any history of legal charges or arrest.

Review of Records

The medical records indicate that the patient presented on the day of her assault with complaints of pain to the left side of her face and head. There was a contusion to the left side of her face and some swelling. The examination was otherwise unremarkable, and she was released to home with standard head injury instructions. Subsequent CT, MRI, PET, and EEG evaluations have been within normal limits. Two neurologists have evaluated the patient, and the only findings have been self-reported complaints. Neurological examinations have been normal. The opinion was that the patient's complaints were disproportional to the known injury and subsequent recommendations for psychiatric treatment were made. The patient received a neuropsychological evaluation, and the consulting neuropsychologist had the opinion that "...the most likely interpretation, in light on [sic] the minimal injury, is that of a malingered profile for both cognitive and emotional residuals from the assault." The patient had an independent psychological evaluation in mm/yyyy, and the psychologist concluded that the patient had PTSD, a pain disorder, and an adjustment disorder with anxiety and depression. He further indicated that though it was probable that the patient was malingering, it was not possible to establish a definitive diagnosis of malingering. As both of these evaluations share many test administrations in common with the current evaluation, reference to specific results will be made in the neuropsychological test result and personality assessment sections of this report. The patient also received a psychological evaluation in mm/yyyy. This evaluation is best described as a psychoeducational evaluation; it focused on presumed acquired losses of basic educational skills in the areas of reading, math, and speech and made recommendations for remediation. This report also stated that the acquired losses of these basic educational skills were a direct result of the physical trauma sustained in the assault on mm/dd/yyyy.

The patient's records contained documentation of psychiatric and psychotherapeutic treatment from multiple providers. She was treated by a nurse practitioner from mm/yyyy to mm/yyyy. A psychiatrist has provided psychiatric treatment and prescribed psychotropic medications and medications for pain from mm/yyyy through the present. Psychiatric diagnoses provided include PTSD, major depressive disorder, and severe chronic head pain. Neurologically, the psychiatrist's diagnoses range from postconcussion syndrome to "functional brain injury from severe beating and concussion." Dr. (name), a psychologist, saw the patient for psychotherapy following his evaluation in mm/yyyy with the last session conducted in mm/yyyy. A licensed clinical social worker treated the patient with individual psychotherapy utilizing cognitive behavior therapy and EMDR from mm/yyyy through mm/yyyy. Additionally, the patient received psychotherapy from two other providers, a clinical psychologist and a licensed clinical social worker, from mm/yyyy until mm/yyyy and from a clinical social worker from mm/yyyy until the time of this evaluation. She also participated in speech and language therapy and received massage therapy. It is noted that with two separate therapists, the recommended treatment approach has been EMDR and the patient has been resistant to engaging in this treatment.

Mental Status

Lisa arrived on time for her appointment and was appropriately dressed and groomed. She was alert, and oriented to person, place, time, and situation. She reported her mood as anxious, fearful, and depressed. Her affect was labile and more intense than ordinarily observed, perhaps best being described as "dramatic." The patient was tearful and emotional throughout the interview, and often during the testing procedures. Her speech was fluent, and normal in rate, prosody, and volume. Suicidal ideation and homicidal ideation were denied. Thought was linear and goal directed. Her movement and gait were observed to be inconsistent from one point in time during a session to another. At times, she moved with a normal gait and with normal ease. At other times, she behaved as if it required great effort to rise from a chair and to walk down the hall. She frequently complained of being too fatigued to continue during testing sessions and would often report that she saw the face of her attacker when test items increased in difficulty. During testing, she performed well on some difficult tasks and contrastingly performed with unusual slowness on easier tasks. The patient's effort and persistence during testing were assessed as poor. The patient often said that she needed to sleep and would place her head on the table during testing. Occasionally, the patient would hold her head in her hands and say, "Why? Why me?" The patient required four 4-h sessions to complete the test battery, whereas in most cases of traumatic brain injury, it would be completed in two such sessions.

Neuropsychological Test Results

As reported above, the patient completed a neuropsychological evaluation with another neuropsychologist in mm/yyyy, and it was the neuropsychologist's opinion that she did not have any neurocognitive impairment secondary to the assault. By contrast, in the psychoeducational evaluation, the examiner indicated that the patient's general intellectual ability is below the patient's estimated pre-morbid IQ and she has various acquired specific learning problems secondary to her assault. Where the two evaluations share administration of similar tests, the data are not remarkably different. A primary difference in the two evaluations is the accepting of the data as being valid by the psychoeducational evaluator and an opinion that it was invalid on the part of neuropsychologist. The neuropsychologist included testing of effort/validity, which the patient failed. The psychoeducational evaluation did not include this type of testing.

The neurocognitive data from the current evaluation are considered invalid for a variety of reasons including the following facts: (1) the patient performed better on some difficult tasks than she did on some easy tasks of the same type; (2) she performed so poorly on some easy items that such performance is considered a reliable sign of malingering; (3) her performance on some very easy tasks was worse during the current evaluation than it had been during the mm/yyyy evaluation; (4) she showed improvement in some areas across evaluations and deterioration in others; (5) the general level of performances was disproportionately poor relative to the known facts of the injury; (6) areas of performance that would be expected to be at or near premorbid levels were not; and (7) the patient's behavior consistently reflected poor effort.

Personality Assessment

The patient completed the MMPI-2. Because she complained of reading difficulties, she was provided with an audio version of the test as well as the print version. The records reflect that the patient completed the MMPI-2 in mm/yyyy for a consulting neuropsychologist and in mm/yyyy for a consulting clinical psychologist, and both were presumably administered using the print versions of the test. Both of these profiles were invalid: the first due to a yea-saying response set and the second due to elevations on the F(B), Fp, and L scales. The data from the mm/yyyy test were available for review and are worthy of additional comment. First, though the data are invalid as per the true response indicator scale, they are also invalid because of a high L scale (T = 81) and because of an elevation on FBS, a validity scale that was not scored when the test was given. The current, third, MMPI-2 clinical profile is invalid because of elevations on scales L, S, and FBS.

Despite the fact that all three profiles are invalid, there is relevant information to be obtained from them. As we currently have complete data on only the mm/yyyy and the mm/yyyy profiles, most of the following comments will be limited to these two profiles.

First, it is important to note that the variable response indicator (VRIN) scale is within normal limits on both of these profiles. This demonstrates that the patient comprehended the test items well enough to answer divergently word questions of similar content in a consistent manner. In other words, her answers to the test questions were made with understanding and thus the elevations on the other validity scales may be considered the result of purposeful responding. The L scale on all three profiles was high enough to indicate that the patient was being dishonest in her responses and claimed unrealistically positive attributes. The elevation on scale S on the third (current) profile adds additional weight to the position that the patient attempted to present herself as virtuous and responsible, and having few or no moral flaws. The S scale on the mm/yyyy profile, though not elevated to the point of invalidating the profile, is high enough to suggest the same self-presentation. On the contrary, the elevations on the FBS scales of profiles 1 and 3, and the elevation of Fp on profile 2, indicate that the patient was endorsing numerous problems. In the case of Fp, these include problems that even serious psychiatric patients generally do not endorse, and in the case of the FBS scale, the endorsement of problems is the one that would be expected from someone attempting to fake or exaggerate problems related to a head injury.

In summary, though the three MMPI-2 profiles are invalid for making comments about the patient's psychological disturbance, these profiles do indicate that the patient understood the test items and that she was dishonest in her responding and answered the test items in a manner so as to simultaneously indicate that she is an exceptionally virtuous person and one who has serious physical, cognitive, and psychological problems. The pattern of problems endorsed, however, further supports the idea that the patient is exaggerating, if not fabricating, her problems.

The patient also completed the MCMI-III in mm/yyyy and mm/yyyy. This test lacks the full range of validity scales available on the MMPI-2, and it is our opinion that in the presence of an invalid MMPI-2, the MCMI-III should also be considered invalid, so we did not administer it during the current evaluation. It is noteworthy that on the first two MCMI-IIIs, the patient presented herself in contrastingly different ways. In January, she basically presented herself as a virtuous individual with relatively few problems of any type and on the second evaluation as an individual with significant impairment.

During the mm/yyyy evaluation by the consulting clinical psychologists, the patient was given the SIRS, a test developed to detect false presentations of serious psychiatric problems. On three of the SIRS primary scales, the patient scored in the range indicating "probable feigning." As the clinical psychologist indicated in his report with three primary scores in the "probable feigning" range, the likelihood that the patient was feigning psychiatric disturbance is 97.9%.

Summary and Conclusions

This 46-year-old female was referred for an evaluation of psychological and neurocognitive functioning as they relate to the incident of mm/dd/yyyy. Lisa was a nurse on assignment at the juvenile detention center where a patient physically assaulted her. She currently complains of cognitive difficulties in the areas of memory, attention, oral language, written language, and math. She also complains of depression and anxiety and reports dramatic PTSD-related symptoms. The patient's effort and persistence during the evaluation were minimal and produced results that do not accurately reflect her true cognitive abilities.

Medical evaluations include normal CT, MRI, and PET scans, normal EEG, and normal neurological evaluations by two neurologists. The descriptions of the assault and physical evidence of injury immediately following are such that if the patient sustained a brain injury of any type it would be classified as mild and it is improbable that any residual neurocognitive impairments would be evidenced this long after the injury. Thus, the patient's claims of neurocognitive deficits and the test performances elicited by us, by an additional independent neuropsychologist, by an independent clinical psychologist, and by an educational psychologist are all incongruent with the injury. On the basis of this analysis, it is my opinion that the neurocognitive problems claimed by this patient are feigned. The feigning of such symptoms leads to one of three possible diagnostic conclusions. The first is that the patient is malingering. The second is that she has a factitious disorder, a condition deliberately feigned for psychological reasons and the benefits that are perceived in taking on a role as a sick, injured, or disabled person. The third possibility is a conversion or other somatoform disorder where the condition is feigned unconsciously for psychological reasons that may or may not be identifiable.

In interviewing the patient, she appears to be in serious psychological distress and has convinced several mental health providers that she suffers from PTSD. However, she has produced invalid MMPI-2 profiles on three different occasions. There is evidence that she understood the test items and responded to them in a discerning manner attempting to simultaneously present herself as virtuous and as having a combination of physical and psychological problems. With scores as high as this patient produced on the MMPI-2, FBS scale studies have shown 100% specificity in separating feigned or exaggerated symptoms from genuine symptoms; in other words, no patients with genuine problems were misclassified as feigning. The bottom line on the MMPI-2 profiles is that the patient was being deceptive. Additionally, the independent clinical psychologist gave the SIRS to the patient during his evaluation in 2003. Her responses on this test indicate a 97.8% chance that she was feigning psychiatric illness.

The facts of her assault are established, and it is in keeping with the role of mental health service providers to accept the believable aspects of a patient's reported response to an assault. However, there is evidence that this patient has feigned or exaggerated symptoms of cognitive, physical, and psychiatric disorders. There is no objective medical or valid psychological test evidence that the patient has any neurocognitive or psychological disturbance. As previously indicated, it is my opinion that the patient does not have neurocognitive deficits from the assault but rather that she is feigning these problems. As discussed above, the question remains whether the patient is malingering, has a factitious disorder, or has a conversion or other somatoform disorder. The patient's established feigning of symptoms on the MMPI-2 and SIRS lends support to the hypothesis that the patient is knowingly exaggerating her problems and thus either is malingering or has a factitious disorder. Although there may be a psychological disturbance related to the assault, the current primary problems are not a consequence of the assault but the patient's exaggerations or feigning. Any residual problems that may be related to the assault cannot be identified or treatment be recommended due to the exaggerations and the patient's self-imposed limitations.

Lyle E. Baade, Ph.D., ABPP CN

Pain Survey Checklist (PSCL)

Full name _____

Date _____

Other names used _____

Birth date _____

Reason for referral _____

Soc. Sec. No. _____

Referral source _____

In state since _____

Place of birth _____

Sex _____

Educational level and
last school attended _____

Race/ethnic group _____

Occupation _____

Employer's name, address, and phone no.

_____

_____

_____

Your residential address and phone no.

_____

_____

_____

Attorney's name, address, and phone no. (for pending legal cases or workers' compensation)

_____

_____

_____

Physical Questions

1 Your height _____

2. Your weight _____

3. Blood type _____

4. List all disorders or diseases you have had in the past.

_____

_____

_____

5. List all significant injuries you have had in the past.

_____

_____

_____

6. List all present medical or psychological conditions.

_____

_____

_____

7. List operations and dates.

_____

_____

_____

8. List hospitalizations and dates.

_____

_____

_____

9. Who is your primary physician?

_____

Address _____

Date of last physical examination _____

10. What other doctor (s) are you seeing?

_____

11. Have you been treated for a psychological concern? What, when, and by whom?

_____

_____

12. Is there a family history of similar pain problems? Please explain.

_____

_____

13. Have you ever been treated for this pain condition in the past? Explain.

_____

_____

14. What is your overall physical condition?

_____

_____

_____

Pain Questions

1. When did your present pain start?

_____

Where was that?

_____

_____

Who was there at the time besides yourself?

_____

What were you doing?

_____

_____

What did you do about the pain?

_____

In your opinion, what do you think was the cause of the pain?

_____

_____

_____

2. Did your pain start

Gradually? _____ Suddenly? _____ Did it spread? _____

Explain any details_____

_____

_____

_____

3. What is the most frustrating thing about your pain?

_____

_____

_____

4. Can you work?_____ Have you changed jobs?_____

5. What do your relatives or acquaintances do when you show pain?

_____

_____

_____

6. What factors seem to bring on or are associated with the pain?

_____

_____

7. Where do you feel your pain now?

_____

8. Is your pain with you all the time? Or does it change during the day? Please explain.

_____

_____

9. Does your pain spread?

_____

_____

10. Does your pain describe a pattern (e.g., continuous, periodic, and brief)?

_____

_____

11. How long does it take for the worst pain to develop?

_____

12. How long does your pain usually last?

_____

13. How many times during a typical day do thoughts of pain cross your mind?

_____

_____

14. How would your future life change if your pain went away for good?

_____

_____

_____

_____

When I experience the following:

	My Pain Is			
	Better	Worse	Same	Comment
Coughing or sneezing				
Alcohol drinking				
Riding in a car				
Waking up in the morning				
Experiencing tension				
Cold				
Dampness				
Middle of night				
Lying on my back				
Urinating				
Defecating				
Having sex				
Sitting (straight chair)				
Sitting (soft chair)				
Being massaged				
Talking with people				
In whirlpool/jacuzzi				
Brushing teeth				
Sleeping or napping				
Standing				
Distracted (T.V., etc.)				
Hearing loud noises				
Middle of the day				
Lying on side with knees bent				

continued

	My Pain Is			
	Better	Worse	Same	Comment
Doing housework	————	————	————	————
Exercising	————	————	————	————
Seeing bright lights	————	————	————	————
Tired	————	————	————	————
Weather changes	————	————	————	————
Drinking coffee or tea	————	————	————	————
Eating a meal	————	————	————	————
Swimming	————	————	————	————
Working at my job	————	————	————	————
Standing after sitting	————	————	————	————
Lifting	————	————	————	————
Walking	————	————	————	————
Running	————	————	————	————
Leaning over	————	————	————	————
Swallowing	————	————	————	————
Elevated blood pressure	————	————	————	————
Certain foods	————	————	————	————
Boredom	————	————	————	————
Being alone	————	————	————	————

1. What medication did you take for any reason before the injury or pain started?

   Medication/purpose   How long did you take it?   How effective was it?

   ——————————   ——————————————   ——————————————
   ——————————   ——————————————   ——————————————
   ——————————   ——————————————   ——————————————
   ——————————   ——————————————   ——————————————

2. What medication have you taken specifically for the pain?

   a. _____ dosage: _____ times a day: _____
   b. _____ dosage: _____ times a day: _____
   c. _____ dosage: _____ times a day: _____
   d. _____ dosage: _____ times a day: _____

3. How well does the medication work?

   _____

   _____

4. What other medication do you take these days?

    a. _____ dosage: _____ times a day: _____
    b. _____ dosage: _____ times a day: _____
    c. _____ dosage: _____ times a day: _____
    d. _____ dosage: _____ times a day: _____

5. What do you do besides taking pain medication to relieve pain?

_____

_____

6. How much alcohol do you drink on the average during the week?

_____

7. What kind of alcohol?

_____

8. Do you mix alcohol with medication (i.e., take at the same time)?

_____

9. What kind of over-the-counter medication do you take?

_____

_____

10. Do you take any illicit drugs? Which kind?

_____

_____

11. Have you ever received a traffic citation for alcohol or drug-related behavior (e.g., DUI)?

What	When	Where	Disposition
_____	_____	_____	_____
_____	_____	_____	_____
_____	_____	_____	_____
_____	_____	_____	_____

12. What other arrests, if any, have you had since 18 years of age?

What	When	Where	Disposition
_____	_____	_____	_____
_____	_____	_____	_____
_____	_____	_____	_____
_____	_____	_____	_____

13. Have you ever received treatment for a drug/alcohol problem?

What	When	Where	Disposition
_____	_____	_____	_____
_____	_____	_____	_____
_____	_____	_____	_____
_____	_____	_____	_____

14. Does drinking coffee or tea bring on or affect the pain?

_____

_____

15. What other factors associated with eating food or drinking liquid affects your pain?

_____

_____

Signs that accompany my pain (mark all which apply)

	Before Pain	During Pain	After Pain
A. Dull ache	_____	_____	_____
B. Sharp pain	_____	_____	_____
C. Burning	_____	_____	_____
D. Steady pain	_____	_____	_____
E. Throbbing pain	_____	_____	_____
F. Deep pain	_____	_____	_____
G. Shooting pain	_____	_____	_____
H. Tingling	_____	_____	_____
I. Pins and needles	_____	_____	_____
J. Tender to touch	_____	_____	_____

continued

(*continued*)

	Before Pain	During Pain	After Pain
K. Vomiting	_____	_____	_____
L. Feeling sick	_____	_____	_____
M. Fear	_____	_____	_____
N. Stress	_____	_____	_____
O. Rapid breathing	_____	_____	_____
P. Dizziness	_____	_____	_____
Q. Heart beating fast	_____	_____	_____
R. Flushed	_____	_____	_____
S. Blurred vision	_____	_____	_____
T. Sweating	_____	_____	_____
U. Fainting	_____	_____	_____
V. Bleeding	_____	_____	_____
W. Skin color change	_____	_____	_____
X. Epileptic seizures	_____	_____	_____
Y. Falling down	_____	_____	_____
Z. Others (specify)	_____	_____	_____

Please give your comments on anything that would help us understand your pain better.

_____

_____

_____

_____

_____

List several people who can be reached for additional information.

Name	Relationship	Address	Phone No.
_____	_____	_____	_____
_____	_____	_____	_____
_____	_____	_____	_____
_____	_____	_____	_____

Pain Chart

1. Please mark all the locations of pain and numbness on your body. Use two different colors of markers, one for pain and the other for numbness.

Front View	Right Side View	Back View	Left Side View

My color code for the above drawing:

The _____ color stands for pain.

The _____ color stands for numbness.

2. Now just for the pain locations, please put letters inside the marked areas to indicate any of the following:
   - Write A to indicate a dull ache.
   - Write B to indicate a sharp pain.
   - Write C to indicate a burning pain.
   - Write D to indicate a steady pain.
   - Write E to indicate a throbbing pain.
   - Write F to indicate a deep pain.
   - Write G to indicate a shooting pain.
   - Write H to indicate a tingling pain.
   - Write I to indicate pins and needles.
3. For traveling pain, draw a line from where it starts to where it ends.
4. For pain you feel right now, show where the pain is with the color marker.

Custody Material to Accompany from Chapter 17 (Martindale and Gould)

Evaluating the Evaluators in Custodial Placement Disputes

In our chapter, we offered the perspectives that follow.

(1) "Ethical reviewers provide feedback that addresses both the strengths and the deficiencies of the work that has been reviewed."

(2) "In the initial stage of a reviewer's work, the task is to educate the retaining attorney."

(3) If a retaining attorney decides that the reviewer can be of most assistance functioning as a trial consultant, "the reviewer can prepare questions for cross-examination, assist at trial, or provide some other type of consultative service."

(4) "If, however, an attorney decides that s/he wishes a reviewer to testify at trial, the reviewer's objective changes and the reviewer implicitly accepts the ethical obligation to function as an educator to the court."

Principle A of the APA Ethics Code (American Psychological Association, 2002) urges psychologists, in their professional actions, to safeguard the rights of those with whom they interact professionally. Principle B admonishes psychologists to "establish relationships of trust with those with whom they work" and to "clarify their professional roles and obligations." Standard 2.01 reminds psychologists to provide services that are within the boundaries of their competence. Standard 3.06 reminds psychologists to refrain from taking on professional roles in which conflicts might impair their effectiveness.

Though APA's *General Guidelines for Providers of Psychological Services* (APA, 1987) may seem dated, Guideline 2.2.2. reminds providers of psychological services to "avoid any action that will violate or diminish the legal or civil rights" of others. Litigants who believe, correctly or incorrectly, that evaluators have erred are entitled to vigorous legal representation; their attorneys are entitled to retain consultants; and the "roles and obligations" of the consultants demand that they be responsive to the adversarial objectives of the attorneys who have retained them, as long as the consultants are not called upon to act unethically.

The characteristics required to perform a task well go beyond education and training; motivation is also required. Among mental health professionals, there are many whose personal values would make it difficult for them to assist attorneys in impeaching other mental health professionals. Just as psychologists should refrain from offering certain services if there is an appreciable risk that inadequacies in education or training may interfere with the competent performance of those services, psychologists should refrain from offering trial consultation services if competing interests or value conflicts will make it difficult for them to serve the needs of one side in an inherently adversarial process.

From the perspective of some colleagues, the "gotcha" tone of many of our cross-examination questions is offensive. Skilled cross-examining attorneys are not likely to be concerned that someone may view their questions as offensive. Their concern—legitimately— is with efficacy, not with tone. Mental health professionals who are uncomfortable generating questions that will make colleagues squirm should not offer their services as trial consultants.

The material presented here was prepared for use by cross-examining attorneys. It is not balanced nor is it intended to be. It is intended to provide cross-examining attorneys with material that will enable them to cast doubt upon the usefulness to the court of the advisory opinions that have been offered by the evaluator.

[1] [**BACKGROUND** > Evaluator appears to excuse a parent's refusal or inability to impose reasonable structure on her children because the parent was raised by a mother and father whom she describes as having imposed too many limits.]

1. Are you familiar with the American Psychological Association's *Guidelines for Child Custody Evaluations in Divorce Proceedings*?
2. Do you recognize the document as authoritative?
3. I present you with a copy of the American Psychological Association's *Guidelines for Child Custody Evaluations in Divorce Proceedings* and ask that you read aloud the highlighted portion.

   ("The focus of the evaluation is on parenting capacity, the psychological and developmental needs of the child, and the resulting fit.")

   To the best of your knowledge, is there anything contained in this document or in any other authoritative document that might suggest that the *reasons* why some parents are more effective than others and better able to meet the needs of their children is of any significance to a forensic evaluator?

4. If an individual has been raised by parents who, in her perception, were unrealistically demanding; if that person—even into adulthood—felt the negative effects of this parenting style; and if, as a result, that individual in parenting her own children is insufficiently demanding, am I not correct that when the law demands that we focus on the best interests of the children, what matters is whether or not this person's parenting style will have a favorable or a detrimental effect upon the children—not how that style developed or what the historical basis for it may be?

[2] [**BACKGROUND** > Evaluator has relied upon a computer-generated report, but has skewed the report's words in a manner favorable to the parent whose position she has supported.]

1. Dr Evaluator, I present you with the computer-generated interpretive report in which Mrs Parent's performance on the Minnesota Multiphasic Personality Inventory (MMPI-2) is described and interpreted. I ask that you read aloud the two sentences that I have highlighted.

   ("Her overly cautious approach to the items suggests that she is concerned with making a good impression and is reluctant to disclose much about her personal adjustment.

Interpretation of the clinical profile should allow for her possible minimization of problems [emphasis added].")

I understand this to mean that Mrs Parent's desire to make a good impression may have caused her to minimize certain problems and that this must be taken into consideration as one endeavors to interpret her test scores. Is my understanding essentially correct?

2. Does the interpretive report suggest that the test data are useless?

3. In describing Mrs Parent's test performance, on page 10 of your report, you write: "Her results were so defensive as to render the results useless." Do you agree that you have dramatically overstated the degree of Mrs Parent's defensiveness?

4. I now present you with the computer-generated interpretive report in which Mr Parent's performance on the MMPI-2 is described and interpreted. I ask that you read aloud the sentence that I have highlighted.

("The client's conscious efforts to influence the outcome of the evaluation and to protect an overly positive self-image produced an MMPI-2 profile that substantially underestimates his psychological maladjustment.")

It seems to me that the words "conscious efforts" are stronger than the words "cautious approach" and that the words "substantially underestimates his psychological maladjustment" are stronger than the words "possible minimization." Would you agree?

5. Mrs Parent's test data are described (on page 10) as "useless." Mr Parent's test data, on the other hand, are described (on page 9) as being "of little value." It seems to me that a higher level of defensiveness is suggested by the word "useless" than by the words "of little value." Would you agree?

6. Am I correct then that defensiveness displayed by Mrs Parent has been accentuated and that defensiveness displayed by Mr Parent has been downplayed?

[3] [**BACKGROUND** > In favoring a father in a custody dispute, an evaluator has emphasized the father's purported need for the children, not their need for him.]

1. Can we agree that the focus of a child custody evaluation is the best interests of the child or children?

2. It would be nice if we could address the best interests of all involved, but the law directs us to focus our attention upon the best interests of the child or children. Is that correct?

3. On page 5 of your report you write that Mr Parent "derives emotional sustenance and a sense of identify from being an involved, hands-on parent." Is that correct?

4. It seems to me that this statement is descriptive of Mr Parent's emotional needs. Would you agree?

5. On page 44 of your report, you indicate that Mr Parent "needs the kids to love him." This, too, is a statement descriptive of Mr Parent's emotional needs. Would you agree?

6. In reading further, I do not see any connection made between the description of Mr Parent's needs and the best interests of the children. Am I correct that no connection is outlined by you?

7. If a parent derives sustenance from his children and if his sense of identity is linked to being a hands-on parent, is there not some risk that he will inadvertently do

things that might delay the arrival of the day when his children no longer require a hands-on parent?

8. Is this risk alluded to anywhere in your report?

9. On page 35 of your report, reference is made to Mrs Paramour's "loneliness and attempt to fill that space with her children." Again, is this not a statement descriptive of the emotional needs of one of the adult participants in this dispute?

10. And if Mrs Paramour is dependent upon her children to fill a void, is it not reasonable to presume that she will also count on the Parent children to meet the same need?

11. In his sessions with you, Mr Parent has made reference to *his* needs. In her sessions with you, Mrs Paramour has made reference to *her* needs. As I reviewed both your notes and your report, I found no reference to an expression by Mrs Parent of her needs. Can you identify something either in your notes or in your report that I missed?

12. In reviewing both your notes and your report, I have been unable to find any reference to a statement by Mr Parent in which he expresses his views concerning his importance to the children. I find only the reference to his views concerning the children's importance to him. Can you identify something in either your notes or your report that I missed?

13. In reviewing both your notes and your report, I have been unable to find any reference to a statement by Mrs Paramour in which she expresses her views concerning her importance to her children. I find only the reference to her need to have the children fill the void created by her loneliness. Can you identify something either in your notes or in your report that I missed?

14. Whether you agree with her concerns or not, am I not correct that, in her first session with you, on February 2, 2002, Mrs Parent explains her motivation not in terms of *her* needs but, rather, in terms of her concern for the children and, in particular, what she believes—rightly or wrongly—to be a harmful environment created by Mr Parent and Mrs Paramour?

15. In reviewing both your notes and your report, I have been unable to find any reference to a statement by Mrs Parent in which she describes *her* needs. I find only references to her concerns—whether realistic in your view or not—regarding the children. Can you identify something either in your notes or in your report that I missed?

[4] [BACKGROUND > Comments appearing in the evaluator's contemporaneously taken notes and opinions expressed in her report suggest that she is unfamiliar with research on parenting styles, and authoritative parenting in particular.]

1. In reading your notes and your report, I get the impression that Mrs Parent displays a limit-setting parenting style. Is my impression essentially correct?

2. Much has been published concerning different parenting styles and the effect of those parenting styles upon children. Is that correct?

3. Do you consider yourself to be fairly familiar with that research?

4. Are there any particular researchers whose research on parenting styles is considered by you in formulating your opinions?

[The most prominent researcher in this area is Baumrind. Whether or not the evaluator mentions Baumrind or other researchers, continue with the questions that follow.]

5. It is my understanding that the parenting style displayed by Mrs Parent is referred to as an authoritative parenting style. Is that correct?

6. It is my understanding that the published research indicates that authoritative parenting tends to produce children who are socially responsible, independent, competent, and self-assured. Is my understanding of the research correct?

7. It is my understanding that the published research indicates that permissive parenting tends to produce children who are poorly socialized and less achievement-oriented than their peers. Is my understanding of the research correct?

8. Though people often say that no child is born bad, it is my understanding that children are, in fact, entirely egocentric at birth—in touch only with their own needs—and that an awareness of the needs of others and a reasonable level of concern for the needs of others requires maturation. Am I essentially correct in my understanding?

9. Am I also correct that, at least in part, children develop a concern for the needs of others when role models such as parents call their attention to the needs of others and, perhaps, explain things that the children can do that will be responsive to the needs of others?

10. The notes taken during your visit at Mr Parent's apartment indicate that he joins the children in bouncing a basketball in the apartment. When children bounce balls in an apartment building, is it not likely that the noise is disturbing to neighbors?

11. Would you not agree that there are several good reasons for instructing children not to bounce a basketball off the walls and floors of an apartment?

12. I am aware that mental health professionals do not like being asked to predict behavior, but we both know that sometimes it is easier than at other times. Can you not reasonably predict that if the children were to play ball in an apartment in their mother's presence that she would curtail the activity?

[5] [**BACKGROUND** > There are indications that the father is attempting to win over the children by not setting any limits on their behavior and that the mother is parenting the children as she has always done.]

1. With only rare exceptions, young children do not really like hearing "you can't do that," is that not true?

2. Is it not also true that in the midst of custody disputes parents are likely to become particularly concerned with how their children view them and what their children might say to an evaluator?

3. Your notes—page 83—reflect that the children agree that at their mother's house there are "lots of rules." Do you have reason to believe that Mrs Parent is unaware that the children view her as imposing "lots of rules"?

4. So, Mrs Parent is aware that her children would prefer fewer rules; she is aware that their father imposes fewer rules; and, she is aware that the custody dispute in which she and Mr Parent are embroiled is, unfortunately, a form of competition. Does it not say something about her concern for the long-term best interests of her children that, in this very difficult time, she still imposes upon the children what she believes to be reasonable rules?

5. Can a parent effectively raise his or her children if the parent's decision making is unduly influenced by a fear that the children will be angry if limits are imposed?

[6] [BACKGROUND: There are indications that the evaluator has applied different standards in making judgments concerning the behaviors of the two parents and the husband's paramour.]

1. In reviewing your report, I find a reference (on page 46) to the fact that {*Jack's*} expression of a desire to spend more time with his father was, in part, attributable to "encouragement"—your word—from Mr Parent. On page 49, you report that Mr Parent "suggested" that {*Sally*} show you some recent pictures. When Mrs Parent tries to stimulate discussion of a recent holiday trip, she is described, in your words, as being "like a cheerleader." Would you agree that words like "encouragement" and "suggested" are neutral in tone but that the phrase "like a cheerleader" is derogatory in tone?

[7] [BACKGROUND > Evaluator appears to excuse certain pertinent behaviors in a parent because the parent declares that she has been diagnosed with attention-deficit hyperactivity disorder (ADHD).]

1. You report that collateral sources and various documents clearly show that Mrs Parent is consistently late for appointments, is forgetful, and is disorganized. Is that correct?
2. You also report that when questioned about this, Mrs Parent informed you that she has been diagnosed with ADHD. Is that correct?
3. You did not seek confirmation of this information, did you?
4. In your commentary, after having alluded to Mrs Parent's tardiness, forgetfulness, and disorganization, you state: "compassion demands that we recognize that these problems are the direct result of a diagnosed condition: ADHD." Am I correct in my understanding that what you are saying, in layman's terms, is that we all need to cut Mrs Parent some slack?
5. Are you familiar with the American Psychological Association's Guidelines for *Child Custody Evaluations in Divorce Proceedings*?
6. Do you recognize the document as authoritative?
7. I present you with a copy of the American Psychological Association's *Guidelines for Child Custody Evaluations in Divorce Proceedings* and ask that you read aloud the highlighted portion.

   (1–3 "psychopathology may be relevant to such an assessment, in so far as it has impact on the child or the ability to parent, but it is not the primary focus.")

   It is my understanding that this guideline is intended to remind evaluators that a parent's having a disorder that is linked to a diagnostic label does not suggest that the parent is impaired in ways that have a direct bearing on parenting capacity. Is that correct?
8. Is not this guideline also pointing out that the primary focus must be the impact upon children of whatever the condition might be?
9. During the course of this evaluation, were you not provided with numerous examples of situations in which the children's lives were adversely affected by their mother's tardiness, forgetfulness, or disorganization?
10. If you are the child, does the reason for the tardiness, forgetfulness, and disorganization matter much from your perspective?

11. So that whether the tardiness, forgetfulness, and disorganization are attributable to an attention deficit, hyperactivity disorder, or to passive aggressive characteristics or to something else, the impact on you—if you are the child—is the same. Is that correct?

12. By informing readers of your report that compassion demands that we all cut Mrs Parent some slack, are you not diverting attention from what we are directed by law to focus on—the best interests of the children—and, in this case, the effects upon the children of their mother's tardiness, forgetfulness, and disorganization?

13. Am I correct that nowhere in your report do you address the issue of the likely effect of Mrs Parent's tardiness, forgetfulness, and disorganization upon the children?

14. Is it fair to say that tardiness, forgetfulness, and disorganization in a parent are likely to have a *negative* effect upon children?

15. Mrs Parent has forgotten her children's dental appointments, has forgotten to pay the electric bill, is tardy, is disorganized; and these behaviors are attributed to ADHD by you. Is it not more important to explore the possible ramifications for the children of these behaviors in Mrs Parent than to label them and discuss them no further?

[8] [**BACKGROUND** > Evaluator has failed to articulate the criteria that were used in assessing the best interests of the child.]

1. I present you with the American Psychological Association's *Guidelines for Child Custody Evaluations in Divorce Proceedings*. Are you familiar with this document?

2. Do you recognize it as authoritative?

3. Would you agree that the issue of what an evaluator should pay attention to in assessing the best interests of the child is an issue concerning which there would likely be differences of opinion?

4. Are you aware that in some states the criteria—the things to attend to—are specified in statutes?

5. In the state of New York, are the criteria specified in our statutes?

6. I ask that you read aloud the portion of the APA guidelines that I have highlighted.

("Recommendations are based on articulated assumptions, data interpretations, and inferences based upon established professional and scientific standards.")

Would you not agree that the words "articulated assumptions" include, among other things, specifying what criteria the evaluator has utilized, if the evaluator is working in a state that does not specify the criteria in its statutes?

[9] [**BACKGROUND** > Evaluator has used descriptive statements taken directly from a computer-generated interpretive report.]

THE LEAD-IN: I would like now to compare some of your statements concerning Mrs Parent with statements appearing in the computer-generated interpretive report.

On page 21 of your report, you opined, based on your analysis of the test data, that Mrs Parent is "not very introspective or insightful about her own behavior." Dr Butcher had written, on page 3, line 4 of his computer-generated interpretive report, that the test-taker is "not very introspective or insightful about her own behavior."

On page 21 of your report, you opined, based on your analysis of the test data, that Mrs Parent is "rigid and inflexible in her approach to problems." Dr Butcher had written, on page 3, line 6 of his computer-generated interpretive report, that the test-taker is "rigid and inflexible in her approach to problems."

On page 21 of your report, you opined, based on your analysis of the test data, that Mrs Parent "may not be open to psychological self-evaluation." Dr Butcher had written, on page 3, line 7 of his computer-generated interpretive report, that the test-taker "may not be open to psychological self-evaluation."

On page 21 of your report, you opined, based on your analysis of the test data, that Mrs Parent is likely to be "somewhat arrogant and intolerant of others' failings." Dr Butcher had written, on page 3, line 8 of his computer-generated interpretive report, that the test-taker is likely to be "somewhat arrogant and intolerant of others' failings."

On page 21 of your report, you opined, based on your analysis of the test data, that Mrs Parent is "likely to blame others for her problems." Dr Butcher had written, on page 5, line 7 of his computer-generated interpretive report, under "mental health considerations," that the test-taker "tends to blame others for her problems."

1. THE QUESTION: Am I correct that your report contained no acknowledgment that the words used by you to describe Mrs Parent were words chosen by Dr Butcher, incorporated into computer software written by him and automatically generated by a computer?
2. Are you familiar with Standard 8.11 of the Psychologists' Ethics Code—the standard that addresses plagiarism?
3. That standard reads: "Psychologists do not present portions of another's work or data as their own, even if the other work or data source is cited occasionally." When, in a formal document such as a report written for the court, you use another person's words and do not indicate that you are doing so, would that not be considered plagiarism, as defined in Standard 8.11?

[10] [BACKGROUND > There are indications that the evaluator has depended upon a computer-generated report and has been inattentive to other information. Additionally, there are indications that the evaluator is unfamiliar with basic principles of test construction.]
1. In your report, on page 20, you state: "The MMPI-2 computer-generated report can serve as a useful source of hypotheses…" Is that correct?
2. According to the information contained on page 1 of your report, your last interview with Mrs Parent was conducted on [3/14/06] and your last interview with Mr Parent was conducted on [3/29/06]. Also, according to the information contained on page 1 of your report, you administered the MMPI-2 to Mrs Parent on [5/10/06] and to Mr Parent on [5/16/06]. Are those dates correct?
3. It is my understanding that psychologists generate hypotheses, test the hypotheses, and then analyze the data in order to see whether the data are or are not supportive of the hypotheses. Is that essentially correct?
4. So if the testing is the last thing done, how is it possible for the test results to facilitate the formulation of hypotheses?
5. After having received the test data from Pearson, you did not meet with Mr and Mrs Parent and offer an explanation of the results to them, did you?

Standard 9.10 of the Psychologists' Ethics Code reads as follows, in its entirety:

Regardless of whether the scoring and interpretation are done by psychologists, by employees or assistants, or by automated or other outside services, psychologists take reasonable steps to ensure that explanations of results are given to the individual or designated representative unless the nature of the relationship precludes provision of an explanation of results (such as in some organizational consulting, preemployment or security screenings, and forensic evaluations), and this fact has been clearly explained to the person being assessed in advance.

6. Was the professional relationship between you and the litigants one that "precludes provision of an explanation of results"?

7. What law, directive from the court, or ethical principle precludes the provision of an explanation of results?

8. The fact that test results would not be explained was not "clearly explained to the [litigants] in advance," was it?

9. The words utilized in Standard 9.10 ("explanations…given") emphasize the imparting of information to those whom one has tested. Would you not agree, however, that if the computer-generated interpretive report is to serve as—to use your words—"a useful source of hypotheses," there should be a posttest session in which test data are reviewed with a test-taker, so that information can be obtained that bears on whatever hypotheses have been formulated?

10. You write, on page 21 of your report: "Mrs Parent tends to deny problems, and is not very introspective or insightful about her own behavior." That sounds to me like a statement and not like a hypothesis that—again, to use your words—"needs to be verified by other sources of clinical information."

11. Does information obtained by you from Dr Helper, Mrs Parent's treating psychologist, fit into the category of "other sources of clinical information"?

12. You acknowledge that the statements appearing in the computer-generated interpretive report are to be viewed as hypotheses that need to be verified. When Dr Helper contradicts the computer's description of Mrs Parent as someone who is "unlikely to seek treatment or to cooperate fully with treatment," does that not suggest that the hypothesis generated by the computer has not been verified?

13. If that is so, then is it not possible that what is being reflected on the test is a transitory mindset and not a deep-seated character trait?

14. I have reviewed the notes of your conversation with Dr Helper, and I do not see anything relating to a tendency on Mrs Parent's part to blame others. Did you ask him whether or not he was in agreement with this statement generated by the computer? On page 4 of the Child Custody Interpretive Report for Mrs Parent, the stability of scores on the Pd scale are discussed. The report says: "Short-term test–retest studies have shown a correlation of 0.79 for this high-point score."

15. When reference is made to "short-term test-retest studies," what is the interval between the first testing and the second testing?

16. The information provided in the interpretive report is provided in order to assist *you*. If you do not understand the information that is provided, how are you able to formulate an opinion concerning the stability of scores on the Pd scale?

17. Where would one find the answer to my question about the interval between the first testing and the second?

18. Are you familiar with the Manual for Administration, Scoring, and Interpretation for the MMPI-2?

    On page 123, *Appendix E* provides *Reliability Data* for the various scales. On that page, the reader of the manual is told that the test–retest data were obtained in a study of 82 males and 111 females and that the average interval was 8.58 days, with a median of 7 days.

19. Does knowing that the scores are stable over a period of roughly 8 days enable you to infer that if Mrs Parent were to take the MMPI-2 a year from today, her score would be essentially the same?

20. What magnitude correlation signifies good test–retest reliability? [The short-term test–retest reliability for the Pd scale is 0.69 for females, according to the manual.]

    The same table that provides the test–retest data for the clinical scales, on page 124, also provides the *standard error of measurement* for each of the scales.

21. Can you explain for the record what the standard error of measurement tells the user of the test manual?

22. The standard error of measurement for the Pd scale is 5.54 for female test-takers. Mrs Parent's score on the Pd scale was 66. What does knowing that the standard error of measurement is 5.54 tell us?

[11] [**BACKGROUND** > Evaluator has seen the father first and last in the interview sequence.]

1. On page 1 of your report, you provide the dates on which the parties were seen. You indicate that the evaluation began with an interview with Mr Parent, on February 10, 2006, followed by an interview with Mrs Parent, on February 15, 2006. Are those dates correct?

2. Are you familiar with the primacy effect?

3. Are you familiar with David Rosenhan's 1973 research, published in *Science* by the title "On being sane in insane places"?

    [She may be familiar with it. It is a study that is widely discussed in psychology courses, even on the introductory level. If she says that she is, follow up.]

4. Can you briefly describe the study and its findings?

5. The dynamics studied by Rosenhan are related to the dynamics of the primacy effect, are they not?

    [It's anyone's guess what her response might be. The answer is "Yes." Rosenhan's research revealed that once normal people, faking psychosis, had been admitted to a mental institution, their actions were perceived as the actions of mental patients, even though the study's volunteers dropped their psychotic "acts" immediately after having been admitted.]

6. Are you familiar with Robert Rosenthal's 1966 research on expectancy effects?

    [Rosenthal found that teachers' grading of students was closely linked to fictitious information that the teachers had been given concerning the children's intellectual ability.]

7. The dynamics that explain the expectancy effect are similar to those that explain the primacy effect is that not so?

    [Clearly, it is. What was learned first—the children's intellectual ability (though fictitious)—affected perceptions of what came later—their performance in school.]

8. Also on page 1, you indicate that your last interview with Mrs Parent was on 3/14/06 and that your last interview with Mr Parent was on 3/29/06. Are those dates correct?

9. Are you familiar with the recency effect?

[If she says that she is, ask that she explain it. If she says that she is not, ask the next question.]

10. Are you familiar with the work of Hermann Ebbinghaus on learning, retention, and recall?

[Unless she has forgotten everything that she learning in graduate school, she should certainly be familiar with Ebbinghaus. His research is certainly high on the list of things that a school psychologist would learn. Assuming that she says she is familiar with Ebbinghaus's research, ask the following question.]

11. Would you please explain, for the record, your understanding of the *serial position effect*?

[Research by Ebbinghaus and many after him has dramatically shown that when information is presented sequentially, the material presented first and the material presented last are the easiest to recall and the material presented midway through the series is the most difficult to recall.]
[Regardless of her answer, ask the next question.]

12. Is it not true that research shows that there are advantages to being the last person to be heard?

13. And there is also an advantage to being the first to be heard, is that not so?

14. Do you dispute that in addition to having the advantage of being the first to be heard, Mr Parent also had the advantage of being the last to be heard?

15. Does giving one party the advantage of being the first to be heard and the advantage of being the last to be heard strike you as being methodologically sound?

[12] [**BACKGROUND** > Evaluator has refused to release test data, in spite of having received a subpoena for her entire file. Her refusal makes it necessary for the attorney to seek a court order.]

1. I am interested in knowing if you are familiar with the *Daubert* decision. Are you?

2. If you recall, what happened to the Daubert family's lawsuit against Merrell Dow Pharmaceuticals after the U.S. Supreme Court decision was handed down?

3. The case was remanded to the 9th Federal Circuit Court, and the evidence proffered by the Daubert family was, again, rejected. It was ruled that courts need to look beyond what experts say and examine the "basis they have for saying it." Does that seem unreasonable to you?

4. Though judges sometimes pose their own questions to witnesses, for the most part, what judges examine is what is brought to their attention by the attorneys on direct examination and cross-examination of witnesses. Would you agree?

5. So if you have made certain statements about Mr Parent and Mrs Parent based on test data and if Judge Justice is to examine the basis for those statements, Mr Adversary and I both must have access to the data and to the computer-generated

reports so that we can question you concerning how the data were used by you in formulating your opinions. Is this not so?

[For your reference: Judge Alex Kozinski: *Daubert v. Merrell Dow Pharmaceuticals, Inc.* (on remand), 43 F.3d. 1311 (9th Cir. 1995). Judge Alex Kozinski, writing for the Court, declared that the Court's task "is to analyze not what the experts say, but what basis they have for saying it." (@ 1316).]

6. Are you aware of your obligations following receipt of a subpoena?
7. When a psychologist receives a subpoena and when one of the items listed is an item that the psychologist believes may be protected from disclosure by privilege, what action is the psychologist expected to take?

    [For your reference: The psychologist is expected to notify the person who may have a basis for asserting privilege and inform the person that s/he has X days in which to formally notify the psychologist of his/her intention to assert privilege. In the absence of such a formal notification, the psychologist must be responsive to the demands of the subpoena.]

8. You indicated in your letter to me that you believed that Mr Parent's test data were protected from disclosure by privilege. What specific privilege did you feel was applicable?

    [Based upon the content of her letter, she is likely to state that she does not know. If she states that psychologist-patient privilege applies, ask the following question.]

9. So it is your understanding that psychologist-patient privilege applies in a situation in which the person tested is not a patient, in which the examination being conducted by you is being conducted under the terms of a court order, and when the results of the testing are alluded to you in your report to the court?
10. Are you familiar with any State statutes or any State case law that supports the notion of protecting a custody litigant's test data from disclosure?
11. So, on what basis did you conclude that the test data should be protected from disclosure?
12. Were you aware that both attorneys in this matter are entitled under the law to examine all the test data and any computer-generated reports?
13. Are you familiar with the provisions of State Rule of Evidence 705?
14. If you are performing forensic psychological activities, is it not incumbent upon you to be aware of the rules of evidence?
    Let me return to the State Annotated Code, 123:45(e), which states: "A licensee shall maintain competence consistent with professional responsibilities…"
15. Is it your position that being familiar with those rules of evidence that directly pertain to the work of custody evaluators is not among your responsibilities?
16. Are you familiar with the Psychologists' Ethics Code?
17. Are you familiar with Standard 4.02—the standard that covers "Discussing the Limits of Confidentiality"?
18. What is your recollection of the content of that standard?
    One element of Standard 4.02 places upon you the obligation to inform those whom you evaluate of "the foreseeable uses of the information generated."

19. How is it possible to meet your obligation under Standard 4.02, to inform others of the foreseeable uses of the information generated if you yourself are not aware of the foreseeable uses of that information?

20. You have been licensed as a psychologist in the State since 1983, is that correct? Were you familiar with the 1992 Ethics Code?

21. As the Ethics Code was undergoing revision, did you follow any of the discussions concerning anticipated changes?

22. Were you aware of the significant change that was made in that portion of the Ethics Code that addresses the release of psychological test data?

23. Are you familiar with the American Psychological Association's *Guidelines for Child Custody Evaluations in Divorce Proceedings*?

24. Are you familiar with the two guidelines that outline the obligations of psychologists to obtain informed consent?
    Guideline 9 admonishes psychologists to inform adult participants "about the possible disposition of the data collected."

25. Did you inform both Mr Parent and Mrs Parent that your file would be subject to discovery?

26. Please tell me what you recall of the second guideline—Guideline 10.

    Guideline 10 declares, in part: "The psychologist informs participants that in consenting to the evaluation, they are consenting to disclosure of the evaluation's findings in the context of the forthcoming litigation and in any other proceedings deemed necessary by the courts."

27. Would you agree that the phrase "disclosure of the evaluation's findings" includes the findings that are derived through psychological testing?

    [In the event that she hesitates or says that she does not agree, ask the following question.]

28. Is there anything in the wording that suggests an exception is to be made for findings derived through testing?

    Guideline 10 also says: "A psychologist obtains a waiver of confidentiality from all adult participants or from their legal representatives." The wording does not refer to confidentiality with respect to notes taken or with respect to documents reviewed. Nothing in the wording suggests that an exception is to be made with respect to confidentiality for test data.

29. Would you not agree that your obligation was to obtain a waiver of confidentiality for the entire contents of your file?

Child Maltreatment Evaluation from Chapter 20 (Manley and Chavez)

Authors' note: The following Parental Assessment has been modified to preserve the parent's confidentiality. All identifiable data have been altered.

Confidential

Child Maltreatment Parental Assessment

Name   : Jane Doe
Date of birth   : 06.09.80
Age   : 24 years old
Evaluator   : XXXX
Date of evaluation : 05.01.06

Reason for Referral

On 01.02.06, an Initial Safe Family Home Report and Service Plan identified harm toward Jo Smith (date of birth: 09.15.05) *via* "threat of physical abuse, and threat of neglect" by mother, Jane Doe, and father, Jo Smith (date of birth: 06.17.55). The report identified the mother's problematic behaviors perpetuating the maltreatment of her child including the areas of mental health, substance abuse, and parenting style.

The report recommended services for Ms. Doe, including a parenting assessment, substance abuse assessment/treatment, domestic violence services, medication management for her psychiatric condition, individual therapy, and a psychological evaluation.

An updated Safe Family Home Report dated 02.15.06 awarded foster custody of Jo Smith to the Department of Human Services (DHS) due to an unsafe family home. The report recommended family supervision of Jo Smith, along with continued domestic violence treatment and counseling for Mother.

On 03.28.06, a Supplemental Safe Family Home Report documented that Ms. Doe was reunified with her daughter, but housing difficulties had resulted in Ms. Doe's request to have Jo Smith placed into Mr. Smith's custody. Mr. Smith was limited to supervised visitations with his daughter and could not legally take custody of her. The child was placed into a state-licensed DHS foster home.

The purpose of this evaluation is to assess and evaluate Ms. Doe's current ability to safely and appropriately parent her child. Her cognitive and learning skills, personality characteristics, emotional state, parenting knowledge, and interpersonal relationships have been reviewed for the following document. Diagnostic impressions and treatment recommendations are offered.

Sources of Information

- Review of DHS referral information including Initial Safe Family Home Guideline Report and Interim Family Service Plan, Safe Family Home Report and Family Service Plan 2, and Supplemental Safe Family Home Report.
- Parent survey summary
- Family status report
- Urinalysis reporting forms dated (five different dates over a 1-year span).
- Treatment center urinalysis result forms dated (10 different dates over a 2-year span)
- Order-granting petition for injunction against harassment against father
- Initial developmental evaluation for Jo Smith
- Mental health centers client contact log, drug use profile, psychiatric evaluation
- Parenting education certificate of completion
- Team conference preliminary report
- Clinical interview and observations
- Mental status examination
- Kaufman Brief Intelligence Test (K-BIT)
- Minnesota Multiphasic Personality Inventory—Second Edition (MMPI-2)

Family Services Background

Hawaii Child Protective Services Background

The following is a chronological account of Ms. Doe's contacts with the Child Protective Services (CPS) in Hawaii.

On 04.21.05, the woman's shelter cited that Ms. Doe had reported that Mr. Smith verbally threatened to kill her. She had also reportedly suffered a miscarriage due to physical abuse from Mr. Smith. Shelter staff reported to the DHS worker that Ms. Doe had difficulties getting along with other residents and staff.

On 05.24.05, Ms. Doe tested positive for delta-9-tetrahydrocannabinol (THC).

On 09.15.05, Ms. Doe gave birth to Jo Smith and was residing at a local woman's shelter. A CPS intake was received for risk concerns. Immediately after childbirth (09.16.05), she was transferred to the psychiatric unit of the hospital for stabilization. According to the supplemental report, Mr. Smith then placed a threatening phone call to the hospital's infant nursery regarding Ms. Doe's situation.

On 09.16.05, Ms. Doe reported to the DHS worker that she had been taking her psychotropic medication until she found out she was pregnant. She discontinued all medications with the exception of antidepressants. She admitted continuing to smoke marijuana throughout her pregnancy. Ms. Doe denied physical abuse between her and her boyfriend but admitted that her boyfriend had exhibited verbal and controlling behaviors toward her. She was released from the hospital with her child.

On 09.20.05, Ms. Doe was observed smoking marijuana at the woman's shelter.

On 09.22.05, Ms. Doe tested positive for THC.

On 10.01.05, Mr. Smith denied any domestic violence toward Ms. Doe to the DHS worker. He agreed to drug testing (urinalysis) but indicated that he would test positive for THC because he used THC as a prescribed medication.

On 10.03.05, Ms. Doe tested positive for THC.

On 10.26.05, the woman's shelter contacted the DHS regarding Ms. Doe's disruptive behavior, breaking shelter rules, and hitchhiking with her infant. Ms. Doe left the shelter and returned later with Mr. Smith's car to retrieve her belongings.

On 10.27.05, temporary DHS family supervision of Jo Smith was awarded by the Court.

On 11.07.05, the DHS social worker reported that Mr. Smith stated that Ms. Doe had not been taking her psychotropic medications. She was reported to have been consuming alcohol. Ms. Doe reported that she was moving back to another state because Mr. Smith was abusive to her. The woman's program reported that the couple drank alcohol during the initial home visit. Poor bonding was observed between Ms. Doe and the baby, Jo Smith.

Minnesota Child Protective Services Background

Prior to the present case, Ms. Doe had numerous contacts with Minnesota Child Protection Services regarding her firstborn, Billy Jones (date of birth: 09.05.01). The information for this section was taken from a file review provided by the referring agency. The following has been provided to add a historical context to the current paternal assessment.

On 11.10.01, a CPS report cited that Ms. Doe and Billy Jones both tested positive for THC. The report noted that Ms. Doe had an alcohol abuse history and continued to be in a violent relationship with her then boyfriend, Jack Jones.

On 11.20.01, A CPS report indicated that Ms. Doe had smoked marijuana during her pregnancy, with daily usage throughout the third trimester. Ms. Doe was observed having bruises and was referred to a women's shelter.

On 11.30.01, the CPS received a report stating that Ms. Doe had been smoking marijuana with Mr. Jones. Then he had allegedly been blowing marijuana smoke into the infant's face and had been aggressive toward Ms. Doe and her son.

On 12.03.01, Ms. Doe reportedly left Billy, then a 3-month-old infant, alone in another room while feeding her son with a baby bottle propped up on a blanket. The CPS worker noted that the infant had a quarter-sized bruise between his eyes. The infant had been wheezing and displayed a neck rash. Ms. Doe explained to the worker that the rash had resulted from milk running out of the propped-up bottle. Ms. Doe admitted smoking marijuana while breastfeeding Billy, commenting that it had made the baby "quiet."

On 01.11.02, the CPS worker found Billy at the family residence in the front room alone. A marijuana "bong" was beside the infant, who was "quietly staring at the wall." Ms. Doe was in a bedroom in the back of the home.

On 05.21.02, a CPS report documented that Ms. Doe rarely held her infant and frequently associated with drug dealers. According to police reports, domestic violence had been ongoing between Ms. Doe and Mr. Jones.

On 06.03.02 and 06.11.02, Ms. Doe reportedly elicited a female adolescent to baby-sit her son. Allegations included the adolescent's inappropriate care of the infant.

On 06.20.02, Mr. Jones allegedly assaulted Ms. Doe and Billy, who was then 7 months old. Allegations included throwing the infant across the room on three occasions. A bruise was observed on the child's right cheek.

On 06.25.02, Ms. Doe requested temporary custody placement of Billy to allow her to become stabilized on her newly prescribed Paxil medication.

On 07.28.02, the CPS received a report that Ms. Doe had abandoned her child. The child was left with a 16-year-old who had minimal interest about caring for the baby.

On 07.30.02, Ms. Doe was allegedly intoxicated with crack-cocaine and LSD. She was unable to care for Billy. It was also reported that Ms. Doe had been intravenously injecting methamphetamine. Billy was observed having a "bump on the back of his head" and was "feverish." Ms. Doe reportedly had left the baby alone in motel rooms on multiple occasions while obtaining drugs.

On 08.22.02, Billy was placed into CPS protective custody.

On 08.25.02, Mr. Jones reported that Ms. Doe had previously shaken and thrown the baby.

On 09.09.02, Billy was relocated to an adjacent county to live with maternal family members.

On 09.16.02, Ms. Doe relinquished the parental rights to her son.

On 04.09.04, Billy was adopted by his paternal aunt and uncle.

Background Information

The following information has been gathered from data collected from collateral sources and the clinical interview.

Ms. Jane Doe was born in La Binder, MN. She reported having a sister 2 years her senior, and an older half-sister and half-brother from her father's previous marriage. In contrast, a prior psychiatric assessment revealed that Ms. Doe had an older sibling, two sisters whom she had never met, and one stepbrother. Reportedly, her father worked as an electrician. Her parents were separated when she was "really young."

Ms. Doe's mother has a 26-year history of heroin abuse. Ms. Doe also reported that her mother was an alcoholic. She noted that her father was a "crack head." Ms. Doe lived with her father and his girlfriend until age four, when her mother, her mother's husband, and another man took her out of state. Reportedly, Ms. Doe's mother had been engaged in prostitution over an extended period of time.

Ms. Doe reported frequent molestations and physical abuse by her mother and mother's husband during a 10-month period. The adults were regularly violent toward each other. The level of violence increased to the point that Ms. Doe and her mother returned to Minnesota.

Ms. Doe's mother contacted the CPS and had her removed from the family home when she was 7 years old. She lived at several group homes and with other family members. At age nine, Ms. Doe was returned to foster care due to her exposure to repeated physical abuse and her mother's heroin addiction. Ms. Doe noted she had lived in approximately 33 foster homes during her childhood.

As a teenager, Ms. Doe displayed frequent anger outbursts and disruptive behaviors. She ran away on multiple occasions. At age 13, she reported that she had found her "family" on the streets and lived under a bridge for a year.

At age 17, Ms. Doe gave birth to her first child, Billy. After Billy's birth, Ms. Doe petitioned the court to have supervised contact with her mother. This contact led to Ms. Doe's increased drug use, as her mother shared drugs with her. Ms. Doe reported that her mother had offered her heroin for menstrual cramps.

During the clinical interview, Ms. Doe was unable to recall whether she had voluntarily given Billy up for adoption, or if the child had been removed by the CPS. She reported that she experienced "emotional loss" after her son was removed.

Currently, Ms. Doe's participation with the CPS-recommended services has been lackluster. She reported noncompletion of her parenting education, missing four sessions because of her marijuana use. She reported that she had completed a domestic abuse educational group, but no supporting documentation was available.

Ms. Doe has been recently referred for individual counseling and skill-building services but has not followed through with her appointments.

Ms. Doe reported that she attended weekly supervised visitation with her daughter.

Education History

Ms. Doe recalled achieving above-average grades in school. English was her best subject; math was her worst subject. She dropped out of high school in the 10th grade and had been "picked on a lot" by her school peers. She denied participation in gang activities.

Employment History

Ms. Doe does not have a consistent work history. She has engaged in short-term employment as a server. She has no viable vocational skills. Ms. Doe does not have plans for future employment and has applied for Social Security benefits.

Mental Health Treatment History

Ms. Doe explained that she has suffered from anxiety and depression throughout her life; she has been previously diagnosed with bipolar disorder. A 2001 psychiatric assessment reported observations of mania, insomnia without fatigue, pressured speech, racing thoughts, distraction, and increased goal-oriented behavior.

Ms. Doe was transferred to a psychiatric ward immediately after her daughter's birth and began medication and treatment for bipolar disorder. She was prescribed Neuronton, Paxil CR, and Abilify. Ms. Doe missed several of her monthly medication management appointments.

Ms. Doe reported that she had attended weekly individual counseling sessions with a psychologist for a few months but dropped out of therapy. Ms. Doe has also attended weekly couples' counseling with Mr. Smith, but the couple had missed their most recent session.

Legal History

During her adolescence, Ms. Doe was arrested for possession of hypodermic syringes. She was incarcerated for one night and later released on her own recognizance. Ms. Doe denied other legal or criminal involvement.

Substance Abuse History

Ms. Doe has an extensive and chronic drug abuse history. She began using methamphetamine when she was 15 years old. By age 17, she reported, "shooting up with crank." She distributed marijuana, cocaine, and methamphetamine until she was arrested at age 19. Ms. Doe noted that she did not sell hallucinogenic drugs, as it was "too risky." Ms. Doe reported using heroin on a single occasion and crystal methamphetamine twice. Collateral information documented regular use of crystal methamphetamine. She denied alcohol use and prescription medication abuse.

At age 20, Ms. Doe entered a substance abuse treatment facility and reportedly completed treatment within seven months. Upon completion, she was reunited with Billy. In contrast, the Initial Safe Family Home Report cited that Ms. Doe dropped out of treatment during her fifth month, was transferred to another facility, and was asked to leave due to rule violations.

Ms. Doe admitted that she continued to use marijuana after drug treatment but had "let go of hard drugs." She admitted she had used cocaine and marijuana in the presence of her infant son.

Ms. Doe reported she recently returned to substance abuse treatment. In contrast, the Supplemental Safe Family Home Report indicated that she received a nonclinical discharge from the program. Ms. Doe reported that she has remained abstinent for 10½ months. She reported attending support group meetings approximately four times weekly, but had not attended any meetings the previous week.

Collateral data indicated that random urinalysis screenings tested negative for the previous 4 months. However, Ms. Doe reported that she did not complete the urinalysis testing the previous month because she refused to "jump through any more hoops." She has not contacted the treatment facility to schedule further urinalysis appointments. The Family Service Plan recommended continuance of the urinalysis program.

Relationship History

Ms. Doe has a history of intimate relationships with violent, drug-abusing men. Collateral information from Minnesota indicated that Jack Jones, the father of Billy Jones, was violent toward Ms. Doe and their child on numerous occasions. In Hawaii, Ms. Doe expressed fear of leaving her daughter alone with Mr. Jones. In contrast, Ms. Doe reported that Mr. Jones took care of their daughter by feeding her and changing her diapers.

Recently, Ms. Doe returned to live with Mr. Smith, the father of Jo Smith. Since then she has experienced increased depression. Ms. Doe reported that her relationship with Mr. Smith has been "on and off," She stated that he "needed to learn to control his anger." Ms. Doe was unable to identify any other friends or viable social support systems, citing that she had returned to Mr. Smith because she had "nowhere else to go."

Psychological Assessment

Mental Status Examination

On 05.01.06, Ms. Doe participated in a 3-h evaluation. She arrived on time for her appointment with her boyfriend, Mr. Smith. During the initial period of introductions, Mr. Smith remained in the room. Ms. Doe presented as nervous, offered minimal eye contact, and displayed tense facial expressions. After Mr. Smith left the room, Ms. Doe was visibly relaxed and established eye contact with the evaluator.

Ms. Doe was oriented to time, place, and reason for meeting. She presented disheveled and had failed to zip up her shorts. Her eyes were bright and clear, and her mood was upbeat throughout the evaluation. She appeared older than her stated age of 24.

During the interview, Ms. Doe exhibited periodic scratching of her arms, yawning, and mumbling her answers. She occasionally displayed a vacant stare when questioned about her childhood. She cried when talking about her childhood sexual molestations and the physical abuse perpetrated by her mother. Her speech was soft-spoken and relaxed during the interview. Ms. Doe was cooperative and reported that she would do "anything" to have her daughter returned to her custody.

Ms. Doe was able to correctly answer several questions regarding current events. She appeared to have concrete reasoning skills. There was no suggestion of cognitive processing errors. Ms. Doe was able to complete tasks of concentration, including simple calculations and serial sevens. Her memory was judged to be intact. She denied ever sustaining a head injury. Her gait and motor activity were observed as normal.

She estimated that her moods were "pretty good" and her appetite seemed "okay." She reported interrupted sleep patterns, waking up three to four times during the night. She denied suicidal or homicidal ideation or history of attempted suicide.

Intellectual Testing

The K-BIT is a brief, individually administered measure of verbal and nonverbal intelligence of a wide range of children, adolescents, and adults, spanning the ages of 4–90 years. The test is designed for circumstances in which a brief screening measure of intelligence will suffice. The K-BIT is well normed among multicultural populations and offers a reliable assessment of intelligence that is based on the measurement of both crystallized and fluid intellectual abilities through two subtests, vocabulary and matrices.

Ms. Doe actively participated in the test administration and appeared interested in achieving her best. She responded to the items presented to her. Ms. Doe's verbal abilities, as measured by the vocabulary subtest, were in the low average range. Her nonverbal abilities, as measured by the matrices subtest, were also in the low average range. Overall, Ms. Doe's intellectual abilities were estimated to be in the low average range.

Psychological Testing

The MMPI-2 is a valid measure of current personality functioning. The interpretive statements that follow are derived primarily from empirical studies of persons with known psychological characteristics whose responses to test items were similar to Ms. Doe, and from actuarial predictions based on combinations of theory and research. These statements are predictions about current functioning and should be considered probabilistic although they may be stated affirmatively. Their accuracy may be affected by this individual's culture, test-taking style, and attitude. They should be interpreted in the context of other information regarding this individual.

Ms. Doe's test protocol suggested that she was open and cooperative during the administration. Ms. Doe endorsed items suggesting social immaturity and superficiality in her interpersonal relationships. Individuals with similar profiles often have not incorporated societal values and standards. She seems to be rebellious toward authority figures. Ms. Doe often experiences conflict in her intimate relationships. Individuals with similar profiles often blame others for their actions while being somewhat dependent and demanding. Ms. Doe can be hostile, irritable, and resentful without consideration of the consequences of her actions. She does not seem to learn from her experiences and instead rationalizes and blames others. Generally, Ms. Doe's profile indicates chronic behavioral problems and mismanagement of angry feelings. She can be passive–aggressive and does not want to discuss her emotional problems. Treatment interventions may be challenging for the therapist as Ms. Doe has difficulty establishing rapport with others.

Diagnosis

Ms. Doe has the following mental conditions as described by criteria outlined in the *Diagnostic Statistical Manual Fourth Edition Text Revision* (DSM-IV-TR):

Axis I:	295.75	Bipolar I disorder, most recent episode unspecified
	304.40	Amphetamine dependence, in early remission
	304.30	Cannabis dependence, in early remission
	304.20	Cocaine dependence, in early remission
	V61.21	Neglect of child
Axis II:	301.83	Borderline personality disorder with antisocial traits
Axis III:		Deferred
Axis IV:		Problems with primary support group, occupational problems, social environment problems, psychosocial problems, legal system—child abuse and neglect
Axis V:		Global assessment of functioning: 41 Serious Symptoms

Summary

Ms. Doe has been identified as having engaged in child maltreatment toward her infant daughter. Recognized safety issues include mental illness, substance abuse, and neglectful parenting. The child was originally placed in a CPS-licensed foster home. Lately, Ms. Doe was reunified with her daughter but could not care for her, resulting in an additional foster placement for the child. Ms. Doe has suffered a tumultuous and abusive childhood and remained in the Minnesota CPS system throughout most of her childhood. As a young mother, she has had numerous interactions with the CPS in two states. In Minnesota, Ms. Doe displayed neglect toward her son, and her parental rights were terminated. During the clinical interview, she continued to display lack of insight about the impact of her actions toward both of her children.

Ms. Doe has a long history of chronic substance abuse, beginning in late childhood. She has abused marijuana, cocaine, methamphetamine, and heroin. She has been referred to several substance abuse treatment programs but did not complete treatment due to her noncompliance. During the interview, Ms. Doe was unable to identify potential triggers for substance abuse relapse. Ms. Doe has not complied with her service plan, and her participation has been erratic. She has not completed her parenting classes, engaged in meaningful therapy, and attended medication management appointments, nor has she presented for random urinalysis testing. She noted that she was tired of "jumping through hoops." Ms. Doe has been diagnosed with several chronic psychological disorders. By history, she was not interested, nor did she have the capacity to consistently attend to her psychiatric needs. Ms. Doe remains in a violent relationship with Mr. Smith. Although she was granted a restraining order of protection against him, she has returned to cohabitate with him. Ms. Doe indicated that the relationship would work "this time," and viewed it as a positive long-term situation.

After considering the available data including collateral documentation, clinical interview, psychological testing, and Ms. Doe's displayed participation in her court-ordered services, it is concluded that she is not ready to be reunited with her daughter at present. Of great concern is Ms. Doe's emotional instability and nonparticipation in medication management for her bipolar disorder. Further, though she reported ongoing abstinence, her current residence with an active cannabis user renders her at significantly high risk for substance relapse.

Recommendations

Along with Ms. Doe's DHS service plan requirements, further recommendations are indicated:

- Maintenance of sobriety
  Goal: Receive and complete substance abuse treatment. Attend Narcotics Anonymous meetings, live in a drug-free environment, and engage in meaningful interactions with a sponsor. Random urinalysis testing is recommended for verification of Ms. Doe's abstinence.
- Psychiatric medication evaluation
  Goal: Attend all medication management appointments. Consistent medication adherence is recommended.
- Continued individual therapy
  Goal: Address sexual abuse history, trauma issues, and monitoring of medication. Specific work on domestic violence and attachment bonding is indicated.
- Visitation
  Goal: Ms. Doe is to continue supervised visits with her daughter.

Respectfully submitted,

_____

XXXXXX
Licensed psychologist

Index

A

abbreviated injury scale (AIS), noncerebral trauma, 587–589

accident history of patient, traumatic brain injury assessment and, 593–594

accommodation/negotiation phase, hostage-barricade crises, 274

accuracy statistics, in forensic deception analysis, 101–103

acquiescence, in mentally retarded offenders, 378

action imperative, in crisis negotiation, 281–282

active listening skills
  crisis negotiation, 274–281
  mitigatory defense and, 365–368

activities of daily living, workers' compensation cases, independent neuropsychological evaluation, 465, 475

actuarial assessment
  juvenile sex offenders
    ethical principles, 425–426
    risk assessment, 429–435
  spousal abuse risk assessment, 179–184

actus rea principle, mitigatory defense and, 347

adaptation model
  forensic deception analysis and, 99–103
  neuropsychological evaluation, 569

adaptive functioning
  IQ scores, 60–61
  post-concussive syndrome, 574

Addington v. Texas, 362–363

adjustment evaluation, independent neuropsychological evaluation, workers' compensation cases, 479–480

Adkins v. Virginia, 354

admissibility of evidence
  hostage-barricade crisis negotiation, 265
  officer-involved violence, 251–253

adolescents
  murderers, Minnesota Multiphasic Personality Inventory group profiles, 400
  pituitary gland injury and developmental delay in, 578–580
  sex offenders, demographics research, 418–421

Adoption and Safe Families Act, 135

Adoption of Nancy, 137

age discrimination, employment case law involving, 559–560

aggravating factors, death penalty jurisprudence, 43–44

aggressive behavior
  domestic abuse evaluation, 196–197
  juvenile sex offenders
    future research issues, 442–444
    treatment evaluation, 440–443
  methamphetamine use and, 19–20
  violence prediction and, 225

Ake v. Oklahoma, 70–73

Albertsons, Inc. v. Kirkingburg, 562

alcohol abuse and dependence, care and protection evaluation, brain impaired patients, 137

Alcohol or Drug Problem Acknowledgment Scale, substance abuse and intoxication, deception analysis, 317

Alcohol or Drug Problem Scale, substance abuse and intoxication, deception analysis, 317

allostatic load, noncerebral trauma, 588

alternative hypotheses, forensic deception analysis and, 117

ambivalence, as suicide by cop risk factor, 247

American Association of Mental Retardation (AAMR) criteria
  IQ variability and, 57–59
  mental retardation, death penalty jurisprudence and, 46

American Law Institute (ALI) Model Penal Code standard
  criminal responsibility negation, 8–13
  deception in criminal responsibility evaluation and, 291–292
  decision path based on, 21–31
  mitigatory defense and, 349, 351

Americans with Disabilities Act (ADA), care and protection evaluation, brain-impaired parents, 140–141

amnesia
  forensic deception analysis and, 114–115
  malingering investigations, 508–518
    contemporary research on, 516–518
    neurobehavioral investigation techniques, 513
  Minnesota Multiphasic Personality Inventory murder profiles, 402
  post-concussive syndrome, 574

amphetamine delusion disorder (ADD), criminal responsibility standard and, 11